TULU ENGLISH
DICTIONARY

TULU ENGLISH
DICTIONARY

REV. A. MANNER
B. M. S.

GYAN

Published by

GYAN

Gyan Publishing House
5, Ansari Road
Daryaganj, New Delhi-110002
Phone: 011-47034999, 9811692060
E-mail: books@gyanbooks.com

Distribution Network
gyanbooks.com
India, USA, Canada, UK, Australia, France

ISBN: 978-81-212-4367-4 (PB)
First Published, 1886

2nd Impression 2020

Printed at: Gyan Press, Delhi.

Tulu-English Dictionary
Author: Rev. A. Manner

PREFACE.

The Tuḷu language, one of the Dravidian family, is spoken only by half a million of people, inhabiting the central part of South-Canara. Until recently there was no literature in this language, except some legends written on palm-leaves in the Malayāḷam character, in the possession of Brahman families. It was only after the arrival of the Basel Missionaries in this district (1834) that some books were written and printed in the Basel Mission Press, the most important being a translation of the New Testament, which was completed in 1847, and of which a new typographical edition was issued in 1859. Other publications intended for the use of the church and schools followed in course of time, and in 1872 Rev. J. Brigel compiled a Tuḷu Grammar, which we recommend to those interested in that language. For writing, a modification of the Malayāḷam alphabet was in vogue till the Basel Mission Press employed Canarese characters in printing.

2. The compilation of a vocabulary was commenced some 30 years ago. The Rev. G. Kammerer, who died in 1858, left a manuscript containing about 2000 words. The author took this vocabulary in hand and continued adding to it from all available sources, without in the least contemplating the printing of the same. In 1883, however, the question of printing a Tuḷu Dictionary was first mooted, and further steps having been taken in the matter, the Government of Madras was pleased to defray the cost of its publication.

3. A Transliterātion in Latin characters of every word will, especially for beginners, facilitate the use of the book. The appended list (p. viii.) will show the rules according to which the transliteration has been made.

4. Special attention should be paid to words **sounding** alike, viz:

ಪಲ್ಲಿ **palli**, a lizard.	ಪಳ್ಳಿ **paḷḷi**, a mosque.
ಆಣೆ **āṇè**, an anna.	ಆನೆ **ānè**, an elephant.
ಮುತ್ತು **muttu**, a pearl.	ಮುದ್ದು **muddu**, a kiss.
ಮಡಿಪು **maḍipu**, a fold.	ಮದಿಪು **madipu**, a consultation.

5. Although it is customary in Dravidian Dictionaries to give the crude form of the Verb, it was thought better to give first the **Infinitive form**, as the conjugation of the verb is dependent on the ending of the Infinitive. The Root, however, is given after the transliteration. The three terminations of the Infinitive are as follows:

1. ಉನಿ **uni**, *as* ಓದ್ + ಉನಿ = ಓದುನಿ **vōduni**, to read;
2. ಪುನಿ **puni**, „ ಮಳ್ + ಪುನಿ = ಮಳ್ಪುನಿ **maḷpuni**, to do;
3. ಪಿನಿ **pini**, „ ತೂ + ಪಿನಿ = ತೂಪಿನಿ **tūpini**, to see.

As the formation of the **Causative form** is sometimes rather intricate and the meaning is often different from that attached to the root, it has been thought best to introduce the causative form as a seperate word.

6. As to the **Adjectives**, only the simple ones have been especially mentioned; all others which are either Adjective-Participles, or Nouns converted into Adjectives either by different terminations, as the Dative, Locative and Genitive, or by adding Adjective-Participles (ಇತ್ತಿ **itti**, ಉಪ್ಪು **uppu**, ಆಯಿ **āyi**, *etc.*), have been omitted, as the student can easily convert any Noun into an Adjective whenever required.

7. In a similiar manner it ought to be stated that all proper **Adverbs** have been specially pointed out; those, however, which are either Datives or Locatives or Nouns with Verbal Participles (ಆದ್ **ādụ**) have been omitted for the above reason.

8. The Tuḷu language does not possess many words with abstract meanings. The Gerund of every verb may, however, be used in this sense, for instance, ಓದುನವು wōdunavu reading, ತೂಪಿನವು tūpinavu observation. Bẹsides this there are some other derivations, as ವೋದಿಗೆ vōdigè of ವೋದುನಿ vōduni, ಹೆಚ್ಚಿಗೆ heččigè of ಹೆಚ್ಚುನಿ heččuni, ಜಪ್ಪೆಲ್ ǰappelu̥ of ಜಪ್ಪುನಿ ǰappuni, ದಿಂಜೆಲ್ diñǰelu̥ of ದಿಂಜುನಿ diñǰuni, ತರ್ತೆ tartè of ತಾರುನಿ tāruni, ಮುರ್ತೆ murtè of ಮೂರುನಿ mūruni, *etc.* Such abstract words, if not found in this Dictionary, can easily be formed by means of the Infinitive.

9. The meanings of many words might have been considerably increased, but for the sake of brevity we have, (especially in the case of words derived from Sanskrit), given only the most usual ones.

10. It should be taken into consideration that not only the different castes of the Tuḷu spẹaking people have their own peculiarities of expression and pronunciation, *e.g.* for "wedding" Brahmans say ಕಲ್ಯಾಣ kalyāṇa, Pariahs say ಬಡತನ baḍatana, and other caste people say ಮದುಮೆ madu̥mè, but that there are also three local distinctions of dialect, viz., a southern, a northern and an eastern one, in which similar peculiarities exist; for instance:

	to cover.	road.	river.	to see.
S.	ಪೊದೆಪಿನಿ podepini,	ಸಾದಿ sādi,	ತುದೆ tudè,	ತೂಪಿನಿ tūpini,
N.	ಪೊದೆಪಿನಿ podepini,	ತಾದಿ tādi,	ಸುದೆ sudè,	ಸೂಪಿನಿ. sūpini,
E.	ಪುದೆಪುನಿ pudepuni,	ಹಾದಿ hādi,	ಹುದೆ hudè,	ಹೂಪಿನಿ hūpini,

11. As to the adoption of Sanskrit, words besides those in common use with the people in connection with their worship, a number of words have been received which are current among Tuḷu Brahmans only, though not all; and there are also some words which owe their introduction to Christianity. The Tuḷu people also use a number of words which were originally Canarese, Malayāḷam and Hindustāni; of these only the most common ones have been introduced here.

12. The names of about 600 Plants will be found in this collection. About half are taken from "Five Hundred Indian

Plants" by C. Stolz, and the others have been obtained in other ways, careful investigation being required in some cases.

13. A **Supplement** of about 200 new words is appended.

14. For List of **Abbreviations** see the following page.

15. In the preparation of this Dictionary the following works have been consulted: Canarese Dictionary by W. Reeve, Malayāḷam Dictionary by Dr. H. Gundert, and Sanskrit Dictionary by Dr. Th. Benfey.

16. In conclusion the author desires to record the great obligations he is under, to the Munshis Messrs. Madhvarāya of Caup, Sītārāma of Mulki, Sarvōttama Pei of Mangalore, and Catechist Israel Aarons for the assistance given him, and among some others, he is also indebted to the corrector of the Mission Press, Mr. Šivarāu, who has been of very great service to him in carrying the work through the press. He nevertheless regrets certain errors which have crept into the work, and for which he craves the forbearance of the critic. These have been noted in the Errata.

Mangalore, October 1886. *A. M.*

Abbreviations.

acc. = accusative.
adj. = adjective.
adv. = adverb.
bet. = better.
bram. = word peculiar to Tuḷu Brahmans.
Chr. = Christian.
cond. = conditional.
c. d. = cum dative.
cf. = confer, compare.
conj. = conjunction.
c. v. = causative verb.
dat. = dative.
dim. = diminutive.
def. v. or *d. v.* = defective verb.
e. g. = for example.
emph. = emphatic.
fem. = feminine.
fg. = figurative.
f. t. = future tense.
gen. = genitive.
gram. = grammatical.
hon. = honorific.
imper. = imperative.
intj. = interjection.
intrg. = interrogative.
lit. = literally.
loc. = locative.
masc. = masculine.
neg. = negative.
n. or *neut.* = neuter.
num. = numeral.
opp. = opposite.
perf. = perfect tense.
part. = participle.
p. or *pers.* = person.
pl. = plural.
postp. = postposition.
pot. = potential.
prep. = preposition.
pron. = pronoun.
pro. = proverb.
p. t. = past tense.
Rom. = Roman Catholic.
s. = substantive.
Sans. = Sanskrit.
sing. = singular.
slg. = slang word.
v. a. = verb active.
v. n. = verb neuter.
v. refl. = verb reflexive.
vlg. = vulgar word.

Transliteration.

a. Vowels.

ಅ	a	*as*	a	*in*	about.
ಆ	ā	„	a	„	far.
ಇ	i	„	i	„	him.
ಈ	ī	„	i	„	police.
ಉ	u	„	u	„	full.
ಊ	ū	„	u	„	rule.
ಋ	rụ, *vocalised* r.				
(ೠ	rū *not used*)				

ಎ	e	*as*	e	*in*	met.
„	è (*final*)	*as*	a	„	mat.
ಏ	ē	*as*	e	„	grey.
ಐ	ei, ai, oi	„	ei	„	height.
ಒ	o (wo)	„	o	„	not.
ಓ	ō (wō)	„	o	„	note.
ಔ	ou, au	„	ou	„	house.
್	ụ (*half* u) *as* e *in* the *French* je.				

b. Medials.

ಂ = ṅ	*before*	ಕ, ಖ, ಗ, ಘ, ಙ.
ń	„	ಚ, ಛ, ಜ, ಝ, ಞ.
ṇ	„	ಟ, ಠ, ಡ, ಢ, ಣ.
n	„	ತ, ಥ, ದ, ಧ, ನ.
ಂ = m	*before*	ಪ, ಫ, ಬ, ಭ.
m̃	„	ಯ, ರ, ಲ, ವ, ಶ, ಷ, ಸ, ಹ.
ಃ = h, *vocalised.*		

c. Consonants.

ಕ	ka	*as*	ka	*in*	kalendar.
ಖ	kha	„	ka		aspirated.
ಗ	ga	„	ga	*in*	gander.
ಘ	gha	„	ga		aspirated.
ಙ	ṅa	„	ng	*in*	singing.
ಚ	ča	„	ch	„	chapter.
ಛ	čha		ča		aspirated.
ಜ	ǰa	„	ǰa	*in*	jam.
ಝ	ǰha		ǰa		aspirated.
ಞ	ńa	„	nya	*in*	bunyan.
ಟ	ṭa	the cerebral ta.			
ಠ	ṭha		ṭa		aspirated.
ಡ	ḍa	the cerebral da.			
ಢ	ḍha		ḍa		aspirated.
ಣ	ṇa	the cerebral na.			
ತ	ta	the dental ta.			
ಥ	tha		ta		aspirated.

ದ	da	the dental da.			
ಧ	dha		da		aspirated.
ನ	na	the dental na.			
ಪ	pa	*as*	pa	*in*	parrot.
ಫ	pha	„	pa		aspirated.
ಬ	ba	„	ba	*in*	bat.
ಭ	bha	„	ba		aspirated.
ಮ	ma	„	ma	*in*	mad.
ಯ	ya	„	ya	„	yam.
ರ	ra	„	ra	„	rag.
ಲ	la	„	la	„	lap.
ವ	va	„	va	„	van.
ಶ	ša	„	sha	„	sham.
ಷ	ša	„	sha	„	marshal.
ಸ	sa	„	sa	„	sat
ಹ	ha	„	ha	„	ham.
ಳ	ḷa	the cerebral l.			

ಕ್ಷ ksha *as* ksha *in* Lakshmi.

A

TULU-ENGLISH

DICTIONARY

ಅ

A

ಅ **a**, The first letter of the alphabet; 2. an interjection of surprise; 3. when prefixed to nouns derived from Sanskrit beginning with a consonant, it denotes negation, *as* ಸತ್ಯ truth, ಅಸತ್ಯ untruth; before a vowel ಅ becomes ಅನ್, as ಅಂತ end, ಅನಂತ endless.

ಅಂಕ **aṅka**, *s.* Fight, war, battle, combat; 2. cock-fight; 3. a mark, sign. —ದಾಯಿ a combatant, wrestler. —ದ ಬಾಕಿಯಾರ್ a field or place for cock-fighting. —ಕಾಡುನಿ to fight, to wrestle.

ಅಂಕಣ **aṅkaṇa**, *s.* The space between two cross beams *or* pillars (supporting a roof); 2. a quadrate, square; 3. a small room, compartment. —ಪಾಡುನಿ to upset.

ಅಂಕಾಯನ **aṅkāyana**, *s.* A temple feast; *see* ಆಯನ.

ಅಂಕಿತ **aṅkita**, *s.* A mark; *adj.* marked. —ಪಾಡುನಿ to affix one's signature to any writing; 2. to dedicate a work; 3. to put a mark.

ಅಂಕುಡೊಂಕು **aṅkuḍoṅku**, *s.* Crookedness; *adj.* bent, crooked.

ಅಂಕುಶ **aṅkuša**, *s.* A goad, hook used to drive an elephant with.

ಅಂಕಿಪುನಿ **aṅkipuni** (ಅಂಕಿ), *v. a.* To cipher, count, reckon (in writing).

ಅಂಕೆ **aṅkè**, *s.* A numerical figure.

ಅಂಕೋಲೆದ ಮರ **aṅkōleda mara**, *s. Alangium decapetalum* (*hexapetalum*).

ಅಂಗ್ **aṅgu̥**, *s.* Greediness, eagerness. —ಬುದ್ಪಿನಿ, —ಇದ್ಪಿನಿ to be greedy, covetous; *cf.* ಅಂಗಿದ್ಪಿನಿ.

ಅಂಗ್‌ಸಾವುನಿ **aṅgu̥sāvuni** (ಅಂಗ್‌ಸಾ), *v.a.* To reproach, despise; 2. to disregard; 3. to arraign; *also* ಅಂಗಿಸಾವುನಿ, ಹಂಗ್‌ಸಾವುನಿ.

ಅಂಗ aṅga, *s.* A limb, member; 2. the body. ಅಂಗಂಗೊಳು the members of the body.

ಅಂಗಕರಣ aṅgakaraṇa, *s.* The instruments of action, *as* ಮನ mind, ವಾಕ್ speech, ಕಾಯ body.

ಅಂಗಜಮೆರಿ aṅgajameri, *s.* The hair of the body.

ಅಂಗಜಾರಿ aṅgajāri, *s.* A name of ಶಿವ, the foe of Cupid.

ಅಂಗಜೆ aṅgajè, *s.* The god of love, ಕಾಮ; 2. a son; 3. desire.

ಅಂಗಡಿ aṅgaḍi, *s.* A shop, stall. –ದಾಯೆ, –ಗಾರೆ a shopkeeper.

ಅಂಗಣ aṅgaṇa, *s.* The space around a temple or demon-shrine; 2. a courtyard, the space in front of a house.

ಅಂಗತಾಪ aṅgatāpa, *s.* Heat of the body; 2. fatigue.

ಅಂಗದನೆ aṅgadanè, *s.* Thirst. –ಕೊಪಿಸಾವಿ to give to drink. –ಪರ್ಪಿನಿ to drink.

ಅಂಗದೆ aṅgade, *s.* The name of a celebrated monkey, the son of ವಾಲಿ.

ಅಂಗಪಂಕ್ aṅgapaṅkụ, *s.* The hair about the privities, *vlg.*

ಅಂಗಪರೀಕ್ಷೆ aṅgaparīkshe, *s.* Anatomy.

ಅಂಗಪೂಜೆ aṅgapūje, *s.* Worshipping the different members of an idol.

ಅಂಗಪ್ರದಕ್ಷಣೆ aṅgapradakshaṇe, *s.* Rolling the body after the car of an idol *or* round a temple, as a penance *or* in fulfilment of a vow; *see* ಮಡಸ್ನಾನ.

ಅಂಗಬೇಸರ್ aṅgabēsarụ, *s.* Fatigue.

ಅಂಗರಕ್ಷೆ aṅgarakshe, *s.* Personal protection, preservation, safety.

ಅಂಗರೇಕೆ aṅgarēke, *s.* A coat, jacket, vesture.

ಅಂಗರೋಮ aṅgarōma, *s.* The hair of the body.

ಅಂಗಲಪ್ಪು, ಅಂಗಲಾಪ aṅgalappu, aṅgalāpa, *s.* Covetousness, inordinate desire, eagerness of gain. –ದಪ್ಪುನಿ to be of inordinate desire; 2. to endeavour, try. –ದಾಯೆ a covetous person.

ಅಂಗವಸ್ತ್ರ aṅgavastra, *s.* An upper garment, a towel.

ಅಂಗಶಿಕ್ಷೆ aṅgaśikshe, *s.* Penance; 2. mortification of the body in penance.

ಅಂಗಶುಚಿ aṅgaśuči *s.* Ceremonial purity; 2. a thrashing, beating.

ಅಂಗಸಂಗ aṅgasaṅga, *s.* Sexual intercourse.

ಅಂಗಸಾಧನೆ aṅgasādhanè, *s.* Gymnastics, bodily exercise.

ಅಂಗಸಿದ್ಧಿ aṅgasiddhi, *s.* Prosperity.

ಅಂಗಸೂತ್ರ aṅgasūtra, *s.* The pulse; 2. a kind of girdle; *see* ಪೊತ್ತು ನೂಲು.

ಅಂಗಸೆ aṅgasè, *s.* A particular kind of building, the front part of which is used as a shop and the back part as a private dwelling; 2. a towel, scarf.

ಅಂಗಸೊನ್ನೆ aṅgasonne, *s.* A sign

made with the finger, head, eye, *etc.*

ಅಂಗಹಿಂಸೆ **aṅgahiṁse,** *s.* Corporal punishment. —ಮಳ್ಪುನಿ to wound, punish.

ಅಂಗಹೀನ **aṅgahīna,** *adj.* Maimed.

ಅಂಗಕ್ಷೇಮ **aṅgakshēma,** *s.* Bodily health.

ಅಂಗಾಂಗ **aṅgāṅga,** *adj.* All, of every kind; *see* ಅಂಙಂಙ.

ಅಂಗಾರ್ **aṅgāru,** *s.* The sole of the foot.

ಅಂಗಾರ **aṅgāra,** *s.* Tuesday.

ಅಂಗಾರಕ **aṅgāraka,** *s.* A black stroke put on the forehead.

ಅಂಗಾರಕೆ **aṅgārake,** *s.* The planet Mars. ಅಂಗಾರಕವಾರ Tuesday.

ಅಂಗಾರೆ **aṅgāre,** *s.* The planet Mars; 2. Tuesday.

ಅಂಗಾವುನಿ **aṅgāvuni,** *c.v.* (*of* ಅಂಗುನಿ), To yawn, gape, open (as the mouth).

ಅಂಗಿ **aṅgi,** *s.* A long gown, *or* coat.

ಅಂಗಿಡ್ಪಿನಿ **aṅgiḍpini** (ಅಂಗಿಡ್), *v. n.* To be greedy, covetous; *see under* ಅಂಗ್.

ಅಂಗಿಪುನಿ **aṅgipuni** (ಅಂಗಿ), *v. a.* To wish, be greedy of.

ಅಂಗಿಸಾವುನಿ **aṅgisāvuni** (ಅಂಗಿಸಾ), *v. a.* To reproach; *see* ಅಂಗ್ಸಾವುನಿ, ಹಂಗ್ಸಾವುನಿ.

ಅಂಗೀಕಾರ **aṅgīkāra,** *s.* Reception, admission; 2. acceptation. —ಮಳ್ಪುನಿ, ಅಂಗೀಕರಿಪುನಿ to accept, receive.

ಅಂಗೀರಸ **aṅgīrasa,** *s.* The name of a Hindoo saint.

ಅಂಗುಟ, ಅಂಗುಷ್ಟ **aṅguṭa, aṅgushṭa,** *s.* The thumb; 2. the great toe; *also* ಉಂಗುಟ.

ಅಂಗುನಿ **aṅguni** (ಅಂಗ್), *v. n.* To open; 2. to be seized with a fit of yawning; *as* ಬಾಯಿ ಅಂಗುಂಡು the mouth opens; 3. to cringe.

ಅಂಗುಲ **aṅgula,** *s.* An inch; 2. a finger, the thumb, great toe; 3. the name of a saint.

ಅಂಗುಸ್ತಾನಿ **aṅgustāni,** *s.* A thimble.

ಅಂಗೆಲ, ಅಂಗೆಳ **aṅgela, aṅgeḷa,** *s.* A native inch equal to about $1\frac{1}{4}$ of the English inch; *see* ಅಂಗುಲ.

ಅಂಗೆಲೆ **aṅgele,** *s.* A greedy person, glutton.

ಅಂಗೈ **aṅgei,** *s.* The palm of the hand. —ಗುಂಡಿ the cavity of the hand. —ರೇಕೆ the lines on the palm of the hand; *see* ಹಸ್ತರೇಕೆ. —ಮುಂಗೈ ನಕ್ಕುನಿ to lick the palm and back of the hand; *fg.* to be greedy.

ಅಂಗೋಪಾಂಗ **aṅgōpāṅga** (ಅಂಗ-ಉಪ-ಅಂಗ), *s.* The members of the body.

ಅಂಗೋಸ್ತ್ರ **aṅgōstra** (ಅಂಗ-ವಸ್ತ್ರ), *s.* An upper garment, a towel.

ಅಂಙಂಙ, ಅಂಙಂಙೊಳು **aṅṅaṅṅa, aṅṅaṅṅoḷu,** *s.* All the limbs; *see* ಅಂಗಾಂಗ.

ಅಂಙಣ **aṅṅaṇa,** *see* ಅಂಗಣ.

ಅಂಙಣ್ಯುನಿ **aṅṅaṇyuni** (ಅಂಙಣ್), *v.a.* To be greedy of, to covet; *cf.* ಅಂಗಿಡ್ಪಿನಿ.

ಅಂಙೆಲೆ, aṅṅele, *see* ಅಂಗೆಲೆ.

ಅಂಚ **ańća**, *adv.* So, thus, like, after that way or manner; 2. *int.* yea, even so. ಅಂಚಂಚಿ there, that side, a little further on. ಅಂಚಾಂಡ if it be so, however. ಅಂಚಾಯಿನೆಡ್ಡ್, ಅಂಚಾ ದುಪ್ಪನೆಡ್ಡ್, ಅಂಚಾಯಿನೆಡ್ಡಾವರ (ಅಂಚ-ಆಯಿನೆಡ್ಡ್, ಅಂಚ-ಆದ್-ಉಪ್ಪನೆಡ್ಡ್, ಅಂಚ-ಆಯಿನಿ-ಎಡ್ಡಾವರ) for that reason, on that account, therefore. ಅಂಚಿತ್ತಿ such.

ಅಂಚದೆ **ańćadè**, *adv.* So, just so.

ಅಂಚನೆ, ಅಂಚೆನೆ **ańćane, ańćene**, *adv.* Just so, even so. –ಮಳ್ಪುನಿ to do so, to do in like manner.

ಅಂಚಲ್ **ańćal**, *s.* The post, tapal. –ಕುದುರೆ a post-horse. –ದಾಯೆ a postman.

ಅಂಚಿ **ańći**, *adv.* Thither, that side; 2. beyond. ಅಂಚಿದ ಪಾಲ್ the other part. ಅಂಚಿಗ ಸಂದುನಿ to die, expire, decease. ಅಂಚಿಂಚಿ here and there, hither and thither, to and fro.

ಅಂಚಿಗೆ, ಅಂಚಿಕೆ **ańćigè ańćikè**, *see* ಅಂಜಿಗೆ.

ಅಂಚಿದಾಯೆ **ańćidāye**, *s.* A postman.

ಅಂಚುನಿ **ańćuni** (ಅಂಚ್), *v. a.* To lurk, *as* ಪುಚ್ಚೆ ಪಕ್ಕಿನ್ ಅಂಚುಂಡು the cat lies in wait for the bird; *v. n.* to be importunate.

ಅಂಜನ **ańjana**, *see* ಅಂಞನ.

ಅಂಜನಾದೇವಿ **ańjanādēvi**, *s.* The wife of ವಾಯು (the god of wind) and mother of ಹನುಮಂತ, the famous monkey general; 2. the black goddess.

ಅಂಜಲ್‌ಮೀನ್ **ańjaḷumīnu**, *s.* A kind of fish.

ಅಂಜಿಗೆ, ಅಂಜಿಕೆ **ańjigè, ańjikè**, *s.* Fear, alarm, fright; 2. shyness. –ಮಳ್ಪುನಿ to fear, be afraid of, be alarmed, be frightened; 2. to be shy. –ದಾಯೆ a coward, timid person.

ಅಂಜಿಯುನಿ, ಅಂಜುನಿ **ańjiyuni, ańjuni** (ಅಂಜಿ, ಅಂಜು), *v. n.* To fear. ಅಂಜುನಾಯೆ a coward, timid person.

ಅಂಜೂರ **ańjūra**, *s.* A fig. –ಪಂರ್ದ್ a ripe fig. –ಮರ the glomerous fig tree.

ಅಂಜೆಲೆ **ańjele**, *s.* A timid fellow.

ಅಂಞನ **aññana** *s.* A collyrium or ointment applied to the eyes (*see* ಕಾಡಿಗೆ); 2. particular applications, *as* lampblack, antimony *etc.*; 3. a kind of medicine for the eyes; *also* ಅಂಜನ. –ದಕಲ್ಲ್ antimony. –ಗಾರೆ, –ದಾಯೆ necromancer, conjurer. soothsayer, *also* ಮಂಜನದಾಯೆ. –ಪಾಡುನಿ to put a sharp medicine *or* collyrium into the eyes; 2. to conjure.

ಅಂಟ್ **aṇṭu**, *s.* Gum, paste, resin; 2. adhesion. –ಪತ್ತುನಿ to come in contact with, to touch; 2. to follow, pursue; 3. to stick, adhere to. –ಪಾಡುನಿ to gum, paste. ಅಂಟಾಪಿನಿ to become adhesive.

ಅಂಟ್‌ಪತ್ತು aṇṭụpattu, *adj.* Adhesive, attractive.

ಅಂಟುನಿ aṇṭuni, *v. n.* To adhere, stick; *v. a.* to paste; 2. to attract.

ಅಂಡ್ aṇḍụ, *s.* The buttocks; ಅಂಡ್‌ಗ ಬಂಜಿ ಮಣಿ a stool to sit upon. ಅಂಡ್‌ದವರ್ a small under garment.

ಅಂಡ aṇḍa, *s.* An egg, that which is oval shaped. –ಜಾತಿ the oviparous class, *as* bird, fish *etc.*

ಅಂಡಸ್ aṇḍasụ, *s.* A kind of fish; *bet.* ಬಂಡಸ್.

ಅಂಡಿ aṇḍi, *s.* A germ of mangoes *etc.* –ಬೂರುನಿ fruits to put forth; *also* ಕಾಯಿ ಕಟ್ಟುನಿ.

ಅಂಡಿಣಾರ್, ಅಂಡಿಪುಣಾರ್ aṇḍiṇārụ, aṇḍipuṇārụ, *s.* The name of a tree, *Carallia integerrima.*

ಅಂಡೆ aṇḍe, *s.* The vessel of a toddy-drawer for putting toddy in; 2. a vessel made of hollow bamboo *or* nut-shell.

ಅಂಣಾವುನಿ aṇṇāvuni (ಅಂಣಾ), *v. a.* To raise or lift up the head or face; 2. to peep.

ಅಂಣುಕಾಯಿ aṇṇukāyi, *s.* Cocoanut and plantains offered to an idol; *see* ಹಂಣುಕಾಯಿ. –ಕೊ ಪ್ಪಿನಿ, –ಮಳ್ಪುನಿ to offer cocoanuts and plantains.

ಅಂಣೆ aṇṇe, *s.* An elder brother; 2. a maternal uncle; 3. an elderly man.

ಅಂತ anta, *s.* End, finale.

ಅಂತಃಕರಣ antahkaraṇa, *s.* The internal sense; 2. the heart, the mind; 3. *fg.* mercy; *also* ಅಂತಸ್ಕರಣ.

ಅಂತಃಪುರ antahpura, *s.* A seraglio, the queen's apartment.

ಅಂತಕೆ antake, *s.* Yama, the Indian Pluto.

ಅಂತದ್‌ರ್ antadụrụ, *s.* A clue, hint, inkling (as of a secret).

ಅಂತಪಂತ antapanta, *s.* Competition, vying; 2. prowess.

ಅಂತರ antara, *s.* Intermediate space, interval; 2. difference, disparity; 3. rank. –ತುತ್ತಿಳ್, –ಕುತ್ತಿಳ್, –ಕುತ್ತ್ಯೊಳು the intermediate posts of a roof.

ಅಂತರಂಗ antaraṅga, *s.* The mind, heart; 2. a secret; 3. secrecy; *in loc.* secretly.

ಅಂತರಗಂಗೆ antaragaṅge, *s. Pistia stratiosa*; *cf.* ನೀರಾಟ.

ಅಂತರಾಂತರ antarāntara, *s.* Distinction of rank.

ಅಂತರಾಟ, ಅಂತ್ರಾಟ, ಅಂತರಾಷ್ಟ್ರ antarāṭa, antrāṭa, antarāshṭra, *s.* Mid-space, mid-air, included space, interval; ಅಂತರಾಟೊಡುಳ್ಳೆ *lit.* 'he is in the atmosphere', *used for* one who has died and has no rest; 2. *fg.* he is in a dilemma, he is not settled.

ಅಂತರಿಪುನಿ, ಅಂತರಿಸ್ಪುನಿ, ಅಂತರಿಯುನಿ, antaripuni, antarisuni, antariyuni (ಅಂತರಿ), *v. n.* To end; 2. to die; 3. to differ.

ಅಂತರ್ದೆಸೆ antardese, *s.* The unknown fate.

ಅಂತರ್ಮಾಡ್ antarmāḍu, *s.* An under roof.

ಅಂತರ್ಯ antarya *s.* The inner part; 2. the heart, mind.

ಅಂತರ್ಸುಣ್ಣ antarsuṇṇa, *s.* The beam on the walls.

ಅಂತುಗ antuga, *s.* Total.

ಅಂತಸ್ತು antastu, *s.* An upper store *or* room; 2. a secret.

ಅಂತ್ಯ antya, *s.* End, completion; *adj.* last, final, ultimate. –ಕಾಲ the time of death.

ಅಂಡ್ anḍu, *d. v.* Yes, yea. –ಆದು ಪ್ಪುನಿ to be true. –ಆಪಿನಿ to be brought up; 2. to be verified, proved. —ಆಯಿ true. –ಆಯಿ ಪಾತೆರ a true word: ಅಂಡಾಯಿ ಪಾತೆರೊಗು ಸಂಡಾಯ ಇಜ್ಜಿ *lit.* there is no gainsaying the truth. –ಮಳ್ಪುನಿ to prove, improve. ಅಂಡಾ is it so? is it true? *also* calling attention.

ಅಂಡ್ಂಡ anduṇḍa (*condl. form of* ಅನ್ಪಿನಿ), *adv.* Namely, that is to say.

ಅಂಡ್ದ್ andudu (*past part. of* ಅನ್ಪಿನಿ *used as*) *conj.* (*lit.* Having said,) that. ಬರ್ಪೆ ಅಂಡ್ದ್ ಪಂಡೆ he said that he would come.

ಅಂದ anda, *s.* Form, shape; 2. beauty, elegance, handsomeness, symmetry; 3. purport. *adj.* beautiful, pretty; –ಗಾರೆ, a handsome man. –ಕೋಪಿನಿ to decay, wane.

ಅಂದಚಂದ andaćanda, *adj.* Very handsome, very pleasant.

ಅಂದಗೆ, ಅಂದಕೆ andage, andake, *s.* A blind man, a man of defective vision; 2. a cripple.

ಅಂದಣ andaṇa, *s.* A kind of palankin.

ಅಂದಯೆ andaye, *see* ಅಂದಾಯಿ.

ಅಂದಸ್ಯ, andasya, *see* ಅಂದೇಶ.

ಅಂದಸ್ಸ andassa, *s.* Darkness, blackness. –ಜಾಗ a very dark place. –ನರಕ hell of darkness.

ಅಂಡಾ anḍā, *see under* ಅಂಡ್.

ಅಂಡಾಜು, ಅಂಡಾಜಿ anḍāju, anḍāji, *s.* Estimate. –ಮಳ್ಪುನಿ to make an estimate.

ಅಂಡಾಯಿ anḍāyi, *see under* ಅಂಡ್.

ಅಂಡಾಯೆ anḍāye (ಅಂಡ್-ಆಯೆ), *s.* A consenter, one who consents; 2. *p. t. of* ಅಂಡಾಪಿನಿ, *cf. under* ಅಂಡ್.

ಅಂದಿಪುನಾರ್ andipunār, *see* ಅಂದಿ ಣಾರ್.

ಅಂದೆ, ಅಂದೇ ande, andē, *int.* of entreaty, addressing, calling attention.

ಅಂದೇಶ, ಅಂದೇಸ andēša, andēsa, *s.* Doubt, hesitation; 2. shyness.

ಅಂಧಕಾರ andhakāra, *s.* Darkness.

ಅಂಧಗೆ andhage (ಅಂಧಕೆ). *s.* A blind man; *see* ಅಂದಗೆ.

ಅಂಧಾದರ್ಬಾರ್ andhādarbāru, *s.* A blind government; 2. tyranny. –ದಾಯೆ a tyrant, mismanager.

ಅಂನ anna, *s.* Food, *esp.* cooked rice. –ದಾನ a gift of food.

ಅಂನಡಿ annaḍi, *s.* A homeless person, pauper; 2. a simpleton; *cf.* ಅಡ್ನಾಡಿ.

ಅಂಪುನಿ ampuni, *see* ಅಂಬುನಿ.

ಅಂಬ, ಅಂಬಾ, ಅಂಬೊ amba, ambā, ambo, *s.* Bellowing, lowing 2. a cry, noise. —ಪಾಡುನಿ to bellow, low (like a calf).

ಅಂಬಟೆ, ಅಂಬಡೆ ambaṭė, ambaḍė, *s.* The wild mango, hogplum. —ಮರ, a hogplum-tree, *Spondias mangifera.*

ಅಂಬರ ambara, *s.* The sky; 2. cloth, apparel; ರಕ್ತಾಂಬರ a purple cloth. ಅಂಬರಾಂಬರ a name of ಶಿವ.

ಅಂಬರಪ್ಪು ambarappu, *s.* Hurry, confusion, perplexity. —ದಾಯೆ a perplexed man. ಅಂಬರಿತ್ ಪೋಪಿನಿ, ಅಂಬೆರಿತ್— to become perplexed.

ಅಂಬರಿ, ಅಂಬಾರಿ ambari, ambāri, *s.* An elephant's saddle, howdah.

ಅಂಬಲ್ ambalu, *s.* Tipsiness, drunkenness; 2. drowsiness: ನಿದ್ರೆದ ಅಂಬಲ್‌ಡ್ ಪಂಡೆ (I *or* he) told (it) in drowsiness of sleep.

ಅಂಬಲ ambala, *see* ಅಂಬಿಲ.

ಅಂಬಾಕಿಲ್ ambākilu, *s.* A kind of verandah; 2. an outer gate *or* door.

ಅಂಬಿ ambi, *s.* Cow-dung.

ಅಂಬಿಗಾರೆ ambigāre, *s.* A boatman; *cf.* ಅಂಬುಗಾರೆ.

ಅಂಬಿಗೆ ambige, *s.* A hunter; *see* ಅಂಬುಗಾರೆ, ಆಂಬಿಗೆ.

ಅಂಬಿಲ ambila, *s.* The place around *or* in front of a temple; 2. a verandah around a temple.

ಅಂಬು ambu, *s.* Water.

ಅಂಬು ambu, *s.* An arrow. —ಗಾರೆ a hunter.

ಅಂಬುಗೆ ambugė, *s.* The flower of *Arum colocosia*; *cf.* ತೇವು.

ಅಂಬುನಿ ambuni (ಅಂ) B., *v.a.* To do, make; *cf.* ಅಂಪುನಿ, ಮಂಪುನಿ, ಮಳ್ಪುನಿ.

ಅಂಬುಲಿ ambuli, *s.* A kind of pap *or* gruel of rāgi *or* rice.

ಅಂಬೆ ambė, *s.* A goddess, ಪಾರ್ವತಿ; ಮೂಕಾಂಬೆ a dumb goddess; *cf.* ಅಂಬ.

ಅಂಬೆಕಾರ್ ambekāru, *s.* Walking *or* crawling on hands and feet. —ಪಾಡುನಿ, —ನಡಪುನಿ to crawl.

ಅಂಬೆಪೂ ambėpū, *s.* Mango blossoms.

ಅಂಬೆಲ ambela, *see* ಅಂಬಿಲ.

ಅಂಬೇ ambē, *see* ಅಂಬ.

ಅಂಬೊಡಿ amboḍi, *s.* A kind of dance *or* mock-fight among the Pariahs.

ಅಂಬೊಡೆ amboḍe, *s.* A kind of fried cake.

ಅಂಬೊತ್ತು ambottu, *s.* Arrogance, pride; *also* ಹಂಬೊತ್ತು. —ತೋಜಾವುನಿ to be arrogant.

ಅಂಮ amma, *s.* A lady; ಮಾರಿಯಂಮ Kāḷi.

ಅಂಮಪದ್ದೆಯಿ ammapaddeyi, *s. euphem. for* Small-pox.

ಅಂಮಯ್ಯ ammayya, *int.* of sorrow *or* pain.

ಅಂಮೆ amme, *s.* A father; ನೇಲ್ಯಂಮೆ, ಪೆರಿಯಂಮೆ an elder uncle; ಶಿದ್ದ್ಯಂಮೆ a younger uncle (father's, not mother's brother); ತಾಂಕಂದಮ್ಮೆ *lit.* nourishing father, foster father, adoptive father; *pl.* ಅಂಮಾಡ್ಳು; *hon. pl.* ಅಂಮೆರ್.

ಅಂಮೊತ್ತು amottu, *see* ಅಂಬೊತ್ತು.

ಅಂಶ aṁśa, *s.* Part, share, portion. —ಮಳ್ಪುನಿ to divide, apportion.

ಅಂಸ aṁsa, *s.* A goose, swan; *also* ಹಂಸ, ಹಂಸಪಕ್ಕಿ.

ಅಂಸಪಾದ, aṁsapāda, *s.* A caret, asterisk; 2. a prop; *cf.* ಹಂಸಪಾದ.

ಅಃ, ಅಹ ah, aha, *int.* Ah! eh!

ಅಕರ, ಅಕಾರ, akara, akāra, *adv.* There, yonder, far; *also* ಆಕರ.

ಅಕಲ್ akalu, *see* ಅಕ್ಕಲ್.

ಅಕಸ್ಮಿಕ akasmika, *adj.* Accidental, sudden, unexpected.

ಅಕಾರ akāra, *s.* The letter ಅ; *cf.* ಅಕರ.

ಅಕಾಲ akāla, *adj.* Untimely, unseasonable. —ಮರಣ premature death.

ಅಕೀರ್ತಿ akīrti, *s.* Infamy, disgrace.

ಅಕೃತ್ಯ akrutya, *s.* Iniquity; *adj.* wicked, bad.

ಅಕೇರಿ, akēri, *s.* End; *in dat. or loc.* at *or* about the end, finally; *also* ಆಖೈರಿ.

ಅಕ್ಕ, ಅಕ್ಕೆ akka, akkè, *s.* An elder sister; 2. an elderly woman.

ಅಕ್ಕಕ್ಕ, ಅಕ್ಕೊಳು akkakka, akkoḷu, *s.* Part; *adv.* asunder. —ದೀಪಿನಿ to put asunder, divide.

ಅಕ್ಕಯ್ಯ akkayya, *s.* An affectionate mode of addressing an elderly woman.

ಅಕ್ಕರ್ akkaru, *s.* An atom; *also* ಅಕ್ಕರ್ದ ಕಡ್ಡಿ; ನಿನ ಅಕ್ಕರ್ದ ಕಡ್ಡಿ ಯಾನ್ ಮುಟ್ಟಯೆ I shall not touch a bit of you.

ಅಕ್ಕರ್ವ akkarva, *s.* The last words of a dying person.

ಅಕ್ಕಲ್ akkalu, *s.* Sense, intellect, understanding; reflection. —ಕೆಟ್ಟುನಿ to be out of wits.

ಅಕ್ಕಿ akki, *s.* Rice, corn, *used only in compos., e.g.* ದಡ್ಡಲಕ್ಕಿ, a coarse kind of rice; ಯೇಲಕ್ಕಿ cardamom; *see* ಅರಿ.

ಅಕ್ಕೀಕ akkīka, *s.* A kind of precious stone, sardius.

ಅಕ್ಕುಡುನಿ akkuḍuni (ಅಕ್ಕುಡಿ), *v.a.* To hang, suspend.

ಅಕ್ರಮ akrama, *s.* Irregularity, abnormity, confusion. ಅಕ್ರಮೂದ irregularly, disorderly. ಅಕ್ರಮೂಯಿ wrong.

ಅಗಣಿತ agaṇita, *adj.* Countless, innumerable.

ಅಗತ್ಯ agatya, *s.* Need, necessity, want; *adj.* urgent, important.

ಅಗಪಾವುನಿ agapāuni, *c.v.* (*of* ಅಗಪುನಿ), To send away, cause to depart.

ಅಗಪುನಿ agapuni (ಅಗ), *v.n.* To remove, depart. *v.a.* to separate; 2. extend.

ಅಗಪೆಲ್ agapelu, *s.* Separation; 2. despatch.

ಅಗಮ agama, *adj.* Fixed, immovable.

ಅಗರ್, ಅಗಳ್ agaru, agaḷu, *s.* A fort ditch, trench, moat; 2. wall; ಉಪ್ಪಡಅಗರ್ a saltpan. –ಕ ಡ್ಪುನಿ to dig a trench.

ಅಗರುಗಂಧ agarugandha, *s.* Red sandal wood, *Aquilaria agallochum.*

ಅಗಸೆನಾರ್ agasenāru, *s.* The lin-plant; 2. flax.

ಅಗಸೆಮರ agasemara, *s.* The name of a tree, *Agati grandiflora.*

ಅಗಸ್ತ್ಯ agastya, *s.* The name of a Hindu saint; 2. necessity, *bet.* ಅಗತ್ಯ.

ಅಗಾತ agāta, *adj.* Not dangerous.

ಅಗಾಧ agādha, *s.* An abyss. *adj.* bottomless, deep; 2. very difficult.

ಅಗಿನಿ agini, *see* ಅಗ್ನಿ.

ಅಗಿಲ್ agilu, *s.* A kind of tree; ಕರಿಅಗಿಲ್ *Agallochum.*

ಅಗುಡೆ aguḍe, *s.* A furnace, fire for warming.

ಅಗುರು aguru, *see* ಅಗರ್.

ಅಗುರುನಿ aguruni (ಅಗುರ್), *v. n.* To totter, stagger.

ಅಗೆಲ್ agelu, *s.* A kind of demon worship with food *etc.* –ತಂಬಿಲ worship of demons and serpents with food-offering. –ತಂಬಿಲ ಕೊರ್ಪಿನಿ to give such offerings to demons, *etc.*

ಅಗೆಲ್-, ಅಗೆಲ-, ಅಗಲ್-ಗಂಧ agelu-, agela-, agalu-gandha, *s.* Aloes; *see* ಅಗರುಗಂಧ.

ಅಗೆಲ agela, *s.* Breadth; *adj.* broad.

ಅಗೆಲುದ್ದ ageludda, *s.* Length and breadth.

ಅಗೊಲಿ, ಅಗೊಳಿ agoli, agoḷi, *s.* A large vessel.

ಅಗೋಚರ agōčara, *adj.* Invisible; 2. incomprehensible.

ಅಗ್ಗ agga *s.* Cheapness. ಅಗ್ಗಡ್ cheaply. ಅಗ್ಗಾಯಿ mean.

ಅಗ್ಗಲಾಸ್, ಅಗ್ಗ್ಸ್ aggalāsu, aggusu, *adj.* Cheap. [ಅಗ್ನಿ.

ಅಗ್ಗಿ aggi, *s.* Hunger; 2. fire; *bet.*

ಅಗ್ಗಿಯುನಿ, ಅಗ್ಯುನಿ aggiyuni, agyuni (ಅಗಿ), *v. a.* To chew, bite.

ಅಗ್ಗೆ agge, *s.* The shoot of a branch.

ಅಗ್ಞಾನ, ಅಗ್ಯನ, ಅಗ್ಯೇನ agñāna, agyana, agyēna, *s.* Ignorance; *bet.* ಅಜ್ಞಾನ.

ಅಗ್ನಿ agni, *s.* Fire.

ಅಗ್ರ agra, *s.* Front, top; 2. a soremouth, aphthae, the thrush; ಕಂಬೊಳಿ ಅಗ್ರ, ಕರಿ ಅಗ್ರ, ಕೊಟ್ಟ ಅಗ್ರ, ಪೂ ಅಗ್ರ, ಸರ್ಪ ಅಗ್ರ, varieties of soremouth. –ಬೇರ್ a kind of root for soremouth.

ಅಗ್ರಗಣ್ಯೆ agraganye, *s.* The chief; 2. one who is regardless of anything.

ಅಗ್ರಸಾಲೆ agrasāle, *s.* A dining hall; 2. a cooking place in temples.

ಅಗ್ರಸ್ತೆ agraste, *s.* A headman, president, manager.

ಅಗ್ರಾರ, ಅಗ್ರಹಾರ agrāra, agrahāra, *s*. A Brahmin village.

ಅಘ agha, *s*. Sin; 2. passion.

ಅಘೋರ aghōra, *adj*. Terrible, fierce, dreadful.

ಅಚಂಚಲ aćańćala, *adj*. Firm, fixed, decided. –ತ್ವ firmness, decidedness.

ಅಚರ aćara, *adj*. Immovable; 2. inanimate.

ಅಚಲ aćala, *s*. A mountain; *adj*. immovable.

ಅಚೋದ್ಯ aćōdya, *adj*. Curious, wonderful.

ಅಚ್ಚ aćća, *adj*. Pure, unmixed, genuine; *cf*. ಸ್ವಚ್ಛ.

ಅಚ್ಚಡೆ aććaḍè, *s*. A peculiar kind of cloth to put on; 2. a wrapper; *cf*. ಪಚ್ಚಡೆ.

ಅಚ್ಚದ, aććada, *s*. A red mark put on the forehead; 2. a mixture of raw rice and red powder; *also* ಅಕ್ಷದ.

ಅಚ್ಚಿ aćći, *s*. A form, model; 2. a weaver's reed. –ಪಾಡುನಿ to print, to coin. –ದ ಮರ a model made of wood; an axle-tree.

ಅಚ್ಚಿಕಟ್ಟ್ aććikaṭṭu, *s*. Convenience, fitness. *adj*. neat, compact commodious.

ಅಚ್ಚಿಬೆಲ್ಲ aććibella, *s*. Country sugar, jaggory made of sugarcane.

ಅಜಂ ajam, *s*. The process of digestion *or* consumption; *also* ಹಜಂ. –ಆಪಿನಿ to be digested; to be exhausted.

ಅಜಂತ ajanta, *adj*. Many, all: ಅಜಂತ ಜನ ಕೂಡುಂಡು plenty people come together.

ಅಜಂತೆ ajante, *s*. An attendant.

ಅಜಕ್ಲ್ ajakulu, *s*. Yawning, gaping. –ಇಡಪಿನಿ to yawn, gape.

ಅಜಕಾಯಿ ajakāyi, *s*. Cocoanut. –ದಪ್ಪುನಿ to break cocoanuts (in a kind of play).

ಅಜಕೆ ajakè, *s*. Idleness. –ದ ಪಾತೆರ idle talk. –ದಾಯೆ a babbler.

ಅಜಕೆಲ್ ajakelu, *s*. Relapse.

ಅಜಕೋಲು, ajakōlu, *s*. The rope *or* cane for putting clothes on.

ಅಜನೆ ajanè, *s*. The noise of a thief, goblin, *etc*.

ಅಜಪು, ಅಜಬ್ ajapu, ajabu, *adj*. Strange, wonderful.

ಅಜಪುನಿ ajapuni (ಅಜ), *v. a*. To select, choose.

ಅಜಪ್ಪು ajappu, *s*. Selection. ಅಜಪ್ಪದ selected.

ಅಜಮಾಸ್ ajamāsu, *s*. Estimate; 2. deliberation; 3. trace, search.

ಅಜಮಿಲ ajamila, *see* ಅಜಾಮಿಳ.

ಅಜಮೈಸುನಿ ajameisuni, *v. a*. To deliberate, trace; 2. to estimate.

ಅಜರ್, ಅಜರ್ಯ ajaru, ajarya, *adj*. Imperishable, not decaying.

ಅಜರ ajara *s*. A kind of moss; *cf*. ಪಾಮಜಿ.

ಅಜಲ್ ajalu, *s*. A portion, part. –ದಾಯೆ a customer.

ಅಜಲಿಪಿ ajalipi, *s*. Fate.

ಅಜಾಗ್ರತೆ ajāgratè, *s.* Carelessness.

ಅಜಾಮಿಳ ajāmiḷa, *s.* The name of a fabulous Brahmin.

ಅಜಾಮೆ ajāme, *s.* A barber; *bet.* ಹಜಾಮೆ.

ಅಜಿಕೆ ajikè, *see* ಅಜಕೆ.

ಅಜಿಕೆಲ್ ajikelụ, *see* ಅಜಕೆಲ್.

ಅಜಿಕುರ್ವೆ ajikurve, *s.* A sower's basket; *also* ಅಜಿಕುರುವೆ.

ಅಜಿಗುಜಿ ajiguji, *s.* A crushing.

ಅಜಿಪ, ಅಜಿಪ್ಪ ajipa, ajippa, *num.* Sixty; *also* ಅಜಿಪ.

ಅಜಿಮೆ, ಅಜ್ಮೆ ajimè, ajmè, *s.* A crook. —ದ ಕಲ್ಲ್ a grinding-stone (for medicine *etc.*).

ಅಜಿರ್ ajirụ, *s.* A blue oyster. —ಕೈ an unfortunate hand. ಅಜಿರ್ದ ಕಬ್ಬ very hard iron.

ಅಜಿಲ್‍ದಾರ್, ಅಜಿಲೆರ್ ajildārụ, ajilerụ, *s.* A title, honorific appellation of a master or manager (particularly applied to a headman of the Bants).

ಅಜೀರ್ಣ, ಅಜೀರ್ತೆ ajīrṇa, ajīrte, *s.* Indigestion.

ಅಜೆ ajè, *s.* The foot-print; 2. footstep, track, trace; 3. a row; 4. the cloth tied over a cradle; *also* ಹಜಿ, ಜೆಜಿ. —ಕಟ್ಟುನಿ to make a row. —ಕೋಲು, *see* ಅಜಕೋಲು. —ಬಳ್ಳ್ a rope for putting clothes on.

ಅಜ್ಜಿ ajji, *s.* A grandmother. —ಕಥೆ a tale, idle story.

ಅಜ್ಜಿಟ್ಟ್ ajjiṭṭụ, *s.* A kind of dough made of rice.

ಅಜ್ಜೆ ajje, *s.* A grandfather.

ಅಜ್ಞಾನ ajñāna, *s.* Ignorance.

ಅಜ್ಞಾನಿ ajñāni, *s.* An ignorant man.

ಅಟ aṭa, *s.* Obstinacy; *bet.* ಹಟ. —ತಾಯಿ, —ನಾರಿ an obstinate person.

ಅಟಕೊಟಲೆ aṭakoṭale, *s.* Constant sickness.

ಅಟಕ, ಅಟಕಾವು aṭaka, aṭakāvu, *s.* Obstacle, hindrance. —ಮಳ್ಪುನಿ, ಅಟಕಾಯಿಸುನಿ to hinder, stop.

ಅಟಮಟ aṭamaṭa, *s.* Deception, pretence.

ಅಟಾರ aṭāra, *adj.* Wide spread, as the branches of a tree.

ಅಟೂರ aṭūra, *s.* *Polycarpaea corymbosa*, *also* ಪಾದೆಮುಳ್ಳು.

ಅಟ್ಟ aṭṭa, *s.* An upper loft, garret, upper room; 2. ceiling.

ಅಟ್ಟಣೆ aṭṭaṇè, *s.* A household; 2. household things; 3. administration. —ಅರಗಣೆ articles to be cooked. —ಜೋಡಣೆ household care.

ಅಟ್ಟಳು aṭṭaḷu, *s.* An upstair-room.

ಅಟ್ಟಹಾಸ, ಅಟ್ಟಾಸ aṭṭahāsa, aṭṭāsa, *s.* Shouting, laughter; 2. pomp, ostentation; 3. delay. —ಮಳ್ಪುನಿ to shout, laugh aloud; to parade, ostentate.

ಅಟ್ಟಾಳ್ aṭṭāḷụ, *s.* A good labourer; 2. a messenger sent after another.

ಅಟ್ಟಿ aṭṭi, *s.* A pile, heap of rice.

ಅಟ್ಟಿಲ್ aṭṭilụ, *s.* Cooking; 2. meal. —ದಾಯಿ a cook.

ಅಟ್ಟುನಿ aṭṭuni (ಅಟ್ಟಿ), *v. a.* To put; ಶೋಸ್ರು ಅಟ್ಟುನಿ to discharge urine, *vlg.*

ಅಟ್ಟೆ, aṭṭè, *s.* The sole of a shoe; 2. support, stand; 3. knot; ಕುತ್ತಟ್ಟ, ಕುತ್ತಟ್ಟೆ an upper loft for storing rice; ಬೆತ್ತದಟ್ಟೆ a knot or ring of a rattan. –ಕಾರ್ bent legs, bandy legs. –ಶೋಯಿಡ್ ಕುಳ್ಳುನಿ, –ಮಡಿತ್ ಕುಳ್ಳುನಿ to sit down on cross legs.

ಅಟ್ಟೆಮಿ, aṭṭemi *s.* The eighth lunar day; ಗೋಕುಲಟ್ಟೆಮಿ the birthday of ಕೃಷ್ಣ; *bet.* ಅಷ್ಟೆಮಿ.

ಅಟ್ಟೆಮುಟ್ಟೆ aṭṭemuṭṭè, *s.* Arms and legs; –ಪೊಲ್ತ್ಂಡ್ hands and legs are broken.

ಅಟ್ಟೊಳಿಗೆ aṭṭoḷigè, *s.* A loft supported on posts, temporary gallery.

ಅಡ್ಪಿನಿ aḍụpini (ಅಡಿ), *v.n.* To cook. ಕಂಡಣ್ಯೆ ಅಡ್ಪಿನಿ to marry a man.

ಅಡಂಗಾಯಿ adaṅgāyi, *s.* A kind of pickle.

ಅಡಕ್, ಅಡಕ aḍakụ, aḍaka, *s.* Hinderance; *also* ಅಟಕ್.

ಅಡಕ, ಅಡ್ಕ, ಅಡ್ಕಜಾಗ್ aḍaka, aḍka, aḍụkajāgụ, *s.* An unclean place; 2. a burying place. –ಕಾಡ್ a wild unclean place.

ಅಡಕಬಾರೆ aḍakabāre, *s.* A kind of fruit, *Cucumis pubescens.*

ಅಡಕಾಯಿಸುನಿ aḍakāyisuni, *v. a.* To hinder.

ಅಡಕುನಿ, aḍakuni (ಅಡಕ್), *v. a.* To throw, cast out; 2. to discharge, fire, *as* ಬೆಡಿ ಅಡಕುನಿ to fire a gun; *also* ಅಡೆಕುನಿ.

ಅಡಗ್ aḍagụ, *s.* A ship; *cf.* ಹಡಗ್, ಕಪ್ಪಲ್.

ಅಡಜಾತಿ aḍajāti, *s.* An out-caste; 2. a mongrel; *adj.* mixed.

ಅಡನ, ಅಡ್ಡಣ aḍana, aḍḍaṇa, *s.* A shield.

ಅಡನಗಾಂಯಿ aḍanagāyi, *see* ಅಡಂಗಾಯಿ.

ಅಡನಾಡಿ aḍanāḍi, *see* ಅಡ್ನಾಡಿ.

ಅಡಪ aḍapa, *s.* A barber's dressing case; 2. a bundle; *also* ಹಡಪ, ಬಾಲ್‌ಮುಟ್ಟು.

ಅಡಪುನಿ aḍapuni (ಅಡ), *v. a.* To plough; *cf.* ದಪ್ಪುನಿ.

ಅಡಬೆ, aḍabè, *s.* An adulteress; *adj.* bastard, illegitimately born; *bet.* ಹಡಬೆ. –ಗ್ ಪುಟ್ಟಿನಾಯೆ a bastard, an illegitimate person, *vlg.*

ಅಡಮೀನ್ aḍamīnụ, *s.* A kind of fish.

ಅಡರ್ aḍarụ, *s.* A thin branch, twig; 2. copse.

ಅಡರುನಿ aḍaruni (ಅಡರ್), *v. n.* To crack.

ಅಡವಿ aḍavi, *s.* A forest, jungle.

ಅಡವು, ಅಡಾವು aḍavu, aḍāvu, *s.* A mortgage, pledge; 2. the thing mortgaged. –ಕೊರ್ಪಿನಿ, –ಪಾಡುನಿ to pawn, pledge, mortgage.

ಅಡಾಯಿಸುನಿ aḍāyisuni, *see* ಅಡಕಾಯಿಸುನಿ.

ಅಡಿ aḍi, *s.* Bottom, base; 2. foot; ಕಾರಡಿ the foot-sole, foot-step. ಅಡಿಕೆಡಿಕ್ ಬೂರುನಿ to fall one upon the other.

ಅಡಿ aḍi, *adj.* Cooked, dressed, prepared. —ಅಟ್ಟಿಲ್ prepared food; a meal ready to be served.

ಅಡಿಂಕರ aḍiṅkara, *s.* A large vessel; *also* ಅಡ್ಡ್ಯರ.

ಅಡಿಕೆಬೂರು aḍikebūru, *s.* A kind of creeper, *Pothas scandens; also* ಅರ್ಕ್ಬೂರು.

ಅಡಿಕೈ aḍikei, *s.* The palm of the hand. *adj.* Defeated, vanquished. —ಆಪಿನಿ, —ಬೂರುನಿ to lie underneath; to be overturned, defeated.

ಅಡಿಗಂಟ್ aḍigaṇṭu, *s.* The binding in the middle of a sack converting it into a "bissac"; the lower part of a "bissac" *or* sack tied in the middle. 2. the lower joints of a reed *or* cane.

ಅಡಿಗುಳು aḍiguḷu, *s.* A cook. 2. a priest.

ಅಡಿಗೆ aḍigè, *s.* Cooking, distilling. 2. emulsion *or* confection prepared from medicinal herbs. —ಭಟ್ಟ a cook.

ಅಡಿಚರಕ್ aḍićaraku, *s.* Ballast.

ಅಡಿನೀರ್ aḍinīru, *s.* Water at the bottom of something, standing water. 2. stored-up-water for irrigation of lower lying fields. —ಕಟ್ಟುನಿ to store up water in a field after the 2nd *or* 3rd crop until rainfall.

ಅಡಿಪತ್ತುನಿ aḍipattuni, *v. a.* To singe, burn.

ಅಡಿಪರೆಲ್ aḍiparelu, *s.* A spurious jewel.

ಅಡಿಪಾಡುನಿ aḍipāḍuni, *v. a.* To stack corn in a straw- (*or* bamboo-mat-) granary in a yard. 2. proceed.

ಅಡಿಪು aḍipu, *s.* Sweeping. —ದಾಯಿ, —ನಾಯಿ a male sweeper. —ನಾಳ್ a female sweeper.

ಅಡಿಪುನಿ aḍipuni (ಅಡಿ), *v. a.* To sweep.

ಅಡಿಬೂರುನಿ aḍibūruni, *v. n.* To submit.

ಅಡಿಮುದೆಲ್ aḍimudelu, *s.* Capital for trading. 2. resources.

ಅಡಿಮೇಲ್ aḍimēlu, *s.* Overturning. —ಆಪಿನಿ, —ಬೂರುನಿ to be overturned. —ಪಾಡುನಿ to upset, turn over.

ಅಡಿಸುಡಿಸಾಮಾನ aḍisuḍisāmāna, *s.* Dressed food.

ಅಡುಂಬು aḍumbu, *s.* The creeper *Ipomoea maritima.*

ಅಡೆ, ಅಡೆಗ್ aḍe, aḍegu, *adv.* There. ಅಡೆಗೇ (*emph.*) just there, to that very place.

ಅಡೆಂಗುನಿ aḍeṅguni, *see* ಅಡೆವುನಿ, ಡೆಂಗುನಿ.

ಅಡೆಕ aḍeka, *adj.* Narrow, close. 2. small, short, brief.

ಅಡೆಕುನಿ aḍekuni, *see* ಅಡಕುನಿ.

ಅಡೆಪು aḍepu, *s.* The act of shutting, closing, finishing. —ಪಾಡುನಿ to shut, close.

ಅಡೆಪುನಿ, ಅಡೆವುನಿ aḍepuni, aḍevuni (ಅಡೆ), *v. n.* To shut, close. 2. to roost, perch: ಕೋರಿ ಅಡೆಯುಂಡು the fowl perches. ಬಿಲೆ ಅಡೆವುನಿ to cost: ದಾನೆ ಅಡೆವು? what's the price? *also* ಅಡೆದ್ ಪೋಪಿನಿ to be shut up, closed.

ಅಡೆಸ್ aḍesu, *adj.* Faded, waned, drooping *or* hanging down (as one's head).

ಅಡೇಕೆ aḍēke, *s.* Obstacle, hinderance. 2. shelter.

ಅಡೇಗೆ aḍēge, *adv.* For nothing, to no purpose. 2. without anything more, barely, merely; *also* ಅಡಿಗೆ.

ಅಡೇವುನಿ, ಅಡೇಯುನಿ aḍēvuni, aḍēyuni (ಅಡೆ), *v. n.* To hide, be concealed.

ಅಡ್ಕ aḍka, *see* ಅಡಕ.

ಅಡ್ಕಲ aḍkala, *s.* A cooking shed. 2. an oven.

ಅಡ್ಡ aḍḍa, *s.* A rafter.

ಅಡ್ಡ aḍḍa, *s.* Obstacle, hinderance. *adj.* Horizontal, intervening. *adv.* Across, athwart. —ಆಪಿನಿ, ಅಡ್ಡಾಪಿನಿ to come across, hinder. —ಕಟ್ಟುನಿ to dam up, shut in; to hinder, interrupt, prevent; to block up a path *or* entrance; to screen. —ಗೀಚುನಿ to cross with lines, underline —ತಲೆವುನಿ to oppose, stop, hinder. —ದೀಪಿನಿ to place across. —ಬರ್ಪಿನಿ to oppose, confront, interrupt. —ಬೂರುನಿ to prostrate, bow down (a kind of salutation). —ಮಳ್ಪುನಿ to hinder, oppose.

ಅಡ್ಡಂತ್ರ aḍḍantra, *s.* The torments supposed to be caused by a demon.

ಅಡ್ಡಕ, ಅಡ್ಕ aḍḍaka, aḍka, *see* ಅಡಕ.

ಅಡ್ಡಕಟ್ಟೆ aḍḍakaṭṭè, *s.* A dam.

ಅಡ್ಡಕತ್ತಿಮುತ್ತಿಗಂಡ aḍḍakattimuttiganḍa, *s.* A female's head-ornament. 2. the head-gear of a devil-dancer.

ಅಡ್ಡಕತ್ತೆರಿ aḍḍakatteri, *s.* A betel-nut-cutter *or* cracker; *also* ಇಡಕತ್ತಿ.

ಅಡ್ಡಕಸಬು aḍḍakasabu, *s.* An improper *or* unnatural profession. *adj.* Unusual, contrary.

ಅಡ್ಡಕಾರ್ aḍḍakāru, *s.* The bent knee, *as* —ಪಾಡ್ದ್ ಕುಳ್ಳುನಿ to squat. 2. a crooked leg. —ಪಾಡುನಿ to interfere with.

ಅಡ್ಡಕೀಲ್ aḍḍakīlu, *s.* A bolt, lock, tenon, linch-pin.

ಅಡ್ಡಕೈ aḍḍakei, *s.* The arm in a posture of defence.

ಅಡ್ಡಕೋಲ್ aḍḍakōlu, *s.* A cross-bar.

ಅಡ್ಡಗಂಧ aḍḍagandha, *s.* A horizontal mark on the forehead made with sandal paste by certain caste people.

ಅಡ್ಡಗೀಟ್, ಅಡ್ಡಗೆರೆ aḍḍagīṭu, aḍḍagerè, *s.* An intersected line, a line across another.

ಅಡ್ಡಗೆಲ aḍḍagela, *s.* Breadth, width, diameter.

ಅಡ್ಡಗೆಲ್ಲ್ aḍḍagellu, *s.* A lateral branch.

ಅಡ್ಡಗೋಡೆ aḍḍagōḍè, *s.* A partition wall.

ಅಡ್ಡಘಾಯ aḍḍaghāya, *s.* An untimely *or* accidental death. ಅಡ್ಡಘಾಯೊಡು ತಿಕ್ಕುನಿ to be caught suddenly, to be in danger of life; to be very afraid.

ಅಡ್ಡಚೌಕ aḍḍačauka, *s.* A box in which the linga is kept.

ಅಡ್ಡಚ್ಚಿ aḍḍačči (ಅಡ್ಡ-ಅಚ್ಚೆ), *s.* An axle.

ಅಡ್ಡಜಾತಿ aḍḍajāti, *see* ಅಡಜಾತಿ.

ಅಡ್ಡಣ aḍḍaṇa, *s.* A shield.

ಅಡ್ಡಣಿ, ಅಡ್ಡಣಿಗೆ aḍḍaṇi, aḍḍaṇigè, *s.* A bench.

ಅಡ್ಡಣೆ aḍḍaṇè, *see* ಅಡ್ಡಣ.

ಅಡ್ಡತರೆ aḍḍatarè, *s.* An ill-formed head.

ಅಡ್ಡತೊಲೆ, ಅಡ್ಡತೋಳ್ aḍḍatolè, aḍḍatōḷụ, *s.* A transverse beam, cross-bar.

ಅಡ್ಡದಂಡಿಗೆ aḍḍadaṇḍigè, *s.* A kind of an open palankin carried sideways.

ಅಡ್ಡದಂಡೆ aḍḍadaṇḍè, *s.* A handcuff. 2. a partition wall, parapet, dam.

ಅಡ್ಡದಬ್ಬೆ aḍḍadabbè, *s.* The bamboo pole with which anything is carried across the shoulder.

ಅಡ್ಡನಾಲಯಿ aḍḍanālayi, *s.* A stammering tongue. 2. lying, gainsaying.

ಅಡ್ಡನೀಟ aḍḍanīṭa, *adv.* Broadwise.

ಅಡ್ಡಪಂತೆ, ಅಡ್ಡಪಂಕ್ತಿ aḍḍapantè, aḍḍapaṅkti, *s.* A line crossing another. –ಕುಳ್ಳುನಿ to sit at meals apart from others (in a siderow).

ಅಡ್ಡಪಾತೆರ aḍḍapātera, *s.* Interrupting one in speaking. 2. contradicting, gainsaying. –ಪಾತೆರುನಿ to interrupt, gainsay.

ಅಡ್ಡಪುದರ್ aḍḍapudarụ, *s.* A nickname.

ಅಡ್ಡಪುದೆ aḍḍapudè, *s.* A load carried on a pole by two *or* more persons. 2. a load carried on the shoulder.

ಅಡ್ಡಬರೆ aḍḍabarè, *see* ಅಡ್ಡಗೋಡೆ.

ಅಡ್ಡಬೇಲಿ aḍḍabēli, *s.* A hedge *or* fence across a path.

ಅಡ್ಡಮರ aḍḍamara, *s.* A cross-bar.

ಅಡ್ಡಮಾರ್ಗ aḍḍamārga, *s.* A crossway, by-path. 2. a false way.

ಅಡ್ಡಮುಡಿ aḍḍamuḍi, *s.* A female's tuft of hair fixed on the side of the head.

ಅಡ್ಡರ, ಅಡ್ಡರೆ aḍḍara, aḍḍarè, *s.* Tetanus; *also* –ರೋಗ.

ಅಡ್ಡಲಿ, ಅಡ್ಡಳಿ aḍḍali, aḍḍaḷi, *s.* A pole placed across.

ಅಡ್ಡವಕ್ಕೆಲ್ aḍḍavakkelụ, *s.* A new *or* temporary tenant *or* lodger.

ಅಡ್ಡಶೆರಂಗ್ aḍḍašeraṅgụ, *s.* The upper end of a woman's cloth drawn over the right shoulder.

ಅಡ್ಡಸಾದಿ aḍḍasādi, *s.* A by-path, cross-way.

ಅಡ್ಡಸಾಲ್ aḍḍasālụ, *s.* A transverse row *or* line. 2. repeated interruptions, interference.

ಅಡ್ಡಳಿಗೆ aḍḍaḷigè, *see* ಅಡ್ಡಣಿಗೆ.

ಅಡ್ಡಾಡುನಿ aḍḍāḍuni (ಅಡ್ಡಾಡ್), *v. n.* To walk to and fro, to parade.

ಅಡ್ಡಾದಿಡ್ಡಿ aḍḍādiḍḍi, *adj.* Awkward, clumsy. 2. topsy-turvy.

ಅಡ್ಡಾಪಿನಿ aḍḍāpini, *see* ಅಡ್ಡ.

ಅಡ್ಡಿ aḍḍi, *s.* Obstacle, stoppage. 2. opposition. —ಮಳ್ಪುನಿ to hinder, prevent, oppose, stop.

ಅಡ್ಡೆಲಿಪುನಿ aḍḍelipuni (ಅಡ್ಡೆಲಿ), *v. a.* To put out, drive out.

ಅಡ್ಡ್ಯರ aḍḍyara, *s.* An earthen jar *or* vessel. ನೀರಡ್ಡ್ಯರ a water pot.

ಅಡ್ಡ್ಯೆ aḍḍyè, *s.* A cake, pudding.

ಅಡ್ಣಾಡಿ aḍṇāḍi (ಅಸ್ಥ-ನಾಡಿ), *adj.* Indifferent, middling. 2. vulgar, low. 3. wild; *cf.* ಅಂನಡಿ.

ಅಡ್ಪಿನಿ, ಅಡ್ಪುನಿ aḍpini, aḍpuni (ಅಡಿ), *see* ಅಡಿಪಿನಿ.

ಅಡ್ಪಿಲ್ಲ್ aḍpillu, *s.* A kitchen.

ಅಡ್ಯೊಣುನಿ, ಅಡ್ಯೊಣ್ದುಪೋಪಿನಿ aḍyoṇuni, aḍyoṇdupōpini, *v. n.* To leave a place at once.

ಅಣಕ aṇaka, *s.* Narrowness, closeness. *adj.* Narrow, small.

ಅಣಕಸಣಕ aṇakasaṇaka, *adj.* Quarrelling.

ಅಣಪು aṇapu, *s.* Need, want. 2. urgency, necessity. 3. hinderance, obstacle. 4. harm.

ಅಣರ್ aṇaru, *s.* Moss, lichen, mouldiness, the green stuff on stagnant water; *cf.* ಪಾಮಜಿ. —ಪತ್ತುನಿ to become mossy, slimy.

ಅಣಸ್ aṇasu, *s.* A handle, hilt.

ಅಣಾವುತ aṇāvuta, *see* ಅನವತ.

ಅಣಾವುನಿ, ಅಣ್ಣಾವುನಿ aṇāvuni, aṇṇāvuni (ಅಣಾ), *v. n.* To look up, lift up the face, gaze.

ಅಣಿ aṇi, *s.* A kind of mask *or* appendage worn by a devil-dancer. 2. a peacock's tail when spread. 3. a small fly. —ಕಟ್ಟುನಿ, —ಪಾಡುನಿ, —ದೀಪಿನಿ to put on a mask *etc.*

ಅಣಿತ aṇita, *adj.* Elastic; *also* ಹಣಿತ.

ಅಣಿಲೆ aṇilè, *see* ಅನಿಲೆ.

ಅಣಿಲೆಕಾಯಿ aṇilekāyi, *s.* The gall-nut, ink-nut.

ಅಣಿಲೆಮರ aṇilemara, *s.* The ink-nut-tree, *Terminalia chebula.*

ಅಣು aṇu, *s.* An atom, any thing extremely small, dust.

ಅಣುಪು aṇupu, *see* ಅಣಪು.

ಅಣುಬೆ aṇubè, *adj.* Soft.

ಅಣೆ aṇè, *int.* Oh! hey.

ಅಣೆ aṇè, *s.* The forehead, *see* ಹಣೆ. 2. steepness. 3. a very steep foot-path. —ಮಿತ್ತಾವುನಿ to ascend a steep path.

ಅಣೆ aṇe, *see* ಅಣಿ.

ಅಣೆಕಲ್ಲ್ aṇekallu, *s.* A certain stone in a temple-yard dedicated to the tutelar demons of a temple.

ಅಣೆಪುನಿ aṇepuni (ಅಣೆ), *v. a.* To press, push, strike against, come in contact.

ಅಣೆಬರವು aṇebaravu, *s.* Fate, destiny. 2. appointed lot; *see* ಹಣೆಬರವು.

ಅಣ್ಜವು, ಅಣ್ಜಾವು aṇjavu, aṇjāvu, *s.* A man, male; *also* ಆಣ್ಜೀವು.

ಅಣ್ಕಿಲ್ aṇkilu, *s.* A very narrow door, a wicket. 2. a lodge. —ಇಟ್ಟೆಡೆ a strait passage.

ಅಣ್ಯ aṇya, *s.* The prow of a vessel.

ಅತಂತ್ರ atantra, *adj.* Unstable, infirm, weak, helpless.

ಅತಂತ್ರೆ atantre, *s.* A dependent, helpless person.

ಅತಿ ati, *pref.* Over, beyond, exceeding, much *etc.*

ಅತಿಕ್ರಮ atikrama, *s.* Transgression, infringement. –ದಾಯಿ a transgressor. –ಮಳ್ಪುನಿ, ಅತಿಕ್ರಮಿಪುನಿ to transgress, encroach, violate.

ಅತಿಥಿ atithi, *s.* A guest.

ಅತಿಥ್ಯ atithya, *see* ಆತಿಥ್ಯ.

ಅತಿಪ್ರಿಯ atipriya, *adj.* Much beloved.

ಅತಿರಿಕ್ತ atirikta, *adj.* Excessive, exceeding.

ಅತಿಶಯ atiśaya, *s.* Pre-eminence. 2. abundance. 3. wonder, marvel.

ಅತಿಸಾರ್ atisāru, *s.* Diarrhœa, dysentery.

ಅತಿಸ್ವಾದ್ atisvādu, *s.* A good flavour.

ಅತುಲ, ಅತುಳ atula, atuḷa, *s.* *Sesamum orientale. adj.* unequalled, incomparable.

ಅತ್ತ್ attu, *def. v.* Not, not so; negation of quality; *cf.* ಇಜ್ಜಿ. –ಇನ್ಪುನಿ to deny, contradict. –ಕಲೆಪಿನಿ to abnegate. ಅತ್ತಂಡ if not, else, or.

ಅತ್ತಂತ್ರ attantra, *s.* Absence of mind, carelessness; *cf.* ಅತಂತ್ರ.

ಅತ್ತಂದಿ attandi, *part.* (*of* ಅತ್ತ್) Not right, unseemly. –ಕೆಲಸ an improper act, a wicked deed.

ಅತ್ತಂಡೆ attandè, *conj.* (*part. of* ಅತ್ತ್) But, besides, except, without, unless.

ಅತ್ತರ್, ಅತ್ತರ attaru, attara, *s.* A kind of mat made of split bamboos.

ಅತ್ತರು attaru, *s.* Otto *or* essence of roses *etc.* 2. perfume.

ಅತ್ತಲ, ಅತ್ತಳ attala, attaḷa, *s.* A kind of cake for the Samārādhane feast.

ಅತ್ತಸಮರ attasamara, *s.* The fig tree, *Ficus religiosa.* ಅತ್ತಸದ ಕಟ್ಟೆ a platform built round the foot of a sacred fig tree; *also* ಅಶ್ವತ್ಥ.

ಅತ್ತಾ attā, *interrog. of* ಅತ್ತ್.

ಅತ್ತಾರ್ attāru, *see* ಅತ್ತರ.

ಅತ್ತಿಗೆ attigè, *s.* An elder brother's wife.

ಅತ್ತೆ attè, *s.* A mother-in-law. 2. an aunt.

ಅತ್ಯಂತ atyanta, *adj.* Excessive, extreme, exceeding.

ಅತ್ಯರ್ಥ atyartha, *adj.* Excessive.

ಅತ್ಯಲ್ಪ atyalpa, *adj.* Very small, trifling.

ಅತ್ಯವಶ್ಯ atyavaśya, *adj.* Very necessary.

ಅತ್ಯಾಶೆ atyāśè, *s.* Greediness, covetousness. 2. lust.

ಅತ್ಯುತ್ತಮ atyuttama, *adj.* Most excellent, best.

ಅತ್ಯೆ atyè, *see* ಅತ್ತೆ.

ಅತ್ರಿ, ಅತ್ರಿಮುನಿ atri, atrimuni, *s.* One of the seven sages, father of Čandra.

ಅತ್ರುವಾಣ, ಅತ್ರುವಾನ atruvāṇa, atruvāna, *s.* Insincerity. 2. machinations.

ಅತ್ರೆಸ atresa, *s.* A kind of sweetened rice-cake.

ಅತ್ರೇಸ atrēsa, *s.* The 9th lunar mansion, (*fr.* ಆಶ್ಲೇಷ). 2. a kind of rain in August.

ಅಥರ್ವ, ಅಥರ್ವಣ atharva, atharvaṇa, *s.* The fourth Vēda.

ಅದ್‌ರ್ adụrụ, *s.* A split, crack, cleft.

ಅದ್‌ರ್‌ಪದ್‌ರ್ adụrụpadụrụ, *s.* The line of cleavage of a rock *or* other formation, which can be separated into slabs *or* scales *or* flakes. 2. shaking and quaking. –ಆಪಿನಿ to go to pieces, be shattered, bruised, split, *etc.* –ಬುದ್ಪಿನಿ to crack.

ಅದ್‌ರಾಟ adụrāṭa, *s.* Shaking, trembling.

ಅದ್‌ರಾವುನಿ adụrāvuni, *c. v.* (*of* ಅದ್‌ರುನಿ), To shake, agitate.

ಅದ್‌ರುನಿ adụruni (ಅದ್‌ರ್), *v.n.* To tremble, quake.

ಅದಗ adaga, *adv.* Then, at that time; *cf.* ಅಪಗ, ಆಪಗ.

ಅದರುನಿ adaruni, *see* ಅದ್‌ರುನಿ.

ಅದರ್ಪುನಿ adarpuni (ಅದರ್), *v. a.* To cause to tremble. 2. to admonish, rebuke, reprove.

ಅದಲ್‌ಬದಲ್ adalụbadalụ, *s.* Exchange. –ಮಳ್ಪುನಿ to exchange.

ಅದಿರ್, ಅದ್‌ರ್ adirụ, adụrụ, *s.* A limit. 2. a boundary wall, parapet.

ಅದುರುನಿ aduruni, *see* ಅದ್‌ರುನಿ.

ಅದೃಢ adrụḍa *s.* Uncertainty. *adj.* Unstable, uncertain; *bet.* ಅದೃಢ.

ಅದೃಶ್ಯ adrụśya, *adj.* Invisible.

ಅದೃಷ್ಟ adrụshṭa, *s.* Fortune, fate.

ಅದೆ adè, *s.* An inner room. 2. a small room.

ಅದೆಕಿ adeki, *s.* Right of management of family-property; *also* ಆದೇಚ. –ದಾಯಿ an heir, the head of a family *etc.* –ಹೆಚ್ಚುನಿ the management *or* administration of the family-property to extend.

ಅದೆಲಿ, ಅದೊಲಿ adeli, adoli, *s.* A kind of chisel.

ಅದೇಲಿ, ಅದೋಲಿ adēli, adōli, *s.* Half an anna; ಜೋಳ್ಳಿದ– half a rupee, an eight anna piece.

ಅದೇಕ್, ಅದೇಕ adēkụ, adēka, *see* ಅಧಿಕ.

ಅದೇಚ adēča, *see* ಆದೇಚ, ಅದೆಕಿ.

ಅದೋಗತಿ, ಅಧೋಗತಿ adōgati, adhōgati, *s.* Perdition.

ಅದೋಮುಖಿ adōmukhi, *s.* Downward tendency. 2. the name of a female Bhūta.

ಅದ್ದನ addana, *s.* Weakness. 2. sickness. 3. affliction; *cf.* ಅಪ್ಪನ, ಅಧ್ಯಾನ. –ದಾಯಿ a weak *or* distressed man.

ಅದ್ದಲಿಪುನಿ, ಅದ್ದೊಲಿಪುನಿ addalipuni, addolipuni (ಅದ್ದಲಿ, ಅದ್ದೊಲಿ), *v. a.* To rebuke. 2. to frighten. 3. to command.

ಅದ್ಪುನಿ adpuni (ಅದ್), *v. n.* To go to stool, *vlg.*

ಅದ್ಭುತ adbhuta, *s.* A phenomenon, miracle, wonder, *adj.* Wonderful, surprising.

ಅದ್ರಿ, adri *s.* A hill. 2. a tree.

ಅದ್ರುಣಿ adruni, *see* ಅಡರುಣಿ.

ಅದ್ವನ advana, *see* ಅಧ್ವನ.

ಅದ್ವಾನ advāna, *see* ಅಧ್ವಾನ.

ಅದ್ವೈತ adveita, *s.* The Vēdānta šāstra *or* the doctrinal system of Šaṅkarāčārya which regards the Supreme Spirit and the human spirit as one.

ಅಧಮ adhama, *adj.* Low, mean, vile. ಅಧಮಿ a low *or* vile person.

ಅಧಿಕ adhika, *adj.* Much, great, more.

ಅಧಿಕಾರ adhikāra, *s.* Authority, power. —ಸ್ತ a head official; a governor; a man of power.

ಅಧಿಪತಿ adhipati, *s.* A ruler, lord, commander.

ಅಧೀನ adhīna, *s.* Possession, control. *adj.* Dependent on. —ತೆ dependence, subjection.

ಅಧೀನೆ adhīne, *s.* An adherent, a dependent.

ಅಧೈರ್ಯ adheirya, *s.* Discouragement, timidity, cowardice.

ಅಧ್ಯಯನ adhyayana, *s.* Study. 2. the reading of sacred books.

ಅಧ್ಯಕ್ಷೆ adhyakshe, *s.* A superintendent, overseer. 2. a bishop, *Chr.*

ಅಧ್ಯಾಯ adhyāya, *s.* Chapter, section; *cf.* ಸಂಧಿ.

ಅಧ್ವಾನ adhvāna, *s.* Labour. 2. immethodical effort. *adj.* Tired. 2. weak. 3. wrong, spoilt. —ದಾಯಿ a hard-working man.

ಅನಂತ ananta, *adj.* Endless, infinite. —ತ್ವ infinity. —ಶಯನೆ Vishṇu, as reclining on the coils of the king of serpents (as in Trivandrum). ಅನಂತೆ the Infinite, God.

ಅನಂತರ anantara, *adv.* Afterwards.

ಅನಪು anapu, *see* ಅಣಪು.

ಅನರ್ anaru, *see* ಅಣರ್.

ಅನರ್ಗ್ಯ anargya, *adj.* Very costly, priceless; *fr.* ಅನರ್ಘ್ಯ.

ಅನರ್ಥ anartha, *s.* Bad fortune, calamity, disaster.

ಅನವತ, ಅನವುತ anavata, anavuta, *s.* Iniquity, transgression. —ದಾಯಿ a transgressor.

ಅನಾಚಾರ anāčāra, *s.* Violation of religious rules *or* practices. 2. misconduct, transgression. 3. irreligion.

ಅನಾಥ anātha, *adj.* Forlorn, helpless, destitute. ಅನಾಥೆ one who is unprotected, helpless, an orphan. ಅನಾಥೆದಿ a widow, poor woman.

ಅನಾದಿ anādi, *adj.* Without beginning, everlasting, eternal.

ಅನಾಧಾರ anādhāra, *s.* Without basis *or* support, want of protection. *adj.* Helpless, unprotected.

ಅನಾಮತಿ anāmati, *s.* Deposit, anything entrusted. 2. all, the whole. 3. keeping in suspense; *cf.* ಅಮಾನತು.

ಅನಿಲೆ anile, *s.* Bud, sprout, germ. 2. soft timber. —ಪರಿಯುನಿ to bud, germinate. ಬಿತ್ತ್ದನಿಲೆ a sprout from a seed.

ಅನಿವಾರ anivāra, *s.* Trouble, hardship. 2. starvation.

ಅನಿಷ್ಟ anishṭa, *s.* Something unpleasant. 2. adversity. 3. displeasure.

ಅನೀತಿ anīti, *s.* Injustice, wrong.

ಅನು anu, *pref.* After, like, under, along *etc.*

ಅನುಕಾಲ, anukāla, *see* ಅನುದಿನ.

ಅನುಕೂಲ anukūla, *s.* Agreement. 2. convenience. 3. help, aid. *adj.* Convenient, helpful. —ಆಪಿನಿ to be convenient. —ಮಳ್ಪುನಿ to make convenient, arrange.

ಅನುಕ್ರಮಣಿಕೆ anukramaṇikè, *s.* Arrangement, order. 2. an index, table of contents.

ಅನುಗ್ರಹ anugraha, *s.* Favour, regard, mercy, grace.

ಅನುತನ anutana, *s.* Opportunity, fitness. —ತೂಪಿನಿ to watch for an opportunity.

ಅನುದಿನ anudina, *adv.* Daily.

ಅನುಪಕಾರ anupakāra, *s.* Unkindness, disfavour.

ಅನುಪತ್ಯ anupatya, *s.* Indigence, necessity, need, want of means. 2. inconvenience.

ಅನುಭವ anubhava, *s.* Enjoyment, suffering 2. experience.

ಅನುಭವಿಪುನಿ, anubhavipuni, *v. a.* To enjoy. 2. to experience.

ಅನುಭೋಗ anubhōga, *s.* Enjoyment.

ಅನುಮತಿ anumati, *s.* Consent, agreement.

ಅನುಮಾನ anumāna, *s.* Doubt, suspicion, conjecture, surmise. 2. fear. —ಮಳ್ಪುನಿ to doubt, suspect.

ಅನುರಾಗ anurāga, *s.* Love, regard, passion.

ಅನುರೂಪ anurūpa, *s.* Likeness, resemblance.

ಅನುಲೇಪ anulēpa, *s.* Anointing, besmearing.

ಅನುವಂದಿಗೆ anuvandigè, *s.* Consent.

ಅನುವಾರ anuvāra, *see* ಅನಿವಾರ.

ಅನುಸಾರ anusāra, *s.* Imitation, following. —ಆದ್ according to.

ಅನೆಪಿನಿ, ಅನೆಪುನಿ anepini, anepuni (ಅನೆ), *v. a.* To touch. 2. to hug, embrace.

ಅನೆವುನಿ anevuni, *see* ಅಣೆವುನಿ.

ಅನೇಕ anēka, *adj.* Much, many, plenty.

ಅನ್ಪಿನಿ anpini (ಅನ್). *v. a.* To say, speak; *cf.* ಅಂದ್ದ್, ಇನ್ಪಿನಿ *etc.*

ಅನ್ಯ anya, *see* ಅನ್ಯೋ.

ಅನ್ಯ anya, *adj.* Foreign, different, strange.

ಅನ್ಯಜಾತಿ anyajāti, *s.* A different class *or* caste. —ದಾಯೆ a person of a different caste *or* creed, a stranger.

ಅನ್ಯದೇಶ anyadēśa, *s.* A foreign country.

ಅನ್ಯಭಾಷೆ anyabhāshè, *s.* A foreign language.

ಅನ್ಯಮನ್ಯ anyamanya, *see* ಅನ್ಯೋನ್ಯ.

ಅನ್ಯಾಯ anyāya, *s.* Injustice,

wrong, iniquity. *adj.* Unjust, unreasonable. —ದಾಯಿ an unjust person.

ಅನ್ಯೋನ್ಯ anyōnya, *s.* Communion, fellowship, friendship.

ಅಪ apa, *pref.* denoting inferiority, privation, separation, contrariety *etc.*; *also* ಅವ.

ಅಪಕಾರ apakāra, *s.* An unkindness, ill-turn, injury. 2. malice, hatred.

ಅಪಕೀರ್ತಿ apakīrti, *s.* Reproach, disgrace, infamy.

ಅಪಗ apaga, *adv.* Then; *also* ಅಪಗ.

ಅಪಚಾರ apaćāra, *s.* Impoliteness, insult. 2. fault.

ಅಪಜಯು apaǰaya, *s.* Defeat, overthrow, loss.

ಅಪದ್ಧ apaddha, *s.* A lie; *see* ಅಬದ್ಧ.

ಅಪನಂಬಿಗೆ apanambigĕ, *s.* Unbelief, distrust. 2. disbelief.

ಅಪಮಾನ apamāna, *s.* Disrespect. 2. disgrace. —ಮಳ್ಪುನಿ to disgrace.

ಅಪರ apara, *adj.* Other, opposite, latter. —ಕ್ರಿಯೆ funeral rites.

ಅಪರಾಂನ, ಅಪರಾಹನ aparānna, aparāhana, *s.* Afternoon.

ಅಪರಾಧ aparādha, *s.* Offence, guilt. 2. a punishment, fine. —ಕೊರ್ಪಿನಿ to pay a fine. —ತುಂಬಾವುನಿ, —ಪಾಡುನಿ to accuse of a crime, to condemn. —ಮಳ್ಪುನಿ to commit an offence, to transgress; to fine.

ಅಪರಿಮಿತ aparimita, *adj.* Unmeasured, boundless, infinite.

ಅಪರೂಪ, ಅಪ್ರೂಪ aparūpa, aprūpa, *adj.* Rare, uncommon. 2. scarce. *adv.* Seldom, rarely.

ಅಪವಾದ apavāda, *s.* Censure, blame. 2. a false accusation. 3. exception (to a rule).

ಅಪವಿತ್ರ apavitra, *adj.* Unclean, impure.

ಅಪಶಕುನ apaśakuna, *s.* A bad omen.

ಅಪಶಬ್ದ apaśabda, *s.* Ungrammatical language, a vulgar expression. 2. bad pronunciation.

ಅಪಸಾಕ್ಷಿ apasākši, *s.* False witness, perjury. 2. a false witness.

ಅಪಸ್ವರ apasvara, *s.* A discordant sound, hoarse voice.

ಅಪಸ್ಮಾರ apasmāra, *s.* Convulsions, epilepsy.

ಅಪಹರಿಪುನಿ apaharipuni (ಅಪಹರಿ), *v. a.* To take by violence, to usurp, plunder, rob, extort.

ಅಪಹಾರ apahāra, *s.* Usurpation, robbery.

ಅಪಹಾಸ್ಯ apahāsya, *s.* Derision, irony.

ಅಪಾತ್ರ apātra, *adj.* Unworthy, undeserving, unfit. ಅಪಾತ್ರೆ an unworthy person.

ಅಪಾಯು apāya, *s.* Danger, peril. 2. misfortune, calamity.

ಅಪಾರ apāra, *adj.* Boundless, infinite.

ಅಪೀಮು apīmu, *see* ಅಫೀಮು.

ಅಪೀಲ್ apīlụ, *s.* An appeal.

ಅಪೂಟು apūṭu, *adj.* Quite, entire, whole.

ಅಪೂರ್ವ apūrva, *adj.* Unprecedented, uncommon.

ಅಪೇಕ್ಷೆ apēkshè, *s.* Wish, desire. 2. expectation, hope. –ಮಳ್ಪುನಿ, ಅಪೇಕ್ಷಿಪುನಿ to desire, wish, request.

ಅಪ್ರೋಲಿ apōli, *s.* Ruin, waste.

ಅಪ್ಪ appa, *int.* of surprise: ದಾನೆ ಅಪ್ಪ what may it be! 2. a mode of calling a mother.

ಅಪ್ಪ appa, an affix of respect added to proper names of men, *as* ತಿಮ್ಮಪ್ಪ, ನಾಗಪ್ಪ, ಬಸಪ್ಪ, ಮುಂಡಪ್ಪ, *etc.*

ಅಪ್ಪ appa, *s.* A kind of cake fried *or* baked.

ಅಪ್ಪಂತಾಯೆ, ಅಪ್ಪಂತೆ appantāye, appante, *s.* An honest, respectable man, a good man.

ಅಪ್ಪಂತಿಗೆ appantigè, *s.* Honesty, fidelity, chastity,

ಅಪ್ಪಡ appaḍa, *see* ಅಪ್ಪಳ.

ಅಪ್ಪಣೆ appaṇè, *s.* Command, order. 2. permission, leave. –ಕೊರ್ಪಿನಿ to command, give order, permit. –ದೆತ್ತೊಣುನಿ to take leave.

ಅಪ್ಪಪ್ಪಾ appappā, *int.* of surprise, sorrow.

ಅಪ್ಪಳ appaḷa, *s.* A very thin round [cake.

ಅಪ್ಪಳಿಪುನಿ appaḷipuni (ಅಪ್ಪಳ), *v. a.* To strike anything with the open hand, to squash.

ಅಪ್ಪಿಯುನಿ appiyuni (ಅಪ್ಪು), *v. a.* To embrace, clasp; *also* ಅಪ್ಪಿದ ಪತ್ತುನಿ.

ಅಪ್ಪುಕೈ, ಅಪ್ಪೈ appukei, appei, *s.* Folding the arms on the breast. –ಪತ್ತುನಿ, –ತೊಟ್ಟುನಿ to cross *or* fold the arms on the breast.

ಅಪ್ಪೆ appè, *s.* Mother. 2. an affix of respect added to proper names of men (*as* ನಾಗಪ್ಪೆ *etc.*); *cf.* ಅಪ್ಪ.

ಅಪ್ಪೊ, ಅಪ್ಪೋಡೆ appo, appōḍè, *s.* A cake made for the performance of funeral rites.

ಅಪ್ರಕಾಶ aprakāša, Absence of light, darkness. 2. obscurity, 3. secrecy.

ಅಪ್ರಮೇಯೆ aprameye, *s.* God, the Incomprehensible.

ಅಪ್ರಯೋಜನ aprayōjana, *s.* Uselessness, unserviceableness.

ಅಪ್ರೋಜಿಗೆ aprōjigè, *s.* A bad man.

ಅಫೀಮು, ಅಫೀನಿ aphīmu, aphīni, *s.* Opium.

ಅಬ aba, *int.* of astonishment.

ಅಬಡ್ abaḍu, *s.* Hoof; *also* ಕಾರಬಡ್. –ಕಾರ್ದಾಯೆ a person with a cleft foot (a kind of deformity).

ಅಬಡೆ abaḍè, *s.* A kind of bean.

ಅಬದ್ಧ abaddha, *adj.* False, incorrect, wrong. –ಪಾತೆರ a false word. –ವರ್ತಮಾನ false news *or* rumours.

ಅಬರ abara, *s.* The stern of a ship.

ಅಬರೆ abarè, *s.* A common country bean, *Lablab vulgaris.*

ಅಬಲ abala, *adj.* Weak, impotent.

ಅಬಲೆ abale, *s.* A weak *or* impotent man.

ಅಬಿಂಡಿಗೆ **abiṇḍigè**, *s.* Perplexity. 2. obstinacy.

ಅಬಿಲಾಸೆ **abilāsè**, *see* ಅಭಿಲಾಷೆ.

ಅಬುರು **aburu**, *s.* Character, respectability, keen feeling of honour; *cf.* ಅಭುರು, ಆಬುರು. —ದಾಯೆ a respectable man. —ದೆಪ್ಪುನಿ to dishonour, rebuke. ನಿನ ಅಬುರು ದಾಯೆಗ್ why are you so overbearing? ಬೇಅಬುರು disrespect, dishonour.

ಅಬುರೋಣಿ **aburōṇi**, *s.* A kind of fish. 2. *see* ಅಬ್ರೋಣಿ.

ಅಬೆಪುನಿ, ಅಬೆಯುನಿ **abepuni, abeyuni** (ಅಬೆ), *v. a.* To beat or pound rice; *also* ಅಬೆಜ್ಜುನಿ. ಅಬೆಯಿ ಅರಿ, ಅಬೆತ್ತಿ ಅರಿ rice well cleared of its husk.

ಅಬೇಸ್ **abēsụ**, *int.* Lift up! pull! an intimation that anything is ready to be lifted up, *e. g.* a basket *or* a bucket from a well *etc.*

ಅಬ್ಬ, ಅಬ್ಬಬ್ಬ, ಅಬ್ಬೋ **abba, abbabba, abbō**, *int.* expressing wonder *or* grief.

ಅಬ್ಬಗೆದಾರಗೆ **abbagedāragè**, *s.* The proper names of female demon twins.

ಅಬ್ಬರ, ಅಬ್ಬರಣೆ **abbara, abbaraṇè**, *s.* Boast, ostentation. 2. sound, noise, cry. —ಮಳ್ಪುನಿ, —ಕುಟ್ಟುನಿ, ಅಬ್ಬರಿಪುನಿ to cry aloud, make noise; to frighten; to boast.

ಅಬ್ಬಲಿಗೆ (ಪೂ) **abbaligè (pū)**, *s.* A kind of flower.

ಅಬ್ಬೆ **abbè**, *s.* An elderly woman, matron.

ಅಬ್ಬೇಸ **abbēsa**, *s.* Study, practice, exercise. 2. familiarity; *fr.* ಅಭ್ಯಾಸ.

ಅಬ್ರೋಣಿ ದೈ **abrōṇi dei**, *s.* A kind of shrub, *Grewia microcos; also* ಅಬುರೋಣಿ.

ಅಭಯ **abhaya**, *s.* Security. 2. promise of protection *or* pardon. 3. confidence.

ಅಭಾವ **abhāva**, *s.* Non-existence. 2. annihilation. 3. a negative (*gram.*).

ಅಭಾಸ **abhāsa**, *adj.* Worthless, vulgar. 2. corrupt; *fr.* ಆಭಾಸ.

ಅಭಿಜನ **abhijana**, *s.* A family, race.

ಅಭಿನ **abhina**, *s.* Mimicry. 2. gesture; *also* ಅಭಿನಯ.

ಅಭಿನೆ **abhine**, *s.* A mimic.

ಅಭಿಪ್ರಾಯ **abhiprāya**, *s.* Design, intention. 2. wish. 3. opinion.

ಅಭಿಮಾನ **abhimāna**, *s.* A keen feeling of honour, pride. 2. regard, affection.

ಅಭಿಲಾಷೆ **abhilāshè**, *s.* Desire, wish, inclination.

ಅಭಿವೃದ್ಧಿ **abhivṛddhi**, *s.* Increase, prosperity. 2. progress, thriving, improvement.

ಅಭಿಷೇಕ **abhishēka**, *s.* Sprinkling with water. 2. consecration by pouring oil, ghee *etc.* 3. unction. ಪಟ್ಟಾಭಿಷೇಕ, ರಾಜಾಭಿಷೇಕ the coronation of a king; ಗುರುಅಭಿಷೇಕ the ordination of a priest. —ಮಳ್ಪುನಿ to anoint, ordain, install.

ಅಭುರು abhuru, *see* ಅಬುರು.

ಅಭ್ಯಂತರ abhyantara, *s.* An interval. 2. delay, vexation. 3. obstacle. 4. offence, scandal. —ಆಪಿನಿ to be an impediment, to be delayed. —ಕೊರ್ಪಿನಿ, —ಮಳ್ಪುನಿ to hinder, object, offend, vex.

ಅಭ್ಯಾಸ abhyāsa, *see* ಅಬ್ಬೇಸ.

ಅಮುಕೆ amakė, *s.* A tendril; 2. a fork.

ಅಮಣಿ, ಅಮನಿ, amaṇi, amani, *s.* A nipple; *also* ಉಮನಿ.

ಅಮುಪುನಿ amapuni, *v. a.* To quiet, press down; *see* ಅಮೆಪುನಿ.

ಅಮರ್ amarụ, *adj.* Twin. 2. double. —ಬಾಳೆಲು twin children.

ಅಮರ amara, *adj.* Immortal. *s.* A deity. 2. an immortal. —ತ್ವ immortality. —ಲೋಕ heaven.

ಅಮರಕೋಶ amarakōśa, *s.* The name of a Sanskrit dictionary of synonyms.

ಅಮರಾವುನಿ amarāvuni (ಅಮರಾ), *v. a.* To push forward. 2. to hold fast.

ಅಮರಿಗೆ amarigė, *s.* A heap; *also* ಯೆಮರಿಗೆ. —ಪಾಡುನಿ to heap up.

ಅಮರಿಯಾದಿ amariyādi, *s.* Disrespect, incivility, dishonour. *adj.* Disrespectful.

ಅಮರಿಯುನಿ, ಅಮರ್ಯುನಿ amariyuni, amaryuni (ಅಮರ್), *v. n.* To aggress. 2. to cleave to.

ಅಮರುನಿ amaruni (ಅಮರ್), *v. n.* To become quiet, calm. *v. a.* To settle, seize, touch, hold.

ಅಮರೆ amarė, *s.* A ditch, canal. —ಶೀಪಿನಿ to make a ditch, dike.

ಅಮರ್ತ amarta, *see* ಅಮೃತ.

ಅಮರ್ಸಾವುನಿ amarsāvuni (ಅಮರ್ಸಾ), *v. a.* To frighten.

ಅಮರ್ಸಿಲ, ಅಮರ್ಸಾಲ amarsila, amarsāla, *s.* Brimstone.

ಅಮಲ್ amalụ, *s.* Intoxication, drunkenness, giddiness. —ಕೋರೆ, —ದಾಯೆ a drunkard. —ಪತ್ತುನಿ, —ಯೇರುನಿ to be intoxicated. —ಮಳ್ಪುನಿ to intoxicate.

ಅಮಸಣಿ amasaṇi, *see* ಅಮುಸಣಿ.

ಅಮಸರ amasara, *s.* Necessity. 2. urgency. 3. hurry *cf.* ಅವಸರ. —ಮಳ್ಪುನಿ to hasten, be in a hurry.

ಅಮಾನತ್ amānatụ, *s.* Deposit. 2. suspension. —ಮಳ್ಪುನಿ to suspend.

ಅಮಾರಿಗೆ amārigė, *s.* A trunk.

ಅಮಾರುನಿ amāruni (ಅಮಾರ್), *v. a.* To suit, fit. 2. to embrace, hold. 3. a plant to twine.

ಅಮಾಸೆ, ಅಮಾವಾಸೆ amāsė, amāvāsė, *s.* The day of the new moon.

ಅಮಿತ amita, *adj.* Immeasurable, boundless, infinite.

ಅಮಿನೆ amīne, *s.* A sheriff's officer; *see* ಆಮಿನೆ.

ಅಮುಸಣಿ amusaṇi, *s.* Pride, arrogance, insolence, haughtiness. —ತೋಜಾವುನಿ to show pride. —ಮಳ್ಪುನಿ to be proud.

ಅಮೂಲ್ಯ amūlya, *adj.* Costly, invaluable.

ಅಮೃತ amrụta, *adj.* Immortal. *s.* Nectar, ambrosia. 2. different fluids as water, milk, palm-wine *etc.* —ಕಾಯಿ a custard-apple. —ಮರ *Anona squamosa,* the custard apple tree, —ಬೂರು *Cocculus cordifolius,* the heart-leaved moon-creeper —ಮಥನ the mythical churning of the sea for nectar. —ವಾಕ್ಯ sweet words *or* speech. —ತ್ವ, ಅಮೃತಿ immortality; *cf.* ಅಮರತ್ವ.

ಅಮೆ amè, *s.* Ceremonial impurity *or* defilement in case of birth.

ಅಮೆಪುನಿ, ಅಮತ್‌ಪತ್ತುನಿ amepuni, amatupattuni (ಅಮೆ), *v. a.* To press, hold in the arms, hug.

ಅಮೇಧ್ಯ amēdhya, *s.* Fæces, ordure.

ಅಮೋಗ amōga, *adj.* Precious, excellent. 2. fruitful.

ಅಮ್ಚಿಕಾಯಿ amćikāyi, *see* ಅಮೃತ ಕಾಯಿ.

ಅಮ್ಮ amma, *s.* A lady. 2. mother. 3. *gen. of* ಅಮ್ಮೆ.

ಅಮ್ಮುನಿ ammuni (ಅಮ್ಮು), *v. a.* To swallow, devour.

ಅಮ್ಮೆ amme, *see* ಅಂಮೆ.

ಅಮ್ಸನಿ amsani, *see* ಅಮುಸನಿ.

ಅಯ aya, *see* ಅಯ್ಯೆ. 2. good luck. 3. a tax.

ಅಯನ ayana, *s.* Going. 2. a path. 3. a half year, that is the course of the sun northward and southward—from solstice to solstice—each of six months.

ಅಯಿಂದಾ ayindā, *adv.* Hereafter, in future.

ಅಯಿಗುಳು ayiguḷu, *see* ಐಗುಳು.

ಅಯಿತ ayita, *s.* Readiness. 2. decoration; *also* ಐತ. —ಮಳ್ಪುನಿ to dress. —ಆಪಿನಿ to be dressed, adorned.

ಅಯಿನ್ ayinu, *see* ಐನ್.

ಅಯಿಬು ayibu, *see* ಐಬು.

ಅಯಿವಜಿ ayivaji, *see* ಐವಜಿ.

ಅಯುಕ್ತ ayukta, *adj.* Improper, unfit.

ಅಯುತ ayuta, *num.* Ten thousand, a myriad.

ಅಯೋಗ್ಯ ayōgya, *adj.* Unfit, unworthy disreputable. —ತೆ unfitness, unworthiness, disrepute.

ಅಯೋಧ್ಯ ayōdhya, *s.* The capital of Rāma, the modern Oude.

ಅಯ್ಯ ayya, *see* ಅಯ್ಯೆ.

ಅಯ್ಯಪ್ಪ ayyappa, *int.* of pain.

ಅಯ್ಯಳ ayyaḷa, *s.* Five seers.

ಅಯ್ಯೆ ayye, *s.* A priest, minister, teacher, master. *Voc.* ಅಯ್ಯ sir. *Plur.* ಅಯ್ಯೆರ್ gods, Brahmins; an affix of respect added to proper names; *see* ಅಪ್ಪ.

ಅಯ್ಯೆರ್ ayyeru, *see* ಐವೆರ್.

ಅಯ್ಯೆಲ್ ayyelu, *s.* Five pairs of oxen *or* buffaloes.

ಅಯ್ಯೋ ayyō, *int.* of grief. Oh, ah, alas, woe. When feeling annoyed, dear me. ಅಯ್ಯಯ್ಯೋ *int.* of grief, pain.

ಅರ ara, *s.* A file. —ತ ಪರು the teeth of a file. —ಪಾಡುನಿ to file, rasp. ಗುಂಡರ a round file.

ಅರಂಕಾವುನಿ arankāvuni, *see* ಅಲಂಕಾವುನಿ.

ಅರಂಟುನಿ araṇṭuni (ಅರಂಟ್), *v. a.* To grope for, grasp. 2. to seek, look for.

ಅರಂಟೆಲೆ araṇṭele, *s.* A greedy person, a miser.

ಅರಂತಡೆ arantaḍè, *s.* A royal residence; *cf.* ಅರಮನೆ.

ಅರಂತುನಿ arantuni (ಅರಂತ್), *v. n.* To feel, grope. 2. to grasp at.

ಅರಂಬುನಿ arambuni (ಅರಂಬ್), *v. a.* To touch. 2. to climb, creep up (plants); *also* ಅರುಂಬುನಿ.

ಅರಕ್ arakụ, *s.* Arrack, country spirit; *cf.* ಗಂಗಸರ, ರಾಕ.

ಅರಕ್ arakụ, *s.* Gum-lac, sealing-wax; ಕಡ್ಡಿ—, ಕೊಂಬು— stick-lac; ಕರಿ— black sealing-wax; ಕೆಂಪು— red sealing-wax; ಪೊಡಿ— seed-lac; ಬಿಲ್ಲೆ— shell-lac. —ದೀಪಿನಿ, —ಪಾಡುನಿ to seal, fasten with sealing-wax.

ಅರಕ್ arakụ, *s.* A fine, white cloth; *also* ಸೈನ್ ಅರಕ.

ಅರಕ್‌ತೇಳ್ arakụtēḷụ, *s.* A large black scorpion, scolopendra.

ಅರಕಲ್ arakalụ, *see* ಅರ್ಕಲ್.

ಅರಕೆ arakè, *adj.* Half filled (*opp. of* ನಿಲಿಕೆ full).

ಅರಖ್, ಅರಖು arakhụ, arakhu, *s.* Essence *or* spirit distilled from any thing; *cf.* ಅರಕ.

ಅರಗಣಿ aragaṇi, *s.* Kitchen furniture.

ಅರಗಿಣಿ aragiṇi, *s.* A talking parrot. 2. a neat *or* tidy woman.

ಅರಗೀಸ್ aragīsụ, *adv.* However, at any rate; *in connection with neg. verbs* by no means, never; ಆಯಿ ಅರಗೀಸ್ ಮಳ್ಪಯಿ he will never do it.

ಅರಗು aragu, *see* ಅರಕ.

ಅರಗುಂಡರ araguṇḍara, *s.* Ruin; *also* ಗುಂಡಾಂತರ.

ಅರಟುನಿ araṭuni (ಅರಟ್), *v. n.* To scramble, fumble. 2. to make a grating noise. 3. to interrupt, blab; *also* ಅಟುರ್ನಿ.

ಅರಟೆ araṭe, *s.* Prate, blabbing, tattle; *also* ಹರಟೆ.

ಅರಡುನಿ araḍuni (ಅರಡ್), *v. a.* To gather up, to grasp. 2. to rub.

ಅರಡೆಕಾಯಿ araḍèkāyi, *see* ಅಡ್ಡೆಕಾಯಿ.

ಅರಣೆ araṇe, *s.* The green lizard, *Lacerta interpunctuala*, said to be poisonous; ಅರಣೆ ತುಚ್ಚಂಡ ಮರಣ if a lizard bites death (is certain). —ಬೂರು a kind of creeper used in medicine. —ಮೀನ್ a kind of fish.

ಅರಣ್ಯ araṇya, *s.* A wilderness, forest. *adj.* Wild.

ಅರತಿ arati, *s.* Anger, passion; displeasure.

ಅರತೆ, ಅರದೆ aratè, aradè, *s.* Heat, burning. 2. impetuosity. —ಜಾಲೆ burning heat; ಅರತಂಡ ಜಾಲೆ ಅಲುರ್ನಿ to burn very much *or* exceedingly.

ಅರದಳ, ಅರದಾಲೆ aradaḷa, aradāle, *s.* Yellow arsenic *or* yellow orpiment. —ಮಣ್ಣ್ yellow ochre.

ಅರದೆರ್ araderụ, *s. pl.* A class of

Mohammedan merchants. 2. policemen, peons; *also* ಹರಡೆರ್.

ಅರನಾರಿ **aranāri,** *see* ಅರೆನಾರಿ.

ಅರಪು, ಅರಪೆಲ್ **arapu, arapelu̧,** *s.* Cooling.

ಅರಪುಚ್ಚೆ **arapuċċe,** *s.* The shoe-flower; *see* ದಾಸನ.

ಅರಪುನಿ **arapuni** (ಅರ), *v.n.* To cool, become calm; ಜಿಟ್ಟ ಅರಪುನಿ to become cool.

ಅರಪೆ **arapè,** *s.* A crack, split; *cf.* ಅರಿಪೆ.

ಅರಬರ ತಿನ್ಪಿನಿ **arabara tinpini,** *v.a.* To eat greedily, devour.

ಅರಬಾಯಿ, ಅರಬೈ **arabāyi, arabei,** *s.* Violent clamour, crying aloud, lamentation. –ಕೊರ್ಪಿನಿ, –ಪೋಪಿನಿ to cry out vehemently, to bawl out, lament. –ದ ಕತ್ತೆ a braying brawler, *vlg.*

ಅರಬಿ **arabi,** *s.* An Arab.

ಅರಬು **arabu,** *s.* Covetousness, desire, eagerness for gain.

ಅರಬೈ **arabei,** *see* ಅರೆಬೈ.

ಅರಮಡಲ್ **aramaḍalu̧,** *see* ಅರೆಮಡಲ್.

ಅರಮನೆ **aramane,** *s.* A palace, royal residence.

ಅರಲ್ **aralu̧,** *s.* Drizzling rain. –ಬೀಜುನಿ to drizzle.

ಅರಲುಣಿ **araluṇi,** *s.* The black bee.

ಅರಲುನಿ **araluni** (ಅರಲ್), *v. n.* To open, expand. 2. to bloom, blossom.

ಅರಲೋಲೆ **aralōle,** *s.* A tender palm-leaf. 2. a kind of ear-ornament.

ಅರವ **arava,** *s.* Tamil. –ಭಾಷೆ the Tamil language. –ದೇಶ the Tamil country.

ಅರವಂಟಿಗೆ, ಅರವಟಿಗೆ **aravanṭigè, aravaṭigè,** *s.* A shed where water is served gratuitously to travellers.

ಅರವಮಣಿ **aravamaṇi,** *s.* A kind of gem.

ಅರವಾಸಿ **aravāsi,** *see* ಅರೆವಾಸಿ.

ಅರವು **aravu,** *s.* Width, breadth. *adj.* Wide, open.

ಅರವುನಿ **aravuni** (ಅರ್), *v.a.* To heap up.

ಅರಸಿನಕುತ್ತ, ಅರಸಿನಮುಂಡ **arasinakutta, arasinamuṇḍa,** *s.* The jaundice.

ಅರಸು **arasu,** *s.* A king, monarch. –ಕುಲ a royal family. –ತನ royalty, kingship. –ಮಗೆ a king's son, royal prince.

ಅರಸುಕುತ್ತ **arasukutta,** *s.* A kind of dropsy.

ಅರಸುಕುರಿ **arasukuri,** *s.* A carbuncle; *also* ಬದೆಂಗಲ, ಭಗಂದಲ.

ಅರಸೆ **arase,** *see* ಅರಸು.

ಅರಳುನಿ **araḷuni,** *see* ಅರಲುನಿ.

ಅರಾಜಕ **arājaka,** *adj.* Kingless. *s.* Anarchy, confusion.

ಅರಾಬಿ **arābi,** *adj.* Broad, large, extensive. –ಇಲ್ಲ a very large house.

ಅರಾಮಿ **arāmi,** *adj.* Unlawful. 2. vicious, restive, *f.i.* a horse; *also* ಹರಾಮಿ.

ಅರಾವು **arāvu,** *see* ಅರವು.

ಅರಾವುನಿ **arāvuni** (ಅರಾ), *v.a.* To gather. 2. to embrace, clasp in the arms. ಅರಾದ್ ಪತ್ತುನಿ to embrace *or* receive with open arms.

ಅರಾಳ್ arāḷu (ಅರೆ-ಆಳ್), *s.* A person doing half a day's work. 2. half a day's wages.

ಅರಿ ari, *s.* An enemy.

ಅರಿ ari, *s.* Rice freed from husk. Some of the principal kinds of rice are: ಅಂಬಡೆ ಅರಿ, ಅಜಿಪ ಸಾಲೆ, ಉರ್ಪೆಲ್ ಅರಿ, ಕಜಿ ಅರಿ, ಕಯಮೆ, ಕಲಮೆದರಿ, ಕಾರ್ತಿದರಿ, ಕೊಳಕೆದರಿ, ಗಂದ ಸಾಲೆ, ಗುಡ್ಡುಬೊಲ್ಯರಿ, ಜೀರಿಸಾಲೆ, ದಡ್ಡ ಅರಿ, ಬೊಳಂತೆ ಅರಿ, ಬೈತರಿ, ಮಸ್ಕತ್ಯರಿ, ಯೇಣೆಲ್ದರಿ, ಸುಗ್ಗಿದರಿ, ಸೋಮಸಲೆ. 2. any small grain, *f. i.* ಸಾಮೆದರಿ. 3. the testicles.

ಅರಿಕಲ arikala, *s.* A place for husking rice; *also* ಬರಕಲ.

ಅರಿಕೆ arike, *s.* Consent. 2. confession. 3. request. —ಮಳ್ಪುನಿ to reveal, confess; to inform, represent; to request.

ಅರಿಗೀಸ್ arigīsu, *see* ಅರಗೀಸ್.

ಅರಿಜೋಳ arijōḷa, *s.* Indian corn, *Sorghum saccharatum.*

ಅರಿತಿ ariti, *see* ಅರ್ತಿ.

ಅರಿದಳ aridaḷa, *see* ಅರದಳ.

ಅರಿಪುನಿ aripuni (ಅರಿ), *v. a.* To sift. 2. to strain, filter.

ಅರಿಪೆ aripe, *s.* A sieve, colander, strainer; ಕಲ್ಲರಿಪೆ a leak (in an earthen vessel).

ಅರಿಯ ariya, *see* ಅರ್ಯ.

ಅರಿಯಂತ್ರ ariyantra, *see* ಅಳಿಯಂತರ.

ಅರಿಯುನಿ ariyuni, *see* ಅರ್ಯುನಿ.

ಅರಿವಾಣ arivāna, *s.* A metal dish; *also* ಹರಿವಾಣ.

ಅರಿವೆ arive, *see* ಅರ್ವೆ.

ಅರಿಷ್ಟ arishṭa, *s.* Misfortune, misery. *adj.* Unfortunate; impious.

ಅರಿಷ್ಟೆ arishṭe, *s.* An unfortunate man, a poor man, a person in distress.

ಅರು aru, *s.* Brim, edge, margin, border. —ಪತ್ತುನಿ to reach the shore, to land; to get out of a difficulty, to be successful; *cf.* ಅರುಗು.

ಅರುಂಬುನಿ arumbuni, *see* ಅರಂಬುನಿ.

ಅರುಗು arugu, *s.* Verge, brink, border, margin; *cf.* ಅರು.

ಅರುಚಿ aruči, *s.* Want of appetite.

ಅರುಣ aruṇa, *adj.* Purple-coloured. *s.* The name of the rising sun.

ಅರುಪು arupu, *see* ಅರುಹು.

ಅರುಬುದ arubuda, *see* ಅರ್ಬುದ.

ಅರುಮುಟ್ಟೆ arumuṭṭe, *s.* The gills of a fish.

ಅರುಮುರಿಯೊಡುನಿ arumuriyoḍuni (ಅರುಮುರಿಯೊಪ್), *v. n.* To weep with loud lamentation and shrieks.

ಅರುವೆ aruve, *s.* The mouth of a river, a seaport; *also* ಅಳುವೆ. —ದ ಬಾಕಿಲ್ a bar, the entrance to a harbour.

ಆರುವೆ aruve, *see* ಅರ್ವೆ.

ಅರುಹು aruhu, *s.* Knowledge. 2. understanding, perception.

ಅರುಳುಮರುಳು aruḷumaruḷu, *adj.* Foolish, simple, childish.

ಅರೂಪ, ಅರೂಪು arūpa, arūpu, *adj.* Formless, invisible. 2. deformed, ugly.

ಅರೆ are, *s.* Half, a moiety; *cf.* ಅರ್ಧ. –ಆಳ್ half a man's height.

ಅರೆಂಚುನಿ areṅcuni (ಅರೆಂಚ್), *v.a.* To rub off, peel, skin.

ಅರೆಂಜಾವುನಿ areñjāvuni, *c.v.* (*of* ಅರೆಂಜುನಿ), To cause to deny. 2. to hide away.

ಅರೆಂಜುನಿ areñjuni (ಅರೆಂಜ್), *v. a.* To deny, gainsay. 2. to conceal; *cf.* ಅಲೆಂಜುನಿ.

ಅರೆಂಜೆಲೆ areñjele, *s.* A denier, disowner.

ಅರೆಂಟೆಲೆ areṇṭele, *see* ಅರಂಟಿಲೆ.

ಅರೆಕಣ್ಣ್ arekaṇṇu, *s.* A half sight, an imperfect glance. 2. squint eyes. 3. eyes partly closed.

ಅರೆಕಾಣಿ arekāṇi, *s.* The hundred and twenty-eighth part of any thing.

ಅರೆಕಾಯಿ arekāyi, *adj.* Half ripe; *also* ಕಸಗಾಯಿ.

ಅರೆಕಾಲ್ arekālu, *s.* The eighth [part.

ಅರೆಕೆ areke, *see* ಅರಕೆ.

ಅರೆಕೊದ್ಯೆಲ್ arekodyelu, *s.* Half salted *or* insufficiently seasoned dish.

ಅರೆಗಂಟ್ areganṭu, *s.* A loose knot; 2. half a load, a small bundle.

ಅರೆಗಾಲ aregāla, *s.* The hot season, summer.

ಅರೆಚಟ್ಟೆ arecaṭṭe, *adj.* Half dead. 2. reduced, thin, lean.

ಅರೆಚಪ್ಪೆ arecappe, *adj.* Tasteless, unsavoury.

ಅರೆಜಾತಿ arejāti, *adj.* Half-caste, mongrel, mixed.

ಅರೆಜೀವ arejīva, *s. lit.* Half the life; the state of being half dead.

ಅರೆಡುನಿ areḍuni (ಅರೆಡ್), *v. a.* To spoil, corrupt, mar, taint. 2. to destroy, ruin.

ಅರೆದಳ aredaḷa, *see* ಅರದಳ.

ಅರೆದುನಿ areduni (ಅರೆದ್), *v. n.* To low.

ಅರೆನಾರಿ arenāri, *s.* A person dressed partly as a male and partly as a female.

ಅರೆನಾಲಾಯಿ arenālāyi, *s.* A stammering tongue.

ಅರೆನಿರೆಲ್ arenirelu, *s.* A slight shadow. 2. an imperfect shade.

ಅರೆಪಾಲ್ arepālu, *s.* Half a share, half part; –ಗಾರೆ a partner *or* shareholder entitled to half a share.

ಅರೆಪಾವು arepāvu, *s.* One half of a quarter, one-eighth of a seer.

ಅರೆಪಾವುನಿ arepāvuni, *c. v.* (*of* ಅರೆಪಿನಿ), To cause to grind. 2. to cause to submit; to subdue.

ಅರೆಪಿನಿ, ಅರೆಪುನಿ arepini, arepuni (ಅರೆ), *v. a.* To pulverize by pounding *or* grinding. 2. *fg.* to oppress. ಅರೆಪ ಕಲ್ಲ್, ಅರೆಪು ಕಲ್ಲ್ a grinding stone.

ಅರೆಪು, ಅರೆಪೆಲ್ arepu, arepelu, *s.* The act of grinding. 2. that which is ground for condiment.

ಅರೆಬಂಜಿ arebañji, *lit.* Half the stomach. *adj.* Half fed, not satisfied, deficiently fed.

ಅರೆಬಂದ arebanda, *adj.* Half cooked.

ಅರೆಬಾಯಿ arebāyi, *see* ಅರಬಾಯಿ.

ಅರೆಬಿರೆಲ್ arebirelu̥, *lit.* Half a finger (measure). *s.* About half an inch.

ಅರೆಬೈ arebei, *s.* Twice thrashed straw.

ಅರೆಮಡಲ್ aremaḍalu̥, *s.* A leaf of a palmyra. 2. one half of a cocoa-palm-leaf.

ಅರೆಮನಸ್ aremanasu̥, *lit.* Half mindedness. *s.* Indecision. 2. reluctance.

ಅರೆಮರ್ಲ್ aremarlu̥, *s.* Craziness, weakness of intellect. *adj.* Half mad.

ಅರೆಮಾಪಲ aremāpala, *s.* A small wild fruit, *Randia longispina.*

ಅರೆಮುಂಡೆ aremuṇḍe, *s.* A widow, whose head has not been shaved.

ಅರೆಮೆಯಿ aremeyi, *adj.* Reduced in body, lean, thin. 2. half inclined, half minded.

ಅರೆವಾಶಿ arevāši, *s.* A half part, a moiety.

ಅರೆಯಾಳ್ areyāḷ, *s.* An honorary name given to a section of the Bant caste.

ಅರೆಯುನಿ, ಅರೆವುನಿ areyuni, arevuni, *see* ಅರೆಪಿನಿ.

ಅರ್ಕ arka, *s.* The sun. 2. a crystal. 3. a shrub, called also the yakkamāle (ಯಕ್ಕಮಾಲೆ).

ಅರ್ಕಂಜಿ arkañji, *s.* Swill, dishwater, the washings of rice *etc.* —ತಪ್ಪು different kinds of leaves chopped and mixed with straw and boiled in a swill for feeding cattle with.

ಅರ್ಕತಿ arkati, *see* ಹರ್ಕತಿ.

ಅರ್ಕಡೆ arkaḍe, *s.* Sunset.

ಅರ್ಕಮೆ arkame, *s.* A strong desire, eagerness. 2. indigestion, flatulency.

ಅರ್ಕರ್ಕ arkarka, *adv.* By degrees. —ತಿನ್ಪುನಿ to eat repeatedly. 2. to gulp down.

ಅರ್ಕಲ್, ಅರ್ಕಳ್ arkalu̥, arkaḷu̥, *s.* A knot, tie. —ಪಾಡುನಿ to tie, make a knot. —ಗಿಡ್ಪುನಿ to loosen a knot, to untie.

ಅರ್ಕಿಲ್, ಅರ್ಕೆಲ್ arkilu̥, arkelu̥, *s.* A handful. ಒಂಜಿ ಅರ್ಕಿಲ್ ಬೈ ಕೊರ್ಲ give (me) a handful of straw.

ಅರ್ಕುನಿ arkuni (ಅರ್ಕ), *v. n.* To become less. 2. to be humbled, depressed.

ಅರ್ಕೆ arkè, *see* ಅರಕೆ.

ಅರ್ಕೆಬೂರು arkebūru, *see* ಅಡಿಕೆ ಬೂರು.

ಅರ್ಗಂಟ್ argaṇṭu̥, *s.* Determination, resolution. 2. obstinacy; 3. malice. —ದಾಯೆ an obstinate man. —ಮಳ್ಪುನಿ to persevere in obstinacy.

ಅರ್ಗಂಟೆ argaṇṭe, *s.* A resolute *or* obstinate person.

ಅರ್ಗಿಲಿಯುನಿ, ಅರ್ಗಿಲ್ಯುನಿ **argiliyuni, argilyuni** (ಅರ್ಗಿಲಿ. ಅರ್ಗಿಲ್), *v. n.* To loathe, be disgusted. ಅರ್ಗಿಲ್ದ್ ತಿನ್ಪುನಿ to eat with aversion.

ಅರ್ಗೀಸ್ **argīsu,** *see* ಅರಗೀಸ್.

ಅರ್ಗುಲೆ **argule,** *s.* Loathsomeness. 2. disgust, aversion.

ಅರ್ಗೆ **argè,** *see* ಅರಿಗೆ.

ಅರ್ಚಕೆ **arćake,** *s.* A worshipper. 2. a priest.

ಅರ್ಚನೆ **arćane,** *s.* Worship, adoration.

ಅರ್ಚಿಪುನಿ **arćipuni,** *v. a.* To worship. *v. n.* To officiate as a priest.

ಅರ್ಜಿ **arji,** *s.* Petition, representation; complaint. —ದಾರೆ a petitioner. —ಕೊರ್ಪುನಿ to present a petition; ಅರ್ಜಿ ಕೊರಂಡ ಮರ್ಜಿ ತಿಕ್ಕು when the petition is presented it will be favourably considered.

ಅರ್ಜಿತ **arjita,** *see* ಆರ್ಜಿತ.

ಅರ್ಜುನೆ **arjune,** *s.* The third son of Pāṇḍu (ಪಾಂಡು).

ಅರ್ಟುನಿ **arṭuni,** *see* ಅರಟುನಿ.

ಅರ್ಡುನಿ **arḍuni,** *see* ಅರಡುನಿ.

ಅರ್ತ **arta,** *see* ಅರ್ಥ.

ಅರ್ತಿ **arti,** *s.* An amusement, sport, fun. 2. novelty, curiosity. 3. fondness. —ದಾಯೆ a merry man, a person given to pleasure. —ಪಡೆಪಾವುನಿ to please, amuse; to fondle.

ಅರ್ತಿ **arti,** *s.* The wild fig tree, *Ficus racemosa.* —ಕಾಯಿ an unripe wild fig.

ಅರ್ಥ **artha,** *s.* Gain, wealth, riches, *esp.* money. 2. meaning. —ಪನ್ಪುನಿ to explain, interpret.

ಅರ್ದಳ **ardaḷa,** *see* ಅರದಳ.

ಅರ್ದಾಯ **ardāya,** *s.* Half the gain.

ಅರ್ದುನಿ **arduni** (ಅರ್ದ್), *v. a.* To wash *or* bleach clothes.

ಅರ್ಧ **ardha,** *s.* Half, a moiety; *cf.* ಅರೆ.

ಅರ್ಧಾಂಶ **ardhāṁśa,** *s.* A half portion.

ಅರ್ನಣ, ಅರ್ನನ **arnaṇa, arnana,** *s.* A male Pariah (*also* ಅಂದರ್ಣ).

ಅರ್ಪಡ **arpaḍa,** *s.* Small-pox; *also* —ರೋಗ. —ದ ಕಲೆ a pock-mark. ಕಲ್ಲರ್ಪಡ a kind of small-pox which leaves scars *or* marks.

ಅರ್ಪಣೆ **arpaṇe,** *s.* An offering. —ಮಳ್ಪುನಿ to offer.

ಅರ್ಪಾಟ **arpāṭa,** *s.* Lamentation.

ಅರ್ಪಿತ **arpita,** *adj.* Presented, offered.

ಅರ್ಪಿನಿ **arpini** (ಅರ್), *v. n.* To weep, cry.

ಅರ್ಪಿಪುನಿ, ಅರ್ಪಿಸುನಿ **arpipuni, arpisuni** (ಅರ್ಪಿ, ಅರ್ಪಿಸ್), *v. a.* To dedicate, offer.

ಅರ್ಪುನಿ **arpuni** (ಅರ್), *v. a.* To efface, waste, obliterate; *cf.* ದರ್ಪುನಿ.

ಅರ್ಪೆಲೆ **arpele,** *s.* A fretful person. 2. one easily moved to tears.

ಅರ್ಪೇಸಿ **arpēsi,** *see* ಅಲ್ಪೇಸಿ.

ಅರ್ಬಟ **arbaṭa,** *see* ಆರ್ಭಟ.

ಅರ್ಬಾಯಿ **arbāyi,** *see* ಅರಬಾಯಿ.

ಅರ್ಬಿ **arbi,** *s.* Water collected in an elevated place. 2. drizzling rain. —ಶೀತುನಿ water to fall in broken streams over a small height. —ಶೀಂತುನಿ water to run out, to fall in broken streams.

ಅಬ್ರುF arbu, *s.* Stinginess, avarice. —ಕುಟ್ಟುನಿ to covet, desire, long. —ದಾಯೆ a greedy man.

ಅಬ್ರುFತ, ಅಬ್ರುFದ **arbuta, arbuda,** *see* ಅದ್ಭುತ.

ಅಬ್ರುFದ **arbuda,** *num.* Ten crores, 100 millions.

ಅಬ್ರುFದರೋಗ **arbudarōga,** *s.* Different swellings, especially cancer.

ಅಮ್ಬ್ರುFಡೆ **armbuḍe,** *s.* A skull-cap made of the spathe *or* capsular bark of the areca palm and worn by a class of Pariahs (called ಮುಗ್ಗೆರ್ಲು).

ಅಯ್ರF **arya,** *s.* A small earthen vessel; ಯೆಂಣೆದಯ್ರF an oil-pot.

ಅಯ್ರFನ **aryana,** *see* ಹರಿವಾಣ.

ಅಯ್ರುFನಿ **aryuni** (ಅರ್), *v. n.* To ooze, drip. 2. to flow, run, as water; *also* ಹರಿಯುನಿ.

ಅರ್ಲ್Fಮರ್ಲ್F **arlụmarlụ,** *see* ಅರುಳು ಮರುಳು.

ಅಲ್ರF **arla,** *s.* Half a seer.

ಅಲ್ರುFನಿ **arluni** (ಅರ್ಲ್F), *v. n.* To burn, blaze. 2. to smart; ಆಯ ಮೋಣೆ ಅಲ್ರುFಂಡು *lit.* his face is burning, *i. e.* he is very angry.

ಅಲ್ರೋFಲೆ **arlōlè,** *s.* A kind of fish.

ಅವ್ರFತ್ತೆ, ಅವ್ರFದೆ **arvatte, arvade,** *s.* A man's sister's son. 2. a son-in-law.

ಅವ್ರೆF **arve,** *s.* A cloth; an old rag. ಕುಂಟುದವ್ರೆF a piece of garment.

ಅವ್ರೆF **arve,** *see* ಅರುವೆ, ಅಳುವೆ.

ಅಸ್ರFಂಡೆ **arsaṇḍè,** *s.* Rejection; disrespect; making light of.

ಅಸ್ರFಯ, ಅಸ್ರಾFಯ **arsaya, arsāya,** *s.* A certain festivity *or* ceremony. ಗೆಂಡಸ್ರFಯ the ceremony of leaping over burning coals, performed by devil-dancers *or* dāsaiyas (ದಾಸಯ್ಯ).

ಅಸ್ರಾFವುನಿ **arsāvuni,** *see* ಆಸ್ರಾFವುನಿ.

ಅಸ್ರೇFವೆ **arsēve,** *see* ಅಸ್ರFಯ.

ಅಲ್ಂಬುಡ, ಅಲ್ಂಬುಡೆ **alụmbuḍa, alụmbuḍe,** *s.* The castor-oil plant. ಕಿನ್ನಲ್ಂಬುಡೆ a smaller kind, called *Ricinus communis.*

ಅಲ್ಂಬೆ **alụmbe,** *s.* Suffering. 2. experience.

ಅಲ್ಂಬೇವುನಿ **alụmbēvuni,** *see* ಅಲ್ಂಭವಿಪುನಿ.

ಅಲ್ಂಭವ **alụmbhava,** *s.* Satisfaction, contentment. 2. experience, knowledge; *see* ಅನುಭವ.

ಅಲ್ಂಭವಿಪುನಿ **alụmbhavipuni** (ಅಲ್ಂಭವಿ), *v. n.* To feel satisfied, content. 2. to experience, enjoy, suffer, to be vexed.

ಅಲ್ಕ್ **alụkụ,** *see* ಅಲ್ಕ್.

ಅಲ್ಗ್ **alụgụ,** *see* ಅಲಗ್.

ಅಲ್ಗೆ **alụge,** *s.* A kind of drum.

ಅಲ್ಪುಚ್ಚೆ **alụpuččе,** *s.* A pole-cat.

ಅಲ್ಬೆ **alụbe,** *a.* Frail, fragile. 2. weak, puny, thin.

ಅಲಂಕ್ alaṅkụ, *s.* An armadillo. 2. a kind of fish.

ಅಲಂಕ್ alaṅkụ, *s.* The dried oil-plant of *Sesamum Indicum* or jinjili seed.

ಅಲಂಕರಿಪುನಿ alaṅkaripuni (ಅಲಂಕರಿ), *v.a.* To adorn, decorate.

ಅಲಂಕಾರ alaṅkāra, *s.* Ornament, decoration. 2. beauty. –ಶಾಸ್ತ್ರ rhetoric.

ಅಲಂಕಾವುನಿ alaṅkāvuni, *c. v.* (*of* ಅಲಂಕುನಿ), To cause to shake, to shake. 2. to perturb, confuse.

ಅಲಂಕುನಿ, ಅಲಂಗುನಿ alaṅkuni, alaṅguni (ಅಲಂಕ್, ಅಲಂಗ್), *v. a.* To shake, agitate, wave, move. 2. to strike *or* knock against, trip up. *v.n.* Be agitated. ಅಲಂಕ್ ನೀರ್ agitated water.

ಅಲಂಗ alaṅga, *s.* A rampart.

ಅಲಂಟುನಿ alaṇṭuni, *see* ಅರಂಟುನಿ.

ಅಲಂಬುಡ alambuḍa, *see* ಅಲಿಂಬುಡ.

ಅಲಂಬುನಿ alambuni (ಅಲಂಬ್), *v. a.* To wash. 2. to shake, be agitated as water; *see* ಲುಂಬುನಿ.

ಅಲಂಭವ alambhava, *see* ಅಲಿಂಭವ.

ಅಲಕ alaka, *s.* The town of Kubēra, the god of wealth. –ಆಪಿನಿ to become wealthy.

ಅಲಗ್, ಅಲಗು alagụ, alagu, *s.* Tremulousness *or* quivering of the voice in singing. –ಸ್ವರ a tremulous voice.

ಅಲಗುನಿ alaguni (ಅಲಗ್), *v. n.* To shake; *cf.* ಅಲಂಕುನಿ.

ಅಲಗೆ alage, *see* ಅಲಿಗೆ.

ಅಲಚುನಿ alačuni (ಅಲಚ್), *v. n.* To move, shake; *cf.* ಅಲಸುನಿ.

ಅಲಜಾವುನಿ alajāvuni, *c. v.* (*of* ಅಲಜುನಿ), To shake; *see* ಅಲೆಜಾವುನಿ.

ಅಲಜುನಿ alajuni, *see* ಅಲಸುನಿ.

ಅಲಪಯಿ alapayi, *s.* Hiring cattle for milking. –ಗೆಪ್ಪುನಿ to take milch cattle on hire. –ಕೊರ್ಪುನಿ to hire out milch cattle.

ಅಲಪುನಿ alapuni *see* ಅಳಪುನಿ, ಲಪ್ಪುನಿ.

ಅಲಮ alama, *see* ಅಲ್ಮ.

ಅಲಮುನಿ alamuni (ಅಲಮ್), *v. a.* To mix with the hand.

ಅಲರುನಿ alaruni, *see* ಅರಲುನಿ.

ಅಲವು alavu, Steel. –ದ ಗಟ್ಟಿ a bar of steel.

ಅಲವುನಿ alavuni (ಅಲ), *v. a.* To mix. 2. to temper. 3. to make even, to level.

ಅಲಸ್ alasụ, *adj.* Old, worn out. 2. bad. 3. mixed; *also* ಹಲಸ್.

ಅಲಸ್‌ಬಲ್ಲ್ alasụballụ, *s.* A thick rope, cable; *see* ಅಲಾತ.

ಅಲಸ alasa, *see* ಆಲಸ್ಯ.

ಅಲಸಲ್, ಅಲಸಿಗೆ alasalụ, alasige, *s.* Fatigue, weariness. 2. vexation.

ಅಲಸುನಿ alasuni (ಅಲಸ್), *v. a.* To agitate, shake. *v. n.* To be fatigued, vexed. 2. to suffer griping pain; ಯೆಂಕ್ ಬಂಜಿ ಅಲಸುಂಡು I have a stomach-ache.

ಅಲಕ್ಷಣ alakshaṇa, *see* ಅವಲಕ್ಷಣ.

ಅಲಕ್ಷ್ಯ, ಅಲಕ್ಷೆ alakshya, alakshe, *s.* Disregard, negligence, indifference.

ಅಲಾ alā, *int.* Behold, lo, there it is; *see* ಎಲಾ.

ಅಲಾಕ್ alāku, *s.* Destruction, ruin; *see* ಹಲಾಕ. —ಮಳ್ಪುನಿ to ruin, spoil, destroy. —ಆದ್ ಪೋಪಿನಿ to go to ruin.

ಅಲಾತ, ಅಲಾದ್ alāta, alādu, *s.* A thick coir-rope, cable; *also* ಅಲಸ್, ಆಲಾತ್.

ಅಲಾಬಿ, ಅಲಾಯಿ alābi, alāyi, *s.* The annual Moharam festival of the Mohammedans. —ಮೀಪಿನಿ to close the festival with bathing.

ಅಲಾಯುನಿ alāyuni (ಅಲಾ) *v. a.* To take away.

ಅಲಾವುನಿ alāvuni, *see* ಅಲವುನಿ.

ಅಲಿಕಿ aliki, *adj.* Inferior, low, mean; *bet.* ಹಲ್ಕ. —ಮಳ್ಪುನಿ to depreciate, disparage, degrade. —ಪಾತೆರ a word of contempt. —ಜನ low people.

ಅಲಿಗೆ alige, *see* ಅಲ್ಗೆ.

ಅಲಿಗೆ alige, *see* ಅಲ್ಲಿ.

ಅಲಿಪುನಿ alipuni, *see* ಅಳಿಪುನಿ.

ಅಲಿಮರ್, ಅಲಿಮಾರ್ alimaru, alimāru, *s.* The tree called *Memecylon.*

ಅಲಿಯುನಿ aliyuni (ಅಲಿ), *v. n.* To dissolve, decay. 2. to perish, die, become extinct; *also* ಅಲಿದ್ಪೋಪಿನಿ.

ಅಲಿವು alivu, *s.* Extinction, ruin.

ಅಲುಂಗುನಿ aluṅguni (ಅಲುಂಗ್), *v. n.* To be soft, as a ripe fruit.

ಅಲುಂಬುಡ alumbuḍa, *see* ಅಲ್ಂಬುಡ.

ಅಲುಂಬುನಿ alumbuni, *see* ಲುಂಬುನಿ.

ಅಲುಗುನಿ aluguni (ಅಲುಗ್), *v. n.* To move; *see* ಅಲಂಕುನಿ.

ಅಲುಬಂಗ alubaṅga, *s.* Vexation, trouble.

ಅಲೆ alè, *s.* Butter-milk; *see* ಅಳೆ. —ತುಲಿಪುನಿ to churn butter-milk.

ಅಲೆ, ಅಲೇ ale, alē, *int.* Behold, lo!

ಅಲೆಂಜಿ aleñji, *s.* Grease *or* oil *etc.* swimming on the surface of water. —ಪತ್ತುನಿ greasy substances to stick to something.

ಅಲೆಂಜುನಿ aleñjuni (ಅಲೆಂಜ್), *v. n.* To turn. ಬಾಯಿ— to hesitate in speaking. 2. to deny; *see* ಅರೆಂಜುನಿ.

ಅಲೆಜಾವುನಿ alejāvuni *c. v.* (*of* ಅಲೆಜುನಿ), To cause to shake, to shake. 2. to cause to mingle.

ಅಲೆಜುನಿ, ಅಲೆಜ್ಜುನಿ alejuni, alejjuni (ಅಲೆಜ್), *v. n.* To be agitated, disturbed. 2. to be turbid. 3. to mix, mingle. 4. to be united.

ಅಲೆಪಾಯಿ alepāyi, *see* ಅಲಪಯಿ.

ಅಲೆಪಾವುನಿ alepāvuni, *c. v.* (*of* ಅಲೆಪುನಿ), To cause to tire, to fatigue.

ಅಲೆಪುನಿ alepuni (ಅಲೆ), *v. a.* To oppress. *v. n.* To be fatigued; *see* ಅಲೆಯುನಿ, ತಲೆಪುನಿ, ಹಲೆಪುನಿ.

ಅಲೆಮಾನಿ alemāni, *s.* A European. 2. a German.

ಅಲೆಯುನಿ, ಅಲೆವುನಿ aleyuni, alevuni (ಅಲೆ), *v. n.* To wander, roam. 2. to be weary. 3. to bethink oneself. ಅಲೆದ್ ತೂಪಿನಿ to stare; *see* ಅಲೇವುನಿ.

ಅಲೇಕಿ, ಅಲೇಖ alēki, alēkha, *s.* An unwritten *or* blank leaf. 2. a blank book of palm leaves.

ಅಲೇವುನಿ alēvuni (ಅಲೇ), *v. n.* To bethink oneself; *see* ಅಲೆವುನಿ.

ಅಲ್ಕ್ alku, *s.* Timidity. *adj.* Timid, frightened; *also* ಹಲ್ಕ್. —ಬೂರುನಿ to shudder.

ಅಲ್ಕಿ alki, *see* ಅಲಿಕಿ, ಹಲ್ಕಿ.

ಅಲ್ಕುನಿ alkuni (ಅಲ್ಕ್), *v. n.* To be afraid. 2. to start, shudder, tremble. ಅಲ್ಕ್‌ದ್ ಬೂರುನಿ, —ಪೋಪಿನಿ to be startled.

ಅಲ್ಗಾವುನಿ algāvuni *c. v.* (*of* ಅಲ್ಗುನಿ), To cause to shake; *cf.* ಅಲಂಕಾವುನಿ.

ಅಲ್ಗುನಿ alguni, *see* ಅಲುಗುನಿ.

ಅಲ್ಡೆಕಾಯಿ aldekāyi, *s.* The gall-nut, ink-nut, *Terminalia chebula.* ಅಲ್ಡೆಮಶಿ a good black ink.

ಅಲ್ಪ alpa, *adj.* Little, small, trifling. 2. mean, low. —ಬುದ್ಧಿ of limited understanding; *cf.* ಅಲ್ಪ.

ಅಲ್ಪೀಸ್ alpīsu, *see* ಅಲ್ಪೇಸಿ.

ಅಲ್ಪುಚ್ಚೆ alpucce, *see* ಅಲ್‌ಪುಚ್ಚೆ.

ಅಲ್ಪೆ alpe, *s.* An unimportant man.

ಅಲ್ಪೇಸಿ alpēsi, *s.* A covetous man, miser. *adj.* Low, mean, stingy.

ಅಲ್ಬಂಗ್ albaṅgu, *see* ಅಲುಬಂಗ.

ಅಲ್ಬೆ albe, *adj.* Thin, weak, lean. 2. good for nothing.

ಅಲ್ಮ alma, *s.* Breed, offspring; ಯೆಡ್ಡೆ ಅಲ್ಮ a good breed.

ಅಲ್ಮಾನ almāna, *see* ಅನುಮಾನ.

ಅಲ್ಮೆ, ಅಲ್ಮೊ alme, almo, *s.* A salutation given to Brahmins *or* Jains by inferiors.

ಅಲ್ಮೆರ್ almeru, *s.* An almeira, a wardrobe.

ಅಲ್ಲ್‌ಕಡ್ಡಿ allukaḍḍi, *s.* A tooth-pick.

ಅಲ್ಲಂಬ್ರ allambra, *s.* Agitation, alarm.

ಅಲ್ಲಾ allā, *s.* The Mohammedan appellation of the Supreme Being. 2. *int.* of surprise.

ಅಲ್ಲಾವುನಿ allāvuni (ಅಲ್ಲಾ), *v. a.* To mix; *cf.* ಅಲವುನಿ.

ಅಲ್ಲಿ, ಅಲ್ಲಿಗೆ alli, allige, *s.* The water-lily; *also* ಅಲ್ಲಿದ ಪೂ. 2. the flower of *Nelumbium speciosum; also* ತಾವರೆ.

ಅಲ್ಲೂದು allūdu, *adj.* Perishable, transient.

ಅಲ್ಲೆ allè, *s.* The side, groin, hip. —ಕೆಲ್ಲ a lateral branch.

ಅವ ava, *pref.* implying diminution, privation.

ಅವ ava, *int.* Behold, lo; *see* ಅವಾ.

ಅವಕಾಶ avakāśa, *s.* Opportunity, leisure; *cf.* ಸಾವಕಾಶ.

ಅವಗಡ avagaḍa, *s.* Calamity, evil, mischief. 2. disorder, confusion. 3. difficulty, danger.

ಅವಗುಣ avaguṇa, *s.* An evil disposition, a vice. 2. the state of growing worse.

ಅವಜೆ avaje, *s.* Sound, noise.

ಅವಡೆ avaḍè, *s.* A kind of country beans; *also* ಆವಡೆ.

ಅವತಾರ avatāra, *s.* Descent, incarnation. ಪತ್ತಾವತಾರ the ten incarnations of Vishṇu (ವಿಷ್ಣು).

—ದೆತ್ತೊಱುನಿ, —ಮಳ್ತೊಱುನಿ, ಅವತರಿತೊಱುನಿ, ಅವತರಿಫುನಿ to become incarnate.

ಅವತ್ತೆ avatte, *see* ಅವಸ್ತೆ.

ಅವತ್ಸರ avatsara, *see* ಅಮುಸರ.

ಅವಧಿ avadhi, *s.* A limit, term, period, fixed time.

ಅವಧೂತೆ avadhūte, *s.* One who has abandoned his family and all earthly desires. ಅವಧೂತ ಮಾರ್ಗ the manner of leading a life of austerity. [ಸ.

ಅವನಂಬಿಕೆ avanambikè, *see* ಅಪನಂಬಿ

ಅವಪತ್ಯ avapatya, *s.* Violation of a prescribed diet. *adj.* Contrary to diet.

ಅವಮತ avamata, *s.* Heterodoxy.

ಅವಮಾನ avamāna, *see* ಅಪಮಾನ.

ಅವಯೋಗ avayōga, *s.* A bad omen, a portent.

ಅವರೆ avarè, *see* ಅಬರೆ.

ಅವಲ್ avalụ, *adj.* Best, first rate. —ತರ the best kind.

ಅವಲಂಬನೆ avalambane, *adj.* Depending on. *s.* Protection, an asylum.

ಅವಲಕ್ಷಣ avalakshaṇa, *s.* An inauspicious sign. 2. ugliness.

ಅವಲೆ avalè, *s.* A rift, cleft. *adj.* Hollow, not solid.

ಅವಶಕುನ avaśakuna, *see* ಅಪಶಕುನ.

ಅವಶ್ಯ avaśya, *s.* Need, necessity. *adj.* Necessary, urgent, requisite. —ದಾಂತಿ unnecessary.

ಅವಸತ್ಯ avasatya, *s.* A lie, falsehood.

ಅವಸರ avasara, *see* ಅಮುಸರ.

ಅವಸಾನ, ಅವಸಾಯು avasāna, avasāya, *s.* End, conclusion, termination. 2. death.

ಅವಸಾರ avasāra, *see* ಅಮುಸರ.

ಅವಸ್ತೆ, ಅವಸ್ಥೆ avaste, avasthe, *s.* State, condition. 2. circumstances, situation. 3. difficulty.

ಅವಾ avā, *int.* Lo! behold; *see* ಅವ.

ಅವಾಂತರ avāntara, *adj.* Intermediate, included. 2. calamitous. *s.* Straits. 2. alarm, confusion. 3. public calamity. 4. foreign invasion.

ಅವಾಚ್ಯ avāćya, *adj.* Not fit to be spoken. 2. obscene.

ಅವಾಲ್ತೆ, ಅವಾಲ್ತಿಗೆ avāltè, avāltigè, *s.* Charge, care; commission, conferred trust; safe keeping. —ಮಳ್ಪುನಿ to give in charge, to entrust another; *also* ಹವಾಲ್ತೆ.

ಅವಿಚಾರ avićāra, *s.* Want of enquiry. 2. indiscretion, rashness. 3. negligence.

ಅವಿಧೇಯ avidhēya, *adj.* Disobedient. —ತ್ವ disobedience.

ಅವಿವೇಕ avivēka, *s.* Indiscretion. 2. imprudence, folly.

ಅವಿಶ್ವಾಸ aviśvāsa, *s.* Distrust, unbelief, unfaithfulness.

ಅವಿಶ್ವಾಸಿ aviśvāsi, *s.* An unbeliever.

ಅವು avu, *pron. dem.* It, that, that thing. —ಅತ್ತಂದೆ besides that. ಅವೋ is it that? ಅವೆ, ಅವ್ವೇ (*emph.*) just that, even that, the very thing.

ಅವುಂಕುನಿ avuṅkuni (ಅವುಂಕ್), *v. a.* To crop. 2. to snatch, 3. to press down: ನಿಕ್ಕ್ ಕೀರುನಾತ್ ಅವುಂಕುದು ತೂಲ press it down as much as you can.

ಅವುಂಟು avuṇṭu, *s.* Pride, haughtiness, arrogance.

ಅವುಂಟುನಿ avuṇṭuni (ಅವುಂಟಿ), *v. n.* To be proud.

ಅವುಂಪುನಿ avumpuni (ಅವುಂ), *v. a.* To press. 2. to mumble.

ಅವುಕಾಸ avukāsa, *see* ಅವಕಾಶ.

ಅವುತನ avutana, *s.* A feast, entertainment, dinner; *also* ಔತಣ. —ಮಳ್ಪುನಿ to give an entertainment. —ದಾಯೆ a guest.

ಅವುಷಧ avushadha, *see* ಔಷಧ.

ಅವುಳು avuḷu, *adv.* There. 2. beyond; *also* ಔಳು. ಅವುಳವುಳು here and there. ಅವುಳೇ (*emph.*) just there, even there, in that very place.

ಅವ್ಯಯ avyaya, *s.* An indeclinable word, *gram.*

ಅವ್ವಲ್ avval, *see* ಅವಲ್.

ಅಶಕ್ತ aśakta, *adj.* Weak, feeble. 2. sick.

ಅಶಕ್ತಿ aśakti, *s.* Weakness, incapacity.

ಅಶಕ್ತೆ aśakte, *s.* A weak *or* sick person.

ಅಶಕ್ಯ aśakya, *adj.* Impracticable, impossible.

ಅಶನ aśana, *s.* Eating. 2. food. ಅಶನಾರ್ಥ maintenance, subsistence; —ಕೊರ್ಪಿನಿ to give maintenance, to feed.

ಅಶರೀರ, ಅಶರೀರಿ aśarīra, aśarīri, *adj.* Incorporeal. —ವಾಕ್ಯ a voice from heaven, an oracle.

ಅಶುಚಿ, ಅಶುದ್ಧ aśuci, aśuddha, *adj.* Impure, unclean, polluted. —ಆಪಿನಿ to become unclean. —ತ್ವ uncleanness, pollution.

ಅಶುಭ aśubha, *adj.* Inauspicious, evil. *s.* Unluckiness, misfortune.

ಅಶೆಮಣೆ aśemaṇe, *s.* A seat for the bride.

ಅಶೋಕ aśōka, *s.* Freedom from grief. 2. the name of a king.

ಅಶೋಕೆ (ಮರ) aśōke (mara), *s.* The tree *Uvaria longifolia.* —ವನ a grove of such trees.

ಅಶ್ರಬ್, ಅಶ್ರಾಪ್ aśrabu, aśrāpu, *see* ಅಸ್ರಾಬ್.

ಅಶ್ಲೇಷ, ಅಶ್ಲೇಸಿ, aślēsha, aślēsi, *see* ಆಶ್ಲೇಷ.

ಅಶ್ವ aśva, *s.* A horse.

ಅಶ್ವತ್ಥ-, ಅಶ್ವತ ಮರ aśvattha-, aśvata mara, *see* ಅತ್ತಸ ಮರ.

ಅಶ್ವಪತಿ aśvapati, *s.* The king of horses. 2. a dynasty at Delhi.

ಅಶ್ವಮೇಧ aśvamēdha, *s.* The ceremony of sacrificing a horse.

ಅಷ್ಟ, ಅಷ್ಟಕ ashṭa, ashṭaka, *adj.* Eight.

ಅಷ್ಟಕಷ್ಟ ashṭakashṭa, *s.* Eight sources of troubles to which man is liable.

ಅಷ್ಟಕಾಂಗ ashṭakāṅga, *s.* A board *or* cloth having eight rows of squares eight in each row; a chess-board.

ಅಷ್ಟಗಜ, ಅಷ್ಟದಿಗ್ಗಜ ashṭagaja, ashṭadiggaja, *s.* The eight elephants which, according to the Hindu Šāstrās, are supposed to support the earth.

ಅಷ್ಟಗೆ ashṭage, *s.* An offering for the dead.

ಅಷ್ಟತಾಳ ashṭatāḷa, *s.* A mode or measure in music.

ಅಷ್ಟದಿಕ್ಕು ashṭadikku, *s.* The eight points of the compass; *also* ಅಷ್ಟಮೂಲೆ. ಅಷ್ಟದಿಕ್ಪಾಲಕರು the guardians of the eight points of the compass.

ಅಷ್ಟದ್ರವ್ಯ ashṭadravya, *s.* An offering of eight ingredients.

ಅಷ್ಟಪಟ್ಟಿ ashṭapaṭṭi, *s.* An octagon.

ಅಷ್ಟಪದಿ ashṭapadi, *s.* A verse with eight feet.

ಅಷ್ಟಬಂಧ ashṭabandha, *s.* A kind of mortar composed of eight ingredients.

ಅಷ್ಟಭಾಗ್ಯ ashṭabhāgya, *s.* The eight requisites to the regal state, *viz.* ರಾಜ್ಯ territory, ಭಂಡಾರ treasure, ದಂಡು forces, ಆನೆ elephant, ಕುದುರೆ horse, ಛತ್ರ ketasol, ಚಾಮರ fly-brush, ಪಲ್ಲಕ್ಕಿ palankeen.

ಅಷ್ಟಭೋಗ ashṭabhōga, *s.* The eight sources of enjoyment, *viz.* ಇಲ್ಲ habitation, ಹಾಸಿಗೆ bed, ಕುಂಟು raiment, ಪದ್ದಾಯಿ jewels, ಜೊಡೆವಿ wife, ಹೂ flower, ಗಂಧ perfumes, ಬಜ್ಜಿರೆಪೂಳು betel-leaf and arecanut.

ಅಷ್ಟಮ ashṭama, *num. adj.* The eighth.

ಅಷ್ಟಮಾಸಿದ್ಧಿ ashṭamāsiddhi, *see* ಅಷ್ಟಸಿದ್ಧಿ.

ಅಷ್ಟಮಿ ashṭami, *see* ಅಟ್ಟಮಿ.

ಅಷ್ಟಸಿದ್ಧಿ ashṭasiddhi, *s.* The eight miraculous attainments.

ಅಷ್ಟಾವಿಧಾನ ashṭāvidhāna, *s.* The eight kinds of devotion.

ಅಷ್ಟಾಕ್ಷರಿಮಂತ್ರ ashṭāksharimantra, *s.* The eight mystical letters used in incantations: ಓಂ ನ ಮೋ ನಾ ರಾ ಯ ಣಾ ಯ.

ಅಷ್ಟೈಶ್ವರ್ಯ ashṭeiśvarya, *see* ಅಷ್ಟಭಾಗ್ಯ.

ಅಸುರು asuru, *see* ಅಸೂರು.

ಅಸಂಖ್ಯ asaṅkhya, *adj.* Innumerable.

ಅಸಂಗತಿ asaṅgati, *s.* An adverse circumstance, an accident.

ಅಸಂದರ್ಭ asandarbha, *s.* Unseasonableness, inconvenience. *adj.* Unconnected, irrelevant; impracticable.

ಅಸಂಬಂಧ asambandha, *s.* Disconnection, incoherence. *adj.* Disconnected, incoherent. 2. absurd.

ಅಸಂಹ್ಯ asaṅhya, *adj.* Disgusting, loathsome. *s.* Molestation, intolerable vexations. 2. disgust, aversion. –ಆಪಿಸಿ to be disgusted with.

ಅಸಕ್ತ asakta, *see* ಅಶಕ್ತ.

ಅಸಡ್ಡೆ asaḍḍe, *s.* Disdain, contempt, scorn. 2. negligence, carelessness. –ತನ the state of being scornful *or* careless. –ಮಾಡು to despise, neglect.

ಅಸತ್ಯ asatya, *adj.* Untrue, false. *s.* Falsehood.

ಅಸದ್ಧ asaddha, *adj.* False. 2. uninspired.

ಅಸದ್ಯ asadya, *see* ಅಸಾಧ್ಯ.

ಅಸಮ, ಅಸಮಾನ asama, asamāna, *s.* Inequality. *adj.* Unequal, dissimilar, unlike. 2. odd, diverse. 3. incomparable.

ಅಸಮಾಧಾನ asamādhāna, *s.* Unsettled state, restlessness, uneasiness, disquietude. 2. dissatisfaction, peacelessness. 3. dissension, quarrel.

ಅಸಯೆ asaye, *see* ಹೊಸಯಿ.

ಅಸಯ್ಯ asayya, *see* ಅಸಂಹ್ಯ.

ಅಸರ್ asaru, *see* ಆಸರಿ.

ಅಸರ್ಮೆ asarmè, *s.* Management of a household.

ಅಸಲ್ asalu, *s.* Root, origin. 2. capital, stock (in trade). 3. prime cost. 4. an original, a fair copy.

ಅಸಲಿ asale, *adj.* First-class, superior. 2. fine, thin, neat.

ಅಸಲೆ asalè, *s.* A split. –ಬುಡ್ಪುನಿ to split, crack. [light.

ಅಸಲೆಮಸಲೆ asalèmasalè, *s.* Twi-

ಅಸಹಿಪುನಿ, ಅಸಹ್ಯಿಸುನಿ asahipuni, asahyisuni (ಅಸಹಿ, -ಹ್ಯ), *v. n.* To loathe, feel disgust at; *cf.* ಅಸಂಹ್ಯ.

ಅಸಾಧ್ಯ asādhya, *adj.* Impracticable, unattainable. *s.* Impractibility.

ಅಸಾಮ್ಯ asāmya, *see* ಅಸಮ.

ಅಸಾರ asāra, *adj.* Sapless, tasteless. 2. worthless; *also* ನಿಸ್ಸಾರ.

ಅಸಿದ್ಧ asiddha, *adj.* Not achieved *or* effected. 2. unprepared, not ready. 3. undecided. 4. improbable.

ಅಸುರ asura, *adj.* Giant-like, gigantic. 2. cruel. –ಕೃತ್ಯ a cruel deed, diabolical action *or* work.

ಅಸುರಿ asuri, *s.* A giantess, the wife of a giant.

ಅಸುರುಸುರು asurusuru, *s.* A deep sigh.

ಅಸುರೆ asure, *s.* A giant.

ಅಸೂಯ asūya, *s.* Envy, jealousy, malignity.

ಅಸೂರ asūra, *adj.* Yellow. 2. unalloyed, as gold.

ಅಸೂರಿ asūri, *adj.* Extra, miscellaneous. –ಕರ್ಚ extra expenses.

ಅಸೂರೆ asūrè, *s.* Daily expenditure; sundry expenses; *also* ಚಿಲ್ಲರೆ ಕರ್ಚ.

ಅಸೆಮಣೆ asemaṇe, *see* ಅಶೆಮಣೆ.

ಅಸೌಖ್ಯ asaukhya, *s.* Uneasiness, unhappiness, ill-health.

ಅಸ್ತ, ಅಸ್ತಮಾನ asta, astamāna, *s.* Sunset.

ಅಸ್ತರ್, ಅಸ್ತ್ರಿ astaru, astri, *s.* The lining of a garment.

ಅಸ್ತಿ asti, *s.* A bone. –ಜರ hectic fever.

ಅಸ್ತಿವಾರ astivāra, *s.* A foundation.

ಅಸ್ತು, ಅಸ್ತುನಾಮ astu, astunāma, *s.* Consent, agreement.

ಅಸ್ತೆ aste, *adv.* Slowly. –ಬುಡ್ಪಿನಿ to breathe heavily; *bet.* ಆಸ್ತೆ.

ಅಸ್ಥಿರ asthira, *adj.* Unsteady, transient, fleeting.

ಅಸ್ರಬ್, ಅಸ್ರಾಪು asrabu, asrāpu, *adj.* Noble.

ಅಸ್ರಬಿದೆ asrabidė (ಅಸುರ ಬೀಜ), (*lit.* a monstrous seed.) *s.* Any grain *etc.*, the cultivation of which exhausts the soil. 2. a wicked person.

ಅಸ್ರಬೆ asrabe, *s.* A nobleman, good man.

ಅಸ್ರೆ asre, *s.* A destroyer; *cf.* ಆಸರ.

ಅಸ್ವಸ್ಥ asvastha, *s.* Sickness, illness. *adj.* Unwell, sick.

ಅಹ, ಅಹಹ aha, ahaha, *int.* of surprise. Ah! aha!

ಅಹಂಕರಿಪುನಿ ahaṅkaripuni (ಅಹಂಕರಿ), *v.n.* To be proud, arrogant, conceited.

ಅಹಂಕಾರ ahaṅkāra, *s.* Self-consciousness. 2. egotism, pride, self-conceit, haughtiness. –ದಾಯೆ a proud, self-conceited *or* insolent man.

ಅಹಂನೀಕ ahannīka, *see* ಆಹ್ನಿಕ.

ಅಹಂಭಾವ ahambhāva, *s.* Self-consciousness, self-confidence, insolence.

ಅಹಂಮತಿ ahammati, *s.* Self-conceitedness, a vain mind.

ಅಹಿ ahi, *s.* A snake.

ಅಹಿತ ahita, *adj.* Disagreeable, unsalutary. *s.* Harm, wrong.

ಅಹೋರಾತ್ರೆ ahōrātre, *s.* A day and a night lasting from sunrise to sunrise.

ಅಳ aḷa, *s.* Measure, capacity.

ಅಳಂಕ್ aḷaṅku, *s.* An ant-eater.

ಅಳಂಕಾವುನಿ aḷaṅkāvuni, *see* ಅಲಂಕಾವುನಿ.

ಅಳಂಕುನಿ aḷaṅkuni, *see* ಅಲಂಕುನಿ.

ಅಳಂಟುನಿ aḷaṇṭuni (ಅಳಂಟಿ), *v. n.* To shake. 2. to move.

ಅಳಕ aḷaka, *s.* A large basket for measuring rice *etc.*

ಅಳಕೆ, ಅಳತೆ aḷakė, aḷatė, *s.* Measurement. –ಮಳ್ಪುನಿ to measure, mete; *cf.* ಅಳತ, ಹಾಳತ.

ಅಳಪುನಿ aḷapuni (ಅಳ್), *v. a.* To measure.

ಅಳಯ alya, *see* ಅಯ್ಯ.

ಅಳವುನಿ aḷavuni (ಅಳ್), *v. n.* To mix.

ಅಳಾ aḷā, *see* ಅಲಾ.

ಅಳಾವು aḷāvu, *see* ಅಲವು.

ಅಳಿಕಟ್ಟ್ aḷikaṭṭu, *s.* Ruin.

ಅಳಿಪುನಿ, aḷipuni (ಅಳಿ), *v. n.* To perish, die. 2. to be destroyed, be ruined; *also* ಅಳಿದ್ ಪೋಪಿನಿ.

ಅಳಿಯ aḷiya, *s.* A son-in-law, nephew; —as a rule a man's sister's son marries the daughter of his mother's brother. *bet.* ಅರ್ವತ್ತು. –ಸಂತಾನ the law of inheritance in the female line. According to this law the family property descends not from a man to his son, but from a woman to her daughter.

ಅಳಿಯಂತರ aḷiyantara, *s.* Ruin, extinction.

ಅಳಿಯುನಿ aḷiyuni, *see* ಅಳಿಪುನಿ.

ಅಳುಕು aḷuku, *s.* Modesty, bashfulness.

ಅಳುವಳಿ aḷuvaḷi, *s.* A daughter's dowry.

ಅಳುವೆ aḷuve, *s.* An instalment. 2. a term of payment; *cf.* ಕಂತ್, ವಾಯಿದೆ.

ಅಳುವೆ aḷuve, *s.* The mouth of a river, a harbour. –ಸಾಯಿರ ಕಟ್ಟಿ a custom-house; *see* ಅರುವೆ.

ಅಳೆ aḷè, *see* ಅಲೆ.

ಅಳೆಂಜಿ aḷeñji, *s.* A kind of weed growing on the surface of stagnant water.

ಅಳೆಜ್ಜುನಿ aḷejjuni, *see* ಅಲೆಜುನಿ.

ಅಳೆಪಾಯಿ aḷepāyi, *see* ಅಲಪಯಿ.

ಅಳೆವುನಿ aḷevuni (ಅಳಿ), *v. n.* To muse, to be absent-minded *or* abstracted. ಅಳೆದ್ ತೂಪಿನಿ to look bewildered, perplexed; *cf.* ಅಲೆವುನಿ.

ಅಳ್ಕುನಿ aḷkuni, *see* ಅಲ್ಕುನಿ.

ಅಳ್ತ್ aḷtụ, *adv.* Thence; *also* ಅಳ್ತ್ಡ್.

ಅಳ್ತ aḷta (*gen. of the adv.* ಅವುಳು), *adj.* Of that place.

ಅಳ್ಪ aḷpa, *adv.* There, in that place. ಅಳ್ಪಳ್ಪ here and there.

ಅಳ್ಯ aḷya, *see* ಅಯ್ಯ್.

ಅಳ್ಳಿ, ಅಳ್ಳಿಗೆ aḷḷi, aḷḷige, *see* ಅಲ್ಲಿ.

ಅಳ್ಳೆ aḷḷe, *see* ಅಲ್ಲೆ.

ಅಕ್ಷ aksha, *s.* The eye. 2. a mark on dice. 3. a die. 4. a wheel. –ಲೀಲೆ, –ಕ್ರೀಡ, –ಕ್ರಿಯ, –ವಿದ್ಯ gambling, playing with dice.

ಅಕ್ಷಂತರಿ akshantari, *s.* A gift of yellow rice.

ಅಕ್ಷತ, ಅಕ್ಷತೆ akshata, akshate, *s.* Raw rice mixed with kuṅkuma (*i.e.* turmeric powder) and used for religious purposes. ಮಂತ್ರಾಕ್ಷತೆ rice over which incantations have been pronounced.

ಅಕ್ಷದ akshada, *s.* A red mark put on the forehead after dinner, chiefly by Brahmins.

ಅಕ್ಷದಾಮ, ಅಕ್ಷಮಾಲೆ akshadāma, akshamālè, *s.* A rosary *or* string of beads, especially of the seeds of *Elaeocarpus*, used in devotion.

ಅಕ್ಷಯ akshaya, *adj.* Imperishable, immortal. –ಪಾತ್ರ a brass vessel for receiving alms. *s.* The last year of the Hindu cycle.

ಅಕ್ಷರ akshara, (*lit.* undecaying). *s.* A letter. –ಮಾಲೆ (*lit.* a garland of letters) the alphabet.

ಅಕ್ಷರಜ್ಞ aksharajña, *s.* A scholar.

ಅಕ್ಷಿ akshi, *s.* The eye. 2. success, prosperity. –ಚಲನೆ moving of the eyes. –ಕೇಳ್ a scorpion.

ಆ Ā

ಆ ā, The second letter of the alphabet.

ಆ ā, *dem. pron.* That; ಆ ಕಡೆ that side *or* party; ಆ ನರಮಾನಿ that man. ಆ ಆ, ಆಯಾ each, every, respective. –ಕಾರ್ಯ each work. 2. when added to two or more consecutive words, the meaning is disjunctive: either–or, whether–or; *as* ಇಂಬೆನಾ ಆಯೆನಾ whether this or that man? 3. it is an affix of interrogation, which changes according to phonetic rules into ನಾ, ಯಾ; *as* ಅಂದ್ yes: ಅಂದಾ is it? ಬತ್ತ್ you came: ಬತ್ತನಾ did you come? ಈ thou, you: ಈಯಾ is it you?

ಆಂಕರಿಯುನಿ āṅkariyuni, *see* ಅಹಂಕರಿಪುನಿ.

ಆಂಕಾರ āṅkāra, *see* ಅಹಂಕಾರ.

ಆಂಕಿತ āṅkita, *see* ಅಂಕಿತ.

ಆಂಕೆ āṅkè, *s.* Force, pressure, compulsion. 2. authority, power, control. 3. support. –ಮಲ್ಪುನಿ to force, compel, to obtain by coaxing. –ದಾಯೆ a strong, powerful man.

ಆಂಗೀರಸ āṅgīrasa, *s.* The sixth year in the Hindu cycle of sixty.

ಆಂಡ್ āṇḍụ, *see* ಆಪಿನಿ.

ಆಂಡ, ಆಂಡಲಾ āṇḍa, āṇḍalā, *see* ಆಪಿನಿ.

ಆಂತರ, ಆಂತ್ರ āntara, āntra, *s.* The bowels, entrails. –ಬಾವು swelling of the scrotum *or* testicles. –ವಾಯು flatulence; hernia.

ಆಂತರ್ಯ āntarya, *s.* The mind; *see* ಅಂತರ್ಯ. 2. sentiment, opinion; *cf.* ಅಂತರಂಗ.

ಆಂದಿ āndi, *s.* Caution. 2. bail, a security. –ಆಯಿನಾಯೆ one who stands security, becomes surety.

ಆಂದ್ರವಾಯು āndravāyu, *see* ಆಂತ್ರವಾಯು.

ಆಂಬಲ್ āmbalụ, *s.* A water-lily which opens after sunset.

ಆಂಬಾಲ āmbāla, *see* ಅಂಬಲ್.

ಆಂಬಿಗೆ āmbige, *see* ಅಂಬುಗೆ.

ಆಂಬುರ, ಆಂಬ್ರ āmbura, āmbra, *see* ಆಮ್ಲ.

ಆಂಬೆ āmbe, *adv.* There, on that side. 2. after. *prep.* Beyond.

ಆಂಬೆರಿಪುನಿ āmberipuni (ಆಂಬೆರಿ), *v. n.* To be drowsy *or* sleepy. 2. to dream. 3. to be confused.

ಆಂಮವಡೆ āmavaḍe, *see* ಅಂಬೊಡೆ.

ಆಂಹಿಕ āmhika, *see* ಆಹ್ನಿಕ.

ಆಕರ ākara, *see* ಅಕರ.

ಆಕರ್ಶ, ಆಕರ್ಷ ākarša, ākarsha, *s.* Attraction, drawing towards each other. –ಶಕ್ತಿ the power of attraction.

ಆಕಾರ ākāra, *s.* Form, shape. 2. the letter ಆ.

ಆಕಾಶ, ಆಕಾಸ ākāśa, ākāsa, *s.* The atmosphere, sky.

ಆಕಿರೆ ākire, *s.* A nettle-plant, *Urtica heterophylla.*

ಆಕುಳು ākuḷu, *dem. pron.* (*pl. of* ಆಯಿ *or* ಆಳ್), They. 2. *it is affixed to adjectives, participles and nouns to convert them into personal nouns, as* ಯೆಡ್ಡೆಂತಿನಾಕುಳು good people, ತೂಪಿನಾಕುಳು those that see, ಬೇಲೆದಾಕುಳು working people *etc.*

ಆಕೃತಿ ākṛuti, *s.* Form, shape.

ಆಕೆರಿ, ಆಕ್ರಿ ākeri, ākri, *see* ಆಖ್ಯೆರಿ.

ಆಖಾತ ākhāta, *s.* An artificial lake.

ಆಖೈರ್, ಆಖೈರಿ ākheiru, ākheiri, *s.* The end, termination. *adj.* Final, last. *adv.* Finally, at last; *see* ಅಕೇರಿ.

ಆಖ್ಯ, ಆಖ್ಯೆ ākhya, ākhye, *s.* A name. 2. the subject of a sentence, *gram.*

ಆಖ್ಯಾತ ākhyāta, *s.* The predicate, *gram.*

ಆಗ್ āgu, (*lit.* fire). *s.* Steam. —ಆಪಿನ to be consumed, to come to an end. —ದ ಗಾಡಿ, *see* ಹುಗೆಗಾಡಿ. ಆಗ್ಬೋಟ್ a steamer.

ಆಗಮ āgama, *s.* Arrival. 2. a work on Hindu ritual *etc.* 3. augment, *gram.*

ಆಗಮನ āgamana, *s.* Advent, arrival.

ಆಗರ, ಆಗಾರ āgara, āgāra, *s.* A habitation, house.

ಆಗರ āgara, *see* ಅಗರ್.

ಆಗ್ನೆ āgne, *see* ಆಜ್ಞೆ.

ಆಗ್ನೇಯ āgnēya, *adj.* South-east.

ಆಗ್ರ agra, *see* ಹಗುರ.

ಆಚಮನೆ ācamane, *s.* The ceremony of sipping a few drops of water and repeating the twenty-four names of Vishṇu (ವಿಷ್ಣು) before performing any religious ceremony.

ಆಚರಣೆ ācaraṇe, *s.* Usage, established custom. 2. observance. 3. performance of religious ceremonies. 4. a ceremony, rite.

ಆಚರಿಪುನಿ ācaripuni (ಆಚರಿ), *v. a.* To observe, practise, perform.

ಆಚಾರ ācāra, *s.* Usage, custom. 2. conduct. ವೃದ್ಧಾಚಾರ traditional observance.

ಆಚಾರಣೆ ācāraṇe, *see* ಆಚರಣೆ.

ಆಚಾರಿ ācāri, *s.* A smith *or* carpenter. —ಬೂರು a kind of creeper.

ಆಚಾರೆ, ಆಚಾರ್ಯೆ ācāre, ācārye, *s.* A spiritual guide, a priest.

ಆಜ āja, An oath, a curse. 2. swearing. —ಕೊಪ್ಪಿನ to swear. —ಪಾಡುನಿ to imprecate, curse. —ಪಿರಿಯುನಿ to deliver from an oath, to revoke a curse.

ಆಜನೆ ājane, *num. adj.* Sixth.

ಆಜರ್ ājar, *s.* Presence; *bet.* ಹಾಜರ್. —ಆಪಿನ to be present. —ಮಳ್ಪುನಿ to produce (a witness *etc.*). —ಜಾಮಿನ್ bail, security for the appearance of another before a court of justice. —ಪಟ್ಟಿ a muster-roll.

ಆಜಳ ājaḷa, *s.* Six seers.

ಆಜಾವುನಿ ājāvuni, *c. v.* (*of* ಆಜುನಿ), To dry *or* drain.

ಆಜಿ āji, *num.* Six.

ಆಜಿಡುನಿ ājiḍuni (ಆಜಿಡ್), *v. a.* To expose clothes *etc.* for drying.

ಆಜಿಪ ājipa, *see* ಅಜಿಪ.

ಆಜಿಯುನಿ, ಆಜುನಿ ājiyuni, ājuni (ಆಜಿ, ಆಜ್), *v.n.* To dry up, drain off; *as*, ಗುವೆಲ್ದ ನೀರ್ ಆಜಿಂಡ್ the well is dry; ಆಜಿದ್ ಪೋಪಿನಿ to be dried up. ಆಜಿದಿ dried, freed from moisture *or* sap. ಆಜಂದಿ undried, wet; ಆಜಂದಿ ಕುಂಟು a wet cloth.

ಆಜೆ āje, *see* ಆಜ.

ಆಜೊಳು ājoḷu, *num. adv.* Six times.

ಆಜ್ಞೆ ājñe, *s.* Command, order. 2. permission. 3. a judicial sentence, doom.

ಆಜ್ಪ ajpa, *num.* Sixty; *see* ಅಜಿಪ.

ಆಟ āṭa, *s.* Amusement, sport, game. 2. a play; —ದಾಯೆ an actor; a gambler. —ಪಾಟ, —ವಾದ್ಯ dancing and playing with music. 3. *when forming the latter part of compounds it signifies continuity; as*, ಅಪ್ಪಾಟ crying *or* weeping long. ಗೋಳಾಟ lamentation.

ಅಟಂಕ್, ಆಟಂಕ aṭaṅkụ, āṭaṅka, *s.* Hinderance, obstacle.

ಅಟಿ aṭi, *s.* The fourth solar month. —ದ ಕತ್ತಲೆ profound darkness. —ಪಂತಿ a kind of grass.

ಆಡ್ āḍụ, *see* ಹಾಡ್.

ಆಡಂಬರ āḍambara, *s.* Pride. 2. pomp, show.

ಆಡಮೋಡೆ āḍemōḍè, *see* ಆಡೆ.

ಆಡಲೋಡ್ āḍalōḍụ, *s.* The Malabar-nut-tree, *Justicia adhadota*.

ಆಡಳಿತೆ, ಆಡಳ್ತೆ āḍaḷite, āḍaḷte, *s.* Administration, management. 2. governing. —ತೂಪಿನಿ to manage. —ತೂಪಿನಾಯೆ an administrator, manager.

ಆಡಾವುನಿ āḍāvuni, *c.v.* (*of* ಆಡುನಿ), To agitate. 2. to shake.

ಆಡಿಗೆ āḍige, *s.* A belch; *bet.* ಆರಿಗೆ.

ಆಡಿಗೆ āḍige, *adv.* In vain, for nothing; *see* ಅಡೇಗೆ.

ಆಡುನಿ āḍuni (ಆಡ್), *v. n.* To move, wave, swing, vibrate. 2. to shake, totter. *v. a.* To move, rock. 2. to shake. Different playful and regular movements are expressed by adding it to verbs; *as*, ನೇತಾಡುನಿ to be swinging. ಅಲ್ಲಾಡುನಿ to be moving to and fro, *etc.*

ಆಡೆ āḍe, *s.* A coward.

ಆಡೆಗ್ āḍegụ, *see* ಅಡೆ, ಅಡೆಗ್.

ಆಡೆಗೆ āḍege, *see* ಆಡಿಗೆ.

ಆಡೆಲೆ āḍele, *s.* An unsteady man. 2. a vagabond.

ಆಡೇವುನಿ āḍēvuni (ಆಡೇ), *v. n.* To be moving, undulating, vibrating. ಆಡೇವುನವು constant motion, oscillation *or* vibration.

ಆಣ್ āṇụ, *adj.* Male. —ಬಾಲೆ a male child, a boy. —ಮರ a male

tree. *s*. A boy, youngster. ಆಣ ಇಲ್ಲ್ the bridegroom's house.

ಆಣ್‌ಗಡಿ **āṇụgaḍi**, *s*. The lower half of a cocoanut-shell.

ಆಣ್‌ಜೋವು **āṇụjōvu**, *s*. A male, man; *also* ಅಣ್ಜವು.

ಆಣ್‌ಪೆಜ **āṇụpeja**, *s*. A male variety of the wild jack-tree.

ಆಣಾ **āṇa**, *s*. The entrance to a harbour. —ಗ್ ಉಂತುನಿ, ಆಣೊಗು ಪೋಪಿನಿ to stand *or* wade in shoal-water for fishing.

ಆಣಿ **āṇi**, *s*. A peg, nail. 2. a wedge. 3. a screw.

ಆಣಿಕಲ್ಲ್ **āṇikallụ**, *s*. The key-stone of an arch.

ಆಣೆ **āṇe**, *s*. An anna.

ಆಣೆ **āṇe**, *s*. An oath.

ಆಣೆಕಲ್ಲ್ **āṇekallụ**, *s*. A hail-stone.

ಆತ್ **ātụ**, *indef. num. adj*. So much. —ಜನ so many people. —ಪೊರ್ತು so much time, so long. 2. as much as: ಇತ್ತಿನಾತ್ ಕೊರ್ಲೆ give all you have. ಆತೇ *emph*. so much only: —ಯಾನ್ ಪಣ್ಪೆನಿ I say only so much. ಆತೆನಾ, ಆತೋ is it only so much? ಆತೇ ಈ ಕೊರ್ಪಿನವೋ, *or* ಈ ಕೊರ್ಪಿನವು ಆತೋ is it only so much that you give? ಆತೆಗ್ for so much.

ಆತ್‌ನೆಂಗೆ, ಆತಾನೆಂಗೆ **ātụneṅge, ātāneṅge**, *see* ಆತೆನೆಂಗೆ.

ಆತಿ **āti**, *see* ಆಪಿನಿ.

ಆತಿಥ್ಯ **ātithya**, *s*. Hospitality. —ಮಳ್ಪುನಿ to entertain a guest.

ಆತುರ **ātura**, *s*. Eagerness, haste.

ಆತೆಕ್ **ātekụ**, *see* ಆತಿ.

ಆತೆನೆಂಗೆ **āteneṅge**, *adv*. Till, as long as.

ಆತ್ಮ, ಆತ್ಮೆ **ātma, ātme**, *s*. Breath, life. 2. the soul, spirit. ಪರಿಶುದ್ಧಾತ್ಮೆ the Holy Ghost, *Chr*. ಪಾಪಾತ್ಮೆ a sinner. ಪುಣ್ಯಾತ್ಮೆ a virtuous *or* fortunate man. ಆತ್ಮಭಾವ spiritual-mindedness, *Chr*. 3. self, *chiefly in comp*: ಆತ್ಮಘಾತಕ suicide. ಆತ್ಮಸ್ತುತಿ self-praise.

ಆದ್ **ādụ**, *see* ಆಪಿನಿ.

ಆದರ **ādara**, *see* ಹಾದರ.

ಆದರಣೆ **ādaraṇe**, *s*. Respect, regard for. 2. protection, support. 3. comfort, consolation.

ಆದರಿಪುನಿ **ādaripuni** (ಆದರಿ), *v. a*. To honor. 2. to support, assist. 3. to console, comfort. ಆದರಿಪುನಾಯೆ a supporter, one who comforts.

ಆದಾಯ **ādāya**, *s*. Gain, profit, income, behoof. —ನಷ್ಟ profit and loss. —ವೆಚ್ಚ receipts and disbursements; management. —ವೆಚ್ಚ ತೂಪಿನಾಯೆ a book-keeper.

ಆದಾರ **ādāra**, *see* ಆಧಾರ.

ಆದಿ **ādi**, *s*. Beginning, origin. *adj*. First, primary; pre-eminent; *e. g*. ಆದಿಕಾರಣ the original cause. 2. *when the latter part of a compound it means*: and others, et cetera, *as* ಮೃಗಾದಿಳು beasts *etc*.

ಆದಿಕ ādika, *see* ಆದಾಯು.

ಆದಿತ್ಯ āditya, *s.* The sun. –ವಾರ Sunday.

ಆದುಪ್ಪುನಿ āduppuni (ಆದ್-ಉಪ್ಪುನಿ), *v. n.* To have become, to be that. ಅಂಚಾದುಪ್ಪುನಗ as *or* when it is so.

ಆದ್ರೆ ādre, *s.* The sixth lunar mansion; *bet.* ಆರ್ದ್ರ.

ಆಧರಿಪುನಿ ādharipuni, *see* ಆದರಿಪುನಿ.

ಆಧಾರ ādhāra, *s.* Support, prop. 2. a basis, foundation. –ಪತ್ರ a title-deed. 2. a security-bond. –ಸ್ಥ a rich man.

ಆಧೀನ ādhīna, *s.* Authority, control. 2. dependence; *cf.* ಅಧೀನ

ಆನಂದ ānanda, *s.* Joy, happiness, pleasure.

ಆನಗ ānaga, *see* ಆಪಿನ.

ಆನರ್ತ ānarta, *see* ಅನರ್ಥ.

ಆನಿ āni, *adv.* Then, at that time. –ಡ್ದ್, –ಡ್ದಂಚಿ from that time, since then. –ಮುಟ್ಟ till then. 2. *affixed to verbs it signifies:* at the time, *as* ಪೋಪಿನಾನಿ at the time of going.

ಆನಿಕೊರಂಟ್ ānikorantu, *s.* A large kernel.

ಆನಿಪುನಿ ānipuni (ಆನಿ), *v. a.* To make lean. 2. to lull.

ಆನೆ āne, *s.* An elephant. –ಕಾಡ್ a thick forest inhabited by elephants. –ಮಾಲ್ an elephant-shed. –ಮಾವುತೆ an elephant keeper. –ಸಂಕಲೆ a chain for fastening an elephant. –ಸುಂಡಿಲ್ the trunk of an elephant.

ಆನೆಂಗೆ ānenge, *see* ಆಪಿನ.

ಆನೆಕಲ್ಲ್ ānekallu, *see* ಆಣಿಕಲ್ಲ್.

ಆನೆಕಾರ್ ānekāru, *s.* The Cochin-leg, elephantiasis.

ಆನೆಕೆದು, ಆನೆಕೆರೆ ānekedu, ānekere, *s.* A large tank.

ಆನೆಗಜ್ಜಿ, ಆನೆಗುಡ್ಡು ānegajji, āneguḍḍu, *s.* A troublesome kind of scab, mange.

ಆನೆಙೋಳಿಸರ āneṅōḷisara, *s.* A kind of aloes.

ಆನೆತಜಂಕ್ ānetajaṅku, *s.* *Cassia occidentalis.*

ಆನೆದೂಜಿ ānedūji, *s.* A large needle.

ಆನೆನೇಗಿಲ್ ānenēgilu, *s.* *Pedalium murex*, a larger variety of caltrops.

ಆನೆಪಾಡುನಿ ānepāḍuni (ಆನೆಪಾಡ್), *v. a.* To lull (a baby).

ಆನೆಬಾಕಿಲ್ ānebākilu, *s.* The entrance gate of a palace. 2. a city-gate. 3. any large gate.

ಆನೆಮಂಜಲ್ ānemañjalu, *s.* *Curcuma zedoaria.*

ಆನೆಮೀನ್ ānemīnu, *s.* A whale; *also* ತಿಮಿಂಗಿಲ.

ಆನೆಮುಂಗು ānemuṅgu, *s.* *Calosanthes indica.*

ಆನ್ಹಿಕ ānhika, *s.* Daily ceremonies.

ಆಪ āpa, *s.* A kind of rice-cake.

ಆಪಗ āpaga, *adv.* Then, at that time. –ನೇ that very moment, instantly. ಆಪಗಾಪಗ now and then, occasionally; gradually.

ಆಪತ್ತ್ āpattu, *s.* Mishap. 2. trouble, calamity, distress. 3. danger, evil. —ಕಾಲ a time of trouble.

ಆಪಿನವು āpinavu, *see* ಆಪಿನಿ.

ಆಪಿನಿ āpini (ಆ), *v. n.* The copula: to be that, to become that. ಬೊಳ್ಳಿನ ಆಪುಂಡು it becomes white. 2. to have origin, grow, *as* ಮರಟ ಕುಕ್ಕು ಆಪುಂಡು mangoes grow on the tree. 3. to happen, occur: ಈ ಸಂಗತಿ ಓಳು ಆಂಡ್ where did this happen? 4. to fit, suit: ಈ ಅಂಗಿ ಯೆಂಕ್ ಆಪುಂಡು this coat fits me. 5. to be possible: ದೆರ್ಪೆರೆ ಆಪುಂಡು it can be lifted. 6. to be related to: ಆಯಿ ಯೆಂಕ್ ಮೆಗ್ಯೆ ಆಪೊಡು he is my younger brother. *It is used as an auxiliary verb, e. g.* ಮಳ್ತ್ದ್ ಆಂಡ್ it is done, *and serves also to form compound verbs:* ಉಂಡಾಪಿನಿ to come into existence, ಅಂದ್ ಆಪಿನಿ to be true, to be proved, *etc.*

ಆಂಡ್, *p. t. 3rd p. sing. neut.* It is done, finished.

ಆವು, *f. t. 3rd p. sing. neut.* It may be *or* may happen: ಬುಳೆ ಯೆಡ್ಡೆ ಆವು the crop is likely to turn out good. 2. when used absolutely as a reply, it is equivalent to "yes"; ಪೋವರೆ ಆವೊ? will you go? ಆವು yes.

The negative forms of these tenses are: *pres. t.* ಆಪುಜಿ, *p. t.* ಆಯಿಜಿ, *perf. t.* ಆತಿಜಿ, *fut. t.* ಆವಂದ್ it may, can, shall *or* will not be—*denoting moral and physical impossibility.* ಆವಂದ್ *added to inf. marks emph. prohibition, as* ಕೆರಿಯೆರೆ ಆವಂದ್ thou shalt not kill. *inter.* ಆವಂದಾ can *or* may it not be?

ಆವಡ್ *imp. 3rd. p.* Let it be, (*neg. 2nd p.* ಆವಡ be not); ಆವಡ್ *when repeated after nouns etc. means* either—or, *as* ಇಂಟೆ ಆವಡ್ ಆಯೆ ಆವಡ್ either this or that man.

ಆತು, *cond.* It should *or* would be. *It is much used as a polite form of request.* ಪೋ ತೆಂಡ ಆತು please go away. ಆಯೆ ಬತ್ತ್ಂಡ ಆತು I should like him to come.

ಆಪಿ, *adj. part. pres. t.,* ಆಯಿ, *p. t.* ಆತಿ, *perf. t.* ಆಪಿ ಸಂಗತಿ a practicable thing; ಆಯಿ *or* ಆತಿ ಕೆಲಸ a finished work. ಮದ್ಮೆ ಆಯಿ married. ಪಾಲಾಯಿ ಭೂಮಿ a divided land. ಆಯಿ, ಆಪಿ *when affixed to nouns and certain verbal forms, they convert them into adjectives, as* ಸಸಾರ ಆಯಿ ಬೇಲೆ an easy work; ಬೋಡಾಯಿ ಸಾಮಾನ the requisite things. *The personal nouns formed of the above, are:* ಆಪಿನಾಯೆ, ಆತಿನಾಯೆ *which are similarly joined to s., adj. etc.*

ಆವಂದಿ, *neg. adj. part.* That which should not be, unbecoming. 2. impracticable. 3. improper, wicked.

ಆದ್, *ger.* (*or adv. part.* Having become, being. 2. *when affixed to s. or adj. it converts them into adv.*, *as* ತಪ್ಪಾದ್ wrongly, ನಿಜ್ಜಯಾದ್ certainly. 3. *affixed to datives and infinitives it means* for, in behalf of, on account of, *as* ಐಕಾದ್ on that account, ಮಳ್ಪುನೆಕಾದ್ in order to make. 4. *affixed to pron. it means* of one's own accord, *as* ಆರಾದ್ ಕೊರಿಯೆರ್ he gave of his own accord (without being requested). ಆವಂದೆ *neg.* having not become, being not.

ಆನಗ When it happens, happened *or* will happen. –ನೇ just when it happens *etc.*

ಆನೆಂಕ Till it happens.

ಆಂಡ, *cond.*, ಆಂಡಲಾ, *emph.* If it becomes, if it be, although it be, ಅಂಚಾಂಡ if it be so. 2. *as a conj.* but, yet, though; at least, even.

ಆವೊಲಿ, *pot.* It can *or* may be.

ಆವೊಡು It must be *or* become. 2. to be related to. ಆರ್ ನಿಕ್ಕ್ ದಾನೆ ಆವೊಡು how is he related to you? ಯೆಂಕ್ ತಮ್ಮಲೆ ಆವೊಡು he is my uncle. ಆವೊಡಿತ್ತಿ what ought to happen, what is necessary.

ಆಪಿನವು, ಆಯಿನವು, ಆತಿನವು, *verbal nouns.* That which happens, *etc.* 2. that which is fit, possible, practicable.

ಆಪುಂಗೆನೇ **āpuṅgene**, *see* ಆಪಗ.

ಆಪುಲೇ **āpulē**, *see* ಆಪೊಲೇ.

ಆಪೆ **āpe**, *adv.* Yonder, opposite. ಆಪೆದ ಇಲ್ಲ್ yonder house. ಆಪೆದಾಯಿ one from the other side. ಆಪೆದಕ್ಕ್ yonder *or* the other side.

ಆಪೇಕ್ಷೆ **āpēkshe**, *see* ಅಪೇಕ್ಷೆ.

ಆಪೊಲೇ **āpolē**, *adv.* Just then; *cf.* ಆಪಗ. ಮಳ್ಪುನಾಪೊಲೇ just when doing.

ಆಪ್ತ **āpta**, *adj.* Dear, attached. 2. trustworthy, confidential.

ಆಪ್ತೆ **āpte**, *s.* An intimate friend. ಆಪ್ತೆರಿಷ್ಟೆರ್ friends and acquaintances.

ಆಫೀಮು **āphīmu**, *see* ಅಫೀಮು.

ಆಬಾದು **ābādu**, *adj.* Populous, inhabited. 2. cultivated. 3. thriving. –ಮಳ್ಪುನಿ to populate; to cultivate; to improve.

ಆಬಾಲ **ābāla**, *adj.* Young.

ಆಬುರು **āburu**, *see* ಅಬುರು.

ಆಭರಣ **ābharaṇa**, *s.* Ornament, jewels.

ಆಮದ್, ಆಮದು **āmadụ, āmadu**, *s.* Import, (*opp.* export). 2. income.

ಆಮರ್ಸುನಿ **āmarsuni**, *see* ಅಮರ್ಸುನಿ.

ಆಮವಡೆ **āmavaḍe**, *see* ಅಂಬೊಡೆ.

ಆಮ್ಲ **āmla**, *s.* Acidity. 2. tamarind. 3. vinegar. *adj.* Sour, acid; *vlg.* ಆಂಬುರ.

ಆಯ **āya**, *s.* A nurse.

ಆಯ **āya**, *s.* Gain; *see* ಅಯ.

ಆಯ **āya**, *s.* A foundation, base. –ಪಾಡುನಿ to lay a foundation.

ಆಯ **āya**, *s.* Measure, proportion. –ಕಟ್ಟುನಿ to regulate *or* fix the limits. –ತೆಪ್ಪುನಿ to measure.

ಆಯಕಟ್ಟ್, ಆಯಿಕಟ್ಟ್ **āyakaṭṭu, āyikaṭṭu**, *s.* Fixing the limits of a field *etc.* 2. regulation, arrangement. *adj.* Choice, excellent. —ದ ಕೆಲಸ a well executed work. —ದ ಜನ select people. —ದ ಪಾತೆರ a choice expression, excellent speech.

ಆಯತ್ತ **āyatta**, *s.* Docility, tractableness.

ಆಯತ್ತ **āyatta**, *s.* Preparation, readiness; *also* ಅಯಿತ.

ಆಯನ **āyana**, *s.* A festival in connexion with a temple.

ಆಯಾ **āyā**, *see* ಆ.

ಆಯಾವುನಿ **āyāvuni** (ಆಯಾ), *v. a.* To dig a foundation.

ಆಯಾವುನಿ **āyāvuni** (ಆಯಾ), *v. a.* To winnow.

ಆಯಾಸ **āyāsa**, *s.* Fatigue, weariness. 2. indisposition. 3. trouble, vexation.

ಆಯಿ **āyi**, *see* ಆಪಿನಿ.

ಆಯಿತ **āyita**, *see* ಆಯತ್ತ.

ಆಯಿದ **āyida**, *see* ಆಯುಧ.

ಆಯಿನವು **āyinavu**, *see* ಆಪಿನಿ.

ಆಯಿಸ **āyisa**, *see* ಆಯುಷ್ಯ.

ಆಯು **āyu**, *see* ಆಯುಷ್ಯ.

ಆಯುಧ **āyudha**, *s.* A weapon, instrument.

ಆಯುನಿ **āyuni** (ಆಯ್), *v. a.* To select, choose. 2. to gather, pick up; *cf.* ಅಜಪ್ಪುನಿ.

ಆಯುನಿ **āyuni** (ಆಯ್), *v. a.* To ford, cross, go over. *v. n.* To blow; ಘಾಳಿ ಆಯುಂಡು the wind blows; *cf.* ಹಾಯುನಿ.

ಆಯುರ್ದಾಯ **āyurdāya**, *s.* Term *or* period of life.

ಆಯುರ್ಬಲ **āyurbala**, *s.* Strength according to age. 2. a good constitution.

ಆಯುಷ್ಯ **āyushya**, *s.* Age, duration of life, term of life.

ಆಯೆ **āye**, *pron.* He. ಆಯಾಯೆ every one, each (man). 2. *it is joined to participles etc. to form personal nouns, as* ಮಳ್ಪುನಾಯೆ one who does, ಮಳ್ತಿನಾಯೆ one who did, ಮಳ್ಪಂದಿನಾಯೆ one who did not do; *cf.* ಆರ್.

ಆಯೆರೆ **āyerè**, *adv.* On that side, beyond (*opp.* ಈಯೆರೆ on this side). ಹುದೆತ ಆಯೆರೆ on that side of the river. ಆಯೆರೆಗ್ ಕಡಪುನಿ to cross a river.

ಆಯ್ಯ **āyya**, *see* ಆಯು.

ಆಯ್ಯೆರ್ **āyyeru**, *see* ಐವೆರ್.

ಆರ್ **āru**, *dem. pron.* (*honorif. pl. 3rd p. of* ಆಯೆ *or* ಆಳ್), They, *i. e.* that person. ಆರೆಡೇ *emph.* himself, none but he. 2. *it is joined to participles to form personal nouns, as* ಪೋಪಿನಾರ್ one who goes, ಪೋಯಿನಾರ್ one who went, ಪೋವಂದಿನಾರ್ one who did not go.

ಆರ **āra**, *A termination occurring in some nouns and meaning* home, place *or* locality, *as* ಬುಡಾರ lodging; ಅಲಿಮಾರ, ಅಡಿಯಾರ, ಪಲಿಮಾರ, ಬೊಳ್ಕಾರ *etc.* names of villages.

ಆರಂಭ ārambha, *s.* Commencement, beginning. —ಮಳ್ಪುನಿ to make a beginning, to begin.

ಆರಂಭಿಪುನಿ ārambhipuni (ಆರಂಭಿ), *v.a.* To begin.

ಆರಗೆ ārage, *see* ಹಾರಗೆ; *cf.* ಕಾರಯಿ.

ಆರಟ, ಆರಡ ārața, ārada, *s.* The concluding part of a temple feast, including bathing the idol.

ಆರಣ್ಯ āraṇya, *see* ಅರಣ್ಯ.

ಆರತಿ ārati, *s.* Wave-offering, consisting in waving lamps *etc.* 2. the lamp for wave-offering. —ಕೊರ್ಪಿನಿ.—ಯೆತ್ತುನಿ to offer, wave frankincense *etc.* ಧೂಪಾರ್ತಿ a censer. ಯೇಕಾರ್ತಿ a lamp with one wick. ಆರತಿತಟ್ಟೆ a metal plate for wave-offering.

ಆರತಿ ārati, *see* ಆರ್ತಿ.

ಆರಭಾರ ārabhāra, *s.* Responsibility, care.

ಆರಭ್ಯ ārabhya, *s.* Beginning, commencement. ಲೋಕಾರಭ್ಯ from the beginning of the world. ನಿಕುಳು ಮಳ್ತಿನಿತ ಆರಭ್ಯ since you began doing; *cf.* ಆರಂಭ.

ಆರವಾರ āravāra, *s.* An usufructuary mortgage. —ಪತ್ರ a deed of such mortgage.

ಆರಾಟ ārāța, *s.* Tottering, shaking; *cf.* ಆರಟ.

ಆರಾದ್‍ಪೋಪಿನಿ ārādupōpini, *v.n.* To walk arm in arm *or* hand in hand.

ಆರಾಧನೆ ārādhane, *s.* Worship, adoration, prayer. —ಮಳ್ಪುನಿ *see* ಆರಾಧಿಪುನಿ.

ಆರಾಧಿಪುನಿ ārādhipuni (ಆರಾಧಿ), *v.a.* To worship, adore.

ಆರಾವುನಿ ārāvuni, *see* ಅರಾವುನಿ.

ಆರಿಗೆ ārige, *s.* A belch. —ಬುಡ್ಪುನಿ to belch; *cf.* ಆಡಿಗೆ.

ಆರಿದೆ āride, *see* ಆರ್ದ್ರೆ.

ಆರಿಯ āriya, *int.* Stop! hold!

ಆರಿಯೆ āriye, *see* ಆಯೆ.

ಆರುಣೆ āruņe, *s.* Contentment, satisfaction.

ಆರುನಿ āruni (ಆರ್), *v.n.* To grow cool, cold *or* dry. 2. to be cool, dry. 3. to distend, grow stout: ಬಂಜಿ ಆರುನಿ the belly to distend *etc.*

ಆರೂಢ ārūḍha, *adj.* Ascended, mounted. *s.* Ascending, climbing.

ಆರೆ āre, *see* ಆಯಿರೆ.

ಆರೆದೇ āredē, *see* ಆರ್.

ಆರೇಕ್ತಿ, ಆರೈಕೆ ārēkti, āreikè, *s.* Protection, care of, nursing, nourishing. —ಮಳ್ಪುನಿ to protect, nurse, nourish.

ಆರೈಸುನಿ āreisuni (ಆರೈಸ್), *v.a.* To expect, wait for, look for. 2. to desire, wish; *bet.* ಹಾರೈಸುನಿ.

ಆರೊಳ್‍ಮೀನ್ ārolumīnu, *s.* A kind of fish.

ಆರೊಳುಮರ ārolumara, *s.* A kind of tree.

ಆರೋಗಣೆ ārōgaņe, *s.* A meal, repast. —ಮಳ್ಪುನಿ to take a meal.

ಆರೋಗ್ಯ ārōgya, *s.* Health, strength. 2. comfort, happiness.

ಆರೋಪ, ಆರೋಪಣೆ **ārōpa, ārōpaṇe,** *s.* Imputation, accusation. 2. a false charge.

ಆರೋಪಿಸುನಿ **ārōpisuni** (ಆರೋಪಿಸ್), *v. a.* To impute, accuse unjustly, charge with.

ಆರೋಹಣ **ārōhaṇa,** *s.* Ascending, climbing, mounting. ದಿವಾರೋಹಣ ಪರ್ಬ Ascension day, *Chr.*

ಆರೋಳಿ **ārōḷi,** *s.* The last leaf of a cocoa-palm-branch.

ಆರ್ಕ **ārka,** *s.* A bow. 2. an arch.

ಆರ್ಕುನಿ **ārkuni** (ಆರ್ಕ್), *v.n.* To cry out, shout.

ಆರ್ಜಿತ **ārjita,** *adj.* Acquired, accumulated, inherited, *as* ಪಿತ್ರಾರ್ಜಿತ patrimonial. ಸ್ವಾರ್ಜಿತ self-acquired. –ಬದ್ಕ್ inherited wealth *or* property.

ಆರ್ತಿ **ārti,** *s.* Pain, distress. *adj.* Afflicted, distressed, sorrowful.

ಆರ್ತೆ **ārtè,** *s.* One who is afflicted.

ಆರ್ದ್ಪೋಪಿನಿ **ārdụpōpini,** *see* ಆರುನಿ.

ಆರ್ದ್ರೆ **ārdre,** *s.* The sixth lunar mansion, *a arionis*, when it rains heavily.

ಆರ್ಬಟ, ಆರ್ಭಟ, ಆರ್ಭಟೆ **ārbaṭa, ārbhaṭa, ārbhaṭe,** *s.* Fearful noise, uproar. 2. a joyful cry, triumph. –ಮಳ್ಪುನಿ to roar, shout, triumph.

ಆರ್ಯ **ārya,** *adj.* Noble, respectable, belonging to the Āryans. ಆರ್ಯಾವರ್ತ the country between the Himālaya and Vindhya mountains.

ಆರ್ಯಯೆರು **āryayeru,** *s.* A castrated buffalo.

ಆರ್ಯೆ **ārye,** *s.* An Aryan. 2. a man of the Ārya caste.

ಆರ್ವದೆ **ārvade,** *see* ಅರ್ವದೆ.

ಆರ್ವಾರ **ārvāra,** *see* ಆರವಾರ.

ಆರ್ಸಾವುನಿ **ārsāvuni** (ಆರ್ಸಾ), *v. a.* To despise, defy, set at naught. 2. to disparage. ಆರ್ಸಾದ್ ಪಾತೆರುನಿ to talk disparagingly *or* defiantly.

ಆಲ **āla,** *s.* The silk-cotton tree, *Salmalia Malabarica*; *also* –ದಮರ. –ದ ಪತ್ತಿ silk cotton.

ಆಲಂಗನೆ **ālaṅgane,** *s.* The act of embracing.

ಆಲಂಬ **ālamba,** *s.* Seizing. 2. killing. 3. a violent death.

ಆಲಡೆ **ālaḍe,** *s.* A kind of demon's shrine.

ಆಲದ ಬಲ್ಲ್ **ālada ballụ,** *see* ಅಲಾದ್.

ಆಲಯ **ālaya,** *s.* An abode, house. 2. any superior edifice. ಘಟಾಲಯ the body. ದೇವಾಲಯ a temple; a church, *Chr.*

ಆಲಸ್ **ālasụ,** *see* ಅಲಾದ್.

ಆಲಸ್ಯ **ālasya,** *s.* Weariness. 2. idleness, laziness, sloth.

ಆಲಾತ್ **ālātụ,** *see* ಅಲಾದ್.

ಆಲಾಪನೆ **ālāpane,** *s.* Humming a tune.

ಆಲಾಪಿಸುನಿ **ālāpisuni** (ಆಲಾಪಿಸ್), *v.n.* To hum a tune, to sing.

ಆಲಾಸ್ **ālāsụ,** *see* ಅಲಾದ್.

ಆಲಿ **āli,** *s.* Breath, life, strength. –ಬಚ್ಚುನಿ to pant, be fatigued, tired. –ಬಚ್ಚಿದ್ ಪೋಂಡು the breath is gone, or exhausted. ಕಣ್ಣದ– visual strength.

ಆಲಿಕಲ್ಲ್, ಆಲಿಪರ್ಂದ್ **ālikallu̥, āliparndu̥**, *s.* Hailstone.

ಆಲೆ **āle**, *s.* A press, mill, *as* ಕಂಬುರ್ದ– a sugarcane mill. –ಪಾಡುನಿ a mill to work.

ಆಲೈಸುನಿ **āleisuni** (ಆಲೈಸ್), *v. n.* To listen to, to hear attentively.

ಆಲೋಕ **ālōka**, *s.* Seeing, a view. 2. light. 3. panegyric. ಆಲೋಕ್ಯ an object of sight.

ಆಲೋಚನೆ **ālōćane**, *s.* Reflection, investigation, thought. –ಮಳ್ಪುನಿ to consider, reflect on. –ಪಣ್ಪುನಿ to advise, to give one's opinion.

ಆವಂದಿ, ಆವಂದೆ, ಆವಡ್ **āvandi, āvandè, āvaḍu̥**, *see* ಆಪಿನಿ.

ಆವಡೆ **āvaḍè**, *s.* A kind of bean, lentil.

ಆವಡೆ **āvaḍe**, *see* ಆಪಿನಿ.

ಆವರ **āvara**, *postp.* On account of. ಐಡ್ದಾವರ on that account. ಉಂಡೆಡ್ದಾವರ on this account.

ಆವರ್ತನೆ **āvartane**, *s.* Revolution. 2. repetition. –ಮಳ್ಪುನಿ to repeat.

ಆವಲ್ **āvalu̥**, *see* ಅವಲ್.

ಆವಲ್ **āvalu̥**, *s.* Yawning. –ಇಡೆಪಿನಿ to yawn, gape.

ಆವಶ್ಯ **āvaśya**, *see* ಅವಶ್ಯ.

ಆವು **āvu**, *see* ಆಪಿನಿ.

ಆವುಸ **āvusa**, *see* ಆಯುಷ್ಯ.

ಆವೆ **āve**, *s.* A potter's kiln, an oven. –ದೆಪ್ಪುನಿ, –ಜಪ್ಪುನಿ to open a kiln. –ಮಣ್ಣ್ clay.

ಆವೆದಿ **āvedi**, *s.* A burnt offering; *cf.* ಆಹುತಿ. –ಕೊರ್ಪಿನಿ to offer a sacrifice.

ಆವೇಶ **āvēśa**, *s.* Possession by spirits, demoniacal possession. –ಆಪಿನಿ to be possessed with a devil, be in a frenzy.

ಆವೊಡು **āvoḍu**, *see* ಆಪಿನಿ.

ಆಶಡ, **āśaḍa**, *see* ಆಷಾಢ.

ಆಶಾಕೃತ **āśākru̥ta**, *adj.* Avaricious, covetous, greedy.

ಆಶಾಮಾರಿ **āśāmāri**, *s.* A covetous person.

ಆಶಿಗೆ **āśige**, *see* ಆಸಿಗೆ, ಹಾಸಿಗೆ.

ಆಶಿಪುನಿ **āśipuni** (ಆಶಿ), *v. a.* To wish, desire.

ಆಶೀರ್ವಚನ, ಆಶೀರ್ವಾದ **āśīrvaćana, āśīrvāda**, *s.* Benediction, blessing. –ಕೊರ್ಪಿನಿ, *see* ಆಶೀರ್ವದಿಪುನಿ.

ಆಶೀರ್ವದಿಪುನಿ **āśīrvadipuni** (ಆಶೀರ್ವದಿ), *v. a.* To bless, confer a blessing.

ಆಶೆ **āśè**, *s.* Desire, longing, wish. 2. expectation, prospect, hope. –ದಾಯೆ a covetous man. –ಉಪ್ಪುನಿ to have a wish. –ಕಡ್ಪುನಿ to be disappointed, to have lost hope, to despair of. –ಕಳೆಪಿನಿ, –ಬುಡ್ಪುನಿ to give up hope, to abandon a wish. –ಪಟ್ಟಾವುನಿ to hold out hope. –ಮಳ್ಪುನಿ to wish, covet, hope.

ಆಶ್ಚರ್ಯ **āśćarya**, *s.* Wonder, surprise. –ಆಪಿನಿ to wonder, be surprised. –ಪಡೆಪಾವುನಿ to astonish, surprise. –ಮಳ್ಪುನಿ to make wonders, perform a miracle. —ದ ಪಾತ್ರ, —ಸಂಗತಿ a wonderful *or* remarkable thing *or* affair.

ಆಶ್ರಮ **āśrama,** *s.* A hermitage. 2. one of the four stages of Brahminical life, *e.g.* ಬ್ರಹ್ಮಚಾರಿ a bachelor, student; ಗೃಹಸ್ಥ a householder; ವಾನಪ್ರಸ್ಥ an anchorite; ಸನ್ಯಾಸಿ an ascetic.

ಆಶ್ರಯ **āśraya,** *s.* Support, refuge. 2. protection, reliance. 3. dependence. —ಕೊರ್ಪಿನಿ to give protection, patronise. —ನಾಡುನಿ to seek shelter. —ಮಳ್ಪುನಿ to depend upon.

ಆಶ್ರಯಿಪುನಿ **āśrayipuni** (ಆಶ್ರಯಿ), *v. a.* To seek shelter.

ಆಶ್ರಿತೆ **āśrite,** *s.* A dependant, client.

ಆಶ್ಲೇಷ **āślēsha,** *s.* The ninth lunar mansion; *also* ಆಸ್ಲೇಸ.

ಆಶ್ವೀಜ **āśvīja,** *s.* The seventh lunar month (September-October).

ಆಷಡ, ಆಷಾಢ **āshaḍa, āshāḍha,** *s.* The fourth lunar month (June-July).

ಆಸ್ **āsu,** *s.* A weaver's warp before starching. 2. a web, texture; *cf.* ಹಾಸ್‌ಪಾಸ್. —ಕಂಬ, —ಮರ the rake of a weaver's warp.

ಆಸ್‌ಪಾಸ್ **āsupāsu,** *s.* Proximity, vicinity, environs, neighbourhood. *adv.* Round about.

ಆಸಕ್ತ **āsakta,** *adj.* Attached, devoted. 2. zealous, active.

ಆಸಕ್ತಿ **āsakti,** *s.* Diligence, devotion, attachment.

ಆಸನ **āsana,** *s.* A stool, seat. ಧರ್ಮಾಸನ the judgment seat. ಸಿಂಹಾಸನ a throne. 2. the anus. —ಕುರಿ, —ಗಂಡಮಾಲೆ an anal fistula.

ಆಸರ್ **āsaru,** *s.* Thirst. 2. that which slakes thirst. —ಕೊರ್ಪಿನಿ to give to drink.

ಆಸರ **āsara,** *s.* Refuge, support. 2. protection, patronage; *cf.* ಆಶ್ರಯ.

ಆಸರ್ಮೆ **āsarme,** *s.* Management of a family, care of a household.

ಆಸಾಡ **āsāḍa,** *see* ಆಷಡ.

ಆಸಾಮಿ **āsāmi,** *s.* A person, an individual. 2. a customer. 3. a debtor.

ಆಸಿಗೆ **āsige,** *s.* A mattress, bed; *also* ಹಾಸಿಗೆ.

ಆಸು **āsu,** *see* ಆಸ್.

ಆಸೆ **asè,** *see* ಆಶೆ.

ಆಸ್ಕಾರ **āskāra,** *s.* Protection, shelter, countenance.

ಆಸ್ತಿ **āsti,** *s.* Property, wealth, estate. —ಬಾಯಿ, —ವಂತೆ a man of property.

ಆಸ್ತೆ **āste,** *adv.* Gently, slowly.

ಆಸ್ಥಾನ **āsthāna,** *s.* An assembly. 2. a hall of audience.

ಆಸ್ಪತ್ರಿ **āspatri,** *s.* An hospital.

ಆಸ್ಪದ **āspada,** *s.* Place to stand on, basis, support. 2. protection, refuge, shelter. 3. means; ಯೆಂಕ್ ದಾಲಾ ಆಸ್ಪದ ಇಜ್ಜಿ I have no means of livelihood.

ಆಸ್ಪಾಸ್ **āspāsu,** *see* ಆಸ್‌ಪಾಸ್.

ಆಸ್ರಣ್ಣೆ āsraṇṇe, *s.* A kind of priest.

ಆಸ್ವದ āsvada, *s.* Ability, power; faculty. 2. estate, property; wealth, riches; *see* ಆಸ್ಪದ.

ಆಹಂಕಾರ āhaṅkāra, *see* ಅಹಂಕಾರ.

ಆಹಾ āhā, *intj.* of joy *or* sorrow.

ಆಹಾರ āhāra, *s.* Food, provision, sustenance.

ಆಹಾಹಾ āhāhā, *intj.* Alas, ha!

ಆಹುತ āhuta, *adj.* Offered as an oblation in fire.

ಆಹುತಿ āhuti, *s.* A sacrifice.

ಆಳ್ āḷu, *s.* A person. 2. a labourer, hired person. 3. a messenger. ಬಲ್ಲಾಳ್ a strong man; a chieftain.

ಆಳ್ āḷu, *pers. pron. fem. sing.* She.

ಆಳ್ āḷu, *see* ಹಾಳ್

ಆಳ āḷa, *s.* Depth. *adj.* Deep, profound.

ಆಳಾ āḷā, *adj.* Ruined, waste; *bet.* ಹಾಳಾ.

ಆಳಿ āḷi, *see* ಆಲಿ.

ಆಳಿಕೆ āḷike, *s.* Reign, government.

ಆಳಿತ āḷita, *see* ಹಾಳಿತ.

ಆಳುನಿ āḷuni (ಆಳು), *v.a.* To rule, govern, reign. ಆಳುನಾಯೆ a governor. ಆಳುನಾಳ್ a governess.

ಆಳುವಿಕೆ, ಆಳ್ವಿಕೆ āḷuvike, āḷvike, *s.* Reign.

ಆಳುವೆ āḷuve, *s.* A family-name of some Bants.

ಆಳ್ಮಗೆ āḷmage, *s.* A servant.

ಆಕ್ಷೇಪ ākshēpa, *s.* Objection. 2. blame, censure.

ಇ

I

ಇ i, The third letter of the alphabet. In MSS. it is very often written ಯಿ. Words not found under this letter should be sought for under ಯಿ.

ಇಂಕ iṅka, *adj.* Base, inferior, mean.

ಇಂಕಿ iṅki, *see* ಇಂಗಿ.

ಇಂಗ್ iṅgu, *see* ಹಿಂಗ್.

ಇಂಗಡ iṅgaḍa, *s.* Separation, distinction. *adj.* Distinct, separate; *also* ಇಂಗಡಿಂಗಡ, ವಿಂಗಡ. —ಮಳ್ಪುನಿ, ಇಂಗಡಿಪುನಿ to divide, separate. —ಆಪಿನ to be divided, separated, as brothers *etc.*

ಇಂಗಲೀಕ iṅgalīka, *see* ಇಂಗಲೀಕ.

ಇಂಗಾವುನಿ iṅgāvuni, *c.v.* (*of* ಇಂಗುನಿ) To cause to dry.

ಇಂಗಿ iṅgi, *adj.* Crooked. 2. false, spurious, as a coin.

ಇಂಗಿಲೀಕ iṅgilīka, *s.* Vermilion.

ಇಂಗಿತ iṅgita, *s.* A hint, shrug, gesture. 2. a secret, secret thought. 3. intent, purpose.

ಇಂಗುಡುನಿ iṅguḍuni (ಇಂಗುಡಿ), *v. n.* To stoop.

ಇಂಗುನಿ iṅguni (ಇಂಗಿ), *v. n.* To absorb, as water, to dry. 2. to sink in, as eyes from disease; *also* ಇಂಗಿದ್ ಪೋಪಿನಿ.

ಇಂಗ್ರೇಜಿ iṅgrēji, *s.* English. 2. a church. –ಬರವು the English writing or language.

ಇಂಚ iñca, *adv.* Thus, so, in this manner; –ಅತ್ತ್ ಅಂಚ not this but that way. –ದಾಯೆ such and such a man. ಇಂಚನೆ, *emph.* just so. ಇಂಚಿತ್ತಿ such, of this kind or sort.

ಇಂಚಿ iñci, *adv.* Here, in this place. –ದಾಯೆ a man of this place, *or* of this age.

ಇಂಚೊಗು iñcogu, *adv.* Lately, recently.

ಇಂಜಾಯಿ iñjāyi, *adj.* Small, little.

ಇಂಜಿನ್ iñjinụ, *s.* An engine, machine.

ಇಂಜೀಲ್ iñjīlụ, *s.* The New Testament, as styled by Mussulmans.

ಇಂದ್ indụ, *see* ಉಂಡು.

ಇಂದ್, ಇಂದ indụ, inda, *see* ಈಂಡ್.

ಇಂದಾ indā, *intj. used to call attention.* Behold, look, take notice, observe. 2. there, take this. ಇಂದೆ please see, come, *or* take.

ಇಂದಿ indi, *s.* Oil-cake; *bet.* ಪುಂಡಿ.

ಇಂದು indu, *dem. pron.* This. ಇಂದೇ *emph.* this alone; *see* ಉಂಡು.

ಇಂದ್ರಜಾಲ indrajāla, *s.* Deception, conjuring. 2. enchantment. 3. artifice, stratagem; *cf.* ಐಂದ್ರಜಾಲ.

ಇಂದ್ರಜಿತು indrajitu, *s.* A son of Rāvaṇa.

ಇಂದ್ರಪ್ರಸ್ಥ indraprasta, *s.* Delhi.

ಇಂದ್ರಬಾಲೆ indrabālè, *s.* A kind of fish.

ಇಂದ್ರಿಯ indriya, *s.* An organ of sense. 2. male power, *semen virile.* 3. sensual desires *or* appetites. ಪಂಚೇಂದ್ರಿಯ the five senses.

ಇಂದ್ರೆ indre, *s.* The chief of the secondary divinities, supposed to preside over the elements, to be the giver of rain, and the guardian of the east (*in Sanskrit* Indra).

ಇಂದ್ರೆ, ಇಂದ್ರ್ಯೆ indre, indrye, *s.* A Jain priest.

ಇಂನೆ inne, *see* ಇನೆ.

ಇಂಪು impu, *s.* Agreeableness, delightfulness, pleasantness.

ಇಂಬಳ್, ಇಂಬಾಳ್ imbaḷụ, imbāḷụ, *see* ಇಂಬೆ.

ಇಂಬಳೆ imbaḷe, *s.* A stout silver *or* gold bracelet.

ಇಂಬು imbu, *s.* Place, room, space. 2. refuge, shelter. 3. opportunity. *adj.* Broad, wide.

ಇಂಬೆ imbe, *dem. pron. m.* This man. ಇಂಬಳ್, ಇಂಬಾಳ್, ಇಂಬೊಳು this woman; *plur.* ಇಂಬೆರ್ this person, *used honorifically, as a polite form of the sing. m. or f.*; *cf.* ಮೇರ್, ಮೋಳು.

ಇಂಬೊಳು imboḷu, *see* ಇಂಜಿ.

ಇಂಮಡ immaḍa, The heel.

ಇಂಮಡಿ, ಇಂಮಡಿಗೆ immaḍi, immaḍige, *adj.* Double, two-fold; *also* ಇಬ್ಬಡಿ.

ಇಂಮುಖ, ಇಂಮೋಣೆ immukha, immōṇe, *adj.* Double faced.

ಇಕರ ikara, *adv.* Hither, this side.

ಇಕ್ಕ್ ikkụ, *see* ಇರ್ಕ್.

ಇಕ್ಕ್ಡಿ ikkụḍi, *s.* Fiction, invention.

ಇಕ್ಕಟ್ಟ್ ikkaṭṭụ, *lit.* two hands. *s.* Narrowness, difficulty, straitness, poverty. —ಆಪಿನಿ to be confined, pent up. 2. to be in troubles. ಇಕ್ಕಟ್ಟಡ್ ತಿಕ್ಕೊಣುನಿ, —ಬೂರುನಿ to encounter difficulties, to be in straits. *adj.* Narrow, strait.

ಇಕ್ಕಡಿ ikkaḍi, *see* ಹಿಕ್ಕಡಿ.

ಇಕ್ಕಡೆ ikkaḍe, *s.* Both sides.

ಇಕ್ಕಲ್ಪ ikkalpa, *see* ವಿಕಲ್ಪ.

ಇಕ್ಕಳೆ ikkaḷe, *see* ಇಕ್ಕುಳಿ.

ಇಕ್ಕಾವುನಿ ikkāvuni, *v. a.* To extinguish, put out, as fire. ಇಕ್ಕಾದ್ ಪೋಪಿನಿ to be extinguished.

ಇಕ್ಕುನಿ ikkuni (ಇಕ್ಕ್), *v. a.* To put, serve up, as food.

ಇಕ್ಕುಳಿ, ಇಕ್ಕುಳೆ ikkuḷi, ikkuḷe, *s.* A pair of pincers *or* tongs.

ಇಕ್ಕೇರಿ ikkēri, *s.* The residence of the late Lingāit kings of Bednore. —ಅರಸ್ತನ, —ಸಂಸ್ಥಾನ the kingdom of these rulers. —ಕೋಲು a measure of two feet and seven inches long. —ವರಹ a gold pagoda worth thirteen gold fanams *or* four rupees.

ಇಕ್ಕೈ ikkei, *s.* Both hands. 2. an ambidexter.

ಇಕ್ಡಿ ikḍi, *see* ಹಿಕ್ಕಡಿ.

ಇಗ್ತಿ igụti, *see* ಯುಕ್ತಿ.

ಇಗಡ igaḍa, *s.* Difference, misunderstanding; *also* ವಿಗಡ.

ಇಗರುನಿ igaruni, *see* ಇಗುರುನಿ.

ಇಗಾದಿ igādi, *see* ಯುಗಾದಿ.

ಇಗುರು iguru, *s.* A bud, germ *or* tender shoot.

ಇಗುರುನಿ iguruni (ಇಗುರ್), *v. n.* To bud, germinate *or* shoot up.

ಇಗ್ಗುನಿ iggụni (ಇಗ್ಗ್), *v. n.* To draw, pull.

ಇಚ್ಚಡಿ iććaḍi, *adj.* Double, two-fold.

ಇಚ್ಚಿರ್ನ iććirna, *s.* Wonder.

ಇಚ್ಚೆ, ಇಚ್ಛೆ ićće, iććhe, *s.* Wish, desire. 2. appetite. 3. relish, delight. ಇಚ್ಛಾನುಸಾರ according to one's desire *or* wish, as one pleases. ಇಚ್ಚೆಪುನಿ, ಇಚ್ಚೈಸುನಿ to wish, long for.

ಇಜ ija, *s.* Trouble. 2. importunity. —ಕೊರ್ಪಿನಿ to trouble, importune; *cf.* ಹಿಜ.

ಇಜಾರ್ ijārụ, *s.* Trousers.

ಇಜಾರ್ದಾಯೆ, ಇಜಾರ್ದಾರೆ ijārụdāye, ijārụdāre, *s.* An abkāri (liquor) contractor. 2. a man wearing trousers.

ಇಜಾರಿಗೆ ijārige, *s.* An abkāri contract.

ಇಜಿಡೆ ijiḍe, *s.* An impotent man.

ಇಜಿನ್ ijinụ, *s.* Cinnamon. —ದ ಮರ the cinnamon tree. —ದ ಯೆಣ್ಣೆ cinnamon oil; *also* ದಾಲ್ಚಿನಿ.

ಇಜ್ಜಿ ijji, *d. v. the neg. of* ಉಂಡು, Negation of existence; not to exist, not to be. It is regularly conjugated only in the present and perfect tenses, through all persons. ಒಂಜಿಲಾ— not even one. ದಾಲಾ— there is nothing. ಯೆಂಕ್ ಪಣವು ಇಜ್ಜಿ I have no money. ನಿಕ್ಕ್ ಬಾಲೆಳು ಉಂಡಾ? ಇಜ್ಜಿ have you any children? no. *Interr.* ಇಜ್ಜಾ? is there not? *Emph.* ಇಜ್ಜೀ ಇಜ್ಜಿ not in the least, not at all. *Used as a disjunctive conjunction:* ಇಜ್ಜಿಡ if not, or; either—or. ಇಜ್ಜಂದಿ not existing, absent. ಇಜ್ಜಂದೆ without; *cf.* ಇದ್ದ್.

ಇಟ್ಟ್ iṭṭụ, *s.* Flour.

ಇಟ್ಟ iṭṭa, *see* ಇಷ್ಟ.

ಇಟ್ಟರೆ, ಇಟ್ಟಿರೆ iṭṭarè, iṭṭire, *s.* A mortice, cavity cut into a piece of timber to receive the end of a beam or plank. 2. a stone placed under a beam.

ಇಟ್ಟಿ iṭṭi, *s.* The jaw; *cf.* ನಿಜ್ಜಿ.

ಇಟ್ಟಿಗೆ iṭṭige, *s.* A brick.

ಇಟ್ಟಿಡೆ iṭṭiḍe, *s.* Narrowness.

ಇಟ್ಟಿರಿ iṭṭiri, *s.* A nightingale.

ಇಟ್ಟೆಯಿ, ಇಟ್ಟೇವು iṭṭeyi, iṭṭēvu, *s.* A kind of medicinal plant.

ಇಡ್ಕಿಡ್ಕ iḍụkiḍka, *adj.* Half ground, coarse, rough.

ಇಡ್ಪುಲು iḍụpulu, *see* ಇಡುಂಬುಲು.

ಇಡ iḍa, *see* ಇಡೆ.

ಇಡಕತ್ತೆರಿ iḍakatteri, *see* ಅಡ್ಡಕತ್ತರಿ.

ಇಡಿ iḍi, *adj.* Entire, whole. —ದಿನ the whole day.

ಇಡಿಮುಡಿ iḍimuḍi, *s.* A stout person. *adj.* Pinioned. —ಕಟ್ಟುನಿ to bind fast, pinion.

ಇಡುಂಬುಲು iḍumbulu, *s.* (*in wrestling*) The act of seizing each other tightly with both hands.

ಇಡೆ iḍè, *s.* Place, room, space. 2. an abode. 3. interval, space between. 4. interval of time, occasion. 5. a split, chasm. —ಬುಡಂದೆ incessantly.

ಇಡೆ, ಇಡೆಗ್ iḍe, iḍegụ, *adv.* Here, hither, so far. —ಮುಟ್ಟ hitherto, so long; so far, thus far; *also* ಇಡ.

ಇಡೆಕಾಜಿ iḍekāji, *s.* A bracelet with an indented brass rim.

ಇಡೆಕೈ iḍekei, *s.* Aid, help. 2. half grown corn (ಇಡೆಕೆಯು).

ಇಡೆತರ iḍetara, *adj.* Middling, 2. inferior. —ತ ದೈ a middle sized tree.

ಇಡೆನಾಳಿ iḍenāḷi, *s.* The inner part of a temple. 2. the three circuits of a temple.

ಇಡ್ತಪಿಡ್ತ iḍtapiḍta, *s.* Experience.

ಇಡ್ಪಿನಿ iḍpini (ಇಡ್), *v.a.* To place, put down.

ಇಣೆ iṇe, *see* ಇನೆ.

ಇತಬಾರ್ itabārụ, *s.* Confidence, trust. —ದೀಪಿನಿ, —ಮಳ್ಪುನಿ to believe, trust.

ಇತಬಾರಿ **itabāri**, *s.* A confident, trustworthy person.

ಇತರ್ **itarụ**, *see* ಇತ್ತರ್.

ಇತಿಹಾಸ **itihāsa**, *s.* History, traditional accounts of former events.

ಇತ್ತಂಡ **ittaṇḍa**, *s.* Both parties *or* sides.

ಇತ್ತಟ್ಟ್ **ittaṭṭụ**, *s.* Both sides *or* places. 2. both banks of a river, *etc.*

ಇತ್ತರ್, ಇತ್ತರ, ಇತ್ತರು **ittarụ, ittara, ittaru**, *adv.* Enough; *cf.* ಇಯ್ಯಾವು.

ಇತ್ತಿ **itti**, *see* ಉಪ್ಪುನಿ.

ಇತ್ತಿಲ್ಲೆ **ittille**, *s.* A written report. —ಮಳ್ಪುನಿ to report in writing.

ಇತ್ತೀರ್ಣ **ittīrna**, *s.* Sickness.

ಇತ್ತೆ **itté**, *adv.* Now, at present. —ನೇ *emph.* just now, this moment, immediately. —ದವು of the present time. —ಏರ now for once, for the present. —ಬಂಜಿ, ಬೊಕ್ಕ ಬಂಜಿ (*lit.*) now one and afterwards another, a proverbial expression for fickleness *or* duplicity, "to blow hot and cold".

ಇತ್ತೆ **itte**, *see* ಉಪ್ಪುನಿ.

ಇತ್ಯರ್ಥ **ityartha**, *s.* Decision, determination, settlement. —ಮಳ್ಪುನಿ to decide, determine, establish.

ಇತ್ಯಾದಿ **ityādi**, These and others, *et cetera.*

ಇದಮುಟ್ಟ **idamuṭṭa**, *adv.* Till now.

ಇದ್ದಿ **iddi**, *see* ಇಜ್ಜಿ.

ಇನ **ina**, *see* ಇನೆ.

ಇನತೆ **inate**, *see* ಎನತೆ.

ಇನಪು **inapu**, *s.* Evil disposition. 2. defeat, discomfiture.

ಇನಾಮ್ **ināmụ**, *s.* A gift, present. —ಕೊರ್ಪಿನಿ to give a present *or* reward.

ಇನಿ **ini**, *adv.* To-day. —ಕ up to *or* for this day. —ಡ್ದ್ from this day.

ಇನೆ **inè**, *s.* A couple, pair. 2. a companion, mate. —ಆಪಿನಿ to be a match. 2. to pair (*obsc.*)

ಇನ್ಕಾರ್ **inkārụ**, *s.* Abnegation. —ಮಳ್ಪುನಿ to abnegate. 2. to refuse.

ಇನ್ಪಿನಿ **inpini** (ಇನ್), *v. a.* To say, tell. 2. to speak; *also* ಅನ್ಪಿನಿ.

ಇಪರೀತ **iparīta**, *see* ವಿಪರೀತ.

ಇಪುನಿ **ipuni**, *see* ಉಪ್ಪುನಿ.

ಇಪ್ಪಡಿತ **ippaḍita**, *s. lit.* Double stripes; a wale, the mark of a rod or whip on animal flesh.

ಇಪ್ಪಕ್ಷ **ippaksha**, *s.* Both parties *or* sides.

ಇಪ್ಪಿಲಿ **ippili**, *s.* Long pepper, *Piper longum*; *also* ತಿಪ್ಪಿಲಿ.

ಇಪ್ಪುನಿ **ippuni** (ಇ), *v. n.* To be, exist; *also* ಉಪ್ಪುನಿ.

ಇಪ್ಪುಲಿ **ippuli**, *see* ಇಪ್ಪಿಲಿ.

ಇಪ್ಪೆ **ippe**, *s.* The olive fruit. —ಮರ the olive tree.

ಇಬೂತಿ **ibūti**, *s.* Sacred ashes with which a Sivite besmears his forehead.

ಇಬ್ಬಿರೆಲ್ **ibbirelụ**, *s.* Two fingers

united by a membrane (web-fingers).

ಇಬ್ಬುಡ್ಳು **ibbuḍḷu,** *s.* A kind of cucumber.

ಇಮ **ima,** *s.* Snow; *bet.* ಹಿಮ.

ಇಮಿನಿ **imini,** *see* ಹಿಮಿನಿ.

ಇಮೆ **imè,** *s.* An eye-lash; *also* ಕಂಣ ಪಿಮೆ; *cf.* ಪಿಮ್ಮೆ.

ಇಯರುನಿ, ಇಯವುನಿ **iyaruni, iyavuni** (ಇಯರ್, ಇಯವ್), *d. v.* To be sufficient; *pres. or fut. 3rd pers. n.* ಇಯರು, ಇಯವು, it will be enough *or* sufficient; *also* ಈಯ್ಯವು. ಆಯೆ ಬರಿಯೆರೆ ಇಯವು he is likely to come; *past.* ಇಯರ್ಂಡ್, ಇಯಾವಾಂಡ್ it is enough; *neg.* ಇಯಂಡ್, ಇಯವಂಡ್ it is not enough *or* sufficient.

ಇಯೆರೆ **iyere,** *s.* This side (of a river).

ಇಯ್ಯೆ **iyye,** *d. v.* Yes; *cf.* ಅಂಡ್.

ಇಯ್ಯೊಡು **iyyoḍu,** *adv.* This year.

ಇರ್ **irụ,** *a prefix signifying* Two, double, both, *e. g.* ಇರ್ಮಡಿ two-fold, ಇರ್ಬಾಯಿ double edged, ಇರ್ಮೆಯಿ both sides; *in some cases the* ರ *assimilates to the consonant following*, *e. g.* ಇಬ್ಬರೆಲ್, ಇಮ್ಮಡಿ *etc.*

ಇರ್ವೆರ್ **irụverụ,** *see* ಇರ್ವೆರ್.

ಇರ್ಸಾಲ್ **irụsālụ,** *s.* A remittance to the treasury.

ಇರಂಬಲ **irambala,** *s.* Twenty seers.

ಇರಕಾಸ್ **irakāsụ,** *s.* Sulphate of iron.

ಇರಿ **iri,** *s.* Abatement of intoxication.

ಇರಿಯುನಿ **iriyuni** (ಇರಿ), *v. n.* To fall, drop, as fruits, leaves *etc.* ಇರಿದ್ ಪೋಪಿನಿ to miscarry. *v. a.* To rub *or* squeeze between the hands, to knead; *see* ಇಲಿಯುನಿ.

ಇರಿಸಾಲ್ **irisālụ,** *see* ಇರ್ಸಾಲ್.

ಇರುಬು **irubu,** *see* ಉಬ್ಬು.

ಇರುವಂತಿಗೆ **iruvantigè,** *s.* An Arabian jessamine.

ಇರುವೆರ್ **iruverụ,** *see* ಇವೆರ್.

ಇರೆ **irè,** *s.* A leaf (of a plant). ಬಾರೆದ– a plantain-leaf. ಬಜ್ಜೆರೆ a betel leaf. ಪುಗ್ಗೆರೆ tobacco.

ಇರೆಕಳ್ಳಿ **irekaḷḷi,** *s.* A kind of milk-hedge-plant, *Euphorbia nivulia.*

ಇರೆಗಿಳಿ **iregiḷi,** *s.* A kind of parrot.

ಇರೆಬಾವೊಲಿ **irebāvoli,** *s.* A bat.

ಇರೆಲ್ **irelụ,** *see* ಅರಲ್. 2. shadow; *also* ನಿರೆಲ್.

ಇರೋಳು **irōḷu,** *see* ಈರೊಳ್.

ಇರ್ಕ್ **irkụ,** *s.* The night. –ಪಗೆಲ್ day and night.

ಇರ್ಕಣ್ಣ್ **irkaṇṇụ,** *s.* Inability to see by night, night-blindness.

ಇರ್ಕಾವುನಿ **irkāvuni,** *c. v.* (*of* ಇರ್ಕುನಿ), To make less. 2. to extinguish. 3. to stop, disturb. ತೂ– to extinguish *or* put out fire.

ಇರ್ಕುನಿ **irkuni** (ಇರ್ಕ್), *v. n.* To abate, lessen, be reduced. 2. to be disturbed. 3. to be quenched; *also* ಇರ್ಕ್‌ದ್ ಪೋಪಿನಿ.

ಇರ್ಕೈ **irkei,** *s.* Both hands. –ಕೂ

ಟುದು ಕೊಪಿನಿ to give a blow with both hands spread out.

ಇದೆ irda, *see* ವಿರೋಧ.

ಇನಾಲಯಿ irnālayi, *s.* Double tongue.

ಇನಾಲಿ irnāli, *s.* A double pulse. 2. a carpenter's boring tool. –ರೋಗ a swelling of the throat.

ಇನೂದು irnūdu, *num.* Two hundred.

ಇನೂಲು irnūlu, *s.* A double [thread.

ಇಪಕ್ಕಿ irpakki, *s.* A bat.

ಇಪಡಕೆ irpaḍakè, *adj.* Ripe and unripe.

ಇಪಡಿ irpaḍi, *s.* Double ration.

ಇಪಲೆ, ಇಪಳೆ irpalè, irpaḷè, *s.* A kind of net. 2. a double leaf. –ದ ಪಜೆ a mat.

ಇಪುಡೆ irpuḍe, *s.* Both sides.

ಇಪುದೆ irpude, *s.* A double load.

ಇಪೆ irpè, *s.* A kind of fish.

ಇಪೊತು irportu, *s.* A whole day (forenoon and afternoon), twice a day. –ದ ಬೇಲೆ a whole day's labour; *cf.* ಒಪೊತು.

ಇಬಡಿ irbaḍi, *adj.* Double, twofold.

ಇಬಲಪ್ಪು irbalappu, *s.* A double growth. 2. a twist. 3. tightness.

ಇಬಲಿಪುನಿ irbalipuni (ಇಬಲಿ), *v. a.* To tie a cloth round the waist, to gird (the loins). 2. to fasten a thatched roof with double ropes over it.

ಇಬಲೆ, ಇಬಳೆ irbalè, irbaḷè, *s.* A double bracelet. 2. double transverse laths *or* slips of bamboos, palms *etc.*

ಇಬಲ್ಯುನಿ irbalyuni (ಇಬಲ್), *v. n.* To be benumbed.

ಇಬಾಯಿ irbāyi, *s.* A double edge. –ದ ಕತ್ತಿ a double edged sword. –ದ ಎಕ್ಕಲೆ a snake, serpent.

ಇಬು irbu, *see* ಉಬು.

ಇಬುಲಿಯುನಿ irbuliyuni (ಇಬುಲ್), *v. n.* To curdle, be decomposed, as milk *etc.*

ಇಮಂಡೆ irmaṇḍe, *s.* Two vessels placed on the same hearth. 2. a large forehead 3. a very large vessel.

ಇಮಡಿಕೆ irmaḍikè, *adj.* Double, two fold; *see* ಇಮ್ಮಡಿ, ಇಬಡಿ.

ಇಮನೆ irmane, *s.* Horripilation. 2. rising up, as of corn shoots.

ಇಮರ್ಳ್ irmarḷu, *s.* Fickle-mindedness, unsteadiness. 2. idiocy.

ಇಮರ್ಲೆ irmarle, *s.* A fickle-minded man. 2. an idiot.

ಇಮಾರ್ಪು irmārpu, *s.* Two fathoms.

ಇಮೀನ್ irmīnu, *s.* A kind of fish.

ಇಮುಣೆ, ಇಮುನೆ irmuṇe, irmune, *s.* A double edge *or* point. –ದ ಕಂಟಾವು a double pointed style used for writing on palmyra leaves.

ಇಮೆನ irmena, *see* ಇಮನೆ.

ಇಮೆಯಿ, ಇಮೈ irmeyi, irmei, *s.* Both sides. 2. a cloth of different colour *or* texture on each side.

ಇರ್ಮೋಣೆ irmōṇè, *see* ಇಂಮುಖ.

ಇರ್ಲ್, ಇರ್ಳ್ irlụ, irḷụ, *s.* Dusk, darkness, night.

ಇರ್ಲ irla, *s.* Two seers. ಇರ್ಲರಿ two seers of rice.

ಇರ್ವ irva, *num.* Twenty. –ನೆ twentieth

ಇರ್ವಂಡೆ irvaṇḍè, *see* ಇರ್ವೊಂಡೆ.

ಇರ್ವಲ irvala, *see* ಇರ್ಲ.

ಇರ್ವಾರ irvāra, *adv.* A second time, twice.

ಇರ್ವೆರ್ irvērụ, (*personal form of the numeral* ರಡ್ಡ್). Two persons.

ಇರ್ವೇರಿ irvēri, *s.* A medicinal plant, *Andropogon muricatum.*

ಇರ್ವೊಂಡೆ irvoṇḍè, *s.* Two kuḍtas *or* eight fluid ounces.

ಇರ್ವೊಳು irvoḷu, *see* ಇರೊಳು.

ಇರ್ವೊಳು irvoḷu, *adv.* Two times, twice; *cf.* ಇರ್ವಾರ.

ಇರ್ಸಾಲ್ irsālụ, *see* ಇರ್‌ಸಾಲ್.

ಇಲಾಕಿ, ಇಲಾಕೆ ilāki, ilāke, *s.* (*in official language*) A department, a branch-office. *adj.* Belonging *or* attached to a department.

ಇಲಾಚಿ ilāči, *s.* A female's cloth.

ಇಲಾತಿ ilāti, *see* ವಿಲಾಯತಿ.

ಇಲಾಲ್ ilālụ, *s.* A large torch, flambeau.

ಇಲಿ ili, *see* ಎಲಿ.

ಇಲಿಜಾರ್ ilijārụ, *see* ಇಳಿಜಾರ್.

ಇಲಿಯುನಿ iliyuni, *v. n.* To fall, tumble, come down.

ಇಲೆ ile, *s.* A hair. 2. a fibre 3. a fold, plait. ಮೂಜಿ– threefold. ಯೇತ– how many fold; *cf.* ಹಿಲೆ.

ಇಲೆ ilè, *see* ಇರೆ.

ಇಲ್ಕುನಿ ilkuni, *see* ಉಲ್ಕುನಿ.

ಇಲ್ಲ್ illụ, *s.* A house, dwelling. 2. a family. ಇಲ್ಲಡ್, ಇಲ್ಲಾಳ್ at home, in the house. ಇಲ್ಲಡೆಗ್ ಪೋಪಿನಿ to go home. –ದಾಕುಲು the inmates of a house. –ಕಟ್ಟುನಿ to build a house.

ಇಲ್ಲಬೂರು illabāru, *s.* A kind of creeper used in thatching roofs and plaiting baskets and small boxes.

ಇಲ್ಲಾಸ್ illāsụ, *see* ವಿಲಾಸ.

ಇಲ್ಲೆ illè, *see* ಹಿಲ್ಲೆ.

ಇಷ್ಟ ishṭa, *adj.* Acceptable, agreeable, pleasant, wished, cherished, beloved. ಇಷ್ಟಾಪಿನಿ to be loved, cherished. –ಕಾರ್ಯ a desired-for event; an object which pleases one. –ಜನ friends. –ಪ್ರಿಯೆ a dearly beloved friend. –ಭೋಜನ savoury food, a favourite dish. *s.* Wish, desire. 2. friendship, familiarity, love. –ಕಡ್ಪುನಿ to break off friendship. –ಮಳ್ಪುನಿ to make friendship, to love, like. ಇಷ್ಟ ಮಳ್ತಿನಾಯಗ್ ಮೂಜಿ ಗುದ್ದು, ಕಷ್ಟ ಮಳ್ತಿನಾಯಗ್ ಮುಕ್ಕೊಂಡೆ ನೈ (*prov.*) three blows to him who makes love, and three measures of ghee to him who causes discord.

ಇಷ್ಟಸಿದ್ಧಿ **ishṭasiddhi**, *s*. Attainment *or* fulfilment of one's desire.

ಇಷ್ಟಾಚಾರ **ishṭāćāra**, *s*. Friendship, familiarity.

ಇಷ್ಟಾನಿಷ್ಟ **ishṭānishṭa**, *adj*. Liked and disliked. 2. good and bad.

ಇಷ್ಟಾನ್ನ **ishṭānna**, *see* ಇಷ್ಟಭೋಜನ.

ಇಷ್ಟಾನ್ಪಿತ್ವೆ **ishṭānpitve**, *s*. Simple imprisonment.

ಇಷ್ಟಾರ್ಥ **ishṭārtha**, *s*. The object of desire. 2. the highest good.

ಇಷ್ಟೆ **ishṭe**, *s*. A friend, companion. —ಕಷ್ಟೆ friend and foe. ಕುಡ್ಡಿರಿಷ್ಟೆರ್ relatives and friends.

ಇಸ್, ಇಸಿ **isụ, isi**, *intj. expressing* disgust.

ಇಸ್ಲ್ **isụlụ**, *s*. Whistling. —ಪಾಡುನಿ to whistle.

ಇಸ **isa**, *see* ವಿಷ.

ಇಸಬಕುಲ್ **isabakulụ**, *s*. The seed of *Plantago Ispaghula*.

ಇಸಮುಂಗಿಲಿ, ಇಸಮುಂಗ್ಲಿ **isamuṅgili, isamuṅgli**, *s*. *Crinum deflexum*.

ಇಸರಬೇರ್ **isarabērụ**, *s*. The root of the plant *Aristolochia Indica*.

ಇಸರೆ **isare**, *see* ಈಶ್ವರೆ.

ಇಸವಿ, ಇಸ್ವಿ **isavi, isvi**, *s*. The Christian era.

ಇಸಾರ, ಇಸಾರತ್ **isāra, isāratụ**, *s*. A sign, hint.

ಇಸೆ, ಇಸೆನ್ **isè, isenụ**, *adv*. Now; at once; *cf*. ಇತ್ತೆ.

ಇಸ್ಕ್ರು, ಇಸ್ಕುರು **iskru, iskuru**, *s*. A screw.

ಇಸ್ತಂಬುಲ್ **istambulụ**, *s*. A Turkish gold coin worth about Rs. 2 As. 8.

ಇಸ್ತಾರ **istāra**, *see* ವಿಸ್ತಾರ.

ಇಸ್ತ್ಯಾರ್, ಇಸ್ತಿಹಾರ್ **istyārụ, istihārụ**, *s*. A notice. —ನಾಮೆ a notification; an advertisement.

ಇಸ್ತ್ರಿ **istri**, *s*. A smoothing iron. —ಮಳ್ಪುನಿ, —ಪಾಡುನಿ to iron washed clothes.

ಇಸ್ಪೀಟ್, ಇಸ್ಪೇಟ್ **ispīṭụ, ispēṭụ**, *s*. Playing cards.

ಇಸ್ಲ್ಗಿಡಿ **islụgiḍi**, *s*. A kind of bird.

ಇಸ್ಸೆ **issè**, *see* ಇತ್ತೆ.

ಇಹ **iha**, *s*. The present state. —ಪರ this world and that to come.

ಇಳಿಜಾರ್ **iḷijārụ**, *s*. A slope, sloping ground. 2. slipperiness.

ಇಳಿಯುನಿ, **iḷiyuni** (ಇಳಿ), *v. n*. To slip out or down, to slide; *also* ಇಳಿದ್‌ಪೋಪಿನಿ.

ಈ Ī

ಈ ī, The fourth letter of the alphabet. In MSS. it is often written ಯಿ.

ಈ ī, *pron. 2nd pers. sing.* Thou; *emph.* ಈಯೇ even thou.

ಈ ī, *dem. pron.* This *or* these; *as* ಈ ಆಣ್ this boy, ಈ ಜನ these people.

ಈಂಗ್ īṅgu, *see* ಇಂಗ್, ಹಿಂಗ್.

ಈಂಗ್ದಾವುನಿ īṅguḍāvuni, *c. v.* (*of* ಈಂಗ್ದುನಿ) To cause to stoop.

ಈಂಗ್ದುನಿ, ಈಂಗುದುನಿ īṅguḍuni, īṅguḍuni, *see* ಇಂಗುದುನಿ.

ಈಂಚಿಲ್ īñcilu, *see* ಈಚಿಲ್.

ಈಂದ್ īndu, *s.* The sago-palm, *Caryota urens.*

ಈಂಬಳ īmbaḷa, *s.* A kind of leech.

ಈಂಬೆ īmbe, *adv.* This side, here; *cf.* ಈಪಿದಕ್ಕ್.

ಈಕ್ಕಣೆ īkkaṇe, *s.* An arrow.

ಈಚಿಲ್ īcilu, *s.* The wild date. —ಮರ the wild date-tree, *Phœnix sylvestris.*

ಈಚುನಿ, ಈಜುನಿ īcuni, ījuni (ಈಚ್, ಈಜ್), *v. n.* To swim.

ಈಟ್ īṭu, *s.* Manure, fertilizer (of land). 2. fat, sap. —ಪಾಡುನಿ to manure.

ಈಟಿ īṭi, *s.* A lance, spear.

ಈಡ್ īḍu, *s.* A pledge, pawn. 2. an equivalent. —ಉಂತುನಿ to stand security. —ಕೊರ್ಪಿನಿ to deposit a pledge, to pawn. —ಆಪಿನಿ to be equal, to match, pair; ಪಾಪೊಗು ಈಡಾಪಿನಿ to be liable to sin.

ಈಡ್ಗೆ, ಈಡೆಗೆ īḍuge, īḍege, *adv.* In vain; *cf.* ಅಡಿಗೆ.

ಈಡಿ īḍi, *see* ಇಡಿ.

ಈಡೆ, ಈಡೆಗ್ īḍe, īḍegu, *see* ಇಡೆ, ಇಡೆಗ್.

ಈಣೆ īṇe, *s.* A lute, a fretted musical instrument of the guitar kind; *also* ಬೀಣೆ, ವೀಣೆ.

ಈತ್ ītu, *indef. num.* So much, so many; *emph.* ಈತೇ just so much, only so much. ಈತೆರ್ *pl.* so many (people), ಈತೆನೆಂಗೆ, ಈತಾನೆಂಗೆ so far, as far as this, up to this. ಈತ್ ಪೊರ್ಲು, ಈತ್‌ಮುಟ್ಟ so far, so long. ಈತೆನಾ is this all? ಈತಾದ್ being so; nevertheless. ಇತಾತ್ (ಈತ್-ಆತ್) so and so much *or* so and so many; *with neg. it denotes unlimitedness*: not a little, inexpressible.

ಈದನೆಂಗೆ, ಈದಮುಟ್ಟ īdaneṅge, īdamuṭṭa, *see* ಈತೆನೆಂಗೆ, ಈತಾನೆಂಗೆ *under* ಈತ್.

ಈಪಿನಿ īpini (ಈಪ್), *v. a.* To shoot (an arrow).

ಈಪೆ īpe, *adv.* This side. —ದ ಜನ people on this side *or* part. —ದಕ್ಕ್ this side.

ಈಬೂತಿ ībūti, *see* ವಿಭೂತಿ.

ಈಯವು īyavu, *see* ಇಯವು.

ಈಯಾವಂದ್, ಈಯ್ಯಂದ್ īyāvandu, īyyandu, *see* ಇಯಂದ್ *under* ಇಯರುನಿ.

ಈಯಾವುನಿ īyāvuni, *see* ಇಯರುನಿ.

ಈಯೆರೆ īyere, *see* ಇಯೆರೆ.

ಈರ್ īru, *pers. pron.* (*pl. of* ಈ), You, *used honorifically in addressing a person.*

ಈರಂಗಡೆ īraṅgaḍe, *s.* Separation.

ಈರಣ īraṇa, *s.* A small drum.

ಈರಿಂಟೆ īrinṭi, *s.* A cricket.

ಈರುನಿ īruni (ಈರ್), *v. a. & n.* To rub off, be worn out. ಈರ್ದ್ ಪೋಪಿನಿ to undergo wear and tear, wear off, be reduced to powder. 2. to pick up.

ಈರುಳ್ಳಿ īruḷḷi, *see* ನೀರುಳ್ಳಿ.

ಈರೊಳ್ īroḷu, *s.* The tender fruit of the palmyra tree.

ಈರ್ಪಡಿ īrpaḍi, *see* ಇರ್ಪಡಿ.

ಈಶೆ īśe, *s.* A lord, master.

ಈಶ್ವರ īśvara, *s.* The eleventh year of the Hindu cycle.

ಈಶ್ವರಬೇರ್ īśvarabēru, *see* ಇಸರ ಬೇರ್.

ಈಶ್ವರೆ īśvare, *s.* The Supreme Being. 2. a name of Śiva.

ಈಸಾತ್‌ಗ್ īsātugu, *adv.* Instantly, this moment.

ಈಸುನಿ īsuni (ಈಸ್), *v. a.* To scrape.

ಉ U

ಉ u, The fifth letter of the alphabet. In MSS. it is often written ವು.

ಉಂಕ uṅka, *s.* Dirtiness, filthiness; *cf.* ವಂಕ.

ಉಂಗಿಲ uṅgila, *s.* A ring. –ಬಿರೆಲ್ the ring-finger. ಗೋಉಂಗಿಲ a plain ring.

ಉಂಗುಟ, ಉಂಗುಷ್ಟ uṅguṭa, uṅgushṭa, *s.* The great toe. –ಬಿರೆಲ್ the thumb.

ಉಂಗುರು uṅguru, *see* ಉಂಬುರು *and* ಉಗುರು.

ಉಂಚಿ uṅci, *see* ಊಂಚಿ

ಉಂಡಾಡಿಬಟ್ಟೆ uṇḍāḍibaṭṭe, *s.* A lazy fellow given to gluttony.

ಉಂಡಾಪಿನಿ, ಉಂಡಾದುಪ್ಪುನಿ uṇḍāpini, uṇḍāduppuni, *see* ಉಂಡು.

ಉಂಡಿ, ಉಂಡಿಚೀಟ್ uṇḍi, uṇḍicīṭu, *s.* A bill of exchange; *bet.* ಹುಂಡಿ.

ಉಂಡಿಗೆ uṇḍige, *s.* A sheaf of straw.

ಉಂಡಿಯೆ uṇḍiye, *see* ಉಂಡೆ, ಉಂಡ್ಯೆ.

ಉಂಡು uṇḍu, *d. v.* There is, *or* exists. 2. *in answer to* ಉಂಡಾ, ಉಂಡೋ is there? *and other questions:* there is, yes. 3. *with the dative case it expresses possession.* ಎಂಕ್ ಉಂಡು I have. ಉಂಡಾಪಿನಿ to come into existence, to spring up, arise; ಉಂಡಾಯಿನವು that which has occurred, what is really a fact, what exists. ಉಂಡಾದುಪ್ಪ ನಿ to exist. —ಮಳ್ಪುನಿ to create, produce; to invent. —ಮಳ್ತಿನಾಯೆ the Creator.

ಉಂಡುಳುಗ uṇḍuḷuga, s. A kind of fried cake.

ಉಂಡೆ uṇḍè, s. A ball, globe. 2. a ball-shaped confection.

ಉಂಡೆ, ಉಂಡ್ಯೆ uṇḍe, uṇḍyè s. A sheaf of straw; cf. ಉಣ್ಪುನಿ.

ಉಂಡ್ಲುಗ uṇḍluga, see ಉಂಡುಳುಗ.

ಉಂತಾವುನಿ untāvuni, c.v. (of ಉಂತುನಿ) To cause to stand up. 2. to detain, stop. ಪಣೊತ್ತು— to allow further time to a debtor to pay his debt.

ಉಂತುನಿ untuni (ಉಂತಿ), v.n. To stand. 2. to remain, stay. 3. to stop, cease.

ಉಂದು undu, pers. pron. neut. This, it. ಉಂದತ್ತಂದೆ besides this, moreover. pl. ಉಂದೆಕುಳು these.

ಉಂನತ unnata, adj. High, lofty, tall, supreme.

ಉಂಬುಗೆ, ಉಂಬುಚ್ಚೆ, ಉಂಬೆ umbuge, umbuċċe, umbe, s. The white flowered thorn-apple, Datura alba; also ಬೊಳ್ದು—; ಕಪ್ಪು— or ಕರಿ— D. fastuosa; see ಉಂಮುತ.

ಉಂಬುಚ umbuċa, s. A kind of bush.

ಉಂಬುಡ umbuḍa, s. A kind of colibry.

ಉಂಬುಡೆ umbuḍe, adj. Globular and small. s. Chewed betel.

ಉಂಬುಡೆಪಕ್ಕಿ umbuḍepakki, s. A kind of bird; cf. ಉಂಬುಡ.

ಉಂಬುರು umburu, s. A kind of small leech; also ಈಂಬಳ.

ಉಂಬೆ umbè, see ಉಂಬುಗೆ.

ಉಂಬೊಳಿ umboḷi, s. A freehold, land granted without rent. 2. any present, donation; gratuitous service.

ಉಂಮ, ಉಂಮಪ್ಪಾ umma, ummappā, int. (when startled), meaning Who knows? 2. I do not know.

ಉಂಮಿ ummi, see ಉಮಿ.

ಉಂಮುಗೆ ummuge, see ಉಂಬುಗೆ.

ಉಂಮುತ ummuta, s. The purple thorn-apple, Datura fastuosa which is said to cause mania. see ಉಂಬುಗೆ.

ಉಂಮುರು ummuru, see ಉಂಬುರು.

ಉಂಡ್ರುಲ urṇḍula, see ಉಂಡುಳುಗ.

ಉಂಡ್ರೆ urṇḍe, s. A lump. 2. a morsel.

ಉಂಡ್ರೆಬೂರು urṇḍebūru, s. The smooth-leaved heart-pea, the creeper Cardiospermum halicababum.

ಉಂಡ್ರೆಲ್ urṇḍelu, adj. Round, circular. —ಪಾಯಸ small rice pastry balls baked or boiled with sugar and milk or cocoanut juice.

ಉಂಡ್ಲ್ರುಗ urṇḍluga, see ಉಂಡುಳುಗ.

ಉಕಾಲ್, ಉಕ್ಕಾಲ್ ukālu, ukkālu, s. Vomiting. 2. an emetic. —ಜುಲಾಬು cholera.

ಉಕ್ಕಡ, ಉಕ್ಕುಡ ukkaḍa, ukkuḍa, s. A small boat. 2. a lookout place between the bounds of two towns.

ಉಕ್ಕಾವುನಿ **ukkāvuni**, *see* ಉಕಾ್ರವುನಿ.

ಉಕ್ಕಿ **ukki**, *s*. Steam; *cf* ಸಿಕ್ಕೆ, ಸಿಜಿ.

ಉಕ್ಕುನಿ **ukkuni** (ಉಕ್ಕ್), *v.n.* To boil, bubble up. 2. to run over in boiling. 3. to swell up, spring up; *cf*. ಉಕರ್ುನಿ.

ಉಗರ್ **ugaru**, *adj*. Brackish; *also* ಒಗರ್.

ಉಗಾದಿ **ugādi**, *see* ಯುಗಾದಿ.

ಉಗಿಪುನಿ **ugipuni** (ಉಗಿ), *v.n.* To spit out.

ಉಗುರಡ್ಡಿಗೆ **uguraddige**, *s*. A necklace with chasings *or* engravings like finger nails.

ಉಗುರು **uguru**, *s*. A nail, claw. –ಸುತ್ತು a whitlow. –ಬೆಚ್ಚ tepid, lukewarm.

ಉಗುರುಬೂರು **ugurubūru**, *s*. The creeper *Daemia extensa.*

ಉಗ್ಗ **ugga**, *s*. Over-boiled rice; *cf*. ಷಗರ್.

ಉಗ್ಗಿ **uggi**, *s*. A handle. 2. a hook. –ಕಟ್ಟುನಿ to fasten a hook; *also* ಒಗ್ಗಿ, ವಗ್ಗಿ.

ಉಗ್ಗುನಿ **ugguni** (ಉಗ್ಗ್), *v.n.* To stammer. 2. to spurt. ನೆತ್ತೆರ್– blood to flow by spurts.

ಉಗ್ಗೆಲ್ **uggelu**, *s*. A well.

ಉಗ್ರ **ugra**, *adj*. Angry, vehement, passionate. 2. cruel. *s*. Wrath, rage. ಉಗ್ರಾಪಿನಿ to be angry.

ಉಗ್ರಾಣ, ಉಗ್ರಾಣಿಗೆ **ugrāṇa, ugrāṇige**, *s*. A storeroom. –ದಾಯೆ; *see* ಉಗ್ರಾಣಿ. ಬಗಸ್– a granary.

ಉಗ್ರಾಣಿ **ugrāṇi**, *s*. A storekeeper, steward. 2. a village peon under a Potail.

ಉಗ್ರೆ **ugre**, *s*. A passionate man.

ಉಚಾಪತಿ **ucāpati**, *s*. Dealings on credit.

ಉಚಾಯಿಸುನಿ **ucāyisuni** (ಉಚಾಯಿಸ್), *v.n.* To exceed the bounds of propriety either in word or deed.

ಉಚಿತ **ucita**, *adj*. Proper, suitable, fit. *s*. A gift. ಉಚಿತಾದ್ freely, gratis.

ಉಚ್ಚಕಚ್ಚ **uccakacca**, *s*. Quarrel, fight. 2. *see* ಉಚ್ಚಿಕಟ್ಟ.

ಉಚ್ಚಕಿಟ್ಟ **uccakiṭṭa**, *see* ಉಚ್ಚಿಕಟ್ಟ.

ಉಚ್ಚಯ **uccaya**, *see* ಉತ್ಸಹ.

ಉಚ್ಚರಿಪುನಿ **uccaripuni** (ಉಚ್ಚರಿ), *v.a.* To utter, pronounce.

ಉಚ್ಚಲ್ **uccalu**, *see* ಉಚ್ಚಾಲ್.

ಉಚ್ಚಾಟನೆ **uccāṭane**, *s*. Exorcising evil spirits.

ಉಚ್ಚಾಯ, **uccāya**, *see* ಉತ್ಸಹ.

ಉಚ್ಚಾರ, ಉಚ್ಚಾರಣೆ, **uccāra, uccāraṇe**, *s*. Pronunciation.

ಉಚ್ಚಾಲ್ **uccālu**, *s*. A hammer.

ಉಚ್ಚಾವ **uccāva**, *see* ಉತ್ಸಹ.

ಉಚ್ಚಿ **ucci**, *s*. A snake. 2. a worm. –ಪಯ್ಯ a kind of fish.

ಉಚ್ಚಿಕಟ್ಟ **uccikaṭṭa**, *s*. A loose knot. 2. spots on the skin of serpents.

ಉಚ್ಚು **uccu**, *s*. A snake, serpent; *cf*. ಉಚು.

ಉಜ **uja**, *s*. A fountain, spring. –ಪತ್ತೊ ಕಂಡ a marshy field; *see* ಉಜಿ.

ಉಜಡೆ **ujaḍe**, *s*. A deserted person.

ಉಜಡೆ ujaḍe, *s.* Light, splendour. —ಆಪಿನಿ to become light.

ಉಜಾಡ್ ujāḍu, *s.* Ruin. —ಆಪಿನಿ to be ruined.

ಉಜಿಲ, ಉಜಿಲಾ ujila, ujilā, *adj.* White. —ಬಣ್ಣ white colour.

ಉಜಿ uje, *see* ಉಜ. —ಪತ್ತುನಿ to ooze, percolate, trickle. 2. to become swampy.

ಉಜ್ಜತು ujjatu, *s.* Force, violence. —ಮಳ್ಪುನಿ to force.

ಉಜ್ಜಾಲ್ ujjālu, *s.* A swing. 2. A hammock.

ಉಜ್ಜುನಿ ujjuni (ಉಜ್ಜ್), *v. a.* To rub; *cf.* ಉದುರ್ನಿ.

ಉಜ್ಜೆರ್, ಉಜ್ಜೇರ್ ujjeru, ujjēru, *s.* A pestle.

ಉಟಾಯಿಸುನಿ, ಉಟಾವುನಿ uṭāyisuni, uṭāvuni (ಉಟಾಯಿಸ್, ಉಟಾ), *v. a.* To raise, lift up; *cf.* ಉಂಟಾವುನಿ.

ಉಟಾರಣೆ uṭāraṇe, *s.* Forgery, fabrication.

ಉಟ್ಟು uṭṭu, *see* ಹುಟ್ಟು.

ಉಟ್ಟೂಟನೆ uṭṭūṭane, *s.* Food and clothing.

ಉಟ್ಟೊಳಿ uṭṭoḷi, *see* ಹುಟ್ಟೊಳಿ.

ಉಡಧಾರ uḍadhāra, *s.* A gold *or* silver girdle; *also* ನ್ಯಾವಳ.

ಉಡರಿಗೆ, ಉಡಾರಿಗೆ uḍarige, uḍārige, *s.* A kind of cake.

ಉಡಲ್, ಉಡಾಲ್ uḍalu, uḍālu, *s.* The belly, stomach. —ಜರ hectic fever.

ಉಡಾಯಿಸುನಿ, ಉಡಾಸುನಿ uḍāyisuni, uḍāsuni (ಉಡಾಯಿಸ್, ಉಡಾಸ್), *v. a.* To deny, contradict. 2. to reject.

ಉಡಿ uḍi, *see* ಪೊಡಿ.

ಉಡಿಗೆರೆ uḍigere, *s.* A gift. ಬಜ್ಜೆಯಿ ಒಂಜಿ— ಆನೆಲಾ ಒಂಜಿ— (*prov.*) a betelnut may be a present as much as an elephant.

ಉಡು uḍu, *s.* An iguana.

ಉಡು uḍu, *s.* A star. 2. water.

ಉಡುಕು uḍuku, *s.* A kind of small drum.

ಉಡುಗೆ uḍuge, *see* ಹುಡುಗೆ.

ಉಡುಗೆರೆ uḍugere, *see* ಉಡಿಗೆರೆ.

ಉಡುಧಾರ uḍudhāra, *see* ಉಡಧಾರ.

ಉಡುಪತಿ uḍupati, *s.* The moon.

ಉಡೆತ್ತೆಲ್ uḍettelu, *s.* Bruise. *adj.* Bruised.

ಉಡೆಪುನಿ, ಉಡೆವುನಿ uḍepuni, uḍevuni (ಉಡೆ), *v. a.* and *n.* To break, split, as pottery *etc.*

ಉಡ್ಡಿ uḍḍi, *s.* Any pile of three, with one on the top, as marbles, seeds *etc.* —ದೀಪಿನಿ to set thus in piles of four each.

ಉಡ್ಡುಡ್ಡನೆ uḍḍuḍḍane, *adv.* In rapid succession, one after another, over and over again. —ಪಣ್ಪುನಿ to speak hastily. —ಬರ್ಪಿನಿ to come or follow in close succession.

ಉಡ್ಸುರೆ uḍsure, *s.* A honorary gift; *cf.* ಉಡಿಗೆರೆ.

ಉಣಪೆ uṇape, *adj.* Little recovering.

ಉಣರ್ uṇaru, *see* ಅಣರ್.

ಉಣಸ್ uṇasu, *s.* A meal, dinner, boiled rice and curry; *also* ಒಣಸ್, ವಣಸ್.

ಉಣಿಲೆ uṇile, *adj.* Small, short, young.

ಉಣುಪಿನಿ, ಉಣ್ಪಿನಿ uṇupini, uṇpini (ಉಣ್), *v. a.* To take one's meal, to dine, eat rice, (in opposition to a slight repast of fruits, cakes *etc*).

ಉಣ್ಕೆಲ್ uṇkelu, *s.* The time of evening. 2. the night-meal.

ಉಣ್ಪು uṇpu, *s.* Boiled rice, solid food; *alsc* ಣುಪ್ಪು.

ಉತಾರ್ utāru, *s.* An antidote.

ಉತ್ತನ uttana, *see* ಉತ್ಥಾನ.

ಉತ್ತಮ uttama, *adj.* Best, chief, superior. 2. excellent, virtuous. ಉತ್ತಮೆ an excellent man. ಉತ್ತಮೋತ್ತಮ the very best; God. —ಪುರುಷ the first person, *gram.*

ಉತ್ತರ uttara, *s.* The north. 2. an answer. 3. (*in law*) a defence. *adj.* (Left), northern; subsequent, later. —ಕ್ರಿಯೆ funeral ceremonies. —ವಾದಿ a surety, bondsman.

ಉತ್ತರಣೆ uttaraṇe, *s.* The shrub *Achyranthes aspera.*

ಉತ್ತರಾಧಿಕಾರಿ uttarādhikāri, *s.* A successor, heir.

ಉತ್ತರಾಯಣ uttarāyaṇa, *s.* The sun's course to the north of the equator.

ಉತ್ತರಾಷಾಡ uttarāshāḍa, *s.* The twenty-first lunar mansion.

ಉತ್ತರಿಗೆ uttarige, *s.* An upper *or* outer garment. 2. a towel.

ಉತ್ತರೆ uttare, *s.* The twelfth lunar mansion, the tail of *Leo.*

ಉತ್ತಾಣ, ಉತ್ತಾವಳಿ, uttāṇa, uttāvaḷi, *s.* Haste, rashness, precipitancy.

ಉತ್ತಾರ uttāra, *see* ಉಥಾನ.

ಉತ್ತಾಸ uttāsa, *s.* Zeal, perseverance. 2. a rash, *or* strenuous exertion.

ಉತ್ತುತ್ತಿ uttutti, *s.* The dried date fruit; *also* ಕಾರೆಕಾಯಿ.

ಉತ್ತುಮ uttuma, *see* ಉತ್ತಮ.

ಉತ್ಥಾನ utthāna, *s.* Rising. 2. resurrection.

ಉತ್ಪತ್ತಿ utpatti, *s.* Birth, origin. 2. produce, profit.

ಉತ್ಪನ್ನ utpanna, *s.* Birth. *adj.* Produced, born.

ಉತ್ಸವ utsava, *s.* A festival, public rejoicing. ರಥೋತ್ಸವ the procession of an idol on a car. —ಮೂರ್ತಿ a moveable idol generally taken abroad during a procession.

ಉತ್ಸಹ, ಉತ್ಸಾಹ utsaha, utsāha, *s.* Festivity, joy, rejoicing 2. energy, strenuous exertion; *it is often interchanged with* ಉತ್ಸವ.

ಉತ್ರಾಣಿ utrāṇi, *see* ಉತ್ತರಣೆ.

ಉಥಾರ್ uthāru, *s.* A free gift, a freehold.

ಉದಕ udaka, *s.* Water.

ಉದಯ udaya, *s.* The rising of the sun, moon, or other heavenly bodies. ಉದಯಕಾಲ. the dawn.

ಉದರ udara, *s.* The belly. 2. the core of any thing. —ಪೋಷಣೆ feeding the belly. —ಶೂಲೆ colic.

ಉದರುನಿ udaruni, *see* ಉದುರುನಿ.

ಉದರ್ಮೆ udarme, *see* ಉತ್ತರ.

ಉದಲ್ **udalụ**, *s.* The white ant.

ಉದಲ್‌ಪುಂಚ **udalụpuñča**, *s.* A white-ant-hill. 2. (*med.*) a cancer; pins *or* pinlike holes on the sole of the foot.

ಉದಲೆ **udalè**, *s.* Saliva, spittle.

ಉದಾತ್ತ **udātta**, *adj.* Liberal. 2. lofty. 3. high, as a note in music. *s.* The acute accent, *gram.*

ಉದಾರ್ **udārụ**, *s.* The credit system, lending.

ಉದಾರ **udāra**, *adj.* Liberal, generous. –ತನ, –ತ್ವ liberality.

ಉದಾರಣೆ, ಉದಾರ್ಣೆ **uḍāraṇe, udārṇe**, *see* ಉದಾಹರಣೆ.

ಉದಾಲ್ **udālụ**, *see* ಉದಲ್.

ಉದಾಸ, ಉದಾಸೀನ **udāsa, udāsīna**, *adj.* Unconcerned, neutral. *s.* Neglect, indifference. –ದಾಯಿ a careless man.

ಉದಾಹರಣೆ **udāharaṇe**, *s.* An answer. 2. an example, illustration.

ಉದಿ **udi**, *see* ಉದಯ.

ಉದಿಪಾವುನಿ **udipāvuni**, *c. v.* (*of* ಉದಿಪಿನಿ) To beget.

ಉದಿಪಿನಿ, **udipini**, *see* ಉದಿಯುನಿ.

ಉದಿಮೆ **udime**, *s.* Merchandise, trade.

ಉದಿಯಬೆನ್ಪಿನಿ **udiyabenpini**, *v. n.* To become rich.

ಉದಿಯುನಿ **udiyuni** (ಉದಿ), *v. n.* To rise, as the sun. 2. to be generated.

ಉದುಪು **udupu**, *s.* The act of coming into existence.

ಉದುರಿಬೂರು **uduribūru**, *s.* The creepers *Asparagus sarmentosus*, and *Asparagus racemosus.*

ಉದುರುನಿ **uduruni**, *v. n.* To fall, drop off. 2. to hang down.

ಉದೆ **ude**, *s.* A sheath.

ಉದೆರಾಗ **uderāga**, *s.* A morning [song.

ಉದೇವುನಿ **udēvuni** (ಉದೇ), *v. a.* To throw out. *v. n.* The hands to shake, as in sickness.

ಉದೊ **udo**, *intj.* A formula used in presenting offerings to a goddess.

ಉದ್ದ **udda**, *s.* Length. 2. distance. *adj.* Long. –ನಾಲಾಯಿದಾಯಿ a prattler, braggart, bully.

ಉದ್ದಕುದ್ದ್ಯ **uddakuddya**, *adj.* (*lit.* long and short) Middle sized. 2. separate. 3. distinct. *adv.* Distinctly.

ಉದ್ದರಿ **uddari**, *see* ಉದಾರ್.

ಉದ್ದಾರ **uḍḍāra**, *see* ಉದ್ಧಾರ.

ಉದ್ದುಮೆ **uddumè**, *see* ಉದಿಮೆ.

ಉದ್ಧಾರ **uddhāra**, *s.* Deliverance. 2. protection. 3. prosperity. –ಆಪಿನಿ to obtain deliverance; to become rich. –ಮಳ್ಪುನಿ to protect, support. –ಕೊರ್ಪಿನಿ to deliver the spirit of a deceased person from the power of a demon by propitiating it.

ಉದ್ಯಾರ್ಚನೆ **udyārčane**, *s.* The biennial ceremony of washing an idol.

ಉದ್ಯೋಗ **udyōga**, *s.* Exertion, industry. 2. business, occupation, employment. –ಸ್ಥ a public servant.

ಉದ್ರಿ udri, *s.* A braid of false hairs.

ಉದ್ರಿ udri, *s.* A match, pair. –ಗಾರ an equal.

ಉದ್ರಿಗೊಂಡೆ udrigoṇḍè, *s.* A hair-ornament. [ಬೂರು.

ಉದ್ರಿಬೂರು udribūru, *see* ಉದುರಿ

ಉದ್ರುನಿ udruni, *see* ಉದುರುನಿ.

ಉದ್ರೇಕ udrēka, *s.* Excess, superabundance. *adj.* Excessive. ಕೋಪೋದ್ರೇಕ outburst of wrath. ಕಾಮೋದ್ರೇಕ excessive lust.

ಉಧಾರಣೆ udhāraṇe, *see* ಉದಾಹರಣೆ.

ಉನಪೆ unape, *see* ಉಣಪೆ.

ಉನಿಲೆ unile *see* ಉಣಲೆ.

ಉನ್ನತ unnata, *see* ಉಂನತ.

ಉಪ upa, *A Sanskrit prefix implying* direction. 2. vicinity. 3. inferiority.

ಉಪಕಥೆ upakathe, *s.* An episode.

ಉಪಕರಣ upakaraṇa, *s.* An appendage. 2. means, materials. 3. an instrument, tool. 4. vessels used in worshipping an idol.

ಉಪಕಾರ, ಉಪಕೃತಿ upakāra, upakr̥ti, *s.* A service, favour, kindness, benefit. ಉಪಕಾರಿ a benefactor.

ಉಪಕ್ರಮ upakrama, *s.* Taking in hand, setting about.

ಉಪಗ್ರಾಮ upagrāma, *s.* Suburb.

ಉಪಚರಣೆ, ಉಪಚಾರ upaćaraṇe, upaćāra, *s.* Politeness, courtesy.

ಉಪಜದ್ರ upajadra, *see* ಉಪದ್ರ.

ಉಪದೇಶ upadēśa, *s.* Instruction, teaching. 2. initiation into the mysteries of religion.

ಉಪದೇಶಿ upadēśi, *s.* A teacher. 2. a catechist, *Chr.*

ಉಪದ್ರ, ಉಪಾತ್ರ, ಉಪಾದಿ upadra, upātra, upādi, *s.* Calamity, adversity, trouble, affliction; *cf.* ಉಪಹತಿ.

ಉಪನಯನ upanayana, *s.* The ceremony of investing a Brahman boy with the sacred thread.

ಉಪಪದ upapada, *s.* The modern grammatical term for article, also any subordinate word in a sentence.

ಉಪಬೋಧಕೆ upabōdhake, *s.* An assistant teacher. 2. a deacon. *Chr.* [division.

ಉಪಭಾಗ upabhāga, *s.* A sub-

ಉಪಮೆ upame, *s.* Resemblance. 2. comparison. 3. simile, parable.

ಉಪಯೋಗ upayōga, *s.* Application, use. 2. advantage, utility.

ಉಪರಾಗ uparāga, *s.* An eclipse.

ಉಪರಾಳಿ uparāḷi, *see* ಉಪ್ರಾಳಿ.

ಉಪರಿ upari, *adv.* Above, over, after; *also* ಉಬರಿ.

ಉಪರ್ಮೆ uparme, *see* ಉಪ್ಪರಿಗೆ.

ಉಪವಾಸ upavāsa, *see* ಉಪಾಸ.

ಉಪಶಮನ upaśamana, *s.* Putting to rest. 2. alleviation. 3. calmness, rest. –ಆಗುನಿ to be alleviated, assuaged. –ಮಳ್ಪುನಿ to appease, pacify.

ಉಪಸರ್ಗ **upasarga**, *s*. A grammatical term for preposition, *e.g.* ಅಪ, ಉಪ *etc*.

ಉಪಸ್ಥ **upastha**, *s*. The parts of generation of either sex.

ಉಪಹತಿ **upahati**, *s*. Mischief, trouble. 2. calamity; *cf*. ಉಪದ್ರ.

ಉಪಾಂಗ **upānga**, *s*. An appendix to ಅಂಗ. 2. a subordinate scientific treatise, of which there are twelve according to the Hindu šāstras.

ಉಪಾಕರ್ಮ **upākarma**, *s*. The annual festival of purification among the Brahmans between July and August when their sacred threads are renewed.

ಉಪಾದಿ **upādi**, *see* ಉಪದ್ರ.

ಉಪಾಯ **upāya**, *s*. An expedient, device, scheme. 2. means. 3. stratagem. [ಪಾಸ.

ಉಪಾಸ **upāsa**, *s*. Fasting; *also*

ಉಪೇಕ್ಷೆ **upēkshe**, *s*. Disregard. 2. want of appetite. 3. reluctance.

ಉಪ್ಪಡ್ **uppaḍu**, *see* ಉಪ್ಪಾಡ್.

ಉಪ್ಪಡ್ **uppaḍu** *imper. of* ಉಪ್ಪುನಿ.

ಉಪ್ಪರಿಗೆ **upparige**, *s*. The upper story of a house.

ಉಪ್ಪಲ **uppala**, *s*. *Macaranga Indica*.

ಉಪ್ಪಲಿಗೆ **uppaligė**, *s*. A kind of tree. *see* ಉಪ್ಪಲ.

ಉಪ್ಪಾಡ್ **uppāḍu**, *s*. Pickles.

ಉಪ್ಪಾರ್ **uppāru**, *see* ಉಬರ್.

ಉಪ್ಪು **uppu**, *s*. Salt. ಉಪ್ಪುಪ್ಪು brackish. —ನೀರ್ salt water. ಅಚ್ಚಿ— refined salt. ಪೊಡಿ— small grained salt. ಕಲ್ಲುಪ್ಪು. rock salt, Bombay salt. ಮಂಣುಪ್ಪು earth salt.

ಉಪ್ಪುಡ **uppuḍa**, *s*. Salted fish; *cf*. ಉಪ್ಪಾಡ್.

ಉಪ್ಪುನಿ **uppuni** (ಉಪ್ಪು), *ir. v*. To be, exist. 2. to abide, live in. 3. to help, support, protect. 4. *c. dat. pers*. to have, possess; *also* ಇಪ್ಪುನಿ, (*past* ಇತ್ತೆ *etc*.)

ಉಪ್ಪುರುನಿ **uppuruni** (ಉಪ್ಪುರು), *v. n*. To faint, stagger.

ಉಪ್ಪೇರುನಿ **uppēruni** (ಉಪ್ಪೇರ್), *v. n*. Cattle to copulate.

ಉಪ್ರಾಲಿ **uprāli**, *s*. Spite. 2. annoyance. —ಮಳ್ಪುನಿ to despise, deride; to annoy.

ಉಬರ್, ಉಬಾರ್ **ubaru**, **ubāru**, *s*. Brackishness. *adj*. High. 2. turbid. *adv*. Above. —ನೀರ್ salt water. —ನೆಲ brackish, *or* barren soil. —ಮಿತ್ತಾವುನಿ fish to ascend a river with the tide. —ಮೂರಿ the stench of (stagnant) sea-water.

ಉಬಳಿಗೆ **ubaḷige**, *s*. A kind of tree.

ಉಬೆ **ubė**, *s*. Steam. —ಕ್ ಪಾಡುನಿ to bleach clothes. 2. to drive out any vermin by smoke. 3. to ripen fruits by artificial heat; *also* ಉಸೆ.

ಉಬೆ, ಉಬ್ಬೆ **ubė**, **ubbė**, *see* ಹುಬ್ಬೆ.

ಉಬೆರುನಿ **uberuni** (ಉಬೆರ್), *v. n*. To become thick.

ಉಬ್ಬರ, ಉಬ್ಬಾರ್ ubbara, ubbāru, *see* ಉಬರ್.

ಉಬ್ಬರ ubbara, *adj.* High. 2. swollen. 3. turbid. *adv.* Aloft,

ಉಬ್ಬಸ ubbasa, *see* ಉಬ್ಬೆಸ.

ಉಬ್ಬಿ ubbi, *s.* Saliva, spittle. —ನೀರ್ viscid spittle. —ಯುನವು a spittoon; [ಪೀಕ್‌ದನಿ.

ಉಬ್ಬಿನ ubbina, *s.* A spittoon; *also*

ಉಬ್ಬಿಯುನಿ ubbiyuni (ಉಬ್ಬಿ), *v. n.* To spit.

ಉಬ್ಬುನಿ, ಉಬ್ಬೇರುನಿ ubbuni, ubbēruni (ಉಬ್ಬು, ಉಬ್ಬೇರ್), *v. n.* To swell. 2. to be elated with joy *or* puffed up with pride.

ಉಬ್ಬೆಸ ubbesa, *s.* Difficulty of breathing, gasping. 2. asthma. —ಬರ್ಪುನಿ to gasp, be breathless; to suffer from asthma; *also* ನೇಸ.

ಉಬ್ಲಪಾತೆರ ublapātera, *s.* Stammering, lisping.

ಉಬ್ಲೆ uble, *s.* A stammerer.

ಉಭಯ ubhaya, *adj.* Both, two. —ತೆರ್, —ಸ್ತೆರ್ both parties. —ತ್ರ on both sides *or* places.

ಉಮನಿ umani, *see* ಅಮಣಿ.

ಉಮಿ umi, *s.* The husk *or* chaff of paddy.

ಉಮಿಲ್ umilu, *s.* A mosquito, gnat. —ದ ಕುಂಟು a musquito-curtain.

ಉಮೆ ume, *s.* The wife of Šiva; *also* ಪಾರ್ವತಿ.

ಉಮೇದ್, ಉಮೇದಿ umēdu, umēdi, *s.* Liking, inclination. 2. expectation, prospect.

ಉಮೇದ್ವಾರೆ umēdvāre, *s.* A volunteer, candidate. 2. a copyist.

ಉಮ್ಮ umma, *see* ಉಂಮ.

ಉಯಿಕ್ uyiku, *s.* Crying like a monkey. [ಲುನಿ.

ಉಯಿಲುನಿ uyiluni, *see* ಊಜುನಿ, ಮ್ಯೆ

ಉಯಿವುಯಿ uyivuyi, *interj. signifying* alarm.

ಉಯ್ಯಾಲ್ uyyālu *see* ಉಜ್ಜಾಲ್.

ಉರ ura, *s.* Ploughing, tillage. —ಬಡು a ploughman's stick. —ಮಳ್ಪುನಿ to plough and level a field a second time; to make a field to hold or retain water.

ಉರಲ್ uralu, *s.* A ploughman's *or* herdman's song. —ಪಾಡುನಿ to sing whilst ploughing; *also* ಒರಲ್.

ಉರಿ uri, *s.* A kind of very small crab.

ಉರಿ uri, *s.* Blaze, flame. 2. heat. 3. acute pain. 4. wrath. —ಗಜ್ಜಿ burning itch. —ಜಾಲ burning heat. —ಮಾರಿ a furious person. —ಮೂತ್ರ urine morbidly heated. —ಬೂಟುನಿ to speak angrily; to take revenge.

ಉರಿಗೆಜ್ಜೆ urigejje, *s.* Small bells strung on a rope and tied round the neck of a he-buffalo.

ಉರಿಪುನಿ uripuni (ಉರಿ), *v. a.* To sound, play upon. ತುತ್ತೂರಿ— to sound a trumpet.

ಉರಿಯುನಿ uriyuni (ಉರಿ), *v. n.* To burn, blaze. 2. to feel a burning sensation, as from fever *or* itch; to feel acute pain. 3. to feel anguish. 4. to be wrath. ಬಂಜಿ– (*lit.* the belly to burn), to be hungry; to feel anguish, to be envious. ಮೈ– (*lit.* the body to burn); to be feverish; to be provoked, be angry. ಉರಿತಿ well-heated, pure, as silver.

ಉರು uru, *s.* Tediousness. *adj.* Idle. –ಆಪಿನಿ to be idle, to feel reluctant. –ಮಳ್ಪುನಿ to procrastinate, put off.

ಉರುಂಟ್, ಉರುಂಡುಲು uruṇṭu, uruṇḍulu, *adj.* Round.

ಉರುಂಟುಚಂಡೆ uruṇṭucaṇḍe, *s.* A kind of drum.

ಉರುಂಡೆಬೂರು uruṇḍebūru, *s.* The smooth-leaved heart-pea, *Cardiospermum Halicababum.*

ಉರುಂಬುನಿ urumbuni (ಉರುಂಬ್), *v.a.* To bore; *also* ರುಮ್ಮುನಿ.

ಉರುದುನಿ uruduni, *see* ಉರ್ದುನಿ.

ಉರುಬು urubu, *see* ಉಬ್ರ್.

ಉರುವೊಲು uruvolu, *see* ಉರೊ, ಉರೊಳು.

ಉರೆ urè, *s.* A deer.

ಉರೆಪುನಿ urepuni (ಉರೆ), *v.a.* To try metals by a touch-stone.

ಉರೆವುನಿ urevuni(ಉರೆ), *v.n.* To be penetrated *or* incrusted, as with salt; *also* ಒರೆವುನಿ.

ಉರೆಸುನಿ uresuni (ಉರೆಸ್), *v.a.* To rub. 2. to polish. 3. *see* ಉರೆಪುನಿ.

ಉರೊ uro, *intj.* Alas. –ಪಾಪನೇ alas, what a pity! –ಪಮ್ಮಯ have pity on me.

ಉರೊ, ಉರೊಳು uro, uroḷu, *s.* A bar across a passage.

ಉರ್ಕಾರುನಿ urkāruni(ಉರ್ಕಾರ್), *v.n.* To bubble up, as boiling water.

ಉರ್ಕಾವುನಿ urkāvuni, *c.v.* (*of* ಉರ್ಕುನಿ) To cause to run over. 2. to put out.

ಉರ್ಕಿ urki, *s.* The shrub *Sida Indica.*

ಉರ್ಕಿಲ್ urkiḷu, *s.* The prickly-heat. 2. a kind of shrub. 3. a rough basket.

ಉರ್ಕು urku, *s.* An amulet. –ಮಣಿ a necklace composed of small glass beads with a big gold bead in the middle.

ಉರ್ಕುಣೆ urkuṇe, *s.* The act of bubbling up.

ಉರ್ಕುನಿ urkuni (ಉರ್ಕ್), *v.n.* To rise; *cf.* ಉಕ್ಕುನಿ.

ಉರ್ಗುನಿ urguni, *v.n.* To curdle. 2. to ferment.

ಉರ್ಚುನಿ urċuni, *v. n.* To go to stool, *vlg.* ಉರ್ಚಾಟ looseness of bowels. ಉರ್ಚಿಲು a filthy woman. ಉರ್ಚಿಲೆ a filthy man.

ಉರ್ಟಿ urṭi, *see* ಉಲ್ಟಿ.

ಉರ್ಡಾಟ urḍāṭa, *s.* Wrestling, combat, struggle.

ಉರ್ಡಾವುನಿ urḍāvuni, *c.v.* (*of* ಉರ್ಡುನಿ) To set persons against each other, to stir up fighting.

ಉರ್ಡುನಿ urḍuni, *v.n.* To wrestle, combat, struggle.

ಉರ್ಣ urṇa, A round shaped cake.

ಉರ್ಣಿ urṇi, *s.* A bulb, protuberance. —ಕಟ್ಟುನಿ to clot, curdle.

ಉರ್ತಿ urti, *see* ಉರಿತಿ *in* ಉರಿಯುನಿ.

ಉರ್ದಿ urdi, *s.* Increase, prosperity.

ಉರ್ದು urdu, *s.* The kidney-bean, *Phaseolus mungo.*

ಉರ್ದುನಿ urduni (ಉರ್ದ್), *v. a.* To rub, file. 2. to polish.

ಉರ್ಪುನಿ urpuni (ಉರ್ಪ್), *v. a.* To blow a wind-instrument; *cf.* ಉರಿಪುನಿ.

ಉರ್ಪೆಲ್ urpeḷu, *s.* Slight boiling. —ಅರಿ rice obtained from boiled paddy and differing from the unboiled (= ಬೊಳಂತೆ).

ಉರ್ಬಿ, ಉರ್ಬು urbi, urbu, *s.* Increase, as of any disease *or* trouble. —ತೆರಿಯುನಿ (*lit.* to perceive trouble), to discern. ಬೇಲೆದ— pressure of work.

ಉರ್ಬುಲಿಯುನಿ urbuliyuni, *see* ಇರ್ಬುಲಿಯುನಿ.

ಉರ್ಯುನಿ uryuni, *see* ಉರಿಯುನಿ.

ಉರ್ಯೆ urye, *s.* A red kind of fowl.

ಉರ್ಲಿ urli, *s.* A brass vessel for preparing curries in.

ಉರ್ಲು urlu, *s.* A noose, snare. —ಗು ತಿಕ್ಕುನಿ to be entrapped in a snare. —ದೀಪಿನಿ to lay a snare. —ಪಾಡುನಿ to put a noose round the neck; to hang. —ಪಾಡೊಣುನಿ to hang oneself.

ಉರ್ಲೆ urle, *s.* A kind of cake.

ಉರ್ವಣೆ urvaṇe, *s.* An instrument for destroying nits.

ಉರ್ವೆ urve, *adj.* Unripe.

ಉಲ ula, *see* ಉಳಾಯಿ.

ಉಲಿ uli, *s.* Nought, nothing. —ಪಾಡುನಿ to annul; *see also* ಉಳಿ, ಪುಲಿ.

ಉಲಿಕುತ್ತು ulikuttu, *s.* A small wound.

ಉಲಿಯುನಿ uliyuni (ಉಲಿ), *v. a.* To instigate, induce. *v. n.* To tremble.

ಉಲುಕು uluku, *see* ಉಳ್ಕು.

ಉಲುಟು uluṭu, *see* ಉರುಂಟ್. 2. fraud, cheating.

ಉಲೆ ule, *s.* A furnace. 2. a deer; *cf.* ಉರೆ.

ಉಲೆವುನಿ ulevuni (ಉಲೆ), *v. n.* To shine.

ಉಲೋ ulō, *see* ಉಳೋ.

ಉಲ್ಕ್ ulku, *see* ಉಳ್ಕು.

ಉಲ್ಕಾಪಾತ ulkāpāta, *s.* The falling of meteors, which is considered a bad sign. 2. an omen.

ಉಲ್ಕು ulku, *see* ಉಳ್ಕು.

ಉಲ್ಕುನಿ, ಉಲ್ಕುದ್‌ಪೋಪಿನಿ, *see* ಉಳ್ಕುನಿ,

ಉಲ್ಟ, ಉಲ್ಟಿ ulṭa, ulṭi, *adj.* Contradictory, opposite, counter. 2. upset; —ಮಳ್ಪುನಿ to take off, upset, *fig.* to lie.

ಉಲ್ಲಾಯೆ, ಉಲ್ಲಾಲ್ದಿ ullāye, ullāldi *see* ಉಳ್ಳಾಯೆ.

ಉಲ್ಲಾಸ ullāsa, *s.* Exultation, happiness. —ಆಪಿನಿ to be cheerful. *adj.* Joyous, blithe.

ಉಲ್ಲಿ ulli, *see* ಉಳ್ಳಿ.

ಉಶ್ವಾಸ uśvāsa, *s.* Breathing out, a sigh; *cf.* ಶ್ವಾಸ.

ಉಷಾರ್ ushārụ, *adj.* Alert, sharp; *bet.* ಹುಷಾರ್.

ಉಷ್ಣ ushṇa, *adj.* Hot, warm. *s.* Heat, warmth.

ಉಸ್, ಉಸ್ಸನೆ usụ, ussane, *s.* A deep sigh.

ಉಸಾರ್ usārụ, *see* ಹುಷಾರ್.

ಉಸುರು, ಉಸುಲು usuru, usulu, *s.* Breath. 2. life. –ಕಟ್ಟುನಿ to hold the breath. –ಪೋಪಿನಿ to die; gases to escape, as from a corked bottle. –ಬುಡುಪಿನಿ to breathe, respire.

ಉಸುಳ್ತಿ usul̤ti, *s.* Collusion, connivance.

ಉಸ್ವಾಸ usvāsa, *see* ಉಶ್ವಾಸ.

ಉಳ ul̤a, Inside, inner part; *cf.* ಉಲ. –ಕೈ the palm of the hand. –ಕೈ ಮಳ್ಪುನಿ to take in, to have a secret. –ಗುಟ್ಟು a latent secret, hidden mystery. –ಬಾಗು a bend; the curve of an arch. –ಮಗೆಲ್ inside. –ಮುಂಬಲ್ the inner square of a house. –ಸಾದಿ a by-path. –ಸೆರಂಗ್ the lower part of a female's garment.

ಉಳಯಿ, ಉಳಾಯಿ ul̤ayi, ul̤āyi, *adv.* In, into. *Some declensions are formed of this adverb; as,* –ದ ಅದೆ a back *or* inner room. ಉಳಯಿಡ್ದ್ from within. ಉಳತವುಳಯಿ, ಉಳಯಿದ್ದುಳಯಿ secretly, privately.

ಉಳವು ul̤avu, *s.* One's secret. 2. design. 3. inclination.

ಉಳಸಂಚಿ ul̤asañci, *s.* Intrigue, conspiracy, secret design; collusion, fraud.

ಉಳಿ ul̤i, *s.* A chisel.

ಉಳಿಯ, ಉಳ್ಳಿಯ ul̤iya, ul̤l̤iya, *s.* A small river-island *or* peninsula.

ಉಳೆ ul̤e, *see* ಉರೆ, ಉಲೆ.

ಉಳೋ ul̤ō, *intj.* Alas!

ಉಳ್ಕಿ ul̤ki, *s.* Remnant, rest.

ಉಳ್ಕು ul̤ku, *s.* A sprain, *or* cramp.

ಉಳ್ಕುನಿ ul̤kuni (ಉಳ್ಕು), *v.n.* To be sprained, *or* cramped; *also* ಉಳ್ಕುದು ಪೋಪಿನಿ.

ಉಳ್ಳ, ಉಳ್ಳೆ ul̤l̤a, ul̤l̤e, *see* ಉಪ್ಪುನಿ.

ಉಳ್ಳಡೆ ul̤lade, *s.* A fisherman.

ಉಳ್ಳಾಯೆ ul̤l̤āye, *s.* A master, lord (*fem.* ಉಳ್ಳಾಳ್ದಿ).

ಉಳ್ಳಿ ul̤l̤i, *s.* A generic name for garlic. ನೀರುಳ್ಳಿ onions, ಬೊಳ್ಳುಳ್ಳಿ garlic.

ಉಳ್ಳೋರಿ ul̤l̤ōri, *s.* A memo. of a receipt given to a tenant for part-payment of rent.

ಊ Ū

ಊ ū, The sixth letter of the alphabet. In MSS. it is often written ಊ.

ಊಂಚಿ, ಊಂಚು ūñci, ūñcu, *adj.* Superior, costly, fine.

ಊಂಟಾವುನಿ ūṇṭāvuni, *c. v.* (*of* ಊಂಟುನಿ) To lift up. 2. to cause a person to get up *or* leave his seat. 3. to insult, despise; *cf.* ಉಟಾಯಿಸುನಿ.

ಊಂಟುನಿ ūṇṭuni (ಊಂಟ್), *v. n.* To get up, press.

ಊಂದುನಿ ūnduni (ಊಂದ್), *v. a.* To press down. ಊಂದುದು ಪತ್ತುನಿ to hold firmly.

ಊಂಬು ūmbu, *see* ತೂಂಬು.

ಊಂಬೆ ūmbe, *s.* A hole.

ಊಜುನಿ ūjuni (ಊಜ್), *v. n.* To ooze; *also* ಊಜಿದ್ ಪೋಪಿನಿ.

ಊಟ ūṭa, *s.* Food, meal.

ಊಟಿ ūṭi, *s.* A spring, fountain.

ಊಟುಪಚಾರ ūṭupacāra, *s.* Hospitality and civility.

ಊಟೆ ūṭe, *see* ತೂಟೆ.

ಊಡಾವುನಿ ūḍāvuni, *c. v.* (*of* ಊಡುನಿ) To fix. 2. to put in order. ಪನಿತ– to fix the boards of a chest.

ಊಡಿಲ್ ūḍilu, *s.* A kind of broom grass.

ಊಡುನಿ ūḍuni (ಊಡ್), *v. a.* To plough; *cf.* ಹೂಡುನಿ. 2. to fix.

ಊಣ ūṇa, *see* ಊನ.

ಊತ ūta, *s.* A weight, burden. 2. a staff. –ಕೋಲು a weighing rod.

ಊದ, ಊದಾ ūda, ūdā, *adj.* Sky-blue.

ಊದು ūdu, *s.* A prop. –ಕೊರ್ಪಿನಿ to prop. –ಕೋಲು a pole used as a prop.

ಊದುಕಾಮೆಲಿ ūdukāmeli, *s.* A malignant kind of jaundice from which particularly children suffer.

ಊದುನಿ ūduni (ಊದ್), *v. a.* To blow, as a pipe. 2. to swell. ಊದಿಲೆ a piper.

ಊದುಬತ್ತಿ ūdubatti, *s.* An aromatic pastille.

ಊನ ūna, *s.* Defect, maim. –ದಾಯಿ, ಊನೆ a cripple.

ಊಯ್ಯಾಲ್ ūyyālu, *see* ಉಜ್ಜಾಲ್.

ಊರ ūra, *adj.* Local. –ಚಾವಡಿ a public office. –ನಡತೆ local custom. –ಸುದ್ದಿ gossip.

ಊರಣೆ ūraṇe, *see* ಉರಣೆ.

ಊರಾವುನಿ ūrāvuni, *c. v.* (*of* ಊರುನಿ) To plant, fix firmly.

ಊರಿಯಾಯೆ ūriyāye, *s.* A stranger; *also* ಊರ್ಯಾಯೆ.

ಊರು ūru, *s.* A town. 2. a village. 3. one's native place. –ದಾಯೆ a countryman. –ಮಂದೆ townsfolk. –ಯೆಳ್ಳ್ country sesamum. ಊರೂರುಗು from village to village; *cf.* ಊರ.

ಊರುಂಬಳಿ ūrumbaḷi, *s.* A village grant.

ಊರುಕೋಲು ūrukōlu, *s.* A walking stick.

ಊರುನಿ ūruni (ಊರ್), *v.a.* To set firmly. 2. to plant in the ground as a seed *or* shrub, *etc.* 3. to gain power. ಕಾರ್– to plant one's foot. ಬೇರ್– to be established firmly, to take root; to grow.

ಊರೊಳು ūroḷu, *s.* A cross bar at the entrance of a garden *etc.*; *cf.* ಉರೊೞ.

ಊರ್ಯ ūrya, *see* ಊರ್ಯ.

ಊರ್ಜಿತ ūrjita, *adj.* Confirmed, established.

ಊರ್ಧ್ವ ūrdhva, *adj.* Aloft, on high. –ಗತಿ ethereal course, heavenly bliss.

ಊರ್ಯ ūrya, *adj.* Strange; *cf.* ಊರಿಯಾಯಿ.

ಊಸಂಟೆ ūsaṇṭè, *s.* A large bug.

ಊಸು ūsu, *s.* A fart.

ಊಸುನಿ ūsuni (ಊಸ್), *v.n.* To ooze; *cf.* ಊಜುನಿ to break wind downwards, *vlg.*

ಊಸೆಲ್ ūselụ, *adj.* Oozing. 2. filthy. 3. breaking wind downwards, *vlg.* ಊಸೆತಿ a man who frequently breaks wind downwards.

ಊಹೆ, ಊಹನೆ ūhe, ūhane, *s.* Supposition, conjecture.

ಊಳಿಗ ūḷiga, *s.* Service. 2. work. –ದಾಯಿ a servant, labourer. –ಮಳ್ಪುನಿ to serve, work.

ಊಳಿಯುನಿ uḷiyuni (ಊಳಿ), *v. n.* To ooze; *cf.* ಊಜುನಿ. 2. the bowels to evacuate frequently; *also* ಊಳಿದ್ಪೋಪಿನಿ.

ಋ RỤ

ಋ rụ, The seventh letter of the alphabet, but seldom used in Tuḷu. It is commonly pronounced like ರು *or* ರಿ, which see for words beginning with ಋ; *as*, ಋಣ = ರುಣ, ಋಷಿ = ರಿಷಿ.

ಎ YE

ಎ **ye,** The eighth letter of the alphabet. In MSS. it is often written ಯೆ.

ಎಂಕ್ **yeṅkụ,** *see* ಯಾನ್.

ಎಂಕುಳು **yeṅkuḷu,** *pers. pro.* We. *This word which is the plural of* ಯಾನ್ *signifies only the persons addressing, and should be distinguished from* ನಮ *which always includes both the persons addressing and addressed.*

ಎಂಚ **yeṅća,** *adv.* How? —ಲಾ, ಎಂಚಾಂಡಲಾ however, anyhow, by all means.

ಎಂಚಿ **yeṅći,** *see* ಎಜ್ಜಿ.

ಎಂಚಿ **yeṅći,** *intg. pro.* What sort of? —ನ, —ನವು, —ತ್ತಿನವು what sort of thing? —ನಾಯೆ, —ತ್ತಿನಾಯೆ what sort of man?

ಎಂಜಿರ್ **yeñjirụ,** *s.* A kind of tree.

ಎಂಟ್ **yeṇṭụ,** *s.* Boasting, pride. 2. craftiness, cunning. —ತೋಜಾವುನಿ to show pride, be cunning. —ಪಾತೆರುನಿ to boast, prattle, play tricks. —ದಾಯೆ a crafty man.

ಎಂಟೆ **yeṇṭe,** *s.* A clod of earth. 2. an unburnt brick; *cf.* ಹೆಂಟೆ.

ಎಂಣಿಗೆ **yeṇṇige,** *s.* Calculation, estimation.

ಎಂಣುನಿ **yeṇṇuni** (ಎಂಣ್), *v. a.* To count. 2. to think, presume. 3. to expect.

ಎಂಣೆ **yeṇṇe,** *s.* Oil. —ದ ಗಾಣ an oil mill. —ಪೂಜುನಿ to rub with *or* apply oil. ಅತ್ತಿ— distilled oil. ಇಜಿನ್ದ— cinnamon oil. ಎಣ್ಮೆದ—, ಎಡ್ಡೆಂಣೆ gingely oil. ಗಂಧದ— sandalwood oil. ತಾರಾಯಿದ— cocoanut oil. ತುಡಾರ್ದ— lamp-oil. ನಾಣಿಲ್ದ— olive oil. ಪರೆಲ್— castor oil. ಪೊಂನೆದ— the oil of the nuts of *Rottleria tinctoria.* ಮಂಣ್ಣೆಂಣೆ kerosene oil. ಸಂಪಿಗೆದ— champaka oil *etc.*

ಎಂಣೆಕಪ್ಪು, ಎಂಣೆಕೆಂಪು **yeṇṇekappu, yeṇṇekempu,** *adj.* Dark red.

ಎಂಣೆಬದನೆ **yeṇṇebadane,** *s.* A species of brinjals.

ಎಂತ್ರ **yentra,** *see* ಯಂತ್ರ.

ಎಂದ್ರುನಿ **yendruni** (ಎಂದ್ರ್), *v. a.* To say fully; *cf.* ಇನ್ಪಿನಿ.

ಎಂನವು **yennavu,** *pro.* Mine; *cf.* ಯಾನ್.

ಎಂನುನಿ **yennuni,** *see* ಎಂಣುನಿ.

ಎಂಪ **yempa,** *see* ಎಪ್ಪ.

ಎಂಮಳು **yemmaḷu,** *s.* A woman. ಕೋಪದ— an angry woman.

ಎಂಮೆ **yemme,** *see* ಹೆಮ್ಮೆ 2. *see* ಎರ್ಮೆ.

ಎಂಮೆಟ್ಟುನಿ **yemmeṭṭuni** (ಎಂಮೆಟ್ಟ್), *v. n.* To turn back. 2. to yield. 3. to abate, as sickness; *cf.* ಹಿಂಮೆಟ್ಟುನಿ.

ಎಕಂಬೆಲ್ **yekambelụ,** *see* ಎಕ್ಕಮಲೆ.

ಎಕರೆ, ಎಕ್ರೆ **yekare, yekre,** *s.* An acre.

ಎಕ್ಕ್ **yekkụ,** *adj.* Nearly dead.

ಎಕ್ಕ್‌ಸಕ್ಕ್ yekkųsakkų, *adv*. Confusedly, indiscriminately. –ಆಪಿನಿ to become confused. –ಪಾತೆರುನಿ to reproach unjustly. –ಮಳ್ಪುನಿ to be perverse.

ಎಕ್ಕ yekka, *see* ಏಕ. 2. the ace.

ಎಕ್ಕಂ yekkam, *s*. The unit of numeration, first place in ciphering.

ಎಕ್ಕಚಕ್ಕ yekkaćakka, *see* ಎಕ್ಕ್‌ಸಕ್ಕ್.

ಎಕ್ಕಡ್ yekkaḍų, *adv*. Then. ಎಕ್ಕಡೆ already. ಒಂತೆ– a little while ago.

ಎಕ್ಕಡಿ yekkaḍi, *s*. A kind of game with cowries, arranged on a board. –ಗೊಬ್ಬುನಿ to play such a game.

ಎಕ್ಕದೆ yekkade, *s*. Hiccough. 2. gasping. –ಕುಟ್ಟುನಿ to hiccough; to gasp; *cf*. ಎಕ್ಕಲೆ.

ಎಕ್ಕನಾಲೆ yekkanāle, *adj*. Lean, thin. *s*. A glutton, greedy man; 2. *see* ಎಕ್ಕಲೆ.

ಎಕ್ಕಮಲೆ, ಎಕ್ಕಮಾಲೆ, ಎಕ್ಕಮೆ yekkamalė, yekkamālė, yekkamė, *s*. The swallow wort, *Calotropis gigantea*.

ಎಕ್ಕಲೆ yekkale, *s*. A cockroach; *also* ಎಕ್ಕಲು; *cf*. ಎಕ್ಕದೆ, ಎಕ್ಕನಾಲೆ.

ಎಕ್ಕಲ್ಯುನಿ yekkalyuni (ಎಕ್ಕಲ್), *v. n*. To stretch the body, *or* stoop down in order to catch *or* pick up anything. 2. to spring *or* jump up.

ಎಕ್ಕಸಕ್ಕ yekkasakka, *see* ಎಕ್ಕ್‌ಸಕ್ಕ್.

ಎಕ್ಕಾವುನಿ yekkāvuni, *c. v*. (*of* ಎಕ್ಕುನಿ) To reach, cause to touch.

ಎಕ್ಕುನಿ yekkuni (ಎಕ್ಕ್), *v. a*. To touch. 2. to gin. *v. n*. To ebb, decline. ಕೈ– to be within reach of the hand. ಜೀವ– to be on the point of death. ಪರ್ತಿ– to gin cotton. ಬಂಜಿ– to be hungry.

ಎಕ್ಕೆ yekke, *s*. The shrub *Aristolochia Indica*.

ಎಗ್ಗೆ yeggė, *s*. A branch, bough.

ಎಗ್ಗೆಲ್ yeggelų, *s*. A small branch. –ಕಡ್ಡ a small piece of wood.

ಎಚಿಪು yećipu, *see* ಎಜಿಪು.

ಎಚ್ಚ yečća, *see* ಹೆಚ್ಚ.

ಎಚ್ಚರಿಕೆ yečćarike, *s*. Wakefulness. 2. care, caution. 3. warning. –ಆಪಿನಿ to be awake. –ಕೊರ್ಪಿನಿ to warn, put on guard. –ದೀಪಿನಿ to take precaution. –ಮಳ್ಪುನಿ to remind. –ಡ್ ಉಪ್ಪುನಿ to be on guard, be alert.

ಎಚ್ಚರಿಪುನಿ, ಎಚ್ಚರಿಸುನಿ yečćaripuni, yečćarisuni (ಎಚ್ಚರಿ), *v. a*. To admonish. 2. to caution, warn against.

ಎಚ್ಚಿ yečći, *s*. Body. –ಡ್ ಪಾಡುನಿ to put on clothes. –ಗ್ ಕೈಪಾಡುನಿ to assult; *see* ಹೆಚ್ಚ.

ಎಚ್ಚಿಗೆ yečćigė, *see* ಹೆಚ್ಚಿಗೆ.

ಎಚ್ಚೆ yečće, *see* ಇಚ್ಛೆ.

ಎಜಮಾನೆ yejamāne, *see* ಯಜಮಾನೆ.

ಎಜಿಪು yejipu, *s*. Endeavour, attempt. –ಕೊರ್ಪಿನಿ to caution, betray. –ಮಳ್ಪುನಿ to try through others.

ಎಜ್ಜ, ಎಜ್ಜಿ yejja, yejji, *s.* A hole. 2. a loophole. 3. the eye of a needle.

ಎಜ್ಜಿ, ಎಜ್ಜೆ yejji, yejje, *see* ಅಜ್ಜ, ಎಜ್ಜ, ಹೆಜ್ಜೆ.

ಎಜ್ಞ yejńya, *see* ಯಜ್ಞ.

ಎಟ್ಟಕುಟ್ಟ yeṭṭakuṭṭa, *s.* Quarrelling and fighting.

ಎಟ್ಟಾವುನಿ yeṭṭāvuni, *c.v.* (*of* ಎಟ್ಟುನಿ) To bend, cause to stoop.

ಎಟ್ಟಿ yeṭṭi, *s.* A prawn.

ಎಟ್ಟಿಬಲ್ಯಾರ್ yeṭṭiballyārụ, *s.* A small kind of shark.

ಎಟ್ಟಿಸುತ್ತ, ಎಟ್ಟಿಸುದ್ದ yeṭṭisutta, yeṭṭisudda, *s.* The sword-fish.

ಎಟ್ಟುನಿ yeṭṭuni (ಎಟ್ಟಿ), *v. a.* To stitch, as leaves. 2. to cause mischief. 3. to box the ear. *v.n.* To stumble, bow down; be hit. ಎಟ್ಟಿದ್‌ಪೋಪಿನಿ to bend down, as a tree laden with fruit.

ಎಟ್ಟೆಲೆ yeṭṭele, *s.* A mischief-maker.

ಎಡ yeḍa, *see* ಯಡ.

ಎಡಂಕ್ yeḍaṅkụ, *adv.* On the left side. —ಪಾತೆರ an offensive word.

ಎಡಂಕುನಿ yeḍaṅkuni (ಎಡಂಕ್), *v. a.* To kick. 2. to hit. 3. to disregard; *see* ದಂಕುನಿ.

ಎಡಪುನಿ, ಎಡುತುರುನಿ yeḍapuni, yeḍuturuni, *see* ಎಡ್ಪುನಿ.

ಎಡವಟ್ಟ್, ಎಡೆವಟ್ಟ್ yeḍavaṭṭụ, yeḍevaṭṭụ, *adj.* Middling, indifferent. 2. dull, stupid. 3. rough, rugged. —ಕೆಲಸ an indifferent work; an objectionable act. —ನರಮಾನಿ a stupid fellow. —ಸಾದಿ a rugged path.

ಎಡುಂಬುರೆ yeḍumbure, *s.* A doll.

ಎಡುಪುನಿ yeḍupuni, *see* ಎಡ್ಪುನಿ.

ಎಡೆ yeḍe, *see* ಇಡೆ.

ಎಡೆದೆಟ್ಟ್ yeḍedeṭṭụ, *see* ಎಡಂಕ್.

ಎಡೆನಾಣ್ಯ yeḍenāṇya, *s.* Paper-money. —ದಾಯೆ a stupid fellow, a man temporarily engaged.

ಎಡೆನಾಳಿ yeḍenāḷi, *s.* An inner wall round a temple.

ಎಡೆಮುಡಿ yeḍemuḍi, *see* ಇಡೆಮುಡಿ.

ಎಡ್ಡೆ yeḍḍe, *s.* Goodness. *adj.* Good, excellent, superior, fair, fine. 2. happy. 3. prosperous. —ಜಾತಿ a superior caste, fine breed. —ದಿನ a festive day, holiday. —ಪೊರ್ತು, —ಮುಹೂರ್ತ, —ವೇಳ್ಯ an auspicious occasion. —ಮುಂಚಿ black pepper. *adv.* Well, very well. —ಆಪಿನಿ to improve in health; to prosper, be happy. —ಆವಡ್ may you, (he *etc.*) be happy. —ಕೊರ್ಪಿನಿ, —ಮಳ್ಪುನಿ to do good, to bless with prosperity. —ತಿನ್ಪಿನಿ (*lit.* to eat good), to enjoy happiness as the fruit of one's good deeds. —ಪಾತೆರುನಿ to speak favourably, fluently, *or* at length; to speak *or* argue ably; to chatter. —ತನ goodness. ಎಡ್ಡಂತಿ of good sort. ಎಡ್ಡೆ

ನೇ good, *emph.* ಎಡ್ಡೇನ copiously, abundantly, heartily; immoderately, severely, violently.

ಎಡ್ಪುನಿ **yeḍpuni** (ಏಡಿ), *v. a.* To thump, strike with the fist. 2. to pound in a mortar.

ಎಣ್‌ಮ, **yeṇụma,** *num.* Eight.

ಎಣ **yeṇa** *s.* A corpse. –ಮುಂಡೆ a good for nothing, *vlg.*

ಎಣಿಕೆ, ಎಣೆ, ಎಣ್ಕೆ **yeṇike, yeṇe, yeṇke,** *s.* Calculation, counting; estimation.

ಎಣೆಲ್ **yeṇelụ,** *adj.* Pertaining to the first crop. –ಬುಳೆ the first crop.

ಎಣ್ಚಿ **yeṇći,** *s.* A ladder.

ಎಣ್ಣೆ **yeṇṇe,** *see* ಎಂಣೆ.

ಎಣ್ಪ **yeṇpa** *num.* Eighty.

ಎಣ್ಮ **yeṇma,** *see* ಎಣ್‌ಮ.

ಎಣ್ಮೆ **yeṇme,** *s.* The gingely-oil seed, *Sesamum orientale.* –ದ ಎಂಣೆ gingely-oil.

ಎತಾ **yetā,** *see* ಎಥಾ.

ಎತಾಸ್ತಿ **yetāsti,** *adj.* Exact, correct. *adv.* Exactly, correctly; *bet.* ಯಥಾಸ್ಥಿತಿ.

ಎತೆ **yete,** *see* ಎಥೆ.

ಎತ್ತ್‌ಗಡಿ, ಎತ್ತ್‌ಗಡೆ **yettụgaḍi, yettụgaḍe,** *s.* Scheme, device. –ಮಳ್ಪುನಿ to scheme, devise.

ಎತ್ತ್‌ತಗ್ಗ್ **yettụtaggụ,** *adj.* Uneven, rugged.

ಎತ್ತನ **yettana,** *see* ಎತ್ನ

ಎತ್ತರ **yettara,** *adj.* High, lofty, tall. *s.* Height.

ಎತ್ತರುನಿ **yettaruni** (ಎತ್ತರ್), *v. a.* To ascend, climb.

ಎತ್ತಾಡುನಿ, ಎತ್ತಾವುನಿ **yettāḍuni, yettāvuni,** *c. v.* (*of* ಎತ್ತುನಿ) To reach, deliver. 2. to gulp, swallow water *etc.* eagerly, *or* in large draughts.

ಎತ್ತಿಗೆ **yettige,** *s.* A collection.

ಎತ್ತುನಿ **yettuni** (ಎತ್ತ್), *v. a.* To raise a subscription *or* tax.

ಎತ್ತುವಳಿ **yettuvaḷi,** *s.* The act of raising a subscription *or* tax.

ಎತ್ನ **yetna,** *s.* Essay, endeavour, effort, exertion; *bet.* ಯತ್ನ.

ಎತ್ವಾಸಿ **yetvāsi,** *s.* Difference, disagreement, variance; *bet.* ವ್ಯತ್ಯಾಸ.

ಎಥಾ **yethā,** *adv.* As, according to. *adj.* Proper, usual. –ಪ್ರಕಾರ as usual. –ಮಾರ್ಗ the usual course *or* way; *bet.* ಯಥಾ.

ಎಥಾರ್ಥ **yethārtha,** *see* ಯಥಾರ್ಥ.

ಎಥೆ **yethe,** *s.* Pain, smart, grief.

ಎಥೇಚ್ಚ, ಎಥೇಷ್ಟ **yethēćća, yethēshṭa,** *see* ಯಥೇಚ್ಛ, ಯಥೇಷ್ಟ.

ಎದ್‌ಪು **yedụpu,** *s.* Beginning. –ದ ಬರ್ಸ the first shower of rain.

ಎದ್‌ರ್, ಎದುರು **yedụrụ, yeduru,** *s.* The front, that which is opposite. 2. presence. –ಚೀಟಿ the counterpart of a deed. –ನುಡಿ, ಎದುರ್ನುಡಿ a conditional deed of sale. –ಬೊಳಂತೆ half boiled rice. –ವಳಿ the counterpart of a lease. –ವಾದಿ an opposite party, opponent. –ಆಪಿನಿ to meet, come face to face. –ಉಂ

ತುನಿ to stand in front, to oppose; to rebel. —ಉಂತಾವುನಿ to set up *or* instigate a person against another. —ಪಾತೆರುನಿ to speak to one's face; to contradict, oppose. —ಬೂರುನಿ to come in sight, be seen; to be overtaken. ಎದ್ರೆದ್ರ್ಗ್ face to face. —ಡ್ before, in presence of.

ಎದಿ **yedi,** *see* ಒದಿ.

ಎದಿಂಕೆ **yediṅke,** *s.* A wing.

ಎದಿಯನೆ **yediyane,** *see* ಎದ್ದೆ.

ಎದುಕೊಣುನಿ **yedukoṇuni** (ಎದು ಕೊಣ್), *v. a.* To advance. 2. to meet, go to meet.

ಎದುರಾಟ **yedurāṭa,** *s.* Antagonism.

ಎದುರಾಳಿ **yedurāli,** *s.* An antagonist.

ಎದೆ **yede,** *s.* The heart, chest, bosom. —ಕಲ್ಲ್ ಮಳ್ಪುನಿ to harden one's heart. —ಕೊಪಿಂಗ್ನಿ to take courage. —ಗುಂಡಿಗೆ courage, boldness.

ಎದ್ದಣಿಗೆ **yeddaṇige,** *see* ಎದ್ದೆ.

ಎದ್ದುಂಬೆ **yeddumbe,** *s.* A kind of plant.

ಎದ್ದುಪು **yeddupu,** *s.* An ambuscade, lying in wait. —ಪಾಡುನಿ to lie in ambush.

ಎದ್ದ್ಯುನಿ **yeddyuni** (ಎದ್ದ್), *v. a.* To fan.

ಎದ್ದೆ, ಎದ್ದೆಣೆ, ಎದ್ದ್ಯನ **yedde, yeddeṇe, yeddyana,** *s.* A fan.

ಎದ್ರ್ **yedrụ,** *see* ಎದ್ರ್, ಎದುರು.

ಎದ್ರೊಳಿ **yedroḷi,** *s.* The creeper *Jasminum angustifolium.*

ಎದ್ರೊಳಿ **yedroḷi,** *see* ಎದ್ರವಳಿ.

ಎನ, ಎನ್ನ **yena, yenna,** *see* ಯಾನ್.

ಎಬುಳಂತೆ **yebulante,** *adj.* Half-boiled. 2. half-witted, silly.

ಎಬ್ಬಾವು **yebbāvu,** *see* ಹೆಬ್ಬಾವು.

ಎಮೆ **yeme,** *see* ಯಮೆ.

ಎಮರಿಕೆ, ಎಮರ್ಗೆ **yemarike, yemarge,** *s.* Storing. —ದೀಪಿನಿ to keep *or* store.

ಎಯಿಪಂಜಿ **yeyipañji,** *s.* A porcupine; *cf.* ಮುಳ್ಳುಪಂಜಿ.

ಎಯ್ಯುನಿ **yeyyuni** (ಎಯಿ), *v. a.* To shoot an arrow.

ಎರಕ **yeraka,** *adj.* Molten, cast, as metal. —ದ ಕೆಲಸ, ಎರಕೊಂತ ಕೆಲಸ molten *or* casting work. —ಮೃಪುನಿ to pour melted metal into a mould.

ಎರಗ್ **yeragụ,** *s.* Fitness.

ಎರಗುನಿ **yeraguni** (ಎರಗ್), *v. n.* To melt. 2. to agree with the stomach.

ಎರಗುನಿ **yeraguni** (ಎರಗ್), *v. a.* and *n.* To bow, prostrate, do obeisance. 2. to fall upon, seize. 3. to alight.

ಎರಡ್ **yeraḍụ,** *num.* Two; *cf.* ರಡ್ಡ್.

ಎರಬಾಯಿ **yerabāyi,** *s.* A kind of fish.

ಎರಲ, ಎರಳ **yerala, yeraḷa,** *see* ಹೇರಳ.

ಎರವು **yeravu,** *s.* The act of lending *or* borrowing anything for temporary use. 2. difference, distinction. —ದ ನಗ a borrowed ornament. —ಗ್ ಕೊಂಡು ಬರ್ಪಿನಿ to borrow.

ಎರಳೆ **yeraḷe,** *s.* An antelope, deer.

ಎರಿ **yeri**, *s*. The glare *or* heat of fire. —ಘಾಳಿ a very hot wind, sultry wind. —ದಪ್ಪುನಿ, —ಪಾಕುನಿ to glare, be affected with the heat of fire; *cf*. ಹಿರಿ.

ಎರಿಯಂಟೆ **yeriyaṇṭe**, *s*. A kind of fish.

ಎರಿಯಾಯೆ **yriyāye**, *see* ಹಿರಿಯಾಯೆ.

ಎರಿಯಾವುನಿ **yeriyāvuni**, *c.v.* (*of* ಎರಿಯುನಿ) To burn, blaze.

ಎರಿಯುನಿ **yeriyuni** (ಎರಿ), *v.n.* To glare. 2. to be hot.

ಎರು **yeru**, *s*. A buffalo. 2. a moth, worm. —ಆಪಿನಿ to be decayed with worms. —ಬರ್ಪಿನಿ to come into manhood.

ಎರುತಾರಿ, ಎರುತಾಳಿ **yerutāri, yerutāḷi**, *s*. A kind of palm tree.

ಎರೆಬಾಯಿ **yerebāyi**, *see* ಎರಬಾಯಿ.

ಎಂದ್ರಲೆ **yerndale**, *s*. A green pigeon.

ಎರ್ಕ್ **yerkụ**, *s*. Rising *or* accumulation, as of water, *etc*. 2. severity. *adj*. Exceeding. —ಪತ್ತುನಿ to be in danger.

ಎರ್ಕ **yerka**, *s*. Fulness. 2. proximity. *adj*. Full; near.

ಎರ್ಕಾವುನಿ **yerkāvuni**, *c.v.* (*of* ಎರ್ಕುನಿ) To tuck up, as clothes, when wading a river *etc*. 2. to hold back, as milk by a cow *etc*.

ಎರ್ಕುನಿ **yerkuni** (ಎರ್ಕ್), *v.n.* To puff up, swell. 2. to rise *or* collect, as water in a place. 3. to be full of milk, as the breast *or* udder. ಬಂಜಿ— the belly to be distended.

ಎರ್ಕೆ, ಎರ್ಕೆಲ್ **yerke, yerkelụ**, *s*. Rising; *cf*. ಎರ್ಕ, ಎರ್ತೆ.

ಎರ್ಗಲೆ, ಎರ್ಗೊಣೆ, ಎರ್ಗೊಲೆ **yergale, yergoṇe, yergole**, *s*. A dull man like a buffalo, a simpleton; a glutton, *vlg*.

ಎರ್ತ **yerta**, *see* ವ್ಯರ್ಥ.

ಎರ್ತೆ **yertè**, *s*. The flood tide; *cf*. ಎರ್ಕ, ಎರ್ಕೆ.

ಎರ್ಪ **yerpa**, *s*. Seventy.

ಎರ್ಪೆನೆ **yerpene**, *s*. A hairpin. *adj*. Old.

ಎರ್ಪುನಿ **yerpuni** (ಎರಿ), *v.a.* To lift up.

ಎರ್ಮೆ **yerme**, *s*. A she-buffalo. —ತರೊಳಿ a kind of bush. —ಪಾಕೊಳು a calf. —ಬಲ್ಯಾರ್ a kind of fish.

ಎಲಕ್ಕಿ **yelakki**, *see* ಏಲಕ್ಕಿ.

ಎಲತ್ರ, ಎಲಸ್ತ್ರ **yelatra, yelastra**, *s*. A handkerchief.

ಎಲಾ **yelā**, *intj*. of surprise.

ಎಲಿ **yeli**, *s*. A rat. —ಪಾಷಾಣ rat's bane, arsenic.

ಎಲಿಕೆಬಿ **yelikebi**, *s*. The herb *Evolvulus emerginatus*.

ಎಲಿಪುನಿ **yelipuni**, *see* ಎಲ್ಪುನಿ.

ಎಲಿಯುನಿ **yeliyuni**, *v.n.* To melt, as any soft substance, butter, *etc*.; *also* ಏಲುನಿ.

ಎಲಿಸೆರಿ **yeliseri**, *s*. A shark; *also* ಏಲಿಸಾರ್.

ಎಲು **yelu**, *s*. A bone. —ಕುತ್ತ a pain in the bones. —ಕೊಟ್ಟೆ, —ಕೊಡೆ a skeleton. —ಬಲೆ a joint of the bones.

ಎಲೆ **yelè**, *s*. A leaf.

ಎಲೆನಾಗೆ yelenāge, *s.* A small but dangerous insect found on betel leaves.

ಎಲೇ yelē, *see* ಎಲಾ.

ಎಲ್ಕೊಡೆ yelkoḍe, *see* ಎಲುಕೊಡೆ.

ಎಲ್ಪುನಿ yelpuni, *v.a.* To melt, as lead, butter, *etc.*

ಎಲ್ಲಂಜಿ yellañji, *adv.* The day after tomorrow.

ಎಲ್ಲಂಮ yellamma, *s.* A name of Kāḷi.

ಎಲ್ಲಿ, ಎಲ್ಲ್ಯ yelli, yellya, *adj.* Little, small, short. 2. inferior, mean. —ಡ್ದ, —ತನೊಡ್ದು from infancy. —ಮಲ್ಲೆ ಮಳ್ಪುನಿ to extol and disparage anything alternately.

ಎಲ್ಲೆ yelle, *adv.* Tomorrow.

ಎಲ್ಲ್ಯಂಣೆ yellyaṇṇe, *s.* A junior elder brother.

ಎಲ್ಲ್ಯಾಯೆ yellyāye, *s.* A youth; 2. a junior, minor. 3. a short man. ಯೆಲ್ಲ್ಯಾವು a small thing.

ಎವಂಚ yevañca, *see* ಜವಂಚ.

ಎವನ yevane, *see* ಜವನ.

ಎಸಳ್ yesaḷu, *s.* The petal of a flower, leaf. —ಪುಳಿ *Garcinia cambogia.* ಪುಗೆರೆದ— a tobacco leaf.

ಎಸ್ಸುನಿ yessuni, *see* ಎತ್ತುನಿ.

ಎಳತ್, ಎಳೆ yeḷatu, yeḷe, *adj.* Tender, green, not fully grown. —ನೀರ್ the water of a tender cocoanut.

ಎಳ್ಪ yeḷpa, *num.* Seventy. —ನೇ seventieth.

ಎಕ್ಷಿ yekshi, *see* ಯಕ್ಷಿ.

ಏ YĒ

ಏ yē, The ninth letter of the alphabet. In MSS. it is often written ಯೇ.

ಏ *is affixed to the words* ಅಂದ್ *and* ಅತ್ತ್ *when addressing or asking honorifically a single person; as,* ಅಂದೇ ರಾಮೆರೇ O Rāmā! ಅಂದೇ ಜೋಕುಳೇ O boys! O children! ಅಂಚತ್ತೇ is it not so? *It is also affixed to nouns, pronouns, and adverbs by way of emphasis.* ನರಮಾನಿಯೇ man only. ಈಯೇ you alone. ಇನಿಯೇ even to day.

ಏಕ yēka, *num.* One, single. 2. solitary. 3. combined, united. —ತಾಳ the accurate adjustment of song and instrumental music. —ತ್ವ unity, unanimity. —ವಚನ singular number, *gram.* —ವರ್ಣ of one colour *or* caste. —ಸ್ಥ a solitary man; a bachelor. —ಸ್ಥರಾದ್ jointly, unanimously; collusively.

ಏಕದಂ yēkadam, *adv.* At once; abruptly.

ಏಕನಾಯಕ yēkanāyaka, *s.* A medical plant.

ಏಕನಾಯಕೆ yēkanāyake, *s.* A monarch.

ಏಕಾ yēkā, *see* ಏಕ. —ಏಕಿ, ಏಕಾಕಿ abruptly, suddenly; without permission. 2. unreasonably, unjustly. —ಪಾತೆರುನಿ to reproach unjustly.

ಏಕಾಂಗಿ yēkāṅgi, *s.* A solitary life. —ಆದ್ alone.

ಏಕಾಂತ yēkānta, *s.* Solitude. 2. secrecy. *adj.* Solitary, secluded; secret. ಏಕಾಂತೊಡು in seclusion, secretly.

ಏಕಾದಶಿ yēkādaši, *s.* The eleventh day of either fortnight in the lunar month, on which Hindus fast.

ಏಕೀನಿ, ಏಖೀನಿ yēkīni, yēkhīni, *s.* Honesty, uprightness. 2. chastity.

ಏಕೋಚಿ yēkōči, *adv.* Alone.

ಏಚನೆ yēčane, *see* ಯೋಚನೆ.

ಏಚ್ಚುನಿ, ಏಚ್ಚ್ಯುನಿ yēččuni, yēččyuni (ಏಚ್ಚ್), *v. n.* To reflect, muse.

ಏಟ್ yēṭu, *s.* A kind of gambling in which a piece of coin is tossed up and a wager laid as to which side it will fall. —ಗೊಬ್ಬುನಿ to gamble in this way.

ಏಡ್ yēḍu, *s.* A goat.

ಏಡಾಮೋಡೆ yēḍāmōḍe, *s.* A stupid [man.

ಏಡಿ yēḍi, *s.* A coward; *cf.* ಹೇಡಿ.

ಏಡೆ yēḍe, *s.* A blockhead.

ಏಣಿ yēṇi, *s.* A ladder; *cf.* ಯೇಣಿ.

ಏತ್ yētu, *intg. pro.* How much? how many? ಏತೆಗಲಾ for any amount, on any account. ಏತೇತ how much each? ಏತೋ how-ever much, how much! —ಸರ್ತಿ how often?

ಏತು yētu, *s.* Annoyance (from goblins); *cf.* ಹೇತು.

ಏತೊಣುನಿ yētoṇuni, *see* ಎತ್ತುನಿ.

ಏತೊಳು yētoḷu, *intg.* How often?

ಏನ್ yēnu, *see* ಯಾನ್.

ಏನಿ yēni, *adv.* When? —ಗಲಾ, —ತೇನಿ ಗಲಾ, ಏನೇನಿಗಲಾ always, for ever.

ಏಪ, ಏಪೊ yēpa, yēpo, *adv.* When? —ಲಾ always, ever.

ಏಪುನಿ yēpuni (ಏಪ್), *v. a.* To catch, as a ball. 2. to take, lift *or* toss up a child in the arms.

ಏಪೊಳು yēpoḷu, *see* ಏಪ.

ಏಮರಿಕೆ, ಏಮರ್ಗೆ yēmarike, yēmarge, *see* ಎಮರಿಕೆ.

ಏಮೆ yēme, *s.* A turtle.

ಏರ್ yēru, *intg. pro.* Who? —ಲಾ, ಏರಾಂಡಲಾ whoever, whosoever, any one. ಏರವು who is that? ಏರೆ ಇಲ್ಲು, ಏರೆನವುಳು at whose house? ಏರೆಗಾದ್ for whom? for whose sake? ಏರಿಂಬೆರ್ (ಏರ್ ಪಿಂಬೆರ್) who knows?

ಏರ್ yēru, *see* ಹೇರ್.

ಏರ್ಪೇರ್ yērupēru, *s.* Difference, distinction. 2. perversion, distortion. 3. reproach.

ಏರಣೆ yēraṇe, *intg.* Who?

ಏರಾವುನಿ yērāvuni, *c. v.* (*of* ಏರುನಿ) To raise, lift up. 2. to increase, enhance; promote. 3. to load; embark. 4. to pet and spoil. ಕರೆಕ್—, ತುದಿಗ್—to flatter; to pet and spoil a child, servant, *etc.* ಬಿಲೆ— to raise the price; to out-bid. ಮರ— to set up a tree. ಶಿಕ್ಷೆ— to enhance punishment. ಸಂಬಳ— to promote, increase one's pay. ಸಾಮಾನ್— to load a cart *or* vessel with goods.

ಏರಿ **yēri,** *s.* A kind of fish. 2. a bed for planting vegetables *etc.*

ಏರುನಿ **yēruni** (ಏರ್), *v.a.* To ascend, climb, mount. *v.n.* To rise. 2. to be increased, be augmented. 3. to be accumulated.

ಏರ್ತೆ **yērte,** *see* ಎರ್ತೆ.

ಏರ್ಲಾಕಿ **yērlāki,** *s.* A part of a boxing match.

ಏರ್ಸಾವುನಿ **yērsāvuni** (ಏರ್ಸಾ), *v. a. see* ಏರಾವುನಿ. 2. to beat, strike. 3. to eat up.

ಏಲ್ **yēlu,** *see* ಏಳ್.

ಏಲಕ್ಕಿ **yēlakki,** *s.* Cardamoms.

ಏಲನ್ನ **yēlanna,** *s.* Weariness. —ಆಪಿನಿ to become weary.

ಏಲಮ್ **yēlamu,** *s.* An auction, public sale. —ಪಾಡುನಿ, —ಮಳ್ಪುನಿ to sell by auction.

ಏಲಾವುನಿ **yēlāvuni,** *c. v.* (*of* ಏಲುನಿ) To cause to melt.

ಏಲುನಿ **yēluni** (ಏಲ್), *v.n.* To melt, as lead, butter *etc.*

ಏವಂಚ **yēvanća,** *adv.* However, at any rate.

ಏವಾರ **yēvāra,** *see* ವ್ಯವಹಾರ.

ಏವುದೆಪ್ಪುದೆ **yēvudeppudė,** *s.* Doubt, perplexity. *adj.* Doubtful.

ಏವುರ **yēvura,** *see* ವೈರ.

ಏಸ **yēsa,** *see* ವೇಷ.

ಏಸಿಗೆ **yēsigė,** *see* ಪೇಶಿಕೆ, ಹೇಸಿಕೆ.

ಏಳ್ **yēlu,** *num.* Seven. ಏಳನೆ seventh.

ಏಳಿಗೆ **yēlige,** *s.* Increase, growth. 2. prosperity. 3. improvement; *cf.* ಹೇಳಿಕೆ.

ಏಳ್ಪ **yēlpa,** *see* ಎಳ್ಪ.

ಏಳ್ಯ **yēlya,** *see* ವೇಳ್ಯ.

ಏಳ್ವೆರ್ **yēlveru,** *s.* Seven persons.

ಐ EI

ಐ **ei,** The tenth letter of the alphabet. Also written ಅಯಿ.

ಐಂದ **einda,** *adv.* Hereafter.

ಐಂದ್ರಜಾಲ, ಐಂದ್ರಜಾಲಿ **eindrajāla, eindrajāli,** *see* ಇಂದ್ರ-, ಮೈಂದ್ರ-.

ಐಕ್ **eiku,** *pro.* (*dal. of* ಅವು) For *or* to it. *emph.* —ಡೆ to *or* for it only. ಐಕಾ is it for it? ಐಕಾಡ owing to it, therefore.

ಐಕುಳು **eikulu,** *pro. neut.* They.

ಐಕ್ಯ **eikya,** *s.* Unity, harmony. 2. diligent application to any pursuit *or* occupation. 3. spiritual communion.

ಐಗಳು, ಐಗುಳು **eigalu, eigulu,** *s.* A schoolmaster.

ಐಗೆರ್ **eigeru,** *see* ಹೈಗರ.

ಐಗೇಣ **eigēna,** *s.* Five spans.

ಐಟ್ eiṭu, *pro.* (*loc. of* ಅವು) In it.

ಐಡ್ದಾವರ eiḍdāvara, *adv.* Owing to it, therefore.

ಐತ eita, *see* ಅಯಿತ.

ಐತ eita, *pro.* (*gen. of* ಅವು), Its, of it.

ಐತಾರ, ಐತ್ವಾರ eitāra, eitvāra, *s.* Sunday.

ಐತಾಳ eitāḷa, *s.* A kind of medicinal plant used for castrated buffaloes.

ಐತಾಳಿ eitāḷi, *see* ಐರ್ತಾಳಿ.

ಐದ ayida, *see* ಆಯುಧ.

ಐನ್ einu, *num.* Five. ಐನನೆ fifth.

ಐನೂದು einūdu, *num.* Five hundred.

ಐಪುನಿ eipuni (ಐ), *v.a.* To tread.

ಐಬು eibu, *s.* A flaw, defect.

ಐಮೂಲೆ eimūlè, *s.* Obliquity, irregularity, as in the foundation of a house.

ಐಯೆ, ಐಯ್ಯೆ eiye, eiyye, *see* ಅಯ್ಯೆ.

ಐಯೊ, ಐಯ್ಯೊ eiyo, eiyyo *intj.* Alas! 2. no, not. ನಿನಡ ಪಣವು ಉಂಡೋ have you got money? ಐಯೊ no.

ಐಯೊ eiyo, *see* ಐಪ.

ಐಯ್ಯೆರ್ eiyeru, *pro.* Five persons.

ಐಯ್ಯೆಲ್ eiyyelu, *see* ಅಯ್ಯಳ.

ಐಯ್ಯೋ eiyyō, *intj.* O! woe!

ಐರ್ತಾಳಿ eirutāḷi, *s.* A kind of necklace worn by a virgin *or* matron.

ಐರಣೆ, ಐರಾಣಿ eiraṇe, eirāṇi, *s.* A new ornamented earthen vessel used by Lingaits during nuptial ceremonies.

ಐರಾಣಾಲಿ eirāṇāli, *see* ಐರ್ತಾಳಿ.

ಐರಾನ, ಐರಾನ್ eirāna, eirānu, *s.* Weariness, affliction; *bet.* ಹೈರಾಣ.

ಐರಾವತ eirāvata, *s.* The elephant of Indra, regent of the eastern quarter.

ಐರುನಿ eiruni (ಐರ್), *v.a.* To wait, stay, stop.

ಐರೊಳು eiroḷu, *s.* A kind of creeper.

ಐಲಾಟ, ಐಲಾಸ್ eilāṭa, eilāsu, *s.* Sport. 2. childishness; *also* ವೈಲಾಟ.

ಐಲಿಸ್ eilisu, *s.* Incivility, impoliteness; *cf.* ನಾಲಿಸ್.

ಐಲೆಸಿ eilesi, *see* ಎಲೆಸರಿ.

ಐವ eiva, *num.* Fifty. —ನೆ the fiftieth.

ಐವಜಿ, ಐವೆಜಿ eivaji, eiveji *s.* Money, wealth, property.

ಐವೆರ್ eiveru, *see* ಐಯ್ಯೆರ್.

ಐಶಬಾಸ್ eiśabāsu, *intj.* Bravo! well done!

ಐಶ್ವರ್ಯ eiśvarya, *s.* Wealth, riches.

ಐಸ್ eisu, *intj.* Ha! alas!

ಐಸ eisa, *see* ಆಯುಷ್ಯ.

ಐಸ್ರ eisra, *s.* Wealth. 2. cheerfulness; *cf.* ಐಶ್ವರ್ಯ.

ಒ WO

ಒ **wo,** The eleventh letter of the alphabet. In MSS. it is often written ಪೊ.

ಒಂಕ್ **woṅkụ,** *adj.* Thin.

ಒಂಕ **woṅka,** *s.* Crookedness. 2. a hole (of rats, snakes *etc.*) *adj.* Crooked, curved.

ಒಂಕದೆ **woṅkade,** *s.* Vomitting. —ಕಟ್ಟುನಿ, —ಬರ್ಪಿನಿ to feel an inclination to vomit.

ಒಂಕಿ **woṅki,** *see* ವಂಕಿ.

ಒಂಗೇರುನಿ **woṅgēruni,** *see* ಓಂಗೆರುನಿ.

ಒಂಚಕೆ **woṅcake,** *s.* A deceiver, cheat; *cf.* ವಂಚಕೆ.

ಒಂಚನೆ, ಒಂಚಲ್ಮೆ **woṅćane, woṅćalme,** *s.* Deceit, fraud, delusion; *also* ವಂಚನೆ. —ಮಳ್ಪುನಿ to cheat, deceive.

ಒಂಚಿ **woṅći,** *adv.* Whence? where? —ಲಾ anywhere. —ಬತ್ತ whence do you come?

ಒಂಚಿಪುನಿ **woṅćipuni** (ಒಂಚಿ), *v. a.* To deceive; *bet.* ವಂಚಿಪುನಿ.

ಒಂಜನೆ, ಒಂಜೆನೆ **woṅjane, woṅjene,** *num.* First; *cf.* ಒಂಜಿ.

ಒಂಜಿ **woṅji,** *num.* One (*mas.* ಒರಿ, *fem.* ಒರ್ತಿ). —ಆಪಿನಿ to be united *or* reconciled. —ವೇಳೆ perhaps. ಒಂಜೊಂಜಿ each, one by one. ಒಂಜಾನೊಂಜಿ some, certain. ಒಂಜಾನೊಂಜಿ ದಿನೊಟು on a certain day.

ಒಂಟ **woṇṭa,** *s.* The hip, waist, loins; *cf.* ಸೊಂಟ.

ಒಂಟಿ **woṇṭi,** *adj.* Alone, single, separated. —ಗೆ a single man.

ಒಂಟಿ **woṇṭi,** *s.* An ear-ring.

ಒಂಟೆ **woṇṭè,** *s.* A camel, dromedary.

ಒಂಡ **woṇḍa,** *s.* A public tank. 2. a hole, pit.

ಒಂಡೆ **woṇḍe,** *see* ಕೊಂಡೆ.

ಒಂತಗಾರೆ **wontagāre,** *s.* A strong man. 2. a clever man.

ಒಂತಿ **wonti,** *s.* Turn, time.

ಒಂತಿಗೆ **wontigè,** *s.* Contribution. —ಎತ್ತುನಿ to collect contributions. —ಕೊರ್ಪಿನಿ, —ಪಾಡುನಿ to contribute.

ಒಂತು **wontu,** *s.* A turn, time. *adv.* Once.

ಒಂತೆ **wontè,** *s.* A little, a bit, smallness. *adj.* Little, few, small, trifling; *also* ಒಂಡ. —ಜನ a few persons. —ದಿನ a few days. —ಪೊರ್ತು a little time. ಒಂತೊಂತೆ very little.

ಒಂದಕೆ **wondakè,** *s.* Urine. —ಮಳ್ಪುನಿ to piss, make water.

ಒಂದನೆ **wondane,** *see* ವಂದನೆ.

ಒಂದಲಿಗೆ, ಒಂದೊಲ್ಮೆ **wondalige, wondolme,** *s.* Congruity.

ಒಂದಾವುನಿ **wondāvuni,** *c. v.* (*of* ಒಂದುನಿ) To gather, collect, join; to heap up.

ಒಂದಿಕೆ, ಒಂದಿಗೆ **wondikè, wondigè,** *s.* Joining, uniting, coalescence; *cf.* ಹೊಂದಿಕೆ.

ಒಂದಿಪುನಿ **wondipuni,** *see* ವಂದಿಪುನಿ.

ಒಂದುನಿ **wonduni** (ಒಂದ್), *v. a. & n.* To gather, accumulate.

ಒಂದೆ **wonde,** *see* ಒಂತೆ.

ಒಂದೊಲುವೆ **wondoluvè,** *s.* Relation.

ಒಂನು **wonnu,** *s.* Gold.

ಒಂನೆ **wonne,** *see* ಹೊಂನೆ.

ಒಂಬು **wombu,** *adj.* Becoming, elegant, graceful.

ಒಂಬುನಿ **wombuni** (ಒಂಬ್), *v. n.* To be suitable, to agree with.

ಒಂಮ **womma,** *intj.* of surprise.

ಒಂಮುಖ, ಒಂಮುಗ **wommukha, wommuga,** *s.* One direction. *adv.* In one direction. —ಆಪಿನಿ, —ಕೂಡುನಿ to assemble for a certain purpose.

ಒಂಮುತ **wommuta,** *adv.* All around; *cf.* ಉಂಬುಗೆ.

ಒಂಮೆ **wommè,** *adv.* Once. 2. together; *cf.* ಒರೋನೆ. —ತನ oneness, unity. —ಮಳ್ಪುನಿ to gather, collect, heap up.

ಒಂಮೆಟ್ಟುನಿ **womeṭṭuni** (ಒಂಮೆಟ್ಟ್), *v. n.* To be gathered.

ಒಂಮೇವುನಿ **wommēvuni** (ಒಂಮೇ), *v. n.* To be united, to be associated.

ಒಂಕುೞ **worṅku,** *s.* A lane, footpath; *also* ಒರಂಕ್.

ಒಂಡೆೞ **worṇḍe,** *s.* A quarter seer; *also* ಒರಂಡೆ; *cf.* ಕೊಂಡೆ.

ಒಂಬೞ **wormba,** *num.* Nine. —ನೆ the ninth.

ಒಂಬುೞನಿ **wormbuni,** *see* ವಂಬುೞನಿ.

ಒಕಲಾತ್ **wokalātụ,** *see* ವಕಾಲತ್.

ಒಕೀಲೆ **wokīle,** *see* ವಕೀಲ್.

ಒಕ್ಕ **wokka,** *s.* The hip, waist. —ನೂಲು a string *or* thin girdle round the waist.

ಒಕ್ಕಟ್ಟ್ **wokkaṭṭụ,** *s.* Concord, unanimity.

ಒಕ್ಕಟ್ಟುನಿ **wokkaṭṭuni** (ಒಕ್ಕಟ್ಟ್), *v. n.* To be in concord.

ಒಕ್ಕಣ, ಒಕ್ಕಣೆ **wokkaṇa, wokkaṇe,** *s.* A heading, title, address. 2. style, composition; *bet.* ವಕ್ಕಣೆ. —ಪಾಡುನಿ to sign.

ಒಕ್ಕಯಿ **wokkayi,** *s.* A single hand.

ಒಕ್ಕುನಿ **wokkuni** (ಒಕ್ಕ್), *v. a.* To scratch.

ಒಕ್ಕೆಲ್ **wokkelụ,** *s.* A tenant. —ಆಪಿನಿ to occupy, reside. —ಪಾಡುನಿ to be tenanted as a house, place *or* garden.

ಒಕ್ಕೆಲ್ಮೆ **wokkelme,** *s.* One of a cultivating class called the Bants, a Bant; *fem.* ಒಕ್ಕೆಂದಿ, ಒಕ್ಕೆಲ್ದಿ.

ಒಗಟ್ **wogaṭụ,** *s.* A riddle, an enigma. 2. mystic language, cant. —ದ ಪಾತೆರ an ambiguous expression.

ಒಗರ್ **wogarụ,** *s.* Brackishness. *adj.* Salty, brackish.

ಒಗರುನಿ **wogaruni** (ಒಗರ್), *v. n.* To become salty *or* brackish.

ಒಗ್ಗಟ್ **woggaṭụ,** *see* ಒಕ್ಕಟ್ಟ್.

ಒಗ್ಗಟ್ಟುನಿ **woggaṭṭuni,** *see* ಒಕ್ಕಟ್ಟುನಿ.

ಒಗ್ಗಡ **woggaḍa,** *s.* Oneness, concord. —ಆಪಿನಿ, *see* ಒಗ್ಗಾಪಿನಿ.

ಒಗ್ಗರಣೆ woggaraṇe, *s.* Seasoning. —ಪಾಡುನಿ to season.

ಒಗ್ಗಾಪಿನಿ woggāpini (ಒಗ್ಗಾ), *v. n.* To become one, be united.

ಒಗ್ಗಿ woggi, *s.* A handle, hook; *cf.* ಉಗ್ಗ. —ಪಲಾಯಿ a piece of plank suspended on both ends, for keeping things. —ಆಪಿನಿ to be of one mind. —ಕಟ್ಟುನಿ to lay wait.

ಒಗ್ಗುಂಡಿ woggunḍi, *s.* Depth.

ಒಚನ wočana, *see* ವಚನ.

ಒಚಿಪುನಿ wočipuni (ಒಚಿ), *v. a.* To wipe off, rub out, efface. 2. to clean.

ಒಚ್ಚಡಿ woččaḍi, *adj.* Single.

ಒಚ್ಚಿ wočči, *s.* A small whetting board; *also* ಒಚ್ಚಿಮಣೆ. —ಪಲಾಯಿ a board for sharpening knives, chisels *etc.*

ಒಚ್ಚಿಯುನಿ woččiyuni (ಒಚ್ಚ್), *v. a.* To deliver, give in charge; *also* ಒಚ್ಚಿದ್ ಕೊರ್ಪಿನಿ; *cf.* ಒಪ್ಪಿಯುನಿ.

ಒಚ್ಚುನಿ woččuni (ಒಚ್ಚ್), *v. a. see* ಒಚಿಪುನಿ. 2. to whet, sharpen (a knife). 3. to row (a boat).

ಒಜ, ಒಜಯ, ಒಜಯೆ, ಒಜಾ, ಒಜೆಡಿ woja, wojaya, wojaye, wojā, wojeḍi, *s.* Deduction, subtraction, remission. —ಪಾಡುನಿ to deduct, remit.

ಒಜನ್, ಒಜನೆ wojanu, wojane, *s.* A load, weight, burden.

ಒಜಿರ, ಒಜ್ರ wjira, wojra, *s.* A diamond; *bet.* ವಜ್ರ.

ಒಜೀರೆ wojīre, *s.* A vizier.

ಒಟಾಯಿಸುನಿ woṭāyisuni (ಒಟಾಯಿಸ್), *v. a.* To gather. 2. to change money, cash a cheque *or* note.

ಒಟಾರ woṭāra, *s.* The enclosure of a house. 2. vicinity.

ಒಟ್ಟ, ಒಟ್ಟವು woṭṭa, woṭṭavu *s.* Discount, agio. 2. premium. ರೂಪಾಯಿದ— discount of a rupee.

ಒಟ್ಟ woṭṭa, *s.* The chin.

ಒಟ್ಟಂ woṭṭam, *s.* Money, cash.

ಒಟ್ಟಾರ, ಒಟ್ಟಾರೆ woṭṭāra, woṭṭārè, *adv.* On the whole; *cf.* ಒಟ್ಟು.

ಒಟ್ಟಿಗೆ woṭṭige, *see* ಒಟ್ಟುಗು.

ಒಟ್ಟು woṭṭu, *s.* Total. 2. amount, sum. 3. the whole. —ಗುತ್ತಿಗೆ the whole contract. —ರಾಶಿ the whole. —ಲೆಖ್ಖ an aggregate account, sum total. —ಮಳ್ಪುನಿ to add, collect, heap, sum up. ಒಟ್ಟುಗು together, with, along with; on the whole.

ಒಟ್ಟುನಿ woṭṭuni (ಒಟ್ಟ್), *v. a.* To press. 2. to heap, pile up.

ಒಟ್ಟೆ woṭṭe, *s.* The lip, mouth.

ಒಟ್ಟೆ woṭṭe, *s.* A fissure, hole. 2. a potsherd. *adj.* Broken, cracked.

ಒಡ್‌ತೆಲ್ woḍutelu, *see* ಉಡೆತ್ತೆಲ್.

ಒಡ woḍa, *postp.* With.

ಒಡಂಬಡಿಕೆ, ಒಡಂಬಡಿಗೆ woḍambaḍikè, woḍambaḍigè, *s.* Agreement, consent, contract, covenant. 2. a treaty.

ಒಡಂಬಡಿಪುನಿ woḍambaḍipuni (ಒಡಂಬಡಿ), *v. a.* To consent, agree, concur. 2. to be pleased.

ಒಡಕ್ woḍakụ, *s.* Bruise, fracture. 2. a leak. —ಬಾಯಿಬಾಯಿ a prater, tell-tale.

ಒಡಕರಿ woḍakari, *see* ಒಡ್ಕದರಿ.

ಒಡತನ woḍatana, *see* ಒಡೆತನ.

ಒಡತಿ woḍati, *s.* A mistress.

ಒಡತೆಲ್ woḍatelụ, *s.* Breaking. *adj.* Broken; *cf.* ಉಡೆತ್ತೆಲ್.

ಒಡಯೆ woḍaye, *s.* A proprietor, master, lord.

ಒಡರ್ woḍarụ, *s.* An additional rafter *or* prop, used for supporting a roof; *also* ಒಡರ್.

ಒಡಲ್ woḍālụ, *see* ಉಡಲ್.

ಒಡವೆ woḍave, *s.* Property in general. 2. an ornament, jewel.

ಒಡಿ woḍi, *s.* A border. 2. division, plot *or* range of rice-fields. —ಕಟ್ಟುನಿ to put borders in a field.

ಒಡಿ woḍi, *s.* A bubo. —ಜಪ್ಪುನಿ —ನೆಗಪುನಿ, —ಲಕ್ಕುನಿ a bubo to break out.

ಒಡಿಪ್ಪುನಿ woḍipuni, *see* ಒಡೆಪುನಿ.

ಒಡಿಯುನಿ woḍiyuni (ಒಡಿ), *v. n.* To break. 2. to stoop, bend, as a branch laden with fruits.

ಒಡಿಲ್ woḍilụ, *see* ಓಡು.

ಒಡಿವೆ woḍive, *see* ಒಡವೆ.

ಒಡು, ಒಡ್ಡು woḍu, woḍḍu, *s.* Iguana. —ನುರಿಯುನಿ, —ಪೊಗ್ಗುನಿ an iguana to get into a house; (*fig.*) to have a bad omen.

ಒಡುಂಕೆಲ್, ಒಡುಂಗೆಲ್ woḍuṅkelụ, woḍuṅgelụ *s.* The end. 2. boundary, limit.

ಒಡುಂಗೆಲುನಿ woḍuṅgeluni (ಒಡುಂಗೆಲ್), *v. n.* To cease to bear fruit.

ಒಡುಂಬು woḍumbu, *s.* Stupidity. 2. uselessness. *adj.* Stupid; useless.

ಒಡುಂಬುಲು woḍumbulu, *see* ಕುಡುಂಬುಲು.

ಒಡುಪುನಿ woḍupuni (ಒಡು), *v. a.* To pluck.

ಒಡೆ, ಒಡೆತಡ್ಡೆ woḍe, woḍetaḍḍye, *s.* A kind of cake.

ಒಡೆ woḍe, *adv.* Where? whither? —ಮುಟ್ಟ how far? how long? ಒಡೆಗ್ whereto?

ಒಡೆತನ woḍetana, *s.* Proprietorship, mastery.

ಒಡೆತರುನಿ woḍetaruni (ಒಡೆತರ್), *v. n.* To suffer from the pain of a boil *etc.*

ಒಡೆಪುನಿ woḍepuni (ಒಡೆ), *v. a.* To break *or* break open.

ಒಡೆಯುನಿ woḍeyuni (ಒಡೆ), *v. n.* To break.

ಒಡೆಯೆ woḍeye, *see* ಒಡಯೆ.

ಒಡೆವೊಟ್ಟು woḍewoṭṭu, *s.* A whole family.

ಒಡ್ಕ woḍka, *s.* End, termination. 2. bruise. *adj.* Broken. —ಬಾಯಿ the last man. ಒಡ್ಕತರಿ, ಒಡ್ಕಲರಿ inferior rice imported from the Ghats, broken rice.

ಒಡ್ಕೆಲ್ woḍkelụ, *s.* Finishing, end.

ಒಡ್ಡ woḍḍa, *adj.* Flowing, —ನೀರ್ flowing water.

ಒಡ್ಡಾವುನಿ woḍḍāvuni, *c. v.* (*of* ಒಡ್ಡುನಿ) To turn, stretch, cast, set.

ನೀರ್‌— to turn flowing water into a field *etc.* ಕೈ— to hold *or* stretch out the hand. ಬಲೆ— to cast a net. ಉರುಲು— to set up a snare.

ಒಡ್ಡಾಳ್‌ woḍḍāḷu, *s.* A stalwart *or* well formed man.

ಒಡ್ಡಿ woḍḍi, *see* ಉಡ್ಡಿ.

ಒಡ್ಡು woḍḍu, *s.* Stubble. 2. *see* ಉಡು, ಒಡು.

ಒಡ್ಡುನಿ woḍḍuni (ಒಡ್ಡಿ), *v. a.* To hold *or* stretch out, as the hand. *v. n.* To flow, run.

ಒಡ್ಡೆ woḍḍe, *s.* Multiplication table.

ಒಡ್ಡೋಲಗ woḍḍōlaga, *s.* A royal assembly, darbār.

ಒಡ್ತ woḍta, *s.* A stroke, beating. 2. gain, emolument.

ಒಡ್ತೆ woḍtè, *s.* A kind of fish.

ಒಡ್ತೆಲ್‌ woḍteḷu, *see* ಒಡತೆಲ್.

ಒಡ್ಪಾವುನಿ woḍpāvuni, *c. v.* (*of* ಒಡ್ಪುನಿ) To cause to pluck, bend, sink in. 2. to lessen, diminish. 3. to drain. ನೀರ್— to drain a rice-field after sowing *or* before reaping. 4. to change, as money.

ಒಡ್ಪು woḍpu, *s.* Plucking.

ಒಡ್ಪುನಿ woḍpuni (ಒಡ), *v. a.* To pluck. 2. to lessen, decrease.

ಒಡ್ಯಣೆ, ಒಡ್ಯಾಣ woḍyaṇe, woḍyāṇa, *s.* A belt *or* girdle, made of gold *etc.* and generally worn by a devil-dancer.

ಒಡ್ಯುಂಗಿಲ woḍyuṅgila, *s.* A ring with engraving worn by females.

ಒಡ್ಯುನಿ woḍyuni, *see* ಒಡ್ಡುನಿ.

ಒಣ್ಂಗೆಲ್‌ woṇuṅgelu, *adj.* Dry, withered; lean, thin; *also* ಉಣಂಗಿಲ್.

ಒಣಕಟ್ಟ್‌, ಒಣಕಟ್ಟೆ woṇakaṭṭu, woṇakaṭṭe, *adj.* Dried. 2. stiff. 3. faded, emaciated; *cf.* ಪುಣಕಟ್ಟ.

ಒಣಕೆಲ್‌ woṇakeḷu, *s.* Dryness. 2. *see* ಉಣ್ಕೆಲ್.

ಒಣಪೆ woṇape, *adj.* Bitter, astringent.

ಒಣರ್‌ woṇaru, *see* ಅಣರ್.

ಒಣಸ್‌ woṇasu, *see* ಉಣಸ್.

ಒಣೆ woṇe, *s.* Bail, security. —ತಾಯಿ a bail, bondsman.

ಒತ್ತ wotta, *see* ಉಅತ.

ಒತ್ತಟ್ಟ್‌ wottaṭṭu, *s.* One side. *adv.* Aside, in a corner. —ದೀಪಿನಿ to keep aside.

ಒತ್ತಯ, ಒತ್ತಾಯ wottaya, wottāya, *s.* Force, compulsion. 2. persuasion, coaxing; *also* ವತ್ತಾಯ. —ಮಳ್ಪುನಿ to force; to persuade.

ಒತ್ತರೆ wottare, *see* ಉತ್ತರೆ.

ಒತ್ತರೆ wottare, *s.* Extremity, corner. 2. order, arrangement. —ದೀಪಿನಿ to keep in a corner, put in order. —ಪೋಪಿನಿ to move aside —ಮಳ್ಪುನಿ to gather.

ಒತ್ತಕ್ಷರ wottakshara, *s.* An under letter.

ಒತ್ತಾಣ wottāṇa, *s.* One place, *or* side.

ಒತ್ತಾವುನಿ wottāvuni, *c. v.* (*of* ಒತ್ತು

ನಿ) To cause to press. 2. to be impressed *or* sealed.

ಒತ್ತಿ **wotti,** *s.* A pawn, pledge. —ದೀಪಿನಿ to pawn.

ಒತ್ತು **wottu,** *s.* The mark of aspiration under a letter; a kerned letter. 2. closeness, thickness. —ದೀಪಿನಿ to place closely, fix firmly; to foment. —ದೀದ್ ಪಣ್ಪುನಿ *or* ಪಾತೆರುನಿ to reproach *or* abuse indirectly.

ಒತ್ತುತ್ತು, ಒತ್ತೊತ್ತು **wottuttu, wottottu,** *adv.* Very closely.

ಒತ್ತುನಿ **wottuni,** *v. a.* To press. 2. shampoo. 3. to seal, stamp. *v. n.* To be close, *or* thick set.

ಒತ್ತೆ **wottè,** *adj.* Single, solitary.

ಒತ್ತೆ **wotte,** *see* ಒತ್ತಿ.

ಒತ್ತೆಲೆ **wottele,** *s.* An oppressor.

ಒದಗ್ **wodagu,** *s.* Haste, speed. —ಮಳ್ಪುನಿ to make haste, to hasten.

ಒದಗಾವುನಿ, **wodagāvuni,** *c. v.* (*of* ಒದಗುನಿ) To procure, supply. 2. to prepare. 3. to assist; *also* ಒದಗಾದ್‌ಕೊರ್ಪಿನಿ.

ಒದಗುನಿ **wodaguni** (ಒದಗ್), *v. n.* To be opportune, *or* ready. 2. to prosper.

ಒದರ್ **wodaru,** *see* ಒದರ್.

ಒದಿ **wodi,** *s.* Phlegm, phlegmatic humour. —ಕಟ್ಟುನಿ phlegm to gather in the throat, to breathe hard; to become hoarse. —ತಲೆಪುನಿ phlegm to rattle.

ಒದೆಯುನಿ **wodeyuni,** *see* ಉದೆವುನಿ.

ಒದ್ದಡ್ಪಾವುನಿ **woddadpāvuni,** *c. v.* (*of* ಒದ್ದಾಡ್ಪುನಿ) To oppress, molest.

ಒದ್ದಾಟ **woddāṭa,** *s.* Hardship, difficulty, misfortune. 2. suffering from any disease.

ಒದ್ದಾಡುನಿ, ಒದ್ದಾಡ್‌ಪುನಿ **woddāḍuni, woddāḍupuni** (ಒದ್ದಾಡಿ), *v. n.* To be in distress, strive with difficulties. 2. to be prostrated from illness.

ಒದ್ದಾವುನಿ **woddāvuni,** *see* ಒಂದಾವುನಿ.

ಒದ್ದುನಿ **wodduni,** *see* ಒಂದುನಿ.

ಒದ್ದೆ **wodde,** *s.* Wetness, moisture. *adj.* Wet; *cf.* ವದ್ದೆ.

ಒನ **wona,** *see* ವನ.

ಒನಪೆ **wonapè,** *see* ಒಣಪೆ.

ಒನರ್ **wonaru,** *s.* An art, skill, cunning. 2. means, device, attempt. —ದಾಯೆ a contriver. schemer; *also* ಹುಂನರ್.

ಒನಾಂತರ **wonāntara,** *see* ವನ.

ಒಪಗೆ, ಒಪ್ಪ, ಒಪ್ಪಗೆ **wopage, woppa, woppage,** *adv.* Jointly, in company with. *adj.* (ಒಪ್ಪ) Joint; accessary; neighbouring. ಒಪ್ಪದಾಯೆ a companion, attendant. ಒಪ್ಪ ಪುಟ್ಟಿನಾಯೆ born of the same parents, a brother.

ಒಪಲಾ **wopalā,** *see* ಒಳ್ಪಲಾ.

ಒಪ್ಪಂದ **woppanda,** *s.* An agreement, contract. 2. an alliance, treaty.

ಒಪ್ಪಸಲೆ **woppasalè,** *s.* Flattery.

ಒಪ್ಪಾವುನಿ, ಒಪ್ಪಿಯಾವುನಿ **woppāvuni, woppiyāvuni,** *c. v.* (*of* ಒಪ್ಪುನಿ) To cause to consent *or* agree. 2. to persuade, prevail upon. 3. to level. ಒಪ್ಪಾವು ಕಂಡ a levelled field.

ಒಪ್ಪಿಗೆ **woppige**, *s.* Consent, assent, agreement; compliance.

ಒಪ್ಪಿಯುನಿ, ಒಪ್ಪಿಯೊಣುನಿ **woppiyuni, woppiyoṇuni** (ಒಪ್ಪಿ), *v. a* To admit, acknowledge; to acquiesce in. *v.n.* To agree to, assent, consent. 2. to comply with. 3. to be fit, suitable. 4. to resemble.

ಒಪ್ಪು **woppu**, *s.* Signature. —ಪಾಪುನಿ to sign.

ಒಪ್ಪೊರ್ತು **wopportu**, *see* ಒಪೊರ್ತು.

ಒಬ್ಬಂಟಿಗೆ, ಒಬ್ಬಂಟೆ **wobbanṭige, wobbanṭe**, *s.* A single man. *adv.* Alone.

ಒಮ್ಮ **womma**, *intj.* of surprise.

ಒಮ್ಮುತ **wommuta**, *see* ಒಂಮುತ. 2. harmony, unanimity. 3. *see* ಉಂಮುತ.

ಒಮ್ಮೆ **womme**, *see* ಒಂಮೆ.

ಒಯನ **woyana**, *see* ವಯನ.

ಒಯಲುನಿ **woyaluni** (ಒಯಲ್), *v. n.* To reel, stagger.

ಒಯಿ **woyi**, *see* ವಹಿ. 2. a pole, staff.

ಒಯಿಟೆ **woyiṭe**, *see* ಒಂಟೆ.

ಒಯಿನ **woyina**, *see* ವಯನ.

ಒಯಿಪನೆ **woyipane**, *s.* A kind of wooden comb to pick lice with; *also* ಊರನೆ.

ಒಯಿಪಾವುನಿ **woyipāvuni**, *c. v.* (*of* ಒಯಿಪುನಿ) To cause to draw *or* pull.

ಒಯಿಪುನಿ **woyipuni**, *v. a.* To draw, pull, drag.

ಒಯಿಮಾಲೆ **woyimālĕ**, *s.* Feigning, pretence; insinuation.

ಒಯಿಲ್ **woyilu**, *s.* The force *or* velocity of a stream *etc.*

ಒಯಿಶೀಲ್ **woyiśīlu**, *see* ಒಶೀಲ್.

ಒಯಿಸುನಿ, ಒಯಿಸೊಣುನಿ **woyisuni, woyisoṇuni**, *see* ವೈಸುನಿ.

ಒಯ್ಯ **woyya**, *intj.* A sound uttered by labourers by way of encouragement when drawing anything very ponderous. —ಪಾಡುನಿ to utter this sound.

ಒಯ್ಯಲುನಿ **woyyaluni**, *see* ಒಯಲುನಿ.

ಒಯ್ಯಾನ **woyyāna**, *see* ವಯನ.

ಒಯ್ಯಾರ **woyyāra**, *s.* Coquetry, affectation, foppery. —ಮಳ್ಪುನಿ, ಒಯ್ಯಾರಿಪುನಿ to be affected *or* foppish.

ಒರ್ **woru**, *num.* One, single, solitary, *esp. in cpds, as* —ಕಣ್ಣ್ one eye *etc.*

ಒರ್ **woru**, *see* ಒರು.

ಒರ **wora**, *adv.* Once, at once. —ಒರ each time, now and then.

ಒರಂಟ್, ಒರಂಟು **woranṭu, woranṭu**, *s.* Hatred, ill-will. 2. retaliation.

ಒರಂಟುನಿ **woranṭuni** (ಒರಂಟ್), *v.n.* To hate. 2. to retaliate.

ಒರಕ **woraka**, *s.* Gold leaf; gilt.

ಒರಕ **woraka**, *s.* A watery place.

ಒರಗ್ **woragu**, *s.* A cushion to lean the back upon. —ಮಣೆ a wooden seat with a back.

ಒರಗುನಿ **woraguni** (ಒರಗ್), *v. n.* To lean the back against *or* upon anything, to recline.

ಒರಟುನಿ **woraṭuni** (ಒರಟ್), *v. n.* To wrangle. 2. to importunate. 3. to haggle; *cf.* ಒರಂಟುನಿ.

ಒರಡ worada, *s.* A collection, subscription; *cf.* ಒಂತಿಗೆ.

ಒರಣ್ woranu, *s.* A pagoda, coin of four Rupees. –ಬಂಗಾ gold below the highest touch. ಇಕ್ಕೇರಿ– a coin of the value of 13 gold fanams.

ಒರತ, ಒರಾತ worata, worāta, *s.* Urgency, necessity; pressure. 2. an urgent demand; importunity. –ಚೀಟಿ a notice of demand for collection of rent. –ಮಳ್ಪುನಿ to demand, importune, urge. ಜೋರು– a peremptory demand.

ಒರತೆ worate, *s.* The name of a female demon.

ಒರದಾಟ woradāta, *s.* Mutual wrangling, disputation, *or* contention.

ಒರದಾಡುನಿ woradāduni (ಒರದಾಡ್), *v. n.* To wrangle, contend, quarrel.

ಒರದಿ woradi, *see* ವರ್ದಿ.

ಒರದುನಿ woraduni, *see* ಒರ್ದುನಿ.

ಒರನ್ woranu, *see* ಒರಣ್.

ಒರಬೆಲ್ worabelu, *s.* Rice once cleared of its husk only.

ಒರಲ್ woralu, *s.* A large mortar. 2. *see* ಒರಳ್.

ಒರಲೆ worale, *s.* A termite, white ant.

ಒರಸರೆ, ಒರಸಳೆ worasare, worasale, *s.* A kind of sham-fight in connection with a temple-festival. –ವೈಪುನಿ, –ಪಾಡುನಿ to play this sham-fight.

ಒರಹ woraha, *see* ಒರಣ್.

ಒರಳ್ woralu, *s.* The ploughman's song. –ಉರಿಪುನಿ, –ಒಯಿಪುನಿ, –ಪಾಡುನಿ to sing such a song.

ಒರಾಡ್, ಒರಾಡ worādu, worāda, *see* ಒರಡ.

ಒರಾಣ್ worānu, *see* ಒರಣ್.

ಒರಿ wori, *adj.* Single, solitary.

ಒರಿಕೆ worike, *see* ಒರಿಪೆ.

ಒರಿಪಾವುನಿ, ಒರ್ಪಾವುನಿ woripāvuni, worpāvuni, *c. v.* (*of* ಒರಿಪುನಿ) To spare. 2. to protect. 3. to assist, help.

ಒರಿಪುನಿ, ಒರಿಯುನಿ woripuni, woriyuni (ಒರಿ), *v. n.* To remain, be left. 2. to survive.

ಒರಿಪೆ, ಒರಿಪೆಲ್ woripe, woripelu, *s.* Remnant. *adj.* Remaining.

ಒರಿಯೆ, ಒರ್ಯೆ woriye, worye, *pro.* A single *or* solitary man. *emph.* –ನೆ, –ದೆ alone, singly.

ಒರು woru, *s.* Features, form, mark, shape. –ಪಗರುನಿ, –ತತ್ತ್ ಪೋಪಿನಿ to be changed, as one's features. –ಪತ್ತುನಿ to recognise, identify.

ಒರುವ woruva, *see* ಒರ್ವ.

ಒರುವಾರ woruvāra, *adv.* Once.

ಒರೆ wore, *s.* A scabbard, sheath.

ಒರೆಂಕುನಿ worenkuni (ಒರೆಂಕ್), *v. n.* To roll on the ground, in the dust *or* mire; *also* ರೆಂಕುನಿ.

ಒರೆಕಲ್ಲ್ workallu, *s.* A touchstone; *also* ಉರೆಕಲ್ಲ್.

ಒರೆಕೊರೆ worekore, *s.* Obliteration.

ಒರೆಗುನಿ **woreguni,** *see* ಒರಗುನಿ.

ಒರೆಪುನಿ **worepuni,** *see* ಉರೆಪುನಿ.

ಒರೆಪೆಲ್ **worepelu,** *see* ಒರಿಪೆಲ್.

ಒರೆವುನಿ **worevuni** (ಒರೆ), *v.a.* To rub, wipe, cause to corrode. 2. to tease, trouble; *cf.* ಉರೆಪುನಿ.

ಒರೆಸುನಿ **woresuni** (ಒರೆಸಿ), *v. n.* To diminish, wear off. 2. to glide. 3. to fail. *v.a.* To rub, wipe.

ಒಕ್ಕಣ್ **workaṇṇu,** *s.* A single eye.

ಒಕ್ಕಡಿ **workaḍi,** *adj.* One sided. 2. partially developed. –ಜೀವ a drooping *or* languid person. –ಕೆತ್ತುನಿ to cut *or* pare on one side of any thing. –ಪಬುರ್ನಿ to develop gradually, as a creeper *or* the kernel of a tender cocoanut. –ತಾರಾಯಿ one half of a cocoanut.

ಒಕ್ಕಡೆ **workade,** *s.* A stick in the manure.

ಒಕ್ಕಾರ್ **workāru,** *s.* A single leg. –ಡ ಉಂತುನಿ to stand on one leg.

ಒಕ್ಕುಂಬೆ **workumbe,** *adv.* Alone.

ಒಕ್ಕೆನ್ನಿ **workenni,** *s.* One of the cheeks *or* temples. –ಕುತ್ತು hemicrania.

ಒಗ್ಗ **worga,** *s.* A class, community; a tribe. 2. a proprietary land. 3. (*merc.*) the ledger (book). 4. transfer, shift. –ಕಾರೆ, –ದಾಯೆ. –ದಾರೆ a proprietor, landlord. –ಆಪಿನಿ to be transferred; *also* ವರ್ಗ.

ಒಗ್ಗಿಪುನಿ **worgipuni** (ಒಗ್ಗಿ), *v. a.* To arrange *or* classify accounts in the ledger; *also* ವರ್ಗಿಪುನಿ.

ಒಗ್ಗುನಿ **worguni** (ಒಗ್ಗ್), *v. n.* To agree (any food) with one's stomach. 2. to have a relish for a particular dish. 3. to agree with a proposition.

ಒಗ್ಗೆಲೆ, ಒಗ್ಗೊಳೆ **worgele, worgole,** *s.* A man who can relish *or* digest anything.

ಒಗ್ಗೋರಿ **worgōri,** *s.* The first of a breed of fowls.

ಒಜ್ಜ **worja,** *see* ವಜ್ಜ.

ಒಜ್ಜಿಪುನಿ **worjipuni,** *see* ವಜ್ಜಿಪುನಿ.

ಒಣ್ಣ **worṇa,** *see* ವರ್ಣ.

ಒತ್ತ **worta.** *see* ಒರತ.

ಒತ್ತಿ **worti,** *pron.* A single woman.

ಒತ್ತೆ **worte,** *see* ಒರತೆ. 2. *see* ಒತ್ತೆ.

ಒದ್ದ **worda,** *adj.* Bent, crooked, tortuous, uneven. –ತೂಪಿನಿ to cast a side-glance, to leer; to squint. –ಪಾಡುನಿ to place crookedly. –ಪಾತೆರುನಿ to talk evasively –ಬೂರುನಿ to fall obliquely; *also* ವದ್ದ.

ಒದ್ದಂಗೆಲ್ **wordaṅgelu,** *adj.* Crooked, curved; inclined, bent.

ಒದ್ದಾವುನಿ **wordāvuni,** *c. v.* (*of* ಒದ್ದುನಿ) To incline, slope, form with a slope.

ಒದ್ದಿ **wordi,** *s.* Report, news, intimation. –ಕೊರ್ಪಿನಿ, ಮುಟ್ಟಾವುನಿ to report, intimate; *also* ವದ್ದಿ.

ಒದ್ದುನಿ **worduni** (ಒದ್ದ್), *v. n.* To bend, bow. 2. to lean on one side.

ಒದೆ೯ಲ್ **wordelu̥**, *adj.* Bent, oblique. *s.* A bend, crook.

ಒದೆ೯ಲೆ **wordele**, *s.* A capricious man.

ಒನ೯ **worna**, *s.* Shape; *see* ವಣ೯. ಒನ೯ದ ಲೆಕ್ಕನೆ as before.

ಒನ೯ಗ **wornaga**, *adv.* Formerly, once upon a time.

ಒನಾ೯ಲಿ **wornāli**, *s.* A single pulse *or* artery. 2. the uvula. 3. a swelling in one of the kernels of the throat; *cf.* ಇನಾ೯ಲಿ.

ಒಪ೯ಲೆ **worpalè**, *s.* A lean, thin man. 2. a single leaf. 3. a mat made of single palmyra leaves. 4. a small mat for one person; *cf.* ಒಬ೯ಳೆ.

ಒಪು೯ಡೆ **worpuḍe**, *s.* Torment, trouble. 2. one side.

ಒಪು೯ದೆ **worpude**, *s.* A single load.

ಒಪೆ೯ **worpe**, *see* ಒರಿಪೆ.

ಒಪೊ೯ತು೯, ಒಪೊ೯ಳ್ತು **worportu, worpoḷtu**, *s.* Half a day. —ದ ಬೇಲೆ half a day's labour; work that can be finished within half a day.

ಒಬ೯ಡಿ **worbaḍi**, *adj.* Single. —ಕುಂಟು a garment, a small piece of cloth. *adv.* Whole, all over, entire.

ಒಬ೯ಲೆ, ಒಬ೯ಳೆ **worbale, worbaḷe**, *s.* A single slip of a bamboo. 2. a bangle.

ಒಬು೯ದ್ಧಿ **worbuddhi**, *s.* Union, harmony.

ಒಬು೯ಳೆ **worbuḷe**, *s.* A single crop.

ಒಭಾ೯ಗ **worbhāga**, *s.* A single part, portion *or* division.

ಒಮ೯ **worma**, *s.* A vital organ *or* member; *also* ಮಮ೯. 2. a secret. —ದ secret; pricking; vital. —ದ ಜಾಗ a vital part. —ದ ಪಾತೆರ a secret that will affect a person.

ಒಮ೯ರ **wormara**, *s.* The trunk of a tree lopped of its branches.

ಒಮೆ೯, ಒಮೆ೯ಲಾ **worme, wormelā**, *adv.* Throughout, everywhere, all over.

ಒಯ೯ **worya**, *s.* Remainder. —ಕಯ೯ conclusion. —ಸಂಕಟ dangerous sickness.

ಒಲ೯ **worla**, *s.* A seer, a measure equal to eighty tolas. —ಬಾರ್ a seer of paddy. —ಬಾರ್ದಾಯೆ (*lit.* a man worth a seer of paddy), a worthless man.

ಒಲು೯ನಿ **worluni**, *see* ಒದು೯ನಿ.

ಒವ೯ **worva**, *s.* Crookedness. *adj.* Oblique, slope; *cf.* ಓರೆ. —ಉಂತುನಿ to stand crookedly. —ಪಾತೆರುನಿ to talk evasively.

ಒವಾ೯ರ **worvāra**, *see* ಒರುವಾರ.

ಒಸ೯ **worsa**, *s.* A year; *also* ವಸ೯.

ಒಲ್ಂಗುನಿ **wolu̥ṅguni** (ಒಲ್ಂಗ್), *v.n.* To move in a circle *or* to and fro.

ಒಲಂಗುನಿ **wolaṅguni** (ಒಲಂಗ್), *v. n.* To incline, lean.

ಒಲಂದಲ, ಒಲಂದಲೆ **wolandala, wolandale**, *s.* Swoon, fainting.

ಒಲಂಪು, ಒಲಪ್ **wolampu, wolapu̥**, *s.* Cleanliness, purity. 2. affectation in walking.

ಒಲಪುನಿ **wolapuni** (ಒಲಿ), *v. a.* To love. 2. to fondle.

ಒಲಮಾಯಿ **wolamāyi**, *s.* Pasture. —ಪಾಡುನಿ to tie cattle for grazing; *also* ಉಳಮಾಯಿ.

ಒಲಮೆ, ಒಲುಮೆ **wolame, wolume**, *s.* Affection, love, kindness.

ಒಲಸ್ **wolasu**, *adj.* Putrid, stinking, dirty, unclean; *also* ಜೊಲಸ್.

ಒಲಾ **wolā**, *intj.* Behold! lo!

ಒಲಿ **oli**, *An affix to verbs meaning* can, *e.g.* ಮಳ್ಪೊಲಿ can make, *or* can be made; ಪೋಪೊಲಿ can go; ಪೋಡೊಲಿ can read, *etc.* (*opp. to* ಬಲ್ಲಿ cannot).

ಒಲಿ **woli**, *s.* A cadjan leaf used to write upon. —ತ ಕುಡ್ಪು a basket made of cadjan leaves.

ಒಲಿಪು **wolipu**, *s.* The skin. 2. the skin of a snake. 3. shape. —ಗೆಪ್ಪುನಿ to cast off the skin, as a snake.

ಒಲಿಪುನಿ **wolipuni** (ಒಲಿ), *v. n.* To be possessed with a demon.

ಒಲಿಪೆ **wolipe**, *s.* Gratuitous supplies to persons of distinction. 2. a present, gift. —ಕೊರ್ಪಿನಿ to give a present; *also* ಉಲಿಪೆ.

ಒಲಿಮದೆ **wolimade**, *s.* A place where devil-dancers are painted.

ಒಲಿಯುನಿ **woliyuni** (ಒಲಿ), *v. n.* To favour, be kind, as superiors to inferiors.

ಒಲುಂಗುನಿ **wolunguni**, *see* ಒಲಂಗುನಿ.

ಒಲೆ **wole**, *pl. of* ಒಲಾ.

ಒಲೆಪ್ಪು **woleppu**, *see* ಲೆಪ್ಪು.

ಒಲ್ಪ **wolpa**, *see* ಓಳು.

ಒಲ್ಪೆ **wolpe**, *s.* Purity; *cf.* ಒಲಂಪು. 2. *see* ಒಲಿಪೆ.

ಒಲ್ಬೆ **wolbe**, *s.* A kind of paddy-field.

ಒಲ್ಮೆ **wolme**, *see* ಒಲುಮೆ.

ಒಲ್ಲಣಿಗೆ **wollaṇigè**, *s.* A cloth covering the privities.

ಒಲ್ಲಾಸ್ **wollāsu**, *see* ಉಲ್ಲಾಸ.

ಒಲ್ಲಿ **wolli**, *s.* The sheet, *i.e.* a broad piece of cloth, used for covering the body in bed. 2. a laced cloth for wearing; *also* ಒಲ್ಲಿ.

ಒಲ್ಲೆ, ಒಳ್ಳೆ **wolle, woḷḷe**, *s.* A water-snake. 2. *see* ಒಲ್ಲಿ.

ಒಲ್ಲೆಕೊಡಿ **wollekoḍi**, *s.* A medicinal plant *Memecylon amplexicaule*.

ಒಲ್ವೆ **wolvè**, *s.* Resemblance, similarity.

ಒವು **wovu**, *intg. pron.* Which? what? ಒವುಲಾ whatever, anything.

ಒವುಳು **wovuḷu**, *see* ಓಳು.

ಒಶ **woša**, *s.* Charge, possession. 2. subjection; *also* ವಶ. —ಆಪಿನಿ to pass into possession, to submit; to be facinated, charmed. —ಮಳ್ಪುನಿ to take charge of; to subject, subdue; to gain over, enchant, charm, decoy.

ಒಶೀಲ್, ಒಶೀಲಿ, ಒಶೇಲಿ **wošīlu, wošīli, wošēli**, *s.* Bias, partiality; *also* ವಶೀಲಿ. —ಮಳ್ಪುನಿ to be partial.

ಒಸಗೆ, ಒಸಯ, ಒಸಯೆ **wosage, wosaya, wosaye**, *s.* News. 2. the ceremony of sending a messenger to a girl's husband *or* parents, with the news of her attaining puberty. –ಕ ಡಪ್ಪುಡುನಿ to send such a message.

ಒಸರ್ wosaru, *s*. A spring, fountain. ತಳ– a fountain-head. ನಂಡ– an oozing *or* trickling spring. ಪಡೆ– a lateral spring.

ಒಸರುನಿ wosaruni (ಒಸರ್), *v. n*. To ooze, leak.

ಒಸೀಲ್ wosīlu, *see* ಒಶೀಲ್.

ಒಸೂಲು wosūlu, *s*. Collection *or* recovery of any dues; *also* ವಸೂಲು. –ಮಳ್ಪುನಿ to collect, recover.

ಒಳ woḷa, *adj*. Inner, internal. 2. secret, private; *also* ವಳ. –ಕೈ intermeddling; collusion, conspiracy.

ಒಳಗಾಪಿನಿ woḷagāpini (ಒಳಗಾ), *v.n*. To submit, obey. 2. to adhere, as to a party.

ಒಳಗುಟ್ಟು woḷaguṭṭu, *s*. A secret, mystery.

ಒಳಚಿಲ್ woḷačilu, *s*. A grove, under-wood; a fenced wood near a house; *also* ಉಜ್ಜಿಲ್.

ಒಳಮಟ್ಟು woḷamaṭṭu, *s*. The internal measurement of a given area, *or* of a hollow thing.

ಒಳಮಾರ್ಗ woḷamārga, *s*. A by-path, footpath; *also* ಉಳಮಾರ್ಗ.

ಒಳವು, ಒಳಾವು woḷavu, woḷāvu, *s*. Curve, bend; inclination. 2. the mind, secret thought.

ಒಳಮುಂದಿಲ್ woḷamundilu, *s*. The inner courtyard of a house.

ಒಳಸಂಚಿ, ಒಳಸಂಚು woḷasañči, woḷasañču, *s*. Collusion, conspiracy, plot.

ಒಳಸೂತ್ರ woḷasūtra, *s*. The inner frame of a door *or* window.

ಒಳಿ woḷi, *s*. Light, splendour.

ಒಳೆಪುನಿ woḷepuni (ಒಳೆ), *v. a*. To call.

ಒಳೆವುನಿ woḷevuni, *see* ಉಲೆವುನಿ.

ಒಳ್ತ್, ಒತ್ತ, ಒಳ್ತು, ಒಳ್ಪ woltu, wolta, woltu, wolpa, *see* ಓಳು.

ಒಳ್ಳೆಕೊಡಿ wollekodi, *see* ಒಲ್ಲೆಕೊಡಿ.

ಓ WŌ

ಓ wō, The twelfth letter of the alphabet. In MSS. it is often written ಶೋ.

ಓ wō, *intj*. O! oh! *as*, ಓ ರಾಮಾ O Rāmā! ಓ ಅಪ್ಪಾ O mother!

ಓಂಕದೆ wōṅkadè, *s*. An effort to vomit, retching. 2. heaving of the belly. –ಕುಟ್ಟುನಿ to vomit.

ಓಂಗೇರುನಿ wōṅgēruni (ಓಂಗೇರ್), *v.n*. To listen. 2. to overhear, eavesdrop.

ಓಂಟಿ wōṇṭi, *see* ಒಂಟಿ.

ಓಂಟೆ wōṇṭe, *s*. A kind of large

thin reed. 2. a pipe made of reed.

ಓಂಟೆ **wōṇṭe**, *see* ಓಟ.

ಓಂಟೆಪುಳಿ **wōṇṭepuḷi**, *s*. The sour fruit of *Garcina cambogia*; *also* ಎಸಳ್ಪುಳಿ, ಕರ್ಕಪುಳಿ.

ಓಂಡು **wōṇḍu**, (*abbr. of* ಓಳುಂಡು) Where is it?

ಓಂತಿ **wōnti**, *s*. A blood-sucker, salamander. —ಕುತ್ತ a swelling of the face. —ಮೀನ್ a kind of fish.

ಓಕಳಿ, ಓಕುಳಿ **wōkaḷi, wōkuḷi**, *s*. Crimsoned turmeric water. —ಆಟ squirting this red liquid upon passers by *etc*. at the conclusion of an important temple festival *or* of a marriage; *also* ಆರದ.

ಓಕೊಣುನಿ **wōkoṇuni** (ಓಕೊಂಡ್), *v. a*. To answer to a call.

ಓಙೊಣುನಿ **wōṅoṇuni**, *see* ಓಂಗೇರುನಿ.

ಓಚಿ **wōči**, *s*. A pair, couple. —ಮಾಡುನಿ to pair, couple.

ಓಜ, ಓಜಸ್ಸ **wōja, wōjassa**, *s*. Light, splendour. 2. strength. 3. bravery, valour.

ಓಜ್ಜಾ **wōjjā**, *intj*. Hailing, calling out to a person at a distance.

ಓಜ್ಜು **wōjju**, *s*. A tie, knot. —ಪಾಡುನಿ to tie.

ಓಟ **wōṭa**, *s*. Running, race. 2. the current of a stream, sailing of a vessel.

ಓಟೆಪುಳಿ **wōṭepuḷi**, *see* ಓಂಟೆಪುಳಿ.

ಓಡ **wōḍa**, *s*. A boat, wherry. —ದಾಯೆ a boatman. —ದ ಬಲೆ a net for throwing from a boat. —ಮರಾಯಿ a boat-shaped wooden trough.

ಓಡರಿ **wōḍari**, *s*. A potter. 2. a term of reproach implying want of sense. —ಕೆಲಸ, —ಬೇಲೆ the potter's work; a clumsy *or* ill-executed work.

ಓಡಿಕಟ್ಟ್ **wōḍikaṭṭu**, *s*. A religious *or* social association of members of the same caste at board, festival, marriage *etc*.; *cf*. ಕೂಡುಗಟ್ಟ್.

ಓಡಿಲ್, ಓಡು **wōḍilu, wōḍu**, *s*. A potsherd. 2. a tile.

ಓಡುನಿ **wōḍuni** (ಓಡ್), *v. n*. To run. ಬೇರ್— roots to spread in every direction.

ಓಡೆ **wōḍe**, *see* ಒಡೆ.

ಓಡೆ, ಓಡೆಗ್ **wōḍe, wōḍegu**, *adv*. Where? *cf*. ಓಳು.

ಓಡ್ರೆಯಿ **wōḍreyi**, *abbr. of* ಓಡಮರಾಯಿ; *see* ಓಡ.

ಓಣಿ **wōṇi**, *s*. A lane, alley.

ಓಣೆ **wōṇe**, *see* ಊನ.

ಓಣೆದಾಯೆ **wōṇedāye**, *s*. An arecanut planter. 2. the name of a caste. 3. a lame man.

ಓದಾವುನಿ **wōdāvuni**, *c. v*. (*of* ಓದುನಿ) To cause to read, to teach how to read.

ಓದಿಗೆ, ಓದು **wōdige, wōdu**, *s*. Reading, perusal.

ಓದುನಿ **wōduni** (ಓದ್), *v. a*. To read, peruse. ಓದದ್ ಪಣ್ಪುನಿ to read over to another.

ಓದ್ಯ **wōdya**, *see* ವಾದ್ಯ.

ಓನಾಮ wōnāma, *s.* The first letters with which a Hindu commences his studies, meaning 'I make obeisance to the Infinite'. 2. an alphabet.

ಓಪಸಾಲೆ wōpasāle, *see* ಒಪ್ಪಸಲೆ.

ಓಪಾದಿ wōpādi, *adv.* Like, according to.

ಓಪು wōpu, *s.* Polish. —ದ ಪೊಯ್ಗೆ a fine kind of sand used for polishing jewellery. —ಕೊರ್ಪುನಿ, —ಪಾಡುನಿ to polish.

ಓಪೆದಾಯೆ wōpedāye, *pro.* What man? *intj. An expression of contempt.*

ಓಬೆಲ್ wōbelu, *s.* The song of women sung while transplanting rice-plants.

ಓಮ wōma, *s.* The seed of bishop's weed, common caraway, *Sison amomum*, *Ptychotis ajowan*. 2. any small seed.

ಓಮ wōma, *see* ಹೋಮ.

ಓಮನ wōmana, *adj.* Darling, dear. *s.* Fondness, tenderness.

ಓಯಿ wōyi, *intj.* A polite form of ಓ used in hailing, *or* in answering the call of a superior person. ಓಯಾ O sir!

ಓಯಿಕ್ಕಣೆ wōyikkaṇe, *s.* A quill of a porcupine.

ಓಯ್ಯ wōyya, *see* ಒಯ್ಯ.

ಓರಾಟ wōrāṭa, *see* ಹೋರಾಟ.

ಓರಿ wōri, *s.* A kind of whisky.

ಓರಿಗೆ wōrige, *s.* Grumbling, howl. 2. tallness, height.

ಓರಿಯಿಲ್ಲ್, ಓರಿಲ್ಲ್ wōriyillu, wōrillu, *s.* A hut. 2. a house with quarrelling inhabitans.

ಓರಿಯುನಿ wōriyuni (ಓರಿ), *v. n.* To grumble; *see* ಒರಿಪುನಿ.

ಓರುನಿ wōruni (ಓರ್), *v. n.* To prate, babble; to wrangle.

ಓರೆ wōre, *adj.* Crooked; bent.

ಓರೆಕೋರೆ wōrekōre, *adj.* Oblique, uneven, irregular.

ಓರೇವುನಿ, ಓರೊವುನಿ wōrēvuni, wōrovuni (ಒರೆ, ಓರೊ), *v. n.* To be grumbling; to quarrel continually.

ಓರ್ಯುನಿ wōryuni, *see* ಓರಿಯುನಿ.

ಓಲಗ wōlaga, *s.* A royal assembly, durbar.

ಓಲಗ wōlaga, *s.* A band of musicians. —ದಾಯೆ a musician. —ಮಳ್ಪುನಿ to play upon musical instruments.

ಓಲಯಿ wōlayi, *s.* Menial service of Pariahs. —ದಾಯೆ a menial servant.

ಓಲಯಿಪುನಿ wōlayipuni (ಓಲಯಿ), *v. a.* To serve. 2. to do homage.

ಓಲಾಯಿ wōlāyi, *adv.* Always, ever.

ಓಲಿ wōli, *s.* A festival in honor of cupid; *bet.* ಹೋಳಿ.

ಓಲಿಗೆ wōlige, *see* ಹೋಲಿಗೆ.

ಓಲಿಯ, wōliya, *s.* A furrow, trench in the earth made by a spade *or* pickaxe. —ಗೆಪ್ಪುನಿ to make a trench.

ಓಲು wōlu, *adv.* As, like. *s.* Likeness, resemblance.

ಓಲೆ wōle, *s.* A metallic ear-ring. 2. a palmyra leaf rolled up and put into the hole of a female's ear. 3. a letter *or* epistle inscribed on a palmyra leaf. –ಗಾರೆ the carrier of such a message. –ಬೆಲ್ಲ jaggory made of palm juice.

ಒಲೆಗ **wōlega,** *see* ಓಲಗ.

ಒಲೆಗುನಿ **wōleguni** (ಒಲೆಗ್), *v.n.* To sit in state. 2. to lean, recline. 3. to tremble as a demon-priest.

ಒಲೆಮಣಂಗ್ **wōlemaṇaṅgụ,** *s.* A kind of fish.

ಒಲ್ಯ **wōlya,** *see* ಓಲಿಯ.

ಒವ್ವು **wōvu,** *intg.* Which? what?

ಒಹೋ **wōhō,** *intj.* Oh! oh!

ಒಳಿಗ್ **wōḷigụ,** *adj.* Flexible, pliable.

ಒಳಿಗೆ **wōḷige,** *see* ಹೋಳಿಗೆ.

ಒಳು **wōḷu,** *adv.* Where? –ಲಾ, ಓಳೋಳುಲಾ, ಓಳಾಂಡಲಾ anywhere, everywhere. ಒಳ್ತ್, ಒಳ್ತು, ಒಳ್ತುದ್ದು wherefrom? whence? ಒಳ್ತ of what place? ಒಳ್ಪ where? whither? in what place? whereabout?

ಒಳೆ **wōḷe,** *see* ಓಲೆ.

ಔ AU

ಔ **au,** The thirteenth letter of the alphabet.

ಔಂಕುನಿ **auṅkuni** (ಔಂಕ್), *v.a.* To press down.

ಔಂಟು **auṇṭu,** *s.* Arrogance, insolence, pride.

ಔಂಪುನಿ **aumpuni** (ಔಂ), *v.a.* To chew, mumble, bite softly.

ಔಟು **auṭu,** *s.* End, termination. –ಆಪಿನಿ to be finished.

ಔಡೆ **auḍe,** *s. Dolichos catjang*; *also* ಅವಡೆ.

ಔತ **auta,** *s.* The letter ಔ in combination with a consonant, as in ಕೌ. –ಕೊರ್ಪಿನಿ to combine it so.

ಔತಣ, ಔತನ **autaṇa, autana,** *s.* A grand dinner. –ಮಳ್ಪುನಿ to give such a dinner.

ಔದಾರ್ಯ **audārya,** *see* ಉದಾರ.

ಔದಿ **audi,** *s. see* ಅವಧಿ.

ಔದ್ರೇಕ **audrēka,** *see* ಉದ್ರೇಕ.

ಔರ **aura,** *adj.* Light, not heavy; *cf.* ಹಗುರ.

ಔಶಕುನ **auśakuna,** *see* ಅಪಶಕುನ.

ಔಶದ, ಔಷಧ, ಔಷಧಿ, ಔಶುಧಿ **auśada, aushadha, aushadhi, auśudhi,** *s.* Medicine. 2. a drug.

ಔಸ **ausa,** *see* ಆಯುಷ್ಯ.

ಔಳು **auḷu,** *see* ಅವ್ವಳು.

ಕ

K

ಕ ka, The fourteenth letter of the alphabet.

ಕಂಕಣ kaṅkaṇa, *s.* A bracelet. 2. a sacred string tied round the right wrist of a bridegroom *or* the left of a bride.

ಕಂಕಣಕಾರ kaṅkaṇakhāra, *s.* Borax used in soldering metal.

ಕಂಕಣಿ, ಕಂಕಣೆ kaṅkaṇi, kaṅkaṇe, *s.* A bracelet of gold *or* shell-lac, with prickly chasings. —ಬಳೆ a shell-lac bracelet of similar form covered with Dutch metal.

ಕಂಕಣೆ kaṅkaṇe, *adv.* On the face, flatwise.

ಕಂಕಪ್ಪೆ kaṅkappè, *s.* A small hammer, especially used by goldsmiths.

ಕಂಕಭಟ್ಟ kaṅkabhaṭṭe *s.* The assumed name of Dharmarājā while residing in disguise with Virāṭarājā.

ಕಂಕರಿಪುನಿ, ಕಂಕರಿಯುನಿ kaṅkaripuni, kaṅkariyuni (ಕಂಕರಿ), *v. n.* To hawk, force up phlegm with a noise; to clear the throat; to hem.

ಕಂಕಿಣಿ kaṅkiṇi, *see* ಕಂಕಣಿ.

ಕಂಕುಷ್ಟ, ಕಂಕೋಷ್ಟ kaṅkushṭa, kaṅkōshṭa, *s.* A kind of fragrant drug, used as a cosmetic.

ಕಂಕುಳ kaṅkuḷa, *s.* The armpit.

ಕಂಕೆ kaṅke, *see* ಕಂಕಭಟ್ಟ.

ಕಂಗ್ kaṅgu, *s.* The areca-nut tree.

ಕಂಗಣ kaṅgaṇa, *see* ಕಂಕಣ.

ಕಂಗಲ್, ಕಂಗಾಲ್ kaṅgalu, kaṅgālu, *adj.* Destitute, poor. 2. weak. 3. inferior. —ತನ poverty, weakness. —ಆಪಿನಿ to be poor; to become weak, *or* decrepit.

ಕಂಗಿಲ್, ಕಂಗಿಲ, ಕಂಗುಲ, ಕಂಗುಳ kaṅgilu, kaṅgila, kaṅgula, kaṅguḷa, *s.* A kind of dancing among pariahs at a particular season. 2. a song sung at the time.

ಕಂಗುರಿ kaṅguri, *s.* Enchased tin foils used in decoration.

ಕಂಞಣ, ಕಂಞಿಲ kaññaṇa, kaññila, *s.* A small plate. —ಪಲ್ಲಯಿ a flat earthen plate. —ಬಟ್ಟಲ್ a hollow plate.

ಕಂಚಲ, ಕಂಚಳ, ಕಂಚಾಲ kańćala, kańćaḷa, kańćāla, *s.* The bitter gourd, *Momordica charantia.*

ಕಂಚಿ kańći, *s.* The town of Conjeveram.

ಕಂಚಿ kańći, *s.* Gong-metal, bell-metal. —ಕಲಶ a vase. —ಕದುಮುಟ್ಟು, metallic utensilsof a demon shrine. —ತಿಪಲೆ a lamp-post with circular tiers of lamps, —ಬಾಜನ a vessel made of that metal.

ಕಂಚಿಕಾಮಾಕ್ಷಿ kańćikāmākshi, *s.* The name of a goddess at Conjeveram.

ಕಂಚಿಕಾಯಿ, ಕಂಚಿಪುಳಿ kańcikāyi, kańcipuḷi, *s.* A kind of bitter orange used in medicine.

ಕಂಚಿಕಾರೆ kańcikāre, *s.* A kind of wasp.

ಕಂಚಿಗಾರೆ kańcigāre, *s.* A worker in bell-metal, brazier.

ಕಂಚಿಣಿ, ಕಂಚಿನಿ kańciṇi, kańcini, *s.* A dancing-girl.

ಕಂಚಿಲ್ kańcilu, *s.* A vow made to a demon.

ಕಂಚು kańcu, *see* ಕಂಚಿ.

ಕಂಜ kańja, *s.* A lotus. 2. *see* ಕಂಜ್ಯ.

ಕಂಜಲಿಗೆ kańjalige, *s.* A kind of tambourine.

ಕಂಜಿ kańji, *s.* A calf. 2. the pestle of a grinding stone. 3. a sheaf of hay.

ಕಂಜೊಳು kańjoḷu, *s.* A kind of bush.

ಕಂಜ್ಯ kańjya, *s.* A bag *or* metallic vessel in which pilgrims put their offerings. 2. a wicker-work used for storing rice *etc.*

ಕಂಟ kanṭa, *see* ಕಂಠ.

ಕಂಟ, ಕಂಟಕ kanṭa, kanṭaka, *s.* Danger, peril.

ಕಂಟವು kanṭavu, *s.* An iron style used for writing upon palm leaves.

ಕಂಟಿ kanṭi, *see* ಕಂಠಿ.

ಕಂಟಿಯಾವುನಿ kanṭiyāvuni, *c. v.* (*of* ಕಂಟಿಯುನಿ) To stir up a quarrel.

ಕಂಟಿಯುನಿ, ಕಂಟ್ಯುನಿ kanṭiyuni, kanṭyuni (ಕಂಟ), *v. n.* To quarrel, fight. ಕಂಟ್ಯಾಟ a quarrel.

ಕಂಟೆಲ್ kanṭelu, *s.* The neck, throat. –ದ್, –ದ ಆಣ swearing by the neck.

ಕಂಟ್ಯೆಲೆ kanṭyele, *s.* A quarrelsome man.

ಕಂಠ kanṭha, *s.* The neck, throat. –ಪ್ರಮಾಣ up to the neck; swearing by the neck. –ಮಾಲೆ an ornament worn round the neck.

ಕಂಠಾಭರಣ kanṭhābharaṇa, *s.* A kind of necklace.

ಕಂಠಾಕ್ಷರ kanṭhākshara, *s.* A guttural letter.

ಕಂಠಿ, ಕಂಠಿಸರ kanṭhi, kanṭhisara, *s.* A necklace of gold beads worn by males.

ಕಂಠಿರಾಯೆ kanṭhirāye, *s.* The name of a certain king. –ವರಾಹ a gold coin issued by him.

ಕಂಡ್, ಕಂಡ್ದಿ kaṇḍu, kaṇḍudi, *adj.* Stolen. –ಕೆಲಸ stealing; adultery. ಕಂಡ್ಪೊಟ್ಟು a woman who has become pregnant by adultery, *vlg.*

ಕಂಡ್ಜಿ kaṇḍuji, *see* ಕಡಂಜಿ.

ಕಂಡ kaṇḍa, *s.* A field.

ಕಂಡ kaṇḍa, *see* ಖಂಡ.

ಕಂಡಣಿ, ಕಂಡಣ್ಯೆ kaṇḍaṇi, kaṇḍaṇye, *s.* A husband.

ಕಂಡಣೆ kaṇḍaṇe, *see* ಖಂಡನೆ.

ಕಂಡಪಿನಿ kaṇḍapini, *abbr. of* ಕೊಂಡು ಬರ್ಪಿನಿ.

ಕಂಡಾಬಟ್ಟೆ kaṇḍābaṭṭe, *adj.* Confused, out of order. 2. unreasonable, improper. *adv.* Confusedly; at random; improperly. –ತಿಂಗುಜಿನಿ to roam about. –ಪಾತೆರುನಿ to prate, prattle; to abuse; to speak nonsense.

ಕಂಡಾವುನಿ **kaṇḍāvuni,** *see* ಕೊಂಡು ಬರ್ಪಿನಿ.

ಕಂಡಿ **kaṇḍi,** *s.* A hole, opening. 2. a window; *cf.* ಖಂಡಿ.

ಕಂಡಿತ **kaṇḍita,** *see* ಖಂಡಿತ.

ಕಂಡಿಮರ **kaṇḍimara,** *s.* The trunk of a tree cut down for sawing.

ಕಂಡು **kaṇḍu,** *s.* A thief. 2. a knave, rogue.

ಕಂಡುಗ **kaṇḍuga,** *see* ಖಂಡುಗ.

ಕಂಡುನಿ **kaṇḍunī** (ಕಂಡ್), *v. a.* To take. 2. to steal.

ಕಂಡೆ **kaṇḍe,** *s.* A bulbous root. 2. the stomach. 3. bottom. –ಕಾರುನಿ (*lit.* the stomach to evacuate), to be hard pressed, bothered; to be done up. –ಪಾರುನಿ, to suffer from colic. –ಮುಗರುನಿ to grow *or* appear above the surface of earth, as the trunk of a cocoanut tree *etc.*

ಕಂಡೆಕುಟ್ಟಿ **kaṇḍekuṭṭi,** *s.* A dwarf.

ಕಂಡೆಗಾರೆ **kaṇḍegāre,** *see* ಕಂಡು.

ಕಂಡೆರಿಯುನಿ **kaṇḍeriyuni** (ಕಂಡೆರ್), *v. a.* To make a cut.

ಕಂಡೆಲ್ **kaṇḍelụ,** *adj.* Thievish, stealing. –ತನ thievishness, theft. ಕಂಡೆಳೆ a male thief. ಕಂಡೆಲು a female thief.

ಕಂಡೊಣುನಿ **kaṇḍoṇuni,** *v. ref.* (*lit.* to take for oneself) To steal, rob.

ಕಂಣ್ **kaṇṇụ,** *s.* The eye; the sight, vision. 2. the nipple of a breast, pap *etc.* 3. a rent, tear. 4. the eye of a needle. 5. the star in a peacock's feather. –ದ ಅಡ್ಡ out of sight. –ದ ಇಮೆ the eye-lashes. –ದ ಕುರುಬು, –ದ ರೆಪ್ಪೆ the eyelids. –ದ ಕೊಡಿ, –ದ ಮುನೆ the outer corner of the eye. –ದ ಗಟ್ಟಿಗೆ, –ದ ಮಣಿ the eye-ball. –ದಡಿ a speck in the eye. –ದ ಪರೆ a film on the eye. –ಪುರ್ಕು the rheum of the eyes. –ದ ಆಲಿ, –ದ ಬೊಂಬೆ, –ದ ಬೋಲೆ the pupil of the eye. –ದ ಸಿಂಮೆ the eye-brows. –ನೀರ್ tears. –ನೀರ್ ದೆಪ್ಪುನಿ to shed tears. –ಬೇನೆ sore eyes. –ಮಲ್ಲ್ liberality, prodigality; eagerness. –ಮುಚ್ಚಿಲೆ a man given to winking. –ಸೊಂನೆ a beck, wink. –ಹಾಳಿತ an estimate made by looking at a thing, a rough calculation. ಓರೆ– a squint, leering. ಕುರುಡು– a blind eye. ಬೇಪೆಲ್– a sickness in which the eyelashes fall off. –ಉಡೆದ್ ಪೋಪಿನಿ, –ಪುಡಾದ್ ಪೋಪಿನಿ to become blind. –ಬತ್ತುನಿ to wink. –ಬತ್ತಾದ್ ಕೊರ್ಪಿನಿ to instigate, encourage by winking. –ಕಟ್ಟುನಿ to blindfold, deceive. –ಕಳೆವುನಿ to stare vacantly, be puzzled. –ಕೊರುನಿ, –ತೂಂಕುನಿ, –ತೂಕಲಿಯುನಿ to doze, be sleepy. –ಜಪ್ಪುನಿ, –ಬುದ್ಪುನಿ, –ಬುಲಾವುನಿ to open the eyes. –ಪಾರುನಿ to swoon. –ಮಲೆಪುನಿ to stare.

ಕಂಣ್ಂಬೆರ್ kaṇṇumberu, *s.* Talking in sleep.

ಕಂಣ್ಕಟ್ಟ್ kaṇṇukaṭṭu, *s.* Blindfolding, deception. 2. jugglery, conjuration. –ದಾಯಿ a juggler.

ಕಂಣ kaṇṇa, *see* ಕಂನ.

ಕಂಣಂಬರುನಿ kaṇṇambaruni (ಕಂಣಂಬರ್), *v. n.* To talk in sleep.

ಕಂಣಡಿ kaṇṇaḍi, *see* ಕಂನಡಿ.

ಕಂಣಡಿಯುನಿ, ಕಂಣಡ್ಯುನಿ kaṇṇaḍiyuni, kaṇṇaḍyuni (ಕಂಣಡ), *v. n.* To be confused, perplexed.

ಕಂಣಮಾಲ್ kaṇṇamālu, *s.* The morbid secretions of the eye.

ಕಂಣಾರೆ kaṇṇāre, *adv.* With one's own eyes. 2. clearly, distinctly. –ತೂಪಿನಿ to see for oneself; to see clearly.

ಕಂಣಿ kaṇṇi, *s.* Fibre. 2. gummy exudation from the outer fibrous covering of a cocoanut. –ಮರ *Caryota urens.*

ಕಂಣುಚ್ಚು kaṇṇuččn, *s.* A kind of insect, infesting the eyes.

ಕಂಣೋಜಿ kaṇṇōji, *see* ಕಂನೋಜಿ.

ಕಂತ್ kantu, *s.* An instalment *or* stipulated period of payment. –ಪತ್ರ a written contract to fulfill an obligation by instalments. –ಮಳ್ಪುನಿ to agree to pay a debt by instalments; to fix, settle.

ಕಂತ್, ಕಂತ kantu, kanta, *s.* Depth. 2. a precipice, steepness. *adj.* Deep. 2. precipitous. *adv.* Deeply. 2. precipitously. –ತೂಪಿನಿ to fathom the depth of water. –ದೀಪಿನಿ to plant deeply. –ನಡಪುನಿ, –ಪೋಪಿನಿ, *see* ಕಂತನೆ ಪೋಪಿನಿ.

ಕಂತನೆ kantanè, *adj.* Inclined, bent downward. –ಕೊಟ್ಟು a spade the edge of which is inclined inward. –ಪೋಪಿನಿ to walk with downcast eyes.

ಕಂತಾವುನಿ kantāvuni, *c. v.* (*of* ಕಂತುನಿ) To cause to fall *or* sink. 2. to prick. 3. to offend.

ಕಂತು kantu, *see* ಕಂತ್.

ಕಂತುನಿ kantuni (ಕಂತ್), *v. n.* To sink, go down. 2. set, as the sun *etc.* 3. to be pricked, as with a thorn, razor *etc.* 4. to take to heart. 5. to be offended.

ಕಂತೆಲ್ kantelu, *s.* Sinking.

ಕಂದ್ kandu, *adj.* Dull, faded. 2. inferior. –ಬೊಳ್ಳಿ inferior silver. –ಪೋಪಿನಿ to fade; to become pale.

ಕಂದ್ಕ, ಕಂದಕ kanduka, kandaka, *s.* A ditch, trench.

ಕಂದಂಬಿ kandambi, *s.* The excrement of a new-born child, calf *etc.*

ಕಂದಾಯ kandāya, *s.* A space of four months. 2. assessment, tax.

ಕಂದಾವುನಿ kandāvuni, *c. v.* (*of* ಕಂದುನಿ) To render dim *or* dull. 2. to deteriorate the actual state *or* quality of a thing.

ಕಂದು kandu, *see* ಕಂದ್.

ಕಂದುನಿ kanduni (ಕಂದ್), *v. n.* To fade, wither; to be wan. 2. to become dim *or* dull. 3. to be vexed, annoyed.

ಕಂದೆಲ್ kandelu, *s*. A pitcher, large pot. —ಜುವಾರಿ a drunkard.

ಕಂದೆಲ್‌ಬೂರು kandelubūru, *s*. A kind of creeper.

ಕಂದೊಡಿ kandodi, *s*. An adder, viper. —ಸಂತಾನ wicked people. ಚಟ್ಟೆ— a broad hooded snake. ತೌಡು— a grey coloured snake. ನೀರ್— a water-snake. ಪಿಲಿ— a yellow spotted snake. —ಬೂರು a kind of creeper.

ಕಂನ kanna, *s*, A hole. —ಕುರೆಪಿನಿ to bore a hole.

ಕಂನಡ kannada, *s*. The Canarese language. *adj*. Of *or* belonging to Canarese *or* Canara.

ಕಂನಡಕ kannadaka, *s*. A pair of spectacles, an eye-glass.

ಕಂನಡಿ kannadi, *s*. Glass. 2. a mirror. 3. a pair of eye-glasses. —ಬಲೆ a network for suspending earthen vessels. —ಬಳೆ a glass bangle.

ಕಂನಡೆಯುನಿ kannadeyuni, *v. n*. To suffer from morbid secretion of the sore eyes.

ಕಂನಡೆರ್ kannaderu, *s*. A class of Canarese speaking Šūdras. ಕಂನಡೆ a man of this class.

ಕಂನಿ kanni, *see* ಕಂಣಿ.

ಕಂನಿಕೆ kannike, *see* ಕನ್ಯೆ.

ಕಂನೋಜಿ kannōji, *s*. A class of professional thieves from the ghauts. 2. a rogue.

ಕಂಪ kampa, *see* ಗಂಪ.

ಕಂಪ kampa, *s*. Agitation, tremor. 2. hesitation. 3. terror. ಭೂ— an earthquake. ಸಭಾ— diffidence in public speaking. ಕಂಪಾದ್ ಬುಡ್ಪಿನಿ to frighten; a fish to draw away the fishing tackle, when it has caught the bait.

ಕಂಪಿಯುನಿ kampiyuni (ಕಂಪಿ), *v. n*. To tremble, quake, as with fear. *v. n*. To make a notch.

ಕಂಬ, ಕಂಭ kamba, kambha, *see* ಕಂಮ.

ಕಂಬದ್, ಕಂಬಾದ್, ಕಂಬಾಪ್ kambadu, kambādu, kambāpu, *see* ಕಾಂಗ.

ಕಂಬಿ kambi *s*. The borders of a cloth. 2. a flat bar of iron. 3. a wire. —ದೆಪ್ಪುನಿ, —ನೀಡುನಿ to run away.

ಕಂಬುಲ, ಕಂಬುಳ kambula, kambula, *s*. A bullock race in a rice-field.

ಕಂಬೆಚ್ಚಿ kambečči, *s*. A steel plate with holes for drawing wires.

ಕಂಬೆರ್ಲು kamberlu, *s*. Demons worshipped by pariahs. —ಕೊಟ್ಯ a hut of such a demon.

ಕಂಬೊಳಿ kāmboli, *s*. A blanket. —ಪುರಿ a species of hairy caterpillar.

ಕಂಮ kamma, *s*. A pillar, post.

ಕಂಮಾರೆ kammāre, *s*. A blacksmith.

ಕಂಮಿ kammi, *adj*. Deficient, defective.

ಕಂಮುಕಿಂಮು kammukimmu, *intj*. Disturbance caused by talking.

ಕಂಮೆನ, ಕಂಮ್ಯನ kammena, kamyana, *see* ಕಮ್ಯನ.

ಕಂಕ karṅka, *s.* The state of being to burnt *or* singed. —ಕೊಪಿನಿ to fry, roast.

ಕಂಕಲ್ಲು karṅkallu, *s.* Gravel, hard sand.

ಕಂಕಾಡುನಿ karṅkāḍuni (ಕಂಕಾಡಿ), *v. a.* To burn.

ಕಂಚಾವುನಿ karṅćāvuni, *c. v.* (*cf.* ಕಂಚುನಿ) To cause to burn to cinders.

ಕಂಚುನಿ karṅćuni (ಕಂಚು), *v. n.* To be burned to cinders.

ಕಂಟ karṇṭa, *s.* Obstinacy; hatred, grudge. —ಪತ್ತುನಿ to be obstinate; to have a grudge.

ಕಂಟಾವುನಿ karṇṭāvuni, *c. v.* (*of* ಕಂಟುನಿ) To blacken, scorch.

ಕಂಟುನಿ karṇṭuni (ಕಂಟಿ), *v. n.* To fade, become pale; to be scorched.

ಕಂಡೆ karṇḍe, *s.* The shrub *Sphaeranthus hirtus.* —ಪುಳಿಮರ the tree *Carissa carandas.*

ಕಂಪಕ್ಕಿ karmpakki, *s.* A kind of small bird frequenting a sugarcane plantation. [cane.

ಕಂಬು karmbu, *s.* The sugar-

ಕಂಬುಡ karmbuḍa, *see* ಕರಿಕಂಬುಡ.

ಕಂಬುನಿ karmbunī (ಕಂಬಿ), *v. a.* To mutter.

ಕಂಬೆಲು karmbelu, *s.* A stingy woman.

ಕಂಸೆ kaṁse, *s.* Krushṇa's uncle.

ಕಕ್ಕ, ಕಕ್ಕಾ kakka, kakkā, *s.* Sediment. ಬೂತಾಯಿದ— putrescence of sardines.

ಕಕ್ಕಾಟ kakkāṭa, *s.* Constant vomiting.

ಕಕ್ಕಾಬಿಕ್ಕಾರೆ kakkābikkāre, *s.* Alarm, fright. *adj.* Crooked.

ಕಕ್ಕಾರೆ kakkāre, *see* ಕೊಕ್ಕರೆ.

ಕಕ್ಕಾವುನಿ kakkāvuni, *c. v.* (*of* ಕಕ್ಕುನಿ) To cause to vomit.

ಕಕ್ಕುನಿ kakkuni (ಕಕ್ಕಿ), *v. a.* & *n.* To vomit. ವಿಷ— to emit poison, as a serpent.

ಕಕ್ಕುಸ್ kakkusu, *s.* A privy. —ಮುಳ್ಪುನಿ to go to stool.

ಕಕ್ಕೆ kakke, *s.* A crow, raven. —ಕೋರಿ a black kind of fowl. —ಮರ್ಗಾಯಿ a kind of black shelled oyster.

ಕಕ್ಕೆ kakke, *s.* *Cassia fistula.* —ಮರ its tree.

ಕಕ್ಕೆಂಡೆಲ್ kakkenḍelu, *s.* The shrub *Canthium parviflorum; Citrullus colocynthis.*

ಕಕ್ಕೋಕಶಾಸ್ತ್ರ kakkōkaśāstra, *s.* A treatise on women.

ಕಙಣ kaṅaṇa, *see* ಕಂಙಣ.

ಕಚಕಚ kaćakaća, *intj.* A sound produced, as when kneading any glutinous substance. —ಕೊಪುನಿ to tread *or* knead anything to a jelly.

ಕಚಕ್ಕ kaćakka, *s.* A sound produced by a stone falling into mud.

ಕಚಪಿಚಿ, ಕಚಿಕುಚಿ kaćapići, kaćikući, *s.* Confusion, disorder. 2. reducing anything to a jelly. *adj.* Gummy, sticky. 3. zigzag; difficult to decipher *or* read.

ಕಚಿತ kaćita, *see* ಖಚಿತ.

ಕಚೂರ kaćūra, *see* ಕಚ್ಚೂರ.

ಕಚೂರೆ kaćūre, *s.* A clever man.

ಕಚೇರಿ kaćēri, *s.* A public office. ತಾಲೂಕ್– the Tahsildar's office. ಹಜೂರ್– the Collector's office.

ಕಚ್ಚಕಡಿ kaććakaḍi, *s.* A tortoise shell.

ಕಚ್ಚಡೆ kaććaḍe, *s.* An outcast.

ಕಚ್ಚಾ kaććā, *adj.* Green, unripe; raw. 2. silly, indiscreet. 3. base, low.

ಕಚ್ಚಾಟ kaććāṭa, *s.* Quarrelling, fighting; dispute.

ಕಚ್ಚಾಡುನಿ kaććāḍuni, *v. a.* To quarrel.

ಕಚ್ಚಾವುನಿ kaććāvuni, *c. v.* (*of* ಕಚ್ಚುನಿ) To join fast.

ಕಚ್ಚಿ kaćći, *see* ಕಚ್ಚಾ.

ಕಚ್ಚಿ kaćći, *s.* A notch, incision. –ಪಾಡುನಿ to make a notch.

ಕಚ್ಚಿಕಡ kaććikaḍa, *see* ಕಚ್ಚಕಡಿ.

ಕಚ್ಚಿದಾಯೆ kaććidāye, *s.* A native of Cutch.

ಕಚ್ಚುನಿ kaććuni (ಕಚ್ಚ್), *v. n.* To be joined fast. *v. a.* To bite.

ಕಚ್ಚೂರ kaććūra, *s.* A fragrant root of the *Zedoary Zerumbet* or *Curcuma Zerumbet; Kæmpferia galanga.*

ಕಚ್ಚೆ kaćće, *s.* The end *or* hem of a lower garment gathered up behind and tucked into the waist-band. –ಕಟ್ಟುನಿ to fasten the under cloth behind; any fluid to run down the rim while tilting; to turn the tail between legs, as a dog.

ಕಜಂಟ್, ಕಜಂಟಿ kajaṇṭu, kajaṇṭi, *see* ಕನಂಟಿ.

ಕಜಂಮದ್ಮೆ kajammadumè, *s.* The tonsure of a child.

ಕಜಕ್ kajaku, *s.* An oyster *or* cockle shell. 2. a cocoanut shell. ಕೋರಿಲು– the shell of a black oyster.

ಕಜಕುರುವೆ kajakuruve, *s.* A kind of basket.

ಕಜಕೆ kajakè, *adj.* Variegated with white and black. –ಕೋರಿ a white fowl streaked with black.

ಕಜನೆ kajanè, *s.* The green stuff floating on stagnant water.

ಕಜರುನಿ kajaruni, *see* ಕಜಿರುನಿ.

ಕಜವು, ಕಜಾವು kajavu, kajāvu, *s.* Rubbish, sweepings. 2. *see* ಕಜಿಲ್.

ಕಜಾನೆ kajānè, *see* ಖಜಾನೆ.

ಕಜಿಪು kajipu, *s.* Curry.

ಕಜಿಲ್ kajilu, *see* ಕಜಿಲ್.

ಕಜೆ kajè, *s.* A kind of grass growing on brackish soil. 2. an acid substance accumulated on the teeth by chewing betel leaves.

ಕಜೆ kaje, *adj.* Dark-red, reddish. –ಅರಿ an inferior kind of rice.

ಕಜೆಪುನಿ kajepuni (ಕಜೆ), *v. a.* To chew. 2. to husk with the teeth *or* beak.

ಕಜೆರುನಿ kajeruni (ಕಜಿರ್), *v. a.* To waste, as time. 2. to lose, as sleep. 3. to delay, put off, as work *or* labour.

ಕಜೆಲ್ kajelu, *s.* The after-birth, *placenta.*

ಕಜೆಲ್ಪುನಿ kajelpuni (ಕಜಿಲ್), *see* ಕದೆಪುನಿ, ಗಜೆಲ್ಪುನಿ.

ಕಜ್ಜಾತ್ kajjātu, *s.* North-west wind.

ಕಜ್ಜಾಯ kajjāya, *s.* A cake made of rice, jaggory and ghee. ಪಂಚ— a sweet preparation consisting of dholl, gingely seed, jaggory, cocoanut, and cardamoms.

ಕಜ್ಜಿ kajji, *see* ಗಜ್ಜಿ.

ಕಜ್ಜೂರ kajjūra, *see* ಗಜಿರ.

ಕಜ್ಜೆ kajje, *s.* Business, work.

ಕಜ್ಜೆರುನಿ kajjeruni (ಕಜ್ಜಿರ್), *v. n.* To be interrupted, procrastinated.

ಕಟ್‌ಕುಟ್ kaṭukuṭu, *s.* The noise produced in biting *or* chewing any hard substance. 2. uneasiness in the bowels.

ಕಟ್‌ಮಸ್ತು kaṭumastu, *see* ಗಟಿಮಸ್ತು.

ಕಟಕಟ kaṭakaṭa, *s.* Babbling, chattering. —ಪಾತೆರುನಿ to chatter; to speak harshly. —ತೆಲಿಪುನಿ to laugh noisily.

ಕಟಕ್ಕನೆ kaṭakkane, *adv.* Readily, suddenly, at once. —ಪಣ್ಪುನಿ to speak harshly.

ಕಟಲೆ kaṭale, *s.* The shopkeeper's open box for putting in cash.

ಕಟಾಕುಟಿ kaṭākuṭi, *s.* Confusion, disorder, disturbance. —ಸಾಮಾನ lumber, things lying in confusion. —ದಾಂತಿನಾಯೆ a quiet man.

ಕಟಾರಿ kaṭāri, *see* ಕಠಾರಿ.

ಕಟಾವು kaṭāvu, *s.* Reaping.

ಕಟಾಕ್ಷ kaṭāksha, *s.* A glance, side-look. 2. mercy, favour. —ತೋಜಾವುನಿ to show mercy. —ದೀಪಿನಿ to regard with favour.

ಕಟಿನ kaṭina, *see* ಕಠಿಣ.

ಕಟಿಪಿಟಿ kaṭipiṭi, *s.* Wrangling. 2. disagreement, misunderstanding. —ಬರ್ಪಿನಿ misunderstanding to arise. —ಮಳ್ಪುನಿ to wrangle; to haggle in making a bargain; to disturb, as by babbling.

ಕಟುರ, ಕಟೂರ, ಕಟೋರ kaṭura, kaṭūra, kaṭōra, *adj.* Harsh, severe, cruel; *cf.* ಕಠಿಣ.

ಕಟ್ಕರೋಹಿಣಿ kaṭkarōhiṇi, *s.* Black hellebore, *Helleborus niger.*

ಕಟ್ಟು kaṭṭu, *s.* A band, hoop. 2. a tie, bandage. 3. a bundle, packet. 4. an order, command; a regulation. 5. a bond. —ಕಟ್ಟಳೆ a law, institute, usage, routine. —ಕೂಲಿ fixed hire. —ಗಿಡ್ಪಿನಿ to loosen a tie. —ಗೆಪ್ಪುನಿ to unfasten; to cancel a rule. —ಮಳ್ಪುನಿ to make a resolution, *or* rule; to excommunicate.

ಕಟ್ಟುಕಂಮ kaṭṭukamma, *s.* A fixed pillar.

ಕಟ್ಟುಕಡ kaṭṭukaḍa, *see* ಕಡಕಟ್ಟು.

ಕಟ್ಟುಕಡಿ kaṭṭukaḍi, *s.* Determination, settlement.

ಕಟ್ಟ್ಕಡೆ kaṭṭụkaḍè, *s.* A final arrangement *or* resolution. –ಕ finally, at last, on the extreme point.

ಕಟ್ಟ್ಕಥೆ kaṭṭụkathè, *s.* A fable, novel, romance.

ಕಟ್ಟ್ಮುಟ್ಟು kaṭṭụmuṭṭu, *see* ಕಡು ಮುಟ್ಟು.

ಕಟ್ಟ್ಲ್ಮೆ kaṭṭụlme, *see* ಕಟ್ಟಲ್ಮೆ.

ಕಟ್ಟ್ವಾಸ್ kaṭṭụvāsụ, *s.* A rough kind of cloth. 2. a piece of cloth to wrap up clothes *etc.*

ಕಟ್ಟ kaṭṭa, *s.* A dam. 2. *see* ಕಟ್ಟೆ.

ಕಟ್ಟ kaṭṭa, *see* ಕಷ್ಟ.

ಕಟ್ಟಣ kaṭṭaṇa, *s.* An embankment. 2. any earth- *or* stonework. 3. a building.

ಕಟ್ಟಣಚೀರವು kaṭṭaṇaćīravu, *s.* A bag with divisions; *also* ಗಟ್ಟಂ ಚೀರವು.

ಕಟ್ಟಪುಣಿ kaṭṭapuṇi, *s.* An embankment between rice-fields *or* across a water-course.

ಕಟ್ಟಲ್ಮೆ kaṭṭalme, *s.* A building.

ಕಟ್ಟಳೆ kaṭṭaḷe, *s.* Custom, practice. 2. an order. 3. a rule, regulation.

ಕಟ್ಟಾಕುಟ್ಟಿ kaṭṭākuṭṭi, *see* ಕಟಾಕಟಿ.

ಕಟ್ಟಾಣಿ kaṭṭāṇi, *s.* A necklace of five *or* seven strings of gold beads, each having a gold coin in the middle.

ಕಟ್ಟಾವುನಿ kaṭṭāvuni, *c. v.* (*of.* ಕಟ್ಟುನಿ) To cause to bind *or* tie. 2. to have a house *etc.* built. 3. to supply. ಪುದೆ– to supply with vegetables.

ಕಟ್ಟಾವುನಿ kaṭṭāvuni (ಕಟ್ಟಾ), *v. a.* To winnow.

ಕಟ್ಟಿಗೆ kaṭṭige, *s.* Fuel, firewood.

ಕಟ್ಟು kaṭṭu, *see* ಕಟ್ಟೆ.

ಕಟ್ಟುತ್ತರ kaṭṭuttara, *s.* Adjustment, settlement. 2. order command. 3. the pacification of a devil.

ಕಟ್ಟುನಿ kaṭṭuni (ಕಟ್ಟಿ), *v. a.* To bind, tie, fasten, secure. 2. to build, construct. 3. to set, as jewels. 4. to amass, as wealth. 5. to deposit, as money. 6. to pay government dues. ಕಟ್ಟಿದ್ ಕೊರ್ಪಿನಿ (*lit.* to tie and give) to erect for another, *as* ಇಲ್ಲ್ ಕಟ್ಟಿದ್ ಕೊರ್ಪಿನಿ to build a house for another; ಕೈಕಟ್ಟಿದ್ ಕೊರ್ಪಿನಿ to submit voluntarily; ನ್ಯಾಯು ಕಟ್ಟಿದ್ ಕೊರ್ಪಿನಿ to refer a dispute for arbitration; ಭೂಮಿ ಕಟ್ಟಿದ್ ಕೊರ್ಪಿನಿ to lease out a land. ಕಟ್ಟಿದ್ ದೀಪಿನಿ to store, amass; to forbear, as from showing one's pride. ಕಟ್ಟಿದ್ ಪಾಡುನಿ to confine. ಕಟ್ಟಿದ್ ಪಾತೆರುನಿ to argue closely a point in dispute, to contest.

ಕಟ್ಟುಮುಟ್ಟು kaṭṭumuṭṭu, *see* ಕಡು ಮುಟ್ಟು.

ಕಟ್ಟೆ kaṭṭe, *s.* A raised seat of earth *or* stone. 2. an altar. 3. an office. ಟಪ್ಪಾಲ್– a post-office. ತೊಳಸಿ– an embankment round the tuḷasi plant. ಸುಂಕದ– a custom-house. –ಪತ್ತುನಿ to suffer loss, be ruined.

ಕಟ್ಟೆವು kaṭṭevu, *s.* A flea.

ಕಟ್ಟೊಣುನಿ kaṭṭoṇuni, *v. refl.* (*of* ಕಟ್ಟುನಿ) To bind for oneself. 2. to supply oneself. ಪಾಪ— to commit sin.

ಕಟ್ಲೆ, ಕಟ್ಳೆ, katle, kaṭle, *see* ಕಟ್ಟಳೆ.

ಕಠಾರಿ kaṭhāri, *s.* A dagger.

ಕಠಿಣ kaṭhiṇa, *adj.* Hard, harsh, severe, difficult. —ನರಮಾನಿ a cruel man. —ಪಾತೆರ a severe expression. —ರೋಗ a serious disease. —ಹೃದಯ a hard heart.

ಕಠೋರ kaṭhōra, *adj.* Severe, horrible.

ಕಡ್‌ಂಚಿಲ್ kaḍųñcilų, *see* ಕಡ್ಚಿಲ್.

ಕಡ್‌ಂಜಿ, ಕಡ್‌ಂಜೆಯಿ kaḍųñji, kaḍųñjeyi, *see* ಗಜಿಗೆ.

ಕಡ್‌ಂಬು kaḍųmbu, *s.* A kind of cake.

ಕಡ್‌ಂಬೆಲೆ kaḍųmbele, *s.* A miser, niggard.

ಕಡ್‌ತ kaḍųta, *s.* A cut, incision. ಒಂಜೇ ಕಡ್ತೊಗು ಕಡ್ತೆ he cut it at one stroke. 2. *see* ಕಡತ.

ಕಡ್‌ತಲೆ kaḍųtale, *see* ಕಡ್ಸಲೆ.

ಕಡ್‌ದ್ kaḍųdų, *see* ಕಡ್ದ್.

ಕಡ್‌ಪುನಿ kaḍųpuni, *see* ಕಡ್ಪುನಿ.

ಕಡ್‌ಮ kaḍųma, *see* ಕಡಮ.

ಕಡ್‌ಮೆ kaḍųme, *s.* Pride, vanity. 2. ostentation, vaunting.

ಕಡ್‌ಸಲೆ, ಕಡ್‌ಸಾಲೆ kaḍųsale, kaḍųsāle, *s.* A devil-dancer's sword.

ಕಡ್‌ಸ್ತನ kaḍųstana, *see* ಗಡ್ಸ್ತನ.

ಕಡ kaḍa, *s.* A loan, debt. —ಕೊಪಿನಿ to lend. —ದೆಪ್ಪುನಿ to borrow.

ಕಡಂದ kaḍanda, *s.* Grinding. —ಕಲ್ಲ್ a grinding stone. —ಕಂಜಿ a grinding pestle.

ಕಡಂಬಲ್ kaḍambalų, *s.* The space behind the hearth.

ಕಡಂಬಳೆ kaḍambaḷe, *s.* A kind of poisonous snake; *also* ಕಡಮಳೆ.

ಕಡಕಟ್ಟ್ kaḍakaṭṭų, *s.* Monetary transactions, lending and borrowing.

ಕಡಕಡ kaḍakḍa, *see* ಗಡಗಡ.

ಕಡಗ kaḍaga, *s.* A bracelet.

ಕಡತ kaḍata, *s.* A cloth covered with a composition of charcoal and gum, and used instead of a slate for writing. 2. the skin.

ಕಡದು kaḍadu, *see* ಕಡ್ದ್.

ಕಡಪ kaḍapa, *s.* Distance. 2. about half a mile.

ಕಡಪಾವುನಿ kaḍapāvuni, *c.v.* (*of* ಕಡಪುನಿ) To cause to pass. 2. to help one to ford a river.

ಕಡಪು kaḍapu, *s.* A ferry. —ಕಲ್ಲ್ a stone placed across a stream for crossing over. —ದಾಯಿ a ferryman.

ಕಡಪು kaḍapu, *s.* A rheumatism of the joints.

ಕಡಪುಡುನಿ kaḍapuḍuni, *c.v.* (*of* ಕಡಪುನಿ) To despatch, forward, send away, dismiss. ಕಡಪುಡ್ದು ಕೊಪಿನಿ to accompany one for a short distance out of civility; to follow the remains of deceased relatives to their last resting place.

ಕಡಪುನಿ kaḍapuni (ಕಡ), *v. a.* To cross, ford, pass. *v. n.* To elapse. 2. to surpass.

ಕಡಪೆಲ್ kaḍapelụ, *s.* That which can be crossed over.

ಕಡಪ್ಯಡೆ kaḍapyaḍe, *see* ಕಡಪು.

ಕಡಮ kaḍama, *s.* A stag, elk.

ಕಡಮೆ kaḍame, *s.* Deficiency, defect. 2. remnant. *adj.* Less, deficient; remaining. ಹೆಚ್ಚ– difference, about. –ಆಪಿನಿ to become less, be diminished. –ಮಳ್ಪುನಿ to lessen, reduce; to deduct.

ಕಡಯಿ kaḍayi, *s.* A boiler of bell-metal.

ಕಡರ kaḍara, *s.* The companions of a bride, bridesmaids. –ಕಟ್ಟುನಿ to choose a bridesmaid. –ದಾಳ್ a bridesmaid. –ದ ಮರಿಯಾದೆ a gift of four rupees to a bridesmaid.

ಕಡರುನಿ kaḍaruni (ಕಡರ್), *v. n.* To croak; to caw.

ಕಡಲ್ kaḍalụ, *s.* The sea, ocean. –ಕಕ್ಕೆ, –ಶಾವೆ the sea-gull. –ನಾಲಾಯಿ the bone of a cuttle-fish. –ನುರೆ the foaming surges of the sea. –ಪಂಜಿ a sea-hog, dolphin. –ಬಾಳೆ a kind of fish. –ಮರಿ a sea-snake. –ಮೀನ್ a sea-fish.

ಕಡಲೆ kaḍalè, *s.* Bengal gram, *Cicer arietinum.* ನೆಲ– the ground-nut, *Arachis hypogaæ.*

ಕಡವು kaḍavu, *s.* A turning-lathe. 2. a wooden shoe. 3. a silver anklet. –ಪಾಡುನಿ to turn in a lathe; to wear anklets, *or* wooden shoes.

ಕಡಸ್ kaḍasụ, *see* ಗಡಸ್.

ಕಡಾಕಡಿ kaḍākaḍi, *adj.* Resolute, decided, strict, exact.

ಕಡಾಯಿ kaḍāyi, *see* ಕಡಯಿ.

ಕಡಾರ kaḍāra, *see* ಕಡರ.

ಕಡಾವು kaḍāvu, *see* ಕಡವು.

ಕಡಿ kaḍi, *s.* An opening, passage. 2. a small fragment, bit. 3. a small passage. –ಕಟ್ಟುನಿ to block up an opening.

ಕಡಿ kaḍi, *s.* Broken rice; *adj.* Broken.

ಕಡಿತ kaḍita, *see* ಕಡ್ತ.

ಕಡಿಚಿಲ್ kaḍicilụ, *see* ಕಡ್ಚಿಲ್.

ಕಡಿಮೆ kaḍime, *see* ಕಡಮೆ.

ಕಡಿಯ kaḍiya, *see* ಕಡಯ.

ಕಡಿಯುನಿ kaḍiyuni (ಕಡಿ), *v. n.* To be cut in two. 2. to break down. 3. to give way, as a dam. 4. to dissolve, as friendship.

ಕಡಿರ್, ಕಡಿರತನ kaḍirụ, kaḍiratana, *see* ಕಡೀರ್.

ಕಡಿವಾಣ kaḍivāṇa, *s.* The bridle of a horse.

ಕಡೀರ್ kaḍīrụ, *adj.* First-born. –ತನ primogeniture. –ದಾಯೆ the first-born son.

ಕಡೀರ್ kaḍīrụ, *s.* The plant *Sida retusa.*

ಕಡು kaḍu, *s.* Pungency; severity. 2. excess; extremity. *adj.* Pungent. 2. extreme, excessive. 3. severe. –ಕಲಪುನಿ, –ಪಾಡುನಿ to poison the fish. –ಕಷ್ಟ excessive trouble. –ಕೈಪೆ

very bitter. —ಕೋಪ excessive passion *or* anger. —ತ್ಯಾಗಿ a very liberal man. —ಪಾಪಿ a great sinner. —ಶೆಕೆ excessive heat.

ಕಡುಂಬರ್ **kaḍumbaru**, *s*. Drowsiness, dreaminess. —ಪಾತೆರುನಿ to talk in sleep; *cf*. ಕಣೊಂಬರ.

ಕಡುಂಬೆ **kaḍumbe**, *see* ಕಡಮ.

ಕಡುಪ, ಕಡುಪು **kaḍupa, kaḍupu**, *see* ಕಡ್ಪು.

ಕಡುಬು **kaḍubu**, *s*. A kind of cake.

ಕಡುಮುಟ್ಟು **kaḍumuṭṭu**, *s*. The extreme point. 2. severity, sharpness. *adj*. Extreme. 2. severe. —ದ ಬೇನೆ travail.

ಕಡುವಾಯಿ **kaḍuvāyi**, *s*. A kind of fish.

ಕಡುವೆ **kaḍuve**, *s*. A hero. 2. a courageous man. 3. a clever man.

ಕಡುಸ್ತನ **kaḍustana**, *see* ಗಡ್ಸ್ತನ.

ಕಡೆ **kaḍe**, *s*. Verge, edge, margin. 2. end, extremity *or* point. 3. place, side, direction. *adj*. Last, final, ultimate. 2. low, mean. —ಕಾಯಿ the fruit of the last crop. —ಕಾಲ (*lit*. last time), end, death; evil; distress. —ಕೊಡಿದಾಂತಿ without head *or* tail; forlorn *or* destitute; stupid, absurd, senseless. —ತಾಯಿ a retainer, adherent. —ದಿನ the last day; the day of judgment. —ನರಮಾನಿ a low, mean, *or* stupid man. —ನೋಟ a side-glance, leer. —ಬಾಯಿ the corners of lips. —ಬೊರ್ಸ್ dis-qualification. —ಸಂದ್ the hip, waist, *esp*. of cattle. —ಕೊಡುನಿ to come to an end. —ತೂಪಿನಿ to witness the end *or* destruction of anything. —ತೋಜಾವುನಿ to threaten with evil. —ಬೂರುನಿ to avoid, escape; to recover; to get through a task. —ಬೋಳುನಿ to pare *or* lop the top. —ಮಳ್ಪುನಿ to conclude, bring to an end. —ಮಾರುನಿ (a woman) to commit adultery, *obsc*. —ಮುಟ್ಟುನಿ, —ಪೊಂದುನಿ to come to a conclusion *or* decision. —ಸೇರುನಿ to finish, terminate. ಕಡೆಕ್ finally, at last. ಕಡೆಕ್ ದೀಪಿನಿ to keep aside. ಕಡೆಕ್ ಮಳ್ಪುನಿ to gather together in one place. ಕಡೆಕ್ ಸೇರುನಿ to be an adherent of. ಕಡೆಕಡೆಕ್ ultimately, finally, at the end. ಕಡೇ the very last, final. ಆ— that side. ಈ— this side. ಉಳಯಿದ— inside. ಪಿದಯಿದ— outside.

ಕಡೆಂಚುನಿ **kaḍeñcuni** (ಕಡೆಂಚ್), *v. a*. To knead.

ಕಡೆಕಣ್ **kaḍekaṇṇu**, *s*. The outer corner *or* angle of the eye. 2. a side-glance, leer. —ಡ್ದ್ ತೂಪಿನಿ to look askance; not to be well disposed.

ಕಡೆಕಟ್ಟ್ **kaḍekaṭṭu**, *s*. The settlement of a dispute. 2. a double cross-beam. 3. a wooden square in front of an upper story, supported on posts.

ಕಡೆಕಾರ್ **kaḍekāru**, *s*. The heel.

ಕಡೆಗುರಿ kaḍeguri, *s.* A pit used by the rope-pullers when working a country water-lift.

ಕಡೆಚ್ಚುನಿ kaḍeććuni, *see* ಕಡೆಂಚುನಿ.

ಕಡೆಪಿನಿ kaḍepini (ಕಡೆ), *v. a.* To bite, champ, gnaw, grind. ಕಾಯಿ– to chew the cud. ಕೂಲಿ– to gnash the teeth. ಕಡೆಪಿಕಲ್ಲ್ a grinding stone.

ಕಡೆಬಲ್ಲ್, ಕಡೆಬಳ್ಳ್ kaḍeballu, kaḍeballu, *s.* The ropes with which a water-lift is worked.

ಕಡೆಯುನಿ, ಕಡೆವುನಿ kaḍeyuni, kaḍevuni (ಕಡೆ), *v. a.* To stir up, turn. 2. *see* ಕಡೆಪಿನಿ.

ಕಡೆರುನಿ kaḍeruni, *see* ಕಡರುನಿ.

ಕಡೆಸ kaḍesa, *s.* Delay.

ಕಡೆಸಾವುನಿ kaḍesāvuni, *c. v.* (*of* ಕಡೆಸುನಿ) To delay, detain, stop.

ಕಡೆಸುನಿ kaḍesuni (ಕಡೆಸ್), *v. n.* To be late, to delay, tarry, linger.

ಕಡೈ kaḍei, *see* ಕಡಯಿ.

ಕಡ್ಗ kaḍga, *s.* A sword.

ಕಡ್ಚಿಲ್ kaḍćilu, *s.* A turning lathe. –ಪಾಡುನಿ to turn in a lathe. –ದಾಯೆ a turner.

ಕಡ್ಡಿ kaḍḍi, *s.* The fibre *or* vein of a leaf. 2. a very small stick. –ಅರಕ್, *see* ಅರಕ್.

ಕಡ್ಡ್ಯ kaḍḍya, *s.* A pitcher, water-pot.

ಕಡ್ಡ್ಯನ kaḍḍyana, *s.* A bridle, reins, bit.

ಕಡ್ತಲೆಬಾಯಿ kaḍtalebāyi, *s.* A quarrelsome person.

ಕಡ್ತೆಲ್ kaḍtelu, *s.* That which is broken.

ಕಡ್ತೆಲು kaḍtelu, *s.* A prattling woman.

ಕಡ್ಡ್ kaḍḍu, *s.* Severity, rigour, harshness. 2. the strength of wine *etc.*; *also* –ಗಾರಿಕೆ. *adj.* Severe, harsh. 2. strong. –ಪಾತೆರ a harsh word. –ಆಪಿನಿ to be severe, strong. –ಮಳ್ಪುನಿ to make strong.

ಕಡ್ಡಾಟ kḍḍāṭa, *s.* Cutting. 2. fighting.

ಕಡ್ಪತ್ತಿ kaḍpatti, *s.* A bill-hook.

ಕಡ್ಪು kaḍpu, *adj.* Excessive, beyond limit, *etc.* –ಅಡ್ಯೆ an oversweet confection. –ಪಾತೆರ a very harsh word. –ಭಂಗಾರ್ gold containing a larger proportion of alloy than usual; *cf.* ಕಡು.

ಕಡ್ಪುನಿ kaḍpuni (ಕಡಿ), *v. a.* To cut; to fell down. ಕಡ್ಪಕಲ್ಲ್ a stone cut from a quarry.

ಕಡ್ಮ kaḍma, *see* ಕಡಮ.

ಕಡ್ಲೆ, ಕಡ್ಳೆ kaḍle, kaḍḷe, *see* ಕಡಲೆ.

ಕಣ kaṇa, *s.* A square piece. ರವಕೆ– the piece of cloth from which a female's bodice is made.

ಕಣ kaṇa, *see* ಕನ.

ಕಣ kaṇa, *v. a.* (*imperat. of* ಕೊಂಡಪಿನಿ) Bring.

ಕಣಂಬರುನಿ kaṇambaruni, *see* ಕಂಣಂಬರುನಿ.

ಕಣಕ್ kaṇaku, *s.* Fuel, firewood.

ಕಣಜ kaṇaja, *s.* A granary, barn.

ಕಣಪಡೆ kaṇapaḍe, *s.* A kind of

tree, having poisonous milky juice.

ಕಣಾಪಣೆ kaṇapaṇe, *s.* A stupid man.

ಕಣಾಪರು kaṇaparu̥, *s.* A jaw-tooth, grinder.

ಕಣಾಪಲಯಿ kaṇapalayi, *s.* A plank for the driver to stand upon in buffalo race.

ಕಣಾಪಿನಿ kaṇapini, *see* ಕೊಂಡಪಿನಿ.

ಕಣಾಪೆ kaṇape, *adj.* Bitter, astringent.

ಕಣಾಲೆ kaṇale, *see* ಕೋಣಾಲೆ.

ಕಣಿ kaṇi, *s.* A ditch, trench.

ಕಣಿಪುನಿ kaṇipuni (ಕಣಿ), *v. n.* To be hardened by burning, as an earthen vessel. 2. to be afflicted. ಮನಸ್– to be depressed, dispirited; the heart to be hardened.

ಕಣಿಮೆ kaṇime, *s.* A defile *or* pass between two mountains.

ಕಣಿಯೆ kaṇiye, *s.* An astrologer.

ಕಣಿಲೆ kaṇile, *s.* A tender bamboo shoot.

ಕಣೆ kaṇe, *s.* A slender bamboo branch.

ಕಣೆ kaṇe, *s.* A blight incidental to rice crops. ಕೆಯಿತ– a blighted ear of corn.

ಕಣೆ kaṇe, *s.* The quill of a porcupine. –ಪಂಜಿ a porcupine.

ಕಣೆಂಗ್, ಕಣೆಂಗಿ kaṇeṅgu̥, kaṇeṅgi, *see* ಕಳೆಂಗ್.

ಕಣೆಪುನಿ kaṇepuni (ಕಣೆ), *v. n.* To have an acrid *or* astringent taste. 2. to rot.

ಕಣೆಪರು kaṇeparu, *see* ಕಣಾಪರು.

ಕಣೆಪೆ kaṇepe, *see* ಕಣಾಪೆ.

ಕಣೆಯುನಿ kaṇeyuni, *see* ಕಣೆಪುನಿ.

ಕಣೆರ್ kaṇeru̥, *s.* Astringency.

ಕಣೆಲ್ kaṇelu̥, *s.* The thick end of grass *or* straw. 2. a small branch of a tree.

ಕಣೆವುನಿ kaṇevuni, *see* ಕಣೆಪುನಿ.

ಕಣೊಪಿನಿ kaṇopini, *see* ಕೊಂಡಪಿನಿ.

ಕಣೊಲೆ kaṇole, *see* ಕೋಣಾಲೆ.

ಕಣ್ಣ್ kaṇṇu̥, *see* ಕಂಣ್.

ಕಣ್ಣಕಟ್ಟ್ kaṇṇakaṭṭu̥, *see* ಕಂಣ್‍ಕಟ್ಟ್.

ಕಣ್ಣನೀರ್ kaṇṇanīru̥, *see* ಕಂಣ್‍ನೀರ್ *under* ಕಂಣ್.

ಕಣ್ಣೋಜಿ kaṇṇōji, *see* ಕಂನೋಜಿ.

ಕತೆ kate, *see* ಕಥೆ.

ಕತ್ತ katta, *s.* The coir *or* fibres of the cocoanut, used to make ropes with.

ಕತ್ತರಿ kattari, *see* ಕತ್ತೆರಿ.

ಕತ್ತಲಿಯುನಿ, ಕತ್ತಲ್ಯುನಿ kattaliyuni, kattalyuni (ಕತ್ತಲ್), *v. n.* To set, as the sun; to get dark. 2. to droop, as one's spirits.

ಕತ್ತಲೆ kattale, *s.* Darkness. ಕರ್–, ಕಸ್ಗತ್ತಲೆ pitch dark. ಮೈ– the twilight.

ಕತ್ತವು kattavu, *see* ಕತ್ತ.

ಕತ್ತಳ್ kattaḷu̥, *s.* Cash, ready money, *vlg.*

ಕತ್ತಿ katti, *s.* A knife; *also* ಕತ್ತೆ.

ಕತ್ತೆ katte, *s.* An ass. 2. a silly creature. –ಕುರ್ಕ a hayena.

ಕತ್ತೆರಿ katteri, *s.* Scissors, shears. 2. an betel-nut cracker. 3. a rat-trap; *also* ಎಲಿ–.

ಕತ್ತೆರಿಯುನಿ, ಕತ್ತೆರುನಿ katteriyuni, katteruni (ಕತ್ತೆರ್), *v.a.* To shear, cut with scissors.

ಕತ್ರಾಣ, ಕತ್ರಾಸ katrāṇa, katrāna, *s.* A composition of chunam and other ingredients used for flooring.

ಕಥೆ, ಕಥನ kathe, kathana, *s.* A story, narrative, narration, history. 2. a fable, tale. *intj.* Ah! ದಾನೆ– wonderful! ಕಥಾ ಪ್ರಸಂಗ narration of a story. ಕಥಾರಸ a delightful *or* pleasant story. ಕಥಾಸಂಗ್ರಹ a collection of stories; a compendium of history.

ಕದ್ಂಪೆ kadųmpe, *see* ಕದಂಪೆ.

ಕದ್ಕ್ಲ್ kadųkųlų, *s.* A vital part of the body, as the heart. 2. the side.

ಕದ್ರ್ kadųrų, *s.* A spindle, distaff.

ಕದಂಪೆ kadampe, *s.* The decayed part of timber. 2. a chip, splinter.

ಕದಂಸರ kadamsara, *s.* A perfumed braid made of the "kēdagi" flower.

ಕದನ kadana, *s.* War, battle.

ಕದನೆ kadane, *s.* A swivel-gun. –ಬುಡ್ಪಿನಿ to fire a swivel-gun.

ಕದರ್, ಕದರು kadarų, kadaru, *see* ಗದ್ರ್.

ಕದಲುನಿ kadaluni, *see* ಕದೆಲುನಿ.

ಕದಲೆ kadale, *s.* A rag. *adj.* Ragged, tattered.

ಕದಿಕೆ kadike, *s.* The *Huriallec* grass, *Cynodon Dactylon.* 2. the name of a village.

ಕದಿಕೆ kadike, *s.* A granary. 2. a depository for the receipt of offerings.

ಕದಿನೆ kadine, *see* ಕದನೆ.

ಕದಿಪು kadipu, *see* ಕದ್ಪು.

ಕದಿಪುನಿ kadipuni, *see* ಕದೆಪುನಿ.

ಕದಿಮೆ kadime, *see* ಕದೀಮೆ.

ಕದಿಯ kadiya, *adv.* Strongly, well. –ಪುಂಟುನಿ to squeeze well.

ಕದಿರ್ kadirų, *s.* An ear of corn. 2. *see* ಕದ್ರ್.

ಕದೀಮ kadīma, *adj.* Of long standing, veteran, experienced.

ಕದೀಮೆ kadīme, *s.* A veteran, an experienced man, a servant of long standing.

ಕದು kadu, *s.* Grit.

ಕದುಪು kadupu, *see* ಕದ್ಪು.

ಕದೆ kade, *s.* Catamenial discharge.

ಕದೆಪುನಿ, ಕದೆಯುನಿ, ಕದೆವುನಿ kadepuni, kadeyuni, kadevuni (ಕದೆ), *v. a.* & *n.* To disjoin. 2. to pull out, strip off.

ಕದೆಲ್ kadelų, *adj.* Loose.

ಕದೆಲುನಿ kadeluni (ಕದೆಲ್), *v. n.* To become loose, slack. 2. to shatter, tatter.

ಕದೊಲಿ kadoli, *s.* A species of plantain, *Musa sapientum.*

ಕದ್ಪು kadpu, *s.* Stealing, theft.

ಕದ್ಪು kadpu, *s.* An ear of ripened corn. –ದಂಗುನಿ an ear of corn to bend from its weight.

ಕದ್ರ್ kadrų, *see* ಕದ್ರ್.

ಕದ್ರೊಳು **kadroḷu,** *s.* A kind of edible grass.

ಕನ **kana,** *s.* A dream. –ತ ರೂಪು a vision; chimera, fancy. –ಮನಸ್ (*lit.* dream and mind); sleep *or* wakefulness, *used negatively* –ಕಟ್ಟುನಿ, *c. dat.* –ತೂಪಿನಿ to dream.

ಕನಂಬರುನಿ **kanambaruni,** *see* ಕಂಣಂ [ಬರುನಿ.

ಕನಕ **kanaka,** *s.* Gold. ಕನಕಾಭಿಷೇಕ showing honour *or* devotion by pouring gold coins on the head. –ಚೂರ್ಣ gold dust.

ಕನಪೆ **kanapè,** *see* ಕಣಪೆ.

ಕನಿಕರ **kanikara,** *s.* Pity, compassion. –ಮಳ್ಪುನಿ to pity, have compassion.

ಕನಿಪುನಿ, ಕನಿಯುನಿ **kanipuni, kaniyuni,** *see* ಕಣಿಪುನಿ.

ಕನಿಮೂರಿ **kanimūri,** *s.* The smell of smoke.

ಕನಿಲೆ **kaṇiḷè,** *see* ಕಣಿಲೆ.

ಕನಿಷ್ಟ **kanishṭa,** *adj.* Small, little. 2. young. 3. base, inferior, low. –ಮ lowest. ಕನಿಷ್ಟೆ a youngster.

ಕನೆ **kane,** *see* ಕಣೆ.

ಕನೆಪಾವುನಿ **kanepāvuni,** *c. v.* (*of* ಕನೆಪುನಿ) To afflict, cause trouble. 2. to harden, as the heart.

ಕನೆಪುನಿ **kanepuni** (ಕನೆ), *v. n.* To be afflicted, troubled. 2. to be hardened; *see* ಕಣೆಪುನಿ.

ಕನೆರ್ **kaneru,** *see* ಕಣೆರ್.

ಕನೆವುನಿ **kanevuni** (ಕನೆ), *v. n.* The skin to be discolored by a blow.

ಕನ್ನ **kanna,** *see* ಕಂನ.

ಕನ್ನಡ **kannaḍa,** *see* ಕಂನಡ.

ಕನ್ನಡಿ **kannaḍi,** *see* ಕಂನಡಿ.

ಕನ್ನಿ **kanni,** *see* ಕಂಣಿ.

ಕನ್ಯ **kanya,** *s.* A virgin, young girl; *also* ಕನ್ಯೆ, ಕನ್ನಿಕೆ, ಕನ್ಯಕೊಂಞು. 2. the sign Virgo in the zodiac; the sixth solar month. –ತ್ವ virginity. –ದ ಅಗೆಲ್ an offering to the dead. –ದ ಕೆಯಿ the first crop. –ದ ಪಜಿರ್ a kind of grass. –ಬೂರು, –ಬೇರ್ the country sarsaparilla, *Hemidesmus indicus*. ಕನ್ಯಾದಾನ giving a girl in marriage.

ಕಪ **kapa,** *see* ಕಫ.

ಕಪಟ **kapaṭa,** *s.* Fraud, deceit; hypocrisy. –ಗಾರೆ, –ದಾಯಿ, –ಸ್ತ್ರೀ, ಕಪಟಿ a hypocrite, dissembler. –ವೇಷ the guise of hypocrisy.

ಕಪಡೆ **kapaḍe,** *s.* A gluttonous woman. 2. cloth.

ಕಪಲ, ಕಪಾಲ **kapala, kapāla,** *s.* The scull. 2. the temples.

ಕಪಾಟ್ **kapāṭu,** *s.* An almirah.

ಕಪಾಯಿ **kapāyi,** *s.* A greedy woman. 2. middling, as liquor.

ಕಪಿ **kapi,** *s.* A monkey, ape. –ಚೇಷ್ಟೆ a monkey's trick; teasing. –ಕಟ್ಟುನಿ to mimic, ape.

ಕಪಿ **kapi,** *s.* A pulley.

ಕಪಿಲ **kapila,** *s.* A tawny colour. *adj.* Tawny. –ಮುನಿ, ಕಪಿಲೆ the founder of the Sāṅkhya philosophy.

ಕಪುರ **kapura,** *see* ಕರ್ಪೂರ.

ಕಪ್ಪ **kappa,** *s.* Tribute, an offer- [ing.

ಕಪ್ಪಂದ **kappanda,** *s.* A sling. —ಕಲ್ಲ a sling stone.

ಕಪ್ಪಡ, ಕಪ್ಪಡಿ, ಕಪ್ಪಡೆ **kappaḍa, kappaḍi, kappaḍè,** *s.* A dirty, tattered cloth.

ಕಪ್ಪಡೆ **kappaḍe,** *s.* A snipe; *cf.* ಕಪ್ಪರಂಟೆ.

ಕಪ್ಪಡೆ **kappaḍè,** *adj.* Dirty. —ಕುಂಟು, *see* ಕಪ್ಪಡ.

ಕಪ್ಪರ್ **kapparu̥,** *s.* A portion of a large earthen pot, potsherd. —ತೆಲ್ಲವು a flat kind of cake, *or* —ರೊಟ್ಟಿ a kind of bread, baked in such a potsherd.

ಕಪ್ಪರ್ **kapparu̥,** *adv.* On the face. —ಬೂರುನಿ to fall on the face.

ಕಪ್ಪರ್‌ಸುತ್ತು **kapparu̥suttu,** *s.* Galvanised iron, zinc.

ಕಪ್ಪರಂಟ್ **kapparaṇṭu̥,** *s.* A fabulous beast. 2. a glutton. 3. a rake, debauchee.

ಕಪ್ಪರಂಟೆ **kapparaṇṭe,** *s.* A tadpole.

ಕಪ್ಪಲ್ **kappalu̥,** *s.* A ship. —ಕೋರಿ a game cock. —ಜೀರಡರಿ a kind of cumin seed, *Nigella sativa.* —ಮಿತ್ತಾವುನಿ, —ಏರುನಿ to go on board a ship.

ಕಪ್ಪು **kappu,** *s.* Blackness, darkness. *adj.* Black, dark. —ಮೋಣೆ a dark *or* dejected face. —ಪಾಡುನಿ to conjure *or* divine by putting a black application on the palm; *cf.* ಕರಿ.

ಕಪ್ಪುತೊಳಚಿ, ಕಪ್ಪುತೊಳಸಿ **kapputoḷaĉi, kapputoḷasi,** *s.* A kind of mint shrub, 'Holy basil,' *Ocimum sanctum.*

ಕಪ್ಪುನಿ **kappuni** (ಕಪ್ಪ್), *v. a.* To eat greedily.

ಕಪ್ಪೆ **kappè,** A frog. —ಕಂಣ್ large eyes. ಪಕ್ಕಿ—, ಪಸಿ— a green frog. —ಕುತ್ತ, —ರೋಗ a disease of cattle, dogs, *etc.* —ರಂಟೆ a tadpole.

ಕಪ್ರಸುತ್ತು **kaprasuttu,** *see* ಕಪ್ಪರ್ ಸುತ್ತು.

ಕಫ **kapha,** *s.* Phlegm. —ಕಟ್ಟುನಿ phlegm to accumulate in the throat. —ಉಪ್ಪುನಿ to expectorate.

ಕಬ್ಚ **kabu̥ĉa,** *s.* A short jacket.

ಕಬ **kaba,** *s.* The space between the fingers; *cf.* ಕಜಿ. —ಕೈ a bifurcated branch.

ಕಬಂಧ **kabandha,** *s.* A headless trunk. 2. water.

ಕಬಂಧೆ **kabandhe,** *s.* The name of a giant. 2. a short-necked man. 3. the moon's ascending node.

ಕಬಕೈ **kabakei,** *see under* ಕಬ.

ಕಬಟ **kabaṭa,** *see* ಕಪಟ. ಕಬಟಿ a dissembling woman.

ಕಬಡ್‌ದಾರ್ **kabaḍu̥dāru̥,** *intj.* Be careful! ಕಬಡ್‌ದಾರಿಕೆ care, caution; control.

ಕಬತ್ **kabatu̥,** *s.* Drill, military exercise.

ಕಬರ್ **kabaru̥,** *s.* A forked *or* lateral branch. 2. a forked stick. 3. a report. 4. news. *adj.* Forked. —ದಾಂತಿನಾಯೆ a heedless *or* negligent man.

ಕಬರಿ **kabari,** *s.* Tufted hair of females.

ಕಬಾಟ್ kabāṭu, *see* ಕಪಾಟ.

ಕಬಿಡುನಿ kabiḍuni (ಕಬಿಡ), *v. a.* To strain, as the gruel of boiled rice.

ಕಬಿಯುನಿ kabiyuni (ಕಬಿ), *v. a.* To besiege, surround, overwhelm. 2. to overspread, as clouds; *also* ಕಬ್ಯುನಿ.

ಕಬೀರ್‌ದಾಸೆ, ಕಬೀರೆ kabīrudāse, kabīre, *s.* A celebrated Hindu saint, once a Mussulman.

ಕಬುಲ್, ಕಬೂಲ್, ಕಬೂಲಿ kabulu, kabūlu, kabūli, *s.* Agreement, consent.

ಕಬುಲೆ kabule, *adj.* Tawny, of a yellowish dark colour. —ಆಪಿನಿ to get ripe, as the gingely oilseed. *s.* A tawny coloured bull.

ಕಬೆ kabe, *s.* A forked stick. *adj.* Cloven, forked. —ಕೈ the cleft between the thumb and the forefinger. —ಕೋಲು a post forked at the top. —ಪಂತಿ a kind of fork-shaped grass.

ಕಬೆತ್ತ್ kabettu, *adj.* Tawny, of a yellowish colour.

ಕಬೆತ್ತಿ kabetti, *s.* A tawny coloured cow.

ಕಬ್ಜ kabča, *see* ಕಬ್ಜ.

ಕಬ್ಬೆ, ಕಬ್ಯ kabbe, kabya, *adv.* Topsyturvy, upside-down. —ಪಾಡುನಿ to overturn. —ಬೂರುನಿ to capsize, upset.

ಕಮಲ kamala, *s.* The lotus, *Nymphea nelumba.*

ಕಮಸ್ kamasu, *see* ಗಮಸ್.

ಕಮಸ್ kamasu, There is none, *vlg.*

ಕಮಸ್ತಾರೆ kamastāre, *s.* A sea-custom superintendent.

ಕಮಾನ್, ಕಮಾನು kamānu, kamānu, *s.* An arch, vault.

ಕಮಾಯಿ kamāyi, *s.* Gain, income.

ಕಮಿಟಿ kamiṭi, *s.* A committee, conference.

ಕಮ್ಮ kamma, *see* ಕಂಮ.

ಕಮ್ಮಿ kammi, *see* ಕಂಮಿ, ಕಡಮೆ.

ಕಮ್ಮೆನ, ಕಮ್ಯನ kammena, kamyana, *s.* Smell, odour, scent, fragrance, savour.

ಕಯ kaya, *s.* Depth, as of water *etc.* 2. swamp. *adj.* Deep; *also* ಕಯಗುಂಡಿ.

ಕಯ kaya, *see* ಕಾಯ.

ಕಯಪ್ಪ kayappa, *adv.* Entirely, wholly, all over. 2. well. —ದಪ್ಪುನಿ to plough well. —ಪೂಜುನಿ to anoint *or* besmear the whole body. —ಮೊರೆಪುನಿ to mix.

ಕಯಮೆ kayame, *s.* A kind of rice; *cf.* ಅರಿ.

ಕಯಲ್ kayalu, *see* ಕಾಯಲ್.

ಕಯಿಪು kayipu, *see* ಕಜಿಪು.

ಕಯಿಪೆ kayipe, *see* ಕೈಪೆ.

ಕಯಿಲ್ kayilu, *see* ಕೈಲ್.

ಕಯಿಲೆ kayile, *see* ಕಾಯಿಲೆ.

ಕರ kara, *s.* An earthen vessel. ಬಂಜಿದ— the stomach. —ಕೈಲ್ cooking utensils.

ಕರ kara, *s.* Pollution from death.

ಕರ kara, *s.* The hand. 2. the trunk of an elephant. 3. a spark, ray of light, *as* ದಿನ— the sun.

ಕರಂಟುನಿ karaṇṭuni, *see* ಕಂಟುೕನಿ.

ಕರಂಡೆ, ಕರಂಡೆಲ್ karaṇḍè, karaṇḍelụ, *see* ಕಂಡೇ.

ಕರಂಪೆ karampè, *s.* A wound. 2. *see* ಕರಪೆ.

ಕರಂಪೆಲ್ karampelụ, *adj.* Perforated, bored; having notches. *s.* The scar of a wound.

ಕರಂಬು karambu, *see* ಕಂಬುೕ.

ಕರಂಬುನಿ karambuni (ಕರಂಬಿ), *v. a.* To prune, cut off, as superfluous branches of a tree; to clear away, as bush, *etc.*; *cf.* ಕಂಬುೕನಿ.

ಕರಂಬೆಲ್ karambelụ, *s.* A kind of coppice.

ಕರಕ karaka, *see* ಕಕೕ.

ಕರಕರ karakara, *s.* The noise made in chewing, sawing, *or* writing.

ಕರಕರಿ, ಕರಕರೆ karakari, karakarè, *s.* Annoyance, trouble. 2. grief, sorrow, distress.

ಕರಗಸ್ karagasụ, *see* ಗರಗಸ.

ಕರಗಾವುನಿ karagāvuni, *c. v.* (*of* ಕರಗುನಿ) To melt, liquefy. 2. to affect the mind, make a person's heart melt. 3. to afflict, cause sorrow.

ಕರಗುನಿ karaguni, *v. n.* To melt, dissolve, liquefy. 2. to become thin *or* lean; to waste. 3. to become affected, softened; to relent, melt with pity; *also* ಕರಗಿದ್ಪೋಪಿನಿ.

ಕರಜಿಕಾಯಿ karajikāyi, *s.* A kind of fruit-shaped cake.

ಕರಡ್ karaḍụ, *s.* Wastage, loss, wear. *adj.* Rough, coarse; worn out. –ಕಾಗದ waste paper. –ನಕ್ಕಲ್ a rough copy. –ಆಪಿನಿ to be worn out. –ಮಳ್ಪುನಿ to waste, spoil.

ಕರಡಿ karaḍi, *s.* A bear. –ಮೆಂಯಿ ತಾಯಿ a hairy man.

ಕರಡಿಗೆ karaḍigè, *s.* A small box.

ಕರಡು karaḍu, *see* ಕರಡ.

ಕರಣ karaṇa, *s.* An organ of sense. 2. cause, instrument *or* means of action. –ತ್ರಯ the three means of action, namely, ಮನೋವಾಕ್ಕಾಯ the mind, speech and body.

ಕರಣಿಕೆ, ಕರಣೀಕೆ karaṇike, karaṇīke, *see* ಕರ್ಣಿಕೆ.

ಕರತಾಳ, karatāḷa, *s.* Cadjan. 2. a mode of beating time with the hands; *also* ಕೈತಾಳ, ಕರತಾಳಿ. –ಓಲೆ cadjan leaf.

ಕರಪುನಿ karapuni, *v. a.* To repulse, drive. 2. to urge. 3. to clear, remove. 4. to digest. 5. to waste. 6. to cause abortion; *cf.* ಕರಗಾವುನಿ.

ಕರಪೆ karapè, *s.* A notch *or* incision.

ಕರಪೆಲು karapelu, *s.* A troublesome *or* mischievous woman.

ಕರಪೆಲೆ karapele, *s.* A troublesome *or* mischievous man.

ಕರಬಸ್ karabasụ, *see* ಕಬಾಸು.

ಕರಯ karaya, *see* ಕರಾಯ.

ಕರಲೆ karalè, *s.* A swelling.

ಕರವಿ karavi, *s.* A mould.

ಕರವುನಿ **karavuni** (ಕರ), *v. n.* To be dissolved, melted. 2. to be digested. 3. to miscarry.

ಕರವೆ **karavė**, *s.* Phlegm. —ಕೋಪೆ pulmonary phthisis.

ಕರಳ್ **karaḷu**, *see* ಕಲ್ಗ.

ಕರಳೆ **karaḷe**, *see.* ಕರಲೆ.

ಕರಾಡಿ **karāḍi**, *s.* A class of Mahratta Brahmins.

ಕರಾಣಿಕೆ **karāṇike**, *see* ಕರ್ಣಿಕೆ.

ಕರಾಬ್ **karābụ**, *adj.* Filthy, dirty, unclean, bad.

ಕರಾಮತ್, ಕರಾಮತಿ, **karāmatụ, karāmati**, *s.* A miracle, wonder. 2. the power of doing wonders, *etc.*

ಕರಾಯ **karāya**, *s.* Phlegm.

ಕರಾರ್, ಕರಾರು **karārụ, karāru**, *s.* An agreement, contract. —ಮಳ್ಪುನಿ to make a contract.

ಕರಾವಳಿ **karāvaḷi**, *s.* The sea-coast, coastline.

ಕರಾವುನಿ **karāvuni**, *see* ಕರವುನಿ.

ಕರಾಳ್ **karāḷu**, *adj.* Frightful, terrible. —ಮೋಣೆ a frightful face.

ಕರಿ **kari**, *s.* Chimney soot. 2. charcoal, or any thing burnt, as the fibrous covering of a cocoanut, straw *etc. adj. see* ಕರಿಯ.

ಕರಿ **kari**, *s.* An elephant.

ಕರಿ **kari**, *s.* A bar with which a door *etc.* is fastened. 2. a pole fastened to a load, by which it is carried on the shoulders.

ಕರಿ **kari**, *s.* Castration. —ಪಾಡುನಿ to castrate.

ಕರಿಂಕ್ **kariṅkụ**, *s.* Sediment.

ಕರಿಂಚುನಿ **kariṅćuni**, *see* ಕಂಚುರ್ನಿ.

ಕರಿಜೀರಿಗೆ **karijīrigė**, *s.* Black cummin seed, *Nigella sativa.*

ಕರಿನೆಲ್ಲಿ **karinelli**, *s.* Country gooseberry.

ಕರಿಪುನಿ **karipuni** (ಕರಿ), *v. a.* To deduct, subtract. 2. to spend. 3. to remove.

ಕರಿಪೆ, ಕರಿಪೆಲ್ **karipė, karipelụ**, *s.* That which is deducted; deduction.

ಕರಿಬೀಟಿ **karibīṭi**, *s.* The real ebony.

ಕರಿಬೇವು, ಕರಿಯಬೇವು **karibēvu, kariyabēvu**, *s. Bergera koenigii*, called the curry-leaf tree, the leaves of which are used for seasoning.

ಕರಿಮರ **karimara**, *s.* Blackwood.

ಕರಿಯ **kariya**, *adj.* Black.

ಕರಿಯ **kariya**, *s.* A ferry.

ಕರಿಯತೊಳಚಿ **kariyatoḷači**, *see* ಕಪ್ಪು ತೊಳಚಿ.

ಕರಿಯದು **kariyadu**, *s.* A black woman.

ಕರಿಯದೆ **kariyade**, *s.* A black man.

ಕರಿಯನೆಕ್ಕಿ **kariyanekki**, *s.* The three leaved chaste tree, *Vitex trifolia.* 2. the plant *Gendarussa vulgaris.*

ಕರಿಯಮಣಿ **kariyamaṇi**, *s.* Black beads.

ಕರಿಯಮುಡ್ಯಲ **kariyamuḍyala**, *s.* An aromatic plant, *Andro-*

pogon Jwarancusa, with fragrant roots.

ಕರಿಯುನಿ kariyuni (ಕರಿ), *v. n.* To elapse, expire, pass as time. *aux. v.* To be able, *or* possible. ಕರಿಯಂದ ಸಂಗತಿ an unavoidable business. ಕರಿದ್ ಪೋಪಿನಿ to die; to drop down; to be over. ಯೆಂಕ್ ಪೋವಂದೆ ಕರಿಯಂದ್ I must go by all means.

ಕರೀದಿ karīdi, *s.* Price, value. –ಮಳ್ಪುನಿ to settle the price; to purchase.

ಕರು karu, *s.* Vulture. 2. *see* ಗರು.

ಕರುಂಬುನಿ karumbuni, *see* ಕೆರಗುನಿ.

ಕರುಕುಂಬುಡ karukumbuḍa, *see* ಕರ್ಕುಂಬುಡ.

ಕರುಕುರು karukuru, *s.* The noise made in chewing any brittle substance.

ಕರುಗೋಂಟು karugōṇṭu, *s.* Boiled and dried areca-nut.

ಕರುಣ karuṇa, *s.* Mercy, pity, kindness. –ಮಳ್ಪುನಿ to show mercy.

ಕರುಪು karupu, *see* ಕರ್ಪು.

ಕರುಬುನಿ karubuni, *see* ಕೆರಗುನಿ.

ಕರುಳು karuḷu, *see* ಕರ್ಲ್.

ಕರೆ karè, *see* ಖರೆ.

ಕರೆ karè, *s.* The seashore, coastline. 2. the bank of a river. 3. land, as opposed to water. 4. border, edge. 5. the coloured border of a cloth. –ಫಾಳಿ land-wind. –ಸಾದಿ by land. –ಒದ್ದುನಿ, –ಪೊಂದುನಿ to touch *or* reach the land; *see* –ಬೂರುನಿ. –ಓಡುನಿ to sail near the shore. –ಕಟ್ಟುನಿ to fasten a selvage; the horizon to become cloudy. –ಪತ್ತುನಿ to sail towards the land. –ಬೂರುನಿ to escape to the shore; to escape from danger; to recover from sickness.

ಕರೆ karè, *s.* The pole to which a bucket is attached in a country water-lift.

ಕರೆ karè, *s.* A parish, a social *or* caste jurisdictional division.

ಕರೆಂಪೆ karempè, *see* ಕರಂಪೆ.

ಕರೆಪಿನಿ karepini *see* ಕರೆಯುನಿ.

ಕರೆಪುನಿ karepuni (ಕರೆ), *v. a.* To make a notch *or* incision.

ಕರೆಮೆದಿ karemedi, *s.* The sides of a border in a rice-field.

ಕರೆಯುನಿ, ಕರೆವುನಿ kareyuni, karevuni (ಕರೆ), *v. n.* To crow.

ಕರೆಲ್ karelụ, *s.* The mark left on the skin by wearing any thing tightly.

ಕರೆಲುನಿ kareluni (ಕರೆಲ್), *v. a.* To leave a mark on the skin, as by dressing tightly *etc.*

ಕರೊಲು karolu, *see* ಕಾರೊಳು.

ಕರೊಳು karoḷu, *pl. of* ಕರ.

ಕರ್ಕ್ karkụ, *s.* A very tender cocoanut. 2. its tender shell.

ಕರ್ಕ್‌ಪುಳಿ karkụpuḷi, *s. Garcina Cambogia.*

ಕರ್ಕ karka, *adv.* At once; suddenly. 2. sharply, violently. –ತುಚ್ಚುನಿ to bite sharply –ಬುಳೆಪುನಿ to grow *or* ripen fast.

ಕರ್ಕಟ karkaṭa, *s.* A crab. 2. the Cancer in the zodiac. ಕರ್ಕಟಿ a female crab.

ಕರ್ಕಡೆಮುಳ್ಳು karkaḍemuḷḷu, *s.* A kind of thorn.

ಕರ್ಕತ್ತಲೆ karkattalè, *see* ಕಾರ್ಗತ್ತಲೆ.

ಕರ್ಕರೆ karkarè, *see* ಕರಕರಿ.

ಕರ್ಕಶ, ಕರ್ಕಸ karkaša, karkasa, *adj.* Violent, harsh, unkind. 2. cruel, hard. 3. intangible. 4. miserly. —ತನ cruelty; hardness; unkindness; intangibility; avarice, niggardliness. ಕರ್ಕಶಿ a violent *or* wicked woman. ಕರ್ಕಶೆ a violent *or* wicked man.

ಕರ್ಕಾಟಕ karkāṭaka, *see* ಕರ್ಕಟ.

ಕರ್ಕುಂಬುಡ karkumbuḍa, *s.* A pumpkin. 2. an ash-gourd.

ಕರ್ಗಂಡಕತ್ತಲೆ, ಕರ್ಗತ್ತಲೆ kargaṇḍakattalè, kargattalè, *see* ಕಾರ್ಗತ್ತಲೆ.

ಕರ್ಗಯಿ kargayi, *see* ಗರ್ಗಯಿ.

ಕರ್ಗಾವುನಿ kargāvuni, *see* ಕರಗಾವುನಿ.

ಕರ್ಗಿ, ಕರ್ಗುಡಿ kargi, karguḍi, *s.* A very black woman.

ಕರ್ಗುಡೆ karguḍe, *s.* A very black man.

ಕರ್ಗೋಟ kargōṭa, *s.* Hardness. 2. hard-heartedness. *adj.* Hard, hard-hearted.

ಕರ್ಗೋಟಿಗೆ kargōṭige, *s.* A hard-hearted man.

ಕರ್ಚಿ karči, *s.* Expenditure, expenses. ಇಲ್ಲದ— household expenses. —ತಾಗುನಿ, —ಪತ್ತುನಿ, —ಬೂರುನಿ to cost. —ಮಳ್ಪುನಿ to expend.

ಕರ್ಚಿಲ್ karčilụ, *see* ಕಡ್ಚಿಲ್.

ಕರ್ಜಾತಿ karǰāti, *s.* A black species. 2. the class of pariahs.

ಕರ್ಜಾಲಿ karǰāli, *s.* The tree *Leucas indica, Phlomis indica.*

ಕರ್ಜೂರ karǰūra, *see* ಗಜ್ಜಿರ.

ಕರ್ಡ್, ಕರ್ಡು karḍụ, karḍu, *see* ಕರಡ.

ಕರ್ಣ karṇa, *see* ಕರ್ನ.

ಕರ್ಣಕುತ್ತ karṇakutta, *adj.* Headlong, topsy-turvy. *s.* A summerset.

ಕರ್ಣಾಟಕ karṇāṭaka, *see* ಕಂನಡ.

ಕರ್ಣಾಟಿಗೆ karṇāṭige, *see* ಕಂನಡೆ.

ಕರ್ಣಿಕೆ karṇike, *s.* The sherastedar, chief ministerial officer of a collector. 2. a secretary.

ಕರ್ಣೆ karṇe, *s.* A half-brother of the Pāṇḍu princes. 2. a hard man. —ಪರ್ವ the story of Karna's exploits as given in the Mahābhārata.

ಕರ್ತ್‌ಪತ್ತುನಿ kartụpattuni (ಕಡಿ ಪತ್ತ್), *v. a.* To set-off. 2. to deduct. 3. to exclude. 4. to give up hope.

ಕರ್ತರಿಪ್ರಯೋಗ kartariprayōga, *s.* Active voice, *gram.*

ಕರ್ತವೆ kartave, *s.* An agent, maker. 2. God, lord. 3. a master, owner. 4. an author; *cf.* ಕರ್ತೃ.

ಕರ್ತಾದಿಗೆ ಕರ್ತುತ್ತಿಗೆ, kartādigè, kartuttigè, *s.* Ownership, proprietorship. 2. dominion, authority.

ಕರ್ತೃ kartrụ, *s.* The nominative of a verb, *gram.* 2. *see* ಕರ್ತವೆ.

ಕರ್ತೊದಿಗೆ kartodigè, *see* ಕರ್ತುತ್ತಿಗೆ.

ಕರ್ದ್ kardu̥, *adj.* Black. —ಬೊಲ್ದು black and white. 2. *see* ಕಡ್ದ್.

ಕರ್ನ karna, *s.* The ear. —ಕುಂಡಲ an ear-ring worn by a woman.

ಕರ್ನ karna, *s.* A black paste composed of dross of iron, kernel of wild liquorice and boiled rice, applied on the right side leather of a finger-drum.

ಕರ್ನಪರ್ವ karnaparva, *see* ಕರ್ಜ.

ಕರ್ನಾಲ್ karnālu̥, *see* ಗನ್ನಾಲ್.

ಕರ್ನಿಕೆ karnike, *see* ಕರ್ಣಿಕೆ.

ಕರ್ನಿರೆಳ್ karnireḷu̥, *s.* A dark shadow.

ಕರ್ಪು karpu, *s.* A pit, hole, ditch. 2. a pit for catching wild beasts.

ಕರ್ಪುರ, ಕರ್ಪೂರ karpura, karpūra, *s.* Camphor. 2. the thick leaved lavender. —ಬೂರು *Levendula carnosa.* ರಸ— crude calomel.

ಕರ್ಪೆಲ್, ಕರ್ಪೆಲು karpelu̥, karpelu, *see* ಕರಪೆಲು.

ಕರ್ಬ karba, *s.* Iron. —ದ ಗಂಟ್ an iron link.

ಕರ್ಬಸ್, ಕರ್ಬಾಸ್ karbasu̥, karbāsu̥, *s.* An ox of superior breed from the up-country. —ಪೆತ್ತ a ghaut cow.

ಕರ್ಬುಲೆ, ಕರ್ಬೊಳ್ಳೆ karbulè, karboḷḷè, *s.* A fowl having white plumage with black spots.

ಕರ್ಮ karma, *s.* An action in general. 2. a religious ceremony. 3. the objective case, *gram.* 4. fate; misfortune. 5. sin, transgression. —ಗತಿ the condition induced by one's deeds. ಕರ್ಮಣಿಪ್ರಯೋಗ the passive voice, *gram.* —ದೋಷ transgression. —ಫಲ the fruit of human actions. ಕರ್ಮಂತ್ರ, ಕರ್ಮಾಂತರ funeral rites. ಕರ್ಮಾಧಿಕಾರಿ a performer of funeral rites. ಕರ್ಮಿ, ಕರ್ಮಿಷ್ಟ a sinner. ಕರ್ಮೇಂದ್ರಿಯ the organ of action, as the hand, foot, *etc.*

ಕರ್ಮಣೆ karmaṇè, *see* ಕಾರ್ಮಣೆ *under* ಕಾರ್.

ಕರ್ಮರ karmara, *see* ಕರಿಮರ.

ಕರ್ಮರ್ karmaru̥, *s.* A superior kind of firewood, *Vatica laccifera.*

ಕರ್ಮುಗಲ್ karmugalu̥, *see* ಕಾರ್ ಮುಗಲ್ *under* ಕಾರ್.

ಕರ್ಮುಡ karmuḍa, *see* ಕರ್ಕುಂಬುಡ.

ಕರ್ಮುಲಿ karmuli, *s.* Thatched grass taken from a roof.

ಕರ್ಯ karya, *s.* A ferry.

ಕರ್ಯಡ, ಕರ್ಯಡೆ karyaḍa, karyaḍè, *s.* The liver, as of a fowl.

ಕರ್ಯುನಿ karyuni, *see* ಕರಿಯುನಿ.

ಕರ್ಲ್ karlu̥, *s.* The bowels. 2. the liver.

ಕರ್ಲ್‌ಕಪ್ಪಡೆ karlu̥kappaḍè, *s.* The intestines, entrails.

ಕರ್ಲೆ karlè, *see* ಕರಲೆ.

ಕರ್ವಾವುನಿ karvāvuni (ಕರ್ವಾ), *v. a.* To burn the downs of a fowl by holding it over the fire.

ಕಲ kala, *s.* A square. 2. a bed

of flowers, *etc.* 3. a place where pariahs assemble. —ಕಟ್ಟುನಿ to make a flowerbed; a group of pariahs to sit in a circle.

ಕಲಂ kalam, *s.* A reed-pen. 2. a paragraph. —ವಾರ್ detailed, item by item.

ಕಲಂಕ್, ಕಲಂಕುನಿ kalaṅkụ, kalaṅkuni, *see* ಕಳಂಕ್.

ಕಲಂತಾನಿ, ಕಲಂದಾನಿ kalamtāni, kalamdānī, *s.* An inkstand. 2. a small box.

ಕಲಂಬಿ kalambi, *see* ಕಳೆಂಬಿ.

ಕಲಂಬುನಿ kalambuni, *v. n.* To quarrel, fight.

ಕಲಕ kalaka, *see* ಕಲ್ಕ.

ಕಲಕಂಬುಲ kalakambula, *s.* A drenched miry floor.

ಕಲಕಲ kalakala, *s.* A confused noise, hum.

ಕಲಕಲ kalakala, *adv.* Brightly. —ಮಿಂಚುನಿ to shine brightly.

ಕಲಡಾವುನಿ kalaḍāvuni, *c. v.* (*of* ಕಲಡುನಿ) To mix. 2, to knead.

ಕಲಡುನಿ kalaḍuni (ಕಲಡ್), *v.n.* To be mixed. 2. to be kneaded.

ಕಲಪುನಿ kalapuni (ಕಲ), *v. a.* To mingle. 2. to knead. ಕಂಡ— to plough a watered field.

ಕಲಪ್ಪು kalappu, *adj.* Mixed. 2. kneaded.

ಕಲಬೆರಕೆ kalaberakè, *s.* Admixture, compound.

ಕಲಮ್ kalamụ, *s.* Grafting —ಮುಳ್ಪುನಿ to graft.

ಕಲಮ್, ಕಲಮು kalamụ, kalamu, *see* ಕಲಂ.

ಕಲಮೆ kalamè, *s.* A kind of rice.

ಕಲಯಿ kalayi, *see* ಕಲಾಯಿ.

ಕಲವು kalavu, *see* ಕಳವು.

ಕಲಶ, ಕಲಸ kalaša, kalasa, *s.* A pitcher, 2. a vase, goblet. 3. a spire. —ಶುದ್ಧಿ purification by pouring water. —ದೀಪಿನಿ to set up a spire.

ಕಲಸೆ kalasè, *s.* A grain measure equal to ten, twelve, fourteen, fifteen, *or* sixteen seers.

ಕಲಹ kalaha, *s.* Quarrel, dispute.

ಕಲಾಪ kalāpa, *s.* A family trial, distress, *or* dispute. 2. an ornament, zone. —ಮಳ್ಪುನಿ to quarrel; to make confusion.

ಕಲಾಯಿ kalāyi, *s.* Tinning. —ಗಾರೆ a person who tins vessels, tinker. —ಕೊರ್ಪಿನಿ, —ಪಾಡುನಿ to tin.

ಕಲಾವು kalāvu, *see* ಕಳವು.

ಕಲಾಶಿ kalāši, *s.* A sailor, lascar.

ಕಲಾಸ್ kalāsụ, *s.* Conclusion, end. 2. consumption, exhaustion. —ಆಪಿನಿ to be finished, *or* consumed. —ಮಳ್ಪುನಿ to complete; to empty.

ಕಲಾಸಿ kalāsi, *see* ಕಲಾಶಿ.

ಕಲಿ kali, *s.* Toddy; liquor.

ಕಲಿ, ಕಲಿಯುಗ kali, kaliyuga, *s.* The fourth *or* iron age of the world; the age of vice.

ಕಲಿಕೆ kalikè, *s.* Dissimulation, dissembling.

ಕಲೆ kalè, *s.* A scar. 2. a mark. blemish, stain.

ಕಲೆಂಗ್, ಕಲೆಂಗಿ kaleṅgụ, kaleṅgi, *s.* Rust, verdigris

ಕಲೆಂಬಿ kalembi, *s.* A chest, coffer. –ಶಾನಿ, –ದಾನಿ, *see* ಕಲಂದಾನಿ.

ಕಲೆಂಬಿ kalembi, *s.* The hindmost sail of a boat.

ಕಲೆಕಾರಣ kalekāraṇa, *s.* A bad affair.

ಕಲೆಕಾರ್ನಿಕ kalekārnika, *see* ಕಾರ್ನಿಕ.

ಕಲೆಪಿನಿ, ಕಲೆಪುನಿ kalepini, kalepuni (ಕಲೆ), *v. a.* To strip off, remove. 2. to subtract, deduct.

ಕಲೆವುನಿ kalevuni (ಕಲೆ), *v. n.* To be stripped. 2. to be deducted.

ಕಲ್ಕ kalka, *s.* Decoction, infusion of any drug. 2. sediment.

ಕಲ್ಕರೆ kalkarè, *s.* A place abounding in latrite stone.

ಕಲ್ಕಿ kalki, *s.* The tenth *or* last incarnation of Vishṇu, expected to put an end to the kali *or* iron age; *also* –ಅವ ತಾರ.

ಕಲ್ಕುಟ್ಟಿ, ಕಲ್ಕುಡೆ kalkuṭṭi, kalkuḍe, *s.* The name of a demon.

ಕಲ್ಕುನಿ kalkuni (ಕಲ್ಕ್), *v. n.* To cry, as a demon *or* one possessed with an evil spirit.

ಕಲ್ಕೆ kalkè, *see* ಕಲಿಕೆ.

ಕಲ್ಕೊರೆ kalkorè, s. A kind of fish.

ಕಲ್ಗಿ ರುಮಾಲ್ kalgi rumālu, *s.* A yellow handkerchief with black spots.

ಕಲ್ತಾಮರ kaltāmara, *s.* A wild kind of lotus growing on stony ground.

ಕಲ್ತೆ kaltè, *s.* Morning, the daybreak; *cf.* ಕಾಂಡೆ. –ಬೈಯ್ಯ morning and evening.

ಕಲ್ತೈಗ್ kalteigu, *adv.* (*lit.* for the mouth of toddy). Something given as a relish when sipping toddy.

ಕಲ್ನಾರ್ kalnāru, *s.* A medicinal drug.

ಕಲ್ಪ kalpa, *s.* A period of time. 2. a sacred work, one of the six Vēdāngas. 3. resolve, purpose. 4. artifice, trickery, cunning.

ಕಲ್ಪಂಡೆ kalpaṇḍè, *see* ಕಲ್ಪಣೆ.

ಕಲ್ಪಡ kalpaḍa, *s.* A fluid measure equal to twelve seers.

ಕಲ್ಪಣೆ kalpaṇè, *s.* A stone quarry.

ಕಲ್ಪನೆ kalpanè, *s.* Fiction, fable. 2. invention, fabrication. 3. producing, forming. –ಮಳ್ಪುನಿ to invent, fabricate, contrive; to produce, form; to establish.

ಕಲ್ಪರುಕ್ಷ, ಕಲ್ಪವೃಕ್ಷ kalparuksha, kalpavr̥ksha, *s.* The tree of Indra's paradise said to yield whatever is desired.

ಕಲ್ಪಾಂತ, kalpānta, *s.* The end of the world.

ಕಲ್ಪಾಂತರ kalpāntara, *s.* Another period of time, eternity.

ಕಲ್ಪಾವುನಿ kalpāvuni, *c. v.* (*of* ಕ ಲ್ಪುನಿ) To teach, instruct. 2. to instigate; *also* ಕಲ್ಪಾದ್‍ಕೊರ್ಪಿನಿ.

ಕಲ್ಪಿಸುನಿ kalpisuni (ಕಲ್ಪಿಸ್), *v. a.* To invent, fabricate.

ಕಲ್ಪುನಿ kalpuni (ಕಲ್), *v. a.* To learn, study.

ಕಲ್ಪೋಕ್ತ kalpōkta, *adv.* According to religious directions.

ಕಲ್ಮಡಿ **kalmaḍi,** *s.* A kind of fish.

ಕಲ್ಮದ **kalmada,** *s.* Bitumen, granulated gypsum from Arabia.

ಕಲ್ಮಷ **kalmasha,** *s.* Corrosion. 2. impurity. 3. sin. 4. the matter of a sore.

ಕಲ್ಯ **kalya,** *see* ಕರಿಯು.

ಕಲ್ಯಂಟೆ **kalyaṇṭè,** *see* ಕಲ್ಲಂಟೆ.

ಕಲ್ಯಾಣ **kalyāṇa,** *s.* Happiness, prosperity, good fortune. 2. marriage.

ಕಲ್ಯಾಣಿ **kalyāṇi,** *s.* The name of a tune. 2. the name of a female.

ಕಲ್ರುಟ್ಟಿ **kalruṭṭi,** *see* ಕಲ್ಲುರುಟಿ.

ಕಲ್ಲ್ **kallụ,** *s.* A stone. —ದ ಉಳಿ a chisel. —ದಕಂಬ,—ದಕಂಮು a stone pillar. —ಕಟ್ಟಣೆ, —ದ ಕಟ್ಟ a stone embankment *or* seat. —ಕಟ್ಟು ನಾಯಿ a mason. —ಪಾಪು a stone put across a stream to pass over. —ದ ಪಲಾಯಿ a slate. —ಸಂಕ a stone bridge. —ಬಸ್ತಿ a Jaina shrine. —ಬಿರು a kind of bow for discharging stones. —ಮರಿಯಿ a stone trough. —ಕಡ್ಪುನಿ to break stones. —ಕೆತ್ತುನಿ to chip stones. —ಕೊಡಿಪುನಿ a stone to grow hard. —ದ, ಕಲ್ಲ stony, made of stones. ಕಲ್ಲಾಟ playing with stones.

ಕಲ್ಲ್ ತೆತ್ತಿ **kallụtetti,** *s.* A rotten egg.

ಕಲ್ಲ್ ಬಾಗೆ **kallụbāgè,** *s.* A kind of tree, the wood of which is used as timber.

ಕಲ್ಲ್ ಬಾರೆ **kallụbārè,** *s.* A kind of plantain tree.

ಕಲ್ಲ್ ಮುಳ್ಳು **kallụmuḷḷụ,** *s.* (*lit.* stones and thorns). The mill-cog. 2. the indented surface of a mill-stone. 3. a rugged path.

ಕಲ್ಲ್ ಸಕ್ಕರೆ **kallụsakkarè,** *s.* Sugar-candy.

ಕಲ್ಲ್ ಸೂಂಟಿ **kallụsūṇṭi,** *s.* Wild ginger, *Zingiber zerumbet.*

ಕಲ್ಲ **kalla,** *s.* A kind of oyster. —ಓಡು its shell; *cf.* ಕಲ್ಲ್.

ಕಲ್ಲಂಕಲ್ಲಿ **kallaṅkalli,** *s.* A kind of bag.

ಕಲ್ಲಂಗೈ **kallaṅgei,** *s.* A kind of small fish.

ಕಲ್ಲಂಟೆ, ಕಲ್ಲಟೆ **kallaṇṭè, kallaṭè,** *s.* The Indian nightshade, *Solanum Indicum.*

ಕಲ್ಲಬಿರು **kallabiru,** *see under* ಕಲ್ಲ್.

ಕಲ್ಲಯಿ **kallayi,** *see* ಕಲ್ಲಂಗೈ.

ಕಲ್ಲರಗ **kallaraga,** *s.* Asphalt.

ಕಲ್ಲರ್ಪಡ **kallarpaḍa,** *s.* Small-pox attacking a person a second time.

ಕಲ್ಲರ್ಪೆ **kallarpè,** *s.* A kind of sieve to remove small stones from earth.

ಕಲ್ಲಾಳೆ **kallāḷe,** *s.* A class of pariahs. 2. their headman.

ಕಲ್ಲಿ **kalli,** *s.* A bag of net-work, made of ropes. 2. a wicker-work. 3. the pods of *cannabis.* 4. *see* ಕಳ್ಳಿ.

ಕಲ್ಲಿತ್ತಿ **kallitti,** *see* ಕಲ್ತೆತ್ತಿ.

ಕಲ್ಲಿರೊಳು **kalliroḷu,** *s.* A hard grown palmyra fruit.

ಕಲ್ಲುಪ್ಪು kalluppu, *s.* Rock-salt, the Bombay salt.

ಕಲ್ಲುರು kalluru, *s.* A kind of fish.

ಕಲ್ಲುರುಞ kalluruña, *adj.* Immature, half-ripe *or* half developed.

ಕಲ್ಲುರುಟಿ kalluruṭi, *s.* The name of a female Bhūta.

ಕಲ್ಲುರುನಿ kalluruni (ಕಲ್ಲುರ್), *v. n.* A stone to press *or* hurt the sole of the foot in walking.

ಕಲ್ಲೆ kallè, *s.* The straw covering of a bundle of rice; *also* ಮುದಿತ–

ಕಲ್ಲೆತ್ತಿ kalletti, *s.* A bag with divisions within.

ಕಲ್ಲೊತ್ತು kallottu, *s.* A foot-sore caused by a stone.

ಕಲ್ಲೋಲ kallōla, *s.* A large wave *or* billow.

ಕವಚ, ಕವಚೆ kavača, kavače, *s.* Armour, a coat of mail. 2. a jacket, short coat.

ಕವಟೆ kavaṭè, *see* ಕಾವಟೆ.

ಕವಡಿ, ಕವಡಿಗೆ, ಕವಡೆ kavaḍi, kavaḍigè, kavaḍè, *s.* A small shell, cowrie. –ಲೆಖ್ಖ calculation with cowries. –ಗೊಬ್ಬುನಿ to play with cowries.

ಕವಣೆ kavaṇè, *s.* A sling. –ಕಲ್ಲ್ a sling-stone.

ಕವತ್ kavatu̥, *see* ಕವಾತ್.

ಕವನ kavana, *s.* Poetry, verse. 2. invention, fabrication. –ಗಾರೆ a poet. –ಕಟ್ಟುನಿ, –ಮಳ್ಪುನಿ to compose verses; to caricature. –ಪಾತೆರುನಿ to exaggerate, invent.

ಕವಳಿಗೆ kavalige, *see* ಕಾಳಿಗೆ.

ಕವಾತ್ kavātu̥, *s.* Drill, military exercise.

ಕವಿ, ಕವೀಶ್ವರೆ kavi, kavīšvare, *s.* A poet.

ಕವಿತೆ, ಕವಿತ್ವ kavitè, kavitva, *s.* Poetry, a poem, verse.

ಕವುಂಡ್ರಸ, ಕವುಡ್ರಸ kavuṇḍrasa, kavuḍrasa, *s.* A cancer on the cheek.

ಕಶಾಯ, ಕಷಾಯ kašāya, kashāya, *s.* A decoction, extract. –ಮಳ್ಪುನಿ to extract, *or* prepare a draught.

ಕಶಿ kaši, *s.* Graft, grafting. –ಮಳ್ಪುನಿ to graft.

ಕಶಿಪಿಶಿ, ಕಶುಕುಶು, ಕಸುಕುಸು kašipiši, kašukušu, kasukusu, *adv.* In bated breath, in a whisper. –ಪಾತೆರುನಿ to whisper.

ಕಶೀದಿ, ಕಶೀಬಿ kašīdi, kašībi, *s.* Embroidery, ornamental needle work.

ಕಶ್ಯಪ kašyapa, *s.* The name of deified sage.

ಕಷ್ಟ kashṭa, *s.* Trouble, hardship. 2. labour, toil. –ಕಾಲ a time of difficulty. –ಕೊರ್ಪುನಿ to give trouble. –ಪಡೆಯುನಿ to be afflicted, to suffer. –ಬುದ್ಪಿನಿ, –ಮಳ್ಪುನಿ to work hard, take pains.

ಕಷ್ಟಿಷ್ಟ kashṭishṭa, *s.* Enmity and friendship; love and hatred.

ಕಸ್ಕಸ್ಕ kasu̥kasu̥ka, *s.* A sound produced when anything is smashed.

ಕಸ್ಕಾಯಿ, ಕಸ್ಗಾಯಿ kasukāyi, kasugāyi, *see* ಕಸ್ಕಾಯಿ.

ಕಸ್ರ್ kasuru, *see* ಕಸರ್.

ಕಸ kasa, *adj.* Brackish. ಉಪ್ಪಿಡ– anything over salted.

ಕಸ kasa, *s.* Sweepings, rubbish.

ಕಸಂಟ್ kasanṭu, *s.* Rancidity. 2. sediment. *adj.* Rancid.

ಕಸಕಸೆ kasakasè, *s.* Poppy seed of *Papaver somniferum.*

ಕಸಕ್ಕ kasakka, *adv.* Forcibly, hardly; deeply. –ಕಂತುನಿ to prick forcibly, as a thorn. –ಪಣ್ಪುನಿ to speak so as to affect another's interest, to betray.

ಕಸಬ, ಕಸಬೆ kasaba, kasabe, *s.* The chief station of a district.

ಕಸಬಿಸಿ kasabisi, *see* ಗಜಿಬಿಜಿ.

ಕಸಬು kasabu, *s.* Profession, trade, business.

ಕಸಮಾಲ್ kasamālu, *see* ಕಸ್ಮಾಲ್.

ಕಸರ್ kasaru, *s.* Remainder. 2. profit. 3. sediment.

ಕಸರ್, ಕಸರಿಗೆ kasaru, kasarigè, *s.* Dross of smelted iron. 2. fissure, flaw, holes. 3. a particle. –ಬೊಳಕುನಿ to remove the fissures of any metallic article.

ಕಸಾಕಸಿ kasākasi, *s.* Haggling.

ಕಸಾಬಿಸಿ kasābisi, *see* ಕಿಶಿಬಿಶಿ.

ಕಸಾಯ kasāya, *see* ಕಷಾಯ.

ಕಸಾಯಿ, ಕಸಾಯಿಗಾರೆ, ಕಸಾಯಿದಾಯೆ kasāyi, kasāyigāre, kasāyidāye, *s.* A butcher.

ಕಸಿ kasi, *see* ಕಶಿ.

ಕಸೀದಿ, ಕಸೂದಿ kasīdi, kasūdi, *see* ಕಶೀದಿ.

ಕಸೆ kasè, *s.* The strings *or* ties of a jacket. –ಕೋಲು a whip. –ಕಟ್ಟುನಿ to fasten the strings of a jacket.

ಕಸ್ಕಾಯಿ kaskāyi, *adj.* Half ripe.

ಕಸ್ತು kastu, *s.* Force, pressure. *adj.* Violent, severe. 2. dangerous. –ಸಂಕಟ dangerous sickness. –ಮಳ್ಪುನಿ to press, force; *also* ಕಷ್ಟು.

ಕಸ್ತೂರಿ kastūri, *s.* Musk. –ಪೂ a species of jessamine. ಮಂಜಳ– *Curcuma zedoaria*; *cf.* ಆನೆ ಮಂಜಳ್. –ಮೃಗ a musk deer. ಕಾಟ– musk-mallow, *Hebicus abelmoschus.*

ಕಸ್ಮಾಲ್ kasmālu, *adj.* Unclean, filthy, loose. –ಕೈನೆ a nasty woman.

ಕಹಳೆ kahaḷè, *s.* A bugle. ರಣ– a large bugle.

ಕಳ kaḷa, *see* ಕಲ.

ಕಳಂಕ್ kaḷanku, *s.* A spot, blemish. 2. turbidness, muddiness. 3. mistake. 4. suspicion. –ನೀರ್ turbid water. –ಮನಸ್ಸ್ a suspicious mind. ಕಳಂಕಾವುನಿ to render turbid. ಕಳಂಕುನಿ to be turbid.

ಕಳಕಳ, ಕಳಪಳ kaḷakaḷa, kalapaḷa, *s.* A confused sort of noise produced as when wading through water, *or* shaking a whole cocoanut.

ಕಳಕಳ kaḷakaḷa, *see* ಕಲಕಲ.

ಕಳಪುನಿ kaḷapuni, *see* ಕಲಪುನಿ.

ಕಳಮೆ kaḷamè, *see* ಕಲಮೆ.

ಕಳವಳ kaḷavaḷa, *s.* Anxiety, alarm. 2. anguish, sorrow. —ಆಪಿನಿ to be anxious, agitated, *or* confused.

ಕಳವು kaḷavu, *s.* Theft, robbery.

ಕಳಸೆ kaḷasè, *see* ಕಲಸೆ.

ಕಳಿ kaḷi, *see* ಕಲಿ.

ಕಳಿಯುನಿ kaḷiyuni, *see* ಕರಿಯುನಿ.

ಕಳು kaḷu, *adj.* False, untrue, not reliable. *s.* Fraud; cheating. 2. trick. 3. a lie, falsehood. —ಪಾತೆರ a falsehood. —ಸಾಕ್ಷಿ perjury, false evidence. —ಪಣ್ಪುನಿ to tell lies.

ಕಳುವೆ kaḷuve, *see* ಕಳ್ವೆ.

ಕಳೆ kaḷe, *see* ಕಲೆ.

ಕಳೆಂಗ್ kaleṅgu, *see* ಕಲೆಂಗ್.

ಕಳೆಪಿನಿ kaḷepini, *see* ಕಲೆಪಿನಿ.

ಕಳೆಯುನಿ, ಕಳೆವುನಿ kaḷeyuni, kaḷevuni (ಕಳೆ), *v. n.* To lapse, pass, as time. 2. to be exhausted, spent, as money. 3. to become loose, as the bands of a box, *etc.*; *cf.* ಕರಿಯುನಿ.

ಕಳ್ಕುನಿ kaḷkuni, *see* ಕಲ್ಕುನಿ.

ಕಳ್ವೆ kaḷve, *s.* A thief, robber.

ಕಳ್ಳ kaḷḷa, *adj.* Deceitful, dishonest, unfair. 2. under, subordinate; additional. *s.* Dishonesty. 2. stealing; *cf.* ಕಳು. —ಕೂಲಿ the swelling gums in teething. —ತಲೆಕೆ an additional piece of split bamboo. —ಮಾಡ್ an under roof.

ಕಳ್ಳಂಟಿ, ಕಳ್ಳಂಟಿಗೆ kaḷḷaṇṭi, kaḷḷaṇṭigè, *s.* Dishonesty. 2. falsehood.

ಕಳ್ಳಿ kaḷḷi, *s.* The milk-hedge, *Euphorbia;* the prickly-pear, *Opuntia dillenii.* 2. the fructification of the hemp plant *or Cannabis sativa.* ಇರೆ—, ಕೋಡ್—, ಜಿಡೆ—, ಮುಳ್ಳು— are its varieties; *cf.* ಕಲ್ಲಿ.

ಕಳ್ಳಿಗೆ kaḷḷigè, *s.* A very tender jack-fruit.

ಕಳ್ಳೆ kaḷḷe, *see* ಕಳ್ವೆ.

ಕಳ್ಳೆ kaḷḷè, *s.* A kind of grass. 2. *see* ಕಲ್ಲೆ.

ಕಕ್ಷಿ kakshi, *s.* Objection *or* reply in argument. 2. wrangling, arguing. 3. one party as opposed to another; *also* —ಗಾರೆ. ಪ್ರತಿ— an opposite party.

ಕಾಂಕರಿಯುನಿ kāṅkariyuni, *v. n.* To hawk, force up phlegm with a noise; to hem.

ಕಾಂಗ್ kāṅgu, *s.* A dark-blue cloth worn by lower classes of people, *or* used for bedding, *etc.*

ಕಾಂಗುನಿ kāṅguni (ಕಾಂಗ್), *v. n.* To be dejected. 2. to become pale.

ಕಾಂಚನ kāñcana, *s.* Gold. 2. money; *also* ಕಾಂಚಾಣ, ಕಾಂಚಾನ.

ಕಾಂಚಿ kāñci, *see* ಕಂಚಿ.

ಕಾಂಟೆ, ಕಾಂಟ್ಯ kāṇṭè, kāṇṭya, *s.* A large basket.

ಕಾಂಡ kāṇḍa, *s.* A section, division of a book.

ಕಾಂಡವ, ಕಾಂಡವನ kāṇḍava, kāṇḍavana, *s.* Indra's garden.

ಕಾಂಡಾಯಿ kāṇḍāyi, *s.* A kind of fish.

ಕಾಂಡಿಲ್ kāṇḍilu, *s.* A kind of tree; *cf.* ಪಾಂಡಿಲ್.

ಕಾಂಡೆ kāṇḍè, *adv.* Early in the morning. *s.* Morning.

ಕಾಂಡೆಯಿ kāṇḍeyi, *see* ಕಾಂಡಾಯಿ.

ಕಾಂಡೆಲ್ kāṇḍelu, *s.* A kind of tree, growing near salt water.

ಕಾಂತನೆ kāntane, *s.* A pot.

ಕಾಂತಿ kānti, *s.* Effulgence, splendour, lustre. 2. beauty, loveliness.

ಕಾಂತೆ kāntè, *s.* A wife. 2. a beloved female.

ಕಾಂಪರ್ kāmparu, *s.* A carcass. 2. a nasty man (*vlg.*) *adj.* Nasty; filthy. 2. pot-bellied.

ಕಾಂಬೋದಿ kāmbōdi, *s.* The name of a tune.

ಕಾಂಕ್ಷೆ kāṅkshe, *s.* Wish, desire. 2. passion, appetite.

ಕಾಕ್, ಕಾಕು kāku, kāku, *adj.* Bad, corrupt. –ಪೋಕ dissolute, vicious. –ಪೋಕೆರ್ wicked people.

ಕಾಕ kāka, *see* ಕಕ್ಕೆ.

ಕಾಕಬಳ್ಳಿ kākaballi, *s.* The creeper *Negretia gigantea.*

ಕಾಕಜಿ kākaji, *see* ಕಾಗಜಿ.

ಕಾಕಿ kāki, *adj.* Black, dark.

ಕಾಕುಳ kākuḷa, *s.* Rashness.

ಕಾಕೆಸೊಪ್ಪು kākesoppu, *s.* The medicinal plant *Phylanthus multiflorus*; *also* ಕಕ್ಕೆಸೊಪ್ಪು.

ಕಾಗಜಿ kāgaji, *s.* Paper. 2. a letter. –ಬರೆಪಿನಿ to write *or* address a letter. ಠಸೆ– stamp-paper.

ಕಾಗಿ kāgi, *s.* A brown colour.

ಕಾಚ್, ಕಾಚಿ kāču, kāči, *s.* Catechu, *Acacia catechu.* 2. the sediment of boiled areca-nut.

ಕಾಚಿಕಲ್ಲಿ kāčikalli, *s.* A money bag of net-work.

ಕಾಚಿಕುಂಬುಡ kācikumbuḍa, *s.* A small species of ash-gourd.

ಕಾಜಿ kāji, *s.* A Mohammedan judge *or* priest.

ಕಾಜಿ kāji, *s.* A glass bangle worn round the wrist; *also* –ಬಳೆ. –ಕಂಣ್ cat-eyed, blue-eyed.

ಕಾಜು kāju, *s.* A brown-coloured dog with black stripes.

ಕಾಟ್ kāṭu, *adj.* Wild, rude. –ಅಶ್ವತ್ಥ the wild peepul tree, *Urostigma arnottianum.* –ಕಂಚಲ the fruit of the creeper *Momordica dioica.* –ಕಲ್ಲ್ a rough stone. –ಕಾಯಿ a wild *or* jungle fruit. –ಕೇನೆ a bulbous root of *Dracontium polyphyllum.* –ಗೋಣ a bull-bison. –ತುರೆ a bottle gourd, *Lagenaria vulgaris.* –ತೇವು wild cocco, *Colocasia nymphaefolia.* –ನರ್ಗಲು the tree *Turnera ulmifolia.* –ಪದೆಂಗಿ wild green-gram, *Phaseolus rostratus.* –ಪುಗೆರೆ wild tobacco, *Lobelia nicotianaefolia.* –ಬಾರೆ a wild plantain tree. –ಮರ a wild tree. –ಯೆರು, *see* ಕಾಟಿ.

ಕಾಟ kāṭa, *s.* Trouble, annoyance, vexation. 2. danger; *also* ಕಾಟಕ. ಪುಚ್ಚೆಗ್ ಆಟ ಯೆಲಿಕ್ ಕಾಟ the cat's play is the death of mice.

ಕಾಟ kāṭa, *s.* A pyre, pile. —ಗೂ ಟುನಿ to prepare a funeral pile.

ಕಾಟಂಣೆ kāṭaṇṇe, *s.* A fowler's idol, consisting of some white-washed stones decorated with flowers. —ಗ ಮುಳ್ಪುನಿ to make an offering to it.

ಕಾಟಕಾಯಿ kāṭakāyi, *s.* Mutiny, rebellion. 2. pillage, plunder.

ಕಾಟಕೆ, ಕಾಟಿಕೆ, ಕಾಟಿಗೆ kāṭake, kāṭike, kāṭige, *s.* A trouble-some fellow.

ಕಾಟರ್ತಿ kāṭarti, *s.* The wild fig-tree, *Bauhinia tomentosa.*

ಕಾಟಾಳೆ kāṭāḷe, *s.* A rude man.

ಕಾಟಿ kāṭi, *s.* A bison.

ಕಾಟೀರ್ kāṭīrụ, *s.* A kind of tree.

ಕಾಟುನಿ kāṭuni, *see* ಕಾಡ್ಯುನಿ.

ಕಾಟೆ kāṭe *s.* A wild untamed beast.

ಕಾಟೆರು kāṭeru, *see* ಕಾಟ.

ಕಾಡ್ kāḍụ, *s.* A jungle, forest. *adj.* Wild, rude; *cf.* ಕಾಟ. —ಕರೆ forest and river-bank. —ಕಾರೊಳು, —ಕಾರೆ the plant *Toddalia aculeata.* —ಕಿಚ್ಚ್ wild fire. —ಕುರಿ a jungle sheep. —ಕೊಂಕಣಿ a lower class of people speaking the Koṅkaṇi language. —ಕೋಳಿ a jungle fowl. —ಜಾತಿ a wild class *or* tribe. —ನರಮಾನಿ a rustic *or* rude man. —ನೀರ್ rain-water rushing through a jungle and washing down all the rubbish in its course. —ಮಾಮೆ (*lit.* a jungle-uncle), a tiger. —ಮೃಗ a wild beast. —ಕಾಡಳಂಬುದ the angular-leaved physic-nut, *Jatropha curcas.*

ಕಾಡ kāḍa, *adj.* Wild, untamed.

ಕಾಡಾಕಡಿ kāḍākaḍi, *see* ಕಡಾಕಡಿ.

ಕಾಡಾನೆ kāḍānè, *s.* A wild elephant.

ಕಾಡಿಕಳ್ kāḍikaḷụ, *s.* A kind of song.

ಕಾಡಿಕೊರಗೆ kāḍikorage, *s.* A man of the Koragar caste living in jungles.

ಕಾಡಿಗೆ kāḍigè *s.* A collyrium of lamp-black and oil. —ಬರಣಿ a collyrium box.

ಕಾಡಿನಾಯೆ kāḍināye, *see* ಕಾಡಿಕೊರಗೆ.

ಕಾಡುಳ್ಳಿ kāḍuḷḷi, *s.* The Indian squill, *Scilla Indica.*

ಕಾಡೆ kāḍè, *s.* A quail, *Tetras coturnix.*

ಕಾಡ್ಯುನಿ kāḍyuni (ಕಾಡಿ), *v. a.* To trouble, torment, importunate; *also* ಗಾಡ್ಯುನಿ.

ಕಾಣ್ಸಾವುನಿ, ಕಾಣಿಸಾವುನಿ kāṇụsāvuni, kāṇisāvuni (ಕಾಣಿಸು), *v. a.* To show, represent, mention.

ಕಾಣಪುರ್ಲಿ kāṇapurli, *s.* The bird *mina.*

ಕಾಣಿ kāṇi, *s.* The fraction one-sixty-fourth.

ಕಾಣಿಕೆ, ಕಾಣಿಗೆ kāṇikè, kāṇigè, *s.* A money offering; a present to a superior. —ಕೊರ್ಪಿನಿ, —ದೀಪಿನಿ, —ಪಾಡುನಿ to make an offering.

ಕಾಣೆ kāṇè, *s.* A kind of fish. —ಕಾರ್ long-legged. —ಕಾರ್ದಾಯೆ a long legged man.

ಕಾತಿ kāti, *see* ಖ್ಯಾತಿ.

ಕಾತೊಣುನಿ kātoṇuni, *refl. v.* (*of* ಕಾಪುನಿ) To wait; to expect.

ಕಾದಾಟ kādāṭa, *s.* A fight, war, battle.

ಕಾದಾಡುನಿ kādāḍuni (ಕಾದಾಡಿ), *v. n.* To fight.

ಕಾದಿ kādi, *see* ಕಾಜಿ.

ಕಾದಿ kādi, *see* ಖಾದಿ.

ಕಾದುನಿ kāduni (ಕಾದ್), *v. n.* To quarrel, fight, wrestle.

ಕಾನ kāna, *s.* A rookery.

ಕಾನ, ಕಾನನ kāna, kānana, *s.* A forest, jungle, wood.

ಕಾನಾಪುರ್ಲಿ kānāpurli, *see* ಕಾಣ ಪುರ್ಲಿ.

ಕಾನೂನ್ kānūnu, *s.* A rule, regulation.

ಕಾನೆ kānė, *see* ಕಾಣೆ, ಖಾನೆ.

ಕಾಪಾಟ kāpāṭa, *s.* The act of watching; guard.

ಕಾಪಾಡುನಿ kāpāḍuni (ಕಾಪಾಡಿ), *v. a.* To protect, preserve.

ಕಾಪಿ kāpi, *s.* Coffee.

ಕಾಪು kāpu, *s.* Protecting 2. watching, tending. 3. brooding; hatching. 4. a scarecrow. —ಗ್ ಕುಳ್ಳುನಿ to brood; to hatch. —ದೀಪಿನಿ to set up some thing in a field *or* garden, to avert the effects of evil eyes; to set up a scarecrow.

ಕಾಪುನಿ kāpuni (ಕಾ), *v. a.* To watch, guard. 2. to keep, preserve, protect. 3. to wait.

ಕಾಪೆಲೆ kāpele, *s.* A watchman.

ಕಾಪ್ಪು kāppu, *see* ಕಾಪು.

ಕಾಮ kāma, *s.* Desire, wish. 2. lust, passion.

ಕಾಮಂಗಾಯಿ kāmaṅgāyi, *s.* A wild species of green gram, *Phaseolus rostratus.*

ಕಾಮಕ, ಕಾಮಕಾ kāmaka, kāmakā, *adv.* Positively certainly.

ಕಾಮಕಸ್ತೂರಿ kāmakastūri, *s.* Sweet Basil, *Ocimum Basilicum.*

ಕಾಮಗಾರಿ, kāmagāri, *s.* Work; *also* ಕಾಮಕಾರಿ, ಕಾಮಗ್ರಿ.

ಕಾಮಚಕ್ರೇಶ್ವರೆ, kāmaćakrēšvare, *see* ಕಾಮೆ.

ಕಾಮದೆ kāmade, *s.* A liberal man.

ಕಾಮಧೇನು kāmadhēnu, *s.* The cow of Indra's paradise, said to give whatever is wished.

ಕಾಮಪಾಲೆ kāmapāle, *s.* A name of Balarāmā, the elder brother of Krishṇa.

ಕಾಮಲಿ kāmali, *see* ಕಾಮೆಲಿ.

ಕಾಮವಿಕಾರ kāmavikāra, *s.* Lust, inordinate affection.

ಕಾಮಾಟಿ kāmāṭe, *s.* A man of the mercantile class. 2. a niggardly *or* cunning man.

ಕಾಮಾತುರ kāmātura, *s.* Lust, inordinate affection. *adj.* Libidinous.

ಕಾಮಾರಿ kāmāri, *s.* Šiva the enemy of Cupid.

ಕಾಮಾರ್ಥ kāmārtha, *see* ಕಾಮ್ಯಾರ್ಥ.

ಕಾಮಾಕ್ಷಿ kāmākshi, *s.* A goddess.

ಕಾಮಿ kāmi, *s.* A debauchee.

ಕಾಮಿತಾರ್ಥ kāmitārtha, *s.* The object of desire.

ಕಾಮಿನಿ kāmini, *s.* A pretty woman.

ಕಾಮಿಲಿ kāmili, *see* ಕಾಮೆಲಿ.

ಕಾಮಿಸುನಿ kāmisuni (ಕಾಮಿಸ್), *v. a.* To covet; to wish.

ಕಾಮುಕ kāmuka, *adj.* Lustful, libidinous. ಕಾಮುಕೆ a libidinous man.

ಕಾಮೆ kāme, *s.* Cupid.

ಕಾಮೆಲಿ kāmeli, *s.* A kind of jaundice. ಊದು– a dropsical kind of jaundice. ಪಿತ್ತ– a salivary kind of jaundice. ಬರಂಟ– jaundice with scab.

ಕಾಮ್ಯ kāmya, *adj.* Desirable, agreeable.

ಕಾಮ್ಯಾರ್ಥ kāmyārtha, *s.* The object of desire.

ಕಾಯ kāya, *s.* The body. –ಕಷ್ಟ bodily exertion. –ಗುಂಡಿ the heart. –ಪುಷ್ಟಿ stoutness. –ದೆಪ್ಪುನಿ to commit suiside. –ಬುಡ್ಪುನಿ to lay down the body, to die.

ಕಾಯಂ, ಕಾಯಮ್ kāyam, kāyamu, *s.* Permanency, settled state. *adj.* Fixed, confirmed, permanent. –ಕೆಲಸ permanent employment. –ಮಳ್ಪುನಿ to confirm, settle, establish.

ಕಾಯಮೆ kāyame, *see* ಕಯಮೆ.

ಕಾಯರ್ kāyaru, *see* ಕಾಯೆರ್.

ಕಾಯಲ್, ಕಾಯಳ್, kāyalu, kāyaḷu, *s.* A folded tender leaf of plants *or* trees. 2. seasoning. –ಇರೆ a tender leaf; *cf.* ಕಾಯೆಲ್.

ಕಾಯಲೆ kāyale, *see* ಕಾಯಿಲೆ.

ಕಾಯಾವುನಿ kāyāvuni, *c. v.* (*of* ಕಾಯುನಿ) To have anything warmed, burned, boiled.

ಕಾಯಿ kāyi, *s.* An unripe fruit of any kind. 2. a cocoanut. 3. the seed. –ಅತ್ರಸ, –ಕಡುಬು a kind of cake. –ಕಂಡೆ vegetables and roots; pulse. –ಕಜಿಪು vegetables in general. –ಕೋಳಿಗೆ a kind of cake. –ಕಡೆಪಿನಿ, –ಕಡೆಯುನಿ to chew the cud. –ಕೋಪಿನಿ to over-boil; to get loose.

ಕಾಯಿದ, ಕಾಯಿದೆ kāyida, kāyide, *s.* Rule, regulation. 2. custom.

ಕಾಯಿಪುನಿ kāyipuni, *c. v.* (*of* ಕಾಯುನಿ) To make hot, warm, as water. 2. to fry, broil.

ಕಾಯಿಪುನಿ kāyipuni, *see* ಕೈಪುನಿ.

ಕಾಯಿಲೆ kāyile, *s.* Sickness.

ಕಾಯಿಳಿತ kāyiḷita, *adj.* Infertile.

ಕಾಯುನಿ kāyuni (ಕಾಯಿ), *v. n.* To burn, to be hot. 2. to get ripe. 3. to be feverish. 4. to become angry. 5. to be tight, *or* fast; *see* ಕಾಯಿಪುನಿ. ಗಂಟ– a knot to be tight *or* fast. ಜೋಂಬು– the sun to be very hot. ನೀರ್– water to boil. ಬಂಜಿ– to be very hungry. ಮೆಯ್– to be feverish *or* hot. ರೊಟ್ಟಿ– bread to bake.

ಕಾಯೆರ್ kāyeru, *s.* Strychnia, *Nux vomica.* *also* –ಕಾಯಿ. –ಮರ the nux vomica tree. –ದ ಬಂದನಿಗೆ *Loranthus loniceroides.*

ಕಾಯೆರ್ಪುಳಿ kāyerupuḷi, *s.* A kind of sour-leafed tree.

ಕಾಯೆಲ್ kāyelu, *s.* The state of being green *or* unripe. 2. seasoning. –ಆಪಿನಿ to become green *or* fresh. –ಕೊಬ್ಬಿನ to season.

ಕಾಯೋಡೆ kāyōḍè, *s.* A kind of cake.

ಕಾರ್ kāṛụ, *s.* The leg. 2. the foot. –ದ ಕಂಕ್ಕು knuckle. –ದ ಬಿರಲ್ the toe. –ನಡಕೆ going *or* walking on foot. –ಪೊಟ್ಟಿ the ancle. ತೇವುದ– the stalk of cocco, *Arum colocasia.* –ಮಣೆ a footstool. –ಊರುನಿ to tread *or* fix the foot. –ಕೊಬ್ಬಿನಿ to run away. –ಜಾರುನಿ to slip the foot, lose balance; to be reduced in one's circumstances. –ತುಡೆ the thigh. –ದೀಪಿನಿ to place the foot. –ನೀಡುನಿ to stretch the leg. –ಪತ್ತುನಿ to prostrate, do obeisance.

ಕಾರ್ kāṛụ, *adj.* Black, dark. –ಮಿಂಚಿ lightning issuing from black clouds. –ಮುಗಲ್ black clouds. –ಕಾಲ *see* ಕಾರ್ಕಾಲ.

ಕಾರ್ಕೂನೆ kāṛụkūne, *s.* A clerk, writer.

ಕಾರ್ಖಾನೆ kāṛụkhānè, *s.* An establishment. 2. a workshop. 3. management.

ಕಾರ್ತುಡೆ kāṛụtuḍè, *s.* The thigh.

ಕಾರ್ಬಾರ್, ಕಾರ್ಬೇರ್ kāṛụbāṛụ, kāṛụbēṛụ, *see* ಕಾಬಾರ್ಬ.

ಕಾರ kāra, *s.* Tasting or smelling hot; *also* ಖಾರ. *adj.* Hot, sharp, pungent. ಪಟ್ಟಿ– alum.

ಕಾರ kāra, *s.* A prison, jail.

ಕಾರ kāra, *A termination affixed to a letter, as* ಅಕಾರ the letter ಅ, *etc.*

ಕಾರಂಗ kāraṅga, *s.* A cutaneous disease which renders the skin black. –ಪತ್ತುನಿ to suffer from such a disease.

ಕಾರಂಜಿ kārañji, *s.* An artificial fountain, a kind of siphon; an underground channel.

ಕಾರಂಟ kāraṇṭa, *see* ಕಾರಕುಂಟ.

ಕಾರಂಡ kāraṇḍa, *adv.* Excessively, exceedingly, very. –ಕೈಪೆ very bitter.

ಕಾರಂಡೆ kāraṇḍè, *see* ಕಂಡೆ.

ಕಾರಕ kāraka, *s.* An agent. 2. acting, doing, *gram.* 3. a tax. –ಕೊಬ್ಬಿನಿ to pay a tax.

ಕಾರಕಣ್ಣ್ kārakaṇṇụ, *s.* The ankle. –ಕುಟ್ಟುನಿ to thump the ankle, as a punishment. –ಮುಟ್ಟ ಕುತ್ತುನಿ to dress down to the ankles, *i. e.* completely; to be foppish.

ಕಾರಕಡ, ಕಾರಗಡಗ kārakaḍa, kāragaḍaga, *s.* A kind of anklet.

ಕಾರಕಾಯಿ kārakāyi, *see* ಕಾರೆಕಾಯಿ.

ಕಾರಕುಂಟ, ಕಾರಕುತ್ತ, ಕಾರಗುಂಟ kārakuṇṭa, kārakutta, kāraguṇṭa, *s.* A disease of cattle, called Epyzootic aphthæ.

ಕಾರಗಂಟ್ kāragaṇṭụ, *s.* The ankle. 2. a corn on the toe. –ಪೊಲಿಪುನಿ to fracture the ankle.

ಕಾರಡಿ kāraḍi, *s.* A footstep. 2. the sole of the foot.

ಕಾರಣ kāraṇa, *s.* Reason, purpose, motive. 2. cause, as opposed to effect.

ಕಾರಣಿಕ kāraṇika, *s.* A miracle. 2. supernatural power. *adj.*

Miraculous, supernatural. —ಋಷಿ a prophet.

ಕಾರಬಾರ್ kārabārụ, *see* ಕಾರ್ಬಾರ್.

ಕಾರವೆ kārave, *s.* One belonging to the class of the Konkaṇi speaking fishermen.

ಕಾರಾಜಿ kārāji, *s.* A low class of pariahs.

ಕಾರಾಡಿಗೆ kārāḍige, *see* ಕರಾಡಿ.

ಕಾರಾವುನಿ kārāvuni, *c.v.* (*of* ಕಾರುನಿ) To cause to vomit.

ಕಾರಿ kāri, *A termination affixed to nouns to signify one's profession*; *as*, ಭಿಕಾರಿ a beggar.

ಕಾರಿ kāri, *s.* A nest. 2. a black bull, ox. *adj.* Black, dark. —ಪೆತ್ತ a black cow. ಕಕ್ಕೆ— a raven-nest. —ಕಟ್ಟುನಿ to build a nest.

ಕಾರುನಿ kāruni (ಕಾರ್), *v. a.* To vomit.

ಕಾರುಪ್ಪು kāruppu, *s.* A strong *or* black sort of salt.

ಕಾರುಬಾರ್ kārubārụ, *see* ಕಾರ್ಬಾರ್.

ಕಾರೂರುನಿ kārūruni, *see* ಕಾರ್.

ಕಾರೆ kāre, *see* ಗಾರೆ.

ಕಾರೆ kārè, *s.* A kind of neck-lace *or* collar. ಪಿತ್ತಲೆದ— a brass collar worn by pariah women.

ಕಾರೆಕಾಯಿ kārekāyi, *s.* A dried date fruit. —ದ ಮುಡ್ಡಿ rotten *or* shrivelled date fruits. —ದ ಮರ a date tree.

ಕಾರೊಳು kāroḷu, *s.* A kind of wild *Cacinia Indica.*

ಕಾರ್ಯ kārya, *see* ಕಾರ್ಯ.

ಕಾರ್ಕಲ kārkala, *s.* The town of Karkal.

ಕಾರ್ಕಾಲ kārkāla, *s.* Cloudy *or* rainy weather.

ಕಾರ್ಗತ್ತಲೆ kārgattalè, *s.* Thick darkness.

ಕಾರ್ಣಿಕೆ kārṇikè, *see* ಕರ್ಣಿಕೆ.

ಕಾರ್ತಿ kārti, *s.* The third solar month. 2. the sign of *Gemini* in the zodiac. —ದ ಬುಳೆ the first crop. —ಪೂಜೆ the worship of an idol, consisting of waving of lamps in fulfilment of a vow.

ಕಾರ್ತಿಕ kārtika, *s.* The eighth lunar month.

ಕಾರ್ತೆಲ್, ಕಾರ್ತೆಳ್ kārtelụ, kārteḷụ, *see* ಕಾರ್ತಿ.

ಕಾರ್ಪಣ್ಯ kārpaṇya, *s.* Trouble, vexation; importunity, dunning. —ಬುಡ್ಪುನಿ to trouble, dun.

ಕಾರ್ಬಾರ್ kārbārụ, *s.* Rule, management, superintendence; control. ಕಾರ್ಬಾರಿ a manager, superintendent.

ಕಾರ್ಮುಗಲ್ kārmugaḷụ, *s.* A dark cloud.

ಕಾರ್ಯ kārya, *s.* Work, business, affair. 2. a ceremony. 3. cause, motive. 4. effect.

ಕಾರ್ವೆ kārve, *see* ಕಾರವೆ.

ಕಾಲ್ kālụ, *s.* A quarter, the fourth part of a unit. *adj.* One-fourth.

ಕಾಲ kāla, *s.* Time, tense of the verb. 2. season. —ಜ್ಞಾನಿ a diviner, seer; an astrologer. —ಚಕ್ರ the revolution *or* circle of time. —ದೋಷ the vicissitude of the times, evil days; misfortune. —ಪುರುಷ the right man in the right place, a man whose life opens a new epoch in human affairs. —ಭೇದ the vicissitude of time; change of seasons. —ಸಂಧಿ the conjunction of two periods of time, as morning, noon, evening. —ಹರಣ, whiling away time, procrastination. —ಕ್ಷೇಪ livelihood, maintenance. —ಕಳಿಯಿಸು, —ದಬ್ಬಿಸು to while away the time; to procrastinate; to live wretchedly. —ಬಹಿರ್ಗಿಸು the end to approach, to die.

ಕಾಲ kāla, *adj.* Black, dark.

ಕಾಲಂಗ್, ಕಾಲಂಗ kālaṅgu, kālaṅga, *s.* A lever. —ಮೀಟುನು to lift with a lever.

ಕಾಲಗತಿ kālagati, *s.* The progress *or* condition of time.

ಕಾಲಜೀರಿಗೆ, ಕಾಲಜೀರ್ದರಿ kālajīrigè, kālajīrdari, *s.* Black cummin seed, *Vernonia anthelmintica.*

ಕಾಲಪಿಲ್ಲಿ kālapilli, *s.* A silver ornament worn on the toes.

ಕಾಲಭೈರವೆ kālabheirave, *s.* One of the sons of Šiva.

ಕಾಲಮಿಣಿಕೆ kālamiṇikè, *s.* A kind of medicine.

ಕಾಲರುದ್ರೆ, ಕಾಲಾಂತಕೆ kālarudre, kālāntake, *s.* Šiva the destroyer.

ಕಾಲಹರಣ kālaharaṇa, *s.* Whiling away time.

ಕಾಲಕ್ಷೇಪ kālakshēpa, *s.* Passing *or* whiling away time. 2. maintenance, support.

ಕಾಲಾಂತರ kālāntara, *s.* The course *or* lapse of time.

ಕಾಲಾವಧಿ kālāvadhi, *s.* The end of a year, season *or* period of time.

ಕಾಲಿ kāli, *see* ಖಾಲಿ.

ಕಾಲಿಗೊಬ್ಬು kāligobbu, *s.* A kind of game. 2. playing for nothing.

ಕಾಲಿವೆ kālivè, *s.* A channel for irrigation. 2. a canal.

ಕಾಲು kālu, *see* ಕಾಳು.

ಕಾಲೆ kālè, *see* ಕುಲೆ.

ಕಾಲೆ kale *s.* A black man. 2. a black dog, *etc.*

ಕಾಲೋಚಿತ kālōcita, *adj.* Opportune, well timed; according to the times.

ಕಾವಂಟೆ, ಕಾವಟೆ kāvaṇṭè, kāvaṭè, *s.* The tree *Zanthoxylon rhetsa.*

ಕಾವಂದೆ kāvande, *s.* A master, lord, proprietor, owner.

ಕಾವಡಿ kāvaḍi, *s.* A split bamboo with ropes suspending from each end, for carrying burdens across the shoulders.

ಕಾವಲ್ kāvalu, *s.* Guard, custody, watch; protection. —ಗಾಯಿ a guard, watchman. —ದೀಪಿಸು to place a guard. —ಮಳ್ಪುನಿ to mount guard.

ಕಾವಲಿ kāvali, *see* ಕಾವೊಲಿ.

ಕಾವಿ kāvi, *s.* Red ochre; *also* —ಕಲ್ಲ್.

ಕಾವು kāvu, *s.* Heat, warmth. 2. the rind *or* scraping of vegetables, *etc.* —ಹೆರೆಸುನಿ to scrape away the skin of vegetables, *etc.*

ಕಾವೆ kāvè, *adj.* Red. —ದ ಕೆಂಟು the red garb of an ascetic.

ಕಾವೆರಮರ kāveramara, *see* ಕಾಯಿರ್ ಮರ.

ಕಾವೇರಿ kāvēri, *s.* The river Kāvēri. 2. a female's name. —ಸಂಕ್ರಾಂದಿ a festival in honor of that river held on the 1st day of the 7th solar month.

ಕಾವೊಲಿ kāvoli, *s.* A frying pan.

ಕಾವ್ಯ kāvya, *s.* Poetry. 2. a poetical work; *cf.* ಕವನ. —ಮಾಲೆ a garland of poetry, poetical anthology.

ಕಾಶಿ kāśi, *s.* Benares. *adj.* White. —ಕಾಗಜಿ a white paper. —ಕಾವಡಿ, *see* ಕಾವಡಿ. —ಗಯಾಳೆ, —ಗ ಯೊಳೆ a Benares priest; an oppressor. —ಜೋಳ the Indian corn. —ದಡಕ a strong, white cloth. —ಭಾಗೀರಥಿ the Ganges water; *also* —ತೀರ್ಥ.

ಕಾಶಿರೋಗ kāśirōga, *s.* Lunacy.

ಕಾಶ್ಮೀರ್ kāśmīrụ, *s.* The province of Cashmere. 2. a superior kind of woollen cloth.

ಕಾಶ್ಯಪ kāśyapa, *s.* A sage of that name.

ಕಾಷಾಯಿ kāshāyi, *s.* The red garb of an ascetic.

ಕಾಸ್ kāsụ, *s.* A cash, an old copper coin worth half a pie. ಕ್ರಿಡಿ— the fraction of a cash. ಕಾಸಂಪ್ರಿ a destitute *or* worthless man.

ಕಾಸರಿಕೆ kāsarikè, *s.* Selfconfession.

ಕಾಸಾ kāsā, *adj.* Own. —ಮೆಗ್ಗಿ one's own younger brother.

ಕಾಸಿ kāsi, *see* ಕಾಶಿ.

ಕಾಸಿಗೆ kāsigè, *adj.* Private, personal. —ಲೆಖ್ಖ private accounts.

ಕಾಸಿತಾಳಿ kāsitāḷi, *s.* The marriage badge worn round the neck of a woman.

ಕಾಹಳ kāhaḷa, *adj.* Black, dark. —ಸರ್ಪ a kind of very poisonous serpent.

ಕಾಹಳೆ kāhaḷè, *see* ಕಹಳೆ.

ಕಾಹಾಳೋರಗೆ kāhāḷōrage, *see* ಕಾಳೋರಗೆ. [*etc.*

ಕಾಳ್ kāḷụ, *s.* A grain, as of rice,

ಕಾಳ kāḷa, *adj.* Black, dark. —ಬೆರು a wild cat. —ಯೆರು a black buffalo. —ರಾತ್ರಿ a very dark night.

ಕಾಳಂಗ್ kāḷaṅgụ, *see* ಕಾಲಂಗ್.

ಕಾಳಕೊಟ್ಟೆ kāḷakoṭṭè, *adv.* Extremely; very. —ಕೈಪೆ extremely bitter.

ಕಾಳಗ kāḷaga, *s.* War, fight, battle.

ಕಾಳಜೀರಿಗೆ kāḷajīrigè, *see* ಕಾಲಜೀರಿಗೆ.

ಕಾಳಮ್ಮ kāḷamma, *s.* A name of Kāḷi. 2. a female's name.

ಕಾಳಿ kāḷi, *s.* Blackness. 2. the goddess Kāḷi. 3. a black cow.

ಕಾಳಿಂಗ kāḷiṅga, *s.* A bird. 2. a snake. 3. an elephant. —ನಾಗೆ, —ಸರ್ಪ a black serpent.

ಕಾಳಿಗ kāḷiga, *see* ಕಾಳಗ.

ಕಾಳಿತಾಕ್ಷಿ kāḷitākshi, *s*. The fifty-second year of the Hindu cycle.

ಕಾಳಿದಾಸೆ kāḷidāse, *s*. A celebrated ancient poet.

ಕಾಳೀಯ kāḷīya, *see* ಕಾಳೋರಗೆ.

ಕಾಳು kāḷu, *s*. A black dog. 2. a man's name. *adj*. Black.

ಕಾಳೆ kāḷe, *s*. Death.

ಕಾಳೋರಗೆ kāḷōrage, *s*. A black [serpent.

ಕಿಂಕನ kiṅkana, *see* ಕಿಣ್ಕಣ.

ಕಿಂಕರೆ kiṅkare, *s*. A man-servant, slave. ಕಿಂಕರತನ servitude, slavery.

ಕಿಂಕಿನಿ kiṅkini, *adj*. Trickish. –ಕೊಬ್ಬು, –ವಿದ್ಯ a trick; trickery. –ಬಿತ್ತ a kind of medicine. *see* ಕಿಣಿಕಿಣಿ.

ಕಿಂಕುನಿ kiṅkuni, *see* ಕಿನ್ಕುನಿ.

ಕಿಂಗುಡೆ kiṅguḍe, *see* ಕೆಂಗುಡೆ.

ಕಿಂಚನಿಲ್ kiṅčanilu, *s*. A red squirrel.

ಕಿಂಡೆ kiṇḍe, *see* ಗಿಂಡೆ.

ಕಿಂಣಿಕಿಟ್ಟಿ kiṇṇikiṭṭi, *s*. Sounding, as a broken bell.

ಕಿಂತನ kintana, *s*. Canvas. 2. linen. –ಕುಂಟು packing cloth.

ಕಿಂತಲ್, ಕಿಂತಲ kintalu, kintala, *s*. The beam of a pair of scales; *also* ಚಿಂತಲ್.

ಕಿಂನರಿ kinnari, *s*. A lute, fiddle. –ರಾಗ, –ಶಬ್ದ the tune of a lute. –ಬಾರಿಸುನಿ to play upon a lute.

ಕಿಂನಿ kinni, *adj*. Small, little, young. *s*. The young of an animal. 2. smallness. ಕೋರಿದ– a chicken. –ನಾಲಾಯಿ uvula, *epiglottis;* a disease under the tongue, called frog. –ಪತಲ್ a small corn; the *Ricinus* seed. –ಬಿತ್ತ a kind of rice. –ಬಿರಲ್ the little finger; *cf.* ಕಿಣ್ಣಬಿರೆಲ್. –ಬುದ್ಧಿ narrow-mindedness; senselessness. –ಮಲ್ಲ old and young. –ಮೋಣೆ a dejected face. –ದೀಪಿನಿ, –ಪಾಡುನಿ to bring forth, yean, as sheep.

ಕಿಂಪುರುಷೆ kimpurushe, *s*. A fabulous bird with a human face.

ಕಿಂಮತ್ kimmatu, *s*. Value, price. –ಕಟ್ಟುನಿ to fix the value.

ಕಿಂಪಿರ್ಲ್ kirmpilu, *see* ಕಿರ್ಪಿಲ್.

ಕಿಂಬರ್ರುನಿ kirmbaruni, *see* ಕಿಂಬುರ್ನಿ.

ಕಿಂಬಾರ್ಟ kirmbāṭa, *s*. An itching sensation. 2. scratching.

ಕಿಂಬಿರ್ಲ್ kirmbilu, *s*. The ear-wax. –ತಟ್ಟುಗ an ear-pick.

ಕಿಂಬಿರ್ಲ್ಲ್ kirmbillu, *see* ಕಿರ್ಪಿಲ್.

ಕಿಂಬುರ್ನಿ kirmbuni (ಕಿಂಬ್ರ್), *v. n.* To itch. *v. a.* To rub, scratch.

ಕಿಂಬೆರ್ಲ್ kirmbelu, *s*. Itching. 2. scratching. –ಕೇವು a kind of nettlish Cocco, *Colocasia nymphæfolia*.

ಕಿಗ್ಗ kigga, *adj*. Little, small.

ಕಿಚಿಕಿಚಿ kičikiči, *s*. Chirping. 2. prattling. *adj*. Bruised, jellied. –ತೊಪ್ಪರ್ನಿ to tread to a jelly. –ಮಲ್ಪುನಿ to chirp; to prattle.

ಕಿಚಿಡಿ, ಕಿಚೆಡಿ kičiḍi, kičeḍi, *s*. Boiled rice mixed with split pulse and jaggory. –ಬಂಣದ ಶೀರೆ a female's brown coloured garment.

ಕಿಚಿತ kićita, *see* ಕಿಚ್ಚಿ.

ಕಿಚ್ಚಡಿ kiććaḍi, *see* ಕಿಚಿಡಿ.

ಕಿಚ್ಚಿ, ಕಿಚ್ಚು, ಕಿಚ್ಚೆ kićći, kićću, kićće, *s.* Fire. 2. envy. 3. indigestion, disorder of the stomach. ಕಾಡ— a jungle fire. ಹೊಟ್ಟೆ— envy, hatred.

ಕಿಚ್ಚಿಡಿ, ಕಿಚ್ಚೊಡಿ kiććiḍi, kiććoḍi, *see* ಕಿಚಿಡಿ.

ಕಿಚ್ಚೆಲಿ kiććeli, *s.* A musk-rat.

ಕಿಜನ್, ಕಿಜಾನ್ kijanų, kijānų, *s.* A kind of fish. —ತರು its spawn.

ಕಿಜಲುನಿ kijaluni, *see* ಗಜಿಲುನಿ.

ಕಿಜಿಕಿಟ್ಟಿ kijikiṭṭi, *s.* A boy's toy; a rattle.

ಕಿಜಿಬಿಜಿ kijibiji, *see* ಗಜಿಬಿಜಿ.

ಕಿಜೆಲುನಿ kijeluni, *see* ಗಜೆಲುನಿ.

ಕಿಟ್ಕ kiṭųka, *see* ಕಿಸ್ಕ.

ಕಿಟ್ಕಿಟ್ kiṭųkiṭų, *s.* Annoyance, disturbance, teasing. —ಗಾರೆ a tormentor. —ಆಪಿನಿ to be vexed. —ಮಳ್ಪುನಿ to vex, disturb.

ಕಿಟಿ kiṭi, *see* ಕಿಡಿ.

ಕಿಟಿಕಿ kiṭiki, *s.* A window.

ಕಿಟಿಕಿಟಿ kiṭikiṭi, *s.* Ticking, as a watch; a small sound produced by tapping on a flat substance. 2. giggling, tittering. —ತೆಲ್ಪುನಿ to titter.

ಕಿಟ್ಟ kiṭṭa, *s.* Sediment of boiled areca-nut. 2. scoria; dross of smelted iron. 3. proximity. *adj.* Near. —ಪಾಡುನಿ to repair *or* cement an earthen *or* stone vessel with the powdered dross.

ಕಿಡಿ kiḍi, *s.* A spark. 2. a small precious stone. —ಆಪಿನಿ to become enraged. —ಪಾರುನಿ, —ರ ಟ್ಟುನಿ, —ರಾಪುನಿ sparks to fly.

ಕಿಣಿ kiṇi, *s.* Wit, keenness, cunning. —ಕೊಬ್ಬುನಿ to play tricks. —ತೋಜಾವುನಿ to show one's cunning.

ಕಿಣಿಕಿಣಿ kiṇikiṇi, *s.* The tinkling of small bells; a clinking sound.

ಕಿಣಿಲ್ kiṇilų, *s.* The noise made by the fall of a small bell, *etc.*

ಕಿಣ್ಕಣ kiṇkaṇa, *adj.* Little. —ಬೆರೆಲ್ the little finger.

ಕಿಣ್ಕುನಿ kiṇkuni, *see* ಕಿನ್ಕುನಿ.

ಕಿಣ್ಣಲ್ kiṇṇalų, *s.* A brass cup.

ಕಿತಾಬ್ kitābų, *s.* A book. 2. the Koran.

ಕಿತ್ತ್ kittų, *see* ಕಿಸ್ತ್.

ಕಿತ್ತ್ kittų, *s.* Lightning. —ಇಡ್ಪಿನಿ lightning to flash.

ಕಿತ್ತಲಿ, ಕಿತ್ತಿಳಿ, ಕಿತ್ಲೆ kittali, kittili, kitlĕ, *s.* An orange.

ಕಿತ್ತುನಿ kittuni (ಕಿತ್ತ್), *v. n.* To flutter; to be in agitation.

ಕಿದ್ಂಕಣ kidųṅkaṇa, *see* ಕಿಣ್ಕಣ.

ಕಿದ್ಂಬ್ರೆ kidųmbrĕ, *s.* A brass ear-ring; *also* ಕೆದುಂಬ್ರು.

ಕಿದ್ಕಿಲ್, ಕಿದ್ಕೆಲ್, ಕಿದ್ಕುಲ್, ಕಿದ್ಕೆಲ್ kidųkilų, kidųkelų, kidkųlų, kidkelų, *s.* The armpit. 2. tickling. —ಆಪಿನಿ to be ticklish. —ಪಾಡುನಿ to tickle.

ಕಿದಂಬುರೆ kidamburĕ, *see* ಕಿದಂಬ್ರು.

ಕಿದಿ kidi, *see* ಕೆದಿ.

ಕಿದೆ kidĕ, *s.* A cow-pen, stall. —ನಡಿ a manger; *cf.* ಜೈವಣೆ.

ಕಿನ್ಕುನಿ kinųkuni, *see* ಕಿನ್ಕುನಿ

ಕಿನ್ರ್, ಕಿನರ್, ಕಿನಲ್ kinųrų, kinarų, kinalų, *s.* A bit, trifle.

ಕಿನಾರೆ kinārė, *s.* Margin, bank, shore. 2. border, edge.

ಕಿನಿಕಿನಿ kinikini, *see* ಕಿಣಿಕಿಣಿ.

ಕಿನ್ಕನ kinkana, *see* ಕಿಣ್ಯಣ.

ಕಿನ್ಕುನಿ kinkuni (ಕಿನ್ಕ್), *v. a.* To pinch.

ಕಿನ್ನರಿ kinnari, *see* ಕಿಂನರಿ.

ಕಿನ್ನಿ kinni, *see* ಕಿಂಞಿ.

ಕಿನ್ಯಪ್ಪೆ kinyappė, *s.* A mother's younger sister.

ಕಿನ್ಯಮ್ಮೆ kinyamme, *s.* A father's younger brother.

ಕಿನ್ಯವು kinyavu, *s.* The young of an animal. 2. a little thing; *cf.* ಕಿಂಞಿ.

ಕಿಪಾಯ, ಕಿಪಾಯತ್, ಕಿಫಾಯಿತಿ kipāya, kipāyatų, kiphāyiti, *s.* Profit, gain, advantage.

ಕಿಪ್ಪಿಲ್ kippilų, *see* ಕಿರ್ಪಿಲ್.

ಕಿಪ್ಪು kippu, *see* ಕೆಪ್ಪಮುಪ್ಪು.

ಕಿಪ್ಪೆ kippė, *s.* A pile, heap. –ಪಾಡುನಿ to heap up.

ಕಿಮ್ಮತ್ kimmatų, *see* ಕಿಂಮತ್.

ಕಿಯುಡೆ kiyuḍe, *see* ಕಿವುಡೆ.

ಕಿರ್ಂಬುನಿ kirųmbuni, *see* ಕಿಂಬುರ್ನಿ.

ಕಿರ್ದ್ kirųdų, *see* ಕಿದ್ರ್.

ಕಿರ್ಬಿಲ್ಲ್ kirųbillų, *see* ಕಿಪಿರ್ಲ್.

ಕಿರಂಚಿ kirañči, *s.* Mire, mud. *adj.* Miry, dirty, foul.

ಕಿರಣ kiraṇa, *s.* A ray *or* beam of light.

ಕಿರಣಿ kiraṇi, *s.* A kind of itch; *also* ಕೆರಣಿ, ಕ್ರಾಣಿ.

ಕಿರಾತೆ kirāte, *s.* A hunter, fowler; a forester.

ಕಿರಿ, ಕಿರು kiri, kiru, *adj.* Small, little, young. 2. low, mean.

ಕಿರಿಕಟ್ಟ್, ಕಿರಿಕಟ್ಟುನಿ kirikaṭṭų, kirikaṭṭuni, *see* ಕೀರಿಕಟ್ಟುನಿ, *under* ಕೀರಿ.

ಕಿರಿಕಿರಿ kirikiri, *s.* Disturbance, annoyance. 2. creaking, as shoes, *etc.*; *cf.* ಕರಕರಿ. –ಪಾತೆರುನಿ to prattle. –ಮಳ್ಪುನಿ to disturb.

ಕಿರಿಗಿ, ಕಿರಿಗೆ kirigi, kirigė, *s.* The garment worn by a girl; *also* ಗಿರಿಗಿ.

ಕಿರಿಗಿ, ಕಿರಿಗೆ kirigi, kirigė, *s.* Annoyance. –ಮಳ್ಪುನಿ to annoy.

ಕಿರಿದ್ kiridų, *see* ಕಿದ್ರ್.

ಕಿರಿಯಾತ್ kiriyātų, *s.* Chirayit gentian, *Ophelia chirata.*

ಕಿರಿಯೆ kiriyė, *s.* Exorcising; charming a demon.

ಕಿರಿಯೆ kiriye, *s.* A junior, younger member.

ಕಿರೀಟ kirīṭa, *s.* A crown, diadem. ಕಿರೀಟಾಧಪತಿ a king.

ಕಿರು kiru, *see* ಕಿರಿ.

ಕಿರೆ kirė, *see* ಕೆರೆ.

ಕಿರೆಂಗ್ kireṅgų, *see* ಕೆರೆಂಗ್.

ಕಿರೆಂಚಿ kireñči, *see* ಕಿರಂಚಿ.

ಕಿರೆಂಚುನಿ kireñčuni, *see* ಕೆರೆಂಚುನಿ.

ಕಿರೆಜುನಿ kirejuni (ಕಿರೆಜ್), *v. a.* To cut, as straw, grass-stumps *etc.* 2. to scrape *or* clear, as the ground.

ಕಿರೆಪಿನಿ, ಕಿರೆಪುನಿ, ಕಿರೆವುನಿ kirepini, kirepuni, kirevuni, *see* ಕೆರೆಪುನಿ.

ಕಿರ್ಕ್ kirkų, *s.* A creaking noise.

ಕಿರ್ಕಳ್, ಕಿರ್ಕಳ kirkaḷu, kirkaḷa, *s.* Annoyance, trouble, teasing. 2. a grain.

ಕಿರ್ಗತ್ತಿ kirgatti, *s.* A small knife. 2. a short sword.

ಕಿರ್ಗುಳ್ಳ kirguḷḷa, *s.* A small kind of brinjal.

ಕಿರ್ತರ kirtara, *s.* An inferior sort *or* kind.

ಕಿರ್ದ್ kirdu, *adj.* Inferior, not fine.

ಕಿರ್ಪಿಲ್, ಕಿರ್ಬಿಲ್ಲ್ kirpilu, kirbillu, *s.* A hut, small temporary shed.

ಕಿರ್ಯಾತ್ kiryātu, *see* ಕಿರಿಯಾತ್.

ಕಿರ್ಸೆ kirsè, *see* ಕೃಷಿ.

ಕಿಲ್ಂಬು, ಕಿಲ್ಬು, ಕಿಲುಮು kilumbu, kilubu, kilumu, *see* ಕಿಲೆಂಬಿ.

ಕಿಲ kila, *s.* The belly. 2. a bag. —ದಂಜಾವುನಿ to fill *or* feed the belly.

ಕಿಲಕಿಲ kilakila, *s.* Chirping. 2. screeching. *adv.* Heartily. —ತೆಲಿಪುನಿ to laugh heartily.

ಕಿಲಿಂಬು, ಕಿಲುಬು kilimbu, kilubu, *see* ಕಿಲೆಂಬಿ.

ಕಿಲಿಕಿಲಿ kilikili, *see* ಕಿಲಕಿಲ.

ಕಿಲೆಂಜಿ kilenji, *s.* A fly.

ಕಿಲೆಂಬಿ, ಕಿಲೆಂಬು kilembi, kilembu, *s.* Rust, verdigris, corrosion.

ಕಿಲೆಂಬಿರಿ kilembiri, *s.* Cream. 2. scum. —ಕಟ್ಟುನಿ, —ಪತ್ತುನಿ froth to form.

ಕಿಲೆಕುನಿ kilekuni (ಕಿಲೆಕ್), *v. a.* To draw out, pull. 2. to irritate, provoke; to stir, move.

ಕಿಲೆಪುನಿ kilepuni, *see* ಕೆಲೆಪುನಿ.

ಕಿಲೆವುನಿ, ಕಿಲೇವುನಿ kilevuni, kilēvuni (ಕಿಲೆ, ಕಿಲೇ), *v. n.* To whistle. 2. to resound.

ಕಿಲೆಸಿ kilesi, *see* ಕೆಲೆಸಿ.

ಕಿಲ್ಬು kilbu, *see* ಕಿಲೆಂಬಿ.

ಕಿಲ್ಲೆ killè, *s.* A fort. —ದಾರೆ the commander of a fort.

ಕಿವಡೆ, ಕಿವುಡೆ kivaḍe, kivuḍe, *s.* A deaf man. ಕಿವುಡು deaf.

ಕಿಶಿಕಿಶಿ kiśikiśi, *s.* A titter, laugh.

ಕಿಸ್, ಕಿಸಿ kisu, kisi, *s.* Grinning. 2. a fragment. 3. trouble. 4. hinderance. —ಕಿಟ್ಟ್, —ಬಾಕಿ a very small balance. —ಬಾಯಿ a grinning face. —ಬಿಸೆ a trifle. —ಒರೆಟುನಿ to give trouble; to haggle. —ಕಟ್ಟುನಿ to hinder.

ಕಿಸ್ಕ kisuka, *s.* Tittering *or* grinning. —ನೆ ತೆಲ್ಪುನಿ to grin, laugh.

ಕಿಸೆ kisè, *s.* The pocket of a jacket.

ಕಿಸ್ತ್, ಕಿಸ್ತೆ kistu, kistè, *s.* A fixed period for payment of revenue. 2. an instalment.

ಕಿಳಿಪಿಳಿ kiḷipiḷi, *s.* The sound of chirping.

ಕೀಚಕೆ kīčake, *s.* The name of an ancient king.

ಕೀಚಬಾವೊಲಿ kīčabāvoli, *s.* A flying fox.

ಕೀಚುಕೀಚು, ಕೀಚುಕೀಟ್ kīčukīču, kīčukīṭu, *s.* The squeaking of rats, *etc.*

ಕೀಚುನಿ kīčuni (ಕೀಚ್), *v. n.* To squeak.

ಕೀಚೆ kīčè, *see* ಕೀಚಕೆ.

ಕೀಜಿ kīji, *s.* White lead.

ಕೀಟ kīṭa, *s.* An insect in general. 2. a worm. 3. *see* ಕಿಟ್ಟ.

ಕೀಟಕೆ, ಕೀಟಗೆ kīṭake, kīṭage, *s.* A base *or* rude fellow.

ಕೀಡ್ kīḍu, *adj.* Inferior.

ಕೀಡ್, ಕೀಡಿ kīḍu, kīḍi, *s.* A worm, insect. –ಆಪಿನಿ, –ಬೂರುನಿ to decay; to become useless.

ಕೀತ್ kītu, *s.* A part, bit; a splinter.

ಕೀತುನಿ kītuni (ಕೀತ್ತಿ), *v. n.* To spirt, sprit; to sprinkle.

ಕೀದುನಿ kīduni (ಕೀದ್ದಿ), *v. a.* To importunate; to dun, tease.

ಕೀಪು kīpu, *s.* A bunch.

ಕೀಬಿಲ್ಲ್ kībillu, *see* ಕಿಪ್ಪಿಲ್.

ಕೀರ್ kīru, *s.* A split, rift; a scratch.

ಕೀರ್ kīru, *adj.* Ancient, old; ಕೀರ್ದ್ ಮೇಲ್ದ್ ಬುದ್ಧಿ a lesson for the past and future.

ಕೀರಿ kīri, *s.* Continuance, incessancy. –ಕಟ್ಟುನಿ to continue, go on without ceasing. –ಕಟ್ಟಿಬರ್ಸ incessant rain.

ಕೀರುನಿ kīruni (ಕೀರ್ದಿ), *v. a.* To scratch; to split; *also* ಗೀರುನಿ.

ಕೀರೆ kīrè, *see* ಕೀರಿ.

ಕೀರೊತ್ತುನಿ kīrottuni (ಕೀರೊತ್ತಿ), *v. a.* To roar, as an elephant.

ಕೀರ್ತನೆ kīrtanè, *s.* Praise; a psalm, hymn. –ಮಳ್ಪುನಿ to sing praises of God.

ಕೀರ್ತಿ kīrti, *s.* Fame, renown, reputation.

ಕೀಲ್ kīlu, *s.* A joint, hinge, peg. 2. a wooden fastening. –ಪಾಡುನಿ to fasten as a door; *also* ಕೀಳ್.

ಕೀಲ್ಂಬ್ kīlumbu, *see* ಕಿಲೆಂಬಿ.

ಕೀಲ್ದವಡೆ kīludavadè, *s.* The lower jaw.

ಕೀಲಿ kīli, *s.* A lock. –ಕೈ the key of a lock.

ಕೀಲ್ಮೇಲ್ kīlmēlu, *adj.* Evil and good. 2. inferior and superior. *adv.* Upside-down.

ಕೀವು kīvu, *s.* Pus, matter of a sore.

ಕೀಸುನಿ kīsuni, *see* ಕೀತುನಿ.

ಕೀಸುಳಿ kīsuḷi, *s.* A carpenter's plane.

ಕೀಳ್ kīḷu, *adj.* Base, low, mean. –ಆಳ್, ಕೀಳಾಳ್ an inferior. –ಜಾತಿ a low class *or* caste. –ತನ baseness, meanness. –ಪಾತೆರ a vulgar expression. –ಬುದ್ಧಿ a mean disposition. –ಮೇಲ್, *see* ಕೀಲ್ಮೇಲ್.

ಕೀಳ್, ಕೀಳು kīḷu, kīḷu, *see* ಕೀಲ್.

ಕು ku, *adj. pref.* Bad, low, small; *as* –ಜನ vulgar people. –ಯುಕ್ತಿ low tricks, *etc.*

ಕುಂಕುಮ kuṅkuma, *s.* A crimsoned powder of turmeric, used by married women for making a mark on their foreheads. –ಕೇಸರಿ *see* ಕೇಸರ.

ಕುಂಕುರು kuṅkuru, *s.* Going on hands and legs, as an infant; *also* ಗೋಂಕುರು. –ಕಪ್ಪೆ a toad. –ಪಾಡುನಿ to stagger, reel.

ಕುಂಕೆ kuṅkè, *see* ಕೂಂಕೆ.

ಕುಂಚ kuńća, *s.* A tassel, flybrush.

ಕುಂಚಿ kuńći, *s.* A kind of children's hood reaching down to the calves of the legs.

ಕುಂಚೆ kuńće, *s.* A weaver's stay.

ಕುಂಜ kuńja, *s.* A heap, accumulation, hoard; assemblage.

ಕುಂಜಾರ್ kuńjāru̥, *s.* A small jungle. 2. the name of a village.

ಕುಂಜಿ kuńji, *see* ಗೂಂಜಿ.

ಕುಂಜಿರ್ಗ kuńjirga, *see* ಕುಂಜಾರ್.

ಕುಂಞ kuńńa, *s.* Genitals, *vlg.*

ಕುಂಟ kuṇṭa, *s.* A peg, post. 2. the stocks. *adj.* Lame, crippled; blunt. —ಕುಸೆಲ್ a cripple's tricks. —ಕಾರ್ a lame leg. —ನಡ್ಪಿನಿ to place *or* fix a post. —ಪಾಡುನಿ to set up a post.

ಕುಂಟಣಿ kuṇṭaṇi, *s.* Vexation. 2. dissoluteness; *cf.* ಕುಟ್ಟಣಿ. —ಗಾರೆ a debauchee.

ಕುಂಟಳ್, ಕುಂಟಾಳ್, ಕುಂಟಾಲ kuṇṭaḷu̥, kuṇṭālu̥, kuṇṭāla, *s.* The tree *Gomphia angustifolia.* —ಪಂದ್ a its fruit.

ಕುಂಟಾವುನಿ kuṇṭāvuni, *see* ಕೋಂಟಾವುನಿ.

ಕುಂಟಿ kuṇṭi, *s.* A female dwarf. *adj.* Short; worn out, wasted; blunt, dull. —ಮೈಪು a worn out broom. —ಬೂರುನಿ to become blunt, *etc.*

ಕುಂಟು kuṇṭu, *s.* Cloth. 2. garment, dress. —ಕುತ್ತುನಿ to dress, clothe. —ಪೊದೆಪುನಿ to cover with clothes, put on clothes.

ಕುಂಟುನಿ kuṇṭuni, *see* ಕೋಂಟುನಿ.

ಕುಂಟೆ kuṇṭe, *s.* A dwarf, short man.

ಕುಂಟೆ kuṇṭè, *s.* The web beam of a loom. —ದ ತೂ fire set up to warm the bleached thread. —ಗೂರುನಿ to set a post *or* peg. ಅಡ್ಡ— the cross-beam of a loom.

ಕುಂಡ kuṇḍa, *s.* A pit, especially of sacrificial fire.

ಕುಂಡಲ kuṇḍala, *s.* A kind of ear-ring; *also* ಗುಂಡಲ.

ಕುಂಡಲಿ kuṇḍali, *s.* A kind of serpent.

ಕುಂಡಿ, ಕುಂಡಿಗೆ kuṇḍi, kuṇḍigè, *s.* A strong trough.

ಕುಂಡೆಲ್ kuṇḍelu̥, *see* ಕೊಂಡೆಲ್.

ಕುಂಣೆ kuṇṇè, *s.* The penis.

ಕುಂತಲ kuntala, *s.* A curl, ringlet. 2. the hair. 3. a drinking cup.

ಕುಂತಿ kunti, *s.* The mother of the Pāṇḍu princes.

ಕುಂದ್ kundu̥, *see* ಕುಂದು.

ಕುಂದ kunda, *s.* A pillar, post. ಕಲ್ಲ ದ— a stone pillar. —ಕಟ್ಟುನಿ to build a pillar.

ಕುಂದಣ kundaṇa, *s.* Pure gold.

ಕುಂದಾವುನಿ kundāvuni, *c. v.* (*of* ಕುಂದುನಿ) To reduce. 2. to boil down. 3. to repress, humble.

ಕುಂದು kundu, *s.* Deficiency, defect, fault. 2. want. 3. loss. —ದಾಯಿ a helper; a companion, comrade. —ಗು to make up a deficiency. —ಕೈ want of money *or* means.

ಕುಂದು kundu, *s.* A child of Pariahs. —ಪಾಡುನಿ to bear, bring forth, as Pariahs.

ಕುಂದುನಿ kunduni (ಕುಂದ್), *v.n.* To decrease, abate, be reduced. 2. to fade, wither. 3. to be boiled down.

ಕುಂದೆಲ್ kundelu, *s.* Deficiency, as in the measurement of grain, *etc.*

ಕುಂದ್ರಿ kundri, *s.* A small craft *or* vessel from the Maldive islands. *adj.* Little, small, short. —ಕುಟ್ಟಿ, —ಬಾಲೆ a puny baby, bantling. —ಕೊಟ್ಟಿ, —ತಾರಾಯಿ a small kind of cocoanut, imported from the Maldive islands.

ಕುಂದ್ರುಕೋಟೆ kundrukōṭè, *s.* An old fort at Mercara.

ಕುಂಪರಿ, ಕುಂಪಾದ್ರಿ kumpari, kumpādri, *s.* A god-father.

ಕುಂಪುನಿ kumpuni, *see* ಕೊಂತುನಿ.

ಕುಂಪೆ kumpè, *see* ಕುಪ್ಪೆ.

ಕುಂಬ kumba, *see* ಕುಂಭ.

ಕುಂಬಕಾರೆ, ಕುಂಬರೆ kumbakāre, kumbare, *see* ಕುಂಬಾರೆ.

ಕುಂಬಟ್ಟ್ kumbaṭṭu, *see* ಕುಂಬು.

ಕುಂಬರುನಿ kumbaruni (ಕುಂಬರ್), *v.n.* To quake, tremble.

ಕುಂಬವ kumbava, *s.* A pumpkin *or* gourd.

ಕುಂಬಸ್ kumbasu, *see* ಕುಂಬು.

ಕುಂಬಾರೆ kumbāre, *s.* A potter; *also* ಓಡರಿ.

ಕುಂಬಿ kumbi, *s.* A mirage. 2. the penis. 3. an elephant.

ಕುಂಬು kumbu, *s.* Rottenness. *adj.* Rotten, carious, decayed. —ಮರ a rotten tree. —ಆಪಿನಿ to rot.

ಕುಂಬುಡ kumbuḍa, A pumpkin *or* gourd, *Cucurbita agenaria.* ಕರ— an ash-gourd. ಕಾಟ—, ಬೋಳ್ಯ— a small kind of ash-gourd. ಬೆಲ್ಲ—, *see* ಕೆಂಬುಡೆ. —ಕೊಯಿಪಿನಿ, —ಬಿಕ್ಕುನಿ to boast, vaunt, *vlg.*

ಕುಂಬೊಟ್ಟು kumboṭṭu, *see* ಕುಂಬು.

ಕುಂಭ kumbha, *s.* The eleventh solar month (Febr.-March). 2. a pot, an earthen vessel. —ಕರ್ಣ the name of a giant, Rāvaṇa's younger brother. —ರಾಶಿ the sign *Aquarius.*

ಕುಂಭ, ಕುಂಭಸ್ಥಲ kumbha, kumbhasthala, *s.* The frontal globe of an elephant's head.

ಕುಂಮಕ್, ಕುಂಮಿಕೆ kummaku, kummikè, *see* ಕುಮಕ್.

ಕುಂಮಾಯ kummāya, *see* ಕುಮಾಯ.

ಕುಂಜಿಲ್ kuṅrjilu, *see* ಕುಕಿಲ್.

ಕುಂಟುನಿ kurṇṭuni (ಕುಂಟ್), *v. n.* To shrivel, shrink.

ಕುಂದು kurndu, *see* ಕೊಂದು.

ಕುಂದೊಡಿ kurndoḍi, *s.* A kind of fish.

ಕುಂಸು kumsu, *see* ಗುಮ್ಸು.

ಕುಕ್ಕು kukku, *s.* A mango. 2. the mourning feast of the Pariahs. —ದ ಮರ a mango tree. —ದ ಮುಡಿ a young mango. —ದ ಉಪ್ಪಡ್, —ದುಪ್ಪಡ್ mango pickle.

—ಕೊಂಡುಪೋಪಿನಿ Pariahs to attend a funeral ceremony.

ಕುಕ್ಕುಲಿ **kukkuli,** *s.* Pecking.

ಕುಕ್ಕುಲಿಯುನಿ **kukkuliyuni** (ಕುಕ್ಕುಲಿ), *v. a.* To peck.

ಕುಕ್ಕೆ **kukke,** *s.* A basket. —ಕುರುವೆ a small basket.

ಕುಗ್ಗುನಿ **kugguni** (ಕುಗ್ಗಿ), *v. n.* To be humbled, depressed. 2. to sink; *see* ಕುಸ್ಕುನಿ.

ಕುಚುಕುಚು **kućukuću,** *s.* A whisper. —ಪಾತೆರುನಿ to whisper.

ಕುಚೆ **kuće,** *see* ಕುಚ್ಚಿ.

ಕುಚೋದ್ಯ **kućōdya,** *s.* Ridicule, derision, mockery.

ಕುಚ್ಚಟ್ **kuććaṭu,** *s.* Shortness, smallness. *adj.* Short, little.

ಕುಚ್ಚಣಿಗೆ, ಕುಚ್ಚಣೆ, ಕುಚ್ಚಾಟ **kuććaṇigè, kuććaṇè, kuććāṭa,** *s.* Reprobation, taunt, upbraiding.

ಕುಚ್ಚಿ **kućći,** *s.* The cropped hair of the head. 2. the stump of a shrub. 3. a tassel. *adj.* Small, short. —ಕಾಡ್ a copse, brushwood. —ಪಂತಿ grass-stump, stubble. —ಮುಳ್ಳು a thicket of thorns. —ಗೀಸುನಿ, —ಕೆಪ್ಪುನಿ to shave the head. ಪಿಲಿ— a kind of fish. ಬರ— an addition made to the tuft of hair on the crown of the head.

ಕುಚ್ಚಿಲೆ **kuććile,** *s.* A taunter.

ಕುಚ್ಚುನಿ **kuććuni,** *see* ಕುಚ್ಚೆಣುನಿ.

ಕುಚ್ಚೆಣುನಿ, ಕುಚ್ಚೊಣುನಿ **kuććeṇuni, kuććoṇuni** (ಕುಚ್ಚೆಣಿ. ಕುಚ್ಚೊಣಿ), *v. refl.* To blame, censure, reprove.

ಕುಚ್ಚೆನ **kuććena,** *see* ಕುಚ್ಚಣಿಗೆ.

ಕುಜ **kuja,** *adj.* Earth-born. *s.* A tree. 2. the planet Mars. —ವಾರ Tuesday.

ಕುಜಂಟಿ **kujaṇṭi,** *see* ಕೊಜಂಟಿ.

ಕುಜರ್ **kujaru,** *s.* The stench of urine; any bad smell.

ಕುಜಲ್ **kujaḷu,** *s.* The hair of the head.

ಕುಜಲುನಿ **kujaluni,** *see* ಕೊಜಲುನಿ.

ಕುಜಿಂಬು, ಕುಜುಂಬು **kujimbu, kujumbu,** *s.* A chip, fragment.

ಕುಟಾಯಿ **kuṭāyi,** *see* ಕೊಟಾಯಿ.

ಕುಟಿ **kuṭi,** *s.* A hut.

ಕುಟಿನಿ **kuṭini,** *s.* A deceitful woman.

ಕುಟಿಲ **kuṭila,** *s.* Trick, imposture, deception. 2. hypocrisy. 3. crookedness. —ದಾಯಿ, ಕುಟಿಲೆ a cheat, imposter.

ಕುಟುಂಬ **kuṭumba,** *s.* A family; a household.

ಕುಟುಂಬಿಗೆ **kuṭumbige,** *s.* A householder, family-man.

ಕುಟುಕು **kuṭuku,** *s.* The game of hide and seek. 2. a female's ear-ornament.

ಕುಟುಕುಟು **kuṭukuṭu,** *s.* The rumbling of the bowels. 2. grinding the teeth.

ಕುಟ್ಟ **kuṭṭa,** *see* ಕೊಟ್ಟ.

ಕುಟ್ಟಣ್ **kuṭṭaṇu,** *s.* A kind of tares. —ಕಂಡ a field overgrown with such tares; a barren field.

ಕುಟ್ಟಣ **kuṭṭaṇa,** *see* ಕುಚ್ಚಣಿಗೆ.

ಕುಟ್ಟಸ್ kuṭṭasu, *see* ಕುಟ್ಟ.

ಕುಟ್ಟಿ kuṭṭi, *s.* A stake, peg, stump. —ಕೋಲು a short stick. —ಕೋಲು ಗೊಬ್ಬುನಿ to play at throwing a stick.

ಕುಟ್ಟಿಲ್ kuṭṭilu, *see* ಕುಟಿಲ.

ಕುಟ್ಟು kuṭṭu, *s.* A blow given with the fist.

ಕುಟ್ಟುನಿ kuṭṭuni (ಕುಟ್ಟಿ), *v. a.* To thump, give a blow, strike with the fist. 2. to crash, pound, bruise.

ಕುಟ್ಟೆ kuṭṭè, *s.* Decay, rottenness. —ಪುರಿ a borer, that destroys trees. —ಪತ್ತುನಿ to decay. —ಪೋಪಿನಿ to be ruined, done up, exhausted.

ಕುಟ್ರು kuṭru, *s.* Cooing. —ಪುದ a spotted dove. —ಪಾಡುನಿ to coo.

ಕುಡ kuḍa, *adv.* Again. —ಲಾ once more. —ಕುಡ again and again, repeatedly.

ಕುಡಂಜಿ kuḍañji, *see* ಕೊಡೆಂಜಿ.

ಕುಡಪುನಿ kuḍapuni, *see* ಕೊಡಪುನಿ.

ಕುಡರಿ kuḍari, *s.* An axe. ಕೈ— a hatchet.

ಕುಡಿಕೋಲ್ kuḍikōlu, *see* ಕುಟ್ಟಿ ಕೋಲು, *under* ಕುಟ್ಟಿ.

ಕುಡಿಚೆಲ್ kuḍićelu, *see* ಕುಡ್ಚೆಲ್.

ಕುಡಿಚೆಲೆ kuḍićele, *see* ಕುಡ್ಚೆಲೆ.

ಕುಡು kuḍu, *s.* Horse-gram, *Dolichos uniflorus.* 2. the testicles of dogs, cats, *etc.* 3. the fresh scars of small-pox. —ಪಾಡುನಿ to feed (cattle) with gram; to cuff, give blows. —ಬಿರ್ಕುನಿ, *lit.* gram to scatter; small-pox to break out.

ಕುಡುಂಬೆ kuḍumbe, *s.* A jungle man. 2. a Koṅkaṇi speaking Roman Catholic.

ಕುಡುತಲೆ kuḍutalè, *see* ಕುಡ್ತಲೆ.

ಕುಡುಪು, kuḍupu, *s.* A strainer, made of wicker-work.

ಕುಡುಪುನಿ kuḍupuni, *see* ಕುಡ್ಪುನಿ.

ಕುಡುಮ kuḍuma, *s.* A ferry. 2. *see* ಕುಟುಂಬ.

ಕುಡುಮೆ kuḍume, *see* ಕುಡುಂಬೆ.

ಕುಡೆ kuḍè, *s.* A rat's hole.

ಕುಡೆಂಜಿ kuḍeñji, *see* ಕೊಡೆಂಜಿ.

ಕುಡೆಂಜಿಮರ kuḍeñjimara, *s.* The tree of oval-leaved rosebay, *Wrightia antidysenterica.*

ಕುಡ್ಕಿ, ಕುಡ್ಕೆ kuḍki, kuḍkè, *s.* A small earthen vessel. —ದುರ್ಸು a kind of firework.

ಕುಡ್ಚುನಿ kuḍćuni (ಕುಡ್ಚಿ), *v. a.* To drink excessively. 2. to swallow liquor.

ಕುಡ್ಚೆಲ್ kuḍćelu, *s.* Drunkenness.

ಕುಡ್ಚೆಲೆ kuḍćele, *s.* A drunkard.

ಕುಡ್ತಲೆ kuḍtalè, *s.* The registered right of paying land revenue.

ಕುಡ್ಪ, ಕುಡ್ಪೆ kuḍpa, kuḍpè, *see* ಕುಡುಪು.

ಕುಡ್ಪಳ್ kuḍpaḷu, *s.* A woman with uncombed hair. 2. the name of a female demon.

ಕುಡ್ಪುನಿ kuḍpuni (ಕುಡ್ಡಿ), *v. n.* To shiver, as from ague. *v. a.* To dust, shake off as the dust of a cloth, *etc.*

ಕುಣಲೆ, ಕುಣಿಲೆ kuṇalè, kuṇile, *see* ಕೊಣಲೆ.

ಕುತ್ತ್‌ರಿ kuttu̥ri, *see* ಕುತ್ತುರಿ.

ಕುತ್ತ kutta, *s.* Sickness. ಅರಶಿನ– jaundice. ನೀರ್– dropsy.

ಕುತ್ತಟ, kuttaṭa, *s.* Pain, as in suppuration of a boil.

ಕುತ್ತಟ್ಟ, ಕುತ್ತ್ಯಟ್ಟ kuttaṭṭa, kuttyaṭṭa, *s.* A granary, store.

ಕುತ್ತನಿ kuttani, *s.* A superior kind of silk cloth.

ಕುತ್ತನೆ kuttanè, *adv.* Headlong.

ಕುತ್ತರಿ kuttari, *see* ಕುತ್ತುರಿ.

ಕುತ್ತರುನಿ kuttaruni (ಕುತ್ತರಿ), *v. n.* To feel a biting *or* itching sensation. 2. to ache.

ಕುತ್ತಲು kuttalu, *see* ಕುತ್ತು.

ಕುತ್ತಲುನಿ kuttaluni, *see* ಕೊಂತಲ್ಯುನಿ.

ಕುತ್ತಲೆ kuttale, *s.* A sickly man.

ಕುತ್ತಾಟ kuttāṭa, *see* ಕುತ್ತಟ.

ಕುತ್ತಾರಿ kuttāri, *see* ಕುತ್ತುರಿ.

ಕುತ್ತಿ kutti, *s.* A liquid measure, as of oil *etc.*

ಕುತ್ತಿ kutti, *s.* The trunk *or* stump of a tree. –ಕಾಣಿಕೆ fees levied for permission to fell trees on government land. –ಕೋಲು a perpendicular post supporting a roof. –ಪೂಜೆ propitiation of demons, supposed to haunt a newly constructed roof. –ಅಳಿಯುನಿ a race *or* family to be extinct. –ಗೆಪ್ಪುನಿ to dig up the stump of a tree. ನಿರ್ಕುತ್ತಿ a post planted in the water for supporting anything.

ಕುತ್ತಿಪುಳಿ kuttipuḷi, *s.* Tamarind.

ಕುತ್ತಿರಿ kuttiri, *s.* A civet cat.

ಕುತ್ತು kuttu, *s.* A prick, puncture; very small hole. 2. a fomentation *or* poultice. 3. a basket-maker's knife; *also* ಕುತ್ತುಕೋಲು. –ಕೊರ್ಪಿನಿ to foment. –ಪಾಡುನಿ to prick, make a hole. –ಬೂರುನಿ to become a hole.

ಕುತ್ತುನಿ kuttuni (ಕುತ್ತಿ), *v. a.* To bore, pierce.

ಕುತ್ತುರಿ kutturi, *s.* A weel for catching fish with. 2. a basket-shaped cage for fowls.

ಕುತ್ತುರುನಿ, ಕುತ್ರುನಿ kutturuni, kutruni, *see* ಕುದುಪುನಿ.

ಕುತ್ತೆಲ್ kuttelu̥, *s.* A kind of brush used by toddy-drawers.

ಕುತ್ತೊಡಿ kuttoḍi, *s.* A cobra emaciated by devouring another species of snake called ‘kandoḍi’.

ಕುತ್ತ್ಯೊಳು kuttyoḷu, *see* ಕುತ್ತಿ ಕೋಲು, *under* ಕುತ್ತಿ.

ಕುದಂಟೆ kudanṭè, *see* ಕೊದಂಟೆ.

ಕುದಡ್ kudaḍu̥, *see* ಕೊದಡ್.

ಕುದಣೆ, ಕುದನೆ kudaṇè, kudanè, *s.* The fruit of *Solanum pubescens.*

ಕುದಿ kudi, *s.* Term, turn. *adj.* Fixed, settled. –ದೀಪಿನಿ to fix a time.

ಕುದಿ kudi, *see* ಕೊದಿ.

ಕುದಿಕಾರ್ kudikāru̥, *s.* Tiptoe.

ಕುದಿಕೆ, kudike, A jackal, fox.

ಕುದಿಪುನಿ, ಕುದಿಯುನಿ kudipuni, kudiyuni (ಕುದ), *v. n.* To repent, regret.

ಕುದಿಪೇವುನಿ **kudipēvuni** (ಕುದಿಪೆ:), *v. a.* To be desiring, wishing. 2. to be anxious.

ಕುದುಂಬು **kudumbu**, *see* ಕೊದುಂಬು.

ಕುದುಂಬುಲು **kudumbulu**, *s.* A quail.

ಕುದುಕೆ **kuduke**, *see* ಕುದಿಕೆ.

ಕುದುಪ **kudupa**, *see* ಖುದುಪ.

ಕುದುಪುನಿ **kudupuni** (ಕುದ್), *v. a.* To cut; to reap.

ಕುದುಪೆ **kudupè**, *s.* A small kind of earthen vessel for boiling rice. 2. (*fig.*) the belly.

ಕುದುಮೆ **kudumè**, *s.* The side *or* cross roof of a house.

ಕುದುರು **kuduru**, *s.* A sand bank. 2. a small island.

ಕುದುರುನಿ **kuduruni** (ಕುದುರ್), *v. n.* To recover from sickness.

ಕುದುರೆ **kudurè**, *s.* A horse. 2. the lock of a gun. —ಗಾರೆ, —ದಾಯಿ a horsekeeper; a rider. —ಜೀನ್ a saddle. —ದ ಜಮ್ಮಿರಿ the mane of a horse. —ಲಾಯು a stable. —ಸವಾರಿ riding. —ಮಿತ್ತ್ರುನಿ, —ಮಿತ್ತಾವುನಿ to mount a horse, to ride.

ಕುದೆ **kudè**, *s.* A piece of wood.

ಕುದ್ಕೆ **kudke**, *see* ಕುದಿಕೆ.

ಕುದ್ದು **kuddu**, *see* ಖುದ್ದು.

ಕುದ್ದೊಣುನಿ **kuddoṇuni**, *see* ಕುಳ್ಳುನಿ.

ಕುದ್ದೊಲಿ **kuddoli**, *see* ಗುದ್ದೊಲಿ.

ಕುದ್ದ್ಯ, ಕುದ್ಯ **kuddya, kudya**, *s.* Shortness. *adj.* Short, small, dwarfish. —ದಾಯಿ a dwarf, short man.

ಕುದ್ಪೆ **kudpè**, *see* ಕುದುಪೆ.

ಕುದ್ರಾಸ್ **kudrāsu̥**, *s.* A square bottle.

ಕುನಲೆ **kunalè**, *see* ಕೊಣಲೆ.

ಕುಪಾಂಡೆ **kupāṇḍè**, *s.* Concealing one's nature, acts, *etc.*; hypocrisy. —ಪಾತೆರುನಿ to talk like a virtuous man; to impose upon.

ಕುಪಾಂದೆ, ಕುಪಾಂದ್ರೆ **kupānde, kupāndre**, *see* ಕುಬೇರೆ.

ಕುಪುಲು, ಕುಪುಳು **kupulu, kupuḷu**, *s.* The crow-pheasant. —ಕಂಣ್ red eyes. —ಬಣ್ಣ reddish colour. —ಮುಂಗ್ a mole-hill.

ಕುಪೇಂದ್ರೆ **kupēndre**, *see* ಕುಬೇರೆ.

ಕುಪ್ಪಸ **kuppasa**, *s.* A petty coat, bodice.

ಕುಪ್ಪಿ **kuppi**, *s.* Glass-ware. 2. china-wares. 3. a pial, bottle.

ಕುಪ್ಪೆ **kuppè**, *see* ಗುಪ್ಪೆ.

ಕುಬಲ್, ಕುಬಾಲ್ **kubalu̥, kubālu̥**, *s.* A pinnacle, the top of a roof.

ಕುಬುಜ **kubuja**, *adj.* Dwarfish; hump-backed.

ಕುಬುಜೆ **kubujè**, *s.* A female dwarf.

ಕುಬುದ್ಧಿ **kubuddhi**, *s.* Foolishness; folly.

ಕುಬೆ **kubè**, *s.* The top of a palm tree.

ಕುಬೇರಮರ **kubēramara**, *s.* The mahogany tree.

ಕುಬೇರೆ **kubēre**, *s.* The Indian Pluto and god of wealth, presiding over the north quarter. 2. a rich man.

ಕುಬ್ಜ kubja, *see* ಕುಬುಜ.

ಕುಬ್ಜೆ kubje, *see* ಕುಬುಜೆ.

ಕುಮಂಡೆ kumaṇḍè, *see* ಕುಪಾಂಡೆ.

ಕುಮಕ್, ಕುಮಿಕಿ, ಕುಮುಕಿ, ಕುಮುಕು, ಕುಮುಕೆ kumakụ, kumiki, kumuki, kumuku, kumukè, *s.* Aid, assistance. —ಜಾಗ unassessed land for the use of cultivation.

ಕುಮಾಂದ್ರ kumāndra, *see* ಕುಳಮಾಂದ್ರ.

ಕುಮಾಯ kumāya, *s.* Chunam, lime. 2. mortar.

ಕುಮಾರಿ, ಕುಮಾರ್ತಿ kumāri, kumārti, *s.* A girl. 2. a virgin. 3. a daughter.

ಕುಮಾರೆ kumāre, *s.* A boy. 2. a son.

ಕುಮುಸಾಲ್ kumusālụ, *s.* Consultation. 2. conspiracy, plot.

ಕುಮೆತೆಲ್ kumetelụ, *s.* Putrid meat *or* fish.

ಕುಮೆವುನಿ kumevuni (ಕುಮೆ), *v. n.* To decay, putrify, as meat, *etc.*

ಕುಮೆರ್, ಕುಮೇರ್ kumerụ, kumērụ, *s.* A waste land cleared for cultivation.

ಕುಮೇರು kumēru, *s.* The south pole.

ಕುಯಿಲಾವುನಿ kuyilāvuni, *see* ಕೊಲಿಯಾವುನಿ.

ಕುಯುಕ್ತಿ kuyukti, *s.* Craft, cunningness.

ಕುಯುಲುನಿ kuyuluni (ಕುಯುಲ್), *v. n.* To inflame, as the eyes, *or* a boil.

ಕುರ kura, *see* ಕೊರಂಬು.

ಕುರಂಗ kuraṅga, *s.* A musk-deer. 2. a monkey.

ಕುರಂಟ್ kuraṇṭụ, *see* ಕೊರಂಟು.

ಕುರಂಟುನಿ kuraṇṭuni, *see* ಕುರುಂಟುನಿ.

ಕುರಂತುನಿ kurantuni, *see* ಕೊರಂತುನಿ.

ಕುರಂದ್ರಕಲ್ಲ್ kurandrakallụ, *s.* A kind of very hard stone.

ಕುರಂಬಿಲ್ kurambilụ, *s.* A kind of grass growing in fields.

ಕುರಂಬು kurambu, *see* ಕೊರಂಬು.

ಕುರಕ್, ಕುರಾಕ್ kurakụ, kurākụ, *s.* Food, sustenance.

ಕುರಡಿ, ಕುರಾಡಿ kuraḍi, kurāḍi, *see* ಕುದರಿ.

ಕುರಡೆ kuraḍe, *see* ಕುರುಡೆ.

ಕುರಾನ್ kurānụ, *s.* The Koran.

ಕುರಿ kuri, *s.* A sheep. —ಜನ foolish people. —ತ ಕಿನ್ನಿ a lamb. —ರೋಮ wool.

ಕುರಿ kuri, *s.* A boil. ಉಮಿ— a small boil.

ಕುರಿಜಾತ್ kurijātụ, *see* ಕುರುಜಾತ್.

ಕುರಿನೀರ್ kurinīrụ, *s.* A mixture of lime and turmeric water.

ಕುರಿಪುನಿ, ಕುರಿಯುನಿ kuripuni, kuriyuni (ಕುರಿ), *v. n.* To decay, rot, putrify.

ಕುರು kuru, *adj.* Little, small.

ಕುರುಂಟು kuruṇṭu, *s.* A small bundle, as of rice *etc.* 2. a lump, as of tamarind *etc.* 3. contraction.

ಕುರುಂಟುನಿ kuruṇṭuni (ಕುರುಂಟು), *v. n.* To contract, shrivel, shrink in.

ಕುರುಂಬಿಲ್ kurumbilụ, *s.* Curled hair. 2. *see* ಕುರಂಬಿಲ್.

ಕುರುಕುಚ್ಚನೆ, ಕುರುಕುಚ್ಚಿ kurukuc̆c̆anè, kurukuc̆c̆i, *s.* Grumbling, murmuring.

ಕುರುಚಿ kuruc̆i, *see* ಕುರ್ಚಿ.

ಕುರುಜಾತ್ kurujātu̥, *s.* A moidore.

ಕುರುಜಿ kuruji, *see* ಗುರ್ಜಿ.

ಕುರುಡ kuruḍa, *adj.* Blind. –ತನ blindness.

ಕುರುಡಾಯಿ kuruḍāyi, *see* ಕುರ್ಡಾಯಿ.

ಕುರುಡು kuruḍu, *adj.* Blind.

ಕುರುಡುಮಣ್ಣ್ kuruḍumaṇṇu̥, *see* ಕುರ್ಡುಮಣ್ಣ್.

ಕುರುಡುಮರಿ kuruḍumari, *see* ಕುರ್ಡುಮರಿ.

ಕುರುಡೆ, ಕುರುತೆ kuruḍe, kurute, *s.* A blind man.

ಕುರುಬಾಕಿಲ್ kurubākilu̥, *s.* A postern, backdoor.

ಕುರುಬು kurubu, *s.* The eyebrow.

ಕುರುಬೆ kurube, *s.* A shepherd.

ಕುರುಲೆ kurulè, *see* ಕುರ್ಲೆ.

ಕುರುವೆ kuruvè, *see* ಕುರ್ವೆ.

ಕುರುಸಾಲ್ kurusālu̥, *s.* Servitude, slavery, bondage.

ಕುರೂಪ, ಕುರೂಪು kurūpa, kurūpu, *s.* Deformity, ugliness. *adj.* Deformed, ugly. ಕುರೂಪಿ an ugly man.

ಕುರೆ kurè, *s.* Filth, dirt. 2. swamp, pool. –ಅಕೆ stinginess in trifles. –ಕಡ್ತ decayed skin. –ಜೀವ a poor life, half-alive. –ಮಣ್ಣ್ filthy soil.

ಕುರೆಪಿನಿ, ಕುರೆಪುನಿ kurepini, kurepuni (ಕುರೆ), *v. a.* To bore, scrape, excavate, drill. 2. *see* ಕೊರೆಪಿನಿ.

ಕುರೆಯುನಿ, ಕುರೆವುನಿ kureyuni, kurevuni (ಕುರೆ), *v. n.* To be worn out, washed away. 2. to decay, rot.

ಕುರೆಲ್ kurelu̥, *s.* The nape of the neck.

ಕುರ್ಕಾವುನಿ kurkāvuni, *c. v.* (*of* ಕುರ್ಕುನಿ) To shake, agitate. 2. to wash well, as clothes.

ಕುರ್ಕಿಲ್ kurkilu̥, *s.* A kind of basket.

ಕುರ್ಕುನಿ kurkuni (ಕುರ್ಕ್), *v. n.* To shake, as a tree *etc.*

ಕುರ್ಕುರು kurkuru, *adv.* Slowly. –ಮುಚ್ಚುನಿ to shut slowly.

ಕುರ್ಕೆ kurkè, *see* ಗುರ್ಕೆ.

ಕುರ್ಣಿ kurṅi, *see* ಕುನ್ನಿ.

ಕುರ್ಚಿ kurc̆i, *s.* A chair, seat.

ಕುರ್ಚಿ kurc̆i, *s.* A kind of fish.

ಕುರ್ಜಾತ್ kurjātu̥, *see* ಕುರುಜಾತ್.

ಕುರ್ಡಾಯಿ kurḍāyi, *s.* A large black beetle that destroys the core of palm-trees.

ಕುರ್ಡಿಬೂರು, ಕುರ್ಡು kurḍibūru, kurḍu, *s.* A kind of creeper.

ಕುರ್ಡು kurḍu, *see* ಕುರುಡು.

ಕುರ್ಡುಮಣ್ಣ್ kurḍumaṇṇu̥, *s.* Soil *or* earth impregnated with the poison of kurḍumari.

ಕುರ್ಡುಮರಿ kurḍumari, *s.* A kind of poisonous vermin.

ಕುರ್ಡೆ kurḍe, *see* ಕುರುಡೆ.

ಕುರ್ತೆ, ಕುರ್ತೆಲ್ kurtè, kurtelu̥, *s.* Dirt, filthiness. *adj.* Dirty.

ಕುರ್ತೆಲೆ kurtele, *s.* A filthy man.

ಕುರ್ನಾಸ್ kurnāsu̥, *s.* Snoring.

ಕುರ್ನಿ **kurni,** *s.* A sore in the eye-lid. –ಕಂಣ್ ಸೋರ್ sore eyes.

ಕುರ್ಪು **kurpu,** *s.* Manure, fertiliser. –ಪತ್ತುನಿ to be fertilised.

ಕುರ್ಪು **kurpu,** *s.* Sharpness, as of a cutting instrument. 2. dissection. –ದೀಪಿನಿ to dissect.

ಕುರ್ಬಿಲ್ **kurbilu,** *see* ಕುರುಂಬಿಲ್.

ಕುರ್ಬು **kurbu,** *see* ಕುರುಬು.

ಕುರ್ಯುನಿ **kuryuni,** *see* ಕುರಿಯುನಿ.

ಕುರ್ಲ್ **kurlu,** *s.* Contraction, shrinking in. 2. parching, drying.

ಕುರ್ಲರಿ, ಕುರ್ಲು **kurlari, kurlu,** *s.* Parched rice.

ಕುರ್ಲುನಿ **kurluni** (ಕುರ್ಲ್), *v. n.* To be contracted, to shrivel, shrink in, as from cold; *also* ಕುರ್ಲ್ದ್ ಪೋಪಿನಿ.

ಕುರ್ಲೆ **kurlè,** *s.* A tender plantain tree. 2. a young pig. 3. the fresh shoots of grains *etc.*

ಕುರ್ಲೆಮರ್ದ್ **kurlemardu,** *s.* A kind of bitter medicinal root.

ಕುರ್ವಾಯಿ **kurvāyi,** *see* ಕುರ್ಡಾಯಿ.

ಕುರ್ವೆ **kurvè,** *s.* A basket. 2. distension. ಬಂಜಿ ಕುರ್ವೆ ಕಟ್ಟುನಿ the belly to distend.

ಕುರ್ಸಂಡಿ **kursaṇḍi,** *s.* A kind of sesamum imported from the ghauts. –ಎಂಣೆ sesamum oil.

ಕುರ್ಸಣಿ **kursaṇi,** *see* ಕುರುಸಾಲ್.

ಕುರ್ಸು **kursu,** *s.* A cross. 2. *see* ಕುರ್ಚಿ.

ಕುಲ **kula,** *s.* Family, race, tribe. –ದೇವೆರ್ a family god. –ಧರ್ಮ, ಕುಲಾಚಾರ duties and customs pertaining to a family *or* caste. –ವಂತೆ one who belongs to a good family. –ಕೆಟ್ಟುನಿ a caste *or* family to be degenerated *or* ruined.

ಕುಲ **kula,** *see* ಕುಳ.

ಕುಲ **kula,** *s.* A sweet preparation consisting of cocoanut juice, jaggory, ripe plantains, and cardamoms; *also* ಕುಳ.

ಕುಲ, ಕುಲವು **kula, kulavu,** *s.* A kind of creeper.

ಕುಲಂಜಿ **kulañji,** *see* ಕುಲೆಂಜಿ.

ಕುಲಯಿ **kulayi,** *s.* A kind of cap.

ಕುಲಾಂಕುಶ **kulāṅkuša,** *adj.* Detailed. 2. whole. *adv.* In detail. 2. wholly.

ಕುಲಾಸ್ **kulāsu,** *s.* Discharge, acquittance, letting go.

ಕುಲಿಪೆ, ಕುಲುಪೆ **kulipè, kulupè,** *see* ಕುಳಿಪೆ.

ಕುಲೀನ **kulīna,** *adj.* Noble, honorable. ಕುಲೀನೆ a nobleman.

ಕುಲೆ **kulè,** *s.* A ghost, apparition. –ಜರ continual fever.

ಕುಲೆಂಜಿ **kuleñji,** *s.* A plot of field.

ಕುಲ್ಪೆ **kulpè,** *see* ಕುಲಿಪೆ.

ಕುಲ್ಲಾ **kullā,** *see* ಖುಲ್ಲಾ.

ಕುಲ್ಲಾವುನಿ **kullāvuni,** *see* ಕುಳ್ಳಾವುನಿ.

ಕುಲ್ಲಿಗೆ **kulligè,** *s.* The buttocks.

ಕುವಕ **kuvaka,** *see* ಕುಹಕ.

ಕುವೆ **kuvè,** *s.* A mast; *also* ಕುವೆ ಮರ.

ಕುವೆ **kuvè,** *see* ಕೂವೆ.

ಕುಶ **kuša,** *s.* The holy grass. *Poa cynosuroides; also* ದರ್ಭೆ.

ಕುಶಲ kušala, *s.* Cleverness, skilfulness. 2. welfare, happiness. *adj.* Clever, expert, able. –ಬುದ್ಧಿ keen wit, quick apprehension.

ಕುಶಾಲ್, kušālụ, *s.* Merriment, pleasure, frolic. –ರೋಗ venereal disease. –ಮಳ್ಪುನಿ to be merry, to lead a debaucherous life.

ಕುಶಿ kuši, *s.* Joy, pleasure; hilarity. 2. will. 3. agreement. ನಿನ– as you like, as you please.

ಕುಶಿಪುನಿ, ಕುಶಿಯುನಿ kušipuni, kušiyuni (ಕುಶಿ), *v. n.* To contract, shrink in.

ಕುಷಿ kushi, *see* ಕುಶಿ.

ಕುಷ್ಟ kushṭa, *see* ಕೊಷ್ಟ.

ಕುಸ kusa, *see* ಕುಶ.

ಕುಸವೆ kusave, *s.* A potter.

ಕುಸಾಲ್ kusālụ, *see* ಕುಶಾಲ್.

ಕುಸಿನ್, ಕುಸಿನಿ kusinụ, kusini, *s.* A kitchen.

ಕುಸಿಪುನಿ kusipuni, *see* ಕುಶಿಪುನಿ.

ಕುಸಿರಿ kusiri, *see* ಕುಸ್ರಿ.

ಕುಸುಂಬೆ kusumbĕ, *s.* The safflower. –ಎಂಣೆ safflower oil. –ಬಂಣ a deep red colour.

ಕುಸುಕುನಿ kusukuni, *see* ಕುಸ್ಕುನಿ.

ಕುಸುಕುಸು kusukusu, *see* ಗುಸು ಗುಸು.

ಕುಸುಬಿ kusubi, *s.* The safflower.

ಕುಸುಮ kusuma, *s.* The filament of a flower. 2. the pollen of a flower.

ಕುಸುರಿ kusuri, *s.* Any thing given to boot, when a person buys commodities. 2. *see* ಕುಸ್ರಿ. –ಕೊ ಪಿಂಡಿ to give something into the bargain.

ಕುಸುರು kusuru, *s.* A bit, trifling. *adj.* Little, few.

ಕುಸುರುನಿ kusuruni (ಕುಸುರ್), *v. n.* To shiver. 2. to shrink in, be afraid.

ಕುಸುಲು kusulu, *s.* The small bead of a nose ornament.

ಕುಸೆಲ್, ಕುಸೇಲ್ kusĕlụ, kusēlụ, *s.* Ingenuity, cunningness, a sly artifice. 2. wittiness, –ಮಳ್ಪುನಿ to play tricks.

ಕುಸ್ಕುನಿ kuskuni (ಕುಸ್ಕ್), *v. n.* To shrink, give way, sink in. 2. to sprain.

ಕುಸ್ತಿ kusti, *s.* Gymnastics, wrestling. –ಕೊಬ್ಬುನಿ, –ಮಳ್ಪುನಿ to wrestle.

ಕುಸ್ರಿ kusri, *s.* The pulp *or* soft part of a fruit. 2. *see* ಕುಸುರಿ.

ಕುಹಕ kuhaka, *adj.* Fraudulent, deceitful. ಕುಹಕೆ a cheat, rogue.

ಕುಳ kuḷa, *s.* A tank *or* pond.

ಕುಳಕ್ kuḷakụ, *see* ಕೊಳಕ್.

ಕುಳಮಾಂದ್ರ kuḷamāndra, *s.* Dried juice of mangoes *or* jackfruit.

ಕುಳವಾರ್ kuḷavārụ, *s.* Details. 2. item by item. 3. a list of creditors, debtors, *etc.*

ಕುಳವು kuḷavu, *see* ಕುಲವು.

ಕುಳಿಗೆ kuḷigĕ, *see* ಗುಳಿಗೆ.

ಕುಳಿಪುನಿ kuḷipuni (ಕುಳಿ), *v. a.* To sting, as an ant.

ಕುಳಿಪೆ kuḷipe, *s.* The large black-ant.

ಕುಳುಂಕುನಿ kuḷuṅkuni (ಕುಳುಂಕ್), *v. a.* To wet, moisten.

ಕುಳುಕುಳು kuḷukulu, *see* ಗುಳುಗುಳು.

ಕುಳುಪು kuḷupu, *s.* A piece of black stone *etc.*, with a device *or* inscription on it to be used as a seal.

ಕುಳುಪು kulupu, *see* ಕುಳಿಪೆ.

ಕುಳುವಾರ್ kuḷuvāru, *see* ಕುಳವಾರ್.

ಕುಳ್ಳಾವುನಿ, ಕುಳ್ಳಪಾವುನಿ kuḷḷāvuni, kuḷḷapāvuni, *c. v.* (*of* ಕುಳ್ಳುನಿ) To make sit, to employ.

ಕುಳ್ಳುನಿ kuḷḷuni (ಕುಳ್ಳ್), *v. n.* To sit, sit down. 2. to lodge, dwell.

ಕೂ kū, *s.* Response, responding to a call. 2. alarm. —ಪಾಡುನಿ to respond to a call; to give alarm.

ಕೂಂಕೆ kūṅkè, *s.* Shortness of breath.

ಕೂಂಕೆ kūṅkè, *s.* The mock tribute given in a kind of game.

ಕೂಂಜ kūñja, *see* ಕುಂಜ.

ಕೂಂಜಿ kūñji, *see* ಗೂಂಜಿ.

ಕೂಂಜೆಲ್ kūñjelu, *s.* A kind of weel for catching fish.

ಕೂಂಟುನಿ kūṇṭuni, *see* ಕೊಟುನಿ.

ಕೂಂಡೆಲ್, ಕೂಂಡೊಲು kūṇḍelu, kūṇḍolu, *s.* A wasp. ಪಿಲಿ— a large yellow wasp.

ಕೂಂತುನಿ, ಕೂಂಪುನಿ kūntuni, kūmpuni (ಕೂಂತ್, ಕೂಂ), *v. a.* To peck, strike with the beak. 2. to prick a hole. 3. to put out.

ಕೂಕೆ kūkè, *see* ಕೂಂಕೆ.

ಕೂಗು kūgu, *s.* A cry, exclamation, outcry.

ಕೂಗುನಿ kūguni (ಕೂಗ್), *v. n.* To cry out.

ಕೂಚಿ kūći, *s.* A small goglet, filled with water and placed in a demon-shrine.

ಕೂಜೆ kūjè, *s.* An earthen goglet.

ಕೂಟ kūṭa, *s.* An assembly, meeting. 2. mixture, amalgamation. —ಕೂಡುನಿ to assemble; to conspire.

ಕೂಟಯಿ kūṭayi, *s.* Storing rice, granary *etc.* —ಪಾಡುನಿ to store rice.

ಕೂಟು kūṭu, *s.* The inner roof of a house. 2. the hip. —ದೀಪಿನಿ, —ಪಾಡುನಿ to place the roof on the wall. —ಪತ್ತುನಿ to construct a roof.

ಕೂಟುನಿ kūṭuni (ಕೂಟ್), *v. a.* To sharpen. 2. to mix, mingle. ಕೂಟಿದ, ಕೂಟುದ sharpened; mixed. ಕೂಟಿಲ್, ಕೂಟೊಲ್ sharpening; mixing.

ಕೂಡ kūḍa, *adv.* With, along with, together with.

ಕೂಡಪನೆ kūḍapanè, *s.* A small country water-lift.

ಕೂಡಾವುನಿ, ಕೂಡಿಸಾವುನಿ kūḍāvuni, kūḍisāvuni, *c. v.* (*of* ಕೂಡುನಿ) To join, connect, unite. 2. to collect, gather. 3. to amass, store. 4. to mix; *also* ಕೂಡಾದ್ ದೀಪಿನಿ.

ಕೂಡಿಗೆ kūḍigè, *s.* Joining; union. 2. collection. 3. assemblage, gathering. 4. storing. 5. mixing.

ಕೂಡಿಸುನಿ **kūḍisuni** (ಕೂಡಿಸ್), *v. a.* To add, sum up.

ಕೂಡು **kūḍu**, *see* ಗೂಡು.

ಕೂಡುಕಟ್ಟ್, ಕೂಡುಗಟ್ಟ್ **kūḍukaṭṭu, kūḍugaṭṭu**, *s.* The association *or* union of the members of the same caste *or* family.

ಕೂಡುನಿ **kūḍuni** (ಕೂಡ್), *v. a.* To join, unite. 2. to cohabit, copulate. 3. to embrace, adopt. *v. n.* To meet, assemble, gather; *also* ಕೂಡ್ದ್ ಬರ್ಪಿನಿ. 2. to be mixed, mingled. 3. *c. dat.* Can, to be able, be possible. ಕೂಡುನವು that which is practicable *or* possible. ಕೂಡಂದ್ cannot, *as* ಎನಡ್ದ್ ಕೂಡಂದ್ I cannot, it is impossible for me. ಕೂಡಂದಿ impracticable, impossible. ಕೂಡಂದಿನವು an impossibility. ಕೂಡಂದೆ not being able, *or* practicable. ಕೂಡಿದಿ, ಕೂಡುದಿ, ಕೂಡ್ಡಿ joint, attached; assembled; *as*, ಕೂಡ್ದಿಜನ the assembled people. ಕೂಡ್ದಿನಾಯೆ a partner; an adherent. ಕೂಡ್ದಿನಾಳ್ a concubine. ಕೂಡೋ is it possible, can I? *etc.*

ಕೂಣಿ **kūṇi**, *see* ಖೂನಿ.

ಕೂಣು **kūṇu**, *s.* Pudenda, *Pudendum muliebre.*

ಕೂತಳೆ **kūtaḷe**, *see* ಕುತ್ತಲೆ.

ಕೂದಿ **kūdi**, *s.* The anus; posteriors. 2. *membrum muliebre.*

ಕೂನಿ **kūni**, *see* ಖೂನಿ.

ಕೂಮಕಿ **kūmaki**, *see* ಕುಮಕ್.

ಕೂಯಿಲುನಿ **kūyiluni**, *see* ಕೂಲಿಯಾವುನಿ.

ಕೂರಂಗೆಲ್ **kūrangeḷu**, *s.* Drowsiness, sleepiness. —ನರಮಾನಿ, ಕೂರಂಗೆಲೆ a drowsy man; a sluggard.

ಕೂರಂಬಿಲ್ **kūrambiḷu**, *s.* A kind of medicinal plant.

ಕೂರಿ **kūri**, *s.* A kind of weel for catching fish. —ದೀಪಿನಿ to set it; *fig.* to ensnare a person. ಕೂರಿಗ್‌ಲಾ ಶಿಕ್ಕಯೆ, ಕುತ್ತರಿಗ್‌ಲಾ ಶಿಕ್ಕಯೆ he will not get into one or the other kind of weel; whatever you do, you will not catch him.

ಕೂಱು **kūṟu**, *s.* Boiled rice; *tlg.* —ಕಾಯಿರ್ rice and curry.

ಕೂರು **kūru**, *s.* The dusty substance contained in the fibrous covering of a cocoa-nut. —ಬುಡ್ಪಾವುನಿ to remove it.

ಕೂರುನಿ **kūruni** (ಕೂರ್), *v. n.* To be drowsy, sleepy. 2. to hesitate.

ಕೂರೆಲೆ **kūrele**, *s.* A sleepy fellow. 2. a sluggard.

ಕೂರ್ತೆ **kūrtè**, *see* ಕೊರತೆ.

ಕೂರ್ನಾಯಿ **kūrnāyi**, *s.* A fierce dog.

ಕೂರ್ಮ **kūrma**, *s.* A turtle, tortoise. —ಅವತಾರ Vishṇu's second incarnation, as a turtle.

ಕೂಲಂಕುಶ **kūlaṅkuša**, *see* ಕುಲಾಂಕುಶ.

ಕೂಲಿ **kūli**, *s.* Hire. —ದಾಯೆ a hireling, labourer.

ಕೂಲಿ kūli, *s.* A tooth. —ಬೇನೆ tooth-ache. —ಕಡೆಯುನಿ to gnash the teeth. ಕಳ್ಳ— swelling of the gums in teething.

ಕೂಲಿಯಾವುನಿ, ಕೂಲ್ಯಾವುನಿ kūliyāvuni, kūlyāvuni (ಕೂಲಿಯಾ, ಕೂಲ್ಯಾ), *v. a.* To make faces, mock, mimic.

ಕೂಲು kūlu, *see* ಕೂರು.

ಕೂಲ್ಯುನಿ kūlyuni, *see* ಕುಯುಲುನಿ.

ಕೂವೆ kūvė, *s.* Arrowroot, *Curcuma angustifolia; also* ಕೂವೆದಪೊಡಿ.

ಕೂವೆ kūvė, *s.* A mast; *also* ಕುವೆ.

ಕೂವೇಕ kūvēka, *see* ಕುಹಕ.

ಕೂಸಂಬ್ರಿ kūsambri, *s.* A kind of condiment made of minced and fried pulse *or* other vegetables.

ಕೂಹಕ kūhaka, *see* ಕುಹಕ.

ಕೂಳ kūḷa, *see* ಖೂಳ.

ಕೂಳಿ kūḷi, *see* ಕೂಲಿ.

ಕೂಳಿಂಗೆ kūḷiṅgė, *s.* An irregular tooth.

ಕೂಳು kūḷu, *see* ಕೂರು.

ಕೃತ krụta, *adj.* Done, made. *s.* Improvement; repairs; addition. —ಮಳ್ಪುನಿ to improve, as land *etc.*

ಕೃತಜ್ಞತೆ krụtajnatė, *s.* Gratitude.

ಕೃತಯುಗ, ಕೃತಾಯುಗ krụtayuga, krụtāyuga, *s.* The primeval golden age of the Hindus.

ಕೃತಾರ್ಥ krụtārtha, *adj.* Successful, fortunate, happy.

ಕೃತಿ krụti, *s.* Verification; literary composition.

ಕೃತಿಕೆ krụtikė, *s.* The Pleiades.

ಕೃತ್ತಿಮ, ಕೃತ್ರಿಮ krụttima, krụtrima, *s.* A trick, artifice, deception. 2. sorcery, witchcraft. *adj.* Fraudulent.

ಕೃತ್ಯ krụtya, *s.* An action, act. 2. duty, conduct. 3. any thing proper to be done.

ಕೃಪೆ krụpė, *s.* Grace, mercy, compassion, favour. ಕೃಪಾನಿಧಿ, ಕೃಪಾಸಾಗರ *lit.* the ocean of mercy; the all-merciful God.

ಕೃಮಿ krụmi, *see* ಕ್ರಿಮಿ.

ಕೃಷಿ, ಕೃಷೆ krụshi, krụshė, *s.* Agriculture, husbandry.

ಕೃಷ್ಣ, ಕೃಷ್ಣೆ krụshṇa, krụshṇe, *s.* Krishṇa, the eighth incarnation of Vishṇu. *adj.* Black. —ಪಕ್ಷ the dark lunar fortnight. —ಮೃಗ a buck antelope. —ಸರ್ಪ a kind of black-serpent.

ಕೆಂ kem, ken, *abbrev. of* ಕೆಂಪು red.

ಕೆಂಗಂಣ್ kengaṇṇụ, *see* ಕೇಂಕಂಣ್.

ಕೆಂಗುಡೆ keṅguḍe, *s.* An obstinate *or* refractory person, blockhead. 2. one who has no feelings, a cruel man.

ಕೆಂಚ, ಕೆಂಚಿ keṅča, keṅči, *adj.* Red. 2. fair. —ಮೀಸೆ red whiskers. —ಕಟ್ಟುನಿ to get red, become red.

ಕೆಂಜರುನಿ keṅjaruni, *see* ಸಿಜಿಲುನಿ.

ಕೆಂಜ keṅja, *see* ಕೆಂಚ.

ಕೆಂಜೆಲ್ keṅjelụ, *s.* The udder.

ಕೆಂಜೋಳ keṅjōḷa, *s.* A red kind of great millet.

ಕೆಂಡ keṇḍa, *see* ಸಿಂಡ.

ಕೆಂದಾವರೆ kendāvarè, *see* ಕೆಂಪಲ್ಲಿ.

ಕೆಂನಿ, ಕೆಂನೆ kenni, kennè, *s.* The cheek.

ಕೆಂಪಟ್ಟ್ kempaṭṭu, *s.* Reddishness. *adj.* Reddish.

ಕೆಂಪಲ್ಲಿ kempalli, *s.* The red kind of water-lily, *Nymphaea rubra.*

ಕೆಂಪು kempu, *s.* Redness. 2. a ruby. 3. chalcedony. –ಕಂಣ್ red eyes; glaring eyes. –ಕುಂಬುಡ squash-gourd, *Cucurbita maxima.* –ಚ್ಚಿ a reddish scurf generally affecting new-born infants. –ತಡ the red wool *or* hair of animals. –ದಪ್ಪೆ a red kind of the vegetable *Amarantus oleraceus.* –ಬಸಳೆ the red spinage, *Basella rubra.* –ಬಣ್ಣ red colour. –ಮಂಣ್ red soil. –ಮೋಣೆ a fair complexion. –ರೋಗ scurf. –ಮಳ್ಪುನಿ to make red. –ಆಟ್ಟುನಿ to turn red.

ಕೆಂಬುಡೆ kembuḍè, *s.* A kind of pumpkin.

ಕೆಂಮ kemma, *see* ತೆಮ್ಮ.

ಕೆಂಮಡೆ kemmaḍè, *s.* Dust. 2. dirt. 3. a kind of red insect; a glow-worm. 4. canker. –ಮೋಪಿನಿ to corrode; to infest.

ಕೆಂಮಮೃಗ kemmamṛuga, *s.* A kind of deer.

ಕೆಂಮರಾಲ್ kemmarālu, *s.* A ruby. 2. a kind of red flower.

ಕೆಂಮೀಸೆ kemmīsè, *s.* Red whiskers.

ಕೆಂರ್ದೆಲ್ kerndelu, *s.* The udder.

ಕೆಕ್ಕಿ, ಕೆಕ್ಕಿಲ್ kekki, kekkilu, *s.* The neck, throat. –ದ ಗುಂಡಿ the pit of the throat; *also* ಕೆಕ್ಕೆಯು, ಕೆಕ್ಕೈ. –ಕೆಬಿ *lit.* the neck and ear; a complete set of jewelry. –ಮುಟ್ಟ up to the neck *or* brim. –ದ ಮುತ್ತು the nape of the neck. –ಕುದುಪುನಿ to cut the throat; to deceive.

ಕೆಜರುನಿ, ಕೆಜಲುನಿ kejaruni, kejaluni, *see* ಗಜಿಲುನಿ, ಗೆಜಿಲುನಿ.

ಕೆಜೆಲ್ಪುನಿ kejelpuni, *see* ಗಜಿಲ್ಪುನಿ.

ಕೆಜ್ಜ kejja, *see* ಗೆಜ್ಜ.

ಕೆಟ್ಟ keṭṭa, *adj.* Bad, base, vile. –ಗುಣ a bad disposition, depraved nature. –ಜಾತಿ a base kind. –ತನ wickedness. –ನಡತೆ bad conduct. –ಪಾತೆರ bad language. –ಸಂಗತಿ a bad thing.

ಕೆಡ, ಕೆಡಕ್ keḍa, keḍaku, *see* ಕೆಡುಕು.

ಕೆಡಕೆ keḍake, *s.* An oppressor.

ಕೆಡಗುನಿ keḍaguni (ಕೆಡಗ), *v. n.* To fall *or* slip down. *v. a.* To ruin, spoil; to deflour. 2. to remain, be left; *also* ಕೆಡಬೂಡುನಿ.

ಕೆಡು keḍu, *s.* A mole, wart.

ಕೆಡುಕು keḍuku, *s.* Nuisance, damage, loss.

ಕೆಡ್ಡಸ keḍḍasa, *s.* A kind of three days' festival among the Tuḷu people about February *or* March, when they go on hunting excursions, and eat fried grains. —ದ ಘೂಳಿ a strong wind blowing during that time.

ಕೆಣಕುನಿ, ಕೆಣ್ಕುನಿ keṇakuni, keṇkuni (ಕೆಣಕ್, ಕೆಣ್ಕ್), *v. a.* To provoke, irritate. 2. to kindle.

ಕೆಣಿ keṇi, *s.* Stratagem.

ಕೆತ್ತರುನಿ, ಕೆತ್ತರ್ಯುನಿ, ಕೆತ್ತಾರುನಿ kettaruni, kettaryuni, kettāruni (ಕೆತ್ತರ್, ಕೆತ್ತಾರ್), *v. n.* To feel pain in the belly.

ಕೆತ್ತಿಗೆ kettigè, *s.* Carving, engraving, chasing. 2. setting, as jewels. —ಕಲ್ಲ್ a carved stone. —ಕೆಲಸ carved work.

ಕೆತ್ತುನಿ kettuni (ಕೆತ್ತ್), *v. a.* To carve, chisel, engrave, chase. 2. to dig slightly. 3. to set, as jewels.

ಕೆತ್ತೆ kettè, *s.* The bark of a tree. 2. a piece, slice, chip.

ಕೆದ್ಂಕೆ, ಕೆದಂಕೆ kedụnkè, kedaṅkè, *s.* The tip of a bird's wing. 2. a thin layer.

ಕೆದ್ಕ್ಲ್ kedụkụlụ, *see* ಕಿದ್ಕಲ್.

ಕೆದರುನಿ kedaruni (ಕೆದರ್), *v. n.* To break out, burst forth. 2. to be excited, irritated.

ಕೆದಿ kedi, *s.* A feather.

ಕೆದು kedu, *s.* An artificial tank, pool, pond.

ಕೆದೊಣುನಿ kedoṇuni (ಕೆದೊಣ್), *v. n.* To lie down, rest.

ಕೆನಕುನಿ kenakuni, *see* ಕೆಣಕುನಿ.

ಕೆನ್ನಿ kenni, *see* ಕೆಂನಿ.

ಕೆಪ್ಪಡೆ keppaḍè, *s.* Swelling of the cheeks. ಕೆಂನಿ— swelling of the temples and cheeks.

ಕೆಪ್ಪತನ keppatana, *s.* Deafness.

ಕೆಪ್ಪರ್ಸೆ kepparse, *see* ಕೆಪ್ಪೆ.

ಕೆಪ್ಪಿ keppi, *s.* A deaf woman. 2. a silly woman.

ಕೆಪ್ಪು keppu, *s.* Deafness. —ಮುಪ್ಪು deafness and old age; dotage. —ಕಟ್ಟುನಿ to behave like a deaf man.

ಕೆಪ್ಪೆ keppe, *s.* A deaf man.

ಕೆಪ್ಪೆ keppè, *s.* The cheek. 2. the temples. —ಗ್ ಹಾಕುನಿ to slap on the cheek. —ಜಾರುನಿ to dislocate the cheek-bone.

ಕೆಬಿ kebi, *s.* The ear. —ಅಡೆಪ್ಪು deafening. —ಕುತ್ತು pain in the ear. —ಕುರು a boil in the ear. —ಕೆಪ್ಪು a deafening noise. —ತಟ್ಟುಗ an ear-pick. —ಪೂರ half deaf. —ತ ಬಂಟಿ, —ನವು a male's large ear-ring. —ತ ಕಂಡೆ the drum *or* tympanum of the ear. —ತ ಕೊಡಂಗೆ a male's ear-ring. —ಬೂರು the rim of the ear. —ತ ಮುರು a male's common ear-ring. —ಒದ್ದಾವುನಿ to give ear, listen. —ಕಿರಂಬುನಿ the ear to itch; to hear with displeasure. —ಕುತ್ತುನಿ to bore the ear. —ಕೇಣುನಿ to hear, listen. —ಕೊರ್ಪಿನಿ to attend, give ear. —ಕೊರ್ದು ಕೇಣುನಿ to listen attentively; to overhear. —ತಿರಂಗಾವುನಿ, —ಪೀಂಟಾವುನಿ to twist the ear. —ಪಿಜಿರಾವುನಿ to turn the ear; to refuse; to be fickle. ನಿಕ್ಕ ಕೆಬಿ ಇಜ್ಜಾ? (*lit.* have you no ears?) don't you hear?

ಕೆಬುರೆ kebure, *s.* A deaf man. 2. an inattentive fellow.

ಕೆಬ್ಬಟ್ಟ್ kebbaṭṭu, *see* ಗೆಬ್ಬಟ್ಟ್.

ಕೆಬ್ಬಟ್ಟುನಿ kebbaṭṭuni, *see* ಗೆಬ್ಬಟ್ಟುನಿ.

ಕೆಬ್ಬು kebbu, *see* ಕೆಪ್ಪ.

ಕೆಮ್ಮ kemma, *see* ಕೆಂಮ.

ಕೆಯಿ keyi, *s.* The standing *or* growing crop in a field. —ಕೊಯಿಪಿನಿ to reap the crop. —ದರ್ಪುನಿ to thrash.

ಕೆರಂಟುನಿ keranṭuni, *see* ಕೆರೆಂಚುನಿ.

ಕೆರಣ kerana, *see* ಗ್ರಹಣ.

ಕೆರಣಿ, ಕೆರಾಣಿ kerani, kerāni, *s.* Warts. 2. a kind of scab; *cf.* ಕ್ರಾಣಿ.

ಕೆರಮ kerama, *see* ಕ್ರಮ.

ಕೆರೆ kerè, *s.* An artificial tank. —ತೂಂಬು the sluice of a tank. —ದೀಪ the illumination of a tank. —ಪೂಜೆ the adoration of a tank with pomp.

ಕೆರೆಂಗ್ kerengu, *s.* A sweet potato, the root *Dioscorea aculeata.*

ಕೆರೆಂಚಿ kerenci, *see* ಕಿರಂಚಿ.

ಕೆರೆಂಚುನಿ kerenćuni (ಕೆರೆಂಚ್), *v.a.* To scratch the ground, as a fowl. 2. to wipe off, as water from the ground. 3. to crush down a clod of earth.

ಕೆರೆಕಿರಿ kerekiri, *see* ಕರಕರೆ.

ಕೆರೆಜುನಿ kereǰuni, *see* ಕಿರೆಜುನಿ.

ಕೆರೆಪುನಿ kerepuni (ಕೆರೆ), *v. a.* To scrape, remove, clear away. 2. to polish.

ಕೆರೆಪೆ kerepè, *s.* Simplicity. 2. a simpleton. 3. a prattler.

ಕೆರ್ಚಿ kerci, *s.* A knot. —ಪಾಡುನಿ to tie two cocoanuts together.

ಕೆರ್ಪ kerpa, *s.* A slope. *adj.* Sloping.

ಕೆರ್ಪಾವುನಿ kerpāvuni, *c. v.* (*of* ಕೆರ್ಪಿನಿ) To cause to kill.

ಕೆರ್ಪಿನಾಯೆ kerpināye, *s.* A murderer, killer.

ಕೆರ್ಪಿನಿ kerpini (ಕೆರ್), *v. a.* To kill, murder, slay.

ಕೆರ್ಪು kerpu, *s.* A kind of ladder. —ದೀಪಿನಿ to place a ladder.

ಕೆರ್ಪುಡುನಿ kerpuḍuni (ಕೆರ್ಪುಡ್), *v. a.* To cause to lean against; to place against.

ಕೆರ್ಪುನಿ kerpuni (ಕೆರ್), *v. a.* To prop, support.

ಕೆರ್ಪೆ kerpè, *s.* A clod of earth. ಸುಗ್ಗಿದ— clods turned up when ploughing after the second crop. —ಬೂರುನಿ to be cloddy.

ಕೆರ್ಬು kerbu, *see* ಕೆರ್ಪು.

ಕೆರ್ಮಲ್ kermalu, *s.* A Pariah virgin.

ಕೆಲ, ಕೆಲವು kela, kelavu, *num.* Some, few, several. —ಜನ a few people.

ಕೆಲಸ kelasa, *s.* Business, work. 2. employment. 3. affair, matter. 4. advantage. ಕೆಲಸೊಗು ಬರಂದ್ it is of no use *or* advantage. ಕೆಟ್ಟ— a bad act *or* affair. ಕೈ— handiwork.

ಕೆಲಸಿ kelasi, *see* ಕೆಲಸಿ.

ಕೆಲೆಂಜಿ kelenji, *see* ಕಿಲೆಂಜಿ.

ಕೆಲೆಂಬು kelembu, *see* ಕಿಲೆಂಬಿ.

ಕೆಲೆಕುನಿ kelekuni, *see* ಕಿಲೆಕುನಿ.

ಕೆಲೆಪುನಿ kelepuni (ಕೆಲೆ), *v. n.* To crow, as a cock. *v. a.* To iron.

ಕೆಲೆಬು kelebu, *see* ಕಿಲೆಂಬಿ.

ಕೆಲೆವುನಿ kelevuni (ಕೆಲೆ), *v. n.* The ears to tingle.

ಕೆಲೆಸಿ, ಕೆಲೆಸೆ kelesi, kelese, *s.* A barber.

ಕೆಲ್ಲ್ kellu̥, *s.* Brink, edge. 2. vicinity. 3. a splinter.

ಕೆಲ್ಲುಗುರು kelluguru, *s.* A toe nail. —ಸುತ್ತು a whitlow. —ಸುತ್ತು ಜಪ್ಪುನಿ a whitlow to rise.

ಕೆವಡೆ, ಕೆವುಡೆ kevaḍe, kevuḍe, *see* ಕಿವುಡೆ.

ಕೆಸರ್ kesaru̥, *s.* Mud, mire. 2. dirt.

ಕೆಸರ್ಕಲ್ಲ್ kesaru̥kallu̥, *s.* A foundation stone. —ಪಾಡುನಿ to lay a foundation.

ಕೆಸರುನಿ kesaruni (ಕೆಸರಿ), *v. n.* To be inflamed, as the eyes.

ಕೆಸರ್ಮೆ kesarmè, *s.* The remaining symptoms of a sickness, before complete recovery.

ಕೇಂಕಂಣ್ kēṅkaṇṇu̥, *s.* Sore eyes, ophthalmia.

ಕೇಂಕಂಣಪಕ್ಕಿ kēṅkaṇṇapakki, *s.* The black Indian cuckoo.

ಕೇಂಕರಿಯುನಿ kēṅkariyuni, *see* ಕಾಂಕರಿಯುನಿ.

ಕೇಂಕ್ರಕಲ್ಲ್, ಕೇಂಕ್ರಾಲ್ kēṅkrakallu̥, kēṅkrālu̥ *s.* A kind of red stone.

ಕೇಕ kēka, *s.* Taking and giving goods on credit. —ದಾಯೆ a customer. —ದಂಗಡಿ a shop supplying goods on credit.

ಕೇಕೆ kēkè, *s.* A shout of joy. 2. a loud laughter. —ಪಾಡುನಿ to shout joyfully; to laugh aloud.

ಕೇಡ್ kēḍu̥, *s.* Mischief, evil. 2. danger, disaster. 3. loss. 4. perdition; *also* ಕೇಡು. —ಕಾಲ evil times. —ಆಪಿನಿ evil *or* danger to happen. —ಮಳ್ಪುನಿ to do mischief. —ಬಸಿಯುನಿ to wish evil.

ಕೇಡಗೆ, ಕೇಡಿಂಗೆ kēḍage, kēḍiṅge, *s.* A mischiefmaker. 2. an instigator. ನಿರೆ— a bad *or* mischievous neighbour.

ಕೇಣುನಿ kēṇuni (ಕೇಣ್ಣ), *v. n.* To hear, be attentive to. 2. to obey. 3. to ask, inquire, request. ಕೇಣುನಾಯೆ a hearer; an inquirer.

ಕೇತ್, ಕೇತು kētu̥, kētu, *s.* The dragon's tail *or* descending node, reckoned by Hindus as the ninth planet. 2. a standard, flag.

ಕೇತೆ kēte, *s.* A glutton.

ಕೇದ್ kēdu̥, *s.* Mud, soft clay.

ಕೇದಯಿ, ಕೇದಾಯಿ kēdayi, kēdāyi, *s.* The flower of the tree *Pandanus odoratissimus*; *also* ಕೇದ್ಗೆ. ಭಂಗಾರ್ದ— a gold head ornament.

ಕೇದರ್ಮೀನ್ kēdaru̥mīnu̥, *s.* A kind of fish.

ಕೇಣೀರ್ kēṇīru̥, *s.* The serous matter of a boil.

ಕೇನೆ kēnè, *s.* A kind of yam, *Arum campanulatum.* ಮುಳ್ಳು– *Dracontium polyphillum.*

ಕೇಪಳೆ kēpaḷè, *see* ಕೇಪುಲ.

ಕೇಪಿಜಿನ್ kēpijinụ, *s.* A red ant.

ಕೇಪು kēpu, *s.* The cap of a musket, *etc.*

ಕೇಪುಲ, ಕೇಪುಳ kēpula, kēpuḷa, *s.* The shrub *Ixora coccinea.* –ಪೂ its flower.

ಕೇಬೊಣ್ಯ kēboṇya, *s.* Hot ashes.

ಕೇಮ kēma, *s.* A blow, hit, box. 2. meal, food.

ಕೇಯಿ kēyi, *see* ಕೆಯಿ.

ಕೇರಳ kēraḷa, *s.* The province of Malabar.

ಕೇರಿ kēri, *s.* A street, lane.

ಕೇರೆ kērè, *s.* A kind of harmless snake.

ಕೇರೆಕಾರ್ kērekārụ, *s.* A scaly-skinned leg.

ಕೇರೆಬೂರು kērebūru, *s.* A kind of creeper.

ಕೇರೆಮೇಯಿ kēremēyi, *s.* A scaly skin.

ಕೇರ್ಲೆ kērle, *s.* A sound, noise. 2. the mid-rib of a sago palm-leaf; *cf.* ತೇಪಲೆ. ನೀರ್ ತೇಪಿ– a kind of scoop for irrigating a field.

ಕೇಲ್ kēlụ, *s.* The abode of a Pariah.

ಕೇವಜಿ kēvaji, *s.* A kind of fish.

ಕೇವಲ kēvala, *adj.* Entire, sole, absolute, excessive. *adv.* Very much, entirely –ಪಾಪಿ a great sinner –ಪ್ರೀತಿ great friendship –ಬಡವೆ a very poor man.

ಕೇವು kēvu, *s.* Boat-hire. –ದ ಓಡ a hired boat. –ದಾಯಿ a boatman.

ಕೇಶ kēša, *s.* The hair of the head.

ಕೇಶರ kēšara, *s.* A filament. 2. pollen. 3. the tree *Mesua ferrea.*

ಕೇಶವೆ kēšave, *s.* Vishṇu, one who is worshipped. 2. a man's name.

ಕೇಸ್ kēsụ, *s.* A male's superior upper garment, made of red silk.

ಕೇಸರಿ kēsari, *s.* A lion. 2. the filaments of a flower. ಕುಂಕುಮ– Spanish saffron. ಪದ್ಮ– the filaments of the lotus.

ಕೇಸರ್ಮೆ kēsarmè, *see* ಕೆಸರ್ಮೆ.

ಕೈ kei, *s.* The hand. 2. a sleeve. 3. the handle of an instrument. 4. a branch *or* leaf of a plantain tree. 5. the arm of a river, *etc.* 6. a key. 7. a lot of five, as nuts, sheaves of hay, *etc.*; *cf.* ಕೆಯಿ. –ಅಮರ್ಕೆ a handful; willingly, liberally. –ಕಾರ್ the hands and legs. –ಕಟ್ಟ್ the hand proper, consisting of the palm and fingers, united by the wrist to the arm. –ತ ಮುಟ್ಟ್ the knuckles of the hand. –ಯುಜಿ, *see* ಕೈಗುಣ. –ತಾತ್ as long as the hand. –ತಿತ್ತ್ subject to, dependent on. –ದೂರ beyond the reach of the hand. ಇಡೆ–, ಒಳ– underhand; collusion. ತುದಿ– the arm of a river. ದಂಬು–, ದಂಮು–, ದತ್ತ–, ಪಿಜ್ಜ– the left hand. ಪುಡ– the handle of a plough. ಪುಡೆ– side by side, closely. ಅಪ್ಪೆ ಪುಡೆಕೈಡ್ ಇತ್ತಿ ಬಾಲೆ a child attached to its mother. ಬಲ–, ಬಲತ– the right hand. ಬೀಗದ– a key. ಮದನ– the ornamental top of a pillar supporting a roof; a roof projecting from the trunk of a tree. ಅಂಗೈ the palm of the hand. ಮುಂಗೈ the elbow. ನೆಲಕೈದರ್ಪುನಿ *lit.* to strike the hands against the ground; to curse. –ತುಂಬ handful; liberally. –ಕ್ ತಿಕ್ಕುನಿ to come to hand, be within reach of the hand; to be caught. –ಕ್ ಬಾಯಿಗ್ ಆಪಿನಿ *lit.* to be serviceable for the mouth and hand; to succour, help, as a grown up son to his parents. –ಕ್ ಬಾಯಿಗ್ ತೂಪಿನಿ *lit.* to glance at the hand and mouth; to covet. –ಕಟ್ಟುನಿ to cross *or* tie the hands. –ಕಾಪುನಿ to expect *or* seek help; to watch. –ಕುದ್ಪುನಿ, –ಕುಡೊತ್ತುನಿ to shake *or* dust off the hand. –ಕೂಡಾವುನಿ to join hands, as in marriage. –ಕೂಡುನಿ to attain, gain; to succeed, prosper. –ಕೊಪಿರ್ನಿ to shake hands; to help, assist. –ಜಾರಾವುನಿ to draw the hand back. –ಜಾರುನಿ the hand to slip; to slip from the hand. –ಜೋಡಾವುನಿ, *see* –ಕೂಡಾವುನಿ. –ಜೋಡುನಿ to close the hands. –ತಟ್ಟುನಿ to clap the hands; to pat on the back. –ತಡೆವುನಿ to stop the hand. –ತತ್ತ್‌ದ್ ದೀಪಿನಿ to misplace, miss; to place out of reach. –ತಿದ್ದುನಿ to settle one's hand in writing. –ತೂಪಿನಿ to feel the pulse; to observe the palm of the hand, as a palmister. –ತೊಂಕುನಿ, –ತೊಲುಂಕುನಿ, –ತೊಳುಂಕುನಿ, –ದೆಕ್ಕುನಿ, –ದೊಳಂಕುನಿ to wash the hand. –ದೀಪಿನಿ to dip *or* place the hand on the head; to ordain. –ದೆರ್ಪುನಿ to lift the hand; to threaten; to assault. –ನಡಪಾವುನಿ *lit.* to direct the hand; to intermeddle; to manage a business. –ನಡಪುನಿ *lit.* the hand to move; to be energetic *or* able to work; to succeed in any undertaking. –ಪಂದಾವುನಿ to move the hands, as when busy. –ಪಂದುನಿ the hand to shake. –ಪತ್ತಾವುನಿ to re-marry a widow *or* divorced woman. –ಪತ್ತುನಿ to stretch out the hand in order to receive; to show the hand; to hold by the hand; to marry; to be blessed with prosperity. –ಪಾಡುನಿ to put *or* thrust the hand into any thing; to undertake; to interfere; to assault; to take liberties, as with a woman. –ಬಚ್ಚುನಿ the hand to get tired. –ಬಪಾರ್ವುನಿ to grope; to give a second coating of plaster; to give permission to eat. —ಬೀಜುನಿ, —ಬೀಪುನಿ, —ಬೀಸುನಿ to move *or* wave the hand; to menace, threaten. —ಬುಡುಪಿನಿ *lit.* to let go the hand; to give over, forsake, desert. —ಬೂರುನಿ *lit.* the hand to fall down; to be unable to work; to meddle, interfere, take part. —ಬೇರುನಿ to lift the hand for striking. —ಮಸೆಲುನಿ to prepare to fight. —ಮಳ್ಪುನಿ to brandish; to assault; to bargain, handsel. —ಮಾರುನಿ to exchange, alter. —ವಿಾರುನಿ to transgress, violate; to menace. —ಮುಗಿಯುನಿ to close the hands out of respect, to salute. —ಮುಟ್ಟುನಿ to touch with the hand; the hand to reach. —ಪೊಚ್ಚುನಿ to rub the hand. —ಪೊಡುಂಗೆಲುನಿ to ease the hands after work. —ಪೊತ್ತುನಿ to press *or* squeeze the hand. —ಪೊಪ್ಪಾವುನಿ to ask permission to eat. —ಶೇರುನಿ to go into one's possession. —ಸೋಪುನಿ the hand to get weary *or* exhausted. —ಪಾಕುನಿ to strike a bargain, to make a cheap bargain; to promise, assure. —ಪೊಂದುನಿ to attain, gain.

ಕೈಅಟ್ಟಿಲ್ kei-aṭṭilu, *s.* Cooking for oneself.

ಕೈಅಕ್ಷರ kei-akshara, *s.* Handwriting.

ಕೈಆಳ್ kei-āḷu, *see* ಕೈಯಾಳ್.

ಕೈಕಂಜಿ keikañji, *s.* Cattle.

ಕೈಕಟ್ಟ್ keikaṭṭu, *s.* A kind of bracelet.

ಕೈಕಡ keikaḍa, *s.* A temporary loan, without interest.

ಕೈಕಷ್ಟ keikashṭa, *s.* Industry, labour, handicraft, husbandry.

ಕೈಕಾಣಿಕೆ keikāṇikè, *s.* A present given to a superior on the occasion of a visit.

ಕೈಕಾರ್ keikāru, *s.* The hands and legs. —ಪತ್ತುನಿ to embrace the hands and feet; to cringe.

ಕೈಕಿಂದೆ, ಕೈಕುಂಟು, ಕೈಕುಂದ keikindè, keikuṇṭu, keikunda, *s.* A piece of cloth to handle heated vessels with.

ಕೈಕುಂದು, ಕೈಕುಂದೆಲ್ keikundu, keikundelu, *s.* Poverty, strait.

ಕೈಕುಡರಿ keikuḍari, *s.* A hatchet.

ಕೈಕುದ್ಯ keikudya, *s.* Shortness of means. 2. poverty, strait.

ಕೈಕೆ keikè, *see* ಕೈಪೆ.

ಕೈಕೆಲಸ keikelasa, *s.* Manual labour, handicraft. —ದಾಯೆ a manual labourer.

ಕೈಕೊಣುನಿ keikoṇuni, *v. refl.* To hold. 2. to accept, receive, take.

ಕೈಕೋರಿ keikōri, *s.* A kind of round *or* long scoop for serving boiled rice with.

ಕೈಕೋಲ್ keikōlu, *s.* A walking stick.

ಕೈಕೋಳ keikōḷa, *s.* Handcuffs.

ಕೈಕ್ರಯ keikraya, *s.* Cash. 2. purchasing for cash.

ಕೈಗಂಟ್ keigaṇṭu, *s.* Money in hand. 2. a hand-bag.

ಕೈಗರ್ಗಸ್ keigargasu, *s.* A hand-saw.

ಕೈಗಾಡಿ keigāḍi, *s.* A wheel-barrow. 2. a go-cart.

ಕೈಗಾರಿಕೆ keigārikè, *s.* Manual skill, dexterity; handi-work.

ಕೈಗುಣ keiguṇa, *s.* The virtue *or* efficiency of the hand. 2. practice. 3. experience.

ಕೈಗುರ್ತ keigurta, *s.* A person's signature.

ಕೈಚಮತ್ಕಾರ keićamatkāra, *s.* Dexterity, sleight of hand. 2. manual skill.

ಕೈಚಳಕ್, ಕೈಚಾಲಕ್ keićaḷaku, keićālaku, *s.* Quickness of hand.

ಕೈತಪಗ್ರ್ keitapaguru, *s.* A gesture made with the hand.

ಕೈತಪ್ಪು keitappu, *s.* A mistake, slip of the hand.

ಕೈತಲೆ keitalè, *s.* A hand-rope to climb a palm tree with.

ಕೈತಡೆಗ್ keitaḍegu *adv.* Towards, [by.

ಕೈತಳ್ keitaḷu, *adv.* Near, by, closely.

ಕೈತಾಂಗ್ keitāṅgu, *s.* A hand rail for supporting when crossing a small bridge.

ಕೈತಾಳ keitāḷa, *s.* A small cymbal.

ಕೈತುಂದ keitunda, *see* ಕೈಕಿಂದ.

ಕೈತುಡರ್ keituḍaru, *s.* A hand-lamp.

ಕೈದ್ keidu, s. A sword, sabre. 2. a prison. 3. arresting. 4. conclusion, end. —ಆಪಿನಿ to conclude, end. —ಡ್ ದೀಪಿನಿ to confine, imprison. —ಮಳ್ಪುನಿ to arrest; to stop, finish, terminate.

ಕೈದಂಡ keidaṇḍa, *s.* An unnecessary loss.

ಕೈದಂಡೆ keidaṇḍè, *s.* A bracelet.

ಕೈದಡ್ಡೈ keidaḍḍyè, *s.* A kind of cake boiled in steam.

ಕೈದಾರೆ keidārè, *s.* A marriage ceremony.

ಕೈದಿ keidi, *s.* A prisoner.

ಕೈದೀಪ keidīpa, *s.* A hand-lamp.

ಕೈದು keidu, *see* ಕೈದ್.

ಕೈನಂಬಿಗೆ keinambigè, *s.* Giving *or* striking the hand in token of a promise *or* assurance.

ಕೈನೆ keinè, A nasty woman, *abus.*

ಕೈನೇನ್ keinēnu, *s.* The knot of a fishing tackle.

ಕೈನೋಟ keinōṭa, *s.* Aim *or* direction of a weapon swung by the hand.

ಕೈಪತ್ತಿನಾಳ್ keipattināḷu, *s.* A wife.

ಕೈಪಾಡ್ keipāḍu, *s.* Gain, advantage.

ಕೈಪು keipu, *see* ಕಜಿಪು.

ಕೈಪುಡೆ keipuḍe, *s.* The name of a certain class of Pariahs.

ಕೈಪುಳು keipuḷu, *s.* A rake.

ಕೈಪುಳು keipuḷu, *pl. of* ಕಜಿಪು.

ಕೈಪೆ keipè, *s.* Bitterness. *adj.* Bitter. 2. envious. —ತನ bitterness; envy. —ತರು a kind of fish. —ಬಾಯಿದಾಯೆ a miser. —ಐರುನಿ, —ಅಕ್ಕುನಿ to be very bitter; to be envious, *fig.*

ಕೈಪೆಲ್ keipelu̥, *s.* Bitterness. *adj.* Bitter.

ಕೈಪೇರಿಪುಳಿ keipēripuḷi, *s.* Bitter orange of *Atalantia monophylla*.

ಕೈಪೊಣ್ಜವು keipoṇjavu, *s.* A single woman.

ಕೈಫೇತ್ keiphētu̥, *s.* A plaint, *law*.

ಕೈಬದಲ್ keibadalu̥, *s.* Exchange. 2. changing hands. —ಮಳ್ಪುನಿ to exchange; to change hands.

ಕೈಬರ್ keibaru̥, *s.* A circle.

ಕೈಬರವು keibaravu, *s.* Hand-writing.

ಕೈಬರ್ಕತ್ keibarkatu̥, *s.* The virtue *or* efficacy of the hand.

ಕೈಬಲಿಕೆ keibalikè, *s.* Avarice, borrowing readily and returning tardily.

ಕೈಬಳೆ kaibaḷè, *s.* A bracelet.

ಕೈಬಾಜಿ keibāji, *s.* A small kind of chisel.

ಕೈಬಿತ್ತ್ keibittu̥, *s.* A handful of seed sown on the fifteenth of Paggu (about the end of April) as a beginning of cultivation operations.

ಕೈಬಿರೆಲ್ keibirelu̥, *s.* The finger.

ಕೈಬಿರ್ಸ್ keibirsu̥, *s.* Sleight of hand. 2. quickness of hand.

ಕೈಬಿಲೆ keibilè, *s.* Cash price.

ಕೈಬುಡ್ತಿನಾಯೆ keibuḍtināye, *s.* A destitute, *or* unhappy man. 2. a wicked man.

ಕೈಬೆಡಿ keibeḍi, *s.* A pistol; a musket.

ಕೈಬೇಡಿ keibēḍi, *s.* Handcuffs.

ಕೈಬೇವು keibēvu, *s.* The neem-tree, margosa.

ಕೈಬ್ಯಾರ keibyāra, *s.* Purchasing for cash.

ಕೈಮ keima, *s.* A small piece. —ಮಳ್ಪುನಿ to chop into small pieces.

ಕೈಮಂಣ್ keimaṇṇu̥, *s.* Fine earth used as a rough plaster. —ಕೊರ್ಪಿನಿ to plaster with it.

ಕೈಮಣಿ keimaṇi, *s.* A hand-bell.

ಕೈಮರ್ಚೆಲ್ keimarčelu̥, *s.* Domestication, taming. *adj.* Domesticated. —ದ ಕೋರಿ a tame fowl. —ಮಳ್ಪುನಿ to domesticate, tame.

ಕೈಮಾಡ keimāḍa, *s.* A funeral ceremony. —ಘಮಾಡ such a cermony performed with magnificence.

ಕೈಮಾಸ್, ಕೈಮಾಸ keimāsu̥, keimāsa, *s.* A slow poison.

ಕೈಮುಟ್ಟ keimuṭṭa, *s.* Urgent need.

ಕೈಮೆ keimè, *see* ಕೇಮೆ.

ಕೈಮೆತ್ತೆ keimettè, *s.* A kind of musical instrument.

ಕೈಮೋಸ keimōsa, *s.* A slip of the hand.

ಕೈಯಾರ keiyāra, *adv.* With one's own hand; by handfuls; willingly; liberally.

ಕೈಯಾಳ್ keiyāḷu̥, *s.* A dependent, an attendant.

ಕೈಯ್ಯಕೈಯ keiyyakeiya, *adv.* Hand in hand.

ಕೈಯ್ಯೆಡ್ಡೆ keiyyeḍḍè, *s.* The virtue

or efficacy of the hand. 2. practice. 3. experience.

ಕೈಯ್ಯೊಪ್ಪಿಗೆ, keiyyoppigè, *s.* A signature.

ಕೈಯ್ಯೊಲಿ keiyyoli, *s.* The mouth of a weel.

ಕೈರ್, ಕೈರಾತ್ keirụ, keirātụ, *s.* Welfare, health. 2. happiness, prosperity.

ಕೈರುಮಾಲ್ keirumālụ, *s.* A handkerchief.

ಕೈಲ್ keilụ, *s.* A spoon, ladle. 2. the handle of a hoe *or* axe. 3. a cluster *or* bunch of fruits. ಕುದರಿದ—, ಮಡುತ— the handle of an axe. ಬಾರೆ— a bunch of plantains. —ಪಾಡುನಿ to fix a handle; to put forth a cluster of fruits, as plantains *etc.*

ಕೈಲಕಡೆ keilakaḍè, *s.* The handle of a ladle pointed towards its end. *adj.* Very thin, as the limbs.

ಕೈಲದೆ keiladè, *s.* A kind of cake. 2. a pigeon hole.

ಕೈಲಪುರ್ಲಿ, ಕೈಲಪುರ್ಳಿ keilapurli, keilapurḷi, *s.* A kind of creeper, the flowers of which are used in curries.

ಕೈಲಪುಳಿರೆ keilapuḷirè, *s.* A kind of creeper; *also* ಕಾಯಿರ್ಪುಳಿರೆ.

ಕೈಲಾಸ keilāsa, *s.* The heaven of Šiva. —ಕರ a loan irrecoverably lost.

ಕೈಲ್ತಾರಿ keiltāri, *s.* The feminine species of palmyra.

ಕೈವಲ್ಯ keivalya, *s.* Heaven; eternal happiness; beatitude. —ಕೆತ್ತುನಿ to attain beatitude. ಕೈವಲ್ಯೊಗು ಪೈಪುನಿ to die.

ಕೈವಶ keivaša, *s.* Possession. 2. subjection, taming. —ಆಪಿನಿ to submit; to get into possession. —ಮಳ್ಪುನಿ to take possession; to subdue.

ಕೈವಾಡ್ keivāḍụ, *s.* Manual skill.

ಕೈವಾರ್ keivārụ, *s.* A pair of compasses. —ಪಾಡುನಿ to use compasses.

ಕೈವೊಡಕ್ keivoḍakụ, *s.* Progress; prosperity.

ಕೈವೊಪ್ಪಿಗೆ, ಕೈವೊಪ್ಪು keivoppigè, keivoppu, *see* ಕೈಯ್ಯೊಪ್ಪಿಗೆ.

ಕೈಶೆರೆ keišerè, *s.* Arrest, capture.

ಕೈಸಟ್ಟಿ keisaṭṭi, *s.* A round, wooden trough with a handle.

ಕೈಸರೆ keisare, *s.* A Cæsar, emperor.

ಕೈಸಾಲ keisāla, *s.* A small *or* temporary loan without a pledge.

ಕೈಸೂಂಬೆ keisūmbè, *s.* A hole in a wall.

ಕೈಸೂರೆ keisūrè, *s.* Plundering, pillaging.

ಕೈಸೊಂನೆ keisonnè, *s.* A sign made with the hand.

ಕೈಹಾಳಿತ keihāḷita, *s.* An estimate made by the hand, *i. e.*, by handling a thing.

ಕೈಹಿಡಿ keihiḍi, *s.* A vade-mecum. 2. a warrant for arresting a person at once.

ಕೊಂಕಣ koṅkaṇa, *s.* The Koṅkaṇa country.

ಕೊಂಕಣಿ koṅkaṇi, *s.* The Koṅkaṇi language.

ಕೊಂಕಣೆ, ಕೊಂಕಣ್ಯೆ koṅkaṇe, koṅkaṇye, *s.* A Koṅkaṇi Brahmin.

ಕೊಂಕೆ koṅkè, *s.* A hook. 2. crookedness; *cf* ಕೊಕ್ಕು. *adj.* Crooked, curved, bent; *also* ಕೂಕೆ. –ಕಂಡ a crooked field; an isolated field.

ಕೊಂಗ್ koṅgu, *s.* Irregularity, crookedness. *adj.* Bent, curved, arched, irregular.

ಕೊಂಗ koṅga, *s.* The declivity of a mountain. 2. a name of the Čēra *or* Kēraḷa country.

ಕೊಂಗರ್ಕೂಲಿ koṅgarukūli, *s.* An irregular tooth; *also* ಕೊಂಜರ್ ಕೂಲಿ.

ಕೊಂಗಿ koṅgi, *see* ಕೋಂಗಿ.

ಕೊಂಗೆರ್ koṅgeru, *s.* The lower class of Tamulians.

ಕೊಂಚಿ końči, *see* ಕುಂಚಿ.

ಕೊಂಟ konṭa, *s.* Viciousness. 2. stupidity. *adj.* Vicious. 2. stupid. –ಕೋಣೆ a vicious buffalo; a stupid fellow. –ಪಾಡುನಿ, –ಬೂರುನಿ to be vicious *or* restive; to limp, halt.

ಕೊಂಟಾವುನಿ konṭāvuni, *see* ಕೋಂಟಾವುನಿ.

ಕೊಂಟು konṭu, *see* ಕೋಂಟು.

ಕೊಂಡ konḍa, *s.* A pit, hole. ತೂತ– a fire-pit.

ಕೊಂಡಪಿನಿ, ಕೊಂಡವುನಿ konḍapini, konḍavuni, *see* ಕೊಂಡುಬರ್ಪಿನಿ.

ಕೊಂಡಾಟ konḍāṭa, *s.* Praise, eulogy, applause.

ಕೊಂಡಾಡುನಿ konḍāḍuni (ಕೊಂಡಾಡ್), *v. a.* To praise, applaud, glorify, celebrate. 2. to boast.

ಕೊಂಡಿ konḍi, *s.* A sting. 2. a hook. 3. the staple that holds the latch of a door, *etc.* 4. the clasp of a bracelet; *also* ಗೊಂಡಿ; *cf.* ಕೊಣೆ.

ಕೊಂಡು konḍu, *past. part.* (*of* ಕೊಳುನಿ.) –ಪಾಡುನಿ to put, lay-down. –ಪಾರುನಿ to run away with. –ಪೋಪಿನಿ to take away, carry, convey. –ಬರ್ಪಿನಿ to bring.

ಕೊಂಡೆ konḍè, *s.* A liquid measure, equal to half a seer, *or* dry measure equal to one-fourth *or* one-sixth of a seer. 2. a hollow piece of a bamboo. 3. the bush *or* socket of a wheel. –ಕೊಡೆ an umbrella with a small bamboo handle.

ಕೊಂಡೊಪಿನಿ, ಕೊಣೊಪಿನಿ konḍopini, koṇopini, *see* ಕೊಂಡುಪೋಪಿನಿ.

ಕೊಂತ konta, *s.* Strength.

ಕೊಂತಳ kontaḷa, *s.* A large boat.

ಕೊಂತಳ್ಯುನಿ kontaḷyuni (ಕೊಂತಳ್), *v. n.* To burn, ache, pain, smart; *also* ಕೊಂತಳಿಯುನಿ.

ಕೊಂತಾನ kontāna, *adj.* Boundless, immeasurable.

ಕೊಂತಿ konti, *s.* A kind of fish.

ಕೊಂತು kontu, *s.* The cross-beam of a hand-water-lift.

ಕೊಂದೆ kondè, *s.* A kind of fish.

ಕೊಂದೆ kondè, *s.* The pudding-pipe tree, *Cassia fistula.*

ಕೊಂದ್ರ kondra, *adj.* Small, little. –ಮಾಲೆ a small garland, rosary.

ಕೊಂಪ, ಕೊಂಪೆ kompa, kompė, *s.* A heap. —ಪಾಡುನಿ to heap up.

ಕೊಂಬ komba, *adj.* Horned. —ಕಾರ the pincers of a crab *etc.* —ತೇರಂಟಿ a kind of centipede. —ತೇಳ್ a scorpion with shears. —ಬಿರೆಲ್ the thumb. —ಮುಟ್ಟಲೆ a kind of cap made of the stalk of an areca-nut branch.

ಕೊಂಬರ್ kombarụ, *s.* A kind of cap worn by Koragars.

ಕೊಂಬರುನಿ kombaruni, *see* ಕುಂಬರುನಿ.

ಕೊಂಬಿಕೋಲ್ kombikōlụ, *see* ಕೊಂಬಿಲ್.

ಕೊಂಬಿರೆಲ್ kombirelụ, *see* ಕೊಂಬ.

ಕೊಂಬಿಮರ kombimara, *s.* A mast.

ಕೊಂಬು kombu, *s.* A horn. 2. a musical horn. 3. a tusk. 4. a branch. 5. spadix, the tender flowerbud of a palm-tree, prepared for the extraction of toddy. ಉರೆತ— the horn of a deer. ಅರಕ—, ಐಬೆ—, ಕೊಕ್ಕೆ—, ತಾಂಟಿ—, ತೂರಲ್—, ದೂಜಿ—, ಪಟಾಲಿ—, ಮೋಡೆ— are varieties of horned buffaloes. ಪಲ್ಲಂಕಿದ— the staff of a palankin. —ದಾಯೆ one who blows the horn; a proud man. —ವಾದ್ಯ music with the wind instruments. —ಸೊಂಡೆ the distance of a horn-sound (about two miles). —ಉರ್ಪುನಿ to blow a horn. —ಬರ್ಪಿನಿ the horns to appear; to become arrogant.

ಕೊಂಬೆ kombė, *s.* A buck deer.

ಕೊಂಬೆಲ್ kombelụ, *s.* A horn used by a toddy-drawer to soften the flowerbud of a cocoanut tree in order to squeeze out toddy from it.

ಕೊಂಮರ್ kommarụ, *see* ಕೊಂಬರ್.

ಕೊಂಮೆ kommė, *s.* Corpulence, fatness. *adj.* Corpulent, fat. —ಬೈದನಾಯೆ a corpulent man; an arrogant fellow. —ಇರಿಯುನಿ to diminish, become thin. —ಜಪ್ಪುನಿ to get fat, become stout. —ಮೂರ್ ಪೋಪಿನಿ to become very fat, as cattle.

ಕೊಂಗಿ korṅgi, *s.* The branch *or* spatha of a sago-palm.

ಕೊಂಗಿ-, ಕೊಂಗು-ಮರ korṅgi-, korṅgu-mara, *s.* The Indian beech tree, *Pongamia glabra.* —ದ ಬೂರು a kind of creeper.

ಕೊಂಗು korṅgu, *s.* A crane, stork.

ಕೊಂಗೆ korṅge, *see* ಕೊಂಗಿ. 2. a white cock.

ಕೊಂಡೆ korṇḍė, *see* ಕೊರಡೆ.

ಕೊಂದು korndu, *s.* The stalk of a cocoanut *or* other palm leaf.

ಕೊಕ್ಕ kokka, *s.* The game of hide and seek. —ದೀಪಿನಿ to play at such a game.

ಕೊಕ್ಕರ್ kokkạrụ, *s.* Roughness.

ಕೊಕ್ಕರ, ಕೊಕ್ಕರೆ, ಕೊಕ್ಕಲೆ kokkara, kokkarė, kokkale, *adj.* Rough. *adv.* On half bended knees. —ಬಿಕ್ಕರೆ rough and crooked. —ಕುಳ್ಳುನಿ to sit on half bended knees. ಬಾಯಿ ಸಕ್ಕರೆ ಕೈ ಕೊಕ್ಕರೆ the words are sweet, but the actions rough.

ಕೊಕ್ಕಾಯಿ kokkāyi, *see* ಕೋಕಾಯಿ.

ಕೊಕ್ಕೆ kokkè, *s.* A hook, clasp; *cf.* ಕೊಲಿಕೆ. —ಪಾತೆರ speaking crossly. —ಕಟ್ಟುನಿ to crouch. —ಡ್ ಬೂರುನಿ to be entangled, get into difficulty.

ಕೊಕ್ಕೆಕಾಯಿ kokkekāyi, *s.* The fruit of the tree *Tabernaemontana coronaria.* —ದ ಮರ its tree.

ಕೊಕ್ಕೆರಿಯುನಿ, ಕೊಕ್ಕೆರುನಿ kokkeriyuni, kokkeruni (ಕೊಕ್ಕೆರ್), *v. n.* The hair to bristle *or* stand erect, to horripilate.

ಕೊಕ್ಕೊ kokko, *s.* Boiled rice. 2. cocoa.

ಕೊಚಕೊಚ kočakoča, *s.* Lisping. —ಪಾತೆರುನಿ to lisp.

ಕೊಚ್ಚರ್ koččaru, *s.* A kind of black crab.

ಕೊಚ್ಚಿಪ್ಪಡ್, ಕೊಚ್ಚಿಲ್, ಕೊಚ್ಚೆಲ್ koččippaḍu, koččilu, koččelu, *s.* A kind of pickle.

ಕೊಚ್ಚುನಿ koččuni (ಕೊಚ್ಚ್), *v. n.* To prate, brag.

ಕೊಜಂಟಿ kojaṇṭi, *s.* The refuse *or* offal of vegetables *etc.*, from which the juice has been expressed.

ಕೊಜಂಟೆ kojaṇṭè, *s.* A thicket of thorns. *adj.* Thorny; impassable.

ಕೊಜಕ್ kojaku, *adj.* Over-ripe. 2. burst, broken.

ಕೊಜಪು kojapu, *s.* Sour milk, curds.

ಕೊಜಪುನಿ, ಕೊಜೆಪುನಿ, ಕೊಜೆಲ್ಪುನಿ kojapuni, kojepuni, kojelpuni (ಕೊಜ, ಕೊಜೆ, ಕೊಜೆಲ್), *v. a.* To spoil. 2. to break, cut in pieces.

ಕೊಜಮೆದ ಬೂರು kojameda-būru, *s.* A kind of creeper.

ಕೊಜರ್ kojaru, *see* ಕುಜರ್.

ಕೊಜಲ್ kojalu, *see* ಕುಜಲ್.

ಕೊಜಲುನಿ, ಕೊಜಿಲುನಿ, ಕೊಜೆಲುನಿ kojaluni, kojiluni, kojeluni (ಕೊಜಲ್, ಕೊಜಿಲ್, ಕೊಜೆಲ್), *v. a.* To burst, break in pieces.

ಕೊಜೆಂಟಿ kojeṇṭi, *see* ಕೊಜಂಟಿ.

ಕೊಜ್ಜೆ kojje, *s.* An eunuch.

ಕೊಟಕೊಟ koṭakoṭa, *adj.* Deficient, short, little. —ನುಪ್ಪು small quantity of rice *or* food. —ಬಳ ಸುನಿ to serve out but little food.

ಕೊಟರೆ koṭarè, *see* ಕೊಟ್ರು.

ಕೊಟರ್ಮೆ koṭarmè, *see* ಕೊಟ್ಟರ್ಮೆ.

ಕೊಟಲೆ, ಕೊಟಳೆ koṭalè, koṭaḷè, *see* ಕೋಟಲೆ.

ಕೊಟ್ಟ koṭṭa, *s.* A hut *or* dwelling of Koragars. 2. leprosy; *cf.* ಕೊಷ್ಟ. —ದಾಯೆ, —ಪತ್ತಿನಾಯೆ a leper, *abus.*

ಕೊಟ್ಟಂಜಿ koṭṭañji, *s.* A fruit without flesh. *adj.* Emaciated.

ಕೊಟ್ಟಯಿ koṭṭayi, *s.* A dried areca-nut. 2. contraction, stiffness, death. —ಕಟ್ಟುನಿ to contract, become stiff, die.

ಕೊಟ್ಟರೆ koṭṭarè, *see* ಕೊಟ್ರು.

ಕೊಟ್ಟರ್ಮೆ koṭṭarmè, *s.* Stewardship.

ಕೊಟ್ಟಾರ koṭṭāra, *s.* A palace, mansion. 2. a store-room.

ಕೊಟ್ಟಾರಿ **koṭṭāri,** *s.* A store-keeper, steward. 2. a sub-division of the Šūdra class.

ಕೊಟ್ಟಿಗೆ **koṭṭigè,** *s.* A kind of cake boiled in steam.

ಕೊಟ್ಟು **koṭṭu,** *s.* A spade. 2. a cock's comb. 3. a peacock's tuft. 4. a veil. –ಪಾಡುನಿ to cover with a veil.

ಕೊಟ್ಟೆ **koṭṭè,** *s.* The kernel of a nut. 2. the testicles. –ಕಟ್ಟುನಿ to harden. –ಗುದ್ದುನಿ to castrate.

ಕೊಟ್ಟೆಅಗ್ರ **koṭṭeagra,** *see under* ಅಗ್ರ.

ಕೊಟ್ಟೆಪಿಜಿನ್ **koṭṭepijinụ,** *s.* A kind of ant.

ಕೊಟ್ಟೆಮುಳ್ಳು **koṭṭemuḷḷu,** *s.* The plant *Zizyphus xylopyrus.*

ಕೊಟ್ಯ **koṭya,** *s.* A shed, stall. ಜಾಲ್– a verandah. ಬೆಂದ್ರ್– a bathroom.

ಕೊಟ್ರಿಂಞಾ **koṭriñña,** *s.* A lark.

ಕೊಟ್ರೆ **koṭrè,** *s,* A spade.

ಕೊಡಂಕತ್ತಿ **koḍaṅkatti,** *s.* A kind of sickle.

ಕೊಡಂಗ್ **koḍaṅgụ,** *see* ಕೊಡಂಜಿ.

ಕೊಡಂಗೆ **koḍaṅgè,** *s.* An ear-ring.

ಕೊಡಂಗ್ಯೆ **koḍaṅgye,** *s.* A buffoon, jester. 2. *see* ಕೊಡಗೆ *under* ಕೊಡಗು.

ಕೊಡಂಜಿ, ಕೊಡಂಜು **koḍañji, koḍañju,** *s.* A large kind of ape, a baboon. ಆಟಿ– a devil dancer going a-begging in the Tuḷu month of ಆಟಿ.

ಕೊಡಂದೆ **koḍandè,** *s.* A kind of fish.

ಕೊಡಂದೆಲ್ **koḍandelụ,** *s.* A snare set up for birds.

ಕೊಡಕ್ಯನ **koḍakyana,** *adj.* Hot *or* strong to the taste.

ಕೊಡಗು **koḍagu,** *s.* Coorg. –ದೇಶ the province of Coorg. –ಭಾಷೆ the Coorg language. ಕೊಡಗೆ a Coorgman; a turbulent fellow.

ಕೊಡಪಣ, ಕೊಡಪನ, ಕೊಡಪಾನ **koḍapaṇa, koḍapana, koḍapāna,** *s.* A metallic waterpot.

ಕೊಡಪಾವುನಿ **koḍapāvuni,** *c. v.* (*of* ಕೊಡಪುನಿ) To weld, forge together.

ಕೊಡಪುನಿ **koḍapuni** (ಕೊಡ), *v. a.* To forge, hammer. 2. to bite, as a serpent. 3. to peck, strike with the beak.

ಕೊಡಪೆ **koḍape,** *s.* A kind of bird, the hoop.

ಕೊಡಮಂದಾಯೆ **koḍamandāye,** *s.* The name of a demon.

ಕೊಡರಿ **koḍari,** *see* ಕುಡರಿ.

ಕೊಡಿ **koḍi,** *s.* Point, end, extremity. 2. a sprout. 3. a flag, ensign. 4. interdict, prohibition. –ಮರ a flag-staff. –ಏರುನಿ to set up a flag in front of a temple as the first ceremony of its car-festival. –ಕಟ್ಟುನಿ to tie, in the name of a demon, a handful of leaves to a tree in a forest *or* plantation, prohibiting its use until their removal. –ಜಪ್ಪುನಿ a flag to be lowered as a concluding ceremony of a car-festival. –ದೆಪ್ಪುನಿ to remove an interdict laid on the use of a forest, *etc.* –ಪಾಡುನಿ to decorate a shed with cloth, *etc.* –ಕಡೆ top and bottom; shelter; progeny, issue. –ದಾಂತಿ issueless. –ದಾಂತಿನಾಯಿ, –ಕಡೆದಾಂತಿನಾಯಿ a vagabond; an issueless man.

ಕೊಡಿಪುನಿ koḍipuni (ಕೊಡಿ), *v. n.* To bud, germinate.

ಕೊಡಿರೆ koḍirè, *s.* The top-leaf.

ಕೊಡುಕು koḍuku, *s.* The hymen. *adj.* Obscene.

ಕೊಡೆ koḍè, *s.* An umbrella.

ಕೊಡೆಂಜಿ koḍeñji, *s.* The inside of the cheeks.

ಕೊಡ್ಡೆಯಿ koḍḍeyi, *s.* A kind of fish.

ಕೊಡ್ಯಣ್, ಕೊಡ್ಯನ್ koḍyaṇu, koḍyanu, *s.* A small kind of fish.

ಕೊಡ್ಡ್ಯೆ koḍḍye, *s.* A bull *or* ox with a tuft of white hair on the tail. –ಲ್ಡಿ a cow with such a tail.

ಕೊಣಜೆ koṇajè, *s.* A fly infesting the eyes.

ಕೊಣಜೆಕಲ್ಲ್ koṇajekallu, *s.* A large rock near Mūḍabidri.

ಕೊಣಪಿನಿ koṇapini, *see* ಕೊಂಡುಬಪಿನಿ *under* ಕೊಂಡು.

ಕೊಣಲೆ, ಕೊಣೊಲೆ koṇalè, koṇolè, *s.* The weed *Papsalum pilosum.* –ದ ಬಿದೆ a bad person. –ದ ಪಕ್ಕಿ a kind of bird with a very long bill.

ಕೊಣಿ koṇi, *s.* A sting. –ಊರುನಿ to sting. *adj.* Cunning, deceitful.

ಕೊಣಿಲೆ koṇilè, *see* ಕೊಣಲೆ.

ಕೊಣುನಿ koṇuni (ಕೊಣ್), *v. n.* To take, hold, keep, *in compounds with other verbs; as,* ಎದು– to meet; ಕೈ– to hold, keep; ತರ– to take to heart; ಪಿದು– to recognise, discern. 2. ಕೊಣುನಿ (ಒಣುನಿ) *is used as an auxiliary verb to form reflexives; as,* ತೂವೊಣುನಿ to be careful; ತಿಕ್ಕೊಣುನಿ to get entangled; ನಡತೊಣುನಿ to walk, behave; ಬಾಳೊಣುನಿ to prosper, do well. ಮಳ್ತೊಣುನಿ to make for one's self. 3. *for its past part. see* ಕೊಂಡು.

ಕೊಣೆ koṇè, *see* ಕೊಣಿ.

ಕೊಣೊಪಿನಿ koṇopini, *see* ಕೊಂಡುಪೋಪಿನಿ.

ಕೊಣ್ಪಿನಿ koṇpini (ಕೊಣ್), *v. n.* To hit.

ಕೊತ್ತಂಬರಿ, ಕೊತ್ತಂಬೆರಿ kottambari, kottamberi, *s.* Coriander, *Coriandrum sativum; also* ಕೊತ್ತುಂಬ್ರಿ, ಕೊತ್ತಿಂಬರಿ. –ಕೊಂಚಿಲ್, –ಬಾವೊಲಿ an ear-ornament of gold, strung with small corals.

ಕೊತ್ತಲ kottala, *see* ಕೊತ್ತಳ, ಕೊತ್ವಾಲೆ.

ಕೊತ್ತಲಕಟ್ಟೆ kottalakaṭṭè, *s.* A police station.

ಕೊತ್ತಲಿಗೆ kottaligè, *s.* A palm branch stripped of its leaves.

ಕೊತ್ತವಾಲೆ kottavāle, *see* ಕೊತ್ವಾಲೆ.

ಕೊತ್ತಳ kottaḷa, *s.* A bastion. 2. bulwarks. 3. a trough. 4. a stone pavement.

ಕೊತ್ತು kottu, *s.* A mark showing the limit of a liquid measure.

ಕೊತ್ತೆ kottè, *s.* Trash, dirt.

ಕೊತ್ವಾಲೆ kotvāle, *s.* A police officer.

ಕೊದಂಟಿ, ಕೊದಂಟಿಗೆ kodaṇṭi, kodaṇṭigè, *s.* A wooden hammer.

ಕೊದಡ್ kodaḍu, *s.* A chopping-block.

ಕೊದಮೆ kodame, *s.* A blockhead, dolt.

ಕೊದಿ kodi, *s.* Greediness, eagerness. –ತಂತುನಿ, –ಬೂರುನಿ to be affected with the evil effects of greediness. –ಗೆಪ್ಪುನಿ to take away the evil effects of greediness by charms. –ಬುಡ್ಪಿನಿ to covet.

ಕೊದಿಪಾವುನಿ kodipāvuni, *c. v.* (*of* ಕೊದಿಪುನಿ) To cause to boil.

ಕೊದಿಪುನಿ, ಕೊದಿಯುನಿ kodipuni, kodiyuni (ಕೊದಿ), *v.n.* To boil, seethe.

ಕೊದಿಪೆಲ್, ಕೊದುಪೆಲ್ kodipelu, kodupelu, *s.* The act of boiling. 2. lisping. –ಬಾರ್ boiled paddy.

ಕೊದುಂಬು kodumbu, *s.* The cymbiform sheath of a bunch of cocoanuts.

ಕೊದ್ದೆ koddè, *s.* Stammering. 2. lisping. –ಬಾಯಿದಾಯಿ a stammerer; one who lisps.

ಕೊದ್ದೆಲ್, ಕೊದ್ಯೆಲ್ koddelu, kodyelu, *s.* A highly seasoned soup of pulse.

ಕೊನಲೆ, ಕೊನಿಲೆ konalè, konilè, *see* ಕೊಣಲೆ.

ಕೊನೆ konè, *s.* A point, end, extremity.

ಕೊಪ್ಪ koppa, *s.* The hut of the lowest grade of Pariahs called "Mārimanšeru"; *cf.* ಕೊಟ್ಟ.

ಕೊಪ್ಪರ, ಕೊಪ್ಪರಿ koppara, koppari, *s.* The dried cocoanut kernel.

ಕೊಪ್ಪರಿಗೆ kopparigè, *s.* A caldron, boiler with a wide mouth. 2. hidden treasure. –ತಿಕ್ಕುನಿ to discover hidden treasure.

ಕೊಪ್ಪಲ koppala, *s.* A cocoanut garden. 2. a village of cocoanut gardens.

ಕೊಪ್ಪಳಿಪುನಿ koppaḷipuni (ಕೊಪ್ಪಳಿ), *v. a.* To gargle, rinse the mouth.

ಕೊಪ್ಪು koppu, *s.* A female's upper earring. –ದ ತಿಂಗಣಿ its screw.

ಕೊಪ್ಪೆ koppè, *see* ಗುಪ್ಪೆ.

ಕೊಬರಿ, ಕೊಬ್ಬರಿ kobari, kobbari, *see* ಕೊಪ್ಪರ.

ಕೊಮ್ಮೆ kommè, *see* ಕೊಂಮೆ.

ಕೊಯ koya, *adv.* Over, out.

ಕೊಯಕೊಯ koyakoya, *adv.* Excessively, exceedingly. –ಬೆಗರುನಿ to have copious perspiration.

ಕೊಯಿಂಪುನಿ koyimpuni, *see* ಕೌಂಪುನಿ.

ಕೊಯಿಂಬುಸುಲು koyimbusulu, *s.* A sigh, long breath. –ದೆಪ್ಪುನಿ, –ಬುಡಪಿನಿ to sigh.

ಕೊಯಿಪಿನಿ koyipini, *see* ಕ್ಯೊಪಿನಿ.

ಕೊಯಿಲ್ koyilu, *s.* Reaping. 2. harvest. 3. a small paddy field; *cf.* ಕೊಂತಿಂಜಿ. –ಪತ್ತುನಿ to begin the harvest work.

ಕೊಯಿಲತ್ತ koyilatta, *s.* The paddy paid to a reaper as wages.

ಕೊಯಿಲತ್ತಿ **koyilatti,** *s.* A scythe *or* sickle.

ಕೊಯಿಲೆ **koyilè,** *s. Pudendum muliebre.* —ಪರಿಯುನಿ to become pubescent, to menstruate.

ಕೊಯ್ಯುನಿ **koyyuni,** *see* ಕ್ಯೊಪಿನಿ.

ಕೊಯ್ಯುಸುಲು **koyyusulu,** *see* ಕೊಯಿಂಬುಸುಲು.

ಕೊಯ್ಯೆಲ್ **koyyeḷu,** *s.* Harvest.

ಕೊಯ್ಯೊಲು **koyyolu,** *s.* Bivalve shell, *Mytilus.*

ಕೊರ **kora,** *adj.* Brief, short.

ಕೊರಂಟ್ **koranṭu,** *s.* The kernel *or* stone of a fruit. 2. the cashew nut. —ಕಟ್ಟುನಿ the kernel to be formed in the stone.

ಕೊರಂಡಿ **koranḍi,** *see* ಕೊರಡೆ.

ಕೊರಂತುನಿ **korantuni** (ಕೊರಂತಿ), *v.a.* To pretend to eat, handle food reluctantly. 2. to pick, as lice from the hair.

ಕೊರಂಪೆ **korampè,** *s.* A bruise, contusion. 2. a welt; *cf.* ಕರಂಪೆ.

ಕೊರಂಬರ **korambara,** *adv.* Abundantly, plentifully. —ಉಣ್ಪುನಿ to eat heartily.

ಕೊರಂಬಿ **korambi,** *s.* A kind of tree.

ಕೊರಂಬಿಲ್ **korambiḷu,** *s.* A protection for a creeper, especially for one of a small kind of cucumber.

ಕೊರಂಬು **korambu,** *s.* A groove shaped umbrella, made of the leaves of the dammer tree. 2. a rib.

ಕೊರಂಬೆ **korambè,** *s.* A swamp.

ಕೊರಗುನಿ **koraguni,** *see* ಕರಗುನಿ.

ಕೊರಗೆ **korage,** *s.* A man of the Koragar caste, a tribe that feeds on carrion and whose women wear leaves.

ಕೊರಜಿ, ಕೊರಜು **koraji, koraju,** *s.* A serpent charmer.

ಕೊರಡ್ **koraḍu,** *s.* A log, stump. ಗಂಧದ— a piece of sandal wood. 2. *see* ಕೊರ್ಪಿನಿ.

ಕೊರಡಿ **koraḍi,** *see* ಕೊಡಿರ್.

ಕೊರಡೆ **koraḍe,** *s.* A pollard.

ಕೊರತಿ, ಕೊರತೆ **korati, koratè,** *s.* Defect. 2. want, need; *cf.* ಕುಂದೆಲ್.

ಕೊರನ್ **koranu,** *s.* A kind of fish.

ಕೊರಪಳು **korapaḷu,** *s.* A Koragar woman. 2. a female's name.

ಕೊರಪುನಿ **korapuni,** *see* ಕೊರೆಪಿನಿ.

ಕೊರಪೆ, ಕೊರಪೆಲೆ **korape, korapele,** *s.* One who snores.

ಕೊರಪೆಲ್ **korapeḷu,** *s.* Snoring.

ಕೊರಲ್ **koraḷu,** *s.* An ear of corn. ಮೂ— a small *or* withered ear of corn. ಮಡಂಡಲ್— an after-ear of corn.

ಕೊರಲೆ **koralè,** *see* ಕೊರಳೆ.

ಕೊರಸಂಡಿ **korasanḍi,** *see* ಕುರ್ಸಂಡಿ.

ಕೊರಳ್ **koraḷu,** *see* ಕೊರಲ್.

ಕೊರಳೆ **koraḷè,** *s.* Cold, catarrh; *cf.* ಕೊರಳೆ.

ಕೊರು **koru,** *s.* A bar of metal. ಭಂಗಾರ್ದ— a bar of gold.

ಕೊರುಂಗು, ಕೊರುಂಗೆ **koruṅgu, koruṅgè,** *see* ಕೊಂಗುರ್.

ಕೊರೆ **korè,** *adj.* Weak. 2. small.

ಕೊರೆಂಗಿ-, ಕೊರೆಂಜಿ-, ಕೊರೆಜಿ-ಮರ koreṅgi-, koreñji-, koreji-mara, *see* ಕೊರ್ಗಮರ.

ಕೊರೆಜುನಿ koreǰuni (ಕೊರೆಜ್), *v. a.* To make a noise.

ಕೊರೆಪಿನಿ, ಕೊರೆಪುನಿ korepini, korepuni (ಕೊರೆ), *v. a.* To bark, roar. 2. to bore; *cf.* ಕುರೆಪಿನಿ.

ಕೊರೆವುನಿ korevuni, *see* ಕುರೆಯುನಿ.

ಕೊರ್ಕಲ್ korkalụ, *s.* A kind of sore.

ಕೊರ್ಜಿ korji, *see* ಕೋಜಿ.

ಕೊರ್ಡಿ, ಕೊರ್ಡೆ korḍi, korḍè, *s.* A whip, scourge.

ಕೊರ್ಪಾಟ korpāṭa, *s.* Giving, distribution.

ಕೊರ್ಪಾವುನಿ korpāvuni, *c. v.* (*of* ಕೊರ್ಪಿನಿ) To cause to give, to give through another.

ಕೊರ್ಪಿನಿ korpini (ಕೊರ್), *v. a.* To give, grant, bestow. 2. to beat, flog.

ಕೊರ್ಮುಕ kormuka, *s.* Startle, sudden alarm.

ಕೊರ್ಸಂಡಿ korsaṇḍi, *see* ಕುರ್ಸಂಡಿ.

ಕೊಲ kola, *see* ಗುಳ.

ಕೊಲಂಬೆ kolambè, *s.* Marshy ground.

ಕೊಲಕ್ kolakụ, *see* ಕೊಳಕ್.

ಕೊಲಕೆ kolakè, *s.* The third crop of rice.

ಕೊಲಮೆ kolamè, *s.* A very deep pit; an abyss, hell.

ಕೊಲವೆ, ಕೊಲಾಯಿ kolavè, kolāyi, *s.* A clasp. 2. the metallic top of a cane. 3. a hollow tube.

ಕೊಲಿಕೆ, kolikè, *s.* A clasp, hook and eye. —ಮೆದಳೆ the upper end of a female's garment tuck up into her necklace.

ಕೊಲೆ kolè, *s.* Murder. 2. *see* ಕುಲೆ. —ಕೊಷ್ಟೆ continual hardship.

ಕೊಲೆಂಜಿ koleñji, *s.* A plot of [paddy field.

ಕೊಲೆಜಿ koleǰi, *s.* A kind of fish.

ಕೊಲ್ಕೆ kolkè, *see* ಕೊಲಿಕೆ.

ಕೊಲ್ಕೋರಿ kolkōri, *s.* A long-legged fowl.

ಕೊಲ್ಚಿ kolći, *s.* Setting on edge.

ಕೊಲ್ಚುನಿ kolćuni (ಕೊಲ್ಚ್), *v. n.* The teeth to be set on edge.

ಕೊಲ್ಡೆ koldè, *see* ಕೊರ್ಡಿ.

ಕೊಲ್ತಳೆ, ಕೊಲ್ತಿಲೆ, ಕೊಲ್ತುಲೆ koltalè, koltilè, koltulè, *s.* A cross beam. 2. a clasp.

ಕೊಲ್ನಿಣೆ kōlninè, *s.* A candle made of a piece of cloth twisted round a stick.

ಕೊಲ್ಪಾವುನಿ kolpāvuni, *c. v.* (*of* ಕೊಲ್ಪುನಿ) To fasten; to touch.

ಕೊಲ್ಪು kolpu, *s.* A sprain. 2. the cramp.

ಕೊಲ್ಪುನಿ kolpuni (ಕೊಲ್), *v. a.* To stick, cleave, come into collision. *v. n.* To touch, reach.

ಕೊಲ್ಮೆ kolme, *s.* Nicety, delicacy. —ದ ಬೇಲೆ delicate workmanship.

ಕೊಲ್ಲತರು kollataru, *s.* A kind of small fish.

ಕೊಲ್ಲಿ kolli, *s.* A bay. 2. a firebrand. —ದೀಪ a firebrand used for a light.

ಕೊಷ್ಟ koshṭa, *s.* Leprosy. —ದಾಯಿ a leper.

ಕೊಸರ್ kosarụ, *see* ಕುಸುರಿ. 2. *see* ಕುಸುರು.

ಕೊಸ್ರಾಕೊಳ್ಳಿ, ಕೊಸ್ರಾಳಿ kosrākoḷḷi, kosrāḷi, *s.* A perverse disposition. 2. tale-bearing. 3. an ill-tempered man. 4. a tale-bearer.

ಕೊಳಂಬೆ koḷambè, *s.* A drain. 2. a bath. *adj.* Decayed, putrid, stinking.

ಕೊಳಕ್ koḷakụ, *s.* Nuisance. *adj.* Filthy, dirty.

ಕೊಳಕೆ koḷakè, *see* ಕೊಲಕೆ.

ಕೊಳಗ koḷaga, *s.* A measure of grain.

ಕೊಳಚಿ koḷaći, *s.* Buffoonery; mimicry, jeering. —ಕಟ್ಟುನಿ to mimic, jest; to play tricks.

ಕೊಳಲ್ koḷalụ, *s.* A fife.

ಕೊಳಲ koḷala, *s.* War, battle.

ಕೊಳವೆ koḷavè, *see* ಕೊಲವೆ.

ಕೊಳ್ಪು koḷpu, *see* ಕೊಲ್ಪು.

ಕೊಳ್ಪುನಿ kolpuni, *see* ಕೊಲ್ಪುನಿ.

ಕೊಳ್ಳಿ koḷḷi, *see* ಕೊಲ್ಲಿ.

ಕೋಂಕೆ kōṅkè, *see* ಕೊಂಕೆ.

ಕೋಂಕೆಕಂಡ kōṅkekaṇḍa, *s.* An uneven field.

ಕೋಂಗಂಣ್ kōṅgaṇṇụ, *s.* A squint eye; *cf.* ಕೋಣ್.

ಕೋಂಗಿ kōṅgi, *s.* Ridicule, jest, mockery. —ಕಟ್ಟುನಿ, —ಮಳ್ಪುನಿ to make fun, to ridicule.

ಕೋಂಚ kōṅća, *s.* Extravagance; *cf.* ಕೋಚ. —ಕಟ್ಟುನಿ to be extravagant.

ಕೋಂಟ್ kōṇṭụ, *see* ಕೋಂಟು.

ಕೋಂಟಂಗೆಲ್ kōṇṭaṅgelụ, *s.* Hobbling. *adj.* Lame.

ಕೋಂಟಾವುನಿ kōṇṭāvuni, *c. v.* (*of* ಕೋಂಟುನಿ) To halt, hobble.

ಕೋಂಟು kōṇṭu, *s.* An angle, corner, crook.

ಕೋಂಟುನಿ kōṇṭuni (ಕೋಂಟಿ), *v. n.* To halt, limp.

ಕೋಂದೆ kōndè, *s.* A stick to which fruits *etc.* are studded.

ಕೋಂದ್ರ, ಕೋಂದ್ರು kōndra, kōndru, *s.* Boasting.

ಕೋಂದ್ರಿ kōndri, *see* ಕುಂದ್ರಿ.

ಕೋಂಬುಲೆ, ಕೋಂಬುಳೆ kōmbulè, kōmbuḷè, *adj.* Soft, delicate. 2. young.

ಕೋಕ kōka, *s.* The game of hide and seek. —ದೆಪ್ಪಿನಿ to play at such a game.

ಕೋಕ್ಕಾಯಿ kōkāyi, *s.* A bill, beak. —ದಾಯೆ a quarrelsome man. —ದಾಳಿ a quarrelsome woman. —ಉರ್ದುನಿ to rub the beak; to quarrel.

ಕೋಕಿಲೆಗಿಳಿ kōkilegiḷi, *s.* A singing parrot.

ಕೋಗಿಲೆ, ಕೋಜಿಲೆ kōgilè, kōjilè, *s.* A cuckoo.

ಕೋಚ, ಕೋಚೆ kōća, kōćè, *s.* Boasting. ಪಟ್ಟವುದ—, ಪನ್ಪಿದ— vainglory.

ಕೋಚಿ kōći, *s.* A kind of mask. —ವೇಷ maskery. —ಕಟ್ಟುನಿ to put on a mask.

ಕೋಟಂಜಿ kōṭañji, *s.* Sexual indulgence.

ಕೋಟಲೆ kōṭalè, *s.* Pain, sickness. 2. the chicken-pox. 3. hardship, distress.

ಕೋಟಿ kōṭi, *s.* A crore, ten millions. 2. remembrance, recollection. 3. the name of a male. —ಕಟ್ಟಳೆ by crores. —ಆಡಿಸಿ to recollect.

ಕೋಟಿ kōṭi, *s.* A store, godown. ಉಪ್ಪಿನ— a salt store.

ಕೋಟಿಯ kōṭiya, *see* ಕೋಟ್ಯ.

ಕೋಟು kōṭu, *s.* Losing a game, *vlg.* —ಆಡಿಸಿ to lose the game. —ಮಳ್ಪುನಿ to defeat.

ಕೋಟೆ kōṭè, *s.* A fort, fortress.

ಕೋಟ್ಯ kōṭya, *s.* A kind of sailing vessel.

ಕೋಡ್ kōḍu, *s.* A horn. 2. a pod. —ಕಳ್ಳಿ the milk-hedge, *Euphorbia antiquorum.*

ಕೋಡಂಗಿ kōḍaṅgi, *see* ಕೊಡಂಗಿ.

ಕೋಡದಬ್ಬು, ಕೋಡಿದಬ್ಬು, ಕೋಡೆದಬ್ಬು kōḍadabbu, kōḍidabbu, kōḍedabbu, *s.* A demon worshipped by Pariahs.

ಕೋಡಿ kōḍi, *adj.* A lot of twenty, a score.

ಕೋಡಿ kōḍi, *s.* Corner. 2. a place, quarter. ದಕ್ಕೆಲ್ದ— fireside. —ದಕ್ಕೆಲ್ the hind part of the fire-place in a bathroom.

ಕೋಡು kōḍu, *see* ಕೋಡ್.

ಕೋಡೆ kōḍè, *adv.* Yesterday. —ದಾಯೆ an upstart; a young, inexperienced man, a griffin.

ಕೋಣ kōṇa, *s.* An angle, corner. 2. *see* ಕೋಣೆ. ತ್ರಿ— a triangle.

ಕೋಣೆ kōṇè, *s.* A room, apartment. 2. a corner.

ಕೋಣೆದಪ್ಪೆ kōṇedappè, *s.* A female demon.

ಕೋಣೇರಿರಾಯೆ kōṇērirāye, *s.* A demi-god.

ಕೋಣ್ಕಲ್ಲ್ kōṇkallu, *s.* A corner stone.

ಕೋತಲೆ kōtalè, *s.* A kind of fishing net. 2. a straight grown tree.

ಕೋತಿ kōti, *s.* A monkey. —ಚೇಷ್ಟೆ the pranks of a monkey; mischief. —ಕಟ್ಟುನಿ to be silly, foolish.

ಕೋದಂಡ kōdaṇḍa, *s.* A rope suspended in schools for punishing boys. 2. a bow.

ಕೋದ್ಲೆ kōdlè, *see* ಕೋಟಲೆ.

ಕೋನ kōna, *s.* A kind of sweetmeat.

ಕೋನೇರಿರಾಯೆ kōnērirāye, *see* ಕೋಣೇರಿರಾಯೆ.

ಕೋಪ kōpa, *s.* Anger, wrath. —ಮಳ್ಪುನಿ to be angry. —ಲಕ್ಕಾವುನಿ to provoke.

ಕೋಪಾರ kōpāra, *s.* Buffoonery, low jesting.

ಕೋಪಿ, ಕೋಪಿಷ್ಠೆ kōpi, kōpishṭhe, *s.* An angry man.

ಕೋಪಿನ್ kōpinu, *s.* A piece of cloth to cover the privities.

ಕೋಪು kōpu, *s.* A cup.

ಕೋಪೆ kōpè, *s.* A string of fruits, fish, *etc.*

ಕೋಮ kōma, *s.* A crowd.

ಕೋಮಟಿ, ಕೋಮಟಿಗೆ kōmaṭi, kōmaṭige, *s.* A class of merchants. 2. cunning, craft. 3. a rogue. —ದಾಯೆ a rogue, crafty fellow.

ಕೋಮಣ kōmaṇa, *s.* A piece of

cloth to cover the privities. 2. the privities.

ಕೋಮಯ kōmaya, *s.* Home-sickness. 2. attachment.

ಕೋಮರೆ kōmarè, *s.* An oracle.

ಕೋಮಲ kōmala, *adj.* Tender, delicate, young. 2. pleasing.

ಕೋಮಲೆ kōmalè, *s.* A handsome woman.

ಕೋಮು kōmu, *s.* A crowd.

ಕೋರ kōra, *s.* Measles.

ಕೋರ kōra, *adj.* Rough, not fine. 2. curved. 3. harsh, jarring. —ಕುಂಟು unbleached lawn cloth. —ದಾಡೆ a curved tusk or fang. —ರಾಗ a discordant song *or* tune.

ಕೋರಂಜಿ kōrañji, *s.* A kind of shrub.

ಕೋರಪಂತಿ kōrapanti, *s.* The fragrant grass, *Mollugo cerviana.*

ಕೋರಯಿ, ಕೋರಾಯಿ kōrayi, kōrāyi, *s.* A basin. 2. lameness, hobbling.

ಕೋರಾವು kōrāvu, *adj.* Lame. —ಕಾರ a lame leg.

ಕೋರಾವುನಿ kōrāvuni (ಕೋರಾ), *v. n.* To halt, limp.

ಕೋರಿ kōri, *s.* A fowl, cock. 2. poultry. 3. a kind of ladle for serving rice. —ಅಬರೆ a small bean, *dolichos.* —ಕಟ್ಟ, —ದ ಅಂಕ cock-fight. —ಕಾರ್ the right foot raised against anything. —ಕೊಟ್ಟು a kind of medicinal plant. —ತಂಮಣಾ an entertainment with fowls. —ದ ಕಿನ್ನಿ a chicken. —ದ ಕೊಟ್ಟು, —ದ ಪೂ a cock's comb. —ದ ಗೂಡು a poultry-yard. —ಪದೆಕ್ಕ a kind of preparation of fowl. —ಬಲ್ಯಾರ್ a kind of fish. —ಕಾರಡ್ ಉಂತುನಿ to stand on the right foot. —ಕಟ್ಟುನಿ to get up a cock-fight. —ಕೆಲೆಪುನಿ to crow. —ನಂಕಿಯುನಿ to crow fast and lustily. ಕಾಡ್— a jungle fowl. ಜಮುಯ— a teal. ಜೀ— a short legged fowl.

ಕೋರಿಕೆ, ಕೋರಿಗೆ kōrikè, kōrigè, *s.* Hope, desire, wish.

ಕೋರುನಿ kōruni (ಕೋರ್), *v. a.* To desire, hope expect. 2. *see* ಗೋರುನಿ.

ಕೋರೆ kōrè, *adj.* Curved, bent; *cf.* ಪೋರೆ.

ಕೋರ್ಜಿ kōrji, *s.* A measure of grain, consisting of forty-two muras of rice. —ಕಟ್ಟಳೆ by kōrjis.

ಕೋರ್ಟು kōrṭu, *s.* A court of justice.

ಕೋರ್ಡೆ kōrḍè, *see* ಕೊಡೆ.

ಕೋರ್ತೆ kōrtè, *s.* Preparing a field for sowing; *also* ಕಂಡದ ಕೋರ್ತೆ.

ಕೋಲ್ kōḷu, *see* ಕೋಲು.

ಕೋಲ kōla, *s.* A devil-dance. —ಕಟ್ಟುನಿ to assume a mask, to act a devil-dance.

ಕೋಲಕಳ್ಳಿ kōlakaḻḻi, *s.* A kind of *Cactus.*

ಕೋಲಯಿ kōlayi, *adv.* In lines. —ದೀಪಿನಿ to place in lines.

ಕೋಲಾಟ kōlāṭa, *s.* A game at which persons make alternate motions and strike mutually short sticks in each others' hands. –ಹೊಯ್ಯುನಿ to play at the above game.

ಕೋಲಾಹಲ kōlāhala, *s.* Pomp, display. 2. din of war.

ಕೋಲಿ kōli, *see* ಕೋರಿ. 2. uproar, bustle.

ಕೋಲು kōlu, *s.* A stick, staff, rod. 2. a sceptre. 3. a measuring rod about two and half English feet. 4. a kind of black oyster. ಅರಸು–, ರಾಜ– a king's sceptre. ಪುರಿಪುದ– a rod with a handle twisted with twine.

ಕೋಲುಕಾರೆ, kōlukāre, *s.* A peon in general. 2. a peon whose duty is to measure salt.

ಕೋಲುದಲ್ kōludalụ, *s.* A kind of white ants.

ಕೋಲುಬೇಲಿ kōlubēli, *s.* A fence of sticks.

ಕೋಲೆ kōlè, *adj.* Hollow, sunken; *cf.* ಕೋಳೆ, ಗೋಳೆ. –ಕಂಣ್ a sunken eye, a large eye.

ಕೊಲ್ಕಾರೆ kolkāre, *see* ಕೋಲುಕಾರೆ.

ಕೋಲ್ಡೆ kōlḍe, *see* ಕೊಡಿಗ.

ಕೋವಣ kōvaṇa, *see* ಕೋಮಣ.

ಕೋವಿ kōvi, *s.* A gun, firelock; *cf.* ಕೋವೆ.

ಕೋವಿಲ್‍ಕಟ್ಟೆ kōvilụkattè, *s.* A mule; *cf.* ಹಾಸರಕಟ್ಟೆ.

ಕೋವೆ kōvè, *s.* A mould. 2. a crucible.

ಕೋವೆತೆಂಮ kōvetemma, *s.* Hooping cough. –ರೋಗ a disease of the bowels of children.

ಕೋವೆಮುಳ್ಳು kōvemuḷḷu, *s.* *Barleria longiflora.*

ಕೋಶ, ಕೋಷ kōša, kōsha, *s.* A glossary, vocabulary, dictionary. 2. the scrotum. ಅಂನ– the stomach.

ಕೋಸ್ kōsụ, *adj.* Oblique, squint. –ಕಂಣ್ a squint eye; *cf.* ಕೋಂ ಗಂಣ್.

ಕೋಸಂಬರಿ, ಕೋಸುಂಬರಿ kōsambari, kōsumbari, *s.* A kind of condiment made of pulse.

ಕೋಳ kōḷa, *s.* The stocks. 2. *see* ಕೋಲ. 3. a veil. –ದಂಡೆ, *see* ಕೋದಂಡ. ಕೈತ– hand-cuffs. ಕೈಕ ಕೋಳ ಎಟ್ಟುನಿ, –ತಿಕ್ಕಾವುನಿ, –ಪಾಡುನಿ to put in stocks.

ಕೋಳಂಬಿ kōḷambi, *s.* A broad spittoon.

ಕೋಳಿ kōḷi, *see* ಕೋರಿ.

ಕೋಳು kōḷu, *see* ಕೋಲು.

ಕೋಳೆ kōḷè, *s.* A kind of cake.

ಕ್ವೈಕುರಿ koikuri, *s.* A kind of sheep with fatty posteriors.

ಕ್ವೈಪಿನಿ koipini, *v. a.* To cut, reap, mow.

ಕ್ವೈಯ್ಯೊಳು koyyoḷu, *s.* Chopping. –ಪದ್ಪೆ a species of the vegetable *Amaranthus tristis.*

ಕ್ವೈಲ್ koilụ, *see* ಕೊಯಿಲ್, ಕೈಲ್.

ಕ್ವೈಸೆರಂಗ್ koiseraṅgụ, *s.* The mode of wearing a shawl by a bridegroom.

ಕೌಂಚ kouṅča, *adv.* Topsy-turvy, upside down. –ಪಾಡುನಿ to upset, overturn.

ಕೌಂಟ್, ಕೌಂಟು kouṇṭų, kouṇṭu, *s.* Rancidity. *adj.* Rancid; *see* ಕಸಂಟಿ.

ಕೌಂಟುನಿ, ಕೌಂಡುನಿ kouṇṭuni, kouṇḍuni (ಕೌಂಟಿ, ಕೌಂಡಿ), *v. n.* To become rancid.

ಕೌಂಡುರಸ kouṇḍurasa, *see* ಕೌಡ್.

ಕೌಂಪುನಿ koumpuni (ಕೌಂ), *v. a.* To bury. ಕೌಂಪು ಜಾಗ a burial ground. ಕೌಂಪುನಾಯಿ a grave-digger; a term of reproach.

ಕೌಂಸನ್, ಕೌಂಸನಿಗೆ kaum̃sanų, kaum̃sanigè, *s.* The scarf-skin, cuticle.

ಕೌಚಣಿಗೆ koućaṇigè, *s.* A kind of comb.

ಕೌಟು kouṭu, *see* ಕೌಂಟಿ.

ಕೌಡ್, ಕೌಡ್ರಸ kouḍų, kouḍųrasa, *s.* A cancer on the cheek.

ಕೌಡಿ kouḍi, *s.* A cowry.

ಕೌಡಿಗೆ, ಕೌಡೆ kouḍigè, kouḍè, *s.* A cowry; *Cypræa moneta.*

ಕೌಡಿಗೆ, ಕೌಡೆ kouḍige, kouḍe, *s.* A milkman. 2. a man bringing contribution for temple feasts.

ಕೌಡುರಸ kouḍurasa, *see* ಕೌಡ್.

ಕೌಮಾರಿ koumāri, *see* ಕುಮಾರಿ.

ಕೌರವೆ kourave, *s.* A descendant of Kuru.

ಕೌರೆ kourè, *s.* A hailstone. —ಬೂರುನಿ to hail.

ಕೌಲ್, ಕೌಲು koulų, koulu, *s.* A special agreement. 2. a document granted by government to a cultivator *etc.* 3. the voucher of a vessel.

ಕೌಲಿ kouli, *see* ಕಾವಲಿ, ಕಾವೊಲಿ.

ಕೌಲೆ koulè, *see* ಕೌಳಿ.

ಕೌಶಲ kouśala, *s.* Happiness, wellfare. 2. skilfulness.

ಕೌಶಿಗೆ kouśige, *s.* A name of the sage Viśvāmitra.

ಕೌಸಲ್ಯೆ kousalyè, *s.* The mother of Rāma.

ಕೌಳಿ, ಕೌಳಿಗೆ kouḷi, kouḷigè, *s.* A drinking vessel. 2. a bundle of twenty *or* twenty-five. ಬಜ್ಜೆರೆದ— a bundle of about twenty-five betel leaves.

ಕೌಳು kouḷu, *s.* Odour, scent, smell. 2. a kind of perfume. 3. stench. 4. the cheek.

ಕೌಳೆ, ಕೌಳ್ಯೆ kouḷè, kouḷyè, *see* ಕೌಳಿ.

ಕ್ಯಾತಿ kyāti, *see* ಖ್ಯಾತಿ.

ಕ್ಯಾದಗೆ kyādagè, *see* ಕೇದಂಯಿ.

ಕ್ಯಾಲ್ kyāḷu, *s.* Diligence. 2. devotion, attention.

ಕ್ರತು kratu, *s.* A sacrifice, oblation.

ಕ್ರಮ krama, *s.* Order, method, regularity. —ಹೀನ irregular, disorderly. —ಪ್ರಕಾರ, ಕ್ರಮೊಡ್ regularly, in order.

ಕ್ರಯ kraya, *s.* Price, value. —ಗಾರೆ a buyer, purchaser. —ಚೀಟಿ a deed of sale; *also* —ಸಾಧನ. —ನಿರ್ಣಯ settlement of price. —ವಿಕ್ರಯ buying and selling; traffic, trade. —ಕಟ್ಟುನಿ, —ಮಳ್ಪುನಿ to fix the price. ಕ್ರಯೊಗು ಕೊರ್ಪಿನಿ to sell. ಕ್ರಯೊಗು ದೆಪ್ಪುನಿ to buy.

ಕ್ರಾಣ krāṇa, *see* ಗ್ರಹಣ.

ಕ್ರಾಣಿ krāṇi, *s.* The erruptive kind of rickets.

ಕೃತ್ತಿಮ krittima, *s.* A trick, artifice, deceit. 2. sorcery, witchcraft.

ಕ್ರಿಮಿ krimi, *s.* An insect, worm.

ಕ್ರಿಯ, ಕ್ರಿಯೆ kriya, kriyè, *s.* An act, action. 2. daily religious ceremonies. 3. obsequies, funeral rites.

ಕ್ರಿಯಾಪದ kriyāpada, *s.* A verb, *gram.*

ಕ್ರಿಯಾಫಲ kriyāphala, *s.* A reward, as the fruit of one's deeds.

ಕ್ರಿಯಾವಿಶೇಷಣ kriyāvišēshaṇa, *s.* An adverb, *gram.*

ಕ್ರೀಡ, ಕ್ರೀಡೆ krīḍa, krīḍè, *s.* Sport, play, amusement.

ಕ್ರುತ kruta, *see* ಕೃತ.

ಕ್ರುಸ್ಸು krussu, *s.* A chair; *cf.* ಕುರ್ಚಿ.

ಕ್ರುಸ್ಸು, ಕ್ರೂಜೆ krussu, krūjè, *s.* A cross.

ಕ್ರೂರ krūra, *s.* Wickedness, cruelty. *adj.* Ferocious, terrible. —ತನ, —ತ್ವ cruelty. —ಭಾವ cruel disposition.

ಕ್ರೈಸ್ತ kreiste, *s.* A Christian.

ಕ್ರೋಧ krōdha, *s.* Wrath, passion.

ಕ್ರೋಧನ krōdhana, *s.* The fifty-ninth year in the Hindu cycle of sixty.

ಕ್ರೋಧಿ krōdhi, *s.* The thirty-eighth year in the Hindu cycle of sixty.

ಕ್ರೌಂಚ krounća, *s.* A curlew. 2. a mountain in the Himālaya range.

ಕ್ಲುಪ್ತ klupta, *adj.* Brief, short. 2. fixed, determined.

ಖ KH

ಖ kha, The fifteenth letter of the alphabet.

ಖಂಜ khañja, *s.* A kind of grass.

ಖಂಡ khaṇḍa, *s.* A piece, part, portion. 2. a continent. 3. a chapter. —ಆಗಿಸು to fall into pieces. —ಮಳ್ಪುನಿ to break into pieces.

ಖಂಡಣೆ khaṇḍaṇè, *s.* Division. 2. dissertation. 3. criticism. —ಮಳ್ಪುನಿ to divide; to decide, settle; to criticise.

ಖಂಡಾಬಟ್ಟೆ khaṇḍābaṭṭè, *see* ಕಂಡಾಬಟ್ಟೆ.

ಖಂಡಿ khaṇḍi, *s.* A weight equal to twenty maunds. 2. *see* ಕಂಡಿ.

ಖಂಡಿತ khaṇḍita, *adj.* Strict, severe. 2. positive, true, certain. *adv.* Strictly; positively.

ಖಂಡಿಸುನಿ khaṇḍisuni (ಖಂಡಿಸಿ), *v. a.* To cut into pieces, to sever. 2. to refute. 3. to criticise. 4. to fix, settle.

ಖಂಡುಗ khaṇḍuga, *s.* A measure of capacity, containing twenty koḷagas.

ಖಂಡೆರುನಿ khaṇḍeruni (ಖಂಡೆರ್), *v. a.*

To chip, cut away a small piece. 2. to square, make right.

ಖಗ khaga, *s.* A bird. —ರಾಜ Garuḍa, the king of birds.

ಖಗೋಳ khagōḷa, *s.* The celestial globe.

ಖಚಿತ khaćita, *adj.* Resolute, positive, decided. *adv.* Resolutely, determinately, positively.

ಖಜಾನ್‌ಜಿ khajānụji, *s.* A treasurer, cash-keeper.

ಖಜಾನೆ khajānė, *s.* A treasury. 2. money. —ಪೆಟ್ಟಿಗೆ a cash chest, cash box.

ಖಜ್ಜಿ khajji, *see* ಗಜ್ಜಿ.

ಖಡಾಖಡಿ khaḍākhaḍi, *see* ಕಡಾಕಡಿ.

ಖಡ್ಗ khaḍga, *s.* A sword. 2. the horn of a rhinoceros. —ಮೃಗ a rhinoceros.

ಖದಿರ್ khadirụ, *see* ಕದರ್.

ಖನಿ khani, *s.* A mine.

ಖಬಡ್, ಖಬರ್ khabaḍụ, khabarụ, *s.* A report, rumour, news, message. 2. caution; *cf.* ಕಬರ್. —ದಾರ್ mind! take care! *cf.* ಕಬಡ್‌ದಾರ್. —ದಾರಿ, —ದಾರಿಕೆ responsibility, control, management.

ಖಯ khaya, *s.* Depth.

ಖರ khara *s.* The twenty-fifth year in the Hindu cycle of sixty. 2. an ass.

ಖರ khara, *adj.* Sharp, hot, harsh.

ಖರಂಚಾವುನಿ kharańćāvuni, *see* ಕಂಚಾರ್ವುನಿ.

ಖರಂಚುನಿ kharańćuni, *see* ಕಂಚುರ್ನಿ.

ಖರಾಬ್ kharābụ, *adj.* Bad, filthy, disgusting.

ಖರಾಮತಿ kharāmati, *see* ಕರಾಮತ್.

ಖರೀದಿ kharīdi, *s.* Value, price. 2. cost. —ಮಳ್ಪುನಿ to settle the price.

ಖರೆ kharė, *adj.* True, correct, certain. —ಮಳ್ಪುನಿ to prove.

ಖರ್ಜೂರ kharjūra, *see* ಗಜ್ಜಿರ್.

ಖಲಾಸಿ khalāsi, *see* ಕಲಾಶಿ.

ಖಲಾಸ್ khalāsụ, *see* ಕಲಾಸ್.

ಖಸಿ khasi, *see* ಕಶಿ.

ಖಸ್ತು khastụ, *see* ಕಸ್ತು.

ಖಾದಿ khādi, *s.* A coarse cloth.

ಖಾನೆ khānė, *s.* A house, dwelling. 2. an office. —ಶುಮಾರಿ census, population. ಛಾಪ— a printing office.

ಖಾರ khāra, *s.* A pungent *or* hot taste. 2. soda. *adj.* Hot, pungent. —ಆಪಿನಿ to burn, feel hot.

ಖಾಲಿ khāli, *adj.* Empty, vacant; unemployed. 2. vain, useless. —ಪಾತೆರ vain talk, useless words. —ಇಲ್ಲ್ an empty house.

ಖಾವಂದೆ khāvande, *s.* A master, owner, proprietor.

ಖಾಸ khāsa, *adj.* Own, private. —ಗತಿ, —ಗಿ one's own. —ಮೆಗ್ಗೆ one's own younger brother, immediate brother.

ಖಿಸ್ತು, ಖಿಸ್ತಿ khistụ, khisti, *see* ಕಿಸ್ತು.

ಖುದುಪ khudupa, *s.* The principal Mohammedan prayer.

ಖುದ್ದು khuddu, *adj.* Own, personal. *adv.* Personally, —ರಾಜಿ

one's own consent. —ಸಂಪಾದನೆ self-acquisition.

ಖುಲಾಸ್ khulāsu, *see* ಕುಲಾಸ್.

ಖುಲ್ಲಾ khullā, *adj.* Open, not closed.

ಖುಶಾಲ್ khušālu, *see* ಕುಶಾಲ್.

ಖುಶಿ khuši, *see* ಕುಶಿ.

ಖುಸ್ತಿ khusti, *see* ಕುಸ್ತಿ.

ಖೂನಿ khūni, *s.* Murder, manslaughter.

ಖೂಳ khūḷa, *adj.* Bad, mean, cruel.

ಖೇಚರೆ khēčare, *s.* A demi-god. ಖೇಚರಭಟ್ಟ, ಖೇಚರಾಳಿ a wandering priest, vagabond, vagrant, beggar.

ಖೋಡಿ khōḍi, *s.* Failing, defect, fault. 2. a simpleton. *adj.* Incorrigible, irreclaimable.

ಖ್ಯಾತಿ khyāti, *s.* Fame, reputation.

ಗ G

ಗ ga, The sixteenth letter of the alphabet.

ಗ, ಗಾ (*mas.*), ಗಲೆ, ಗಳಿ (*fem.*) *are affixed to verbs in addressing Pariahs, as* ಬಲ್ಲಗ, ಬಲ್ಲಗಾ come (man); ಬಲ್ಲಗಳಿ come (woman).

ಗಂಗ, ಗಂಗಾ, ಗಂಗೆ gaṅga, gaṅgā, gaṅgè, *s.* The river Ganges. 2. a female's name. ಗಂಗಾಧರೆ Šiva, who received the Ganges on his head. ಗಂಗಾಯಾತ್ರೆ pilgrimage to the Ganges. ಗಂಗಾಸ್ನಾನ bathing in the Ganges water.

ಗಂಗರ, ಗಂಗಸರ gaṅgara, gaṅgasara, *s.* Arrack, liquor.

ಗಂಚಕ್ಕರ್ gaṅčakkaru, *s.* A hoax, humbug. —ಮಳ್ಪುನಿ, —ಡ್ ಪಾಡುನಿ to hoax. —ಡ್ ಬೂರುನಿ to be hoaxed.

ಗಂಜಣಿಗೆ gañjaṇigè, *s.* A fragrant grass.

ಗಂಜನಿ gañjani, *see* ಗಜಿಬಿಜಿ.

ಗಂಜಲಿ gañjali, *s.* A kind of parasite.

ಗಂಜಿ gañji, *s.* Gruel, rice water. 2. starch. 3. porridge.

ಗಂಜಿಪ್ಪು, ಗಂಜೀಪ್ gañjippu, gañjīpu, *s.* A kind of playing cards.

ಗಂಜುಪ್ಪು gañjuppu, *s.* Purified salt, table salt.

ಗಂಟ್ gaṇṭu, *s.* The ankle. 2. a knot. 3. a bundle. 4. money; riches. —ಗುಜ್ಜೆ a small kind of jack fruit. —ಕಳುವೆ, —ಕಳ್ವೆ a pickpocket. —ಪರೆಂಗಿ a variety of syphilis in which the joints are affected. —ಮುದ್ರೆ a sealed bundle. —ಕಟ್ಟುನಿ to pack; to amass wealth. —ಗೆರ್ಪುನಿ, —ಬುಡುಪಾವುನಿ to untie. —ತೀರಿಸುನಿ, —ಸಂದಾವುನಿ to settle a debt. —ಪಾಡುನಿ to tie, bind, knit. —ಬೂರುನಿ to form a knot; to come in contact with; to attack. —ಮಳ್ಪುನಿ to make a marriage alliance. ಬಜೀ— a fabrication, false story.

ಗಂಟ ganṭa, *see* ಕಂಟವು.

ಗಂಟಪುಚ್ಚೆ ganṭapuččè, *s.* A male cat; *also* ಗಂಟ.

ಗಂಟಾಮಣಿ ganṭāmaṇi, *s.* A large bell.

ಗಂಟಾಶೆ ganṭāšè, *s.* Avarice, covetousness.

ಗಂಟಿ ganṭi, *s.* A kind of earring.

ಗಂಟಿಸುತ್ತು ganṭisuttu, *s.* A child's necklace of beads.

ಗಂಟು ganṭu, *s.* The knot *or* joint of a reed *or* cane. 2. *see* ಗಂಟಿ.

ಗಂಟೂಸ್ ganṭūsu, *s.* Stinking produced by breaking wind downwards.

ಗಂಟೆ ganṭè, *s.* A bell, gong. 3. a clock. 4. an hour. 5. *see* ಗಂಟ. —ಹಾಕುನಿ to ring the bell, strike the hour.

ಗಂಡ್‌ಕಾಯಿ ganḍukāyi, *s.* Papaw, the fruit of *Carica papaya.* 2. manliness.

ಗಂಡ್‌ಮೃಗ ganḍumrṳga, *s.* A rhinoceros.

ಗಂಡ್‌ಸ್ತನ ganḍustana, *s.* Manliness, bravery.

ಗಂಡಗಣ ganḍagaṇa, *s.* A host of demons. 2. a band of heroes.

ಗಂಡಬೇರುಂಡಪಕ್ಕಿ ganḍabēruṇḍapakki, *s.* A fabulous bird with two heads.

ಗಂಡಮಾಲೆ ganḍamālè, *s.* Scrofula. 2. ulcers on the neck.

ಗಂಡಸ್ತನ ganḍastana, *see* ಗಂಡ್ಸ್ತನ.

ಗಂಡಕ್ಷರ ganḍakshara, *s.* An aspirated letter.

ಗಂಡಾಂತರ ganḍāntara, *s.* Danger, peril.

ಗಂಡಾಗಾಲಿ ganḍāgāli, *s.* Intercourse, intimacy. 2. interference. 3. slander, defamation. 4. a report. ಆಯು ಗಂಡಾಗಾಲಿ ಜೊಡ್ಡಿ I will have nothing to do with him.

ಗಂಡಾಗುಂಡಿ ganḍāguṇḍi, *s.* Audacity, barefacedness.

ಗಂಡಿ ganḍi, *s.* A hole, opening, gap; *cf.* ಕಂಡಿ. —ಮಳ್ಪುನಿ to bore a hole.

ಗಂಡಿದ ganḍida, *see* ಖಂಡಿತ.

ಗಂಡಿಪುನಿ ganḍipuni, *see* ಖಂಡಿಸುನಿ.

ಗಂಡು ganḍu, *adj.* Male. 2. brave, valiant. 3. large, stout. —ಕತ್ತರಿ large scissors.

ಗಂಡುಸು ganḍusu, *s.* A husband.

ಗಣ್ಯ gaṇṇya, *s.* Esteem, regard, attention. 2. estimate. *adj.* Numerable; honorable. —ಮಳ್ಪುನಿ to esteem, regard, revere, care for.

ಗಂತ್ gantṳ, *see* ಕಂತ್.

ಗಂತಿ, ಗಂತೆ ganti, gantè, *s.* Rags, patched clothes.

ಗಂದ, ಗಂಧ ganda, gandha, *s.* Sandal wood, *Santalum album.* 2. smell, odour. ಶ್ರೀ— a superior kind of sandal. —ದ ಎಂಣೆ, —ದ ತೈಲ sandal oil. —ದ ಕಲ್ಲ್ a stone for grinding sandal on. —ದ ಕೊರಡ್ a piece *or* log of sandal wood. —ದ ಬಿಲ್ಲೆ a cake of sandal powder. —ದ ಬೊಟ್ಟ್ a sectarian mark of sandal on the forehead. –ಭಟ್ಟಿ the distillary of sandal oil. –ದ ಮರ sandal tree, sandalwood. –ಮಸಾಲೆ a sandal paste prepared with other ingredients. –ಲೇಪ smearing sandal on the person. –ಸರಕ್ spices. –ಪೂಜುನಿ to smear sandal on the person.

ಗಂಧಕ gandhaka, *s.* Sulphur, brimstone.

ಗಂಧಗಿರಿ gandhagiri, *s.* A kind of timber tree.

ಗಂಧಮುಣ್ಚಿ gandhamuṇći, *s.* Cubebs, *Piper cubeba.*

ಗಂಧರ್ವ gandharva, *s.* A horse. 2. a musician of the demigods, having a human face and a horse's body. –ಸ್ತ್ರೀ a handsome woman.

ಗಂಧಸಾಲೆ gandhasālè, *s.* A superior kind of table-rice.

ಗಂನ ganna, *s.* A sugar-cane.

ಗಂನಕತ್ತೆರಿ gannakatteri, *s.* A burglar's instrument; *also* ಕನ್ನ ಕತ್ತರಿ. 2. a deceiver.

ಗಂನ್ಯ gannya, *see* ಕಂಙ್ಯ.

ಗಂಪ gampa, *s.* Mire, mud. *adj.* Muddy, sticky. –ಕಂಡ a fertile paddy-field. –ಜ್ಯೆಲ್ a large tract of fertile land.

ಗಂಭೀರ gambhīra, *adj.* Honorable, revered, venerable. 2. deep, profound. –ತ್ವ honorableness; profoundness. –ದಾಯಿ an honourable man.

ಗಂಮ್ gammu, *s.* A good *or* bad smell.

ಗಂಮತ್ gammatu, *s.* Merriment. 2. happiness. –ಮಳ್ಪುನಿ to be merry.

ಗಕ್ಕನೆ gakkanè, *adv.* Quickly.

ಗಗ್ಗಂಧ gaggandha, *adj.* Very dark.

ಗಗ್ಗರ, ಗಗ್ಗರೆ gaggara, gaggarè, *s.* A petticoat. 2. a bell-ornament. 3. a kind of liquor.

ಗಗ್ಗಲ್ಲ್ gaggallu, *s.* A rock.

ಗಗ್ಗುರ, ಗಗ್ಗುರು gaggura, gagguru, *s.* A kind of curry.

ಗಗ್ಗುರಿಯುನಿ gagguriyuni (ಸಗ್ಗುರಿ), *v. n.* To bark. *v. a.* To frighten.

ಗಗ್ಗೆರಾವುನಿ gaggerāvuni (ಸಗ್ಗೆರಾ), *v. a.* To frighten, alarm. 2. to censure, scold.

ಗಗ್ಗೆಲ gaggela, *s.* Fulmination, denouncement; *cf.* ಸಡ್ಡಿಲ.

ಗಗ್ಗೆಲ್ಯುನಿ gaggelyuni (ಸಗ್ಗೆಲ್), *v. n.* To roar, cry. *v. a.* To frighten.

ಗಜ್ಜಿ, ಗಜ್ಜು gaćći, gaćću, *s.* Mortar, plaster. 2. a lump. –ಕುಳ್ಳುನಿ to stick fast.

ಗಜ gaja, *s.* An elephant. *adj.* Elephantine. –ಮುಖ Gaṇēśa, with the head of an elephant.

ಗಜ, ಗಜೆ gaja, gajè, *s.* A yard measure. 2. a ramrod. –ಕಂಮ a flag-staff. –ಕಟ್ಟಳೆ a standard in purchasing elephants. –ಕೋಲು a yard measure.

ಗಜಂಟ್ gajaṇṭu, *see* ಕಸಂಟ.

ಗಜಗಜ gajagaja *s.* Jostling, jolting. 2. trembling.

ಗಜನಿ gajani, *s.* Poor *or* infertile

ground. —ಜಾಗ, —ಭೂಮಿ an infertile land.

ಗಜಪುನಿ gajapuni, *see* ಗಜಿಲ್ಪುನಿ.

ಗಜಲ್ gajalu, *adj.* Confused, distracted. 2. filthy, foul. 3. rough, not fine. —ಅರಿ a foul *or* rough sort of rice. —ಜಾಗ a filthy place.

ಗಜಲುನಿ gajaluni, *see* ಗಜಿಲುನಿ.

ಗಜಲ್ಪುನಿ gajalpuni, *see* ಗಜಿಲ್ಪುನಿ.

ಗಜಾಲ್ gajālu, *adj.* Boasting.

ಗಜಿಗೆ gajigè, *s.* The Molucca bean, *Guilandina bonduc.*

ಗಜಿಪುನಿ gajipuni (ಗಜಿ), *v.a.* To fasten, strengthen.

ಗಜಿಬಿಜಿ gajibiji, *s.* Complication, entanglement, confusion. —ಬರವು bad hand-writing, scribbling. —ಮಾರ್ಗ a miry road.

ಗಜಿರ್ gajiru, *see* ಗಜ್ಜಿರ.

ಗಜೆ gajè, *see* ಗಜ.

ಗಜೆಕಂಪ gajekampa, *s.* A stick for flogging.

ಗಜೆನಿ gajeni, *see* ಗಜನಿ.

ಗಜೆಪುನಿ gajepuni, *see* ಗಜಿಲ್ಪುನಿ.

ಗಜೆಲುನಿ gajeluni (ಗಜಿಲ್), *v. n.* A sore to form *or* suppurate.

ಗಜೆಲ್ಪುನಿ gajelpuni (ಗಜಿಲ್), *v.a.* To cause a sore to form *or* suppurate.

ಗಜ್ಜಿ gajji, *s.* Itch, scab. —ಪಾಡುನಿ, *see* ಗದ್ದಪುನಿ. ಗಜ್ಜಿ ಇತ್ತಿನಾಯಗ ಲಜ್ಜಿ ಇಜ್ಜಿ he who suffers from itch has no shame.

ಗಜ್ಜಿರ gajjira, *s.* The marsh date tree. —ಪಂದ್ also its fruits.

ಗಜ್ಜೆ gajjè, *see* ಗೆಜ್ಜೆ.

ಗಟ gaṭa, *see* ಘಟ.

ಗಟಗಟ gaṭagaṭa, *s.* A gurgling noise, as produced when drinking.

ಗಟಣಿ gaṭaṇi, *see* ಘಟ್ಟಣೆ.

ಗಟ್ಟ gaṭṭa, *see* ಘಟ್ಟ.

ಗಟ್ಟಣಿ, ಗಟ್ಟಣಿಗೆ, ಗಟ್ಟಣೆ gaṭṭaṇi, gaṭṭaṇigè, gaṭṭaṇè, *s.* The foundation of a building.

ಗಟ್ಟಳೆ gaṭṭaḷè, *see* ಕಟ್ಟಳೆ.

ಗಟ್ಟಿ gaṭṭi, *adj.* Firm, secure. 2. solid, hard. 3. clever, able, strong. —ಉಳಿ a narrow, thick chisel. —ಕೆಲಸ substantial work. —ಬಾಯಿ a loud speaker, a talkative person. —ಕಟ್ಟುನಿ to coagulate, curdle, freeze. —ಪತ್ತುನಿ to hold fast. —ಮಲ್ಪುನಿ to make strong, fix firmly; to bake a kind of cake; *cf.* ಗಟ್ಟಿ.

ಗಟ್ಟಿಗಟ್ಟಿ gaṭṭigaṭṭi, *s.* Clot after clot, clod after clod. *adj.* Very cloddy, very hard.

ಗಟ್ಟಿಗೆ gaṭṭige, *s.* A clever man. ಗಟ್ಟಿಗತನ cleverness, ability, skill.

ಗಟ್ಟಿಯುನಿ, ಗಟ್ಟ್ಯುನಿ gaṭṭiyuni, gaṭṭyuni (ಗಟ್ಟಿಯ್), *v. a.* To wipe off.

ಗಟ್ಟೆ gaṭṭè, *s.* A kind of cake. 2. a clod, lump.

ಗಟ್ಳೆ gaṭḷè, *see* ಕಟ್ಟಳೆ.

ಗಡ್ಸ್ gaḍusu, *adj.* Powerful, strong, able. 2. clever. 3. brave, firm, gallant. 4. severe, strict. —ತನ severity, strictness, strength; ability. —ದಾಯಿ, ಗಡಿಸಿ an able *or* wealthy man.

ಗಡಂಗ್ gaḍaṅgu, *s.* A godown, store-room. 2. a toddy-shop.

ಗಡಂಬಲೆ gaḍambalè, *s.* A poisonous snake.

ಗಡಕ, ಗಡಗ gaḍaka, gaḍaga, *see* ಕಡಗ.

ಗಡಕ್ಕ gaḍakka, *adv.* Suddenly.

ಗಡಗಡ gaḍagaḍa, *s.* A chattering noise. —ನಡುಗುನು to shiver, tremble with cold.

ಗಡಬಡಿ gaḍabaḍi, *see* ಗಡಿಬಿಡಿ.

ಗಡಯಿ, ಗಡಾಯಿ gaḍayi, gaḍāyi, *s.* A long pole with spherical bells, shaken in temples; *cf.* ಗಗ್ಗರ. 2. a hillock, hill. —ಕಲ್ಲ್ the name of a rocky hill.

ಗಡಸ್ gaḍasu, *s.* A heifer, young cow.

ಗಡಾಬಾಜಿ gaḍābāji, *s.* A rocket. 2. an independent person. 3. heedlessness, recklessness, disregard.

ಗಡಿ gaḍi, *s.* An incision, cut. 2. the half of a cocoanut. 3. a limit, boundary, frontier. 4. authority, power. 5. appointment of a headman *or* chieftain. ಅಡಂಗ್ಯೆಡ— a piece of mango-pickles. —ಕಲ್ಲ್ a boundary stone, land-mark. —ನಿಡಿ, —ನುಡಿ nomination and appointment of a headman with certain privileges in a demon shrine. —ಪಾರ್ banishment, transportation. —ಪಾರ್ ಮಳ್ಪುನಿ, —ದಾಂಟಿಸುನಿ to banish. —ಕೊರ್ಪಿನಿ to appoint a headman. —ದಾಂಟುನಿ to transgress, violate the bounds. —ಪಾಡುನಿ to make an incision, mark out a tree to be cut down. ಜಾರ್— a slip. ಚತುಸ್ಗಡಿ the boundary of a land.

ಗಡಿಗೆ gaḍige, *s.* A small earthen ware, a pot.

ಗಡಿಪುನಿ gaḍipuni (ಗಡಿ), *v. n.* To agree, harmonize, be in unison. 2. to suit, be convenient. ಪುಗೆ ಪತ್ತಿ ಇಲ್ಲ್ ಗಡಿಪಂದ್ a house black with smoke will not suit, (said of a restless *or* fickle-minded man). ಮೋಕುಳೆಗ್ ಗಡಿಪುಜಿ they do not agree together.

ಗಡಿಬಿಡಿ gaḍibiḍi, *s.* Bustle confusion, disorder, tumult, disturbance. —ಮಳ್ಪುನಿ to bustle; to disturb; *cf.* ಗಲಿಬಿಲಿ.

ಗಡಿಮ gaḍima, *s.* A large piece of any thing.

ಗಡಿಯಾಳ್ gaḍiyāḷu, *s.* A watch, clock. —ದಾಯೆ a watchmaker.

ಗಡಿಯುನಿ gaḍiyuni, *see* ಗಡಿಪುನಿ.

ಗಡು gaḍu, *s.* A term, fixed time *or* place. —ಗಡು periodically, now and then. —ದೀಪಿನಿ, —ಪಾಡುನಿ to fix a time.

ಗಡುವಾಡ್ gaḍuvāḍu, *s.* Halt, stay. —ಜಾಗ a halting place.

ಗಡುಸ್ತನ gaḍustana, *s.* Bravery, manliness. 2. power, strength, greatness; *cf.* ಗಂಡುಸ್ತನ.

ಗಡ್ಡ gaḍḍa, *s*. The chin. 2. the beard. —ಪತ್ತಿದ ನಟ್ಟೊಳುನಿ to entreat a person by taking hold of his beard in token of respect.

ಗಡ್ಡಯಿ gaḍḍayi, *s*. Compulsion, force. *adj*. Compulsory; *also* ಕಡ್ಡಾಯಿ. —ದ ಕೆಲಸ compulsory work. —ಕಟ್ಟುನಿ to compel, force.

ಗಡ್ಡಿ gaḍḍi, *see* ಕಡ್ಡಿ.

ಗಡ್ಡೆ gaḍḍè, *s*. A bulbous root. 2. a lump, clod. —ಕಟ್ಟುನಿ to coagulate, curdle.

ಗಡ್ಸ್ತನ gaḍsụtana, *see* ಕಡಸ್.

ಗಣ gaṇa, *s*. A flock, host, multitude. 2. a retinue, train of attendants. 3. a class of spirits. 4. a foot of three syllables. 5. a number, *arith*. 6. series of asterisms classed under three heads, ನರ— human, ರಾಕ್ಷಸ— infernal, and ದೇವ— divine. —ಪತಿ Gaṇēša the leader of Šivā's retinue. ಕಂದ— evil spirits. ದೂತ— angels.

ಗಣಂಬ್ gaṇṇaṅụ, *s*. A tinkling sound.

ಗಣಕಲೆಪಿನಿ gaṇakalepini (ಗಣಕಲೆ), *v. n*. To be pensive, thoughtful and sad.

ಗಣಗಟಿ gaṇagaṭi, *s*. Leg ornaments.

ಗಣನೆ gaṇanè, *s*. Regard, esteem. 2. calculation.

ಗಣಸ್ gaṇasụ, *s*. The link of a chain. 2. a hook.

ಗಣಾಲ್ gaṇālụ, *see* ಗಣಿಲ್.

ಗಣಿತ gaṇita, *s*. Arithmetic, calculation. *adj*. Counted, numbered. —ವಿದ್ಯ arithmetic.

ಗಣಿಪುನಿ gaṇipuni, *see* ಕೆಣಪುನಿ, ಗುಣಿಪುನಿ.

ಗಣಿಲ್ gaṇilụ, *s*. Tinkling. —ಆಪಿನಿ to tinkle.

ಗಣೆ gaṇè, *s*. A pole, staff. 2. an arrow. ದೊಂಬರೆ— a tumbler's pole; *cf* ಕಣೆ.

ಗಣೇಶ, ಗಣೇಶೆ gaṇēša, gaṇēše, *s*. The chief of demi-gods and remover of obstacles. He is invoked at the commencement of auspicious ceremonies; *also* ಗಣಪತಿ.

ಗಣ್ಯ gaṇya, *see* ಗಣ್ಯ.

ಗತ್ gatụ, *s*. Fatigue, weariness, trouble. ಬೆಂದ್ ಬೆಂದ್ ಗತಿ ಆಯೆ he is done up by working continuously.

ಗತ gata, *adj*. Past, gone, antecedent. —ಆಪಿನಿ to expire. ಜೀವ— suicide, extinction of life. ಮನೋ— intention, wish, purpose.

ಗತಿ gati, *s*. Destiny, fate, fortune, condition. 2. protection, support. 3. means, resources, income. 4. motion, course. —ಗೋತ್ರ means and family. —ಗೋತ್ರದಾಂತಿನಾಯೆ a poor, helpless man. ಅಧೋ— a downward course; perdition. ಊರ್ಧ್ವ— an upward *or* heavenward course; salvation. ಕಾಲ— the progress of time. ಗ್ರಹ— the motion of planets, their influence on the human destiny. ದುರ್– a bad condition; future misery. ದೈವ– fate, destiny. –ಮಳ್ಪುನಿ to help, show means; to make funeral ceremonies. ಎಂಕ್ ಏರ್– who will protect *or* save me? ಎಂಕ್ ದಾನೆ– what support have I? what is to become of me? ಎಂಕ್ ಗತಿ ಇಜ್ಜಿ I have no means *or* support.

ಗತು **gatu,** *see* ಗತಿ.

ಗದ **gada,** *see* ಗದೆ.

ಗದಗದ **gadagada,** *s.* A crackling noise. –ಅಲುಗನಿ to burn *or* blaze with a crackling noise.

ಗದರ್ **gadaru,** *s.* A lump. 2. an object of love.

ಗದಿಪುನಿ **gadipuni,** *see* ಗೆದಿಪುನಿ.

ಗದುಕುನಿ, ಗದ್ಕುನಿ **gadukuni, gadkuni** (ಗದಿ), *v. n.* To lap, jolt.

ಗದೆ **gade** *s.* A weapon; a club, mace.

ಗದ್ದಲ **gddala,** *s.* Confusion, disturbance, noise. –ಮಳ್ಪುನಿ to make noise, to reprove, rebuke; to exhibit magnificence, grandeur.

ಗದ್ದವು, ಗದ್ದಾವು **gaddavu gaddāvu,** *s.* An earthen plate.

ಗದ್ದಾವುನಿ **gaddāvuni,** *c. v.* (*of* ಗದ್ದುನಿ) To shake, move, rock.

ಗದ್ದಿಗೆ **gaddigė,** *s.* A throne, seat of honour.

ಗದ್ದುನಿ **gadduni** (ಗದ್ದಿ), *v. n.* To shake, quiver, be agitated.

ಗದ್ದೆಲ **gaddela,** *see* ಗದ್ದಲ.

ಗದ್ಯ **gaddya,** *s.* Prose. –ಪದ್ಯ prose and verse.

ಗಧೆ **gadhe,** *see* ಗದೆ.

ಗನ **gana,** *see* ಘನ.

ಗನಾಗಟ್ಟಿ **ganāgaṭṭi,** *s.* A tinkling article. 2. anklets and toe-ornaments. *adj.* Powerful.

ಗನ್ನಕತ್ತೆರಿ **gannakatteri,** *see* ಗಂನ ಕತ್ತರಿ.

ಗಪ್ **gapu,** *s.* Concealing; suppression. 2. misappropriation. –ಚಿಪ್, –ಚೀಪು silence, quietness. –ಮಳ್ಪುನಿ to hide; to misappropriate.

ಗಪಲತ್ತ್ **gapalatu,** *s.* A lie, falsehood. 2. shuffling, as cards. 3. misplacing.

ಗಪೆ, ಗಪ್ಪಿ, ಗಪ್ಪೆ **gapė, gappi, gappė,** *s.* A lie, falsehood. 2. a hoax, humbug. –ಬುಡ್ಪುನಿ, –ಹಾಕುನಿ to tell a lie; to hoax. –ಮಳ್ಪುನಿ to hide, conceal, suppress.

ಗಪ್ಪ **gappa,** *adj.* Silent, quiet; *cf.* ಗಪೆ.

ಗಬಗಬ **gabagaba,** *s.* Gulping, swallowing. –ತಿಪ್ಪುನಿ to gulp, swallow up.

ಗಬ್ಬ **gabba,** *see* ಗರ್ಭ.

ಗಮಗಮ **gamagama,** *s.* Fragrance, odour; *cf.* ಗಂಮ್.

ಗಮತ್ **gamatu,** *see* ಗಂಮತ್.

ಗಮನ **gamana,** *s.* Going, moving, motion, course.

ಗಮಸ್ **gamasu,** *s.* Fragrance, odour. 2. stink, stench.

ಗಮಸುನಿ gamasuni (ಗಮಸಿ), *v. n.* To smell, scent; stink.

ಗಮಾಯಿಸುನಿ gamāyisuni (ಗಮಾಯಿಸಿ), *v. n.* To be fragrant, odoriferous. 2. to strike, flag.

ಗಮೆಯುನಿ, ಗಮೆಲುನಿ, ಗಮೆವುನಿ gameyuni, gameluni, gamevuni (ಗಮೆ, ಗಮೆಲ್, ಗಮೆ), *v. n.* To be hot, feel hot, as in a fit of fever.

ಗಯ gaya, *see* ಕಯ.

ಗಯ gaya, *s.* A place of pilgrimage. –ವಾಳೆರ್ the people of Gaya –ಕ್ಷೇತ್ರ the sacred place at Gaya.

ಗಯಾಳ್ gayāḷu, *adj.* Prodigal, extravagant. –ತನ prodigality. ಗಯಾಳಿ an extravagant woman. ಗಯಾಳೆ an extravagant man.

ಗಯಿಳ್ gayiḷu, *see* ಕೈಳ್.

ಗರ್, ಗರ, ಗರಗರ garu, gara, garagara, *s.* A whirling noise, turning with rapidity. –ತಿರಂಗುನಿ to turn round with rapidity, as a top.

ಗರಕೆನ garakena, *adj.* Clean, clear.

ಗರಗರಿ garagari, *see* ಗರಿ.

ಗರಗಾಸ್ garagāsu, *see* ಗರ್ಗಾಸ್.

ಗರಡಿ garaḍi, *see* ಕರಡಿ, ಗರೊಡಿ.

ಗರಡೆ garaḍe, *see* ಗರುಡೆ.

ಗರಣ garaṇa, *see* ಗ್ರಹಣ.

ಗರಮ್ garamu, *adj.* Hot, warm. *s.* Heat, warmth; *cf.* ಗರ್ಮಿ. –ಮಸಾಲೆ spices for curry.

ಗರಸ್ತೆ garaste, *see* ಗೃಹಸ್ತೆ.

ಗರಾಬು garābu, *see* ಕರಾಬ್.

ಗರಿ gari, *s.* A wing, feather.

ಗರಿಮಿ garimi, *see* ಗರ್ಮಿ.

ಗರಿಮೆ garime, *s.* Severity, strictness.

ಗರಿಯುನಿ gariyuni (ಗರಿ), *v. n.* To break off, give way; *cf.* ಗರ್ಪುನಿ.

ಗರೀಬ್ garību, *adj.* Poor. ಗರೀಬೆ a poor man.

ಗರು garu, *s.* A rafter. 2. a mould; *cf.* ಕರು. *adj.* Rough.

ಗರುಗ garuga, *see* ಗರ್ಗ.

ಗರುಡ, ಗರುಡೆ garuḍa, garuḍe, *s.* The son of Kašyapa, having a human form, with a bird's bill and wings, and described to be Vishṇu's vehicle. 2. the Brahmany kite, eagle; *also* –ಪಕ್ಷಿ. ಗರುಡವಾಹನ a wooden form of Garuḍa, used to carry an idol in procession. ಗರುಡಸ್ತಂಭ a post *or* pillar in front of a temple, with the figure of Garuḍa on its top. ಗರುಡಾಸನ a seat of an idol with the figure of Garuḍa –ಪಾತಾಳ a kind of bush, *Ophiorrhiza mungos.* ಪಾತಾಳ– a drag to catch things under water; an outer part of a palm-leaf.

ಗರುಪುಟ್ಟ garupuṭṭa, *s.* A crucible.

ಗರೆ garè, *s.* The shaft of a country water-lift; *cf.* ಕರೆ. –ತ ಓಡು a broken tile.

ಗರೆಯಾಟ gareyāṭa, *s.* A kind of game.

ಗರೊಡಿ garoḍi, *s.* The shrine of

the demons called ಬ್ರೈದೆಲುರ್. 2. a veranda. 3. a fencing school, gymnasium. —ಸಾಧನೆ gymnastic exercise.

ಗರ್ರನೆ garranè, *see* ಕರಕರ.

ಗರ್ಕ garka, *adv.* Suddenly.

ಗರ್ಗ garga, *s.* A kind of medicinal plant, *Eclipta erecta.*

ಗರ್ಗಂಡ gargaṇḍa, *adj.* Profound, 2. thick. —ಕತ್ತಲೆ thick darkness.

ಗರ್ಗಯಿ gargayi, *adj.* Half-ripe, half-grown, as an arecanut *etc.*

ಗರ್ಗಾಸ್ gargāsu, *s.* A saw. —ದ ಕೂಲಿ the teeth of a saw.

ಗರ್ಜನೆ garjanè, *s.* Roaring. —ಮ ಳ್ಪುನಿ to roar, bellow.

ಗರ್ಜಿ garji, *s.* Need, necessity, occasion. —ದ ಪೊತುರ್ a time of difficulty.

ಗರ್ತಿ garti, *s.* A married woman. 2. a chaste *or* continent woman.

ಗರ್ನಾಲ್ garnālu, *s.* A mortar. 2. a bomb, cannon.

ಗರ್ಪುನಿ garpuni (ಕರ್), *v. a.* To dig.

ಗರ್ಪೆಲ್ garpelu, *s.* Scooping, burrowing.

ಗರ್ಬ garba, *see* ಗರ್ಭ.

ಗರ್ಬೀಜ garbīja, *s.* A melon, the fruit of *Cucumis melo.*

ಗರ್ಭ garbha, *s.* The womb, uterus. 2. pregnancy. 3. embryo. —ಸಿಲೆ, —ಸೂಲ disorder in the womb; colic. —ಆಪಿನಿ, —ಉಂ ತುನಿ to be conceived. —ದೆಪ್ಪುನಿ to cause abortion. —ಪೋಪಿನಿ to miscarry. ಗರ್ಭೊಗು ತಾಗುನಿ, —ಪತ್ತುನಿ to be afraid; to touch the vitals.

ಗರ್ಭಸುತಿ garbhasuti, *s.* A web of cloth woven with red and black thread. —ರುಮಾಲ್ a turban of this kind. —ಶೀರೆ a female's garment of this kind.

ಗರ್ಭಿಣಿ garbhiṇi, *s.* A pregnant woman.

ಗರ್ಮಸಾಲೆ garmasālè, *see under* ಗರಮ್.

ಗರ್ಮಿ, ಗರ್ಮು garmi, garmu, *s.* Heat, burning, warmth; zeal.

ಗರ್ಯುನಿ garyuni, *see* ಕರಿಯುನಿ.

ಗರ್ವ garva, *s.* Pride, arrogance. —ದಾಯೆ a proud *or* arrogant man. —ಮಳ್ಪುನಿ to be proud, haughty. —ಕಟ್ಟುನಿ to subdue one's pride with effort.

ಗರ್ವಿ, ಗರ್ವಿಷ್ಟೆ garvi, garvishṭe, *s.* A proud man.

ಗಲ್ಗುಲ್ galugulu, *s.* A rumbling in the stomach.

ಗಲಗಲ galagala, *s.* A noise caused by bracelets.

ಗಲಬು galabu, *s.* Tumult, confusion, noise.

ಗಲಮೆನ galamena, *see* ಗಲ್ಮೆನ.

ಗಲಸುನಿ galasuni (ಕಲ), *v. a.* To use, employ.

ಗಲಾಸ್ galāsu, *s.* A tumbler. 2. a swinging glass lamp.

ಗಲಿಜ, ಗಲೀಜ್ galija, galīju, *s.* Dirt, filth, nuisance. —ಮಳ್ಪು ನಿ to soil, make filthy.

ಗಲಿಬಿಲಿ galibili, *s*. Disorder, confusion, tumult; anarchy; *cf*. ಗದಿಬಿದಿ. –ಆಪಿನಿ to be confused. –ಮಳ್ಪುನಿ to disturb.

ಗಲಿಮೆ galimè, *s*. Acquirement.

ಗಲುಕು, ಗಲ್ಕ್, ಗಲ್ಕು galuku, galkų, galku, *s*. A noise produced as when sinking *or* diving.

ಗಲ್ಜುನಿ galjuni (ಗಲ್ಜಿ), *v. a*. To confuse, disturb.

ಗಲ್ತಿ galti, *s*. Error, mistake. 2. misplacing.

ಗಲ್ಪಾಸ್ galpasų, *see* ಗಳ್ಪಸ್.

ಗಲ್ಮೆನ galmena, *s*. Freshness, briskness, vigour.

ಗಲ್ಲ್ gallų, *see* ಗಲ್ಲಾ.

ಗಲ್ಲ galla, *s*. The lower part of the cheek. –ಮೀಸೆ whiskers on the lower part of the cheek; *also* ಗಲ್ಮೀಸೆ.

ಗಲ್ಲಾ, ಗಲ್ಲು gallā, gallu, *s*. The gallows. ಗಲ್ಲೊಗು ಪಾಡುನಿ to hang, execute a person.

ಗಲ್ಲಿ galli, *s*. A street.

ಗವ gava, *s*. Sense, sensation, consciousness. –ತಪ್ಪುನಿ to be out of senses, be disturbed.

ಗವಲ gavala, *s*. A handful, mouthful. 2. a buffalo's horn; *also* ಕವಲೆ, ಕಬಳೆ.

ಗವಸಣಿಗೆ gavasaṇigè, *s*. The case *or* cover of a fiddle, *etc*.

ಗವಿ gavi, *s*. A cave, hole, cell.

ಗವುಡಿ gavuḍi, *see* ಗೌಡಿ.

ಗವುಡೆ gavuḍe, *see* ಗೌಡೆ.

ಗವುತಮ gavutama, *see* ಗೌತಮ.

ಗವುಲೆ gaule, *see* ಗೌಲೆ.

ಗವ್ಯ gavya, *s*. The product of a cow. *adj*. Of *or* belonging to a cow; *cf*. ಪಂಚಗವ್ಯ.

ಗವ್ವೆ gavve, *adj*. Very tender.

ಗಸಂಟ್ gasaṇṭų, *see* ಕಸಂಟ.

ಗಸಗಸ gasagasa, *s*. Coarseness, roughness. *adj*. Coarse, rough. *adv*. Coarsely, roughly. –ಅರೆಪಿನಿ to grind coarsely.

ಗಸರ್ gasarų, *see* ಕಸರ್.

ಗಸಿ gasi, *s*. The sediment of oil, pickles, *etc*.

ಗಸೆಯುನಿ gaseyuni (ಗಸೆ), *v. n*. To rub.

ಗಸೇನಿ gasèni, *s*. Difficulty. *adj*. Narrow, strait.

ಗಸ್ತಿ gasti, *s*. A patrole. –ದಾಯಿ a patrole, watchman. –ತಿರ್ಂಗುನಿ to patrole.

ಗಳಗಳ gaḷagaḷa, *s*. A noise, as in drinking fast *or* by shaking a cocoanut.

ಗಳಮೆನ gaḷamena, *see* ಗಲ್ಮೆನ.

ಗಳಸುನಿ gaḷasuni, *see* ಗಲಸುನಿ.

ಗಳಿಗೆ gaḷigè, *s*. A fold, crease, wrinkle. 2. *see* ಘಳಿಗೆ. –ಪತ್ತುನಿ to arrange folds. –ಮಳ್ಪುನಿ to fold, double.

ಗಳು, ಗಳೆ gaḷu, gaḷè, *see* ಗರು.

ಗಳ್ಪಸ್ gaḷpasų, *s*. A halter round the neck, a noose. 2. death by hanging. 3. a lie, falsehood.

ಗಳ್ಪು gaḷpu, *see* ಗಪು.

ಗಾಂಜಾ gāñjā, *s*. The hemp plant, *Cannabis sativa*, whose leaves and fructification are smoked, *or* ground in water and drunk for inebriating purposes.

ಗಾಂಟಿ gāṇṭi, *s*. A kind of sweetmeat.

ಗಾಂಡ್, ಗಾಂಡು gāṇḍu, gāṇḍu, *s*. A coward. 2. a man without self-respect.

ಗಾಂಡಾಗೌಜಿ gāṇḍāgouji, *s*. Much fuss, much ado.

ಗಾಂಡಿಯುನಿ gāṇḍiyuni, *see* ಕಾಡ್ಯುನಿ.

ಗಾಂತ್, ಗಾಂತರ, ಗಾಂತ್ರ gāntu, gāntara, gāntra, *s*. Depth. *adj*. Deep.

ಗಾಂದಾಯೆ gāndāye, *see* ಗಾಣದಾಯೆ.

ಗಾಂದಾರಿ, ಗಾಂದಿನಿ gāndāri, gāndini, *s*. A roving woman.

ಗಾಂವ್ಟಿ gāṅvṭi, *adj*. Local, country.

ಗಾಗ್ರ gāgra, *s*. A child's petticoat.

ಗಾಜಿ, ಗಾಜು gāji, gāju, *s*. Glass ware. 2. China ware. 3. *see* ಕಾಜಿ; *cf*. ಗಾರೆ.

ಗಾಟ್, ಗಾಟಿ gāṭu, gāṭi, *adj*. Hot, pungent.

ಗಾಡ್, ಗಾಡ gāḍu, gāḍa, *s*. Torment, vexation.

ಗಾಡಿ gāḍi, *s*. A bandy, cart, coach. –ಗಾರೆ, –ದಾಯೆ a coachman. –ಕಟ್ಟುನಿ to harness horses *or* bullocks to a coach, cart *or* bandy. –ದೇರುನಿ to drive a cart.

ಗಾಡಿಯುನಿ, ಗಾಡ್ಯುನಿ gāḍiyuni, gāḍyuni, *see* ಕಾಡ್ಯುನಿ.

ಗಾಡಿಯುಳಿ gāḍiyuḷi, *s*. A small chisel.

ಗಾಢ gāḍha, *adj*. Strong, firm. 2. excessive, much, great. –ನಿದ್ರೆ sound sleep.

ಗಾಣ gāṇa, *s*. An oil-mill. 2. a sugar-mill. –ದ ಎಂಣೆ oil expressed in a mill. –ದ ಕಣೆ, –ದ ಗಣೆ the perpendicular roller of a mill. –ದ ಜಿಡ್ಡೆ the excavated trunk of a tree, used as the body of a mill. –ದಾಯೆ an oilman. –ಪಾಡುನಿ to work a mill.

ಗಾಣಿಗೆ gāṇige, *s*. An oil-miller.

ಗಾಣುನಿ gāṇuni (ಗಾಣ್ಣ), *v. n*. To smoke, burn to cinders, glow; *cf*. ಗಮೆಲುನಿ.

ಗಾತ, ಗಾತಕ, ಗಾತಿ gāta, gātaka, gāti, *see* ಘಾತ.

ಗಾತಕೆ, ಗಾತುಗೆ gātake, gātuge, *s*. A treacherous man.

ಗಾತ್ರ gātra, *s*. The body. 2. a member *or* limb. *adj*. Stout, thick.

ಗಾದಿನಿ, ಗಾದಿವಿ gādini, gādivi, *see* ಗಾಂದಾರಿ.

ಗಾದೆ, ಗಾಧೆ gādè, gādhè, *s*. A proverb, adage.

ಗಾನ gāna, *s*. Psalmody, music. –ವಿದ್ಯ the science of psalmody.

ಗಾಪು gāpu, *see* ಗಾಬು.

ಗಾಬಡಿ gābaḍi, *s*. A leak, hole in a vessel. –ಪಾಡುನಿ to repair a leak. –ಲಕ್ಕುನಿ a vessel to leak.

ಗಾಬರಿ, ಗಾಬಿರಿ gābari, gābiri, *s*. Perplexity, confusion, alarm, perturbation. –ಆಪಿನಿ to be perplexed, alarmed, confused. –ಮಳ್ಪುನಿ to alarm, perplex.

ಗಾಬಿ gābi, *s.* Darkness.

ಗಾಬಿಡಿ, ಗಾಬುಡಿ gābiḍi, gābuḍi, *see* ಗಾಬುಡಿ.

ಗಾಬು, ಗಾಬೆ gābu, gābè, *s.* Agitation, commotion, disturbance, ferment. 2. rumour. ಗಾಬೆದ ಗಾಬು rumour upon rumour.

ಗಾಬ್ರಿ gābri, *see* ಗಾಬರಿ.

ಗಾಮಿನಿ gāmini, *s.* Confluence, junction.

ಗಾಯ gāya, *see* ಘಾಯ.

ಗಾಯಕೆ gāyake, *s.* A singer, musician.

ಗಾಯತ್ರಿ gāyatri, *s.* The most sacred incantation of the Brahmans, namely ಓಂ ಭೂರ್ಭುವಃ ಸ್ವಃ ತತ್ಸವಿತುರ್ವರೇಣ್ಯಂ ಭರ್ಗೋದೇವಸ್ಯ ಧೀಮಹೀ ಧಿಯೋಯೋನಃ ಪ್ರಚೋದಯಾತ್. [sic; *cf.* ಗಾನ.

ಗಾಯನ gāyana, *s.* Singing, music.

ಗಾರ್ gāru, *adj.* Dry. 2. hot. –ಕಂಡ a dry field. –ಆಪಿನಿ to be dried, heated.

ಗಾರಣೆ, ಗಾರನೆ gāraṇè, gāranè, *s.* Whitewashing *or* painting walls, *etc.* –ಕೊರ್ಪಿನಿ, –ಪಾಡುನಿ, –ಮಳ್ಪುನಿ to whitewash *or* paint them.

ಗಾರಿಗೆ gārigè, *s.* A kind of cake *or* fritter.

ಗಾರಿಪುನಿ gāripuni, *see* ಗಾಲಿಪುನಿ.

ಗಾರೆ gārè, *s.* Lime plaster, a composition of lime, earth, *etc.*

ಗಾರೆ gāre, *An affix of nouns denoting* profession, employment, *etc.*; *as*, ಕುದುರೆ– a horsekeeper. ಚಾಡಿ– a backbiter. ಬಳೆ– a seller of bracelets. ಸುಳ್ಳು– a liar.

ಗಾರ್ಗಂಡಕತ್ತಲೆ, ಗಾರ್ಗತ್ತಲೆ gārgaṇḍakattalè, gārgattalè, *see* ಕಾರ್ಗತ್ತಲೆ.

ಗಾರ್ಸನ್, ಗಾರ್ಸಿ gārsanu, gārsi, *s.* A store, provision.

ಗಾಲ್‌ಮೇಲ್ gālumèlu, *adv.* Headlong, topsyturvy.

ಗಾಲ gāla, *see* ಗಾಳ.

ಗಾಲಿ gāli, *s.* A wheel. 2. *see* ಗಾಳಿ. –ತಿರಂಗುನಿ the wheel to turn round. ಗಾಡಿದ– a cart wheel.

ಗಾಲಿಪುನಿ gālipuni (ಗಾಲಿ), *v. a.* To strain, filter.

ಗಾಲಿಯುನಿ, ಗಾಲ್ಯುನಿ gāliyuni, gālyuni (ಗಾಲಿ), *v. n.* To be strained, filtered.

ಗಾಲಿಸುನಿ gālisuni (ಗಾಲಿಸ್), *v. a.* To separate grain from refuse by washing. 2. to strain, filter.

ಗಾವಳೆ gāvaḷè, *s.* Jugglery. –ದಾಯಿ a juggler. –ವಿದ್ಯ conjuration.

ಗಾವು gāvu, *s.* Heat. 2. fomentation. 3. glare; *cf.* ಕಾವು.

ಗಾವುದ gāvuda, *s.* A stage *or* distance of twelve miles.

ಗಾಸಿ gāsi, *s.* Fatigue, exhaustion, toil, pain, trouble. 2. the state of being emptied. 3. end, termination, death. –ಆಪಿನಿ to be distressed, wearied; to be confused, dissatisfied.

ಗಾಳ gāḷa, *s.* An angle, fishhook.

ಗಾಳಿ gāḷi, *s.* Wind, air. 2. breath. –ಗಂಟಿ a falsehood. –ಪಟ a paper kite. –ವರ್ತಮಾನ, –ಸುದ್ದಿ an unfounded rumour, a false report. —ಪಾಡುನಿ to fan. —ಬೀಜುನಿ wind to blow.

ಗಾಳಿಯುನಿ, ಗಾಳ್ಯುನಿ gāḷiyuni, gāḷyuni, *see* ಗಾಲಿಯುನಿ.

ಗಿಂಡಿ, ಗಿಂಡ್ಯ, ಗಿಂಡ್ಯೆ giṇḍi, giṇḍya, giṇḍyè, *s.* A goblet, small metal vessel.

ಗಿಂಣಲ್ giṇṇalụ, *s.* A goglet, cup of bell-metal.

ಗಿಂಪು gimpu, *see* ಗಿಡ್ಪು.

ಗಿಂಮ, ಗಿಂಮು gimma, gimmu, *see* ಗುಂಮ, ಗುಂಮು.

ಗಿಜರ್, ಗಿಜ್ಜರ್ gijarụ, gijjarụ, *see* ಕಿರಂಜಿ.

ಗಿಜಿಕಿಟ್ಟಿ gijikiṭṭi, *see* ಕಿಜಿಕಿಟ್ಟಿ.

ಗಿಜಿಗಿಜಿ gijigiji, *adj.* Soft, pulpous. *s.* A chirping noise. 2. a rattle, toy. —ದೈ the shrub *Crotoloria verrucosa.*

ಗಿಜಿಬಿಜಿ gijibiji, *see* ಗಜಿಬಿಜಿ.

ಗಿಜಿಲ್ gijilụ, *s.* Confusion; *also* ಗಿಜಿಲಾಟ. *adj.* Confused. —ಆದ್ ಪೋಪಿನಿ to become confused.

ಗಿಜ್ಜ gijja, *adj.* Thick, full. *s.* A heap, mass, crowd.

ಗಿಟ್ಟ್, ಗಿಟ್ಟ, ಗಿಟ್ಟಿ giṭṭụ, giṭṭa, giṭṭi, *s.* Scoria, dross of smelted iron. —ಪಾಡುನಿ to repair an earthen vessel with its paste; *cf.* ಕಿಟ್ಟ.

ಗಿಟ್ಟ giṭṭa, *adj.* Proximate, near.

ಗಿಟ್ಟೆ giṭṭè, *see* ಗಿಟ್ಟ.

ಗಿಡ್ಂಗ್, ಗಿಡ್ಕ್ giḍụṅgụ, giḍụkụ, *see* ಗಿಡ್ಕ್.

ಗಿಡ್ಗೆ, ಗಿಡಗೆ giḍụgè, giḍagè, *see* ಗಿಡಿ.

ಗಿಡ್ಪು giḍụpu, *see* ಗಿಡ್ಪು.

ಗಿಡ್ಪುನಿ giḍụpuni, *see* ಗಿಡಿಪುನಿ.

ಗಿಡ giḍa, *s.* A shrub. —ಮೂಲಿಗೆ a medicinal drug.

ಗಿಡಕ giḍaka, *see* ಗಿಡ್ಕ.

ಗಿಡಿ giḍi, *s.* The falcon *or* hawk; an eagle. —ಆಟ a kind of game. —ದೀರುನಿ to play at such a game. ಕಾರಿ— a black eagle *or* hawk. ಕೆಂಪು— a red eagle.

ಗಿಡಿಕಿ, ಗಿಡಿಕೆ giḍiki, giḍikè, *see* ಗಿಡ್ಕೆ.

ಗಿಡಿಪುನಿ giḍipuni (ಗಿಡಿ), *v. a.* To make fast.

ಗಿಡಿಬಿಡಿ giḍibiḍi, *s.* A small drum played by turning it up and down in the hand.

ಗಿಡಿಯಾವುನಿ giḍiyāvuni, *c. v.* (*of* ಗಿಡಿಯುನಿ) To cause to run, to drive, race.

ಗಿಡಿಯುನಿ giḍiyuni (ಗಿಡಿ), *v. n.* To run. ಗಿಡ್ತೊಂಡ್ದು ಬರ್ಪಿನಿ to attack, assail.

ಗಿಡೆ giḍè, *s.* A partner in a game. 2. *see* ಜಿಡೆ. —ಪತ್ತುನಿ to choose a partner.

ಗಿಡ್ಕ್ giḍkụ, *s.* A stopper, cork. 2. a mouthful, draught. —ನೀರ್ a mouthful of water.

ಗಿಡ್ಕೆ giḍkè, *s.* A blind *or* screen, made of palm leaves. 2. a rib.

ಗಿಡ್ಡ giḍḍa, *adj.* Small, short. —ತನ smallness.

ಗಿಡ್ಡಿ, ಗಿಡ್ಡು giḍḍi, giḍḍu, *s.* A short woman.

ಗಿಡ್ಡೆ, ಗಿಡ್ಡೆಲೆ, ಗಿಡ್ಯೆ, ಗಿಡ್ಯೆಲೆ giḍḍe, giḍḍele, giḍye, giḍyele, *s.* A dwarf, short man,

ಗಿಡ್ಡ giḍḍa, *s.* A kind of tonsure.

ಗಿಡ್ಡೆರು giḍḍeru, *s.* A race-buffalo.

ಗಿಡ್ಪು giḍpu, *s.* Thickness. *adj.* Thick, stout.

ಗಿಡ್ಯೆ giḍye, *s.* A kind of cock. *adj.* Short; *cf.* ಗಿಡ್ಡೆ.

ಗಿಡ್ಯೆದಯೆರು giḍyedayeru, *see* ಗಿಡ್ಡೆರು.

ಗಿಣಿ giṇi, *see* ಗಿಳಿ.

ಗಿಣಿಗಿಣಿ, ಗಿಣಿಲ್ giṇigiṇi, giṇilụ, *s.* The tinkling sound of a small bell.

ಗಿದ್‍ಪುನಿ, ಗಿದ್‍ರುನಿ, ಗಿದುರುನಿ, ಗಿದ್ರುನಿ gidụpuni, gidụruni, giduruni, gidruni, *see* ಗಿರ್ಪುನಿ.

ಗಿದಿಪುನಿ gidipuni, *see* ಕೆದಿಪುನಿ. 2. *see* ಜಡಿಪುನಿ.

ಗಿದ್ಪು gidpu, *s.* Loosening.

ಗಿರವು, ಗಿರಾವು giravu, girāvu, *s.* Epilepsy; *also* ಗಿರವುರೋಗ. —ಪತ್ತುನಿ to suffer from it. ಪಂಜಿ— a kind of epilepsy.

ಗಿರಾಕಿ, ಗ್ರಾಕಿ girāki, grāki, *s.* A customer, purchaser.

ಗಿರಾಗತಿ girāgati, *s.* Family affairs. 2. influence of evil stars upon one's fortune, fate.

ಗಿರಿ giri, *s.* A mountain.

ಗಿರಿಕೋಲ್ girikōlụ, *see* ಗಿರ್ಕೋಲು.

ಗಿರಿಗಿ girigi, *s.* A female's underdress of striped cloth.

ಗಿರಿಗಿಟ್ಟಿ girigiṭṭi, *s.* A child's toy, with wheels whirling round by means of a string between them. 2. a kind of gambling by turning round a ball, dotted with figures, in a plate.

ಗಿರಿಗಿರಿ girigiri, *s.* Creaking. *adv.* Quickly, speedily. —ತಿರಂಗುನಿ to turn round with great speed.

ಗಿರಿದ್‍ಪೋಪಿನಿ giridụpōpini, *see* ಗಿರ್ಪುನಿ. 2. *see* ಗಿರಿಯುನಿ.

ಗಿರಿಯಂತ್ರ giriyantra, *s.* Ruin.

ಗಿರಿಯಾಟ giriyāṭa, *s.* Wandering; vagabondage.

ಗಿರಿಯುನಿ giriyuni (ಗಿರಿ), *v. n.* To wander, roam. 2. to suffer from giddiness. ತರೆ— to be giddy.

ಗಿರಿಯೆಲೆ giriyele, *s.* A wanderer, vagabond.

ಗಿರ್ಕ್ giṛkụ, *see* ಗಿಲ್ಕ್.

ಗಿರ್ಕಾಲ್ girkālụ, *s.* The smallest fraction of a coin.

ಗಿರ್ಕೋಲ್ girkōlụ, *s.* A wooden [peg.

ಗಿರ್ಪುನಿ girpuni (ಗಿರ್), *v. a.* To loosen, untie, break, pull down. ಇಲ್ಲ್— to pull down a house. *v. n.* To be loose, be pulled down, to break.

ಗಿರ್ಬುದಾರಿ girbudāri, *s.* Fate, misfortune.

ಗಿಲ್ಂಬಿ gilụmbi, *see* ಜಿಲ್ಬಿ.

ಗಿಲಿಕಿಟ್ಟಿ gilikiṭṭi, *see* ಕಿಜಿಕಿಟ್ಟ.

ಗಿಲ್ಕ್, ಗಿಲ್ಕಿ gilkụ, gilki, *s.* Fear; trembling.

ಗಿಳಿ giḷi, *s.* A parrot; *cf.* ಗಿಣಿ. —ಕುಕ್ಕು a kind of mango. —ತವಾಳೆ, —ಬಾವೊಲಿ kinds of ear-ornament.

ಗಿಳಿಗಿಳಿ giḷigiḷi, *s.* A jingling sound.

ಗಿಳಿಗೆಜ್ಜೆ giḷigejjè, *s.* A necklace.

ಗಿಳಿಮೂಕು giḷimūku, *s.* A hooked nose. 2. an ornamental carving on door posts.

ಗೀಚುನಿ gîćuni (ಗೀಚ್), *v. a.* To draw lines, to rule. 2. to scratch over with a pen, scrawl, erase; *cf.* ಕೀಚುನಿ.

ಗೀಟ್ gîṭu, *s.* A line, stroke, mark. –ಪಾಡುನಿ to draw a line.

ಗೀತ್ gîtu, *see* ಕೀತ್.

ಗೀತ gîta, *s.* A song, hymn.

ಗೀರ್, ಗೀರು gîru, gîru, *s.* A scratch, superficial wound *or* mark, slight incision.

ಗೀರುನಿ gîruni (ಗೀರ್), *v. a.* To scratch, wound slightly by the nails, *etc.*

ಗೀಲ್ gîlu, *see* ಕೀಲ್.

ಗೀಸುನಿ gîsuni (ಗೀಸ್), *v. a.* To pare, strip off, shave, scrape. ತರೆ– to shave the head. ಗೀಸು ನಾಯಿ a barber.

ಗೀಸುಳಿ gîsuḷi, *see* ಕೀಸುಳಿ.

ಗುಂಗೆ guṅgè, *s.* Mould, downy substance –ಪತ್ತುನಿ to mould, get mouldy.

ಗುಂಜಿ guñji, *see* ಗೂಂಜಿ.

ಗುಂಟ, ಗುಂಟಿ, ಗುಂಟೆ guṇṭa, guṇṭi, guṇṭè, *see* ಗೂಂಟ.

ಗುಂಟಕೆ guṇṭake, *s.* A bastard.

ಗುಂಡ guṇḍa, *s.* The idol's apartment in a pagoda. 2. a closet, small room. 3. a kind of cake *or* pudding boiled over steam.

ಗುಂಡಲ guṇḍala, *s.* An ear-ornament.

ಗುಂಡಾಂತರ guṇḍāntara, *s.* Sapping the foundation, undermining, ruining.

ಗುಂಡಿ guṇḍi, *s.* An abyss, gulf, great depth. –ಕಂಣ್ದಾಯಿ one with deep *or* large eyes.

ಗುಂಡಿಗೆ guṇḍigè, *s.* The breast, heart. 2. bravery, courage.

ಗುಂಡು guṇḍu, *s.* A ball, bullet. anything round. *adj.* Round, globular. –ಕಲ್ಲ್ a grinding stone, roller. –ಗೂಜಿ a pin. –ರುಮ round. –ಸರ a necklace of large gold beads. –ಹಾಳಿತ guess, surmise. –ಪಾಡುನಿ, –ಹಾಕುನಿ to fire with a bullet,

ಗುಂಡುಳಿ guṇḍuḷi, *s.* A round chisel.

ಗುಂಡೆ guṇḍe, *s.* Courage. *adj.* Round. –ಕಾಯಿ the heart.

ಗುಂಪು gumpu, *adj.* Secret, concealed.

ಗುಂಪು gumpu, *s.* A flock, assemblage, crowd, multitude, heap. –ಕೂಡಾವುನಿ to collect. –ಕೂಡುನಿ to assemble. –ಗುಂಪಾದ್ in crowds, flocks.

ಗುಂಮ್ gummu, *see* ಗುಂಮು.

ಗುಂಮ gumma, *s.* Stench, stinking. 2. a quick, sharp noise. –ಅಪಿನಿ to make a sudden, sharp noise; to stink.

ಗುಂಮ gumma, *adj.* Unequal, irregular. –ಮಣೆ an irregular stool.

ಗುಂಮಟೆ, ಗುಂಮಡೆ gummaṭe gummaḍe, *s.* A statue of Buddha. 2. a kind of drum.

ಗುಂಮು gummu, *s.* A noise produced, as in firing a gun. 2. cooing, as a wild dove. 3. a cuff, blow.

ಗುಂಮುನಿ gummuni (ಗುಂಮ್), *v.n.* To blow, cuff.

ಗುಂಮೆ gummè, *s.* An owl. 2. a bugbear. —ಮೀನ್ a kind of fish. —ಕೂರುನಿ to hoot. ಗಾಡಿ ಡ— the nave of a wheel.

ಗುಂಮೆಯುನಿ gummeyuni (ಗುಂಮೆ), *v.n.* To rise.

ಗುಂಸು gumsu, *see* ಗುಮುಸು.

ಗುಂಪೆ, ಗುಂಬೆ gurmpè, gurmbè, *s.* A pond, pool, puddle.

ಗುಂಬು gurmbu, *see* ಕೊರಂಬು.

ಗುಕ್ಕಿ gukki, *see* ಮುಕ್ಕಿ.

ಗುಗ್ಗಿಲ್ guggilu, *s.* Damp soil.

ಗುಗ್ಗುರಿ gugguri, *s.* Soaked grain.

ಗುಗ್ಗುರು gugguru, *s.* A small insect infesting grain *or* corn.

ಗುಗ್ಗುಳ guggula, *s.* Bdellium, a fragrant gum of the tree *Boswellia glabra.*

ಗುಚಿ guci, *s.* Buttress, stay.

ಗುಚ್ಚಿ gucci, *see* ಕುಚ್ಚಿ.

ಗುಜರಾಣಿ, ಗುಜರಾನ್, ಗುಜಾರ್, ಗುಜಾರ gujarāṇi, gujarāṇu, gujāru, gujāra, *s.* The mode of passing time. 2. livelihood, living, life. —ಮಳ್ಪುನಿ to live according to one's means.

ಗುಜಿ, ಗುಜು guji, guju, *adj.* Short and stout. 2. whispering, speaking in an under tone. —ಕುಂಟಿ, —ಗುಂಟಿ a stout dwarf. —ಪಾತೆರ talking in whispers.

ಗುಜುಗುಜು gujuguju; *s.* A boiling *or* bubbling noise. —ಕೊಂಡ್ಪುನಿ to bubble up.

ಗುಜೆ guje, *see* ಗುಜ್ಜೆ.

ಗುಜ್ಜನಿಗೆ gujjanigè, *s.* A metallic oil-pot with a tapering mouth.

ಗುಜ್ಜನೆ gujjanè, *s.* Quarreling.

ಗುಜ್ಜರಿ gujjari *adj.* Fruitful.

ಗುಜ್ಜರೆ gujjare, *s.* A native of Guzerat.

ಗುಜ್ಜಿ gujji, *see* ಗುಜಿ.

ಗುಜ್ಜಿ, ಗುಜ್ಜು gujji, gujju, *s.* A pole *or* post fixed in water. 2. conversing in whisper. —ಪಾಡುನಿ to fix a pole in water.

ಗುಜ್ಜಿರ್ gujjiru, *adj.* Curled. —ಕುಜಾಲ್, —ತರೆ curled hair.

ಗುಜ್ಜೆ gujjè, *s.* A tender *or* half-ripe jack-fruit. 2. a kind of buffalo. —ಕಳ್ಳಿಗೆ a very tender jack fruit. ದೀಪಿ— the fruit of *Artocarpus incisa*, bread-fruit.

ಗುಟಿಗೆ guṭigè, *s.* A kind of drum.

ಗುಟುಕ, ಗುಟುಕು guṭuka, guṭuku, *s.* A single gulp, a draught; *cf.* ಗಡ್ಕ.

ಗುಟ್ಟು guṭṭu, *s.* A secret, mystery. 2. one's private affairs. *adj.* Secret. —ದಾಯೆ a reserved man. —ಪತ್ತುನಿ to find out a secret, to trace. —ಮಂಡ್ಪುನಿ to consult secretly.

ಗುಟ್ಟೆ guṭṭè, *see* ಕುಟ್ಟೆ.

ಗುಡ guḍa, *s.* Coarse sugar.

ಗುಡದಿ guḍadi, *see* ಗುಡ್ಡಿ.

ಗುಡಾಕ್ guḍākụ, *s.* A narcotic composition of tobacco and other ingredients, used for smoking *or* snuff.

ಗುಡಾನ gudāna, *s.* A large vessel with small mouth; *cf.* ಗುಕ್ಕ.

ಗುಡಾರ guḍāra, *s.* A tent.

ಗುಡಿ guḍi, *s.* A small pagoda *or* shrine.

ಗುಡಿಗಾರೆ guḍigāre, *s.* A turner and cabinet maker.

ಗುಡಿಗುಡಿ guḍiguḍi, *see* ಗುಡುಗುಡಿ.

ಗುಡಿಚಿಲ್, ಗುಡಿಸಲ್, ಗುಡಿಸಿಲ್ guḍičilụ, guḍisalụ, guḍisilụ, *s.* A hut, shed.

ಗುಡಿದಿ guḍidi, *see* ಗುಡ್ಡಿ.

ಗುಡಿಸಿ guḍisi, *see* ಗುಡ್ಸಿ.

ಗುಡುಂಬು guḍumbu, *s.* Gulping. 2. the noise of anything falling into a well *etc.*

ಗುಡುಗುಡಿ guḍuguḍi, *s.* A hubble-bubble, hooka.

ಗುಡುಗುಡು guḍuguḍu, *s.* A rumbling noise, as of thunder. 2. a noise made in smoking tobacco in a hubble-bubble. 3. a noise made in shaking a cocoanut whose kernel has dried within. –ಜಾಂಬು, *see* ಜಮ್ ನೀರೊಳು.

ಗುಡುಸು guḍusu, *see* ಗುಡ್ಸು.

ಗುಡೆ guḍè, *see* ಕುಡೆ.

ಗುಡ್ಕ್, ಗುಡ್ಕ guḍkụ, guḍka, *see* [ಗಿಡ್ಕ.

ಗುಡ್ಕುಗುಡ್ಕು guḍkuguḍku, *adv.* Hastily, hurriedly.

ಗುಡ್ಕೆ guḍke, *s.* A crooked man. 2. a small earthen vessel.

ಗುಡ್ಚಿಲ್ guḍčilụ, *see* ಗುಡಿಚಿಲ್.

ಗುಡ್ಡುಮಲ್ಲಿಗೆ guḍḍumalligè, *s.* A short, thick kind of jassamine.

ಗುಡ್ಡೆ guḍḍè, *s.* A hill. –ಅಂಬು a kind of mushroom. –ಮಿತ್ತಾವುನಿ to ascend a hill; to forget what is learnt.

ಗುಡ್ಡೆಟ್ಟಿ guḍḍeṭṭi, *s.* A kind of small prawn.

ಗುಡ್ಡೆಲೆ guḍḍele, *s.* A cultivator, peasant.

ಗುಡ್ದಮ್ guddamụ, *s.* A blow, cuff, box.

ಗುಡ್ಡಲಾಮ್ guḍḍalāmụ, *s.* An artifice, expedient, shift. 2. fraud, deception. 3. a kind of mint.

ಗುಡ್ಡಿ guḍḍi, *s.* The stopper of a small phial.

ಗುಡ್ಯಲೆ gudyale, *see* ಗುಡ್ಡೆಲೆ.

ಗುಡ್ಸಿ guḍsi, *s.* The embodied form of letter ಇ *or* ಈ, as in ಕಿ, ಕೀ.

ಗುಡ್ಸಿಲ್ guḍsilụ, *see* ಗುಡಿಚಿಲ್.

ಗುಡ್ಸು guḍsu, *s.* A kind of broom. 2. a fetid smell, stench. –ಬೆಯಿಪಿನಿ to stink.

ಗುಡ್ಸೊಲು guḍsolu, *s.* Hitting from a distance. –ಪಾಡುನಿ to hit *or* strike from a distance.

ಗುಣ guṇa, *s.* A quality, property, attribute. 2. temper, disposition. 3. excellence, merit. 4. moral *or* physical improvement, recovery from sickness, restoration to health. 5. use, advantage. –ದೋಷ good and evil. –ವಂತೆ an excellent man. –ಆಪಿನಿ to recover from sickness; to win, gain. —ತಿಕ್ಕುನಿ to derive benefit. —ಮಳ್ಪುನಿ to cure a disease; to decide in one's favour.

ಗುಣಕ guṇaka, s. The multiplier, *arith.*

ಗುಣಗಾರೆ, ಗುಣಾದಿಗೆ guṇagāre, guṇādige, s. A good *or* virtuous man. —ದಿ a virtuous woman.

ಗುಣಾಕಾರ guṇākāra, s. Multiplication. —ಮಳ್ಪುನಿ to multiply.

ಗುಣಿತ guṇita, *see* ಗಣಿತ.

ಗುಣಿತೊಣುನಿ guṇitoṇuni, *v. refl.* To be pondering, thinking. 2. to be calculating, reckoning.

ಗುಣಿಪುನಿ guṇipuni (ಗುಣಿ), *v. a.* To multiply; to calculate.

ಗುಣುಗುಟ್ಟು, ಗುಣುಗುಣು guṇuguṭṭu, guṇuguṇu, s. Murmuring, muttering, grumbling.

ಗುಣುಗುಟ್ಟುನಿ guṇuguṭṭuni (ಗಣುಗುಟಿ), *v. n.* To mutter, murmur, grumble; *also* ಗುಣುಗುಣು ಪಾತೆರುನಿ.

ಗುಣ್ಪಣ್ಣೆ guṇpaṇṇe, s. One who murmurs.

ಗುಣ್ಯ guṇya, s. The multiplicand.

ಗುತ್ತ guttạ, *see* ಗುಪಿತ, ಗುಪ್ಪುನಿ.

ಗುತ್ತದಾರೆ guttadāre, *see* ಗುತ್ತೆದಾರೆ.

ಗುತ್ತಯ guttaya, s. A stipulated supply, as of liquor.

ಗುತ್ತಿ gutti, *see* ಕುತ್ತಿ.

ಗುತ್ತಿಗೆ guttigė, s. An ale-house, liquor-shop. —ದಾಯಿ the keeper of an ale-house *or* liquor-shop

ಗುತ್ತಿನಾಯೆ guttināye, s. A Bant. 2. the holder of a manor *or* landed property with certain privileges attached to it.

ಗುತ್ತು guttu, s. A manor-house with certain privileges attached to it. 2. a leap, jump. 3. a stride. —ದಾಯಿ, *see* ಗುತ್ತಿನಾಯೆ, —ದೀಪಿನಿ to take strides. —ಲಾಗ್ಯುನಿ to jump.

ಗುತ್ತೆದಾರೆ guttedāre, s. The holder of a monopoly, a liquor contractor.

ಗುತ್ರುನಿ guttruni, *see* ಗುಪ್ಪುನಿ.

ಗುದಣೆ, ಗುದನೆ gudaṇė, gudanė, s. *Solanum pubescens*, a kind of thorny shrub used in medicine. —ಕಾಯಿ its fruit.

ಗುದಿಗೆ gudigė, s. A club, cudgel. —ಪೆಟ್ಟು a blow, hit with a cudgel. —ಶಾಸ್ತ್ರ resorting to force, transgressing law.

ಗುದಿಪುನಿ gudipuni, *see* ಕುದಿಪುನಿ.

ಗುದುಗುದು gudugudu, *see* ಗುಜು ಗುಜು.

ಗುದ್ದಣ್ guddaṇụ, s. A long pole. ಪೋಂಡ ಪೊಂಜಿ ಗುದ್ದಣ್, ಬತ್ತ್ಂಡ ಪೊಂಜಿ ಕುಕ್ಕು if lost it will be a stick, if gained it will be a mango (said of a doubtful enterprise).

ಗುದ್ದಲಿ guddali, *see* ಗುದ್ದೊಲಿ.

ಗುದ್ದಳ್ guddaḷụ, s. A worn out plough.

ಗುದ್ದಾಟ, ಗುದ್ದ್ಯಾಟ guddāṭa, guddyāṭa, s. Boxing cuffing, thumping.

ಗುದ್ದು guddu, s. A blow, box, cuff. —ಕಲ್ಲ್ a stone used by

toddy-drawers, a pounding stone.

ಗುದ್ದುನಿ gudduni (ಗುದ್ದ್), *v. a.* To box, cuff, beat.

ಗುದ್ದೊಲಿ guddoli, *s.* A kind of pickaxe. —ಕೆರೆಂಗ್ a kind of sweet potatoes. —ನಂಗ್ a kind of fish. —ಪಾಡುನಿ to burrow, dig; to dig a pit as the first ceremony of the Moharam festival; to ramp, leap and frisk about in play.

ಗುದ್ದೊಲಿಪುನಿ guddolipuni (ಗುದ್ದೊಲಿ), *v. a.* To dig with a pick-axe.

ಗುನುಗುನು gunugunu, *see* ಗುಣು ಗುಟ್ಟು.

ಗುಪಿತ, ಗುಪ್ತ gupita, gupta, *adj.* Hidden, concealed, secret.

ಗುಪ್ಪುನಿ guppuni (ಗು), *v. a.* To pour, shed, spill; *also* ಗೂಚುನಿ, ಗೂಸುನಿ.

ಗುಪ್ಪೆ guppè, *s.* A heap.

ಗುಬಿತ gubita, *see* ಗುಪಿತ.

ಗುಬ್ಬಿ, ಗುಬ್ಬೆ gubbi, gubbè, *s.* A stud, ornamental knob. 2. a button. 3. *see* ಗುಬಿರ್.

ಗುಮ್ಸು gumṳsu, *see* ಗುಮುಸು.

ಗುಮಟೆ gumaṭe, *see* ಗುಂಮಟೆ.

ಗುಮಾನ gumāna, *s.* Doubt, suspicion. 2. regard, notice. —ಮಳ್ಪುನಿ to suspect; to take notice, attend.

ಗುಮಾನಿ gumāni, *adj.* Suspicious, doubtful. —ಜನ suspicious people.

ಗುಮಾಸ್ತಿಗೆ gumāstigè, *s.* Clerkship, writership.

ಗುಮಾಸ್ತೆ gumāste, *s.* A clerk, writer. 2. an assistant.

ಗುಮುಗುಮು gumugumu, *s.* Noise of a multitude. —ಬೂರುನಿ to box, cuff, beat.

ಗುಮುಟು gumuṭu, *s.* Fighting, cuffing.

ಗುಮುಲು gumulu, *s.* Fire burning in embers.

ಗುಮುಲುನಿ gumuluni, *see* ಗಮೆಯುನಿ.

ಗುಮುಸು gumusu, *s.* A stroke, cuff, box. —ಕೊರ್ಪಿನಿ, —ಪಾಡುನಿ to strike, box. ನಿಕ್ಕ್ ಒಂಜಿ ಗುಮುಸುಕ್ಕೈ ಕೊರ್ಪೆ ತೂಲ mind, I will slap you, if you do not look out.

ಗುಮುಸುನಿ gumusuni (ಗುಮುಸ್), *v. a.* To box, strike.

ಗುಮ್ಮೆ gumme, *see* ಗುಂಮೆ.

ಗುರ್ಂಪೆ gurṳmpe, *s.* A temporary reservoir in a dry field for the use of crop. 2. a puddle.

ಗುರಗುಟ್ಟುನಿ guraguṭṭuni, *see* ಗುರ್ಗುಟ್ಟುನಿ.

ಗುರನೆ guranè, *s.* The snarling of a dog.

ಗುರಿ guri, *s.* A hole, pit. —ದೆಪ್ಪುನಿ to dig a hole, a pit *or* a grave.

ಗುರಿ guri, *s.* An aim, mark, butt. 2. liability, responsibility. —ಆಪಿನಿ to be liable. —ತೂಪಿನಿ, —ಪತ್ತುನಿ to aim, mark.

ಗುರಿಕಾರೆ gurikāre, *see* ಗುರ್ಕಾರೆ.

ಗುರಿಗುಂಪು gurigumpu, *s.* Unevenness, roughness.

ಗುರಿಯಾಳ guriyāḷa, *s.* A game of the Pāṇḍu princes.

ಗುರು guru, *s.* A spiritual preceptor, teacher, guide, priest. 2. the planet Jupiter, Bṛhaspati. *adj.* Heavy, weighty; venerable. –ಉಪದೇಶ the instruction given by a Guru. –ಕಾಣಿಕೆ a present *or* gift to a Guru. –ಜನ venerable persons. –ತ್ವ, –ತನ the position of a Guru; respectability, dignity; heaviness, gravity. –ಪಾದ the foot of a Guru. –ಭಕ್ತಿ devotion to him. –ಮಠ his house *or* residence, especially of a Lingaita priest. –ಲಘು heavy and light; great and small. –ವಾರ Thursday. –ಸೇವೆ service due to a Guru. –ಕೈಪತ್ತುನಿ to get a blessing from a Guru.

ಗುರುಂಪು, ಗುರುಂಪೆ gurumpu, gurumpè, *see* ಗುಂಪೆ.

ಗುರುಂಬೆ gurumbè, *s.* Anything hollow.

ಗುರುಕು guruku, *see* ಗುರ್ಕು.

ಗುರುಕುಂಜಿ, ಗುರುಗುಂಜಿ gurukuñji, guruguñji, *see* ಗುರ್ಗುಂಜಿ.

ಗುರುಕುಟ್ಟುನಿ gurukuṭṭuni (ಗುರುಕುಟ್ಟಿ), *v.n.* To snore. 2. to purr. 3. to coo. 4. phlegm to rattle in the throat. 5. to roar.

ಗುರುಕೆ gurukè, *see* ಗುರ್ಕೆ.

ಗುರುಗುಟ್ಟು guruguṭṭu, *s.* Snoring. 2. *see* ಗುಱುಗುಟ್ಟು.

ಗುರುಗುರು guruguru, *s.* Snoring. 2. the rattling of phlegm in the throat.

ಗುರುತ guruta, *see* ಗುರ್ತ.

ಗುರುತ್ವ gurutva, *see under* ಗುರು.

ಗುರುದ guruda, *see* ಗುರ್ದ.

ಗುರುಬಿ gurubi, *s.* A sparrow; *cf* ಗುಬ್ಜಿ, ಗುಬ್ಬಿ.

ಗುರುವಾರ guruvāra, *s.* Thursday.

ಗುರೆಪುನಿ gurepuni, *see* ಕುರೆಪುನಿ.

ಗುರೇಟುನಿ gurēṭuni (ಗುರೇಟಿ), *v.a.* To hit a mark.

ಗುರ್ರುಕೊರೆಪುನಿ gurrukorepuni (ಗುರ್ರುಕೊರೆ), *v. n.* To bark, growl. 2. to snore.

ಗುರ್ಕಲ್ಲ್ gurkallụ, *s.* Standing steadily *or* motionless.

ಗುರ್ಕಾಯಿಸುನಿ, ಗುರ್ಕಾಯ್ಸುನಿ gurkāyisuni, gurkāysuni (ಗುರ್ಕಾಯಿಸ್ಸಿ), *v. a.* To frown, knit the brows. 2. to grunt, growl. 3. to menace, frighten. 4. to snore

ಗುರ್ಕಾರೆ gurkāre, *s.* A head-man, foreman, manager, master. –ದಿ a mistress, matron.

ಗುರ್ಕು, ಗುರ್ಕುಗುರ್ಕು gurku, gurkugurku, *s.* Roar of a tiger. 2. grunting of a pig. –ಕುಟ್ಟುನಿ to roar, as a tiger; to grunt, as a pig. –ಪೈಪುನಿ phlegm to rattle in the throat.

ಗುರ್ಕುಟ್ಟುನಿ gurkuṭṭuni (ಗುರ್ಕುಟಿ), *v.n.* To grunt. 2. *see* ಗುರುಕುಟ್ಟುನಿ.

ಗುರ್ಕೆ gurkè, *s.* A very large water-vessel.

ಗುರ್ಗುಂಜಿ, ಗುರ್ಗೊಂಜಿ gurguñji, gurgoñji, *s.* The seed of the country liquorice, *Abrus precatorius.*

ಗುರ್ಜಿ gurji, *s.* A temporary halting place for idols, decorated with leaves, flags *etc.* 2. a temporary shed covered with awning for offering oblations to the manes of the deceased Šudrās. *adj.* Fine, small, short, little. –ಮೋವೆ offering rice *etc.* to the manes. –ಕಟ್ಟುನಿ to erect a temporary shed decorated with leaves, flags *etc.*

ಗುರ್ತ **gurta,** *s.* A mark, sign, token, symbol. 2. acquaintance, recognition. –ಆಪಿನಿ to become acquainted. –ತಿಕ್ಕುನಿ to identify, recognise. –ತೋ ಜಾವುನಿ to point out. –ದೀಪಿನಿ to mark. –ಪಣ್ಪುನಿ to describe. –ಪತ್ತುನಿ to recognise. –ಪಾಡುನಿ to sign, make a mark. –ಮ ಳ್ಪುನಿ to note, mark.

ಗುದು **gurdu,** *s.* Sounding lead. 2. a buoy. 3. a post planted in water to mark the spot where a net is spread. –ಪಾಡುನಿ to fathom water; to plant a post as a mark.

ಗುಬಿ **gurbi,** *s.* A sparrow. ಅಂ ಗಡಿ–, ಬಜ್ಜಯಿ– the ordinary sparrow. ತಾರಿ– a species of sparrow which builds a hanging nest.

ಗುಲ **gula,** *s.* Condensation. 2. condensed sugar ready for putting in forms.

ಗುಲಾಬಿ, ಗುಲಾಬು **gulābi, gulābu,** *s.* A rose. –ತಾನಿ, –ದಾನಿ a goglet for sprinkling rosewater. –ನೀರ್ rose-water.

ಗುಲಾಮಲಿ **gulāmali,** *s.* A buffoon, jester.

ಗುಲಾಮೆ **gulāme,** *s.* A slave. ಗು ಲಾಮತನ slavery, servitude.

ಗುಲಾಲ್ **gulālu,** *s.* A crimson powder used at the Hōḷi festival; *also* –ಪೊಡಿ. –ಬಂಣ crimson colour.

ಗುಲಿ **guli,** *see* ಗುಳಿ.

ಗುಲುಂಬು **gulumbu,** *see* ಗುಳುಂ.

ಗುಲ್ಕಂದ್ **gulkandu,** *s.* Confection of roses.

ಗುಲ್ಮ, ಗುಲ್ಮವಾಯು, ಗುಲ್ಮೆ **gulma, gulmavāyu, gulmè,** *s.* A disease of mesenteric glands; a kind of colic. 2. *see* ಗುರ್ಂಪೆ.

ಗುಲ್ಮು **gulmu,** *see* ಗುಳುಂ.

ಗುಲ್ಲ **gulla,** *s.* A kind of small mollusk. 2. *see* ಗುಳ್ಳ.

ಗುಲ್ಲಿ **gulli,** *see* ಕುಳ್ಳಿ.

ಗುಲ್ಲು **gullu,** *s.* A great noise, shout, uproar.

ಗುಲ್ಲೆ **gullè,** *see* ಗುಳ್ಳೆ.

ಗುವೆಲ್ **guvelu,** *s.* A well; *cf.* ಉ ಗ್ಗೆಲ್.

ಗುಸು **gusu,** *s.* A whisper. –ಗು ಟ್ಟುನಿ, –ಗುಸುಪಾತೆರುನಿ to whisper, lisp, talk in a low tone.

ಗುಸ್ಸುನಿ **gussuni,** *see* ಗುಪ್ಪುನಿ.

ಗುಹ **guha,** *s.* A name of Gaṇapati.

ಗುಹಾನಿಪುನಿ **guhānipuni** (ಗುಹಾನಿ), *v. n.* To meditate.

ಗುಹೆ **guhè,** *s.* A cave, cavern, grotto. 2. a den, lair.

ಗುಹೆಲಿ **guheli,** *see* ಗುವೆಲ್.

ಗುಳ guḷa, *see* ಕುಳ.

ಗುಳಿ guḷi, *s.* A pit. 2. loss, ruin. 3. end, death. –ಆಪಿನಿ to sink in, disappear; to fall into ruin; to die. –ಮಳ್ಪುನಿ to ruin another.

ಗುಳಿಗೆ guḷigè, *s.* A pill, globule, bolus. 2. the name of a demon. 3. the son of Saturn. –ದ ಘುಳಿಗೆ a fatal hour, inauspicious time; a bad omen. ಅಂತರ– a demon haunting the air.

ಗುಳುಂ, ಗುಳುಕು, ಗುಳುಮ್ gulum, guḷuku, guḷumu, *s.* A noise made by the falling of a stone *etc.* into a well. 2. loss. 3. cheating, fraud. –ಘಾತಗೆ a cheat, defrauder. –ಆಪಿನಿ to fall into water; to be lost. –ಮಳ್ಪುನಿ to defraud.

ಗುಳುಗುಳು guḷuguḷu, *s.* A noise made, as in filling a pitcher with water.

ಗುಳ್ಳ guḷḷa, *s.* A kind of round brinjal, *Solanum Jacquini*. –ಬದನೆ *Solanum ferox*.

ಗುಳ್ಳೆ, guḷḷè, *s.* A bubble. 2. blister, pustule, vesicle. 3. *see* ಕೂಳೆ.

ಗೂಂಗು gūṅgu, *s.* The cry of an owl.

ಗೂಂಜಿ gūñji, *s.* The stalk in the midst of a jackfruit. 2. the germ-matter of a boil. ತಿಗಲೆದ– the core of the heart.

ಗೂಂಟ, ಗೂಂಟಿಗೆ gūṇṭa, gūṇṭigè, *s.* A peg, pin, stake. –ಕೆತ್ತುನಿ to make a peg. –ಜದಿಪುನಿ, –ಜದಿಯುನಿ, –ಬೊಟ್ಟುನಿ to drive in a peg.

ಗೂಗೆ gūgè, *see* ಗುಂಮೆ.

ಗೂಚುನಿ gūčuni, *see* ಗುಪ್ಪುನಿ.

ಗೂಜಾವುನಿ gūjāvuni, *c. v.* (*of* ಗೂಜುನಿ) To cause to ooze.

ಗೂಜುನಿ gūjuni (ಗೂಜಿ), *v. n.* To ooze; *cf.* ಊಜುನಿ.

ಗೂಜೆ gūjè, *s.* A goglet made of cocoanut shell.

ಗೂಟ, ಗೂಟೆ gūṭa, gūṭè, *see* ಗೂಂಟ.

ಗೂಡಾಕ್ gūḍāku, *see* ಗುಡಾಕ್.

ಗೂಡು gūḍu, *s.* A nest. 2. a cocoon. 3. a bird-cage. 4. the hollow in a seal for receiving a stone. –ಕಟ್ಟುನಿ to build a nest. ತಿಗಲೆದ– the hollow of the chest.

ಗೂಡೆ gūḍè, *s.* A kind of basket.

ಗೂದೆ gūdè, *s.* Prolapsus of the anus. 2. *see* ಗುದನೆ.

ಗೂನು gūnu, *s.* A hump. 2. a mushroom. ಗೂನೆ a hunchback.

ಗೂರು gūru, *s.* Asthma. 2. cough. –ಉಚ್ಛ್ವಾಸ asthmatic breathing.

ಗೂರುನಿ gūruni (ಗೂರ್), *v. a.* To pile up, as rice, firewood, stones, *etc.*; *also* ಗೂರುದೀಪಿನಿ. 2. to stick in, fix. 3. to hoot. 4. to make a plough ನಾಯೆರ್– to stick the pole of a yoke into the ploughshare; to make a ploughshare.

ಗೂರ್ಕೆ gūrkè, *see* ಗುರ್ಕೆ.

ಗೂರ್ಮೆ gurme, *s.* A kind of bird.

ಗೂಸುನಿ gūsuni, *see* ಗುಪ್ಪುನಿ.

ಗೂಳೆ gūḷè, *s*. People leaving a place *en masse* on account of invasion *or* famine.

ಗೃಹ gr̥ha, *s*. A house, mansion. *adj*. Domestic. –ಕೃತ್ಯ household affairs. –ಛಿದ್ರ domestic trouble *or* quarrel.

ಗೃಹಸ್ತಲಿಗೆ, ಗೃಹಸ್ತೊಲಿಗೆ gruhastaligè, gr̥hastoligè, *s*. Respectability, honesty. –ದಾಯಿ a honest, upright man. –ದಾಳ್ an honest, upright woman.

ಗೃಹಸ್ತೆ gr̥haste, *s*. A householder, married *or* family man. 2. an honest man. –ದಿ a respectable woman.

ಗೆ gè, *a particle signifying*, It is said, they say *etc*.; *also* ಕೆರೆ. ಬತ್ತ್‌ಗೆ, ಬತ್ತ್‌ಕೆರೆ it is said that he came. ಬರ್ಪೆ‌ಗೆ, ಬರ್ಪೆ‌ಕೆರೆ he says that he is coming. –ಸುದ್ದಿ a rumour.

ಗೆಂಡ genḍa, *s*. A live *or* burning coal. –ಅಸ್ಗಯ a dance upon burning coals; *also* –ಸೇವೆ.

ಗೆಂದ genda, *adj*. Reddish. –ತಾರೆ, *see* ಕೆಂದಳಿ. –ಪೆತ್ತ, *see* ಕೆಂದಿ.

ಗೆಂದಳಿ, ಗೆಂದಳೆ gendaḷi, gendaḷè, *s*. A reddish coloured cocoanut tree. –ರೋಗ a kind of red eruptions on the skin.

ಗೆಂದಿ gendi, *s*. A reddish cow.

ಗೆಂದುನಿ genduni, *v. a*. To win, conquer. *v. n*. To be hot, to burn.

ಗೆಂದೆ gende, *s*. A reddish coloured ox. ಅರ್ಕಗೆಂಜಿ– a tawny coloured cocoanut.

ಗೆಗ್ಗರ geggara, *see* ಸಗ್ಗರ.

ಗೆಜೆಲುನಿ gejeluni, *see* ಗಜಿಲುನಿ.

ಗೆಜ್ಜ, ಗೆಜ್ಜೆ gejja, gejjè, *s*. A small round bell, tinkling ornament. –ಕತ್ತಿ, –ತ್ತಿ a knife *or* sword with the handle ornamented with spherical bells, *etc*. –ಕಲ್ಲ್ small stones, iron-ore. –ಕೋಲು a stick with bells attached to it. –ಟಿಕ್ಕಿ a neck ornament of gold with chasings. –ಪೂಜೆ the act of worshipping gingling bells when put on dancing girls for the first time.

ಗೆಟ್ಟಿ, ಗೆಟ್ಟೆ geṭṭi, geṭṭè, *s*. A lump, clod.

ಗೆಟ್ಟಿಮಂಡೆಲೆ geṭṭimanḍele, *s*. A wagtail.

ಗೆಣಿಕೆ geṇikè, *s*. Calculation, estimation. 2. regard, esteem.

ಗೆಣಿಪುನಿ geṇipuni, *v. a*. To count, reckon, number.

ಗೆಣೆ geṇè, *s*. Coupling; *cf*. ಇಣೆ. –ಗಾರೆ an associate.

ಗೆತ್ತೊಣುನಿ gettoṇuni, *see* ಕೆಪ್ಪುನಿ.

ಗೆದ್ಂಗಾವುನಿ geduṅgāvuni, *c. v*. (*of* ಗೆದ್ಂಗುನಿ) To get rammed, stuffed in.

ಗೆದ್ಂಗುನಿ, ಗೆದಿಪುನಿ geduṅguni, gedipuni (ಗೆದ್ಂಗ್, ಗೆದಿ), *v. a*. To stuff, push in, ram.

ಗೆದರುನಿ gadaruni, *see* ಕೆದರುನಿ.

ಗೆದಿಯುನಿ gediyuni (ಗೆದಿ), *v. n*. To be rammed, stuffed.

ಗೆಪ್ಪುನಿ geppuni (ಗೆ), *v. a*. To take, receive. 2. to buy, purchase.

3. to draw, pull out. 4. to steal. 5. to draw back, open. 6. to dismiss, discharge. 7. to dig, excavate. 8. to remove, take away. 9. to excommunicate, interdict. 10. to press, express. 11. to dishonour; to ruin. ಒರಿಯ ಇಲ್ಲ್— to ruin a person. ಕಿಸೆಡ್ದ್ ಜೇರ ವು— to draw out the purse from the pocket. ಕೂಲಿ— to knock out a tooth. ಗಂಟ— to steal a bundle. ಗುರಿ— to dig a pit. ಚಾಕ್ರಿ— to discharge from service. ಜಾತಿ— to excommunicate. ಪುದರ್— to take one's name; to dishonour one. ಬಾಕಿಲ್— to open the door. ಮುಳ್ಳ— to draw out a thorn. ರಸ— to express juice. ಸಾಮಾನ್— to purchase articles. ಸಾಲ— to borrow.

ಗೆಬ್ಬಟ್ಟ್ gebbaṭṭu, *s.* Confusion, perplexity.

ಗೆಬ್ಬಟ್ಟಾವುನಿ gebbaṭṭāvuni, *c. v.* (*of* ಗೆಬ್ಬಟ್ಟುನಿ) To perplex, confuse.

ಗೆಬ್ಬಟ್ಟುನಿ gebbaṭṭuni (ಗೆಬ್ಬಟ್ಟಿ), *v.n.* To be confused, perplexed.

ಗೆಬ್ಬು gebbu, *s.* The temples. —ಗು ಕೊರ್ಪಿನಿ, —ಗು ಕೇರಾವುನಿ, —ದರ್ಪುನಿ to beat on the temples.

ಗೆಯಿಪಿನಿ geyipini, *see* ಗೈಪಿನಿ.

ಗೆರಂತಿ geranti, *see* ಗ್ರಾಂತಿ.

ಗೆರಚಾರ geračāra, *see* ಗ್ರಾಚಾರ.

ಗೆರತ್ತೆ geratte, *see* ಗೃಹಸ್ತೆ.

ಗೆರಮ gerama, *see* ಗ್ರಾಮ.

ಗೆರವು geravu, *see* ಗಿರವು.

ಗೆರಸ್ತೆ geraste, *see* ಗೃಹಸ್ತೆ.

ಗೆರೆ gerè, *s.* A line, row. 2. a stroke. —ಪಾಡು ಕೋಲು a ruler. —ಪಾಡುನಿ,—ವೈಪುನಿ to draw a line, to rule. —ಮುಟ್ಟುನಿ to insist.

ಗೆರೆಪುನಿ, ಗೆರೆವುನಿ gerepuni, gerevuni, *see* ಗ್ರಹಿಪುನಿ.

ಗೆರ್ಪುನಿ gerpuni, *v. a.* To raise, lift up; *bet.* ದೆರ್ಪುನಿ.

ಗೆಲವು gelavu, *s.* Sprightliness, liveliness, vivacity, courage.

ಗೆಲಿಪುನಿ, ಗೆಲ್ಪುನಿ gelipuni, gelpuni, *see* ಗೆಂದುನಿ.

ಗೆಲ್ಕಾಯಿ gelkayi, *s.* Victory, winning. *adj.* Victorious.

ಗೆಲ್ಪು gelpu, *s.* Victory, gain. —ಸೋಲ್ಪು gain and loss.

ಗೆಲ್ಲ್ gellu, *s.* A branch, twig.

ಗೇಡ್ gēḍu, *see* ಕೇಡ್.

ಗೇಣ್, ಗೇಣ gēṇu, gēṇa, *s.* A span from the tip of the thumb to that of the little finger. —ಉದ್ದ a span long.

ಗೇಣಿ gēṇi, *s.* Rent, contract. ಕಾಯಂ—, ಮೂಲ— a permanent lease, perpetual rent. —ಚೀಟಿ a lease. —ಗಾರೆ,—ದಾಯೆ a tenant, contractor. ಚಾಲ— tenancy at will, annual rent. ವಾಯಿದೆ— rent for a fixed time. —ಕಟ್ಟುನಿ to fix the amount of rent. —ಗ್ ಕಟ್ಟಿದ್ ಕೊರ್ಪಿನಿ to lease out. —ಪೊಕ್ಕೆಲ್ a tenant.

ಗೇನ gēna, *see* ಜ್ಞಾನ.

ಗೇರ್‌ಕಾಯಿ, ಗೇರೆಕಾಯಿ gērukāyi,

gēme ? i.e. 166 keime

gērekāyi, *s.* The marking nut. —ದ ಮರ the tree *Semicarpus anacardium.*

ಗೇರ gēra, *adv.* Around. —ಪಾಡುನಿ to surround.

ಗೇಜ಼ gērja, *s.* A kind of bird; *also* —ಪಕ್ಕಿ.

ಗೇಲಿ gēli, *s.* Ridicule, jest, mockery, insult.

ಗೈಂದಳೆ geindaḷè, *see* ಕೆಂದಳೆ.

ಗೈಪಿನಿ geipini (ಗ್ಯ), *v. a.* To do, fulfil.

ಗೈಬು gaibu, *s.* Missing, disappearing. 2. *see* ಗರೀಬ್. 3. *see* ಖರಾಬ್. —ಆಪಿನಿ to disappear.

ಗೈರ್ geiru, *adj.* Unoccupied. *adv.* Not, without. —ಹಾಜರ್ absence. —ಹಾಜರ್ ಆಪಿನಿ to be absent.

ಗೈರೆಯ geireya, *s.* Red chalk.

ಗೈಲ್ geilu, *s.* A bell-sound.

ಗೊಂಗ goṅga, *s.* A large cowrie, shell.

ಗೊಂಗುಕ goṅguka, *s.* An oil tree. 2. a bunch.

ಗೊಂಚಿ, ಗೊಂಚಿಲ್ gońci, gońcilu, *s.* A bunch, cluster.

ಗೊಂಜು goñju, *s.* A tassel.

ಗೊಂಡ goṇḍa, *see* ಕೊಂಡ.

ಗೊಂಡಿ goṇḍi, *s.* A button.

ಗೊಂಡೆ goṇḍè, *s.* A cluster, tassel, topknot. —ದ ಜಲ್ಲಿ a fringe with tassels. —ಪೂ a kind of flower resembling the marigold. ಉದರಿದ— an ornament put in the hair of females.

ಗೊಂತು gontu, *s.* Knowledge, understanding, acquaintance. —ಆಪಿನಿ to become acquainted. —ಉಪ್ಪುನಿ to know. —ಮಲ್ಪುನಿ to find out, ascertain. ಯೆಂಕ್ ಗೊಂತಿಜ್ಜಿ I do not know.

ಗೊಂದಲಪೂಜೆ, ಗೊಂದ್ಲುಪೂಜೆ gondalapūjè, gondlupūjè, *see* ಗೋಂದಳ ಪೂಜೆ.

ಗೊಂಬೆ gombè, *s.* An image, puppet, doll; *also* ಬೊಂಬೆ.

ಗೊಜ್ಜರಂನ gojjaranna, *see* ಗುಜರಾಣಿ.

ಗೊಜ್ಜಿ gojji, *s.* Boiled juice *or* pulp of any fruit, mixed with cocoanut, salt, chillies *etc.*, seasoned, and eaten with boiled rice to make it savoury.

ಗೊಜ್ಜೆ gojje, *see* ಕೊಜ್ಜೆ.

ಗೊಟ್ಟ goṭṭa, *see* ಕೊಟ್ಟ.

ಗೊಟ್ಟಾನ goṭṭāna, *see* ಗುಟ್ಟು.

ಗೊಟ್ಟಿ goṭṭi, *s.* A kind of play.

ಗೊಟ್ಟು goṭṭu, *s.* The kernel of a nut, as cocoanut, almond, castor oil seed *etc.*

ಗೊಡವೆ goḍavè, *s.* Interference, connection, intercourse, concern with.

ಗೊಡ್ಡು goḍḍu, *adj.* Barren, sterile. —ತನ barrenness, sterility.

ಗೊಡ್ಡುಸಾರ್ goḍḍusāru, *s.* A kind of pepper-water made of tamarind, chillies *etc.*

ಗೊಡ್ಡೆ goḍḍe, *s.* A Pariah. *pl.* ಗೊಡ್ಡೆರ್, ಗೊಡ್ಡೆಲುಜ the name of a sub-division of Pariahs.

ಗೊಣಸ್ goṇasu, *see* ಗಣಸ್.

ಗೊತ್ತು gottu, *see* ಗೊಂತು.

ಗೊತ್ತೆ gottè, *s.* Sweepings, rubbish.

ಗೊದಗೊದ godagoda, *see* ಕೊಚ ಕೊಚ.

ಗೊದ್ದುನಿ godduni (ಗೊದ್ದ್), *v. a.* To pick *or* devour, as a fowl.

ಗೊದ್ದೆ goddè, *s.* Lisping, stammering. –ಬಾಯಿದಾಯೆ a lisper, stammerer.

ಗೊನೆ gonè, *s.* A bunch of fruits, as plaintains, cocoanuts.

ಗೊಪ್ಪು goppu, *see* ಕೊಪ್ಪು.

ಗೊಪ್ಪೆ goppè, *see* ಗಪೆ.

ಗೊಬ್ಬರ gobbara, *s.* Manure, sweepings. –ಪಾಡುನಿ to manure.

ಗೊಬ್ಬಾಟ gobbāṭa, *s.* Diversion, amusement.

ಗೊಬ್ಬಾವುನಿ gobbāvuni, *c. v.* (*of* ಗೊಬ್ಬುನಿ) To make one play.

ಗೊಬ್ಬು gobbu, *s.* A play, dance, game. –ಜಾಗೆ a play-ground.

ಗೊಬ್ಬುನಿ gobbuni (ಗೊಬ್ಬ್), *v. a.* To play. 2. to trifle with, mock.

ಗೊಬ್ಬುಲಿ gobbuli, *s.* A bubble.

ಗೊಬ್ಬೆ gobbè, *see* ಬೊಬ್ಬೆ.

ಗೊರಂಟೆ, ಗೊರಟೆ goranṭè, goraṭè, *see* ಗೋರಂಟಿ.

ಗೊರಕು goraku, *see* ಗೊರ್ಕೆ.

ಗೊರಸ್ತಲಿಗೆ gorastaligè, *see* ಗೃಹಸ್ಥಲಿಗೆ.

ಗೊರಾಜನ gorājana, *see* ಗೋರೋಜನ.

ಗೊರ್ಕೆ gorkè, *s.* Snoring.

ಗೊರ್ತೆ gortè, *s.* The final preparation of a field for sowing.

ಗೊಲಂಬುಡೆ, ಗೊಲ್ಲುಂಬುಡೆ, ಗೊಲ್ಲುಮುಂಡೆ golambuḍè, gollumbuḍè, gollumuṇḍè, *s.* The angular leaved physic-nut, *Jatropha curcas*.

ಗೊಲ್ಲೆ gollè, *s.* A man of the cowherd *or* milkman caste. –ದಿ a female of this caste. –ರ್ cowherds.

ಗೊಳಕ goḷaka, *see* ಕೊಳಗ.

ಗೋ gō, *s.* A cow. –ಕಲ್ಲ್ a block of stone set up by the roadside for cattle to rub themselves against. –ದಾನ a gift of cattle. –ಮಯ cowdung. –ಮುಖ a spout *or* fountain, made like a cow's head. –ಮೇಧ the sacrifice of a cow.

ಗೋಂಕು gōṅku, *s.* A cashew fruit. –ದ ಮರ the cashew tree, *Anacardium occidentale*.

ಗೋಂಕುರು, ಗೋಂಕ್ರು gōṅkuru, gōṅkru, *s.* Rocking, as a child does on its legs and hands. 2. a lullaby used when so rocking. *adj.* Large, great; *cf.* ಗೋಂಪರ.

ಗೋಂಟು gōṇṭu, *adj.* Dried. –ತಾರಾಯಿ a cocoanut the kernel of which has dried within. –ಪೂಜು an unripe dried betel-nut. –ಕಟ್ಟುನಿ to get dried.

ಗೋಂದಳಪೂಜೆ, ಗೋಂದ್ಲುಪೂಜೆ gōndaḷapūjè, gōndlupūjè, *s.* A special worship of Durgā in fulfilment of a vow, performed by decorating her image indoors and by dancing in the outer court, with music and lights.

ಗೋಂದು gōndu, *s.* Gum; the gum arabic of *Acacia arabica*. –ತಾಗಾವುನಿ to gum.

ಗೋಂಪರ್ gōmparu, *adj.* Large, great. —ಕಪ್ಪೆ, *see* ಕೋಂಪೆ. —ತಿಪ್ಪಿ a large cocoanut shell. —ಮುಟ್ಟಲೆ a large kind of cap made of the areca leaf-stem.

ಗೋಂಪೆ gōmpè, *s.* A toad, paddock. 2. *see* ಕೋಪೆ.

ಗೋಕರ್ಣ gōkarṇa, *s. lit.* A cow's ear. 2. a celebrated place of pilgrimage in North Canara.

ಗೋಕು gōku, *see* ಕೋಂಕು.

ಗೋಕುಲ gōkula, *s.* Cattle. 2. a station of cowherds. 3. the place of Kṛushṇa's early life; *also* ನಂದಗೋಕುಲ. —ಅಷ್ಟಮಿ the birthday of Kṛushṇa. ಗೋಕುಲಾಟ Kṛushṇa's frolics when at Gōkula.

ಗೋಚರ, ಗೋಚಾರ gōčara, gōčāra, *s.* Perception, conception, penetration. 2. an object *or* organ of sense. —ಆಪಿನಿ to be visible; to comprehend, understand.

ಗೋಜಿ gōji, *s.* Interference. 2. intercourse. 3. confusion. —ಡ್ ಪೋಪಿನಿ to forget. ಆಯ ಗೋಜಿಗ್ ಪೋವಡ have nothing to do with him.

ಗೋಟು gōṭu, *s.* Embroidery; lace. —ದೀಪಿನಿ to put on a lace border *etc. adj. see* ಕೋಂಟು.

ಗೋಡ gōḍa, *s.* A horse; *bet.* ಘೋಡ.

ಗೋಡಾಮುಖೆ, ಗೋಡಾಮೃಗ gōḍāmukhe, gōḍāmrụga, *s.* A dunce, fool, simpleton.

ಗೋಡಿ gōḍi, *adj.* Erect, straight, direct. —ಪೋಪಿನಿ to go straight.

ಗೋಡಿಯಾವುನಿ gōḍiyāvuni, *c. v.* (*of* ಕೋಡಿಯುನಿ) To join, knit together. 2. to prepare, get ready.

ಗೋಡಿಯುನಿ gōḍiyuni (ಕೋಡಿ), *v. n.* To join, connect.

ಗೋಡೆ gōḍè, *s.* A wall. —ದೀಪಿನಿ to raise a wall.

ಗೋಣ gōṇa, *s.* A he-buffalo; *see* ಕೋಣ.

ಗೋಣಿ gōṇi, *s.* A sackcloth, gunny bag. 2. a malignant kind of small-pox. —ತಟ್ಟ sacking. —ಮಿಾರುನಿ to fall a victim to malignant small-pox, *abus.*

ಗೋಣೆ gōṇe, *s.* A he-buffalo. 2. *fig.* a stupid fellow.

ಗೋತ್ರ gōtra, *s.* A family, tribe, lineage. ಗತಿ ಗೋತ್ರ ದಾಂತಿನಾಯೆ a destitute man.

ಗೋದಾವರಿ gōdāvari, *s.* A river so called. 2. the name of a woman.

ಗೋದಿ, ಗೋಧಿ gōdi, gōdhi, *s.* Wheat. —ಕುಕ್ಕು a kind of mango.

ಗೋದಿಕ್ಕೆ gōdikke, *s.* An unmarried Pariah. 2. a nickname.

ಗೋದುಡಿ gōduḍi, *s.* A quilted bed sheet.

ಗೋಪಾಲೆ gōpāle, *s.* A herdsman. 2. Kṛushṇa. 3. a beggar. 4. the name of a man.

ಗೋಪಿ gōpī, *s.* A herdswoman. 2. yellow ochre; *also* ಕೋಪಿಚಂದನ, —ಮಣ್ಣ್.

ಗೋಪು gōpu, *s.* A thin girdle.

ಗೋಪುನಿ gōpuni (ಗೋ), *v. n.* To hold fast a tree with hands *or* with a rope. 2. to join.

ಗೋಪುರ gōpura, *s.* A tower.

ಗೋಪೆ gōpe, *s.* A chief of herdsmen.

ಗೋಪ್ಯ gōpya, *adj.* Secret, hidden, preserved. –ಸಂಗತಿ a secret. ಗೋಪ್ಯೊಡು secretly.

ಗೋಬಿ gōbi, *s.* A cabbage.

ಗೋಮು gōma, *s.* A peevish woman.

ಗೋಮಂತ, ಗೋಮೇಧಿಕ gōmanta, gōmēdhika, *s.* A gem of a yellowish *or* tawny colour, topaz, onyx.

ಗೋರಂಟೆ, ಗೋರಟೆ gōraṇṭè, gōraṭè, *s.* The prickly amaranth, *Barleria prionitis*.

ಗೋರಟ್ gōraṭu, *see* ಕೊರಂಟೆ.

ಗೋರಜಿನ gōrajina, *see* ಗೋರೋಜನ.

ಗೋರಬಲೆ gōrabalè, *s.* A large hand-net.

ಗೋರಲೆ gōralè, *s.* A small hand-net.

ಗೋರಾಜನ gōrājana, *see* ಗೋರೋಜನ.

ಗೋರಿ gōri, *s.* A grave. 2. a burial ground.

ಗೋರುನಿ gōruni (ಗೋರಿ), *v. a.* To dig from, out, *or* up, as coals *etc.* 2. to gather, collect, pile up. 3. to catch fish by a hand-net. 4. to level a ploughed field with a plank.

ಗೋರೆ gōrè, *see* ಕೋರೆ.

ಗೋರೆಲ್ gōrelu, *see* ಗೋರಲೆ.

ಗೋರೇಯುನಿ gōrēyuni (ಗೋರೆ), *v. a.* To drive together.

ಗೋರೋಜನ gōrōjana, *s.* Gall of cattle, *Calculus cysticus*.

ಗೋರ್ತೆ gōrte, *see* ಕೋರ್ತೆ.

ಗೋರ್ಲೆ gōrlè, *see* ಗೋರಲೆ.

ಗೋಸಾರ್ವುನಿ gōrsāvuni, *v. a.* To threaten.

ಗೋಲ್ gōlu, *adj.* Round. –ಕೆತ್ತುನಿ to make round.

ಗೋಲಂದಾಸ್ gōlandāsu, *s.* A gunner.

ಗೋಲಂಬುಡೆ gōlambuḍè, *see* ಕೊಲಂಬುಡೆ.

ಗೋಲಿ gōli, *see* ಗೋಳಿ.

ಗೋಲಿಕೊಟ್ಟೆ gōlikoṭṭè, *s.* The great great grand-father.

ಗೋಲಿಮರ gōlimara, *see* ಗೋಳಿಮರ.

ಗೋಲು gōlu, *s.* Grief, lamentation. –ತಾಗುನಿ, –ದರ್ಪುನಿ to be affected with the evils of another's grief.

ಗೋಲುಂಗಿಲ gōluṅgila, *s.* A plain ring, a guard ring.

ಗೋಲೆ gōlè, *see* ಗೋಳೆ.

ಗೋವತೆ gōvatè, *see* ಗೋಹತ್ಯ.

ಗೋವರ್ಧನ gōvardhana, *s.* The name of a mountain.

ಗೋವಲೆ, ಗೋವಲಿಗೆ, ಗೋವಾಲೆ gōvale, gōvalige, gōvāle, *s.* A herdsman; *cf.* ಗೋಪಾಲೆ, ಗೋಪೆ.

ಗೋವಿಂದೆ gōvinde, *s.* A name of Vishṇu. 2. the name of a man.

ಗೋವು gōvu, *see* ಗೋ.

ಗೋವೆ gōvè, *s.* Goa.

ಗೋಶ್ವಾರಿ, ಗೋಶ್ವಾರೆ gōšvāri, gōšvārè, *s.* An abstract, summary; *also* ಗೋಸ್ವಾರಿ.

ಗೋಷ್ಟಿ gōshṭi, *s.* Conversation, discourse.

ಗೋಸ್, ಗೋಸು gōsu̥, gōsu, *adv.* Leeward. 2. seaward. –ಕಟ್ಟುನಿ to shift the sail in order to direct the vessel seaward. –ಪತ್ತುನಿ, –ಕೋಪಿನಿ to steer seaward.

ಗೋಸಂಪಯಿ, ಗೋಸಂಪಿಗೆ gōsampayi, gōsampigè, *s.* The flower of the wild *champaka* tree, *Plumeria acuminata.*

ಗೋಸಾಯಿ gōsāyi, *s.* A sect of Śivites. 2. a religious mendicant.

ಗೋಹತ್ಯ gōhatya, *s.* Killing of a cow.

ಗೋಳ gōḷa, *s.* A globe.

ಗೋಳಕೆ gōḷake, *s.* An illegitimate son of a widow.

ಗೋಳಾಕಾರ gōḷākāra, *adj.* Globular, spherical.

ಗೋಳಾಟ gōḷāṭa, *see* ಕೋಲು.

ಗೋಳಿ gōḷi, *s.* A marble. 2. a ball, bullet. –ಫೈರ್ gun fire.

ಗೋಳಿದಮರ gōḷidamara, *s.* The large banyan tree, *Ficus Indica.*

ಗೋಳಿಪದ್ಪೆ gōḷipadpè, *s.* A kind of potherb, *Nyctanthes tristis.*

ಗೋಳು gōḷu, *see* ಕೋಲು.

ಗೋಳೆ gōḷè, *s.* Hollowness. *adj.* Hollow, void within. –ಮರ a hollow tree.

ಗೌಂಡಿ gouṇḍi, *s.* A female slave, maid servant.

ಗೌಂಡು gouṇḍu, *s.* Swelling. –ಕಟ್ಟುನಿ the body to be puffed up.

ಗೌಂಡೆ gouṇḍe, *see* ಗೌಡೆ.

ಗೌಜಿ gouji, *s.* A noise, tumult, uproar. 2. alarm agitation. 3. magnificence, grandeur. –ಕುಟ್ಟುನಿ to make noise; to threaten. –ಮುಳ್ಪುನಿ to shout; to be magnificent.

ಗೌಡ gouḍa, *s.* The district of Gour. 2. *see* ಗೌಡೆ.

ಗೌಡಿ gouḍi, *see* ಗೌಂಡಿ.

ಗೌಡು gouḍu, *adj.* Peevish, fretful.

ಗೌಡುಬಂಗಾಳಿ gouḍubaṅgāḷi, *s.* A trick, artifice, stratagem. 2. a trickster, cheat.

ಗೌಡೆ gouḍe, *s.* The headman of a village, *etc.* 2. a man of a caste of farmers.

ಗೌಣಾದಿಕೆ gouṇādikè, *s.* Greatness.

ಗೌಣೆ gouṇè, *see* ಕವಣೆ.

ಗೌತಮ, ಗೌತಮೆ goutama, goutame, *s.* A name of Sakya Muni, Buddha; *cf.* ಗುಂಮಟೆ.

ಗೌದಿಗೆ goudigè, *s.* The seat of a demon.

ಗೌರಿ gouri, *s.* A name of Pārvati. 2. the name of a woman. –ಹೂ balsamine.

ಗೌರಿಪಾಷಾಣ gouripāshāṇa, *s.* A tawny coloured mineral poison.

ಗೌಲೆ goule, *adj.* Tender, unripe, sapless, as a sugarcane.

ಗೌಸಣಿಗೆ gousaṇigè, *s.* A bag, case, cover.

ಗೌಳ್ಗೌಳ್ gouḷu̥gouḷu̥, *s.* Chewing *or* eating voraciously, as betel leaves *etc.*

ಗೌಳ, ಗೌಳಾಸ್ goul̥a, goul̥āsu̥, *s.* Digestion. —ಆಪಿನಿ to be digested.

ಗೌಳಿ goul̥i, *s.* A kind of lizard. —ಶಕುನ the chirp of a lizard, considered ominous. —ಶಾಸ್ತ್ರ a treatise on the omens presaged by the chirps *etc.* of a lizard.

ಗೌಳಿಗೆ goul̥ige, *s.* A milkman. 2. *see* ಕೌಳಿಗೆ.

ಗೌಳು goul̥u, *see* ಗೌಳ್‌ಗೌಳ್.

ಗೌಳೆ goul̥è, *see* ಗೌಲೆ.

ಗ್ಞಾನ gńāna, *see* ಜ್ಞಾನ.

ಗ್ಞಾನಿ gńāni, *see* ಜ್ಞಾನಿ.

ಗ್ಞಾಪಕ gńāpaka, *see* ಜ್ಞಾಪಕ.

ಗ್ರಂಥ grantha, *s.* A book, work, composition.

ಗ್ರಸ್ತಲಿಗೆ, ಗ್ರಸ್ತೊಲಿಗೆ grastaligè, grastoligè, *see* ಗೃಹಸ್ತಲಿಗೆ.

ಗ್ರಹ graha, *s.* A planet. 2. an evil spirit. —ಕುಂಡಲ an astrological diagram *or* table. —ಕೂಟ conjunction of planets. —ಗತಿ, —ಚಾರ the motion of the planets; their influence on the human destiny; fate, luck. —ರಾಶಿ the mansions of the planets. ನವ— the nine planets as enumerated by Hindus; *viz*, ಸೂರ್ಯ the sun, ಚಂದ್ರ the moon, ಮಂಗಳ Mars, ಬುಧ Mercury, ಬೃಹಸ್ಪತಿ Jupiter, ಶುಕ್ರ Venus, ಶನಿ Saturn, ರಾಹು the ascending node, ಕೇತು the descending node. ಬಾಲ— convulsion of children.

ಗ್ರಹಣ grahaṇa, *s.* Reception, acceptance. 2. comprehension. 3. an eclipse. —ಕಾಲ the occasion of an eclipse.

ಗ್ರಹಣಿ grahaṇi, *s.* Rickets, a wasting disease.

ಗ್ರಹಿಕೆ grahikè, *s.* Understanding, comprehension.

ಗ್ರಹಿಪುನಿ, ಗ್ರಹಿಸುನಿ grahipuni, grahisuni (ಗ್ರಹಿ), *v. n.* To understand, comprehend, perceive. 2. to consider, ponder.

ಗ್ರಾಂತಿ grānti, *s.* Habit, practice. 2. appetite, longing, eager desire.

ಗ್ರಾಚಾರ grācāra, *see under* ಗ್ರಹ.

ಗ್ರಾಣ grāṇa, *see* ಗ್ರಹಣ.

ಗ್ರಾಣಿ grāṇi, *see* ಗ್ರಹಣಿ.

ಗ್ರಾಮ grāma, *s.* A village, hamlet. —ಕಟ್ಟಳೆ the custom of a village. —ಕೂಟ a village council. —ದಾಯೆ, —ಸ್ಥ a villager. ಗ್ರಾಮ್ಯ rural, rustic, unpolished, inelegant.

ಗ್ರಾಸ grāsa, *s.* A mouthful of food. 2. food, subsistence.

ಗ್ರಾಸ್ತೆ grāste, *see* ಗೃಹಸ್ತೆ.

ಘ GH

ಘ **gha,** the seventeenth letter of the alphabet.

ಘಂಟ **ghaṇṭa,** *see* ಕಂಟವು.

ಘಂಟಿ **ghaṇṭi,** *see* ಗಂಟಿ.

ಘಂಟೆ **ghaṇṭè,** *s.* An hour. 2. a clock; *see* ಗಂಟೆ.

ಘಂಡಿ **ghaṇḍi,** *see* ಗಂಡಿ.

ಘಂಮ್ **ghamu,** *see* ಗಂಮು.

ಘಟ **ghaṭa,** *s.* A large earthen water-jar. 2. the body.

ಘಟಕ್ಕನೆ **ghaṭakkanè,** *see* ಗಡಕ್ಕ.

ಘಟನೆ **ghaṭanè,** *s.* Contact. 2. assemblage, bringing together.

ಘಟಸರ್ಪ **ghaṭasarpe,** *s.* A large snake.

ಘಟ್ಟ **ghaṭṭa,** *s.* A ghaut, defile, pass.

ಘಟ್ಟಣೆ **ghaṭṭaṇè,** *see* ಘಟನೆ.

ಘಟ್ಟಿ **ghaṭṭi,** *see* ಗಟ್ಟಿ.

ಘಡಾವನೆ **ghaḍāvanè,** *s.* Joining, uniting. 2. invention, manufacture, coining. 3. fabrication, concoction.

ಘಡಿ **ghaḍi,** *see* ಗಡಿ.

ಘಣಘಣ **ghaṇaghaṇa,** *s.* The sound of a ringing bell.

ಘನ **ghana,** *s.* Respectability, honour, dignity. 2. hardness. 3. solidity, substance. *adj.* Heavy. 2. noble, great. –ತೆ greatness, nobility, glory. –ಮೂಲ the cube root.

ಘಮ **ghama,** *s.* Fragrance, odour.

ಘರಿಮ್, ಘರ್ಮಿ **gharimu, gharmi,** *see* ಗರ್ಮಿ.

ಘಳಿಗೆ **ghaḷigè,** *see* ಗಳಿಗೆ.

ಘಾಟ್ **ghāṭu,** *see* ಗಾಟಿ.

ಘಾತ, ಘಾತಕ, ಘಾತಗ **ghāta, ghātaka, ghātaga,** *s.* Murder, slaughter, killing. 2. treachery, fraud. ಆತ್ಮ– suicide. ಜೀವ– destroying life, murder; suicide. ವಿಶ್ವಾಸ– treachery, breach of trust. ಘಾತಕೆ, ಘಾತಗೆ a murderer; an executioner; a cheat.

ಘಾತಿ **ghāti,** *s.* A matter becoming serious. ಅತಿ ಅತಿ ಘಾತಿ ಆಂಡ್ what was meant for a joke, has become serious.

ಘಾದ **ghāda,** *s.* Depth.

ಘಾಬರಿ **ghābari,** *see* ಗಾಬರಿ.

ಘಾಯ **ghāya,** *s.* A wound.

ಘಾರ **ghāra,** *see* ಗಾರ್.

ಘಾಸಿ **ghāsi,** *s.* Fatigue, trouble, toil. 2. conclusion, exhaustion, termination, death. –ಆಪಿನಿ to be troubled, fatigued; to die; to conclude, finish.

ಘಾಳಿ **ghāḷi,** *s.* Air, wind, breeze.

ಘೋಡ **ghōḍa,** *s.* A horse.

ಘೋರ **ghōra,** *adj.* Frightful, horrible, dreadful.

ಙ Ṅ

ಙ ṅa, The eighteenth letter of the alphabet. No words begin with this letter.

ಚ Č

ಚ ća, The nineteenth letter of the alphabet.

ಚಂಗ್ ćaṅgụ, *s.* Guimbard, Jew's-harp.

ಚಂಗ, ಚಂಗನೆ, ಚಂಗಮಂಗ, ಚಂಗೈಮಂಗೈ ćaṅga, ćaṅganè, ćaṅgamaṅga, ćaṅgeimaṅgei, *s.* A frolic, gambol. 2. hoax, humbug, deceit. –ಮಳ್ಪುನಿ to deceive, impose upon.

ಚಂಗಾಯಿ čaṅgāyi, *s.* A friend. 2. friendship.

ಚಂಗುಲಿ čaṅguli, *s.* A preparation consisting of jackfruit, jaggory, the juice of cocoanut and rice.

ಚಂಚ čam̃ča, *s.* A spoon.

ಚಂಚಲ čañčala, *adj.* Fickle, wavering, unsteady. –ತನ, –ತ್ವ fickleness. –ಮನಸ್ fickle mindedness. ಚಂಚಲೆ a fickle man.

ಚಂಡ್ čaṇḍụ, *see* ಚೆಂಡ್.

ಚಂಡ čaṇḍa, *s.* Vehemence, fierceness, obstinacy. 2. offspring. 3. host, multitude. *adj.* Vehement, fierce, obstinate. 2. quarrelsome.

ಚಂಡಾಡುನಿ čaṇḍāḍuni, *see* ಚೆಂಡಾಡುನಿ.

ಚಂಡಾಲೆ čaṇḍāle, *s.* An outcast, Pariah. 2. a wicked man.

ಚಂಡಿ čaṇḍi, *s.* Wetness. *adj.* Wet, moist, humid. –ಪುಂಡಿ very wet. –ಮಳ್ಪುನಿ to wet.

ಚಂಡಿ, ಚಂಡಿಕೆ ćaṇḍi, ćaṇḍikè, *s.* A name of Pārvati.

ಚಂಡು čaṇḍu, *see* ಚೆಂಡ್.

ಚಂಡೆ ćaṇḍè, *s.* A kind of drum.

ಚಂಡೆಮರ ćaṇḍemara, *see* ತೆಂಡೆ.

ಚಂದ ćanda, *s.* Beauty, elegance.

ಚಂದಗ, ಚಂದುಕ, ಚಂದುಗ ćandaga, čanduka, čanduga, *s.* A small box.

ಚಂದನ ćandana, *s.* Sandal, *Santalum album.*

ಚಂದ್ರ ćandra, *s.* The moon. –ಕಲೆ a digit of the moon. –ಕಾವಿ the colour of the rising moon, red. –ಕೆರಣ, –ಗ್ರಹಣ an eclipse of the moon. –ಬಿಂಬ the moon's disk.

ಚಂದ್ರಕ čandraka, *s.* The eye in a peacock's tail.

ಚಂದ್ರಕಾಂತ čandrakānta, *s.* A kind of gem. 2. alabaster.

ಚಂದ್ರಕಾಂತಿ čandrakānti, *s.* The moon-flower, *Ipomoea grandiflora.*

ಚಂದ್ರಜೋತಿ čandrajōti, *s.* A blue light, a kind of firework.

ಚಂದ್ರನಾಗೆ čandranāge, *s.* A serpent with a crescent-like stripe on its head.

ಚಂದ್ರಬಾರೆ čandrabārè, *s.* A red kind of plantain tree.

ಚಂದ್ರಬಾವಲಿ čandrabāvali, *s.* A kind of ornament for females.

ಚಂದ್ರಮಂಡಲ čandramaṇḍala, *s.* The moon's orb. 2. an idol's whirling car.

ಚಂದ್ರಮಡಕೆ čandramaḍakè, *s.* A kind of fish.

ಚಂದ್ರಮುರು čandramuru, *s.* A female's ear-ornament in the form of a half-moon.

ಚಂದ್ರವಂಶ čandravaṁśā, *s.* The lunar race.

ಚಂದ್ರಾಯುಧ čandrāyudha, *see* ಚಕ್ರ.

ಚಂದ್ರಾರಿ čandrāri, *s.* Kētu, the ascending node.

ಚಂದ್ರಾವತಿ čandrāvati, *s.* The name of a city. 2. the name of a woman.

ಚಂದ್ರಿಕೆ čandrikè, *s.* Moonlight. 2. the covering of a letter written on a palm leaf. 3. palm leaves rolled and tied up.

ಚಂದ್ರೆ čandre, *s.* The moon.

ಚಂನ čanna, *adj.* Red. 2. handsome, well.

ಚಂನನಾಯಿ čannanāyi, *s.* A wolf.

ಚಂನಳಿಗೆ čannaḷige, *s.* The red jasmine.

ಚಂನಾಬೂರು, ಚಂನೆಬೂರು čannābūru, čannebūru, *s.* A kind of creeper.

ಚಂನೆ čanne, *s.* A kind of game with cowries. –ಮಣೆ a board with two rows of seven holes for arranging the cowries. –ಕೊಬ್ಬುನಿ to play at such a game.

ಚಂಪಕ čampaka, *s.* The flower of *Michelia champaka; bet.* ಸಂಪಯಿ.

ಚಂಪೆ čampè, *see* ಚಪ್ಪೆ.

ಚಂಬ, ಚಂಬು čamba, čambu, *s.* A small water-pot; *cf.* ಚೆಂಬು. 2. a barge, fishing boat.

ಚಂಬಾರೆ čambāre, *see* ಚಂಮಾರೆ.

ಚಂಬಿಗೆ, ಚಂಬುಗೆ čambigè čambugè, *s.* A shoe. 2. a bad smell.

ಚಂಬೇಲಿ čambēli, *s.* A cunning female.

ಚಂಬೊಡಿ, ಚಂಮಡಿ čambodi, čammaḍi, *s.* A sledge hammer. 2. skin, leather. 3. a scourge, whip.

ಚಂಮಾರೆ čammāre, *s.* A shoemaker, chuckler; *cf.* ಸಮಗಾರೆ.

ಚಂಮಿ čammi, *s.* Dampness, moisture. 2. a kind of water-plant.

ಚಂಬುೞ čarmbu, *s.* A blossom without setting fruit. *adj.* Thin.

ಚಂಬುೞರಿ čarmburi, *see* ಚಮುೞರಿ.

ಚಕ್ čakụ, *see* ಚಕ್ಕು.

ಚಕ್ಬಂದಿ čakụbandi, *see* ಚಕ್ಕುಬಂದಿ.

ಚಕ್ಮುಕಿ ಚಕಮುಕಿ, čakṳmuki, čakamuki, *s.* The steel with which fire is struck. —ಕಲ್ಲ a flint stone. —ಹಾಕುನಿ to strike fire with a flint and steel.

ಚಕಂದ čakanda, *see* ಚಕ್ಕಂದ.

ಚಕಚಕ್ čakačakṳ, *adj.* Slow. *adv.* Shortly, suddenly.

ಚಕೋತ್ರ čakōtra, *see* ಚಕ್ಕುಲ್ಲಿ.

ಚಕ್ಕ್ čakkṳ, *adj.* Hollow, without kernel. 2. stunted, short, lean. 3. flat. —ತಾರಾಯಿ a hollow cocoanut. —ಮಂಡೆ a flat head. —ಮಣೆ a low seat. —ಮೂಕು a flat nose; *also* ನಂದ್‌ಮೂಕು.

ಚಕ್ಕ čakka, *adv.* Quickly, at once. —ಕುಳ್ಳುನಿ to sit at once, without observing where.

ಚಕ್ಕಂದ čakkanda, *s.* Plausibleness, speciousness. *adj.* Plausible, specious. —ದಾಯೆ a plausible man. —ಪಾತೆರ a plausible speech, flattery. —ಪಾತೆರುನಿ to say what is plausible, to flatter.

ಚಕ್ಕಟ್ಟ್ čakkaṭṭṳ, *adj.* Low.

ಚಕ್ಕಪ್ಪ čakkappa, *adv.* Down, below.

ಚಕ್ಕಮ್ čakkamṳ, *see* ಜಖಮ್.

ಚಕ್ಕಮುಕ್ಕಿ čakkamukki, *see* ಚಕ್ ಮುಕಿ.

ಚಕ್ಕರೆ čakkarė, *s.* Sugar.

ಚಕ್ಕಿ čakki, *s.* An ornament worn by female children.

ಚಕ್ಕು čakku, *see* ಚಕ್ಕ್.

ಚಕ್ಕುಬಂದಿ čakkubandi, *s.* Boundary-stones. 2. jurisdiction.

ಚಕ್ಕುಲಿ čakkuli, *s.* A cake made of rice flour, salt *etc.*, and fried in oil; *also* ಕಂಕಣವಡ್ಡೆ.

ಚಕ್ಕುಲಿಮರ čakkulimara, *s.* The Manilla tamarind tree, *Inga dulcis.*

ಚಕ್ಕುಲ್ಲಿ čakkulli, *s.* The pumplemose *or* shaddock, *Citrus decumana.*

ಚಕ್ಕೆ čakke, *see* ಚಿಕ್ಕೆ.

ಚಕ್ಕೆಲ್ čakkelṳ, *s.* The bosom.

ಚಕ್ರ čakra, *s.* A quarter rupee. 2. a wheel, circle. 3. a potter's wheel, coach wheel. 4. a discus. —ಗಡಿ two equal parts, as of a cocoanut. —ತುಂಡು a kind of small white cloth. —ಬಾಣ a wheel shaped firework. —ವಾದ್ಯ a mendicant's drum. —ಸರ a necklace of gold ringlets.

ಚಕ್ರವರ್ತಿ čakravarti, *s.* An emperor. —ನಿ an empress.

ಚಕ್ರಿ čakri, *s.* Vishṇu. 2. a potter. 3. a snake.

ಚಗನೆ čaganė, *see* ಚಂಗ.

ಚಗುಳೆ čaguḷė, *s.* A bug.

ಚಚ್ಚರ čaččara, *s.* Haste, speed, hurry.

ಚಚ್ಚೌಕ čaččouka, *s.* A square, quadrangle.

ಚಟ್ čaṭṳ, *intj.* Fie, fie! *adj.* Useless, excessive. ಪುಳಿಚಟಿ very sour. —ಪಟಿ, *see* ಚಟಿಪಟಿ.

ಚಟ್ಕ čaṭṳka, *s.* A snapping sound. *adv.* Quickly, briskly. —ಪೋಪಿನಿ to walk briskly.

ಚಟ್ಕ್ಕನೆ ćaṭukkane, *adv.* Harshly, rudely. —ಪಣ್ಪುನಿ to say rudely.

ಚಟ čaṭa, *s.* Energy, vigour. 2. the germ of a disease, the remaining symptoms of a disease. —ದೆಪ್ಪುನಿ to eradicate a disease. —ಪೋಪಿನಿ to lose energy, be tired, weary.

ಚಟಕ ćaṭaka, *s.* A summary method of offering to the manes of departed ancestors.

ಚಟಕ್ಕ ćaṭakka, *s.* A slapping *or* cracking sound; *cf.* ಚಟಕ.

ಚಟಚಟ, ಚಟಪಟ ćaṭaćaṭa, ćaṭapaṭa, *s.* Noise produced, as in slapping *or* cracking a whip.

ಚಟಿಣಿ ćaṭiṇi, *s.* Grain *or* fruit pounded, made into a thick paste with chillies, salt, *etc.* and eaten as a condiment with curry; chatney.

ಚಟಿಪಿಟಿ ćaṭipiṭi, *adv.* For nothing, uselessly.

ಚಟೀಲ čaṭīla, *s.* A cracking sound.

ಚಟ್ಟ್ ćaṭṭu, End, dissolution, termination, death. 2. exhaustion, consumption, ruin, demolition, extinction. —ಕಟ್ಟುನಿ, —ದೆಪ್ಪುನಿ, —ಮಳ್ಪುನಿ to exhaust, spend away, tire.

ಚಟ್ಟ ćaṭṭa, *s.* A litter, sort of a palanquin. 2. a bier. 3. a window frame. —ಕಟ್ಟುನಿ to prepare a bier.

ಚಟ್ಟನೆ ćaṭṭane, *adv.* Suddenly; *cf.* ಪಕ್ಕನೆ.

ಚಟ್ಟಿ čaṭṭi, *s.* A broad-mouthed spittoon. 2. a chamber pot.

ಚಟ್ಟಿಣಿ čaṭṭini, *see* ಚಟಿಣಿ.

ಚಟ್ಟು čaṭṭu, *s.* A country pony. 2. *see* ಚಟ್ಟ್.

ಚಟ್ಟೆ čaṭṭe, *adj.* Flat, level, without inclination. —ಕಲ್ಲ್ a flat stone.

ಚಟ್ಟೆಗಾರೆ čaṭṭegāre, *s.* A native who assumes European dress.

ಚಟ್ಣಿ, ಚಟ್ನಿ čaṭṇi, ćaṭni, *see* ಚಟಿಣಿ.

ಚಡ್ಚಡ್ čaḍućaḍu, *adv.* Quickly, speedily. —ಏಣಿಗ್ ಮಿತ್ತಾರುನಿ to mount a ladder quickly.

ಚಡ್ತ, ಚಡತ čaḍuta, čaḍata, *see* ಚತ್ರ.

ಚಡತಿ čaḍati, *s.* Dissimulation. 2. *see* ಸತಿರ.

ಚಡಾಚಡಿ čaḍāčaḍi, *see* ಚಟಚಟ. 2. *see* ಚಡ್ಚಡ್.

ಚಡಾಯಿಸುನಿ čaḍāyisuni (ಚಡಾಯಿಸ್), *v. a.* To increase, raise *or* bid higher, as price. 2. to beat, strike, flog. ಕೋಳ— to put in stocks. ಗಂಗಸರ— to swallow liquor. ಚುಟ್ಟ— to smoke excessively.

ಚಡಾವು čaḍāvu, *s.* An ascent, uphill. 2. increase, enhancement. 3. a kind of country shoes. —ಮಳ್ಪುನಿ to raise, enhance, as the price; *cf.* ಚಡಾಯಿಸುನಿ.

ಚಡಾವುನಿ čaḍāvuni, *v. a.* To ascend, climb.

ಚಡಾಸುನಿ čaḍāsuni, *see* ಚಡಾಯಿಸುನಿ.

ಚಡಿ čaḍi, *s.* A notch, indentation. 2. a whip, stripe. —ದೆಪ್ಪುನಿ,

—ಮಳ್ಪುನಿ to make a notch. —ಪಾಡುನಿ to whip. —ತ ಮಣಿ a joining bench, groove-plane, jointer.

ಚಡು ćaḍu, *s.* The belly. 2. a pleasing discourse.

ಚಡುಗು ćaḍugu, *adj.* Bad, depraved.

ಚಡುತ ćaḍuta, *s.* Persistency, obstinacy. 2. a bet *or* wager. —ಪಾತೆರುನಿ to speak persistently, to provoke.

ಚಡೆ ćaḍe, *s.* A kind of bag.

ಚಡ್ತ čaḍta, *s.* Daily *or* regular observance of rites *or* customs; *cf.* ಚರ್ಯ. 2. *see* ಚಡುತ. ದಿನ— a diary.

ಚಡ್ಪು ćaḍpu, *s.* Leanness, thinness.

ಚಣ ćaṇa, *see* ಕ್ಷಣ.

ಚಣಿಲ್ ćaṇilụ, *see* ಚನಿಲ್.

ಚತ್ರೆಂಗಿ ćatụreṅgi, *see* ಜಮಕನ್.

ಚತುರ್ ćaturụ, *num.* Four. —ಸ ದಿ the four sides *or* boundaries of a land *etc.*

ಚತುರ ćatura, *adj.* Clever, dexterous.

ಚತುರಂಗ čaturaṅga, *s.* Chess.

ಚತುರಂಗಬಲ ćaturaṅgabala, *s.* An army consisting of infantry, cavalry, elephants and war chariots.

ಚತುರೆ čature, *see* ಚಾತುರೆ.

ಚತುರ್ಥಿ čaturthi, *adj.* Fourth. *s.* The fourth day of the lunar fortnight. —ವಿಭಕ್ತಿ the dative case, *gram.*

ಚತುರ್ದಶಿ čaturdaši, *s.* The fourteenth day of the lunar fortnight.

ಚತುರ್ವರ್ಗ ćaturvarga, The four objects of pursuit: justice, wealth, pleasure, and heaven.

ಚತುರ್ವರ್ಣ ćaturvarṇa, *s.* The four castes.

ಚತುರ್ವೇದ ćaturvēda, *s.* The four Vēdas *or* ancient scriptures of the Hindus.

ಚತುಷ್ಪಾದ ćatushpāda, *adj.* Quadruped.

ಚದ್ರ್, ಚದರ್, ಚದರ ćadụrụ, ćadarụ, ćadara, *s.* Dispersion, dissipation, scattering. —ಆಪಿನಿ to be dispersed, scattered. —ಮಳ್ಪುನಿ to disperse, scatter.

ಚದರಾವುನಿ, ಚದರಿಪುನಿ ćadarāvuni, ćadaripuni, *c. v.* (*of* ಚದರುನಿ) To disperse, scatter.

ಚದರುನಿ ćadaruni (ಚದರ್), *v. n.* To be scattered, dispersed; *also* ಚದರ್ದ್ ಪೋಪಿನಿ.

ಚದಿ čadi, *s.* Obstinacy, pertinacity. —ಮಳ್ಪುನಿ to be obstinate. ಚದಿಕ್— revenge, retaliation.

ಚದುಪು čadupu, *s.* Skill, ingenuity, cunning. —ತೋಜಾವುನಿ to play tricks.

ಚದುರ ćadura, *see* ಚತುರ, ಚಾತುರ್ಯ.

ಚದುರೆ čadure, *see* ಚಾತುರೆ.

ಚದೆ čade, *s.* Severe fighting. 2. destruction of life.

ಚನಾನಿ čanāni, *s.* Great harm. 2. quarrel, riot. 3. desolation, waste, ruin.

ಚನಿ ćani, *see* ಸನಿ.

ಚನಿಲ್ čanilụ, *s.* A squirrel. 2. [*see* ಸನಿಲ್.

ಚನ್ನ čanna, *see* ಚಂದ.

ಚಪಚಪ čapačapa, *s.* A noise made with the mouth, as a pig in eating.

ಚಪಟೆ čapaṭe, *see* ಚಟ್ಟಿ.

ಚಪರಾಸ್ čaparāsụ, *see* ಚಪ್ರಾಸಿ.

ಚಪಲ, ಚಪಳ čapala, čapaḷa, *adj.* Waving, moving. 2. fickle, unsteady. 3. swift, quick. –ತನ, –ತ್ವ fickleness; quick perception. –ಸರಮಾನಿ a man of quick perception *or* apprehension. –ಮನಸ್ fickle-mindedness. ಚಪಲೆ a woman with quick and moving eyes. 2. Laxmi, the goddess of wealth.

ಚಪಾಯಿಸುನಿ čapāyisuni, *see* ಛಪಾಯಿಸುನಿ.

ಚಪಾವು čapāvu, *see* ಛಪಾವು.

ಚಪ್ಡಿ čapḍi, *see* ಚಪ್ಪುಡಿ.

ಚಪ್ಪ čappa, *adv.* Fast, firmly. 2. suddenly. –ಪೊತ್ತುನಿ to stick fast. –ಹಾಕುನಿ to fix firmly.

ಚಪ್ಪ čappa, *see* ಚೆಪ್ಪೆ.

ಚಪ್ಪಂಗ čappaṅga, *s.* The sappan tree, *Caesalpinia sappan.*

ಚಪ್ಪಟ್ čappaṭụ, *adj.* Tasteless, insipid. 2. bad, worthless.

ಚಪ್ಪಟೆ čappaṭe, *s.* A worthless person. *adj. see* ಚಪ್ಪೆ.

ಚಪ್ಪಟ್ಟೆ čappaṭṭe, *s.* Cooling.

ಚಪ್ಪಡಾಚಿ čappaḍāči, *s.* Coaxing, flattering. 2. fabrication, invention.

ಚಪ್ಪಡಿ čappaḍi, *see* ಚಪ್ಪುಡಿ.

ಚಪ್ಪನ್ನ čappanna, *adj.* Fifty-six. –ದೇಶ the fifty-six countries enumerated by the Hindu writers.

ಚಪ್ಪರ್ čapparụ, *s.* A kind of dried fish.

ಚಪ್ಪರ್ čapparụ, *adj.* Low, cast down. –ಕೊಂಬು an ornament of a devil-dancer. –ಬೂರುನಿ to be low.

ಚಪ್ಪರ čappara, *s.* A shed, pandal. –ಮಂಚ a cot with posts and curtains. –ಪಾಡುನಿ to put up a temporary shed.

ಚಪ್ಪರಿಪುನಿ čappariputi (ಚಪ್ಪರ್), *v. a.* To smack the lips.

ಚಪ್ಪಲ್, ಚಪ್ಪಳ್ čappalụ, čappaḷụ, *s.* A shoe, sandal.

ಚಪ್ಪಳಿ čappaḷi, *s.* Clapping the hands.

ಚಪ್ಪಳಿಪುನಿ čappaḷipuni (ಚಪ್ಪಳಿ), *v. a.* To clap the hands.

ಚಪ್ಪಾಯಿಸುನಿ čappāyisuni, *see* ಛಪಾಯಿಸುನಿ.

ಚಪ್ಪಾವು čappāvu, *see* ಛಪಾವು.

ಚಪ್ಪಿ, ಚಪ್ಪೆ čappi, čappe, *s.* A stamp, seal, mark.

ಚಪ್ಪುಡಿ čappuḍi, *s.* Concealing. 2. legerdemain, jugglery; *also* –ಗಲಿ. 3. the play of 'hide and seek'.

ಚಪ್ಪೆ čappe, *adj.* Tasteless, insipid, unsavoury. 3. cool, vapid. 4. trifling, worthless. –ಚಾರ್ quite worthless.

ಚಪ್ರಾಸ್ čaprāsụ, *s.* A kind of drill cloth.

ಚಬಕಾರ, ಚಬುಕಾರ čabakāra, čabukāra, *s.* Soap; fuller's earth; *also* ಸಬುಕಾರ್, ಸಾಬೂನು.

ಚಬುಕ್‌ಮರ čabukụmara, *see* ತವುಕ ಚಮರ.

ಚಬುಕು čabuku, *s.* A whip. –ದ ಮರ a *Casuarina* tree.

ಚವುಕಾನ್ čamụkānụ, *see* ಜಮ್ಕಾನ್.

ಚಮ್‌ಗಾರೆ čamụgāre, *s.* A shoemaker, chuckler. –ರ ಉಳಿ a chuckler's awl; *also* ಸಮ್ಗಾರೆ.

ಚವ್‌ಚ čamụča, *see* ಚಮ್ಚ.

ಚಮಟಿಗೆ čamaṭige, *s.* A sledge hammer.

ಚಮಡ čamaḍa, *s.* The skin, leather,

ಚಮತ್ಕಾರ čamatkāra, *s.* Cleverness, dexterity, artifice. 2. astonishment, surprise. 3. wit, eloquence. 4. anything curious, ingenious *or* extraordinary; *also* ಚಮತ್ಕಾರಿಕೆ.

ಚಮತ್ತಿಗೆ, čamattigè, *s.* The flower of *Pyrethrum indicum.*

ಚಮರಿಮೃಗ čamarimrụga, *s.* The yak, *or bos-grunniens.*

ಚಮಾನ್ čamānụ, *see* ಜಮ್ಕಾನ್.

ಚಮಿಪುನಿ čamipuni, *see* ಕ್ಷಮಿಪುನಿ.

ಚಮ್ಚ čamča, *s.* A spoon, ladle.

ಚಯ čaya, *see* ಕ್ಷಯ.

ಚಯಿ čayi, *see* ಚಐ.

ಚಯಿಲ čayila, *see* ತೈಲ.

ಚರ್ಂಬು čarụmbu, *see* ಚಂಬುರ್.

ಚರ čara, *adj.* Moveable, locomotive. –ಜಿಂದಿಗೆ, ಚರಾಸ್ತಿ moveable *or* personal property, chattels.

ಚರಕ್, ಚರಕು čarakụ, čaraku, *s.* Merchandise, cargo. 2. goods, articles; *bel.* ಸರಕ್.

ಚರಕ್ čarakụ, *s.* Machinery. –ತಿಂಗಾರ್ಪುನಿ to set a machine in motion.

ಚರಚರ čaračara, *s.* A noise made in spurting *or* throwing water from a pump. 2. *see* ಚಿರಿಚಿರಿ. –ನೀರ್ an even accumulation of water in a field. –ಪಾತೆರುನಿ to prattle.

ಚರಟೆ čaraṭè, *s.* What is coarse; leavings *or* stalks.

ಚರಣ čaraṇa, *s.* The foot. 2. a foot in poetry. –ಸೇವೆ, *see* ಪಾದ ಸೇವೆ.

ಚರಣೆ čaraṇè, *s.* Pasturage, grazing.

ಚರಾಚರ čarāčara, *adj.* Moveable and immoveable. –ವಸ್ತುಳು animate *or* inanimate things; the creation, world.

ಚರಾಸ್ತಿ čarāsti, *see under* ಚರ.

ಚರಿಗೆ čarigè, *s.* A cooking utensil of copper *or* brass. 2. *see* ಸರಿಗೆ.

ಚರಿಗೆ čarigè, *see* ಚುಯರ್.

ಚರಿತ, ಚರಿತ್ರ, ಚರಿತ್ರೆ čarita, čaritra, čaritrè, *s.* A history, story, narrative. 2. conduct, behaviour.

ಚರಿಪು čaripu, *s.* An offering presented to an idol and then distributed among the people present.

ಚರಿಪುನಿ čaripuni (ಚರಿ), *v. a.* To quake, tremble, shudder, shiver; *cf.* ದರಿಪುನಿ.

ಚರಿಪುನಿ čaripuni (ಚರಿ), *v. n.* To move; wander.

ಚರು, ಚರುವ čaru, čaruva, *s.* An oblation of rice and other ingredients to the gods *or* demons. 2. a small fish.

ಚರುಬು čarubu, *see* ಚಂಬುರ್.

ಚರೆ čarè, *s.* Small shots. 2. the head; *bet.* ತರೆ.

ಚರ್ಕ čarka, *adv.* Straightly, directly. –ರಟ್ಟುನಿ to splash off, as mud.

ಚರ್ಕಿ čarki, *see* ಚರಕ್.

ಚರ್ಚಿ, ಚರ್ಚೆ čarči, čarče, *s.* Dispute, wrangling. –ಮಳ್ಪುನಿ to dispute, reason, argue.

ಚರ್ದಿ čardi, *s.* Vomiting.

ಚರ್ಪಟ್, ಚರ್ಪಟ್ಟ್, ಚರ್ಪಾಟ್ čarpaṭu, čarpaṭṭu, čarpāṭu, *adj.* Watery.

ಚರ್ಪು čarpu, *see* ಚರಿಪು.

ಚರ್ಬಿ čarbi, *s.* Fat, grease. 2. arrogance, pride, *fig.*

ಚರ್ಮ čarma, *s.* The skin, hide, leather. –ಜಾರಾವುನಿ to flay, peel, skin, bark.

ಚರ್ಮುರಿ čarmuri, *s.* Parched rice.

ಚರ್ಯ, ಚರ್ಯೆ čarya, čaryè, *s.* Observance of rites *or* customs. 2. conduct, demeanour. ದಿನ– a diary, chronicle.

ಚರ್ವ čarva, *see* ಚರು.

ಚರ್ವಣ čarvaṇa, *s.* Chewing betel.

ಚಲ್‌ಪಟ್ čalupaṭu, *see* ಚಪ್ಪಟೆ.

ಚಲ čala, *see* ಛಲ.

ಚಲಕ್ čalaku, *s.* Dexterity, particularly of the hand *or* tongue.

ಚಲಚಲ čalačala, *s.* A noise in wading through water, as children make while playing.

ಚಲನೆ čalanè, *s.* Motion, movement. *adj.* Wandering, roaming.

ಚಲಪಟ್ čalapaṭu, *see* ಚಪ್ಪಟೆ.

ಚಲವಲ čalavala, *s.* Alarm, consternation, agitation. 2. exhaustion, weariness; *cf.* ತಳಬಲ.

ಚಲಾಪಲ čalāpala, *s.* Agitating water.

ಚಲಾವಣಿ čalāvaṇi, *s.* Currency, genuineness, as of a coin. ಹುಂಡಿ– drawing a bill of exchange. –ದ ನಾಣ್ಯ a current coin. –ಮಳ್ಪುನಿ to make pass *or* current.

ಚಲಿ čali, *s.* Cold, chilliness, shivering, as in ague. *adj.* Cold, chilly; *also* ಸಲಿ. –ಕಾಲ the cold season. –ಗೆಜ್ಜಿ, *see* ಚಲ್ಲಿಕೆ. –ಘಾಳಿ cold wind. –ಜರ ague. –ಕಯಿಪುನಿ to warm. –ಕಯಿತೊಂಬುನಿ to be warming oneself. –ಪತ್ತುನಿ to catch cold; to be afraid. –ಬುದ್ದುಪೋಪಿನಿ to be relieved of cold; fear to depart.

ಚಲಿಪುನಿ čalipuni (ಚಲಿ), *v. a.* To shake, move.

ಚಲಿಮಿ, ಚಲ್ಮಿ čalimi, čalmi, *see* ಚಿಲಿಂಬಿ.

ಚಲ್ಪಟ್ಟೆ čalpaṭṭe, *see* ಚಲ್ಲೆ.

ಚಲ್ಲ್ čallu, *adj.* Stupid, dull. 2. timid, timorous. 3. imbecile, weak, useless.

ಚಲ್ಲ್‌ಕೆ čalluke, *s.* A kind of small bell.

ಚಲ್ಲ čalla, *s.* A noise of a fall with force.

ಚಲ್ಲಂಗಾಯಿ čallangāyi, *s.* The Sepistan plum, *Cordia myxa.*

ಚಲ್ಲಂಟೆ čallaṇṭe, *s.* A kind of crab.

ಚಲ್ಲಣ, ಚಲ್ಲನ, ಚಲ್ಲಾನ čallaṇa, čallana, čallāna, *s.* Short breeches, reaching only to the middle of the thighs. 2. a mat of straw rope. 3. a covering for a horse.

ಚಲ್ಲಾಪಿನಿ čallāpini (ಚಲ್ಲಾ), *v. n.* To get weak. 2. to become useless. 3. to fail, lose; *cf.* ಚಲ್ಲ.

ಚಲ್ಲಾಪಿಲ್ಲಿ čallāpilli, *s.* Confusion, disorder. 2. dispersion, scattering.

ಚಲ್ಲಿ čalli, *s.* A chip. 2. a reed. 3. a potsherd. 4. a kind of grass.

ಚಲ್ಲುನಿ čalluni (ಚಲ್ಲ್), *v. n.* To spill, shed; to disperse.

ಚಲ್ಲೆ čalle, *s.* A weak *or* timid man. 2. the name of a man.

ಚಲ್ಲೆಪಿಲ್ಲೆ čallepille, *s.* Youngsters. ಈ ಚಲ್ಲೆಪಿಲ್ಲೆನ್ ಯಾನ್ ವೊಡೆಗ್ ಕೊಂಡು ಪೋಪಿನಿ where shall I take these little ones?

ಚವಡಿಗೆ čavaḍige, *see* ಚಾಡಿಗೆ.

ಚವಣೆ čavaṇe, *s.* An instrument for drawing wire, pincers, tweezers. —ಡ್ ಪಾಡ್ದ್ ವೈಪುನಿ to draw wire through it.

ಚವರ čavara, *s.* A fly-brush. 2. *see* ಕ್ಷೌರ.

ಚವಲ čavala, *s.* Half a rupee. 2. the ceremony of tonsure of a child. —ಬಡ್ಡಿ interest at $12\frac{1}{2}$ per cent.

ಚವಿ čavi, *s.* A disease of newly born infants.

ಚವುಂಟು čavuṇṭu, *see* ಚಾಂಟು.

ಚವುಂಟುನಿ čavuṇṭuni, *see* ಚಾಂಟುನಿ.

ಚವುಕ čavuka, *see* ಚಾಕ.

ಚವುಕಳಿ čavukaḷi, *see* ಚಾಕಳಿ.

ಚವುಕಾಸ, ಚವುಕಾಸಿ čavukāsa, čavukāsi, *s.* Cleverness in dealings, marketing with judgment. 2. leisure, respite; *bet.* ಸಾವಕಾಶ.

ಚವುಕಿ, ಚವುಕೆ čavuki, čavuke, *see* ಚಾಕಿ.

ಚವುರ čavura, *see* ಚಾರ.

ಚವುರಾಸ್ čavurāsu, *s.* A square bottle.

ಚವುರಿ čavuri, *see* ಚಾರಿ.

ಚವುಲಿ, ಚವುಳಿ čavuli, čavuḷi, *adj.* Cold. —ನೀರ್ cold water. —ಚಂಡಿರ್ very cold water.

ಚವುಳ್, ಚವುಳು čavuḷu, čavuḷu, *adj.* Brackish, saline. —ಭೂಮಿ poor *or* infertile land. —ಉಪ್ಪು. nitre; earth salt.

ಚವುಳಿಕಾಯಿ čavuḷikāyi, *s.* The vegetable *Dolichos fobas formis.*

ಚಹಲ್, ಚಹಾರ್ čahalu, čahāru, *s.* Expertness, dexterity. 2. conduct.

ಚಳಕ್ čaḷaku, *see* ಚಲಕ್.

ಚಳಕಿ čaḷaki, *s.* A kind of bracelet, made of gold and coral beads.

ಚಳಚಳ čaḷačaḷa, *s.* A bubbling noise. 2. glittering. —ಮಿಂಚುನಿ to glitter, glimmer, shine.

ಚಳತುಂಪ್, ಚಳ್ತುಂಬು čaḷatummu, čaḷtumbu, *s.* A double cone-shaped ear-ornament worn by females.

ಚಳಿ čaḷi, *see* ಚಲಿ.

ಚಳ್ಳ್ čaḷḷu, *see* ಚಲ್ಲ್.

ಚಳ್ಳ čaḷḷa, *see* ಚಲ್ಲ.

ಚಳ್ಳಮರ čaḷḷamara, *s.* The monkey-fruit tree.

ಚಾ čā, *s.* The tea plant, *Thea viridis.* 2. lemon grass, *Andropogon schoenanthus.* 3. infusion *or* decoction of the leaves of tea or any medicinal plant. –ತಪ್ಪು the tea leaves. –ಮಳ್ಪುನಿ to prepare tea.

ಚಾಂಟ್ čāṇṭu, *see* ಚಾಟಿ.

ಚಾಂಟೆ čāṇṭe, *adj.* Lame, crippled. –ಕಾರ್ a lame leg.

ಚಾಂಡಾಲೆ čāṇḍāle, *see* ಚಂಡಾಲೆ.

ಚಾಂಡುನಿ čāṇḍuni (ಚಾಂಡಿ), *v. a.* To fling *or* dart a spear.

ಚಾಂಪಾಡುನಿ čāmpāḍuni (ಚಾಂಪಾಡಿ), *v. a.* To withdraw, get out.

ಚಾಂಪು čāmpu, *s.* A knot, as of an angling tackle.

ಚಾಂಬುನಿ čāmbuni (ಚಾಂಬಿ), *v. n.* To flee, escape, run away. 2. to close, shut, shrivel, as a flower. *v. a.* To lift with a lever.

ಚಾಕ್ čāku, *s.* Chalk.

ಚಾಕಟ್ಟ್ čākaṭṭu, *s.* A kind of bracelet made of coral and gold beads. 2. a packet of tea. –ದ ಮಣಿ, ಚಾಕಟ್ಟಿಕಾಯಿ a bead of such a bracelet.

ಚಾಕರಿ, ಚಾಕ್ರಿ čākari, čākri, *s.* Service, employment. –ದಾಯೆ a servant. –ಮಳ್ಪುನಿ to do service.

ಚಾಚುನಿ čāčuni (ಚಾಚ್), *v. a.* To stretch out, hold out. 2. to bow.

ಚಾಟ್ čāṭu, *s.* Exchange, barter; *also* ಸಾಟಿ. –ಮಳ್ಪುನಿ to barter, exchange.

ಚಾಟ್ čāṭu, *s.* Force, current. ನೀರ್ದ– current of water.

ಚಾಟಕ, ಚಾಟಕಮಂತ್ರ čāṭaka, čāṭakamantra, *s.* An incantation for destroying *or* subjugating a person.

ಚಾಟಿ, ಚಾಟೆ čāṭi, čāṭe, *see* ಚಾಟಿ.

ಚಾಡಿ čāḍi, *s.* Defamation, slander. 2. talebearing. –ಗಾರೆ a slanderer, talebearer. –ತ ರಳಿ, –ಪಾತೆರ, –ಸುದ್ದಿ slanderous report.

ಚಾಡಿಯುನಿ čāḍiyuni (ಚಾಡಿ), *v. a.* To slander.

ಚಾತಪ್ಪು čātappu, *see* ಚಾ.

ಚಾತಿ čāti, *see* ಛಾತಿ.

ಚಾತುರೆ čāture, *s.* A clever, dexterous person.

ಚಾತುರ್ಯ čāturya, *s.* Eloquence. 2. dexterity. 3. cleverness; *also* ಬುದ್ಧಿ–. *adj.* Skilful, clever. –ದಾಯೆ a dexterous man.

ಚಾನಾಹಾನಿ čānāhāni, *see* ಚನಾನಿ.

ಚಾನು čānu, *see* ಚೇನ್.

ಚಾನೂಲು čānūlu, *s.* A woman's neck ornament.

ಚಾಪಕಾನೆ čāpakāne, *see* ಛಾಪಖಾನೆ.

ಚಾಪಣೆ čāpaṇė, *s.* A lever. 2. *see* ಛಾಪು. 3. *see* ಸ್ಥಾಪನೆ.

ಚಾಪಿಸುನಿ čāpisuni *see* ಛಾಪಿಸುನಿ.

ಚಾಪು čāpu, *s.* The cock, as of a gun. 2. a piece of a cloth *or* web, containing several garments *etc.* 3. a shop; *bet.* ಶಾಪು. —ದ ಪಲಾಯಿ a thin metal plate. ಅಂಗೋಸ್ತ್ರದ—, ಎಲ ತ್ರದ— a piece of cloth containing several towels *or* handkerchiefs.

ಚಾಪೆ čāpė, *s.* A mat; *bet.* ಪಡಿ. 2. *see* ಛಾಪೆ. —ಪಲಾಯಿ a kind of window-shutter.

ಚಾಮು čāma, *see* ಕಾಮು. 2. *see* ಜಾಮು.

ಚಾಮರ čāmara, *s.* A fly-brush of the hair of yak *or bos grunniens.*

ಚಾಮೀಕರ čāmīkara, *s.* Gold.

ಚಾಮುಂಡಿ čāmuṇḍi, *s.* A goddess so called, a form of Durgi. 2. the name of a female demon.

ಚಾಮೆ čāmė, *see* ಸಾಮೆ.

ಚಾಯು, ಚಾಯೆ čāya, čāyė, *see* ಛಾಯೆ.

ಚಾಯಿ čāyi, *s.* Ink. 2. *see* ಛಾಯೆ.

ಚಾರ್ čāru, *s.* A kind of pepper-water; *also* ಸಾರ್.

ಚಾರ čāra, *see* ಚರ.

ಚಾರಗೆ čārage, *s.* A cocoanut.

ಚಾರಣಿ, ಚಾರಣೆ čāraṇi, čāraṇė, *s.* Smearing a wall *or* floor with mud, chunam *or* cow-dung.

ಚಾರಿ čāri, *s.* A traveller. ಪಾದ— a traveller on foot.

ಚಾರಿತ್ರ čāritra, *see* ಚರಿತ.

ಚಾರುಕಾನೆಶೀರೆ čārukānešīrė, *see* ಚಾರ್ಖಾನೆಶೀರೆ.

ಚಾರೆ čārė, *s.* Features. 2. food. 3. a cocoanut tree; *cf.* ತಾರೆ.

ಚಾರ್ಖಾನೆಶೀರೆ čārkhānešīrė, *s.* A female's cloth with interwoven flowers.

ಚಾರ್ವಾಕ čārvāka, *adj.* Sceptical. 2. sophistical. 3. opposed to the Hindu scriptures. —ಮತ scepticism. ಚಾರ್ವಾಕೆ a sceptic; a sophist.

ಚಾಲ್ čālu, *see* ಚಾಲಿ. 2. *see* ಶೀಲ. —ಚಲಾನಿ behaviour.

ಚಾಲಗೇಣಿ čālagēṇi, *s.* Rent for one year. —ಚೀಟಿ a written agreement for one year's rent.

ಚಾಲಾಕ್ čālāku, *s.* Dexterity, cleverness. —ದಾಯಿ a dexterous man.

ಚಾಲಿ čāli, *s.* Nature. 2. habit. 3. conduct. 4. scorn, mockery, scoffing. —ಮಳ್ಪುನಿ to mock.

ಚಾಲಿಪುನಿ čālipuni (ಚಾಲಿ), *v. a.* To mock, ridicule, jest.

ಚಾಲಿಮರ čālimara, *s.* The tree *Ocimum gratissimum.*

ಚಾಲಿಯೆ čāliye, *see* ತಾಲಿಯೆ.

ಚಾಲೀಸ್ čālīsu, *num.* Forty. *adj.* Weak *or* near sighted. *s.* A pair of spectacles.

ಚಾಲ್ತಿ, ಚಾಲ್ದಿ čālti, čāldi, *adj.* Of daily occurrence, practical. *s.* A routine of business.

ಚಾವಡಿ čāvaḍi, *s.* An open hall, *or* veranda in front of a house.

2. a public place where business is transacted. 3. a lodging place for travellers. 4. a demon shrine.

ಚಾವಲ čāvala, *see* ಚವಲ.

ಚಾಳಿಪುನಿ cāḷipuni, *see* ಚಾಲಿಪುನಿ.

ಚಿಂಗರ čiṅgara, *s.* Ornament, decoration, embellishment; beauty; *bet.* ಶೃಂಗಾರ.

ಚಿಂಗಿರಿ čiṅgiri, *s.* A kind of fish.

ಚಿಂಗ್ಲಿಕೆ čiṅglike, *s.* A large kind of ape.

ಚಿಂಚಿಂಸಕ್ಕರೆ čiṁčiṁsakkarĕ, *see* ಕಲ್ಲ ಸಕ್ಕರೆ.

ಚಿಂತಾಕ್ರಾಂತೆ čintākrānte, *s.* A man overwhelmed with sorrow *or* anxiety.

ಚಿಂತಾಮಣಿ čintāmaṇi, *s.* A fabulous gem which gratifies its possessor's wishes. —ಪುಸ್ತಕ a book on omens. —ಮಂತ್ರ an incantation supposed to gratify one's desires. —ಮಾತ್ರೆ a kind of pill. —ಯಂತ್ರ a talisman.

ಚಿಂತೆ čintĕ, *s.* Thought, reflection, consideration. 2. distress, grief, sorrow. 3. anxiety, care, uneasiness. —ಡುಪ್ಪುನಿ to be anxious *or* sorrowful. —ಮಳ್ಪುನಿ to reflect; to care.

ಚಿಂದಿ čindi, *s.* A rag.

ಚಿಂದಿಡಿ čindiḍi, *adj.* Spotted. —ರುಮಾಲ್ a spotted turban of black *or* red colour.

ಚಿಂನ činna, *s.* Gold.

ಚಿಂನಾಳಿ činnāḷi, *s.* An immodest *or* incontinent woman.

ಚಿಂಪು čimpu, *see* ಚೀಂಪಿ. 2. *see* ಚಿಪ್ಪಿ. 3. a bunch, cluster. ಬಾರೆದ— a bunch of plantains.

ಚಿಂಮ čimma, *see* ಸಿಮ.

ಚಿಕ್ cikụ, *intj.* Fie!

ಚಿಕ್ರ್ čikụrụ, *see* ಚಿಗರ್, ತಿಗರ್.

ಚಿಕರ čikara, *see* ಚೀಕರ.

ಚಿಕಿಣಿ cikiṇi, *adj.* Tender, young, small. *s.* A chicken. —ಪೂಳು a piece of tender, boiled arecanut. —ಕೋರಿ a young fowl.

ಚಿಕಿತ್ಸೆ cikitsĕ, *s.* The practice of medicine.

ಚಿಕ್ಕ್ cikkụ, *see* ತಿಕ್ಕ್.

ಚಿಕ್ಕ čikka, *adj.* Little, young, small, short.

ಚಿಕ್ಕಾಣಿ cikkāṇi, *see* ಚುಕಾಣಿ.

ಚಿಕ್ಕಾಸ್ čikkāsụ, *s.* A cash, trifle. —ದ trifling, worthless. —ದ ಬುದ್ಧಿ a mean disposition.

ಚಿಕ್ಕೆ čikkĕ, *s.* A dwarf; the name of a man.

ಚಿಕ್ನೋಳಿ ciknōḷi, *s.* A syringe.

ಚಿಗ್ತೆ čigụtĕ, *s.* A slit of a leaf, *etc.*; *bet.* ತಿಸ್ತ.

ಚಿಗ್ರ್ čigụrụ, *s.* A sprout, bud, germ.

ಚಿಗ್ರುನಿ, ಚಿಗುರುನಿ čigụruni, čiguruni (ಚಿಗರ್, ಚಿಗುರ್), *v. n.* To sprout, bud, germinate.

ಚಿಗಲಿಸ್ čigalisụ, *s.* A method of treating diseases by oils and ointments. 2. *see* ಚಿಕಿತ್ಸೆ. —ಮಳ್ಪುನಿ to treat a patient by that method.

ಚಿಟ್ ciṭụ, *s.* The influence of

evil eyes. —ಪಾಡುನಿ to be affected by evil eyes.

ಚಿಟ್ಕ್, ಚಿಟಿಕಿ, ಚಿಟ್ಕ čiṭuku, čiṭiki, čiṭka, *s.* A snap of the fingers. 2. a pinch, as of snuff. —ಪಾಡುನಿ to snap fingers.

ಚಿಟಿ čiṭi, *see* ಚಿಟ್ಟಿ.

ಚಿಟಿಚಿಟಿ čiṭičiṭi, *s.* The throbbing pain of a boil, when suppurating *or* forming. 2. a crashing *or* crackling noise.

ಚಿಟ್ಟಿ čiṭṭi, *s.* A small spot *or* speck. *adj.* Spotted, speckled.

ಚಿಟ್ಟೆ čiṭṭè, *s.* The foundation *or* platform of a house. 2. the register of a land. 3. a rough, daily account. —ನಂಬರ್ the registered number of a land.

ಚಿಟ್ಟೆ čiṭṭè, *adj.* Small, little. —ನರಮಾನಿ a small man. —ಕೋರಿ a small cock.

ಚಿತ, ಚಿತಾ, ಚಿತಿ, ಚಿತೆ čita, čitā, čiti, čitè, *s.* A funeral pile. —ಕಾಷ್ಟ the wood for burning it. —ಭಸ್ಮ the ashes of a funeral pile. —ಭಸ್ಮಧಾರಿ Šiva, smeared with the ashes of burnt bodies.

ಚಿತಿ čiti, *see* ಸ್ಥಿತಿ.

ಚಿತ್ಕಾರ čitkāra, *s.* The whirling noise of a war-car. 2. the notes of superior birds.

ಚಿತ್ತ್ čittu, *s.* A blot *or* erasure. —ನಕಲ್ a rough copy, draft. —ಮಳ್ಪುನಿ to blot, erase.

ಚಿತ್ತ čitta, *s.* Will, desire, wish, inclination, disposition, pleasure. —ಶುದ್ಧ correctness of disposition, purity of heart. —ಪ್ರಕಾರ as one pleases.

ಚಿತ್ತಿರ čittira, *see* ಚಿತ್ರ.

ಚಿತ್ತುರ್ಲಿ čitturli, *s.* An orange.

ಚಿತ್ಯ čitya, *see* ಚಿತ.

ಚಿತ್ರ čitra, *s.* A picture, painting, carving. —ಗಾರೆ a painter. —ದಗೊಂಬೆ a painted picture; appearances. —ವಿಚಿತ್ರ a curiosity, rarity, wonder. —ವಿಚಿತ್ರ ಮಳ್ಪುನಿ to work wonders; to make much of a thing; to mystify.

ಚಿತ್ರಕೂಟ čitrakūṭa, *s.* A mountain so called, to which Rāma retired in exile.

ಚಿತ್ರಭಾನು čitrabhānu, *s.* Fire. 2. the sun. 3. the sixteenth year of the Hindu cycle of sixty.

ಚಿತ್ರಮೂಲ čitramūla, *s.* The lead-wort. ಕೆಂಪು— rose-coloured lead-wort, *Plumbago rosea.* ಬೊಳ್ದು— the Ceylon lead-wort, *Plumbago zeylanica.*

ಚಿತ್ರಾನಕ್ಷತ್ರ, ಚಿತ್ರೆ čitrānakshatra, čitrè, *s.* The fourteenth lunar mansion.

ಚಿತ್ರಾಪೂರ್ಣಮಿ čitrāpūrṇami, *s.* The full moon of the first lunar month ಚೈತ್ರ, which is observed as a holiday.

ಚಿತ್ಲಿಪುಳಿ čitlipuḷi, *s.* A kind of orange.

ಚಿದ್ರ čidra, *see* ಛಿದ್ರ.

ಚಿನಿಮಿಟ್ಟಿ činimiṭṭi, *adj.* Trifling. —ಕೆಲಸ trifling work.

ಚಿನಿವಾರೆ, ಚಿನವಾರ್ದೆ činivāre, činavārde, *s.* A money-changer, jeweller. ಚಿನಿವಾರ್ಗಿಕೆ money changing, dealing in jewelry.

ಚಿನ್ನ činna, *see* ಚಿಂನ.

ಚಿನ್ಪಿಟ್ činpiṭu, *see* ಚಿನಿಮಿಟ್ಟಿ.

ಚಿಪುಲ್, ಚಿಪುಲ್ಕೊಟ್ಟೆ, ಚಿಪುಲೊಟ್ಟೆ ćipulu, čipulukoṭṭè, cipuloṭṭè, *s.* The poisonous seed of the drug *Cocculus suberosus.*

ಚಿಪ್ಪಲೆ čippalè, *see* ತಿಪಲೆ. 2. a clamp used for torture.

ಚಿಪ್ಪಿ cippi, *s.* A cocoanut shell. 2. an oyster shell. 3. a pearl; *also* ತಿಪ್ಪಿ.

ಚಿಪ್ಪಿಗೆ cippige, *s.* A tailor.

ಚಿಪ್ಪು cippu, *s.* A crust, scurf, scale.

ಚಿಬ್ಬು cibbu, *s.* White spots on the body; *also* ಸುಬ್ಬು.

ಚಿಮಟಿ, ಚಿಮಿಟಿ čimaṭi, čimiṭi, *s.* Tongs, tweezers, pincers.

ಚಿಮಿಚಿಮಿ čimičimi, *adj.* Faint. —ಪಾತೆರ prattle. —ಬೊಳ್ಪು a faint light.

ಚಿಮುಕುನಿ čimukuni (ಚಿಮುಕ್), *v.a.* To press, throng, throb. 2. to pinch.

ಚಿಮುಚಿಮು čimučimu, *adj.* Nervous, weak. 2. throbbing, painful. —ಬೇನೆ pain caused by a slight wound; a nervous pain; throbbing.

ಚಿರ čira, *s.* A long time. *adj.* Lasting, durable, firm. —ಕಾಲ a long time, always, ever. —ಜೀವಿ, ಚಿರಂಜೀವಿ long lived; a crow; a younger member of a family.

ಚಿರವು čiravu, *see* ಚೀರವು.

ಚಿರಾಕ್ čirāku, *s.* A lamp.

ಚಿರಿಚಿರಿ čiričiri, *s.* Gabble, babble. 2. drizzle. 3. a certain game played by boys, tip-cat. —ಬರ್ಸ a drizzling rain. —ಪಾತೆರುನಿ to babble.

ಚಿರ್ಕ čirka, *see* ಸಿರ್ಕ.

ಚಿರ್ಕೆ čirke, *see* ತಿರ್ಕೆ.

ಚಿರ್ತೆಪಿಲಿ čirtepili, *s.* A leopard.

ಚಿರ್ಪಲೆ čirpalè, *see* ಚಿಪ್ಪಲೆ.

ಚಿರ್ವೆ čirve, *adj.* Tender, green.

ಚಿಲ್ಂಬಿ čilumbi, *s.* The fire bowl of a hooka.

ಚಿಲ್ಕ್, ಚಿಲ್ಕು čiluku, čilku, *s.* Lifting, raising; a push. 2. the catch *or* bolt of a window. ಕುಟ್ಟಿ— a wooden pin used in playing at tip-cat.

ಚಿಲಿಂಬಿ, ಚಿಲಿಮೆ, ಚಿಲ್ಮೆ čilimbi, čilimè, čilmè, *s.* A small tank; 2. *see* ಚಿಲ್ಂಬಿ.

ಚಿಲೀಲ್ čililu, *see* ಚಿಲ್ಲೀಲ್.

ಚಿಲುವಾನ čiluvāna, *s.* The odd money, over a round sum. *adj.* Little, small, trifling, mean, low.

ಚಿಲೆ čilè, *s.* A fishing rod.

ಚಿಲ್ಕುನಿ čilkuni (ಚಿಲ್ಕ್), *v.a.* To lift up. 2. to flay.

ಚಿಲ್ಲ್ čillu, *s.* A small round piece, a piece for playing at draughts. 2. *see* ಚಿಲ್ಲಿ.

ಚಿಲ್ಲರೆ čillarè, *s.* Small money, change, trifle. *adj.* Little, trifling. —ಅಂಗಡಿ a petty wareshop. —ಖರ್ಚ trifling *or* contingent expenses. —ಕೆಲಸ little work. —ಬಾಯಿ a man of inferior mind, a simpleton. —ಬುದ್ಧಿ mean understanding.

ಚಿಲ್ಲಾ, ಚಿಲ್ಲೆ čillā, čillè, *see* ಜಿಲ್ಲಾ.

ಚಿಲ್ಲಿ, ಚಿಲ್ಲೆ čilli, čillè, *s*. A leaf stitched *or* folded in the form of a spoon *or* funnel. 2. a kind of cucumber. —ಪಿಲ್ಲೆ scattered, dispersed; *cf*. ಚಲ್ಲೆ ಪಿಲ್ಲೆ. —ಯೆಟ್ಟುನಿ to stitch a leaf into the form of a spoon.

ಚಿಲ್ಲೀಲ್ čillīlụ, *s*. The screech of an eagle.

ಚಿಲ್ಲೇಲಿ čillēli, *s*. A sharp stick to dart a fish with.

ಚಿಲ್ವಾನ čilvāna, *see* ಜಿಲುವಾನ.

ಚೀ, ಚೀಚೀ čī, čīčī, *intj*. Fie!

ಚೀಂಕರಿ, ಚೀಂಕಿರಿ čīṅkari, čīṅkiri, *s*. The stalk of a cocoanut leaf. 2. thin splitters of bamboo used for stitching leaves *etc*. together; *also* ಶೀಂಕಿರಿ, ಸೀಂಕಿರಿ. —ತೆಲ್ಲವು a kind of cake.

ಚೀಂಚೀಂ čīṅčīṅ, *s*. The chirping of birds. —ತೆಲ್ಲವು, —ಪಕ್ಕಿ a spongy cake; *cf*. ಚೂಂಚೂಂ. ಚೀಂಚೀಂಪಕ್ಕಿಗ್ ಮುಂನೂದು ಕಂಣ್ the čīṅčīṅ cake has many (*lit*. 300) eyes *or* holes.

ಚೀಂಚುನಿ čīṅčuni (ಚೀಂಚ್), *v. n*. To chirp. 2. to be scorched, burnt.

ಚೀಂಟುನಿ čīṅṭuni, *see* ಸೀಂಟುನಿ.

ಚೀಂತುನಿ čīntuni (ಚೀಂತ್), *v. n*. To burn. 2. to roast as a fruit.

ಚೀಂಪಿ, ಚೀಂಪು čīmpi, čīmpu, *s*. A bolt, bar, latch. 2. a kind of sail.

ಚೀಕಡೆ čīkaḍè, *s*. A kind of fish.

ಚೀಕರ čīkara, *adj*. Not pungent; sweetish.

ಚೀಕಾರಿ čīkāri, *see* ಚೀಮಾರಿ.

ಚೀಟ್, ಚೀಟಿ čīṭụ, čīṭi, *s*. A note, short letter. 2. a bill, bond. 3. a ticket, label, stamp. 4. chintz, coloured cloth. ಅಂಗಡಿದ— a shop-bill. ಟಪಾಲ್— a postage stamp. ಮೇಲ್— a transfer deed, a mortgage of title-deed. ಹುಂಡಿ— a bill of exchange. —ಪತ್ತಾವುನಿ to paste a stamp. —ಬರೆಪಿನಿ to write a note.

ಚೀನ čīna, *s*. The empire of China; *also* —ದೇಶ. —ಕಾಗಜಿ Chinese paper. —ದಾಯಿ a Chinese. —ಪಾವು a kind of medicine. —ಮುಂಚಿ a kind of pepper.

ಚೀನಿ čīni, *adj*. Chinese. —ಕಂಣಡಿ a telescope. —ಕಾರ alum. —ಬೆಡಿ a blue light. —ವಾದ್ಯ a kind of music, used especially among Muhammedans. —ಸಕ್ಕರೆ white sugar.

ಚೀನೆಕೋಲು čīnekōlu, *s*. A music band of Māpḷas.

ಚೀಪಿ, ಚೀಪು čīpi, čīpu, *see* ಚೀಂಪಿ.

ಚೀಪು čīpu, *s*. A wedge, wooden peg. 2. a comb *or* cluster of plantains. 3. *see* ಚೀಂಪು. 4. *see* ಉರ್ವಣೆ.

ಚೀಮಾರಿ čīmāri, *s*. A loathsome woman

ಚೀರ čīra, *s*. Lead. 2. bark, rind. 3. a cloth made of bark.

ಚೀರವು čīravu, *s.* A bag, purse, pocket.

ಚೀರ್ಣಿಕೆ čīrnikè, *s.* Carved *or* chiselled workmanship. –ದಾಯಿ an artist. –ಬುಡ್ಡಾವುನಿ to carve, chisel.

ಚೀರ್ಲೊ čīrlo, *s.* Responding to a call in a game. [ಸೀಳ್.

ಚೀಲ್ čīlụ, *s.* A split, splinter; *bet.*

ಚೀಲೆರ್ čīlerụ, *s.* Forced converts to Mohammedanism.

ಚು ču, *see* ಚೂ.

ಚುಂಕ čuṅka, *see* ಸುಂಕ.

ಚುಂಗಾಣಿ čuṅgāṇi, *s.* A tobacco-pipe. 2. *see* ಚುಕ್ಕಾಣಿ.

ಚುಂಗುಡಿ čuṅguḍi, *s.* A trifling sum, odds, small coins, change. 2. anything of little value. –ಬ್ಯಾರ a petty trade. –ಸಾಲ a trifling debt.

ಚುಂಗೆ čuṅgè, *s.* A kind of rice. 2. awn.

ಚುಂಚುಂ čumčum, *see* ಚುಮ್ಚುಮ್.

ಚುಂಣ čuṇṇa, *see* ಸುಂಣ.

ಚುಂಣೈ čuṇṇei, *s.* A kind of cloth. 2. scab, scurf. 3. shabbiness.

ಚುಂಬನ čumbana, *s.* Kissing.

ಚುಂಮ čumma, *see* ಚುಮ್ಚುಮ್.

ಚುಂಯಿಚುಂಯಿ čuñyičuñyi, *s.* The hissing noise of a heated metal dipped into water.

ಚುಕ್‌ಚುಕ್ čukụčukụ, *s.* Chirping of birds.

ಚುಕಾಣಿ, ಚುಕ್ಕಾಣಿ čukāṇi, čukkāṇi, *s.* The rudder, helm of a ship.

ಚುಗುಡೆ čuguḍe, *s.* A smart man; *also* ಸುಕುಟ.

ಚುಗುಳಿ čuguḷi, *s.* The rind of a fruit *or* vegetable.

ಚುಚ್ಚುಕು čuččuku, *see* ಚುಕ್‌ಚುಕ್.

ಚುಚ್ಚುನಿ čuččuni (ಚುಚ್ಚ್), *v. a.* To pierce, bore. 2. to bite; *cf.* ಕುತ್ತುನಿ, ತುಚ್ಚುನಿ.

ಚುಟಿ čuṭi, *adj.* Smart, clever. 2. sharp, pungent.

ಚುಟ್ಟ čuṭṭa, *s.* A cheroot, cigar.

ಚುಟ್ಟಿ čuṭṭi, *s.* A span. 2. *see* ಚುಟಿ. 3. *see* ಚುರುಕು.

ಚುದ್ರ čudra, *see* ಛುದ್ರ.

ಚುಮ್‌ಚುಮ್ čumụčumụ, *s.* Pain caused by the sting of an insect. 2. sleeping of the hand *or* leg; *cf.* ಜಿಮುಜಿಮು.

ಚುಮುಲ, ಚುಮ್ಲ čumula, čumla, *see* ಜುಮ್ಲ.

ಚುಯಿಚುಯಿ čuyičuyi, *see* ಚುಂಯಿಚುಂಯಿ.

ಚುರುಕು čuruku, *s.* Quickness, haste, speed. 2. sharpness. 3. zeal, activity. *adj.* Quick, vigorous, zealous. 2. vivid. –ಬುದ್ಧಿ quick understanding, wit.

ಚುರುಚುರು čuručuru, *s.* A hissing noise caused by frying, burning, *etc.*

ಚುಲಕ čulaka, *adj.* Light; *cf.* ಸುಲಭ.

ಚುವು čuvu, *see* ತೂ.

ಚುಳಿ čuḷi, *see* ಸುಳಿ.

ಚುಳ್ಳಿ čuḷḷi, *s.* The plant of *Barleria obovata.*

ಚೂ čū, *s.* Setting on a dog. 2. driving a dog away. 3. *see* ತೂ.

ಚೂಂ čūm, *see* ಚುಮ್ಚುಮ್.

ಚೂಟಿ, ಚೂಟು čūṭi, čūṭu, *s.* Escaping from the grasp in wrestling. 2. aim; device. 3. perception. 4. cessation from work, leisure.

ಚೂಟೆ čūṭè, *see* ತೂಟೆ.

ಚೂಡ čūḍa, *s.* The lock of hair left on the head at the time of tonsure. ಚೂಡಾಕರ್ಮ the ceremony of tonsure.

ಚೂಡ, ಚೂಡಗ čūḍa, čūḍaga, *s.* A kind of gold bracelet.

ಚೂಡಾಮಣಿ čūḍāmaṇi, *s.* A jewel worn in a crest *or* diadem.

ಚೂಡಿ čūḍi, *s.* The coil of a rope. 2. a bundle, as of fagots, betel leaves *etc.*; *also* ಸೂಡಿ.

ಚೂಡು čūḍu, *s.* Heat, warmth. 2. zeal. *adj.* Hot, warm.

ಚೂಡೆ čūḍè, *see* ಚೂಡ.

ಚೂಣಿ čūṇi, *s.* The front, van. 2. strength. *adj.* Former. *adv.* Before.

ಚೂಣ್ಯ čūṇya, *see* ಸೂಣ್ಯ.

ಚೂರಿ čūri, *s.* A knife, small sword.

ಚೂರು čūru, *s.* A piece, bit, small fragment. —ಮಳ್ಪುನಿ to pulverise, cut into small pieces *or* bits. —ಚೂರಾಪಿನಿ to break to pieces.

ಚೂರ್ಣ čūrṇa, *s.* Powder, dust, any pulverised substance, medicinal powder. 2. *see* ಸೂರಣ.

ಚೂಲಿ čūli, *see* ಚೋಲಿ.

ಚೆಂಗಣಿ čeṅgaṇi, *s.* A friend. 2. *see* ಚುಂಗಾಣಿ.

ಚೆಂಡ್ čeṇḍu, *s.* A ball. —ಗೊಬ್ಬುನಿ to play with ball.

ಚೆಂಡ್ಮಲ್ಲಿಗೆ čaṇḍumalligè, *s.* A species of clustered jasmine.

ಚೆಂಡಾಡುನಿ čeṇḍāḍuni (ಚೆಂಡಾಡ್), *v. a.* To play with ball. 2. to destroy, ruin.

ಚೆಂಡೆ čeṇḍè, *s.* A large drum; a kettle-drum. —ಬೊಟ್ಟುನಿ to beat a drum.

ಚೆಂಡೆಮರ čeṇḍemara *s.* The tree *Cerbera odollam*; *also* ತೆಂಡೆಮರ. —ದ ಬಿತ್ತ್ its poisonous seeds.

ಚೆಂಡೆಮುಳಿ čeṇḍemuḷi, *see* ತೆಂಡೆಮುಳಿ.

ಚೆಂಡೆಲ್ čeṇḍelu, *see* ತೆಂಡೆಲ್.

ಚೆಂನನಾಯಿ čennanāyi, *see* ಚಂನನಾಯಿ.

ಚೆಂನೆ čennè, *see* ಚಂನೆ.

ಚೆಂನೆಬೂರು čennebūru, *see* ಚಂನಾಬೂರು.

ಚೆಂಬಟೆ čembaṭe, *s.* A coppersmith.

ಚೆಂಬು čembu, *s.* Brass, latten. 2. a small copper *or* brass pot. —ಕುಟ್ಟಿ a coppersmith.

ಚೆಕ್ಕ್ čekku, *see* ಚಕ್ಕ್.

ಚೆಕ್ಕಟ್ čekkaṭu, *adj.* Thin, lean.

ಚೆಕ್ಕರ್ಮೆ čekkarme, *see* ತಿಕ್ಕರ್ಮೆ.

ಚೆಕ್ಕಿ čekki, *see* ಚಕ್ಕಿ.

ಚೆಕ್ಕಿ, ಚೆಕ್ಕೆ čekki, čekkè, *s.* A chip, split, splinter.

ಚೆಕ್ಕುಬಂದಿ čekkubandi, *see* ಚಕ್ಕುಬಂದಿ.

ಚೆಕ್ಕೆಲ್ čekkelu, *see* ಚಕ್ಕೆಲ್.

ಚೆಟ್ಟಿ čeṭṭi, *see* ಚಟ್ಟಿ.

ಚೆಟ್ಟೆ čeṭṭè, *see* ಚಟ್ಟಿ.

ಚೆಡಿ čeḍi, *see* ಚಡಿ.

ಚೆಪ್ಪೆ čeppè, *s.* A splinter, chip, slice, paring. 2. disappointment, failure. *adj. see* ಚಪ್ಪೆ. —ಆಪಿನಿ, —ಬೂರುನಿ to fail; to rest, lie down.

ಚೆರಡ್ čeraḍu, *s.* The ear. —ಪತ್ತ್ದ್ ಪಿಂಟಾವುನಿ to twist the ear.

ಚೆರಿಗೆ cerigè, *see* ಚರಿಗೆ.

ಚೆರೆ cerè, *see* ಚರೆ.

ಚೆರ್ಚೆ čerčè, *see* ಚರ್ಚೆ.

ಚೆರ್ಬಿ cerbi, *see* ಚರ್ಬಿ.

ಚೆರ್ವ červa, *see* ಚರು.

ಚೆಲವೆ čelavè, *adj.* Damp, moist.

ಚೆಲುವಿಕೆ čeluvikè, *s.* Beauty, comeliness.

ಚೆಲುವೆ čeluve, *s.* A beautiful *or* handsome man.

ಚೆಲ್ಲಾಟ čellāṭa *s.* Scattering, dispersing. 2. spilling, shedding.

ಚೆಲ್ಲುನಿ čelluni (ಚೆಲ್ಲ್), *v. a.* To sprinkle. 2. to spill, shed. *v. n.* To spill, drop, shed.

ಚೆಲ್ವಯಿ čelvayi, *s.* Dyed cotton.

ಚೆಲ್ವೆ čelve, *see* ಚೆಲುವೆ.

ಚೇ čē, *see* ಛೇ.

ಚೇಕರೆ čēkarè, *see* ತಿಕ್ಕರೆ.

ಚೇಟೆ, ಚೇಟ್ಟೆ čēṭè, čēṭṭè, *see* ಚೇಷ್ಟೆ.

ಚೇಡಿ čēḍi, *see* ಚೀಡಿ.

ಚೇಣ್ čēṇu, *s.* An awl, chisel. *adj.* Even, smooth. —ಪಾಡುನಿ to chisel.

ಚೇತನ čētana, *see* ಚೈತನ.

ಚೇದನ, ಚೇದನೆ čēdana, čēdanè, *see* ಛೇದ.

ಚೇದಿ čēdi, *s.* One of the fiftysix countries of the Hinduwriters.

ಚೇನ್ čēnu, *see* ಚೇಣ್.

ಚೇಪಂಗೆಲ್ čēpaṅgelu, *adj.* Curved, inclined; *cf.* ತೇಪಂಗೆಲ್.

ಚೇಪು čēpu, *see* ತೇಪು.

ಚೇಲಕಡೆ čēlakaḍè, *s.* The Indian turnsole, *Tiaridium Indicum.*

ಚೇಲೆ cēlè, *see* ಸೇಲೆ.

ಚೇಲ್ಗೊಂಡಿ cēlgoṇḍi, *s.* The sting of a scorpion.

ಚೇಲ್ಗೊಂಡಿಮರ cēlgoṇḍimara, *see* ಚೇಲಕಡೆ.

ಚೇವು čēvu, *see* ತೇವು.

ಚೇಷ್ಟೆ čēshṭè, *s.* A grimace, trick, gesture. 2. jest, mockery, joke. ಕು— ridiculous grimaces. —ಗಾರೆ one who makes grimaces, a jester, mocker, wag; a humorist. —ಮಳ್ಪುನಿ to make gestures, to mock; to joke.

ಚೇಳ್ čēḷu, *see* ತೇಳ್. —ಬಗ್ಗ್ನವು a kind of sport.

ಚೈ čei, *see* ಚವಿ.

ಚೈತನ, ಚೈತನ್ಯ čeitana, čeitanya, *s.* Strength, liveliness, vigour, animation. 2. life. —ದಾಯಿ, —ವಂತೆ a vigorous man. —ಕುಂದುನಿ to lose strength.

ಚೈತ್ರ ceitra, *s.* The first lunar month, corresponding to March-April.

ಚೈಲ čeila, *see* ತೈಲ.

ಚೈಲಿ čeili, *see* ತೈಲ್.

ಚೈಲೆ čeile, *s.* A pair of large cymbals.

ಚೊಂಟಿ čonṭi, *see* ಚೊಟ್ಟಿ.

ಚೊಂಪುಡಿ čompuḍi, *s.* Copper powder. 2. verdigris. 3. *see* ಜೋಂಪುಡಿ.

ಚೊಂಬಟೆ čombaṭe, *see* ಚೆಂಬಟೆ.

ಚೊಂಬಟ್ಟಲ್ čombaṭṭalu, *s.* Brazen pot and plate.

ಚೊಂಬು čombu, *see* ಚೆಂಬು.

ಚೊಕ್ಕ čokka, *adj.* Pure, genuine. 2. neat. —ಬೊಳ್ಳಿ pure silver.

ಚೊಕ್ಕಟ čokkaṭa, *adj.* Neat, choice, agreeable. ಚೊಕ್ಕಟಿಗೆ beauty, handsomeness.

ಚೊಕ್ಕಲೆ čokkalè, *see* ಚೊಕ್ಕೆ. 2. *see* ಸೊರ್ಕೆಲೆ.

ಚೊಕ್ಕಾಟ čokkāṭa, *see* ಚೊಕ್ಕಟ.

ಚೊಕ್ಕು čokku, *adj.* Stupid, silly. —ಚೊಕ್ಕು well riped.

ಚೊಕ್ಕೆ čokke, *s.* A stupid man.

ಚೊಗರ್ čogaru, *adj.* Astringent. —ಆಪಿನಿ to be astringent, to have an acrid taste.

ಚೊಟ್ಟ čoṭṭa, *s.* A Pariah's hut; *also* ಚಿಟ್ಟೊ. *adj. see* ಚೊಟ್ಟು.

ಚೊಟ್ಟಿ čoṭṭi, *s.* A woman with a maimed hand.

ಚೊಟ್ಟು čoṭṭu, *adj.* Handless, maimed *or* deformed in the hand.

ಚೊಟ್ಟೆ čoṭṭe, *s.* A man with a maimed hand.

ಚೊಟ್ಟೆತೆ čoṭṭete, *s.* The headman of Pariahs.

ಚೊಣಂಗಿನಾಯಿ čoṇanginâyi, *s.* A greyhound.

ಚೊಣಿಂಕೆ, ಚೊಣ್ಕೆ čoṇinkè, čoṇkè, *s.* The scab of itch *etc.*

ಚೊಪ್ಪಿ čoppi, *s.* A cap, hat.

ಚೊಪ್ಪು čoppu, *see* ತಪ್ಪು, ಸೊಪ್ಪು.

ಚೊರ್ಪಟ್ čorpaṭu, *adj.* Loose *or* thin, as cowdung *etc.*

ಚೊರ್ಪು čorpu, *see* ಚರಿಪು.

ಚೊರ್ಪುನಿ čorpuni, *see* ತೊರ್ಪುನಿ.

ಚೊಲಕೆ, ಚೊಲಿಕೆ, ಚೊಲ್ಕೆ ಚೊಲುಂಪೆ čolakè, čolikè, čolkè, čolumpè, *see* ಚೋಲಿ.

ಚೊಲ್ಲೆ čollè, *adj.* Halt, crippled. —ಮೃಗ a hyæna.

ಚೋಂಕಟ್ಟ್ čōṅkaṭṭu, *adj.* Lank, lean, thin. —ಪೋಪಿನಿ to become thin.

ಚೋಂಕರ čōṅkara, *see* ಚೊಗರ್.

ಚೋಂಕು čōṅku, *see* ಸೋಂಕು. *adj. see* ಚೋಕು.

ಚೋಂಕುನಿ čōṅkuni, *see* ತೇಪುನಿ.

ಚೋಂಚಿ čōñči, *s.* The beak of a bird.

ಚೋಂಟು čōṇṭu, *see* ಚೋಟು.

ಚೋಂಟೆ čōṇṭè, *see* ಸೋಂಟೆ.

ಚೋಕು čōku, *adj.* Sapless, unfruitful; exhausted, old. *s.* An unfruitful *or* old tree.

ಚೋಕೊಲಿ čōkoli, *s.* A merry man.

ಚೋಗರ್ čōgaru, *see* ಚೊಗರ್.

ಚೋಗೆ čōgè, *s.* A leaf *or* branch of a palm tree; *bet.* ಸೋಗೆ.

ಚೋಟಾ čōṭā, *adj.* Short, small, petty.

ಚೋಟು, ಚೋಟ್ಟು čōṭu, čōṭṭu, *s.* A span from the tip of the thumb to that of the fore-finger.

ಚೋದಿಕ, ಚೋದ್ಯ čōdika, čōdya, *s.* A curiosity. 2. surprise. *adj.* Curious, wonderful. –ಆಪಿನಿ to wonder, to be surprised; *bet.* ಸೋದ್ಯ.

ಚೋಪಟ್ಟ್ čōpaṭṭụ, *s.* A kind of pitching *or* calking a boat. –ಕೊರ್ಪಿನಿ, –ಪಾಡುನಿ to calk a boat with a mixture of tallow (ಚೊಲಕ್) and chalk.

ಚೋಪಾವುನಿ čōpāvuni, *see* ಸೋಪಾವುನಿ.

ಚೋಪು čōpu, *see* ಸೋಪು.

ಚೋಪೆ čōpe, *s.* A scrap, scratch.

ಚೋಯಿ čōyi, *s.* Milk. –ತಿಪ್ಪುನಿ to suck the breast.

ಚೋರಟ್ čōraṭụ, *see* ಚೊರ್ಪಟಿ.

ಚೋರಣ čōraṇa, *s.* A festoon of leaves and flowers, hung over the door-way *or* across the highway on a joyful *or* triumphant occasion, a triumphal arch; *bet.* ತೋರಣ. –ಕಟ್ಟುನಿ to put up a festoon.

ಚೋರತನ, ಚೋರಿ čōratana, čōri, *s.* Theft, robbery. –ಮಳ್ಪುನಿ to steal, rob.

ಚೋರೆ čōre, *s.* A thief, robber, rogue.

ಚೋಲಿ čōḷi, *s.* Skin, bark, rind. –ಗೆಪ್ಪುನಿ to peel, skin, pare off.

ಚೋಲೆ čōle, *see* ಚೊಲ್ಲೆ.

ಚೋಳದೇಶ, ಚೋಳರಾಜ್ಯ čōḷadēša, čōḷarājya, *s.* The Coromandel coast; the ancient kingdom on the Kāveri delta.

ಚೌಂಟು čounṭu, *see* ಸೌಂಟು.

ಚೌಂಟುನಿ čounṭuni (ಚೌಂಟಿ), *v. a.* To pinch, nip.

ಚೌಂಡಿ čounḍi, *see* ಚಾಮುಂಡಿ.

ಚೌಕ čouka, *s.* A square. 2. the linga box. *adj.* Square. –ಮಣೆ a square stool. –ದರ್ಪ a square piece of cloth. ಚ– quadrate.

ಚೌಕಟ್ಟ್ čoukaṭṭụ, *s.* A door-frame.

ಚೌಕಡಿ, ಚೌಕಣಿ čoukaḍi, čoukaṇi, *adj.* Quadrangular. *s.* A quadrangle.

ಚೌಕಸ čoukasa, *see* ಸಾವಕಾಶ.

ಚೌಕಳಿ čoukaḷi, *adj.* Square. *s.* An earring set with four pearls. –ಶೀರೆ a female's garment with small square patterns.

ಚೌಕಾಸ್, ಚೌಕಾಸ čoukāsụ, čoukāsa, *see* ಚವುಕಾಸ್.

ಚೌಕಿ čouki, *s.* A railed veranda, pial. 2. a watch-house. –ದಾರೆ a guardsman.

ಚೌಕುಳಿ čoukuḷi, *see* ಚೌಕಳಿ.

ಚೌಕೆ čouke, *s.* A stool, chair.

ಚೌಕ್ಕಿಲ್ čoukkilụ, *s.* A kind of earring; *cf.* ಚೌಕಳಿ.

ಚೌಟು, čouṭu, *see* ಸೌಂಟು.

ಚೌಡಾಲ್ čouḍālụ, *s.* A square shield.

ಚೌಡಿಗೆ čouḍigè, *s.* A one-stringed guitar formed by a small barrel, open at one end and covered with a skin at the other. 2. a peculiar kind of neck-ornament. 3. a kind of ear-ring. —ದಾಯಿ a man playing upon such a guitar.

ಚೌತಟುನಿ čoutaṭuni (ಚೌತಟೆ), *v. a.* To sing a lullaby.

ಚೌತಿ čouti, *see* ಚತುರ್ಥಿ.

ಚೌಪದ čoupada, *s.* A quadruped. 2. a kind of verse.

ಚೌರ čoura, *s.* Shaving; *bet.* ಕ್ಷೌರ.

ಚೌರಕೆ, ಚೌರದಾಯೆ čourake, čouradāye, *s.* A barber.

ಚೌರಿ čouri, *s.* The tail of the yak. 2. a fly-brush.

ಚೌಲ čoula, *see* ಚವಲ.

ಚೌಲಿ čouli, *see* ಚವುಲಿ.

ಚೌಳ čouḷa, *adv.* At once. —ನೆ ಪೋಯೆ he went at once. —ಚೌಳ again and again, one after another.

ಚೌಳಿಕಾಯಿ čouḷikāyi, *see* ಚವುಳಿಕಾಯಿ.

ಚೌಳು čouḷu, *see* ಚವುಳ್.

ಛ ČH

ಛ čha, *s.* The twentieth letter of the alphabet.

ಛಂದ čhanda, *see* ಚಂದ.

ಛಟಛಟ čhaṭačhaṭa, *see* ಚಟಚಟ.

ಛಟಾಲ čhaṭāla, *s.* The noise of a slap *or* lash. —ಹಾಕುನಿ to beat *or* strike heavily.

ಛಡಾವು čhaḍāvu, *see* ಚಡಾವು.

ಛಡಾಳಿ čhaḍāḷi, *s.* A stupid fellow.

ಛಡಿ čhaḍi, *see* ಚಡಿ.

ಛತ್ರ čhatra, *s.* An umbrella; *also* ತತ್ರ. 2. an inn, choultry.

ಛತ್ರಾಂತರ čhatrāntara, *s.* Wandering.

ಛತ್ರಾಧಿಪತಿ čhatrādhipati, *s.* A king, sovereign. ಯೇಕ— an emperor.

ಛತ್ರಿ čhatri, *s.* A barber. 2. *see* ಕ್ಷತ್ರಿ. 3. *see* ಛತ್ರ.

ಛಪಾಯಿಸುನಿ čhapāyisuni (ಛಪಾಯಿಸ್), *v. a.* To conceal, secrete. 2. to deceive, defraud.

ಛಪಾವು čhapāvu, *s.* Concealment, secretion. 2. absconding. 3. deceit, fraud. —ಆಪಿನಿ to abscond. —ಮಳ್ಪುನಿ to conceal.

ಛಪ್ಪ čhappa, *see* ಚಪ್ಪ.

ಛಪ್ಪಂನ čhappanna, *num.* Fifty-six. —ದೇಶ fifty-six countries enumerated by Hindu writers.

ಛಪ್ಪಕ čhappaka, *adv.* Backwards, on the back. —ಬೂರುನಿ to fall backwards.

ಛಪ್ಪರಿಗೆ čhapparigè, *see* ಕಿಪ್ಪರಿಗೆ.

ಛಪ್ಪರಿಪುನಿ čhappariṗuni, *see* ಚಪ್ಪರಿಪುನಿ.

ಛರಛರ čharačhara, *see* ಚರಚರ.

ಛಲ čhala, *s.* Fixed purpose, firmness, determined resolution. 2. obstinacy. —ತ ಮುದ್ದೆ exceedingly obstinate. —ವಾದಿ a resolute *or* obstinate person. —ಸಾಧನೆ perseverance in a purpose. –ಪಟ್ಟುನಿ, –ಮಳ್ಪುನಿ to be obstinate; to persevere.

ಛಲಕ್ čhalakụ, *see* ಚಲಕ್.

ಛಳಛಳ čhaḷačhaḷa, *s.* Glitter; brandish.

ಛಳಿ čhaḷi, *see* ಚಳಿ.

ಛಾಡಿ čhāḍi, *see* ಚಾಡಿ.

ಛಾತಿ čhāti, *s.* The breast, bosom. 2. courage, bravery. –ವಂತೆ a brave man; a bold trader *or* practitioner.

ಛಾದರ čhādara, *s.* A silk garment, a shawl.

ಛಾನಸ್, ಛಾನಸಿ čhānasụ, čhānasi, *s.* Being peculiar *or* singular in what one does; nicety, fastidiousness. 2. accuracy, precision.

ಛಾಪಿಸುನಿ čhāpisuni (ಛಾಪಿಸ್), *v. a.* To stamp, seal. 2. to print.

ಛಾಪು čhāpu, *see* ಚಾಪು.

ಛಾಪು, ಛಾಪೆ čhāpu, čhāpe, *s.* A printing press. 2. a shop.

ಛಾಯಿ, ಛಾಯೆ čhāyi, čhāye, *s.* Shadow, shade. 2. colour, tint, dye. ಕಪ್ಪು– black colour.

ಛಿಂದಿ čhindi, *see* ಚಿಂದಿ.

ಛಿಂನ čhinna, *adj.* Cut, divided. ಛಿಂನಾಭಿಂನ broken, fractured, as a limb.

ಛಿದ್ರ čhidra, *s.* A hole, vacuity, perforation. 2. flaw, defect. 3. disaster, trouble. 4. sorcery, witchcraft. –ಬಾಯಿ a sorcerer, wizard; a defective man. –ಮಳ್ಪುನಿ to assume an air; to bewitch, enchant. ಗೃಹ– domestic quarrel *or* dispute.

ಛೀ, ಛೀಛೀ čhī, čhīčhī, *intj.* Fie! –ಪಡಿಕೆ fie, fie, it is bad. –ಕಳುವಾ fie, you rogue!

ಛುದ್ರ čhudra, *adj.* Small, little. 2. low, mean. *s.* Smallness; baseness. 2. sorcery, witchcraft; *bet.* ಕ್ಷುದ್ರ.

ಛುದ್ರೆ čhudre, *s.* A base man. 2. a sorcerer.

ಛೇದ čhēda, *s.* Loss, ruin.

ಛೇದ, ಛೇದನೆ čhēda, čhēdane, *s.* Cutting, dividing. –ಮಳ್ಪುನಿ to cut, divide; to circumcise. ಪರಿ– a part, fragment; circumcision.

ಛೇದಿಪುನಿ čhēdipuni (ಛೇದಿ), *v. a.* To cut, divide. 2. to circumcise.

ಜ J̌

ಜ ǰa, The twenty-first letter of the alphabet.

ಜಂ ǰam, *s.* Rust. —ಕೊಡಿಪುನಿ to become rusty.

ಜಂಕ್ ǰanku̥, *see* ಪೆತ್ತಕಜಂಕ್.

ಜಂಕಾನೆ, ಜಂಖಾನೆ ǰaṅkānè, ǰaṅkhānè, *see* ಜಮ್‌ಕಾನ್.

ಜಂಗ ǰaṅga, *s.* Being across, transverseness. 2. a ceiling of boards *etc.* over a fireplace.

ಜಂಗಮ ǰaṅgama, *adj.* Locomotive, moveable. 2. of *or* belonging to a Lingait priest. —ಮಠ the residence of a Lingait priest. —ಸಾಲ a debt, which is urgently demanded. —ವಸ್ತು a moveable thing.

ಜಂಗಮೆ ǰaṅgamè, *s.* A Lingait.

ಜಂಗಮೆಮರ ǰaṅgamemara, *see* ಪೆಜ್ಜಿ ಪಂರ್ದ್.

ಜಂಗಲ್, ಜಂಗಾರ್, ಜಂಗಾಲ್ ǰaṅgalu̥, ǰaṅgāru̥, ǰaṅgālu̥, *s.* A wooden platform placed on boats. —ಪಟ್ಟಿ the rafts of a ferry boat to carry large *or* heavy things. —ಪಚ್ಚೆ a green colour, the subacetate of lead.

ಜಂಗಾಯಿ ǰaṅgāyi, *see* ಚಂಗಾಯಿ.

ಜಂಗಿ ǰaṅgi, *s.* Force, compulsion, oppression, —ನಡಪುಡುನಿ to force; to plunder, pillage; to rebel.

ಜಂಗೆ, ಜಂಘೆ ǰaṅge, ǰaṅghe *s.* The calf of the leg. 2. an old man. —ಜಾರುನಿ the calf of the leg to be disjointed.

ಜಂಗ್ಲಿ ǰaṅgli, *s.* A forest, jungle, waste land. *adj.* Wild. —ಇಲಾಖೆ the forest department.

ಜಂಞಾಯಿ ǰaññāyi, *see* ಚಂಗಾಯಿ.

ಜಂಜರ, ಜಂಜರಿ ǰañǰara, ǰañǰari, *s.* Fetters. —ಜಾಮಿನ್ a bail for a prisoner.

ಜಂಜರ ǰañǰara, *adj.* Serial, ordinal. —ನಂಬರ್ serial numbers.

ಜಂಜಾಟ ǰañǰāṭa, *s.* Trouble, annoyance, grief.

ಜಂಜಾರ ǰañǰāra, *see* ಸಂಚಾರ.

ಜಂಜಾಲಿ ǰañǰāli, *s.* A wall-piece *or* long swivel gun. 2. flattering, fawning.

ಜಂಜಾಲೆ ǰañǰāle, *s.* A talkative man; a boaster.

ಜಂಜುಂ ǰamǰum, *s.* A sound, utterance. —ಪಣ್ಪುಜೆ he does not say a word.

ಜಂಡ್ ǰaṇḍu̥, *see* ದಂಡ್.

ಜಂಡೆ ǰaṇḍè, *s.* Delay. 2. a tassel on the tail of a tiger in a masquerade. 3. an ensign, standard, flag. —ಮಳ್ಪುನಿ to hinder, stop. [ಝುಣ್.

ಜಂಣ್‌ಜಂಣ್ ǰaṇṇu̥ǰaṇṇu̥, *see* ಝುಣ್

ಜಂತ ǰanta, *s.* Ivory, the tusk of an elephant. 2. *see* ದಂತ.

ಜಂತಗ ǰantaga, *s.* A halter-bandage.

ಜಂತರ್ ǰantaru̥, *s.* A kind of ointment.

ಜಂತಿ ǰanti, *s.* A rafter, a piece of timber crossing a rafter.

ಜಂತು J̌antu, *s.* A creature, animal. 2. a worm.

ಜಂತೆ J̌antè, *see* ಜಂತಿ.

ಜಂತ್ರ J̌antra, *see* ಯಂತ್ರ.

ಜಂತ್ರಿ J̌antri, *s.* A calender. 2. a table of interest. [ಕೊಶ್.

ಜಂನೀರೊಳ್ J̌annīroḷụ, *see* ಜಂಬುನೀ

ಜಂನೆ J̌anne, *s.* A burnt offering.

ಜಂಪಮರ ಜಂಪೆಮರ J̌ampamara, J̌ampemara, *see* ತಬುಕು.

ಜಂಪೆತಾಳ J̌ampètāḷa, *s.* A mode of beating time in music.

ಜಂಬ J̌amba, *see* ಜಂಭ.

ಜಂಬರ, ಜಂಬಾರ J̌ambara, J̌ambāra, *s.* An affair, business. —ದಾಯಿ a busy man. —ತೀರಿಸಾವುನಿ to finish a business. [ಕಾನ್.

ಜಂಬುಖಾನ್ J̌ambukhānụ, *see* ಜವ್

ಜಂಬುದ್ವೀಪ J̌ambudvīpa, *s.* India.

ಜಂಬುನೀರೊಳ್, ಜಂಬುನೀರೊಳಿ J̌ambunīroḷụ, J̌ambunīroḷi, *s.* The rose-apple, *Syzigium jambolanum.* 2. *Jambosa malaccensis.*

ಜಂಬುಮೂರಿ J̌ambumūri, *s.* An offensive smell.

ಜಂಬುಲಿ J̌ambuli, *s.* A kind of basket made of date leaves.

ಜಂಭ J̌ambha, *s.* Pomp, ostentation, display. 2. foppery; *also* ಜಂಭಾಟ. [Indra.

ಜಂಭಾರಿ J̌ambhāri, *s.* A name of

ಜಂಭೆ J̌ambhè, *s.* A giant.

ಜಂಮ J̌amma, *see* ಜನ್ಮ.

ಜಂಮನಿಗೆ J̌ammanigè, *s.* Headmanship among Pariahs. 2. idle talk.

ಜಂಮನೆ J̌ammanè, *s.* A demon priest. 2. a headman of Pariahs.

ಜಕಂ J̌akam, *see* ಜಖಮ್.

ಜಕಣಿ J̌akaṇi, *see* ಜಕ್ಕಿಣಿ.

ಜಕ್, ಜಕ್ಕ, ಜಕ್ಕಡಿ J̌akkụ, J̌akka, J̌akkaḍi, *adj.* Worthy. 2. youthful. 3. *see* ಚಕ್ಕ. —ಜವ್ವನೆ a youthful man. —ಪಕ್ಕಿ the ruddy goose. —ಬೂರುನಿ, —ಮಾರುನಿ to undersell.

ಜಕ್ಕಿಣಿ J̌akkiṇi, *s.* A married woman who dies in her husband's lifetime, and causes demoniac possession.

ಜಕ್ಕು J̌akku, *see* ಜಕ್ಕ.

ಜಕ್ಕುಲಿ J̌akkuli, *see* ಚಕ್ಕುಲಿ.

ಜಕ್ಕೆ J̌akkè, *s.* Vanity, foppishness. —ದಾಯಿ a fop. —ದಾಳ್ a coquette. —ನಲಿಕೆ strut, affectation of diginity in walking. —ಪಾತೆರುನಿ to boast.

ಜಕ್ಕೆಲ್ J̌akkelụ, *s.* The lap; *cf.* ಮಟ್ಟೆಲ್. —ಪೊಯ್ಯುನಿ to tarry, linger.

ಜಕ್ರಿ J̌akri, *s.* Plenty.

ಜಖಮ್ J̌akhamụ, *s.* A wound. —ಆಪಿನಿ to be wounded, bruised.

ಜಗ J̌aga, *see* ಜಗೆ.

ಜಗ, ಜಗತ್ತ್, ಜಗತ್ಯ J̌aga, J̌agattụ, J̌agatya, *s.* The world, universe.

ಜಗಂನಾಥ J̌agannātha, *s.* A celebrated place of pilgrimage.

ಜಗಂನಾಥೆ J̌agannāthe, *s.* The lord of the universe. 2. a name of Vishṇu.

ಜಗಜಗ ǰaga, ǰaga, *see* ಝಗಝಗ.

ಜಗಲಿ ǰagali, *s.* An open veranda.

ಜಗಳ, ಜಗಳಾಟ ǰagaḷa, ǰagaḷāṭa, *s.* Quarrel, fight, dispute. —ಗಂಟಿ a vixen, shrew.

ಜಗುಡೆ ǰaguḍe, *s.* An old man.

ಜಗುಳ್ ǰaguḷu, *see* ಜಗಳ.

ಜಗೆ ǰagè, *s.* A sigh, groan, ejaculation; *cf.* ಜಗ್ಗ. —ಕಟ್ಟುನಿ to be unable to breathe, to breathe hard. —ಬುಡ್ಪಿನಿ to groan, sigh.

ಜಗ್ಗ್ ǰaggu, *s.* A kind of small fish. 2. delay, postponement. —ಗ್‍ಪಾಡುನಿ to delay. —ನರಮಾನಿ a sluggard, lazy fellow; *also* ಜಗ್ಗ.

ಜಗ್ಗಾವುನಿ ǰaggāvuni, *see* ತಗ್ಗಾವುನಿ.

ಜಗ್ಗೆ ǰaggè, *s.* Stooping, bending. 2. *see* ಜಗೆ. 3. *see under* ಜಗ್.

ಜಜ್ಜುನಿ ǰaǰǰuni (ಜಜ್ಜ್), *v. a.* To bruise, squash, crush, pound.

ಜಟ್‍ಪಟ್ ǰaṭupaṭu, *adv.* Smartly, promptly, speedily.

ಜಟ ǰaṭa, *see* ಜಡ.

ಜಟಾಜಟ, ಜಟಾಪಟಿ ǰaṭāǰaṭa, ǰaṭāpaṭi, *s.* Strife. 2. hurry, confusion.

ಜಟಾಮಾಂಸಿ ǰaṭāmāṁsi, *s.* The Indian spikenard, *Nardostachys jatamansi.*

ಜಟಿಲೆ ǰaṭile, *s.* A hermit, ascetic, devotee.

ಜಟೆ ǰaṭè, *see* ಜಡೆ.

ಜಟ್ಕ ǰaṭka, *adj.* Soon; *cf.* ಜದ್ಕ.

ಜಟ್ಟಿ ǰaṭṭi, *s.* A waist-band, belt. 2. a wrestler, boxer. —ಕಾಳಗ a boxers' combat. —ಗೆ a brave man; the tutelar god of wrestlers. —ಮುರು a pair of earrings.

ಜಠರ ǰaṭhara, *s.* The belly, stomach. 2. womb. *adj.* Firm, hard. ಜಠರಾಗ್ನಿ digestive power, digestion.

ಜಡ್ ǰaḍu, *s.* Origin, root. —ಬುನಾದಿ the ultimate source.

ಜಡ ǰaḍa, *s.* Fatigue, weariness. 2. dullness. *adj.* Sick. 2. dull, stupid. 3. inanimate. 4. cold. —ಕಾಲ cold weather. —ಗುಣ sluggish disposition. —ಭರಿತ full of dullness. ಜಡಾಮತಿ a very stupid man. —ಕಲೆಪಿನಿ to stretch oneself.

ಜಡಾಯಿಸುನಿ ǰaḍāyisuni, *see* ಜಡಿಪಿನಿ.

ಜಡಿ ǰaḍi, *see* ದಡಿ. 2. *see* ದಡಿಕೆ.

ಜಡಿತ, ಜಡ್ತ ǰaḍita, ǰaḍta, *s.* Ramming, stuffing. —ಪಾಡುನಿ, *see* ಜಡಿಪಿನಿ.

ಜಡಿತಿ ǰaḍiti, *see* ಝಡಿತಿ.

ಜಡಿಪಿನಿ, ಜಡಿಪುನಿ, ಜಡಿಯುನಿ ǰaḍipini, ǰaḍipuni, ǰaḍiyuni (ಜಡಿ, ಜಡಿಯ್), *v. a.* To ram, stuff, 2. to load, as firearms. 2. to drive cattle. 3. to rain incessantly. ಜಡಿದ್‍ಕುಳ್ಳಾವುನಿ to drive in, fix.

ಜಡು ǰaḍu, *s.* Apathy. 2. fright, shyness.

ಜಡೆ ǰaḍè, *s.* Matted *or* clotted hair. 2. plaited hair. 3. the hood of a serpent. —ಕಳ್ಳಿ a kind of *cactus.* —ಬಿಲ್ಲೆ small, circular, ornamented, gold plates attached in succession on *or* along with a woman's plaited hair. —ಗೊಂಡೆ ornamented tassels suspended at the end of a woman's plaited hair. —ಕಟ್ಟುನಿ to fasten braided *or* matted hair. —ಜಡೆ in clots, braids.

ಜಡೆಪುನಿ Jaḍepuni, *see* ಜಡಿಪಿನಿ.

ಜಡ್ಕ Jaḍka, *adv.* At once.

ಜಡ್ಡ್ Jaḍḍụ, *s.* Callosity, hardness, as of the skin of the hand, *etc.* from much use; *also* ದಡ್ಡ್. *adj. see* ಜಿಡ್ಡ್.

ಜಡ್ಡಿ Jaḍḍi, *s.* Land subject to be overflowed by salt water; *bet.* ಜಡ್ಡಿ.

ಜಡ್ತಿ Jaḍti, *see* ಝಡತಿ.

ಜಣ್ಜಣ್ Jaṇụjaṇụ, *see* ಝಣ್ಝಣ್.

ಜತ Jata, *see* ಜತೆ.

ಜತನ Jatana, *s.* Carefulness. *adj.* Secure, careful, fast.

ಜತಿ Jati, *see* ಯತಿ.

ಜತೆ Jatè, *s.* A pair, couple. 2. a set. 3. equality of shape, size, *etc. adj.* Equal. —ಗಾರೆ, —ತಾಯೆ a companion, colleague. —ಕಟ್ಟುನಿ to make a pair.

ಜತ್ನ Jatna, *see* ಯತ್ನ.

ಜದರುನಿ, ಜದುರುನಿ Jadaruni, Jaduruni, *see* ಚದರುನಿ.

ಜದ್ರ Jadra, *s.* Poverty, want, penury, distress. 2. ailment, indisposition. *adj.* Poor, indigent, distressed. 2. mean, worthless. —ದಾಯೆ an unfortunate *or* worthless man. —ಪಾತೆರ vulgar speech. —ಪತ್ತುನಿ to be indisposed.

ಜನ Jana, *s.* Man, individually *or* collectively; people, population, community. —ಮಾನಿ persons, both old and young, mankind. ಜನ ಮುಲ್ಪ ಜಾತ್ರೆ ಮುಲ್ಪ is it the people or festival that attracts most?

ಜನಕಬಾರೆ Janakabārè, *s.* A kind of plantain tree.

ಜನಕೆ Janake, *s.* A progenitor, father.

ಜನಜನ Janajana, *s.* Every one. —ಪಾತೆರುನಿ be talked of by every one.

ಜನಜನಿತ Janajanita, *adj.* Rumoured abroad, generally known.

ಜನನ Janana, *s.* Birth; *cf.* ಜನ್ಮ. —ಮರಣ birth and death.

ಜನನಿ Janani, *s.* A mother.

ಜನರಂಜನ Janarañjana, *s.* Popular, pleasing to people in general.

ಜನಾಂಗ Janāṅga, *s.* A nation, body of people; generation.

ಜನಾಪವಾದ Janāpavāda, *s.* Public censure. 2. disgrace, infamy.

ಜನಿಪುನಿ Janipuni (ಜನಿ), *v. n.* To arise; to be born.

ಜನಿಲ್ Janilụ, *see* ಗಣಿಲ್.

ಜನಿವಾರ Janivāra, *s.* The brahminical thread. —ಪಾಡುನಿ to put on the brahminical thread.

ಜನ್ಮ Janma, *s.* Birth, nativity, state of existence. —ಕರ್ಮ, —ಪಾಪ inherent sin. —ಪತ್ರಿಕೆ a horoscope.

ಜನ್ಮಾಂತರ **ǰanmāntara**, *s.* Another birth. 2. regeneration. 3. transmigration.

ಜನ್ಮಿಪುನಿ **ǰanmipuni** (ಜನ್ಮ), *v. a.* To beget.

ಜಪ **ǰapa**, *s.* Repeating prayers, incantations *or* the names of the gods, as an act of adoration. –ತಪ religious devotions. –ಮಾಲೆ, –ಸರ a rosary. –ಕರಿಪುನಿ, –ಮಳ್ಪುನಿ to pray, to repeat prayers, *etc.*

ಜಪಾಸನ **ǰapāsana**, *see* ಜೋಪಾಸನ.

ಜಪಿಪುನಿ, ಜಪಿಸುನಿ **ǰapipuni, ǰapisuni**, (ಜಪಿ), *v. a.* To repeat prayers *etc.*, as an act of adoration.

ಜಪುಡಾವುನಿ **ǰapuḍāvni**, *c. v.* (*of* ಜಪುಡುನಿ) To cause to let down, to lower.

ಜಪುಡುನಿ **ǰapuḍuni**, *v. a.* (ಜಪುಡಿ) To let down, lower.

ಜಪ್ತಿ **ǰapti**, *s.* Confiscation, sequestration. 2. attachment, *law.* –ಮಳ್ಪುನಿ to attach, confiscate.

ಜಪ್ಪಂಗೆಲ್ **ǰappaṅgelu**, *s.* Goods *etc.* remaining after selection.

ಜಪ್ಪು **ǰappu**, *s.* Selection, choosing; *cf.* ಅಜಪ್ಪು.

ಜಪ್ಪುನಿ **ǰappuni** (ಜ), *v. a.* To open. 2. to descend, come down, alight. 3. to select, choose; *cf.* ಅಜಪ್ಪುನಿ. ಬಾಕಿಲ್– to open the door. ತಿರ್ತ– to descend, dismount.

ಜಪ್ಪೆಲ್ **ǰappelu**, *s.* A descent, slope. 2. ebb.

ಜಬರ್‍ಜಾಸ್ತಿ, ಜಬರ್‍ದಸ್ತ್, ಜಬರ್‍ದಸ್ತಿ **ǰabaruǰāsti, ǰabarudastu, ǰabarudasti**, *s.* Violence, force, urgency; *also* ಜಬ್ಬರುದಸ್ತು. –ಮಳ್ಪುನಿ to force; to dun, set on.

ಜಬರ್‍ಮೆಯಿ **ǰabarumeyi**, *s.* A stout body. *adj.* Stout.

ಜಬಾಬು **ǰabābu**, *see* ಜವಾಬ್.

ಜಬುಲು **ǰabulu**, *adj.* Slack.

ಜಬ್ತಿ **ǰabti**, *see* ಜಪ್ತಿ.

ಜಬ್ಬಿ, ಜಬ್ಬು **ǰabbi, ǰabbu**, *s.* An old woman, a hag.

ಜಬ್ಬು **ǰabbu**, *s.* Delay. *adj.* Hollow, empty within, not solid. 2. old, infirm.

ಜಬ್ಬೆ **ǰabbe**, *s.* An old man.

ಜಮ್‍ಕಾನ್, ಜಮಕನ್, ಜಮಕಾನ್ **ǰamukānu, ǰamakanu, ǰamakānu**, *s.* A carpet. 2. a blanket.

ಜಮ್‍ನೀರೊಳು **ǰamunīroḷu**, *see* ಜಂಬುನೀರೊಳ್.

ಜಮನ್ **ǰamanu**, *s.* A kettle.

ಜಮಬಂದಿ, ಜಮಾಬಂದಿ **ǰamabandi, ǰamābandi**, *s.* Settlement of the assessments. –ಮಳ್ಪುನಿ to settle assessments.

ಜಮಲ್‍ಕೊಟ್ಟೆ **ǰamalukoṭṭe**, *s.* Croton seed.

ಜಮಾಕರ್ಚಿ, ಜಮಾಖರ್ಚಿ **ǰamākarči, ǰamākharči**, *s.* The receipts and disbursements,

ಜಮಾಯಿಸುನಿ **ǰamāyisuni** (ಜಮಾಯಿಸಿ), *v. a.* To collect.

ಜಮಿಪುನಿ **ǰamipuni** (ಜಮಿ), *v. a.* To utter incantations, in order to gain the favour of an evil spirit *or* demon, *or* to charm it away.

ಜಮಿ಼ಾನ್ **ǰamīnụ**, *s.* The soil, ground, land. —ದಾರೆ a landholder, zemindar.

ಜಮುಕು **ǰamuku**, *s.* Rashness, inconsiderateness. 2. pride, haughtiness; *cf.* ದಿಮಾಕ್, ಮುಡುಕು.

ಜಮುಕುನಿ **ǰamukuni** (ಜಮುಕ್), *v. a.* To brandish. 2. to smack. 3. to frighten, threaten.

ಜಮೆ **ǰamė**, *s.* A collection, gathering, assemblage. 2. assessment. 3. receipts. 4. cognizance. 5. lurking. 6. overhearing. —ಕರ್ಜ್, *see* ಜಮಾಕರ್ಜ್. —ತೂಪಿನಿ to lurk, spy; to overhear; to estimate. —ಮಳ್ಪುನಿ to collect, gather, assemble.

ಜಮೆದಾರೆ **ǰamedāre**, *s.* A native military officer.

ಜಮೆಪುನಿ **ǰamepuni** (ಜಮೆ), *v. a.* To assemble, collect. 2. to reckon, estimate; to meditate; *also* ಜಮೆದ್‌ಪತ್ತುನಿ.

ಜಮೆರಿ **ǰameri**, *s.* The hair about the body. —ಗುಡ್ಡೆ a hairy man.

ಜಮ್ನೀರುಳಿ **ǰamnīruḷi**, *see* ಜಂಬುನೀರೊಳಿ.

ಜಮ್ಮನ್ಯೆ **ǰammanye**, *see* ಜಂಮನೆ.

ಜಮ್ಮು **ǰammu**, *see* ಜಂಫ.

ಜಯ **ǰaya**, *s.* Conquest, victory, success, triumph. —ಜಯ hail! vivat! —ಧ್ವನಿ the sound *or* shout of victory. —ಭೇರಿ a war-drum. —ಆಪಿನಿ to conquer, succeed, gain.

ಜಯಂತಿ **ǰayanti**, *s.* The public rejoicing on the birthday of a god. ರಾಮ— the festivity of Rāma's advent.

ಜಯಮಿನಿ **ǰayamini**, *see* ಜೈಮಿನಿ.

ಜಯವಂತೆ, ಜಯಶಾಲಿ **ǰayavante, ǰayaśāli**, *s.* A conqueror, victor.

ಜಯವಿಜಯೆರ್ **ǰayaviǰayerụ**, *s.* The door-keepers of Vishṇu's heaven.

ಜಯಾಜಯ **ǰayāǰaya**, *s.* Victory and defeat.

ಜಯಿನಾದಿಗೆ **ǰayinādigė**, *see* ಜೈನಾದಿಗೆ.

ಜಯಿನೆ **ǰayine**, *see* ಜೈನೆ.

ಜಯಿಪುನಿ, ಜಯಿಸುನಿ **ǰayipuni, ǰayisuni**, *see* ಜೈಪುನಿ.

ಜಯಿಲ್ **ǰayilụ**, *see* ಜೈಲ್.

ಜರ **ǰara**, *s.* Fever. ಉಡಲ್— a hectic fever. ಉಷ್ಣ— a fever from morbid heat in the body. ಪಿತ್ತ— bilious fever. ಮಾರಿದ— small-pox. ವಾತ— rheumatic fever. ಸಂನಿಪಾತ— typhus fever. ಸಳಿ—, ಸೀತ— fever with ague. —ಬರ್ಪಿನಿ to be attacked with fever. —ಬುಡ್ಪಿನಿ fever to abate *or* leave.

ಜರ **ǰara**, *s.* Old age, decrepitude. 2. hardness.

ಜರಕಂಡೆ **ǰarakaṇḍė**, *s.* Enlargement of the spleen, ague-cake.

ಜರಕ್ಕ **ǰarakka**, *see* ಜರ್ರ.

ಜರಜರ **ǰaraǰara**, *see* ಚರಚರ.

ಜರಡ್ **ǰaraḍụ**, *adj.* Vain, unsubstantial.

ಜರತಾರ್, ಜರತಾರಿ **ǰaratārụ, ǰaratāri**, *see* ಜಲತರ.

ಜರನೆ **ǰaranė**, *see* ಜರ್ರ.

ಜರಬು, ಜರಾಬ್ jarabu, jarābu, *see* ಜರ್ಬು.

ಜರಾಬರಿ jarābari, *s.* Tall and stout, well-proportioned.

ಜರಾಮರಣ jarāmaraṇa, *s.* Old age and death; death in old age.

ಜರಾಸಂಧೆ jarāsandhe, *s.* A king of Māgadha.

ಜರಿ jari, *s.* A precipice, slope. 2. gold *or* silver thread *or* lace. 3. cuttings. 4. grit, granule. 5. sand. –ಬೂರುನಿ, *see* ಜರಿಪುನಿ.

ಜರಿಪುನಿ jaripuni (ಜರಿ), *v. a.* To insult, jeer, despise. 2. to shake, make tremble; *cf.* ಜರಿಪುನಿ.

ಜರಿಯುನಿ jariyuni (ಜರಿ), *v. n.* To fall *or* slip down. 2. to wear away. 3. to shiver, tremble. –ದ ಬೂರುನಿ to fall off, drop off; to be cut away.

ಜರೂರು jarūru, *s.* Necessity, occasion, urgency. 2. want. 3. pressure. *adj.* Necessary, urgent. ಜರೂರ್ದ pressing, urgent. ಜರೂರುಡು urgently.

ಜರೆ jare, *see* ಜರ.

ಜರೆಪುನಿ jarepuni, *see* ಜರಿಪುನಿ.

ಜರ್ರ jarra, *adv.* Suddenly, quickly. –ಜಾರುನಿ to slide down suddenly.

ಜರ್ಕ jarka, *see* ಚರ್ಕ.

ಜರ್ತೊಣುನಿ jartoṇuni, *see* ಜಿಪ್ಪುನಿ.

ಜರ್ಪು jarpu, *see* ದರ್ಪು.

ಜರ್ಪುನಿ jarpuni, *see* ಜರಿಪುನಿ. 2. *see* ಜಿಪ್ಪುನಿ.

ಜರ್ಬು jarbu, *s.* Oppression, undue authority, overbearing conduct. –ಗಾರೆ a tyrant, oppressor. –ಡು ಪಾತೆರುನಿ to speak in an overbearing tone. –ಡು ಪೋಪಿನಿ to walk with a haughty mien. –ಮಳ್ಪುನಿ to show undue authority.

ಜಲ್ಂಬೆವುನಿ jalumbevuni (ಜಲ್ಂಬೆ), *v. n.* To be born. 2. to be pregnant.

ಜಲ್ಜಲ್ jaljalu, *adv.* Brightly. 2. *see* ಜುಳ್ಜುಳ್.

ಜಲ jala, *s.* Water. –ಕ್ರೀಡೆ sporting in water. –ಪಾನ water beverage. –ಯಂತ್ರ a water-pump.

ಜಲಕ್ jalaku, *s.* Glitter, gleam. –ಪಾಕುನಿ to glitter, gleam.

ಜಲಕ jalaka, *s.* Bathing, ablution. –ಮಳ್ಪುನಿ to bathe.

ಜಲಕಾವುನಿ jalakāvuni, *c. v.* (*of* ಜಲಕುನಿ) To cause to shine.

ಜಲಕುನಿ jalakuni (ಜಲಕ್), *v. n.* To shine.

ಜಲಗಾರೆ jalagāre, *s.* A man searching for gold in sweepings, *etc.*

ಜಲಚರ, ಜಲಜಂತು jalačara, jalajantu, *s.* An aquatic animal.

ಜಲತರ, ಜಲತಾರ jalatara, jalatāra, *s.* Gold *or* silver thread, *or* lace. –ದ ಪಗಡಿ a turban with gold lace.

ಜಲದ್ jaladu, *see* ಜಲ್ದಿ.

ಜಲದಾರೆ jaladāre, *see* ಜಲಗಾರೆ.

ಜಲಪ್ರವಾಹ jalapravāha, *s.* An inundation *or* stream of water.

ಜಲಪ್ರಳಯ ǰalapraḷaya, *s.* The deluge; a flood.

ಜಲಮಟ್ಟ ǰalamaṭṭa, *s.* A level; a mason's level.

ಜಲಮಲಕ್ ǰalamalakụ, *s.* A complete set of ornaments.

ಜಲಾಲಿಬಿಲಾಲಿ, ಜಲಾಲಿಬುಲಾಲಿ ǰalālibilāli, ǰalālibulāli, *s.* A masquerade at the Moharam.

ಜಲಿಪುನಿ, ಜಲಿಯುನಿ ǰalipuni, ǰaliyuni, *see* ಜ್ವಲಿಪುನಿ.

ಜಲ್ದಿ ǰaldi, *adv.* Quickly, speedily, soon.

ಜಲ್ಮ ǰalma, *see* ಜನ್ಮ. 2. honour. —ಪಿತುವೆ imprisonment for lifetime. —ದೆಪ್ಪುನಿ to dishonour.

ಜಲ್ಮಟ್ಟ ǰalmaṭṭa, *see* ಜಲಮಟ್ಟ.

ಜಲ್ಮಿಯುನಿ, ಜಲ್ಮೆವುನಿ ǰalmiyuni, ǰalmevuni (ಜಲ್ಮಿ, ಜಲ್ಮೆ), *v. n.* To be born, come into existence.

ಜಲ್ಲ ǰalla, *s.* A boatman's pole.

ಜಲ್ಲಿ ǰalli, *s.* A chaplet of flowers. 2. anything dangling *or* hanging loosely. 3. boast, bragging. 4. broken stones. ಕುಂಟುದ— clothes loosely worn. ಪೂತ— a chaplet of flowers; flowers dangling down the head, *etc.* —ಕೊಚ್ಚುನಿ, —ಪಾತೆರುನಿ to boast, brag. —ಜಪ್ಪಡುನಿ to wear flowers loosely; to suspend a garland of flowers. —ನೇಲುನಿ flowers to hang loosely.

ಜಲ್ಲಿಯುನಿ ǰalliyuni (ಜಲ್ಲಿ), *v. n.* To boast, brag.

ಜಲ್ಲೆ, ಜಲ್ಲೆದೊಲ್ಲೆ ǰallè, ǰallèdollè, *see* ಡೊಲ್ಲೆ.

ಜವಣೆ, ಜವನೆ, ಜವನ್ಯೆ ǰavaṇe, ǰavane, ǰavanye, *s.* A youth, young man.

ಜವಣ್ತನ, ಜವನ್ತನ, ಜವಣ್ಡಿಗೆ, ಜವನ್ದಿಗೆ ǰavaṇtana, ǰavantana, ǰavaṇdigè, ǰavandigè, *s.* Manhood, manliness, courage, hardiness.

ಜವಣ್ಡಿ, ಜವನ್ದಿ ǰavaṇdi, ǰavandi, *s.* A young woman.

ಜವನ ǰavana, *see* ಜವ್ವನ.

ಜವಳಿ ǰavaḷi, *see* ಜಾಳಿ.

ಜವಳೆ ǰavaḷe, *see* ಜಾಳೆ.

ಜವಾದಿ ǰavādi, *s.* Civet. —ದ ಪುಚ್ಚೆ a civet cat.

ಜವಾನ್, ಜವಾನೆ ǰavānụ, ǰavāne, *s.* A peon. 2. a servant, porter.

ಜವಾಬ್, ಜವಾಬು ǰavābụ, ǰavābu, *s.* An answer, reply. —ಕೊರ್ಪಿನಿ to answer, reply.

ಜವಾಬ್ದಾರಿಗೆ, ಜವಾಬುದಾರಿಗೆ ǰavābụdārigè, ǰavābudārigè, *s.* Responsibility, accountability, liability. ಜವಾಬುದಾರೆ a responsible man.

ಜವುಳಿ ǰavuḷi, *see* ಜಾಳಿ.

ಜವೆಗೋಧಿ ǰavegōdhi, *s.* Barley.

ಜವ್ವನ ǰavvana, *s.* Youth, virility, maturity; *bet.* ಯೌವನ. —ಜಾರುನಿ to fade, get old.

ಜವ್ವನೆ ǰavvane, *see* ಜವಣೆ.

ಜಳಕ ǰaḷaka, *see* ಜಲಕ.

ಜಳಬಳ ǰaḷabaḷa, *s.* A noise made by agitating water; bubbling, as of boiling water.

ಜಳ್ಳ ǰaḷḷa, *see* ಜಲ್ಲ.

ಜಾಂಕಿ ǰāṅki, *s.* Prattling, chattering.

ಜಾಂಗಟಿ jāṅgaṭi, *see* ಜಾಗಂಟಿ.

ಜಾಂಗಲಿ jāṅgali, *see* ಜಂಗ್ಲಿ.

ಜಾಂತನ jāntana, *see* ಜಾಣತನ *under* ಜಾಣ.

ಜಾಂಪರ್ jāmparu, *see* ಕಾಂಪರ್.

ಜಾಂಬ jāmba (*abbr. of* ಜಾನೆ ಮಳ್ಪ), What will you do? what are you doing?

ಜಾಂಬವಂತೆ jāmbavante, *s.* The king of bears. 2. a fat old man; *fem.* ಜಾಂಬೆಲು a fat old woman.

ಜಾಂಬವೆ jāmbave, *s.* A bear. 2. a strong, bold man. 3. a hairy man.

ಜಾಂಬಿಗೆ, ಜಾಂಮ್ಗೆ jāmbigė, jāmmugė, *s.* A flower twig of the wild jack. 2. a piece of coir rope used for igniting a gun, *etc.*

ಜಾಂಬೆ jāmbe (*abbr. of* ಜಾನ್ಂಬೆ), What is he doing?

ಜಾಂಬೆಲ್ jāmbelu, *adj.* Large. —ಮಿರೆ a large breast.

ಜಾಕಿನ jākina, *s.* Regard of person. 2. partiality. 3. respect, consideration. 4. kindness, compassion; *bet.* ದಾಕ್ಷಿಣ್ಯ.

ಜಾಕ್ಟೆ jākṭė, *see* ಜಾಗಂಟಿ.

ಜಾಕ್ತಿ jākti, *see* ಜಾಜಿಕಾಯಿ.

ಜಾಗ್ jāgu, *s.* A place, dwelling, station. 2. space, room. 3. land, ground.

ಜಾಗಂಟೆ jāganṭė, *s.* A circular gong.

ಜಾಗರ, ಜಾಗರಣೆ jāgara, jāgaraṇė, *s.* Waking, watchfulness. —ಪಾಸ the eleventh day of the first half of the lunar month Kārtika, which is observed by the Hindus as a day of fasting and wakefulness. —ಆ ದುಪ್ಪುನಿ to be awake. —ಕುಳ್ಳುನಿ to keep awake.

ಜಾಗಿನಪಟ್ಟೆ jāginapaṭṭė, *s.* A kind of garment worn by females.

ಜಾಗೀರ್ jāgīru, *s.* A rent-free land, a freehold; *cf.* ಉಂಬಳಿ.

ಜಾಗೆ jāge, *see* ಜಾಗ್.

ಜಾಗ್ರತೆ jāgratė, *s.* Caution, carefulness, vigilence. 2. diligence, assiduity. —ಆದುಪ್ಪುನಿ, —ದುಪ್ಪುನಿ to be careful, cautious.

ಜಾಜ್, ಜಾಜಿ jāju, jāji, *s.* A ship.

ಜಾಜಿ jāji, *s.* The great flowered jasmine, *Jasminum grandiflorum.* —ಕಲ್ಲ್ red chalk. —ಪೂ jasmine flower.

ಜಾಜಿಕಾಯಿ jājikāyi, *s.* The nutmeg. —ಮರ the nutmeg-tree *Myristica moschata.*

ಜಾಜಿಪತ್ರೆ jājipatrė, *s.* Mace.

ಜಾಡ್ jāḍu, *s.* A broom, bisom.

ಜಾಡ್ jāḍu, *see* ಝಾಡ್.

ಜಾಡ್ಮಲ್ಲಿ jāḍumalli, *s.* A sweeper. 2. a scavenger. 3. a servant in charge of a travellers' bungalow.

ಜಾಡಣೆ jāḍaṇė, *s.* Purging, looseness of bowels. 2. sweeping. 3. *see* ಝಾಡ್.

ಜಾಡದಾಯೆ jāḍadāye, *see* ಜಾಡೆ.

ಜಾಡಪುರಿ jāḍapuri, *s.* A spider.

ಜಾಡಿ jāḍi, *s.* A large earthen vessel.

ಜಾಡಿಪುನಿ jāḍipuni (ಜಾಡಿ), *v. a.* To shake off. 2. to sweep, clear.

ಜಾಡಿಮಲೆ jāḍimale, *see* ಜಾಡ್‌ಮಲ್ಲಿ.

ಜಾಡೆ, ಜಾಡ್ಯೆ jāḍe, jāḍye, *s.* A weaver. 2. a spider.

ಜಾಡ್ಯ jāḍya, *s.* Carelessness, negligence. 2. sickness, disease. 3. heaviness. 4. folly, stupidity.

ಜಾಣ jāṇa, *s.* Skill, wisdom; *cf.* ಜ್ಞಾನ. –ತನ skilfulness, ability.

ಜಾಣಕಿ jāṇaki, *see* ಜಾನಕಿ.

ಜಾಣಾದಿಗೆ jāṇādigè, *s.* Cleverness, skilfulness.

ಜಾಣಿ, ಜಾಣೆ jāṇi, jāṇe, *s.* A wise man.

ಜಾತ್ jātụ, *see* ದಾತ್. 2. *see* ದಾಸ್ತಾನ.

ಜಾತ jāta, *adj.* Born, produced. –ಕರ್ಮ the ceremonies performed on the birth of a child.

ಜಾತಕ jātaka, *s.* A horoscope. ನಷ್ಟ– a horoscope cast up without sufficient data. ಮರಣ– a horoscope prognosticating one's death.

ಜಾತಿ jāti, *s.* Kind, sort, class, tribe, caste. 2. birth. 3. social position, status. *adj.* Pure, unadulterated; superior, highbred. –ಕಟ್ಟಿ, –ಕ್ರಮ the rules regulating a caste. –ಕರ್ಮ ceremonies peculiar to a caste. –ಕುದುರೆ a horse of a superior breed. –ದ್ವೇಷ, –ವೈರ the mutual jealousy of castes. –ಧರ್ಮ, –ನೀತಿ, –ಪದ್ಧತಿ, –ಮರಿಯಾದಿ, –ರಿವಾಜಿ the usage and custom of a caste. –ಭ್ರಷ್ಟ, –ಕೆಟ್ಟನಾಯಿ an outcaste. –ಮರ teakwood. –ಹೀನೆ a man of low caste. –ಕೆಟ್ಟುನಿ to lose caste. –ಡ್ದ ದೆಪ್ಪುನಿ to excommunicate. –ಗ ಸೇರಾವುನಿ to admit into a caste. –ವಾರ order of castes; according to castes.

ಜಾತಿ, ಜಾತಿಕ ಮರ jāti, jātika mara, *see* ಜಾಜಿ.

ಜಾತಿಪತ್ರಿ jātipatri, *see* ಜಾಯಿಪತ್ರಿ.

ಜಾತಿಫಲ jātiphala, *see* ಜಾಯಿಕಾಯಿ.

ಜಾತ್ರೆ jātrè, *s.* The annual festival of a temple; *cf.* ಯಾತ್ರೆ. –ದ ಪರಷೆ the people attending a festival, pilgrims.

ಜಾದ್, ಜಾದು jādụ, jādu, *s.* Sorcery, conjuration. –ಮಳ್ಪುನಿ to conjure.

ಜಾದಿ jādi, *see* ಜಾಜಿ.

ಜಾನ jāna, *see* ಜ್ಞಾನ. 2. *see* ಧ್ಯಾನ.

ಜಾನಕಿ jānaki, *s.* Sīta, daughter of Janaka.

ಜಾನಿ jāni, *see* ಜ್ಞಾನಿ.

ಜಾನಿಪುನಿ, ಜಾನುನಿ jānipuni, jānuni, *see* ಧ್ಯಾನಿಪುನಿ.

ಜಾನೆ jānè, *see* ದಾನೆ.

ಜಾಪಾವುನಿ jāpāvuni, *c. v.* (*of* ಜಾಪಿನಿ) To put down, as a load; to unload, lighten.

ಜಾಪಕ jāpaka, *see* ಜ್ಞಾಪಕ.

ಜಾಪಿನಿ, ಜಾಪುನಿ jāpini, jāpuni (ಜಾ), *v. n.* To be unloaded, lightened.

ಜಾಪು Jāpu, *s.* A kind, sort, form. –ಜಾಪು different sorts.

ಜಾಪೆಲ್ jāpelu, *s.* Putting down, as a load. 2. unloading. 3. a stone pillar for placing a load temporarily. 4. a halting place.

ಜಾಪ್ಯ jāpya, *s.* Delay, loitering. *adj.* Slow, backward, lingering, loitering.

ಜಾಮ್ಗೆ jāmugè, *see* ಜಾಂಬಿಗೆ.

ಜಾಮ jāma, *s.* A watch *or* a period of three hours. –ದ ಕೋಳಿ a cock crowing at three in the morning; *cf.* ಜಾಮು.

ಜಾಮದಾನಿ jāmadāni, *s.* A knapsack; *cf.* ನಾಗಜಾಪು.

ಜಾಮೀನ್ jāmīnu, *s.* Bail, security. –ದಾಯಿ a surety, security.

ಜಾಮುಗೆ jāmugè, *see* ಜಾಂಬಿಗೆ.

ಜಾಮೆ jāme, *s.* A cunning *or* artful man. ಜಾಮಕಳುವೆ a great thief.

ಜಾಯಿಕಾಯಿ jāyikāyi, *s.* The nutmeg.

ಜಾಯಿನಾಯಿ jāyināyi, *s.* A greyhound.

ಜಾಯಿಪತ್ರಿ jāyipatri, *s.* Mace.

ಜಾಯೆ jāye, *see* ದಾಯಿ.

ಜಾರ, ಜಾರತ್ವ jāra, jāratva, *s.* Adultery, incontinence.

ಜಾರಂಗೆ jāraṅgè, *see* ಜಾರಿಗೆ.

ಜಾರಂಗೆಲ್ jāraṅgelu, *s.* Slipperiness, glibness, smoothness.

ಜಾರಂದಾಯೆ jārandāye, *s.* The name of a demon.

ಜಾರಜಾತ jārajāta, *adj.* Illegitimate.

ಜಾರಾವುನಿ jārāvuni, *c. v.* (*of* ಜಾರು ನಿ) To let slip. 2. to strip off, as clothes, *etc.*; to bark, peel, flay. 3. to lop off, as the branches of a tree. 4. to steal. ಮಾಡ– to remove the thatching of a roof. ಕೆಪ್ಪೆ– to turn the cheek-bone by a slap. ಬಾಕಿಲ್– to leave the door ajar. ಮಂಣ್– to throw earth, as into a pit, *etc. or* fill it with earth.

ಜಾರಿ jāri, *s.* Enforcement, execution. –ನಡಪುನಿ, –ಮಳ್ಪುನಿ to put into operation; to enforce, execute.

ಜಾರಿಗೆ jārigè, *s.* The Mysore gamboge tree, *Garcinia pictoria.* –ಪುಳಿ its fruit. –ಮೋಣೆ an ugly face.

ಜಾರುನಾಯೆ jārunāye, *s.* An unsteady man, a backslider.

ಜಾರುನಿ jāruni (ಜಾರ್), *v. n.* To slide, slip down; to move further. 2. to be slippery *or* smooth. 3. to tumble, fall down. 4. to be dislocated, as a limb. 5. to shrink, hesitate; to backslide. 6. to flee, run away. 7. to stretch, as the lobe of the ear *etc.*

ಜಾರುಪಡಿ jārupaḍi, *see* ಜಾರ್ಪಡಿ.

ಜಾರೆ jāre, *s.* An adulterer, whoremonger.

ಜಾರೆಲೆ jārele, *s.* A runaway. 2.

an unsteady man. 3. a backslider. 4. a coward.

ಜಾರ್ಗೆ jārgè, *see* ಜಾರಿಗೆ.

ಜಾರ್ತೆ, ಜಾರ್ದೆ jārtè, jārdè, *s.* The sign Scorpio, the eighth Tuḷu month.

ಜಾರ್ಪಡಿ jārpaḍi, *s.* Running away, decampment, retreat. —ಮಳ್ಪುನಿ to run away, decamp; to slink, escape.

ಜಾಲ್ jāḷu, *s.* A thrashing floor. 2. a courtyard.

ಜಾಲ jāla, *s.* A net. 2. the lattice of a window. 3. magic, conjuration, illusion. 4. pride. ಇಂದ್ರ— producing, by magic art, supernatural appearances. ಮಹೇಂದ್ರ— bringing into existence, by sorcery, any thing required.

ಜಾಲರ್ jālaru, *s.* A fringe, network. 2. the borders of a garment, *etc.*

ಜಾಲಾ jālā, *see* ಚಾಲಾ.

ಜಾಲಾಂದ್ರ jālāndra, *s.* Any wood work with bored holes. 2. an ornament worked into small perforations *or* holes.

ಜಾಲಿ jāli, *see* ಜಾಲೆ.

ಜಾಲಿಕಟ್ಟ jālikaṭṭa, *s.* Black stripes on the throat of a cobra.

ಜಾಲಿಪುನಿ jālipuni, *see* ಗಾಲಿಪುನಿ.

ಜಾಲಿಮರ jālimara, *s.* The tree *Ocymum gratissimum.*

ಜಾಲೆ jālè, *s.* Heat. 2. burning sensation. 3. pity, compassion, sorrow; *cf.* ಜ್ವಾಲೆ.

ಜಾವ jāva, *see* ಜಾಮು.

ಜಾವಕಲ್ಲ್ jāvakallu, *s.* A block of stone by the road-side to rest a load upon, a porter's rest.

ಜಾವಕುದುರೆ jāvakudurè, *s.* A grasshopper.

ಜಾವಡಿ jāvaḍi, *s.* A kind of verse. 2. *see* ಚಾವಡಿ.

ಜಾವಳನಾಯಿ jāvaḷanāyi, *s.* A wolf-dog.

ಜಾವಾವುನಿ jāvāvuni, *see* ಜಾಪಾವುನಿ.

ಜಾವಿಗೆ, ಜಾವುಗೆ jāvigè, jāvugè, *see* ಜಾಂಬಿಗೆ.

ಜಾವುನಿ jāvuni (ಜಾ), *see* ಜಾಪಿನಿ.

ಜಾವೆಲ್ jāvelu, *see* ಜಾಪೆಲ್.

ಜಾಸ್ತಿ jāsti, *s.* Increase, addition. 2. injustice, violence. —ಡ್ದ ದೆತ್ತೊಣುನಿ to take by force. —ಪಾತೆರುನಿ to speak in a violent tone, to abuse. —ಮಳ್ಪುನಿ to force, compel; to increase, promote; to raise, as rent *etc.*

ಜಾಹಿರ್ jāhiru, *s.* Representation, showing, informing. *adj.* Obvious, plain, clear. —ಆಪಿನಿ to become known; to be clear —ಮಳ್ಪುನಿ to explain, inform.

ಜಾಳ್ jāḷu, *see* ಜಾಲ್.

ಜಾಕ್ಷಣ jākshaṇa, *see* ದಾಕ್ಷಿಣ.

ಜಿಂಕೆ jiṅkè, *s.* An antelope.

ಜಿಂಗಿರಿ jiṅgiri, *see* ಬಿಂಗ್ರಿ.

ಜಿಂಜ jiñja, *see* ದಿಂಜ.

ಜಿಂಜಾವುನಿ jiñjāvuni, *see* ದಿಂಜಾವುನಿ.

ಜಿಂಜಿಗೆ jiñjigè, *see* ಜಿಂದಿಗೆ.

ಜಿಂಜುನಿ jiñjuni, *see* ದಿಂಜುನಿ.

ಜಿಂದಗಾನಿ, ಜಿಂದಿಗಾನಿ ǰindagāni, ǰindigāni, *s.* Treasure, treasury, wealth.

ಜಿಂದಿಗೆ ǰindigè, *s.* Property, estate. ಚರ– moveable property. ಸ್ಥಿರ– immoveable property.

ಜಿಂನೆ, ಜಿಂನೇಶ್ವರೆ ǰinne, ǰinnēśvare, *s.* The name of a personage peculiar to the Jaina sect, who is ranked by them as superior to the gods of other sects. 2. a teacher. 3. a saint.

ಜಿಂಬುನಿ ǰimbuni, *see* ಜುಂಬುನಿ.

ಜಿಂಬುಲಿ, ಜಿಂಬ್ಲಿ ǰimbuli, ǰimbli, *see* ಬಿಂಬಿಲಿ.

ಜಿಂಮ ǰimma, *adv.* Suddenly.

ಜಿಂಹೆ ǰiñhè, *see* ಜಿಹ್ವೆ.

ಜಿಕಿರ್ ǰikiru̥, *s.* Care, anxiety. 2. interference.

ಜಿಗ ǰiga, *see* ತಿಗ.

ಜಿಗಜಿಗ, ಜಿಗಿಜಿಗಿ ǰigaǰiga, ǰigiǰigi, *s.* The jingling noise of dancing.

ಜಿಗಾರ್ ǰigāru̥, *see* ಜುಗಾರ್.

ಜಿಜ್ಞಾಸ ǰiǰñāsa, *s.* Asking, inquiring. 2. search, investigation.

ಜಿಟ್ಟಿ ǰiṭṭi, *see* ದೃಷ್ಟಿ.

ಜಿಟ್ಟು ǰiṭṭu, *see* ಜುಟ್ಟು.

ಜಿಟ್ಟೆ ǰiṭṭè, *s.* A lump, unshapen mass.

ಜಿಡೆ ǰiḍè, *see* ಜಡೆ.

ಜಿಡ್ಡ್, ಜಿಡ್ಡ ǰiḍḍu̥, ǰiḍḍa, *s.* Rancidity, mustiness. *adj.* Rancid, musty. 2. *see* ದಿಡ್ಡಿ. –ಯೆಂಣೆ rancid oil.

ಜಿಡ್ಡಿ ǰiḍḍi, *adj.* Back, postern. *s.* A small, raised platform. –ಬಾಕಿಲ್ a back door; a small gate.

ಜಿಡ್ಡೆ ǰiḍḍè, *s.* A kind of mortar. 2. *see* ಜಿಡ್ಡ್. ಅರಿಮೆದ್ಪು– a wooden mortar for pounding rice.

ಜಿತ ǰita, *adj.* Conquered, subdued, overcome. –ಪಾಠ learning a lesson by heart. –ಬುದ್ಧಿ a disposition under discipline; a firm mind.

ಜಿತೇಂದ್ರಿಯೆ ǰitēndriye, *s.* One who has subdued his passions. 2. an ascetic. 3. a sage.

ಜಿತ್ತೆಕಳ್ಳಿ ǰittekaḷḷi, *see* ಜಡೆಕಳ್ಳಿ *under* ಜಡೆ.

ಜಿದ್ದ್ ǰiddu̥, *s.* Enmity, hatred.

ಜಿದ್ದಾಜಿದ್ದ್ ǰiddāǰiddu̥, *s.* Mutual hatred.

ಜಿದ್ದು ǰiddu, *see* ಜಿಡ್ಡ್.

ಜಿನ್ಸ್, ಜಿನಸ್ ǰinu̥su̥, ǰinasu̥, *s.* A thing, article, goods, provisions.

ಜಿನ್ಸಾರ ǰinu̥sāra, *s.* Variety, diversity. *adj.* Various, diverse.

ಜಿಬಳು, ಜಿಬುಲು, ಜಿಬುಳು ǰibaḷu, ǰibulu, ǰibuḷu, *s.* Boiled, tender areca nuts.

ಜಿಬುಳಿ ǰibuḷi, *s.* A kind of boys' game, similar to hopscotch.

ಜಿಬ್ಬ ǰibba, *see* ಜುಬ್ಬ.

ಜಿರಾಸಾಲೆ ǰirāsālè, *see* ಜೀರಸಾಲೆ.

ಜಿರೆ ǰirè, *adj.* Little, small. –ದಾಲೆ light red.

ಜಿಲ್ಂಬಿ jilụmbi, *see* ಜುಲುಮ್.

ಜಿಲಿಜಿಲಿ jilijili, *s.* Splashing.

ಜಿಲೇಬಿ, ಜಿಲ್ಬಿ jilēbi, jilbi, *s.* A kind of sweetmeat; *also* ಜಿಲಿಬಿಲಿ, ಜಿಲೇಬ್.

ಜಿಲುಪು, ಜಿಲುಬು, ಜಿಲ್ಪು jilupu, jilubu, jilpu, *s.* Locks of hair left above the ear as an ornament.

ಜಿಲ್ಮೆ jilmè, *see* ಜುಲುಮ್.

ಜಿಲ್ಲಾ, ಜಿಲ್ಲೆ jillā, jillè, *s.* A district, collectorate.

ಜಿಲ್ಲಾಟಿಗೊಬ್ಬು jillāṭigobbu, *s.* A kind of game; *cf.* ಜಿಲ್ಲ್.

ಜಿಲ್ಲ್ಯ jillya, *s.* A curl. —ದೀಪಿನಿ to dress the hair in curls; *cf.* ಜಿಲ್ಪು.

ಜಿಹ್ವೆ jihvè, *s.* The tongue.

ಜೀ jī, *adj.* Small, little, short. —ಕೋರಿ a short legged fowl. —ನರಮಾನಿ a dwarf. —ನಾಯಿ a lapdog; a small kind of dog.

ಜೀಕ್ jīkụ, *s.* Creaking, as sandaḷs, shoes, *etc.* when walking in them. —ದ ಮುಟ್ಟು creaking sandals.

ಜೀಟಿಗೆ jīṭigè, *s.* A torch, flambeau. —ದಾಯೆ a torch-bearer.

ಜೀತ್ jītụ, *s.* Advantage, gain. *adj.* Profitable, advantageous. —ಲಕ್ಕುನಿ to win, gain.

ಜೀನ್, ಜೀನಿ jīnụ, jīni, *s.* A saddle. —ಕಟ್ಟುನಿ, —ಪಾಡುನಿ to saddle.

ಜೀನ್ಸ್ jīnụsụ, *see* ಜಿನ್ಸ್.

ಜೀನ jīna, *adj.* Niggardly, parsimonious, stingy. —ತನ parsimony, stinginess.

ಜೀನೆ jīne, *s.* A miser, niggard.

ಜೀಪುನಿ jīpuni, *see* ದೀಪಿನಿ.

ಜೀರ್ jīrụ, *see* ಜೀರ್ಣ.

ಜೀರದರಿ jīradari, *s.* The seed *Cuminum Cyeninum.*

ಜೀರಸಾಲೆ jīrasālè, *s.* A superior kind of rice, a fine table rice.

ಜೀರಿಗೆ jīrigè, *see* ಜೀರದರಿ. *adj.* Small, short. —ಮುಂಚಿ, —ಮುಚ್ಚಿ a small species of capsicum (perhaps bird-pepper) of a stronger taste than other sorts.

ಜೀರುನಿ jīruni, *see* ಗೀರುನಿ.

ಜೀರೆ jīre, *s.* A hero, brave man.

ಜೀರೆವಾಲೆ, ಜೀರ್ವಾಲೆ jīrevālè, jīrvālè, *s.* A wasted palm-leaf. 2. a worn out ear-ornament,

ಜೀರ್ಗೆ jīrgè, *see* ಜೀರಿಗೆ.

ಜೀರ್ಣ jīrṇa, *s.* Digestion. *adj.* Digested. 2. tattered, old, worn out; *cf.* ಕ್ಷೀಣ. —ಶಕ್ತಿ the power of digestion. —ಆಪಿನಿ to be digested; to be worn out, reduced. —ಮಳ್ಪುನಿ to digest.

ಜೀರ್ಣಧಾರ, ಜೀರ್ಣೋದ್ಧಾರ jīrṇadhāra, jīrṇōddhāra, *s.* Reparation, renovation.

ಜೀರ್ಣೆ jīrṇè, *see* ಜೀರ್ಣ.

ಜೀರ್ದರಿ jīrdari, *see* ಜೀರದರಿ.

ಜೀರ್ನ jīrna, *see* ಜೀರ್ಣ.

ಜೀರ್ಸಾಲೆ jīrsālè, *see* ಜೀರಸಾಲೆ.

ಜೀವ jīva, *s.* Life, existence. 2. vitality, strength. 3. a living creature. —ಅತಾಗತಿ, —ಅತಿಗತಿ languor, prostration. —ದ ಗಂಟೆ dear, fond. —ಜೀವ full of life; fresh. —ದಾಂತೆ

lifeless. —ದ ಮೂರ್ಛೆ fainting. —ಮರ್ಕೊಗು at the risk of life. —ಆಪಿನಿ to be quickened, animated. —ಕಳೆಪಿನಿ, —ಗೆಪ್ಪುನಿ, —ದೆಪ್ಪುನಿ to take away life, to kill. —ಕಳೆವೊಂಟುನಿ, —ದೆತೊಂಟುನಿ to commit suicide; to bother oneself. —ಪತ್ತುನಿ to be animated; to spring, sprout. —ಪಾರುನಿ to swoon, faint; to be alarmed. —ಪೋಪಿನಿ to die, expire. —ಬುಡ್ಪಿನಿ to die; to endeavour, aspire after. —ಮಳ್ಪುನಿ to revive, renovate. —ಲಕ್ಕುನಿ to be envious. ನೇಲ್ಯ— vital powers. ಜೀವೊಗು ಜೀವ ಕೊರ್ಪಿನಿ to help at the risk of one's life.

ಜೀವಂತೆ **jīvante,** *s.* A living man.

ಜೀವಕಲೆ, ಜೀವಕಳೆ **jīvakalè, jīvakaḷè,** *s.* Animation, vitality. —ಕೊರ್ಪಿನಿ, —ದಿಂಜಾವುನಿ —ಪುಟ್ಟಾವುನಿ to animate, *i. e.* consecrate an idol.

ಜೀವಕಾಂತೆ **jīvakānte,** *s.* A husband.

ಜೀವಕಾಲ **jīvakāla,** *s.* The lifetime, existence.

ಜೀವಘಾತ, ಜೀವಘಾತಗ **jīvaghāta, jīvaghātaga,** *s.* Danger to life. 2. murder. 3. treachery. ಜೀವಘಾತಗೆ a murderer; a betrayer, treacherous man.

ಜೀವಜಂತು **jīvajantu,** *s.* A living creature, animal.

ಜೀವದಾನ **jīvadāna,** *s.* Gift of life.

ಜೀವದಾಶೆ **jīvadāśè,** *s.* Care for life.

ಜೀವನ **jīvana,** *s.* Subsistence, livelihood. 2. life, existence. 3. means of sustenance. —ದೆಪ್ಪುನಿ to deprive one's means of livelihood. —ಮಳ್ಪುನಿ to live; to earn one's livelihood; to follow a trade.

ಜೀವನಾಥೆ **jīvanāthe,** *s.* A husband. 2. Yama.

ಜೀವಮಾನ **jīvamāna,** *s.* Duration of life, lifetime.

ಜೀವರಾಶಿ **jīvarāśi,** *s.* The animal kingdom, living creatures.

ಜೀವಸಂಕಡ **jīvasaṅkaḍa,** *s.* Fatigue, weariness. 2. languor, exhaustion. —ಆಪಿನಿ to be fatigued, exhausted.

ಜೀವಸ್ಥಾನ **jīvasthāna,** *s.* A vital part.

ಜೀವಾತ್ಮ **jīvātma,** *s.* The sentient soul, spirit. 2. life; *cf.* ಪ್ರಾಣ. ಜೀವಾತ್ಮೆ man, as a sentient being.

ಜೀವಾದಿ **jīvādi,** *s.* Living creatures, animal kingdom.

ಜೀವಾಕ್ಷರ **jīvākshara,** *s.* A vowel.

ಜೀವಿ **jīvi,** *s.* A living creature. 2. a worm, an insect.

ಜೀವಿತ **jīvita,** *adj.* Living, alive, existent.

ಜೀವಿಸುನಿ **jīvisuni** (ಜೀವಿಸಿ), *v. n.* To live, exist, subsist.

ಜೀವು **jīvu,** *see* ದೀವು.

ಜುಂಜುಂ **jumjum,** *see* ಜುಮುಜುಮು.

ಜುಂಬುನಿ **jumbuni** (ಜುಂಬಿ), *v. n.* To suck, sip, lick.

ಜುಂಬುಲಿ, ಜುಂಬುಳಿ **jumbuli, jumbuḷi,** *see* ಬಿಂಬುಲಿ.

ಜುಂಮು jumma, *s.* A sudden stunning *or* smarting sensation.

ಜುಂಮೆ jummè, *s.* Custody, charge.

ಜುಂಯಿ juñyi, *s.* A boiling *or* bubbling noise.

ಜುಕಾಸುನಿ jukāsuni (ಜುಕಾಸಿ), *v. n.* To nod, be drowsy, sleepy.

ಜುಕುತಿ jukuti, *see* ಯುಕ್ತಿ.

ಜುಕ್ಕು jukku, *s.* A measure of seven sticks in a game.

ಜುಗ juga, *s.* A pair. 2. twins. 3. *see* ಯುಗ.

ಜುಗಾರ್, ಜುಗಾರಿ jugāru, jugāri, *s.* Gaming, gambling. –ಗೊಬ್ಬು ನಾಯಿ a gamester, gambler. –ಗೊಬ್ಬುನಿ to gamble.

ಜುಟ್ಟು juṭṭu, *s.* A tuft of hair of the head, cue. –ಕಟ್ಟುನಿ, –ಗಂಟ ಪಾಡುನಿ to tie the hair into a knot.

ಜುಡ್ಡೆ juḍḍè, *see* ಜಿಡ್ಡೆ.

ಜುಬ್ಬ jubba, *s.* A short jacket.

ಜುಬ್ಬು jubbu, *s.* A spheroid, globule.

ಜುಮ್‌ಜುಮ್ jumjum, *s.* Numbness, sleeping of the limb. 2. a throbbing pain. 3. horripilation. –ಆಪಿನಿ a limb to be benumbed; to be horrified; to feel pain, as when a boil suppurates.

ಜುಮಾದಿ jumādi, *s.* A demon so called.

ಜುಮುಲ jumula, *see* ಜುಮ್ಲ.

ಜುಮ್ಮ jumma, *see* ಜುಂಮು.

ಜುಮ್ಮೆ jummè, *see* ಜುಂಮೆ.

ಜುಮ್ಲ jumla, *s.* Total, whole.

ಜುರುಂಗುನಿ juruṅguni (ಜುರುಂಗಿ), *v. n.* To hesitate, be reluctant.

ಜುರುಮಾನೆ jurumānè, *see* ಜುಲುಮಾನೆ.

ಜುಲಾಬು julābu, *s.* Purging, looseness of bowels. 2. a purgative. –ಆಪಿನಿ to purge. –ಕೊರ್ಪಿನಿ to administer a purgative. –ದೆಪ್ಪುನಿ to take a purgative. –ಪೋಪಿನಿ to suffer from looseness of bowels. ಉಕ್ಕಾಲ್– vomiting and diarrhœa, cholera.

ಜುಲಿಪೆ, ಜುಲುಪು, ಜುಲ್ಪು julipè, julupu, julpu, *see* ಜಿಲ್ಪು.

ಜುಲುಮ್, ಜುಲ್ಮು julumu, julmu, *s.* Oppression, tyranny, injustice; *also* ಜುಲುಮಿ, ಜುಲ್ಮೆ. –ಜಾಸ್ತಿ tyrannical procedure, violent measures.

ಜುಲುಮಾನೆ, ಜುಲ್ಮಾನ್, ಜುಲ್ಮಾನೆ julumānè, julmānu, julmānè, *s.* A fine, penalty. –ಮಳ್ಪುನಿ to fine.

ಜುವಾದಿ juvādi, *see* ಜೇವಾದಿ.

ಜುವಾಳಿ juvāḷi, *s.* A kind of reed.

ಜುಳ್‌ಜುಳ್ juḷuj uḷu, *s.* The noise of falling water.

ಜೂಜಿ, ಜೂಜು jūji, jūju, *s.* Gaming, a wager, as with cocoanuts. –ಕಟ್ಟುನಿ to gamble. –ಗಾರೆ a gambler. –ದ ಕೋರಿ a fighting cock.

ಜೂಟ್, ಜೂಟು jūṭu, jūṭu, *s.* A lie, falsehood.

ಜೂಡಿಪುಗೆರೆ jūḍipugerè, *s.* A kind

of tobacco imported from the Ghauts.

ಜೂತಿ jūti, *s.* Shoes.

ಜೂಲ್ jūlu̥, *s.* The cover of a saddle, horse-cloth.

ಜೂಲಿ jūli, *s.* A funnel, pipe, spout. —ಪ ಕರ a distilling pot with a pipe. —ಚೆಂಬು a pot with a spout.

ಜೆಂಬಿಲ್, ಜೆಂಬುಲಿ jembilu̥, jembuli, *see* ಜಂಬುಲಿ.

ಜೆಂಬೆ jembè, *adj.* Insipid, tasteless.

ಜೆಕ್ಣಿ jekṇi, *see* ಜಕ್ಕಿಣಿ.

ಜೆಕ್ಕೆಲ್ jekkelu̥, *see* ಜಕ್ಕೆಲ್.

ಜೆಗೆ jegè, *see* ಜಗೆ.

ಜೆಗ್ಗ್ jeggu̥, *see* ಜಗ್ಗ್.

ಜೆಗ್ಗೆ jegge, *see* ಜಗ್ಗೆ.

ಜೆಟ್ಟಿ jeṭṭi, *see* ಜಟ್ಟಿ.

ಜೆಡಿ jeḍi, *s.* A speck in the eye; *bet.* ಜಡಿ.

ಜೆಡಿಪುನಿ jeḍipuni, *see* ಜಡಿಪಿನಿ. 2. *see* ಗೆದಿಯುನಿ.

ಜೆಡೆ jeḍè, *see* ಜಡೆ.

ಜೆಪ್ಪುನಿ, ಜೆರ್ಪುನಿ jeppuni, jerpuni (ಜೆ), *v. n.* To lie down. 2. to sleep, rest; *also* ಜೆತ್ತೊಣುನಿ.

ಜೆಪ್ಪೆ jeppè, *s.* The last cowrie put in an empty hole of a playing board (ಚಂನೆಮಣೆ) at the end of one's turn.

ಜೆಮೆ jemè, *see* ಜಮೆ.

ಜೆರ್ jēru̥, *see* ಜೇರ್.

ಜೆಷ್ಟೆ jèshṭè, *s.* Misfortune, calamity.

ಜೇಂಕಾವುನಿ jēṅkāvuni, *c. v.* (*of* ಜೇಂಕುನಿ) To detain, stop. 2. to delay, put off.

ಜೇಂಕುನಿ jēṅkuni (ಜೇಂಕ್), *v. n.* To delay, be deferred. 2. to hesitate, waver; *cf.* ತೇಂಕುನಿ.

ಜೇಂಕೆ jēṅkè, *see* ಸೇಂಕೆ.

ಜೇಗ್ jēgu̥, *see* ದಾಯಿಗ್.

ಜೇಡಿ jēḍi, *s.* Glutinous clay, chalk, a kind of white earth; *also* ಸೇಡಿ.

ಜೇದಿ jēdi, *ir. past part. of* ಜಪ್ಪುನಿ *or* ಜೆಪ್ಪುನಿ.

ಜೇಪು, ಜೇಬು jēpu, jēbu, *s.* A pocket.

ಜೇರ್ jēru̥, *s.* A Pariah's child.

ಜೇರ್, ಜೇರ jēru̥, jēra, *s.* Descent, declivity, precipice.

ಜೇರ್ಕಾಯಿ jēru̥kāyi, *see* ಗೇರ್ಕಾಯಿ.

ಜೇರ್ಲು jērlu, *s.* Pariah children.

ಜೇವು jēvu, *s.* A child. 2. a lad, youth. ಆಣ್— a male, man. ಪೊಣ್— a female, woman.

ಜೇಲ್ jēlu̥, *see* ಜೈಲ್.

ಜೇಷ್ಟ jēshṭa, *see* ಜ್ಯೇಷ್ಠ.

ಜೇಷ್ಟಮಧು jēshṭamadhu, *see* ಜ್ಯೇಷ್ಠಮಧು.

ಜೇಷ್ಟೆ jēshṭe, *see* ಜ್ಯೇಷ್ಠೆ.

ಜೈತ್ತ, ಜೈತ್ಯೆ jeitta, jeitye, *see* ಚೈತ್ಯ.

ಜೈನಾದಿಗೆ jeinādigè, *s.* Abstinence from meat and liquor.

ಜೈನೆ jeine, *s.* A Jain.

ಜೈಪಾನ jeipāna, *adj.* Invulnerable.

ಜೈಪುನಿ, ಜೈಸುನಿ jeipuni, jeisuni (ಜೈ), *v. a.* To conquer, win, be successful.

ಜೈಮಿನಿ jeimini, *s.* A sage so called.

ಜೈಲ್ jeilu̥, *s.* A jail, prison.

ಜೊಂಕೆ, ಜೊಂಕೆಲ್ jonkè, jonkelu, *s.* A bunch, cluster.

ಜೊಂಪಡಿ, ಜೊಂಪುಡಿ jompaḍi, jompuḍi, *s.* A shed, hut.

ಜೊಗ್ಗು joggu, *see* ಜಗ್ಗ್.

ಜೊಗ್ಗುರ joggura, *adj.* Overripe.

ಜೊತೆ jotè, *see* ಜತೆ.

ಜೊತ್ತೆ jottè, *past t. of* ಜಪ್ಪುನಿ, *or* ಜೆಪ್ಪುನಿ.

ಜೊಲ್ಲೆ jollè, *s.* Spittle; *cf.* ಜೊಲ್ಲ್.

ಜೋಂಪುಡಿ jōmpuḍi, *see* ಜೊಂಪಡಿ.

ಜೋಕು jōku, *s.* Ostentation, display; vanity, foppery.

ಜೋಕುಮ್ jōkumu, *s.* Danger, risk. *adj.* Dangerous.

ಜೋಕುಳು jōkuḷu, *s.* Children; *cf.* ಜೋವು. ಜೋಕುಳಾಟಿಕೆ childishness.

ಜೋಕೆ jōkè, *s.* Care, heed, caution; safety. —ಮಳ್ಪುನಿ to take care.

ಜೋಗ jōga, *s.* Abstraction of mind; *see* ಯೋಗ. —ಆಪಿನಿ to be in ecstasy. —ಬರ್ಪಿನಿ to be seized with demoniac frenzy.

ಜೋಗಂಮ jōgamma, *s.* A female devotee.

ಜೋಗಟ್ಟೆ jōgaṭṭè, *s.* Sitting cross-legged. —ಪೊಯ್ಯುಪಿನಿ to sit on cross-legs.

ಜೋಗಿ jōgi, *s.* A religious mendicant. 2. the name of a caste. 3. the name of a man; *also* ಯೋಗಿ.

ಜೋಗಿಪಂದ್ರ್ jōgiparndu, *s.* A kind of fruit.

ಜೋಗಿಪುರ್ಸೆ jōgipurse, *s.* The name of a demon. [flower.

ಜೋಗಿಪೂ jōgipū, *s.* A kind of

ಜೋಗಿಮರ jōgimara, *s.* The portia tree, *Thespasia populnea*; *also* ಜೋಗಿ ಅತ್ತಸದ ಮರ.

ಜೋಗು jōgu, *s.* A water-fall, cataract. [vessel.

ಜೋಗುಣಿ jōguṇi, *s.* A drinking

ಜೋಗುಳ, ಜೋಗುಳಿ jōguḷa, jōguḷi, *s.* A lullaby.

ಜೋಜಪಾಡುನಿ jōjapāḍuni (—ಪಾಡ್), *v. a.* To sing a lullaby; to lull.

ಜೋಜಿಯುನಿ, ಜೋಜುನಿ jōjiyuni, jōjuni (ಜೋಜಿ, ಜೋಜ್), *v. n.* To lull to sleep.

ಜೋಜೋ jōjō, *intj. expressive of blessing*, Be happy, *etc.* It terminates every song of certain lullabies.

ಜೋಟಿ jōṭi, *s.* A plait.

ಜೋಡಣೆ jōḍaṇè, *s.* Joining, uniting, union, collecting. —ಮಳ್ಪುನಿ to join; to get ready, prepare. [ಜೋಡು.

ಜೋಡಾಪಿನಿ jōḍāpini, *see under*

ಜೋಡಾವುನಿ jōḍāvuni, *c. v.* (*of* ಜೋಡಿಯುನಿ) To make join, unite.

ಜೋಡಿ jōḍi, *see* ಜೋಡು.

ಜೋಡಿಗೆ jōḍigè, *see* ಜೋಡಣೆ.

ಜೋಡಿಪುನಿ jōḍipuni (ಜೋಡಿ), *v. a.* To join, pair, unite.

ಜೋಡಿಯುನಿ jōḍiyuni (ಜೋಡ್), *v. n.* To be joined, united.

ಜೋಡು jōḍu, *s.* A pair, yoke, match, couple. 2. a pair of sandals. *adj.* Equal, like. —ಜೋಡು two and two. —ಆಪಿನಿ,

ಜೋಡಾಪಿನಿ to join, couple, pair. –ಮಳ್ಪುನಿ to join, pair, unite. 2. to assist, countenance, patronise. ಕೈ– a pair of gloves. ಪಾಪಸ್– a pair of slippers. ಮೆಯಿ– a pair of stockings.

ಜೋಡ್ಣೆ jōḍṇe, *see* ಜೋಡಣೆ.

ಜೋತಾಡುನಿ jōtāḍuni (ಜೋತಾಡ್), *v. n.* To wave, move, oscillate.

ಜೋತಿ jōti, *see* ಜ್ಯೋತಿ.

ಜೋತಿಕೋಲು jōtikōlu, *s.* A long walking stick.

ಜೋತಿಷ, ಜೋತಿಸ jōtisha, jōtisa, *see* ಜ್ಯೋತಿಷ.

ಜೋತಿಷ್ಯ jōtishye, *see* ಜ್ಯೋತಿಷ್ಯ.

ಜೋತ್ರ jōtra, *see* ದೋತ್ರ.

ಜೋನಗೆ jōnage, *s.* A wicked person; a lewd fellow.

ಜೋಪಡಿ jōpaḍi, *see* ಜೊಂಪಡಿ.

ಜೋಪನೆ, ಜೋಪಸನ, ಜೋಪಾನ jōpane, jōpasana, jōpāna, *s.* Care, circumspection. *adj.* Cautious, careful. –ಮಳ್ಪುನಿ to take care of; to keep carefully.

ಜೋಮಾಲೆಸರ jōmālesara, *s.* A kind of gold necklace.

ಜೋಯಿ jōyi, *see* ಜೋಗಿ.

ಜೋಯಿಸೆ jōyise, *s.* An astrologer.

ಜೋರ jōra, *see* ಜೇರ್.

ಜೋರು, ಜೋರಾವರಿ jōru, jōrāvari, *s.* Force, pressure, violence. 2. importunity. 3. power, strength. 4. severity, harshness; *also* ಜೋರ್, ಜೋರಿ. –ಆಪಿನಿ to become importunate; to become powerful, to be affected with liquor, tobacco, *etc.*; to be harsh. –ಉಪ್ಪುನಿ to be hard. –ಮಳ್ಪುನಿ to force, compel.

ಜೋಲ jōla, *see* ಜೋಳ.

ಜೋಲಂಗಿ jōlaṅgi, *see* ದಾರಂಗಿ.

ಜೋಲಾಟ jōlāṭa, *s.* Oscillation, hanging.

ಜೋಲಿ, ಜೋಲಿಗೆ jōli, jōligè, *s.* A small bag for receiving alms. 2. a piece of cloth suspended by a woman down her shoulders to carry about her baby in it.

ಜೋಲು jōlu, *adj.* Soft, moist. 2. pendent, flapping. –ಬೆಲ್ಲ a soft *or* moist kind of jaggory.

ಜೋವು jōvu, *s.* A child, baby, youth, youngster. 2. a female child. –ಕುಳು, ಜೋಕುಳು children.

ಜೋಳ jōḷa, *s.* The great millet, *Sorghum vulgare.* ಅರಿ– a small kind of millet, *Sorghum saccharatum*, the Chinese sugar-cane.

ಜೋಳಿ jōḷi, *see* ಇಜೋಲಿ.

ಜೋಳಿ, ಜೋಳಿಗೆ jōḷi, jōḷigè, *see* ಜೋಲಿ.

ಜೌಳಿ jouḷi, *s.* Cloth. –ದಾಯಿ a cloth merchant, draper.

ಜೌಳೆ jouḷè, *adj.* Tasteless, insipid.

ಜ್ಞಾನ jṅāna, *s.* Knowledge, wisdom.

ಜ್ಞಾನಿ jṅāni, *s.* A wise, learned man, a sage.

jñāvanā pan excuse

ಜ್ಞಾನುನಿ ǰñānuni, *see* ಧ್ಯಾನಿಪುನಿ.

ಜ್ಞಾಪಕ ǰñāpaka, *s.* Memory, recollection.

ಜ್ಯೇಷ್ಠ ǰyēshṭha, *s.* The third lunar month. *adj.* Best, excellent. 2. elder-born; *cf.* ಜ್ಯೇಷ್ಠ.

ಜ್ಯೇಷ್ಠಮಧು ǰyēshṭhamadhu, *s.* Liquorice root.

ಜ್ಯೇಷ್ಠೆ ǰyēshṭhe, *s.* The eighteenth lunar mansion. 2. an elder sister. 3. the goddess of poverty (ಕಲಿಲಕ್ಷ್ಮಿ), misfortune.

ಜ್ಯೇಷ್ಠೆ ǰyēshṭhe, *s.* The elder son *or* brother.

ಜ್ಯೋತಿ ǰyōti, *s.* Light, lustre. 2. a star. —ಶಾಸ್ತ್ರ astrology.

ಜ್ಯೋತಿಷ ǰyōtisha, *s.* The science of astronomy; astrology.

ಜ್ಯೋತಿಷ್ಯೆ ǰyōtishye, *s* An astronomer, astrologer.

ಜ್ವರ ǰvara, *see* ಜರ.

ಜ್ವಾಲಾಮುಖಿ ǰvālāmukhi, *s.* A volcano.

ಜ್ವಾಲೆ ǰvālė, *s.* Flame. 2. heat, warmth. 3. inflammation.

ಝ ǰH

ಝ ǰha, The twenty-second letter of the alphabet.

ಝಂಕಾರ ǰhaṅkāra, *see* ಝೇಂಕಾರ.

ಝಂಝಂ ǰhamǰham, *see* ಝುಮ್ ಝುಮ್.

ಝಂಪೆತಾಳ ǰhampetāḷa, *see* ಜಂಪೆ [ತಾಳ.

ಝಕಾಯಿಸುನಿ ǰhakāyisuni (ಝಕಾಯಿಸ್), *v. n.* To bluster, tyrannise.

ಝಗಝಗ ǰhagaǰhaga, *s.* Brilliancy. —ಮಿಂಚುನಿ to shine brilliantly.

ಝಗಳ ǰhagaḷa, *see* ಜಗಳ.

ಝಗ್ಗನೆ ǰhaggane, *adv.* Quickly, hastily. —ಮಿಂಚುನಿ to flash, as lightning.

ಝಟಾಪಟಿ ǰhaṭāpaṭi, *see* ಜಟಾಜಟ.

ಝಡಿತಿ, ಝಡ್ತಿ ǰhaḍiti, ǰhaḍti, *s.* Examination, as of accounts. 2. search, rummage.

ಝಡಿಪುನಿ ǰhaḍipuni, *see* ಜಡಿಪಿನಿ.

ಝಣ್‌ಝಣ್, ಝಮ್‌ಝಮ್ ǰhaṇuǰhaṇu, ǰhamuǰhamu, *s.* The tinkling of ornaments when walking.

ಝಮೆರಿ ǰhameri, *see* ಜಮೆರಿ.

ಝರಿ ǰhari, *s.* A spring. 2. a cascade, waterfall.

ಝಲ್ಲ್ ǰhallu, *s.* Sudden terror. 2. palpitation.

ಝಾಡ್, ಝಾಡಾ ǰhāḍu, ǰhāḍā, *s.* Settlement *or* payment in full. 2. completion, termination. —ಆಪಿನಿ to be settled *or* paid fully, to be over, finished. —ಮಳ್ಪುನಿ to pay entirely, to finish.

ಝಾಡನೆ ǰhāḍane, *see* ಜಾಡನೆ.

ಝಾಮ, ಝಾವ ǰhāma, ǰhāva, *see* ಜಾಮ.

ಝಾಲರ್, ಝಾಲರಿ jhālarụ, jhālari, *see* ಜಾಲರ.

ಝಾಳಿಗೆ jhāḷigè, *see* ಜೋಲಿ.

ಝೇಂಕಾರ jhēṅkāra, *s.* The buzzing *or* humming of bees.

ಝೋಂಪಡಿ jhōmpaḍi, *see* ಜೋಂಪಡಿ.

ಞ Ń

ಞ ńa, The twenty-third letter of the alphabet.

ಞಂಬ್, ಞಕ್ಕ್ ńaṅṅụ, ńakkụ, *s.* Crushing, bruising into a jelly *or* mass. —ಆಪಿನಿ to be crushed into a mass. —ಮಳ್ಪುನಿ to crush into a mass.

ಞಕ್ಕಞಕ್ಕ ńakkańakka, *adv.* Quickly, swiftly; coarsely.

ಞಕ್ಕಟ್, ಞಗಪಟ್ ńakkaṭụ, ńagapaṭụ, *adj.* Lean, thin, stunted, faded.

ಞಪ್ಪೆ ńappè, *see* ಞಂಬ್. 2. *see* ನಪೆ.

ಞರ್ಞರ್ ńarụńarụ, *see* ಜಿರಿಜಿರಿ. 2. *see* ನರಿನುರು.

ಞರಞರ, ಞರ್ಕಞರ್ಕ ńarańara, ńarkańarka, *adj.* Slight, little. —ಬೇನೆ slight pain.

ಞರ್ಕೆ ńarke, *see* ನರ್ಕೆ.

ಞವುಳಿಞಪುಳಿ, ಞೋಳಿಞಪ್ಪುಳಿ ńavuḷińapuḷi, ńōḷińappuḷi, *adv.* Indiscriminately. —ತಿಪ್ಪಿನಿ to eat indiscriminately.

ಞಾನಿ ńāni, *see* ಜ್ಞಾನಿ.

ಞೊಂಬು ńoṅṅu, *adj.* Shrivelled, contracted.

ಞೋಲಿ ńōli, *s.* Anything sticky, gummy glutinous, viscous. 2. saliva. —ಸರ *Aloe litoralis*. —ಕಾರುನಿ to vomit phlegm.

ಟ Ṭ

ಟ ṭa, The twenty-fourth letter of the alphabet.

ಟಂಕ್‌ಟಂಕ್ ṭaṅkụṭaṅkụ, *s.* Pit-a-pot, twang, as of a wire, *etc.*

ಟಂಕಣ ṭaṅkaṇa, *s.* Borax.

ಟಂಕಸಾಲೆ ṭaṅkasālè, *see* ಠಂಕಸಾಲೆ.

ಟಂಕಾರ್ ṭaṅkārụ, *see* ಠಕ್ಕೆ.

ಟಂಕು ṭaṅku, *s.* The twang of a bow-string.

ಟಂಗ್ ṭaṅgụ, *s.* A saddle girth.

ಟಂಟಣ್ ṭanṭaṇụ, *s.* A noise made in sounding a brass vessel, *etc.*, with the knuckles. 2. the striking of a clock.

ಟಕಾಯಿಸುನಿ ṭakāyisuni, *see* ಠಕಾಯಿಸುನಿ.

ಟಕಾರ್, ಟಕಾರಿ ṭakārụ, ṭakāri, *see* ಠಕ್ಕೆ.

ಟಕ್ಕ್, ಟಕ್ಕು ṭakkṳ, ṭakku, *see* ತಕ್ಕ್.

ಟಕ್ಕೆ ṭakke, *see* ತಕ್ಕೆ.

ಟಗರ್ ṭagarṳ, *s.* A ram.

ಟಪ್ಪ ṭappa, *adv.* Flatly. –ಪಾಡುನಿ to drop down flatly. –ಬೂರುನಿ to fall flatly.

ಟಪ್ಪಾಲ್ ṭappālṳ, *s.* The post. 2. a relay of bearers, bullocks, *etc.*; *also* ಟಪ್ಪೆ. –ಕಟ್ಟ the post-office. –ಕಾಗಜಿ a letter-paper; a post-letter. –ಕುದುರೆ a post-horse.

ಟಮಟೆ, ಟಮ್ಕಿ ṭamaṭè, ṭamki, *s.* A tambour. 2. proclamation by beat of tomtom. –ಹಾಕುನಿ to proclaim in such a manner.

ಟರಾಯಿಸುನಿ ṭarāyisuni, *see* ತರಾಯಿಸುನಿ.

ಟರಾವಣೆ ṭarāvaṇè, *see* ತರಾವಣೆ.

ಟವಣೆ ṭavaṇè, *see* ತವಣೆ.

ಟಸೆ, ಟಸ್ಸೆ ṭasè, ṭassè, *see* ತಸೆ.

ಟಾಂಕ್ ṭāṅkṳ, *s.* The nib of a pen. 2. basting down a stuffed bed, to make it secure. –ಪಾಡುನಿ, –ಕುತ್ತುಪಾಡುನಿ to nib a pen; to baste down a stuffed bed.

ಟಾಂಕನ್, ಟಾಂಕನಿ ṭāṅkanṳ, ṭāṅkani, *see* ಟಾಕಣ್.

ಟಾಂಕಿ ṭāṅki, *s.* A trough, *or* cistern.

ಟಾಂಕಿನಿ ṭāṅkini, *see* ಟಾಕಣ್.

ಟಾಕ್ ṭākṳ, *see* ಟಾಂಕ್.

ಟಾಕಣ್, ಟಾಕನ್ ṭākaṇṳ, ṭākanṳ, *s.* A Pegu pony.

ಟಾಕಾಟಾಕ್, ಟಾಕೋಟಾಕ್ ṭākāṭākṳ, ṭākōṭākṳ, *adj.* Quick, hurried, hasty.

ಟಾಣೆ, ಟಾಣ್ಯ ṭāṇe, ṭāṇya, *see* ಠಾಣ.

ಟಾಪು, ಟಾಪುಪಿತುವೆ, ಟಾಪೆ ṭāpu, ṭāpupituvè, ṭāpe, *s.* Banishment, transportation. –ಆಪಿನಿ to be punished with transportation.

ಟಾರ್ ṭārṳ, *see* ತಾರ್.

ಟಾರ ṭāra, *see* ತಾರ್.

ಟಾವು, ಟಾವುಟಿಕಾಣ್ ṭāvu, ṭāvuṭikāṇṳ, *see* ಠಾವು.

ಟಾಳಿ ṭāḷi, *s.* A lie, deceit.

ಟಾಳಿಪುನಿ ṭāḷipuni (ಟಾಳಿ), *v. a.* To deceive, cheat; *cf.* ಚಾಲಿಪುನಿ.

ಟಿಂಕ್ ṭiṅkṳ, *s.* The sound of a stringed, musical instrument, as a guitar, *etc.*; *also* ಟಿಂಕಿಣಿ.

ಟಿಞ್ಟಿಞ್ ṭiñṳṭiñṳ, *s.* Tinkling.

ಟಿಕ್ ṭikṳ, *s.* The sound, as of a pendulum. –ಆಪಿನಿ to tick.

ಟಿಕಾಣ್, ಟಿಕಾಣಿ ṭikāṇṳ, ṭikāṇi, *see* ಠಿಕಾಣ್.

ಟಿಕ್ಕಿ ṭikki, *s.* Hitting one marble with another in a game of marbles. –ಪಾಡುನಿ to hit a marble.

ಟಿಕ್ಕೆ ṭikke, *see* ತಕ್ಕೆ.

ಟಿಟ್ಟಿಭ ṭiṭṭibha, *s.* A lapwing.

ಟಿಪ್ಪಣೆ ṭippaṇè, *s.* A commentary; an explanatory note.

ಟಿಬ್ಬಿ ṭibbi, *see* ಟೀವು.

ಟಿಲ್ಲಿ tilli, *s.* The spleen, milt; liver.

ಟೀಕ್, ಟೀಕು ṭīkṳ, ṭīku, *s.* Meaning, interpretation, glossary. ಟೀಕಿಸುನಿ to translate, interpret, explain.

ಟೀಕ್ ṭīku, *see* ಠೀಕ್.

ಟೀಕಿ ṭiki, *s.* A small precious object; a small bell; *cf.* ಗೆಜ್ಜೆ. —ಮಣಿ a gold necklace.

ಟೀಪು ṭīpu, *s.* A stitch; *also* ಟೀಪು ಪೊಲಿಗೆ. —ಹಾಕುನಿ to stitch.

ಟೀವಿ ṭīvi, *see* ಠೀವಿ.

ಟುಕ್ಕುಟುಕ್ಕು, ಟುಕ್ಟುಕ್ ṭukkuṭukku, ṭukṭuku, *adv.* Rapidly, quickly. —ಲಾಗ್ಯುನಿ to dart, flit, fly.

ಟೆಂಕಸಾಲೆ, ಟೆಂಕ್ಸಾಲೆ ṭeṅkasālè, ṭeṅksālè, *see* ಠಂಕಸಾಲೆ.

ಟೇವಣಾತಿ, ಟೇವಣಿ ṭēvaṇāti, ṭēvaṇi, *see* ಠೇವಣಾತಿ.

ಟೊಂಕ ṭoṅka, *s.* The loins, hip. —ದೆಪ್ಪುನಿ, —ಪಾಡುನಿ to hop, leap on one leg.

ಟೊಪ್ಪಿ ṭoppi, *s.* A cap, hat, *or* helmet. 2. fraud, cheating. 3. failure, defeat. —ಆಪಿನಿ to fail. —ದೀಪಿನಿ a hat to put on. —ಪಾಡುನಿ to cheat.

ಟೊಳ್ಳು ṭoḷḷu, *see* ಡೊಳ್ಳು.

ಟೋಕ್, ಟೋಕು ṭōku, ṭōku, *s.* Cash, ready money. 2. total, aggregate; *also* ಟೋಂಕು, ಟೋಕಿ. —ಪಣವು money in cash. —ರೂಪಾಯಿ total rupees.

ಠ TH

ಠ ṭha,. The twenty-fifth letter of the alphabet.

ಠಂಕಸಾಲೆ ṭhaṅkasālè, *s.* A mint.

ಠಕಾಯಿಸುನಿ ṭhakāyisuni (ಠಕಾಯಿಸ್), *v. a.* To deceive, cheat. 2. to gain time by false representations.

ಠಕಾರಿ ṭhakāri, *adj.* Spurious, false, counterfeit. —ಮುತ್ತು a mock-pearl.

ಠಕ್ಕ್, ಠಕ್ಕು ṭhakku, ṭhakku, *s.* Dissimulation, deceit, pretence, hypocrisy, fraud. —ತನ chicanery; hoaxing. —ಪಣ್ಪುನಿ to lie; to pretend. —ಮಳ್ಪುನಿ to cheat, deceive, defraud.

ಠಕ್ಕೆ ṭhakke, *s.* A cheat, dissembler.

ಠಗರ್ ṭhagaru, *see* ಟಗರ್.

ಠರಾಯಿಸುನಿ ṭharāyisuni (ಠರಾಯಿಸ್), *v. a.* To compose, execute any literary work. 2. to fix, determine, settle.

ಠರಾವಣೆ ṭharāvaṇe, *s.* Composition, combination of the parts of any literary work *or* discourse; diction, style. 2. settlement, determination.

ಠವಣೆ ṭhavaṇè, *s.* Simple and compound addition. —ಕೂಡಾವುನಿ to add up figures. —ಪಾಡುನಿ to write down figures for adding.

ಠಸೆ, ಠಸ್ಸೆ ṭhasè, ṭhassè, *s.* A seal, stamp. 2. stamp duty. —ಕಾಗಜಿ a stamp paper.

ಠಾಣ, ಠಾಣ್ಯ ṭhāṇa, ṭhāṇya, *s.* A place, station; lodging; a garrison, police-station.

ಠಾರ್ ṭhāru, *adv.* At one stroke; completely, fully.

ಠಾವು ṭhāvu, *s.* A place, abode, lodging. 2. cause, occasion; *also* ಠಾವುಠಿಕಾಣ.

ಠಿಕಾಣ್, ಠಿಕಾಣಿ ṭhikāṇu, ṭhikāṇi, *s.* Resort, residence, station. 2. means, room, opportunity.

ಠೀಕ್, ಠೀಕು ṭhīku, ṭhīku, *adj.* Proper, fit. 2. exact, complete. 3. true. –ದ ವಣಸ್ a sumptuous meal.

ಠೀಪು ṭhīpu, *see* ಟೀಪು.

ಠೀವಿ ṭhīvi, *s.* Ostentation, display. 2. condition, state. 3. gait, figure, mien.

ಠೆಂಕಾರ, ಠೇಂಕಾರ ṭheṅkāra, ṭhēṅkāra, *s.* The twang of a bow. 2. haughtiness, pride.

ಠೇವಣಾತಿ, ಠೇವಣಿ ṭhēvaṇāti, ṭhēvaṇi, *s.* Deposit of cash. 2. ready-cash. 3. keeping money in a bank. –ದೀಪಿನಿ to deposit, keep money in a bank.

ಡ D

ಡ ḍa, The twenty-sixth letter of the alphabet.

ಡ ḍa, *a conditional particle affixed to verbs, signifying:* If. ಆಯೆ ಬತ್ತ್ಂಡ if he should come. ಬರ್ಪುಜಿಡ if he does not come.

ಡಂ ḍam, *see* ಡಮ್.

ಡಂಕ್, ಡಂಕ, ಡಂಕಣಿ ḍaṅku, ḍaṅka, ḍaṅkaṇi, *s.* A large, double drum. ಡಂಕಾಬಾಜಿ a drummer.

ಡಂಕಾರ ḍaṅkāra, *s.* The sound of a double drum.

ಡಂಕೆ ḍaṅkè, *see* ಡಂಕ್.

ಡಂಗ್, ಡಂಗು ḍaṅgu, ḍaṅgu, *s.* Surprise, wonder. –ಆಪಿನಿ to be surprised, stunned, overpowered.

ಡಂಗ, ಡಂಗರ ḍaṅga, ḍaṅgara, *see* ಡಂಗ್ರ.

ಡಂಗಡಂಗ ḍaṅgaḍaṅga, *adv.* Hastily.

ಡಂಗುನಿ ḍaṅguni, *see* ಡಂಗುನಿ

ಡಂಗೆ ḍaṅgè, *see* ಡಂಕೆ.

ಡಂಗ್ರ ḍaṅgra, *s.* Proclamation by beating of a gong *etc.* –ಹಾಕುನಿ to proclaim in such a manner.

ಡಂಡಣ್ ḍaṇḍaṇu, *s.* The sound of a large drum *or* gong.

ಡಂಬ ḍamba, *see* ಡಂಭ.

ಡಂಬರ ḍambara, *s.* Pomp, grandeur.

ಡಂಬರೆ ḍambarè, *see* ಡೆಂಬರೆ.

ಡಂಭ ḍambha, *s.* Ostentation, display. –ಕೊಚ್ಚುನಿ to boast, brag.

ಡಂಭಾಚಾರ, ಡಂಭಾಟ ḍambhācāra, ḍambhāṭa, *s.* Ostentation, empty show.

ಡಕ್ಕ, ಡಕ್ಕೆ ḍakka, ḍakkè, *s.* A large kind of double drum, shaped like an hour-glass. —ದ ಬಲಿ carrying an idol in procession round its temple with beating of such a drum. —ದಾಯಿ a drummer. *adv. see* ಡಕ್ಕ.

ಡಣಡಣ ḍaṇaḍaṇa, *s.* The sound of a large bell.

ಡಪ್ಪು ḍappu, *s.* A small drum beaten on one side; a tabret.

ಡಬ್ಬ ḍabba, *s.* A noise of anything falling into water. —ಬೀಳುವುದು to fall into water with a noise.

ಡಬ್ಬ ḍabba, *s.* A tin box, as of kerosine oil.

ಡಬ್ಬಿ ḍabbi, *s.* A small box, chest. 2. a box kept in temples, for receiving offerings. ಪೊಡಿ— a snuff box.

ಡಬ್ಬು ḍabbu, *s.* A lie, falsehood. 2. a boast, brag. 3. a half anna piece. —ಗಾರೆ a liar; a braggart. —ಹಾಕುವಿ to tell a lie; to brag.

ಡಮ್ ḍam, *s.* The noise of firing a gun. —ಡಮ್ the noise of a drum.

ಡಮರ್, ಡಮರುಕ, ಡಮರುಗ ḍamarụ, ḍamaruka, ḍamaruga, *s.* A small drum, shaped like an hour-glass.

ಡಮಾನ, ಡಮಾರ ḍamāna, ḍamāra, *s.* A kettle-drum.

ಡಮಾಮಿ ḍamāmi, *s.* A hollow sound, empty noise. 2. false dignity; ostentation, empty show.

ಡಲಾಯಿತೆ ḍalāyite, *s.* A belted peon.

ಡವಾಲ್, ಡವಾಲಿ ḍavālụ, ḍavāli, *s.* A peon's belt. —ಪಾಡೋಳುವಿ to put on a belt.

ಡವುಲು ḍavulu, *see* ಡೌಲು.

ಡಾಂಬಿಕೆ, ಡಾಂಭಿಗೆ ḍāmbike, ḍāmbhige, *s.* A pedant, one given to affectation. 2. a hypocrite.

ಡಾಕ್ ḍākụ, *s.* Vaccination. —ಪಾಡುವಿ to vaccinate.

ಡಾಮ್‌ಡುಮ್ ḍāmḍum, *see* ಧಾಮ್‌ಧುಮ್.

ಡಾಲ್ ḍālụ, *s.* A shield.

ಡಾಲ್ಚಿನಿ ḍālćini, *see* ದಾಲ್ಚಿನಿ.

ಡಾಳಿ ḍāḷi, *s.* An army.

ಡಿಂಕಿ diṅki, *s.* A gymnastic feat.

ಡಿಂಡಿಂಡಿ ḍiṇḍiṇḍi, *s.* The knolling of a bell.

ಡಿಂಡಿಮ, ಡಿಡಿಮ ḍiṇḍima, ḍiḍima, *s.* A small drum.

ಡಿಬ್, ಡಿಬ್‌ಡಿಬ್ ḍib, ḍibḍib. *s.* The noise of a violent blow.

ಡಿಬ್ಬು dibbu, *s.* A push with the leg.

ಡೀಲ್ ḍīlụ, *adj.* Loose, not tight. 2. free, unrestrained; *also* ಡಿಲ, ಡೀಲು.

ಡುಕ್ ḍuk, *see* ಟುಕ್ಕುಟುಕ್ಕು.

ಡುಗ್ಗು ḍuggu, *s.* Uneasiness.

ಡುಬಾಯಿಸುನಿ ḍubāyisuni (ಡುಬಾಯಿಸುನಿ), *v.a.* To drown 2. to cause loss. 3. to deceive, cheat.

ಡುಬ್ಡುಬ್ ḍubḍub. *s.* The sound of a small drum.

ಡುಬ್ಬ ḍubba, *see* ಡಬ್ಬ.

ಡುಮ್ಡುಮ್ ḍumḍum, *s.* The sound of a large drum. 2. *see* ಡಮ್.

ಡುರ್ಕುಡುರ್ಕು ḍurkuḍurku, *s.* The noise of breaking wind downward.

ಡೆಂಸನ ḍennana, *see* ಪಾಡ್ದನ.

ಡೇರೆ ḍērè, *s.* A tent. –ಪಾಡುನಿ. –ಹಾಕುನಿ to pitch a tent.

ಡೈಮಾನ್ ḍeimānu, *s.* Diamond in cards.

ಡೊಂಕ್, ಡೊಂಕು ḍoṅku, ḍoṅku, *s.* Crookedness. *adj.* Crooked, curved. 2. perverse, cross. –ಪಾಡುನಿ to limp, hobble.

ಡೊಂಕ ḍaṅka, *see* ಟೊಂಕ.

ಡೊಂಕೆಲ್ ḍoṅkelu, *s.* Crookedness.

ಡೊಂಣೆ ḍoṇṇe, *s.* A cudgel, club.

ಡೊಂಬರಾಟ, ಡೊಂಬಾಟ ḍambarāṭa, ḍombāṭa, *see* ಡೊಂಬರಾಟ.

ಡೊಂಬಾರೆ ḍombāre, *see* ಡೊಂಬೆ.

ಡೊಂಬಿ, ಡೊಂಬೆ ḍombi, ḍombe, *see* ಡೊಂಬಿ.

ಡೊಂಬೆರ್ ḍomberu, *see* ಡೊಂಬೆರ್.

ಡೊಂಬೆಲ್ ḍombelu, *see* ಡೊಂಬೆಲ್.

ಡೊಕ್ಕ, ಡೊಕ್ಕಾಲ್, ಡೊಗ್ಗಲ್, ಡೊಗ್ಗಾಲ್, ಡೊಗ್ಗು ḍokka, ḍokkālu, ḍoggalu, ḍoggālu, ḍoggu, *see* ಡೊಗ್ಗಲ್, ಡೊಗ್ಗು.

ಡೊಪ್ಪ ḍoppa (-ದ-ಒಪ್ಪ), *postp.* With, together with. ಆಯು– with him. ನರಮಾನ್ಯ– with man; *cf.* ಒಪ್ಪ.

ಡೊಪ್ಪೆ ḍoppe, *see* ಡೊಪ್ಪೆ.

ಡೊಳ್ಳು ḍoḷḷu, *adj.* Fat, stout, large. 2. void, hollow. *s.* A pot-belly.

ಡೊಳ್ಳೆ ḍoḷḷe, *s.* A pot-bellied man.

ಡೋಕು ḍōku, *see* ಢೋಕು.

ಡೋಬಿ ḍōbi, *s.* A washerman.

ಡೋಲ್ ḍōlu, *see* ಡೌಲು.

ಡೋಲಂಗಿ ḍōlaṅgi, *see* ಡೌಲಂಗಿ.

ಡೋಲಿ ḍōli, *s.* A dooly *or* litter.

ಡೋಲು, ಡೋಳು ḍōlu, ḍōḷu, *see* ದೋಲು.

ಡೋಳಾ ḍōḷā, *s.* The eye. *adj.* Stout.

ಡೌಲತ್ ḍoulatu, *see* ದೌಲತ್.

ಡೌಲು ḍoulu, *s.* An estimate, valuation. 2. appearance; mien; air; demeanor.

ಢ DH

ಢ ḍha, The twenty-seventh letter of the alphabet.

ಢಂಕ ḍhaṅka, *see* ಡಂಕ.

ಢೇರೆ ḍhērè, *see* ಡೇರೆ.

ಢೋಕು ḍhōku, *s.* Injury, defect. 2. fear, alarm.

ಣ N̤

ಣ ṇa, *s.* The twenty-eighth letter of the alphabet.

ಣಪ್ಪಡ ṇappaḍa, *s.* Weariness, exhaustion; harassing. —ಪೋಪಿನಿ to be done up, harassed.

ಣಳ ṇaḷa, *adj.* Smooth.

ತ T

ತ ta, *s.* The twenty-ninth letter of the alphabet.

ತಂಕ taṅka, *s.* The lungs. 2. the liver. 3. *see* ಸಂಕ. —ಕಡಿಯುನಿ, —ಪುಡಾವುನಿ to be very much fatigued.

ತಂಕಿ taṅki, *see* ಟಾಂಕಿ.

ತಂಗ್ taṅgụ, *see* ಶಾಂಗ್.

ತಂಗಡ taṅgaḍa, *see* ಸಂಗಡ.

ತಂಗಡಿ taṅgaḍi, *s.* A male's younger sister; *also* ತಂಗಿ.

ತಂಗದ taṅgada, *adv.* Together.

ತಂಗಾಳಿ taṅgāḷi, *s.* A cool breeze.

ತಂಗೀಸ್ taṅgīsụ, *adj.* Cold, chill. *s.* A fishing tackle, fishing line.

ತಂಗುಳಿ taṅguḷi, *see* ಚಂಗುಲಿ.

ತಂಙಣೆಮಂಙಣೆ taṅṅaṇemaṅṅaṇè, *s.* Deception, imposition, pretence. —ಮಳ್ಪುನಿ to impose upon; to pretend.

ತಂಚಿ taṅči, *s.* A bag, purse.

ತಂಜ taṅja, *s.* Evening, sunset, night. —ದ ಬೊಳ್ಳಿ the evening star.

ತಂಙಾನ taṅṅana, *s.* Rice boiled in the preceding evening, stale food.

ತಂಟಾವುನಿ taṇṭāvuni, *see* ಶಾಂಟಾವುನಿ.

ತಂಟುನಿ taṇṭuni, *see* ಶಾಂಟುನಿ.

ತಂಟೆ taṇṭe, *s.* Annoyance, trouble, difficulty. 2. mischief. 3. interference, meddling, connection. —ಗಾರೆ, —ಲ್ಯಾರಿ a troublesome, mischievous *or* obstinate man. —ತಕ್ರಾರ್ vexation, molestation. —ತರಕ್, —ಸರಕ್ bad goods; rotten things. —ಮಳ್ಪುನಿ to annoy, trouble. ಆಕ್ಲೆಡಯು ತಂಟೆ ಬೊಡ್ಚಿ have nothing to do with him.

ತಂಡ್ taṇḍụ, *s.* Whole. 2. *see* ದಂಡ್. *adj.* Entire, whole.

ತಂಡ್, ತಂಡ taṇḍụ, taṇḍa, *s.* Multitude, crowd, host, army. 2. a side, party.

ತಂಡಾತುಂಡು taṇḍātuṇḍu, *see* ತುಂಡು ತುಂಡು.

ತಂಡಾಸ್ taṇḍāsụ, *s.* A privy on the bank of a river.

ತಂಡಿ taṇḍi, *see* ಚಂಡಿ.

ತಂಡಿಗೆ taṇḍigè, *see* ದಂಡಿಗೆ.

ತಂಡುತುಂಡು taṇḍutuṇḍu, *see* ತುಂಡು ತುಂಡು.

ತಂಡುಲ taṇḍula, *s.* Rice in a raw state.

ತಂಡೆ taṇḍè, *s.* A silver anklet.

ತಂಡೆಲ್, ತಂಡೆಲೆ taṇḍelụ, taṇḍele, *s.* The captain of a native vessel; a boatman, tindal.

ತಂಣ taṇṇa, *see* ಸಂಣ.

ತಂಣನ, ತಂಣ್ಮೆಣ taṇṇana, taṇṇụmeṇa, *see* ತಲ್ಲೈನ.

ತಂಣಾಸ್ taṇṇasụ, *see* ತಣಾಸ್.

ತಂಣಿ taṇṇi, *adj.* Cold; *cf.* ಸಂಣಿ. ತಂಣೀರ್ cold water.

ತಂತ್, ತಂತು tantụ, tantu, *s.* Thread. 2. pulse, vein, nerve. ತಂತ್ ಮಾತ್ರ ಪಂಡುಂಡು only the pulse beats.

ತಂತಿ tanti, *s.* Wire. 2. the string of a musical instrument. —ಟಪ್ಪಾಲ್ the telegraph.

ತಂತ್ರ tantra, *s.* Craft, cunning, device, trick, intrigue, plot. 2. worship performed by hand without formulas. 3. a religious treatise on formulas, rites, *etc.* for the worship of the deities. 4. the part of the Vēdas treating of magical and mystical formulas. 5. subservience, service, dependance. —ಗಾರೆ, —ದಾಯೆ, —ಮೂರ್ತಿ a crafty man. —ದಾರ್, *see* ತಂತ್ರಿ. —ಮಳ್ಪುನಿ to play tricks, to deceive.

ತಂತ್ರಜ್ಞೆ tantrajńe, *s.* A man of art.

ತಂತ್ರಿ, ತಂತ್ರಿಕೆ tantri, tantrike, *s.* One versed in mystical formulas, rites, *etc.* for the worship of the deities.

ತಂದ್ tandụ, *see* ಸಂದ್.

ತಂದ್ಪುಡಿ, ತಂದ್ಮುಡಿ tandụpuḍi, tandụmuḍi, *see* ತಂದೊಡಿ.

ತಂದನ tandana, *s.* An unmeaning sound, used in humming a tune. 2. red sandal; *cf.* ಚಂದನ. *adj.* Small. 2. deteriorated, reduced, worn out ಈ ನಗ ತಂದನ ಆಂಡ್ this ornament is worn out.

ತಂದೆಲ್ tandelụ, *s.* A cudgel, club; *also* —ಗುದಿಗೆ.

ತಂದೊಡಿ tandoḍi, *s.* The handle of a plough.

ತಂದೊಳಿಗೆ tandoḷigè, *s.* The white dammer tree *Vateria Indica.*

ತಂನನ tannana, *see* ಚಂದನ.

ತಂನವು tannavu, *pron.* One's own; his own.

ತಂನಾತೆ, ತಂನಾತೆಗ್ tannāte, tannātegụ, *pron.* For oneself, himself, itself. *adv.* Of one's own accord, by itself. —ನಡತೊಂಬುನಿ to walk for oneself, *i. e.* to act as one likes.

ತಂನಾಯೆ tannāye, *s.* One's own man; a dependant; a friend, favourite.

ತಂನಿಮಾಣಿಗ tannimāṇiga, *s.* The name of a female demon.

ತಂನೆ tannè, *adv.* Near, by, close, *s.* A bystander. —ಉಂತುನಿ to stand by one. —ತೊರಪುನಿ to vex. —ಬರ್ಪಿನಿ to come together.

ತಂನೆನ tannena, *adj.* Cold, cool.

ತಂನೆಪಿಂನೆ tannèpinnè, *s.* The old and young. 2. box and dice.

ತಂನೇಡೆ **tannēḍe**, *see* ತೇಡೆ.

ತಂಪಡೆ **tampaḍe**, *s.* Two slips of a bamboo placed close to each other, and tied together.

ತಂಪು **tampu**, *s.* Coolness, cold. *adj.* Cool, cold. —ಘಾಳಿ cool breeze. —ಆಪಿನಿ to become cool; to be appeased, pacified. —ಮಳ್ಪುನಿ to cool; to appease, pacify.

ತಂಬಕ್ **tambakụ**, *s.* The prince's metal, an alloy of certain metals, pinchbeck. 2. tobacco

ತಂಬಟ, ತಂಬಟೆ **tambaṭa, tambaṭe**, A tambourine, war-drum. 2. boast, bragging. 3. *see* ಚಂಬೊಡಿ. —ಕೊಟ್ಟುನಿ to brag.

ತಂಬಡ **tambaḍa**, *s.* A large drum.

ತಂಬರ **tambara**, *s.* Coriander. 2. *see* ಸಂಬಾರ.

ತಂಬರಂಡೆ **tambaraṇḍe**, *s.* Garlic.

ತಂಬಾಕ್ **tambākụ**, *see* ತಂಬಕ್.

ತಂಬಿಗೆ **tambige**, *s.* A small, round, metal vessel.

ತಂಬಿಲ **tambila**, *s.* An ordinary offering to demons, *etc.* ಅಗೆಲ್— *see under* ಅಗೆಲ್. ನಾಗ— an offering to serpents. ಭೂತ— a grand offering to demons. —ಕೊರ್ಪಿನಿ to give such offerings.

ತಂಬು **tambu**, *s.* A tent. —ಪಾಡುನಿ, —ಹಾಕುನಿ to pitch a tent; to remain, stay; to delay. —ಪೊಯಿಪಿನಿ to halt, stop in a march.

ತಂಬುರಿ, ತಂಬೂರಿ **tamburi, tambūri**, *s.* A five-stringed guitar. 2. a soldier's drum.

ತಂಬುಳಿ **tambuḷi**, *s.* A kind of chaṭni *or* sauce, prepared of cocoanut milk, condiments *etc.* with *or* without greens, and eaten with rice.

ತಂಬುಳು **tambuḷu**, *s.* Tamil.

ತಂಬೇರ್ **tambērụ**, *s.* A kind of reckoning in the game of yekkaḍi (ಎಕ್ಕಡಿ).

ತಂಬೇರುನಿ **tambēruni**, *eee* ತೆಂಬೇರುನಿ.

ತಂಬೊಡಿ, **tamboḍi**, *see* ತಂಬಟ. 2. *see* ಚಂಬೊಡಿ.

ತಂಬೊಳಿ **tamboḷi**, *see* ತಂಬುಳಿ.

ತಂಮಟೆ **tammaṭe**, *see* ತಂಬಟ.

ತಂಮಣ **tammaṇa**, *s.* Hospitality, entertainment; dinner. —ದ ಒಣಸ್ a grand wedding dinner. —ಪಾಡುನಿ to give a dinner to a pregnant women. —ಮಳ್ಪುನಿ to give a dinner to a wedding party.

ತಂಮಣಿಪುನಿ, ತಂಮಣ್ಯುನಿ, ತಂಮನಿಪುನಿ **tammaṇipuni, tammaṇyuni, tammanipuni** (ತಂಮಣಿ, ತಂಮನಿ), *v. a.* To entertain a guest, to give a dinner.

ತಂಮಲೆ **tammale**, *s.* A maternal uncle. 2. a father-in-law. 3. a kind of tare growing among corns *etc.* ಕುಡುತ— a kind of tare found in gram.

ತಂಮುಗೆ **tammuge**, *see* ತಂಮ್ಮಿಗೆ.

ತಂಮೆಣ **tammeṇa**, *see* ತಲ್ಮೆನ.

ತಂಮೆಪುನಿ **tammepuni**, *see* ತಮೆಪುನಿ.

ತಂಮೆರ್, ತಂಮೆರಿ **tammerụ, tammeri**, *see* ತಮೆರ್.

ತಂಮೆಲುನಿ tammeluni, *see* ತಮೆಲುನಿ.

ತಂಮ್ಮೆಯ tammeiya, *s.* An affectionate form of addressing a younger brother.

ತಂಮ್ಗೆ tammgė, *s.* A kind of rice.

ತಂಟುರ್ನಿ tarnṭuni (ತಂಟ್ರ್), *v. n.* To shrivel.

ತಕತ್ತ್ takattu, *s.* A throne.

ತಕತಕ, ತಕಪಕ takataka, takapaka, *s.* Agility in dancing, *etc.* 2. bubbling in boiling. *adv.* Nimbly, briskly.

ತಕ್ಕ takka, *adj.* Fit, suitable, proper, deserving, worthy. —ತನ fitness. —ಪಾತೆರ a proper word. —ಸಮಯ a good opportunity, favourable season. ತಕ್ಕಾದ್ suitably, properly, deservedly.

ತಕ್ಕಂದ takkanda, *see* ಚಕ್ಕಂದ.

ತಕ್ಕಟ್, ತಕ್ಕಟ್ಟ್ takkaṭu, takkaṭṭu, *adj.* As much as is suitable; adequate, sufficient.

ತಕ್ಕಡಿ takkaḍi, *s.* Large scales. —ದಾಯಿ one who cheats in weighing; a rogue.

ತಕ್ಕಣ, ತಕ್ಕನ takkaṇa, takkana, *s.* A small spoon. 2. a small kind of mat; *also* ತಕ್ಕನಪಜೆ. *adj.* Little. ಅರಿಯುನಡೆಗ್ ತಕ್ಕಣ ಪತ್ತುನಾಯಿ *lit.* one who holds a spoon where (anything) drops, *i. e.* one who takes advantage of another's weakness, a stingy man.

ತಕ್ಕೆಯಿಮುಂಗ್ಯೆ takkeyimuṅgei, *s.* The upper arm and forearm.

ತಕ್ಕೆಲಗ್, ತಕ್ಕೆಲೊಗು takkelagu, takkelogu, *see* ತಶ್ಯಾಲೊಗು *under* ತಶ್ಯಾಲ.

ತಕ್ಕೊನ takkona, *see* ತಕ್ಕಣ.

ತಕ್ರಾರ್ takrāru, *s.* Interference, hinderance. 2. dispute, quarrel.

ತಕ್ರೀರ್ takrīru, *s.* Objection, protest. —ಅರ್ಜಿ a counter petition. —ಮಳ್ಪುನಿ to object, protest, quarrel.

ತಕ್ಶೀರ್ takšīru, *s.* An offence, crime, fault.

ತಗಡ್ tagaḍu, *s.* A thin metal plate. —ಭಂಗಾರ pure gold. ಭಂಗಾರದ— a gold leaf.

ತಗರು tagaru, *see* ಟಗರ್.

ತಗರುನಿ tagaruni (ತಗರ್), *v. n.* To draw near.

ತಗವು, ತಗಾದಿ, ತಗಾದೆ, ತಗಾವು tagavu, tagādi, tagādė, tagāvu, *s.* Dunning for payment. 2. peremptory demand.

ತಗುಮೆ tagume, *see* ತಗ್ಗೆ.

ತಗುಲೆ tagulė *s.* A bug.

ತಗೆ tagė, *s.* A female's elder brother.

ತಗ್ಯೆರ್, ತಗ್ಯೆರೆ tageiru, tageirė, *s.* Discharge, dismissal. —ಮಳ್ಪುನಿ to turn out, dismiss.

ತಗೊರಿ tagori, *s.* The potter's wheel.

ತಗ್ಗ್ taggu, *s.* Low ground, a dale, valley, descent, declivity. *adj.* Low, depressed. —ತನ lowliness, humility.

ತಗ್ಗಾವುನಿ taggāvuni, *c. v.* (*of* ತಗ್ಗು

ನಿ) To lower, humble. 2. to diminish, lessen. 3. to level down.

ತಗ್ಗುನಿ tagguni (ತಗ್ಗ), *v. n.* To be humble, modest. 2. to incline, lean.

ತಗ್ಗೆಲೆ taggele, *s.* A lowly *or* humble man; *also* ತಗ್ಗದಿನಾಯಿ.

ತಗ್ಮಳ್ tagmaḷụ, *s.* A female slave, maid-servant.

ತಗ್ಮೆ tagme, *s.* A male slave, man-servant.

ತಜಂಕ್ tajaṅkụ, *s.* The plant *Cassia tora.*

ತಜಪು tajapu, *s.* Notching, indentation. *adj.* Indented, notched. —ಪಾಡುನಿ to cut into a row of teeth.

ತಜಪುನಿ tajapuni (ತಜ), *v. a.* To chop, cut in pieces.

ತಜಿಬಿಜಿ tajibiji, *s.* Endeavour, effort, exertion. 2. cogitation, reflection. —ಮುಳ್ಪುನಿ to endeavour, try; to reflect; to get out of a scape by unlawful means.

ತಟ್ಗ tatụga, *s.* A ladle.

ತಟಿ taṭa, *s.* A shore, bank.

ತಟಕ್ taṭakụ, *s.* A drop.

ತಟಕ್ಕ taṭakka, *see* ತಟ್ಟನೆ.

ತಟಪಟ taṭapaṭa, *s.* A slapping sound. 2. loquacity.

ತಟಪ್ಪ taṭappa, *adv.* Heavily, with a jerk. 2. suddenly. —ಬೂರುನಿ to fall heavily *or* suddenly.

ತಟಾನೆ taṭāne, *see* ತಟ್ಟನೆ.

ತಟಾಲ್, ತಟಾಲ, ತಟಾಲಿ taṭālụ, taṭāla, taṭāli, *see* ಥಟಾಲ.

ತಟಾವು taṭāvu, *s.* A lake, pond.

ತಟೀಲ taṭīla, *s.* A snapping noise.

ತಟ್ಟ್ taṭṭụ, *s.* A country pony, a pack-horse. *also* —ಕುದುರೆ. 2. the forearm; *also* ಕೈತಟ್ಟ. *adj.* Serious, critical. —ತಡವು much delay. —ಸಂಕಡ a serious illness. ಮುಂಡೆಯಿದ— the stalk of screw pine.

ತಟ್ಟವಸ್ taṭṭụvasụ, *see* ತಟ್ಟಾಸ.

ತಟ್ಟ taṭṭa, *see* ತಟ್ಟನೆ.

ತಟ್ಟ taṭṭa, *see* ಚಟ್ಟ.

ತಟ್ಟಂಕ್ taṭṭaṅkụ, *s.* Hinderance, obstacle.

ತಟ್ಟನೆ taṭṭane, *adv.* Speedily, quickly. 2. suddenly, unexpectedly, without premeditation. —ನಡಪುನಿ, —ಪೋಪಿನಿ to go quickly *or* suddenly. —ಪಣ್ಪುನಿ to say instantly *or* without premeditation.

ತಟ್ಟಪ್ಪ taṭṭappa, *see* ತಟಪ್ಪ.

ತಟ್ಟಾವುನಿ taṭṭāvuni, *c. v.* (*of* ತಟ್ಟುನಿ) To cause to hit, strike.

ತಟ್ಟಾಶಿ, ತಟ್ಟಾಸ್ taṭṭāśi, taṭṭāsụ, *see* ತಟ್ಟಾಸ.

ತಟ್ಟಿ taṭṭi, *s.* A screen *or* blind made of split bamboos, cadjan palm leaves. *etc.* 2. a honeycomb. ಅತ್ತರದ— a mat made of split canes. ಕೈ— a small, low kind of wooden trough. —ಕುಡುಪು a wicker strainer, sieve. —ತಮ್ಮುಡ್ಜಿ the wooden lid and the strainer of a culinary vessel. —ಕಟ್ಟುನಿ to put up a screen *or* blind as protection from rain.

ತಟ್ಟಿಮುಟ್ಟು tāṭṭimuṭṭu, *s.* A vessel for distilling liquor. 2. culinary utensils. 3. household stuff.

ತಟ್ಟು taṭṭu, *see* ತಟ್ಟಿ.

ತಟ್ಟುಗ taṭṭuga, *s.* A flat kind of trough for serving boiled rice.

ತಟ್ಟುನಿ taṭṭuni, *see* ತಟ್ಟೊಣುನಿ.

ತಟ್ಟುಮುಟ್ಟು taṭṭumuṭṭu, *s.* Strait, dilemma; *cf.* ತಟ್ಟಿಮುಟ್ಟು.

ತಟ್ಟೆ taṭṭe, *adj.* Empty, void within. —ಸರಕ್ good and bad things.

ತಟ್ಟೊಣುನಿ taṭṭoṇuni *v. refl.* To (*of* ತಟ್ಟುನಿ), carry on the haunch, as natives do a child.

ತಟ್ವಾಸ್ taṭvāsu, *s.* Unevenness, inequality, variation, as in weighing.

ತಡ್ಪೆ taḍupe, *see* ತಪ್ಪೆ.

ತಡ್ತೊಣುನಿ taḍutoṇuni, *v. refl.* (*of* ತಡಿಪುನಿ) To quarrel *or* dispute mutually.

ತಡ taḍa, *see* ತಡವು.

ತಡ taḍa, *s.* Wool, fur. 2. skin with soft hair.

ತಡಕ್ taḍaku, *s.* Intoxication.

ತಡಪು taḍapu, *see* ತಡೆಪ್ಪು.

ತಡಮಾಟ taḍamāṭa, *s.* Fumbling.

ತಡಮೆ taḍame, *s.* A kind of stile *or* narrow entrance to a garden.

ತಡಯಿ taḍayi, *s.* A small earthen cup *or* plate.

ತಡವ taḍava, *see* ಜಡಾವು.

ತಡವು taḍavu, *s.* Delay, hinderance, impediment. 2. a slow-coach *or* dilatory person. —ಆಪಿನಿ to get late, to be delayed. —ಮಳ್ಪುನಿ to delay, linger.

ತಡಿ taḍi, *s.* An inferior kind of saddle. —ದಪ್ಪುನಿ to join imperceptibly.

ತಡಿಪುನಿ taḍipuni (ತಡಿ), *v. a.* To quarrel, dispute, contend, struggle. ನ್ಯಾಯೊ— to dispute, argue.

ತಡೆ taḍe, *s.* Hinderance, obstacle. 2. charm for serpents. —ಕಟ್ಟುನಿ, —ದೀಪಿನಿ to stop the motion of a serpent by incantations; to obstruct, hinder. —ತಪ್ಪಾವುನಿ to remove the charm, to break a spell. —ಪಾಡುನಿ to hinder, impede; to charm.

ತಡೆಪಾವುನಿ taḍepāvuni, *c. v.* (*of* ತಡೆಪಿನಿ) To hinder, impede, obstruct.

ತಡೆಪಿನಿ, ತಡೆಪುನಿ taḍepini, taḍepuni, (ತಡೆ), *v. a.* To hold off: to hinder, keep back, prevent, stop; to oppose.

ತಡೆಪ್ಪು taḍeppu, *s.* Stoppage, resistance. 2. anything put up to stop a passage.

ತಡೆಯಿ taḍeyi, *see* ತಡಯಿ.

ತಡೆಯುನಿ, ತಡೆವುನಿ taḍeyuni, taḍevuni (ತಡೆ), *v. n.* To halt, stop, tarry. 2. to bear, endure, suffer. ಯೆನಡ್ಡ್ ನನ ತಡೆವೆರೆ ಬಲ್ಲಿ I can bear it no more.

ತಡೆವು taḍevu, *s.* A halt, stopping, tarrying. 2. impediment, hinderance.

ತಡೆವೊಣುನಿ taḍevoṇuni, *v. refl.* (*of* ತಡೆಯುನಿ) To bear, suffer; to be patient.

ತಡ್ಪು taḍpu, *s.* A foreign cloth. —ಮಗ್ಗ a kind of loom.

ತಡ್ಪುನಿ taḍpuni, *see* ತದಿಪುನಿ.

ತಡ್ಪೆ taḍpè, *s.* A sieve for cleansing grain, *etc.* —ಮುಂಡಾಸ್ a large turban. —ಮೈಪು *lit.* a sieve and a brom: a bad omen; a cruel woman.

ತಡ್ಯ, ತಡ್ಡ್ಯ taḍya, taḍḍya, *s.* A step, stair. ಇಡೆತಡ್ಯ the middle step. ತಿರ್ತ್‌ಡ್ಯ the lower step, threshold. ಮಿತ್ತಡ್ಯ the lintel of a door.

ತಣಸ್ taṇasu, *s.* Wetness, dampness. *adj.* Wet. —ನೆಲ wet ground.

ತಣಿಪುನಿ taṇipuni (ತಣಿ), *v. a.* To cool, pacify, soothe, comfort.

ತಣಿಯುನಿ taṇiyuni (ತಣಿ), *v. n.* To become cool, calm.

ತಣಿಲ್ taṇilu, *see* ಚಣಿಲ್.

ತಣು taṇu, *s.* Coolness, cold. 2. quenching, appeasement. —ಮಳ್ಪುನಿ to cool; appease, as hunger, *etc.*

ತತ್ಕ್ಷಣ tatkshaṇa, *adv.* Instantly.

ತತಂಗ tatanga, *s.* Obstacle, hinderance, complication, entanglement.

ತತ್ಲೈಲಸ tateilasa, *s.* A joyous dance.

ತತ್ಕಾಲ tatkāla, *adj.* The time then *or* now. ತತ್ಕಾಲೊಗು for the present, for the time being.

ತತ್ತ tatta, *s.* A shuffle, artifice; 2. jesting, joking. *adv.* Shufflingly. 2. jestingly. —ಪಾತೆರುನಿ to speak shufflingly *or* jestingly.

ತತ್ತಾರ tattāra, *see* ತತ್ವಾರ.

ತತ್ತಿ tatti (*past part. of* ತಪ್ಪುನಿ), *adj.* Missed, beyond reach, failed. —ವಿಷಯ, —ಸಂಗತಿ what is past; a lost opportunity; a mistake.

ತತ್ರ tatra, *s.* An umbrella.

ತತ್ವ tatva, *s.* Essential nature, real nature of the soul. 2. the Supreme Being. 3. truth, reality, substance. 4. mind, intellect. 5. identity. —ಬೋಧನೆ instruction in the real nature of the Supreme and human spirit; *cf.* ಸತ್ವ.

ತತ್ವಾದಿ tatvādi, *s.* Mystical theology.

ತತ್ವಾರ tatvāra, *s.* Destitution, [want.

ತತ್ವಾರ್ಥ tatvārtha, *s.* The essential purpose.

ತದನಂತರ tadanantara, *adv.* Afterwards, subsequently.

ತದಿಗಿಣ tadigiṇa, *s.* Beating time in dancing to music. 2. intrigue, plot. 3. upsetting, fall. —ಪಾಡುನಿ to dance; to be overturned. —ಮಳ್ಪುನಿ to intrigue.

ತದಿಗೆ **tadigè**, *s.* The third day of the lunar fortnight.

ತದ್ದ್ **taddụ**, *s.* Retch, qualm.

ತದ್ದು **taddu**, *s.* An eruption *or* swelling, erysipelas.

ತದ್ದುನಿ **tadduni** (ತದ್ದ್), *v. n.* To retch, puke, to be qualmish.

ತನ **tana**, *An affix to form abstract nouns*; *e.g.* ಯೆಡ್ಡೆ good, ಯೆಡ್ಡೆತನ goodness. 2. *genit. of* ತಾನ್.

ತನಕಿ, ತನಿಖಿ **tanaki, tanikhi**, *s.* Examination, investigation, inquiry.

ತನಸ್ **tanasụ**, *see* ತಣಸ್.

ತನಿಪುನಿ **tanipuni**, *see* ತಣಿಪುನಿ.

ತನಿಯುನಿ **taniyuni**, *see* ತಣಿಯುನಿ.

ತನು **tanu**, *see* ತಣು. 2. the body.

ತನುಕುಳು **tanukuḷu**, *pron. hon. plur. of* ತಾನ್.

ತನೆ **tanè**, *s.* Conceiving, breeding, as cattle, sheep, *etc.* —ಆಪಿನಿ to be conceived. —ಏರುನಿ, —ದಿಂಜುನಿ to be big with young. ಮೈ— the incipient stage of being with young.

ತನೆಯುನಿ **taneyuni** (ತನೆ), *v.n.* Cattle *or* animals to be big with young.

ತಪ **tapa**, *see* ತಪಸ್.

ತಪತಪ **tapatapa**, *s.* Palpitation.

ತಪರಾಕ್, ತಪರಾಕೆ, ತಪರಾತ್ **taparākụ, taparākè, taparātụ**, *s.* Slapping the cheek *or* temple.

ತಪಲ **tapala**, *s.* A spear, lance.

ತಪಲೆ **tapalè**, *s.* A large metallic cooking vessel, saucepan.

ತಪಶೀಲ್ **ṭapaśīlụ**, *see* ತಫ್ಸೀಲ್.

ತಪಸ್ **tapasụ**, *s.* Prayer, devotion, religious austerities. ತಪಸಿ a devotee, ascetic. ತಪೋಬಲ power of devotion.

ತಪಾಲ್ **tapālụ**, *see* ಟಪ್ಪಾಲ್.

ತಪಾವತ್ **tapāvatụ**, *s.* Difference, discrepancy. 2. cheating, deceit. 3. prevarication, equivocation, evasion.

ತಪಿಯುನಿ **tapiyuni** (ತಪಿ), *v.n.* To burn, be inflamed, hot.

ತಪೋಧನೆ **tapōdhane**, *s.* An ascetic.

ತಪೋನಿಷ್ಠ **tapōnishṭha**, *s.* The practice of religious austerities.

ತಪೋಬಲ **tapōbala**, *see under* ತಪಸ್.

ತಪ್ತ **tapta**, *adj.* Heated, inflamed, boiling, burnt. 2. affected with pain *or* grief. —ದೇಹ heated body. —ಮನಸ್ mind affected with grief.

ತಪ್ಪ್ **tappụ**, *see* ತಪ್ಪು.

ತಪ್ಪ **tappa**, *s.* Sap; *cf.* ತಪ, ಸಪ.

ತಪ್ಪಂಗಾಯಿ **tappaṅgāyi**, *s.* Scrambling for cocoanuts thrown into a crowd of people. —ಉರ್ದುನಿ to gamble with cocoanuts.

ತಪ್ಪಡತಪ್ಪಡ, ತಪ್ಪಡಪ್ಪ **tappaḍatappaḍa, tappaḍappa**, *adv.* Occasionally, now and then, alternately.

ತಪ್ಪಡೆಪ್ಪು **tappaḍeppu**, *s.* Concealing one's fault.

ತಪ್ಪಡೆಸುನಿ **tappaḍesuni** (ತಪ್ಪಡೆಸ್), *v.a.* To hide, conceal, as one's fault. *v.n.* To escape, evade.

ತಪ್ಪರಿಗೆ **tapparigè**, *see* ತೆಪ್ಪರಿಗೆ.

ತಪ್ಪಳಿಪುನಿ **tappaḷipuni,** *see* ತಪ್ಪೊಲಿಯುನಿ.

ತಪ್ಪಾವುನಿ **tappāvuni,** *c. v.* (*of* ತಪ್ಪುನಿ) To cause to err, evade. 2. to extricate, disentangle, deliver.

ತಪ್ಪು **tappu,** *s.* A fault, mistake, error. 2. an offence, crime. —ತುಂಬಾವುನಿ to accuse, charge with a fault *or* crime. —ಮಳ್ಪುನಿ to err; to commit a crime.

ತಪ್ಪು **tappu,** *s.* A leaf, foliage. 2. vegetables, greens.

ತಪ್ಪುಡುನಿ **tappuḍuni** (ತಪ್ಪುಡ್), *v. a,* To beat the bush in hunting.

ತಪ್ಪುತಿಪ್ಪು **tapputippu,** *see* ತಬ್ಬಿಬ್ಬು.

ತಪ್ಪುನಿ **tappuni** (ತ), *v. n.* To mistake, err, sin. 2. to miss, escape, slip. 3. to fail in an engagement *or* promise; *also* ತತ್ತ್ಪೋಪಿನಿ. ಯೆನಡ್ದ್ ತತ್ತ್ಂಡ್ I made a mistake; I missed. ಎಂಕ್ ತತ್ತ್ಂಡ್ it slipped from me, *or* I have lost.

ತಪ್ಪೆರಿಗೆ **tapperige,** *see* ತೆಪ್ಪರಿಗೆ.

ತಪ್ಪೊಲಿಯುನಿ **tappoliyuni** (ತಪ್ಪೊಲ್), *v. n.* To be covered with foliage as a tree, to grow to leaf.

ತಪ್ಶೀಲ್ **tapšīlu,** *s.* An analysis, detail, the particulars of an account.

ತಬಕ್ **tabaku,** *s.* A salver *or* plate, [a tray.

ತಬಕುನಿ **tabakuni** (ತಬಕ್), *v. a.* To desire, wish, covet. *v. n.* To be allured, enticed, tempted.

ತಬಟ್ **tabaṭu,** *s.* Unsavouriness, acerbity. —ಪತ್ತುನಿ to be unsavoury.

ತಬಟುನಿ **tabaṭuni** (ತಬಟ್), *v. n.* To be unpalatable to the taste; to remain as after-taste.

ತಬಟೆ **tabaṭè,** *s.* A kind of fish.

ತಬಟೆ **tabatè,** *s.* The name of a creeper. —ಪಂದ್ the fruit of it, (eaten by children).

ತಬಲಿ **tabali,** *see* ತಬ್ಬುಲಿ.

ತಬಿ **tabi,** *s.* Flavour, taste; *also* ಸಬಿ. *adj.* Savoury, delicious.

ತಬಿಟೆ **tabiṭe,** *see* ತಮಟೆ.

ತಬಿಪುನಿ **tabipuni** (ತಬಿ), *v. a.* To appease, as the appetite. 2. to smack. 3. *see* ತಜಪುನಿ.

ತಬಿಮೆ **tabimè,** *s.* A follower.

ತಬುಕು **tabuku,** *see* ತಬಕ್.

ತಬುಕುದಮರ **tabukuda-mara,** *see* ತವುಕುದಮರ.

ತಬುದಿಪ್ಪು **tabudippu,** *see* ತಬ್ಬಿಬ್ಬು.

ತಬುರಿ **taburi,** *s.* A pot.

ತಬುರು **taburu,** *s.* A kind of red [ant.

ತಬುಲಿ **tabuli,** *see* ತಬ್ಬುಲಿ.

ತಬುಲೆ **tabule,** *see* ತಗುಲೆ.

ತಬೆಪುನಿ **tabepuni** (ತಬೆ), *v. n.* To long, eagerly desire.

ತಬೆರುನಿ **taberuni** (ತಬೆರ್), *v. a.* To threaten.

ತಬೆಲ **tabela,** *s.* A stable.

ತಬ್ತ **tabta,** *see* ತಪ್ತ.

ತಬ್ದಿಲ್ **tabdilu,** *s.* Change, alteration, variation.

ತಬ್ಬಿಬ್ಬು **tabbibbu,** *s.* Distraction, confusion. 2. variation, difference. *adj.* Irregular.

ತಬ್ಬಿಲ್ **tabbilu,** *see* ತಬ್ದಿಲ್. 2. *see* ತಬ್ಬುಲಿ.

ತಬ್ಬಿಲ **tabbila**, *see* ತಬೆಲ.

ತಬ್ಬಿಲಿ **tabbili**, *see* ತಬ್ಬುಲಿ.

ತಬ್ಬುನಿ **tabbuni** (ತಬ್), *v. a* To feel, grope.

ತಬ್ಬುದಿಬ್ಬು **tabbudibbu**, *see* ತಬ್ಬಿಬ್ಬು.

ತಬ್ಬುಲಿ **tabbuli**, *s.* An orphan. *adj.* Low, vulgar. 2. weak, infirm. 3. cowardly, timid.

ತಮ **tama**, *s.* Darkness. 2. mental darkness, ignorance. 3. worldly delusion.

ತಮಕೆ **tamakè**, *s.* Leisure, respite, opportunity. 2. delay, procrastination. —ಕೊರ್ಪಿನಿ, —ದೀಪಿನಿ, —ಪಾಡುನಿ to delay, put off, postpone.

ತಮಟೆ **tamaṭè**, *s.* A tambour. 2. a little drum.

ತಮನಿಯುನಿ **tamaniyuni**, *see* ತಂಮ ಣಿಪುನಿ.

ತಮರ್, ತಮರ **tamarụ, tamara**, *s.* Tin.

ತಮರ್, ತಮರಿ, ತಮರೆ **tamarụ, tamari, tamare**, *see* ತಮಿರ್.

ತಮಸ್ **tamasụ**, *see* ತಮ.

ತಮಾಮ್, ತಮಾಮು **tamāmụ, tamāmu**, *s.* The whole. *adj.* All.

ತಮಾಶೆ, ತಮಾಸೆ **tamāśè, tamāsè**, *s.* A show, fun, sport, amusement. —ಗಾರೆ a pantomime, one fond of show *or* amusements; a wag. —ಪಾತೆರುನಿ to crack jokes. —ಮಳ್ಪುನಿ to make fun.

ತಮಿರ್ **tamirụ**, *s.* A gimlet. 2. *see* [ತಮಿರ್.

ತಮುಳ್, ತಮುಳು **tamuḷụ, tamuḷu**, *s.* Tamil.

ತಮೂಸಕ್ **tamūsakụ**, *s.* A bond.

ತಮೆಪುನಿ **tamepuni** (ತಮೆ), *v. a.* To pour, spill. 2. to cast into a mould.

ತಮೆಪೆಲ್ **tamepelụ**, *s.* Effusion, issue.

ತಮೆಯುನಿ **tameyuni**, *see* ತಮೆಲುನಿ.

ತಮೆರ್ **tamerụ**, *s.* One who gives a bride away in marriage; a guardian.

ತಮೆರಿಯುನಿ **tameriyuni** (ತಮೆರ್), *v. n.* To extricate, disentangle, save.

ತಮೆರುನಿ **tameruni**, *see* ತಬೆರುನಿ.

ತಮೆಲುನಿ, ತಮೆವುನಿ **tameluni, tamevuni**, *v. n.* To overflow, run over *or* out. 2. to menstruate.

ತಮೋಗುಣ **tamōguṇa**, *s.* The quality of darkness; ignorance; passionate *or* angry disposition; *cf.* ತಮ.

ತಯಪುನಿ **tayapuni**, *see* ತಜಪುನಿ.

ತಯಾರ್ **tayārụ**, *s.* Preparation, readiness. *adj.* Ready. —ಆಪಿನಿ to become ready. —ದೀಪಿನಿ to keep ready. —ಮಳ್ಪುನಿ to prepare, make ready.

ತಯಿ **tayi**, *see* ತೈ.

ತಯಿಲ **tayila**, *see* ತೈಲ.

ತಯಿಲಿ **tayili**, *see* ತೈಲಿ.

ತರ **tara**, *s.* Kind, sort, class, grade. 2. manner, mode. 3. a line, row, range. —ತರ variety; variegation; gradation, order, method. ತರೊಕು ತರ a good match.

ತರಂಕ್, ತರಂಗ್ taraṅkụ, taraṅgụ, *see* ಸರಂಗ್.

ತರಂಟುನಿ taranṭuni, *see* ತಂಟುಗ್ನಿ.

ತರಕ್ taraku, *see* ಸರಕ್.

ತರಕಾರಿ tarakāri, *s.* Vegetables in general.

ತರಕೊಣುನಿ tarakoṇuni (ತರಕೊಣ್), *v. refl.* To receive, accept. 2. to hear, listen, mind.

ತರಡ್ taraḍu, *see* ತಡ್ಗ್.

ತರಣ taraṇa, *s.* Fording, crossing, passing over.

ತರತಮ್ಯ taratamya, *see* ತಾರತಮ್ಯ.

ತರತ್ರ taratra, *see* ತರೆತ್ರ.

ತರಪು tarapu, *s.* A side, party. 2. care, custody. *adv.* Towards.

ತರಪುನಿ tarapuni (ತರ), *v. a.* To rivet, fasten firmly. *v. n.* To be riveted, fixed.

ತರಪೊಳಿ tarapoḷi, *see* ಸರಪೊಳಿ.

ತರಬೇತ್, ತರಬೇತಿ tarabētụ, tarabēti, *s.* Training, education. —ಮಳ್ಪುನಿ to train, instruct.

ತರವಾಳಿ taravāḷi, *see* ತರಾವಳಿ.

ತರಸ್ tarasụ, *see* ತ್ರಾಸ್.

ತರಳೆ taraḷè, *s.* Slander, calumny. 2. backbiting, talebearing. —ದ ಒಟ್ಟಿ a mischievous backbiter. —ಗಾರೆ a slanderer, talebearer. —ಪಣ್ಪುನಿ to slander, backbite.

ತರಾಂತರ tarāntara, *see* ತಲಾಂತರ.

ತರಾತರ tarātara, *s.* Variety in goods. 2. distinction of rank, *etc.*; *cf.* ತರ.

ತರಾತುರಿ ṭarāturi, *s.* Haste, speed.

ತರಾಬಳಿ, ತರಾವಳಿ tarābaḷi, tarāvaḷi, *s.* Kind, species; variety, diversity. *adj.* Various, diverse.

ತರಿಪುನಿ taripuni (ತರಿ), *v. a.* To lop off, as the superfluous branches of a tree; to clear, as a jungle.

ತರಿಯುನಿ tariyuni (ತರಿ), *v. n.* To stay, stop, tarry, delay.

ತರು taru, *s.* A small kind of fish; any little fish. —ಬುತ್ತ್, —ಬುರುದೆ a swamp with such fishes. —ಬೂತಯಿ a small kind of sardine.

ತರುಂಬು tarumbu, *s.* A bunch of betelnuts.

ತರುಣಿ taruṇi, *s.* A girl, young woman. 2. a wife.

ತರುಣೆ taruṇe, *s.* A youth, young man.

ತರುವ taruva, *see* ಚರು.

ತರೆ tarè, *s.* The head, top. 2. the hair of the head. 3. generation. —ಡ್ದ ತರೆ from generation to generation. —ತಿರ್ಗ ಕಾರ್ ಮಿತ್ತ್ upside down, topsyturvy, headlong. —ಪಣವು poll-tax. —ಪುರೆ a head-load. —ಬಂಗಾರ್ head-ornaments. —ಬೇನೆ headache. —ಕಡ್ಪುನಿ to behead, decapitate; to injure, ruin. —ಕಲೆಪಿನಿ to leave the head bare. —ಕೊರ್ಪಿನಿ *lit.* to offer the head; to undertake, engage in; to submit; to take the risk. —ಗಿರಿಯುನಿ, —ತಿಂಗುಣಿ to be giddy, confused; to be tipsy; to become proud. —ಕ್ ಪಾಡುನಿ to impute, attribute.

—ಪಂಡುನಿ *lit.* the head to shake; to be improved in one's circumstances; to gain power. —ಬಗ್ಗಾವುನಿ to bow the head; to humiliate; to be modest, polite. —ಬಗ್ಗುನಿ the head to be bowed down; to be ashamed; to be humiliated. —ಬಜರ್ನಿ to comb the hair. —ಮುದಿಪುನಿ to introvert the tuft-knot. —ಅಕ್ಕಾವುನಿ to thrive, prosper. —ಸೆಡಿಪುನಿ the head to ache. ಯೆಂಕ್ ತರೆ ಇಜ್ಜಿ *lit.* I have no head; I have a severe headache.

ತರೆತ್ರ taretra, *s.* A turban, head-dress.

ತರೆನೀರ್ tarenīru, *s.* Spring *or* fountain on the top of a hill, irrigating the land below. 2. amniotic fluid *or* fruitwater. —ಪರಿಯುನಿ the amnios to burst *or* break.

ತರೆಪುನಿ tarepuni (ತರೆ), *v. a.* To grind, rub. 2. to try, assay metal.

ತರೆಬಿಲೆ tarebilè, *s.* Exorbitant price, overcharge. 2. the price fetched by the first sale of goods.

ತರೆಮಂಡೆ taremaṇḍè, *s.* The skull. —ಪಕೊರ್ಣುನಿ to quarrel; to break one's head over a business.

ತರೆಮುರಿ taremuri, *s.* Determination, resolution. —ಪಣ್ಪುನಿ to say definitely, decisively; to make known one's resolution.

ತರೆಯುನಿ tareyuni (ತರೆ), *v. n.* To be rubbed off; to abrade; wear away, to become thin, wasted.

ತರೆಲ್ tarelu, *adj.* Worn out. —ಕತ್ತಿ a blunt *or* worn out billhook.

ತರೆವುನಿ tarevuni, *see* ತರೆಯುನಿ.

ತರೊಳಿ taroḷi, *s.* A kind of creeper; *also* ಕಕ್ಕೆ—. 2. the tree *Rhynchoglossum obliq.*, the leaves of which are used for cleansing the head in bathing. ಯೆಮ್ಮೆ— a larger species of the same. 3. a milky plant, *Ericyne.*

ತರೊಳು taroḷu, *s.* A kind of tree the leaves of which are used by toddy-drawers to rub the horn of palm trees. ಬೊಳ್ದು— a white species of the same.

ತರೋತರ tarōtara, *see* ತರಾತರ.

ತರ್ರ tarra, *see* ಸರ್ರ.

ತರ್ಕ tarka, *s.* Dispute, discussion, reasoning. 2. logic. —ವಾಯಿ a disputant, sophist. —ವಿದ್ಯೆ, —ಶಾಸ್ತ್ರ the science of logic. —ಮಳ್ಪುನಿ to dispute, discuss, argue.

ತರ್ಕತ್ತಿ, ತರ್ಕತ್ತೆ tarkatti, tarkattè, *s.* The curved knife of a toddy-drawer.

ತರ್ಕೊಣುನಿ tarkoṇuni (ತರ್ಕೊಂಡ್), *v. a.* To hold up in one's arms, as a sick person; *cf.* ತರಕೊಣುನಿ.

ತರ್ಕೊಲ್, ತರ್ಕೋಲು tarkolu, tarkōlu, *s.* A key. 2. a midwife. 3. assisting a woman in labour. —ಕುಳ್ಪುನಿ to assist a woman in labour.

ತರ್ಗಯಿ **targayi,** *see* ನರ್ಗಯಿ.

ತರ್ಗೊಡೆ **targoḍè,** *s.* Leanness, thinness. 2. a lean man.

ತರ್ಜಿಮೆ, ತರ್ಜುಮೆ **ṭarjimè, tarjumè,** *s.* Translation. —ಮಳ್ಪುನಿ to translate, interpret.

ತರ್ಡ್ **tarḍu,** *s.* The testicles.

ತರ್ಪಣ **tarpaṇa,** *s.* Satisfaction. 2. a religious rite, presenting water to the manes of the deceased *or* to the gods. —ಕೊರ್ಪಿನಿ to present such water; to satisfy, please.

ತರ್ಪಾವುನಿ, ತರ್ಪುಡುನಿ **tarpāvuni, tarpuḍuni,** *c. v.* (*of* ತರ್ಪುನಿ) To cause to bring, send for. 2. to get, obtain.

ತರ್ಪುನಿ **tarpuni** (ತರ್), *v. a.* To rivet, fix firmly. 2. to depress, humble. *v. n.* To be riveted. 2. to be depressed.

ತರ್ಮೆಣ **tarmeṇa,** *see* ತಲ್ಮೆನ.

ತರ್ವ **tarva,** *see* ಚರು.

ತರ್ವೆಲ್ **tarvelụ,** *s.* Holding up in arms.

ತರ್ಳೆ **tarḷè,** *see* ತರಳೆ.

ತಲ **tala,** *see* ತಳ & ಸ್ಥಳ.

ತಲಂಬು **talambu,** *s.* The sunhemp, *Crotalaria juncea.*

ತಲಕೆ **talakè,** *s.* A slip *or* lath of a bamboo. ಕೈತ— the bone between the wrist and elbow.

ತಲಗುಳ್ಳೆ **talaguḷḷè,** *see* ಗುಳೆ.

ತಲಪುನಿ **talapuni** (ತಲ), *v. n.* To arrive, reach; *cf.* ತಲ್ಪುನಿ.

ತಲಬು, ತಲವು **talabu, talavu,** *s.* Pay, wages. 2. a tribute in a game of cards.

ತಲರ **talara,** *s.* A kind of whitlow between the toes.

ತಲಸುನಿ **talasuni,** *see* ತಲಾಸ್‌ಮಳ್ಪುನಿ *under* ತಲಾಸ್.

ತಲಾಂತರ, ತಲಾಂತ್ರ **talāntara, talāntra,** *s.* A generation; an age; *cf.* ಸ್ಥಳಾಂತರ.

ತಲಾವು **talāvu,** *s.* A large tank.

ತಲಾಸ್ **talāsụ,** *s.* Inquiry, search. 2. procuring, providing —ಮಳ್ಪುನಿ to search; to procure.

ತಲಿಪು **talipu,** *s.* Sprinkling. 2. *see* ತಲಿಪು.

ತಲಿಪುನಿ **talipuni** (ತಲಿ), *v. a.* To sprinkle.

ತಲು **talu,** *adj.* Thrashed, beaten. —ಬೈ thrashed straw.

ತಲುಕುಪಡಿಕ **talukupaḍika,** *s.* A topaz.

ತಲೆ **talè,** *s.* A rop, for climbing palm trees. ಕೈ— the hand-rope, ಕಾರ್— the foot rope, —ಕೊಡಂಙ್ the whole apparatus of a toddy drawer.

ತಲೆಂಬು **talembu,** *s.* A pillow.

ತಲೆನೀರ್ **talenīrụ,** *see* ತರೆನೀರ್,

ತಲೆಪಟ್ಟ **talepaṭṭa,** *s.* A head-ornament of a devil-dancer.

ತಲೆಪು **talepu,** *s.* Interruption, stoppage.

ತಲೆಪುನಿ **talepuni** (ತಲೆ), *v. a.* To interrupt, hinder, stop, detain, delay.

ತಲೆಮಣಿ **talemaṇi,** *s.* A head ornament worn by a devil-dancer. —ಚಾಕುಳ a tasselled headband of a demon-priest.

ತಲೆಮರ **talemara,** *s.* The frame of a thrashing stool.

ತಲ್ಕತ್ತಿ **talkatti,** *see* ತರ್ಗತ್ತಿ.

ತಲ್ಕು **talku,** *s.* An ambush.

ತಲ್ಕುನಿ **talkuni,** *see* ತಲ್ಲುನಿ.

ತಲ್ಪುನಿ **talpuni** (ತಲ್), *v. a.* To drop. 2. to knock, shake off, as fruit from a tree. 3. to thrash, as paddy. ತಲ್ಪು ಬೋರಿ a thrashing ox.

ತಲ್ಮೆನ **talmena,** *s.* Refreshment, revival, relief. *adj.* Cool, cold, refreshing, bracing. —ಘಾಳಿ a cool breeze.

ತಲ್ಲಣ **tallaṇa,** *adj.* Wavering, vexed.

ತಲ್ಲಿ **talli,** *s.* A kind of cucumber pickle.

ತಲ್ಲುನಿ **talluni** (ತಲ್), *v. a.* To penetrate, push in, press through. 2. to hide, conceal.

ತಲ್ಲೆ **talle,** *see* ತಳ್ಳೆ, ಥಲ್ಲೆ, ಥಲ್ಲಿ. —ನಕ್ಕೆರುನಿ to be proud, arrogant.

ತಲ್ಲೆಪಿಲ್ಲೆ **tallèpillè,** *see* ತಂಡೆಪಿಂಡೆ.

ತಲ್ವಾರ್ **talvāru,** *s.* A scimitar.

ತವರ **tavara,** *s.* Tin.

ತವಾಯಿ **tavāyi,** *s.* Delay, detention. 2. halting in a journey. —ಮುಳ್ಪುನಿ to halt, stop, delay.

ತವು- **tavu-,** *see under* ತಾ.

ತವುಂಕು **tavuṅku,** *s.* Agitation.

ತವುಕುದಮರ **tavukuda-mara,** *s.* A kind of fruit tree. ತವುಕ್ದ ಪಂಡ್ its fruit.

ತವುಡು **tavuḍu,** *see* ತಾಡು.

ತವುತೆ **tavutè,** *see* ತಾತೆ.

ತವುರುನಿ **tavuruni** (ತವುರ್), *v. a.* To cut away any leaves *or* brushwood, to clear a bush.

ತಸಾರ **tasāra,** *see* ಸಸಾರ.

ತಸಿಬಿ **tasibi,** *see* ತಸ್ಪಿ.

ತಸ್ಕ್, ತಸ್ಕರ **tasku, taskara,** *s.* A trick, wile, pretext. 2. a mistake, error.

ತಸ್ಕರ್ **taskaru,** *s.* Theft, robbery; *also* ತಸ್ಕರತನ.

ತಸ್ಕರೆ **taskarè,** *s.* A thief, robber.

ತಸ್ತ್, ತಸ್ತು **tastu, tastu,** *s.* A basin, broad mouthed vessel.

ತಸ್ತಿಕ್, ತಸ್ತಿಗ್, ತಸ್ತೀಕ್, ತಸ್ತಿಗೆ **tastiku, tastigu, tastīku, tastige,** *s.* A government allowance for a temple.

ತಸ್ಪಿ, ತಸ್ಬಿ **taspi, tasbi,** *s.* The rosary of Mohammedans.

ತಹ, ತಹಾ **taha, tahā,** *s.* Consent, agreement. 2. a contract; *also* ತಹಾನಾಮೆ. —ಮುಳ್ಪುನಿ to agree; to contract.

ತಹಶೀಲ್ **tahaśīlu,** *s.* Collection of revenue. —ದಾರೆ the revenue officer of a taluk, a tahsildar. ತಹಶೀಲಿಕೆ the post of a tahsildar.

ತಳ **taḷa,** *s.* Low ground, base, bottom. 2. *see* ತಲೆ. —ಊರುನಿ to find out a place for a building. —ಕಟ್ಟುನಿ to lay a foundation. —ಪತ್ತುನಿ to lie flat on the ground; to be in a great calamity; to be drowned.

ತಳತಂತ್ರ **taḷatantra,** *s.* Ruin, desolation, destruction.

ತಳತಳ taḷataḷa, *s.* Glitter, lustre. —ಮಿಂಚುನಿ to glitter, flash, sparkle.

ತಳಪಟ, ತಳಪಟ್ಟ್ taḷapaṭa, taḷapaṭṭu, *s.* Ruin; *cf.* ತಳತಂತ್ರ. *adj.* Vacant, empty, deserted, waste. —ಮಳ್ಪುನಿ to devastate, desert.

ತಳಪಳ taḷapaḷa, *see* ಚಳಚಳ.

ತಳಬಳ, ತಳಮಳ taḷabaḷa, taḷamaḷa, *s.* Alarm, agitation. 2. exhaustion, weariness.

ತಳವಾರೆ taḷavāre, *s.* A village watchman.

ತಳಾಂತರ taḷāntara, *see* ಸ್ಥಳಾಂತರ.

ತಳಾರ taḷāra, *s.* A sore in the toes.

ತಳಿಪುನಿ taḷipuni, *see* ತಲಿಪುನಿ.

ತಳಿರ್ taḷiru, *s.* A sprout, bud, shoot. —ದರೆ a tender leaf.

ತಳು taḷu, *see* ತಳ.

ತಳೆಪುನಿ taḷepuni, *see* ತಲಿಪುನಿ, ತಲೆಪುನಿ.

ತಳ್ಪುನಿ taḷpuni, *see* ತಲ್ಪುನಿ.

ತಳ್ಮೆನ taḷmena, *see* ತಲ್ಮೆನ.

ತಳ್ಳಿ taḷḷi, *s.* Slander, calumny, defamation. 2. intercourse, interference, association. 3. *see* ತಲ್ಲಿ. *adj.* Slanderous. 2. anonymous. —ಅರ್ಜಿ an anonymous petition.

ತಳ್ಳುನಿ taḷḷuni, *see* ತಲ್ಲುನಿ.

ತಳ್ಳೆ taḷḷè, *s.* A heap. 2. plunder. —ಪಿಳ್ಳೆ, *see* ತಂಡೆಪಿಂಡೆ.

ತಾಂಕಣ tāṅkaṇa, *s.* Fosterage, fostering. —ದಂಮೆ a foster father. —ದಪ್ಪೆ a foster mother. —ದ ಬಾಲೆ a foster child.

ತಾಂಕಾವುನಿ tāṅkāvuni, *c. v.* (*of* ತಾಂಕುನಿ) To cause to nurse. 2. to cause to give (*said by Pariahs*).

ತಾಂಕುನಿ tāṅkuni (ತಾಂಕ್), *v. a.* To take care of, nourish, bring up, foster, nurse, feed; shelter. 2. to give (*said by Pariahs*).

ತಾಂಗ್ tāṅgu, *s.* A support, prop. —ಕೊರ್ಪಿನಿ, —ಪಾಡುನಿ to prop, support, provide with support. —ತರ್ಪೆಲ್ supporting by holding up in arms.

ತಾಂಗುನಿ tāṅguni (ತಾಂಗ್), *v. a.* To assist, help. 2. to prop, support, sustain.

ತಾಂಗೊಳಿಪುನಿ tāṅgoḷipuni (ತಾಂಗೊಳಿ), *v. a.* To support.

ತಾಂಙುನಿ tāññuni, *see* ತಾಂಗುನಿ.

ತಾಂಚ tāñča, *see* ಸಾಂಚ.

ತಾಂಚಾವುನಿ tāñčāvuni, *see* ತಾಂಟಾವುನಿ.

ತಾಂಚುನಿ tāñčuni, *see* ತಾಂಟುನಿ.

ತಾಂಟ್ಮೋಂಟ್ tāṇṭumōṇṭu, *adj.* Crooked, bent. 2. vain, useless. *s.* Debris, fragments.

ತಾಂಟಾವುನಿ tāṇṭāvuni, *c. v.* (*of* ತಾಂಟುನಿ) To make touch, to bring into collision or contact. 2. to set one person against another.

ತಾಂಟುನಿ tāṇṭuni (ತಾಂಟ್), *v. n.* To touch, hit, come into collision *or* contact with. 2. to quarrel, fight.

ತಾಂಟೆ tāṇṭè, *adj.* Lean, thin, slender. —ಕಾರ್ lean slender

legs. —ಮೋಂಟೆ a cripple, a decrepit person. —ಕೊಂಬು a slender horn.

ತಾಂಡೇಲೆ tāṇḍēle, *see* ತಂಡೆಲ್.

ತಾಂತಂಣ್ಣೆ tāntaṇṇe, *s.* A glutton.

ತಾಂತ್ರಿಕೆ tāntrike, *see* ತಂತ್ರಿ.

ತಾಂಬಟಿ, ತಾಂಬಟೆ tāmbaṭi, tāmbaṭe, *see* ಚೆಂಬಟೆ.

ತಾಂಬಾಣ tāmbāṇa, *s.* A metallic dish *or* tray.

ತಾಂಬೂಲ tāmbūla, *s.* Betel leaf and areca nut. —ಚರ್ವಣ chewing betel.

ತಾಂಬ್ರ tāmbra, *s.* Copper. *adj.* Copper-coloured. —ದ ಚೆಂಬು a copper-pot. —ದ ತಗಡ್ a copper plate. —ಭಸ್ಮ, —ಸಿಂಧೂರ calx *or* oxide of copper.

ತಾಕಟೆಮರ tākaṭemara, *s.* The tree *Morinda citrifolia.*

ತಾಕಿಕ tākika, *s.* True report, correct information.

ತಾಕಿತ್, ತಾಕಿದ್, ತಾಕಿದಿ tākitu, tākidu, tākidi, *s.* An order, command, injunction. —ಕೊಪಿಂಣಿ, —ಮಳ್ಪುನಿ to order, direct.

ತಾಕುತೋಕು, ತಾಕುದೋಕು tākutōku, tākudōku, *s.* Responsibility; risk, liability. *adj.* Responsible; liable.

ತಾಕುನಿ tākuni (ತಾಕ್), *v. n.* To hit, touch; *cf.* ತಾಗುನಿ.

ತಾಗ tāga, *adv.* Pointedly, directly; explicitly. —ಪಣ್ಪುನಿ to say directly, refer pointedly.

ತಾಗಾವುನಿ tāgāvuni, *c. v.* (*of* ತಾಗುನಿ) To cause to touch, make hit. ಒರಿಯನ್ ಒಯ್ಯಗ್— to set one against another.

ತಾಗುನಿ tāguni (ತಾಗ್), *v. a.* To touch, hit, come in collision *or* contact with. *v. n.* To be impressed, sensible. ಆಯಗ್ ಪಂಡಿನವು ತಾಗಂಡ್ he was impressed by what was said.

ತಾಚುನಿ tāčuni (ತಾಚ್), *v. n.* To come in collision.

ತಾಜಾ tājā, *adj.* Fresh, new; genuine. 2. fair, correct. —ಕಲಮ್ *nota bene*, a postscript. —ಪ್ರತಿ a fair copy. —ಮಾಲ್ a genuine article.

ತಾಜೀಪ್ tājīpu, *adj.* Marvellous.

ತಾಟಂಕ tāṭaṅka, *s.* An ear-ornament.

ತಾಟಕಿ tāṭaki, *s.* A female giant. 2. a quarrelsome woman.

ತಾಟಿ tāṭi, *s.* Clapping the hands; applause. —ಬೊಟ್ಟುನಿ to clap the hands; to applaud.

ತಾಟೆ tāṭe, *s.* A kind of fish.

ತಾಡನೆ tāḍane, *s.* Beating, whipping.

ತಾಡಿ tāḍi, *see* ಚಾಡಿ.

ತಾಡು tāḍu, *s.* Goring; *also* ತಾಡಾಟ.

ತಾಡುನಿ tāḍuni (ತಾಡ್), *v. a.* To gore with the horns; to butt.

ತಾಡೆಲ್ tāḍelu, *s.* The act of goring *or* butting.

ತಾಣ tāṇa, *s.* A place; *cf.* ಸ್ಥಾನ. —ದಿಸೆ, —ದ ತುದರ್ a lampstand.

ತಾತಯಿ, ತಾತಾಯಿ tātayi, tātāyi, *s.* Caraway seed, *Curum carui*; *cf.* ಜೀರದರಿ.

ತಾತಿ tāti, *s.* A kind of ornament; *also* ತಾತಿಮಣಿ. 2. *see* ತಾಟಿ.

ತಾತುರಿ tāturi, *s.* Eloquence, ability, cleverness; *cf.* ಚಾತುರ್ಯ. 2. love, affection; *cf.* ತಾತ್ಪರ್ಯ.

ತಾತೆ tāte, *s.* A grand-father. 2. Brahma.

ತಾತ್ಪರ್ಯ, ತಾತ್ಪರ್ರ್ಯ tātparya, *s.* Sentiment, opinion, notion. 2. love, affection. 3. purport, meaning. 4. object, intent, design, purpose. —ಪಣ್ಪುನಿ to tell one's opinion. —ದೀಪಿನಿ to care, favour.

ತಾತ್ಸಾರ tātsāra, *s.* Slight, disrespect, contempt.

ತಾದಿ tādi, *see* ಸಾದಿ.

ತಾನ್ tānu, *s.* A web of piece-goods.

ತಾನ್ tānu, *pron.* Self, one's self.

ತಾನ tāna, *see* ಸ್ಥಾನ.

ತಾನಿಕೆ tānike, *see* ಸ್ಥಾನಿಕೆ.

ತಾಪ tāpa, *s.* Heat, burning. 2. fever, inflammation. 3. anguish, distress.

ತಾಪತ್ರ, ತಾಪತ್ರಯ tāpatra, tāpatraya, *s.* Grief, distress, trial, trouble.

ತಾಪಿ tāpi, *s.* A trowel.

ತಾಪಿಪುನಿ tāpipuni (ತಾಪಿ), *v. a.* To burn. 2. *see* ಸ್ಥಾಪಿಪುನಿ.

ತಾಪು tāpu, *s.* A watchman's stand in a field. 2. an ambush.

ತಾಬುಲು tābulu, *s.* A tinsel, brass leaf. 2. the cuts, as of a precious stone.

ತಾಬೂತು tābūtu, *s.* The cage made of paper and tinsel by Mussalmans at the Moharam.

ತಾಬೆ tābe, *s.* Control. 2. charge, care. ನಿನ ತಾಬೆಡ್ ಉಳ್ಳೆ he is in your charge.

ತಾಮಕಾಯಿ tāmakāyi, *see* ತಮಕೆ.

ತಾಮಣಿ tāmaṇi, *see* ತಲೆಮಣಿ.

ತಾಮಯಿ tāmayi, *see* ತವಾಯಿ.

ತಾಮರೆ tāmare, *s.* The lotus flower, *Nymphæa pubescens*; *also* ತಾಮರೆಪೂ. —ಮಣಿ the seed of a lotus. —ದಂಡ್ the stalk of a lotus.

ತಾಮರೆರೋಗ tāmareroga, *s.* A wasting disease of children. 2. green sickness.

ತಾಮಸ tāmasa, *s.* Laziness, indolence. 2. delay, procrastination. 3. anger, passion. —ದಾಯೆ, ತಾಮಸಿ a sluggard; a passionate man.

ತಾಮಿಸ್ರ tāmisra, *s.* Great darkness. —ಪಕ್ಷ the dark half of the lunar month.

ತಾಮೆ tāme, *see* ಸಾಮೆ.

ತಾಮೆರ್ tāmeru, *see* ತಮೆರ್.

ತಾಮ್ರ tāmra, *see* ತಾಂಬ್ರ.

ತಾಯಿ tāyi, *s.* Mother.

ತಾಯಿಗಂಡೆ tāyigaṇḍe, *s.* A rogue, cheat, scoundrel, *obsc.*

ತಾಯಿಬೇರ್ tāyiberu, *s.* The principal root of a tree, taproot.

ತಾರ್ tāru, *s.* A rivulet. 2. tar.

ತಾರ tāra, *s.* A star. 2. two pie. 3. crossing, passing over.

ತಾರಣ tāraṇa, *s.* The eighteenth year of the Hindu cycle. 2.

the act of crossing. 3. persecution. 4. a raft, float.

ತಾರತಮ್ಯ **tāratamya**, *s.* Rank, state, condition. 2. distinction, discrimination.

ತಾರಾಯಿ **tārāyi**, *s.* A cocoanut. –ದ ಶಿಪ್ಪಿ, –ದ ಬುರುಡೆ the shell of a cocoanut. ರಂಕದ– a large cocoanut. ಕೋರಿ– a small hard cocoanut. ದೀವುದ– a cocoanut of the (Laccadive) isles. ಗೆಂಡೆ–, *see* ಗೆಂಡಳಿ. –ಕಟ್ಟುನಿ to play with cocoanuts by knocking one against the other, the person who breaks the cocoanut of the other gains it.

ತಾರಾವುನಿ **tārāvuni**, *c. v.* (*of* ತಾರುನಿ) To drive in. 2. to immerse.

ತಾರಿ **tāri**, *s.* The palmyra, *Borassus flabelliformis.* –ಕಂಡೆ the bulb of a fragrant grass, *Cyperus rotundus.* –ದ ಕಳಿ palmyra toddy. –ದ ಕುಜಿಲ a vessel for palm-wine. –ಗುಬ್ಬಿ a kind of sparrow, building its pendent nest on a palm tree. –ಪಂತಿ a kind of grass, *Cyperus hexastachyus.* –ಪಂಡ್ a the fruit of the palmyra tree. –ದ ಬೆಲ್ಲ jaggory made from palm juice. –ಮಡಲ a poisonous snake. –ದ ಮದೊಡಿ the midrib of a palm-leaf.

ತಾರಿಣಿ **tāriṇi**, *s.* A goddess peculiar to the Jains.

ತಾರೀಕ್, ತಾರೀಕು **tārīkụ, tārīku**, *s.* A date, day of the month.

ತಾರೀಪು **tārīpu**, *s.* Praise, commendation. 2. novelty, rarity. –ಮಳ್ಪುನಿ to commend, praise.

ತಾರುಣ್ಯ **tāruṇya**, *s.* Youth, manhood.

ತಾರುನಿ **tāruni** (ತಾರ್), *v. n.* To sink in, plunge. ಕಾರ್– feet to sink, as in mire.

ತಾರುಮಾರ್ **tārumārụ**, *s.* Confusion, disorder. –ಆಪಿನಿ to become confused.

ತಾರೆ **tārè**, *s.* The cocoanut palm, *Cocos nucifera.* ಗುಜ್ಜ– a short cocoanut palm. ಜೇ–, ದೀವುದ– a species from the (Laccadive) isles, bearing small cocoanuts. ರಂಕ– a species, bearing large cocoanuts. –ದ ಕೊತ್ತಳಿಗೆ the stalk *or* midrib of a cocoanut leaf.

ತಾರೊಳಿ **tāroḷi**, *see* ತರೊಳಿ.

ತಾರ್ಕಣೆ **tārkaṇè**, *s.* Substantiation, proof, demonstration. 2. apparition. –ಕೊಪಿನಿ, –ಮಳ್ಪುನಿ to substantiate.

ತಾರ್ಕಿಕೆ **tārkike**, *s.* A sophist, disputant.

ತಾರ್ಕೊಲ್ **tārkolụ**, *see* ತರ್ಕೊಲ್.

ತಾರ್ಮಾರ್ **tārmārụ**, *see* ತಾರುಮಾರ್.

ತಾಲ **tāla**, *s.* The metallic lid of a cooking utensil. 2. *see* ತಾಳ.

ತಾಲಂಗಡಿ **tālaṅgaḍi**, *s.* The wooden peg by which a water-lift is fastened to the stem.

ತಾಲವ್ಯ **tālavya**, *s.* A palatal letter, *gram.*

ತಾಲಾಂಕೆ **tālāṅke**, *s.* A name of Balarāma.

ತಾಲಿ tāli, *s*. The marriage badge, worn by a female. 2. a metal tumbler *or* small pot. 3. a kind of grass. –ಕಟ್ಟುನಿ to tie the marriage badge to the neck. –ತಪ್ಪ a kind of climbing shrub.

ತಾಲಿಯೆ tāliye, *see* ತಾಲ್ಯೆ.

ತಾಲೀಮು tālīmu, *s*. Gymnastics, athletic exercise. –ಕೊಬ್ಬುನಿ to practise gymnastics.

ತಾಲು ṭālu, *s*. The throat. 2. the palate.

ತಾಲುಕು tāluku, *s*. The division of a district.

ತಾಲುನಿ tāluni (ತಾಲ್), *v. n*. To fall off, drop down; *cf*. ತಾಳುನಿ.

ತಾಲೆ tāle, *see* ತಾಲ್ಯೆ.

ತಾಲ್ಪುನಿ tālpuni, *see* ತಲ್ಪುನಿ.

ತಾಲ್ಯತುಂಡು tālyatuṇḍu, *s*. A special cloth worn only by weavers.

ತಾಲ್ಯಪಟ್ಟ್ tālyapaṭṭu, *s*. A cobweb.

ತಾಲ್ಯಪುರಿ tālyapuri, *s*. A spider.

ತಾಲ್ಯೆ tālye, *s*. A weaver. 2. a spider.

ತಾವಜಿ tāvaji, *s*. A metallic tube for keeping an amulet, money, *etc*.

ತಾವರೆ tāvarė, *see* ತಾಮರೆ. 2. *see* ಅಲ್ಲಿ.

ತಾವು tāvu, *s*. A sheet of paper. 2. death; *cf*. ಸಾವು. 3. place, room.

ತಾಷ tāsha, *s*. A kind of drum.

ತಾಸ್ tāsu, *s*. An hour.

ತಾಸಯಿ tāsayi, *see* ತಾಶಾಯಿ.

ತಾಸಯೆ tāsaye, *see* ದಾಸಯೆ.

ತಾಸೀಲ್ದಾರೆ tāsīldāre, *see* ತಹಶೀಲ್ ದಾರೆ *under* ತಹಶೀಲ್.

ತಾಸೆ tāse, *see* ತಾಷ.

ತಾಸೆಮಿ tāsemi, *see* ದಾಸೆಮಿ.

ತಾಹ tāha, *see* ತಹ.

ತಾಳ tāḷa, *s*. A cymbal. 2. tune, beating time in music. –ಮೇಳ music and play. –ಬೊಟ್ಟುನಿ to beat time.

ತಾಳಿ tāḷi, *see* ತಾರಿ. 2. *see* ತಾಲಿ.

ತಾಳುನಿ tāḷuni (ತಾಳ್), *v. n*. To bear, endure, suffer, forbear, have patience.

ತಾಳೆ tāḷė, *see* ತಾರೆ.

ತಾಳ್ಮೆ tāḷmė, *s*. Patience, forbearance. 2. endurance.

ತಿಂಕಿ tiṅki, *see* ತಿಂಗಿ.

ತಿಂಕಿರಿ, ತಿಂಕೆರಿ tiṅkiri, tiṅkeri, *s*. A very small piece *or* strip of anything. *adj*. Thin, fine, wiry.

ತಿಂಕೆ tiṅkė, *see* ತಿರ್ಕೆ.

ತಿಂಕ್ರಿ tiṅkri, *see* ತಿಂಕಿರಿ.

ತಿಂಗಪುರಿ tiṅgapuri, *s*. A larva, moth.

ತಿಂಗಬಾರೆ tiṅgabārė, *see* ಬಿಂಗಬಾರೆ.

ತಿಂಗರ tiṅgara, *s*. Ornament, decoration. 2. *see* ಪಿಂಗರ.

ತಿಂಗಿ tiṅgi, *s*. Poison. –ಕಲಪುನಿ *lit*. to mix poison; to foment a quarrel. –ಪಾಡುನಿ to poison; to taint.

ತಿಂಗೊಡೆ tiṅgoḍė, *s*. The first day of a solar month, which is considered unlucky.

ತಿಂಗೊಳು tiṅgoḷu, *s*. The moon. 2. a month. ಪಗ್ಗ April. ಬೇಷ್ಯ May. ಕಾರ್ತೆಲ್ June. ಆಟಿ July. ಸೋಣ August. ಕನ್ಯೆ *or* ನಿರ್ನಾಲ September. ಬೊಂತೆಲ್ *or* ಪುಣಿ October. ಜಾರ್ದೆ November. ಪೆರಾರ್ದೆ December. ಪುಯಿಂತೆಲ್ January. ಮಾಯಿ February. ಸುಗ್ಗಿ March. —ಪುರಿ a kind of large worm. —ದ ಬೊಳ್ಪು moon-light, moon-shine. —ದ ಸಂಬಳ monthly pay *or* salary.

ತಿಂಣ tiṇṇa, *s*. Repetition.

ತಿಂದಡ tindaḍa, *s*. A rag.

ತಿಂದ್ರುನಿ tindruni (ತಿಂದ್ರಿ), *v. a.* To eat all, guzzle; *cf*. ತಿನ್ಪುನಿ.

ತಿಂಬಟ್ tимbaṭu, *adj*. Worthless.

ತಿಂಬಟ್ಟೆ timbaṭṭe, *s*. A vagabond, worthless man.

ತಿಂಬರೆ timbarè, *see* ತೆಂಬರೆ.

ತಿಂಬುಳು timbuḷu, *s*. A thimble.

ತಿಂಬೆಲೆ timbele, *s*. A glutton.

ತಿರ್ಗ್ದ್ tirṅguḍu, *past part.* (*of* ತಿರ್ಗುನಿ) Having turned. *adv*. Again, once more. —ಪೋಪಿನಿ to return, go back, go again. —ಬರ್ಪಿನಿ to come again; to return from a walk. —ಬೂರುನಿ to be upset, overturned; to rebel, revolt.

ತಿರ್ಗಣೆ tirṅgaṇè, *s*. A pivot, hinge, swivel. 2. a screw.

ತಿರ್ಗಮುರ್ಗ tirṅgamurṅga, *adv*. topsy-turvy, pell-mell.

ತಿರ್ಗಾಟ tirṅgāṭa, *s*. Excursion, walk, roaming. 2. turning, change.

ತಿರ್ಗಾವುನಿ tirṅgāvuni, *c. v.* (*of* ತಿರ್ಗುನಿ) To turn, whirl, make return. 2. to change, convert, gain over. ನಾಲಾಯಿ— to break a promise; to deny. ಮನಸ್— to change the mind. ಸಾಕ್ಷಿ— to gain over a witness.

ತಿರ್ಗುನಾಯೆ, ತಿರ್ಗೆಲೆ tirṅgunāye, tirṅgele, *s*. A rover, vagabond. 2. a backslider, unsteady man.

ತಿರ್ಗುನಿ tirṅguni (ತಿರ್ಗಿ), *v. n.* To turn, revert, revolve, whirl, turn back. 2. to shift, as the wind. 3. to move, wander, travel about. ತರೆ— to be giddy; to become proud. ತಿರ್ಗರೆ ಪೋಪಿನಿ to go for a walk, take a walk; *cf*. ತಿರ್ಗಡ್.

ತಿರ್ಟುನಿ tirṇṭuni, *see* ತಿರ್ಂಟುನಿ.

ತಿರ್ಬಿ tirmbi, *s*. A kind of fern; *also* ತಿರ್ಬಿಪಂತಿ.

ತಿಕಾಣಿ tikāṇi, *see* ಠಿಕಾಣಿ.

ತಿಕ್ಕ್ tikku, *s*. Entanglement, intricacy, perplexity. 2. difficulty, distress, trouble. 3. *see* ಟಿಕ್ಕಿ. —ಕಟ್ಟುನಿ to get entangled. —ಬೂರುನಿ to be entangled.

ತಿಕ್ಕಟ್ಟ್ tikkaṭṭu, *s*. A labyrinth, maze, intricacy.

ತಿಕ್ಕಟುನಿ tikkaṭuni (ತಿಕ್ಕಟಿ), *v. n.* To be matted, as hair. 2. to be entangled; to be intricate.

ತಿಕ್ಕಲೆ tikkalè, *adj*. Short and thin.

ತಿಕ್ಕಾವುನಿ tikkāvuni, *c. v.* (*of* ತಿಕ್ಕುನಿ) To ensnare, entangle. 2. to fix. 3. to button.

ತಿಕ್ಕುನಿ tikkuni (ತಿಕ್ಕ್), *v. a.* To rub, brush, polish. *v. n.* To be ensnared, caught. 2. to be seized, apprehended. *c. dat.* To find, get, obtain.

ತಿಕ್ಕೊಟೆ tikkoṭe, *see* ತಿಕ್ಕೋಟೆ.

ತಿಗ್ತೆ tigụtè, *s.* A split, splinter, slip, piece. —ಮಳ್ಪುನಿ to split, divide, saw.

ತಿಗ್ಪುನಿ tigụpuni, *see* ತಿಗಿಪುನಿ.

ತಿಗ್ರುನಿ tigụruni, *see* ತಿಗುರುನಿ.

ತಿಗ tiga, *s.* A beehive. 2. honey. —ತ ಕೆಲಂಜಿ bees. —ತ ತಟ್ಟ್, —ತ ಪಟ್ಟ a honeycomb. —ತ ನೆಯ್ಯಿ honey. —ತ ಮಾಯಿನ bees' wax. —ತ ಮೊಜಂಟೆ a small kind of bee.

ತಿಗಡಿ tigaḍi, *s.* The Indian jalap, *Ipomœa turpethum.*

ತಿಗಡಿಬಿಗಡಿ tigaḍibigaḍi, *s.* Confusion, tumult.

ತಿಗತೆ, ತಿಗತ್ತಿ tigatè, tigatti, *see* ತಿಗ್ತೆ.

ತಿಗಲೆ tigalè, *s.* The breast, chest, heart. 2. courage. —ಗಂಟೆ a giant; a big, lazy fellow; a desparado. —ದ ಗೂಂಜಿ, —ದ ಗೂಡು, —ದ ನಿಡಿಪು the hollow of the breast; bravery. —ಬೇನೆ pain in the chest. —ದ ರಾಪು anger, wrath. —ಕೊರ್ಪಿನಿ to brave, encounter with courage; to be bold. —ಡ್ ದೀಪಿನಿ to give in charge; to hold responsible. —ನಲಿಪುನಿ the heart to palpitate. —ಸುರ್ಪುನಿ the heart to break; to labour hard. —ಡ್ ಬೂರುನಿ to have charge. —ಸುದುಪುನಿ to suffer from heart-burn.

ತಿಗಿತೆ tigitè, *see* ತಿಗ್ತೆ.

ತಿಗಿಪುನಿ, ತಿಗುಪುನಿ tigipuni, tigupuni (ತಿಗಿ, ತಿಗ್), *v. a.* To split, slit, cut, saw, tear.

ತಿಗುರುನಿ, ತಿಗ್ರುನಿ, ತಿಗುಲುನಿ tiguruni, tigruni, tiguluni (ತಿಗುರ್, ತಿಗ್ರ್), *v. n.* To sprout, shoot, germinate. 2. to split.

ತಿಗ್ತೆ tigtè, *see* ತಿಗ್ತೆ.

ತಿಟ್ಟಿ tiṭṭi, *s.* White spots on leaves; *cf.* ಚಿಟ್ಟ.

ತಿಟ್ಟೆ tiṭṭè, *see* ಜಿಡ್ಡಿ.

ತಿಟ್ಟೇಸಿ tiṭṭēsi, *s.* Interference, intermeddling. 2. annoyance, trouble; *also* ಚಿಟ್ಟೇಸಿ.

ತಿಣೆ tiṇè, *s.* A small open veranda.

ತಿತಿ titi, *see* ಸ್ಥಿತಿ.

ತಿತ್ತಿರಿ tittiri, *s.* Playing upon a pipe, *etc.* 2. a top. 3. a partridge. —ಗೊಬ್ಬುನಿ to play at tops.

ತಿತ್ತಿರಿಬಿತ್ತಿರಿ tittiribittiri, *s.* An unfair dealing.

ತಿಥಿ tithi, *s.* A lunar day. 2. the annual ceremony performed to one's deceased ancestors.

ತಿದ್, ತಿದಿ tidụ, tidi, *adj.* Small.

ತಿದ್ಂಕರ tidụṅkara, *s.* Sitting on the feet. —ಕುಳ್ಳುನಿ to sit on the feet.

ತಿದಿ tidi, *see* ತಿದ್. 2. *see* ಸಿದಿ.

ತಿದಿಪಂಚ tidipañca, *adj.* Dwarfish, short.

ತಿದ್ದಾವುನಿ **tiddāvuni,** *c. v.* (*of* ತಿದ್ದುನಿ) To get corrected, rectified, altered.

ತಿದ್ದಿಗೆ **tiddigè,** *s.* Correction, training, renovation. –ಕಂಬು an erect pillar. –ಬರವು settled hand-writing.

ತಿದ್ದುನಿ **tidduni** (ತಿದ್ದ್), *v. a.* To correct, mend, reform, rectify, alter. ಕೈ– *lit.* to correct the hand; to acquire a good penmanship.

ತಿದ್ದುಪಡಿ, ತಿದ್ದುಪಾಟ **tiddupaḍi, tiddupāṭa,** *s.* Correction, amendment, modification. 2. reformation. –ಮಳ್ಪುನಿ to correct, amend, modify.

ತಿದ್ದ್ಯ **tiddya,** *adj.* Junior, younger. –ಪ್ಪೆ an aunt, *i. e.* mother's younger sister, *or* younger uncle's wife. –ಅಮೆ an uncle, *i. e.* father's younger brother, *or* aunt's husband.

ತಿದ್ದ್ಯಾಯೆ **tiddyāye,** *s.* A young man.

ತಿದ್ಪು **tidpu,** *see* ತಿಪ್ಪು.

ತಿದ್ಮ **tidma,** *s.* A kind of fish.

ತಿನಸ್ **tinasụ,** *see* ತಿನಸ್.

ತಿನೆ **tinè,** *see* ತಿಣೆ.

ತಿನ್ಪಾವುನಿ **tinpāvuni,** *c. v.* (*of* ತಿನ್ಪಿನಿ) To feed, nurse.

ತಿನ್ಪಿನಿ **tinpini** (ತಿನ್), *v. a.* To eat, consume. 2. to destroy, waste. 3. to receive, as bribes, blows, *etc.* ಪೆಟ್ಟ್– to get blows. ಲಂಚ– to take bribes.

ತಿನ್ಪೆಲೆ **tinpele,** *s.* A glutton.

ತಿಪಲೆ **tipalè,** *s.* The creeper *Clypea Burmanni.* 2. an application for the head, generally prepared of the leaves of this plant.

ತಿಪಿಲ, ತಿಪುಲೆ **tipila, tipulè,** *see* ತಿಬಿಲ.

ತಿಪ್ಪ **tippa,** *adj.* Small.

ತಿಪ್ಪಿ **tippi,** *s.* A cocoanut shell. –ಕೋಲ್ *lit.* a cocoanut shell and a stick; beggary. –ಕೋಲ್ ಪತ್ತ್‌ದ್ ನಟ್ಟುನಿ to come down to beggary. –ಮಿರೆ a small breast, resembling a cocoanut shell. ಅಡಿ– the lower half of a shell. ಕೊಂಬು– the upper half of a shell. ತರೆ– the skull.

ತಿಪ್ಪಿಲಿ **tippili,** *s.* A kind of borer.

ತಿಪ್ಪಿವೊಕ್ಕೆಲ್, ತಿಪ್ಯೊಕ್ಕೆಲ್ **tippivokkelụ, tipyokkelụ,** *s.* A poor tenant.

ತಿಪ್ಪು **tippu,** *see* ಚಿಪ್ಪು.

ತಿಪ್ಪೆ **tippè,** *s.* A heap, pile. 2. a hill.

ತಿಬಿಲ **tibila,** *s.* A hand-lamp, night-lamp.

ತಿಬುರು **tiburu,** *s.* A crack, split. –ಬುಡ್ಪಿನಿ, ತಿಬುರುನಿ, *see* ತಿಗುರುನಿ.

ತಿಬ್ಬಿ, ತಿಬ್ಬೆ **tibbi, tibbè,** *s.* Hemming.

ತಿಬ್ರಾಲ್ **tibrālụ,** *s.* Treble distilled arrack.

ತಿಮರೆ **timarè,** *s.* The Pennywort, *Hydrocotyle asiatica.*

ತಿಮಿಂಗ್‌ಲ್ **timiṅgụlụ,** *s.* A whale.

ತಿಮುಕುಡುನಿ **timukuḍuni** (ತಿಮುಕುಡ್), *v. a.* To jostle, push; to try to escape from a crowd.

ತಿಮುಕುನಿ, ತಿಮುರುನಿ **timukuni, timuruni** (ತಿಮುಕ್, ತಿಮುರ್), *v. n.* To throng, crowd. [ಉ.

ತಿಮೆಕೋಲು **timekōlu,** *see* ಸೀಮೆ ಕೋ

ತಿಯರ **tiyara,** *see* ಸೀಕರ.

ತಿರ್ಂಗುನಿ **tirṇguni,** *see* ತಿಂಗುನಿ.

ತಿರ **tira,** *see* ಸ್ಥಿರ.

ತಿರಸ್ **tirasụ,** *see* ತ್ರಾಸ್.

ತಿರಸ್ಕಾರ **tiraskāra,** *s.* Contempt, disrespect, reproach, affront.

ತಿರಿ **tiri,** *s.* A sprout, shoot, sprig, germ; the tender branch of a palm. 2. the wick of a lamp; *cf.* ಶಿರಿ. –ಬಾಯಿ a harelip. –ಮೈ a thin body. –ಅಡೆವುನಿ to cease to sprout. –ಪುಡಾವುನಿ, –ಬರ್ಪಿನಿ to sprout, shoot. ಉಗುರುದ– the point of the nail.

ತಿರಿಕಟ್ಟ್ **tirikaṭṭụ,** *see* ತಿರ್ಕಟ್ಟ್.

ತಿರಿಯರ **tiriyara,** *adv.* Within reach of the hand; below, beneath.

ತಿರು **tiru,** *s.* A bow string. 2. a short stick used to tighten, as the string of a bow, *etc.* –ಕಟ್ಟುನಿ, –ಪಾಡುನಿ to tie a bow-string.

ತಿರು **tiru,** *adj.* Holy. –ಸಭೆ the holy church.

ತಿರುಂಗುನಿ **tiruṅguni,** *see* ತಿಂಗುನಿ.

ತಿರುಗಣೆ **tirugaṇè,** *see* ತಿಂಗಣೆ.

ತಿರುದಣ **tirudaṇa,** *see* ತಿರುವಣ.

ತಿರುಪ, ತಿರುಪೆ **tirupa, tirupè,** *s.* Alms, charity.

ತಿರುಪತಿ **tirupati,** *s.* A celebrated place of pilgrimage in North Arcot.

ತಿರುಪು **tirupu,** *see* ತಿರ್ಪು.

ತಿರುಬಂಜಿ **tirubañji,** *see* ತಿರ್ಬಂಜಿ.

ತಿರುಮುರು **tirumuru,** *s.* Property, wealth. 2. exchange.

ತಿರುಮೂರ್ತಿ **tirumūrti,** *see* ತ್ರಿಮೂರ್ತಿ.

ತಿರುವ **tiruva,** *see* ತಿರ್ವ.

ತಿರುವಣ **tiruvaṇa,** *s.* A nitpick.

ತಿರುವೆ **tiruvè,** *see* ತೀವೆ.

ತಿರುಳಿ **tiruḷi,** *s.* A kind of round chisel *or* gimlet.

ತಿರೆ, ತಿರೆಕಜಿಪು **tirè, tirekajipu,** *see* ಸಿರೆಕಜಿಪು.

ತಿರ್ಕ್ **tirkụ,** *s.* A band, tie made of the fibre taken from the flat side of the cocoanut branch; *cf.* ಸಿರ್ಕ್. –ಪಾಡುನಿ to fasten the cocoanut blossom with such a tie.

ತಿರ್ಕಟ್ಟ್ **tirkaṭṭụ,** *s.* The slip-knot of a rope used for drawing water. 2. *see* ತಿಕ್ಕಟ್ಟ್. –ಪಾಡುನಿ to fasten a band, peg, *etc.*

ತಿರ್ಕಡೆ **tirkaḍè,** *s.* The lower part of any thing.

ತಿರ್ಕಾಯಿ **tirkāyi,** *see* ತಿರ್ಕೈ.

ತಿರ್ಕಾವುನಿ **tirkāvuni,** *c. v.* (*of* ತಿರ್ಕುನಿ) To make lean, to weaken.

ತಿರ್ಕಾಸ್ **tirkāsụ,** *adj.* Oblique, slant, sloping. *adv.* Obliquely, aslant.

ತಿರ್ಕುಂಟು **tirkuṇṭu,** *s.* An under-garment.

ತಿರ್ಕುನಿ **tirkuni** (ತಿರ್ಕ್), *v. n.* To be lean, weak; *also* ಸಿರ್ಕುನಿ.

ತಿರ್ಕೆ **tirkè,** *s.* A split, splinter; *also* ಸಿರ್ಕೆ.

ತಿರ್ಕೈ **tirkei,** *s.* A water jar, pitcher. 2. a handful. –ಪತ್ತುನಿ

to join the hands for receiving anything. ಕೈ– a small pitcher.

ತಿರ್ಕೊಟೆ tirkoṭè, *s.* A lean *or* weak man.

ತಿರ್ಕೋಲು tirkōlu, *see* ತ್ರಿಶೂಲ.

ತಿರ್ಗಣೆ tirgaṇè, *see* ತಿಂಗಣೆ.

ತಿರ್ಗುನಿ tirguni, *see* ತಿಂಗುನಿ.

ತಿರ್ಙಣೆ tirṅaṇè, *see* ತಿಂಗಣೆ.

ತಿರ್ತ್ tirtu̥, *adv.* Down, beneath, below, under. *adj.* Lower, subordinate. –ಮತ್ತ್ topsy-turvy. –ಬೂರುನಿ to fall down.

ತಿರ್ತಟ್ಟ್ tirtaṭṭu̥, *s.* Lower side *or* level. –ದ ಕಂಡ a lower field.

ತಿರ್ತಡ್ಯ tirtaḍya, *s.* The threshold, lower step, under frame.

ತಿರ್ತಣೆ tirtaṇè, *s.* The lower part of a slope; *cf.* ಅಣೆ.

ತಿರ್ತರ tirtara, *s.* An inferior kind. *adj.* Lower, inferior. *adv.* Below, under.

ತಿರ್ಥಟ್ಟ್ tirthaṭṭu̥, *see* ತಿರ್ತಟ್ಟ್.

ತಿರ್ದುನಿ tirduni (ತಿದ್ದ್), *v. n.* To turn. 2. *see* ತಿದ್ದುನಿ.

ತಿರ್ಪಣಾತ್ರೆ tirpaṇatrè, *s.* A place near Cochin; the former residence of the Cochin kings.

ತಿರ್ಪಣಿ tirpaṇi, *s.* A fund for the repairs of a temple.

ತಿರ್ಪತಿ tirpati, *see* ತಿರುಪತಿ.

ತಿರ್ಪಲಿ tirpali, *s.* Long pepper.

ತಿರ್ಪಲೆ tirpalè, *see* ತಿಪಲೆ.

ತಿರ್ಪಾವುನಿ tirpāvuni, *c. v.* (*of* ತಿರ್ಪು ನಿ) To get made, settled. 2. *see* ತೀರ್ಪಾವುನಿ. ಭಂಗಾರ್– to make gold ornaments.

ತಿರ್ಪು tirpu, *s.* A swivel. –ದ ಪೂ a head-ornament.

ತಿರ್ಪುನಿ tirpuni (ತಿರ್ದ್), *v. a.* To twirl round.

ತಿರ್ಬಂಜಿ tirbañji, *s.* The abdomen, bowels.

ತಿರ್ಬೆ tirbè, *s.* A piece, chip; *cf.* ತಿರ್ಕೆ.

ತಿರ್ಮುರು tirmuru, *s.* Exchange.

ತಿರ್ಯಂಡೆ tiryaṇḍè, *s.* A kind of fish.

ತಿರ್ಯರ tiryara, *adj.* Low. *adv.* Below, downward, under.

ತಿರ್ಲ್ tirlu̥, *s.* The core, heart of a tree. –ಕೂಡುನಿ to come to age, to be full-grown.

ತಿರ್ಲೆ tirle, *s.* A full-grown, strong man.

ತಿರ್ವ tirva, *s.* A kind of timber [tree.

ತಿರ್ಸೆ tirsè, *see* ತೃಷೆ.

ತಿರ್ಳಿ tirḷi, *s.* The bandage *or* crown of a stack of corn.

ತಿಲ್ tilu̥, *s.* The spleen, milt. 2. *see* ದಿಲ್.

ತಿಲ tila, *s.* The gingely oil seed, *Sesamum indicum.* –ಕುಸುಮ the sesamum flower. –ತರ್ಪಣ, ತಿಲೋದಕ sesamum seed and water, presented as an offering to the manes of the departed ancestors. –ತೈಲ gingely oil. –ದಾನ, ತಿಲಾದಾನ a gift of sesamum.

ತಿಲಕ tilaka, *s.* A sectarian *or* ornamental mark on the forehead. 2. a freckle, mole.

ತಿಲವುನಿ tilavuni, *see* ತೆಲವುನಿ.

ತಿಲಾಣ tilāṇa, *see* ತಿಲ್ಲಾಣ. 2. *see* ತೆಲ್ಲೆನ.

ತಿಲಾವು tilāvu, *see* ತಿಲವು.

ತಿಲೋದಕ tilōdaka, *see under* ತಿಲ.

ತಿಲ್ಲಾಡುನಿ tillāḍuni (ತಿಲ್ಲಾಡ್), *v. a.* To dissipate, disperse, scatter.

ತಿಲ್ಲಾಣ tillāṇa, *s.* Humming a tune.

ತಿವಾಸ್, ತಿವಾಸಿ tivāsu, tivāsi, *s.* A kind of carpet, a rug. 2. a cushion.

ತಿಳಿ tiḷi, *adj.* Transparent, clear. 2. distilled; *cf.* ತೆಳಿ, ಸೆಳಿ. —ನೀರ್ clear, *or* filtered water.

ತಿಳುವಳಿಕೆ, ತಿಳುವಳಿಗೆ tiḷuvaḷikè, tiḷuvaḷigè, *s.* Understanding, intellect; knowledge, information.

ತಿಳ್ಳಪಿಳ್ಳ tiḷḷapiḷḷa, *see* ಚಿಲ್ಲಾಪಿಲ್ಲಿ.

ತಿಳ್ಳೆ tiḷḷè, *see* ಚಿಲ್ಲೆ.

ತೀಂಕಿರಿ, ತೀಂಕೆರಿ, ತೀಂಕ್ರಿ tīṅkiri, tīṅkeri, tīṅkri, *s.* Preparing for the festival of the female demons ಅಬ್ಬಗೆ ದಾರಗೆ. 2. *see* ಸೀಂಕಿರಿ.

ತೀಂಕು tīṅku, *see* ತೀಕ್.

ತೀಂಕೆಲ್ tīṅkelu, *see* ತಿಂಕಿರಿ.

ತೀಂಟುನಿ tīṇṭuni, *see* ಸೀಂಟುನಿ.

ತೀಂತಾಟ tīntāṭa, *see* ಸೀಂಟಾಟ.

ತೀಂತಾರ, ತೀಂಥಾರ tīntāra, tīnthāra, *s.* Dispersion, dissipation. 2. ruin, waste. —ಆಪಿನಿ to become dispersed; to be ruined. —ಮಳ್ಪುನಿ to waste.

ತೀಂತಾರೆ tīntāre, *s.* A destitute *or* miserable man.

ತೀಂತಾವುನಿ tīntāvuni, *c. v.* (*of* ತೀಂತುನಿ) To cause to splash.

ತೀಂತುನಿ tīntuni (ತೀಂತ್), *v. n.* To splash; *also* ಸೀಂತುನಿ.

ತೀಂಪು tīmpu, *see* ಚೀಂಪು.

ತೀಂಪುನಿ tīmpuni (ತೀಂ), *v. n.* To snort, breathe heavily. 2. to snivel; *cf.* ತುಯಿಂಪುನಿ.

ತೀಂಪೆಲೆ tīmpele, *s.* A sniveller; *cf.* ತುಯಿಂಪೆಲೆ.

ತೀಂಟ್ರುನಿ tīrṇṭuni, *see* ತಿಳಿಂಟುನಿ.

ತೀಕ್ tīku, *adj.* Tasteful, savoury.

ತೀಕರ, ತೀಕೆರ್ tīkara, tīkeru, *adj.* Sweetish; not pungent, not properly seasoned.

ತೀಕೊಡೆ tīkoḍè, *s.* A kind of fish.

ತೀಗೆ tīgè, *see* ಸೀಗೆ.

ತೀಡುನಿ tīḍuni (ತೀಡ್), *v. a.* To rub, press. 2. to irritate.

ತೀನ್, ತೀನಿ tīnu, tīni, *s.* Food, meal, diet. 2. a glutton.

ತೀಪಲೆ tīpalè, *see* ತಿಪಲೆ.

ತೀಪೆ tīpè, *s.* Sweetness. *adj.* Sweet, fresh. —ಕಡ್ಡಿ the liquorice. —ಕೆರೆಂಗ್ sweet potato, Goa potato, *Dioscorea aculeata.*

ತೀಮುಳ್ಳು tīmuḷḷu, *s.* A kind of touch-me-not, *Cæsalpina mimosoides.*

ತೀರ್ tīru, *s.* A nit. 2. the egg of a bug. 3. *see* ತೀರ್ಪು. —ಪೇನ್ a small louse. —ಪೋಪಿನಿ, *see* ತೀರುನಿ. ತಟ್ಟ— a crushed nit.

ತೀರ tīra, *adj.* Entire, whole. *adv.* Wholly, entirely. 2. decidedly, positively.

ತೀರಂದಿ tīrandi, *see under* ತೀರುನಿ.

ತೀರಟೆ tīraṭè, *see* ತೀರಂಟೆ.

ತೀರಾವುನಿ tīrāvuni, *see* ತೀರಿಸಾವುನಿ.

ತೀರಿ tīri, *see* ತೀರಿ.

ತೀರಿಕೆ tīrikè, *s.* Conclusion, end.

ತೀರಿನಾತ್ tīrinātụ, *see* ತೀರುನಾತ್.

ತೀರಿಸಾವುನಿ, ತೀರಿಸುನಿ tīrisāvuni, tīrisuni, *c. v.* (*of* ತೀರುನಿ) To finish, conclude, complete. 2. to settle, decide, determine. 3. to pay off, as a debt.

ತೀರುನಾತ್ tīrunātụ, *adv.* As far as practicable, to the extent of one's ability.

ತೀರುನಿ tīruni (ತೀರ್), *v. n.* To be finished, settled. *c. dat.* To be able. ತೀರಂದಿ (*neg. part.*) incapable, infeasible, unsettled; endless, inexhaustible. ತೀರಂದಿ ಬಳಕೆ work beyond one's ability to perform. ಆಯಗ್ ತೀರುಜಿ he is not well. ಆಯಡ್ದ್ ತೀರಂದ್ heit not able to do it. ತೀರ್ಂಡ್ is is done. ತೀರ್ಪೋಪಿನಿ, ತೀರ್ದ್ ಪೋಪಿನಿ to end, expire, die.

ತೀರುಮಾನ tīrumāna, *s.* Conclusion, settlement, completion. *adj.* Complete, final. *adv.* Finally. —ದ ಬಿಲೆ, —ಕ್ರಯ the lowest price. —ಮಳ್ಪುನಿ to settle, resolve, determine.

ತೀರುವಿಕೆ tīruvikè, *see* ತೀರ್ವಿಕೆ.

ತೀರೆ tīrè, *see* ತೀರ.

ತೀರೆಲ್ tīrelụ, *s.* Termination, conclusion.

ತೀರ್ಗಡೆ tīrgaḍè, *s.* Completion. 2. *see* ತೀರ್ಗಡೆ.

ತೀರ್ತ, ತೀರ್ಥ tīrta, tīrtha, *s.* Pure water, sacred water in which an idol is bathed; a bathing place of pilgrimage. 2. a bathing place. —ಯಾತ್ರೆ pilgrimage to a sacred river. —ಸ್ನಾನ bathing in sacred water. —ಕೊರ್ಪಿನಿ to administer sacred water, to give water to drink. —ಬರ್ಪಿನಿ to spring forth, as water from a fountain.

ತೀರ್ನಿಕೆ, tīrnikè, *see* ಜೀರ್ನಿಕೆ.

ತೀರ್ಪಾವುನಿ tīrpāvuni, *see* ತೀರಿಸಾವುನಿ.

ತೀರ್ಪು tīrpu, *s.* Settlement, adjustment, decision, decree. —ಆಪಿನಿ to be settled. —ಮಳ್ಪುನಿ to decide, adjudge.

ತೀರ್ಪುನಿ tīrpuni, *see* ತೀರಿಸಾವುನಿ.

ತೀರ್ವಿಕೆ tīrvikè, *s.* Conclusion, settlement, adjustment.

ತೀರ್ವೆ tīrvè, *s.* Land assessment, tax.

ತೀರ್ಸಾವುನಿ tīrsāvuni, *see* ತೀರಿಸಾವುನಿ.

ತೀಸ tīsa, *see* ಸೀಸ.

ತೀಕ್ಷಣ, ತೀಕ್ಷ್ಣ tīkshaṇa, tīkshṇa, *s.* Haste, hurry. 2. heat, warmth, pungency. *adj.* Sharp, quick; hot, warm, pungent.

ತುಂಕುನಿ tuṅkuni, *see* ತೂಂಕುನಿ.

ತುಂಗ tuṅga, *s.* The river Tuṅga. 2. height, loftiness. *adj.* High, lofty. —ಭದ್ರ the river formed by the junction of Tuṅga and Bhadra.

ತುಂಗಯೆ tuṅgaye, *s.* A tall man.

ತುಂಗಯೆ tuṅgayè, *s.* A kind of seed.

ತುಂಗಾಯಿ tuṅgāyi, *s.* A fragrant kind of grass.

ತುಂಗು tuṅgu, *see* ತೂಂಗು.

ತುಂಟ tuṇṭa, *adj.* Mischievous, impudent, wicked. –ತನ impudence, wickedness.

ತುಂಟಿ, ತುಂಟೆದಿ tuṇṭi, tuṇṭedi, *s.* A mischievous *or* impudent woman.

ತುಂಟೆ tuṇṭe, *s.* A wicked *or* impudent man.

ತುಂಡು tuṇḍu, *s.* A piece, slice, bit. –ಕುಂಟು a rag. –ಗುದಿಗೆ, –ಗುದ್ದಣ a short cudgel. –ತುಂಡು pieces, fragments. –ಪತ್ತಾವುನಿ to patch, join pieces. –ಪಾಡುನಿ to fell a tree in blocks. –ಮಳ್ಪುನಿ to cut into pieces.

ತುಂಡೆ tuṇḍè, *s.* The cover of leaves round the loins, as worn by Koragar women. –ನೆಕ್ಕಿ a black kind of the five-leaved chaste-tree.

ತುಂಣ tuṇṇa, *see* ಸುಂಣ.

ತುಂಣಂಗ್, ತುಂಣೈ tuṇṇaṅgu, tuṇṇei, *s.* The scurf *or* mealy crust of the body.

ತುಂಬ tumba, *adj.* Full, complete.

ತುಂಬಾವುನಿ tumbāvuni, *c. v.* (*of* ತುಂಬುನಿ) To cause to fill, load, lade. 2. to accuse, impute, attribute.

ತುಂಬಿ tumbi, *s.* The blackbee. 2. *see* ತುಂಬೆ. ಆನೆದ–, *see* ಸುಂದಿಲ್.

ತುಂಬಿಲ್ tumbilu, *s.* Sneezing. –ಬರ್ಪಿನಿ, –ಅಪ್ಪುನಿ to sneeze.

ತುಂಬುನಿ tumbuni (ತುಂಬ್), *v. a.* To bear, carry, as a load. 2. to fill. 3. to endure, suffer. *v. n.* To be filled, full. ಅಪವಾದ–, ಪಾತರ– to suffer from a false accusation. ಪಾಪೊತ್ತು– to be guilty. ಪುಡೆ– to carry a load. ಸಾಲ– to be in debt. ತುಂಬುದು ಬಲಿ ಬರ್ಪಿನಿ to carry an idol in procession, round its temple.

ತುಂಬುರು tumburu, *see* ತಂಬರ.

ತುಂಬುರು, ತುಂಬುರೆ tumburu, tumbure, *s.* A celestial chorister.

ತುಂಬೆ tumbè, *s.* The plant *Phlomis indica.*

ತುಂಬೆನೆಕ್ಕಿಲ್ tumbenekkilu, *s.* Wild vegetation. –ಕೊಡಿಪುನಿ wild vegetation to grow; to fall in ruins.

ತುಂಬೊಣುನಿ, ತುಂಮೊಣುನಿ tumboṇuni, tummoṇuni, *refl. v.* (*of* ತುಂಬುನಿ) To bear *or* suffer for one's self, to be patient.

ತುಂಬುರ್ tumbu, *see* ತುರುಂಬು.

ತುಕಡಿ tukaḍi, *s.* A piece, rag, fragment, bit. 2. the division of a district. 3. rank and file. –ಮಳ್ಪುನಿ to divide, to put into files.

ತುಕ್ಕುತುಕ್ಕು tukkutukku, *s.* Skipping; strutting. 2. arrogance, haughtiness. –ಲಾಗ್ಯುನಿ to skip; to strut.

ತುಕ್ರೆ tukre, *see* ಕುಕ್ರೆ.

ತುಗಡಿ, ತುಗುಡಿ tugaḍi, tuguḍi, *see* ತುಕಡಿ.

ತುಗಲ್ tugalu, *s*. The skin, bark, rind. –ಕಳೆಪಿನಿ, –ಜಾರಾವುನಿ, –ದೆಪ್ಪುನಿ to skin, pare, peel.

ತುಚ್ಚ tučča, *adj*. Small, little, mean. 2. void, empty, deserted. –ತನ contempt, scorn, vileness. –ಬುದ್ಧಿ low-mindedness. –ಮಳ್ಪುನಿ to despise, scorn.

ತುಚ್ಚಾಟ tuččāṭa, *s*. Biting. 2. dispute, quarrel. –ಮಳ್ಪುನಿ to dispute *or* abuse mutually.

ತುಚ್ಚಾವುನಿ tuččāvuni, *c. v.* (*of* ತುಚ್ಚುನಿ) To cause to bite, chase. 2. to join, unite.

ತುಚ್ಚಿ tučči, *see* ತುಚ್ಚ.

ತುಚ್ಚುನಿ tuččuni (ತುಚ್ಚ್), *v. a.* To bite. 2. to be joined, united.

ತುಚ್ಚೆಲ್ tuččelu, *s*. A vicious animal; a biting animal. *adj*. Vicious; biting.

ತುಜ್ಜಿ tujji, *see* ತೊಜ್ಜಿ.

ತುಟಿ, ತುಟ್ಟಿ tuṭi, tuṭṭi, *s*. Dearth, scarcity. *adj*. Dear, scarce, rare.

ತುಡ tuḍa, *adj*. Bored, scooped out; *cf*. ತೋಡ. –ಮರಯಿ a trough made of a palm stump.

ತುಡರ್, ತುಡಾರ್ tuḍaru, tuḍāru, *s*. A light; a lamp. ಕಕ್ಕೆ– an iron hand-lamp. –ಯೆಣ್ಣೆ lamp oil. –ಬಲಿ the lamp-light procession of an idol, *etc*. –ಪೊತ್ತಾವುನಿ to light a lamp.

ತುಡಲೆ tuḍalè, *see* ತೊಡಲೆ.

ತುಡಿ tuḍi, *see* ದುಡಿ.

ತುಡುಪಿನಿ tuḍupini, *see* ಸುಡುಪಿನಿ.

ತುಡೆ tuḍè, *s*. The thigh, shank, side piece; *cf*. ತುಡ. –ಕರಂಡೆ the hip. –ಪಲಂಯಿ a side plank. –ಬಳ, –ಬಾಳ a bubo, venereal ulcer; *cf*. ತೊಡೆವಾಳ್.

ತುಡೆಪುನಿ tuḍepuni, *see* ತೊಡೆಪುನಿ.

ತುಣಾಂಗ್ tuṇaṅgu, *see* ತುಂಣಂಗ್.

ತುಣೆ tuṇè, *s*. The gummy juice exuding from the stalk, *etc*. of certain fruits. 2. arrogance, pride. –ಪುಟ್ಟುನಿ to be arrogant.

ತುತಿ tuti, *s*. A sort of drone corresponding a bagpipe. 2. *see* ಸ್ತುತಿ.

ತುತ್ತಾರಿ tuttāri, *see* ತುತ್ತೂರಿ.

ತುತ್ತಾವುನಿ tuttāvuni, *c. v.* (*of* ತುತ್ತುನಿ) To cause to dress, clothe.

ತುತ್ತು tuttu, *s*. Dressing. –ಕುಂಟು clothes, raiment. –ಪೊದೆಪು dress, clothing, covering.

ತುತ್ತುನಿ tuttuni (ತುತ್), *v. a.* To dress, wear, clothe.

ತುತ್ತೂರಿ tuttūri, *s*. A trumpet, horn, pipe. –ದಾಯೆ a trumpeter, piper. –ಊರಿಪುನಿ to blow a horn *or* trumpet.

ತುದಿ tudi, *s*. Point, end, extremity, top. –ಕೈ the arm from the elbow. –ಮುಟ್ಟ complete-ly; up to the top. –ಮುದೆಲ್ top and bottom. –ಮುದೆಲ್ ಇಜ್ಜಂದೆ aimless, purposeless. –ಬೂರುನಿ to be sufficient, convenient. –ಮುಟ್ಟುನಿ to finish, complete. ಕೈದಡ– the point of a sword.

ತುದುಂಕರ tuduṅkara, *see* ತಿದಂಕರ.

ತುದೆ tudè, *s.* A river, stream. –ಬರಿ the bank of a river. –ಕ ಡಪುನಿ, –ದಾಂಟುನಿ to ford a river.

ತುದೆಚುಳ್ಳಿ tudečuḷḷi, *s.* The holly-leaved acanthus, *Dilivaria ilicifolia.*

ತುದೆಮದಿರೆಂಗಿ tudemadireṅgi, *s.* The tree *Cratæva nirvala.*

ತುನುಸು, ತುನುಸೆ tunusu, tunusè, *s.* A kind of grass *or* nettle. *Tragia involucrata.*

ತುನೆ tunè, *see* ತುಜಿ.

ತುಪಾಕ್, ತುಪಾಕಿ tupāku, tupāki, *s.* A gun, musket.

ತುಪ್ಪಟಿ tuppaṭi, *see* ದುಪ್ಪಟಿ.

ತುಪ್ಪೆ tuppè, *s.* A stack, heap of corn *or* rice. ತಿರ್ಗ– a stack with a crown of twisted rope of straw and ears of paddy. ಶಿರಿ– the crown of a stack. –ಕೆರೆಂಗ್ a kind of yam, *Dioscorea atropurpurea.* –ಮದಿತ್ ಕುಳ್ಳುನಿ to sit in a coil, as a serpent.

ತುಫಾನ್ tuphānu, *s.* A cyclone, storm. 2. calamity, misfortune. 3. a serious imputation.

ತುಬ್ಬು tubbu, *see* ಸುಬ್ಬು.

ತುಬ್ಬು tubbu, *s.* Discovery, as of stolen property; detection, as of an offence.

ತುಮುಕು tumuku, *s.* Pressure, throng.

ತುಮುಕುನಿ tumukuni, *see* ತಿಮುಕುನಿ.

ತುಯಿ tuyi, *s.* A feather, quill, the plume of birds.

ತುಯಿಂಪುನಿ, ತುಯಿಂಬುನಿ tuyimpuni, tuyimbuni (ತುಯಿಂ, ತುಯಿಂಬ್), *v. n.* To hiss. 2. to grow angry. 3. to blow the nose; *cf.* ಸುಯಿಂಬುನಿ.

ತುಯಿಂಪೆಲೆ tuyimpele, *s.* A fretful person. 2. a sniveller.

ತುಯಿಲ್ tuyilu, *see* ಸುಯಿಲ್.

ತುರಂಗ turaṅga, *see* ಸುರಂಗ. 2. *see* ತುರುಂಗು.

ತುರಣ turaṇa, *see* ತೃಣ.

ತುರಲ turala, *see* ತೂರೊಳು.

ತುರಲೆ turalè, *see* ತೊರಲೆ.

ತುರಾಯಿ turāyi, *s.* A crest-like head-ornament worn by males. 2. a crest, plume of feathers.

ತುರಿ turi, *s.* A cramp-iron, brace.

ತುರಿತ turita, *see* ತುರ್ತ.

ತುರಿಪಿನಿ, ತುರಿಪುನಿ turipini, turipuni (ತುರಿ), *v. a.* To string, as beads. 2. to bore, perforate. ಕೆಬಿ– to bore the ears; to whisper; to backbite.

ತುರಿಯುನಿ turiyuni (ತುರಿ), *v. n.* To be stringed. 2. to be bored, perforated. ತುರಿದ್ ಬೂರುನಿ to fall, as powder from decayed wood.

ತುರುತುರು turu, *adv.* Violently, strongly. –ವೈಪುನಿ to pick flesh from a carcass, as a vulture, *etc.*; to vie as puppies when sucking, *etc.*

ತುರುಂಗು turuṅgu, *s.* A prison, jail.

ತುರುಂಬು turumbu, *s.* Chaff. –ತೂಪುನಿ to winnow.

ತುರುಟು turuṭu, *see* ತುರ್ಟ.

ತುರುಣ turuṇa, *see* ತೃಣ.

ತುರುತ turuta, *see* ತುರ್ತ.

ತುರುತುರು turuturu, *adv.* Swiftly, quickly.

ತುರುಪು turupu, *s.* Cavalry. 2. a trump *or* winning card.

ತುರುಪುನಿ turupuni, *see* ತುರಿಪಿನಿ.

ತುರುವಯಿ turuvayi, *see* ತುರಾಯಿ.

ತುರುವುನಿ turuvuni, *see* ತುರಿಯುನಿ.

ತುರುವೊಣುನಿ turuvoṇuni, *v. refl.* To embrace, take in.

ತುರೂದು turūdu, *adv.* Fast, tightly. —ಪತ್ತುನಿ to hold fast.

ತುರೆ turè, *s.* A water-gourd, pumpkin. —ತ ಅಂಡೆ a large calabash used by toddy-drawers for collecting toddy, *or* by mendicants as a vessel. —ತ ಪೋಡು the shell of an over-grown gourd. —ತ ಬೂರು the creeper of water-gourd.

ತುರ್ಕಮತ turkamata, *s.* Mohammedanism.

ತುರ್ಕಲಿ turkali, *s.* Distention, puffing. 2. pride, insolence. —ಪೋಪಿನಿ to be proud, insolent; to be troublesome.

ತುರ್ಕಲ್ಯುನಿ turkalyuni (ತುರ್ಕಲ್), *v. n.* To be distended, as an overloaded stomach.

ತುರ್ಕೆ turke, *s.* A Turk, Mussulman.

ತುರ್ಟು turṭu, *s.* A female's hair tied into a knot.

ತುರ್ಣ turṇa, *see* ತೃಣ.

ತುರ್ತ, ತುರ್ತು turta, turtu, *s.* Swiftness, haste, speed. *adj.* Quick, hasty, swift. —ಮಳ್ಪುನಿ to hasten, accelerate, be quick.

ತುರ್ಲಿ turli, *s.* Obeisance.

ತುಲ tula, *s.* A balance. 2. similarity. 3. *see* ತುಲಾ.

ತುಲಚಿ, ತುಲಸಿ tulaċi, tulasi, *s.* The holy basil, *Ocimum sanctum*; *also* ತೊಲಸಿ. —ಕಟ್ಟೆ the embankment round a basil plant. —ಪೂಜೆ worship paid to it. —ಮಣಿ beads made of wood of the holy basil. —ಮಾಲೆ, —ಸರ a necklace of those beads. —ಮುರು a kind of earring. ನಾಯಿ— the wild basil, *Ocimum album*.

ತುಲಾ tulā, *s.* The sign Libra. 2. the seventh solar month.

ತುಲಾವುನಿ tulāvuni, *see* ಸುಲಾವುನಿ.

ತುಲಾಸ್ tulāsu, *see* ತ್ರಾಸ್.

ತುಲಿ tuli, *adj.* Sweet, fresh. —ನೀರ್ fresh water.

ತುಲಿಪುನಿ, ತುಲಿಯುನಿ tulipuni, tuliyuni (ತುಲಿ), *v. a.* To churn, make butter.

ತುಲಿಯುನಿ tuliyuni, *see* ಸುಲಿಯುನಿ.

ತುಲೆ tulè, *see* ತೊಲೆ.

ತುಲೆಬಾರ tulebāra, *s.* Weighing one's self against gold, *etc.* —ತೂಕಾವುನಿ to get one's self weighed against gold and distribute it in charity.

ತುಲ್ಯ tulya, *adj.* Comparable, analogous, equal.

ತುಲ್ಲತುಲ್ಲ tullatulla, *see* ತುಳ್ಳತುಳ್ಳ.

ತುಲ್ಲಿ tulli, *see* ಚುಲ್ಲಿ.

ತುಲ್ಲುನಿ tulluni, *see* ತುಳ್ಳುನಿ.

ತುಲ್ಲೆಲ, ತುಲ್ಯಾಲ tullela, tullyāla, *see* ತುಳ್ಳೆಲ್.

ತುವ tuva, *s.* Overflowing, running over.

ತುವ್ವಿ tuvvi, *see* ತುಂಬು.

ತುಸ್ಕು tusku, *adj.* Useless, vain, unmeaning; *also* ಪುಸ್ಕು.

ತುಳಸಿ tuḷasi, *see* ತುಲಜಿ.

ತುಳಾಪಿನಿ, ತುಳಾವುನಿ tuḷapini, tuḷāvuni (ತುಳಾ), *v. a.* To row, paddle, steer; *cf.* ಸುಲಾವುನಿ.

ತುಳಿ tuḷi, *see* ಸುಳಿ.

ತುಳಿಪುನಿ tuḷipuni, *see* ಸುಳಿಪುನಿ.

ತುಳಿಯುನಿ tuḷiyuni, *see* ಸುಲಿಯುನಿ.

ತುಳು tuḷu, *s.* Tuḷu. *adj.* Of *or* belonging to Tuḷu. —ಜನ the Tuḷu people. —ದೇಶ the Tuḷu country. —ಭಾಷೆ the Tuḷu language.

ತುಳುಕುನಿ tuḷukuni, *see* ದೊಲಂಕುನಿ.

ತುಳುತಾಯೆ tuḷutāye, *s.* A native of the Tuḷu country.

ತುಳುವೆ tuḷuve, *s.* Softness, as that of a variety in fruit, *etc.* *adj.* Soft, as a fruit, *etc.* —ಕುಕ್ಕು a soft kind of mango.

ತುಳುವೆ tuḷuve, *s.* A Tuḷu man. —ಎರು an ox born and bred up in the Tuḷu country.

ತುಳ್ಪುನಿ tuḷpuni, *see* ಸುಳಿಪುನಿ.

ತುಳ್ಪೆ tuḷpe, *s.* A shell, skin, rind.

ತುಳ್ಯ tuḷya, *see* ತುಲ್ಯ.

ತುಳ್ಳತುಳ್ಳ tuḷḷatuḷḷa, *adv.* In an outspoken manner, straightforwardly. 2. suddenly, hurriedly. —ಪಣ್ಪುನಿ to speak out *or* straightforwardly.

ತುಳ್ಳಿ tuḷḷi, *see* ಜುಳ್ಳಿ.

ತುಳ್ಳುನಿ tuḷḷuni (ತುಳ್ಳ್), *v. n.* To roll, turn. 2. to leap, jump.

ತುಳ್ಳೆಲ್ tuḷḷeḷu, *s.* A marriage among Pariahs; *also* ಉಳ್ಳೆಲ್.

ತೂ tū, *s.* Fire. *adj.* Fiery. 2. bright. 3. ardent. —ತ ಕಡ್ಡಿ matches. —ತ ಕರಿ soot. —ತ ಕಲೆ the scar of a burn. —ತ ಕಲ್ಲ್ a flint stone. —ತ ಕಿಟಿ, —ತ ಕಿಡಿ, —ತ ಮೆಂಗ್ a spark. —ತ ಕುಂಡ, —ತ ಕೊಂಡ, —ತ ಗೊಂಡ a fire pit. —ತ ಕೊಳ್ಳಿ a firebrand. —ತ ಗೆಂಡ burning coals. —ತ ನಾಲಾಯಿ flame. —ತ ಪುಗೆ smoke. —ತ ಪೆಟ್ಟಿಗೆ a box of matches. —ತ ಪೊಕ್ಕೆ, —ಪೊಕ್ಲ, —ತ ಪೊಕ್ಳೆ a burn, scald, blister. —ತ ಸೆಕೆ the heat of fire. —ಅಲ್ಗುನಿ fire to burn. —ಉರಿಪುನಿ to blow fire. —ಒಕ್ಕುನಿ to poke fire. —ಕೊರೆಪುನಿ fire to blaze. —ಗಾನುನಿ fire to burn fitfully. —ತೆಕ್ಕಾವುನಿ to quench *or* extinguish fire. —ತೆಕ್ಕುನಿ fire to extinguish. —ತೊಪ್ಪುನಿ, —ದೊಂಕುನಿ to tread on fire; to smother. —ದೀಪಿನಿ, —ಪಾಡುನಿ to set fire. —ಪೊತ್ತಾವುನಿ to light, kindle a fire. —ಮೋಯುನಿ fire to smoulder

ತೂಂಕಣ tūṅkaṇa, *s.* Swinging. 2. dependence.

ತೂಂಕಲಿಯುನಿ tūṅkaliyuni, *see* ತೂಕಲಿಯುನಿ.

ತೂಂಕಿ tūṅki, *see* ತೂಂಕಣ.

ತೂಂಕು tūṅku, *s.* Swinging. 2. drowsiness. 3. reeling. 4. deliberation.

ತೂಂಕುನಿ, ತೂಂಗುನಿ **tūṅkuni, tūṅguni** (ತೂಂಕ್, ತೂಂಗ್), *v. a.* To swing, toss. *v. n.* To reel. 2. to doze, be drowsy. 3. to deliberate.

ತೂಂಗಲ್ **tūṅgalu**, *adj.* Awny, full of beard, as corn. —ಬಾರ್ awny paddy.

ತೂಂಗು **tūṅgu**, *s.* The beard of barley, *etc.*

ತೂಂಚಿ **tūñci**, *adj.* Thin, fine, small. 2. *see* ದುಂಚಿ.

ತೂಂಜಿ **tūñji**, *see* ದೂಜಿ.

ತೂಂಟಿ **tūṇṭi**, *see* ಸೂಂಟಿ.

ತೂಂಡಲ್ **tūṇḍalu**, *s.* A nest of red ants. 2. *see* ತುಂಡೆ.

ತೂಂಡುನಿ **tūṇḍuni** (ತೂಂಡ್), *v. a.* To aim, point at.

ತೂಂಡೆಲ್ **tūṇḍelu**, *s.* Pointing, directing.

ತೂಂಬರ್ **tūmbaru**, *s.* A big hole. 2. *see* ಸೂಂಬು.

ತೂಂಬರ **tūmbara**, *s.* The eye of a spade; *cf.* ಮುರಿಲ್.

ತೂಂಬು, ತೂಂಬೆ **tūmbu, tūmbè**, *see* ಸೂಂಬು.

ತೂಂಬೊ **tūmbo**, *see* ಸೂಂಬೊ.

ತೂಕ **tūka**, *s.* Weight; weighing. —ದ ಗುಂಡು a plummet; weights. —ತೂಪಿನಿ to ascertain the weight. —ಮಳ್ಪುನಿ to weigh.

ತೂಕ **tūka**, (*imperat. first pers. pl. of* ತೂಪಿನಿ). Let us see!

ತೂಕರ **tūkara**, *s.* Turbulence. —ತೋಪಿನಿ to be turbulent.

ತೂಕಲ **tūkala**, *see* ತೂಕುಲ.

ತೂಕಲಿಯುನಿ, ತೂಕಲ್ಯುನಿ **tūkaliyuni, tūkalyuni** (ತೂಕಲ್), *v. n.* To doze, be drowsy.

ತೂಕಾವುನಿ **tūkāvuni**, *c. v.* (*of* ತೂಕುನಿ) To cause to weigh. 2. to hang up.

ತೂಕಿರಿ **tūkiri**, *see* ತೂಕುಲಿ.

ತೂಕು **tūku**, *s.* Hanging. —ತುದರ್ a hanging lamp.

ತೂಕುನಿ **tūkuni** (ತೂಕ್), *v. a.* To weigh. 2. to hang suspend. 3. to swing, rock, as a cradle; *cf.* ತೂಕಲಿಯುನಿ.

ತೂಕುಲ **tūkula**, *s.* A hanging lamp.

ತೂಕುಲಿ, ತೂಕ್ರಿ **tūkuli, tūkri**, *s.* Annoyance, distraction. —ತೋಪಿನಿ to annoy, distract.

ತೂಗಡಿ **tūgaḍi**, *s.* Drowsiness, sleepiness. 2. *see* ತುಕಡಿ.

ತೂಗಡಿಪುನಿ **tūgaḍipuni** (ತೂಗಡಿ), *v. n.* To be drowsy, sleepy.

ತೂಗುನಿ **tūguni**, *see* ತೂಕುನಿ.

ತೂಟಣ್ **tūṭaṇu**, *s.* A mixture of rubbish and earth, burnt and used as manure.

ತೂಟೆ **tūṭè**, *s.* A torch, made of palm leaves, *etc.* 2. a fierce, quarrelsome woman; *also* ಸೂಟೆ. —ಕಾಳಗ, —ದರ a mock-fight with torches. —ಮಾಕಾಳಿದ a quarrelsome woman.

ತೂಟುಕೋಲು **tūṭukōlu**, *s.* A soldering rod.

ತೂಡಿ **tūḍi**, *see* ಸೂಡಿ.

ತೂಣ **tūṇa**, *see* ತೂನ.

ತೂತಿ **tūti**, *s.* Appetite; desire.

ತೂತೂ **tūtū**, *int.* Fie! shame!

ತೂನ **tūna,** *s.* A stake, post. —ಕೆರೆಂಗ್ a kind of yam, *Dioscorea alata.*

ತೂಪಣ **tūpaṇa,** *s.* A sign.

ತೂಪಾವುನಿ **tūpāvuni,** *c. v.* (*of* ತೂಪಿನಿ & ತೂಪುನಿ) To show, point out. 2. to cause to winnow.

ತೂಪಿನಿ **tūpini** (ತೂ), *v. a.* To see, look, observe. 2. to try, test, examine. 3. to visit. 4. to seek; to consider, regard. 5. to take care.

ತೂಪು **tūpu,** *s.* Winnowing, as grain.

ತೂಪುನಿ **tūpuni** (ತೂ), *v. a.* To winnow, fan. 2. to blame, abuse; *see* ತೂಕುನಿ.

ತೂಬೆ **tūbè,** *s.* A hole.

ತೂರ **tūra,** *s.* A contract, particularly for toddy. —ದ ಕಲಿ toddy supplied according to contract. —ದ ಬೈದೆ a toddy-drawer who has contracted to supply toddy. —ದ ಕಲಿ ಮೈಪುನಿ to consign toddy according to contract.

ತೂರಿ **tūri,** *s.* An earthen water-pot; *cf.* ಚೂರಿ. —ಪೊಟ್ಟೆ a man with a dropsical belly.

ತೂರಿಮುಳ್ಳು **tūrimuḷḷu,** *s. Ziziphus œnoplia.* —ಪಾಡುನಿ to instigate.

ತೂರು **tūru,** *s.* A crack, chap, fissure. —ಬುಡ್ಪಿನಿ to crack, chap.

ತೂರುನಿ **tūruni** (ತೂರ್), *v. n.* To crack, as a vessel.

ತೂರೊಳು **tūroḷu,** *s.* A kind of rattan, *Calamus rotang*; *cf.* ಸೂರೊಳು. —ದ ಕಂಡೆ the root of the same. —ದ ಬಲ್ಲ a thicket of the same. —ದ ಬೆತ್ತ a walking stick made of the same.

ತೂರ್ಯ **tūrya,** *s.* A musical instrument.

ತೂಲ **tūla,** (*imperat. 2nd pers. sing. of* ತೂಪಿನಿ) See! 2. *see* ಸೂಲ.

ತೂಲಂಗಿ **tūlaṅgi,** *see* ಸೂಲೆಂಗಿ.

ತೂಲಾವುನಿ **tūlāvuni,** *see* ಸುಲಾವುನಿ.

ತೂಲಿ **tūli,** *see* ಚೋಲಿ.

ತೂಲುನಿ **tūluni** (ತೂಲ್), *v. n.* To totter, reel; to nod, be drowsy.

ತೂಲೆಂಗಿ **tūleṅgi,** *see* ಸೂಲೆಂಗಿ.

ತೂಳ **tūḷa,** *s.* Inspiration; enthusiasm, ecstacy.

ತೂಳಂ **tūḷam,** *s.* A kind of cotton.

ತೂಳು **tūḷu,** *see* ಧೂಳು.

ತೃಟ್ **truṭu,** *s.* An instant.

ತೃಣ **truṇa,** *s.* Grass, hay, straw. 2. a bit. *adj.* Light *or* trifling, as a straw. —ಪ್ರಾಯು contemptible; short life.

ತೃಪ್ತಿ **trupti,** *s.* Satisfaction, gratification, contentment. —ಆಪಿನಿ to be satisfied. —ಪಡೆಪಾವುನಿ to satisfy.

ತೃಷೆ **trushè,** *s.* Thirst. 2. wish, desire.

ತೆಂಕಾಯಿ **teṅkāyi,** *see* ತೆನ್ಕಾಯಿ.

ತೆಂಕ್ರಾಲ್ **teṅkrāḷu,** *s.* A red kind of stone.

ತೆಂಗ್ **teṅgu,** *s.* The cocoanut tree. 2. a swelling.

ತೆಂಡ್ **teṇḍu,** *see* ಚೆಂಡ್.

ತೆಂಡೆ **teṇḍè,** *see* ಚೆಂಡೆಮರ.

ತೆಂಡೆವುಲಿ, ತೆಂಡೆಮುಳಿ tendemuli, tendemuli, *s.* A species of thatch grass.

ತೆಂಡೆಲ್ tendelu, *s.* A very young cocoanut just out of bud. –ಮೋಣೆ a shrivelled *or* wan face. –ಕಟ್ಟುನಿ the face to shrivel.

ತೆಂನ್ tennu, *adv.* Now.

ತೆಂನಸ್ tennasu, *see* ತೆನಸ್.

ತೆಂಬರ, ತೆಂಬರೆ tembara, tembarè, *s.* A small drum. –ಬೊಟ್ಟುನಿ to drum.

ತೆಂಬಿ tembi, *s.* The lower part of a cocoanut shell. 2. the back of the head.

ತೆಂಬಿರಿ, ತೆಂಬೆರಿ tembiri, temberi, *s.* A burning sensation in the throat. 2. a raw taste, as of imperfect seasoning of food.

ತೆಂಬೆರಿಯುನಿ temberiyuni (ತೆಂಬೆರ್), *v. n.* To feel a burning sensation in the throat. 2. to taste raw, as imperfectly seasoned food.

ತೆಂಬುಡ tembuda, *adv.* Yet, still, up to this time.

ತೆಂಬೆ tembè, *see* ಬೆಂಡೆಮರ.

ತೆಂಬೆರೆ temberè, *see* ತೆಂಬರ.

ತೆಂಬೆಲ್ tembelu, *see* ದೆಂಬೆಲ್.

ತೆಂಮ temma, *s.* A cough, cold. ಕಪ್ಪೆ– the whooping cough. ಕೋಪೆ– cough with dyspnœa, bronchitis. ಮುಕ್ಕ– a catarrhal cough. –ಅಪ್ಪುನಿ to cough, hawk.

ತೆಕ್ಕ್ tekku, *see* ತೆಕ್ಕಿ.

ತೆಕ್ಕರೆ tekkarè, *s.* A cucumber, *Cucumis sativa.*

ತೆಕ್ಕರ್ಮೆ tekkarmè, *s.* A kind of ornament; *also* ಚಕ್ಕಿ. 2. *see* ತೆಕ್ಕರೆ.

ತೆಕ್ಕಳೆ tekkalè, *see* ತೆಕ್ಕರೆ.

ತೆಕ್ಕಾವುನಿ tekkāvuni, *c. v.* (*of* ತೆಕ್ಕುನಿ) To quench, put out, smother.

ತೆಕ್ಕಿ tekki, *s.* Teakwood, *Tectona grandis.* –ದ ಮರ the teak tree.

ತೆಕ್ಕುನಿ tekkuni (ತೆಕ್ಕ್), *v. n.* To be extinguished. 2. to be calm, be pacified. ತೂ ತೆಕ್ಕ್ಯಂಡ್ the fire is quenched. ಕೋಪ– anger to be pacified.

ತೆಕ್ಕೆ tekkè, *see* ಚಕ್ಕಿ. 2. *see* ಚಿಕ್ಕಿ.

ತೆಕ್ಕೆರೆ tekkerè, *see* ತೆಕ್ಕರೆ.

ತೆಗುಲ್ tegulu, *s.* A sprout, bud.

ತೆಗುಲುನಿ teguluni (ತೆಗಿಲ್), *v. n.* To sprout, shoot, bud.

ತೆಗುನಿ teguni (ತೆಗಿ), *v. a.* To take. 2. to abuse, revile. ತೆಗೇ making a threatening noise.

ತೆಗೆಲುನಿ tegeluni, *see* ತೆಗಿಲುನಿ.

ತೆಗೆಲೆ tegelè, *s.* Abusing, reviling. –ತೆಗುನಿ to abuse.

ತೆಟ್ಟ್ tettu, *adj.* Bad, wicked. 2. rotten, decayed; *also* ಕೆಟ್ಟ್.

ತೆಟ್ಟಾವುನಿ tettāvuni, *c. v.* (*of* ತೆಟ್ಟುನಿ) To cause to be damaged, corrupted *or* failed; *also* ಕೆಟ್ಟಾವುನಿ.

ತೆಟ್ಟುನಿ tettuni (ತೆಟ್ಟ್), *v. n.* To rot, decay, be damaged. 2. to become corrupt. 3. to fail; *also* ಕೆಟ್ಟುನಿ.

ತೆಡಿ teḍi, *see* ಕೆಡಿ.

ತೆಡಿಲ್ teḍilu, *s.* Thunder, thunderbolt, thunderclap. —ಮಿಂಚಿ a flash of lightening. —ಕೊರೆ ಪುನಿ, —ಪೊರೆಲುನಿ, —ಮುರೆಸುನಿ to thunder. —ದರ್ಪುನಿ, —ನೋಪುನಿ, —ಹಾಕುನಿ to be struck by lightening; to be thunderstruck.

ತೆಣಸ್ teṇasu, *see* ತೆನಸ್.

ತೆತ್ತಿ tetti, *s.* An egg.

ತೆತ್ತುನಿ tettuni (ತೆತ್ತಿ), *v. n.* To throb *or* distend, as the kidneys from accumulation of urine.

ತೆನ್ tenu, *see* ತೆಂನ್.

ತೆನ್‌ಕಾಯಿ, ತೆನ್ಕಾಯಿ tenukāyi, tenkāyi, *s.* South. *adj.* Southern. 2. the Malabar province.

ತೆನಸ್ tenasu, *s.* Food, feeding.

ತೆನಿ teni, *see* ತಣು.

ತೆನ್ಕೆರೆ tenkere, *irregular gerund of* ತಿನ್ಪಿನಿ.

ತೆಪ್ಪ teppa, *s.* A float, raft. 2. a shoal of fish. *adj.* Dense; *cf.* ಜಪ್ಪ. —ಕಟ್ಟುನಿ to make a float.

ತೆಪ್ಪರಿಗೆ tepparigè, *s.* A cloth-like substance which wraps round the base of the cocoanut branches.

ತೆಪ್ಪು teppu, *s.* The fibrous covering of certain nuts. 2. *see* ಕೆಪ್ಪು.

ತೆಪ್ಪೆ teppè, *see* ಕೆಪ್ಪೆ.

ತೆಬಟುನಿ tebaṭuni, *see* ತಬುಟುನಿ.

ತೆಬಟೆ tebaṭè, *s.* A kind of fish.

ತೆಬ್ಬು tebbu, *s.* A bow string.

ತೆಬ್ಬುಬ್ಬು tebbubbu, *see* ತಬ್ಬಿಬ್ಬು.

ತೆಮತಿಗೆ tematigè, *see* ಕೇಮತಿಗೆ.

ತೆಮ್ಮ temma, *see* ತೆಂಮ.

ತೆಯಿ, ತೆಯ್ಯ teyi, teyya, *s.* Beating time in dancing.

ತೆಯ್ಯ teyya, *see* ದೆಯ್ಯ.

ತೆರಂಟೆ teranṭè, *see* ತೇರಂಟೆ.

ತೆರಕಯಿ terakayi, *s.* Breadth. 2 making way. *adj.* Broad, wide; *also* ತೆರಕಾಯಿ.

ತೆರಡುನಿ teraḍuni, *see* ತೆರೆಡುನಿ.

ತೆರಣ teraṇa, *see* ತ್ರಾಣ.

ತೆರಪು terapu, *s.* Space, room.

ತೆರಸ್ terasu, *see* ತ್ರಾಸ್.

ತೆರಿಗೆ terigè, *s.* Taxes.

ತೆರಿಪಾವುನಿ teripāvuni, *c. v.* (*of* ತೆರಿಯುನಿ) To make known, communicate, inform. 2. to explain, expose.

ತೆರಿಪುನಿ teripuni, *see* ತೆರಿಯುನಿ.

ತೆರಿಯ teriya, *s.* A cirular pad of wicker or straw, placed under a vessel to make it steady.

ತೆರಿಯು teriyu, *s.* A circle.

ತೆರಿಯುನಿ teriyuni (ತೆರಿ), *v. n.* To be known, understood, comprehended. *c. dat.* To understand. 2. to be able. 3. to feel, perceive, conceive. ಯೆಂಕ್ ತೆರಿಯುಂಡು I know, *or* I can. ಆಯಗ್ ತೆರಿಜಿ he did not know, he could not.

ತೆರುಂಟುನಿ teruṇṭuni, *see* ತೆಳೆಂಟುನಿ.

ತೆರುವೆ teruvè, *see* ತೀರ್ವೆ.

ತೆರೆ terè, *see* ಕೆರೆ.

ತೆರೆಕಾಯಿ terekāyi, *see* ತೆರಕಯಿ.

ತೆರೆಡುನಿ **tereḍuni** (ತೆರೆಡ್), *v. n.* To be confounded, confused. 2. to roll down.

ತೆರ್ಪುನಿ **terpuni** (ತೆರ್), *v. a.* To separate. ತೆರ್ಪ್‍ಡ್ ಪಾಡುನಿ to make one sit in a cross line as an outcaste at dinner. ತೆರ್ಪೆ ದೀಪಿನಿ to keep separate; to interdict, excommunicate.

ತೆರ್ಪೆ **terpè**, *s.* Sod thrown up by ploughing; *cf.* ತೇಪೆ.

ತೆರ್ವೆ **tervè**, *see* ತೀವೆ.

ತೆಲ್ಂಟುನಿ **teluṇṭuni**, *see* ತೆಳ್ಂಟುನಿ.

ತೆಲವು, ತೆಲಾವು **telavu, telāvu**, *s.* A young *or* half grown cock.

ತೆಲವುನಿ, ತೆಲಾವುನಿ **telavuni, telāvuni** (ತೆಲ, ತೆಲಾ), *v. n.* To go aside, make way. 2. to avoid, shun.

ತೆಲಾಂಟ್ **telāṇṭu**, *s.* Coming beforehand.

ತೆಲಿ **teli**, *s.* Gruel, rice water. 2. *see* ಸೆಲಿ.

ತೆಲಿಕೆ **telikè**, *s.* A laugh, smile, laughter. 2. ridicule, derision. ಮುಗುರು— a gentle smile.

ತೆಲಿಪಾವುನಿ **telipāvuni**, *c. v.* (*of* ತೆಲಿಪುನಿ) To make laugh.

ತೆಲಿಪುನಿ **telipuni** (ತೆಲ್), *v. n.* To laugh, smile. *v. a.* To deride.

ತೆಲಿಯಾವುನಿ **teliyāvuni**, *see* ಸೆಲಿಯಾವುನಿ.

ತೆಲಿಯುನಿ **teliyuni**, *see* ಸೆಲಿಯುನಿ.

ತೆಲು **telu**, *see* ತೆಲ್ಪು.

ತೆಲುಂಗು, ತೆಲುಗು **teluṅgu, telugu**, *s.* Telugu.

ತೆಲುಂಗೆ **teluṅge**, *s.* A Telugu man.

ತೆಲುಂಟುನಿ **teluṇṭuni**, *see* ತೆಳ್ಂಟುನಿ.

ತೆಲ್ಪು **telpu**, *s.* Thinness. *adj.* Thin, lean. 2. few, little.

ತೆಲ್ಪುನಿ **telpuni**, *see* ತೆಲಿಪುನಿ.

ತೆಲ್ಲವು, ತೆಲ್ಲಾವು **tellavu, tellāvu**, *s.* A thin, flat kind of cake, made of rice flour, *etc.*

ತೆಲ್ಲುನಿ **telluni** (ತೆಲ್ಲ್), *v. a.* To winnow, sift.

ತೆಲ್ಲೆ **tellè**, *see* ಸೆಲ್ಲೆ.

ತೆಲ್ಲೆನ **tellena**, *adj.* Thinnish; *cf.* ತೆಲ್ಪು.

ತೆವಲ್ **tevaḷu**, *s.* Desire, wish. 2. attachment.

ತೆಳ್ಂಟುನಿ **teḷuṇṭuni** (ತೆಳ್ಂಟ್), *v. n.* To contract, shrivel. 2. to wither, grow thin.

ತೆಳಿ **teḷi**, *see* ತೆಲಿ.

ತೆಳಿಯುನಿ **teḷiyuni**, *see* ಸೆಲಿಯುನಿ.

ತೇಂಕುನಿ **tēṅkuni**, *see* ಸೇಂಕುನಿ.

ತೇಂಕೆ **tēṅkè**, *see* ಸೇಂಕೆ.

ತೇಕ್‌ಮುರ್ಕ್, ತೇಕಮುರ್ಕ **tēkumurku, tēkamurka**, *s.* Cloying, palling, satiation.

ತೇಕ **tēka**, *see* ಸೇಕ.

ತೇಕೆ **tēkè**, *adj.* Brimful, up to the brim only. —ಅರಿ about three quarter seer of rice. —ಅಳಪುನಿ to mete up only to the brim of a measure.

ತೇಗ್ **tēgu**, *s.* Belching.

ತೇಗುನಿ **tēguni** (ತೇಗ್), *v. n.* To belch.

ತೇಜ, ತೇಜಸ್ಸ್ **tēja, tējassu**, *s.* Lustre, light, splendour. 2. glory, fame.

ತೇಜಿ tēji, *s.* A gift; *cf.* ಸೇಜ.

ತೇಜಿ tēji, *s.* A horse of superior breed. *adj.* Swift, fast. 2. sharp, as a knife.

ತೇಟ್ tēṭụ, *s.* The beard of grass; *cf.* ತೂಂಗು. *adj.* Pure, clear; glaring, downright. –ದಾಯಿ a tall man. –ಯೆಂಣೆ pure oil. –ಸುಳ್ಳು a glaring lie.

ತೇಟಿಲ, ತೇಟ್ಲ tēṭila, tēṭla, *s.* A kind of vegetable, *Caladium nymphacifolium.*

ತೇಟೆ tēṭė, *see* ಚೇಷ್ಟೆ.

ತೇಡಯಿ tēḍayi, *s.* A base woman, [*vlg.*

ತೇಡಾಯಿ tēḍāyi, *see* ತೇಡೆ.

ತೇಡಿ tēḍi, *see* ಸೇಡಿ.

ತೇಡು, ತೇಡೆ tēḍu, tēḍė, *s.* A slice, piece, as of a jack fruit; *cf.* ಸೇಡು.

ತೇಡೆ tēḍė, *s.* A kind of fish. ಕಪ್ಪ–, ಬೆಂಗೊಡಿ–, ಬೊಲ್ಯ–, ಮಂಜಲ್–, ಮುಂಗುಲಿ– are its different species.

ತೇಡೆಮುಳ್ಳು tēḍemuḷḷu, *s.* A kind of tree. –ಪಂರ್ದ್ the fruit of the same.

ತೇದಿ tēdi, *s.* A day of the solar month.

ತೇಪಂಗಾಯಿ tēpaṅgāyi, *see* ತಪ್ಪಂಗಾಯಿ.

ತೇಪಂಗೆಲ್ tēpaṅgelụ, *s.* Any article with an inclined surface.

ತೇಪಕಲ್ಲ್ tēpakallụ, *s.* A polishing stone, whetstone.

ತೇಪಣೆ tēpaṇė, *s.* Rubbing, polishing, as a precious stone.

ತೇಪಲೆ tēpalė, *s.* A kind of trough *or* bucket used for watering trees, *etc.*

ತೇಪು tēpu, *s.* Rubbing, whetting, polishing, as a precious stone. –ಕಲ್ಲ್ a polishing stone; a corundum. –ಗಾರೆ a polisher. –ಪಲಂಯಿ a whetting board. –ಪತ್ಡಾವುನಿ to polish, cut, as a precious stone.

ತೇಪುನಿ tēpuni (ತೇ), *v. a.* To throw water with a bucket *or* trough. 2. to irrigate. 3. to rub, polish.

ತೇಬಟೆ tēbaṭė, *see* ತಬಟೆ.

ತೇಮತಿಗೆ tēmatigė, *see* ಶೇಮತಿಗೆ.

ತೇಮನ, ತೇಮಾನ tēmana, tēmāna, *s.* Loss in assaying metals, waste caused by rubbing *or* polishing metals.

ತೇಮಯಿ, ತೇಮೆ tēmayi, tēmė, *see* ಸೇಮಯಿದಡ್ಡೆ.

ತೇಯ tēya, *see* ತಂಯಿ.

ತೇರ್ tērụ, *s.* An idol-car. 2. the car-festival. –ವೈಪುನಿ to draw a car in procession.

ತೇರ್ tērụ, *s.* Bark, rind, peel. –ಕಲೆಪಿನಿ, –ದೆಪ್ಪುನಿ, –ಲಕ್ಕಾವುನಿ, –ವೈಪುನಿ to peel, bark, flay. ತೌತೆದ– the peelings of cucumber.

ತೇರಂಟೆ tēranṭė, *s.* A centipede, millepede.

ತೇರಾಟ tērāṭa, *s.* A car festival.

ತೇರು tēru, *see* ತೇರ್.

ತೇರೆ tērė, *see* ತೇರ್.

ತೇರೆದಮರ tēreda-mara, *s.* The

marking-nut tree, *Semecarpus Anacardium.*

ತೇರ್ಗಡೆ tērgaḍè, *s.* Settlement; conclusion; acquittal. 2. passing, as an examination.

ತೇರ್ಪೆ tērpè, *s.* Mire sticking to a plough.

ತೇರ್ಬೀದಿ tērbīdi, *s.* The street through which an idol-car is drawn; the car-street.

ತೇಲ್ tēlų, *see* ತೇಳ್.

ತೇಲಾವುನಿ tēlāvuni, *see* ತೆಲವುನಿ.

ತೇಲುನಿ tēluni (ತೇಲ್), *v. n.* To float.

ತೇವು tēvu, *s.* A kind of yam, *Arum colocasia*; *Calladium esculentum.*

ತೇಳ್ tēḷų, *s.* A scorpion. –ಗುಂಡಿ the hook of a chain, to which a coin *etc.* is suspended. –ಕಾಕುನಿ a scorpion to sting.

ತೈ tei, *see* ದೈ.

ತೈನಾತಿ teināti, *s.* Being in one's charge *or* care. 2. a peon attending on a superior officer; an orderly.

ತೈಪಿನಿ teipini, *see* ಸೈಪಿನಿ.

ತೈರಣೆ teiraṇè, *see* ಸೈರಣೆ.

ತೈರುನಿ teiruni, *see* ತರಿಯುನಿ.

ತೈಲ್ teilų, *s.* A money bag, purse.

ತೈಲ, ತೈಲೆ teila, teilè, *s.* Oil, ointment.

ತೈಲಸ teilasa, *see* ತತ್ತೈಲಸ.

ತೈಲಿ teili, *see* ತೈಲ್.

ತೊಂಕೆ toṅkè, *s.* Void, vacuum.

ತೊಂಗೆ, ತೊಂಗೆಲ್ toṅgè, toṅgelų, *s.* A cluster of blossoms; a bunch of fruits, *etc.*

ತೊಂಡೆ toṇḍè, *see* ತುಂಡೆ 2. *see* ದೊಂಡೆ.

ತೊಂಡೆಕಲ್ಪು toṇḍekalpu, *s.* The northern frontier of the Tuḷu land. ತೊಂಡೆಕಲ್ಪುಡ್ದು ಕಾಸರ್ಗೋಡುದ ಕಡವು ಮುಟ್ಟ ತುಳು ದೇಶ the Tuḷu country extends from Toṇḍekalpu down to the ford of Kāsargōḍ.

ತೊಂಡ್ತಿನಿ toṇḍtini, *see* ತೊಡ್ತಿನಿ.

ತೊಂದಪ್ಪೆ tondappè, *s.* A tadpole.

ತೊಂದರೆ tondarè, *s.* Entanglement, confusion. 2. perplexity, annoyance, trouble, vexation. 3. misfortune, distress.

ತೊಂದುನಿ tonduni (ತೊಂದ್), *v. a.* To work hard, labour; *cf.* ಸೊಂದುನಿ.

ತೊಂದುರು, ತೊಂದೊರು tonduru, tondoru, *s.* A baking pan; a copper vessel for baking cakes by steam.

ತೊಂದೆ tondè, *adj.* Big, distended. –ಬಂಜಿ a big belly. –ಪುರಿ a tadpole. –ಮೀನ್ a kind of fish.

ತೊಂಬರ tombara, *adj.* Abundant, much. *adv.* Heartily, freely. –ಉಣ್ಪುನಿ to eat heartily.

ತೊಂಬಾಕ್ tombākų, *see* ತಂಬಾಕ್.

ತೊಂಮೆ tommè, *s.* The lobe of the ear.

ತೊಗರಿ, ತೊಗರೆ togari, togarè, *s.* The pigeon-pea, *Cajanus*

indicus. –ಜೇಳಿ, –ಸಲಾಯಿ doll, split pigeon-pea.

ತೊಗಲ್ togaḷu, *see* ತುಗಲ್.

ತೊಗೊರಿ togori, *see* ತೊಗರಿ.

ತೊಜಂಕ್ tojaṅku, *see* ತಜಂಕ್.

ತೊಜಕೆ, ತೊಜಕಡೆ tojakè, tojakaḍè, *s.* Malice. –ಪಾತೆರುನಿ to talk maliciously; to give vent to malice.

ತೊಜ್ಜಿ tojji, *s.* Itching, scratching. 2. the scum of water, collected into bubbles.

ತೊಟಿ toṭi, *s.* An old woman.

ತೊಟೆ toṭe, *s.* An old man.

ತೊಟ್ಟಿ toṭṭi, *s.* A bucket, trough, tub.

ತೊಟ್ಟಿಲ್ toṭṭiḷu, *s.* A cradle, cot. –ಪಕ್ಕಿ a bat. –ಪಾಂತೆ a large kind of butterfly. –ತೂಂಕುನಿ to rock a cradle.

ತೊಟ್ಟು toṭṭu, *s.* The stem *or* stalk of a leaf *or* fruit. 2. the nipple of a breast.

ತೊಟ್ಟುನಿ, ತೊಟ್ಟೊಣುನಿ toṭṭuni, toṭṭoṇuni (ತೊಟ್ಟ್, ತೊಟ್ಟೊಣ್), *v. a.* To embrace, hug, hold fast; *cf.* ತಟ್ಟೊಣುನಿ.

ತೊಟ್ಟೆ toṭṭè, *s.* A basket made of cocoanut leaves. 2. a honeycomb; *cf.* ತಟ್ಟೆ. –ಕೊಂಗುರ್ a kind of crane.

ತೊಟ್ರಯಿ toṭrayi, *s.* A wooden trough.

ತೊಟ್ಲಲೆ toṭlalè, *s.* A child in the cradle; *also* ತೊಟ್ಟಿಲ್‌ಬಾಲೆ. –ಪೋಪಿನಿ a wife to return to her husband's house, with the new-born child.

ತೊಡ್ಂಬೆ toḍumbè, *s.* A cluster of flowers.

ತೊಡಂಕ್ toḍaṅku, *s.* A clasp, hook.

ತೊಡಕ್ toḍaku, *s.* Entanglement; obstacle, hinderance.

ತೊಡಗುನಿ toḍaguni (ತೊಡಗ್), *v. n.* To begin, commence. 2. to undertake.

ತೊಡಗೆಲ್ toḍageḷu, *s.* Beginning, commencement.

ತೊಡಮಣೆ toḍamaṇè, *s.* Entertaining a son-in-law *or* a mother-in-law for the first time.

ತೊಡರ್, ತೊಡರು toḍaru, toḍaru, *s.* Entanglement, obstacle.

ತೊಡಲೆ toḍalè, *s.* The funeral dinner. 2. hardship, trouble. –ದ ನುಪ್ಪು food earned with hardship.

ತೊಡಿ toḍi, *see* ತೊಡು.

ತೊಡಿಗೆ toḍigè, *s.* Clothes, dress. 2. ornaments. 3. avidity, eagerness.

ತೊಡು, ತೊಡುವೆಲ್ toḍu, toḍuveḷu, *s.* Greediness. ತೊಡುವೆಲೆ a greedy man.

ತೊಡೆ toḍè, *see* ತುಡೆ.

ತೊಡೆಪುನಿ toḍepuni (ತೊಡೆ), *v. a.* To anoint. 2. to paint. 3. to smear, rub.

ತೊಡೆವಾಳ್ toḍevāḷu, *s.* A bubo.

ತೊಡ್ಡುವೆ toḍḍuvè, *s.* A large bee. 2. a beehive, honeycomb. 3. a lump of musty flour. –ಕಟ್ಟುನಿ to build a beehive; to become musty. –ಗೆಪ್ಪುನಿ to extract honey from a beehive.

ತೊಡ್ಡೆ toḍḍè, *s.* A large kind of bee. 2. its hive; *cf.* ತೊಡ್ಡುವೆ.

ತೊಡ್ಡೆಲ್ toḍḍelụ, *s.* Greediness. 2. a large bee.

ತೊಡ್ಡೆಲಿ toḍḍeli, *see* ತೊಡ್ತಿನಿ.

ತೊಡ್ಡಲೆ, ತೊಡ್ತೆಲೆ toḍḍele, toḍtele, *s.* A greedy man.

ತೊಡ್ತಿನಿ toḍtini, *s.* A greedy woman.

ತೊತ್ತು tottu, *s.* A maid servant.

ತೊದಲೆ todale, *s.* A stammerer.

ತೊದಳೆ todaḷè, *s.* Stammering. 2. indistinct pronunciation. 3. untruth. —ಪಾತೆರುನಿ to stammer; to lisp; *cf.* ದದಲುನಿ.

ತೊದುಂಕರ toduṅkara, *see* ತಿದ್ಂಕರ.

ತೊದುಂಗೈಲ್ toduṅgeilụ, *s.* Longing, eagerness.

ತೊದುಪು todupu, *s.* A vain hope *or* desire.

ತೊಪ್ಪಳಿಪುನಿ toppaḷipuni, *see* ತಪ್ಪಿಲಿಯುನಿ.

ತೊಪ್ಪಿ toppi, *s.* A cap, hat.

ತೊಪ್ಪು toppu, *see* ತಪ್ಪು.

ತೊಯಳಿ toyaḷi, *s.* A washerwoman.

ತೊಯಿಪುನಿ toyipuni, *see* ತ್ಯೊಪುನಿ.

ತೊಯಿಲ toyila, *see* ತ್ಯೊಲ್.

ತೊಯಿಲಿ toyili, *see* ತೊಯಳಿ.

ತೊರ tora, *see* ಸ್ವರ.

ತೊರಂಗ್ toraṅgụ, *see* ತುರುಂಗ.

ತೊರಕೆ torakè, *s.* A large flat seafish, a skate, thornback. ಪಕ್ಕಿ—, ಪಿಲಿ— different species of thornback.

ತೊರಗೆ toragè, *see* ಸೊರಗೆ.

ತೊರಣ toraṇa, *see* ತೋರಣ.

ತೊರಪುನಿ torapuni, *v. a.* To wash superficially. 2. to flatter. 3. to heal a disease by incantations, fumigation, *etc.*; *also* ತೊರತಿದಪ್ಪುನಿ.

ತೊರಲಿ torali, *see* ತರೊಳಿ.

ತೊರಲೆ toralè, *s.* The mucus of the nose.

ತೊರಿಪುನಿ toripuni, *see* ತೊರ್ಪುನಿ.

ತೊರೆಲ್ torelụ, *s.* Abandonment.

ತೊರೆವುನಿ torevuni (ತೊರೆ), *v. a.* To abandon, give up.

ತೊರ್ಕಲಿಯುನಿ torkaliyuni, *see* ಸೊರ್ಕಲುನಿ.

ತೊರ್ಕುನಿ torkuni (ತೊರ್ಕ್), *v. a.* To play. 2. *see* ಸೊರ್ಕುನಿ.

ತೊರ್ಕೆಲ್ torkelụ, *see* ಸೊರ್ಕೆಲ್.

ತೊರ್ಪು torpu, *s.* A kick.

ತೊರ್ಪುನಿ torpuni (ತೊರ್), *v. a.* To kick. 2. to tread.

ತೊಲ್ಂಬೆ tolụmbè, *see* ತೊಲುಂಬೆ.

ತೊಲಂಗ tolaṅga, *see* ತೋಳಂಗ್.

ತೊಲಗುನಿ tolaguni (ತೊಲಗ್), *v. n.* To depart, move away; to leave, forsake, desert.

ತೊಲಾಧಾರಿ tolādhāri, *s.* A weigher.

ತೊಲಿಕೆ tolikè, *s.* The skin, bark, rind.

ತೊಲುಂಕುನಿ toluṅkuni, *see* ದೊಲಂಕುನಿ.

ತೊಲುಂಬೆ tolumbè, *s.* A bunch, cluster.

ತೊಲುವೆ toluvè, *s.* A hole. —ತೋಡುನಿ to bore a hole.

ತೊಲೆ tolè, *s.* The weight of a rupee. 2. a beam, log.

ತೊಲ್ಕೆಲ್ tolkelụ, *see* ಸೊರ್ಕೆಲ್.

ತೊಲ್ಪುನಿ **tolpuni** (ತೊಲ್), *v. a. & n.* To prick. 2. to open, as a boil. 3. to split, as a tender cashew nut.

ತೊಲ್ಲು **tollu**, *s.* Substance, property. –ಕುಡ್ಪುನಿ to dissipate.

ತೊಲ್ಲುನಿ **tolluni** (ತೊಲ್ಲ್), *v. a.* To pluck out, as hair, feathers, *etc.*

ತೊಳಚಿ **toḷači**, *see* ತುಲಚಿ.

ತೊಳಿಂಬೆ, ತೊಳುಂಬೆ **toḷimbè, toḷumbè**, *see* ತೊಲುಂಬೆ.

ತೊಳಿಲ್ **toḷilu**, *s.* Trade, business. 2. *see* ತೊಯಳ್.

ತೊಳು **toḷu**, *s.* A hole. *adj.* Empty.

ತೊಳುಂಕುನಿ **toḷuṅkuni**, *see* ದೊಲಂಕುನಿ.

ತೊಳೆ **toḷè**, *see* ತೊಲೆ.

ತೊಳ್ಕೆ **toḷkè**, *see* ಚೋಲಿ, ತೊಲಿಕೆ.

ತೊಳ್ಳುನಿ **toḷḷuni**, *see* ತೊಲ್ಲುನಿ.

ತೊಳ್ಳೆ **toḷḷè**, *see* ದೊಳ್ಳು.

ತ್ರೊಯ್ಪುನಿ **toipuni** (ತ್ರೊಯ್), *v. a.* To strike, beat. 2. to wash, as clothes.

ತ್ರೊಯಂಬು **toimbu**, *adj.* Large, tall. 2. fat, stout.

ತ್ರೊಯಿಲ್ **toilu**, *s.* Plenty, abundance.

ತೋಂಕು **tōṅku**, *see* ತೋಕು.

ತೋಂಕುನಿ **tōṅkuni**, *see* ಸೋಂಕುನಿ.

ತೋಂಕೆ **tōṅkè**, *see* ಜೊಂಕೆ, ತೊಂಗೆ.

ತೋಂಕೆಲ್ **tōṅkelu**, *see* ತೋಕೆ.

ತೋಂಗೆ **tōṅgè**, *see* ತೊಂಗೆ.

ತೋಂಬೆ **tōmbè**, *see* ಸೂಂಬು.

ತೋಂಬುರ್ **tōrmbu**, *see* ತುರುಂಬು.

ತೋಕು **tōku**, *s.* Danger, risk. 2. collision.

ತೋಕುಲು **tōkulu**, *see* ತೋಕೊಲು.

ತೋಕೆ, ತೋಕೆಲ್ **tōkè, tōkelu**, *s.* A slope, declivity. *adj.* Secluded, retired.

ತೋಕೊಲು **tōkolu**, *s.* A kind of bait.

ತೋಕ್ಕಾಳೆ **tōkkāḷè**, *see* ಸೊರ್ಕಲೆ.

ತೋಜಾವುನಿ **tōjāvuni**, *c. v.* (*of* ತೋಜುನಿ) To show, point out.

ತೋಜುನಿ **tōjuni** (ತೋಜ್), *v. n.* To appear, be seen. *c. dat.* To seem, think. ತೋಜಂದೆಪೋಪಿನಿ to disappear, vanish; to miss.

ತೋಟ **tōṭa**, *s.* A garden, orchard, plantation. –ದಾಯೆ a gardener, planter. ಕಾಪಿ– a coffee plantation. ತಾರೆದ– a cocoa-nut garden.

ತೋಟಿ **tōṭi**, *s.* A scavenger; a sweeper.

ತೋಟಿಗೆ **tōṭige**, *s.* A class of Brahmins, working in plantations.

ತೋಟು **tōṭu**, *see* ಚೋಟು.

ತೋಡ **tōḍa**, *s.* Faintness exhaustion. 2. *see* ತೋಡು. –ಬೂರುನಿ to be exhausted.

ತೋಡಂಗೆಲ್ **tōḍaṅgelu**, *adj.* Scooped, burrowed.

ತೋಡಮರಯಿ **tōḍamarayi**, *s.* A trough scooped out of a single log of wood.

ತೋಡಾವುನಿ **tōḍāvuni**, *c. v.* (*of* ತೋಡುನಿ) To cause to dig, to have dug.

ತೋಡು **tōḍu**, *s.* A drain, sewer, gutter. 2. a brook, water-course, canal.

ತೋಡುನಿ **tōḍuni** (ತೋಡ್), *v. a.* To dig, burrow, mine. ಗುವೆಲ್– to dig *or* sink a well.

ತೋಡ್ತಿನಿ **tōḍtini**, *see* ತೊಡ್ತಿನಿ.

ತೋಣ **tōṇa**, *see* ಸೋಣ.

ತೋತ್ರ **tōtra**, *see* ಸ್ತೋತ್ರ.

ತೋಪಣ **tōpaṇa**, *s.* A drain *or* opening on the border of a garden to let out rain water; *cf.* ಸೋಪಣ.

ತೋಪಿ **tōpi**, *see* ತೊಪ್ಪಿ.

ತೋಪು **tōpu**, *s.* A grove, clump of trees. 2. a cannon. 3. a red coloured cloth. *adj.* Red. –ಶೀರೆ a female's garment of red colour.

ತೋಪೆಲ್ **tōpelu**, *see* ತೋಪೆ.

ತೋಪ್ರ, ತೋಬ್ರ **tōpra, tōbra**, *s.* A gram-bag for horses.

ತೋಬ **tōba**, *s.* A fault, crime. –ತೋಬ ಆಪಿನಿ to be harassed, *or* defeated. –ಪಣ್ಪಿನಿ to plead guilty.

ತೋಬೆ, ತೋಬೆಲ್ **tōbè, tōbelu**, *adj.* Big, large. –ಬಂಜಿ a pot-belly.

ತೋಮ **tōma**, *see* ಸೋಮ. 2. ಸ್ತೋಮ.

ತೋಮರ **tōmara**, *s.* An iron crow. 2. an arrow. 3. a javelin.

ತೋಯ **tōya**, *s.* Water.

ತೋಯಿಪುನಿ **tōyipuni**, *see* ತೊಯ್ಪುನಿ.

ತೋರ **tōra**, *s.* Stoutness, thickness. *adj.* Thick, stout, large.

ತೋರಣ **tōraṇa**, *s.* A festoon of leaves, flowers, *etc.* hung over a doorway *or* across the highway, a triumphal arch. –ಕಟ್ಟುನಿ to put up a triumphal arch.

ತೋರಿಕೆ, ತೋರಿಗೆ **tōrikè, tōrigè**, *s.* Appearance, show, exhibition.

ತೋರು **tōru**, *s.* Leaking.

ತೋರುನಿ **tōruni** (ತೋರ್), *v. n.* To leak, ooze, run. 2. *see* ತೋಜುನಿ.

ತೋಲು **tōlu**, *see* ತೋಳು.

ತೋಲ್ಪುನಿ **tōlpuni**, *see* ಸೋಲ್ಪುನಿ.

ತೋವಾಳೆ **tōvāḷe**, *s.* A cultivator, gardener.

ತೋವು **tōvu**, *see* ಸೋವು.

ತೋವೆ **tōvè**, *s.* Boiled pigeon-peas.

ತೋಷ **tōsha**, *s.* Joy, delight, pleasure.

ತೋಷೆಖಾನೆ, ತೋಸ್ಖಾನೆ **tōshekhānè, tōskhānè**, *s.* A treasury.

ತೋಳ್ **tōḷu**, *see* ತೋಳು.

ತೋಳ್ **tōḷu**, *s.* The arm. 2. a wolf; *also* ತೋಳಮೃಗ. –ಬಲ strength of arm. –ಸರಿಗೆ an ornament worn on the arm. –ಬೀಜುನಿ to wave the arm.

ತೋಳಂಗ್ **tōḷaṅgu**, *s.* Shaking of the arm.

ತೋಳು **tōḷu**, *s.* A beam.

ತೋಳೆ **tōḷè**, *see* ತೊಳೆ.

ತೊಯ್– **toi-**, *see after* ತೊಳ್ಳೆ.

ತೌ– **tou-**, *see* ತವು–.

ತೌಂಟುನಿ **touṇṭuni** (ತೌಂಟ್), *v. a.* To shake, wave.

ತೌಕು touku, *see* ತಬಕ.

ತೌಜಿ touji, *see* ತಾವಜಿ.

ತೌಡ touḍa, *see* ತೌಡು.

ತೌಡಂಗೆ touḍaṅgè, The creeper *Asparagus sarmentosus*

ತೌಡು touḍu, *s.* Bran, husk. —ಬಂಣ brown, ruddy colour. —ಕಂಡೊಡಿ a kind of viper.

ತೌಡುಗೋಳಿ touḍugōḷi, *s.* A kind of wild fig tree.

ತೌತಿ touti, *see* ಚೌತಿ.

ತೌತೆ toutè, *s.* A cucumber.

ತೌರುನಿ touruni (ತೌರ), *v. a.* To strip off, as the leaves of a tree *etc.*, to remove.

ತೌರ್ಯ, ತೌರ್ಯ್ಯ tourya, *s.* Music.

ತೌಲಿ, ತೌಳಿ touli, touḷi, *see* ಚವುಲಿ.

ತ್ರಾಣ trāṇa, *s.* Power, strength, ability. —ದಾಯಿ a strong man.

ತ್ರಾಣಿಕೆ trāṇike, *s.* A strong man.

ತ್ರಾಸ್ trāsu, *s.* A balance, pair of scales.

ತ್ರಾಹಿ trāhi, *imperat.* Nourish, protect (*poetic*).

ತ್ರಿಕಡು trikaḍu, *s.* A medicine composed of three ingredients (ಯೆಡ್ಡೆಮುಂಚ್ಚಿ, ಇಪ್ಪಿಲಿ, ಸೂಂಟಿ).

ತ್ರಿಕರಣ trikaraṇa, *s.* Thought, word and deed.

ತ್ರಿಕಾಲ trikāla, *s.* Morning, noon and night. 2. past, present, and future tenses.

ತ್ರಿಕೋಣ trikōṇa, *s.* A triangle. *adj.* Triangular.

ತ್ರಿಗುಣ triguṇa, *s.* The three qualities, *i.e.*, truth, passion, and ignorance. *adj.* Threefold, treble.

ತ್ರಿಜಾಯಿ trijāyi, *s.* A third part.

ತ್ರಿತೀಯ tritīya, *adj.* Third. —ವಿಭಕ್ತಿ the instrumental case.

ತ್ರಿದಿವ tridiva, *s.* Heaven.

ತ್ರಿನಾಮ trināma, *s.* The sectarian mark worn on the forehead by Vaishṇavaits.

ತ್ರಿಫಲ triphala, *s.* Three kinds of fruits, *i. e.* ಅಲ್ಡೆ, ನೆಲ್ಲಿ, ತಾಂತಿಕಾಯಿ, used in medicine.

ತ್ರಿಭುವನ tribhuvana, *s.* The three worlds, heaven, earth and hell.

ತ್ರಿಮರ trimara, *s.* A holy tree; *also* ತಿರುಮರ.

ತ್ರಿಮೂರ್ತಿ trimūrti, *s.* The Hindu triad, Brahma Vishṇu, and Śiva.

ತ್ರಿಮೂಲ trimūla, *s.* Three kinds of medicinal roots.

ತ್ರಿಯೇಕ triyēka, *adj.* Triune.

ತ್ರಿಲಿಂಗ triliṅga, *s.* The three genders, namely: masculine, feminine, and neuter.

ತ್ರಿಲೋಕ trilōka, *see* ತ್ರಿಭುವನ.

ತ್ರಿವರ್ಗ trivarga, *s.* The three human objects, namely: love, duty, and wealth.

ತ್ರಿವಿಕ್ರಮೆ trivikrame, *s.* A name of Vishṇu.

ತ್ರಿವಿಧ trividha, *s.* Three kinds. *adj.* Threefold.

ತ್ರಿವುಡೆ trivuḍè, *s.* A kind of metre.

ತ್ರಿಶೂಲ triśūla, *s.* The trident of Śiva.

ತ್ರೇತಯುಗ trētayuga, *s.* The second *or* silver age of the world.

ತ್ರೈಲೋಕ್ಯ treilōkya, *see* ತ್ರಿಭುವನ.

ತ್ವಕ್ಕ್ tvakkụ, *s.* The skin; the rind, bark, as of fruits, trees, *etc.*

ತ್ವರಿತ tvarita, *s.* Haste, speed, quickness.

ಥ TH

ಥ **tha,** The thirtieth letter of the alphabet.

ಥಗ್ಡೆ **thagụḍe,** *see* ದಗಡಿ.

ಥಟಾಲ **thaṭāla,** *s.* The sound of an unexpected slap.

ಥಟ್ಟ್ **thaṭṭụ,** *see* ತಟ್ಟ್.

ಥಟ್ಟನೆ **thaṭṭane,** *see* ತಟ್ಟನೆ.

ಥಟ್ಟಿ **thaṭṭi,** *see* ತಟ್ಟಿ.

ಥಟ್ಟುಗ **thaṭṭuga,** *see* ತಟ್ಟುಗ.

ಥಟ್ಟೆತರಕ್ **thaṭṭetarakụ,** *s.* Household furniture.

ಥರ **thara,** *see* ತರ.

ಥಳ **thaḷa,** *see* ತಳ.

ಥಳಥಳ **thaḷathaḷa,** *see* ತಳತಳ.

ಥಾಂಟುನಿ **thāṇṭuni,** *see* ತಾಂಟುನಿ.

ಥಾಟು **thāṭu,** *s.* Gaiety, mirth, festivity.

ಥಾಟುನಿ **thāṭuni,** *see* ತಾಂಟುನಿ.

ಥಾಟೆ **thāṭe,** *see* ತಾಟಿ.

ಥಾಡುನಿ **thāḍuni,** *see* ತಾಡುನಿ.

ಥಾಡೆ **thāḍe,** *s.* An ox that gores.

ಥಾಣೆ **thāṇe,** *see* ಠಾಣ.

ಥಾಸ **thāsa,** *s.* Heat, burning. 2. inflammation, fever. 3. anguish, distress.

ಥೇಡಿ **thēḍi,** *see* ಸೇಡಿ.

ದ D

ದ **da,** The thirty-first letter of the alphabet.

ದಂ **dam,** *see* ದಾಮ್.

ದಂಕಾವುನಿ **dankāvuni,** *c. v.* (*of* ದಂಕುನಿ) To cause to kick, *etc.*

ದಂಕಿಯುನಿ **dankiyuni,** *see* ದಂಕ್ಯುನಿ.

ದಂಕುನಿ **dankuni** (ದಂಕ್), *v. a.* To kick, *or* throw with the foot, as a ball. 2. to despise, treat with contempt. 3. to flaunt, strut. ದಂಕ್‌ದ್ ಪಾತೆರುನಿ to speak defiantly. ಬೆರ್ಮೆ– to mock at fear. ಹಿರಿಯಾಕುಳೆನ್ ದಂಕೆರೆ ಆವಂದ್ elders should not be despised.

ದಂಕ್ಯುನಿ **dankyuni** (ದಂಕ್), *v. n.* To crow lustily, as a cock. 2. mucus to discharge from the nose; to suffer from catarrh.

ದಂಗ್ daṅgṳ, *s.* The arm.

ದಂಗ daṅga, *see* ಡಂಕಿ.

ದಂಗಾಪಿನಿ daṅgāpini, *see under* ಡಂಗ್.

ದಂಗಾವುನಿ daṅgāvuni, *c. v.* (*of* ಡಂಗುನಿ) To cause to bend, bow.

ದಂಗಿ daṅgi, *see* ಡಂಕಿ.

ದಂಗಿ, ದಂಗಿದಿ daṅgi, daṅgidi, *adj.* Bent, inclined. —ಮರ a bent tree. ಪ್ರಾಯ— bent with age; old, infirm; *cf.* ಡಂಗುನಿ.

ದಂಗು daṅgu, *see* ಡಂಗ್.

ದಂಗುನಿ daṅguni (ಡಂಗ್), *v. n.* To bend, incline.

ದಂಗೆ daṅgè, *s.* Rebellion, mutiny. —ಮಳ್ಪುನಿ, —ಲಕ್ಕಾವುನಿ to rebel.

ದಂಗೆಲ್ daṅgelṳ, *adj.* Bent, inclined. *s.* Bending, inclination.

ದಂಟ್ daṇṭṳ, *s.* The stalk of certain grains and vegetables. 2. any pot-herb, as spinage, *etc.*

ದಂಟಾವುನಿ daṇṭāvuni, *c. v.* (*of* ಡಂಟುನಿ) To cause to stumble, trip. 2. to give offence.

ದಂಟುನಿ daṇṭuni (ಡಂಟೆ), *v. n.* To stumble. *v. a.* To throw with the foot, as a ball. ಡಂಟೆದ್ ಬೂರುನಿ to stumble; to be offended.

ದಂಟೆ daṇṭè, *s.* A walking staff, stick.

ದಂಡ್ daṇḍṳ, *s.* A spring of water. 2. an army. —ತೀರ್ಥ a sacred bathing place near Uḍapi. —ದಾಯಿ a soldier. —ನಾಯಕೆ a general. ನೀರ್ದ— a spring of water. —ಕಟ್ಟುನಿ to levy an army. —ಸೋಗಿಯುನಿ to go to war.

ದಂಡ್ daṇḍṳ, *s.* The stalk, as of a plantain leaf. 2. an oar, paddle. —ಜೀರುನಿ, —ವೈಪುನಿ to row, paddle.

ದಂಡ daṇḍa, *s.* A staff, stick; *also* ದಂಡಕೋಲು. 2. punishment, fine. 3. obeisance, salutation; *also* ದಂಡವತ್ತ್. 4. loss, waste. —ಕಾಷ್ಟ an ascetic's staff. —ದಾಯಿ a worthless fellow. —ನೀತಿ polity; ethics. —ಆಪಿನಿ to become worthless; to be wasted. —ಕೊರ್ಪಿನಿ to pay fine *or* damages. —ಮಳ್ಪುನಿ to waste.

ದಂಡಕ daṇḍaka, *s.* A sort of metre. 2. the name of a forest mentioned in the Rāmāyaṇa.

ದಂಡನೆ daṇḍanè, *s.* Punishment, pain, torment. ದೇಹ— penance, mortification.

ದಂಡಸ್ daṇḍasṳ, *s.* A blacksmith's tongs; a large pair of pincers.

ದಂಡಿ daṇḍi, *s.* A mace-bearer. 2. an ascetic.

ದಂಡಿಗೆ daṇḍigè, *s.* A kind of open palanquin. 2. a palanquin pole. 3. a sunbeam.

ದಂಡಿಪುನಿ, ದಂಡಿಸುನಿ daṇḍipuni, daṇḍisuni (ದಂಡಿ), *v. a.* To punish. 2. to mortify, as the body.

ದಂಡಿಯಾವುನಿ daṇḍiyāvuni, *c. v.* (*of* ದಂಡಿಯುನಿ) To cause to stretch out the hand, as by offering to give something, to offer; *also* ದಂಡ್ಯಾವುನಿ.

ದಂಡಿಯುನಿ **daṇḍiyuni** (ದಂಡಿ), *v. a.* To put forth, stretch the hand to receive anything; *also* ದಂಡ್ಯುನಿ.

ದಂಡೆ **daṇḍè**, *s.* Ornament worn on the arm. 2. a dam, mound, bank, bar. 3. the back of a pial. —ಮರ a log of wood placed across the brink of a well to stand upon.

ದಂಡ್ಯೆ **daṇḍyè**, *see* ದಂಡಿಗೆ.

ದಂತ **danta**, *s.* A tooth, tusk. 2. ivory.

ದಂತಾವಳೆ, ದಂತಿ **dantāvaḷè, danti**, *s.* An elephant.

ದಂತ್ಯ **dantya**, *adj.* Dental.

ದಂಪತಿ **dampati**, *s.* A married couple. 2. a household. —ತ್ಯ, *see* ದಾಂಪತ್ಯ. —ಪೂಜೆ adoration *or* honour paid to a married couple.

ದಂಬ **damba**, *see* ದಂಭ. 2. *see* ದಂಮ.

ದಂಬಟೆ **dambaṭi**, *see* ತಂಬಟ.

ದಂಬಡಿಗೆ **dambaḍigè**, *s.* Delight, pleasure. 2. love, good will. 3. acquiescence. 4. persuasion. —ಮಳ್ಪುನಿ, *see* ದಂಬಡಿಪುನಿ.

ದಂಬಡಿಪುನಿ, ದಂಬಡಿಯುನಿ, ದಂಬಡಿಸುನಿ **dambaḍipuni, dambaḍiyuni, dambaḍisuni** (ದಂಬಡಿ), *v. a.* To please, delight. 2. to reconcile, appease, bring to acquiescence. 3. to persuade, convince.

ದಂಬಡೆ **dambaḍè**, *see* ತಂಬಟ.

ದಂಬಡ್ಯುನಿ **dambaḍyuni**, *see* ದಂಬಡಿಪುನಿ.

ದಂಬತ್ತಿ **dambatti**, *see* ದಂಪತಿ.

ದಂಬಿಲ **dambila**, *see* ತಂಬಿಲ.

ದಂಬು **dambu**, *see* ದಂಮು.

ದಂಬುಡಿ **dambuḍi**, *s.* A pie.

ದಂಬುಳಿ, ದಂಬೊಳಿ **dambuḷi, damboḷi**, *s.* A thunder bolt.

ದಂಬೆ **dambè**, *s.* The hollow slip of a palm *or* bamboo used as a drain.

ದಂಬೆಲ್ **dambelụ**, *see* ಡೆಂಬೆಲ್.

ದಂಭ **dambha**, *see* ಡಂಭ.

ದಂಮ **damma**, *see* ಧರ್ಮ.

ದಂಮ **damma**, *adj.* Left. 2. *see* ದಪ್ಪ. —ಕೈ the left hand. —ಕೈತಾಯಿ a left-handed man.

ದಂಮಂತೆ, ದಂಮಯಂತೆ **dammantè, dammayantè**, *see* ದಮಯಂತಿ.

ದಂಮಯ **dammaya**, *s.* An humble mode of entreaty; craving mercy *or* indulgence; *also* ದಂಮಯದಕ್ಕಯ. —ಪಣ್ಪುನಿ to crave mercy. —ಪಾಡುನಿ to entreat, importunate, dun.

ದಂಮಾರ್ **dammārụ**, *see* ದಾಮರ್.

ದಂಮಾರೆ **dammāre**, *see* ಚಂಮಾರೆ.

ದಂಮು **dammu**, *s.* Breath, hard breathing. —ಕಸರತ್ gymnastics. —ಕಟ್ಟುನಿ to hold one's breath; to be silent. —ಪತ್ತುನಿ to hold one's breath. —ಪಾರುನಿ to die. —ಬುಡ್ಪುನಿ to breathe; to sigh. —ಮುಕ್ಕುನಿ to breathe in. —ವೈಪುನಿ breathe hard; to smoke.

ದಂಮುಡಿ **dammuḍi**, *see* ದಂಬುಡಿ.

ದಂಷ್ಟ್ರ daṁshṭra, *s.* A tusk, fang, large canine tooth. —ಕರಾಳೆ a person having projecting teeth; a demon so called.

ದಂಶ, ದಂಸ daṁśa, daṁsa, *s.* A gadfly. 2. a bee. 3. *see* ಧ್ವಂಸ.

ದಕ್ಕ್ದಿಕ್ಕ dakkụdikka, *adv.* Soon, quickly.

ದಕ್ಕ dakka, *s.* Trouble. —ತಿಕ್ಕುನಿ to get into trouble.

ದಕ್ಕತಿ dakkati, *s.* Possession, control. 2. appropriation. 3. digestion. —ಆಪಿನಿ to be appropriated; to be digested.

ದಕ್ಕಾ dakkā, *s.* Weight. 2. Difficulty. —ದೀಪಿನಿ to place a weight upon anything; to press; to condense.

ದಕ್ಕಾವುನಿ dakkāvuni, *c. v.* (*of* ದಕ್ಕುನಿ) To cause to throw, expel. *v. n.* To place a weight upon anything.

ದಕ್ಕಾವೊಣುನಿ dakkāvoṇuni, *refl. v.* (*of* ದಕ್ಕಾವುನಿ) To retain, digest anything eaten. 2. to misappropriate successfully. 3. to carry a load *or* burden. 4. to take charge of.

ದಕ್ಕಿತ dakkita, *see* ದಕ್ಕತಿ.

ದಕ್ಕುನಿ dakkuni (ದಕ್ಕ್), *v. a.* To cast out, throw away, expel. 2. to reject; *also* ದಕ್ಕುದುನಿ. *v. n.* *see* ದಕ್ಕ್ಸುನಿ. ದಕ್ಕ್ದ್ಪೋಪಿನಿ to be thrown away, lost. ಬೆಡಿ— to shoot.

ದಕ್ಕೆ dakkè, *s.* A quay, pier, embankment. 2. *see* ಡಕ್ಕೆ.

ದಕ್ಕೊತಿ dakkoti, *see* ದಕ್ಕತಿ.

ದಕ್ಸಾವುನಿ dạksāvuni, *c. v.* (*of* ದಕ್ಸುನಿ) To bring into another's possession. *v. a.* To defend, retain, *or* appropriate to one's self what belongs to another; *also* ದಕ್ಸಾವೊಣುನಿ.

ದಕ್ಸುನಿ daksuni (ದಕ್ಸ್), *v. n.* To be retained, digested, as food medicine, *etc.* 2. To be misappropriated successfully.

ದಗ್ಡಿ dagụḍi, *s.* A rogue, impostor. 2. a termagant, vixen.

ದಗ daga, *see* ದಗೆ.

ದಗಣೆ dagaṇè, *s.* An amazon, masculine woman. *adj.* Bold, masculine. 2. ill-tempered. —ಬಾಯಿ an aggressive *or* quarrelsome tongue *or* temper.

ದಗದಗ, ದಗಬಗ dagadaga, dagabaga, *adv.* Brightly. —ಅಲುಗ್ನಿ to blaze.

ದಗರೆ dagarè, *s.* A funeral drum; *also* ದಗರೆದೋಲು.

ದಗಲ್ಬಾಜಿ dagalụbāji, *s.* A rogue, cheat, impostor. 2. roguery, dishonesty, imposture.

ದಗಲೆ dagalè, *s.* A coat; livery. —ಪಾಡುನಿ to put on a livery.

ದಗಸ್ dagasụ, *s.* Corn, grain in general.

ದಗೆ dagè, *s.* Deceit, trickery, imposture. —ಗಾರೆ, —ತಾಯೆ a deceiver, impostor. —ಮಳ್ಪುನಿ to deceive, cheat; to disappoint.

ದಗ್ಗ, ದಗ್ಗನೆ dagga, daggaṇè, *adv.* Suddenly. —ಅಲುಗ್ನಿ to blaze up suddenly.

ದಚ್ಚ dačča, *see* ದಟ.

ದಚ್ಚಣೆ daččaṇè, *see* ದಕ್ಷಿಣೆ.

ದಜ್ಜುನಿ dajjuni, *see* ದಜರ್ನಿ.

ದಟ daṭa, *s.* Thickness. 2. coarseness. 3. closeness. *adj.* Thick, stout, coarse. 2. close.

ದಟಾಯಿಸುನಿ daṭāyisuni (ದಟಾಯಿ ಸ್), *v. a.* To fix, make firm.

ದಟ್ಟಿ daṭṭi, *s.* A waist-band.

ದಟ್ಟಿಯುನಿ, ದಟ್ಟ್ಯುನಿ daṭṭiyuni, daṭṭyuni (ದಟ್ಟಿ), *v. a.* To rub out, obliterate, wash off. *v. n.* To be dense, crowded.

ದಡ್ daḍụ, *see* ದಡ್ಡ್.

ದಡ್ಂಬಾಸ್, ದಡ್ಕ್ daḍụmbāsụ, daḍụkụ, *adj.* Coarse. –ಕುಂಟು a coarse cloth.

ದಡ್ಜಡ್ಡ್ daḍụjaḍḍụ, *s.* Callosity. *adj.* Callous.

ದಡ daḍa, *s.* A shore, bank.

ದಡಕ್ಕ daḍakka, *adv.* Suddenly. –ಬೂರುನಿ to fall suddenly.

ದಡದಡ daḍadaḍa, *s.* The noise of fast walking *or* talking. –ನಡಪುನಿ to walk very fast. –ಪಾತೆರುನಿ to speak *or* talk rapidly.

ದಡಬಡ, ದಡಬಡಿ daḍabaḍa, daḍabaḍi, *s.* Rapidity, hurry; *cf.* ದಡದಡ. 2. the noise of falling suddenly. –ತನ hurry, haste. –ದಾಯೆ a bouncer, blusterer. –ಬೂರುನಿ to fall suddenly.

ದಡಲ್ daḍalụ, *adj.* Talkative, loquacious. –ಬಾಯಿ loquacity.

ದಡಲೆ daḍalè, *see* ದಡಿಕೆ.

ದಡವಂತೆ daḍavante, *s.* A strong, powerful *or* influential man.

ದಡಾದಡಿ daḍādaḍi, *adj.* Quick, active, smart. *adv.* In hot haste.

ದಡಿ daḍi, *s.* A speck in the eye. 2. anger, rage. 3. *see* ದಡೆ. 4. *see* ತಡಿ. –ಬೂರುನಿ to have a speck in the eye. –ಬೊಟ್ಟುನಿ to stamp the ground with the foot.

ದಡಿಕೆ daḍikè, *s.* A kind of rash, blotch.

ದಡಿಪುನಿ, ದಡಿಯುನಿ daḍipuni, daḍiyuni (ದಡಿ), *v. a.* To drive away. 2. *see* ಜಡಿಪಿನಿ.

ದಡಿಲ daḍila, *adv.* Suddenly. –ಮಗುರುನಿ to drop suddenly.

ದಡುಬಡು daḍubaḍu, *see* ದಡಬಡ.

ದಡೆ daḍè, *s.* An obstacle, hinderance. 2. a screen, blind. 3. a charm. 4. a scaffold, platform. 5. a roller, lever. 6. a weight equal to seven pounds. –ಕಟ್ಟುನಿ to charm a serpent; to hinder by witchcraft. –ಟಿ ದೀಪಿನಿ to postpone; to come to terms. –ಟಿ ಪಾಡುನಿ to lift upon a scaffold. –ಮಳ್ಪುನಿ to prolong.

ದಡ್ಡ್ daḍḍụ, *s.* Short stubble left in the ground. 2. worthless paddy. 3. callosity, hardness, as of the skin of the palm from manual work, *etc. adj.* Dull, stupid, idle; void. –ಕತ್ತಿ a blunt knife. –ತನ stupidity, idleness. –ಫರಂಗಿ indolent syphilitic ulcers. –ಅರಿ a bad kind of rice. –ಮುಂಡೆ

ಯಿ a kind of wild screw-pine. —ಪೊರ್ಗಲಿಯುನಿ an indolent sore to suppurate.

ದಡ್ಡ dadda, *adv.* Suddenly; *cf.* ದಡಕ್ಕ. —ಮಗ್ರುನಿ to fall suddenly.

ದಡ್ಡಲ್ daddalu, *s.* The tree *Careya arborea.*

ದಡ್ಡಲಕ್ಕಿ daddalakki, *s.* An inferior kind of rice.

ದಡ್ಡಿ daddi, *s.* A stupid woman. 2. *see* ದಡ್ಡೊಲಿ.

ದಡ್ಡಿಯುನಿ daddiyuni, *see* ಗಡಿಯಾವುನಿ.

ದಡ್ಡೆ dadde, *s.* A stupid fellow. 2. a sow.

ದಡ್ಡೊಲಿ daddoli, *s.* The American aloe.

ದಡ್ಮೆನ dadmena, *s.* Sluggishness, torpor. 2. indigestion.

ದಣಲ್ danalu, *s.* The sound of a bell.

ದಣಿ dani, *see* ಧನಿ. 2. *see* ಧ್ವನಿ.

ದಣಿಕೆ danikè, *s.* Fatigue, weariness, exhaustion. —ಆಪಿನಿ to become weary, fatigued, tired.

ದಣಿಪಾವುನಿ danipāvuni, *c. v.* (*of* ದಣಿಯುನಿ) To fatigue, weary, satiate.

ದಣಿಯ daniya, *adj.* Heavy.

ದಣಿಯುನಿ daniyuni (ದಣಿ), *v. n.* To be fatigued, tired, exhausted. 2. satiated, satisfied; *also* ದಣಿಪುನಿ.

ದಣು danu, *s.* Fatigue, weariness, exhaustion.

ದತ್ತ್ dattu, *s.* The left side.

ದತ್ತ datta, *adj.* Left. —ಕೈ the left hand.

ದತ್ತ datta, *s.* Adoption. 2. a gift. *adj.* Given, presented, made over. 2. adopted. —ಪುತ್ರ, —ಮಗೆ an adopted son. —ಸ್ವೀಕಾರ adoption. ದತ್ತೋಲೆ a deed of adoption. —ಗೆಪ್ಪುನಿ, —ಮಳ್ಪುನಿ to adopt.

ದತ್ತಾಪಹಾರ dattāpahāra, *s.* Taking back a gift.

ದತ್ತೆ datte, *s.* An adopted son.

ದತ್ತೋಜಿ dattōji, *see* ದಸ್ತೈವಜಿ.

ದತ್ತೋಲೆ dattōlè, *see under* ದತ್ತ.

ದದಲುನಿ dadaluni (ದದಲ್), *v. a.* To give, distribute. *v. n.* To tremble. 2. to boast. 3. to stammer.

ದದೆವುನಿ dadevuni (ದದೆ), *v. n.* To become hard, get stiff.

ದದ್ದು daddu, *s.* The ringworm, *herpes.* —ಮರ್ದ್ the shrub *cassia alata.*

ದನ dana, *see* ಧನ.

ದನಿ dani, *see* ಧನಿ. 2. *see* ಧ್ವನಿ.

ದನು danu, *s.* A daughter of Daksha. 2. *see* ಧನು.

ದಪನ dapana, *s.* Burying. —ಮಳ್ಪುನಿ to bury, commit to earth.

ದಪೆ, ದಫೆ dapè, daphè, *s.* A turn, time. —ದಪೆ every time, again and again, frequently.

ದಪೆದಾರೆ dapedāre, *see* ದಫೆದಾರೆ.

ದಪ್ತರ್, ದಪ್ತಾರ್ daptaru, daptāru, *s.* A bundle of papers tied together in a cloth; records. —ಪೂಜೆ an annual ceremony observed by merchants on closing their old and opening their new accounts on the 1st day of Vikramāditya's era.

ದಪ್ತಿ **dapti**, *see* ದಫ್ತರಿ.

ದಪ್ಪ **dappa**, *s.* Thickness. *adj.* Thick, stout. –ಕುಂಟು a thick *or* coarse cloth.

ದಪ್ಪು **dappu**, *s.* Occasion, convenience, opportunity; making room *or* forming an open file in a gathering of people. 2. ploughing. 3. an umbrella stripped of its leafy covering.

ದಪ್ಪುನಿ **dappuni** (ದ), *v.a.* To plough.

ದಫನ **daphana**, *see* ದಪನ.

ದಫೇದಾರೆ **daphēdāre**, *s.* A head peon.

ದಬಕ್ಕ **dabakka**, *adv.* Suddenly. 2. headlong. –ಬೂರುನಿ to fall suddenly. –ಲಾಗ್ಯುನಿ to jump down suddenly.

ದಬಡೆ **dabaḍè**, *s.* A capacious leathern bottle.

ದಬದಬ **dabadaba**, *s.* Palpitation of the heart. –ಲಾಗ್ಯುನಿ to palpitate.

ದಬನ **dabana**, *see* ದಬ್ಬಣ.

ದಬರೆ **dabarè**, *s.* A kind of brazen pot. 2. confusion, disorder.

ದಬರ್ದಸ್ತಿ **dabardasti**, *see* ಜಬರ್ ಜಾಸ್ತಿ.

ದಬಾಯಿಸುನಿ, ದಬಾಸುನಿ **dabāyisuni, dabāsuni** (ದಬಾಯಿಸ್), *v. a.* To menace. 2. to force. 3. to chide, frighten. 4. to stop, detain. 5. to keep under, press down.

ದಬಿ **dabi**, *s.* Sense. –ತಪ್ಪುನಿ to lose one's senses, become insensible.

ದಬಿಲಿ **dabili**, *see* ತಬ್ಬಿಲಿ.

ದಬುತಿ **dabuti**, *see* ದವುತಿ.

ದಬುರಸ್ **daburasu**, *see* ದರ್ಬಾರ್.

ದಬುರಿ **daburi**, *s.* Division of profit. 2. a writer. 3. *see* ತಬುರಿ.

ದಬ್ತರ್ **dabtaru**, *see* ದಪ್ತಾರ್.

ದಬ್ತಿ **dabti**, *see* ದವುತಿ.

ದಬ್ಬದಬ್ಬನೆ **dabbadabbanè**, *see* ಡಬ್ಬ.

ದಬ್ಬಣ **dabbaṇa**, *s.* A bodkin, a large packing needle.

ದಬ್ಬರದಿಬ್ಬರ **dabbaradibbara**, *adj.* Disorderly, confusedly. –ಮಾಡುನಿ to put into confusion. –ಪಾತೆರುನಿ to speak incoherently.

ದಬ್ಬಿ **dabbi**, *see* ಡಬ್ಬಿ.

ದಬ್ಬಿಲಿ **dabbili**, *see* ತಬ್ಬಿಲಿ.

ದಬ್ಬು **dabbu**, *s.* A crack, break. 2. *see* ಡಬ್ಬು.

ದಬ್ಬುಡಿ **dabbuḍi**, *s.* The wicker-work of a cart.

ದಬ್ಬುಳಿ **dabbuḷi**, *see* ತಬ್ಬುಲಿ.

ದಬ್ಬೆ **dabbè**, *s.* A splinter, slip of bamboo, *etc.* *adj.* Cracked, split.

ದಬ್ಬೆಲ್ **dabbelu**, *s.* A split, cleft, chink. *adj.* Cracked, split.

ದಮಯಂತಿ **damayanti**, *s.* The name of Naḷa's wife.

ದಮಾನ್ **damānu**, *s.* The large sail of a boat.

ದಮಾಮಿ **damāmi**, *s.* The noise of a drum.

ದಮಾಸ್ **damāsu**, *s.* A stamper, beater, large wooden block with a handle, used to level the ground.

ದಮಾಸ **damāsa**, *s.* Damask cloth.

ದಮುಕಾವುನಿ **damukāvuni**, *c. v.* (*of* ದಮುಕುನಿ), To cause bluster, tumult, noise.

ದಮುಕುನಿ **damukuni**, *v. n.* To bluster, storm, swagger.

ದಮ್ಮಯ **dammaya**, *see* ದಂಮಯ.

ದಯ **daya**, *s.* Kindness, favour; compassion, pity, goodness. –ದೀಪಿನಿ to favour, condescend, oblige. –ಮಳ್ಪುನಿ to honour with a visit; to give; to come; to sit down; to go.

ದಯಸುನಿ **dayasuni** (ದಯಸ್), *v. n.* To suit, be fit.

ದಯಾಕರ **dayākara**, *adj.* Kind, compassionate.

ದಯಾನಿಧಿ **dayānidhi**, *s.* The treasure of kindness, God.

ದಯಾವಂತೆ **dayāvante**, *s.* A kind *or* generous man.

ದಯಾಸಾಗರ **dayāsāgara**, *s.* The ocean of kindness, God.

ದಯಾಳು **dayāḷu**, *adj.* Kind hearted, merciful, compassionate. –ದೇವೆರ್ the merciful God.

ದರ **dara**, *s.* Price, rate.

ದರ **dara**, *s.* Fear, terror. 2. a hole in the ground.

ದರಕಾರ **darakāra**, *s.* Power, authority; right.

ದರಕಾಸ್, ದರಕಾಸ್ತ್ **darakāsu, darakāstu**, *see* ದರ್ಕಾಸ್ತ್.

ದರಗ್ **daragu**, *see* ದೊರಗ್.

ದರಜಿ **daraji**, *see* ದರ್ಜಿ.

ದರಣ **daraṇa**, *s.* Bursting, splitting. 2. *see* ಧರಣ.

ದರದರ **daradara**, *s.* A noise, sound. –ವೈಪುನಿ to drag with a noise.

ದರಬರ **darabara**, *adv.* Greedily, voraciously. –ತಿನ್ಪುನಿ to eat voraciously; *cf.* ಅರಬರ.

ದರಬಾರ್ **darabāru**, *see* ದರ್ಬಾರ್.

ದರಸಿಗೆ **darasigè**, *s.* A kind of grass.

ದರಸೆ **darasè**, *s.* The day of the new moon.

ದರಿ **dari**, *s.* Coloured border of a cloth; *cf.* ಜರಿ. 2. a window blind. 3. railing. –ಕುಂಟ the peg of a railing; a wooden post to fasten a racing buffalo.

ದರಿದ್ರ **daridra**, *adj.* Poor, indigent. *s.* Poverty. –ತನ the state of poverty.

ದರಿದ್ರೆ **daridre**, *s.* A poor, destitute man.

ದರಿಪುನಿ **daripuni** (ದರಿ), *v. a.* To shudder, shiver, tremble (as a demon priest); *cf.* ಜರಿಪುನಿ.

ದರಿಯ **dariya**, *s.* The sea. –ಬಾದರ್‌ಗಡ a small island off the coast of Uḍapi, called the St. Mary's Island.

ದರಿಯಾಪ್ತಿ **dariyāpti**, *s.* Enquiry, investigation, trial, examination. –ಮಳ್ಪುನಿ to make an enquiry.

ದರಿಯುನಿ **dariyuni** (ದರಿ), *v. n.* To break, burst, spring open; *also* ದರಿದ್ಪೋಪಿನಿ.

ದರಿಶನ **darišana**, *s.* A necklace of shells. 2. *see* ದರ್ಶನ.

ದರು **daru**, *s.* A door. 2. *see* ದರ.

ದರುಣಿ **daruṇi**, *see* ಧರಣಿ.

ದರುದುರು **daruduru**, *adj.* Rough, coarse. —ಪಣ್ಪುನಿ to speak evasively.

ದರುಬುರು **daruburu**, *s.* Sipping.

ದರುಶನ **darušana**, *see* ದರ್ಶನ.

ದರೆ **darè**, *s.* A fence, parapet, wall; *cf.* ಬರೆ. —ಪಾಡುನಿ to fence, raise a wall.

ದರೋಬಸ್ತು **darōbastụ**, *adj.* All, whole.

ದರ್ಕಾರ್ **darkārụ**, *see* ದರಕಾರ.

ದರ್ಕಾಸ್ತು, ದರ್ಖಾಸ್ತು **darkāstụ, darkhāstụ**, *s.* A tender for the cultivation of land; an offer for liquor contract. —ಮಳ್ಪುನಿ to bid for a farm, *etc.*

ದರ್ಗ **darga**, *s.* A tomb supposed to work miracles.

ದರ್ಜಿ **darji**, *s.* A tailor.

ದರ್ಜುನಿ **darjuni** (ದರ್ಜ್), *v.a.* To mumble.

ದರ್ಣ **darṇa**, *see* ಧರಣ.

ದರ್ತೆಲ್ **dartelụ**, *s.* Breakage, what is broken.

ದರ್ತೆಲೆ **dartele**, *s.* A striker, breaker; *also* ದರ್ಪೆಲೆ; *cf.* ದರ್ಪುನಿ.

ದರ್ತೊಣುನಿ **dartoṇuni**, *refl. v.* (*of* ದರ್ಪುನಿ) To beat one's self in sorrow, *etc.* ತಿಗಲೆಗ್— to beat the breast; to mourn.

ದರ್ಪ **darpa**, *s.* Pride, arrogance. —ಬಾಯಿ a proud, arrogant man.

ದರ್ಪಣ **darpaṇa**, *s.* A mirror, looking glass.

ದರ್ಪು **darpu**, *s.* Swelling, inflammation.

ದರ್ಪುನಿ **darpuni** (ದರ್), *v. a.* To thrash, beat, strike, break. *v. n.* To swell, inflame. ಸೆಲ ಕೈ— to curse, anathematise.

ದರ್ಬಾರ್ **darbārụ**, *s.* An audience. 2. an audience hall, a court. 3. grandeur, pomp, ostentation, show.

ದರ್ಬೆ, ದರ್ಭೆ **darbè, darbhè**, *s.* Sacrificial grass, *Poa cynosuroides.*

ದರ್ಮ **darma**, *see* ಧರ್ಮ.

ದರ್ಯಾಪ್ತಿ **daryāpti**, *see* ಪರಿಯಾಪ್ತಿ.

ದರ್ಶನ, ದರ್ಸನ **daršana, darsana**, *s.* A vision, sight. 2. a visit, advent.

ದಲ **dala**, *adj.* Stout, strong, robust, thick.

ದಲವಾದ್, ದಲವಾದಿ **dalavādụ, dalavādi**, *see* ದಳವಾಯಿ.

ದಲಾದಿ **dalādi**, *s.* Depth. *adj.* Deep. —ನೀರ್ deep water.

ದಲಾಲ್, ದಲಾಲಿ **dalālụ, dalāli**, *see* ದಲ್ಲಾಲಿ.

ದಲಿ **dali**, *see* ದರಿ.

ದಲ್ಲ್ **dallụ**, *see* ದಡ್ಡ್.

ದಲ್ಲಾಲಿ, ದಲ್ಲಾಳಿ **dallāli, dallāḷi**, *s.* A broker, agent. 2. agency, commission, brokerage.

ದಲ್ಲಿಯ **dalliya**, *s.* A foot-cloth.

ದಲ್ಲಿಯುನಿ **dalliyuni** (ದಲ್ಲ್), *v. a.* To slap, beat. 2. to smear. ಗೋಡೆಗ್ ಮಂಣ್— to smear a wall with mud; *cf.* ಸಾರಣೆ.

ದವಡೆ **davaḍè**, *s.* The jaw, cheek.

ದವಣಿ, ದವಣೆ **davaṇi, davaṇè**, *s.* A fixed term of payment. —ನಾರೆ

one who pays by installments. —ಚೀಟಿ a written agreement fixing installments.

ದವಣೆಬಲ್ಲ್ davaṇeballu, *s.* A long rope to which cattle are tied in rows.

ದವತಿ davati, *s.* An inkstand; *also* ದಾತಿ.

ದವನ davana, *s.* A kind of fragrant shrub.

ದವರ್ davaru, *s.* The flapping selvedge of a garment. —ಹೊಲಿವದೆ hemming the selvedge of a garment.

ದವರು davaru, *adj.* Loose. —ಚಲ್ಲನ loose breeches.

ದವಸ davasa, *s.* Produce of the field; corn, grain in general.

ದವಾಲಿ davāli, *s.* A peon's belt.

ದವುಡು davuḍu, *s.* Expedition; march, speed. 2. a gallop.

ದವುಡೆ davuḍe, *see* ದವಡೆ.

ದವುತಿ davuti, *see* ದವತಿ.

ದವುರಂಗಿ davurangi, *s.* A loose jacket, long coat.

ದವುರು davuru, *see* ದವರು.

ದಶ daśa, *num.* Ten. —ಮ tenth. —ವಿಧ ten kinds *or* sorts.

ದಶಮಿ daśami, *s.* The tenth day of the lunar fortnight.

ದಶಮುಖೆ daśamukhe, *s.* Rāvaṇa the ten-faced giant.

ದಶಮೂಲ daśamūla, *s.* A medicine composed of ten ingredients.

ದಶರಥೆ daśarathe, *s.* The father of Rāma.

ದಶಾಂಗ daśānga, *s.* A composition of ten fragrant substances, used as perfumery.

ದಶಾಂಶ daśāmśa, *s.* The tenth part, tithe.

ದಶಾವತಾರ daśāvatāra, *s.* The ten incarnations of Vishṇu. —ಆಟ a dramatic performance exhibiting puranic episodes.

ದಶೆ daśe, *s.* Condition, fortune, luck, influence of the planets; *cf.* ದೆಶೆ.

ದಶೆವುನಿ, ದಸಿಯುನಿ daśevuni, dasiyuni (ದಶೆ, ದಸಿ), *v. a.* To tread down, press in.

ದಷ್ಟಿಯುನಿ dashṭiyuni (ದಷ್ಟಿ), *v. a.* To clean, as a slate.

ದಸ dasa, *see* ದಶ.

ದಸಬಸ dasabasa, *see* ಬಸಬಸ.

ದಸರಿ dasari, *s.* A kind of striped linen cloth worn by Brahmin females when cooking *or* during meals. 2. *see* ದಸ್ರು.

ದಸರೆ dasarè, *see* ದಸ್ರು.

ದಸಾಲ್ dasālu, *see* ಬಸಾಲ್.

ದಸಿ dasi, *s.* A painted palmyra stick.

ದಸೆ dasè, *see* ದಶೆ, ದೆಶೆ.

ದಸೆಮೀನ್ dasemīnu, *s.* A kind of fish.

ದಸ್ಕತ್ daskatu, *s.* A signature. —ಪಾಡುನಿ, —ಮಳ್ಪುನಿ to sign.

ದಸ್ತ್ dastu, *s.* A parole.

ದಸ್ತ dasta, *s.* A quire of paper. 2. a pack of cards.

ದಸ್ತಕ್ dastaku, *s.* A passport, permit. 2. a summons.

ದಸ್ತೂರಿ dastūri, *s.* Custom, usage. 2. likeness, similarity. 3. a signature. 4. fees, duty. ಟಪ್ಪಾಲ್— postage

ದಸ್ತೈವಜಿ, ದಸ್ತೋಜಿ dasteivaji, dastōji, *s.* A legal paper, voucher, document, exhibit.

ದಸ್ಯ dasya, *see* ದಾಸತ್ವ.

ದಸ್ಯು dasyu, *s.* A demon. 2. an enemy. 3. a barbarian.

ದಸ್ರ, ದಸ್ರೆ dasra, dasrè, *s.* A popular festival observed in honour of Durga for the first nine days of the lunar month Āśvīja.

ದಸ್ರಿ dasri, *see* ದಸರಿ.

ದಹನ dahana, *s.* Fire. 2. burning, especially of a corpse. 3. digestion. —ಬಲಿ a burnt offering.

ದಹಿಪುನಿ dahipuni (ದಹಿ), *v. a.* To burn, consume.

ದಳ daḷa, *s.* An army. 2. bottom. 3. the shore of a river, *etc.* 4. the petal of a flower. 5. a fragment. *adj.* Thick, stout, robust; *cf.* ದಪ್ಪ. —ಕೊಡಿಪುನಿ to foam, bubble up. ದಳ ಆವೊಡು ದಪ್ಪ ಆವೊಡು it must be thick and stout.

ದಳಂಕ್ dalaṅku, *see* ದೊಳಂಕ್.

ದಳಂಕೆ dalaṅkè, *adj.* Large. 2. loose. —ಕಾಜಿ a loose bracelet *or* bangle.

ದಳಬಳ dalabaḷa, *adj.* Thin, clear, lucid. 2. loose.

ದಳವಾಡ dalavāḍa, *s.* Artizan's tools. 2. an assembly of people. 3. an army.

ದಳವಾಯಿ daḷavāyi, *s.* The general of an army.

ದಳಸರಿ daḷasari, *s.* Strength, thickness, robustness.

ದಳಿ daḷi, *s.* A line of reepers *or* splits of bamboos. 2. wooden *or* iron railings; *cf.* ದರಿ. —ತ ಚಾವಡಿ a travellers' inn. —ಕಟ್ಟುನಿ to erect a frame work of railings.

ದಳಿಯ daḷiya, *s.* A mode of purifying clothes on account of pollution from birth *or* death of a relative; *also* ಉದ್ದೆ.

ದಳೇನ daḷēna, *adj.* Torpid, inactive, as the stomach.

ದಳ್ಮೆನ daḷmena, *see* ತಲ್ಮೆನ.

ದಕ್ಷಿಣ dakshiṇa, *s.* South. *adj.* Southern.

ದಕ್ಷಿಣಾಯನ dakshiṇāyana, *s.* The sun's course south of the equator.

ದಕ್ಷೆ dakshe, *s.* A son of Brahma.

ದಾ dā, *intg. pron.* What? which? *cf.* ವಾ. ದಾನೆ what? ದಾಯೆಗ್ why? ದಾಲಾ anything. *intj.* A sound for calling cattle.

ದಾಂಟುನಿ dāṇṭuni (ದಾಂಟಿ), *v. a.* To cross, ford, pass by; *also* ದಾಂಟಿದ್‌ಪೋಪಿನಿ.

ದಾಂಡಿ dāṇḍi, *s.* A stone-mark on the seashore.

ದಾಂಡಿಗೆ dāṇḍige, *s.* A strong, stalwart man.

ದಾಂಡಿಮರ **dāṇḍimara,** *see* ಕಾಂತಿ ಮರ.

ದಾಂತಿ **dānti,** *neg. part.* What is not; destitute; less. ಜನ– uninhabited. ಫಲ– fruitless. ಬುದ್ಧಿ– senseless, imprudent. ದಾಲಿ ದಾಂತಿನಾಯಿ a man without means. ಯಾನ್ ದಾಂತಿ ಪೊರ್ತು during my absence.

ದಾಂತೆ **dāntè,** *neg. ger.* Without, except, not being. ಪೋಡಿಗೆ– without fear, fearlessly.

ದಾಂನಾ **dānnā,** *intg. pron.* Whether. 2. I know not what. ಆಯಿ ಮಳ್ಪೆನಾ– I doubt whether he will do *or* not. ಅವು ಆವುಂ ದಾ– I doubt (*or* I cannot say) whether it will happen *or* not.

ದಾಂಪತ್ಯ **dāmpatya,** *s.* Married state.

ದಾಂಬುನಿ **dāmbuni,** *see* ದಾನುನಿ.

ದಾಕ್ **dāku,** *see* ಡಾಕ್.

ದಾಕಿನ **dākina,** *see* ದಾಕ್ಷಿಣ.

ದಾಖಲ್, ದಾಖಿಲ್ **dākhalu, dākhilu,** *s.* Arrival. 2. entry in a book *or* register. –ಆಪಿನಿ to arrive; to be registered *or* put on record, as a petition, *etc.* –ಮಳ್ಪುನಿ to make an entry; to file, register; to produce.

ದಾಖಲೆ, ದಾಖ್ಲೆ **dākhalè, dākhlè,** *s.* Demonstration, proof, documentary evidence. –ಕೊರ್ಪಿನಿ to give proof.

ದಾಗ್ **dāgu,** *s.* A scar. 2. disgrace, infamy.

ದಾಗದೂಜಿ **dāgadūji,** *s.* Repairs. –ಮಳ್ಪುನಿ to repair.

ದಾಗಯಿ **dāgayi,** *s.* The left hand.

ದಾಡಿ **dāḍi,** *s.* The beard.

ದಾಡಿ **dāḍi,** *s.* Harm, risk.

ದಾಡುನಿ **dāḍuni,** *see* ತಾಡುನಿ.

ದಾಡೆ **dāḍè,** *s.* A tusk, fang.

ದಾತ್ **dātu,** *see* ಧಾತು.

ದಾತಾರಿ **dātāri,** *s.* Protection, support. 2. *see* ದಾತೆ.

ದಾತಿಕೆ, ದಾತಿಗೆ **dātike, dātige,** *s.* A strong, courageous man. 2. a thriving, prosperous man.

ದಾತು **dātu,** *see* ಧಾತು.

ದಾತೃತ್ವ **dātṛutva,** *s.* Liberality, generosity.

ದಾತೆ **dāte,** *s.* A generous *or* liberal man.

ದಾತ್ವಾರಿ **dātvāri,** *see* ದಾತಾರಿ.

ದಾದವು **dādavu,** *intg. pron.* Which, what?

ದಾನ **dāna,** *s.* A gift, donation. –ಧರ್ಮ liberality, charity. –ಪತ್ರ a deed of gift. –ಮಾನ gifts and honours. –ಶೀಲ generous, liberal. –ಕೊರ್ಪಿನಿ, –ಮಳ್ಪುನಿ to bestow alms.

ದಾನವೆ **dānave,** *s.* A demon, giant.

ದಾನಿ **dāni,** *see* ದಾನೆ.

ದಾನಿ **dāni,** *s.* A giver, donor. 2. an elephant.

ದಾನುನಿ **dānuni,** *def. v.* What is to be done? ದಾನುವ what are you doing?

ದಾನೆ **dānè,** *intg. pron.* What? —ಬತ್ತ what did you come for?

ದಾನೆಂದ್ ಂಡ **dānendụṇḍa,** *conj.* (*lit.* If you say what), namely, thus, as follows, because, for.

ದಾಪು **dāpu,** *see* ತಾಪು.

ದಾಬಣಿಬಲ್ಲ್ **dābaṇiballụ,** *see* ದವ ಣಿಬಲ್ಲ್.

ದಾಬಳಿ **dābaḷi,** *s.* A kind of white blanket.

ದಾಬು **dābu,** *s.* A child's girdle, a silver belt.

ದಾಬುಡಿ **dābuḍi,** *s.* A joint-piece.

ದಾಬೆ **dābè,** *s.* A pigeon-loft. 2. bodily care.

ದಾಮ್ದುಮ್ **dāmụdumụ,** *see* ಧಾಮ್ ಧುಮ್.

ದಾಮರ್ **dāmarụ,** *see* ದಮರ್. 2. *see* ರಾಳ.

ದಾಮಸ್ **dāmasụ,** *see* ದಮಾಸ್.

ದಾಮಾದಿ **dāmādi,** *see* ದಾಯದ್ಯೆ.

ದಾಮಾಶಾಯಿ **dāmāšāyi,** *s.* Proportion, apportionment.

ದಾಮಿಸ್ **dāmisụ,** *adj.* Useless, worthless. 2. worn out.

ದಾಮೋದರೆ **dāmōdare,** *s.* A name of Krishṇa.

ದಾಯ **dāya,** *s.* Heritage, inheritance. 2. a gift, present from relations.

ದಾಯಕೆ **dāyake,** *s.* A giver, donor.

ದಾಯಣ **dāyaṇa,** *s.* Illusion.

ದಾಯದ್ಯೆ, ದಾಯಾದಿ **dāyadye, dāyādi,** *s.* A kinsman, relation, coparcener.

ದಾಯೆ **dāye,** (-ದ -ಆಯೆ) *see under* ಆಯೆ.

ದಾಯೆ, ದಾಯೆಗ್ **dāye, dāyegụ,** *intg. pron.* Why, for what purpose?

ದಾಯೆಗಂದ್ ಂಡ **dāyegandụṇḍa,** *conj.* (*lit.* Why, if you say) Wherefore, because.

ದಾರ್ **dārụ,** *see* ದಾರೆ.

ದಾರ್ದೂರು **dārụdūru,** *see* ದಾರುದೂರು.

ದಾರ **dāra,** *s.* A thread, string. 2. a wife. —ಪಾಡುನ to stitch.

ದಾರಂದ **dāranda,** *s.* A door frame. —ಪಟ್ಟಿ a lintel.

ದಾರಗೆ **dāragè,** *s.* The second of the female twin demons; *cf.* ಅಬ್ಬಗೆ.

ದಾರಣೆ **dāraṇè,** *s.* Price, value, charge; *cf.* ದರ. 2. *see* ಧಾರಣೆ.

ದಾರಯ **dāraya,** *s.* A star. 2. *see* ತಾರಯಿ.

ದಾರಿ **dāri,** *s.* Road, way, path.

ದಾರುದೂರು **dārudūru,** *s.* A false accusation; slander.

ದಾರೆ **dārè,** *see* ಧಾರೆ.

ದಾರೆ **dāre,** *A personal affix denoting* an office bearer, holder, *etc.*; *as,* ತಹಶಿಲ್‌ದಾರೆ, ಜಮೆ ದಾರೆ, ದಫೆದಾರೆ, *etc.*; *cf.* ಗಾರೆ.

ದಾರೆಪೀರೆ **dārepīrè,** *s.* The fruit of *Cucumis acutangula,* a variety of ಪೀರೆ.

ದಾರೆಪುಳಿ **dārepuḷi,** *s.* The carambola fruit, *Averrhoa carambola.*

ದಾರೆಮಣೆ **dāremaṇè,** *s.* A seat occupied by bride and bridegroom during the marriage ceremony.

ಡಾರೇಕಳ್ಳಿ dārēkaḷḷi, *s.* A kind of striped milk-hedge, *Euphorbia antiquorum.*

ಡಾರ್ಣೆ dārṇe, *see* ಡಾರಣೆ.

ಡಾಬರ್ಡಾಡ್ dārbāḍḍu, *see* ಡಬ್ಬಾರ್.

ಡಾಲಚಿನಿ dālacini, *see* ಡಾಲ್ಚಿನಿ.

ಡಾಲಾ dālā, *s.* Anything; *cf.* ಡಾ. –ಇಜ್ಜಿ, ಡಾಲಿಜ್ಜಿ there is nothing.

ಡಾಲಾಲಿ dālāli, *see* ದಲ್ಲಾಲಿ.

ಡಾಲಿಂಬ, ಡಾಲಿಂಬಿ dālimba, dālimbi, *see* ದಾಳಿಂಬ.

ಡಾಲಿಜ್ಜಿ dālijji, *see under* ಡಾಲಾ.

ಡಾಲ್ಚಿನಿ dālcini, *s.* Cinnamon.

ಡಾವ dāva, *see* ಡಾ, ಡಾನೆ, ವಾ. 2. *see* ಡಾವೆ.

ಡಾವಣಿಬಲ್ಲ್ dāvaṇiballu, *see* ದವಣೆ [ಬಲ್ಲ್.

ಡಾವತಿ dāvati, *s.* Grief, sorrow, distress, suffering. 2. weariness, fatigue.

ಡಾವಳಿ dāvaḷi, *see* ದಾಬುಳಿ.

ಡಾವು dāvu, *s.* Glare, lustre, heat, warmth.

ಡಾವೆ dāve, *s.* A suit, claim; complaint. 2. enmity, spite. –ದಾರೆ a complainant. –ಮಳ್ಪುನಿ to claim; to complain.

ಡಾಸತ್ವ dāsatva, *s.* Slavery, bondage, servitude.

ಡಾಸನ dāsana, *s.* The shoe-flower plant, *Hibiscus rosa sinensis*; *also* ದಾಸನಪೂ.

ಡಾಸಪಂತಿ dāsapanti, *s.* A kind of grass, used as a blister.

ಡಾಸಯ dāsaya, *see* ಅನ್ವಯ.

ಡಾಸಯೆ, ಡಾಸಯ್ಯೆ dāsaye, dāsayye, *s.* A Vishṇuite mendicant.

ಡಾಸಿ dāsi, *s.* A female slave, maid servant.

ಡಾಸಿನ dāsina, *s.* The colouring of the teeth. 2. a kind of grass. 3. *see* ಉದಾಸ.

ಡಾಸೆ dāse, *s.* A slave, servant. 2. a mendicant; *cf.* ದಾಸಯೆ.

ಡಾಸೆಮಿ dāsemi, *s.* Mustard.

ಡಾಸ್ತನ, ಡಾಸ್ತಾನ್ dāstana, dāstānu, *s.* A store, storing. –ದೀಪಿನಿ to store. –ಮಳ್ಪುನಿ to collect, make ready.

ಡಾಸ್ಯತ್ವ dāsyatva, *see* ದಾಸತ್ವ.

ಡಾಹ dāha, *s.* Burning. 2. thirst, ardent desire. –ತೀರ್ಪುನಿ to quench thirst.

ಡಾಳಿ dāḷi, *s.* Marauding, plunder, sacking.

ಡಾಳಿಂಬ dāḷimba, *s.* The pomegranate.

ಡಾಕ್ಷಿಣ, ಡಾಕ್ಷಿಣ್ಯ dākshiṇa, dākshiṇya, *s.* Regard, respect, considerateness. 2. partiality. ಮುಖ– regard of person.

ದಿ di, *A feminine affix of nouns*; *as*, ಜವನೆ a youth; ಜವನೆದಿ, ಜವಂದಿ a maiden. ಯಜಮಾನೆ a master; ಯಜಮಾನೆದಿ a mistress.

ದಿಂಗುಡುನಿ, ದಿಂಗುನಿ diṅguḍuni, diṅguni, *see* ನಿಂಗುನಿ.

ದಿಂಜ diñja, *s.* Plenty, abundance. *adj.* Full, complete, replete. 2. much. 3. violent, severe. *adv.* Very, often. –ಜನ plenty of people. –ಬೇನೆ severe pain. –ಸರ್ತಿ often, many times.

ದಿಂಜಾವುನಿ diñjāvuni, *c. v.* (*of* ದಿಂಜುನಿ) To cause to fill, load, heap.

ದಿಂಜುನಿ diñjuni (ದಿಂಜ್), *v. n.* To be filled, full, replete. *v. a.* To fill. ಬಂಜಿ– *lit.* to fill the belly; to earn one's livelihood; to be pleased.

ದಿಂಜೆಲ್ diñjelụ, *s.* Fullness. 2. flood-tide.

ದಿಂಡ್ diṇḍụ, *s.* The festival of illumination, when the idol of a temple is carried in procession. –ಕಟ್ಟುನಿ to decorate; to prepare for an illumination.

ದಿಂಡ್ diṇḍụ, *adj.* Strong, stout. 2. rash. –ತನ, *see* ದಿಂಡಾಟಿಗೆ. –ಶಾಸ್ತ್ರದಾಯೆ a tyrant, bully.

ದಿಂಡ್ diṇḍụ, *s.* The tender stalk inside a plantain tree.

ದಿಂಡ diṇḍa, *adj.* Proud, mischievous, impudent; *cf.* ದಿಂಡೆ.

ದಿಂಡಾಟಿಗೆ diṇḍāṭigė, *s.* Mischief, impudence. 2. stupidity.

ದಿಂಡು diṇḍu, *see* ದಿಂಡ್.

ದಿಂಡೆ diṇḍe, *s.* A strong, stout man; a mischievous fellow. –ತಾರೆ a large cocoanut tree.

ದಿಂಣ diṇṇa, *see* ದುಂಣ.

ದಿಂದಿಗೆ dindigė, *see* ಜಿಂದಿಗೆ.

ದಿಂನೆ dinnė, *s.* A hillock, eminence. –ತಗ್ಗ್ hill and dale, ups and downs.

ದಿಂಮ dimma, *s.* The sound of a small finger-drum.

ದಿಂಮನೆ dimmanė, *adv.* Quickly, suddenly.

ದಿಂಮಾಕ್ dimmākụ, *see* ದಿಮಾಕ್.

ದಿಂಮೆ dimmė, *s.* A wedge; a stopple, plug.

ದಿಂಮ್ಸ್‌ಕಾಯಿ dimmskāyi, *see* ಗುಮುಸು.

ದಿಕ್ಕ್ dikkụ, *s.* Direction, side, region *or* quarter of the world. 2. refuge, shelter, protection. ನಾಲ್– four points of the compass. –ದಾಂತಿ destitute, helpless. –ದಾಂತಿನಾಯೆ a destitute man, an orphan. –ದಾಂತೆ without protection. –ಭ್ರಮೆ giddiness, confusion; roaming, wandering. –ತಪ್ಪುನಿ to miss the direction.

ದಿಕ್ಕ dikka, *adv.* Quickly, speedily.

ದಿಕ್ಕರಿಪುನಿ dikkaripuni (ದಿಕ್ಕರಿ), *v. a.* To despise, condemn, censure, reproach. 2. to disdain, reject.

ದಿಕ್ಕಳ್ dikkaḷụ, *see* ದಿಕ್ಕೊಳು.

ದಿಕ್ಕಾಪಾಲ್ dikkāpālụ, *s.* Dispersion, dissipation, ruin. –ಆದ್ ಪೋಪಿನಿ to be dispersed, dissipated, ruined.

ದಿಕ್ಕಾಮಲ್ಲಿ dikkāmalli, *s.* A kind of resin tree, *Gardenia lucida.*

ದಿಕ್ಕಾರ dikkāra, *s.* Disrespect, insult, contempt; disdainment, rejection.

ದಿಕ್ಕಿ dikki, *see* ದಿಕ್ಕೆ.

ದಿಕ್ಕಿಜ್ಜ್ಯಂದೆ dikkijjyandė, *see* ದಿಕ್ಕ್ ದಾಂತೆ *under* ದಿಕ್ಕ್.

ದಿಕ್ಕೆ dikke, *s.* A Pariah.

ದಿಕ್ಕೆ, ದಿಕ್ಕೆಲ್ dikkė, dikkelụ, *s.* A hearth, fireplace. –ದ ತಿಟ್ಟ the front of a hearth. ದಿಕ್ಕೆದಂಗಲ್ the hearth-place.

ದಿಕ್ಕೊಳ್ dikkoḷu (*fem. of* ದಿಕ್ಕೆ), *s.* A Pariah woman.

ದಿಕ್ಪಾಲಕೆ dikpālake, *s.* The guardian of one of the eight points of the compass.

ದಿಗ್ರ್ digụrụ, *s.* Disregard, indifference. 2. resentment. *adj.* Adverse, contrary. —ಪಾತರ, —ಸವಾಲ್ an adverse statement *or* reply. —ಮುಳ್ಪುನಿ to resent; to disregard.

ದಿಗಂತ diganta, *s.* The horizon.

ದಿಗಂತರ digantara, *s.* A foreign country.

ದಿಗಂಬರ digambara, *adj.* Naked, uncovered. ದಿಗಂಬರೆ a nude man; a recluse, anchorite.

ದಿಗಿಲ್ digilụ, *s.* Fear, alarm. 2. cowardice.

ದಿಗ್ಗಜ diggaja, *s.* One of the fabulous elephants supporting the globe.

ದಿಗ್ಬಂಧನ digbandhana, *s.* A general charm to keep off all evils.

ದಿಗ್ಭ್ರಮ digbhrama, *s.* Unsteadiness.

ದಿಗ್ವಾರ್ತೆ digvārtè, *s.* News from different directions.

ದಿಗ್ವಿಜಯ digvijaya, *s.* Universal conquest.

ದಿಟ diṭa, *see* ದೃಢ.

ದಿಟ್ಟ diṭṭa, *adj.* Confident, bold. —ತನ boldness.

ದಿಟ್ಟಿ diṭṭi, *see* ದೃಷ್ಟಿ.

ದಿಟ್ಟೆ diṭṭe, *s.* A bold, *or* clever man.

ದಿಡ್ಂಬು diḍụmbu, *adj.* Corpulent.

ದಿಡ್ಂಬೆರ್ diḍụmberụ, *s.* A deified bull, an ox belonging to a Śiva temple. 2. Śiva's steed.

ದಿಡ್ಕ diḍụka, *see* ದಿಡ್ಕ.

ದಿಡ್ದಿಡ diḍụdiḍa, *adv.* Quickly.

ದಿಡ್ಮೆನ diḍụmena, *see* ದಡ್ಕೆನ.

ದಿಡ diḍa, *see* ದೃಢ.

ದಿಡಿಕ diḍika, *see* ದಿಡ್ಕ.

ದಿಡುಂಬು diḍumbu, *s.* A big drum. *adj. see* ದಿಡ್ಂಬು.

ದಿಡುಂಬೆರು diḍumberu, *see* ದಿಡ್ಂಬೆರ್.

ದಿಡ್ಕ diḍka, *adv.* Immediately, quickly; suddenly.

ದಿಡ್ಡ್ diḍḍụ, *s.* An elevated ground, a mound. 2. rancidity.

ದಿಡ್ಡೆ diḍḍè, *see* ಜಿಡ್ಡೆ.

ದಿಡ್ಮೆನ diḍmena, *see* ದಡ್ಕೆನ.

ದಿದಂಮೆ, ದಿದಪ್ಪೆ didamme, didappè, *see* ತಿದ್ದ್ಯಂಮೆ, ತಿದ್ಯಪ್ಪೆ, *under* ತಿದ್ದಿ.

ದಿನ್ಸ್ dinụsụ, *s.* Likeness. 2. kind, sort.

ದಿನ್ಸಾರ dinụsāra, *s.* Different kinds *or* sorts, as of goods, *etc.*

ದಿನ dina, *s.* A day. —ಕಟ್ಟಳೆ daily routine. —ಕೂಲಿ daily wages. —ಚಡ್ತ daily. —ಚರಿ, —ವಾರಿ a diary, day-book, chronicle. —ಚರ್ಯೆ daily conduct. —ದಿನೊಕು daily. —ಮಾನ the length of a day, a day in general; the times. —ಹರಣ passing time. ಇತ್ತೆದ— the present time. —ಕೆಪ್ಪುನಿ to spend time, to live.

ದಿನಂಪ್ರತಿ dinamprati, *adv.* Daily, every day.

ದಿನಸ್ dinasụ, *see* ಜಿನಸ್.

ದಿನಾನದಿನ **dinānadina,** *s.* A certain day.

ದಿನಾಲಾ **dinālā,** *adv.* Daily.

ದಿಬ್ಬಣ **dibbaṇa,** *s.* A bridal party, a marriage procession. —ದಾ ಕುಳು, ದಿಬ್ಬಣಿಗರ್ persons belonging to a marriage party.

ದಿಬ್ರಾಲ್ **dibrālu,** *see* ದುಬ್ರಾಲ್.

ದಿಮುಸ್ಕಾಯಿ **dimusˈkāyi,** *see* ಗುಮುಸು.

ದಿಮಾಕ್ **dimāku,** *s.* Haughtiness, arrogance, pride, disdain.

ದಿಮಿಟಿ **dimiṭi,** *s.* A kind of stout, white cotton cloth, ribbed *or* figured; dimity.

ದಿಮಿದಿಮಿ **dimidimi,** *s.* Agility, dancing nimbly.

ದಿಯ್ಯ, ದಿರ್ರ **diyya, dirra,** *adv.* Suddenly, at once; *cf.* ದಿಕ್ಕ.

ದಿಲ್ **dilu,** *s.* The mind, heart.

ದಿವ, ದಿವಸ **diva, divasa,** *see* ದಿನ.

ದಿವಾಕರೆ **divākare,** *s.* The sun.

ದಿವಾನ್, ದಿವಾನೆ **divānu, divāne,** *s.* The minister *or* secretary of a native state. 2. an idiot, fool.

ದಿವಾರಾತ್ರೆ **divārātrè,** *s.* Day and night. *adv.* By day and night.

ದಿವಾರೋಹಣ **divārōhaṇa,** *s.* Ascension.

ದಿವಾಳಿ **divāḷi,** *s.* Bankruptcy. 2. *see* ದೀಪಾಳಿ. —ಕೋರೆ a bankrupt; a spendthrift. —ಆಪಿನಿ, —ದೆಪ್ಪುನಿ to become insolvent.

ದಿವಿ **divi,** *s.* Heaven, the sky.

ದಿವಿಟಿ **diviṭi,** *see* ಜೀಟಿಗೆ.

ದಿವಿದಿವಿಮರ **dividivimara,** *s.* The dividivi tree, *Cæsalpina coriara.*

ದಿವ್ಯ **divya,** *adj.* Divine, celestial. 2. beautiful, agreeable, excellent, supernatural. —ಗುಣ excellent disposition. —ಜ್ಞಾನ divine knowledge. —ಮೂರ್ತಿ the Divine Being, God. —ರತ್ನ a rare gem. —ರಸ quicksilver; *also* ಪಾದರಸ. —ಲೋಕ heaven. —ವಸ್ತು an excellent substance; a holy being.

ದಿಶಾಂತರ **diśāntara,** *see* ದೇಶಾಂತರ.

ದಿಶಾಟನೆ **diśāṭanè,** *see* ದೇಶಾಟನೆ.

ದಿಶೆ **diśè,** *s.* Direction, side, space, region; *cf.* ದಿಕ್ಕ, ದೆಶೆ.

ದಿಷ್ಟ **dishṭa,** *s.* Fate, destiny, fortune.

ದಿಷ್ಟಿ **dishṭi,** *see* ದೃಷ್ಟಿ. —ಮಣಿ glass beads put on the neck of an infant to ward off the effect of evil eyes.

ದಿಸೆ **disè,** *s.* Fortune, luck. —ಲಕ್ಕುನಿ to be lucky. ಯಿಡ್ಡೆ— good luck. ಪದಿಕೆ— bad luck.

ದೀಟಿಗೆ **dīṭigè,** *see* ಜೀಟಿಗೆ.

ದೀನ್ಸ್ **dīnusu,** *see* ಜಿನಸು.

ದೀನ **dīna,** *adj.* Poor, indigent, needy, 2. modest, humble, cringing.

ದೀನೆ **dīne,** *s.* A poor *or* weak man. 2. an humble man.

ದೀಪ **dīpa,** *s.* A lamp; a light. —ಪೂಜೆ lighting lamps in a temple as an act of devotion.

ದೀಪನ **dīpana,** *s.* Hunger.

ದೀಪಾಳಿ, ದೀಪಾವಳಿ **dīpāḷi, dīpāvaḷi,** *s.* (*lit.* A row of lights), a festival with nocturnal illuminations in honour of a god.

ದೀಪಾವುನಿ dīpāvuni, *c.v.* (*of* ದೀಪಿನಿ) To cause to place, keep, put, *etc.*

ದೀಪಾವೊಣುನಿ dīpāvoṇuni, *refl. v.* (*of* ದೀಪಾವುನಿ) To keep, *etc.* for one's self. 2. to keep a concubine, *vlg.*

ದೀಪಿಕೆ dīpikè, *see* ದೀಪ.

ದೀಪ್ತಿ dīpti, *s.* Light, lustre. 2. fire. 3. a lamp kept burning near an idol.

ದೀಪಿನಿ dīpini (ದೀ), *v. a.* To place, keep, put, reserve, lay by.

ದೀಯ dīya, *see* ದಿಯ್ಯ.

ದೀರೆ dīre, *see* ಧೀರೆ.

ದೀರ್ಘ dīrgha, *adj.* Long. *s.* The long form of a vowel, the letter ೯. —ಆಯುಷ್ಯ a long life. —ದರ್ಶಿ a prophet, seer. —ಶಯನ death. —ಶಾಂತಿ long suffering, patience.

ದೀರ್ಸಾಲೆ dīrsālè, *s.* A superior kind of rice.

ದೀವಟಿ dīvaṭi, *see* ಜೀಟಿಗೆ.

ದೀವಳಿ dīvaḷi, *see* ದೀಪಾಳಿ.

ದೀವಿ, ದೀವು dīvi, dīvu, *s.* An island. —ದಗುಜ್ಜಿ the bread fruit, *Artocarpus incisa.*

ದೀಕ್ಷಾಂತ dīkshānta, *s.* The fulfilment of a vow *or* austerities.

ದೀಕ್ಷೆ dīkshè, *s.* The initiatory ceremony of a sacrifice, *etc.* 2. a vow, resolve to accomplish anything. 3. undertaking a service, austerities, *etc.* —ಪತ್ತುನಿ to take a vow; to undertake any pious work.

ದುಂಕುನಿ duṅkuni, *see* ಡೊಂಕುನಿ.

ದುಂಚಿ duñci, *s.* Shag, nap, as of a cloth. —ಕಟ್ಟುನಿ to hem a garment. —ಲಕ್ಕುನಿ to become woolly *or* shaggy.

ದುಂಚೆಲ್ duñcelu, *adj.* Shaggy, woolly, as a cloth.

ದುಂಡು duṇḍu, *adj.* Round, globular. —ಬಳೆ a kind of bracelet worn by females. —ಮಲ್ಲಿಗೆ a kind of round jasmine, *Jasminum sambac.*

ದುಂಡೆ duṇḍè, *see* ದೊಂಡೆ.

ದುಂಣ duṇṇa, *s.* Heaviness. *adj.* Heavy.

ದುಂದು dundu, *adj.* Prodigal, wasteful. —ಗಾರಿಕೆ, —ತನ prodigality, waste. —ಗಾರೆ a prodigal, squanderer.

ದುಂದುಭಿ dundubhi, *s.* The fifty-sixth year of the Hindu cycle of sixty. 2. a kettle-drum.

ದುಂನ dunna, *see* ದುಂಣ.

ದುಂನೊಂಚಿ dunnoñci, *s.* A kind of earring.

ದುಂಪಿಯುನಿ dumpiyuni (ದುಂಪಿ), *v.n.* To stumble.

ದುಂಬಗ್ dumbagu, *adv.* In future, next year; *cf.* ದುಂಬು.

ದುಂಬತ್ತ dumbatta, *adv.* First, at first.

ದುಂಬಿನಾನಿ dumbināni, *adv.* The day before, previous day.

ದುಂಬು dumbu, *s.* Front. 2. past time. 3. futurity. *adv.* In front. 2. early, beforehand. 3. at first, in the beginning. 4. formerly. 5. in future, hereafter; *also* ದುಂಬಗ್. —ಬಾಯಿ the first man, firstborn. —ಪೋ ಪಿನಿ to go in advance. —ಪಿರವು before and behind, front and rear.

ದುಂಮ್ಮಾನ **dummāna,** *s.* Grief, sorrow.

ದುಂಯಿ **duṁyi,** *s.* The sound of a mosquito.

ದುಂಶ, ದುಂಸ **duṁśa, duṁsa,** *see* ಧ್ವಂಸ.

ದುಃ **duḥ,** *see* ದುರ್.

ದುಃಖ **duḥkha,** *s.* Sorrow, grief, affliction. —ಕೊರ್ಪಿನಿ to afflict, grieve, tease. —ಮಳ್ಪುನಿ to mourn, lament.

ದುಃಖಿಯುನಿ **duḥkhiyuni** (ದುಃಖಿ), *v. n.* To mourn, lament. ದುಃಖಿ ದುಃಖಿದ್ ಅರ್ಪಿನಿ to sob, weep bitterly.

ದುಃಶಕುನ **duḥśakuna,** *s.* A bad omen.

ದುಕಾನ್ **dukāṇu,** *s.* A shop.

ದುಕ್ಕ **dukka,** *adv.* Suddenly, at once, quickly; *cf.* ಡಿಕ್ಕ. —ಲಕ್ಕು ನಿ to get up at once.

ದುಖ್ಖ **dukkha,** *see* ದುಃಖ.

ದುಗಣೆ, ದುಗ್ಗಾಣಿ **duganè, duggāṇi,** *s.* Two pie.

ದುಟ್ಟ **duṭṭa,** *see* ದುಷ್ಟ.

ದುಡಿ **duḍi,** *s.* The lip.

ದುಡಿತ, ದುಡಿತೆ **duḍita, duḍitè,** *s.* Gain, acquisition. 2. property. —ಮಳ್ಪುನಿ, *see* ದುಡಿಯುನಿ.

ದುಡಿಯುನಿ, ದುಡಿಪಿನಿ **duḍiyuni, duḍipini** (ದುಡಿ), *v. a.* To acquire, gain, earn, obtain.

ದುಡುಂಬುನಿ **duḍumbuni** (ದುಡುಂಬ್), *v. a.* To drive.

ದುಡುಕು, ದುಡುಕುತನ **duḍuku, duḍukutana,** *s.* Hurry, rashness. 2. violence, injustice. 3. pride, haughtiness.

ದುಡುಕುನಿ **duḍukuni** (ದುಡುಕ್), *v. n.* To be rash *or* hasty. 2. to be violent, haughty. *v. a.* To defy.

ದುಡುತ **duḍuta,** *see* ದುಡಿತ.

ದುಡ್ಡಾಟ **duḍḍāṭa,** *s.* The game of chuckfarthing.

ದುಡ್ಡಾಶೆ **duḍḍāśè,** *s.* Covetousness.

ದುಡ್ಡು **duḍḍu,** *s.* A copper coin worth four pie. 2. copper coin in general. 3. money, cash. ಆನೆ—, ಗಟ್ಟಿ— a thick copper coin that was current in former days.

ದುಣಿಪುನಿ **duṇipuni** (ದುಣಿ), *v. n.* To struggle, strive. 2. to flutter, flap the wings in agitation, as a bird. 3. to bustle, be in a hurry.

ದುಣಿಪೆಲ್ **duṇipeḷu,** *adj.* Struggling, striving, fluttering. 2. bustling.

ದುಣಿಪೆಲೆ **duṇipele,** *s.* A bustler, busybody.

ದುಣ್ಣ **duṇṇa,** *see* ದುಂಣ.

ದುತ್ತು **duttu,** *see* ದುಸ್ತು.

ದುಪ್ಪ **duppa,** *adv.* Suddenly; quickly.

ದುಪ್ಪಟಿ, ದುಪ್ಪಟೆ **duppaṭi, duppaṭè,** *s.* A laced *or* other cloth loosely thrown over the body. 2. a sheet, tablecloth.

ದುಪ್ಪೆ duppè, *see* ತುಪ್ಪೆ.

ದುಬರಾಲ್ dubarālu, *see* ದುಬ್ರಾಲ್.

ದುಬಲಾಕ್ dubalāku, *adj.* Twice distilled; double.

ದುಬಾರಿ dubāri, *adj.* Double. 2. needless, useless. —ಕರ್ಚು double *or* needless expense. 3. *see* ದುಬ್ರಾಲ್.

ದುಬಾಸಿ dubāsi, *s.* An interpreter. 2. a broker, agent, *etc.*

ದುಬ್ರಾಲ್ dubrālu, *s.* Twice distilled arrack.

ದುಮುಕುನಿ dumukuni (ದುಮುಕ್), *v. a.* To jump down; to alight quickly.

ದುಮುಸು dumusu *see* ಗುಮುಸು.

ದುಯಮ್ duyamu, *adj.* Secondary, subordinate. 2. middling, second-hand.

ದುರ್, ದುಸ್ dur, dus, *Prefixes denoting* Bad, ill, wicked. 2. difficult. 3. inferior, vile.

ದುರಂಗಿ durangi, *adj.* Differently coloured on both sides, as some cloths.

ದುರಭ್ಯಾಸ durabhyāsa, *s.* A bad habit *or* practice.

ದುರಯ duraya, *see* ದ್ರವ್ಯ.

ದುರಾಚಾರ durācāra, *s.* A bad custom *or* usage. 2. wicked conduct.

ದುರಾತ್ಮೆ durātme, *s.* An evil spirit. 2. a wicked man.

ದುರಾಲೋಚನೆ durālōcanè, *s.* Wicked thoughts.

ದುರಾಶೆ durāśè, *s.* Covetousness. 2. a vain *or* forlorn hope, unattainable desire.

ದುರಿತ durita, *s.* Sin, transgression.

ದುರುಜಿ duruji, *see* ಗುಜಿರ್.

ದುರುಡ duruda, *see* ದೃಢ.

ದುರುಬಿ durubi, *adj.* Inebriating. 2. surfeiting. —ತನ inebriation; surfeit.

ದುರುಬಿನಿ durubini, *see* ದುರ್ಬಿನಿ.

ದುರುಬೀಜ durubīja, *see* ದುರ್ಬೀಜ.

ದುರುಸು durusu, *see* ದುಸುರು.

ದುರುಸ್ತು durustu, *s.* Repairs, improvement. *adj.* Proper, well, right. —ಮಳ್ಪುನಿ to repair, mend, put in order.

ದುರುಳ durula, *adj.* Wicked. —ತನ wickedness.

ದುರುಳೆ durule, *s.* A wicked man.

ದುರ್ಗ durga, *s.* A castle, hill-fort. 2. *see* ದುರ್ಗೆ.

ದುರ್ಗಂಧ durgandha, *s.* A stench, fetid smell.

ದುರ್ಗಟ, ದುರ್ಘಟ durgata, durghata, *adj.* Difficult of attainment, insurmountable. —ಕಾರ್ಯ an object difficult to accomplish.

ದುರ್ಗತಿ durgati, *s.* A bad destiny, misery. 2. hell.

ದುರ್ಗಾಲಯ durgālaya, *s.* A temple of Durgi.

ದುರ್ಗಿ durgi, *s.* A name of Pārvati. 2. the name of a female.

ದುರ್ಗುಣ durguna, *s.* A bad disposition *or* temper, corrupt nature. *adj.* Ill-natured.

ದುರ್ಗೆ durgè, *see* ದುರ್ಗ.

ದುರ್ಚಿ durči, *s.* A sheet of paper. 2. *see* ದೊರ್ಜಿ.

ದುರ್ಜನ durǰana, *s.* Wicked people.

ದುರ್ಜಾತಿ durǰāti, *s.* A disreputable caste.

ದುರ್ಜಿ durǰi, *see* ಗುರ್ಜಿ. 2. *see* ದೊರ್ಜಿ.

ದುರ್ಜಿಲ್ durǰilu, *see* ದೊರ್ಜಿ.

ದುರ್ದಶೆ durdaśè, *s.* Misfortune, ill-luck.

ದುರ್ನಡತೆ durnaḍatè, *s.* Bad conduct.

ದುರ್ನುಡಿ durnuḍi, *s.* A bad word.

ದುರ್ಬಲ durbala, *s.* Weakness, impotency. *adj.* Weak, impotent; helpless.

ದುರ್ಬಿನಿ durbini, *s.* A telescope.

ದುರ್ಬೀಜ durbīja, *s.* *lit.* A bad seed. *adj.* Of bad family, of disreputable descent.

ದುರ್ಬುದ್ಧಿ durbuddhi, *s.* A wicked mind, bad disposition. 2. folly, want of sense.

ದುರ್ಬೋಧನೆ durbōdhanè, *s.* Bad advice.

ದುರ್ಭಿಕ್ಷೆ durbhikshè, *s.* Scarcity, famine.

ದುರ್ಮತಿ durmati, *s.* The fifty-fifth year of the Hindu cycle of sixty. 2. an evil mind.

ದುರ್ಮನಸ್ durmanasu, *s.* A bad mind.

ದುರ್ಮರಣ durmaraṇa, *s.* An untimely death, death by accident.

ದುರ್ಮಾರ್ಗ durmārga, *s.* Wickedness, vice.

ದುರ್ಮಿತ್ರ durmitre, *s.* A bad friend.

ದುರ್ಮುಖ durmukha, *s.* An angry face.

ದುರ್ಮುಖಿ durmukhi, *s.* The thirtieth year in the Hindu cycle of sixty.

ದುರ್ಯೋಧನೆ duryōdanè, *s.* The elder of the Kuru princes.

ದುರ್ಲಭ durlabha, *adj.* Difficult of attainment, scarce, rare.

ದುರ್ವಾರ್ತೆ durvārtè, *s.* Bad news.

ದುರ್ವಾಸನೆ durvāsanè, *s.* A stink, stench.

ದುರ್ವ್ಯಯ durvyaya, *see* ದುರ್ವ್ರಯ.

ದುರ್ವ್ಯಸನ durvyasana, *s.* A bad habit, evil practice.

ದುರ್ವ್ರಯ durvraya, *s.* A useless expense, squandering, waste.

ದುರ್ಸು dursu, *s.* Rockets; *also* ದುರ್ಸುಬಾಣ. 2. *see* ದುರುಸ್ತು. —ಬಿಡು to fire rockets.

ದುಲ್ಲೊಡಿ dulloḍi, *s.* A kind of necklace.

ದುಶ್ಮಾನೆ duśmāne, *s.* An enemy, opponent. ದುಶ್ಮಾನಿಗೆ enmity, hostility.

ದುಶ್ಶೀಲ duśśīla, *s.* A bad disposition *or* practice.

ದುಷ್ಕರ್ಮ dushkarma, *s.* An evil deed, crime, sin. ದುಷ್ಕರ್ಮಿ a wicked man.

ದುಷ್ಕಳೆ dushkaḷe, *s.* A great thief.

ದುಷ್ಕಾಲ dushkāla, *s.* An evil time. 2. famine, scarcity.

ದುಷ್ಕೀರ್ತಿ dushkīrti, *s.* Infamy, bad name.

ದುಷ್ಟ, dushṭa, *adj.* Bad, wicked, depraved. 2. low, vile. –ಗುಣ, –ಭಾವ a bad disposition. –ತನ wickedness, depravity. –ಬುದ್ಧಿ an evil mind; a minister so called. –ಮಾರ್ಗ wicked conduct. –ಮೃಗ a wild beast, mischievous animal.

ದುಷ್ಟೆ, dushṭe, *s.* A wicked *or* bad man.

ದುಸ್ತರ dustara, *adj.* Difficult, trying, hard.

ದುಸ್ತಲೆ dustale, *s.* An unhappy man; a bad man.

ದುಸ್ತು dustu, *s.* A suit of clothes.

ದುಸ್ವಭಾವ dusvabhāva, *s.* An evil disposition, ill-nature.

ದುಸ್ಸಂಗ dussaṅga, *s.* Bad company *or* intercourse; evil companions.

ದೂಂಟ dūṇṭa, *see* ಗೂಂಟ.

ದೂಂಡೆ dūṇḍe, *see* ಬೊಂಡೆ.

ದೂಂಬೆ, ದೂಂಬೆಲ್ dūmbe, dūmbeḻu, *see* ಸೂಂಬು.

ದೂಜಿ dūji, *s.* A needle, pin. –ಕಲ್ಲ್ a magnet. –ಮರ the tinian pine.

ದೂಡುನಿ dūḍuni, *see* ನೂಕುನಿ.

ದೂತಿ dūti, *s.* A pimp, procuress. 2. a female messenger.

ದೂತೆ dūte, *s.* A messenger, spy. ದೇವ– an angel. ಯಮ– the messenger of death.

ದೂದು dūdu, *see* ಜೂಜಿ. 2. *see* ಕೂರು.

ದೂಪ, ದೂಪನ dūpa, dūpana, *see* ಧೂಪ.

ದೂಪೆ dūpè, *s.* Food laid out for the dead; a mound marking the burial place of a Šūdra. 2. a temporary shed, covered with awnings, for offering oblations to the manes of deceased Šūdra. –ದ ಕಂಡ a field in which such a mound *or* shed has been raised. –ದ ನುಪ್ಪು oblations of boiled rice offered to the manes of a deceased Šūdra. –ಗ ಮಳ್ಪುನಿ to prepare such food. –ಗ ಮೆತ್ತುನಿ to serve such food; to serve a person with a large quantity of food.

ದೂಬಿನ dūbina, *s.* A comb.

ದೂರ dūra, *s.* Distance. *adj.* Distant, remote. ದೂರೊಗು– very far. –ದಾಯೆ a low-caste man; a man come from a distance. –ದಾಳ್ a female in her menses; a low-caste woman. –ದೃಷ್ಟಿ foresight; long-sighted. –ಮಾರ್ಗ, –ಸಾದಿ a long way. –ಉಂತುನಿ to stand at a distance. –ಪೋಪಿನಿ to go far, move further. –ಬೂರುನಿ to be deferred, delayed. –ಮಳ್ಪುನಿ to separate; to shun.

ದೂರಾಟ dūrāṭa, *s.* Aspersing, calumniating; complaining.

ದೂರು dūru, *s.* Aspersion, blame, reproach. 2. a complaint. –ಕೊರ್ಪಿನಿ, –ಪನ್ಪುನಿ to complain. –ಪಾಡುನಿ to accuse, blame, censure.

ದೂರುನಾಯೆ dūrunāye, *s.* An accuser, censurer, complainant.

ದೂರುನಿ dūruni (ದೂರ್), *v. a.* To accuse, complain; to blame, reproach, censure.

ದೂರೆಲೆ dūrele, *see* ದೂರುನಾಯಿ.

ದೂರ್ತತನ dūrtatana, *s.* Craftiness.

ದೂರ್ತೆ dūrte, *s.* A deceiver.

ದೂಷಕೆ dūshake, *s.* A blasphemer.

ದೂಷಣೆ dūshaṇè, *s.* Cursing. 2. censure, reproach. ದೇವ– blasphemy.

ದೂಷಿಪುನಿ dūshipuni (ದೂಷಿ), *v. a.* To blaspheme. 2. to blame, censure, reproach.

ದೂಸು dūsu, *s.* Fine powder; *cf.* ದೂಸೆಲ್.

ದೂಸುನಿ dūsuni (ದೂಸ್), *v. a.* To spill, sprinkle.

ದೂಸೆಲ್ dūselṳ, *s.* Powder, dust. *adj.* Powdered, dusty.

ದೂಳಿ dūḷi, *see* ಧೂಳು. 2. a dispicable person. 3. a high number. –ಪಟಿ, –ಪಡೆ unreliable.

ದೂಳು dūḷu, *see* ಧೂಳು.

ದೃಕ್ drṳkṳ, *s.* The eye. 2. sight, seeing.

ದೃಢ drṳḍha, *s.* Firmness, stability. 2. certainty. *adj.* Firm, stable. –ತ್ವ firmness; truthfulness. –ಮಳ್ಪುನಿ to affirm, declare; to fix, make certain.

ದೃಢೀಕರಣ drṳḍhīkaraṇa, *s.* Confirmation.

ದೃಷ್ಟ drṳshṭa, *adj.* Visible, apparent.

ದೃಷ್ಟಾಂತ drṳshṭānta, *s.* An example, illustration, evidence. –ತೋಜಿಪುನಿ to exemplify, illustrate.

ದೃಷ್ಟಿ drṳshṭi, *s.* Sight, seeing. 2. an eye.

ದೆಂಗ್ deṅgṳ, *s.* A hiding place.

ದೆಂಗಾವುನಿ deṅgāvuni, *c. v.* (*of* ದೆಂಗುನಿ) To cause to be hidden, concealed; hide, conceal.

ದೆಂಗುನಿ deṅguni (ದೆಂಗ್), *v. n.* To be hidden, concealed, lie in ambush.

ದೆಂಗೆಲೆ deṅgele, *s.* One who hides, a refugee.

ದೆಂಜಿ deñji, *s.* A crab. –ಬಾಷ an abscess between the thumb and the forefinger. ಕಡಲ–, ಕುಮುರೆ–, ಕಲ್ಲ–, ಬಳ್ಪುನಿ–, ಮಡಕೆ–, ಮುಕ್ಕುರು–, ಮೆತ್ತಿ–, ಪಕಾರ–, are some of the species of crab.

ದೆಂಜೆಲಿ deñjeli, *s.* A kind of umbrella made of palm leaves.

ದೆಂಟ್ deṇṭṳ, *see* ದಂಟ.

ದೆಂನಣ dennaṇa, *see* ವಾರ್ಧನ.

ದೆಂಬು dembu, *see* ದೊಂಬು.

ದೆಂಬೆಲ್ dembelṳ, *see* ದೊಂಬೆಲ್.

ದೆಕ್ಕಟ್ಟುನಿ dekkaṭṭuni (ದೆಕ್ಕಟ್ಟ್), *v. a.* To shuffle, *or* move in a slovenly manner, as a person in a tight dress *or* when the foot is entangled in anything.

ದೆಕ್ಕತ್ತಿ dekkatti, *s.* A kind of nutcracker used for cutting the areca-nut into pieces.

ದೆಕ್ಕಯಿ dekkayi, *s.* The betrothal badge. –ಕಟ್ಟುನಿ to put the same on the person of a bride.

ದೆಕ್ಕರೆ, ದೆಕ್ಕಾರ್, ದೆಕ್ಕಾರು dekkarė, dekkāru, dekkāru, *s.* The space between the legs, when they are apart. *adv.* Between the legs.

ದೆಕ್ಕಾಜಿ dekkāji, *s.* A kind of bracelet.

ದೆಕ್ಕಾಣೆ dekkāṇè, *adv.* Tightly.

ದೆಕ್ಕಾವುನಿ dekkāvuni, *c. v.* (*of* ದೆಕ್ಕುನಿ) To cause to wash.

ದೆಕ್ಕಿ dekki, *s.* Space, room, place.

ದೆಕ್ಕುನಿ dekkuni (ದೆಕ್ಕ್), *v. a.* To wash (anything except clothes), lave, cleanse.

ದೆಕ್ಕುಳು dekkuḷu, *see* ದಕ್ಕಿನಾಕುಳು.

ದೆಕ್ಕುಲಿ dekkuli, *s.* Irregular teeth, projecting teeth.

ದೆಕ್ಕೆ dekkè, *see* ಜೊಂಕೆ.

ದೆಪ್ಪಾವುನಿ deppāvuni, *c. v.* (*of* ದೆಪ್ಪುನಿ) To cause to take.

ದೆಪ್ಪು deppu, *see* ತೆಪ್ಪು. 2. *see* ದೆಪ್ಪುನಿ.

ದೆಪ್ಪುನಿ deppuni (ದೆ), *v. a.* To take, receive; *cf.* ಕೆಪ್ಪುನಿ. ದೆತ್ತ್‌ದ್ ಪಾಡುನಿ to abolish, take away, put aside; to pull out; to remove, dismiss.

ದೆಬ್ಬೆ debbè, *see* ದಬ್ಬೆ.

ದೆಯ್ಯ deyya, *see* ದೈಯ. 2. *see* ದೈವ. 3. *see* ದೆವ್ವ.

ದೆಯಿವ deyiva, *see* ದೈವ.

ದೆರಂಗಯಿ deraṅgayi, *see* ಗೇರ್‌ಕಾಯಿ.

ದೆರ್ಪುನಿ derpuni (ದೆರ್), *v. a.* To lift, raise.

ದೆವ್ವ devva, *s.* A demon, evil spirit.

ದೆಶೆ, ದೆಸೆ deśè, desè, *s.* Condition, state. 2. fortune, luck.

ದೆಶೆಡ್ದು deśeḍḍu, *postp.* From, by, on account of, for.

ದೇಕಿ dēki, *s.* Nicety. 2. management *or* foresight. *adj.* Nice, good.

ದೇಗ್ dēgu, *see* ದಾಯಿ.

ದೇಜ dēja, *see* ತೇಜ.

ದೇಬೆ dēbè, *s.* A quarrelsome woman.

ದೇರಾಟ dērāṭa, *s.* Driving.

ದೇರುನಿ dēruni (ದೇರ್), *v. a.* To drive, drive away.

ದೇಲ dēla, *s.* A small temple. 2. God. —ಗುಂಡ the idol's apartment in a temple. ಬಾಲೆ ಸೈತಿನಾಯೆ ದೇಲ ದೂರುವೆ a man bereft of his child blasphemes against God.

ದೇಲಂತೊಟ್ಟು dēlantoṭṭu, *s.* A Brahmin's house.

ದೇಲಂದಪುದ, ದೇಲಪುದ dēlandapuda, dēlapuda, *s.* A temple pigeon.

ದೇವ dēva *see* ದೇಹ. 2. the male organ.

ದೇವಂದ dēvanda, *adj.* Pertaining to temples. —ಓಡು a small kind of tiles.

ದೇವಕಿ dēvaki, *s.* Kṛushṇa's mother.

ದೇವಗಣ dēvagaṇa, *s.* The race of gods.

ದೇವಡಿಕೆ, ದೇವಡಿಗೆ dēvaḍike, dēvaḍige, *s.* One of the caste of musicians.

ದೇವತಾರ್ಚನೆ dēvatārčanè, *s.* Worship of a god.

ದೇವತೆ dēvatè, *s.* A demi-god.

ದೇವತ್ವ dēvatva, *s.* Divinity; godhead.

ದೇವದತ್ತ dēvadatta, *adj.* Given by God.

ದೇವದಾರ್, ದೇವದಾರೆ dēvadārụ, dēvadārè, *s.* A cedar.

ದೇವದೂತೆ dēvadūte, *s.* An angel.

ದೇವದ್ರೋಹ dēvadrōha, *s.* Apostacy, heresy.

ದೇವನಾಮು dēvanāma, *s.* The name of God,

ದೇವನಿಂದೆ dēvanindè, *s.* Blasphemy.

ದೇವಪೂಜೆ dēvapūjè, *s.* Adoration of God, divine worship.

ದೇವಪ್ರತಿಷ್ಠೆ dēvapratishṭhè, *s.* The consecration of an idol.

ದೇವಬಾರೆ dēvabārè, *s.* A superior kind of plantains.

ದೇವಭಕ್ತಿ dēvabhakti, *s.* Piety, devotion.

ದೇವಭಕ್ತೆ dēvabhakte, *s.* A pious man, a devotee.

ದೇವಮಂದಾರ dēvamandāra, *s.* A kind of flower.

ದೇವಮಾರ್ಗ dēvamārga, *s.* God's ways. 2. pious behaviour.

ದೇವರಂಗ dēvaraṅga, *s.* The centre of a temple.

ದೇವರಾಜೆ dēvarāje, *s.* Indra.

ದೇವಲೋಕ dēvalōka, *s.* Heaven.

ದೇವಲ್ಯ dēvalya, *see* ದೇವಾಲಯು.

ದೇವಸ dēvasa, *s.* Temple-lands *or* property.

ದೇವಸಮರಂಗ dēvasamaraṅga, *s.* Presence; God's presence.

ದೇವಸಮರ್ಪಣೆ dēvasamarpaṇè, *s.* Offering to God.

ದೇವಸ್ಥಾನ dēvasthāna, *s.* A temple.

ದೇವಾಂಗ dēvāṅga, *s.* A Lingāyat class of weavers. 2. an ape. –ಬಾಯಿ one of the weaver class.

ದೇವಾಧೀನ dēvādhīna, *s.* Death. *adv.* In God's disposal. –ಆಪಿಸಿ to die.

ದೇವಾರಾಧನೆ dēvārādhanè, *s.* Divine worship.

ದೇವಾಲಯು dēvālaya, *s.* A church; a temple.

ದೇವಿ dēvi, *s.* A goddess. 2. Pārvati. 3. a queen. –ಪೂಜೆ the Šakti worship.

ದೇವಿರಿ, ದೇವಾರಿ dēviri, dēvāri, *s.* A Brahmin's dress.

ದೇವೆರ್ dēverụ, *s.* God. 2. an honorific title, applied to persons of rank. ದೇವೆರೆ ಕಾರ್ಯ a sacred work *or* undertaking.

ದೇವೇಂದ್ರೆ dēvēndre, *s.* Indra.

ದೇಶ dēśa, *s.* A country, land, territory, district, region. –ಗೇಡಿ one who has left his country, an exile. –ತಿಂಗುಣಿ to travel.

ದೇಶಭಾಷೆ dēśabhāshè, *s.* The language of a country.

ದೇಶಭ್ರಷ್ಟ dēśabhrashṭa, *s.* Transportation, expatriation.

ದೇಶಸ್ಥೆ dēśasthe, *s.* A native, inhabitant. 2. a class of Brahmins.

ದೇಶಾಂತ್ರ dēśāntra, *s.* A foreign country.

ದೇಶಾಂತ್ರಿ dēśāntri, *s.* A foreigner; a traveller.

ದೇಶಾಚಾರ dēšācāra, *s.* The custom of a country, local usage.

ದೇಶಾಟನ dēšāṭana, *s.* Travels; travelling.

ದೇಶಾಧಿಕಾರಿ, ದೇಶಾಧಿಪತಿ dēšādhikāri, dēšādhipati, *s.* A sovereign ruler.

ದೇಶಾಯಿ dēšāyi, *s.* A chief man among the Lingāyats.

ದೇಶಾವರ, ದೇಶಾವಾರ dēšāvara, dēšāvāra, *adj.* Foreign, exotic. *s.* A present, gift, alms.

ದೇಶೆ dēšė, *see* ದೆಶೆ.

ದೇಶ್ಯ dēšya, *adj.* Local, of *or* belonging to a country. –ಭಾಷೆ, *see* ದೇಶಭಾಷೆ.

ದೇಹ dēha, *s.* The body. –ದಂಡಣೆ corporal punishment, penance, mortification.

ದೇಹಿ dēhi, *adj.* Having a body, corporeal.

ದೈ dei, *s.* A plant, young tree.

ದೈಂಡಿ deiṇḍi, *s.* The name of a tree. 2. a staff, stick.

ದೈಂಡೆ deiṇḍe, *see* ದಿಂಡೆ.

ದೈಂಡೆ deiṇḍė, *see* ದಂಡಿಗೆ.

ದೈತ್ಯ, ದೈತ್ಯೆ deitya, deitye, *s.* A titan, demon, giant. –ಕರ್ಮ a giant's deed; a wicked act.

ದೈನ, ದೈನ್ಯ deina, deinya, *s.* Meanness, humility, servility. 2. poverty. *adj.* Mean, humble, lowly. 2. cringing, servile. –ಭಾವ humble disposition.

ದೈಪುನಿ deipuni, *see* ಜೈಪುನಿ.

ದೈಯ deiya, *see* ದೈವ. –ಕಾಣಿಗೆ a gift *or* offering to demons. –ಮುಡಿಪು treasure devoted to a deity.

ದೈಯಂಕಡೆ deiyaṅkaḍė, *adv.* Towards god or a demon. *s.* An inclosure of an idol. 2. the name of a village.

ದೈಯಾರೆ deiyāre, *s.* The name of a demon.

ದೈರ್ಯ, ದೈರ್ಯ deirya, *see* ಧೈರ್ಯ.

ದೈವ deiva, *s.* A deity; God. 2. an evil spirit, a demon. 3. destiny, fate. *adj.* Divine, celestial. –ಕೃತ್ಯ –ತಂತ್ರ a divine act. –ಕಲ್ಪನೆ, –ಸಂಕಲ್ಪ divine origin, God's will. –ಕಲ್ಪಿತ ordained by God. –ಗತಿ, –ಯತ್ನ, –ಯೋಗ fate, God's decree. –ಗುಣ divine nature. –ಘಟನೆ, –ಸಂಘಟನೆ God's help. –ಬಲ divine strength. –ಮುಖ the face of God; divine grace.

ದೈವಾಧೀನ deivādhīna, *adj.* Subject to God's will. *s.* Fate, God's decree; death.

ದೈವೀಕ deivīka, *adj.* Divine.

ದೈಸುನಿ deisuni, *see* ಜೈಸುನಿ. 2. *see* ದಯಸುನಿ.

ಡೊಂಕ doṅka, *see* ಟೊಂಕ.

ಡೊಂಕ doṅka, *adj.* Tall. –ಬಳಪುನಿ to grow tall.

ಡೊಂಕಾವುನಿ doṅkāvuni, *c. v.* (*of* ಡೊಂಕುನಿ) To cause to tread, trample.

ಡೊಂಕಾಸ್ doṅkāsu, *see* ಡೊಂಕ.

ಡೊಂಕುನಿ doṅkuni (ಡೊಂಕ್), *v. a.* To tread, trample. ಮುಳ್ಳ– a Pariah woman to become pubescent, *vlg*.

ದೊಂಕೆ, ದೊಂಕೆಲ್ doṅkè, doṅkelụ, *see* ಜೊಂಕೆ.

ದೊಂಕೆಲ್ doṅkelụ, *s.* What has been trodden. *adj.* Trodden, trampled.

ದೊಂಗುನಿ doṅguni, *see* ಡಂಗುನಿ.

ದೊಂಟೆ doṇṭè, *see* ದೋಂಟೆ.

ದೊಂಡಿ doṇḍi, *see* ದುಂಡು.

ದೊಂಡೆ doṇḍè, *s.* The throat. –ನನೆಪುನಿ (*lit.* to wet the throat) to drink, allay thirst.

ದೊಂಣ doṇṇa, *s.* Self-confidence. –ಗಾರೆ a man carrying a club; a self-confident man.

ದೊಂಣಪ್ಪೆ doṇṇappe, *s.* A self-confident *or* conceited man.

ದೊಂಣೆ doṇṇè, *s.* A cudgel, club, mace.

ದೊಂದಪ್ಪೆ dondappe, *s.* A companion.

ದೊಂದಿ dondi, *s.* A small torch made of a rag.

ದೊಂದು dondu, *s.* A couple, pair. 2. *see* ದೊಂದಪ್ಪೆ.

ದೊಂದೆಪುರಿ dondepuri, *see* ತೊಂದೆಪುರಿ *under* ತೊಂದೆ.

ದೊಂನೆ donnè, *s.* A cup made of plantain leaves, *etc.* –ಹೆಟ್ಟುನಿ to make such a cup.

ದೊಂಪ dompa, *s.* A pandal, shed, temporary covering of matted palm leaves, *etc.*; *cf.* ಚಪ್ಪರ. 2. a frame-work of bamboos, *etc.* erected for training a creeper. –ದ ಅಬರೆ *Cynamopsis psoraloides*, a kind of bean. –ದ ಬಲಿ the annual festival of a demon celebrated under a pandal. –ದ ಬೂರು the succulent creeper purslane, *Basella rubra; cf.* ಬಸಳೆ.

ದೊಂಪಿಯುನಿ dompiyuni (ದೊಂಪಿ), *v. n.* To stumble.

ದೊಂಬಿ dombi, *s.* A mob, rabble. 2. a riot, uproar. –ಗಾರೆ a rioter, turbulent man.

ದೊಂಬು dombu, *s.* Sunshine, heat of the sun. –ಕುದುರೆ mirage. –ಅರಪುನಿ the heat to decrease. –ಗು ಪಾಡುನಿ to expose to the sun. –ಬೂರುನಿ the sun to shine. –ಹಾಕುನಿ the sun to strike. ಕಡು– very hot. ನೆಸರ್– the morning sun. ಸೆಯ್ಯ–, the evening sun. ಪನಿ– twilight.

ದೊಂಬುಡಿ dombuḍi, *see* ದೊಂಬೆಲ್.

ದೊಂಬೆ dombe, *s.* A tumbler, rope-dancer. –ರಾಟ tumbling, rope-dancing. –ರೆ ಚೆಂನಿ a female tumbler.

ದೊಂಬೆಲ್, ದೊಂಬೊಲಿ dombelụ, domboli, *s.* A chap, cleft in the surface of the earth.

ದೊಂಮರೆ dommare, *see* ದೊಂಬೆ.

ದೊಂಸ doṁsa, *see* ಧ್ವಂಸ.

ದೊಕ್ಕಿನಾಕುಳು, ದೊಕ್ಕುಳು dokkinākuḷu, dokkuḷu, *s.* A mode of addressing high caste people by Pariahs.

ದೊಕ್ಕೆ dokkè, *s.* Breath; breathing. –ಆಪಿನಿ, –ಕೊಡುನಿ, –ಬರ್ಪಿನಿ –ನ ಆಪಿನಿ to revive. –ಕಡಿಯುನಿ, –ಪಾರುನಿ to cease to breathe; to expire. –ಯೆಕ್ಕುನಿ, –ನಲಿಪುನಿ to palpitate.

ದೊಗ್ಗಲ್ doggaḷu, *s.* Kneeling. —ಪಾಡುನಿ, —ಬೂರುನಿ to kneel.

ದೊಗ್ಗು doggu, *adj.* Kneeling. —ಸಲಾಂ *lit.* saluting on one's knees; submission, yielding. —ಸಲಾಂ ಪಾಡುನಿ to submit, yield.

ದೊಗ್ಗುನಿ dogguni (ದೊಗ್ಗ್), *v. n.* To kneel.

ದೊಗ್ಗೊಲಿ ಪದ್ಪೆ doggoli padpè, *s.* A short kind of the vegetable *Amarantus oleraceus.* 2. the purslane.

ದೊಜ್ಜಲ್ dojjaḷu, *s.* Uncleanliness; rubbish.

ದೊಜ್ಜುನಿ dojjuni (ದೊಜ್ಜ್), *v. n.* To stammer; to hesitate.

ದೊಜ್ಜೆ dojje, *s.* A stammerer.

ದೊಟ್ಟೆ doṭṭe, *see* ದುಷ್ಟೆ.

ದೊಡಕ್ doḍaku, *adj.* Perplexed, confused. 2. broken, damaged.

ದೊಡೆ doḍe, *s.* A greedy man; *cf.* ತೊಡು. 2. *see* ಜೋಡೆ. 3. *see* ತುಡೆ. —ತನ greediness.

ದೊಡ್ಡ doḍḍa, *adj.* Great, large.

ದೊಡ್ಡಣ್ಣೆ doḍḍaṇṇe, *s.* An elder brother.

ದೊಡ್ಡಂತಿ doḍḍanti, *s.* Birthday.

ದೊಡ್ಡಣದಾಯೆ doḍḍaṇadāye, *s.* A powerful man.

ದೊಡ್ಡಪ್ಪಯೆ, ದೊಡ್ಡಯೆ doḍḍappaye, doḍḍaye, *s.* A father's elder brother.

ದೊಡ್ಡರೆ doḍḍarè, *s.* A kind of rice.

ದೊಡ್ಡಲೆ, ದೊಡ್ಲೆ doḍḍalè, doḍlè, *s.* A wild orange, *Atalantia Monophylla.*

ದೊಡ್ಡಸ್ತಿಗೆ doḍḍastigè, *s.* Greatness, loftiness. 2. riches, power. 3. ostentation, pride.

ದೊಡ್ಡು doḍḍu, *see* ದುಡ್ಡು. 2. *see* ಕಾಟಿ.

ದೊಡ್ಡೆ doḍḍe, *see* ದಡ್ಡೆ.

ದೊಣೆಲ್ doṇeḷu, *s.* A club.

ದೊಣ್ಣ doṇṇa, *see* ದೊಂಣ.

ದೊದ್ದೆ doddè, *see* ಗೊದ್ದೆ.

ದೊನೆಲ್ doneḷu, *see* ದೊಣೆಲ್.

ದೊಪ್ಪೆ doppe, *s.* A kind of grass.

ದೊಬಾರಿ dobāri, *see* ದುಬಾರಿ.

ದೊಬ್ಬಿ dobbi, *see* ಡಬ್ಬಿ.

ದೊಬ್ಬು dobbu, *s.* Pushing, shoving.

ದೊಬ್ಬುನಿ dobbuni (ದೊಬ್ಬ್), *v. n.* To push, shove, put off.

ದೊರಂಕ್ doraṅku, *see* ದೊರಗ್.

ದೊರಂಕುನಿ doraṅkuni, *see* ದೊರಕುನಿ.

ದೊರಂಗ್ doraṅgu, *see* ದೊರಗ್.

ದೊರಂದಳಿಗೆ, ದೊರಂದೊಲಿಗೆ dorandaḷigè, dorandoligè, *s.* Self-praise, egotism, elation.

ದೊರಕಾವುನಿ dorakāvuni, *c. v.* (*of* ದೊರಕುನಿ) To cause to obtain; to procure.

ದೊರಕುನಿ dorakuni (ದೊರಕ್), *v. n.* & *c. dat.* To be got, obtained, procured, found.

ದೊರಕೆ dorakè, *see* ತೊರಕೆ.

ದೊರಗ್ doragu, *adj.* Coarse, rough.

ದೊರಸ್ತ್ dorastu, *see* ದುರುಸ್ತು.

ದೊರಿ dori, *adj.* Poured, as corn, *etc.*; *cf.* ದೊರಿಯುನಿ.

ದೊರಿಪಾವುನಿ doripāvuni, *c. v.* (*of* ದೊರಿಪುನಿ) To cause to flow down, run out, *or* run over as corn, *etc.*

ದೊರಿಪುನಿ **doripuni** (ದೊರಿ), *v. a.* To shoot out as corn, *etc.*, from a sack *or* bundle.

ದೊರಿಯುನಿ **doriyuni** (ದೊರಿ), *v. n.* To flow down, run out, *or* run over as corn, *etc.*, from a sack *or* bundle. 2. to fall, as rain, to shower. 3. to feel a limb heavy.

ದೊರೆ **dorè**, *see* ಧೊರೆ.

ದೊರ್ಜಿ, ದೊರ್ಜಿಲ್ **dorji, dorjilu**, *s.* A kind of rafter.

ದೊರ್ತೆಲ್ **dortelu**, *adj.* Partially empty *or* loose, as a bundle of rice.

ದೊರ್ಪುನಿ, ದೊರ್ಬುನಿ **dorpuni, dorbuni**, *see* ದೊರಿಪುನಿ.

ದೊಲಂಕುನಿ **dolaṅkuni** (ದೊಲಂಕ್), *v. a.* To relax, loosen.

ದೊಲ್ಲು **dollu**, *adj.* Useless, unprofitable, vain. 2. empty, void. 3. *see* ದೊಳ್ಳು.

ದೊಲ್ಲೆ **dollè**, *s.* Saliva, spittle. —ಕಾರುನಿ to cough hard.

ದೊಳಂಕ್, ದೊಳುಂಕು **dōḷaṅku, doḷuṅku**, *adj.* Loose, lax. *s.* Looseness; *also* ದೊಳುಂಕೆಲ್. —ಕಟ್ಟುನಿ to tie loose; to slacken.

ದೊಳುಂಕುನಿ **doḷuṅkuni** (ದೊಳುಂಕ್), *v. n.* To be loose, lax; be bruised.

ದೊಳೆ **doḷè**, *see* ತೊಳೆ.

ದೊಳ್ಪುನಿ **doḷpuni**, *see* ತೊಲ್ಪುನಿ. 2. *see* ತೊರ್ಪುನಿ.

ದೊಳ್ಳು **doḷḷu**, *see* ದೊಳ್ಳು.

ದೊಳ್ಳೆ **doḷḷè**, *see* ದೊಲ್ಲೆ.

ದೋಂಟಾಸ್ **dōṇṭāsu**, *s.* A tall man; *cf.* ದೋಂಟೆ.

ದೋಂಟಿ **dōṇṭi**, *s.* A long pole with a hook to pluck fruit.

ದೋಂಟೆ **dōṇṭe**, *s.* Tallness, length. 2. a tall man. *adj.* Tall, long. —ಕಾರ್. long legs. —ಪುರಿ a long worm.

ದೋಂದಳ **dōndaḷa**, *see* ಗೋಂದಳಪೂಜೆ.

ದೋಕು **dōku**, *see* ಧೋಕು.

ದೋಗ **dōga**, *s.* Crawling.

ದೋಗುನಿ **dōguni** (ದೋಗ್), *v. a.* To crawl on hands and knees *or* in a sitting posture. 2. to grub up grass.

ದೋಟ **dōṭa**, *see* ತೋಟ.

ದೋಟೆ **dōṭè**, *see* ದೋಂಟೆ.

ದೋಡಣೆ **dōḍaṇè**, *s.* Furniture, *etc.*

ದೋಡಿಯುನಿ **dōḍiyuni** (ದೋಡಿ), *v. n.* To arrange. 2. to collect, gather, provide, store; *cf.* ದು ಡಿಯುನಿ.

ದೋಡೆ **dōḍè**, *s.* A talkative woman.

ದೋಣಿ **dōṇi**, *s.* A boat. 2. a spirited *or* quarrelsome woman.

ದೋಣೆ **dōṇè**, *see* ದೊಂಣೆ.

ದೋತ್ರ **dōtra**, *s.* A Hindu's lower garment, the cloth wrapped round the loins. —ದ ಕೆಂಬಿ the colored borders of such a garment.

ದೋದು **dōdu**, *adj.* Thin, watery. 2. *see* ಜೂಜಿ.

ದೋದೆಲ್ dōdelụ, *s.* Thinness.

ದೋಬಿ dōbi, *s.* A washerman.

ದೋರ dōra, *see* ದ್ವಾರ.

ದೋರಕ dōraka, *see* ದ್ವಾರಕ.

ದೋರಣೆ dōraṇè, *see* ತೋರಣ

ದೋರಿ dōri, *s.* A rope.

ದೋರೆ dōrè, *s.* A kind of gold bracelet. 2. the thread used for fastening a knife to the legs of a cock in cock-fighting.

ದೋರೆಕಾಯಿ dōrekāyi, *s.* A ripe fruit.

ದೋರ್ಗಂಡ dōrgaṇḍa, *see* ದುರ್ಗಟ.

ದೋಲಂಟೆ, ದೋಲಗಂಟೆ dōlaṇṭè, dōlagaṇṭè, *s.* A drum and bell, bell-drum.

ದೋಲಿ dōli, *see* ಡೋಲಿ.

ದೋಲು dōlu, *s.* A drum. –ಬಂಜಿ a pot-belly. –ದ ಕರ the hollow cylinder *or* hemisphere of a drum.

ದೋಲೆ dōle, *s.* A man with a pot-belly.

ದೋಷ, ದೋಸ dōsha, dōsa, *s.* Fault, defect, blemish. 2. sin, offence, crime. 3. error, mistake. –ರಹಿತ a man of unblemished character.

ದೋಸೆ dōsè, *s.* A cake of rice flour.

ದೋಸ್ತಿ dōsti, *s.* Friendship, intimacy. 2. a friend.

ದೋಳಾ dōḷā, *s.* Desire. 2. the lin plant.

ದೋಳಿ dōḷi, *see* ಡೋಲಿ.

ದೋಳು dōḷu, *see* ಡೋಲು.

ದೋಳ್ಕಿ dōḷki, *s.* A small drum.

ದೌಂಸ douṅsa, *see* ಧ್ವಂಸ.

ದೌಡು douḍu, *s.* A gallop. 2. a quick motion. 3. arrogance. 4. speed, haste. ದೌಡಾದೌಡಿ great haste.

ದೌಡೆ douḍè, *s.* The jaw, cheek. –ಗೆ ಕೊಡ್ಡನಿ to slap the cheek.

ದೌತ douta, *s.* Loss, destruction. –ಮಳ್ಪುನಿ to destroy.

ದೌತಿ douti, *s.* An ink-stand.

ದೌರಂಗಿ, ದೌಲಂಗಿ douraṅgi, doulaṅgi, *s.* A long coat

ದೌಲತ್, ದೌಲೊತು doulatụ, doulotu, *s.* Rule, government. 2. pomp, ostentation.

ದೌಲು doulu, *see* ಡೌಲು.

ದೌವೆ douvè, *adj.* Toothless.

ದ್ರವಿಡ dravida, *see* ದ್ರಾವಿಡ.

ದ್ರವ್ಯ dravya, *s.* Wealth, property, substance. 2. elementary substance, *namely:* earth, water, fire, air, ether, time, space, soul, intellect.

ದ್ರವ್ಯಾಶೆ dravyāśè, *s.* Love of gold, avarice.

ದ್ರಾವಿಡ drāviḍa, *adj.* Dravidian *or* Tamil. –ದೇಶ properly the country from Madras to Cape Comorin. –ಬ್ರಾಹ್ಮಣ a Brahmin, native of the South of the Vindya mountains. –ಭಾಷೆ one of the Dravidian languages.

ದ್ರಾಕ್ಷ, ದ್ರಾಕ್ಷೆ drāksha, drākshè, *s.* Grapes. –ತೋಟ a vineyard. –ಬೂರು the grape vine. –ರಸ wine.

ದ್ರೋಹ drōha, *s.* Treason, treachery, rebellion, revolt. ದೈವ– apostasy. ಸ್ವಾಮಿ– treason. ದ್ರೋಹಿ an apostate, traitor, betrayer.

ದ್ವಂದ್ವ dvandva, *s.* A couple, pair. 2. strife, dispute. –ಯುದ್ಧ single combat. –ಸಮಾಸ a form of grammatical combination of words.

ದ್ವಾರ dvāra, *s.* A door. –ಕ, –ಪಾಲಕ a doorkeeper.

ದ್ವಾರಕ dvāraka, *s.* The city where Krushṇa, reigned.

ದ್ವಿ dvi, *adj.* Two

ದ್ವಿಜ dvija, *adj.* Twice born. *s.* The oviparous class of animals, as birds, snakes, fish, *etc.*, which are first born in the shell *or* egg and then produced from it.

ದ್ವಿಜಾತಿ dvijāti, *s.* One of the twice born castes.

ದ್ವಿಜೆ dvije, *s.* A Brahmin, whose investiture with the sacred thread is supposed to constitute a second birth.

ದ್ವಿತೀಯ dvitīya, *adj.* Second. –ವಿಭಕ್ತಿ the accusative case.

ದ್ವಿಪದೆ dvipadè, *s.* A metrical composition in couplets.

ದ್ವಿಪಾದಿ dvipādi, *s.* A biped.

ದ್ವಿವಚನ dvivačana, *s.* The dual number, *gram.*

ದ್ವಿವಿಧ dvividha, *adj.* Twofold.

ದ್ವೀಪ dvīpa, *s.* An island.

ದ್ವೇಷ dvēsha, *s.* Hatred, enmity. –ಮಾಡು to hate, detest.

ದ್ವೈತ dveita, *s.* Dualism. –ಮತ a sect that regards God and matter as distinct. ದ್ವೈತಿ one of this sect.

ಧ DH

ಧ dha, The thirty-second letter of the alphabet.

ಧಕ್ಕ dhakka, *see* ದಕ್ಕ. –ಮುಕ್ಕಿ a peremptory demand.

ಧಕ್ಕೆ dhakkè, *see* ದಕ್ಕೆ.

ಧಡೆ dhaḍè, *see* ದಡೆ. 2. *see* ತಡೆ.

ಧಣಿ dhaṇi, *see* ಧನಿ.

ಧಣೆ dhaṇè, *see* ತನೆ.

ಧನ dhana, *s.* Riches, wealth, property. –ಪತಿ, ಧನಾಧಿಪತಿ Kubēra; a wealthy person. –ವಂತ a rich man.

ಧನಿ dhani, *s.* A proprietor, master, lord. 2. a wealthy man. 3. *see* ಧ್ವನಿ.

ಧನಿಕೆ dhanike, *s.* A wealthy man.

ಧನು, ಧನುಸ್ಸು dhanu, dhanussu, *s.* A bow. 2. the ninth solar month. –ರಾಶಿ the sign *Sagittarius.* ಧನುರ್ಧಾರಿ an archer.

ಧಮ್‌ಧುಮ್ dhamụdhumụ, *see* ಧಾಮ್‌ಧುಮ್.

ಧರ dhara, *see* ದರ.

ಧರಣ್ dharaṇu, *s.* An old coin equivalent to one Rupee.

ಧರಣ dharaṇa, *see* ಧಾರಣೆ.

ಧರಣಿ, ಧರಿತ್ರಿ, ಧರೆ dharaṇi, dharitri, dharè, *s.* The earth. ಧರಣಿಪತಿ a king.

ಧರಿಸುನಿ, ಧರಿತೋಣುನಿ dharisuni, dharitoṇuni (ಧರಿ), *v. a.* To wear, dress, put on, assume a form. 2. to retain in mind, hold. ಅವತಾರ– to become incarnate. ಗರ್ಭ– to become pregnant. ಮೌನ– to be silent.

ಧರ್ಮ dharma, *s.* Justice. 2. charity, liberality. 3. duty, obligation. 4. usage, practice. 5. fitness, propriety. 6. virtue, merit. –ಧಾರೆ a wedding in which the bridegroom incurs no expense. –ಪತ್ನಿ a wedded wife. –ರಾಯೆ the oldest of the Pāṇḍu princes; Yama. –ಶಾಸ್ತ್ರ a code of laws. –ಕೊರ್ಪಿನಿ, –ಮಳ್ಪುನಿ to give alms. –ಮಳ್ಪುನಿ to do justice.

ಧರ್ಮಾನುಜೆ dharmānuje, *s.* A charitable man.

ಧರ್ಮಾರ್ತ, ಧರ್ಮಾರ್ಥ dharmārta, dharmārtha, *adj.* Gratuitous, charitable, free. ಧರ್ಮಾರ್ತಾದ್, ಧರ್ಮಾರ್ತೊಗು gratuitously, freely, gratis.

ಧರ್ಮಾಧರ್ಮ dharmādharma, *s.* Right and wrong.

ಧರ್ಮಾಧಿಕಾರಿ dharmādhikāri, *s.* A judge.

ಧರ್ಮಿ, ಧರ್ಮಿಷ್ಠೆ dharmi, dharmishṭhe, *s.* A charitable *or* liberal man.

ಧವಳ dhavaḷa, *adj.* White, fair. –ವರ್ಣ white colour.

ಧವಳಿ dhavaḷi, *s.* A white cow.

ಧಾತ್, ಧಾತು dhātu, dhātu, *s.* The pulse. 2. any constituent part of the body, as flesh, blood, *etc.* 3. a primary *or* elementary substance, as earth, air, *etc.* 4. the property of a primary element, as odour, colour, *etc.* 5. a grammatical root. 6. a fossil *or* mineral. 7. the tenth year in the Hindu cycle of sixty. –ನಷ್ಟ spermatorrhoea, *emissio seminis.* –ಪುಷ್ಟಿ full pulse; strength.

ಧಾನ್ಯ dhānya, *s.* Grain, corn in general.

ಧಾಮ್‌ಧುಮ್ dhāmudhumu, *s.* Prodigality, dissipation. 2. the noise of a drum *or* a gun.

ಧಾರ dhāra, *see* ದಾರ.

ಧಾರಣೆ dhāraṇè, *s.* Price, charge. 2. holding, having, maintaining, wearing. 3. keeping the mind collected, breath suspended, and all natural wants restrained.

ಧಾರಾದತ್ತ dhārādatta, *adj.* Given by pouring water on the hand. –ಮಳ್ಪುನಿ to give by pouring water on the hand.

ಧಾರೆ dhārè, *s.* Sharpness, as of a knife, *etc.* 2. the stream of a jet of water poured. 3. a wedding ceremony. –ಪತ್ತುನಿ

to pour water *etc.* in a stream. —ಮೈಪುನಿ to solemnise a wedding by pouring water on the hands of the bride and bridegroom.

ಧಾವತಿ **dhāvati,** *s.* Thirst, desire, ardour, heat, hotness.

ಧಾವು **dhāvu,** *s.* Heat, warmth. 2. purse-pride, pride of wealth. 3. being care-worn from excessive love of money.

ಧಾವೆ **dhāvè,** *see* ದಾವೆ.

ಧೀಮತಿ, ಧೀಮತೆ **dhīmati, dhīmate,** *s.* A wise *or* intelligent man.

ಧೀರ **dhīra,** *adj.* Brave. 2. firm. steady. —ತ್ವ bravery, boldness, firmness.

ಧೀರೆ **dhīre,** *s.* A hero.

ಧುಕ್ಕ್ **dhukkụ,** *see* ದುಕ್ಕ. 2. *see* ದುಃಖ.

ಧುತ್ತು **dhuttu,** *adj.* Reproached, reviled. 2. abandoned, deserted.

ಧುನಿ **dhuni,** *s.* A river.

ಧುಬುದುಬು **dhubudubu,** *see* ದುಬ್ಬುದುಬು.

ಧುರ **dhura,** *s.* War.

ಧುರಂಧರ **dhurandhara,** *adj.* Powerful, able. ಧುರಂಧರೆ a strong *or* powerful man.

ಧುರಿ, ಧುರಿಕೆ **dhuri, dhurikè,** *s.* A burden.

ಧುರೀಣ **dhurīṇa,** *s.* A bad disposition *or* mind.

ಧುರು **dhuru,** *s.* A yoke.

ಧುಕ್ಷು **dhukshu,** *adj.* Elevated.

ಧೂಪ **dhūpa,** *s.* Incense. —ದ ಕಲಸ, —ಬಟ್ಟಲ್ a censer. —ದ ಮರ the dammer tree *Vateria indica*; *cf.* ತಂದೊಳಿಗೆ. —ದ ಮಾಯನ its resin. —ಸುದ್ಪಿನಿ to burn incense.

ಧೂಪಂಬುತ್ತಿ **dhūpambutti,** *see* ಉಂಬುತ್ತಿ.

ಧೂಪಾರತಿ, ಧೂಪಾರ್ತಿ, ಧೂಪುಂಡಿ **dhūparati, dhūpārti, dhūpuṇḍi,** *s.* A censer.

ಧೂಪಿಪುನಿ **dhūpipuni** (ಧೂಪಿ), *v. a.* To offer incense, burn incense.

ಧೂಮ **dhūma,** *s.* Smoke. —ಕೇತು a comet.

ಧೂಮಲ **dhūmala,** *see* ಧೂಮ್ರ.

ಧೂಮಾವತಿ **dhūmāvati,** *see* ಜುಮಾದಿ.

ಧೂಮ್ರ **dhūmra,** *s.* A sort of purple colour compounded of black and red. —ಪತ್ರ tobacco.

ಧೂಮ್ರೆ **dhūmre,** *s.* The name of a demon.

ಧೂರ್ತ **dhūrta,** *adj.* Fraudulent, crafty. —ತನ, —ಲಕ್ಷಣ craftiness; dissimulation. ಧೂರ್ತೆ a deceitful man.

ಧೂಸು **dhūsu,** *see* ದೂಸು.

ಧೂಸೆಲ್ **dhūselụ,** *see* ದೂಸೆಲ್.

ಧೂಳು **dhūḷu,** *s.* Dust. —ಪನಿ mildew; *cf.* ದೂಳಿ.

ಧೇನು **dhēnu,** *s.* A milch cow.

ಧೇನುಕಾರಿ, ಧೇನುಕೆ **dhēnukāri, dhēnuke,** *s.* A name of Krụshṇa.

ಧೈರ್ಯ **dheịrya,** *s.* Courage, bravery. 2. firmness, steadiness. —ದಾಯಿ a courageous man, adventurer. —ಹೀನೆ a timid man, coward. —ಮಳ್ಪು ನಿ to take courage.

ಧೊಡೆ dhoḍè, *see* ಡೊಡೆ.

ಧೊರಂದರಿಗೆ, ಧೊರಂದಲಿಗೆ dhorandarigè, dhorandaligè, *see* ದೊರಂದ ಳಿಗೆ.

ಧೊರೆ dhorè, *s.* A master, lord, king, ruler. 2. a European. —ತನ sovereignty, lordship, mastership. —ಸಾನಿ a lady, mistress.

ಧೋಕು dhōku, *see* ಢೋಕು.

ಧೋಡೆ dhōḍè, *see* ಡೋಡೆ.

ಧೋರಣೆ dhōraṇè, *s.* Manner, way, mode. 2. display. 3. prowess. 4. ability.

ಧೌತ dhouta, *adj.* Washed, cleansed, white. —ಅಂಬರ washed cloth.

ಧ್ಯಾನ dhyāna, *s.* Meditation, reflection. —ಮಳ್ಪುನಿ to meditate.

ಧ್ಯಾನಿಪುನಿ dhyānipuni (ಧ್ಯಾನಿ), *v. n.* To meditate, reflect.

ಧ್ವಂಸ dhvaṁsa, *s.* Loss, destruction, extinction. —ಮಳ್ಪು ನಿ to destroy, desolate, annihilate.

ಧ್ವಜ dhvaja, *s.* A flag, standard, banner.

ಧ್ವನಿ dhvani, *s.* Sound, voice, noise, report.

ನ N

ನ na, The thirty-third letter of the alphabet.

ನಂಕ್ naṅku, (*pron. dat. plur. of* ನಮ) To us.

ನಂಗ್ naṅgu, *s.* A kind of fish. —ಬಾರ್ useless paddy.

ನಂಗರ್, ನಂಗಲ್ naṅgaru, naṅgalu, *s.* An anchor.

ನಂಜಿ, ನಂಜು nañji, nañju, *s.* Poison. 2. puerperal convulsions. 3. impurity in the blood, scrofulous tendency. 4. the after-birth. 5. envy, jealousy. 6. *see* ನಂಡ. *adj.* Poisonous, impure, unwholesome. —ಕಾಯಿ *Menispermum cocculus;* any unwholesome fruit. —ದಾಯಿ a man with a scrofulous constitution; a malicious man. —ಮರ a poisonous tree. —ಮುಳ್ಳು a poisonous thorn. —ರೋಗ a scrofulous disease. —ಪದಾರ್ಥ, —ವಸ್ತು anything tending to deteriorate the quality of blood. —ಏರುನಿ, —ಮಾರುನಿ to have puerperal convulsions.

ನಂಜುಂಡೆ nañjuṇḍe, *s.* A name of Śiva.

ನಂಟ್, ನಂಟಸ್ತಿಗೆ, ನಂಟು naṇṭu, naṇṭastigè, naṇṭu, *s.* Kin, relationship.

ನಂಡ್ naṇḍu, *adj.* Chronic, virulent, festering. 2. shrunken, shrivelled; *also* ನಂಡ. —ಪಸಿ

dampness. —ಪುಣಿ a festering sore. —ಮೂಕು a shrivelled nose. —ಪಸರ್ a slender spring *or* fountain. —ಕಟ್ಟುನಿ to become shrunken *or* shrivelled. —ಗ ಬೂರುನಿ to become indurated.

ನಂದ **nanda,** *s.* The foster-father of Krishṇa; *also* ನಂದಗೋಪೆ, ನಂದರಾಯಿ. —ಗೋಕುಲ Krishṇa's birth-place.

ನಂದನ **nandana,** *s.* Delight, joy. 2. the twenty-sixth year in the Hindu cycle of sixty. 3. Indra's garden; a pleasure garden; *also* ನಂದನವನ.

ನಂದನೆ **nandane,** *s.* A son.

ನಂದರಿಕೆ **nandarikè,** *s.* A class of Brahmins.

ನಂದಲ **nandala,** *s.* A lamp-post in front of a temple.

ನಂದಾದೀಪ **nandādīpa,** *s.* A lamp always kept burning before an idol.

ನಂದಿ **nandi,** *s.* A bull. 2. one of Śiva's principal attendants; *also* ನಂದಿಕೇಶ್ವರೆ. 3. joy, pleasure. 4. the name of a man. —ಗೋಣೆ the name of a demon; the statue of a bull. —ಬಟ್ಟಲ್ a kind of white flower.

ನಂದಿನಿ **nandini,** *s.* A daughter. 2. a celestial cow.

ನಂಬಯೆ **nambaye,** *see* ನಂಬಿ.

ನಂಬರ್ **nambaru,** *s.* A number. 2. a suit, case. 3. any criminal proceedings. 4. an imputation, charge.

ನಂಬರಾಪು **nambarāpu,** *see* ಅಂಬರಪ್ಪು.

ನಂಬಾವುನಿ **nambāvuni,** *c. v.* (*of* ನಂಬುನಿ) To make believe, inspire with confidence. 2. to hoax, deceive.

ನಂಬಿ **nambi,** *s.* A Vaishṇava priest; *also* ನಂಬಿಯಾಯೆ, ನಂಬಿಯಾರೆ.

ನಂಬಿಗೆ **nambigè,** *s.* Fidelity, faithfulness, honesty, loyalty. 2. trust, confidence, belief, faith. —ದಾಯೆ a confidential *or* trustworthy man.

ನಂಬುಡಿ **nambuḍi,** *see* ನಂಬೂರಿ.

ನಂಬುನಿ **nambuni** (ನಂಬಿ), *v. a.* To believe, trust, rely upon, place confidence *or* faith in.

ನಂಬೂರಿ **nambūri,** *s.* A Brahmin of Malabar.

ನಂಬೊಲಿಗೆ **namboligè,** *see* ನಂಬಿಗೆ.

ನಂಮವು **nammavu,** *see* ನಮ.

ನಂಮೀಕೆ **nammīkè,** *see* ನಂಬಿಗೆ.

ನಂಮುನಿ **nammuni,** *see* ನಂಬುನಿ.

ನಕ **naka,** *s.* The shell of a fish. *cf.* ಕಡಲ್‌ನಾಲಯಿ. 2. *see* ನಖ. —ಗಂಧ a kind of perfume.

ನಕರಿಯುನಿ **nakariyuni,** *see* ನಕೆರುನಿ.

ನಕಲ್ **nakalu,** *s.* A copy, transcript. —ದೆಪ್ಪುನಿ, —ಬರೆಪಿನಿ to copy, transcribe; to take a copy. —ಮಳ್ಪುನಿ to make a rough copy.

ನಕಲಿ **nakali,** *s.* Ridicule, satire, caricature; imitation. *adj.* Spurious, counterfeit. —ದಾಯೆ a buffoon, satirist. —ಮಳ್ಪುನಿ

to ridicule, caricature; to imitate.

ನಕಾರಿ nakāri, *adj.* Useless, worthless. *adj.* Inferior.

ನಕುಲ nakula, *s.* A mungoose. 2. the fourth of the five Pāṇḍu princes.

ನಕೆರ nakera, *s.* A nail, claw. *adj.* Claw-like

ನಕೆರುನಿ nakeruni (ನಕೆರ್), *v. n.* To neigh. 2. to titter, giggle.

ನಕ್ಕಾಮುಟ್ಟಿ nakkāmuṭṭi, *s.* A sort of gambling.

ನಕ್ಕಾವುನಿ nakkāvuni, *c. v.* (*of* ನಕ್ಕುನಿ) To cause to lick.

ನಕ್ಕುನಿ nakkuni (ನಕ್ಕ್), *v. a.* To lick, lap.

ನಕ್ಕುರು nakkuru, *s.* An earthworm. ಪಾಲ್– a red worm.

ನಕ್ಕೆರುನಿ nakkeruni, *see* ನಕೆರುನಿ.

ನಕ್ಕೆಲು nakkelu, *see* ನಕ್ಕೆಲ್ದಿ.

ನಕ್ಕೆಲೆ nakkele, *s.* A man who licks, especially the plate in which food had been served. 2. a greedy man.

ನಕ್ಕೆಲ್ದಿ nakkeldi, *s.* An abandoned woman. 2. *the fem. of* ನಕ್ಕೆಲೆ.

ನಕ್ರ nakra, *s.* A crocodile.

ನಕ್ರಜಿತ್ತು nakrajittu, *s.* Vishṇu's weapon.

ನಕ್ರಮದ್ದೊಲಿ nakramaddoli, *s.* A [kettle-drum.

ನಕ್ರು nakru, *see* ನಕ್ಕುರು.

ನಕ್ಲಿ nakli, *see* ನಕಲಿ.

ನಖ nakha, *s.* A nail, talon, claw. 2. a fragrant substance resembling a nail.

ನಖಗುತಿ nakhaguti, *s.* A market tax.

ನಖಾವಳಿ nakhāvaḷi, *s.* A row, as of nails.

ನಖಿ nakhi, *s.* A perfume. *adj.* Having claws.

ನಗ್‌ಪುನಿ nagụpuni, *see* ನಿಗಪುನಿ.

ನಗ naga, *s.* Jewels, ornaments. 2. goods, property. 3. a mountain. 4. a sailing vessel *or* craft. –ಧರೆ Vishṇu.

ನಗಡ್ nagaḍụ, *adj.* Fibrous; nappy. 2. overgrown.

ನಗದ್, ನಗದಿ nagadụ, nagadi, *s.* Ready money, cash. –ಕೊರ್ಪಿನಿ to pay in cash.

ನಗರ್, ನಗರ nagarụ, nagara, *s.* A city, town. 2. the name of a town. –ವಾಸಿ a citizen, townsman.

ನಗರಿ, ನಗಾರಿ, ನಗಾರೆ nagari, nagāri, nagārė, *s.* A large kettle-drum.

ನಗೆ nagė, *s.* Mouldiness, rottenness. –ಪತ್ತುನಿ to moulder, become mouldy; to be rotten.

ನಗೆಪುನಿ nagepuni (ನಗೆ), *v. n.* To mould, get rusty.

ನಗ್ಗ್ naggụ, *adj.* Stunted, not fully developed. –ಬಾರ್ stunted paddy.

ನಗ್ಗ್‌ನುಗ್ಗು naggụnuggu, *adj.* Stunted, diminutive.

ನಚ್ಚ načča, *s.* Pricking. 2. pecking. 3. *see* ನಚೆ. –ಬೆಪ್ಪುನಿ to prick, peck.

ನಚ್ಚತ್ರ naċċatra, *see* ನಕ್ಷತ್ರ.

ನಚ್ಚೆ naċċe, *see* ನಕ್ಷೆ.

ನಜರ್ najarụ, *s.* Sight, seeing. 2. estimate, value. 3. a present to a superior. —ಬಂದಿಡ್ ದೀಪಿನಿ to keep in surveillance.

ನಟ naṭa, *see* ನಟ್ಟ.

ನಟನಟ naṭanaṭa, *adv.* Briskly, nimbly. 2. with a crackling noise. —ನಲಿಪುನಿ to frisk, gambol.

ನಟನೆ naṭanè, *s.* A dance, dancing. 2. sham respect *or* attentions.

ನಟಾವು naṭāvu, *see* ನಟ್ಟಾವು.

ನಟುಕು, naṭuku, *s.* Cracking the fingers.

ನಟ್ಟ್, ನಟ್ಟ naṭṭụ, naṭṭa, *adj.* Begging; beggarly. —ಪುರಿ sores about the underlip, believed to be curable only by partaking of food earned by begging.

ನಟ್ಟ naṭṭa, *see* ನಷ್ಟ.

ನಟ್ಟ naṭṭa, *adj.* Middle, central. 2. trifling. —ನಡೀರ್ midnight. —ಪನಿ a trifling, bit. —ಮಧ್ಯಾನ midday.

ನಟ್ಟಾ, ನಟ್ಟಾವು naṭṭā, naṭṭāvu, *s.* A loan, lending. ನಟ್ಟಾವುಗು ಕೊರ್ಪಿನಿ to lend.

ನಟ್ಟಾವುನಿ naṭṭāvuni, *c. v.* (*of* ನಟ್ಟುನಿ) To cause to beg; to send for begging.

ನಟ್ಟಿ naṭṭi, *s.* Planting, transplanting. —ಪುಗೆರೆ a kind of tobacco grown in South-Canara.

ನಟ್ಟುನಾಯೆ, ನಟ್ಟೆಲೆ naṭṭunāye, naṭṭele, *s.* A beggar; a beggarly man.

ನಟ್ಟುನಿ naṭṭuni (ನಟ್ಟಿ), *v. a.* To beg, request, apply, pray.

ನಟ್ಟೊಗುಕೊರ್ಪಿನಿ naṭṭogukorpini, *see under* ನಟ್ಟಾ.

ನಡ್ಪಿನಿ naḍụpini, *see* ನಡ್ಪಿನಿ.

ನಡಕೆ naḍakè, *s.* Walking. 2. pace, gait. ಕಾರ್— travelling on foot.

ನಡತರ naḍatara, *see* ನಡುತರ.

ನಡತೆ naḍatè, *s.* Behaviour, conduct. 2. intercourse, familiarity. ಆಕುಳೆಗ್ ನಡತೆ ಉಬ್ಜಿ they have no intercourse with each other.

ನಡತೊಣುನಿ naḍatoṇuni, *refl. v.* (*of* ನಡಪುನಿ) To behave, conduct one's self.

ನಡಪಾಟ naḍapāṭa, *s.* Walking, exercise. 2. behaviour, conduct.

ನಡಪಾವುನಿ, ನಡಪುಡುನಿ naḍapāvuni, naḍapuḍuni, *c. v.* (*of* ನಡಪುನಿ) To cause to walk. 2. to manage, direct, guide, lead.

ನಡಪು naḍapu, *see* ನಡಪಾಟ.

ನಡಪುನಿ naḍapuni (ನಡ), *v. n.* To walk, proceed, go on. 2. to behave.

ನಡಮಡ naḍamaḍa, *s.* Noise, crying.

ನಡರಿ naḍari, *s.* The periodical feast of a temple.

ನಡರೆ naḍarè, *s.* A native hearth.

ನಡವರಿ naḍavari, *see* ನಡರಿ.

ನಡವಳಿಕೆ naḍavaḷikè, *s.* Intercourse, familiarity. 2. management, control.

ನಡಾವಳಿ naḍāvaḷi, *s.* A grand festival occurring once in 12 years at Dharmasthala.

ನಡಿ naḍi, *s.* Behaviour, conduct, walk. ನುಡಿ–, *see under* ನಡೆ.

ನಡಿಕೆ, ನಡಿಗೆ naḍikè, naḍigè, *see* ನಟ್ಟಿ. 2. ನಡಕೆ.

ನಡಿಯುನಿ naḍiyuni (ನಡಿ), *v. n.* To be planted, *or* transplanted.

ನಡಿರ್ naḍiru, *see* ನಡೀರ್.

ನಡಿಲ್ಲ್ naḍillu, *s.* The middle room of a house.

ನಡೀರ್, ನಡೀರ್ಲ್ naḍīru, naḍīrlu, *s.* Midnight.

ನಡು naḍu, *s.* Centre, middle. 2. the waist, loins. *adj.* Central, middle. –ಗೋಡೆ a middle *or* cross wall. –ಜಾಲ್ the courtyard before a house. –ತರೆ, –ನೆತ್ತಿ the crown of the head. –ಠಾಯೆ one who is in the middle; an intermediate son *or* brother. –ತುಂಡು a middle piece. –ದಂಗ್ the middle arm. –ದೊಂಬು the midday-sun. –ಮುಳ್ಳು the backbone. –ರಾತ್ರಿ midnight. –ಸಾಲ್ the middle row. –ಕಟ್ಟುನಿ to gird up the loins. –ಕಡೆಪುನಿ to have pain in the loins. –ಪತ್ತುನಿ to hold by the waist.

ನಡುಂಬುಳು naḍumbuḷu, *see* ನಡುಪು[ಲು.

ನಡುಗುನಿ naḍuguni (ನಡುಗ್), *v. n.* To tremble, shake, shiver, quake, totter.

ನಡುಗುರೋಗ naḍugurōga, *s.* The palsy, tremor.

ನಡುತರ naḍutara, *adj.* Middling moderate.

ನಡುಪುನಿ naḍupuni, *see* ನಡಪುನಿ.

ನಡುಪುಲು naḍupulu, *s.* The waist, loins.

ನಡುವಂತಾಡಿ naḍuvantāḍi, *s.* The residence of a priest.

ನಡುವಡಿ naḍuvaḍi, *s.* Conduct. 2. a customary observance.

ನಡುವಣೆ naḍuvaṇè, *adj.* Central, middle. –ದಾಯೆ the intermediate brother.

ನಡುವಣ್ಡಿ naḍuvaṇḍi, *s.* The intermediate daughter *or* sister.

ನಡುವೆ naḍuvè, *see* ನಡು.

ನಡೆ naḍè, *s.* Walk, step, gait. 2. conduct, behaviour. 3. a closet, side-room. 4. the lower space between the two verandas of a house *or* temple. –ವಳಿಯೆ a cloth spread on the road for a procession to pass over. –ನುಡಿ conduct and speech, *or* word and deed.

ನಡ್ಡಂತಾಡಿ naḍḍantāḍi, *see* ನಡುವಂತಾಡಿ.

ನಡ್ಪಿನಿ naḍpini (ನಡ್), *v. a.* To plant.

ನಣವರೆ naṇavarè, *see* ನೆನವರಿಕೆ.

ನಣಿಲ್, ನಣಿಲೆ naṇilu, naṇilè, *see* ನಾಣಿಲ್.

ನಣೆ naṇè, *adj.* Wet, moist.

ನತ್ತ್, ನತ್ತು, ನತ್ರು nattu, nattu, nartu, *s.* A female's ornament for the nose.

ನತ್ತಿಂಗೆ nattinge, *s.* An owlet. 2. a man who is partially dumb.

ನದ್ರ್, ನದರ್ nadru, nadaru, *see* ನಜರ್.

ನದಿ nadi, *s.* A river.

ನನ, ನನಲಾ nana, nanalā, *adv.* Yet, still, once more, farther on. ಉಂಡೆನ್ ನನ ಮಳ್ಪಯಿ I shall no more do this. ನನಲಾ ಬತ್ತಿಜಿ he has not yet come.

ನನಪಿನಿ nanapini, *see* ನೆನೆಪುನಿ.

ನನವರಿಕೆ nanavarikè, *see* ನೆನವರಿಕೆ.

ನನಿಕೆ nanike, *s.* A brother-in-law.

ನನೆಪಾವುನಿ nanepāvuni, *c. v.* (*of* ನನೆಪಿನಿ) To make wet, to moisten, soak.

ನನೆಪಿನಿ, ನನೆಪುನಿ, ನನೆಯುನಿ, ನನೆವುನಿ nanepini, nanepuni, naneyuni, nanevuni (ನನೆ), *v. n.* To be moist, wet, damp. ಕೈ ನನೆಂಡ ಕೊಂಡೆಲಾ ನನೆವು *lit.* if the hand be wet, the throat also will be wet; if you work, you will eat.

ನನೆರಿ naneri (ನನೆಅರಿ), *s.* Wet rice.

ನಪಾಸ್ napāsu, *see* ನಾಪಾಸ್.

ನಪುಂಸಕ napuṁsaka, *adj.* Neuter. –ತ್ವ impotency. –ಲಿಂಗ the neuter gender. ನಪುಂಸಕೆ a eunuch.

ನಪೆ napè, *see* ನಫೆ.

ನಪ್ಪಡ nappaḍa, *see* ಅಪ್ಪಡ.

ನಪ್ಪು nappu, *s.* Injury, degradation.

ನಪ್ಪೆ nappè, *see* ಇಂಜರ್. 2. *see* ನಫೆ.

ನಫೆ naphè, *s.* Profit, gain, advantage; *also* ನಫ.

ನಬಾಬ್ nabābu, *see* ನವಾಬ್.

ನಬೆ nabè, *see* ನಫೆ.

ನಭ, ನಭಸ್ಸು nabha, nabhassu, *s.* The sky, atmosphere. 2. a cloud. ನಭೋಮಂಡಲ the firmament.

ನಮ nama, *pron.* (*pl. of* ಯಾನ್) We, *including the person or persons addressed*; *cf.* ಯೆಂಕುಳು. ನಂಮವು ours. ನಂಮಾಯಿ one of us, one of our party.

ನಮನ namana, *s.* The act of prostrating.

ನಮನಟ್, ನಮನಮ namanaṭu, namanama, *s.* Union. –ಆಪಿನಿ to unite.

ನಮರ್ namaru, *see* ನಮ್ರು.

ನಮಸ್ಕರಿಪುನಿ namaskaripuni (ನಮಸ್ಕರಿ), *v. n.* To bow, make obeisance.

ನಮಸ್ಕಾರ, ನಮಸ್ಯ namaskāra, namasya, *s.* Salutation, prostration, obeisance; *also* ನಮಾಜಿ. –ಪಾಡುನಿ to prostrate, fall down. –ಮಳ್ಪುನಿ to salute, bow, do obeisance.

ನಮಿಪುನಿ, ನಮಿಸುನಿ namipuni, namisuni (ನಮಿಸ್), *v. a.* To bow, reverence, do obeisance.

ನಮುನೆ, ನಮೂನೆ namunè, namūnè, *s.* A pattern, sample, model, form.

ನಮೂದಿಸುನಿ **namūdisuni** (ನಮೂದಿಸ್), *v. a.* To mark; to mention, state, show.

ನಮೂದು **namūdu,** *s.* Appearance, mark. 2. mentioning, stating, showing. –ಆಪಿನಿ to appear, be mentioned. –ಮಳ್ಪುನಿ to mention, show.

ನಮೆಪುನಿ **namepuni,** *see* ನಮಿಪುನಿ.

ನಮೆಯುನಿ **nameyuni** (ನಮೆ), *v. n.* To wear away. 2. to become poor.

ನಮೆಲುನಿ **nameluni,** *see* ಗಮೆಯುನಿ.

ನಮ್ಮ **namma,** *see* ನಮ.

ನಮ್ರ **namra,** *adj.* Humble, submissive, gentle. –ತೆ, –ತ್ವ humility, submissiveness, gentleness.

ನಯ **naya,** *s.* Gentleness, meekness. 2. kindness. 3. fineness, polish, softness, delicacy. 4. a bait to catch alligators. 5. cheapness. 6. *see* ನ್ಯಾಯ. *adj.* Fine, soft, smooth, glossy. 2. gentle, meek. 3. kind. 4. cheap. –ಗುಣ, –ಶೀಲ an amiable *or* gentle disposition. –ನುಡಿ, –ಪಾತೆರ an elegant expression *or* kind word.

ನಯಿಕುಂಬು **nayikumbu,** *adj.* Half cotton and half woollen. 2. *see* ಬೊಂಡು. 3. *see* ಬೊಳುಂಬು.

ನಯಿಕೂಲಿ **nayikūli,** *s.* The tree *Wrightia tinctoria.*

ನಯಿಕೆ **nayike,** *see* ನಾಯಕೆ. 2. *see* ನೇಯಿಕೆ.

ನಯಿಪಿಲಿ **nayipili,** *see* ನಾಯಿಪಿಲಿ.

ನರ್ನುರು **narṇuru,** *s. see* ನರುಗುರು. *adj.* Bruised.

ನರ **nara,** *s.* A vein, nerve, tendon.

ನರ **nara,** *s.* A man. *adj.* Human. –ಜನ್ಮ, –ಜಲ್ಮ human existence. –ಜಾತಿ mankind. –ಬಲಿ human sacrifice. –ಲೋಕ the earth, nether world. –ಹತ್ಯ murder.

ನರಂಗುನಿ **naraṅguni** (ನರಂಗ್), *v. n.* To waver, hesitate, be reluctant.

ನರಂಡ್ **naraṇḍu,** *see* ನರಡ್.

ನರಂಬು **narambu,** *s.* A sinew, nerve, pulse. –ವೈಪುನಿ sinews to contract, to feel cramped.

ನರಕ **naraka,** *s.* Hell, hades. 2. dirt, filth. –ದ ಕೊಂಡ the abyss of hell. –ದ ತೂ the hell-fire. –ವೇದನೆ hell-torments.

ನರಕಾಂತಕೆ **narakāntake,** *s.* A name of Vishṇu.

ನರಕಾಧಿಪತಿ **narakādhipati,** *s.* Yama.

ನರಕಿ **naraki,** *adj.* Hell-worthy. 2. dirty, filthy.

ನರಕುನಿ **narakuni** (ನರಕ್), *v. a.* To sigh, groan, moan, grumble.

ನರಕೆಲೆ **narakele,** *s.* A grumbler.

ನರಗುಡುನಿ **naraguḍuni** (ನರಗುಡ್), *v. a.* To bruise, crush; to torment.

ನರಗುನಿ **naraguni,** *see* ನರಕುನಿ.

ನರಗುರಿ **naraguri,** *s.* A sheepish man, coward.

ನರಗೋಳಿ **naragōḷi,** *see* ತಾಡುಗೋಳಿ.

ನರಟುನಿ **naraṭuni** (ನರಟ್), *v. n.* To grumble; *cf.* ನರಕುನಿ.

ನರಡ್ naraḍu, *s.* Roughness. 2. a wart, protuberence. 3. stuntedness. 4. false pregnancy. *adj.* Rough, craggy, stunted.

ನರದೇವ, ನರಪತಿ naradēva, narapati, *s.* A human ruler.

ನರನರ naranara, *adj.* Slow, gentle. –ಬೇನೆ slow labour.

ನರಪುರಿ narapuri, *s.* A mortal.

ನರಮಾನಿ, ನರಮಾನೆ, ನರಮಾನ್ಯೆ naramāni, naramāne, naramānye, *s.* Man; a mortal.

ನರಯೆ naraye, *s.* A kind of crane. 2. a grey-haired man. 3. a white-spotted ox. *adj.* Grey. 2. white-spotted.

ನರಲುನಿ naraluni, *see* ನರಕುನಿ.

ನರವು naravu, *see* ನರ.

ನರಸಿಂಹ narasiṁha, *s.* The fourth incarnation of Vishṇu.

ನರಳುನಿ naraḷuni, *see* ನರಕುನಿ.

ನರಾಧಮೆ narādhame, *s.* The meanest of mankind.

ನರಾಧಿಪತಿ narādhipati, *s.* The ruler of men.

ನರಿ nari, *s.* A jackal, fox.

ನರಿಕೆ narikè, *see* ನರ್ಕೆ.

ನರಿಪು naripu, *see* ನರ್ಪು.

ನರುಗುರು, ನರುನುರು naruguru, narunuru, *s.* A crack, crash. 2. a sound produced while eating anything crisp.

ನರುವೊಲು naruvolu, *s.* A kind of aromatic tree of which the leaves are used for curry *or* medicine, *Saccharum Munja.*

ನರೆ narè, *see* ನರ.

ನರೆ narè, *s.* Greyness, hoariness. *adj.* Grey, hoary. –ಕುಜಲ್, –ತರೆ grey hair. –ಶಾಯಿ a grey-haired man. –ಬರ್ಪಿನಿ to become grey.

ನರೆಂಗಿ nareṅgi, *see* ನೇರೆಂಗಿ.

ನರೆಂಗುನಿ nareṅguni (ನರೆಂಗ್), *v. a.* To hesitate; *cf.* ನರಕುನಿ.

ನರೆಂಗೆಲೆ nareṅgele, *s.* A dull, tardy, slow, hesitating man.

ನರೆತಿ nareti, *s.* A white-spotted cow.

ನರೆಲುನಿ nareluni, *see* ನರಕುನಿ.

ನರೆವುನಿ narevuni (ನರೆ), *v. n.* Hair to become grey, grow white.

ನರೇಂದ್ರೆ narēndre, *s.* A king.

ನರ್ಕ narka, *see* ನರಕ.

ನರ್ಕುನಿ narkuni, *see* ನರಕುನಿ.

ನರ್ಕೆ narkè, *s.* The skin, hide, bark.

ನರ್ಗಾಟ nargāṭa, *s.* Bruising.

ನರ್ಗಾವುನಿ nargāvuni, *c. v.* (*of* ನರ್ಗುನಿ) To bruise, crush.

ನರ್ಗುನಿ narguni (ನರ್ಗ್), *v. n.* To be bruised, crushed. 2. to be close, as a cluster of fruits.

ನರ್ಗುರು narguru, *see* ನರುಗುರು.

ನರ್ಗೆಲೆ nargele, *s.* A grumbler.

ನರ್ತ್ನುರ್ತು nartṇurtu, *adv.* Forcibly; by dint of perseverance.

ನರ್ತ narta, *adj.* Soft, pure.

ನರ್ತಗೆ nartage, *s.* A dancer, actor.

ನರ್ತನ nartana, *s.* Dancing, acting. –ಮಳ್ಪುನಿ to dance.

ನರ್ತೆ nartè, *s.* A bivalved shell-fish, mollusk.

ನರ್ನರ narnara, *see* ನರುಗುರು.

ನರ್ನುರ್ತೆಲ್ narnurtelụ, *adj.* Half boiled.

ನರ್ಪು narpu, *s.* Deserting, forsaking. 2. disgust, dislike.

ನರ್ಪುನಿ narpuni (ನರ್), *v. a.* To desert, forsake. 2. *see* ನೆರ್ಪಿನಿ. *v. n.* To be disgusted.

ನರ್ಮ narma, *s.* Sport, amusement, pleasure.

ನರ್ಮದ narmada, *s.* The river Nerbuda.

ನರ್ಲುನಿ narluni (ನರ್ಲ್), *v. n.* To rattle, as phlegm in the throat. 2. *see* ನರಕುನಿ.

ನರ್ವಂಟೆ narvaṇṭe, *s.* A small univalved shell-fish, mullusk.

ನರ್ವೊಲು narvolu, *see* ನರುವೊಲು.

ನಲ್, ನಲ nalụ, nala, *adj.* Good. 2. cheap.

ನಲ nala, *see* ನಳ.

ನಲಗುನಿ nalaguni (ನಲಗ್), *v. n.* To grumble, murmur. 2. to fade, wither. 3. to be prostrated, reduced from sickness; *cf.* ನರಕುನಿ.

ನಲಿ nali, *s.* Dent, dimple, as of a metallic vessel. –ದೆಪ್ಪುನಿ to remove the dimple of such a vessel. –ಬೂರುನಿ to be indented.

ನಲಿಕೆ nalikè, *s.* Dancing, jumping. –ದಾಯೆ a dancer; one of the class of demon-dancers.

ನಲಿಗೆ naligè, *see* ನಳಿ.

ನಲಿನ nalina, *s.* The lotus.

ನಲಿಪುನಿ nalipuni (ನಲಿ), *v. n.* To dance, leap; to turn round. *v. a.* To let fall, as a vessel. 2. to indent, bruise.

ನಲಿಯುನಿ naliyuni (ನಲಿ), *v. n.* To be indented, dimpled, as a metallic vessel.

ನಲಿಯೆ naliyè, *see* ನಲ್ಲಿಕೆ.

ನಲೆ nale, *see* ನಳೆ.

ನಲೆಂಚಿ naleṅči, *see* ನೆಲೆಂಚಿ.

ನಲ್ಕೆ, ನಲ್ಪು nalkè, nalpu, *see* ನಲಿಕೆ.

ನಲ್ಪುನಿ nalpuni, *see* ನಲಿಪುನಿ.

ನಲ್ಮೆ nalmè, *s.* Goodness, friendship.

ನಲ್ಲ್ nallụ, *s.* A kind of flea which infests poultry, cats, *etc.* 2. a sprain.

ನಲ್ಲಿ nalli, *s.* The bone of the leg below the knee, shinbone. 2. *see* ನಲ್ಲ್.

ನಲ್ಲಿಗೆ, ನಲ್ಲೆ, ನಲ್ಲ್ಯೆ nalligè, nallè, nallyè, *s.* A weed, tare, *Paspalum pilosum.* 2. a hollow. –ಬೂರುನಿ to be dimpled, depressed.

ನವ nava, *adj.* New, fresh. *num.* Nine.

ನವಗ್ರಹ navagraha, *s.* The nine planets, *viz.*, the Sun, Moon, Mars, Mercury, Jupiter, Venus, Saturn, Rāhu (*Caput draconis*), and Kētu (*Cauda draconis*).

ನವದಾರ, ನವದ್ವಾರ navadāra, navadvāra, *s. lit.* The nine doors. 2. the human body which has nine inlets *or* outlets, as the nostrils, ears, mouth, *etc.*

ನವಧಾನ್ಯ **navadhānya,** *s.* Nine kinds of corn, as ಬಾರ್ paddy, ಗೋದಿ wheat, ಕಡಲೆ Bengal gram, ತೊಗರಿ dholl, ಕುಡು gram, ಎಣ್ಣೆ gingely seed, ಅಬರೆ country beans, ಉರ್ದ್ black gram, and ಪದೆಂಗಿ green gram.

ನವನೂತನ **navanūtana,** *adj.* Very beautiful, handsome; singular.

ನವಪತ್ತ್ **navapattu,** *s.* Fungosity. 2. music accompanied with beating of drums. *adj.* Fungous, excrescent.

ನವಮ **navama,** *num.* Ninth.

ನವಮಾಸ **navamāsa,** *s.* Nine months, the period of pregnancy.

ನವಮಿ **navami,** *s.* The ninth lunar day of either fortnight.

ನವರ **navara,** *s.* A kind of grain; *cf.* ನವರೆ.

ನವರತ್ನ **navaratna,** *s.* Nine kinds of precious stones *or* gems, *viz.*, ಮುತ್ತು pearl, ಕೆಂಪು ruby, ವಜ್ರ diamond, ವೈಡೂರ್ಯ cat's eye *or* beryl, ಗೋಮೇಧಿಕ onyx, ಪುಷ್ಯರಾಗ topaz, ನೀಲ sapphire, and ಪಚ್ಚೆ emerald.

ನವರಾತ್ರಿ **navarātri,** *s.* A festival observed for the first nine days of the seventh lunar month in honour of the goddess Durga.

ನವರೆ **navare,** *s.* A kind of rice.

ನವಸಾಗರ, ನವಸಾರ **navasāgara, navasāra,** *s.* The salt *Sal ammoniac.*

ನವಾಬೆ **navābe,** *s.* A Nabob, governor.

ನವಾಯಿತೆ **navāyite,** *s.* A Konkaṇi speaking class of Mohammedan cloth-merchants.

ನವಾರ್, ನವಾರ್ದಪಟ್ಟಿ **navāru, navāruda-paṭṭi,** *s.* Tape, band, fillet.

ನವಿಲ್ಪಕ್ಕಿ **navilupakki,** *s.* A peacock; *also* ಮೈರ.

ನವೀಕರಣ **navīkaraṇa,** *s.* Renewal, renovation. –ಮಳ್ಪುನಿ to renew.

ನವೀನ **navīna,** *adj.* New, fresh, excellent.

ನವುಂಟೆ **navuṇṭa,** *s.* Itching, irritation in the throat. –ಪತ್ತುನಿ, ನವುಂಟುನಿ, *see* ನೌಂಪುನಿ.

ನವುಂಪುನಿ **navumpuni,** *see* ನೌಂಪುನಿ.

ನವೆ **nave,** *see* ನಗ.

ನಶಿಪುನಿ **naśipuni** (ನಶಿ), *v.a.* To destroy, ruin. *v.n.* To perish, decay. 2. to work hard, exert one's self beyond one's strength.

ನಶೀಬ್, ನಶೀಬು **naśību, naśību,** *s.* Fate, destiny.

ನಶೆ **naśe,** *s.* Snuff, medicinal snuff. –ಡಬ್ಬಿ a snuff box.

ನಷ್ಟ **nashṭa,** *s.* Loss, damage, injury. *adj.* Lost, destroyed, damaged. –ಆಪಿನಿ to be lost; *c.dat.* to lose.

ನಸ್ಕ್ **nasuku,** *see* ನಸ್ಯ.

ನಸಪಾಣಿ, ನಸರಾಣಿ, ನಸ್ರಾಣಿ **nasapāṇi, nasarāṇi, nasrāṇi,** *s.* A Nazarene *or* Syrian Christian. 2. a nasty, base, mean, *or* worthless fellow.

ನಸಿ **nasi,** *see* ನಸಿ.

ನಸಿಯುನಿ **nasiyuni** (ನಸಿ), *v. n.* To submit, subdue.

ನಸೀಯತ್ **nasīyatu,** *s.* Punishment.

ನಸುಕು **nasuku,** *see* ನಸ್ಕು.

ನಸುಡಿ **nasuḍi,** *s.* The forehead.

ನಸೆ **nasè,** *adj.* Soft, gentle. 2. moist, damp, humid. *s.* Moistness. 2. softness. –ಗಾರೆ a man in good circumstances.

ನಸ್ಕು **naskụ,** *s.* Twilight, dawn, early morning.

ನಸ್ಕ್ಯತ್ರ **naskyatra,** *see* ನಕ್ಷತ್ರ.

ನಸ್ಯ **nasya,** *see* ನಶೆ.

ನಳ **naḷa,** *s.* The fiftieth year of the Hindu cycle of sixty. 2. *see* ನಳೆ. –ಪಾಕ superior cooking.

ನಳಕಂಭ **naḷakambha,** *s.* A pole planted in the middle of a stack of straw.

ನಳಿ **naḷi,** *see* ನಲಿ.

ನಳಿ, ನಳಿಗೆ **naḷi, naḷigè,** *s.* A tube, pipe. 2. the barrel of a gun.

ನಳಿನ **naḷina,** *see* ನಲಿನ.

ನಳಿಪುನಿ **naḷipuni,** *see* ನಲಿಪುನಿ.

ನಳಿಯುನಿ **naḷiyuni,** *see* ನಲಿಯುನಿ.

ನಳೆ **naḷe,** *s.* A celebrated king, the husband of Damayanti.

ನಳ್ಮೆ **naḷme,** *see* ನಲ್ಮೆ.

ನಳ್ಯೆ **naḷyè,** *see* ನಲ್ಲಿಗೆ.

ನಳ್ಳು **naḷḷụ,** *see* ನಲ್ಲು.

ನಳ್ಳಿ **naḷḷi,** *s.* A spool. –ಸುಂದುನಿ to spool.

ನಕ್ಷ, ನಕ್ಷೆ **naksha, nakshè,** *s.* A map, plan, chart. 2. a painting, picture, photograph. ಸಂತಾನದ– a genealogical table, pedigree.

ನಕ್ಷತ್ರ **nakshatra,** *s.* A star, planet. 2. a constellation *or* lunar mansion. –ಮಂಡಲ, –ಲೋಕ the planetary system. ನಕ್ಷತ್ರಾನುಕೂಲ favourable conjunction of natal stars.

ನಾ **nā,** *An interrogative particle affixed to nouns, pronouns adjectives, verbs and adverbs; as,* ರಾಮೆನಾ is it Rāma? ಆಯೆನಾ is it he? ಯೆಡ್ಡೆನಾ is it good? ಪೋಪನಾ are you going? ಕೋಡೆನಾ was it yesterday?

ನಾಂಚುನಿ **nāñcuni** (ನಾಂಚ್), *v. n.* To dance.

ನಾಂಟುನಿ **nāṇṭuni,** *see* ನಾಟುನಿ.

ನಾಂಡೆ **nāṇḍè,** *s.* A measure of grain, equal to one-sixteenth *or* one-twentieth of a seer.

ನಾಂಣ್ಯ **nāṇṇya,** *see* ನಾಣ್ಯ.

ನಾಂತ **nānta,** *see* ನಾತ.

ನಾಂದಿ **nāndi,** *s.* Benedictory verses recited at the commencement of an auspicious ceremony. 2. a ceremony performed to preserve a marriage party from the pollution of birth *or* death in the family.

ನಾಂಬು nāmbu, *see* ಲಾಂಬು.

ನಾಕ nāka, *s.* Heaven, paradise, sky, atmosphere. 2. *see* ನಾಕು. —ಬಲಿ a sacrifice to all the gods on the fifth day of a marriage.

ನಾಕಾರಿ nākāri, *see* ನಕಾರಿ.

ನಾಕು nāku, *s.* A female calf.

ನಾಗ nāga, *s.* A snake, serpent. 2. a class of demi-gods. 3. the image of a serpent. —ಕನ್ಯೆ a class of demi-goddesses. —ಕಲ್ಲ the stone image of a serpent. —ಕುರುಳೆ, —ಮರಿ the young of a serpent. —ಗುಂಡಲ an ear-ornament in the form of a serpent's hood. —ಜಡೆ the hood of a serpent. —ಲೋಕ the infernal regions.

ನಾಗ nāga, *see* ನಗ.

ನಾಗಕುಷ್ಟ nāgakushṭa, *s.* A kind of leprosy.

ನಾಗಜಿಡೆಪೂ nāgajiḍepū, *s.* A head ornament like the extended hood of a serpent.

ನಾಗತಾಳಿ nāgatāḷi, *s.* The cactus *Trichosanthes anguina.*

ನಾಗದಂಡ್ nāgadaṇḍụ, *s.* Stagnant water of yellowish color.

ನಾಗನಗರಿ nāganagari, *s.* A kind of drum.

ನಾಗಪಟ್ಟ nāgapaṭṭa, *s.* A kind of serpent-worship.

ನಾಗಬಣ, ನಾಗಬನ nāgabaṇa, nāgabana, *s.* A grove haunted by, *or* sacred to, serpents.

ನಾಗಬೀದಿ nāgabīdi, *s.* A locality, affecting the health of those dwelling there, *or* the purity of any thing, as water, *etc.*

ನಾಗಬೆತ್ತ nāgabetta, *s.* A species of cane with black spots about the joints.

ನಾಗಮಲ್ಲಿಗೆ nāgamalligè, *s.* The flower *Justicia nasuta.*

ನಾಗರ್‌ಸುತ್ತು nāgarụsuttu, *s.* A gold *or* silver thread.

ನಾಗರ nāgara, *s.* Dry ginger. 2. the cobra. 3. *see* ನಗರ. —ಪಂಚಮಿ a feast on the fifth day of the fifth lunar month. —ಬರವು the Nāgari *or* Sanskrit character. ಜೀವ— the Bengal Nāgari character. ನಂದಿ— the Peninsula Nāgari character.

ನಾಗರಿಕ nāgarika, *adj.* Civilized, refined, cultured. 2. elegant. 3. prudent. —ತನ civilization; elegance; prudence. ನಾಗರಿಕೆ a civilized, neat, *or* prudent man.

ನಾಗವಂದಿಗೆ nāgavandigè, *s.* A shelf.

ನಾಗವಳ್ಳಿ nāgavaḷḷi, *s.* A very pungent species of betel leaf, piper betel.

ನಾಗಸಂಪಿಗೆ, ನಾಗಸಂಪೈ nāgasampigè, nāgasampei, *s.* The flower *Mesua speciosa.*

ನಾಗಸರ, ನಾಗಸ್ವರ nāgasara, nāgasvara, *s.* A pipe answering to the drone of the bagpipe; a snake pipe with two holes.

ನಾಗೆ nāge, *s.* A serpent. 2. the image of a serpent. ಕಲೆ— a spotted serpent. ಮುಸೆ—, ಯಿಲೆ—, *see* ಎಲೆನಾಗೆ.

ನಾಗೆರ್ nāgeru, *s.* Native Roman Catholics, so called by Pariahs.

ನಾಗೇಂದ್ರೆ nāgēndre, *s.* The chief of the serpents. 2. the name of a man.

ನಾಗೋಳೆ nāgōlè, *s.* The concluding ceremony of a marriage among Brahmins.

ನಾಚ್ nācu, *s.* Dancing, a nautch.

ನಾಚಿಕೆ, ನಾಚಿಗೆ nāćikè, nāćigè, *s.* Shame, modesty, blushing. –ಗೇಡ್ shameless, impudent. –ಆಪಿನಿ to be ashamed, modest; to blush.

ನಾಚಿಕೆದೈ, ನಾಚಿಗೆದೈ nāćikedei, nāćigedei, *s.* The sensitive plant *Mimosa pudica.*

ನಾಚುನಿ nācuni (ನಾಚ್), *v. n.* To blush, be ashamed.

ನಾಜರ್, ನಾಜರೆ nājaru, nājare, *s.* A sheriff.

ನಾಜಿ nāji, *s.* A kind of dance.

ನಾಜೂಕು nājūku, *adj.* Delicate, fine, soft. –ಕೆಲಸ delicate workmanship.

ನಾಜ್ರೆ nājre, *see* ನಾಜರ.

ನಾಟ nāṭa, *s.* A pole used for a hedge. 2. a pole used for supporting a plantain tree, *or* for training up a creeper.

ನಾಟಕ, ನಾಟಗ nāṭaka, nāṭaga, *s.* A play, drama. 2. a theatrical performance. –ದಾಯೆ, ನಾಟಿಗೆ an actor. –ಶಾಲೆ a theatre.

ನಾಟಾವುನಿ nāṭāvuni, *c. v.* (*of* ನಾಟುನಿ) To cause to affect *or* operate.

ನಾಟಿ nāṭi, *s.* Fixing, pitching, planting.

ನಾಟಿರಾಗ nāṭirāga, *s.* A prelude.

ನಾಟುನಿ nāṭuni (ನಾಟ್), *v. a.* To affect, impress, move. 2. to operate, act upon, as a medicine. ನಿಕ್ಕ್ ದಾಲಾ ನಾಟುಜಾ will nothing move you? *or* will all the telling be lost upon you?

ನಾಟೆ nāṭè, *see* ನಾಟ.

ನಾಟ್ಯ nāṭya, *s.* Dancing, acting.

ನಾಡ್ nāḍu, *s.* A district, village.

ನಾಡಾವುನಿ nāḍāvuni, *c. v.* (*of* ನಾಡುನಿ) To cause to search.

ನಾಡಿ nāḍi, *s.* The pulse. 2. a blood-vessel, artery, *or* vein. 3. vital air *or* breath. 4. an astrological term connected with natal stars. –ಕೂಟ the planetary conjunction consulted by astrologers when matrimonial alliances are to be formed. –ಪರೀಕ್ಷೆ examination of the pulse. –ಉಂತುನಿ the pulse to cease. –ತೂಪಿನಿ to feel the pulse. –ನಡಪುನಿ, –ಪಂಡುನಿ the pulse to beat.

ನಾಡಿಗೆ nāḍige, *s.* One of the cultivating classes in the northern part of Canara.

ನಾಡು nāḍu, *see* ನಾಡ್.

ನಾಡುನಿ nāḍuni (ನಾಡ್), *v. a.* To search, seek.

ನಾಡೆ nāḍè, *s.* A cord, rope.

ನಾಣ್, ನಾಣ nāṇu, nāṇa, *s.* Nakedness, nudity. 2. the buttocks.

ನಾಣಪರ್ವೆಸಿ, ನಾಣಪ್ರವೇಸಿ nāṇaparvesi, nāṇapravēsi, *see* ನಾನಪರವರ್ಷಿ.

ನಾಣಿಲ್ nāṇilu, *s.* A species of olive. –ದ ಯೆಂಣೆ oil prepared from its fruit.

ನಾಣ್ಯ nāṇya, *s.* Money, coin. ಇಂಗ– a counterfeit coin.

ನಾಣ್ಮೆ nāṇmè, *s.* Manipulation.

ನಾತ nāta, *s.* Smell, odour. 2. stink, stench; *also* ಪಡಿಕೆ ನಾತ, –ಕುಲ a base family.

ನಾತಪೂ nātapū, *s.* The plant *Lantana aculeata.*

ನಾತು nātu, *see* ನಾತ; *cf.* ನಾದುನಿ.

ನಾಥೆ nāthe, *s.* A husband, master, lord, protector.

ನಾದ nāda, *s.* A sound, report, noise *or* note. ಮೇಘ– thunder. ಸಿಂಹ– the roar of a lion; a war cry.

ನಾದಾನಿ nādāni, *adj.* Stupid, thoughtless.

ನಾದಾರಿ, ನಾಧಾರಿ nādāri, nādhāri, *s.* Poverty, pauperism. 2. bankruptcy, insolvency. *adj.* Indigent, poor. 2. bankrupt.

ನಾದುನಿ nāduni (ನಾದ್), *v.n.* To smell, stink.

ನಾದ್ರೆ nādre, *see* ನಜೀರ್.

ನಾನಪರವರ್ಷಿ nānaparavarshi, *s.* A pension, gratuity; superannuation.

ನಾನಾ nānā, *adj.* Various, diverse, different. –ತರ different sorts. –ವರ್ಣ diverse colours. –ವಿಧ various ways.

ನಾನುನಿ nānuni (ನಾನ್), *v. n.* To shrink; *cf.* ಉದುರುನಿ.

ನಾನ್ಯ nānya, *s.* Likeness. 2. kind.

ನಾಪಸ್, ನಾಪಾಸ್, ನಾಪೆ, ನಾಪೆಸ್ nāpasu, nāpāsu, nāpè, nāpesu, *adj.* Worthless, useless. 2. powerless, helpless. 3. stingy, miserly.

ನಾಪಿಕೆ nāpike, *s.* A barber.

ನಾಭಿ nābhi, *s.* The navel. 2. the holes in the leaves of a palm book, to string them together.

ನಾಮ nāma, *s.* A name, appellation. 2. a sectarian mark on the forehead. –ಕರಣ the ceremony of naming a child after birth. –ದ ಕಾಜಿ a kind of bangles. –ವಾಚಕ a noun. –ಸ್ಮರಣೆ invoking *or* repeating the name of God. –ಅಪಿನಿ, –ಬೂರುನಿ to fail, be defeated. –ಪಾಡುನಿ to put on the sectarian mark; to cheat, deceive.

ನಾಮದಬೇರ್ nāmadabēru, *s.* Country sarsaparilla, *Hemidesmus Indicus.*

ನಾಮರದ್ nāmaradu, *adj.* Peevish. 2. impotent.

ನಾಮರ್ದೆ nāmarde, *s.* A eunuch, impotent man. 2. a sneak, coward.

ನಾಮಾಂಕಿತ nāmānkita, *s.* A name. *adj.* Dedicated, as a work to a person.

ನಾಮುಸ್ nāmusu, *s.* Disgrace. 2. shame.

ನಾಮೇಸ nāmēsa, *s.* Nothing, a bit.

ನಾಯ nāya, *see* ನ್ಯಾಯ.

ನಾಯಕೆ nāyake, *s.* A guide, leader. 2. a chief, head, general. 3. an honorary title given to a Roman Catholic *or* a Konkani.

ನಾಯರೆ nāyare, *see* ನಾಯಿಮಾರೆ.

ನಾಯಿ nāyi, *s.* A dog. –ಪರೆಂಗಿ an acute form of syphilis. ನೀರ್– an otter.

ನಾಯಿಕಿನಿ nāyikini, *s.* A mistress.

ನಾಯಿಕೆ nāyike, *see* ನಾಯಕೆ.

ನಾಯಿತೊಳಚಿ nāyitoḷači, *s.* The white basil *or* country tea, *Ocimum album.*

ನಾಯಿಪಲ್ಲೆ nāyipallè, *s.* A kind of tree.

ನಾಯಿಪಿಲಿ nāyipili, *s.* A hyena.

ನಾಯಿಬಾದಮ್ nāyibādamu, *s.* The wild almonds.

ನಾಯಿಮಾರೆ nāyimāre, *s.* A Nāyar of Malabar.

ನಾಯಿಯುಳ್ಳಿ nāyiyuḷḷi, *see* ಬೊಗ್ಗುಳ್ಳಿ.

ನಾಯಿಸೊಣಂಗ್ nāyisoṇaṅgu, *s.* The plant *Mucuna pruriens.*

ನಾಯೆರ್ nāyeru, *s.* A plough. 2. *see* ನಾಯಿಮಾರೆ. –ಕತ್ತಿ, *see* ನಾರಕತ್ತಿ. –ದ ಗುದ್ದಲ್, –ದ ಗುದ್ದೊಳು a worn out plough.

ನಾರ್ nāru, *s.* The hemp of plants, fibrous bark of trees, *etc.*; linen. –ದ ಕುಂಟು, –ಮುಡಿ a linen cloth. –ದ ಬಳ್ಳಿ a hempen rope. –ಕಟ್ಟುನಿ to become stringy *or* tough. –ಪಿಜಿಪ್ಪುನಿ to twist hemp *or* fibre into ropes.

ನಾರಂಗಾಯಿ nāraṅgāyi, *see* ನಾರೆಂಗಿ.

ನಾರಂಗೆ nāraṅgè, *see* ನಾರೆಂಗಿ.

ನಾರಕತ್ತಿ, ನಾರತ್ತಿ nārakatti, nāratti, *s.* A kind of sword used by the Nāyars.

ನಾರದೆ nārade, *s.* A celebrated sage and legislator, the son of Brahma, and inventor of the lute. 2. a tell-tale, slanderer.

ನಾರಸ್ nārasu, *s.* A very thin wire. 2. the hook of a native woman's nose-ring. *adj.* Thin, lean, emaciated. 2. stingy, miserly. ಕಲಸೆ– a rod with which the measure of a (ಕಲಸೆ) kalasè is struck.

ನಾರಸಿಂಹ nārasiṁha, *see* ನರಸಿಂಹ.

ನಾರಾಯಣ, ನಾರಾಯಣೆ nārāyaṇa, nārāyaṇe, *s.* A name of Vishṇu. 2. the name of a man. –ಕವಚ a kind of amulet.

ನಾರಾಯಣಿ nārāyaṇi, *s.* The wife of Vishṇu and goddess of prosperity. 2. the wife of Śiva and goddess of destruction. 3. the river Ganges.

ನಾರಿ nāri, *s.* A woman.

ನಾರು nāru, *see* ನಾರ್.

ನಾರೆಂಗಿ nāreṅgi, *s.* A kind of orange.

ನಾರೆಸ್ nāresu, *s.* An instrument to make either gold *or* silver wire. 2. *see* ನಾರಸ್.

ನಾರ್ಡೆ nārdè, *see* ನೇರ್ಡೆ.

ನಾಲ್ nālu, *num.* Four. –ಊರು, ನಾಲೂರು *lit.* four towns; some countries *or* parts of the world. ನಾಲ್ ಊರು ತಿಂಗೊಡು one should travel abroad. –ಕೈತಾಯಿ the name of a demon. –ದಿಕ್ಕು the four points of the compass. –ನೂದು, ನಾಲ್ನೂದು four hundred. –ಮೂಲೆ four corners, a square. –ವೇದ the four Vēdas.

ನಾಲ್ nālu, *s.* A horse-shoe; *cf.* ಲಾಲ್. –ಬಂದ್ a farrier, shoe-smith; farriery. –ಕಟ್ಟುನಿ,–ಹಾಕುನಿ to shoe a horse, *etc.*

ನಾಲಂಗ nālaṅga, *s.* The hands, legs, eyes, and ears.

ನಾಲನೆ nālane, *adj.* Fourth.

ನಾಲಯಿ, ನಾಲಾಯಿ nālayi, nālāyi, *s.* The tongue. –ದ ವಾಶಿ faithfulness to a promise. ಅರೆ– speaking faintly, as a sick person. ಇರ್– *lit.* double tongued; hoarseness; duplicity, equivocation. ಕಿಂನಿ–, ಕಿರಿ– the uvula. –ಪಂಡುನಿ to be able to speak. –ಪಿಜಿರುನಿ *lit.* to retract one's tongue, to break a promise. –ಬೂರುನಿ to falter, cease to speak, as a dying person; to pledge one's word. –ಮಗರುನಿ to speak fluently; to break a promise.

ನಾಲಾವರ್ತಿ nālāvartī, *s.* The four seasons. *adv.* Four times.

ನಾಲಿ nāli, *s.* The throat, windpipe. 2. a pipe, tube. 3. the stalk of a lotus. 4. *see* ನಾಡಿ.

ನಾಲಿಸ್ nālisu, *s.* Disparagement, detraction, censure. 2. dishonour, disgrace. –ಮಳ್ಪುನಿ to disparage, censure; to disgrace.

ನಾಲೆ nālè, *s.* A sewer, drain. 2. a pipe.

ನಾಲ್ಕೊಳು nālkoḷu, *adv.* Four times; *also* ನಲ್ಕೊಳು.

ನಾಲ್ಕೋಂಟು nālkōṇṭu, *s.* Four corners.

ನಾಲ್ಪ nālpa, *num.* Forty.

ನಾಲ್ಪಾಮರ nālpāmara, *s.* The bark, *etc.* of four kinds of milky trees used in medicine, namely:. ಗೋಳಿ, ಅತ್ತಸ, ಅರ್ತಿ, and ಬಿದಿಗೋಳಿ.

ನಾಲ್ಲಾ nāllā, *s.* A fourfold ploughing. 2. *see* ನಾವೊಳ.

ನಾಲ್ಲೆ nāllè, *see* ನಾಲೆ.

ನಾಲ್ವೆರ್ nālveru, *s.* Four persons.

ನಾವಡೆ nāvaḍe, *s.* A man belonging to a tribe so called. 2. the claw of cattle, beasts *or* birds.

ನಾವಳ nāvaḷa, *see* ನಾವೊಳ.

ನಾವಿಕೆ, ನಾವಿಗೆ nāvike, nāvige, *s.* A sailor.

ನಾವೆ nāvè, *s.* A ship, vessel.

ನಾವೊಳ nāvoḷa, *s.* Four seers.

ನಾಶ, ನಾಶನ nāśa, nāśana, *s.* Destruction, ruin, loss. 2. annihilation, death. –ಕೆ a destroyer. –ರಹಿತ God, the immortal. –ಆಪಿನಿ, –ಆದ್ ಪೋಪಿನಿ to be destroyed; to fall in ruins; to die. –ಮಳ್ಪುನಿ to destroy, ruin.

ನಾಷ್ಟ, ನಾಷ್ಟೆ nāshṭa, nāshṭè, *s.* Breakfast. 2. luncheon.

ನಾಸ್ **nāsų**, *s*. Snuff.

ನಾಸಾಗ್ರ **nāsāgra**, *s*. The top of the nose. 2. *see* ನವಸಾಗರ.

ನಾಸಿಕ **nāsika**, *s*. The nose.

ನಾಸ್ತಿ **nāsti**, *s*. Denial, refusal.

ನಾಸ್ತಿಕ **nāstika**, *adj*. Infidel, heretical. –ತನ infidelity, atheism, heresy.

ನಾಸ್ತಿಕೆ **nāstike**, *s*. An atheist, infidel, heretic.

ನಾಳ್ **nāḷų**, *see* ನಾಲ್. 2. *see* ಲಾಲ್.

ನಾಳ, ನಾಳಿ **nāḷa**, **nāḷi**, *see* ನಾಲಿ.

ನಾಳಿಕೇರ **nāḷikēra**, *s*. A cocoanut tree.

ನಿಂಕುನಿ **niṅkuni**, *see* ನಿಲ್ಕುನಿ.

ನಿಂಗಲ್ **niṅgalų**, *s*. Broken rice, grit. ಮೂಕು– very fine grit.

ನಿಂಗುಡುನಿ, ನಿಂಗುನಿ **niṅguḍuni**, **niṅguni** (ನಿಂಗುಡ್, ನಿಂಗ್), *v. a*. To swallow.

ನಿಂಗೊಳು **niṅgoḷu**, *see* ನಿಂಗಲ್.

ನಿಂಣಿ **niṇṇi**, *see* ನಿಂನಿ.

ನಿಂದಿಪುನಿ, ನಿಂದಿಸುನಿ, ನಿಂದುನಿ **nindipuni**, **nindisuni**, **ninduni** (ನಿಂದ್, ನಿಂದಿಸ್), *v. a*. To abuse, reproach. 2. to blame, censure. 3. to mock, ridicule. 4. to blaspheme.

ನಿಂದೆ **nindè**, *s*. Abuse, blame, censure, reproach. 2. mockery, ridicule. 3. blasphemy. –ಗಾರೆ, –ದಾಯೆ an abuser, censurer, scoffer, blasphemer.

ನಿಂನ, ನಿಂನವು **ninna**, **ninnavu**, *see* ನಿನ.

ನಿಂನಿ **ninni**, *s*. An echo, reverberation. 2. mimicry. –ಶಬ್ದ the sound of an echo. –ಪಾತೆರುನಿ to mimic.

ನಿಂನೇವುನಿ **ninnēvuni** (ನಿಂನೇ), *v. n*. To echo.

ನಿಂಬೆ **nimbè**, *see* ಲಿಂಬೆ.

ನಿಕ **nika**, *s*. A marriage among Mohammedans. –ಮಳ್ಪುನಿ to marry a Mohammedan woman.

ನಿಕುಳು **nikuḷu**, *pron*. (*pl. of* ಈ) You.

ನಿಖಿಲ, ನಿಖಿಳ **nikhila**, **nikhiḷa**, *adj*. All, the whole, entire, complete.

ನಿಗ್ದಿ **nigųdi**, *s*. Instalment. 2. a fixed period *or* sum for payment, as the assessment on land. 3. fixing, settlement. ಸರ್ಕಾರ್– government assessment. –ಮಳ್ಪುನಿ to resolve, determine.

ನಿಗ್ಪುನಿ **nigųpuni**, *see* ನಿಗಾಪುನಿ.

ನಿಗಚುನಿ **nigaćuni** (ನಿಗಚ್), *v. n*. To stretch.

ನಿಗಡ **nigaḍa**, *see* ನೆಗಡ.

ನಿಗಡಿ, ನಿಗಡೆ **nigaḍi**, **nigaḍè**, *see* ನೆಗಡಿ.

ನಿಗದಿ **nigadi**, *see* ನಿಗ್ದಿ.

ನಿಗಪುನಿ **nigapuni**, *see* ನೆಗಪುನಿ.

ನಿಗಮ **nigama**, *s*. The Vēdas. 2. a fair.

ನಿಗಯಿನೇನ್ **nigayinēnų**, *s*. A cord *or* rope for fastening a buoy.

ನಿಗರ್ **nigarų**, *see* ನೆಗರ.

ನಿಗರಿಗೆ **nigarigè**, *see* ನೆಗರಿಗೆ.

ನಿಗರುನಿ **nigaruni**, *see* ನೆಗರುನಿ.

ನಿಗರ್ವಿ nigarvi, *s.* An unassuming, modest person. *adj.* Unassuming, modest.

ನಿಗವು nigavu, *s.* A buoy.

ನಿಗಸ್ nigasụ, *s.* Food, victuals. 2. disregard, disdain.

ನಿಗಳ್ nigaḷụ, *see* ನೆಗಳ್.

ನಿಗಾಸ್ nigāsụ, *s.* Glitter, shining.

ನಿಗಿಪಾವುನಿ nigipāvuni, *c. v.* (*of* ನಿಗಿಪುನಿ) To cause to level.

ನಿಗಿಪುನಿ nigipuni (ನಿಗಿ), *v. a.* To level. 2. *see* ನುಗಿಪುನಿ.

ನಿಗಿಯುನಿ nigiyuni (ನಿಗಿ), *v. n.* To be levelled. 2. to be filled up, as a pit.

ನಿಗುರುನಿ niguruni, *see* ನೆಗರುನಿ.

ನಿಗೃಹ nigṛha, *see* ನಿಗ್ರಹ.

ನಿಗ್ಗ್, ನಿಗ್ಗಿರ niggụ, niggira, *s.* Inelegance. 2. filthiness, nastiness. 3. disgust. *adj.* Unpleasant, filthy. —ದಾಯೆ a filthy man. —ಮಳ್ಪುನಿ to make foul, render filthy.

ನಿಗ್ಗೀಸ್ niggīsụ, *s.* An unclean man; *also* ನಿಗ್ಗಿರದಾಯೆ.

ನಿಗ್ಗ್ಯ್, ನಿಗ್ಗ್ಯ niggyụ, niggya, *s.* Fullness, completeness. *adj.* Full, complete.

ನಿಗ್ರ nigra, *see* ನಿಗ್ಗಿರ.

ನಿಗ್ರಹ nigraha, *s.* Punishment. 2. killing; *also* ನಿಗ್ಗಿರಹ. —ಮಳ್ಪುನಿ to punish; to kill.

ನಿಗ್ರುನಿ nigruni, *see* ನೆಗರುನಿ.

ನಿಘಂಟ್, ನಿಘಂಟು nighaṇṭụ, nighaṇṭu, *s.* A dictionary, vocabulary, glossary.

ನಿಚ್ಚ nicca, *see* ನಿತ್ಯ.

ನಿಚ್ಚಯ niccaya, *see* ನಿಶ್ಚಯ.

ನಿಚ್ಚಲ niccala, *see* ನಿಶ್ಚಲ.

ನಿಜ nija, *s.* Condition, circumstances in life. *adj.* Own. —ರೂಪು one's own *or* natural form. ಪೊರಿಯ ನಿಜ ತಿಕ್ಕುನಿ to understand a man's disposition *or* character.

ನಿಜ nija, *s.* Truth, veracity, certainty, reality. *adj.* True, certain, sure, real. —ಆದ್, ನಿಜಾದ್ truly, certainly. —ತ್ವ certainty. —ದಾಂತಿ uncertain, unreliable. —ಪಾತೆರ a true word *or* statement, a fact. —ತಿಕ್ಕುನಿ to ascertain the truth. —ಮಳ್ಪುನಿ to prove.

ನಿಜಿಕತ್ರುನಿ, ನಿಜಿಕಾವುನಿ, ನಿಜ್ಕಾವುನಿ nijikatruni, nijikāvuni, nijkāvuni, (ನಿಜಿಕತ್ರ್, ನಿಜಿಕಾ, ನಿಜ್ಕಾ), *v. n.* To grin; *also* ಕೊಲಿಬುಡ್ಪುನಿ.

ನಿಜಿಕುನಿ nijikuni (ನಿಜಿಕ್), *v. n.* To appear, seem.

ನಿಜ್ಜಿ nijji, *s.* The gums. —ಮೋಣೆ a toothless mouth.

ನಿಟಿಲ niṭila, *s.* The forehead.

ನಿಟ್ಟ niṭṭa, *s.* Pleasure. *adj.* Pleasant. 2. *see* ನಿಷ್ಠ.

ನಿಟ್ಟಣಿಗೆ niṭṭaṇigè, *s.* A ladder. 2. a pile, heap. 3. a row, line. 4. the name of a village.

ನಿಟ್ಟುರ, ನಿಟ್ಟೂರ niṭṭuṙa, niṭṭūra, *see* ನಿಷ್ಠುರ.

ನಿಟ್ಟುಸುರ್ niṭṭusurụ, *s.* A deep sigh; loud sobbing.

ನಿಟ್ಟೆ niṭṭe, *see* ನಿಷ್ಠೆ. 2. *see* ನೆಂಟೆ.

ನಿಟ್ಟೆಲ್ niṭṭelu, *s.* The hip, loins, waist. 2. the bosom.

ನಿಡಂಕುನಿ niḍaṅkuni (ನಿಡಂಕ್), *v. n.* To incline; *cf.* ಬಂಕುನಿ.

ನಿಡಿ niḍi, *adj.* Straight, high, lofty. –ಕಲ್ಲ್ a lofty stone, an erect stone. –ಯರಿ (ಅರಿ) rice not broken by pounding.

ನಿಡಿಪ niḍipa, *see* ನಿಡ್ಪ.

ನಿಡಿಯುನಿ, ನಿಡಿಪಿನಿ niḍiyuni, niḍipini (ನಿಡಿ), *v. a.* To wash. ಮೋಣೆ– to wash the face.

ನಿಡು niḍu, *adj.* Long, tall, high.

ನಿಡುಂಬರೆ niḍumbarè, *s.* Barracks; *also* ನಿಡುಂಬುರ.

ನಿಡುಪ್ಪ niḍuppa, *s.* Tallness, length. 2. *see* ನಿಡ್ಪ.

ನಿಡ್ಡಾಡಿತರು, ನಿಡ್ಯರು, ನಿಡ್ಯೆಡಿ niḍḍāḍitaru, niḍyaru, niḍyeḍi, *s.* A kind of small fish.

ನಿಡ್ಪ niḍpa, *see* ನಿಡ್ಪ.

ನಿಣೆ niṇè, *see* ನಿನೆ.

ನಿತಂಬ nitamba, *s.* The buttocks. 2. a mountain side.

ನಿತಿಂಗ nitiṅga, *adj.* Strong, hard. 2. serious, dangerous. –ಸಂಕಟ a serious illness.

ನಿತಿಂಜ nitiñja, *see* ನೀತಿಂಜ.

ನಿತ್ತೆಲ್ nittelu, *see* ನಿಟ್ಟೆಲ್.

ನಿತ್ಯ nitya, *adj.* Eternal, constant, perpetual, everlasting. 2. daily, regular. –ಕರ್ಜ daily expenses. –ಕರ್ಮ daily ceremonies. –ಕೃತ್ಯ daily observance. –ಜೀವ eternal life. –ನೈಮಿತ್ತಿಕ daily and occasional.

ನಿತ್ಯತ್ವ nityatva, *s.* Eternity.

ನಿತ್ಯಾತ್ಮೆ nityātme, *s.* The eternal Spirit, God.

ನಿತ್ಯಾನಂದ nityānanda, *s.* Everlasting happiness.

ನಿತ್ಯಾನಿತ್ಯ nityānitya, *s.* Eternal and temporal.

ನಿತ್ರಾಣ nitrāṇa, *s.* Weakness, debility. *adj.* Weak, faint. ನಿತ್ರಾಣೆ a weak man.

ನಿದ್ಪ nidupa, *see* ನಿಡ್ಪ.

ನಿದ್ಪುಡುನಿ nidupuḍuni, *see* ನಿಡ್ಪುಡುನಿ.

ನಿದರ್ಶನ nidaršana, *s.* An example, illustration, evidence, instance.

ನಿದಾನ nidāna, *s.* Ascertaining the cause; the study of symptoms with a view to trace the remote *or* proximate causes, as of a disease. 2. a work on pathology. 3. *see* ನಿಧಾನ.

ನಿದಿ nidi, *see* ನಿಧಿ.

ನಿದ್ಧಿ niddhi, *s.* Abundance, plenty. –ಬರ್ಪಿನಿ to prosper.

ನಿದ್ಪ nidpa, *adj.* Straight, upright, erect. *adv.* Straightly, erectly. –ಉಂತುನಿ to stand erectly.

ನಿದ್ಪುಡುನಿ nidpuḍuni (ನಿದ್ಪುಡ್), *v. a.* To erect, set up, stay. 2. *see* ನಿಲ್ಪುಡುನಿ.

ನಿದ್ರೆ nidrè, *s.* Sleep, drowsiness. –ಗಾರೆ, –ದ ಕುರ್ನಾಸ್, ನಿದ್ರಾಲೋಲೆ a sleepy man. ಪತ್ತುನಿ, –ಬರ್ಪಿನಿ to become drowsy. –ಮಳ್ಪುನಿ to sleep.

ನಿದ್ರೆಡ್ಪಿನಿ nidreḍpini (ನಿದ್ರೆಡ್), *v. n.* To sleep, be asleep; to go to bed.

ನಿಧಾನ nidhāna, *s.* Caution, deliberation, calmness, quietness. 2. slowness, dilatoriness. *adj.* Cautious, deliberate. 2. calm, quiet. 3. slow, dilatory. —ಆಲೋಚನೆ a careful consideration, deliberate judgment. —ಗುಣ quiet disposition. —ನಡಕೆ slow motion. ನಿಧಾನೊಡು carefully, quietly, slowly.

ನಿಧಾನಿಪುನಿ nidhānipuni (ನಿಧಾನಿ), *v. a.* To consider, examine carefully.

ನಿಧಾರ nidhāra, *see* ನಿರ್ಧಾರ.

ನಿಧಿ nidhi, *s.* Concealed *or* buried treasure. 2. a receptacle, place of accumulation. —ಪುರುಷೆ an opulent man.

ನಿನ nina, *s.* The serum of the flesh. 2. the marrow of the bones.

ನಿನ nina, *pro.* (*gen. of* ಈ) Thy. ನಿನಾತೆಗ್ by *or* of thyself. ನಿನವು, ನಿಂನವು thine.

ನಿನೆ ninè, *s.* A wick. 2. a very young fruit.

ನಿನೆಪು ninepu, *see* ನೆನೆಪು.

ನಿನೊಶ ninoša (ನಿನ ವಶ), Thy care *or* charge.

ನಿಪಾತ್ nipātụ, *s.* Ruin.

ನಿಪಾತ nipāta, *s.* Falling, coming down, alighting. *adj.* Irregularly formed, *gram.* ನಿಪಾತಾವ್ಯಯ interjection.

ನಿಪುಣ nipuṇa, *adj.* Clever, skillful, conversant. —ತ್ವ skill, proficiency in any art, *etc.*

ನಿಪುಣೆ nipuṇe, *s.* A clever man.

ನಿಪುತ್ರೆ niputre, *s.* A sonless man.

ನಿಬಂಧನೆ nibandhanè, *s.* Order, mandate. 2. appointment, engagement.

ನಿಬಾಸುನಿ, ನಿಭಾಸುನಿ, ನಿಭಾಯಿಸುನಿ nibāsuni, nibhāsuni, nibhāyisuni, *v. a.* (ನಿಬಾಸ್, ನಿಭಾಸ್, ನಿಭಾಯಿಸ್), To bear, endure. 2. to manage, sustain.

ನಿಬ್ಬಣ nibbaṇa, *see* ದಿಬ್ಬಣ.

ನಿಭಾವಣೆ nibhāvaṇè, *s.* Endurance, toleration. 2. undertaking, sustaining.

ನಿಮಾಜಿ nimāji, *s.* A Mussulman's ritual *or* form of prayer.

ನಿಮಿತ, ನಿಮಿತ್ತ, ನಿಮಿತ್ಯ nimita, nimitta, nimitya, *s.* Cause, reason. 2. object, motive, purpose. 3. consulting stars, an omen, *or* fate-book. *postp.* For, on account of. —ಕೋಡಿ result of soothsaying. —ದಾಯಿ an astrologer, soothsayer. —ತೂಪಿನಿ to consult stars *or* a fate-book.

ನಿಮಿಷ nimisha, *s.* The twinkling of an eye, a second, instant, minute.

ನಿಮುರುನಿ nimuruni (ನಿಮುರ್), *v. n.* To become straight.

ನಿಯತ್ niyatụ, *s.* Restraining the natural appetites and passions; good morals *or* conduct.

ನಿಯತ niyata, *adj*. Checked, restrained, as the natural appetites and passions.

ನಿಯಮ niyama, *s*. An agreement. contract, engagement. 2. a religious observance in general; voluntary penance. 3. a rule, law; *cf*. ನೇಮ.

ನಿಯುಕ್ತ niyukta, *adj*. Appointed, ordered. 2. attached to.

ನಿಯೋಗ niyōga, *s*. An order, command. 2. authority, appointment. 3. occupation, engagement.

ನಿಯೋಗಿಪುನಿ niyōgipuni (ನಿಯೋಗಿ), *v. a*. To order, command. 2. to authorize, appoint.

ನಿರ್, ನಿಸ್ nirų, nisų, *prefixes implying* Certainty. 2. negation, want. 3. out, without; *as:* ನಿರಪರಾಧ innocence; ನಿರ್ದೋಷ blamelessness; ನಿಸ್ಸಂತಾನ childless; ನಿಸ್ಸಂದೇಹ undoubted.

ನಿರಂಜನ nirañjana, *adj*. Immaculate, pure, spotless. 2. absorbed in. —ವಸ್ತು, ನಿರಂಜನೆ God, the immaculate one.

ನಿರಂತರ nirantara, *adj*. Continued, continuous, perpetual. 2. unimpeded, constant. *adv*. Ever, always, generally, frequently.

ನಿರಕ್ nirakų, *s*. Current *or* fixed price. 2. assize *or* tariff.

ನಿರಡಿ niradi, *see* ನೀರಟು.

ನಿರಪರಾಧ niraparādha, *s*. Innocence.

ನಿರಪರಾಧಿ niraparādhi, *s*. An innocent person. *adj*. Innocent, not guilty.

ನಿರಪು nirapu, *s*. A frame of boards, fitted with planks, as a shutter *or* a door. [ತು.

ನಿರವು niravu, *s*. The anus; *cf*. ನಿರ

ನಿರಸ nirasa, *s*. Want of flavour *or* passion. 2. dryness, want of juice. *adj*. Insipid, tasteless.

ನಿರಹಂಕಾರ nirahaṅkāra, *s*. Absence of pride, humility, modesty. ನಿರಹಂಕಾರಿ a modest person, one without egotism.

ನಿರಾಕರಿಪುನಿ, ನಿರಾಕರಿಸುನಿ nirākaripuni, nirākarisuni (ನಿರಾಕರಿ, ನಿರಾಕರಿಸ್), *v. a*. To transgress, disobey, disregard. 2. to reject, set aside, refuse, decline.

ನಿರಾಕಾರ nirākāra, *s*. Shapelessness, absence of form. 2. censure. 3. denial, negation. *adj*. Shapeless, formless. ನಿರಾಕಾರೆ God, who has no material form.

ನಿರಾಖ್ nirākhų, *see* ನಿರಕ್.

ನಿರಾಜಿ nirāji, *s*. A kind of cloth with gold borders.

ನಿರಾತಂಕ nirātaṅka, *adj*. Uninterrupted, unmolested.

ನಿರಾಧಾರ nirādhāra, *adj*. Unsupported, unsustained. 2. poor, destitute. ನಿರಾಧಾರಿ a destitute person.

ನಿರಾನಿ nirāni, *s*. A kind of eruption on the skin, eczema.

ನಿರಾಪರಾಧಿ nirāparādhi, *see* ನಿರಪರಾಧಿ.

ನಿರಾಮಯ nirāmaya, *adj.* Well, hale, free from sickness.

ನಿರಾಯಾಸ nirāyāsa, *adj.* Easy, unfatiguing.

ನಿರಾಯುಧ nirāyudha, *adj.* Unarmed, defenceless.

ನಿರಾರ nirāra, *see* ನಿರಾಹಾರ.

ನಿರಾವು nirāvu, *see* ನಿರವು. 2. *see* ನೆರವು.

ನಿರಾಶೆ nirāśè, *s.* Despair, despondency. 2. disappointment. —ಆಪಿನಿ to be disappointed. —ಮಳ್ಪುನಿ to despair.

ನಿರಾಶ್ರಯ nirāśraya, *adj.* Without refuge, asylum *or* support; helpless, destitute.

ನಿರಾಸಿ nirāsi, *see* ನಿರಾಶೆ.

ನಿರಾಹಾರ nirāhāra, *s.* Fasting.

ನಿರಾಕ್ಷೇಪ, ನಿರಾಕ್ಷೇಪಣೆ nirākshēpa, nirākshēpaṇè, *adj.* Unquestionable, unobjectionable.

ನಿರಿ niri, *see* ನೆರಿ.

ನಿರೀಕ್ಷಿಪುನಿ nirīkshipuni (ನಿರೀಕ್ಷಿಸಿ), *v. a.* To hope, desire, look for, expect.

ನಿರೀಕ್ಷೆ nirīkshè, *s.* Hope, expectation, waiting.

ನಿರುದ್ಯೋಗಿ nirudyōgi, *s.* A man without employment, a lazy man.

ನಿರುದ್ಧ niruddha, *adj.* Obstructed.

ನಿರೂಪ nirūpa, *s.* A letter, epistle, representation in writing.

ನಿರೆ nirè, *s.* Neighbourhood; *also* ನಿರೆಕರೆ. *adj.* Neighbouring, adjoining. —ಕೇಡಿಂಗೆ a bad neighbour. —ತಾಯಿ a neighbour.

ನಿರೆಪು nirepu, *see* ನಿರವು.

ನಿರೆಲ್ nireḷu, *s.* A shadow, resemblance. 2. shade, shelter.

ನಿರೆವುನಿ nirevuni (ನಿರೆ), *v. n.* To be ready; *cf.* ನೆರೆವುನಿ.

ನಿರೋಗಿ nirōgi, *s.* A man who is free from sickness, a healthy man.

ನಿರೋಧ nirōdha, *s.* Loss, destruction.

ನಿರ್ಕಂಡೆ nirkaṇḍè, *s.* A soft root.

ನಿರ್ಕಕ್ಕೆ nirkakkè, *s.* The sea-gull.

ನಿರ್ಕಣೆ nirkaṇè, *s.* A small branch of bamboo.

ನಿರ್ಕನ್ಯ nirkanya, *s.* A water-nymph.

ನಿರ್ಕುಂಟ nirkuṇṭa, *s.* A post fixed in water.

ನಿರ್ಕುಂಟು nirkuṇṭu, *see* ನೀರ್ಕುಂಟು.

ನಿರ್ಕುಜೆಲುನಿ nirkujeluni (ನಿರ್ಕುಜೆಲ್), *v. n.* To curdle, coagulate.

ನಿರ್ಕುತ್ತ nirkutta, *s.* Dropsy.

ನಿರ್ಕುತ್ತಿ nirkutti, *s.* The post of a watering-machine.

ನಿರ್ಕೂವೆ nirkūve, *s.* A kind of arrowroot.

ನಿರ್ಗ್ nirgu, *see* ನರ್ಗುನಿ.

ನಿರ್ಗಂಧ nirgandha, *adj.* Inodorous, without smell.

ನಿರ್ಗಮ nirgama, *s.* Setting out, exit. 2. total loss *or* departure.

ನಿರ್ಗುಣ nirguṇa, *adj.* Void of all properties. 2. destitute of the qualities incident to humanity. 3. having no good qualities, bad, worthless.

ನಿಜನ nirjana, *adj.* Lonely, uninhabited. –ಪ್ರದೇಶ, –ಭೂಮಿ a deserted country.

ನಿಜಲ nirjala, *adj.* Waterless.

ನಿಜೀವ nirjīva, *adj.* Lifeless, inanimate. 2. weak, helpless. 3. inactive, lazy. ನಿಜೀವಿ a dead body.

ನಿಣಯ nirṇaya, *s.* Resolution, determination. 2. certainty, positive conclusion. 3. settlement, final arrangement. –ಮಳ್ಪುನಿ to resolve, settle, fix.

ನಿಣಯಿಸುನಿ nirṇayisuni (ನಿಣಯಿಸಿ), *v.a.* To resolve, decide, settle.

ನಿತ nirta, *see* ನೆತ.

ನಿದಯ nirdaya, *s.* Unkindness.

ನಿದಾಕ್ಷಿಣ್ಯ nirdākshiṇya, *s.* Disregard, want of attention. 2. severity, strictness.

ನಿದೋಷ nirdōsha, *s.* Blamelessness, innocence. 2. freedom from blemish. *adj.* Innocent, sinless. 2. unblemished.

ನಿಧಾರ nirdhāra, *s.* Certainty, ascertainment. 2. determination, resolution.

ನಿನಾಮ nirnāma, *s.* Extirpation, eradication.

ನಿನಾಯಿ nirnāyi, *s.* An otter.

ನಿನಾಲ nirnāla, *s.* The sixth Tuḷu month between September and October.

ನಿನಾಲಿ nirnāli, *s.* A water-spout.

ನಿನಿರೆಲ್ nirnirelu, *see* ನೀರ್‌ನಿರೆಲ್.

ನಿಪಟ್ಟ್ nirpaṭṭu, *adj.* Moist, wet. 2. diluted. –ಪೇರ್ diluted milk.

ನಿಬಂಧ, ನಿಬಂಧನ nirbandha, nirbandhana, *s.* Violence, oppression, force, constraint. –ಮಳ್ಪುನಿ to constrain, *or* oppress.

ನಿಬುದ್ಧಿ nirbuddhi, *s.* Foolishness.

ನಿಬೆ, ನಿಭೆ nirbè, nirbhè, *s.* A kind of oblation given to a priest. –ಪತ್ತುನಿ to prepare.

ನಿಭಯ, ನಿಭೀತಿ nirbhaya, nirbhīti, *s.* Fearlessness. *adj.* Fearless, undaunted.

ನಿಮದೆ nirmadè, *adj.* Uncovered.

ನಿಮಲ nirmala, *s.* Purity, cleanliness. *adj.* Pure, transparent, pellucid, clear.

ನಿಮಾಣ nirmāṇa, *s.* Creation, manufacture, production, invention. –ಮಳ್ಪುನಿ to create, produce, invent.

ನಿಮಿತ nirmita, *adj.* Made, invented. 2. fabricated. 3. artificial. –ಜಿಪ್ಪುನಿ to produce, invent.

ನಿಮಿಸುನಿ nirmisuni (ನಿಮಿಸಿ), *v.a.* To create, produce. 2. to manufacture, invent. 3. to fabricate.

ನಿಮುನೆ nirmunè, *s.* An apparatus for watering a field. *adj.* Blunt.

ನಿಮುರುಂಗೆಲೆ nirmuruṅgele, *s.* An arrogant man.

ನಿಮೂಲ nirmūla, *s.* Extirpation, eradication. –ಮಳ್ಪುನಿ to extirpate, eradicate.

ನಿರ್ಮೋಹ **nirmōha,** *s.* Want of affection *or* love.

ನಿರ್ಯಾಣ **niryāṇa,** *s.* Death, demise; final beatitude.

ನಿರ್ಲಜ್ಜೆ **nirlajje,** *s.* Impudence, shamelessness.

ನಿರ್ಲೇಪಿ **nirlēpi,** *adj.* Undefiled, untainted. 2. innocent, blameless.

ನಿರ್ವಂಚನೆ **nirvañcanè,** *s.* Sincerity, ingenuousness.

ನಿರ್ವಹಿಸುನಿ **nirvahisuni** (ನಿರ್ವಹಿಸ್), *v. a.* To manage, transact, sustain, effect.

ನಿರ್ವಾಕ, ನಿರ್ವಾಹ **nirvāka, nirvāha,** *s.* Management, power *or* ability to perform, execute, sustain, *etc.*; *also* ನಿರ್ವಾ. –ದಾಂತೆ without power to manage, *etc.*; unavoidably.

ನಿರ್ವಾಣ **nirvāṇa,** *s.* Nakedness. 2. reunion of the soul with the deity, final beatitude.

ನಿರ್ವಾದ, ನಿರ್ವಿವಾದ **nirvāda, nirvivāda,** *adj.* Undisputed, unquestionable, unobjectionable.

ನಿರ್ವಿಷ **nirvisha,** *s.* An antidote for poison. 2. the plant *Curcuma ferumbet.*

ನಿರ್ವೆ **nirvè,** *see* ನಿಬೆರ್.

ನಿರ್ವೇದ **nirvēda,** *s.* Humility. 2. despair. 3. weariness. 4. *see* ನಿಬೆರ್.

ನಿರ್ಸಾಣಿ **nirsāṇi,** *see* ನಿಶಾನಿ.

ನಿಲ **nila,** *see* ನೆಲ.

ನಿಲಂ **nilam,** *s.* Ballast. 2. the bottom of a vessel.

ನಿಲಂಕಾರ **nilaṅkāra,** *s.* Disfigurement. 2. ruin.

ನಿಲಕರ **nilakara,** *see* ನೆಲಕರ.

ನಿಲಕಾರ್ **nilakārụ,** *s.* Stretching. –ದೈಪುನಿ to stretch out the forelegs, to scrape along the ground.

ನಿಲಗಡೆ **nilagaḍè,** *s.* Settlement, adjustment, conclusion, determination. 2. cessation, intermission.

ನಿಲವು, ನಿಲಾವು **nilavu, nilāvu,** *see* ನಿಲೆವು. 2. *see* ಮಿಲಾವು.

ನಿಲಿಕೆ, ನಿಲೀಕೆ **nilikè, nilīkè,** *adj.* Full, replete.

ನಿಲಿಪುನಿ **nilipuni,** *see* ನಿಲ್ಪುನಿ.

ನಿಲುವಂಗಿ **niluvaṅgi,** *s.* A long coat.

ನಿಲೆ **nilè,** *s.* The bottom, as of a well, *etc.*; depth, profundity. 2. a secret, mystery. *adj.* Firm, fast, abiding. 2. quiet, still, calm. –ಆದುಪ್ಪುನಿ to be firm, steadfast. –ಆಪಿನಿ to be quiet.

ನಿಲೆಂಚಿ **nileñci,** *see* ನೆಲೆಂಚಿ.

ನಿಲೆಪ್ಪು **nileppu,** *s.* State. 2. posture, station.

ನಿಲೆವು **nilevu,** *s.* Balance, arrears. 2. standing, residence.

ನಿಲೆವುನಿ **nilevuni** (ನಿಲೆ), *v. n.* To be steadfast.

ನಿಲ್ಕಾವುನಿ **nilkāvuni,** *c. v.* (*of* ನಿಲ್ಕುನಿ) To cause to peep. 2. to cause to reach.

ನಿಲ್ಕುನಿ **nilkuni** (ನಿಲ್ಕ್), *v. n.* To peep, look slily, get a glimpse of. 2. to reach.

ನಿಲ್ಕೆ nilke, *see* ನಿಲಿಕೆ.

ನಿಲ್ಗಡೆ nilgaḍè, *see* ನಿಲಗಡೆ.

ನಿಲ್ಪು nilpu, *s.* A pause, stop, interruption. 2. stay, duration.

ನಿಲ್ಪುಡುನಿ nilpuḍuni, *c. v.* (*of* ನಿಲ್ಪುನಿ) To put a stop, cause to stop, make stand.

ನಿಲ್ಪುನಿ nilpuni (ನಿಲ್), *v. n.* To stay. 2. to cease; to become quiet.

ನಿಲ್ಲಾವುನಿ nillāvuni, *see* ಪಿಲ್ಯಾವುನಿ.

ನಿವರ್ತನೆ nivartanè, *s.* Cessation. 2. remission, forgiveness.

ನಿವಾಜಿ, ನಿವಾದಿ nivāji, nivādi, *see* ನಿಮಾಜಿ.

ನಿವಾರಣೆ nivāraṇè, *s.* A remedy. 2. averting. 3. deliverance. 4. prevention.

ನಿವಾಸ nivāsa, *s.* A habitation, dwelling.

ನಿವಾಸಿ nivāsi, *s.* A citizen, inhabitant.

ನಿವಾಳಿ nivāḷi, *s.* Taking away the effects of evil eyes.

ನಿವಾಳಿಪುನಿ, ನಿವಾಳಿಸುನಿ nivāḷipuni, nivāḷisuni (ನಿವಾಳಿ, ನಿವಾಳಿಸ್), *v. a.* To take away the effects of evil eyes.

ನಿವೃತ್ತಿ nivrutti, *s.* Cessation. 2. abandoning. 3. repose, rest.

ನಿವೇದನ nivēdana, *s.* An offering. 2. an address. 3. informing.

ನಿಶ niša, *s.* Inebriation, intoxication. —ಜೋರೆ an inebriate man.

ನಿಶಾಚರೆ nišāčare, *s.* A fiend, goblin. 2. a night-walker.

ನಿಶಾನಿ, ನಿಶಾನೆ nišāni, nišānè, *s.* A mark, sign. 2. a flag, standard, banner.

ನಿಶಿ niši, *see* ನಿಶೆ.

ನಿಶಿಂ nišiñ, *adv.* Together with, also.

ನಿಶೂದಿ nišūdi, *s.* A bill of acquittance.

ನಿಶೆ nišè, *s.* Night, midnight.

ನಿಶ್ಕರ್ಷ niškarsha, *see* ನಿಷ್ಕರ್ಷ.

ನಿಶ್ಚಯ niščaya, *s.* Certainty, ascertainment, positive conclusion. 2. resolution, determination. —ತಾಂಬೂಲ a present of betel, *etc.*, at the settlement of a marriage. —ದಾಂತಿ uncertain. —ಮಳ್ಪುನಿ, ನಿಶ್ಚಯಿಸುನಿ to resolve, settle, determine; to ascertain. —ಮಲ್ತ್‌ತೋಜಿಪುನಿ to prove.

ನಿಶ್ಚಲ niščala, *s.* Firmness stability. *adj.* Firm, steady, fixed.

ನಿಶ್ಚಿಂತೆ niščintè, *s.* Ease, freedom from care *or* anxiety.

ನಿಶ್ಚಿತ niščita, *adj.* Determined, settled.

ನಿಶ್ತೀಕ ništīka, *see* ನಿಸ್ತೂಕ.

ನಿಶ್ಶಬ್ದ nišśabda, *adj.* Noiseless, still, quiet.

ನಿಷಿದ್ಧ nishiddha, *adj.* Prohibited, forbidden.

ನಿಷೇಧ nishēdha, *s.* Negation, prohibition. 2. the negative mood, *gram.*

ನಿಷ್ಕಪಟ nishkapaṭa, *s.* Sincerity. *adj.* Frank, sincere.

ನಿಷ್ಕರುಣ nishkaruṇa, *adj.* Pitiless, cruel, harsh.

ನಿಷ್ಕರ್ಷ, ನಿಷ್ಕರ್ಷೆ nishkarsha, nishkarshè, *s.* Determination, settlement. 2. certainty.

ನಿಷ್ಕಲಂಕ್, ನಿಷ್ಕಳಂಕ್ nishkalaṅkụ, nishkaḷaṅkụ, *adj.* Irreproachable, spotless, unblemished.

ನಿಷ್ಟುರ, ನಿಷ್ಠೂರ nishṭura, nishṭūra, *adj.* Cruel, harsh, severe. *s.* Harshness, severity.

ನಿಷ್ಪ್ರಯೋಜನ nishprayōjana, *s.* Uselessness. *adj.* Useless, vain, bootless.

ನಿಷ್ಫಲ nishphala, *adj.* Fruitless, vain.

ನಿಸರ್ಗ nisarga, *s.* The natural condition.

ನಿಸಾನಿ nisāni, *see* ನಿಶಾನಿ.

ನಿಸ್ತರಿಪುನಿ nistaripuni (ನಿಸ್ತರಿ), *v. a.* To endure, bear, sustain. 2. to cross *or* pass over.

ನಿಸ್ತೂಕ nistūka, *adj.* Critical, serious, as the turn of a disease.

ನಿಸ್ಸಂಗ nissaṅga, *s.* Separation. 2. seclusion, retirement. 3. indifference.

ನಿಸ್ಸಂಗಿ nissaṅgi, *s.* A man who mortifies himself to the world, a recluse.

ನಿಸ್ಸಂತಾನ nissantāna, *adj.* Childless, issueless, heirless: —ಆಪಿನಿ to die childless; to be ruined, annihilated.

ನಿಸ್ಸಂದೇಹ, ನಿಸ್ಸಂಶಯ nissandēha, nissaṁśaya, *s.* Confidence. *adj.* Undoubted.

ನಿಸ್ಸಾರ nissāra, *s.* Worthlessness. *adj.* Sapless, pithless, dry; worthless. —ಭೂಮಿ unfertile, barren land.

ನಿಸ್ಸುನಿ nissuni, *see* ಸುಧರಿಪುನಿ.

ನಿಕ್ಷಯ nikshaya, *see* ನಿಶ್ಚಯ.

ನಿಕ್ಷೇಪ nikshēpa, *s.* Hidden *or* buried treasure. 2. a deposit.

ನೀಂದಾಟ nīndāṭa, *s.* Swimming. 2. floating.

ನೀಂದಾವುನಿ nīndāvuni, *c. v.* (*of* ನೀಂದುನಿ) To set afloat. 2. to cause to swim.

ನೀಂದುನಿ nīnduni (ನೀಂದ್), *v. n.* To swim. 2. to float.

ನೀಕಲಿಯುನಿ nīkaliyuni (ನೀಕಲಿ), *v.a.* To peep.

ನೀಕಾವುನಿ nīkāvuni, *c. v.* (*of* ನೀಕುನಿ) To grin. ಕೂಲಿ— to show the teeth, as dogs, monkeys.

ನೀಕುನಿ nīkuni (ನೀಕ್), *v. n.* To appear, as the projecting teeth.

ನೀಗುನಿ nīguni, *see* ನೆಗರುನಿ.

ನೀಚ nīca, *adj.* Mean, low, base, vile, abject. —ಜಾತಿ low caste. —ತನ, —ತ್ವ meanness, baseness, vulgarity. —ನರಮಾನಿ a mean man. —ವಾತೆರ a mean, vulgar expression.

ನೀಚತಾಡನೆ nīcatāḍanè, *s.* A kind of beating.

ನೀಚುನಿ nīcuni (ನೀಚ್), *v. n.* To go through, pierce. 2. to extend; *cf.* ನೀಂಡುನಿ.

ನೀಚೆ nīce, *s.* A mean fellow. 2. a demon so called.

ನೀಟ nīṭa, *adj.* Long, extended, high, upright. 2. straight, direct. ಅಡ್ಡ— lengthwise and crosswise, zigzag; confounding.

ನೀಟಾನೀಟಿ nīṭānīṭi, *adv.* Straightly. 2. lengthwise.

ನೀಟಾವುನಿ nīṭāvuni, *c. v.* (*of* ನೀಟುನಿ) To cause to stretch, lengthen, *etc.*; *also* ನೀಡಾವುನಿ.

ನೀಟು nīṭu, *see* ನೀಟ.

ನೀಟುನಿ, ನೀಡುನಿ nīṭuni, nīḍuni (ನೀಟ್, ನೀಡ್), *v. a.* To stretch out *or* forth, hold out, lengthen. ಕೈ— to stretch out the hand.

ನೀತಿ nīti, *s.* Morality; righteousness, justice, equity. —ಕೇಡ್ injustice, iniquity. —ಧರ್ಮ morals. —ದಾಯಿ, —ವಂತ a just man. —ನಿರ್ಣಯ justification. —ಪಾತೆರ a just word, moral saying. —ಬೋಧನೆ moral teaching. —ಮಾರ್ಗ the way of righteousness, upright conduct. —ಶಾಸ್ತ್ರ moral philosophy, ethics. —ಸಾರ essence of morality; a treatise on ethics. —ಹೀನ immoral.

ನೀತಿಂಗ nītiṅga, *see* ನಿತಿಂಗ.

ನೀತಿಂಜ nītiñja, *see* ನೀತಿಹೀನ *under* [ನೀತಿ.

ನೀರ್ nīru, *s.* Water. —ಅದ್ಯರ a water jar. —ಆನೆ a whale. —ಉಪ್ಪರ a water bubble. —ಓಳ್ಯ, ನೀರೋಳ್ಯ furrows between a row of plants, *etc.*, for watering them. —ಕಂಡೊಡಿ a water snake. —ಕಕ್ಕೆ a sea-gull, shag. —ಕೋರಿ a water-fowl. —ತೆಲ್ಲವು a kind of cake. —ತೇವು a species of yam. —ಧಾರೆ a falling stream of water. —ದಾಯಿ a water-carrier. —ನಂಜಿ poison in water, miasma. —ನಾಯಿ an otter. —ನಿರೆಲ್, —ನೀರ್ perspiration; fatigue. —ಪಣಿ a drop of water. —ಪಾಲ್, ನೀರ್ಪಾಲ್ fixed hire for watering rice fields. ಅಮೆ— a mode of watering rice fields. ಉಪ್ಪು— salt water. ಎಡ್ಡೆ— fresh water. ಕಂಣ— tears. ಕಂಣೀರ್ ಗೆಪ್ಪುನಿ to weep, shed tears. ಕಡಲ— sea water. ಕುರಿ— yellow water. ಚಾಳಿ— cold water. ಚೌಳು— brackish water. ತುಲಿ—, ತುಳಿ— sweet water. ತೆಲಿ—, ತೆಳಿ— clear *or* filtered water. ಧಾರೆ— rain water falling down from a roof. ಪೋಂಕುರು— muddy water. ಬೆಚ್ಚ— hot water. ಸೀಂತೆಲ್— putrid water. ಮೆಯಿ— sweat; urine. —ಅರಿಯುನಿ, —ಊಜುನಿ, —ಪೀರ್ಯುನಿ to leak, ooze. —ಆಪಿನಿ to melt, dissolve. —ಓಲುನಿ to water a rice field. —ಕಟ್ಟುನಿ to turn the course of water on a land. —ಕೈಪುನಿ, —ಕೊದಿಪುನಿ water to boil. —ಕೋಲುನಿ to water. —ಕೊಂಡುನಿ water to be very hot. —ಗಿಡಿಯಾವುನಿ to squirt, spirt. —ಗುಡ್ಡುನಿ water to run down. —ತಲಿಪುನಿ to sprinkle water. —ತೆಳಿಯುನಿ, —ನೆಳಿಯುನಿ water to become clear. —ತೇಪುನಿ to water. —ದೀಪಿನಿ *lit.* to lay water; *c. dat.* to involve one in difficulties; to ruin. —ಪರಪುನಿ water to flow. —ಪುಂಟುನಿ water to wring out. –ಬಚ್ಚ್ನಿ water to dry up. –ಬುದ್ಪಿನಿ to irrigate *or* water, as a field. –ದೆಗಪುನಿ, –ದೂಪುನಿ, –ಪೈಪುನಿ to draw water from a well *or* tank. –ಮ್ಯೈಪು ನಿ to pour water.

ನೀರಂಡೆ nīraṇḍè, *s.* A small syringe.

ನೀರಕೊಳಂಬೆ nīrakoḷambè, *s.* The damp *or* swampy ground.

ನೀರಗುಳ್ಳೆ nīraguḷḷè, *s.* A bubble.

ನೀರಜ nīraja, *s.* A lotus.

ನೀರಟ, ನೀರಡಿ nīraṭa, nīraḍi, *s.* A water plant, *Pistia stratiotes; also* ಅಂತರಗಂಗೆ.

ನೀರಸುಳಿ nīrasuḷi, *s.* A whirlpool.

ನೀರಳೆ nīraḷè, *s.* Butter-milk diluted with water.

ನೀರಾಟ nīrāṭa, *s.* Bathing for sport. 2. *see* ನೀರಟ.

ನೀರುಪ್ಪಡ್ nīruppaḍụ, *s.* Green fruits pickled in salt-water.

ನೀರುಳ್ಳಿ nīruḷḷi, *s.* Onions.

ನೀರ್ಕುಂಟ nīrkuṇṭa, *see* ನಿರ್ಕುಂಟ.

ನೀರ್ಕುಂಟು nīrkuṇṭu, *s.* Waterproof cloth. 2. a small piece of cloth put on in mourning.

ನೀರ್ಕುತ್ತ nīrkutta, *s.* Dropsy. –ದಾಯಿ a man suffering from dropsy.

ನೀರ್ನೀರೆಲ್ nīrnīrelụ, *s.* Water poured on a corpse, a funeral ceremony.

ನೀರ್ಪಟ್ nīrpaṭụ, *adj.* Watery, thin.

ನೀರ್ಪಾಲ್ nīrpālụ, *see under* ನೀರ್.

ನೀರ್ಮುತ್ತು nīrmuttu *s.* An inferior kind of pearl.

ನೀಲ nīla, *s.* Blue colour. 2. the sapphire; *also* ನೀಲಕಲ್ಲ್. 3. *see* ನೀಲಿ. *adj.* Blue, dark blue. –ಬಂಣ, –ವರ್ಣ blue colour.

ನೀಲಕಂಠೆ nīlakaṇṭhe, *s.* The blue necked Śiva. 2. a peacock.

ನೀಲಗಿರಿ nīlagiri, *s.* A blue mountain; the Nilagiris.

ನೀಲಾಂಜನ nīlāñjana, *s.* Blue vitriol. 2. a small lamp.

ನೀಲಿ nīli, *s.* The indigo plant. 2. blue colour. –ಪಣ್ಪನಿ to mock at. –ಪತ್ತ್ನಿ to become blue.

ನೀಲೆ nīle, *s.* One of the monkey chiefs. 2. the planet Saturn. – ಕೋರಿ a dark *or* black fowl.

ನುಂಗ nuṅga, *see* ನುಂಗು.

ನುಂಗಾವುನಿ nuṅgāvuni, *c. v.* (*of* ನುಂಗುನಿ) To get dried, cause to dry.

ನುಂಗು nuṅgu, *s.* A species of mite, tick, which infests cattle.

ನುಂಗುನಿ nuṅguni (ನುಂಗ್), *v. a.* & *n.* To dry up, become dried; *also* ನುಂಗುದುಪೋಪಿನಿ.

ನುಂಗೆಲ್ nuṅgelụ, *s.* Drying. *adj.* Dry, dried. –ಕುಂಟು a dry cloth. –ಮೀನ್ dry fish, salted fish. –ನೆಲ dry ground.

ನುಕುಡುನಿ nukuḍuni, *see* ನುಗುಡುನಿ.

ನುಕ್ಕುನಿ nukkuni (ನುಕ್ಕ್), *v. a.* To bruise; *cf.* ನುರಿಪುನಿ. *v. n.* To decay, rot.

ನುಗ್ದಿ nugụdi, *see* ನಿಗ್ದಿ.

ನುಗ nuga, *s.* A yoke.

ನುಗತೆ nugatè, *see* ನುಗುತೆ.

ನುಗಪಣೆ nugapaṇè, *s.* The jointpiece of a watering machine.

ನುಗಿಪುನಿ **nugipuni** (ನುಗಿ), *v. a.* To fill up, as a pit.

ನುಗಿಯುನಿ **nugiyuni** (ನುಗಿ), *v. n.* To be filled up.

ನುಗುಡುನಿ **nuguḍuni** (ನುಗುಡ್), *v. n.* To labour. 2. to become rich; *cf.* ನುಗುರುನಿ.

ನುಗುತೆ **nugutè**, *s.* A dot over a letter, as in Persian. 2. softness.

ನುಗುಪುನಿ **nugupuni** (ನುಗು), *v. a.* To throng, press. 2. to accumulate. 3. to loosen. 4. to fill up; *cf.* ನುಗಿಪುನಿ.

ನುಗುರುನಿ **nuguruni** (ನುಗುರ್), *v. a.* To loosen, slacken, make loose.

ನುಗ್ಗಿಯುನಿ **nuggiyuni** (ನುಗ್ಗ್), *v. a.* To press. *v. n.* To be filled up.

ನುಗ್ಗು **nuggu**, *adj.* Small, little; *also* ಮುಗ್ಗು.

ನುಗ್ಗೆಲ್ **nuggelu**, *s.* Smallness.

ನುಗ್ರು **nuggru**, *see* ನುಗ್ಗು.

ನುಚ್ಚಿ, ನುಚ್ಚು **nuĉĉi, nuĉĉu**, *see* ನೊಚ್ಚಿ.

ನುಜ್ಜಿ, ನುಜ್ಜು **nujji, nujju**, *s.* A contusion, bruise.

ನುಡಿ **nuḍi**, *s.* A word, speech, saying. —ಕಟ್ಟ an oracle, as uttered by a demon-dancer. ಯೆದುರು— the counter-part of a deed *or* document. ನಡೆ— conduct and speech.

ನುಡಿಪಾವುನಿ **nuḍipāvuni**, *c. v.* (*of* ನುಡಿಪುನಿ) To cause to speak, speak through another. 2. to play on a musical instrument.

ನುಡಿಪಿನಿ **nuḍipini** (ನುಡಿ), *v. a.* To speak, talk.

ನುಡಿಯುನಿ **nuḍiyuni** (ನುಡಿ), *v. n.* To pronounce, utter.

ನುಪ್ಪು **nuppu**, *s.* Boiled rice.

ನುಪ್ಪುನಿ **nuppuni** (ನುಪ್ಪ್), *v. a.* To twist.

ನುಬ್ಬು **nubbu**, *adj.* Mouldy, musty. —ತೊಗರಿ ಸಲಾಯಿ musty split dholl.

ನುರಿಗೆ **nurigè**, *s.* The drum-stick tree, *Hyperanthera moringa.*

ನುರಿತೆಲ್ **nuritelu**, *s.* Bruising. 2. chips.

ನುರಿಪಾವುನಿ **nuripāvuni**, *c. v.* (*of* ನುರಿಪುನಿ) To cause to crush. 2. to press into a hole.

ನುರಿಪುನಿ **nuripuni** (ನುರಿ), *v. a.* To break, powder, granulate, pulverize.

ನುರಿಯುನಿ **nuriyuni** (ನುರಿ), *v. n.* To break, go to pieces. 2. to decay; *also* ನುರಿದ್‌ಪೋಪಿನಿ. ನುರಿದಿ ಹೃದಯ a broken heart.

ನುರುಂಟು **nuruṇṭu**, *see* ಮುರುಂಟು.

ನುರುಂಟುನಿ **nuruṇṭuni**, *see* ಮುರುಂಟುನಿ.

ನುರುಂಪೆ **nurumpè**, *s.* A hole; *cf.* ಗುಂಪೆ. —ತೋಡುನಿ to make a hole.

ನುರುಂಬು **nurumbu**, *s.* Alluvium; wood-dust; iron-rust. [ನಿ.

ನುರುಂಬುನಿ **nurumbuni**, *see* ರುಂಬುನಿ

ನುರುನುರು **nurunuru**, *s.* A cracking noise; *cf.* ನರುಗುರು.

ನುರೆ **nurè**, *s.* Foam, froth, scum. —ಬಂಗುಡೆ a small kind of fish,

—ಕಾರುನಿ to vomit froth. —ರುಂಬುನಿ to foam, froth.

ನುರೆಕಾಯಿ nurekāyi, *s.* The soap-nut, *Sapindus emarginatus.*

ನುರ್ಕ nurka, *adv.* Suddenly.

ನುರ್ಕಲ್ಲ್ nurkallu, *s.* A kind of pebbles found in rice.

ನುರ್ಕುನಿ nurkuni (ನುರ್ಕ್), *v. a.* To press on. 2. to elbow, push, make way.

ನುರ್ಗುನಿ nurguni (ನುರ್ಗ್), *v. n.* To pass over. 2. to sprain. 3. to decay; *also* ನುರ್ಗುದುಪೋಪಿನಿ.

ನುರ್ಗೆ nurgè, *see* ನುರಿಗೆ.

ನುರ್ತಿಂಗೆ nurtiṅge, *s.* A malicious *or* spiteful man.

ನುರ್ತೆಂಗಿ nurteṅgi, *s.* A climbing shrub, *Bryonia scabrella.*

ನುರ್ತೆಲ್ nurtelu, *see* ನುರಿತೆಲ್.

ನುರ್ಪುನಿ, ನುರ್ಪುಡುನಿ nurpuni, nurpuḍuni, *see* ನುರಿಪುನಿ.

ನುರ್ಲುನಿ nurluni (ನುರ್ಲ್), *v. a.* To wind up, fold, shrink.

ನುಲಿ nuli, *s.* A bit, fragment.

ನುಲಿಯುನಿ nuliyuni (ನುಲಿ), *v. n.* To be broken, shattered.

ನುಸುಲು nusulu, *see* ಉಸುಲು.

ನೂಂಗು nūṅgu, *see* ನುಂಗು.

ನೂಕತಾಕ nūkatāka, *s.* Fighting.

ನೂಕುನಿ nūkuni (ನೂಕ್), *v. a.* To thrust, push. 2. to reject.

ನೂಟಾವುನಿ nūṭāvuni (ನೂಟಾ), *v. a.* To show.

ನೂತನ nūtana, *adj.* Fresh, new, recent. *s.* Newness, freshness.

ನೂತ್ರ nūtra, *adj.* All. 2. a hundred.

ನೂದನೆ nūdanè, *num. adj.* The hundredth.

ನೂದು nūdu, *num.* A hundred.

ನೂನತೆ nūnatè, *see* ನ್ಯೂನತೆ.

ನೂಪುನಿ nūpuni (ನೂ), *v. a.* To spin, twist, string.

ನೂಪುರ nūpura, *s.* An ornament of the leg, foot-ring.

ನೂರುನಿ nūruni (ನೂರ್), *v. n.* To creep in, enter with difficulty.

ನೂಲು nūlu, *s.* Thread, yarn. ನಯು— fine thread. ಸಂಣ— thin *or* short thread. —ಪಿಜಿಪುನಿ to spin. —ಸುಂದುನಿ to spool. —ಸುತ್ತುನಿ to twist thread.

ನೂಲೊಡು nūlodu, *s.* A spindle.

ನೃಪೆ nrupe, *s.* A king, sovereign. ನೃಪಾಸನ a royal throne.

ನೃತ್ತ, ನೃತ್ಯ nrutta, nrutya, *s.* A dance; dancing.

ನೆಂಗೆ (-ಎಂಗೆ) neṅgè (-eṅgè), *postp.* Till, until, as long as. ಬಂ— till one comes. ಮಳ್ಪ— till it is done.

ನೆಂಟಸ್ತಿಗೆ neṇṭastigè, *s.* Relationship.

ನೆಂಟೆ neṇṭe, *s.* A relation.

ನೆಂಪು nempu, *see* ನೆನಪು.

ನೆಕ, ನೆಕ್ಕ್ neka, nekku, (*contraction of* ಇಂಚಿಕ್) To *or* for this.

ನೆಕ್ಕರೆ, ನೆಕ್ಕಾರ್ nekkarè, nekkāru, *s.* The plant *Melastoma malabathrica.* ಪಿಲ— a kind of grass.

ನೆಕ್ಕಿ nekki, *s.* Five leaved chaste tree, *Vitex trifolia.* ಕರಿ—*Vitex negundo.* ತುಂಬೆ–, ನೀರ್– *Clerodendrum inerme.* –ತಪ್ಪು its leaves, used by Koragar women for clothing, and by some other castes for certain ceremonies.

ನೆಕ್ಕಿಲ್‌ಪದ್ಪೆ **nekkilupadpè,** *s.* A variety of *Amarantus.*

ನೆಗಡ **negaḍa,** *adv.* Near.

ನೆಗಡಿ, ನೆಗಡೆ **negaḍi, negaḍè,** *s.* Cold in the head, catarrh. –ಪತ್ತುನಿ to catch cold.

ನೆಗತ್ತ್ **negattu,** *s.* Overflowing, running over.

ನೆಗಪುನಿ **negapuni** (ನೆಗ), *v. n.* To overflow, run over. 2. to ooze. 3. to perspire.

ನೆಗರ್ **negaru,** *s.* Loitering, lingering, as a sick person. 2. a sea-animal, the vehicle of Varuṇa. 3. a whirlpool, eddy. –ತೈಪುನಿ to be caught in a current.

ನೆಗರಿಗೆ **negarigè,** *s.* Lingering.

ನೆಗರುನಿ **negaruni** (ನೆಗರ್), *v. n.* To linger, loiter. 2. to procrastinate.

ನೆಗವು **negavu,** *see* ನಿಗವು.

ನೆಗಳ್ **negaḷu,** *s.* An alligator, crocodile. 2. *see* ನೆಗರ್.

ನೆಗಿ **negi,** *see* ನೆಗ್ಗಿ. 2. *see* ಗಿಡ್ಪು.

ನೆಗಿಪುನಿ **negipuni** (ನೆಗ), *v. a.* To leap, jump, spring up. 2. *see* ನಿಗಿಪುನಿ. ನೆಗಿದ್ ಪೊಲ್ಲುನಿ to sew tight.

ನೆಗಿಯುನಿ **negiyuni** (ನೆಗ), *v. n.* To rise, come up.

ನೆಗಿಲ್‌ಮುಳ್ಳು **negilumuḷḷu,** *see* ನೇಗಿಲ್‌ಮುಳ್ಳು.

ನೆಗ್ಗಿ **neggi,** *s.* Shyness; shame,

ನೆಗ್ಗಿ, ನೆಗ್ಗ್ಯ **neggi, neggya,** *adj.* Full, complete.

ನೆಟ್ಟ್ **neṭṭu,** (*abbr. of* ಉಂಡೆಟ್) In this, herein.

ನೆಟ್ಟಗೆ **neṭṭagè,** *adj.* Straight, upright. *adv.* Straightly; properly.

ನೆಟ್ಟಳಿಗೆ **neṭṭaḷigè,** *s.* The ground-floor of a storied house.

ನೆಟ್ಟಿ **neṭṭi,** *see* ನೆತ್ತಿ.

ನೆಟ್ಟು **neṭṭu,** *s.* A deep breath.

ನೆಟ್ಟೆಲ್ **neṭṭelu,** *see* ನಿಟ್ಟೆಲ್.

ನೆಡಂಕ್ **neḍaṅku,** *see* ಮೊಡಂಕ್.

ನೆಡಂಕುನಿ **neḍaṅkuni,** *see* ನಿಡಂಕುನಿ.

ನೆಡಿ **neḍi,** *adj.* Long; *cf.* ನಿಡಿ. –ಕೋಲು a long stick, pole.

ನೆಡಿಪಿನಿ, ನೆಡಿಪುನಿ **neḍipini, neḍipuni,** *see* ನಿಡಿಯುನಿ. 2. *see* ನಡ್ಪಿನಿ.

ನೆಡಿಲ್ **neḍilu,** *s.* A kind of bush.

ನೆಡ್ದ್ **neḍḍu** (*abbr. of* ಇಂದೆಡ್ದ್), From this, herefrom.

ನೆಡ್ಪುನಿ **neḍpuni,** *see* ನಡ್ಪಿನಿ.

ನೆಣೆ **neṇè,** *see* ನಿಣ. 2. *see* ನಿಣೆ.

ನೆತ್ತ **netta,** (*abbr. of* ಇಂಚೆತ್ತ್) Of this.

ನೆತ್ತಿ **netti,** *s.* The forehead; the crown of the head. 2. the front, vertex. 3. a whirlpool. 4. cracking the fingers. 5. the tender stalk of fragrant screw-pine. ನಡು– top, vertex. –ತೆಪ್ಪುನಿ to crack the fingers. –ಪುಪ್ಪುನಿ to make the fingers crack.

ನೆತ್ತಿಕಂಡೆ nettikaṇḍè, *s.* Dysentery.

ನೆತ್ತೆ nette, *see* ಮೆತ್ತೆ; *cf.* ನೆತ್ತಿ.

ನೆತ್ತೆರ್ netterụ, *s.* Blood. ಕರ್ನೆತ್ತೆರ clotted blood. —ದ ಕೊಳಲ, —ದ ಪೋಕುಳಿ a stream of blood. —ಸಂಬಂಧ consanguinity. —ಅರಿಯುನಿ to bleed. —ನುಪ್ಪುನಿ to shed blood. —ಜಪ್ಪುನಿ blood to run out. —ತಮಿಲುನಿ to menstruate. —ಪೋಪಿನಿ to have bloody stools.

ನೆದ್ಪ nedụpa, *see* ನಿದ್ಪ.

ನೆದೆ nedè, *see* ನಿದ್ರೆ.

ನೆನಪು nenapu, *see* ನೆನೆಪು.

ನೆನವರಿಕೆ nenavarike, *see* ನೆನೆವರಿಗೆ.

ನೆನೆತೊಣುನಿ, ನೆನೆಪಿನಿ nenetoṇuni, nenepini, *see* ನೆನೆಪುನಿ.

ನೆನೆಪು nenepu, *s.* Thought, intention. 2. remembrance, recollection, memory. ಯೆಂಕ್ ನೆನೆಪು ಇಜ್ಜಿ I do not remember. —ಪುಟ್ಟಾವುನಿ to remind, bring to recollection. —ಮಳ್ಪುನಿ to remember, recollect.

ನೆನೆಪುನಿ nenepuni (ನೆನೆ), *v. n.* To think, imagine, mind, reflect, intend. 2. to recollect, remember.

ನೆನೆವರಿಗೆ nenevarigè, *s.* Remembrance, recollection; recognition.

ನೆಪ nepa, *see* ನೆನೆಪು.

ನೆಯಮ neyama, *see* ನಿಯಮ. 2. *see* ನೇಮ.

ನೆಯಿ neyi, *s.* Clarified butter, ghee; grease, fat.

ನೆಯಿಗಾರೆ neyigāre, *s.* A weaver.

ನೆಯಿಗೆ neyigè, *s.* Weaving. 2. texture.

ನೆಯಿಪಿನಿ neyipini (ನೆಯ್), *v. a.* To weave, plait, braid.

ನೆಯಿಪಂತಿ nayipanti, *s.* A smooth kind of grass, soft straw.

ನೆಯಿಮುಲಿ neyimuli, *s.* Soft grass.

ನೆಯಿಮೆ neyimè, *adj.* Fine. —ಕುಂಟು a fine cloth.

ನೆಯಿಲ್ neyilụ, *s.* A peacock.

ನೆಯಿಲುನಿ neyiluni (ನೆಯಿ), *v. n*, To fade, as a bunch of cocoanut. 2. *see* ನೇಲುನಿ.

ನೆಯಿಸ್ರೆ neyisrè, *s.* A cloth used for cleaning an oilmill.

ನೆಯುನಿ neyuni (ನೆಯ್), *v. a.* To weave, as a spider.

ನೆಯ್ಯ neyya, *see* ನೈಯ.

ನೆಯ್ಯೊಳಿ neyyoḷi, *s.* A tender palm-leaf.

ನೆರ nera, *see* ನಿರೆ.

ನೆರಡೆ neraḍè, *s.* Abuse, bad language; nickname. —ದ ಪಾತೆರ abusive language.

ನೆರಪು nerapu, *see* ನಿರಪು.

ನೆರವಣಿಗೆ neravaṇigè, *see* ಮೆರಣಿಗೆ.

ನೆರವು neravu, *s.* The privities of the male sex.

ನೆರಿ neri, *s.* A fold *or* gather in clothes, wrinkle, crease; *also* ನೆರಿಗೆ. —ದಾಂತಿನಾಯೆ an upright man. —ಪತ್ತುನಿ to gather into folds. —ಮಳ್ಪುನಿ to fold; to rumple.

ನೆರಿಯುನಿ, ನೆರೆವುನಿ neriyuni, nerevuni (ನೆರಿ, ನೆರೆ), *v. n.* To be full. 2. to assemble. 3. to be attached. 4. to be *in coitu.*

ನೆರೆ nerè, *see* ನಿರೆ.

ನೆರೆಲ್, ನೆರೆಳ್ nerelu, nerelu, *see* [ನಿರೆಲ್.

ನೆರ್ತ nerta, *adj.* Straight. 2. true. *adv.* Straightly. 2. truly.

ನೆರ್ತಮ nertama, *s.* Straight ploughing.

ನೆರ್ತ್ರುನಿ nertruni, *see* ನೆರ್ಪಿನಿ.

ನೆರ್ಪಡೆ, ನೆರ್ಪಣಿ, ನೆರ್ಪಾಟ nerpadè, nerpani, nerpāta, *see* ನೆರಡೆ.

ನೆರ್ಪಾವುನಿ nerpāvuni, *c.v.* (*of* ನೆರ್ಪಿನಿ) To cause to abuse.

ನೆರ್ಪಿನಿ nerpini (ನೆರ್), *v. a.* To abuse, revile. 2. to give nicknames.

ನೆರ್ಪೆಲೆ nerpele, *s.* An abuser, [reviler.

ನೆರ್ಬೆ nerbè, *see* ನಿರ್ಬೆ.

ನೆರ್ಲುನಿ nerluni, *see* ನರಕುನಿ.

ನೆರ್ವೆ nervè, *see* ನೇಮೆ.

ನೆಲ್ಂಟುನಿ nelunṭuni, *see* ತೆಳಿಂಟುನಿ.

ನೆಲ nela, *s.* Earth, soil, floor, ground. 2. bottom. —ಗಟ್ಟ the foundation of a building. —ಗಡೆ, *see* ನಿಲಗಡೆ. —ದಿರಾಟ an earthquake; *cf.* ಭೂಕಂಪ. —ಮಾಳಿಗೆ a ground floor, cellar, —ದಾಂತಿ bottomless. —ಕೈದವುನಿ to curse, im- precate. —ಪಾರಾವುನಿ to bury.

ನೆಲಕಂಚಿ nelakanči, *s.* The plant *Naregamia alata.*

ನೆಲಕಡಲೆ nelakadalè, *s.* The ground-nut, *Arachis hypogæa.*

ನೆಲಕರ nelakara, *s.* Fertility of land.

ನೆಲಕಲೆ nelakalè, *s.* A mark on the ground. 2. *see* ನಿಲಗಡೆ.

ನೆಲಕಾರ್ nelakāru, *see* ನಿಲಕಾರ್.

ನೆಲಕಾಲೆ nelakālé, *s.* Palsy affecting on one side of the body.

ನೆಲಕುಂಬುಡ nelakumbuda, *s.* The vegetable *Batatas paniculata.*

ನೆಲಗಡೆ nelagadè, *see* ನಿಲಗಡೆ.

ನೆಲನಾಲಿಗೆ nelanāligè, *s.* A medicinal plant.

ನೆಲನೆಕ್ಕರೆ nelanekkarè, *see* ನೆಕ್ಕರೆ.

ನೆಲನೆಲ್ಲಿ nelanelli, *s.* *Phyllanthus maderaspatensis, P. niruri.*

ನೆಲಪಾಲೆ nelapālé, *s.* A kind of creeper.

ನೆಲಬಸಲೆ nelabasalè, *s.* The spreading hogweed, *Bœrhavia diffusa.*

ನೆಲಬೇವು nelabēvu, *s.* A sort of [gentian.

ನೆಲಮುಂಡ nelamunda, *s.* A kind of fern, *Curculigo orchioides.*

ನೆಲಮುಚ್ಚಿಲ್ nelamuččilu, *s.* A kind of medicinal plant.

ನೆಲಸಂಪಯಿ nelasampayi, *s.* *Kampferia rotunda.*

ನೆಲೆ nelè, *see* ನಿಲೆ.

ನೆಲೆಂಚಿ neleñči, *s.* Dysentery. —ಪೋಪಿನಿ to have dysentery.

ನೆಲೆಂಟುನಿ nelenṭuni, *see* ತೆಳಿಂಟುನಿ.

ನೆಲೆಕಲೆ nelekalè, *see* ನೆಲಕಲೆ.

ನೆಲ್ಪುಡುನಿ nelpuduni, *c. v.* (*of* ನೆಲ್ಪುನಿ) To hang.

ನೆಲ್ಪುನಿ nelpuni (ನೆಲ್), *v. n.* To be hung, suspended.

ನೆಲ್ಲಿ nelli, *s.* The emblic myrobalan, country gooseberry, *Phylanthus emblica.* ನೆಲ್ಲಿಂಟೆ pickle made of emblic myrobalan. —ಚಟ್ಟ its dried fruit.

ನೆಲ್ಲಿರ್ತಾಯೆ nellirtāye, *s.* A demon so called.

ನೆವನ nevana, *s.* Pretence, pretext, trick. –ಪಣ್ಪುನಿ to make excuses; to pretend.

ನೆವಲ, ನೆವಳ nevala, nevaḷa, *see* ನೇವಳ.

ನೆವೇದ್ಯ nevēdya, *see* ನೈವೇದ್ಯ.

ನೆಸ್ರ್ nesụrụ, *adj.* Morning. –ದೊಂಬು the morning sun.

ನೆಸರ್, ನೆಸಲ್ nesarụ, nesalụ, *s.* Seasoning. –ಕೊರ್ಪಿನಿ, –ಪಾಡುನಿ to season.

ನೆಸಲ್ nesalụ, *s.* The forehead; *cf.* ನೆಸರ್. –ಬರವು fate, fortune.

ನೆಸಲೆ, ನೆಸಳೆ nesalè, nesaḷè, *s.* A silly fellow. 2. a large, broad, frying pan; *also* ಬಿಸಲೆ.

ನೆಸಿಪುನಿ nesipuni (ನೆಸಿ), *v. a.* To press down, make tight.

ನೇಂದ್ರಬಾರೆ nēndrabārè, *s.* The Malabar plantain.

ನೇಗ nēga, *s.* Beauty, nicety. *adj.* Beautiful, nice, fair.

ನೇಗಿಲ್ nēgilụ, *s.* Small caltrops, *Tribulus lanuginosus.* –ಮುಳ್ಳು its thorn.

ನೇಜಿ nēji, *s.* A nursling, young plant of rice, *etc.* –ದ ಕಂಡ, –ದ ಕಳ a nursery. –ನಡ್ಪಿನಿ to transplant. –ಪಾಡುನಿ to sow in a nursery.

ನೇಟಿ nēṭi, *see* ನೆತ್ತಿ.

ನೇಣ, ನೇಣು nēṇa, nēṇu, *s.* A cord, rope; a bow-string.

ನೇತಾಟ nētāṭa, *s.* Hanging; swinging. 2. entanglement.

ನೇತಾಡುನಿ nētāḍuni (ನೇತಾಡ್), *v. n.* To be pendent, to hang, swing; to depend. 2. to be involved in difficulties.

ನೇತ್ರ nētra, *s.* An eye. –ರೋಗ ophthalmia.

ನೇತ್ರಮುಕ್ಕುಳಿ nētramukkuḷi, *s.* A demon so called.

ನೇತ್ರಾವತಿ nētrāvati, *s.* A river so called.

ನೇದ್ಯ ṇēdya, *see* ನೈವೇದ್ಯ.

ನೇನು nēnu, *see* ನೇಣು.

ನೇಪಾಳಬೇರ್ nēpāḷabērụ, *s.* The root of swallow-wort, *Asclepias asthmatica.*

ನೇಪಿನಿ nēpini, *see* ನೆಯಿಪಿನಿ.

ನೇಮ nēma, *s.* The annual festival of a demon. 2. *see* ನಿಯಮ. –ದೆಜ್ಜಿದ್ a priest seized with a demon.

ನೇಮಕ nēmaka, *s.* Regulation, rule, law; determination, choice. 3. appointment, nomination to a post. –ಮಳ್ಪುನಿ to appoint, fix.

ನೇಮಿಸುನಿ nēmisuni (ನೇಮಿಸ್), *v. a.* To determine. 2. to appoint.

ನೇಯ nēya, *see* ನೈಯ.

ನೇಯಿ nēyi, *see* ನೆಯಿ.

ನೇಯಿಗೆ nēyigè, *see* ನೆಯಿಗೆ.

ನೇಯುನಿ nēyuni, *see* ನೆಯಿಪಿನಿ.

ನೇಯಿಸ್ರೆ nēyisrè, *see* ನೆಯಿಸ್ರೆ.

ನೇರಿ nēri, *see* ಏರಿ.

ನೇರಿಂಕೆನಟ್ಟಿ, ನೇರಿಂಕೆಪುಗೆರೆ nēriṅkenaṭṭi, nēriṅkepugerè, *s.* A variety of country tobacco.

ನೇರೆ nērè, *s.* Straightness. 2. justice, truth. 3. agreement. *adj.* Straight; just, true; even, like; thin, delicate.

ನೇರೆಂಗಿ nēreṅgi, The name of a village. —ನಟ್ಟಿ, *see* ನೇರಿಂಕೆನಟ್ಟಿ.

ನೇರೊಲ್, ನೇರೊಳು nērolụ, nēroḷu, *s.* The newel fruit, *Syzyg jambolanum.* ಜಂಬು— the rose apple, *Jambosa vulgaris.*

ನೇರ್ಡೆ nērḍè, *adv.* Early in the morning.

ನೇರ್ಮೆ nērmè, *adj.* Fine, thin, delicate. —ದಾಯೆ a delicate man.

ನೇಲ, ನೇಲಂಗ್ nēla, nēlaṅgụ, *s.* A hanging rope. 2. a square piece of white cloth tied over a cradle, to divert *or* amuse the baby in it. —ಪಾಡುನಿ to hang a rope for drying clothes upon it; *fig.* to make frequent visits.

ನೇಲಂಗಿ nēlaṅgi, *see under* ನೇಲ್ಯ.

ನೇಲಾವುನಿ nēlāvuni, *c. v.* (*of* ನೇಲುನಿ) To hang, suspend.

ನೇಲಿ nēli, *see* ನೇಲ್ಯ.

ನೇಲಿಕೆ nēlikè, *s.* Hanging, swinging.

ನೇಲುನಿ nēluni (ನೇಲ್), *v. n.* To hang, be suspended; to swing, vibrate. 2. to hang on, stick.

ನೇಲೆ nēlè, *see* ನೇಲ.

ನೇಲ್ಯ nēlya, *adj.* Great, large, extensive. —ಅಂಗಿ, ನೇಲಂಗಿ a long coat. —ಮ್ಮೆ uncle, father's elder brother, husband of mother's elder sister. —ಪ್ಪೆ aunt, wife of father's elder brother, mother's elder sister.

ನೇವರಿಪುನಿ nēvaripuni (ನೇವರಿ), *v.a.* To fondle, caress.

ನೇವಳ nēvaḷa, *s.* A silver *or* gold girdle worn round the loins.

ನೇವುರಿ nēvuri, *s.* A kind of cake.

ನೇಸ nēsa, *s.* Asthma.

ನೇಳೆ nēḷè, *see* ನೇಲ.

ನೈ nei, *see* ನೆಯಿ.

ನೈಕೂಲಿ neikūli, *s.* The tree *Wrightia tinctoria.* 2. *see* ಪುಚ್ಚೆಕೂಲಿ.

ನೈದಿಲೆ neidilè, *s.* The water-lily.

ನೈಪುಣ್ಯ neipuṇya, *s.* Cleverness, skill.

ನೈಯ neiya, *adj.* Soft. —ದೊಂಬು the evening sun.

ನೈವೇದ್ಯ neivēdya, *s.* Food presented to an idol, an oblation to a deity.

ನೈಸರಂಗ್ neisaraṅgụ, *see* ನಾಯಿಸೊಣಂಗ್.

ನೊಂಣ, ನೊಂಣಗೆ noṇṇa, noṇṇagè, *adj.* Soft, nice.

ನೊಕ್ಕುನಿ nokkuni (ನೊಕ್ಕ್), *v. a.* To stroll about.

ನೊಕ್ಕೆ nokkè, *s.* Sweepings, rubbish. 2. the name of a woman. —ನೊರಡ್ all rubbish.

ನೊಕ್ಕೆಲೆ nokkele, *s.* A trifling *or* destitute man.

ನೊಗ noga, *see* ನುಗ.

ನೊಚ್ಚ nočča, *see* ನಚ್ಚ. 2. *see* ನಿಂಗಲಿ.

ನೊಚ್ಚಿ nočči, *s.* Rice cooked with ghee, cocoanut, *etc.* 2. *see* ನೆಕ್ಕಿ. –ಇರೆ a leaf used for various ceremonies.

ನೊಚ್ಚು, ನೊಚ್ಚೆ nočču, noččè, *adj.* Minute. 2. light. 3. beneath notice, paltry.

ನೊಣ್ಣ noṇṇa, *see* ನೊಂಣ.

ನೊಯಿರ್ noyirụ, *s.* Whiting, lady-fish; *cf.* ಕಾಣಿ.

ನೊರಡ್ noraḍụ, *s.* Rubbish.

ನೊರೆ norè, *see* ನುರೆ.

ನೊಲ್ಲು nollu, *s.* A kind of water-snake.

ನೋಂಪು nōmpu, *s.* Any meritorious act of devotion. 2. a festival, especially the one observed on the 14th day of the 6th lunar month in honor of Ananta.

ನೋಂಬು nōmbu, *s.* Fasting among the Mohammedans; fast, penance. ನೊಂಬುನಿ to fast.

ನೋಕಟೆ, ನೋಕೊಟೆ nōkaṭè, nōkoṭè, *s.* The name of a tree.

ನೋಕು, ನೋಗು nōku, nōgu, *adj.* Small; inferior. 2. bad.

ನೋಟ nōṭa, *s.* Sight, vision, view. 2. aim. –ಗಾರೆ a fortune-teller; one who hits the mark. –ನಿಮಿತ್ಯ fortune-telling; guess, surmise. –ಸಲೆ aiming. –ದೀಪಿನಿ, ಪತ್ತುನಿ to aim; to hit. –ಪಾಡುನಿ to watch, look after.

ನೋಟಿಸ್ nōtice, *s.* Notice, intimation.

ನೋಟು nōṭu, *s.* A bill of exchange; a promissory note; a currency note.

ನೋಡದ್ರುನಿ, ನೋಡಾವುನಿ nōḍadruni, nōḍāvuni, *v. a.* To point at, show. 2. to rake up, stir.

ನೋಡಿಲ್ nōḍilụ, *s.* ನಡಿಲ್.

ನೋಣೆ nōṇè, *s.* Saliva, spittle.

ನೋಪಾವುನಿ nōpāvuni, *c. v.* (*of* ನೋಪುನಿ) To cause to beat *or* strike.

ನೋಪಿನಿ, ನೋಪುನಿ nōpini, nōpuni (ನೊ), *v. a.* To beat, strike, flog, knock. 2. *see* ನೋಯಿಪಿನಿ.

ನೋಪುನಾಯೆ, ನೋಪೆಲೆ nōpunāye, nōpele, *s.* A beater, striker.

ನೋಯಿ nōyi, *see* ನೋಹಿ.

ನೋಯಿಪಿನಿ nōyipini (ನೋಯ್), *v. n.* To ache, pain.

ನೋರು nōru, *s.* Freight, fare, hire. 2. *see* ನೊಯಿರ್. –ಬಾಡಯಿ fixed hire.

ನೋರೆ nōrè, *s.* A kind of water-plant. 2. a kind of tare. –ದೆಪ್ಪುನಿ to root out the tares.

ನೋರೆ nōrè, *s.* A kind of crane.

ನೋಲಿ nōli, *see* ಇಸೋಲಿ.

ನೋಲಿಸರ nōlisara, *s.* A species of aloe, *Aloe litoralis*.

ನೋಲು nōlu, *see* ನೋರು.

ನೋಲೆ nōlè, *adj.* Very sour.

ನೋವು nōvu, *s.* Pain, ache. 2. distress.

ನೋಹಿ nōhi, *s.* A meritorious act *or* vow.

ನೌ nou, *adj.* Naval.

ನೌಂಟಾವುನಿ nouṇṭāvuni, *c. v.* (*of* ನೌಂಟುನಿ) To cause to pinch.

ನೌಂಟು nouṇṭu, *s.* Pinching.

ನೌಂಟುನಿ nouṇṭuni (ನೌಂಟಿ), *v. a.* To pinch.

ನೌಂತು nōuntu, *s.* Squeezing, pinching, crushing. 2. chewing. –ತಿನ್ಪಿನಿ to masticate, ruminate. –ಬಿಡಿಪಿನಿ to loosen slowly.

ನೌಂತುನಿ nountuni (ನೌಂತಿ), *v. a.* To chew.

ನೌಂಪು noumpu, *see* ನೋಂಪು.

ನೌಂಪುನಿ noumpuni (ನೌಂ), *v. a.* To chew. 2. to entangle.

ನೌಕ nouka, *s.* A ship.

ನೌಕರ, ನೌಕಾರೆ noukare, noukāre, *s.* A servant. 2. a lascar.

ನೌಜಿ nouji, *s.* A spear, lance.

ನೌಟ್ nouṭu *see* ನೌಂಟು.

ನೌಟಾಂಗ್ nouṭāṅgu, *s.* A weight equal to about three Rupees *or* one-eighth of a seer.

ನೌಟು nouṭu, *see* ನೌಂಟು.

ನೌಡಿ nouḍi, *s.* Kubera's nine gems; *also* ನವನಿಧಿ. –ಮಾಣಿಕ್ಯ the imaginary gem on the head of a serpent.

ನೌಮಿ noumi, *see* ನವಮಿ.

ನೌಲುನಿ nouluni (ನೌಲ್), *v. n,* To itch, be irritated. 2. to be distressed. *v. a.* To covet, desire eagerly.

ನೌಳು nouḷu, *s.* Longing, hope; *cf.* ವನೌಳು.

ನ್ಯಾಂಡೆ nyāṇḍè, *s.* One-sixth of a seer.

ನ್ಯಾಡ್ nyāḍu, *s.* Pain, aching.

ನ್ಯಾಯ nyāya, *s.* Justice, equity, propriety, fitness. 2. law. 3. logic. 4. morality. 5. quarrel. *adj.* Right, just, proper, reasonable. –ಗಾರೆ a logician; a lawyer; a quarrelsome man. –ತೀರಿಕೆ, –ತೀರ್ಪು a judgment, decision, verdict. –ಶಾಸ್ತ್ರ logic; a work on law. –ಸ್ಥಾನ a court of justice, judgment seat. –ತರಿಪುನಿ, –ಮುಳ್ಪುನಿ to quarrel, fight, dispute.

ನ್ಯಾಯಾಧಿಪತಿ nyāyādhipati, *s.* A judge, tribunal.

ನ್ಯಾವಳ nyāvaḷa, *see* ನೇವಳ.

ನ್ಯಾಸ nyāsa, *s.* Abandonment. 2. a deposit, pledge. 3. mental appropriation, accompanied with certain prayers and gesticulations.

ನ್ಯೂನ nyūna, *adj.* Blamable. 2. less, deficient, defective.

ನ್ಯೂನತೆ nyūnatè, *s.* Defect, deficiency; omission.

ಪ P

ಪ pa, The thirty-fourth letter of the alphabet.

ಪಂಕ್ paṅkụ, *s.* The hair about the privities.

ಪಂಕ paṅka, *s.* A fan, pankah. 2. mud, mire. 3. evil, sin.

ಪಂಕಜ paṅkaja, *s.* The lotus.

ಪಂಕಾಸ್ pankāsụ *s.* Sprinkling.

ಪಂಕಿಲ paṅkila, *adj.* Muddy.

ಪಂಕ್ತಿ paṅkti, *see* ಪಂತಿ.

ಪಂಖ paṅkha, *see* ಪಂಕ.

ಪಂಗ paṅga, *see* ಪಂಙ.

ಪಂಗಡ paṅgaḍa, *adj.* Distinct, apart. *s.* A division, part, portion. 2. a group.

ಪಂಗಡಿಪುನಿ paṅgaḍipuni (ಪಂಗಡ), *v. a.* To straddle; to place apart.

ಪಂಗಿದನ paṅgidana, *see* ಪಾಂಗಿದನ.

ಪಂಗು paṅgu, *adj.* Lame, cripple. *s.* A cripple.

ಪಂಗುಲ paṅgula, *s.* A horse of a silvery white colour. 2. a cripple.

ಪಂಗುಲಿ paṅguli, *adj.* Soft, slippery. 2. *see* ಚಂಗುಲಿ. —ಪಾತೆರ a soft word.

ಪಂಚ pañca, *s.* A rice field. 2. a breed, sort, kind. ಯೆಡ್ಡೆ— a good breed. ಕಿರು— a small kind.

ಪಂಚ pañca, *adj.* Five, consisting of five. —ಕ five, made of five; a pack of five, as of paper.

ಪಂಚಕಜ್ಜಯ pañcakajjaya, *s.* An aggregate of five articles: dholl, gingely seed, jaggory, cocoanut and cardamoms, as an offering to Gaṇēša.

ಪಂಚಕುರ್ವೆ pañčakurvé, *s.* A wicker basket *or* box.

ಪಂಚಗಜ್ಜೆಯಿ pañcagajjeyi, *see* ಪಂಚಕಜ್ಜಯ.

ಪಂಚಗವ್ಯ pañcagavya, *s.* Five articles derived from the cow: *viz.*, milk, curds, ghee, urine, and dung, mixed together and drunk as a means of purification.

ಪಂಚತಂತ್ರ pañcatantra, *s.* A popular book of fables in five chapters, containing stories illustrative of five qualities necessary to kings and great men.

ಪಂಚತತ್ವ pañčatatva, *see* ಪಂಚಭೂತ.

ಪಂಚನಿ pañčani, *s.* A variegated colour.

ಪಂಚನೆಕ್ಕರೆ, ಪಂಚನೆಕ್ರಿ pañčanekkarè, pañčanekri, *s.* A nettle creeper.

ಪಂಚಪಕೀರೆ pañčapakīre, *s.* A pauper, vagabond.

ಪಂಚಪತ್ರೆ pañčapatre, *s.* The wormwood plant.

ಪಂಚಪಾಂಡವೆರ್ pañčapāṇḍaverụ, *s.* The five Pāṇḍu princes.

ಪಂಚಪಾತಕ pāñčapātaka, *see* ಪಂಚಮಹಾಪಾತಕ.

ಪಂಚಪಾತ್ರೆ pañčapātrè, *s.* A small metal tumbler, cup.

ಪಂಚಪಾಪಿ pañčapāpi, *see under* ಪಂಚಮಹಾಪಾತಕ.

ಪಂಚಪ್ರಾಣ pañčaprāṇa, *s.* The five vital airs in the body.

ಪಂಚಬಲಿ pañčabali, *s.* An offering to the five elements.

ಪಂಚಭೂತ pañčabhūta, *s.* The five elements: earth, air, fire, water, and ether.

ಪಂಚಮ pañčama, *adj.* Fifth.

ಪಂಚಮಹಾಪಾತಕ pañčamahāpātaka, *s.* The five most heinous sins: murdering a Brāhman, stealing gold, drinking spirits, seducing the wife of one's spiritual preceptor, and associating with a person who has committed such sins. ಪಂಚಮಹಾಪಾತಕೆ, ಪಂಚಪಾಪಿ one guilty of these sins.

ಪಂಚಮಾಲ್ pañčamāl̤u, *s.* The local market of a town.

ಪಂಚಮಿ pañčami, *s.* The fifth day of a lunar fortnight.

ಪಂಚಮುಖೆ pañčamukhe, *s.* Śiva with five faces.

ಪಂಚಮೂಲ pañčamūla, *s.* A medicine of five ingredients.

ಪಂಚರಂಗ pañčaraṅga, *see* ಪಂಚವರ್ಣ.

ಪಂಚರತ್ನ pañčaratna, *s.* A poem of five verses. 2. five principal gems: diamond, emerald, pearl, ruby, and sapphire.

ಪಂಚರಿಯೆರ್ pañčariyeru̥, *see* ಪಂಚೇಂದ್ರಿಯ.

ಪಂಚರೆಂಗಿ pañčarèṅgi, *see* ಪಚ್ಚೆರೆಂಗಿ.

ಪಂಚಲೋಹ pañčalōha, *s.* The five chief metals: gold, silver, copper, iron, and lead; *or* copper, brass, tin, led, and iron. 2. a metallic composition, bell-metal.

ಪಂಚವರ್ಗ pañčavarga, *s.* The five classes of letters in the alphabet from ಕ to ಮ.

ಪಂಚವರ್ಣ pañčavarṇa, *s.* Five colours: white, black, red, yellow, and green.

ಪಂಚವಳಿಬಚ್ಚಿರೆ pañčavaḷibaččirè, *see* ಪಂಚೊಳಿ.

ಪಂಚವಾದ್ಯ pañčavādya, *s.* Five principal musical instruments: the lute, cymbals, drum, trumpet, and a kind of hautboy.

ಪಂಚಾಂಗ pañčāṅga, *s.* An almanac. 2. the foundation of a building.

ಪಂಚಾತಿಗೆ pañčātigè, *see* ಪಂಚಾಯಿತಿ.

ಪಂಚಾತ್ಮ pañčātma, *s.* The conscience.

ಪಂಚಾಪಾಡ್ pañčāpāḍu̥, *s.* Dispersion, scattering. 2. waste, ruin.

ಪಂಚಾಮೃತ pañčāmru̥ta, *s.* The aggregate of five articles, used in bathing an idol: milk, curds, butter, honey, and water.

ಪಂಚಾಯಿತಿ, ಪಂಚಾಯಿತಿಗೆ pañčāyiti, pañčāyitigè, *s.* Arbitration. 2. an assembly composed of five *or* more persons to settle a matter by arbitration. ಪಂ

ಚಾಯಿತೆರ್ arbitrators. —ಮಳ್ಪುನಿ to settle by arbitration.

ಪಂಚಾಲಿ pańćāli, *see* ಪಂಚಾಳಿ.

ಪಂಚಾಲಿಬಚ್ಚಿರೆ pańćālibaccirè, *see* ಪಂಚೊಳಿ.

ಪಂಚಾಲೆರ್ pańćāleru, *see* ಪಂಚಾಳೆರ್.

ಪಂಚಾಶತಿ pańćāšati, *s.* Pentecost.

ಪಂಚಾಳಿ pańćāḷi, *s.* A braggart, talkative man.

ಪಂಚಾಳೆರ್ pańćāḷeru, *s.* The five classes of artificers: goldsmiths, blacksmiths, carpenters, braziers, and masons. 2. the name of a warrior tribe.

ಪಂಚೇಂದ್ರಿಯ pańćēndriya, *s.* The five organs of sense: the eye, ear, nose, tongue, and skin.

ಪಂಚೇರ್ pańćēru, *s.* One-eighth of a maund, 3½ pounds.

ಪಂಚೈವೆರ್ pańćeiveru, *see* ಪಂಚಾಯಿತೆರ್ *under* ಪಂಚಾಯಿತಿ.

ಪಂಚೊಳಿ pańćoḷi, *s.* A very pungent kind of betel leaf.

ಪಂಜ pańja, *s.* The hand with fingers extended. 2. a representation of the same carried in procession at the Moharam, supposed to represent the hand of Āli. 3. the tuft of a bird.

ಪಂಜ pańja, *s.* Scarcity. 2. famine.

ಪಂಜರ pańjara, *s.* A cage. 2. a skeleton.

ಪಂಜಾರ pańjāra, *s.* A fritter. 2. a kind of amulet.

ಪಂಜಿ pańji, *s.* A pig, hog. 2. a torch. —ಬಿದರ್ a male bamboo, *Bambusa stricta.* —ತುಂಡು, *see* ಪಂಜಿ. —ಮುಂಡೆಯಿ, *see* ದಡ್ಡೊಲಿ. ಐಯಿ—; ಕಣೆ—, ಮುಳ್ಳು— a porcupine. ಕಡಲ— a porpoise. ಕೈ— a hand-lamp. ಪಿಲ— the country pig.

ಪಂಜು pańju, *s.* A torch.

ಪಂಜುರ್ಲಿ pańjurli, *s.* The name of a demon.

ಪಂಜೆ pańjè, *s.* A kind of towel

ಪಂಟ್ paṇṭu, *see* ಪವನ್.

ಪಂಡ್ದ್‌ಕೊರ್ಪಿನಿ, ಪಂಡ್‌ಕೊರ್ಪಿನಿ paṇḍudu korpini, paṇḍukorpini, *see under* ಪಣ್ಪುನಿ.

ಪಂಡ paṇḍa, *s.* Discernment, learning, wisdom, understanding. 2. articles *or* things in general.

ಪಂಡಿತೆ paṇḍite, *s.* A learned man. 2. a teacher. 3. a doctor, physician.

ಪಂಡಿಲಿ paṇḍili, *s.* A musk-rat.

ಪಂಡೊಣುನಿ paṇḍoṇuni, *see* ಪಣ್ಪುನಿ.

ಪಂಣವು paṇṇavu (*abbr. of* ಪಂಡಿನವು), *see under* ಪಣ್ಪುನಿ. 2. *see* ಪಣವು.

ಪಂಣಿ paṇṇi, *see* ಪಂನಿ.

ಪಂಣೆ paṇṇè, *s.* A bunch of plantains.

ಪಂಣೊಳಿಗೆ paṇṇoḷigè, *s.* A basket *or* wooden trough for drawing water.

ಪಂಣ್ಯ paṇṇya, *s.* A comb.

ಪಂತ್ pantu, *s.* A trap.

ಪಂತ panta, *s.* A purpose, vow,

resolution. 2. a bet *or* wager. ಪೌರುಷತ್ವದ– a manly resolution. –ಉಪ್ಪುನಿ to be resolute. –ಪಾ ಡುನಿ to bet. –ಸೋಣುನಿ to lose a wager. ಪಂತೊಗು resolutely, positively, purposely.

ಪಂತಿ **panti,** *s.* Grass. 2. a dauble nail.

ಪಂತಿರೆಂಗಿ **pantireṅgi,** *see* ಪಟ್ಟಿರೆಂಗಿ.

ಪಂತುರ **pantura,** *see* ಪಂಜರ.

ಪಂತೆ **pantè,** *s.* A line, row, range. –ಕುಳ್ಳುನಿ to sit in a line. ಮ ರ– the succeeding line of guests at a meal.

ಪಂತೋಜಿ **pantōji,** *s.* A schoolmaster, teacher.

ಪಂತ್ಯೆ **pantyè,** *s.* A small lamp. ಲಕ್ಷ– mud lamps used at an illumination (ಲಕ್ಷದೀಪ).

ಪಂಥ **pantha,** *see* ಪಂತ.

ಪಂದಡೆ **pandaḍè,** *s.* Fructification, productiveness of a tree. *adj.* Dense.

ಪಂದಾವುನಿ **pandāvuni,** *c. v.* (*of* ಪಂ ದುನಿ) To rock, swing, move, wave, shake, oscillate.

ಪಂದಿ **pandi,** *adj.* Reserved, cautious. –ನರಮಾನಿ a reserved man.

ಪಂದಿಲಿ **pandili,** *s.* A kind of mouse; *also* ಕಿಚ್ಚಿಲಿ; *cf.* ಪಂದಿಲಿ.

ಪಂದುನಿ **panduni** (ಪಂದ್), *v. n.* To shake, be loose, wave, move, be agitated, oscillate, vibrate.

ಪಂದ್ರಾಲಿ **pandrāli,** *s.* A very talkative man.

ಪಂಧುರಾಳಿರಾಗ **pndhurāḷirāga,** *s.* The name of a tune.

ಪಂಣ **panna,** *see* ಪಂಣಿ.

ಪಂನಂಬರ, ಪಂನಂಬುರ **pannambara, pannambura,** *s.* Ambergris. 2. affectation, ado. 3. mystery, mystification. –ಮಳ್ಪುನಿ to make a mystery of anything.

ಪಂನಗ **pannaga,** *s.* A serpent.

ಪಂನಿ **panni,** *s.* Bragging, boasting. 2. egotism, self-conceit. 3. *see* ಅತಿಗ. –ಬೆಂನಿ profession and practice, exhortation and example; advice, admonition. –ಬೆಂನಿ ಕೇಣುಜೆ he cares neither for exhortation nor for example. –ದಕೋಟಿ a braggart, an idler. –ಕಡ್ಪುನಿ, –ಕೊಚ್ಚುನಿ, –ಪಾತೆ ರುನಿ, –ಬಿರ್ಕುನಿ to boast, brag.

ಪಂನೀರ್ **pannīru,** *s.* Rose water. –ತಳಿಪುನಿ to sprinkle rose water.

ಪಂನೀರ **pannīra,** *adj.* Rose-scented. –ಗಂಧ rose-cented sandal wood.

ಪಂಣೆ **pannè,** *see* ಪಂಜೆ.

ಪಂಣೆ **pannè,** *s.* The cheek. 2. tonsure at the forehead in the form of a comb. 3. *see* ಪಲ್ಲೆ. *adj.* Small. 2. worn-out. –ಕೊ ಟ್ಟು –ಕೊಟ್ರ a worn-out spade. –ತತ್ರ a parasol. –ಜಾರುನಿ the cheeks to fall in. –ತಿರ್ದುನಿ to ornament the beard *or* the hair about the face with tweezers. –ಮಿರೆಯುನಿ to become proud.

ಪಂಬದೆ **pambade,** *s.* A devildancer belonging to a low class of Šudrās.

ಪಂಬು **pambu,** *see* ಪಣ್ಪುನಿ.

ಪಂಮ pamma, *s.* Fraud, trick.

ಪಂಕುನಿ parṅkuni (ಪಂಕ್), *v. a.* To pluck out, scratch with nails.

ಪಂಗೊಟ್ಟೆ parṅgoṭṭè, *s.* A cashew-nut.

ಪಂಚುನಿ parṅcuni (ಪಂಚ್), *v. a.* To trouble.

ಪಂಚೆಲೆ parṅcele, *s.* A troublesome man.

ಪಂದ್ parndu, *s.* Ripeness. 2. a ripe fruit. 3. ripe plantains. *adj.* Ripe. 2. gray.

ಪಂದಾವುನಿ parndāvuni, *c. v.* (*of* ಪಂದುನಿ) To ripen. 2. to persuade.

ಪಂದುನಿ parnduni (ಪಂದ್), *v. n.* To be ripe, mature. 2. the hair to turn gray.

ಪಂಬುನಿ parmbuni, *see* ಪಮ್ಬುನಿ.

ಪಕ್ಡಿ pakuḍi, *s.* A long, narrow turban.

ಪಕಡ್ pakaḍu, *s.* Seizure; fetching.

ಪಕತ್ pakatu, *adv.* Only, merely, simply. 2. entirely, wholly. —ಸುಳ್ಳು a daring lie.

ಪಕಪಕ pakapaka, *adv.* Quickly; much, excessively. —ಆಗ್ಪುನಿ to palpitate, as the heart; to pant; to leap, hop.

ಪಕರ pakara, *s.* Sap, juice. 2. use, profit. ಬಾಲಾ ಪಕರ ಇಜ್ಜಿ it is good for nothing.

ಪಕಲ, ಪಕಳ pakala, pakaḷa, *s.* Coral. ಸಕಲ ಕಲ್ತ್‌ದ್ ಪಕಲ ನಿಂಗಿಯೆ *lit.* having learned everything, he swallowed a coral (bead); he is a jack of all trades and master of none.

ಪಕಾಲಿ pakāli, *s.* A leathern water bag carried on a bullock, *etc.* 2. one who supplies water in such a manner; a water carrier.

ಪಕಾಸ್ pakāsu, *see* ಪಕ್ಕಾಸ್.

ಪಕೀರೆ pakīre, *s.* A fakir, mendicant.

ಪಕುರು pakuru, *s.* A rascal.

ಪಕ್ಕ, ಪಕ್ಕನೆ pakka, pakkanè, *adv.* Suddenly, unexpectedly. 2. immediately.

ಪಕ್ಕ pakka, *adj.* Foreign, of another country. 2. *see* ಪಕ್ಕಾ. 3. *see* ಪಕ್ಷ. 4. *see* ಪಕ್ಷಿ. —ದಾಯೆ a foreigner.

ಪಕ್ಕಲೆ pakkale, *s.* A glutton. 2. a small net. 3. *see* ಪಗೆಲೆ; *cf.* ಬಕ್ಕಲೆ.

ಪಕ್ಕಸ್ pakkasu, *s.* A rafter.

ಪಕ್ಕಾ pakkā, *adj.* Ripe, mature. 2. fit, proper. 3. substantial, solid. 4. exceeding, perfect, complete. —ಕಳು a consummate falsehood. —ಕಳುವೆ a downright rogue. —ಕೆಲಸ a clever stroke of business; excellent workmanship. —ನರಮಾನಿ a clever man. —ಪಾತೆರ a proper word; an apt reply. —ಶಿಪಾಯಿ a valiant soldier.

ಪಕ್ಕಾಲಿ pakkāli, *see* ಪಕಾಲಿ.

ಪಕ್ಕಿ pakki, *s.* A bird. ಕೇಂಕಂಣ— a kind of partridge. —ತೊರಕೆ, —ಮೀನ್ kinds of fish. —ದಾಯೆ a fortune-teller. —ಪಲಾಯಿ a lintel, headpiece of a door frame. —ರೋಗ croup, bronchitis, peculiar to children. —ಸಲೆ a hawk.

ಪಕ್ಕು **pakku**, *see* ಪಕ್ವ.

ಪಕ್ಕೆ **pakke**, *s.* A rogue, rascal, cunning fellow. 2. a clever man.

ಪಕ್ಕೆ **pakkė**, *s.* The side; *cf.* ಪಕ್ಷ. 2. a banner. —ಎಲು a rib.

ಪಕ್ತಾ **paktā**, *see* ಪಕಡ.

ಪಕ್ವ **pakva**, *adj.* Mature, ripe, fit, suitable, proper; cooked. —ಆಪಿನಿ to ripen.

ಪಗ್ಡಿ **pagụḍi**, *see* ಪಕಡಿ.

ಪಗ್ಮಲ್ **pagụmalụ**, *see* ತಗ್ಮಳ್.

ಪಗ್ರ್ **pagụrụ**, *s.* Cleverness, skill. 2. trickery, cunning. 3. *see* ಪಗರ್.

ಪಗಡೆ **pagaḍė**, *s.* An ace, one in games, dice. —ಗೊಬ್ಬುನಿ to play at dice.

ಪಗತೆ **pagatė**, *s.* Exchange, return; revenge. —ಗ್ in exchange, instead of. —ಗ್ ಪಗತೆ like for like.

ಪಗದಿ **pagadi**, *s.* Tribute, tax, custom.

ಪಗಪುನಿ **pagapuni** (ಪಗ), *v. a.* To change, exchange, substitute.

ಪಗರ್ **pagarụ**, *s.* Time, turn. 2. making signs with the hand. 3. hire, rent, wages.

ಪಗರ **pagara**, *s.* Exchange. 2. trickery.

ಪಗರಾಟ **pagarāṭa**, *s.* Changing, exchanging.

ಪಗರಿ **pagari**, *s.* An arrow, dart.

ಪಗರುನಿ **pagaruni** (ಪಗರ್), *v. n.* To be infected. 2. to shift, change place. ರೋಗ— to take the infection.

ಪಗರ್ಚೆ **pagarćė**, *see* ಪಗತೆ.

ಪಗಲ್ **pagalụ**, *see* ಪಗೆಲ್.

ಪಗಲ, ಪಗಳ **pagala, pagaḷa**, *see* ಪಕಲ.

ಪಗಲೆ **pagale**, *see* ಪಗೆಲೆ.

ಪಗಿ **pagi**, *s.* A rent, splint, split.

ಪಗಿಡಿ **pagiḍi**, *see* ಪಕಡಿ.

ಪಗಿಪುನಿ **pagipuni** (ಪಗಿ), *v. a.* To rend, split.

ಪಗಿಪೆಲ್ **pagipelụ**, *see* ಪಗ್ತೆಲ್.

ಪಗಿಯುನಿ **pagiyuni** (ಪಗಿ), *v. n.* To split, rend; to crumble, fall in pieces; to give way.

ಪಗೆ **pagė**, *s.* Hatred, enmity, malice, hostility. —ನಾಯಿ a foe, adversary. —ಪಗರಿ antipathy, spite. —ಪತ್ತುನಿ to entertain hatred. —ಮಳ್ಪುನಿ to hate. —ಬೂಟುನಿ, —ಸಾದಿಯುನಿ to seek revenge.

ಪಗೆಲ್ **pagelụ**, *s.* The day-time. —ಬತ್ತಿ a blue light.

ಪಗೆಲೆ **pagelė**, *s.* A kind of harmless snake.

ಪಗ್ಗು **paggu**, *s.* The first Tuḷu month; the sign *Aries* in the zodiac.

ಪಗ್ತೆಲ್ **pagtelụ**, *s.* A rent, slit.

ಪಚಕ್ಕ **pacakka**, *s.* Plash, splash. —ಬೂರುನಿ to fall with a splashing noise.

ಪಚನ **paćana**, *s.* Cooking. 2. digestion. —ಆಪಿನಿ to be digested. —ಮಳ್ಪುನಿ to dress food; to digest.

ಪಚಪಚ **paćapaća**, *s.* Licking. 2. a clacking noise. *adj.* Little, scanty. —ನೀರ್ scanty water. —ತಿಪ್ಪುನಿ to lick, eat with a clacking noise.

ಪಚಾರ pačāra, *s.* Punishment, castigation. 2. a fine, penalty. —ಮಳ್ಪುನಿ to fine; to reverence.

ಪಚಿಲೆ pačilè, *s.* A kind of oyster.

ಪಚೀತಿ pačīti, *s.* Plight, predicament; trouble, distress. 2. disgrace.

ಪಚ್ಚ paččа, *s.* An emerald. *adj.* Green. 2. fresh. —ಪಗೆಲ್ broad daylight.

ಪಚ್ಚಂಗ್ರಿ paččangri, *see* ಪಚ್ಚಿರೆಂಗಿ.

ಪಚ್ಚಂದಿಗೆ paččandigè, *see* ಪಂಚಾಯಿತಿ.

ಪಚ್ಚಕರ್ಪೂರ paččakarpūra, *s.* A superior kind of camphor.

ಪಚ್ಚಟ್ paččaṭu, *see* ಪಚೀತಿ.

ಪಚ್ಚಡಿ paččaḍi, *s.* Minced vegetables, salad.

ಪಚ್ಚಡೆ paččaḍè, *s.* A silk cloth worn by males; a shawl.

ಪಚ್ಚನ paččana, *see* ಪಚನ.

ಪಚ್ಚನೆಕ್ಕಿರೆ paččanekkirè, *see* ಪಚ್ಚಿರೆಂಗಿ.

ಪಚ್ಚಲ paččala, *s.* The buttocks.

ಪಚ್ಚಾರಿಗೆ paččārigè, *see* ಪಚಾರ.

ಪಚ್ಚಿರ್, ಪಚ್ಚಿರೆ paččiru, paččirè, *s.* The pulp enclosing the seed of a jackfruit. ಕಂಣಿ— a small layer of it.

ಪಚ್ಚಿರೆಂಗಿ paččirengi, *see* ಪಚ್ಚಿರೆಂಗಿ.

ಪಚ್ಚಿಲ paččila, *s.* A medicinal plant.

ಪಚ್ಚೀಸ್ paččīsu, *s.* A kind of game with dice *or* cowries.

ಪಚ್ಚೆ paččè, *s.* Greenness, freshness. *adj.* Green; fresh; *cf.* ಪಚ್ಚ. —ಬಂಣ green colour.

ಪಚ್ಚೆಕೊರಲ್ paččekoralu, *s.* A kind of fragrant flower.

ಪಚ್ಚೆರೆಂಗಿ paččerengi, *s.* A kind of nettle, *Tragia involucrata.*

ಪಚ್ಚ್ಯ paččya, *see* ಪಚ್ಚ.

ಪಜಕ್ pajaku, *s.* A bag made of [mat.

ಪಜಕಾಯಿ pajakāyi, *see* ಪಜಕಾಯಿ. 2. *see* ಅದ್ಯಬಾರೆ.

ಪಜಿ paji, *adj.* Wet, damp. 2. full of sap. 3. green, fresh. —ಕೊಡಿ green grass, tender shoot, sprout. —ಪಜಿ quite raw, green. —ಮರ a tree *or* timber in a fresh state. —ಮರಿ a green whip-snake. —ರೆ a green leaf. —ಏರುನಿ to revive, as a faded plant. —ಪತ್ತುನಿ, —ಪುಟ್ಟುನಿ to grow green, become stout.

ಪಜಿರ್ pajiru, *s.* Grass.

ಪಜಿರೆ pajirè, (*abbrev. of* ಪಜಿ ಇರೆ) A green *or* fresh leaf.

ಪಜೀತಿ pajīti, *see* ಪಚೀತಿ.

ಪಜೆ pajè, *s.* A mat. ಇರ್ಪಳೆ— a mat plaited with double leaves. ಒರ್ಪಳೆ— a mat plaited with single leaves. ತಕ್ಕಣ— a very small mat. —ಪಜಕ್ಕ a worn-out mat. ಮಂಚವುದಾರೆದ— a fine mat. —ಪತ್ತುನಿ to be confined to bed from sickness; to be very sick.

ಪಜೆಮಡಿಪೆಲೆ pajemaḍipele, *s.* A large kind of bee.

ಪಜ್ಜಿ pajji, *see* ಪಜಿ.

ಪಜ್ಜೆ pajje, *see* ಅಜ್ಜೆ.

ಪಟ್ paṭụ, *adj.* Sharp, skilful, clever, strong. —ಕಡಿ a dodge.

ಪಟ pata, *see* ಪಠ.

ಪಟಂಗ paṭaṅga, *see* ಪಟ್ಟಂಗ.

ಪಟಕ್ಕ paṭakka, *see* ಪಟಾಲ.

ಪಟಣೆ, ಪಟನೆ paṭaṇè, paṭanè, *s.* Reading, perusal, recitation.

ಪಟಪಟನೆ paṭapaṭanè, *s.* A flapping *or* rattling sound.

ಪಟಲ paṭala, *see* ಪಟ್ಲ.

ಪಟಲಾಮ್ paṭalāmụ, *s.* A regiment, army, battalion. —ದಾಯಿ a soldier, sepoy.

ಪಟಲ್ಕೋಡು paṭalkōḍu, *see* ಪಟ್ಲಕಾಯಿ.

ಪಟವಸುತ್ತು paṭavasuttu, *s.* A kind of drum.

ಪಟಾಕಿ paṭāki, *s.* A squib, cracker. —ಬುಡ್ಪಿನಿ to let off a cracker, to crack up; to tell fibs.

ಪಟಾಕಿಲ paṭākila, *see* ಪಟ್ಲಕಾಯಿ.

ಪಟಾಟೆ paṭāṭè, *see* ಬಟಾಟೆ.

ಪಟಾಣಿ paṭāṇi, *s.* A class of Mohammedans. 2. *see* ಬಟಾಣಿ.

ಪಟಾನ್‌ದಾಯೆ paṭānụdāye, *s.* A fisherman.

ಪಟಾಲ paṭāla, *adv.* Smartly, sharply. —ಹಾಕುನಿ to strike sharply.

ಪಟಾಲಂ paṭālam, *see* ಪಟಲಾಮ್.

ಪಟಾಲಿ paṭāli, *see* ಪಟಾಳಿ.

ಪಟಾವು paṭāvu, *see* ಪಟ್ಟಂಗ.

ಪಟಾಳಿ paṭāḷi, *s.* A buffalo with wide-spread horns. 2. a palanquin bearer.

ಪಟಿ paṭi, *s.* A rafter. ತಾರಿದ— a palmyra rafter.

ಪಟಿಂಗ paṭiṅga, *adj.* Roguish, knavish. —ತನ roguery, knavery; prodigality.

ಪಟಿಂಗೆ paṭiṅge, *s.* A rogue, rascal, knave, scoundrel. 2. a prodigal.

ಪಟಿಕಾರ paṭikāra, *s.* Alum.

ಪಟಿಕೆ, ಪಟಿಗೆ paṭikè, paṭigè, *s.* Urine.

ಪಟಿಲ್‌ಕಾಯಿ paṭilụkāyi, *see* ಪಟ್ಲ [ಕಾಯಿ.

ಪಟೇಲ್, ಪಟೇಲೆ paṭēlụ, paṭēle, *s.* The headman of a village.

ಪಟ್ಟ್ paṭṭụ, *s.* A nest. 2. abundance. —ಗ ಕೈಪಾಡುನಿ *lit.* to thrust hand into a nest; to divulge a secret. ಮುಳ್ಳುಪ— abounding in thorns. —ಕಟ್ಟುನಿ to build a nest. —ಗಿದ್ಯುನಿ a nest to be pulled down; to be dispersed; a secret to be divulged.

ಪಟ್ಟ paṭṭa, *s.* A metal plate with astrological inscriptions, fastened on the forehead of a Brahman, to avert the consequences of having been born under an unlucky star. 2. crowning, anointing, installation, ordination. 3. a throne, office, rank. 4. title *or* appointment of office. 5. a deed of lease *or* gift, a grant. —ದ ಮುದ್ರೆ a royal seal. ಪಟ್ಟಾಭಿಷೇಕ anointing a king, *or* priest, coronation, ordination. —ಸಾಲೆ. *see* ಪಡಸಲೆ. —ಆಳುನಿ

to reign, rule. —ಕಟ್ಟುನಿ, —ಕೊಡಿಪಿನಿ to crown; to ordain.

ಪಟ್ಟ paṭṭa, *adv.* Suddenly. 2. *see* ಪಟ್ಟ. —ಪರಕೆ a vow suddenly made when in trouble. —ಪುಡಾವುನಿ to break suddenly.

ಪಟ್ಟಂಙ, ಪಟ್ಟಂಗ paṭṭanña, paṭṭanga, Bragging, boasting. —ಪಾತೆರುನಿ, —ಪಾಕುನಿ to talk idly and falsely.

ಪಟ್ಟಂಗೆ paṭṭange, *s.* A braggart.

ಪಟ್ಟಂಬರ paṭṭambara, *s.* A robe of state.

ಪಟ್ಟಡಿ paṭṭaḍi, *s.* A kind of necklace.

ಪಟ್ಟಡೆ paṭṭaḍe, *see* ಪಟ್ಟಡೆ.

ಪಟ್ಟಣ paṭṭaṇa, *s.* A city, town.

ಪಟ್ಟದಾನೆ paṭṭadāne, *s.* A royal elephant.

ಪಟ್ಟದೇವಿ paṭṭadēvi, *s.* A queen.

ಪಟ್ಟನೆ paṭṭane, *see* ಪಟ್ಟ.

ಪಟ್ಟಬಂಧ paṭṭabandha, *s.* Coronation.

ಪಟ್ಟಯ paṭṭaya, *see* ಪಟ್ಟ.

ಪಟ್ಟವಾಳಿ paṭṭavāḷi, *s.* A striped silk cloth.

ಪಟ್ಟವು paṭṭavu, *see* ಪಟ್ಟ.

ಪಟ್ಟಾಂಗ paṭṭānga, *see* ಪಟ್ಟಂಗ.

ಪಟ್ಟಾಣಿ paṭṭāṇi, *see* ಬಟಾಣಿ.

ಪಟ್ಟಾಣ್ಯೆ paṭṭāṇye, *see* ಪಟಾನ್‌ದಾಯಿ.

ಪಟ್ಟಾಭಿಷೇಕ paṭṭābhishēka, *see under* ಪಟ್ಟ.

ಪಟ್ಟಾಯಿಪಿಲಿ paṭṭāyipili, *s.* A royal tiger.

ಪಟ್ಟಾರಿ paṭṭāri, *s.* Ruin. —ಪೋಪಿನಿ to go to ruin.

ಪಟ್ಟಾಲ paṭṭāla, *see* ಪಟಾಲ.

ಪಟ್ಟಾವು paṭṭāvu, *see* ಪಟ್ಟಂಗ.

ಪಟ್ಟಾವುನಿ paṭṭāvuni, *c. v.* (*of* ಪಟ್ಟುನಿ) To cause to be distributed, *etc.*

ಪಟ್ಟಿ paṭṭi, *s.* A list, catalogue, voucher. 2. a note, short letter. 3. the fastenings of a box, *etc.*; *cf.* ಪಟ್ಟಿ. 4. a strip of cloth, collar of a coat. 5. a lathe. 6. a kind of tonsure. 7. a bundle of betel leaves; *also* ಪಟ್ಟಬಜ್ಜೆರೆ. —ಕಾಜಿ a kind of glass bangles. —ಕಟ್ಟುನಿ to apply a bandage *or* ligature. —ಕೊರ್ಪಿನಿ to appoint. —ಗೀಸುನಿ to shave the head in stripes. —ಬರೆಪಿನಿ to write a list, note, *etc.*

ಪಟ್ಟಿಂಗ, ಪಟ್ಟಿಂಗೆ paṭṭinga, paṭṭinge, *see* ಪಟಿಂಗ.

ಪಟ್ಟಿಗೆ paṭṭige, *see* ಪಟಿಕೆ.

ಪಟ್ಟಿಮುರು paṭṭimuru, *s.* A kind of earring.

ಪಟ್ಟು paṭṭu, *see* ಪಟ್ಟೆ.

ಪಟ್ಟುನಿ paṭṭuni (ಪಟ್ಟಿ), *v. a.* To divide, distribute, apportion.

ಪಟ್ಟೆ paṭṭe, *s.* A strip, stripe. 2. silk. 3. a document specifying a grant of land, *etc.*; *cf.* ಪಟ್ಟ. 4. a slip *or* strip of a palm tree. 5. a piece of cloth; a tape. —ಕಂಜಿ a silk border. —ಗಾರೆ a silk merchant; a dealer in silk. —ನೂಲು raw silk, silk thread. —ಶೀರೆ a female's silk garment. ಕರಿಯ— a black stripe. ಬಾರೆ— a black *or* yellow coloured cloth.

ಪಟ್ಟೊಣುನಿ paṭṭoṇuni, *refl. v.* (*of* ಪಟ್ಟುನಿ) To share, divide, *etc.*

ಪಟ್ಟ್ಯೆ paṭṭyè, *see* ಪಟ್ಟಿ. 2. *see* ಪಟ್ಟಿ.

ಪಟ್ಣ paṭna, *see* ಪಟ್ಟಣ.

ಪಟ್ಲಕಾಯಿ, ಪಟ್ಲಕೋಡು paṭlakāyi, paṭlakōḍu, *s.* The snake-gourd, *Trichosanthes anguina.*

ಪಠ paṭha, *s.* A picture, drawing. 2. a boy's kite. *adv.* Much. —ಪತ್ತುನಿ to fear much. —ಪಾರಾವುನಿ to let fly a kite.

ಪಡ್ಚ, ಪಡ್ಚಿ paḍụča, paḍụči, *see* ಪಟ್ಟ.

ಪಡ್ಪ್, ಪಡ್ಪು paḍụpụ, paḍụpu, *see* ಪಣ್ಪು.

ಪಡ್ಪೆ paḍụpe, *see* ಪಡಪೆ.

ಪಡ paḍa, *adj.* Not sufficiently sloping. 2. placing *or* laying. —ಮಾಡ್ a flat roof. —ಬೂರುನಿ to fall *or* lie at length.

ಪಡ paḍa, *s.* A boat.

ಪಡಂಗ paḍanga, *see* ಪಾಡಂಗ.

ಪಡಂಬು paḍambu, *s.* A rough canvas cloth.

ಪಡಂಬೊಳಿ paḍamboḷi, *s.* A liar. 2. *see* ದಡ್ಡೊಲಿ.

ಪಡಚ paḍača, *see* ಪಟ್ಟ.

ಪಡಪಡ paḍapaḍa, *see* ಪಟಪಟ.

ಪಡಪುನಿ paḍapuni, *see* ಪಡೆರುನಿ. 2. *see* ಪಡೆಪಿನಿ. 3. *see* ಬಡವುನಿ.

ಪಡಪೆ paḍapè, *s.* A whore; a whoremonger.

ಪಡಪೆರದ್ paḍaperadụ, *s.* A kind of grass.

ಪಡಪೋಸ್ paḍapōsụ, *adj.* Superficial, shallow, not profound. —ದಾಯೆ a flatterer.

ಪಡಪ್ಪೆ paḍappè, *see* ಪಡಪೆ.

ಪಡಯ paḍaya, *adv.* One upon another. —ಬೂರುನಿ to fall one upon another.

ಪಡರಿ paḍari (ಪದಿಅರಿ), *see under* ಪದಿ.

ಪಡರುನಿ paḍaruni (ಪಸರ್), *v. n.* To creep.

ಪಡವು paḍavu, *s.* A vessel. 2. *see* ಪಡಾವು.

ಪಡಸ್ paḍasụ, *see* ಪೊಡಸ್.

ಪಡಸಾಲೆ paḍasālè, *s.* A veranda, reception hall.

ಪಡಾಯಿ paḍāyi, *s.* Trouble. 2. *see* ಪದ್ದಾಯಿ.

ಪಡಾವು paḍāvu, *s.* An imputation, charge.

ಪಡಿ paḍi, *s.* A daily allowance of food, extra pay to servants when travelling. 2. alms in kind. 3. a small weight. 4. a thrashing frame; *also* ಪಡಿ ಮುಂಚವು. 5. a door *or* shutter made of slips of bamboos tied together. —ಅರಿ rice for charity. —ಪುರೆ a building over a gateway, a porter's lodge. —ಕಟ್ಟುನಿ to be reduced. —ಕೊರ್ಪಿನಿ, —ಅಪ್ಪುನಿ to pay allowance to labourers, *etc.*; to distribute alms. —ಟ ದರ್ಪುನಿ to thrash.

ಪಡಿಕೆ paḍikè, *s.* Wickedness, corruption, depravity; *also* —ತನ. *adj.* Bad, corrupt.

ಪಡಿಕೆಂತಿ paḍikenti, *adj.* Bad, wicked, corrupt.

ಪಡಿಕೊಂಡಾಯೆ paḍikondāye, *s.* The name of a demon.

ಪಡಿಚ, ಪಡಿಚಿ paḍiča, paḍiči, *see* ಪಡ್ಚ.

ಪಡಿಚಾರೆ, ಪಡಿಚಾರಕೆ paḍičāre, paḍičārake, *s.* A peon, attendant.

ಪಡಿತ paḍita, *s.* A stripe, streak. 2. a wale, mark of a whip, *etc.*, as on a bullock.

ಪಡಿಪುನಿ paḍipuni (ಪಡಿ), *v. a.* To learn. 2. to plunge. 3. to swell. 4. *see* ಪಡೆಪಿನಿ. ಪಾಠ– to learn a lesson, exercise.

ಪಡಿಬಾಟ್ಲು paḍibāṭlu, *s.* Straits, difficulty, trouble.

ಪಡಿಲ್ paḍilu, *s.* Waste land. *adj.* Waste, barren, unfruitful, fallow. 2. fallen in ruins.

ಪಡು paḍu, *adj.* Pure. 2. *see* ಪಡ್ಡಯಿ. –ಕಲಿ pure palm wine.

ಪಡುಂಬು paḍumbu, *see* ಪೊಡುಂಬು.

ಪಡುಪು paḍupu, *see* ಪಡ್ಪು.

ಪಡೆ paḍè, *s.* A multitude, mob, rabble. 2. an army. –ತಲವಿ the general of an army. –ನಾಯಿ a stray dog, *abus.* –ಕೂಡಾವುನಿ to raise an army. –ತಡೆಯುನಿ an army to halt.

ಪಡೆಂಗಿ paḍeṅgi, *adj.* Old. –ಯೆರ್ಮೆ a very old she-buffalo.

ಪಡೆತಲೆ paḍetalè, *s.* The helix *or* border of the ear.

ಪಡೆನಾಳಿ paḍenāḷi, *s.* Leanness. –ಕಟ್ಟುನಿ to become lean, *or* weary.

ಪಡೆಪಾವುನಿ paḍepāvuni, *c. v.* (*of* ಪಡೆಯುನಿ) To cause, occasion. 2. to inflict. ದುಃಖ– to inflict pain, cause sorrow. ಸಂತೋಷ– to make glad.

ಪಡೆಪಿನಿ paḍepini (ಪಡೆ), *v. a.* To get, attain, acquire, obtain. 2. to possess, have. 3. to beget, bear, bring forth.

ಪಡೆಯುನಿ, ಪಡೆವುನಿ paḍeyuni, paḍevuni (ಪಡೆ), *v. n.* To suffer, feel, experience, enjoy. ದುಃಖ– to suffer grief. ಸಂತೋಷ– to enjoy pleasure.

ಪಡ್ಕಣತಾಯೆ paḍkaṇatāye, *see* ಪಡಿಕೊಂದಾಯೆ.

ಪಡ್ಚ paḍča, *s.* Settlement, arrangement. 2. determination, disposing. 3. clearance, consumption. –ಆಪಿನಿ to be settled *or* disposed of. –ಮಳ್ಪುನಿ to settle; to dispose.

ಪಡ್ಡಣೆ paḍḍaṇè, *adj.* Sloping, flat.

ಪಡ್ಡಯಿ, ಪಡ್ಡಾಯಿ paḍḍayi, paḍḍāyi, *s.* The west.

ಪಡ್ಯ, ಪಡ್ಡ್ಯ paḍya, paḍḍya, *s.* A spittoon, especially an earthen one.

ಪಡ್ತ paḍta, *see* ಪಡಿತ.

ಪಡ್ಪು paḍpu, *s.* A plain. 2. waste ground.

ಪಡ್ಪೆ paḍpè, *see* ಪದಪೆ.

ಪಡ್ಪೊಸಿ, ಪಡ್ಪೊಳಿ paḍposi, paḍpoḷi, *see* ಫಡ್ಪೋಸ್.

ಪಡ್ಯೆಲೆ paḍyele, *s.* An honorific title among the Jains.

ಪಣ paṇa, *s.* Senselessness.

ಪಣಕೆ paṇakè, *s.* Pairing together with a rope, as cattle.

ಪಣಜ paṇaja, *s.* A kind of grass.

ಪಣತೂಕ panatūka, *s.* The weight of a gold fanam.

ಪಣವು, ಪಣಾವು panavu, panāvu, *s.* A quarter rupee. 2. money in general. 3. wealth, riches in specie.

ಪಣಿ pani, *s.* Dew, fog, mist, snow. 2. *see* ಫಣಿ. –ಕಡಿಯುನಿ to be moist. –ಜಪ್ಪುನಿ dew to fall.

ಪಣಿತ panita, *s.* Praise. *adj.* Praiseworthy. –ಮಳ್ಪುನಿ to praise, eulogise.

ಪಣಿಪುನಿ panipuni (ಪಣಿ), *v. a.* To give a shape. *v. n.* To drizzle. ಕರ– to shape a vessel.

ಪಣಿಯಾರ paniyāra, *see* ಪನಿಯಾರ.

ಪಣೆ pane, *s.* The forked stem of a water-lift; *also* ಪಣೆಕುತ್ತಿ, ಪಣೆಮರ.

ಪಣೆ pane *adj.* Proper, due. *adv.* Duly. –ತೂಕ due weight.

ಪಣೆಕಾಯಿ panekāyi, *s.* The fruit of palmyra.

ಪಣೆಳ್ panelu, *s.* A kind of tree.

ಪಣೊರು panoru, *s.* A ploughshare.

ಪಣೊಲಿ panoli, *s.* A kind of palmyra tree. 2. a kind of umbrella made of palmyra leaves.

ಪಣ್ಣೆ panne, *see* ಪಂಣೆ.

ಪಣ್ಪಾವುನಿ panpāvuni, *c. v.* (*of* ಪಣ್ಪುನಿ) To cause to say, let say, inform.

ಪಣ್ಪಿನಿ panpini (ಪಣ್), *v. a.* To say, tell, inform, narrate, relate, recite. 2. to teach, instruct. ಪದ– to recite a verse, sing a song. ಪಂಡದ್‌ಕೊರ್ಪಿನಿ to teach, advise, instigate; to backbite. ಪಂಡಿನವು, ಪಂಣಾವು what was said. ಪಂಡೊಂಬುನಿ to talk to one's self; to address, represent, announce. ಪಂಡದ್‌ಕಡಪುಡುನಿ to send word.

ಪಣ್ಯೆ panye, *see* ಪಂಣೆ.

ಪತ್ patu, *see* ಪದಿ.

ಪತ pata, *s.* Maintenance, support, alimony. 2. *see* ಪಥ. –ನಡಪುಡುನಿ to maintain.

ಪತಂಗ patanga, *s.* A bird; a winged moth.

ಪತಂಗೆಲ್ patangelu, *s.* Harmony, fitness. 2. adherence. –ಆಪಿನಿ to fit.

ಪತಂಜಲಿ patañjali, *s.* The name of a celebrated teacher of the Yōga philosophy.

ಪತನ patana, *adj.* Falling, liable to fall.

ಪತಾಕಿ patāki, *s.* A standard, flag.

ಪತಾಯಿ patāyi, *s.* A large chest, coffer.

ಪತಿ pati, *s.* A husband, master, owner. 2. a match, equal. –ಪ್ರಕಾಧರ್ಮ faithfulness to a husband. –ಸೊರತೆ, –ವ್ರತೆ a virtuous wife. ದಂ– husband and wife.

ಪತಿ pati, *s.* Similarity, equality; *cf.* ಪ್ರತಿ. –ಗ್ ಪತಿ equal to.

ಪತಿತ patita, *adj.* Fallen, overthrown, defeated. 3. wicked.

ಪತಿತೆ patite, *s.* A sinner. 2. an outcast, a heretic.

ಪತಿನಿ patini, *see* ಪತ್ನಿ.

ಪತೆಂಗಲ **pateṅgala,** *see* ಪತಂಗೆಲ್.

ಪತೆಮಾರ್ **patemāru,** *see* ಪತ್ತೆಮಾರಿ.

ಪತ್ತ್ **pattu,** *num.* Ten. *s.* A nail, peg, pin, particularly used for a plough.

ಪತ್ತ **patta,** *adv.* Quite, fully, entirely wholly, effectually; at all. –ಆಜುನಿ to be quite dry. –ಬೇಪಾವುನಿ to boil fully. –ಲಾ ಇಜ್ಜಿ there is nothing at all.

ಪತ್ತಂಗೆಲ್ **pattaṅgelu,** *s.* Tightness; *cf.* ಪತಂಗೆಲ್.

ಪತ್ತನಜೆ, ಪತ್ತನದ್ಯ, ಪತ್ತನಾಜಿ **pattanaje, pattanadya, pattanāji,** *s.* The tenth day of the Tuḷu month Bēšya. 2. a feast celebrated at Dharmasthala.

ಪತ್ತನೆ **pattanè,** *adj.* Tenth.

ಪತ್ತಯ, ಪತ್ತಾಯ, ಪತ್ತಾಯಿ **pattaya, pattāya, pattāyi,** *see* ಪತಾಯಿ.

ಪತ್ತಾ **pattā,** *see* ಪತ್ತ.

ಪತ್ತಾವಳೆ, ಪತ್ತಾಳಿ **pattāvaḷè, pattāḷi,** *s.* Bribery; *cf.* ಪತ್ರಾವಲಿ.

ಪತ್ತಾವುನಿ **pattāvuni,** *c.v.* (*of* ಪತ್ತುನಿ) To cause to join, stick, attach, adhere, affix. 2. to cause to hold, seize, catch.

ಪತ್ತಾಸ್ **pattāsu,** *s.* A kind of sweetmeat. 2. *see* ಪತಾಯಿ.

ಪತ್ತಿ **patti,** *s.* A trace.

ಪತ್ತಿಗೆ **pattigè,** *see* ಪತ್ತೆ.

ಪತ್ತುನಿ **pattuni** (ಪತ್ತ್), *v. a.* To hold, catch. *v. n.* To adhere, stick, be joined, united. ಗೆರಂತಿ– to contract a habit. ಮರ್ಲ್– to turn mad.

ಪತ್ತೆ, **pattè,** *s.* A patch. 2. trace, discovery. 3. *see* ಪತ್ಯ. –ದೀಪಿನಿ to patch.

ಪತ್ತೆಮಾರಿ **pattemāri,** *s.* A pattemar, sailing vessel with one mast.

ಪತ್ತೊಂಜಿ **pattoñji,** *num.* Eleven.

ಪತ್ತೊಂಜನೆ **pattoñjenè,** *adj.* Eleventh.

ಪತ್ತೊಲಿ **pattoli,** *see* ಪತ್ತಾವಳೆ.

ಪತ್ನಿ **patni,** *s.* A wife.

ಪತ್ಯ **patya,** *s.* Regimen, diet. 2. *see* ಪತ್ತೆ. *adj.* Suitable, agreeing with. –ಆಪಿನಿ to suit, agree with. –ಮಲ್ಪುನಿ to observe diet.

ಪತ್ಯೆ **patyè,** *see* ಪತ್ತೆ.

ಪತ್ರ **patra,** *s.* The leaf of a tree *or* book. 2. a written bond. 3. *see* ಪತ್ರಿಕೆ. 4. a passport. –ದ ಅಡ್ಡೆಯ, *see* ಪತ್ರೊಟ್ಟೆ. –ಮಲ್ಪುನಿ to execute a bond.

ಪತ್ರಾಜಿ **patrāji,** *s.* Bragging, boasting.

ಪತ್ರಾವಲಿ, ಪತ್ರಾಳಿ **patrāvali, patrāḷi,** *s.* A plate formed of leaves stitched together.

ಪತ್ರಿ **patri,** *see* ಪತ್ರ.

ಪತ್ರಿಕೆ **patrikè,** *s.* An epistle, letter. 2. a memorandum of some important event. ಮರಣ– a testament, will.

ಪತ್ರೆ **patrè,** *s.* A twig with the leaves on. 2. mace.

ಪತ್ರೊಟ್ಟೆ, ಪತ್ರೋಡೆ **patroṭṭè, patrōḍè,** *s.* A kind of cake made of the leaves of yam *or* other pot-herbs.

ಪಥ patha, *s.* A path, road, way.

ಪಥ್ಯ pathya, *see* ಪಠ್ಯ.

ಪದ್ರ್ padyru, *s.* A fold, layer, stratum. 2. a plait.

ಪದ್ರಾಟ, ಪದರಾಡ್ padyrāṭa, padarāḍu, *s.* Flight, retreat. ಪದ್ರಾಡ್‌ಪಾಡುನಿ to run away, decamp.

ಪದ್ರಾಡ್ padyrāḍu, *num.* Twelve. ಪದ್ರಾಡನೆ twelfth.

ಪದ್ರುನಿ padyruni, *see* ಪನೆರುನಿ.

ಪದ pada, *s.* A foot, step. 2. a foot-mark. 3. a word; a connected sentence. 4. a verse, song. –ಪಣ್ಪುನಿ to sing a song.

ಪದ pada, *s.* Abatement, subsidence; tranquillity. –ಆಪಿನಿ to abate, as storm *or* rain.

ಪದಂಕ padaṅka, *s. see* ಪದಿಕ. *adj. see* ಪದಕರ.

ಪದಂಕರ padaṅkara, *adv.* In a stooping posture. 2. *see* ಪದಕರ. –ಕುಳ್ಳುನಿ to cower, crouch, stoop.

ಪದಂಜನೆ padaññane, *s.* A lazy fellow.

ಪದಂಜಿ padañji, *see* ಪದೆಂಗಿ.

ಪದಂಪುನಿ padampuni (ಪದಂಪ್), *v. n.* To become wet.

ಪದಕ padaka, *s.* An ornamental breast-plate. 2. meditation. 3. *see* ಪದಿಕ. –ಕುಳ್ಳಾವುನಿ to set a breast-plate with precious stones.

ಪದಕರ್ padakaru, *s.* Breadth. –ದ ಕೊರಂಬು a kind of concave umbrella made of leaves.

ಪದಕರ padakara, *adj.* Dense, thick. *adv.* Densely, thickly, closely. –ಬೂರುನಿ to fall thickly.

ಪದಣುನಿ, ಪದನುನಿ padaṇuni, padanuni (ಪದಣ್, ಪದನ್), *v. n.* To become soft. 2. to get wet, be chilly.

ಪದನ, ಪದನಪ್ಪ padana, padanappa, *adv.* Well, nicely. –ಪೂಜುನಿ to smear well.

ಪದನಿಯುನಿ padaniyuni, *see* ನನೆಪಿನಿ.

ಪದನಿಯೆ padaniye, *s.* A wealthy man.

ಪದಪದ್ಯ padapadya, *s.* Singing; *cf.* ಪದ.

ಪದಪ್ಪು padappu, *s.* The temples. 2. *see* ಪದೆಪು.

ಪದರ್ padaru, *s.* Ambiguity, vagueness. *adj.* Ambiguous, vague. –ಪಾತೆರ an ambiguous statement; speaking vaguely.

ಪದರ padara, *see* ಪದ್ರ್.

ಪದರಾಜಿ padarāji, *see* ಪತ್ರಾಜಿ.

ಪದವಿ padavi, *s.* Wealth, property, possession. 2. rank, degree, grade. 3. road, path. 4. fortune, luck.

ಪದವು padavu, *s.* A plateau, table-land.

ಪದಸ್ತೆ padaste, *s.* A moderate man.

ಪದಾಂಗ padāṅga, *s.* A syllable.

ಪದಾಟಿಗೆ padāṭigè, *see* ಪಾದಾಟಿಗೆ.

ಪದಾಣ padāṇa, *see* ಪದನ.

ಪದಾತಿ, ಪದಾದಿ padāti, padādi, *s.* A foot-soldier.

ಪದಾರ್ಚನೆ padārčanè, *s.* Homage paid by falling at one's feet.

ಪದಾರ್ತಿ padārti, *s.* A class of drummers, attached to the service of a temple.

ಪದಾರ್ಥ padārtha, *s.* A thing, article. 2. vegetable curry, sauce. 3. the meaning of a word *or* sentence.

ಪದಿ padi, *s.* A basket.

ಪದಿ padi, *num.* Ten, *esp. used in comp.*; *as*, –ನಾಜಿ sixteen. –ನಾಲ್ fourteen. –ನೆಣ್ಮ eighteen. –ನೇಳ್ seventeen. –ನೈನ್ fifteen. –ನೊಂಬ್ಯ nineteen. –ಮೂಜಿ thirteen.

ಪದುಮ paduma, *see* ಪದ್ಮ.

ಪದುಮುಖ padumukha, *s.* A kind of medicine.

ಪದೆಂಗಿ, ಪದೆಂಜಿ padeṅgi, padeñji, *s.* Green gram, *Phaseolus mungo.* ಕಿಂನಿ–, ನೇಲ್ಯ–, ಪಜ್ಜೆ–, ಪೇರ್– are varieties of it.

ಪದೆಕ padeka, *s.* Collection; recovery.

ಪದೆಚ್ಚಿಲ್ padeččilu, *see* ಪಯುಕೆಲ್. 2. *see* ಪೈಚಿಲ್.

ಪದೆತಿ padeti, *s.* A midwife.

ಪದೆಪದೆ padepadè, *see* ಪದೇಪದೆ.

ಪದೆಪಿನಿ padepini (ಪದೆ), *v. a.* To collect, recover.

ಪದೆಪು padepu, *s.* The crown of the head.

ಪದೆಯುನಿ padeyuni (ಪದೆ), *v. n.* To sink down. 2. to become invisible.

ಪದೇಪದೆ padēpadè, *adv.* Frequently, again and again.

ಪದೊಲಿ, ಪದೊಳಿ padoli, padoḷi, *s.* The principal hall of a house. –ಕೊಟ್ಟ್ಯ an out-house.

ಪದ್ದಂಟಿಗೆ, ಪದ್ದಂತಿಗೆ, ಪದ್ದತಿ paddaṇṭigè, paddantigè, paddati, *see* ಪದ್ಧತಿ; *cf.* ರಿವಾಜಿ.

ಪದ್ದುನಿ padduni (ಪದ್), *v. n.* To sneak, crouch, hide, lurk. 2. to be afraid, perplexed, depressed.

ಪದ್ದೇಯಿ paddēyi, *s.* Ornaments, jewels.

ಪದ್ದೊಲಿ paddoli, *see* ಪದೊಲಿ.

ಪದ್ಧತಿ paddhati, *s.* Custom, practice, habit, rule.

ಪದ್ಪು padpu, *s.* A particle, atom; a very small quantity. 2. a dot, clotted blood on the skin. –ಇಜ್ಜಿ nothing at all.

ಪದ್ಪೆ padpè, *s.* The common herb *Amaranthus oleraceus.* ಕೆಂಪು– a red kind of the same. ಬೊಳ್ದು– a white kind of the same.

ಪದ್ಮ padma, *s.* A lotus, *Nelumbium speciosum.* 2. the Egyptian *or* Pythagorian bean. 3. coloured marks on the throat of a serpent *or* on the face and trunk of an elephant. –ಕೇಸರ the filament of a lotus. –ನಾಭ a name of Vishṇu. –ರಾಗ a ruby. –ಸಾಲೆ a weaver. ಪದ್ಮಾಕ್ಷ the seed of a lotus.

ಪದ್ಮಿನಿ padmini, *s.* One of the four classes of females.

ಪದ್ಯ padya, *s.* A verse, metre.

ಪನ, ಪನಪಾನ pana, panapāna, *see* ಪನಿ.

ಪನಂಬರ panambara, *s.* Ambergris. 2. boasting, making a mountain of a mole-hill. –ಮಳ್ಪುನಿ to boast, make a great ado about trifles.

ಪನಿ pani, *s.* Drizzling rain. 2. *see* ಪಣಿ. *adj.* Little, small. 3. few; *cf.* ಪಿನಿ. –ಕಪ್ಪೆ a small kind of frog. –ಕತ್ರ a small umbrella. –ದೊಂಪ a temporary shed. –ಬರ್ಸ drizzling rain. –ಬೂರುನಿ to drizzle. –ಕಡಿಯುನಿ to abate, as a drizzle.

ಪನಿಪುನಿ panipuni (ಪನಿ), *v. n.* To drizzle, shower.

ಪನಿಯಾರ paniyāra, *s.* An offering to a god, *etc.*, consisting of preparations of fruits and vegetables.

ಪನೂರು, ಪನೊರು, ಪನೋರು panūru, panoru, panōru, *see* ಪಜೊರು.

ಪನೆ, ಪನೆಕುತ್ತಿ pane, panekutti, *see* ಪಣೆ.

ಪನೆಮಾಡೆ panemāḍe, *s.* A demon so called.

ಪನೊಳಿ panoḷi, *see* ಪಜೊಳಿ.

ಪನ್ಕೋರಿ pankōri, *s.* A kind of fish.

ಪನ್ನಿ panni, *see* ಪಂನಿ.

ಪನ್ನೆ panne, *see* ಪಂನೆ.

ಪನ್ಪು panpu, *see* ಬಜ್ಪು.

ಪಪ್ಪಡ, ಪಪ್ಪಳ pappaḍa, pappaḷa, *s.* Pappaḍam, a very thin kind of cake made of pulse, salt, *etc.*

ಪಪ್ಪು pappu, *s.* A carcass, carrion.

ಪಬ್ಬ pabba, *see* ಪರ್ಬ.

ಪಯ paya, *s.* An ear of rice, *etc.* 2. gum, resin. 3. *see* ಪಾಯ. –ಆಪಿನಿ an ear of rice to shoot.

ಪಯಕೆಲ್, ಪಯಚೆಲ್, ಪಯಚ್ಚೆಲ್ payakelu, payačelu, payaččelu, *s.* The time of shooting of the ears of corn.

ಪಯಣ payaṇa, *see* ಪ್ರಯಾಣ.

ಪಯತಾಯೆ payatāye, *s.* A thriving man.

ಪಯರಂದ್ತಾಯೆ payarandutāye, *s.* A demon so called.

ಪಯವುನಿ, ಪಯಾವುನಿ payavuni, payāvuni (ಪಯ, ಪಯಾ), *v. n.* To shoot, as an ear of corn.

ಪಯಸ್ payasu, *s.* Water 2. milk.

ಪಯಿ payi, *s.* An ear of corn; *cf.* ಪಯ.

ಪಯಿಚಿಲ್ payičilu, *s.* A bag made of palm-leaves.

ಪಯಿಚ್ಚಿಲ್ payiččilu, *see* ಪಯಕೆಲ್.

ಪಯಿಜಾನ್, ಪಯಿಞಾನ್ payijānu, payiñānu, *s.* A kind of silver anklet.

ಪಯಿಞಾಲಿ, ಪಯಿನಾಲಯಿ, ಪಯಿನಾಳಿ payiñāli, payinālayi, payināḷi, *see* ಪೈಂಞಾಲಿ.

ಪಯಿಟಿನ್ಶೀರೆ payiṭinuširė, *see* ಪೈಟಿನಿಶೀರೆ.

ಪಯಿತೋಟ payitōṭa, *s*. A young garden *or* plantation.

ಪಯಿಲ್ payilu, *see* ಪಯ್ಯೋಲ್.

ಪಯಿಲ್‌ಮಾನಿಗೆ payilumānigė, *see* ಪೈಲ್‌ಮಾನಿಗೆ.

ಪಯೆಚೆಲ್ payečelu, *s*. Subscription, contribution. 2. *see* ಪಯಕೆಲ್.

ಪಯೆಬೆಲ್ payebelu, *see* ಪೈಂಬೆಲ್.

ಪಯೊಲಿ payoli, *see* ಪೈಯ್ಯೆರ್.

ಪಯ್ಯ, ಪಯ್ಯೆ payya, payyė, *see* ಪೈಯ್ಯೆ.

ಪಯ್ಯನ payyana, *adj*. Gently, softly, quietly; *cf*. ಪಯಣ. –ದೆಂಗಾವುನಿ to conceal quietly. –ಪಾಡುನಿ to put gently.

ಪಯ್ಯೆರ್ payyeru, *s*. A horse. 2. *see* ಪೈಯ್ಯೆರ್.

ಪಯ್ಯೋಲ್, ಪಯ್ಯೋಲಿ payyolu, payyoli, *s*. A horse. 2. riding, galloping. –ಎಪ್ಪಾವುನಿ to gallop.

ಪರ para, *adj*. Distant, remote. 2. subsequent, after, following. 3. other, different. 4. more, exceeding. 5. before. –ಊರು a strange place, foreign country.

ಪರ para, *adj*. Old, worn out. –ಕುಂಟು worn out clothes.

ಪರ para, *s*. Regard, respect. –ದಾಂತಿನಾಯೆ a careless man. –ಉಪ್ಪುನಿ to have regard *or* respect. –ಪರಿಪುನಿ to lose respect. –ಮದಪುನಿ be careless, regardless. –ಮಳ್ಪುನಿ to regard, give attention. ನಿಕ್ಕ್ ದಾಲಾ ಪರ ಇಜ್ಜಾ have you no regard? do you not care?

ಪರಂಕುನಿ paraṅkuni, *see* ಪಂಕುನಿ.

ಪರಂಗ್ paraṅgu, *see* ಪರಂಗೆಲ್.

ಪರಂಗಿ paraṅgi, *see* ಪರೆಂಗಿ.

ಪರಂಗುನಿ paraṅguni (ಪರಂಗ್), *v. n*. To become stale, musty; to decay; *also* ಪರಂಗದ್‌ಪೋಪಿನಿ.

ಪರಂಗೆಲ್ paraṅgelu, *s*. Staleness, decay. *adj*. Stale, decayed, decrepit. ಪರಂಗೆಲೆ a decrepit man.

ಪರಂಚುನಿ parañčuni, *see* ಪರೆಂಚುನಿ.

ಪರಂಚೆನ, ಪರಂಚೆಲ್ parañčena, parañčelu, *s*. Prattling. 2. grumbling, murmuring.

ಪರಂಚೆಲೆ parañčele, *s*. A prattler, babbler. 2. a grumbler.

ಪರಂಜಿ parañji, *see* ಪರೆಂಜಿ.

ಪರಂಜ್ಯೋತಿ parañjyōti, *s*. The Supreme Being, Light of lights.

ಪರಂಟ್ paraṇṭu, *s*. A bull frog.

ಪರಂಟ paraṇṭa, *s*. Murmuring, grumbling. –ಪಾತೆರುನಿ to grumble, talk nonsense.

ಪರಂಟಳ್, ಪರಂಟಳಿಗೆ paraṇṭaḷu, paraṇṭaḷigė, *s*. A kind of creeper.

ಪರಂಟುನಿ paraṇṭuni (ಪರಂಟಿ), *v. a*. To gripe, grasp, seize, lay hold of. 2. *see* ಪರೆಂಚುನಿ.

ಪರಂಟೆ paraṇṭė, *s*. An old buffalo.

ಪರಂಟೆಲೆ paraṇṭele, *s*. A prattler, grumbler.

ಪರಂಡ paraṇḍa, *s*. Murmuring, grumbling.

ಪರಂಡುನಿ paraṇḍuni, *see* ಪರಡುನಿ.

ಪರಂಧಾಮ parandhāma, *s*. Vishṇu's paradise.

ಪರಂಪರೆ paramparè, *s.* Succession; race, lineage, descent. *adj.* Successive, proceeding from one to another, hereditary.

ಪರಂಬುನಿ parambuni, *see* ಪಬ್ಬುನಿ.

ಪರಕ್ paraku, *see* ಫರಕ್.

ಫರಕಟ್ parakaṭu, *see* ಪರ್ಕಟ್ಟ್.

ಪರಕಳೆ, ಪರಕಾಳಿ parakaḷè, parakāḷi, *s.* A long cloth.

ಪರಕಾಯ parakāya, *s.* Another body. —ಪ್ರವೇಶ transmigration.

ಪರಕಿ paraki, *see* ಪರ್ಕಿ.

ಪರಕೆ parakè, *s.* A vow made in trouble; beseeching. 2. *see* ಪರಾಕೆ. —ಪಣ್ಪುನಿ to vow, make a vow. —ಪಾಡುನಿ, —ಕೊರ್ಪಿನಿ to fulfil a vow. —ಸಂದಾವುನಿ to do a work carelessly. ಸಂದುನಿ a vow to be fulfilled.

ಪರಕೈ parakei, *s.* Depositing with another, as the stake of a wager. —ಕಟ್ಟುನಿ to deposit in this way.

ಪರಗಂತೆ paragantè, *see* ಪರ್ಕಟ್ಟ್.

ಪರಗತಿ paragati, *s.* Future destiny.

ಪರಜನ parajana, *s.* Strangers.

ಪರಜಾತ parajāta, *adj.* Adopted, fostered by a stranger.

ಪರಜಾತಿ parajāti, *s.* A foreign tribe *or* caste.

ಪರಜಿ paraji, *see* ಪರೆಂಜಿ.

ಪರಡಿ paraḍi, *see* ಪರೊಡಿ.

ಪರಡುನಿ paraḍuni (ಪರಡಿ), *v. n.* & *a.* To grope. 2. to spread.

ಪರಡೆಲೆ paraḍele, *s.* One who gropes about. 2. a lazy man, *etc.*

ಪರತ್ paratu, *adj.* Old, worn out. —ಆಪಿನಿ to become old.

ಪರತಂತ್ರ paratantra, *adj.* Dependent, obedient, subservient.

ಪರತರುನಿ, ಪರತುರುನಿ parataruni, paraturuni (ಪರತರ್, ಪರತುರ್), *v. n.* To spread, extend, diffuse. 2. to creep, as an ant, *etc.*

ಪರತಿ parati, *see* ಪರ್ತಿ.

ಪರದಿ, ಪರದೆ paradi, paradè, *s.* A curtain, blind, screen. —ಕಟ್ಟುನಿ, —ಪಾಡುನಿ to put up a blind.

ಪರದೇವತೆ paradēvatè, *s.* A foreign deity.

ಪರದೇಶ paradēša, *s.* A foreign country.

ಪರದೇಶಿ paradēši, *s.* A foreigner. 2. a vagrant, vagabond.

ಪರದೈಸ್ paradeisu, *s.* Paradise.

ಪರನಾರಿ paranāri, *s.* Another's wife.

ಪರನಿಂದೆ paranindè, *s.* Abusing others.

ಪರನೀರ್ paranīru, *s. lit.* Old water. 2. flowing water. 3. a perennial fountain. 4. water stored the preceding day.

ಪರಪಂಚ parapañča, *see* ಪ್ರಪಂಚ.

ಪರಪಕ್ಷ parapasha, *s.* Partiality. —ಮಳ್ಪುನಿ to show partiality, be biased.

ಪರಪರ parapara, *s.* The noise of rending cloth.

ಪರಪು **parapu,** *s.* A sand bed. *adj.* flowing, running.

ಪರಪುನಿ **parapuni** (ಪರ), *v. n.* To flow, as water. 2. to creep, crawl on hands and legs. 3. to spread, as a creeper.

ಪರಬಾರಿ **parabāri,** *s.* Assignment. *adv.* Separately. 2. indirectly. —ಪಾತೆರುನಿ to speak indirectly. —ಕೋಪಿನಿ to avoid, as a place in a journey, and go another way. —ಮಳ್ಪುನಿ to transfer, deliver over to another.

ಪರಬು **parabu,** *s.* An old woman.

ಪರಬೆ **parabe,** *s.* An old man.

ಪರಬ್ರಹ್ಮ **parabrahma,** *s.* The Supreme Being.

ಪರಮು **parama,** *adj.* Best, most excellent. 2. principal, chief, supreme. —ಗತಿ a blessed condition, salvation. —ಗುಣ an excellent disposition. —ಗುರು a supreme, religious guide. —ಘಾತಕೆ, —ದುಷ್ಟ a very wicked man. —ಜ್ಞಾನ superior understanding. —ಪದವಿ heavenly bliss.

ಪರಮಂಡಲ **paramaṇḍala,** *s.* Heaven, the sky.

ಪರಮತ **paramata,** *s.* A strange religion. 2. another's intention.

ಪರಮಾಂನ, ಪರಮಾಯನ **paramānna, paramāyana,** *s.* Rice *or* wheat boiled in milk with sugar, *etc.*

ಪರಮಾತ್ಮೆ **paramātme,** *s.* The Supreme Being.

ಪರಮಾನಂದ **paramānanda,** *s.* Great happiness, heavenly bliss.

ಪರಮಾಪ್ತೆ **paramāpte,** *s.* A best friend, intimate friend.

ಪರಮಾರ್ಥ **paramārtha,** *s.* Chief object *or* intention. 2. truth, fact.

ಪರಮಾರ್ಥಿ **paramārthi,** *s.* A truthfull, honest man.

ಪರಮಾರ್ಥೆ **paramārthe,** *s.* God.

ಪರಮಾಸ್ **paramāsu̧,** *adj.* Best, excellent.

ಪರಮಾಸಿ **paramāsi,** *s.* Command, mandate, order; will, pleasure.

ಪರಮೆ **parame,** *s.* A clever man. 2. a cunning, tricky fellow.

ಪರಮೇಶ್ವರೆ **paramēšvare,** *s.* The Supreme Lord. 2. a name of Šiva.

ಪರಮೇಷ್ಟಿ **paramēshṭi,** *s.* The Creator. 2. a name of Brahma.

ಪರಯೆ **paraye,** *see* ಪಲಯಿ.

ಪರರಾಜ್ಯ **pararājya,** *s.* A foreign territory.

ಪರಲ್ **paralu̧,** *see* ಪೊರಲ್.

ಪರಲೋಕ **paralōka,** *s.* The next world, heaven.

ಪರವ **parava,** *s.* Concern, care, regard, respect; *cf.* ಪರ್ವ.

ಪರವಂಚ **paravañca,** *see* ಪ್ರಪಂಚ.

ಪರವಡವೆ **paravaḍave,** *s.* Another's property *or* thing.

ಪರವಶ **paravaša,** *s.* Subservience, dependence. 2. ecstacy. 3. absence of mind.

ಪರವಾಸ **paravāsa,** *s.* Residence in a foreign land, exile.

ಪರವಿ paravi, *see* ಪರಬು.

ಪರವೆ parave, *s.* A man belonging to a low class of devil-dancers.

ಪರವೇಷ paravēsha, *s.* Personation. 2. *see* ಪ್ರವೇಶ.

ಪರಶು parašu, *s.* A hatchet, an axe. 2. the philosopher's stone; *also* ಪರಶುಕಲ್ಲ. –ರಾಮ the sixth incarnation of Vishṇu, who is said to have peopled the coast of Malabar.

ಪರಶೆ parašè, *s.* Pilgrims going to *or* assembled at any sacred place *or* festival of an idol.

ಪರಸ್ parasụ, *s.* Benediction.

ಪರಸಾಧಕ parasādhaka, *s.* Means of obtaining heaven.

ಪರಸೆ parasè, *s.* The perforations of a small machine for making a kind of vermicelli (ಶೇ ಮಯಿಡ ಅಡ್ಡೆ). 2. *see* ಪರಶೆ.

ಪರಸೇವೆ parasēvè, *s.* Serving another.

ಪರಸ್ಥಳ parasthaḷa, *s.* A strange place, foreign country.

ಪರಸ್ತ್ರೀ parastrī, *s.* The wife of another.

ಪರಸ್ಪರ paraspara, *adj.* Mutual, reciprocal. –ವೈರ mutual hatred. –ಸ್ನೇಹ mutual friendship.

ಪರಸ್ವ parasva, *s.* Another's property.

ಪರಸ್ವಾಧೀನ parasvādhīna, *see* ಪರಾಧೀನ.

ಪರಹಿಂಸೆ parahimsè, *s.* Persecution.

ಪರಹಿತ parahita, *s.* Kindness to strangers, benevolence.

ಪರಳೊಪ್ಪ paraḷoppa, *adv.* Wholly, totally, fully.

ಪರಾ parā, *pref. implying* Supremacy. 2. liberation. 3. invested order. 4. pride. 5. excess. 6. encounter. 7. overcoming. 8. going. 9. destroying.

ಪರಾಂಙ್ಮುಖ parāṅṅmukha, *s.* An averted face.

ಪರಾಂನ parānna *s.* Living on others; food supplied by another.

ಪರಾಂಬರಿಕೆ parāmbarikè, *s.* Care, protection. 2. enquiry, investigation.

ಪರಾಂಬರಿಪುನಿ parāmbaripuni (ಪರಾಂಬರಿ), *v. a.* To take care of, watch over, nurse. 2. to investigate, consider.

ಪರಾಕ್ parākụ, *see* ಪ್ರಾಕ್.

ಪರಾಕೆ parākè, *intj.* Attention! 2. calling attention while addressing a superior.

ಪರಾಕ್ರಮ parākrama, *s.* Power, valour. 2. exertion. –ದಾಯಿ, –ಶಾಲಿ a powerful man, hero.

ಪರಾಖತ್ parākhatụ, *see* ಫರಾಖತ್.

ಪರಾಜಯ parājaya, *s.* Conquest, defeat.

ಪರಾಙ್ಮುಖ, parāṇmukha, *see* ಪರಾಂಙ್ಮುಖ.

ಪರಾತ್ಪರೆ parātpare, *s.* The Supreme Being, God.

ಪರಾಧೀನ parādhīna, *s.* Possession by another, alienation. *adj.*

Dependant on, subject to another. —ಮಳ್ಳುನಿ to alienate, as property.

ಪರಾನ್ನ parānna, *see* ಪರಾಂದ.

ಪರಾಪರವಸ್ತು parāparavastu, *see* ಪರಾತ್ಪರೆ.

ಪರಾಭವ parābhava, *s*. The fortieth year of the Hindu cycle of sixty. 2. discomfiture. 3. destruction.

ಪರಾಬರಿ parābari, *see* ಪರಬಾರಿ.

ಪರಾಮರಿಕೆ, ಪರಾಮರ್ಶ parāmarikè, parāmarša, *see* ಪರಾಂಬರಿಕೆ.

ಪರಾಯಿ parāyi, *adj*. Strange, foreign. —ಜನ foreign people. —ವಸ್ತು another's things.

ಪರಾರಿ parāri, *see* ಫರಾರಿ.

ಪರಾರ್ಥ parārtha, *s*. The property of another. 2. another meaning. *adv*. On account of another.

ಪರಾಶ್ರಯ parāšraya, *s*. Taking refuge with another.

ಪರಿ pari, *s*. A path, way. 2. an opening, gap; a vacant space. ಮುಗೆರಿದ—a rabbit's path. —ಕಟ್ಟುನಿ, —ನುಗ್ಗುನಿ to repair, as a gap in a hedge. —ತೂಪಿನಿ to seek a way; to track the path. —ಪತ್ತುನಿ to go one's way; to escape. —ಪಾಡುನಿ to plant again where the previous plants have perished; to repair a hedge. —ಮಳ್ಳುನಿ to take care. —ಮುತ್ತುನಿ, —ಮುರಿಯುನಿ a path to be out of repair.

ಪರಿ pari, *pref*. *implying* Ubiquity. 2. part, portion. 3. abandonment. 4. end, term. 5. sickness, infirmity. 6. stress. 7. separateness, distribution. 8. encircling. 9. depreciation, exposure of faults. 10. respect. 11. rejection, turning off *or* away. 12. ornament. 13. diffusion. 14. sign. 15. sorrow. 16. cessation; impediment. 17. truth. 18. an exclamation of pleasure *or* satisfaction.

ಪರಿಂಕಿಗಡ್ಡೆ pariṅkigaḍḍè, *s*. The Telinga potato, *Arum campanulatum*.

ಪರಿಂಕುನಿ pariṅkuni, *see* ಪಂಕುರ್ನಿ.

ಪರಿಂಗೊಟ್ಟೆ pariṅgoṭṭè, *see* ಪಂಗೊರ್ಟ್ಟೆ.

ಪರಿಕಾಳೆ parikāḷè, *see* ಪರಕಳೆ.

ಪರಿಕಿ pariki, *see* ಪರ್ಕಿ.

ಪರಿಕೆ parikè, *see* ಪರಕೆ. 2. *see* ಪರೀಕ್ಷೆ.

ಪರಿಖ್ಯಾತಿ parikhyāti, *see* ಪ್ರಖ್ಯಾತಿ.

ಪರಿಗ pariga, *s*. An iron club.

ಪರಿಚಯ, ಪರಿಚರ್ಯ, ಪರಿಚಿತಿ, ಪರಿಚಿತೆ paricaya, paričarya, paricíti, paricítè, *s*. Acquaintance, knowledge; intimacy.

ಪರಿಚಾರಕೆ paricārake, *s*. An attendant, servant.

ಪರಿಚ್ಛೇದನೆ paričchēdanè, *s*. Division, section, as of a book. 2. circumcision.

ಪರಿಜನ parijana, *s*. Dependence. 2. retinue.

ಪರಿಜಿತಿ, ಪರಿಜೆ parijiti, parijè, *see* ಪರಿಚಯ.

ಪರಿಣಾಮ, ಪರಿಣೇಮ pariṇāma, parinēma, *see* ಪರ್ಣಾಮ.

ಪರಿತ್ಯಾಗ parityāga, *s.* Separation, abandonment.

ಪರಿಧಾವಿ paridhāvi, *s.* The forty-sixth year of the Hindu cycle of sixty.

ಪರಿನಾಮ parināma, *see* ಪರ್ಣಾಮ.

ಪರಿಪಕ್ಷ paripaksha, *see* ಪರಪಕ್ಷ.

ಪರಿಪರಿ paripari, *adj.* Diverse, various.

ಪರಿಪಾಲನೆ paripālanė, *s.* Protection, care, fostering.

ಪರಿಪುನಿ paripuni (ಪರಿ), *v. a.* To tear, rend.

ಪರಿಪೂರ್ಣ paripūrṇa, *adj.* Complete, full.

ಪರಿಪೂರ್ತಿ paripūrti, *s.* Fulness, completion, satisfaction.

ಪರಿಬಂಧ paribandha, *s.* Relationship. —ದಾಯಿ a kinsman.

ಪರಿಭ್ರಮೆ paribhramė, *s.* Turning round, flurry.

ಪರಿಮಳ parimaḷa, *s.* Fragrance, perfume. —ವಸ್ತು perfumery. —ನೀರ್ fragrant water.

ಪರಿಮಾಣ parimāṇa, *s.* Measure, amount, quantity.

ಪರಿಮಾಳ್ parimāḷu, *s.* An honorific title amongst Bants.

ಪರಿಮಿತ parimita, *adj.* Measured, meted. *s.* Estimate, value.

ಪರಿಮುಣ್ಚಿ parimuṇči, *s.* Country chilli.

ಪರಿಮುದಿ parimudi, *s.* Perishing.

ಪರಿಯ pariya, *adj.* Plenty, exceeding, much.

ಪರಿಯಂತರ pariyantara, *adv.* Till, until.

ಪರಿಯಾಟನೆ pariyāṭanė, *s.* Wandering, roaming; revolution. —ಮಳ್ಪುನಿ to wander, roam; to revolve.

ಪರಿಯಾಯ pariyāya, *s.* Order, arrangement. succession. 2. opportunity, occasion. 3. a grand festival once in two years at Uḍipi, celebrating the occasion of a Svāmi's succession to the management of Krishṇa's temple there.

ಪರಿಯುನಿ pariyuni (ಪರಿ), *v. n.* To run, flow. 2. to rend.

ಪರಿಯೊಳು pariyoḷu, *s.* A kind of fish.

ಪರಿವಾರ parivāra, *s.* Followers, retinue; army.

ಪರಿಶುದ್ಧ pariśuddha, *adj.* Sacred, holy, pure. —ದಾಯಿ, —ವಂತ, ಪರಿಶುದ್ಧೆ a holy man. —ಮಳ್ಪುನಿ to sanctify.

ಪರಿಶುದ್ಧಾತ್ಮ pariśudhātme, *s.* The Holy Ghost, Holy Spirit.

ಪರಿಶೆ pariśė, *see* ಪರಸೆ.

ಪರಿಶೋಧನೆ pariśōdhanė, *s.* Examination, investigation. 2. temptation. —ಮಳ್ಪುನಿ, ಪರಿಶೋಧಪುನಿ to investigate; to tempt.

ಪರಿಶ್ರಮ pariśrama, *s.* Fatigue, difficulty, exhaustion. 2. practice, exercise.

ಪರಿಸಾನ parisāna, *s.* Death.

ಪರಿಹರಿಪುನಿ pariharipuni (ಪರಿಹರಿ), *v. a.* To forgive, absolve, pardon. 2. to clear, as a debt.

ಪರಿಹಾರ parihāra, *s*. Removal. 2. healing, relief. 3. absolution, pardon. –ಮಳ್ಪುನಿ to heal, relieve; to pardon, absolve; to propitiate, as an evil spirit, *etc*.

ಪರಿಹಾಸ, ಪರಿಹಾಸ್ಯ parihāsa, parihāsya, *s*. Jeer, mocking, raillery, sport. –ಮಳ್ಪುನಿ to jeer; to sport.

ಪರೀಯ pariya, *see* ಪರಿಯ.

ಪರೀಕ್ಷೆ parīkshè, *s*. Trial, experiment, investigation, examination, test, discrimination. –ದಾಯೆ, ಪರೀಕ್ಷಕೆ an experimenter; examiner; a tempter. –ತೂಪಿನಿ, –ಮಳ್ಪುನಿ, ಪರೀಕ್ಷಿಸುನಿ to examine, test, try.

ಪರು paru, *s*. The teeth, as of a beast, saw, file, *etc*. –ಕಣಿ a tooth-pick. –ಅಡೆವುನಿ to set teeth on edge. –ಉದುರುನಿ, –ಕದೆವುನಿ the teeth to fall out. –ಉರ್ದುನಿ to file the teeth of a saw. –ಕಡೆಪಿನಿ, –ಕಡೆಯುನಿ to gnash the teeth. –ಪಾಡುನಿ to furnish a saw, *etc*., with teeth. –ಬರ್ಪುನಿ to teeth.

ಪರುಕತ್ತಿ parukatti, *see* ಪರ್ಗತ್ತಿ.

ಪರುಕು paruku, *see* ಪರ್ಗ್.

ಪರುವ paruva, *see* ಪರ್ವ.

ಪರುವೆಲ್ paruvelu, *s*. Food, meal, as of a Pariah. 2. *see* ಪೊರುವೆಲ್.

ಪರುಶ, ಪರುಶು paruša, parušu, *see* ಪರಶು.

ಪರೆ parè, *s*. A cataract *or* web on the eye. 2. *see* ಪಾರೆ.

ಪರೆಂಗಿ parengi, *s*. A Frank *or* Portuguese. 2. an European. *adj*. European; foreign. –ಪೆಲಕಾಯಿ ananas, pine-apple. –ಮುಳ್ಳ್ Spanish pepper, *Capsicum annuum*. –ರೋಗ syphilis. ಗಂಟು–, ತೊಜ್ಜಿ–, ನಾಯಿ–, ಪುಟ– are some of the different kinds of venereal diseases.

ಪರೆಂಗೆಲೆ parengele, *s*. A syphilitic man. 2. *see* ಪರೆಂಚೆಲೆ.

ಪರೆಂಚಣ, ಪರೆಂಚಾಟ parenčaṇa, parenčāṭa, *s*. Prattle. 2. twaddle.

ಪರೆಂಚುನಿ parenčuni (ಪರೆಂಚ್), *v. n*. To prate, prattle. 2. to find fault with, censure.

ಪರೆಂಚೆಲೆ parenčele, *s*. A prattler, tattler. 2. one given to fault-finding.

ಪರೆಂಜಿ, ಪರೆಜಿ parenji, pareji, *s*. A scaffold, temporary platform. –ಕಟ್ಟುನಿ to erect a scaffold.

ಪರೆಲ್ parelu, *s*. A grain of sand, grit, gravel; a bit of glass, *etc*. 2. a grain of corn, *etc*. –ಕಲ್ಲ್ a pebble. ಬೆಡಿತ– small shot. –ಮಡ್ಯೆ a washerman-barber of low class.

ಪರೆಲುನಿ pareluni, *see* ಪಲುಗನಿ.

ಪರೆಲ್ದೆಂಣೆ pareldeṇṇè, *s*. Castor oil.

ಪರೆಳ್ parelu, *see* ಪರೆಲ್.

ಪರೇಜಿ, ಪರೇಜು parēji, parēju, *adj*. Equal, corresponding with; *cf*. ಪರೆಂಜಿ.

ಪರೇತೆ parētè, *s*. Crawling on hands and feet.

ಪರೇಶೆ parēše, *see* ಪರೇಜಿ.

ಪರೊಡಿ paroḍi, *s.* Dissimulation, hypocrisy. 2. skill, craft, scheme. —ಗಾರೆ a hypocrite. —ಮಳ್ಪುನಿ to simulate, pretend; to play tricks.

ಪರೋಪಕಾರ parōpakāra, *s.* Kindness to strangers, benevolence. ಪರೋಪಕಾರಿ a philanthropist.

ಪರ್ರಾಯೆ parrāye, *s.* A stranger, foreigner.

ಪರ್ಕ್, ಪರ್ಕಟ್ಟ್, ಪರ್ಕಟೆ, ಪರ್ಕಟ್ಟೆ parkų, parkaṭṭų, parkaṭè, parkaṭṭè, *adj.* Old, worn out, ragged.

ಪರ್ಕಡ್, ಪರ್ಕಡೆ parkaḍų, parkaḍè, *adj.* Grinding *or* gnashing of teeth. —ತುಜ್ಜುನಿ to grind *or* gnash teeth.

ಪರ್ಕಡಿ, ಪರ್ಕಡ್ಡಿ parkaḍi, parkaḍḍi, *s.* A tooth-pick.

ಪರ್ಕತ್ತಿ, ಪರ್ಕತ್ತೆ parkatti, parkattè, *s.* A scythe, sickle.

ಪರ್ಕಾವುನಿ parkāvuni (ಪರ್ಕಾ), *v. a.* To draw in, call in. 2. to confiscate. 3. *c. v. of* ಪರ್ಕುನಿ.

ಪರ್ಕಿ, ಪರ್ಕೀಸ್, ಪರ್ಕೆಲ್ parki, parkīsų, parkelų, *adj.* Destitute, wretched.

ಪರ್ಕುನಿ parkuni, *see* ಪಂಕ್ರುನಿ.

ಪರ್ಕೆ parkè, *see* ಪರಕೆ.

ಪರ್ಕೆ parkè, *s.* Bedding. 2. sleep, rest. —ಪಡಿ the mat under a bed, *etc.*

ಪರ್ಕೊಟೆ, ಪರ್ಕೊಟ್ಟ್ parkoṭè, parkoṭṭų, *see* ಪರ್ಕಟ್ಟ್.

ಪರ್ಕೊಡೆಯುನಿ parkoḍeyuni (ಪರ್ಕೊಡೆ), *v. a.* To grin, gnash.

ಪರ್ಗಣೆ pargaṇè, *see* ಪಿರ್ಗೆ.

ಪರ್ಚರ್ಯ, ಪರ್ಚಿತ parćarya, parćita, *see* ಪರಿಚಯ.

ಪರ್ಜಿ parji, *see* ಪರೆಂಜಿ.

ಪರ್ಣ parṇa, *see* ಪರ್ನ.

ಪರ್ತಿ parti, *s.* Cotton, *Gossypium indicum.*

ಪರ್ತೆ partè, *s.* Sharpness, edge. *adj.* Sharp, quick, keen. —ಮಳ್ಪುನಿ to whet, sharpen.

ಪರ್ತೆ, ಪರ್ತೆಲ್ partè, partelų, *s.* A rent, tear, as in clothes, *etc.* *adj.* Torn, tattered, old.

ಪರ್ತೆಲೆ partele, *s.* A man in rags.

ಪರ್ದತ್ತಿ pardatti, *see* ಪರ್ಕತ್ತಿ.

ಪರ್ದಿ pardi, *see* ಪಲಿ.

ಪರ್ದಿ, ಪರ್ದೆ pardi, pardè, *see* ಪರದ.

ಪರ್ದೇಶಿ pardēśi, *see* ಪರದೇಶಿ.

ಪರ್ನ parna, *s.* A leaf. 2. a feather.

ಪರ್ನಶಾಲೆ parnaśālè, *s.* A hut made of leaves, hermitage. 2. a booth. 3. a bower.

ಪರ್ನಾಮ parnāma, *s.* Health, welfare. 2. prosperity. *adj.* Thriving, prosperous.

ಪರ್ಪಾಟ parpāṭa, *s.* Drinking.

ಪರ್ಪಾಟಕ parpāṭaka, *s.* The shrub *Mullugo cerviana.*

ಪರ್ಪಾವುನಿ parpāvuni, *c. v.* (*of* ಪಪಿನಿ *or* ಪರ್ಪುನಿ) To cause to drink. 2. to have pulled out, cause to pluck *or* pull.

ಪರ್ಪಿನಿ parpini (ಪರ್), *v. a.* To drink, sip. 2. to take food, as a Pariah.

ಪರ್ಪು parpu, *see* ಪರಪು.

ಪರ್ಪುನಿ parpuni (ಪರ್), *v. a.* To

pluck, pull out, as roots, grass, *etc.*; *cf.* ಪೊಪ್ಪುನಿ.

ಪರ್ಪೆಲೆ parpele, *s.* A drunkard.

ಪರ್ಬ parba, *s.* A festival, feast, holiday.

ಪರ್ಬಾವುನಿ parbāvuni, *c. v.* (*of* ಪರ್ಬುನಿ) To cause to spread, extend, diffuse.

ಪರ್ಬು parbu, *see* ಪ್ರಭು.

ಪರ್ಬುನಿ parbuni (ಪರ್ಬ್), *v. n.* To spread, multiply, diffuse; to flow.

ಪರ್ಮನ parmana, *see* ಪರಮಾಂನ.

ಪರ್ಮರಿ parmari, *see* ಪೆರ್ಮರಿ.

ಪರ್ಮಾನ್ parmānụ, *s.* A pole attached to a boat's sail.

ಪರ್ಮಾಸ್ parmāsụ, *see* ಪರಮಾಸ್.

ಪರ್ಮಾಳೆ parmāḷè, *s.* The name of a hill.

ಪರ್ಯ parya, *see* ಪರಿಯ.

ಪರ್ಯಾಟಣೆ paryāṭaṇè, *see* ಪರಿಯಾಟಣೆ.

ಪರ್ಯಾಯ paryāya, *see* ಪರಿಯಾಯ.

ಪರ್ಯುನಿ paryuni, *see* ಪರಿಯುನಿ.

ಪರ್ಲುನಿ parluni (ಪರ್ಲ್), *v. n.* To be washed, as a dam *or* reservoir. *v. a.* To cut sharply, as a knife.

ಪರ್ವ parva, *s.* Awe, fear, reverence, respect, regard; *cf.* ಪರ.

ಪರ್ವ parva, *s.* A knot, joint of a cane. 2. a name given to certain days in the lunar month, as the full and change of the moon. 3. division of a year, as the equinox, solstice, *etc.*; *cf.* ಪರ್ಬ. 4. a section, division, chapter. 5. stage *or* degree of ripeness in fruits. —ಕಾಲ a holy day.

ಪರ್ವಂದ parvanda, *adj.* Honorary. —ಪಟ್ಟೆ a robe of honor.

ಪರ್ವತ parvata, *s.* A mountain, hill.

ಪರ್ವೆಲ್, ಪರ್ವೆಲಿ parvelụ, parveli, *s.* A feast *or* meal among Pariahs. 2. *see* ಪರಿಯೊಳು.

ಪರ್ಶೆ parśè, *see* ಪರಶೆ.

ಪರ್ಳೆಪ್ಪು parḷeppu, *see* ಪರಳೊಪ್ಪು.

ಪಲ pala, *see* ಫಲ.

ಪಲಂಕೆನ palaṅkena, *adv.* Early. 2. *see* ಪಣಕೆ.

ಪಲಂಗ್ palaṅgụ, *see* ಪಲ್ಲಂಗ.

ಪಲಂಬರ palambara, *s.* Fulness. 2. *see* ಪನಂಬರ.

ಪಲಂಬರುನಿ palambaruni (ಪಲಂಬರ್), *v. n.* To be full. 2. *see* ಕಂಣಂಬರುನಿ.

ಪಲಂಬುನಿ palambuni (ಪಲಂಬ್), *v. a.* To lament.

ಪಲಟುನಿ palaṭuni (ಪಲಟ್), *v. n.* To be altered, changed.

ಪಲಪು palapu, *s.* A boundary, limit.

ಪಲಯಿ palayi, *s.* A plank, board. —ಮೀನ್ the Indian cod.

ಪಲಯೆ palaye, *s.* An elder brother.

ಪಲವು palavu, *see* ಫಲಾವು.

ಪಲಾನ palāna, *see* ಫಲಾನೆ.

ಪಲಾಯನ palāyana, *s.* Flight, retreat. —ಮಳ್ಪುನಿ to retreat, decamp.

ಪಲಾಯಿ palāyi, *see* ಪಲಯಿ.

ಪಲಾಯೆ palāye, *see* ಪಲಯೆ.

ಪಲಾರ palāra, *see* ಫಲಾರ.

ಪಲಾಶ palāša, *s.* The tree *Butea frondosa.*

ಪಲಿ pali, *s.* An elder sister.

ಪಲಿ pali, *see* ಪರಿ. 2. *see* ಪಳಿ.

ಪಲಿಕೆ palikè, *s.* A valley, declivity. 2. a pond, ditch.

ಪಲಿತ palita, *see* ಫಲಿತ.

ಪಲಿತ, ಪಲಿಪು palita, palipu, *s.* Effect, virtue, efficacy, as of a hand, medicine, *etc.* 2. durability, survivance

ಪಲಿಪುನಿ palipuni, *see* ಫಲಿಪುನಿ.

ಪಲು palu, *s.* Ripening, as of fruit. 2. *see* ಪಲಿಕೆ. *adj.* Half ripe.

ಪಲೆ pale, *see* ಪಲಯೆ.

ಪಲ್ಕುನಿ palkuni (ಪಲ್ಕ್), *v. n.* To be very soft, as an over-ripe fruit. 2. to be pliant, flexible.

ಪಲ್ಗಸೆಡಿ palgseḍi, *see* ಪಸ್ಕಟ್ಟ.

ಪಲ್ಗೇಡಿ palgēḍi, *s.* A base, mean fellow.

ಪಲ್ದಿ paldi, *see* ಪಲಿ.

ಪಲ್ನೀರ್ palnīru, *see* ಪಂನೀರ್.

ಪಲ್ಲ್ pallu, *see* ಪಲ್ಲು.

ಪಲ್ಲ palla, *s.* A small enclosure of wicker work for keeping cooked food during an entertainment. 2. *see* ಪಳ್ಳ.

ಪಲ್ಲಂಗ pallaṅga, *s.* A canopy over a couch *or* bedstead.

ಪಲ್ಲಕಿ pallaki, *s.* ಪಲ್ಲೆಂಕಿ.

ಪಲ್ಲಟ pallaṭa, *adj.* Overwhelmed. 2. altered. 3. misplaced. —ಆಪುನಿ to be altered. —ಮಳ್ಪುನಿ to alter.

ಪಲ್ಲನ pallana, *s.* Rags. 2. patch-work of a garment. —ಪಾರಾವುನಿ to wear patched garments.

ಪಲ್ಲಯಿ pallayi, *s.* An earthen dish.

ಪಲ್ಲವ pallava, *s.* A sprout, shoot.

ಪಲ್ಲಾ pallā, *s.* A port. 2. *see* ಪಳ್ಳ.

ಪಲ್ಲಾಡುನಿ pallāḍuni (ಪಲ್ಲಾಡ್), *v. n.* To be unsteady.

ಪಲ್ಲಿ palli, *s.* A house lizard. 2. a fork. 3. a rake. —ಪತ್ತುನಿ to grasp one's hands in a children's game.

ಪಲ್ಲು pallu, *adj.* Stupid, simple. 2. timid, spiritless, wanting boldness; *cf.* ಚಲ್ಲ್. 3. *see* ಪೊಲ್ಲು. —ಕುಡುಕೆ a mad *or* howling jackal. —ನರಮಾನಿ a weak fellow; a stupid man.

ಪಲ್ಲೆ pallè, *s.* The spleen. 2. the large bean of *Entada monastachya*; *also* —ಕಾಯಿ. ಮೊರಂಪು ಡ— the knee-cap. —ದ ಪೈಮುಡಿ a bundle of the said beans. —ಬೂರು the creeper of *Entada monastachia.* —ಗೊಬ್ಬುನಿ to play with *Entada* seeds.

ಪಲ್ಲೆಂಕಿ palleṅki, *s.* A palankeen.

ಪಲ್ಲೆಕ್ಕಿರೋಗ pallekkirōga, *s.* Rickets.

ಪವನ್ pavanu, *s.* A gold coin equal to twenty shillings.

ಪವನ pavana, *s.* A sieve, strainer.

ಪವನ, ಪವಮಾನ pavana, pavamāna, *s.* Air, wind.

ಪವಲ, ಪವಳ pavala, pavaḷa, *see* ಪಕಲ.

ಪವಿತ್ರ pavitra, *adj.* Clean, pure, purified. *s.* Sacrificial (*or* kuša) grass, *Poa cynosuroides.* 2. a ring of kuša grass put on the fourth finger by a Brahman while performing a ceremony.

ಪವುಂಚಿ pavuṅči, *s.* A bracelet of gold beads.

ಪವುಂಜಿ pavuṅji, *s.* The Dasara festival.

ಪವುಂಜಿಗಾರೆ pavuṅjigāre, *s.* A fop, dandiprat; a vain *or* proud man.

ಪವುಜಿ pavuji, *see* ಫವುಜಿ.

ಪವೊಲಿ pavoli, *see* ಪಾವೊಲಿ.

ಪಶಪಶ pašapaša, *see* ಪಚಪಚ.

ಪಶು pašu, *s.* An animal in general. 2. a beast. 3. horned cattle.

ಪಶೆ pašè, *see* ಪಸೆ.

ಪಶ್ಚಾತಾಪ, ಪಶ್ಚಾತ್ತಾಪ pasčātāpa, pasčāttāpa, *s.* Contrition, repentance, remorse, sorrow. 2. pity, compassion. –ಆಪಿನಿ to be penitent. –ಪಡೆವೊಂಁಬುನಿ, –ಮಳ್ಪುನಿ to repent.

ಪಸ್ಂಬೆ, ಪಸಂಬೆ pasụmbè, pasambè, *s.* A sack *or* bag made of coir.

ಪಸಂಗರಿ pasaṅgari, *s.* A kind of condiment.

ಪಸಂತ್, ಪಸಂದ್ pasantụ, pasandụ, *adj.* Comely, handsome, well, pleasing, nice.

ಪಸಂತ್ರ, ಪಸಂದ್ರ pasantra, pasandra, *s.* Vicinity, neighbourhood, environ.

ಪಸಕ್ಕ pasakka, *see* ಪಚಕ್ಕ.

ಪಸರಿಯುನಿ pasariyuni, *see* ಪಸೆರುನಿ.

ಪಸಲ್ pasalụ, *s.* The share of a fisherman.

ಪಸಲಿ pasali, *see* ಫಸಲಿ.

ಪಸಾಡಿ pasāḍi, *see* ಪಾಸಾಡಿ.

ಪಸಾದ್ pasādụ, *s.* Transpiring, becoming public.

ಪಸಾರ್ pasārụ, *see* ಪಸ್ಸರ.

ಪಸಾರಿ pasāri, *s.* A druggist.

ಪಸಿ pasi, *s.* A boy. 2. a child.

ಪಸಿಂಕರ pasiṅkara, *s.* Dampness, wetness. 2. yielding, softness.

ಪಸಿಗೆಟ್ಟಿ, ಪಸಿಗೆಟ್ಟೆ pasigeṭṭi, pasigeṭṭè, *see* ಪಸ್ಕಟ್ಟಿ.

ಪಸು pasu, *see* ಪಸಿ.

ಪಸೆ pasè, *s.* Moisture, wetness, dampness. 2. greasiness, oiliness. 3. essence, substance, strength. ನೀರದ– dampness. ನೆಯಿತ– greasiness of ghee. ಪುಗೆರೆದ– the strength of tobacco.

ಪಸೆರುನಿ paseruni (ಪಸೆರ್), *v. n.* & *a.* To extend, diffuse, spread.

ಪಸ್ಕ್ paskụ, *s.* Collection, fee. –ಎತ್ತುನಿ to collect a fee.

ಪಸ್ಕಟ್ಟಿ, ಪಸ್ಕೆಟ್ಟಿ paskaṭṭi, paskeṭṭi, *s.* Turf, sod, sward, removed from the earth for covering a wall, *etc.*, with it.

ಪಸ್ಕಾರ್ paskārụ, *see* ಪಚಾರ.

ಪಸ್ಕಿ paski, *s.* Punishing a boy

by making him to stand and sit alternately with both ears seized by his fingers cross-armed.

ಪಸ್ಕುತ್ತ **paskutta,** *s.* Sickliness. –ದಾಯೆ a sickly man, invalid.

ಪಸ್ಕೆಡಿ **paskeḍi,** *see* ಪಸ್ಕಟ್ಟಿ.

ಪಸ್ಪು **paspu,** *adj.* Clear. 2. wet; *cf.* ಪಸೆ. 3. *see* ಪದ್ಪು.

ಪಸ್ಸರ್ **passaru,** *s.* Clipping, cutting asunder. 2. killing, murdering.

ಪಸ್ಸುನಿ **passuni,** *see* ಪತ್ತುನಿ.

ಪಳಂಕ್, ಪಳಂಗ್ **paḷaṅku, paḷaṅgu,** *see* ಪಲ್ಲಂಗ.

ಪಳಂಕೆನ **paḷaṅkena,** *see* ಪಲಂಕೆನ.

ಪಳಂತಿಗೆ **paḷantigè,** *s.* Declivity.

ಪಳದ್ಯ **paḷadya,** *s.* Sauce *or* pepper-water with *or* without vegetables.

ಪಳಪಳ **paḷapaḷa,** *s.* The rippling noise of water. *adv.*, *see* ಥಳಥಳ.

ಪಳಾನೆ **paḷānè,** *see* ಫಲಾನೆ.

ಪಳಿ **paḷi,** *s.* A long rice-field. 2. *see* ಪಲಿ.

ಪಳಿಕೆ **paḷikè,** *see* ಪಲಿಕೆ.

ಪಳೆಂಕುನಿ **paḷeṅkuni** (ಪಳೆಂಕ್), *v. a.* To upset, overturn.

ಪಳ್ಕುನಿ **paḷkuni,** *see* ಪಲ್ಕುನಿ.

ಪಳ್ಳ **paḷḷa,** *s.* A shallow stream, pond, ditch. 2. a hollow, low spot. 3. a hole, pit. –ತೆಂಜುನಿ to roll in a pond; to fill up a hollow.

ಪಳ್ಳಿ **paḷḷi,** *s.* A mosque. 2. *see* ಹಳ್ಳಿ.

ಪಳ್ಳು **paḷḷu,** *see* ಪಲ್ಲು.

ಪಳ್ಳೆ **paḷḷè,** *see* ಪಲ್ಲೆ.

ಪಳ್ಳೆನ **paḷḷena,** *s.* Light, shine. 2. *see* ಪಣಕೆ. –ಆಪಿನಿ to become light; to shine.

ಪಕ್ಷ **paksha,** *s.* The dark *or* bright half of the lunar month. 2. a side, flank. 3. a party. 4. partiality. 5. an argument; a position advanced *or* to be maintained. –ದಾಯೆ a partisan, adherent. –ಪಾತ, ಪರ– partiality. –ಪಾತಿ a partial person. –ರಾವು, –ವಾತ paralysis. –ವಾತದಾಯೆ a paralytic. ಕೃಷ್ಣ– the dark lunar fortnight. ಶುಕ್ಲ– the bright lunar fortnight. ಪಕ್ಷೊಗು ಪೋಪಿನಿ, ಪಕ್ಷೊಗು ಸೇರುನಿ to take a side.

ಪಕ್ಷವಾತ, ಪಕ್ಷವಾಯು **pakshavāta, pakshavāyu,** *s.* Paralysis.

ಪಕ್ಷಾಂತರ **pakshāntara,** *s.* Another side *or* part. 2. the opinion of a party.

ಪಕ್ಷಿ **pakshi,** *see* ಪಕ್ಕಿ.

ಪಕ್ಷಿವಾಲ್ **pakshivālu,** *see* ಪಕ್ಷದಾಯೆ *under* ಪಕ್ಷ.

ಪಾಂಕ್ **pāṅku,** *s.* A kind of musical instrument.

ಪಾಂಕ **pāṅka,** *see* ಪಂಕ.

ಪಾಂಗಳ **pāṅgaḷa,** *s.* A portion, share. –ಹಾಕುನಿ to divide; to mark.

ಪಾಂಗಿತನ, ಪಾಂಗಿದನ, ಪಾಂಗಿದಾನ **pāṅgitana, pāṅgidana, pāṅgidāna,** *s.* Scorn, mockery, jeering, despising.

ಪಾಂಗಿಯಾವುನಿ **pāṅgiyāvuni,** *c. v.* (*of* ಪಾಂಗಿಯುನಿ) To despise, jeer, mock.

ಪಾಂಗಿಯುನಿ, ಪಾಂಗ್ಯುನಿ **pāṅgiyuni, pāṅgyuni** (ಪಾಂಗಿ), *v. n.* To be despised, jeered, mocked.

ಪಾಂಗೀಲ **pāṅgīla,** *adj.* Precious.

ಪಾಂಗು **pāṅgu,** *s.* Sickness. 2. a share. 3. proportion.

ಪಾಂಚಾಲೆರ್ **pāñcāleru̥,** *see* ಪಂಚಾಳೆರ್.

ಪಾಂಜ **pāñja,** *adj.* Oblique, sloping.

ಪಾಂಜರ, ಪಾಂಜಾರ **pāñjara, pāñjāra,** *s.* A den, cave, cavern. 2. a cage.

ಪಾಂಟ್, ಪಾಂಟು **pāṇṭu̥, pāṇṭu,** *s.* Fatigue, weariness. –ಕಟ್ಟುನಿ to get weary.

ಪಾಂಟೆ **pāṇṭe,** *s.* A spool. [man.

ಪಾಂಟೆ **pāṅṭe,** *s.* A stiff, stunted

ಪಾಂಟೆಲ **pāṇṭela,** *s.* Stiffness; stuntedness.

ಪಾಂಡ **pāṇḍa,** *see* ಪಾಂಡಿ.

ಪಾಂಡರ **pāṇḍara,** *s.* Pale *or* yellowish white.

ಪಾಂಡವಬಜ್ಜೆಯಿ **pāṇḍava bajjei,** *s.* A large kind of areca nut.

ಪಾಂಡವು, ಪಾಂಡವೆ **pāṇḍavu, pāṇḍave,** *s.* A pigeon, dove.

ಪಾಂಡವೆರ್ **pāṇḍaveru̥,** *s.* The five Pāṇḍu princes.

ಪಾಂಡಿ **pāṇḍi,** *s.* A country in the south of India, comprehending part of the modern Tamil provinces. –ತುಂಡು, –ಮುಂಡು a male's garment manufactured there. –ಮರ, *see* ಪಾಂಡಿಲ್.

ಪಾಂಡಿಲ್, ಪಾಂಡೆಲ್ **pāṇḍilu̥, pāṇḍelu̥,** *s.* A kind of tree; *cf.* ಬಾಂಡೀಲ್. –ಕೆಬಿ large ears.

ಪಾಂಡು **pāṇḍu,** *s.* The father of the five Pāṇḍu princes and sovereign of ancient Delhi. *adj.* Pale, yellowish white, piebald. –ಪಿತ್ತ liver complaint. –ರೋಗ the white leprosy.

ಪಾಂಡ್ಯ **pāṇḍya,** *see* ಪಾಂಡಿ.

ಪಾಂಣೆರೆ **pāṇṇere,** *see* ಪಾಡ್ಣೆರೆ *under* ಪಾಡುನಿ.

ಪಾಂತ **pānta,** *adj.* Linear, regular, methodical.

ಪಾಂತುನಿ **pāntuni** (ಪಾಂತಿ), *v. n.* To be eager, impatient. 2. to vie, compete. ಪಾಂತಿಪಾಂತಿದ್ eagerly, ardently. ಪಾಂತ್ಪಾಂತ್ದ್ ಗೆಪ್ಪುನಿ to purchase eagerly.

ಪಾಂತೆ **pānte,** *s.* A butterfly.

ಪಾಂದವ, ಪಾಂದವು **pāndava, pāndavu,** *s.* A thin strip of a cocoanut branch *or* of other fibrous trees, generally used as a band *or* tie. –ದ ಬಳ್ಳಿ a string *or* cord made of such strips.

ಪಾಂದಿಲ್, ಪಾಂದೆಲ್ **pāndilu̥, pāndelu̥,** *s.* A kind of bush.

ಪಾಂಪು **pāmpu,** *see* ಪಾವು.

ಪಾಂಬೊಲ್ **pāmbolu̥,** *s.* A kind of flat, long fish. *adj.* Long, slender. –ಕೇರೆ a rat-snake.

ಪಾಕ್ **pāku̥,** *adv.* Once a day. –ಮೂರುನಿ to cut once; to tap, as a palm-tree.

ಪಾಕ **pāka,** *adj.* Some, several,

a few. –ಜನ a few persons. –ಸಮಯ some time.

ಪಾಕ pāka, *s*. Maturity, the state of being boiled *or* ripened. –ಆಪಿನಿ to be fully ripe; to be properly prepared, as food, *etc*. –ಮಳ್ಪುನಿ to cook, boil.

ಪಾಕು pāku, *see* ಪಾಕ.

ಪಾಕುಟ್ಟಿ pākuṭṭi, *s*. A knife for cutting betel-nuts.

ಪಾಗರ, ಪಾಗಾರ pāgara, pāgāra, *s*. An inclosure, fence; a rampart.

ಪಾಗೆ pāgè, *s*. A kind of tree.

ಪಾಚ pāca, *s*. The lungs of fish. 2. the skin of the leg.

ಪಾಚಿ pāci, *s*. A sponge. 2. *see* ಪಾಚ.

ಪಾಚಿಗೆ, ಪಾಚು pācigè, pācu, *s*. A kind of pill.

ಪಾಚಿಲ್, ಪಾಚಿಲೆ pācilu, pācilè, *s*. A bivalve shell, *Mythilus*.

ಪಾಚೆ pācè, *see* ಪಾಚ. 2. *see* ಪಾರೆ.

ಪಾಛ್ಛಾಯೆ, ಪಾಜಾವು pāccāye, pājāvu, *s*. A pasha, sovereign, ruler. –ಅರಸ್ಥನ royalty of a pasha.

ಪಾಜಿ pāji, *s*. A servant, menial. ಕಾಜಿ ಪೋದು ಪಾಜಿ ಆವೆ even a Kāzi may become a menial; misfortune may reduce a great man to obscurity.

ಪಾಜೆ, ಪಾಜೆಯಿ pājè, pājeyi, *s*. Algae, lichen. –ಪತ್ತುನಿ algae to grow.

ಪಾಜೆಯಿ, ಪಾಜೇವು pājeyi, pājēvu, *s*. The tree *Ficus conglomerata*; *also* ಗರ್ಗಸ ತಪ್ಪು.

ಪಾಟ್ pāṭu, *see* ಪಾಡ್.

ಪಾಟ pāṭa, *see* ಪಾಠ.

ಪಾಟಲ pāṭala, *s*. Pale red, rose colour. 2. the trumpet flower plant; *also* ಪಾಟಲಿ. –ಪೂ the trumpet flower.

ಪಾಟಾಳಿ pāṭāḷi, *s*. The manager *or* warden of a temple.

ಪಾಟಿ pāṭi, *s*. A gang of workmen, particularly working on roads. 2. road-work; *also* ಪಾಟಿದ ಬೇಲೆ. 3. a party, set of people.

ಪಾಠ pāṭha, *s*. A lesson, task. 2. reading. –ಶಾಲೆ a school. –ಕಲ್ಪುನಿ to commit to memory. –ಕೊರ್ಪಿನಿ to deliver a lesson. –ಮಳ್ಪುನಿ to learn *or* commit to memory, as a lesson; to practise, do frequently; to contract a habit.

ಪಾಡ್ pāḍu, *s*. Likeness, similarity, mode, form, order.

ಪಾಡ pāḍa, *s*. An oil vessel. 2. a liquid measure equal to about one maund.

ಪಾಡಗ pāḍaga, *s*. An anklet.

ಪಾಡಲ್ pāḍalu, *see* ಪದಿಲ್.

ಪಾಡಾರಿ pāḍāri, *adj*. Destitute, poor. 2. extravagant, reckless, ruinous.

ಪಾಡಾವಳ್ಳಿ pāḍāvaḷḷi, *see* ತಿಪಲೆ.

ಪಾಡಾವುನಿ pāḍāvuni, *c. v.* (*of* ಪಾಡುನಿ) To cause to throw, place, put.

ಪಾಡಿ pāḍi, *s*. An under-wood, small forest; *also* ಹಾಡಿ.

ಪಾಡುಗ pāḍuga, *see* ಪಾಡಗ.

ಪಾಡುಣಿಯೆರೆ pāḍuṇiyerè, *see under* ಪಾಡುನಿ.

ಪಾಡುನಿ pāḍuni (ಪಾಡ್), *v. a.* To throw, cast, fling; to discharge, as a missile weapon *or* fire-arm. 2. to place, put. 3. to put on, dress. 4. to pour. ಅಂಗಿ– to put on a coat. ಗುಂಡು– to shoot. ಪುದರ್– to name. ಕಡ್ಯಡ್– to pour into a pot. ಗುವೆಲ್ಡ್– to throw into a well. ಪೆಟ್ಟಿಗೆಡ್– to put into a box. ಪಾಡಿ thrown, discharged; worn; poured. ಪಂಡಿ ಬೇಲೆ ಪಾಡಿ ನುಪ್ಪು *lit.* the task set and the food doled out; slavery which exacts the largest quantity of labour for the least pay. ಪಾಡುಣಿಯೆರೆ, ಪಾಡ್ಣೆರೆ, ಪಾಂಜಿರೆ *lit.* put for eating; any thing serving as sauce *or* pepper-water.

ಪಾಡೆನಾಯಿ pāḍenāyi, *see* ಪಡೆನಾಯಿ.

ಪಾಡೊಣುನಿ pāḍoṇuni, *refl. v.* (*of* ಪಾಡುನಿ) To wear, dress; to put on a mask.

ಪಾಡ್ಣೆರೆ pāḍṇerè, *see under* ಪಾಡುನಿ.

ಪಾಡ್ದನ pāḍdana, *s.* A legendary account of the demons and heroes of the Tuḷu country in verse. ಜುಮಾದಿ– the tale of the demon Jumādi. –ಪಣ್ಪುನಿ to recite such verses.

ಪಾಡ್ಯ pāḍya, *s.* The first lunar day of either fortnight.

ಪಾಡ್ರುನಿ pāḍruni, *see* ಪಾಡುನಿ.

ಪಾಣಿ pāṇi, *s.* The hand. –ಗ್ರಹಣ a marriage.

ಪಾಣಿ pāṇi, *s.* A large water-pot.

ಪಾಣಿನಿ pāṇini, *s.* A celebrated Sanskrit grammarian.

ಪಾಣೆ pāṇè, *s.* A large earthen pot.

ಪಾಣ್ಣೆರೆ pāṇṇerè, *see under* ಪಾಡುನಿ.

ಪಾತ, ಪಾತನ pāta, pātana, *see* ಪತನ.

ಪಾತಕ, ಪಾತಗ pātaka, pātaga, *s.* Sin, crime. ಪಾತಕಿ, ಪಾತಕೆ, ಪಾತಗೆ a sinner.

ಪಾತಾಳ pātāḷa, *s.* The infernal regions, hell. –ಗರುಡ, –ಗರುಡೆ a drag to catch things under water; *cf.* ಗರುಡಪಾತಾಳ *under* ಗರುಡ. –ಗುಳಿಗೆ a demon so called. –ಗ್ರಹಣ an eclipse below the horizon. –ಭೈರವೆ a demon so called.

ಪಾತಿ pāti, *s.* A small boat. 2. a trough *or* bathing tub. 3. a spout, drain, sluice, tube. 4. a nursery for plants.

ಪಾತಿತ್ಯ pātitya, *s.* A lapse, fall. 2. loss of caste.

ಪಾತಿರಿ pātiri, *s.* A priest. 2. a demon priest.

ಪಾತಿವ್ರತ್ಯ pātivratya, *s.* Chastity.

ಪಾತು pātu, *adj.* Bent. –ಪೋಪಿನಿ to bend, be curved.

ಪಾತುನಿ pātuni, *see* ಪಾಪಾವುನಿ.

ಪಾತೆರ pātera, *s.* A word, speech, saying. 2. language. 3. a promise. –ಕೊರ್ಪಿನಿ to promise.

ಯೆಂಕ್ ಬಂಜಿ ಪಾತೆರ ಉಂಡು I have something to say.

ಪಾತೆರಾವುನಿ, ಪಾತೆರ್ಪಾವುನಿ pāterāvuni, pāterpāvuni, *c.v.* (*of* ಪಾತೆರುನಿ) To cause to speak. 2. to make reproach.

ಪಾತೆರಿ pāteri, *see* ಪಾತಿರಿ.

ಪಾತೆರುನಿ pāteruni (ಪಾತೆರ್), *v. n.* To speak, say, converse, talk. *v. a.* To reproach, scold, abuse.

ಪಾತ್ರ pātra, *adj.* Worthy, fit, suitable. *s.* Worth.

ಪಾತ್ರ, ಪಾತ್ರೆ pātra, pātrè, *s.* A vessel in general; a plate, cup, jar. —ತುರೆ a round kind of water-gourd.

ಪಾತ್ರಿ pātri, *see* ಪಾತಿರಿ.

ಪಾದ pāda, *s.* A foot. 2. the foot *or* line of a stanza. —ತೀರ್ಥ water in which a spiritual guide has washed his feet; a foot-bath. —ಪೀಠ a foot-stool. —ಪೂಜೆ worshipping the feet, as of a guru. —ರಕ್ಷೆ a sandal, shoe. —ಸೇವೆ prostration; personal service.

ಪಾದಟ್ಟಿಗೆ pādaṭṭigè, *s.* The pedestal of a column.

ಪಾದರಸ pādarasa, *s.* Quicksilver, mercury.

ಪಾದರಿ pādari, *s.* The tree *Bignonia chelonoides.* 2. *see* ಪಾದ್ರಿ.

ಪಾದಾಟಿಗೆ pādāṭigè, *see* ಪಾದಟ್ಟಿಗೆ.

ಪಾದಾರ pādāra, *s.* A pair.

ಪಾದುಕೆ, ಪಾದುಗೆ pādukè, pādugè, *s.* Wooden sandals.

ಪಾದೆ pādè, *s.* A rock. —ಪೂ a flower growing on rocks. —ಮುಳ್ಳು *Polycorpaea corymbosa*; *cf.* ಅಟೂರ.

ಪಾದ್ಯ pādya, *s.* Water for washing the feet.

ಪಾದ್ರಿ, ಪಾದ್ರೆ pādri, pādrè, *s.* An European clergyman. 2. a Christian missionary, minister.

ಪಾನ್ pāṇu, *s.* A page.

ಪಾನ pāna, *s.* Drinking. ಮದ್ಯ— drinking spirituous liquors.

ಪಾನಕ pānaka, *s.* The cooling drink made from jaggory, pepper, and water mixed together, lemonade. —ಪೂಜೆ offering such a drink to a deity.

ಪಾನಪಾತ್ರ pānapātra, *s.* A drinking vessel, cup.

ಪಾನಸ್, ಪಾನಾಸ್ pānasu, pānāsu, *s.* A lantern.

ಪಾನಿ pāni, *s.* Water.

ಪಾನೆ pānè, *s.* A kind of brass vessel. ಒಲಿತ— a vessel made of palmyra leaves. —ಪತ್ತುನಿ to make a small basket of leaves.

ಪಾಂಕ pānka, *see* ಪಾನಕ.

ಪಾಪ pāpa, *s.* Sin, fault, transgression, iniquity, crime, guilt, wickedness, evil. 2. pity. *adj.* Vile, mischievous. 2. pitiable. ಅಯ್ಯೋ— alas! what a sin! what a pity! —ಕರ್ಮ a wicked act. —ಗುಣ a depraved nature. —ಸಂಕೀರ್ತನೆ, —ದರಿಕೆ confession of sin. —ನಾಶನ, —ಹರಣ —ಪರಿಹಾರ pardon, atonement of sin, absolution from sin. —ಸಂಕಟ distress occasioned by sin. —ಪುಣ್ಯ vice and virtue. —ಕಟ್ಟುನಿ to commit evil; to incur guilt. —ತಟ್ಟೊಣುನಿ to be hardened in sin. —ಮಳ್ಪುನಿ to sin.

ಪಾಪಟೆ **pāpaṭe**, *s.* The parting of the hair on a female's forehead.

ಪಾಪತು **pāpatu**, *see* ಪಾಪೊತ್ತು.

ಪಾಪರಿ **pāpari**, *s.* Pauperism, destitution. 2. a pauper. *adj.* Insolvent.

ಪಾಪಸ್ **pāpasu**, *s.* Shoes, slippers.

ಪಾಪವುನಿ **pāpavuni**, *see* ಪಾಪಾವುನಿ.

ಪಾಪರಿಗೆ **pāparige**, *s.* Insolvency.

ಪಾಪಾತ್ಮೆ **pāpātme**, *s.* A sinner, criminal.

ಪಾಪಾವು **pāpāvu**, *adj.* Bent.

ಪಾಪಾವುನಿ **pāpāvuni** (ಪಾಪಾ), *v. a.* To bow, bend. *v. n.* To be sufficient, enough.

ಪಾಪಾಸ್ **pāpāsu**, *see* ಪಾಪಸ್.

ಪಾಪಿ, ಪಾಪಿಷ್ಟೆ **pāpi, pāpishṭe**, *s.* A sinner. 2. a destitute man.

ಪಾಪು **pāpu**, *s.* A small bridge; a stone *or* log of wood, *etc.*, serving for a bridge.

ಪಾಪು **pāpu**, *adj.* Enough.

ಪಾಪೆ **pāpe**, *s.* An image, statue, puppet, doll. *adj.* Bent, inclined. —ಮರ a bent tree. —ದೀಪಿನಿ, —ಪಾಡುನಿ to offer a representation of one's self as a thank-offering to a deity.

ಪಾಪೊತ್ತು **pāpottu**, *adj.* Suffering innocently. —ನರಮಾನಿ an innocent sufferer.

ಪಾಮಚ್ **pāmaču**, *s.* A small wooden bridge.

ಪಾಮಚ್ಚ **pāmačča**, *s.* A kind of scab.

ಪಾಮಜಿ, ಪಾಮಜು **pāmaji, pāmaju**, *s.* Moss. 2. a green substance floating on stagnant water. —ಪತ್ತುನಿ to become mossy.

ಪಾಮರ **pāmara**, *adj.* Ignorant, stupid, foolish. 2. wicked, vile, base, rude. —ಜನ low, ignorant people. —ತನ ignorance, rudeness.

ಪಾಮರಿ **pāmari**, *adj.* Vile. 2. scabby. —ರೋಗ scabbiness; itch, eczema.

ಪಾಯ **pāya**, *s.* Foundation. 2. gain, profit; *cf.* ಪಾಯಿದ. —ತೂಪಿನಿ to look to one's own advantage. —ತೋಡುನಿ, —ದೆಪ್ಪುನಿ to dig a foundation. —ಪಾಡುನಿ to lay a foundation. —ಮಳ್ಪುನಿ to gain.

ಪಾಯ **pāya**, *s.* Coming into existence, *or* being delivered of a child, as among Pariahs, *etc.* 2. *see* ಪಯ. —ಆಪಿನಿ, ಪಾಯಾಪಿನಿ to be born, delivered of a child.

ಪಾಯಸ **pāyasa**, *s.* A preparation consisting of rice, milk, and sugar.

ಪಾಯಾಪಿನಿ **pāyāpini**, *see under* ಪಾಯ.

ಪಾಯಾವುನಿ pāyāvuni, *c. v.* (*of* ಪಾಯುನಿ) To ripple, agitate the surface of water.

ಪಾಯಿ pāyi, *s.* A sail. 2. a mat. 3. *see* ಪಾಯ. –ಕಟ್ಟುನಿ, –ಮಡಿಪುನಿ to take the sails in; to decamp, run away. –ಕೊರ್ಪಿನಿ, –ಪಾಡುನಿ, –ಬುದ್ಪಿನಿ to set sail.

ಪಾಯಿಕಾನೆ, ಪಾಯಿಖಾನೆ pāyikānè, pāyikhānè, *s.* A privy.

ಪಾಯಿದ, ಪಾಯಿದೆ pāyida, pāyidè, *s.* Profit, advantage, gain. 2. ready money.

ಪಾಯಿದಳ pāyidaḷa, *s.* Infantry.

ಪಾಯಿನಾಳಿ pāyināḷi, *see* ಪಯಿಞಾಲಿ.

ಪಾಯಿಲ್ಮಾನೆ pāyilumāne, *see* ಪೈಲ್ವಾನೆ.

ಪಾಯಿಸ್ pāyisu, *adj.* Public, published, known. 2. *see* ಪಾಯಸ. 3. *see* ಪೈಸ್. –ಮಳ್ಪುನಿ to publish, advertise, notify, make known.

ಪಾಯಿಸ pāyisa, *see* ಪಾಯಸ.

ಪಾಯುನಿ pāyuni (ಪಾಯಿ), *v. n.* To ripple, be agitated, as the surface of water. 2. to be diffused, as molten metal, *etc.*, in a mould.

ಪಾಯೆಕ್ಕೆಲ್ pāyekkelu, *see* ಪಯಕೆಲ್.

ಪಾಯೆಸ್ pāyesu, *see* ಪೈಸ್.

ಪಾಯ್ಯನ pāyyana, *see* ಪಯ್ಯನ.

ಪಾರ್ pāru, *s.* An islet.

ಪಾರ್ pāru, *s.* The opposite bank of a river. 2. end, extremity. –ಆಪಿನಿ to pass, ford, cross over; to get through *or* over a difficulty. –ಮಳ್ಪುನಿ to make pass *or* cross over; to deliver from a difficulty.

ಪಾರ್ಪೋಪಿನಿ pārupōpini, *see* ಪಾರುನಿ.

ಪಾರ pāra, *s.* Guard, custody, keeping. –ಕಾಪುನಿ, –ಮಳ್ಪುನಿ to guard. –ಕುಳ್ಳುನಿ to guard, watch. –ದೀಪಿನಿ, –ಪಾಡುನಿ to place a guard. –ದಾಯೆ a sentry, guard. ಪಾರೊಡು ದೀಪಿನಿ to put in a lockup.

ಪಾರ pāra, *s.* Brooding, hatching, incubation. ಪಾರೊಡು ಕುಳ್ಳುನಿ to brood, sit on eggs. ಪಾರೊಗು ದೀಪಿನಿ to place the eggs for brooding *or* incubation. ಪಾರೊಗು ಬರ್ಪಿನಿ to prepare to sit on eggs after a fowl has finished laying them.

ಪಾರಂಪರೆ, ಪಾರಂಪರ್ಯ pāramparè, pāramparya, *s.* Continuous order *or* succession. 2. tradition.

ಪಾರಜಾತ pārajāta, *see* ಪರಿಜಾತ.

ಪಾರದಾಯೆ pāradāye, *s.* A guard, sentry, *or* watchman.

ಪಾರಮಾರ್ಥಿಕ pāramārthika, *s.* One intent upon another world. *adj.* Real, true, sincere.

ಪಾರಾಟ pārāṭa, *s.* Running, a race.

ಪಾರಾಯಣ pārāyaṇa, *s.* Reading from a sacred book the lesson for the day.

ಪಾರಾವುನಿ pārāvuni, *c. v.* (*of* ಪಾರುನಿ) To cause to run; to drive.

ಪಾರಿ **pāri**, *s.* A milk pot. 2. water. 3. *see* ಪಾಲಿ.

ಪಾರಿಗೆ **pārigè**, *see* ಪಾರಾಟ.

ಪಾರಿಜಾತ **pārijāta**, *s.* One of the trees of paradise, *Nyctanthes arbor tristis.* 2. the tree yielding every wish.

ಪಾರಿಶ **pāriša**, *see* ಪಾರ್ಶಿ.

ಪಾರು **pāru**, *see* ಪಾರ್. 2. *see* ಪಾರ.

ಪಾರುನಿ **pāruni** (ಪಾರ್), *v. n.* To run. 2. to fly. 3. to escape. ಜೀವ— to expire. ಪಾರುನಾಯಿ, *see* ಪಾರೆಲೆ.

ಪಾರುಪಣಿ **pārupaṇi**, *s.* A drizzling [rain.

ಪಾರುಪತ್ಯ **pārupatya**, *s.* Management, superintendence. —ಗಾರೆ a manager, superintendent.

ಪಾರುಳು **pāruḷu**, *see* ಪಾರೊಳು. 2. *see* ಪೊಲ್ಯ.

ಪಾರೆ **pārè**, *s.* The hip, haunch. 2. the shoulder. 3. the scomber, a kind of fish; *also* ಪಾರೆಮೀನ್. 4. *see* ಪಾರ. 5. *see* ಪೊರ್ವೆಲ್. —ಜಾರುನಿ the hip *or* shoulder to be dislocated.

ಪಾರೆಂಗಿ **pāreṅgi**, *s.* An iron crowbar, used for digging. 2. a lever.

ಪಾರೆಂಜಿ **pāreñji**, *see* ಪರೆಜಿ.

ಪಾರೆಲ್ **pārelụ**, *s.* A fugitive animal. 2. *see* ಪಾರೊಳು.

ಪಾರೆಲೆ **pārele**, *s.* A runner; a run-away, truant; a fugitive.

ಪಾರೊಳು **pāroḷu**, *s.* A young she-buffalo.

ಪಾರ್ಕಣೆ **pārkaṇè**, *s.* Paying into a government treasury the revenue collected by a village officer. 2. examination of coins, assaying.

ಪಾರ್ತೆ **pārtè**, *see* ಪರ್ತೆ.

ಪಾರ್ಥ **pārtha**, *s.* A name of Arjuna. —ಸಾರಥಿ Kruṣhṇa.

ಪಾರ್ದನ **pārdana**, *see* ಪಾಡ್ದನ.

ಪಾರ್ಪಡಿಲ್ **pārpaḍilụ**, *adj.* Empty.

ಪಾರ್ವಣ **pārvaṇa**, *s.* A particular funeral ceremony. 2. a cake used at a funeral ceremony.

ಪಾರ್ವತಿ **pārvati**, *s.* The wife of Šiva.

ಪಾರ್ಶಿ **pārši**, *s.* A Parsee. 2. the Persian language. —ದೇಶ, —ಸ್ಥಾನ the kingdom of Persia.

ಪಾರ್ಶ್ವ **paršva**, *s.* A side. 2. a part. ಬಲ— the right side. ಯಡ— the left side.

ಪಾಲ್ **pālụ**, *s.* A share, portion, part, division. —ಗಾರೆ, —ದಾಯಿ a partner. ದಿಕ್ಕಾ— on all sides; dispersion. —ಆಪಿನಿ to be divided. —ಕೊರ್ಪಿನಿ to give a part, portion *or* share. —ತಿರ್ಪುನಿ to apportion. —ದೀಪಿನಿ, —ಮಳ್ಪುನಿ to divide. ಪಾಲ್ *is sometimes added to cardinal numbers for the purpose of forming multiplicatives; as*, ನಾಲ್—quadruple.

ಪಾಲಕಿ **pālaki**, *see* ಪಲ್ಲಂಕಿ.

ಪಾಲಕೆ **pālake**, *s.* A keeper, guardian; a protector, preserver. ದ್ವಾರ— a doorkeeper, porter. ದಿಕ್ಪಾಲಕೆರ್ the regents of the eight points of the compass.

ಪಾಲನೆ pālanè, *s.* Cherishing, protecting, nourishing, nursing; *see* ಪರಿಪಾಲನೆ.

ಪಾಲಸ, ಪಾಲಾಸೆ pālasa, pālāsè, *see* ಪಲಾಶ.

ಪಾಲಿ pāli, *s.* Invoking, addressing in prayer. 2. a vow. –ಪಣ್ಪುನಿ to implore; to make a vow.

ಪಾಲಿಪುನಿ, ಪಾಲಿಯುನಿ, ಪಾಲಿಸುನಿ pālipuni, pāliyuni, pālisuni (ಪಾಲಿ, ಪಾಲಿಸ್), *v. a.* To nourish, cherish, protect, keep. 2. to bestow, give, grant, distribute, vouchsafe.

ಪಾಲೆ, ಪಾಲೆಂಬು pālè, pālembu, *s.* The spatha of palm-blossoms *or* of an areca branch. 2. a cap made of areca spatha. 3. the sole of the foot. 4. the tree *Alstonia scholaria*. ಕಂಚಿ– the stalk of a spatha. –ದೀಪಿನಿ to put on a cap; to be in servitude. –ಪತ್ತುನಿ to hold a spatha; to beg. –ಲಕ್ಕುನಿ the spatha of an areca branch to fall off. ನೆಲ– a kind of grass.

ಪಾಲೆವು pālevu, *s.* A large tortoise.

ಪಾಲ್ಗುಣ pālguṇa, *see* ಫಾಲ್ಗುಣ.

ಪಾಲ್ಯ pālya, *s.* A grant. 2. *see* ಪಾಳ್ಯ.

ಪಾವಟೆ pāvaṭè, *s.* A step *or* stair. –ಕಟ್ಟುನಿ to erect steps.

ಪಾವಟೆ pāvaṭè, *s.* The bush *Pavetta Indica.*

ಪಾವಡೆ pāvaḍè, *s.* A foot-cloth; cloth spread on the floor at a wedding for the bride and bridegroom to tread upon. 2. a girl's garment, skirt. 3. a cover. 4. the cloth put on the back of a buffalo. ಕಸ– a petticoat.

ಪಾವಣ್ pāvaṇu, *see* ಪವನ್.

ಪಾವಣೆ, ಪಾವಾಣೆ pāvaṇè, pāvāṇè, *s.* A quarter anna, three pie.

ಪಾವತಿ pāvati, *s.* An acknowledgment. 2. payment. –ಚೀಟಿ a receipt.

ಪಾವನ pāvana, *s.* Purification. 2. penance. *adj.* Pure, purified.

ಪಾವಲಿ pāvali, *see* ಪಾವೊಲಿ.

ಪಾವು pāvu, *s.* A quarter seer. 2. curing, as tobacco, *etc.*; *see* ಅರೆಪಾವು. –ಕೊಡಿಗನಿ to cure, as tobacco, *etc.*

ಪಾವುಪೈಚಿಲ್ pāvupeičilu, *s.* A subscription given to a demon.

ಪಾವೊರಿ pāvori, *s.* A leech. ಯಿಮ್ಮೆ– a larger kind of leech.

ಪಾವೊಲಿ pāvoli, *s.* A quarter rupee.

ಪಾಶ pāśa, *s.* A fetter, chain, bond, tie. 2. a noose, snare.

ಪಾಶಿ pāśi, *s.* Hanging by the neck. 2. algae. 3. a kind of glass beads. 4. bleeding of the nose *or* the gums. –ಕಂಮ gallows. –ಗ ಕೊಡಿಗನಿ to hang.

ಪಾಶು pāśu, *s.* A mattress.

ಪಾಶುಪತ pāśupata, *s.* A Śivite sect. ಪಾಶುಪತಾಸ್ತ್ರ a kind of

charmed weapon; Šiva's trident.

ಪಾಶ್ವ pāšva, *see* ಪಾರ್ಶ್ವ.

ಪಾಷಂಡ pāshaṇḍa, *s.* Heresy, imposture.

ಪಾಷಂಡೆ pāshaṇḍe, *s.* A heretic, impostor. 2. a bigot, enthusiast.

ಪಾಷಾಣ pāshāṇa, *s.* A stone in general. 2. arsenic. —ಭೇದಿ the plant *Frianthema pentantra.* ಎಲಿ— white arsenic. ಗೌರಿ—, ಸಂಕ— are some of its varieties.

ಪಾಸ್ pāsụ, *s.* The warp of a loom. 2. *see* ಪಾಶು. —ಪಟ್ಟ a border. —ಜಪ್ಪುನಿ to prepare the warp. —ಪಾಡುನಿ to fix the warp in a loom.

ಪಾಸ್ pāsụ, *s.* Passing, as an examination *or* test. —ಆಪಿನಿ, ಪಾಸಾಪಿನಿ to pass, as an examination.

ಪಾಸ್‍ಪರಿಕೆ, ಪಾಸ್‍ಪಳಿಕೆ pāsụparikè, pāsụpaḷikè, *s.* A mattress, *etc.* 2. sound sleep. 3. cohabitation, conjugal harmony.

ಪಾಸ pāsa, *s.* Fasting; *cf.* ಉಪಾಸ. 2. the eleventh lunar day of either fortnight.

ಪಾಸಾಂತ್ರ pāsāntra, *s.* Neighbourhood, vicinity, suburbs.

ಪಾಸಾಡಿ pāsāḍi, *postp.* With, *a sign of the social case*; *as*, ಆಯ ಪಾಸಾಡಿ ಪೋಲ go with him. —ದಾಯಿ a companion, associate. —ಪೋಪಿನಿ to accompany.

ಪಾಸಾಣ pāsāṇa, *see* ಪಾಷಾಣ.

ಪಾಸಾಪಿನಿ pāsāpini, *see under* ಪಾಸ್.

ಪಾಸಿ pāsi, *see* ಪಾಶಿ.

ಪಾಸೆ pāsè, *s.* A kind of grass.

ಪಾಸ್ಪು pāspu, *see* ಪಾಮಜ್ಜ.

ಪಾಳ್ pāḷụ, *see* ಹಾಳ್.

ಪಾಳಿ pāḷi, *s.* A rag, shred. 2. *see* ಪಾಲಿ.

ಪಾಳಿ, ಪಾಳೆ pāḷi, pāḷè, *s.* The tip of the ear.

ಪಾಳೆ pāḷè, *see* ಪಾಲೆ.

ಪಾಳ್ಯ, ಪಾಳ್ಯೆ pāḷya, pāḷyè, *s.* An army. 2. a halting place. ತುಂಡುಪಾಳ್ಯಗಾರೆ a petty chieftain.

ಪಿಂಗ piṅga, *see* ಪಿಂಗಲ.

ಪಿಂಗಣ, ಪಿಂಗಣಿ piṅgaṇa, piṅgaṇi, *see* ಪಿಂಗಾಣಿ.

ಪಿಂಗರ, ಪಿಂಗರೆ piṅgara, piṅgarè, *s.* The blossom of the areca tree.

ಪಿಂಗರಿ piṅgari, *s.* Dissipation.

ಪಿಂಗಲ, ಪಿಂಗಳ piṅgala, piṅgaḷa, *s.* The fifty-first year of the Hindu cycle of sixty. 2. tawny colour; gold colour.

ಪಿಂಗಳೆ piṅgaḷe, *s.* A demi-god, called Yaksha. 2. fire.

ಪಿಂಗಾಣಿ piṅgāṇi, *s.* A small plate; porcelain, China ware.

ಪಿಂಗಾರ piṅgāra, *see* ಪಿಂಗರ.

ಪಿಂಙಣ, ಪಿಂಙಾಣಿ piṅṅaṇa, piṅṅāṇi, *see* ಪಿಂಗಾಣಿ.

ಪಿಂಚಿ piṅči, *s.* Parsimony, stinginess. *adj.* Parsimonious, stingy, miserly. —ಕಾಸ್ a miser, pinchpenny.

ಪಿಂಜರ, ಪಿಂಜಿರ, piṅjara, piṅjira, *s.* A bird's cage. 2. the body.

ಪಿಂಜರಿ piñjari, *adj.* Dejected, spiritless. 2. timorous; timid.

ಪಿಂಟ, ಪಿಂಟಂಗೆಲ್ piṇṭa, piṇṭangelu, *see* ಪೀಂಟ.

ಪಿಂಡ piṇḍa, *s.* A lump, heap, quantity. 2. a ball, globe. 3. a mouthful. 4. an oblation to the manes, as a ball *or* lump of rice mixed with milk, *etc.* 5. the fœtus *or* embryo, in the early period of gestation. 6. the body. ಪಿಂಡಾಧಿಕಾರಿ a man entitled to make oblations to the manes of his deceased relations. ಪಿಂಡೋತ್ಪತ್ತಿ the formation of the foetus.

ಪಿಂಡಾಂಡ piṇḍāṇḍa, *s.* The body.

ಪಿಂಡಿ piṇḍi, *s.* A bundle, parcel, burden. 2. what is squeezed *or* ground. 3. *see* ಪುಂಡಿ. –ಮರ್ದನ harassing, dunning, teasing. ಕುಂಟುಡ– a bundle of cloth. ಬಜ್ಜೆರೆಡ– a bundle of betel leaves. –ಕಟ್ಟುನಿ to tie into a parcel *or* bundle.

ಪಿಂಡು piṇḍu, *see* ಪುಂಡು.

ಪಿಂಡೆ piṇḍe, *see* ಪಿಂಡಿ.

ಪಿಂದ pinda, *see* ಪಿನ್ನಿನಿ.

ಪಿಂದಿನವು, ಪಿಂದಿನಾಯೆ, ಪಿಂದೊಣುನಿ pindinavu, pindināye, pindoṇuni, *see under* ಪಿನ್ನಿನಿ.

ಪಿಂನಿ pinni, *see* ಪಿನಿ.

ಪಿಂನೆ pinne, *s.* A hole. 2. the eye of a needle, *etc.* –ಕಡಿಯುನಿ the eye of a needle to break.

ಪಿಂಬಿಲಿ pimbili, *see* ಬಿಂಬಿಲಿ.

ಪಿಂಯಂವು piñyañvu, *adj.* Small, little.

ಪಿಕಿರ್ pikiru, *see* ಫಕಿರ.

ಪಿಕಿಲಾಟ, ಪಿಕ್ಲಾಟ pikilāṭa, piklāṭa, *s.* Cheating; wheedling, dishonest dealing. –ಮಳ್ಪುನಿ to cheat, deal dishonestly.

ಪಿಕ್ಕ pikka, *adj.* Fast, as colour.

ಪಿಕ್ಕಸ್, ಪಿಕ್ಕಾಸ್ pikkasu, pikkāsu, *s.* A pickaxe.

ಪಿಕ್ದಾನಿ pikdāni, *see* ಪೀಕದಾನಿ.

ಪಿಚಿಪಿಚಿ pičipiči, *adj.* Miry, muddy. 2. oozing, trickling. –ನೀರ್ oozing water.

ಪಿಚ್ಚ piċċa, *adj.* Left. –ಕೈ left hand.

ಪಿಚ್ಚಂಡ, ಪಿಚ್ಚಂಡಿ, ಪಿಚ್ಚಡಿ, ಪಿಚ್ಚಾಂಡಿ, ಪಿಚ್ಚಾಡಿ piċċaṇḍa, piċċaṇḍi, piċċaḍi, piċċāṇḍi, piċċāḍi, *s.* The hind part. 2. fetters. –ಬಲ್ಲ್ a rope to tie a horse's hind legs. –ಕಟ್ಟುನಿ to pinion, tie the hands behind.

ಪಿಚ್ಚಲಿ piċċali, *see* ಕಿಚ್ಚಲಿ.

ಪಿಚ್ಚಿ piċċi, *s.* Mammon; *also* ಪಿಚ್ಚಿದೇವೆರ್. 2. the testicles of animals. 3. a nut, especially the cashew nut; *also* –ಕೊರಂಟ. –ಮಾರ್ a nursery field. –ಗೊಬ್ಬುನಿ to play with cashew nuts. –ದೆಪ್ಪುನಿ to castrate.

ಪಿಚ್ಚೆ piċċe, *adj.* Left. –ಕೈ left hand.

ಪಿಚ್ಚೊಲಿ piċċoli, *see* ಪೆಚ್ಚಲಿ.

ಪಿಜ pija, *see* ಪಿಜ.

ಪಿಜಕ್ರೆ pijakrè, *see* ಬಿಜಕ್ರೆ.

ಪಿಜಿ piji, *s.* A twist.

ಪಿಜಿಂಕೆ pijinkè, *see* ಪಿಜಿಕೆ.

ಪಿಜಿಂಟ್ pijinṭu, *s.* Twisting, writhing.

ಪಿಜಿಂಟಾವುನಿ pijinṭāvuni, *c. v.* (*of* ಪಿಜಿಂಟುನಿ) To twist, writhe.

ಪಿಜಿಂಟುನಿ pijinṭuni (ಪಿಜಿಂಟಿ), *v. n.* To be twisted, writhed. 2. to be distorted, deformed. ಮೋಣಿ— the face to be distorted; to make a wry face.

ಪಿಜಿಂಟೆಲೆ pijinṭele, *s.* A man whose features are distorted, a deformed man.

ಪಿಜಿಕೆ pijikè, *s.* A kind of tree. 2. a twist.

ಪಿಜಿಕ್ರೆ pijikrè, *see* ಬಿಜಕ್ರೆ.

ಪಿಜಿನ್ pijinu, *s.* An ant. ಕೇ—, ನೆಯಿ—, ಮಂಡೆ—, ಮರ—, ಮರ್ಲ್— are some kinds of ants.

ಪಿಜಿಪುನಿ pijipuni (ಪಿಜಿಪ್), *v. a.* To twist, as a rope, yarn, *etc.*

ಪಿಜಿರ್ pijiru, *s.* A thin ear-ring.

ಪಿಜಿರಿಗೆ pijirigè, *s.* The matrix of a screw.

ಪಿಜಿರುನಿ pijiruni (ಪಿಜಿರ್), *v. n.* To turn, return. 2. to abate, subside; as rain, fever, *etc.*

ಪಿಜ್ಜಿ pijji, *s.* A great grandmother.

ಪಿಜ್ಜೆ pijje, *s.* A great grandfather.

ಪಿಜ್ರಿ pijri, *s.* The corner end of a female's cloth.

ಪಿಟಾರೆ piṭārè, *s.* A chest *or* trunk of rattan.

ಪಿಟಿ piṭi, *s.* Fear. 2. regard.

ಪಿಟಿಪಿಟಿ piṭipiṭi, *s.* A small noise. —ನಡಪುನಿ to walk with short, rapid steps, as a child. —ಲಾಗ್ಯುನಿ to hop, skip, jump.

ಪಿಟಿಲ್ piṭilu, *s.* A fiddle.

ಪಿಟ್ಟ್, ಪಿಟ್ಟ piṭṭu, piṭṭa, *s.* The tartar of the teeth. —ಪತ್ತುನಿ the teeth to be incrusted with tartar.

ಪಿಟ್ಟಸ್, ಪಿಟ್ಟಾಸ್ piṭṭasu, piṭṭāsu, *adj.* Brittle, fragile. 2. not properly baked *or* burnt. 3. delicate, frail, thin. 5. sordid, stingy, mean. —ಕರ a half baked earthen vessel. —ತಾರಾಯಿ a thin-shelled cocoanut. —ನರಮಾನಿ a man of delicate constitution; a mean person. —ಸಾಮಾನ್ brittle ware.

ಪಿಟ್ಟೆಲೆ piṭṭele, *s.* A miser, stingy man.

ಪಿಡಿತ, ಪಿಡಿತ್ತ, ಪಿಡ್ತ piḍita, piḍitta, piḍta, *s.* Discrimination, judgment; *bet.* ಹಿತ್ತ ಪಿಡ್ತ.

ಪಿಡಿತೆ piḍitè, *see* ಪಗರ್.

ಪಿಡಿಬಾಳ್ piḍibāḷu, *s.* A kind of razor.

ಪಿಡ್ಕ್ piḍku, *s.* Indisposition, indigestion.

ಪಿತ, ಪಿತೃ pita, pitru, *s.* A father. 2. the manes *or* deceased progenitors of mankind. —ತರ್ಪಣ, —ಕಾರ್ಯ worship of the manes by oblation of water, food, *etc.* —ತಿಥಿ the day on which offerings are made to the manes of an ancestor.

—ಲೋಕ the peculiar region *or* habitation of departed ancestors. —ವನ a cemetery. —ಸ್ಥಾನ like a father; a father's place.

ಪಿತಾಂಬ್ರ **pitāmbra,** *see* ಪೀತಾಂಬರ.

ಪಿತಾಮಹಿ, ಪಿತಾಮಿ **pitāmahi, pitāmi,** *s.* A paternal grandmother.

ಪಿತಾಮಹೆ, ಪಿತಾಮೆ **pitāmahe, pitāme,** *s.* A paternal grandfather. 2. Brahma, the great progenitor.

ಪಿತುಲಾತ್ **pitulātu̥,** *see* ಪಿಕಿಲಾಟ.

ಪಿತೂರಿ **pitūri,** *see* ಫಿತೂರಿ.

ಪಿತೆ **pite,** *see* ಪಿತ.

ಪಿತ್ತ್ **pittu̥,** *s.* Bile. 2. shifting, changing position; fickleness. —ದೀಪಿನಿ to shift, change position.

ಪಿತ್ತ **pitta,** *adj.* Bilious, choleric. —ಕಾಮೆಲಿ a jaundice producing salivation. —ಜರ bilious fever. —ಶರೀರ a bilious constitution *or* temperament. —ಪತ್ತುನಿ, —ಕೆದರುನಿ, —ಯೇರುನಿ to be bilious; to be irritated.

ಪಿತ್ತಪ್ಪೆ **pittappe,** *s.* A man of bilious *or* irritable temper; a crack-brained man.

ಪಿತ್ತರ **pittara,** *see* ಪಿದರ.

ಪಿತ್ತಲೆ **pittalè,** *s.* Brass. 2. tinsel. —ಕೆಬಿದಾಯಿ one who listens to tales. ಪೇರ್— pure brass, the mixture of copper and zink.

ಪಿತ್ತೂರಿ **pittūri,** *see* ಫಿತೂರಿ.

ಪಿತ್ರೆ **pitre,** *see* ಪಿತ.

ಪಿದ **pida,** *adj.* Outer. 2. lucky; *cf.* ಪಿದಯಿ. —ಕೈ allurement, a lucky hand. —ಕೈಮಳ್ಪುನಿ to allure, entice. —ತರ outside, external.

ಪಿದಂಕೆ **pidaṅkè,** *see* ಪೆದಂಕೆ.

ಪಿದಂಗರ **pidaṅgara,** *see* ಪೆದಂಗರ.

ಪಿದಂಬು **pidambu,** *see* ಪೆದಂಬು.

ಪಿದಕೈ **pidakei,** *s.* A water-vessel; *cf.* ಪೆದಂಗರ. 2. *see under* ಪಿದ.

ಪಿದಮಾಲೆ **pidamālè,** *see* ಪೆದಮಲೆ.

ಪಿದಯಿ **pidayi,** *adv.* Out, outside, abroad. *adj.* Outer. —ದ ಕಂಣ್ a covetous eye. —ದಾಯೆ an outsider, stranger, outcaste, heathen. —ದಾಳ್ a strange woman; a woman in menstruation. —ಆಪಿನಿ to be in monthly course. —ಪೋಪಿನಿ to go to stool.

ಪಿದರ **pidara,** *s.* The tie-beam of a roof, a beam resting on the pillars of a veranda.

ಪಿದಲುನಿ **pidaluni** (ಪಿದಲ್), *v. n.* To stumble, be sprained, introverted.

ಪಿದಾಡಾವುನಿ **pidāḍāvuni,** *c. v.* (*of* ಪಿದಾಡುನಿ) To cause to start, depart.

ಪಿದಾಡುನಿ **pidāḍuni** (ಪಿದಾಡ್), *v. n.* To start, depart.

ಪಿದಾರ **pidāra,** *see* ಪಿದರ.

ಪಿದುಕೊಣುನಿ **pidukoṇuni** (ಪಿದುಕೊ), *v. refl.* To know, understand, comprehend, ascertain, for one's self.

ಪಿನಾರಿ **pināri,** *see* ಪೀನಾರಿ.

ಪಿನಾಶಿ pināši, *s.* A cold affecting the nose. 2. a disease of the nasal membrane.

ಪಿನಿ pini, *adj.* Little, small, slight, trifling. –ಪಿನಿ very slight; *as*, –ಪಿನಿ ಬರ್ಸ a very slight drizzle.

ಪಿನ್ಕಟ್ pinkaṭu, *s.* An atom, mite, tittle.

ಪಿನ್ಪಾವುನಿ pinpāvuni, *c. v.* (*of* ಪಿನ್ಪಿನಿ) To make known, communicate, inform, report, reveal.

ಪಿನ್ಪಿನಿ pinpini (ಪಿನ್), *v. a.* To know, understand, comprehend. ಪಿಂದಿನವು what is known; knowledge, acquaintance, information. ಪಿಂದಿನಾಯೆ a man who is informed; a learned *or* wise man, scholar. ಪಿನಂದಿನಾಯೆ an ignorant man, a simpleton. ಪಿಂದೋಣುನಿ to know for one's self. ಪಿನಯು (you) don't know, (you) don't understand.

ಪಿಪ್ಪಲಿ pippali, *s.* Long pepper. *Piper longum.*

ಪಿಪ್ಪಿ pippi, *see* ಪೆಪ್ಪಿ.

ಪಿಯ್ಯ piyya, *see* ಪೀಯ್ಯೊ.

ಪಿರ pira, *adv.* Behind, after, *as to either situation, or time*; *cf.* ಪಿರವು. 2. again, back. –ಕೈ support, help; *as*, –ಕೈ ಕೊರ್ಪಿನಿ to support, help. –ಬುದ್ಧಿ an after-thought. –ಭಾಗ the hind part. –ಮುಖ abatement. ಮುಂಬು– front and rear. –ಆವುನಿ to abate, subside. –ಕೊರ್ಪಿನಿ to give back. –ಜಾರುನಿ to backslide; to with-draw. –ದೀಪಿನಿ to place behind, lay aside; to postpone, put off, defer. –ಪಾಡುನಿ to throw *or* put behind; to defeat, vanquish. –ಪೋಪಿನಿ to go back, return. –ಬರ್ಪಿನಿ to come back. –ಬೂರುನಿ to lag behind; to fall back; to be defeated, vanquished; to be put off, deferred. –ಮಳ್ಪುನಿ to do again; to delay, dilate. ಆಯೆ ಪಿರ ಜಾರಯೆ he will not shrink back; he can be relied on.

ಪಿರಂಕ್ pirañku, *see* ಪಿರಂಟ್.

ಪಿರಂಗಿ pirangi, *s.* A cannon. 2. *see* ಪರಂಗಿ.

ಪಿರಂಟ್, ಪಿರಂತ್ pirantu, pirantu, *see* ಜಿರಂತ್.

ಪಿರಕ piraka, *see* ಪ್ರಾಕ.

ಪಿರಡುನಿ piraḍuni, *see* ಪೆರೆಡುನಿ.

ಪಿರಣ piraṇa, *see* ಪ್ರಾಣ.

ಪಿರತ pirata, *see* ಪೆರತ.

ಪಿರತಿ pirati, *see* ಪ್ರತಿ.

ಪಿರದನೆ piradanè, *see* ಪೆರದನೆ.

ಪಿರಪ pirapa, *adv.* Back; again.

ಪಿರವು piravu, *adv.* Behind, in the rear. –ಕಾಜಿ a kind of bracelet. –ಬರ್ಪಿನಿ to follow. –ಪೋಪಿನಿ to go back, retreat, return.

ಪಿರಿ piri, *s.* A twist. 2. the spiral thread, as of a screw. 3. cure, healing. 4. abatement, removal. *adj.* Curing, healing. –ಮರ್ದ an antidote.

ಪಿರಿಕಟ್ಟ್ pirikaṭṭu, *s.* Cancellation, revocation, repealing, as an interdict, oath, *etc.*

ಪಿರಿಕೆ pirikè, *s.* Twisting; winding. 2. the state of being shaped like the spiral thread of a screw.

ಪಿರಿತಿನಿ piritini, *s.* A ceremony at Dharmasthala.

ಪಿರಿಪಾವುನಿ piripāvuni, *c. v.* (*of* ಪಿರಿ ಪುನಿ) To turn, twist.

ಪಿರಿಪಿನಿ piripini, *see* ಪಿರಿಯುನಿ.

ಪಿರಿಪಿರಿ piripiri, *adv.* In a continuous drizzle. 2. pratingly, loquaciously. —ಪಾತೆರುನಿ to prattle, prate. —ಬರ್ಸ ಬರ್ಪಿನಿ to rain, drizzle continuously.

ಪಿರಿಪು piripu, *s.* Abatement, removal; cessation. 2. antidote.

ಪಿರಿಪುನಿ piripuni (ಪಿರಿ), *v. a.* To twist, as a rope. 2. to cancel, repeal, revoke, as an interdict, oath, *etc.* 3. to counteract; to abate, remove.

ಪಿರಿಯ piriya, *see* ಪ್ರಿಯ. 2. *see* ಪಿರಿ.

ಪಿರಿಯಾದಿ piriyādi, *see* ಫಿರ್ಯಾದಿ.

ಪಿರಿಯುನಿ piriyuni (ಪಿರಿ), *v. n.* To be sober, sane, *or* lucid, as after being drunk *or* insane. 2. to be cancelled, repealed, as an interdict *or* oath. ಪರ್ಸಗ ಬಂಜಿ ಪಿರ್ಸಗ ಬಂಜಿ indicates a changeable character.

ಪಿರೀತಿ pirīti, *see* ಪ್ರೀತಿ.

ಪಿರೆಡುನಿ pireḍuni, *see* ಪೆರೆಡುನಿ. 2. *see* ಪೊರೆಡುನಿ.

ಪಿರೆಪುನಿ pirepuni, *see* ಪಿರೆಸುನಿ.

ಪಿರೆಯುನಿ, ಪಿರೆವುನಿ pireyuni, pirevuni (ಪಿರೆ), *v. n.* To ache, gripe, as the belly *or* bowels.

ಪಿರೆಸುನಿ piresuni (ಪಿರೆಸ್), *v. a.* To peel, scrape *or* pare off, as the outer coatings of certain nuts; tò grate, as a nutmeg *or* cocoanut.

ಪಿರ್ಪು pirpu, *see* ಪೆರ್ಪು.

ಪಿರ್ಮರ pirmara, *see* ಬೆರ್ಮರ.

ಪಿರ್ಮರಿ pirmari, *see* ಪೆರ್ಮರಿ.

ಪಿರ್ಯಾದಿ piryādi, *see* ಫಿರಿಯಾದಿ.

ಪಿಲ pila, *see* ಪಿಲಿ.

ಪಿಲಿ pili, *s.* A tiger. —ಕಂಡೊಡಿ a big viper. —ಕೊಂಡೆಲ್, —ಕೊಂಡೊಲು a large kind of wasp. —ತೊರಕೆ a spotted thornback. ನಾಯಿ— a hyena.

ಪಿಲಿಂಬಿ, ಪಿಲಿಂಬೆ pilimbi, pilimbè, *s.* A low ground.

ಪಿಲಿಕುಚ್ಚಿ pilikučči, *s.* A kind of fish.

ಪಿಲಿಕುತ್ತ pilikutta, *s.* Swelling of the head.

ಪಿಲಿಸ್ pilisu, *s.* A span.

ಪಿಲೆ pilè, *s.* Impurity from birth. 2. the menstrual. 3. humility. —ಕಟ್ಟುನಿ to humiliate. ಅಮಿ— defilement, especially on account of birth *or* death in a family.

ಪಿಲ್ಚಂಡಿ pilčaṇḍi, *s.* A demon so called.

ಪಿಲ್ಲಿ, ಪಿಲ್ಲೆ pilli, pillè, *s.* A silver-ring worn on the toes. —ಮೆಂಟೆ the same ornament consisting of four silver rings

ಪಿಲ್ಲಿಯಾವುನಿ, ಪಿಲ್ಲ್ಯಾವುನಿ pilliyāvuni, pillyāvuni (ಪಿಲ್ಲ್ಯ), *v.a.* To despise, scorn, slight.

ಪಿಶಾಚಿ pišāči, *s.* A demon, evil spirit.

ಪಿಶುಣೆ pišuṇe, *s.* A talebearer, informer, spy, calumniator.

ಪಿಸ್ರ್ pisṛṛu, *s.* Displeasure, anger. 2. self-conceit, arrogance. —ದೆಪ್ಪುನಿ to humiliate, humble. —ಬಪಿನಿ, —ಮಲ್ಪುನಿ to be angry, offended.

ಪಿಸಂಟ್ pisaṇṭu, *s.* Fretfulness, peevishness. 2. anger, displeasure. —ಕಟ್ಟುನಿ to be fretful.

ಪಿಸಂಟೆ, ಪಿಸಂಟೆಲೆ pisaṇṭe, pisaṇṭele, *s.* A fretful or peevish man.

ಪಿಸಂಡೆ pisaṇḍè, *s.* A kind of broom.

ಪಿಸರ್ pisaru, *see* ಪಿಸ್ರ.

ಪಿಸಿಂಟೆ pisiṇṭe, *see* ಪಿಸಂಟೆ.

ಪಿಸ್ಕಾರಿ piskāri, *s.* A syringe.

ಪಿಸ್ಕಾವುನಿ piskāvuni, *c.v.* (*of* ಪಿಸ್ಕುನಿ) To take by force, extort. 2. to compel payment.

ಪಿಸ್ಕುನಿ piskuni (ಪಿಸ್ಕಿ), *v. a.* To squeeze, press. 2. to pay on compulsion, pay in ready cash.

ಪಿಸ್ನಾರಿ pisnāri, *see* ಪೀನಾರಿ.

ಪಿಳಪಿಳ, ಪಿಳಿಪಿಳಿ piḷapiḷa, piḷipiḷi, *adj.* Sparkling, twinkling, glittering. —ಕಂಣ್ sparkling eyes.

ಪಿಳ್ಳೆ, piḷḷè, *s.* A child, baby.

ಪೀ pī, *s.* The ordure, excrements of human beings, dogs, pigs, *etc.*

ಪೀಂಕಣ್, ಪೀಂಕನ್ pīṅkaṇu, pīṅkanu, *s.* The buttocks.

ಪೀಂಕಾಡ್ರುನಿ, ಪೀಂಕಾವುನಿ pīṅkāḍruni, pīṅkāvuni, *c. v.* (*of* ಪೀಂಕುಡುನಿ) To cause to slip, move *or* fly out. 2. to press out, as tamarind seeds *or* the testicles of animals. 3. to get on the sly.

ಪೀಂಕುಡುನಿ, ಪೀಂಕುನಿ pīṅkuḍuni, pīṅkuni (ಪೀಂಕ್, ಪೀಂಕುಡ್), *v. n.* To escape, slip out.

ಪೀಂಕ್ರಟ್ pīṅkraṭu, *see* ಪೀಕ್ರಟ್.

ಪೀಂಗುಳುನಿ pīṅguḷuni, *see* ಪೀಂಕುಡುನಿ.

ಪೀಂಚಿಕಾಯಿ pīñčikāyi, *see* ಪೊಂಗರೆ.

ಪೀಂಚಿಲ್ pīñčilu, *adj.* Thin, slender. 2. bent *or* crooked. —ಕಾರ್ thin *or* bandy legs.

ಪೀಂಚೆಲ್ pīñčelu, *adj.* Without a handle. —ಕತ್ತಿ a knife without a handle.

ಪೀಂಜಾರ್ pīñjāru, *see* ಪಿಂಜರ.

ಪೀಂಜಿಲ್ pīñjilu, *see* ಪೀಂಚಿಲ್.

ಪೀಂಟ್ pīṇṭu, *s.* A twist; distortion.

ಪೀಂಟಂಗೆಲ್, ಪೀಂಟೆಲ್ pīṇṭaṅgelu, pīṇṭelu, *adj.* Twisted, distorted.

ಪೀಂಟಾವುನಿ pīṇṭāvuni, *c. v.* (*of* ಪೀಂಟುನಿ) To cause to twist *or* distort. ಮೋಣೆ— to make grimaces.

ಪೀಂಟುನಿ pīṇṭuni (ಪೀಂಟಿ), *v. a.* To twist, turn, wring.

ಪೀಂಟೆಲ್‌ತನ pīṇṭelụtana, *s.* The state of being twisted *or* distorted. 2. perverseness, crossness, wryness.

ಪೀಂಬಿಲಿ, ಪೀಂಬುಲಿ pīmbili, pīmbuli, *see* ಬಿಂಬುಲಿ.

ಪೀಕದಾನಿ pīkadāni, *s.* A spittoon.

ಪೀಕ್ರಟ್ pīkraṭụ, *see* ಪಿಸ್ಕಟಿ.

ಪೀಙಾದಮರ pīṅadamara, *s.* The pine tree.

ಪೀಠ pīṭha, *s.* A seat; a throne; a pulpit. ರಜತ— the seat of Uḍipi Svāmis.

ಪೀಠಿಕೆ pīṭhikè, *s.* A preface, preamble, introduction.

ಪೀಡಣೆ, ಪೀಡನೆ pīḍaṇè, pīḍanè, *s.* Vexation, pain, suffering, anguish; *cf.* ಪೀಡೆ.

ಪೀಡಿಪುನಿ, ಪಿಡಿಸುನಿ pīḍipuni, pīḍisuni (ಪೀಡಿ, ಪೀಡಿಸ್), *v. a.* To vex, annoy, molest.

ಪೀಡಿಯುನಿ pīḍiyuni (ಪೀಡಿ), *v. n.* To be vexed, annoyed; to suffer.

ಪೀಡೆ pīḍè, *see* ಪೀಡಣೆ.

ಪೀತ pīta, *adj.* Yellow.

ಪೀತರ್ಮಣಿ pītarụmaṇi, *s.* A kind of medicine, *Veratram album.* 2. antimony.

ಪೀತಾಂಬರ pītāmbara, *s.* A yellow silk cloth. —ಧಾರಿ Krụshṇa, as wearing such a garment.

ಪೀನಸ್ pīnasụ, *see* ಪಿನಾಶಿ.

ಪೀನಾರಿ pīnāri, *adj.* Stinking, emitting a disagreable odour. —ನರಮಾನಿ a miser, niggard. —ಮರ the poon tree, *Sterculia foetida, Ailanthus.* —ರೋಗ, *see* ಪಿನಾಶಿ.

ಪೀಪ, ಪೀಪಾಯಿ pīpa, pīpāyi, *s.* A cask, tub.

ಪೀಪಿ pīpi, *s.* A kind of pipe.

ಪೀಪುನಿ pīpuni, *see* ಪಿಜಿಪುನಿ.

ಪೀಬಾಲೆ pībālè, *s.* A little child.

ಪೀಮಂಣ್ pīmaṇṇụ, *s.* Miry earth.

ಪೀಯವು pīyavu, *s.* A small chicken.

ಪೀಯ್ಯೊ pīyyo, *intj.* An expression of ridicule, mockery, generally accompanied with clapping of hands.

ಪೀರಿಯುನಿ, ಪೀರುನಿ pīriyuni, pīruni (ಪೀರಿ, ಪೀರ್), *v. n.* To ooze, percolate. 2. *see* ಪೇರುನಿ.

ಪೀರೆ pīrè, *s.* A potherb, *Luffa acutangula.* ಕಂನಡ—, ಗೊಂಚಿಲ್—, ದಾರೆ— are varieties of the same.

ಪೀರೆಂಗಿ pīreṅgi, *see* ಪಿರಂಗಿ.

ಪೀಲಿ pīli, *s.* Pith, a kind of rush used as corks. 2. a peacock's feather. *adj.* Dry, thin, light. —ಕಂಡೆ the soft part of a bird's tail. —ಅಳಿಯುನಿ to die out. —ದ ಕಂಣ್ the star in a peacock's feather. —ಕಟ್ಟುನಿ to be stunted, to grow lean.

ಪೀಸ್ pīsụ, *see* ಫೀಸ್.

ಪೀಸುನಿ pīsuni, *see* ಪಿಸ್ಕುನಿ.

ಪುಂಕ್, ಪುಂಕು puṅkụ, puṅku, *see* ಪೂಂಕೆ.

ಪುಂಕಣ್ puṅkaṇụ, *see* ಮೊಂಕಣ್.

ಪುಂಗವೆ **puṅgave,** *s.* An excellent *or* pre-eminent man. ಮುನಿ– the chief of sages.

ಪುಂಗಿ, ಪುಂಗು **puṅgi, puṅgu,** *s.* A sort of drone *or* bagpipe.

ಪುಂಗು **puṅgu,** *s.* The Indian beech, *Pongamia glabra.* 2. *see* ಪುನುಗು.

ಪುಂಗುನಿ **puṅguni** (ಪುಂಗ್), *v. a.* To rock, toss, as a boat, *etc.*

ಪುಂಗೆ, ಪುಂಗೆಲೆ **puṅge, puṅgele,** *s.* A fickle-minded man.

ಪುಂಙಟ್ **puṅṅaṭụ,** *adj.* Tender, young.

ಪುಂಚ **puñča,** *s.* A white-ant-hill. 2. a snake's hole. 3. a kind of poison. –ಕಂಡ a very good rice-field. –ದ ಮಂಣ್ the termite soil used for chemical processes. –ಪೂ a kind of protuberance.

ಪುಂಚಲ್ **puñčalụ,** *see* ಪೂಂಚ.

ಪುಂಚಲ **puñcala,** *s.* A kind of fly-brush, held by a devil-dancer.

ಪುಂಜ **puñja,** *s.* A heap, collection. 2. property consisting of ready money.

ಪುಂಟಾವುನಿ **punṭāvuni,** *c. v.* (*of* ಪುಂಟುನಿ) To cause to wring, press *or* express.

ಪುಂಟುನಿ **punṭuni** (ಪುಂಟ್), *v. a.* To wring, as a wet garment. 2. to press *or* express, as juice from fruits, *etc.*

ಪುಂಡ **puṇḍa,** *adj.* Mischievous, quarrelsome, wicked. –ತನ mischievousness.

ಪುಂಡದೆ **puṇḍadè,** *s.* A kind of water-fowl.

ಪುಂಡರಿ **puṇḍari,** *see under* ಪುಂಡಿ.

ಪುಂಡಾಟ, ಪುಂಡಾಟಿಗೆ **puṇḍāṭa, puṇḍāṭigè,** *s.* Mischievousness, wickedness.

ಪುಂಡಿ **puṇḍi,** *s.* The fist. 2. a handful. 3. the refuse of expressed cocoanut, *etc.*, oil-cake. –ಅರಿ, ಪುಂಡರಿ spare rice. ಆನೆದ– the dung of an elephant. –ಕಲ್ಲ್, *see* ಪುಣಿಕಲ್ಲ್. ಕೋರಿ– fowl curry and rice balls boiled in steam, and served on particular occasions.

ಪುಂಡಿತ್ತ್ **puṇḍittụ,** *see* ಪುಂಡಿಬಿತ್ತ್.

ಪುಂಡಿತಪ್ಪು **puṇḍitappu,** *s.* The red sorrel, *Hibiscus sabdariffa.*

ಪುಂಡಿನಾರ್ **puṇḍinārụ,** *s.* Jute.

ಪುಂಡಿಬಿತ್ತ್ **puṇḍibittụ,** *s. lit.* A handful of seed. 2. a mode of sowing seed in the third rice crop (ಕೊಳಕೆ).

ಪುಂಡಿಯುನಿ **puṇḍiyuni,** *see* ಪುಂಟುನಿ.

ಪುಂಡು **puṇḍu,** *s.* A crowd, herd, flock, swarm.

ಪುಂಡುಗಾರಿಗೆ, ಪುಂಡುತನ **puṇḍugārigè, puṇḍutana,** *see* ಪುಂಡಾಟ.

ಪುಂಡೆ **puṇḍè,** *s.* A bush, thicket. –ದ ಪಕ್ಕಿ, *see* ಪುಂಡದೆ. ಬೆದ್ರ್‌ದ– a thicket of bamboos.

ಪುಂಡೆಲ್ **puṇḍelụ,** *see* ಪೂಂಡೆಲ್.

ಪುಂಣಮೆ **puṇṇamè,** *s.* The day of full moon.

ಪುಂತೆ puntè, *see* ಪೊಂತೆ.

ಪುಂದಿ pundi, *adj*. Sapless.

ಪುಂಕಟ್ pur̃kaṭu, *s*. Storing, keeping. 2. *see* ಪುಂಗಟ್.

ಪುಂಕು pur̃ku, *see* ಪುಕ್ಕು.

ಪುಂಗಟ್ pur̃gaṭu, *s*. Fermentation. 2. decomposition, decay. *adj*. Fermented. 2. decomposed.

ಪುಂಗಾವುನಿ pur̃gāvuni, *c. v*. (*of* ಪುಂಗುನಿ) To cause *or* allow to ferment *or* decompose.

ಪುಂಗುನಿ pur̃guni (ಪುಂಗ್), *v. n*. To ferment, undergo fermentation. 2. to decompose, decay.

ಪುಂಗೆಲ್ pur̃gelu, *adj*. Fermented. 2. decomposed, decayed, mouldy.

ಪುಂಗೆಲೆ pur̃gele, *s*. A dirty man.

ಪುಂಚುನಿ pur̃čuni (ಪುಂಚ್), *v. a*. To squeeze, as a lemon, *etc*.

ಪುಂಡೆ pur̃ḍè, *s*. A thorny bush; *cf*. ಪುಂಡೆ. *adj*. Shaped like a bush. 2. distended, enlarged. –ಕಟ್ಟುನಿ to be shaped like a bush. ಬಂಜಿ ಪುಂಡೆ ಕಟ್ಟುನಿ the belly to distend.

ಪುಂಸ puṁsa, *s*. Manhood, virility.

ಪುಕಲಾಯಿಸುನಿ pukalāyisuni, *see* ಪುಸಲಾಯಿಸುನಿ.

ಪುಕಾರ, ಪುಕಾರಿ pukāra, pukāri, *s*. Rumour, report. 2. alarm, noise. –ಮಳ್ಪುನಿ, –ಲಕ್ಕಾವುನಿ to raise an uproar.

ಪುಕುಸಾಟೆ pukusāṭè, *adj*. Vain, useless. 2. false, untrue. *adv*. For nothing, in vain; *cf*. ಪೊಕ್ಕಡೆ.

ಪುಕುಳಿ pukuḷi, *s*. The anus.

ಪುಕ್ಕ್ pukku, *see* ಪುಕ್ಕು.

ಪುಕ್ಕಟೆ pukkaṭè, *see* ಪುಕುಸಾಟೆ.

ಪುಕ್ಕಲೇರ್ಸಾವುನಿ pukkalērsāvuni, *see* ಪುಕ್ಲೇರ್ಸಾವುನಿ.

ಪುಕ್ಕಳಿಯುನಿ pukkaḷiyuni, *see* ಮುಕ್ಕಳ್ಯುನಿ.

ಪುಕ್ಕು pukku, *s*. Fear, timidity. *adj*. Timid. ಪೋಡಿಗೆದ– being easily overcome by fear; a frightened goose. –ತನ cowardice.

ಪುಕ್ಕೆ, ಪುಕ್ಕೆಲೆ pukke, pukkele, *s*. A timid man, coward, sneak.

ಪುಕ್ಲಾಯಿಸುನಿ puklāyisuni, *see* ಪುಸಲಾಯಿಸುನಿ.

ಪುಕ್ಲೇರ್ಸಾವುನಿ puklērsāvuni, *c. v*. To instigate, incite.

ಪುಗತೆ, ಪುಗರಿಗೆ pugarigè, *s*. Praise, eulogium, flattery.

ಪುಗರುನಿ, ಪುಗಳುನಿ pugaruni, pugaḷuni (ಪುಗರ್, ಪುಗಳ್), *v. a*. To praise, laud, eulogise, flatter.

ಪುಗೆ pugè, *s*. Smoke, vapour, fume. –ಮಾಯಿಲೆ –ತ ಕಪ್ಪಲ್ a steamer. –ತ ಗಾಡಿ a railway train. –ತೂಪಿನಿ to wish for one's ruin. –ಪತ್ತುನಿ to be affected with smoke. –ಪಲಾಯಿ a shelf in the kitchen. –ಟಿ ದೀಪಿನಿ, –ಪಾಡುನಿ to expose to smoke; to fumigate.

ಪುಗೆಪುನಿ pugepuni (ಪುಗೆ), *v. a*. To expose to smoke; to fumigate.

ಪುಗೆಯುನಿ pugeyuni (ಪುಗೆ), *v. n.* To smoke, reek.

ಪುಗೆರೆ pugerè, *s.* Tobacco. ನಟ್ಟಿ–, ಬಿತಯಿ–, ಸರ್ಸುರಡಿ– are some kinds of tobacco.

ಪುಗೆಲ್, ಪುಗ್ಗೆಲ್ pugelu̥, puggelu̥, *s.* The shoulder. –ಕೊರ್ಪುನಿ to give shoulder; to help, assist.

ಪುಚುಕ್ಕು pučukku, *s.* The force, as of spitting. –ಉಬ್ಬಿಯುನಿ to spit out with force.

ಪುಚ್ಚಾಡಿ puččāḍi, *s.* The hind part.

ಪುಚ್ಚೆ puččè, *s.* Braiding *or* plaiting hair. 2. braided hair. –ಭಂಗಾರ್ ornaments worn in the braids of hair. –ನೇಪಿನಿ to plait, braid.

ಪುಚ್ಚೆ puččé, *s.* A cat. ಅರ– a wild cat. ಘುಂಟ– a male cat. ಪುಣುಂಗು– a civet cat. –ಮೀನ್ a cat-fish. –ಮುಟ್ಟು a kind of tree.

ಪುಚ್ಚೆಕೂಲಿ puččekūli, *s.* A tooth growing after the eightieth year.

ಪುಚ್ಚೆಪಂದ್ರ್ puččeparndu̥, *s.* The fruit of *Pavetta Indica.*

ಪುಟ puṭa, *s.* A page of a book. 2. folding *or* doubling. 3. a pair. 4. the purifying *or* calcining of metals, *etc.*, by fire. ಕರ– the hands joined, as in supplication, *etc.* ನಾಸಾ– both nostrils. ಭಂಗಾರ್ ಪುಟೊಗು ದೀಪಿನಿ *or* ಪಾಡುನಿ to subject gold to the process of purification.

ಪುಟಾಣಿ puṭāni, *see* ಪೈಟಣಿ.

ಪುಟ್ಟ puṭṭa, *adj.* Small, little, diminutive. –ಕೊಡಂಗೆ a small kind of earring.

ಪುಟ್ಟಣ್ puṭṭaṇu̥, *s.* A kind of grass.

ಪುಟ್ಟನ puṭṭana, *s.* A thistle.

ಪುಟ್ಟಾವುನಿ puṭṭāvuni, *c. v.* (*of* ಪುಟ್ಟುನಿ) To produce, originate, give birth to, cause to be born, cause to take place.

ಪುಟ್ಟಿ puṭṭi, *s.* A small round basket. –ಬುಟ್ಟಿ a wickered bottle.

ಪುಟ್ಟು puṭṭu, *s.* Cowries; *also* –ಕಾಯಿ. 2. *see* ಹುಟ್ಟು. –ಗೊಬ್ಬುನಿ to play with cowries.

ಪುಟ್ಟುನಿ puṭṭuni (ಪುಟ್ಟಿ), *v. n.* To be born, come into existence. 2. to arise, originate, spring up *or* from, be produced. ಕರುಣ– to feel pity. ದುಃಖ– to be sorry. ಬಾಲೆ– a child to be born. ಸುದ್ದಿ– a report to be afloat.

ಪುಟ್ಟೆ puṭṭè, *s.* A fox, jackal.

ಪುಟ್ಲ puṭla, *s.* A bubble, blister, pustule. –ಲಕ್ಕುನಿ a blister to rise.

ಪುಠ puṭha, *see* ಪುಟ.

ಪುಡ puḍa, *see* ಪುಡು.

ಪುಡತೆಲ್ puḍatelu̥, *s.* A bruise, crack. *adj.* Bruised, broken, cracked.

ಪುಡಪುನಿ puḍapuni (ಪುಡ), *v. a.* To break, burst.

ಪುಡಯಿ puḍayi, *s.* A basket.

ಪುಡಸ್ puḍasu, *see* ಪೊಡಸ್.

ಪುಡಾಡುನಿ puḍāḍuni (ಪುಡಾಡಿ), *v. a.* To prostrate, bow, salute.

ಪುಡಾಯಿ puḍāyi, *see* ಪುದಯಿ.

ಪುಡಾವುನಿ puḍāvuni (ಪುಡಾ), *v. n.* To break, burst. 2. to ache, smart. ಕಂಣ್– *lit.* the eye to break, smart; to lose one's sight, *abus.* ಕುರಿ– a boil to open. ತರೆ– to have headache. ದೊಂಡೆ– to have sore throat; to become hoarse.

ಪುಡಿ puḍi, *s.* A sore, ulcer, abscess. 2. *see* ಪೊಡಿ.

ಪುಡಿ puḍi, *s*, A handle, haft, hilt; *cf.* ಪುಡು.

ಪುಡಿಕೆ puḍikè, *s.* A small basket.

ಪುಡಿಪು puḍipu, *s.* Covering, clothing. 2. *see* ಪುರಿಪು.

ಪುಡಿಪುನಿ puḍipuni (ಪುಡಿ), *v. a.* To offend, provoke. 2. to quarrel, fight; *cf.* ತಡಿಪುನಿ. ಪುಡಿತೊಣುನಿ to be offended; to quarrel with each other.

ಪುಡು puḍu, *s.* Holding, grasping, handling. –ಕೈ the shaft of a plough. –ಬಲ್ಲ್ a rope attached to the yoke of a plough, to serve as the reins.

ಪುಡುಕು puḍuku, *s.* Slight, disparagement, depreciating. 2. insult, indignity.

ಪುಡುಕುನಿ puḍukuni (ಪುಡುಕ್), *v. n.* To be afflicted, grieved.

ಪುಡುತ puḍuta, *adj.* Foolish.

ಪುಡುಪುನಿ puḍupuni, *see* ಪುಡಿಪುನಿ.

ಪುಡೆ puḍè, *s.* Border, edge, brink, margin, brim. 2. interval, space. ಕಂಡದ– the border of a field. ಕಂಣ್ದ– the eye-lid. ಗುವೆಲ್ದ– the brink of a well. ಗೋಡೆದ– the side of a wall. –ತೊತ್ತುನಿ to trim the borders, as of a field. –ಮುಟ್ಟ up to the brim.

ಪುಡೆಕುನಿ puḍekuni, *see* ಪೊಡೆಕುನಿ.

ಪುಡೆಪುನಿ puḍepuni (ಪುಡೆ), *v. a.* To winnow, fan.

ಪುಡೆರುನಿ puḍeruni (ಪುಡೆರ್), *v. n.* To suppurate, break, burst. 2. to be haughty.

ಪುಡ್ಕೆ puḍkè, *adj.* Plump, fat. –ಬಾಲೆ a plump child.

ಪುಡ್ಕೆ puḍke, *s.* A stout man.

ಪುಡ್ಪುನಿ puḍpuni, *see* ಪುಡಿಪುನಿ.

ಪುಡ್ಪೆಲೆ puḍpele, *s.* A quarrelsome man.

ಪುಡ್ಯಾಡುನಿ puḍyāḍuni, *see* ಪುಡಾಡುನಿ.

ಪುಣ puṇa, *s.* A dead body, corpse. *adj.* Dead. 2. inactive. –ಕಟ್ಟುನಿ to grow stiff. –ಕಾಂಪುನಿ to bury a corpse.

ಪುಣಕಟ್ಟ್ puṇakaṭṭu, *adj.* Emaciated, slender, reduced to skin and bone.

ಪುಣಕೆ puṇakè, *see* ಪಣಕೆ.

ಪುಣರಪುಳಿ puṇarapuḷi, *s.* The mate mangosteen, *Garcinia purpurea.*

ಪುಣಲ್ puṇalu, *s.* Floating.

ಪುಣಲುನಿ puṇaluni, *see* ಪುಲಾವುನಿ.

ಪುಣಿ puṇi, *s.* The border of a field.

ಪುಣಿಕಲ್ಲ್ puṇikallụ *s. lit.* A hand-stone (ಪುಂಡಿಕಲ್ಲ್). 2. a small pestle for grinding turmeric, *etc.*

ಪುಣಿಕೆ puṇikè, *s.* Tamarind. –ಮರ the tamarind tree.

ಪುಣಿಕೊಟ್ಟೆ puṇikoṭṭè, *s.* A tamarind seed.

ಪುಣುಂಗು, ಪುಣುಗು puṇuṅgu, puṇugu, *s.* Civet. –ದ ಪುಚ್ಚೆ a civet cat.

ಪುಣೆ puṇè, *s.* Security, bail. –ತಾಯಿ a surety.

ಪುಣೆಪಿನಿ, ಪುಣೆಪುನಿ, ಪುಣೆವುನಿ puṇepini, puṇepuni, puṇevuni (ಪುಣೆ), *v. a.* To persevere till one has avenged himself; to contest to the last, as a suit. 2. to compete, vie.

ಪುಣೆವು puṇevu, *s.* Resoluteness.

ಪುಣ್ಯ puṇya, *s.* Religious merit, virtue. 2. a good action. 3. purity, purification. *adj.* Virtuous, good, meritorious. 2. pure. –ಕರ್ಮ a virtuous deed; a meritorious act. –ಕಾಲ an auspicious occasion. –ತೀರ್ಥ a sacred river. –ದಿನ a sacred day. –ಫಲ the fruit of one's merits. –ಲೋಕ heaven. –ವಂತ a virtuous man. –ಸ್ಥಳ, –ಕ್ಷೇತ್ರ a sacred place of pilgrimage. –ಮಳ್ಪುನಿ to perform holy *or* virtuous acts.

ಪುಣ್ಯಾತ್ಮೆ, ಪುಣ್ಯಾದಿಗೆ puṇyātme, puṇyādige, *s.* A virtuo usman, a fortunate man.

ಪುಣ್ಯಾದಿಗೆ puṇṇyādigè, *s.* Goodness; well being; good fortune, prosperity.

ಪುಣ್ಯಾಹ puṇyāha, *s.* A lucky day. 2. purifying. –ವಾಚನೆ purifying a house, *etc.*, after accouchement, *etc.*

ಪುತ್ತ, ಪುತ್ತು, ಪುತ್ತೆ putta, puttu, puttè, *s.* A darling. *adj.* Darling, beloved.

ಪುತ್ತಲಿ, ಪುತ್ತೊಳಿ puttali, puttoḷi, *s.* A gold coin. –ಗೊಂಬೆ an image, puppet. –ಭಂಗಾರ್ gold of 12 carats. –ಸರ a string of such coins, worn by females.

ಪುತ್ರೆ putre, *s.* A son. ದತ್ತ– an adopted son. ಪುತ್ರಸಂತಾನ having a family. ಪುತ್ರಸ್ವೀಕಾರ adoption of a son.

ಪುದ puda, *s.* A dove, pigeon.

ಪುದಂಗರ, ಪುದಕಡಲೆ pudaṅgara, pudakaḍalè, *see* ಪೆದಂಗರ.

ಪುದಕೆ pudakè, *see* ಪೊದಕೆ. 2. *see* ಪೊದಿಕೆ.

ಪುದಕೈ pudakei, *s.* A kind of game by making alternate motions and mutually clapping each other's hands. –ಹಾಕುನಿ, –ಗೊಬ್ಬುನಿ to play at such a game.

ಪುದಬಾರೆ pudabārè, *s.* A demon so called.

ಪುದರ್ pudarụ, *s.* A name, appellation, designation. 2. fame, celebrity, reputation. –ಆಪಿನಿ, –ಲಕ್ಕುನಿ to become known. –ಗೆಪ್ಪುನಿ to utter a person's name; to bring one's reputation into discredit. —ಪಾಡುನಿ to name. —ಪೋ ಪಿನಿ to be celebrated.

ಪುದಾಪಿನಿ **pudāpini,** *see* ಪೊದು ಆಪಿನಿ *under* ಪೊದು.

ಪುದಿನ **pudina,** *s.* A kind of mint.

ಪುದುಕು **puduku,** *s.* Boasting.

ಪುದುಕ್ಕು **pudukku,** *adv.* Suddenly, at once. —ಬೊರಿಯುನಿ to pour suddenly, as a bag of rice.

ಪುದುಬಾರ್ **pudubārụ,** *s.* New [paddy.

ಪುದೆ **pudè,** *s.* A load, burden.

ಪುದೆಪುನಿ **pudepuni,** *see* ಪೊದೆಪುನಿ.

ಪುದೆಲ್ **pudelụ,** *s.* A bush, shrub.

ಪುದ್ದಾರ್ **puddārụ,** *s.* The harvest feast; a ceremony observed in partaking of new produce for the first time.

ಪುದ್ದೆ **pudde,** *see* ಪೊದ್ದೆ.

ಪುನಃ **punah,** *adv.* Again, once more.

ಪುನರಪುಳಿ **punarapuḷi,** *see* ಪುಣರಪುಳಿ.

ಪುನರುತ್ಥಾನ **punarutthāna,** *s.* Resurrection.

ಪುನರ್ಜನ್ಮ, ಪುನರ್ಜಲ್ಮ **punarjanma, punarjalma,** *s.* Being born again; regeneration. 2. transmigration of the soul.

ಪುನರ್ವಸು **punarvasu,** *s.* The seventh of the lunar mansions.

ಪುನರ್ವಿಚಾರಣೆ **punarvičāraṇè,** *s.* Reconsideration, review.

ಪುನರ್ವಿವಾಹ **punarvivāha,** *s.* Remarriage.

ಪುನಲುನಿ **punaluni,** *see* ಪುಲಾವುನಿ.

ಪುನಶ್ಚರಣೆ **punaščaraṇè,** *s.* Repetition of mystic formulas *or* incantations.

ಪುನಸ್ಥಾಪನೆ **punasthāpanè,** *s.* Reformation.

ಪುನಹ **punaha,** *see* ಪುನಃ.

ಪುನಿಕೆ **punikè,** *see* ಪುಣಿಕೆ.

ಪುನೀತ **punīta,** *adj.* Free from sin, purified. —ಮಳ್ಪುನಿ to absolve, purify; to justify.

ಪುನುಗು **punugu,** *see* ಪುಣುಂಗು.

ಪುಪ್ಪಳ **puppaḷa,** *see* ಪಪ್ಪಡ.

ಪುಪ್ಪಿ, ಪುಪ್ಪು **puppi, puppu,** *s.* Decay, rottenness.

ಪುಯಿಂತೆಲ್ **puyintelụ,** *s.* The tenth Tuḷu month.

ಪುರ **pura,** *s.* A city, town. 2. a house *or* any receptacle. —ವಾಸಿ a citizen.

ಪುರ **pura,** *see* ಪುರು.

ಪುರಂದರೆ **purandare,** *s.* A name of Indra. ಪುರಂದರದಾಸೆ a celebrated Canarese poet.

ಪುರಕೆ **purakè,** *s.* A bad smell.

ಪುರತ್ **puratụ,** *s.* A dowry.

ಪುರಮರ್ದನೆ **puramardane,** *s.* Rubbing of the body with an unguent.

ಪುರಮೆ **purame,** *see* ಪುಂಣಮೆ.

ಪುರಮೆಯಿ **purameyi,** *s.* A mucous body.

ಪುರಲ್, ಪುರಲೆ **puralụ, puralè,** *see* [ಪೊರಲ್.

ಪುರಸ್ **purasụ,** *see* ಪೊಲಸ್.

ಪುರಸ್ಕಾರ **puraskāra,** *s.* Reverence, honour.

ಪುರಾಕೃತ **purākrụta**, *see* ಪ್ರಕೃತ.

ಪುರಾಣ **purāṇa**, *s.* A sacred and political work comprising the Hindu theology. *adj.* Old; ancient. —ಕಥೆ an old story. —ಪುರುಷ God. There are eighteen acknowledged Purāṇās, namely, ಬ್ರಹ್ಮ—, ಪದ್ಮ—, ಬ್ರಹ್ಮಾಂಡ—, ಅಗ್ನಿ—, ವಿಷ್ಣು—, ಗರುಡ—, ಬ್ರಹ್ಮಕೈವರ್ತ—, ಶಿವ—, ಲಿಂಗ—, ನಾರದ—, ಸ್ಕಾಂದ—, ಮಾರ್ಕಂಡೇಯ—, ಭವಿಷ್ಯತ್—, ಮತ್ಸ್ಯ—, ವರಾಹ—, ಕೂರ್ಮ—, ವಾಮನ—, ಭಾಗವತ—.

ಪುರಾಣಿಕೆ **purāṇike**, *s.* One who reads *or* narrates sacred history.

ಪುರಾತನ **purātana**, *adj.* Ancient, old.

ಪುರಿ **puri**, *see* ಪುರ.

ಪುರಿ **puri**, *s.* A worm, mite, moth. 2. skin parasite. 3. twining, twisting, as threads. 4. coir yarn. —ತಪ್ಪು mulberry leaves. —ಬಲ್ಲಿ coir. —ಕೈಪುನಿ to twine coir yarn. —ಮುಳ್ಪುನಿ to prepare a rope from cocoanut fibre. —ಮೇಪಿನಿ to suffer from ringworm.

ಪುರಿಂಗುನಿ **puriṅguni**, *see* ಪುಂಗುರ್ನಿ.

ಪುರಿಗಂಟ್ **purigaṇṭụ**, *s.* Anything eaten *or* perforated by worms. *adj.* Worm-eaten. 2. envious, jealous. 3. obstinate, stubborn. —ನರಮಾನಿ, ಪುರಿಗಂಟಿ an envious *or* obstinate fellow.

ಪುರಿಜಂತ್ರ **purijantra**, *s.* Malice, envy. 2. mischief. 3. obstinacy, self-will. —ಪಾತೆರುನಿ to talk maliciously.

ಪುರಿಪು **puripu**, *s.* The twist, as of a rope *or* cord. —ದ ಬಡು a bullock-driver's whip *or* rod with its handle twisted with rope.

ಪುರಿಯೊಲು **puriyolu**, *s.* An eel.

ಪುರು **puru**, *s.* A snail. *adj.* Small, tender. 2. snail-like. —ನಿಜಿ a tender fruit, bud. —ಬಾಲೆ a suckling. —ಜಾರುನಿ to be very slippery; to glide like a snail.

ಪುರುಂಕುನಿ **puruṅkuni**, *see* ಪುಂಚುರ್ನಿ.

ಪುರುಂಗುನಿ **puruṅguni**, *see* ಪುಂಗುರ್ನಿ.

ಪುರುಂಗೆಲೆ **puruṅgele**, *see* ಪುಂಗೆರ್ಲೆ. 2. a sickly person. 3. a reluctant worker. 4. a stingy man.

ಪುರುಂಡೆ **puruṇḍè**, *see* ಪುಂಡೆರ್.

ಪುರುಕು **puruku**, *see* ಪುರ್ಕು.

ಪುರುಕುಚ್ಚಣ, ಪುರುಕುತ್ಸೆ **purukućća-ṇa, purukutsé**, *see* ಕುರುಕುಚ್ಚನೆ.

ಪುರುಬು **purubu**, *see* ಪುರ್ಬು.

ಪುರುಷತ್ವ **purushatva**, *s.* Manhood, manliness.

ಪುರುಷರತ್ನ **purusharatna**, *s.* A kind of medicinal plant, *Ionidium suffruticosum.*

ಪುರುಷಾರ್ಥ **purushārtha**, *s.* Human desire, object of life. 2. benefit, use.

ಪುರುಷೆ **purushe**, *s.* A man, male. 2. a husband.

ಪುರುಷೋತ್ತಮೆ **purushōttame**, *s.* The best of mankind. 2. a name of Vishṇu. 3. the name of a man.

ಪುರುಸತ್ತು purusattu, *see* ಪುರ್ಸತ್.

ಪುರೆ purė, *s.* A roof, ceiling. ಮೇಲ್— the upper part of a roof; *pl.* ಪುರೆಕುಳು materials of a roof.

ಪುರೆಂಚುನಿ, ಪುರೆಚುನಿ pureńćuni, purećuni, *see* ಪುಂಚುರ್ನಿ.

ಪುರೆಪುನಿ purepuni (ಪುರೆ), *v. a.* To roll, turn over. 2. to retract, recant. 3. to impute, attribute.

ಪುರೆಲುನಿ, ಪುರೆಯುನಿ pureluni, pureyuni (ಪುರೆ), *v. n.* To roll, turn. ಕಿಂಞಿ— to come out, as a young bird from the egg-shell.

ಪುರೆಸುನಿ, ಪುರೈಸುನಿ puresuni, pureisuni (ಪುರೆಸ್, ಪುರೈಸ್), *v. n.* To complete, fulfil. 2. to afford. 3. to be satisfied. ಎಂಕ್ ಪುರೆಸುಜಿ I cannot afford.

ಪುರೋಹಿತೆ purōhite, *s.* A family-priest.

ಪುರ್ಕ purka, *s.* Remains, residue, saving. 2. frugality, economy.

ಪುರ್ಕಂಣ್ purkaṇṇu, *s.* Purulent eyes.

ಪುರ್ಕಟ್, ಪುರ್ಕಟೆ purkaṭu, purkaṭė, *adj.* Diminutive, small.

ಪುರ್ಕಾವುನಿ purkāvuni, *c. v.* (*of* ಪುರ್ಕುನಿ) To bake in embers, half bake. 2. to save, lay up, rake, hoard. ಪುರ್ಕಾದ್ ದೀಪಿನಿ to spare, save, reserve; to lay out frugally.

ಪುರ್ಕಾಸ್ purkāsu, *s.* A very small thing.

ಪುರ್ಕು purku, *s.* The rheum of the eye.

ಪುರ್ಕುನಿ purkuni (ಪುರ್ಕು), *v. n.* To be half baked. 2. to become soft. 3. to rot, decay, become putrid.

ಪುರ್ಗ purga, *s.* Sour gruel *or* pap.

ಪುರ್ಗಟ್ purgaṭu, *see* ಪುರಿಗಂಟಿ.

ಪುರ್ಗುನಿ purguni (ಪುರ್ಗ), *v. n.* To be well boiled, as rice.

ಪುರ್ಚುನಿ purčuni, *see* ಪುಂಚುರ್ನಿ.

ಪುರ್ಜಂತರ purjantara, *see* ಪುರಿಜಂತ್ರ.

ಪುರ್ಪ purpa, *s.* The tender areca blossoms. 2. *see* ಪುಷ್ಪ.

ಪುರ್ಬು purbu, *s.* The eye-brows.

ಪುರ್ಯೊಲು puryolu, *see* ಪುರಿಯೊಲು.

ಪುರ್ಲಿ purli, *s.* The wild hog-plum. 2. *see* ಕಾಣಿಪುರ್ಲಿ.

ಪುರ್ಸತ್, ಪುರ್ಸತ್ತು pursaṭu, pursattu, *s.* Leisure, opportunity, occasion, time. 2. relief, rest; *also* ಪುಸೋರ್ದು. —ಪುಪ್ಪುನಿ to be at leisure. —ಗೆತೊಣುನಿ to take time. —ಮುಳ್ಪುನಿ to find an opportunity.

ಪುರ್ಸಾದ pursāda, *see* ಪ್ರಸಾದ.

ಪುಲ pula, *s.* Pasturage, grazing ground. 2. reminiscences, recollection of old associations. —ಎಂಣುನಿ cattle to low for their old pasturage; to call to mind old associations.

ಪುಲಂಕೆನ pulaṅkena, *see* ಪುಲ್ಲಿ.

ಪುಲಂಪುನಿ pulampuni (ಪುಲಂ), *v. a.* To set afloat; *cf.* ಪುಲಾವುನಿ.

ಪುಲಕ pulaka, *s.* Horripilation, erection of the hair from ecstasy. 2. rejoicing, festivity. –ಅಭಿಷೇಕ, ಪುಲಕಾಭಿಷೇಕ bathing an idol in scented water on a festive occasion.

ಪುಲಪಾವುನಿ pulapāvuni, *c. v.* (*of* ಪುಲಾವುನಿ) To cause to float.

ಪುಲಬು, ಪುಲಮೆ pulabu, pulamè, *see* ಪೊಲಬು.

ಪುಲವಾಡ್, ಪುಲಾಡಿ pulavāḍu, pulāḍi, *s.* Pasturage, grazing-ground.

ಪುಲಾವುನಿ pulāvuni (ಪುಲಾ), *v. n.* To float.

ಪುಲಿ puli, *s.* Acidity. 2. a sour fruit. 3. tamarind. 4. leaven. 5. pride, arrogance. *adj.* Sour, acid. –ಕೊಟ್ಟೆ a tamarind seed. –ಒದ್ರು, –ಕಂಟೆ, –ಗಂಟೆ, –ಚಟೆ anything very sour. –ಕೊಚ್ಚಿಲ್ sauce, condiments, *etc.* mixed with acids, boiled and seasoned. –ಮೋಣೆ a wry face. –ತೋಜಾವುನಿ to be arrogant. –ಪುಃಟುನಿ to squeeze a lemon *or* other sour fruit; to check one's arrogance, to humiliate. ಎಸಲ್–, ಓಂಟೆ–, ಕಂಚಿ–, ಕರಂಡೆ–, ಕರ್ಗ–, ಕಾಯಿಬ್–, ಜಾರಿಗೆ–, ದಾರೆ–, ದೊಡ್ಡಾಯಿ–, ನಾರಂಗಾಯಿ–, ಪುಜಾರ–, *or* ಬಡ್ದ–, ಪುಣಿಕೆ–, ಬಿಂಬುಲಿ–, ಮರ್ಗ–, ಲಿಂಬೆ– are varieties of sour fruits.

ಪುಲಿ puli, *see* ಪುರಿ.

ಪುಲಿಜಂತ್ರ pulijantra, *see* ಪುರಿಜಂತ್ರ.

ಪುಲಿಪಾವುನಿ pulipāvuni, *c. v.* (*of* ಪುಲಿಯುನಿ) To make sour; to leaven.

ಪುಲಿಪು, ಪುಲುಪು pulipu, pulupu, *s.* Money.

ಪುಲಿಪುನಿ pulipuni (ಪುಲಿ), *v. a.* To irritate, itch.

ಪುಲಿಪುನಿ, ಪುಲಿಯುನಿ pulipuni, puliyuni (ಪುಲಿ), *v. n.* To become sour; to be leavened.

ಪುಲಿಪ್ಪೆನ pulippena, *adj.* Sour.

ಪುಲಿಸ್ pulisu, *s.* Policē. 2. money, cash.

ಪುಲೆಯಿ puleyi, *s.* A skin. ಉರೆತ– a deer's skin.

ಪುಲೆಯುನಿ, ಪುಲೆವುನಿ puleyuni, pulevuni (ಪುಲೆ), *v. n.* To smart, feel sharp pain.

ಪುಲೆವು pulevu, *s.* A crack. 2. a patch. 3. a crook, bend, curve. –ದೆಪ್ಪುನಿ to remove the same.

ಪುಲ್ಕ pulka, *see* ಪುಲಕ.

ಪುಲ್ಕಡಿ pulkaḍi, *s.* A handful of grass given by a vendor to the purchaser of cattle in token of striking the bargain.

ಪುಲ್ಕೊಟ್ಟೆ pulkoṭṭè, *s.* Tamarind seed.

ಪುಲ್ಪು pulpu, *adj.* Tepid, lukewarm; *also* ಪುಲ್ಪುಬೆಚ್ಚ, ಉಗುರುಪುಲ್ಪು.

ಪುಲ್ಯ pulya, *see* ಪುಲ್ಲ್ಯ.

ಪುಲ್ಲಡಿ pullaḍi, *s.* A place overgrown with rushes.

ಪುಲ್ಲಯಿ pullayi, *s.* A kind of cap.

ಪುಲ್ಲಾವುನಿ pullāvuni, *see* ಪುಲಾವುನಿ.

ಪುಲ್ಲಿ pulli, *s.* A sheet of paper. 2. *see* ಪುಳ್ಳಿ.

ಪುಲ್ಲಿಂಗ pulliṅga, *s.* The masculine gender, *gram.*

ಪುಲ್ಲು pullu, *s.* A rush. 2. a kind of grass. –ಗಡಿ, *see* ಪುಲ್ಲಡಿ. –ನೀರ್ grass and water, cattle fodder. –ಪಡೆ a mat made of rush. –ಪುದೆಲ್ a bush of rushes, bulrush. –ಒಡ್ಪುನಿ to pluck out a grass blade; to twist the ear. –ಜಾರಾವುನಿ to pluck the feathers.

ಪುಲ್ಲೆ pullè, *s.* An off-shoot. 2. a split, splint. 3. *see* ಪುಲ್ಲುಶಿ. –ಮೃಗ a kind of deer. –ಪುದಾವುನಿ, –ದೀಪಿನಿ, –ಲಕ್ಕುನಿ to sprout, bud.

ಪುಲ್ಲೆಯಿ pulleyi, *s.* A kind of whale.

ಪುಲ್ಲೆಲ್ pulleḷu, *s.* Abundance, increase. 2. gluttony.

ಪುಲ್ಯ, ಪುಲ್ಯಕೆಲ, ಪುಲ್ಯಕೊಲೆ pulya, pulyakela, pulyakolè, *s.* Morning, day-break. *adv.* Early in the morning.

ಪುವಳು, ಪುವೊಳು puvaḷu, puvoḷu, *s.* The navel.

ಪುಷ್ಕಟ್ pushkaṭu, *see* ಪುಸ್ಕಟೆ.

ಪುಷ್ಕಲ pushkala, *adj.* Copious, full, complete. 2. much, many. 3. excellent, eminent, best.

ಪುಷ್ಟ pushṭa, *adj.* Nourished, fed. 2. strong, stout.

ಪುಷ್ಟಿ pushṭi, *s.* Increase, thriving. 2. stoutness, strength.

ಪುಷ್ಪ pushpa, *s.* A flower, blossom.

ಪುಷ್ಯ pushya, *s.* The tenth lunar month.

ಪುಷ್ಯರಾಗ pushyarāga, *s.* The topaz, chrysolite.

ಪುಷ್ಯೆ pushyè, *s.* The eighth of the lunar mansions.

ಪುಸಲಾಯಿಸುನಿ, ಪುಸಲ್ಯಾಸುನಿ pusalāyisuni, pusalyāsuni, (ಪುಸಲಾಯಿಸ್, ಪುಸಲ್ಯಾಸ್), *v. a.* To coax, cajole, persuade, fawn.

ಪುಸ್ಕ್, ಪುಸ್ಕು pusku, pusku, *see* ಪುಸ್ಸ್.

ಪುಸ್ಕಟ್, ಪುಸ್ಕಟೆ puskaṭu, puskaṭè, *adj.* Vain, useless, feigned. 2. empty. *adv.* In vain, for nothing.

ಪುಸ್ತಕ pustaka, *s.* A book, volume.

ಪುಸ್ತಿ pusti, *s.* Instigation, abetment, incitement. 2. help, support. 3. a portfolio for keeping loose papers in *or* for placing under a paper while writing on it. –ಕೊರ್ಪಿನಿ to instigate, back up.

ಪುಸ್ಸ್, ಪುಸ್ಸು pussu, pussu, *s.* The hissing sound of a flash in the pan, when the gun does not go off. 2. unsuccessful termination of an undertaking, coming to nothing, defeat.

ಪುಳ pulạ, *see* ಪುಲ.

ಪುಳಕ puḷaka, *see* ಪುಲಕ.

ಪುಳಬ್ಬು puḷabbu, *see* ಪೊಲಬು.

ಪುಳಿ puḷi, *see* ಪುರಿ. 2. *see* ಪುಲಿ.

ಪುಳಿಂದೆ puḷinde, *s.* A hunter, forester, savage.

ಪುಳಿಕಂಟ್ pulikanṭu, *see under* ಪುಲಿ.

ಪುಳಿಚಾರ್ puḷičāru, *s.* A sour kind of sauce.

ಪುಳಿಪು puḷipu, *s.* Acidity.

ಪುಳಿಯಾರಲ್ puḷiyāralu, *s.* The yellow wood-sorrel, *Oxalis corniculata.*

ಪುಳುಕು puḷuku, *s.* Slipping out, anything soft *or* greasy.

ಪುಳೆವುನಿ puḷevuni, *see* ಪುಲೆವುನಿ.

ಪುಳ್ಕು puḷku, *see* ಪುರ್ಕ.

ಪುಳ್ಕೊಟ್ಟೆ pulkoṭṭè, *see* ಪುಲ್ಕೊಟೆ.

ಪುಳ್ಳ puḷḷa, *see* ಪುಲ.

ಪುಳ್ಳಿ puḷḷi, *s.* A grand-child.

ಪುಳ್ಳು puḷḷu, *see* ಪುಲ್ಲು.

ಪುಳ್ಳೆನ puḷḷena, *see* ಪುಲ್ಲ್ಯ.

ಪೂ pū, *s.* A flower, blossom. 2. a cataract in the eye. –ಅಗ್ರ a sore mouth. –ಕಾಯಿ a very young fruit. –ತ ಮಾಲೆ a garland of flowers. –ತೊಳಂಬೆ a bunch of flowers, nosegay. –ಮೂರಿ a disagreable smell of flowers. –ಅರಲುನಿ, –ಪೋಪಿನಿ, –ಬಿರ್ನಿ to flower, bloom, blossom. –ಮುಡಿಪುನಿ to wear flowers.

ಪೂಂಕೆ pūṅkè, *s.* Mould, mildew. –ಕೊಡಿಪುನಿ, –ಪತ್ತುನಿ to become mouldy.

ಪೂಂಗುನಿ pūṅguni (ಪೂಂಗ್), *v. n.* To shake.

ಪೂಂಜೆ pūñje, *s.* A cock. 2. a family-name among Bants. –ಕೆಲೆಪುನಿ a cock to crow.

ಪೂಂಟುನಿ pūṇṭuni, *see* ಪುಂಟುನಿ.

ಪೂಂಡೆಲ್ pūṇḍelu, *s.* A thicket, clump, as of bamboos. 2. matter from a sore.

ಪೂಂತೆ pūntè, *adj.* Light, very light, not heavy.

ಪೂಂಬೆ pūmbè, *s.* The flower bud of a plantain.

ಪೂಕರೆ pūkarè, *s.* An ornamental structure, as the stake of a bullock race. –ಪಾಡುನಿ to fix a post of such a structure; to ornament the ridge of a racing field.

ಪೂಕಿ pūki, *s.* A fart.

ಪೂಕುಟೆ pūkuṭè, *adj.* Empty, void. *s.* An empty mouth.

ಪೂಕುರು, ಪೂಕ್ರು pūkuru, pūkru, *adj.* Tender, young, little. 2. sallow.

ಪೂಕ್ರೆ pūkre, *s.* A sickly man.

ಪೂಗ pūga, *s.* A betel-nut.

ಪೂಚೆ pūčè, *see* ಪುಚ್ಚೆ.

ಪೂಜಾರಿ pūjāri, *s.* A demon priest. 2. a Billavar *or* toddy-drawer.

ಪೂಜಾರ್ಮೆ pūjārmè, *s.* The office of a priest. ಜರಿಪು–, ದರಿಪು– a demon priest who is also the devil-dancer.

ಪೂಜಾವುನಿ pūjāvuni, *c. v.* (*of* ಪೂಜುನಿ) To cause to smear *or* apply.

ಪೂಜಿತ pūjita, *adj.* Worshipped, reverenced.

ಪೂಜುನಿ pūjuni (ಪೂಜ್), *v. a.* To smear, rub, daub, apply.

ಪೂಜೆ pūjè, *s.* Worship, adoration; prayer. ಮಹಾ– principal worship in a temple. –ಕರಿಪುನಿ, –ಮಳ್ಪುನಿ to worship.

ಪೂಜ್ಯ pūjya, *adj.* Worshipful, adorable, venerable. 2. blank, void. *s.* A cipher. –ತೆ dignity, nobleness.

ಪೂಟಿ pūṭi, *s. Membrum muliebre.*

ಪೂಡು pūḍu, *see* ಪೂಳು.

ಪೂತ pūta, *a.* Of *or* belonging to a flower. 2. purified, cleansed. 3. *see* ಪೂಂತೆ.

ಪೂತನಿ pūtani, *s.* A giantess killed by Krishṇa. ಪೂತನಾರಿ Krishṇa.

ಪೂನಿಣೆ pūniṇè, *s.* A very tender fruit.

ಪೂನೀರ್ pūnīrụ, *s.* Flower and water placed in a demon shrine. –ದೀಪಿನಿ to place flower and water before a demon.

ಪೂಪುನಿ pūpuni (ಪೂ), *v. n.* To break wind, fart, *vlg.*

ಪೂಪೆಲೆ pūpele, *s.* One who farts frequently, *vlg.*

ಪೂಬಾರೆ pūbārè, *s.* A kind of plantain.

ಪೂಮಾಲೆ, ಪೂಮಾಲಿಕೆ pūmālè, pūmālikè, *see under* ಪೂ.

ಪೂಮೀನ್ pūmīnụ, *s.* A trout.

ಪೂರ pūra, *see* ಪೂರ್ಣ. 2. ಪುರಾತನ; *cf.* ಪೂರ್ವ.

ಪೂರಂಡ pūranḍa, *adj.* Vindictive. 2. implaccable, unappeasable. –ಪಗೆ implaccable hatred.

ಪೂರತ್ತರ pūrattara, *see* ಪೂರ್ವೋತ್ತರ.

ಪೂರಪ್ಪರ pūrappara, *adj.* Clear *or* full understanding.

ಪೂರಾ pūrā, *see* ಪೂರ್ಣ.

ಪೂರಿತ pūrita, *adj.* Filled, complete.

ಪೂರೈಸುನಿ pūreisuni, *see* ಪುರೆಸುನಿ.

ಪೂರೋತ್ತರ pūrōttara, *see* ಪೂರ್ವೋತ್ತರ.

ಪೂರ್ಣ pūrṇa, *adj.* Full, filled, complete. 2. all, entire. 3. able, powerful. *adv.* Wholly, completely. –ತೆ, –ತ್ವ fulness; the whole; ability.

ಪೂರ್ಣಮಿ, ಪೂರ್ಣಮೆ pūrṇami, pūrṇamè, *see* ಪುಂಣಮಿ.

ಪೂರ್ತಿ pūrti, *s.* Fulness, completion. –ಮಳ್ಪುನಿ to complete, fulfil.

ಪೂರ್ವ pūrva, *adj.* Former, prior, first, before, in front of. 2. east, eastern. *s.* Ancient times, days of old; the east. –ಕರ್ಮ former actions. –ಕಾಲ former time. –ಜರ್ progenitors, ancestors. –ಪದ the first member of a compound word, sentence *or* verse, *gram.* ಪೂರ್ವೋಡು in olden times.

ಪೂರ್ವಪಕ್ಷ pūrvapaksha, *s.* A proposition, assertion, the first part of an argument.

ಪೂರ್ವಾಪರ pūrvāpara, *s.* Past and future, former and latter. –ಸಂಗತಿ past and future circumstances.

ಪೂರ್ವಾಭಾದ್ರೆ pūrvābhādrè, *s.* The twenty-fifth lunar mansion.

ಪೂರ್ವಾಷಾಢ pūrvāshāḍha, *s.* The twentieth lunar mansion.

ಪೂರ್ವಾಹ್ನ pūrvāhna, *s.* The early part of the day, forenoon.

ಪೂರ್ವಿಕೆ pūrvike, *s*. An ancestor, progenitor.

ಪೂರ್ವೋತ್ತರ pūrvōttara, *s*. Circumstances, particulars of a person *or* event.

ಪೂವರಿ pūvari, *s*. Rice used at the worship of a demon. —ದಕ್ಕುನಿ to throw rice on a demon priest.

ಪೂವೆ pūvè, *s*. The day preceding the full moon.

ಪೂವೊಳು pūvoḷu, *s*. The navel. 2. a thin film between the pulp and seed of a jack fruit.

ಪೂಶರ pūšara, *s*. A kind of garland.

ಪೂಷಣ, ಪೂಷಣೆ pūshaṇa, pūshaṇè, *see* ಪೋಷಣ.

ಪೂಸುನಿ pūsuni, *see* ಪೂಜುನಿ.

ಪೂಳಂದಾಯೆ pūḷandāye, *s*. A demon so called.

ಪೂಳು pūḷu, *s*. A chip, small piece of anything. 2. a piece of betel nut. —ಕಜಿಪ a vegetable curry. —ಪೂಳು small pieces. ಕಾಯಿದ— a piece of a fruit. ನುಂಗೆಲ್— a piece of dry betel nut. ಬಜ್ಜೆಯಿದ— a piece of fresh *or* preserved betel-nut. —ದೀಪಿನಿ, —ಮಳ್ಪುನಿ to slice, chip, cut.

ಪೃಥಿವಿ, ಪೃಥ್ವಿ pru̥thivi, pru̥thvi, *s*. The earth.

ಪೃಷ್ಠ pru̥shṭha, *s*. The back. 2. the rear, last. 3. the back *or* hind part of anything.

ಪೆಂಗಂಣೆ peṅgaṇṇe, *see* ಪೆಂಗೆ.

ಪೆಂಗತನ peṅgatana, *s*. Silliness, stupidity, foolishness.

ಪೆಂಗರೆ, ಪೆಂಗಾರ peṅgarè, peṅgāra, *see* ಪಿಂಗರ.

ಪೆಂಗು peṅgu, *adj*. Blackish.

ಪೆಂಗೆ, ಪೆಂಞೆ peṅge, peññe, *s*. A fool, stupid fellow, simpleton.

ಪೆಚ್ಚ pečča, *see* ಬೆಜ್ಜ.

ಪೆಜ peja, *s*. The wild jack, *Artocarpus pubescens*. —ಕಾಯಿ its fruit.

ಪೆಜಂಕುನಿ, ಪೆಜಕುನಿ pejaṅkuni, pejakuni, *see* ಪೊಜಂಕುನಿ.

ಪೆಜಿಪಿನಿ, ಪೆಜ್ಜುನಿ pejipini, pejjuni (ಪೆಜಿ, ಪೆಜ್ಜ್), *v. a.* To select, choose. 2. to pick up. 3. to pick *or* remove stones *or* paddy from rice, *etc*.

ಪೆಜಿರೆನಾಯೆ pejirenāye, *s*. A demon so called.

ಪೆಜ್ಜೆ pejjè, *s*. Gruel, rice water, porridge. —ತ ಪೂ, *see* ಜಾಂಬಿಗೆ.

ಪೆಟ್ಟ್ peṭṭu̥, *s*. A blow, slap, cuff. —ಕೊರ್ಪಿನಿ to beat, slap, cuff. —ತಿನ್ಪಿನಿ to receive blows, be beaten. —ಪಾಡುನಿ to eat greedily.

ಪೆಟ್ಟ್‌ಗ್ peṭṭugu̥, *adv*. Immediately, directly.

ಪೆಟ್ಟಂಕ್ peṭṭaṅku̥, *see* ತಜಂಕ್.

ಪೆಟ್ಟಿಗೆ peṭṭigè, *s*. A box, chest. —ಕುಂದ a square pillar *or* post.

ಪೆಟ್ಟಿಗೆ peṭṭigè, *see* ಪಟ್ಟಿಗೆ.

ಪೆಟ್ಲ peṭla, *see* ಪೇಟ್ಲ.

ಪೆಟ್ಲುಪ್ಪು peṭlupu, *see* ಪಟ್ಲುಪ್ಪು.

ಪೆತ್ತ petta, *s*. A cow. —ತೊಜಂಕ್ a kind of *Cassia tora*; *cf*. ತಜಂಕ್.

ಪೆದ್ಮೆದಿ pedu̥medi, *see* ಪಿದ್ಮೆದಿ.

ಪೆದಂಕೆ pedaṅkè, *s.* Stumbling, tripping. 2. sprain. —ಬೂರು ನಿ to be sprained.

ಪೆದಂಗ್ pedaṅgụ, *adv.* Behind the back. —ಕಟ್ಟುನಿ to pinion behind, as the hands.

ಪೆದಂಗರ, ಪೆದಂಗಾಯಿ, ಪೆದಂಗೈ pedaṅgara, pedaṅgāyi, pedaṅgei, *s.* A water-pot placed outside a house for washing purpose.

ಪೆದಂಬು pedambu, *adv.* Obliquely, not directly. —ಕುದುಪುನಿ to cut, shave, *etc.*, obliquely.

ಪೆದಕಾಲೆ pedakāle, *s.* A demon so called.

ಪೆದಮಾಲೆ pedamālè, *see* ಪಿದಮಲೆ.

ಪೆದ್ದೊಲ್ದಿ peddoldi, *see* ಪೆದ್ಮೆದಿ.

ಪೆದ್ಪಾವುನಿ pedpāvuni, *c. v.* (*of* ಪೆದ್ಪಿನಿ) To assist a woman in child-birth, serve as a midwife.

ಪೆದ್ಪಿನಿ, ಪೆದ್ದುನಿ pedpini, pedduni (ಪೆದ್), *v. a.* To bear, bring forth, as a child.

ಪೆದ್ಮೆದಿ pedmedi, *s.* A woman in child-bed, lying-in woman.

ಪೆನ್ಸ್ pensụ, *s.* The lungs.

ಪೆನ್ಸಿಲ್ pensilụ, *s.* A slate *or* led pencil.

ಪೆಪ್ಪು, ಪೆಪ್ಪೆ peppu, peppè, *s.* Dumbfoundedness, speechlessness, as from amazement, *etc.* —ಪಾತೆರುನಿ to stammer; to speak hesitatingly.

ಪೆಬ್ಬೆ pebbe, *s.* A dolt.

ಪೆರಂಗಾಯಿ peraṅgāyi, *see* ಪೇರಂಗಾಯಿ.

ಪೆರಂಟ್ perantụ, *see* ಬೆರಂಟಿ.

ಪೆರಂತ್ perantụ, *see* ಬೆರಂತ್.

ಪೆರಡೆ peradè, *s.* A hen. —ಕರೆಪುನಿ, —ಕಿರೆಪುನಿ, —ಕೆರೆಪುನಿ to cluck.

ಪೆರತ perata, *s.* A ceremony performed in behalf of females who have become pubescent. 2. *see* ಪ್ರೇತ.

ಪೆರತಿ perati, *see* ಪ್ರತಿ.

ಪೆರದನೆ, ಪೆರಮಣೆ peradanè, peramaṇè, *s.* A grater, scraper. —ಪೂ a kind of moss.

ಪೆರದೆ peradè, *see* ಪರದೆ.

ಪೆರಸ್ತನ perastana, *see* ಪ್ರಯತ್ನ.

ಪೆರಾರ್ತೆ perārtè, *see* ಪೆರತ.

ಪೆರಾರ್ದೆ perārdè, *s.* The ninth Tuḷu month.

ಪೆರಿ peri, *see* ಪೆರಿಯ.

ಪೆರಿಕೆ perikè, *s.* A bullock's load. 2. any burden. —ಪಾಡುನಿ to load. —ಬೂರುನಿ, *see* ಪೆರ್ಯೆ.

ಪೆರಿಯ periya, *adj.* Large, great, high, superior. —ನೆಯಿ honey. —ಸಾದಿ a highway.

ಪೆರಿಯಮ್ಮೆ periyamme, *s.* A father's elder brother, *or* a mother's elder sister's husband.

ಪೆರಿಯಪ್ಪೆ periyappè, *s.* A mother's elder sister, *or* a father's elder brother's wife.

ಪೆರಿಯೆ periyè, *s.* A heap, pile.

ಪೆರಿಯೊಳು periyoḷu, *s.* An eel.

ಪೆರಿಸ್ತ್ peristụ, *s.* The contents of a book, library, *etc.* —ಬರೆಪಿನಿ to write such contents.

ಪೆರುಮಾರಿ **perumari,** *see* ಪೆರ್ಮಾರಿ.

ಪೆರೆಡುನಿ **pereḍuni** (ಪೆರೆದ್), *v. n.* To roll, move, wallow. 2. to scrape, shave.

ಪೆರೆಪಿನಿ **perepini** (ಪೆರೆ), *v. a.* To grate, scrape. 2. to bore, perforate.

ಪೆರೆಮಣೆ **peremaṇè,** *see* ಪೆರಡನೆ.

ಪೆರೆವುನಿ **perevuni** (ಪೆರೆ), *v. n.* To be grated, scraped. 2. to be bored, perforated.

ಪೆರೆಸುನಿ **peresuni** (ಪೆರೆಸ್), *see* ಪಿರೆಸುನಿ.

ಪೆರ್ಕೆ, ಪೆರ್ಗೆ **perkè, pergè,** *see* ಪೆರಿಕೆ.

ಪೆರ್ಗ **perga,** *s.* Winnings made in a game of ಚಂಪೆಮಣೆ. 2. profit, gain. ಇನಿ ಆಯಗ್ ಪೆರ್ಗ he had a good meal to-day.

ಪೆರ್ಗಡೆ **pergaḍè,** *s.* A chieftain, headman. 2. an honorary title.

ಪೆರ್ಗುಡೆ **perguḍè,** *s.* A bandicoot, large rat. —ಲಾಂಬು a kind of mushroom.

ಪೆರ್ಗೆ **pergè,** *s.* A kind of bag. 2. *see* ಪುಂಕೆರ್ಲ್.

ಪೆರ್ಚಿ **perči,** *s.* Shying, starting suddenly. —ಕಟ್ಟುನಿ to shy, as a horse, *etc.*

ಪೆರ್ಚುನಿ **perčuni** (ಪೆರ್ಚ್), *v. n.* To shy, start aside suddenly. 2. to rise, increase.

ಪೆರ್ಜೀವ **perjīva,** *s.* Life, spirit.

ಪೆರ್ಜುನಿ **perjuni** (ಪೆರ್ಜ್), *v. n.* To increase.

ಪೆರ್ನಾಮ **pernāma,** *see* ಪರ್ನಾಮ.

ಪೆರ್ನಾಲ್, ಪೆರ್ನಾಳ್ **pernālu, pernāḷu,** *s.* A festival on the conclusion of fasting among the Mussulmans.

ಪೆರ್ಪು **perpu,** *s.* Anything put into milk in order to curdle it. —ಆಪಿನಿ, *see* ಪೆರ್ಪನಿ. —ಕೊಟುನಿ, —ಪಾಡುನಿ to put in milk any thing to curdle *or* turn it sour.

ಪೆರ್ಪುನಿ **perpuni** (ಪೆರ್), *v. n.* To be curdled, as milk.

ಪೆರ್ಮಾರಿ **permari,** *s.* A boa *or* large serpent. 2. sheaves of straw placed in the form of a ring to serve as a granary. —ಕಟ್ಟುನಿ to make such a granary.

ಪೆರ್ಮೆ **permè,** *s.* Sluggishness, laziness. 2. haughtiness.

ಪೆರ್ಯ **perya,** *s.* A large bee. 2. *see* ಪೆರಿಯ. —ದ ತಟ್ಟೆ a beehive, honey-comb. —ಬೂರುನಿ to become dense; to fall densely.

ಪೆರ್ಯಾದಿ **peryādi,** *s.* A highway, public road.

ಪೆರ್ಯೆ **peryè,** *s.* The toadstool, mushroom. 2. a rush.

ಪೆಲ **pela,** *s.* The jack, *Artocarpus integrifolia.* —ಕಾಯಿ the jack-fruit. —ತರಿ the seed of the jackfruit. —ಮರ the jack-tree, jack-wood. ತುಳುವೆ—, ಬರ್ಕೆ—, ಮುಂಡೆ— are varieties of jackfruit

ಪೆಲಂಬು **pelambu,** *see* ಪೊಲಂಬು.

ಪೆಲಿ **peli,** *see* ಪಿಲಿ.

ಪೆಲೇಗು **pelēgu,** *adj.* Rude, mean.

ಪೇಂಚಿ **pēñči,** *s.* Filth, dirt.

ಪೇಂಟಿ **pēṇṭi,** *s.* A good meal.

ಪೇಂಟೆ **pēṇṭè,** *s.* The mercantile part of a town, bazaar, market.

ಪೇಚಾಟ pēcāṭa, *s.* Effort, exertion. 2. affliction, distress, trouble.

ಪೇಚಾಡುನಿ pēcāḍuni (ಪೇಚಾಡ್), *v.n.* To try, exert, strive. 2. to be in distress, trouble.

ಪೇಚಿಲ್ pēcilu, *see* ಬೇಚಿಲ್.

ಪೇಚುನಿ pēcuni, *see* ಪೇಶಿಯುನಿ.

ಪೇಟ, ಪೇಟ್ಲ, ಪೇಟ್ಲೆ pēṭa, pēṭla, pēṭlè, *s.* A pop-gun. —ಬುಡ್ಪುನಿ to shoot a pop-gun.

ಪೇಟೆ pēṭè, *see* ಪೇಂಟೆ.

ಪೇಡೆ pēḍè, *s.* A kind of thorn-bush.

ಪೇತ್, ಪೇತು pētu, pētu, *s.* Parturition, child-bed. 2. fear.

ಪೇತಲೆ pētale, *s.* A greedy man.

ಪೇತ್ರಿ, ಪೇತ್ರಿಕಲ್ಲ್ pētri, pētrikallu, *s.* A large stone.

ಪೇದೆ pèdè, *s.* A peon; *also* ಪ್ಯಾದೆ.

ಪೇನ್ pēnu, *s.* A louse. 2. a pen. ಕೊಟ್ಟ—, ಜಮಾಯಿ— a very large louse. ಶಿದ್— a small louse. ಬೊಳ್ಳ— a white-nit found on dirty clothes; *see* ಬೊಲ್ಲೆ.

ಪೇಪೆ pēpè, *see* ಪಿರಿಯುಪ್ಪ.

ಪೇಮೆ pēme, *see* ಪಿರಿಯುಂಮೆ.

ಪೇಯಿ pēyi, *s.* A demon.

ಪೇರ್ pēru, *s.* Milk. 2. cocoanut-juice. 3. the milky juice of plants. —ದಾಯೆ a milkman. ಪೇರಬಿಸಲೆ a milk-pail.

ಪೇರಂಗಾಯಿ pērangāyi, *s.* The guava fruit, *Psidium pomiferum.*

ಪೇರಣೆ pēraṇè, *see* ಪ್ರೇರಣೆ.

ಪೇರಾಟ pērāṭa, *s.* Lading, freighting, shipping.

ಪೇರಾವಡೆ pērāvaḍè, *s.* A kind of *Phaseolus trilobus.*

ಪೇರಾವುನಿ pērāvuni, *c.v.* (*of* ಪೇರುನಿ) To lade, load, burden.

ಪೇರಿತ pērita, *see* ಪ್ರೇರಿತ.

ಪೇರುನಿ pēruni (ಪೇರ್), *v. a.* To load, burden.

ಪೇರೆಂಗೆಲ್ pērengelu, *s.* A kind of creeper.

ಪೇರೇಪಣೆ pērepaṇè, *see* ಪ್ರೇರೇಪಣೆ.

ಪೇರೊಣಾಸ್ pēroṇasu, *s.* The meal just preceding the celebration of a wedding.

ಪೇರ್ಗ pērga, *see* ಪೆರ್ಗ.

ಪೇರ್ಗೆ pērgè, *see* ಪೆರ್ಗೆ.

ಪೇರ್ಚಿ pērci, *see* ಪೆರ್ಚಿ.

ಪೇರ್ಚುನಿ pērcuni, *see* ಪೆರ್ಚುನಿ.

ಪೇರ್ಮೆ pērmè, *s.* Fame, glory. 2. *see* ಪೆರ್ಮೆ.

ಪೇರ್ವೆ pērvè, *adj.* Outside. —ಮುಂದಿಲ್ an outer court.

ಪೇಶಿಗೆ pēśigè, *s.* Disgust, loathing. 2. dirt, filth. —ಮಳ್ಪುನಿ to be disgusted.

ಪೇಶಿಯುನಿ pēśiyuni (ಪೇಶಿ), *v. a.* To loathe, be disgusted.

ಪೇಷ್ಕಾರ್, ಪೇಷ್ಕಾರೆ peshkāru, pēshkāre, *s.* A subordinate revenue officer.

ಪೇಸಿಗೆ pēsigé, *see* ಪೇಶಿಗೆ.

ಪೈ pei, *s.* A pie, one-twelfth of an anna.

ಪೈಂಗು peingu, *s.* Pegu.

ಪೈಂಚೆಲ್ peiṅcelu, *s.* Ten pairs.

ಪೈಂದನಿ peindani, *see* ಪಯಿಜಾನ್.

ಪೈಂದಲೆ, ಪೈಂದ್ಲೆ peindalè, peindlè, *s.* A notch, nick.

ಪೈಂಬಳ **peimbaḷa**, *s.* Ten seers.

ಪೈಂಬಳೆ **peimbaḷe**, *s.* A flatterer. 2. a potbelly. 3. a glutton.

ಪೈಂಬೆ **peimbe**, *s.* A bag.

ಪೈಕ್, ಪೈಕ **peiku, peika**, *s.* A pouch, scrip made of rushes *or* palm leaves.

ಪೈಕಿ **peiki**, *postp.* Of, out of. 2. concerning, respecting. ಅ— out of it. ಮೋಕುಳೆ— of *or* respecting these persons.

ಪೈಕುನಿ **peikuni** (ಪೈಕ್), *v. n.* To contract, shrivel.

ಪೈಕೋರಿ **peikōri**, *s.* A kind of fowl; game fowl.

ಪೈಚಿಲ್ **peićilu**, *see* ಪಯಕೆಲ್.

ಪೈಜಾಣ್, ಪೈಜಾಣಿ **peijāṇu, peijāni**, *see* ಪಯಿಜಾನ್.

ಪೈಜಾರ್ **peijāru**, *s.* Shoes, slippers.

ಪೈಞಾಲಿ **peiñāli**, *s.* Bragging, boasting. 2. hoaxing, deceiving. —ಕಡ್ಪುನಿ, —ಪಾತೆರುನಿ to brag.

ಪೈಟಣಿ **peiṭini**, *s.* A country so called. —ಶೀಲೆ a female's cloth made of silk and cotton.

ಪೈತ, ಪೈತ್ಯ **peita, peitya**, *s.* Biliousness. *adj.* Bilious. —ಗಾರೆ a man of irritable temper; a lunatic, fool.

ಪೈತ್ರ್ **peitru**, *see* ಪಿತ್ರ್.

ಪೈದ, ಪೈದೆ **peida, peide**, *see* ಪಾಯಿದ.

ಪೈದಾಸ್ತ್ **peidāstu**, *s.* Produce, crop. —ಆಪಿನಿ to grow, produce. —ಮಳ್ಪುನಿ to grow, raise a crop.

ಪೈನ **peina**, *see* ಪಯಾಣ.

ಪೈನಲೆ **peinale**, *see* ಪೈಂದಲೆ.

ಪೈನಾಲಿ **peināli**, *see* ಪೈಞಾಲಿ.

ಪೈನೀರ್ **peiniru**, *s.* Turbid water of a river.

ಪೈಪುನಿ **peipuni** (ಪೈ), *v. a.* To cut, reap; *cf.* ಬೈಪುನಿ.

ಪೈಮಾಲೆ **peimāle**, *see* ಪೈಞಾಲಿ.

ಪೈಮಾಶಿ, ಪೈಮಾಸಿ **peimāśi, peimāsi**, *s.* Measurement of land, survey.

ಪೈಮುಡಿ **peimuḍi**, *see under* ಪಲ್ಲ.

ಪೈಯೆರ್, ಪೈಯ್ಯೆರ್ **peiyeru, peiyyeru**, *see* ಪೈಯ್ಯ.

ಪೈಯ್ಯ **peiyya**, *s.* A child. —ಜ ಕಾರ್ a small cloud.

ಪೈಯ್ಯಾನೆ **peiyyāne**, *s.* A kind of medicinal tree, *Bignonia longifolia.*

ಪೈಯ್ಯೆ **peiyye**, *s.* A child, boy; a Pariahs child. 2. a kind of fish.

ಪೈರ್ **peiru**, *s.* Standing *or* growing corn. 2. goods *or* cattle imported from the ghauts.

ಪೈಲ್ **peilu**, *see* ಫೈಲ್.

ಪೈಲ್ವಾನಿಗೆ **peiluvānige**, *s.* Tumbling, rope-dancing, gymnastics.

ಪೈಲ್ವಾನೆ **peiluvāne**, *s.* A tumbler, acrobat, gymnast.

ಪೈಲಾಂಡಿ **peilāṇḍi**, *s.* Brag, boast. —ಪಾತೆರುನಿ to brag.

ಪೈವಸ್ತ್, ಪೈವಸ್ತೆ **peivastu, peivaste**, *s.* Endorsement of a letter, specifying the date of its receipt. —ಪಾಡುನಿ, —ಮಳ್ಪುನಿ to endorse.

ಪೈಸ್ **peisu**, *adj.* Distant, remote. *intj.* Get away, make way.

ಪೈಸ peisa, *s.* Four pie. 2. money.

ಪೈಸಲ್, ಪೈಸಲೆ, ಪೈಸುಲ್ peisalu, peisalè, peisulu, *s.* Settlement, adjustment. 2. decision, decree.

ಪೊಂಕ poṅka, *adj.* Handsome, [pretty.

ಪೊಂಕರ poṅkara, *see* ಪೋಂಕರ.

ಪೊಂಕು poṅku, *s.* A kind of boil *or* sore; *cf.* ಪೊಂಗಡೆ.

ಪೊಂಕುರು poṅkuru, *see* ಪೋಂಕುರು.

ಪೊಂಕೆ poṅke, *see* ಪೊಂರ್ಕೆ.

ಪೊಂಗ್ poṅgu, *see* ಬೊಂಗ್.

ಪೊಂಗಡೆ poṅgaḍè, *s.* Proud flesh. —ಪಿಂಕುನಿ proud flesh to form.

ಪೊಂಗರೆ poṅgarè, *s.* The Indian coral tree, *Erythrina indica.*

ಪೊಂಗಾಯಿ poṅgāyi, *s.* A canoe.

ಪೊಂಗಾರ poṅgāra, *s.* Borax. 2. *see* ಪೊಂಗರೆ.

ಪೊಂಗಾವುನಿ poṅgāvuni, *c. v.* (*of* ಪೊಂಗುನಿ) To cause to rock *or* tumble, as a boat.

ಪೊಂಗು poṅgu, *see* ಬೊಂಗು.

ಪೊಂಗುನಿ poṅguni (ಪೊಂಗ್), *v. n.* To rock, reel, tumble, toss, as a boat.

ಪೊಂಗೆ poṅge, *s.* An unsteady [man.

ಪೊಂಗೆಲ್ poṅgelu, *s.* Tumbling, rocking. 2. unsteadiness. ಪೊಂಗೆತೆ a fickle man, dolt.

ಪೊಂಬಣ್ poṅṅaṇu, *see* ಪೊಂಗಡೆ.

ಪೊಂಣ ponṇa, *adj.* Female, feminine. 2. bridal. —ಕೋಡಿ a bride's parental home. —ತಿಂಕುಳು a bridal cartege. —ಶೀಲ a female's conduct *or* disposition.

ಪೊಂಣಂಬುರ poṇṇambura, *see* ಪಂನಂಬುರ.

ಪೊಂಣು poṇṇu, *s.* A girl, female, maid. —ಗಡಿ the upper half of a cocoanut. —ಜಾತಿ the female sex. —ಬಾಲೆ a female child.

ಪೊಂಣೆ poṇṇè, *see* ಪೊಂನೆ.

ಪೊಂಣೊಳಿಗೆ poṇṇoḷigè, *see* ಪೊಂನಳಿಗೆ.

ಪೊಂಣ್ಜವು poṇṇjavu, *see* ಪೊಣ್ಜವು.

ಪೊಂಜು poñju, *s.* A purse *or* bundle of money.

ಪೊಂತನ pontana, *s.* Favourableness, auspiciousness.

ಪೊಂದ್ಯನಿ ponduni, *see* ಹೊಂದುನಿ.

ಪೊಂನಣಿ ponnaṇi, *s.* A kind of medicine.

ಪೊಂನಳಿಗೆ ponnaḷigè, *s.* A kind of jungle tree. —ತಪ್ಪು leaves of this tree used as medicine.

ಪೊಂನಾಂಕಂಣಿ ponnāṅkaṇṇi, *s.* A kind of vegetable, *Alternanthera sessilis.*

ಪೊಂನು ponnu, *s.* Gold. 2. *see* ಪೊಂಣು.

ಪೊಂನೆ ponnè, *s.* The tree *Rottlera tinctoria.* ಶಿರಿ— *Boswellia thurifera; Calophyllum apetalum.*

ಪೊಂಬಟ್ಟೆ pombaṭṭè, *s.* A yellow cloth.

ಪೊಂಬಡೆ pombade, *see* ಪಂಬಡೆ.

ಪೊಂಬರಿಯುನಿ pombariyuni (ಪೊಂಬರಿ), *v. n.* To start, wince, shudder; to be startled, amazed, astounded.

ಪೊಂರ್ಕ್, ಪೊಂರ್ಕು porṅkų, pornku, *adj.* Slovenly, dirty, filthy.

ಪೊಂರ್ಕಾವುನಿ porṅkāvuni, *c. v.* (*of* ಪೊಂರ್ಕುನಿ) To cause to roll. 2. *see* ಪೊಂರ್ಗಾವುನಿ.

ಪೊಂರ್ಕುನಿ porṅkuni (ಪೊಂರ್ಂಡ್), *v. a.* To roll, run over. 2. to make fun. 3. *see* ಪೊಂರ್ಗುನಿ.

ಪೊಂರ್ಕೆ, ಪೊಂರ್ಕೆಲೆ porṅke, porṅkele, *s.* A dirty man.

ಪೊಂರ್ಕೆಲ್ porṅkelų, *s.* Dirtiness, filthiness.

ಪೊಂರ್ಗಾವುನಿ porṅgāvuni, *c. v.* (*of* ಪೊಂರ್ಗುನಿ) To make stiff, harden.

ಪೊಂರ್ಗುನಿ porṅguni (ಪೊಂರ್ಂಗ್), *v. n.* To become stiff *or* hard.

ಪೊಂರ್ದನ porndana, *s.* A Pariah woman.

ಪೊಂರ್ಬಾಟ pormbāṭa, *s.* Strife, struggle. 2. wrestling. 3. wrangling.

ಪೊಂರ್ಬುನಿ pormbuni (ಪೊಂರ್ಂಬ್), *v. a.* To wrestle, strive.

ಪೊಂರ್ಬೆಲೆ pormbele, *s.* A wrestler, wrangler. 2. a quarrelsome man.

ಪೊಕಂಕುನಿ pokaṅkuni (ಪೊಕಂಕ್), *v. a.* To learn by looking on others.

ಪೊಕ್ಕಡೆ pokkaḍè, *adv.* Without cause, reason, *or* meaning. 2. for nothing. 3. gratis, gratuitously. 4. for pastime. 5. without success. *adj.* False, vain, mere, empty.

ಪೊಕ್ಕು pokku, *s.* A game of throwing pebbles in the air and catching them as they fall down. –ದ ಕಲ್ಲ್ pebbles used in this game. –ಗೊಬ್ಬುನಿ to play at such a game.

ಪೊಕ್ಕೆ pokkè, *s.* A sore, ulcer; a blister, pustule. –ದ ಕಲೆ the scar of a sore. –ಲಕ್ಕುನಿ a vesicle *or* blister to form.

ಪೊಕ್ಕೆಲೆ pokkele, *see* ಪುಕ್ಕೆ.

ಪೊಗತೆ pogatè, *see* ಪುಗತೆ.

ಪೊಗರುನಿ, ಪೊಗಳುನಿ pogaruni, pogaḷuni, *see* ಪುಗರುನಿ.

ಪೊಗುತಿ poguti, *s.* A shameless woman.

ಪೊಗುಳು poguḷu, *s.* Praise, eulogium. 2. renown.

ಪೊಗೆ pogè, *see* ಪುಗೆ.

ಪೊಗೆಪುನಿ pogepuni, *see* ಪುಗೆಪುನಿ.

ಪೊಗ್ಗಾವುನಿ poggāvuni, *c. v.* (*of* ಪೊಗ್ಗುನಿ) To cause to enter, penetrate *or* interfere. 2. to pierce.

ಪೊಗ್ಗುನಿ pogguni (ಪೊಗ್ಗ್), *v. a.* To enter, penetrate. 2. to interfere.

ಪೊಗ್ಪಾವುನಿ pogpāvuni, *see* ಪೊಗ್ಗಾವುನಿ.

ಪೊಜಂಕುನಿ, ಪೊಜಕುನಿ pojaṅkuni, pojakuni, *see* ಪೊಜಿಂಕುನಿ.

ಪೊಜಕ್ pojakų, *see* ಪಜಕ್.

ಪೊಜಕೊಣುನಿ pojakoṇuni, *v. refl.* To be grieved. 2. to be distorted, as from pain. 3. to rub the face, as in grief *or* shame.

ಪೊಜಿಲ್ pojilų, *s.* A germ, sprout, bud. –ಅರಿ rice made of germinated paddy. –ಕೊರಂಟೆ a germinated cashew-nut.

–ಬಿತ್ತ್ malt, grain steeped in water.

ಪೊಜೆಂಕಾವುನಿ pojeṅkāvuni, *c. v.* (*of* ಪೊಜೆಂಕುನಿ) To strangulate. 2. to cause to knead.

ಪೊಜೆಂಕುನಿ, ಪೊಜೆಕುನಿ pojeṅkuni, pojekuni (ಪೊಜೆಂಕ್), *v. a.* To knead. 2. to shampoo, rub. 3. to squeeze. 4. to strangle. ಕೆಕ್ಕಿಲ್– to strangle.

ಪೊಜೆಂಕಲೆ pojeṅkele, *s. lit.* A squeezer. 2. a sycophant, a man seeking to please.

ಪೊಜೆಕಾವುನಿ pojekāvuni, *see* ಪೊಜೆಂಕಾವುನಿ.

ಪೊಜ್ಜ pojja, *see* ಬೊಜ್ಜ.

ಪೊಟೀರ poṭīra, *see* ಚಕ್ಕುಲ್ಲಿ.

ಪೊಟ್ಟಂಗೆಲ್ poṭṭaṅgelu, *s.* Anything useless.

ಪೊಟ್ಟಡ್ಯೆ poṭṭaḍyè, *s.* A kind of cake made without jaggory.

ಪೊಟ್ಟಿ poṭṭi, *s.* A dumb *or* taciturn woman. 2. a silly woman.

ಪೊಟ್ಟು poṭṭu, *s.* Husk, chaff. 2. a fruit *or* seed without kernel. 3. a blighted ear of corn, *etc.* 4. a crack, hurt. *adj.* Dumb. 2. empty, useless. 3. stupid. 4. injured. –ಗುಂಡಿಲ್ a dry well. –ತಾರಾಯಿ an empty cocoanut. –ಪಂಡಿ vain bragging. –ಬಾರ್ blighted paddy. –ಕಂಣ್ a blind eye. –ಕಂಣಿ a blind man.

ಪೊಟ್ಟುಗಟ್ಟಿ poṭṭugaṭṭi, *see* ಪೊಟ್ಟಡ್ಯೆ.

ಪೊಟ್ಟುತಟ್ಟೆ, ಪೊಟ್ಟುದಡ್ಡ್ poṭṭutaṭṭè, poṭṭudaḍḍu, *s.* Blighted corn. (ಪೊಡೆತಿದ) ಮಿಡ್ಡೆಂತಿನೆನ್ ಮಾರಿಯೆ, ಪೊಟ್ಟುತಟ್ಟೆ ಮಾತ್ರ ಒರಿಂಡ್ he sold the grain and kept the chaff.

ಪೊಟ್ಟೆ poṭṭe, *s.* A dumb man. 2. a demon so called.

ಪೊಟ್ಟೆ poṭṭè, *s.* The calf of the leg; *also* ಕಾರಪೊಟ್ಟೆ. 2. a tender ear of corn. 3. the hollow of a stalk *or* tree. 4. pregnancy, *vlg.* 5. thickness, as that of a blade of a knife. –ಮಸೆಯುನಿ to whet the thick part of a knife.

ಪೊಟ್ಟೆದಾಳ್ poṭṭedāḷu, *s.* A pregnant Pariah woman.

ಪೊಟ್ಟೆಬಂಜಿ poṭṭebañji, *s.* A pot belly. 2. a corpulent man.

ಪೊಟ್ಲ poṭla, *s.* A pustule, blister. 2. swelling of the gums. 3. *see* ಪೋಟ್ಲ.

ಪೊಡ್ತೊಣುನಿ poḍutoṇuni, *v. refl.* To struggle, strive. 2. to flutter, flap the wings, as a bird. 3. to bustle, be in a hurry.

ಪೊಡತರೆ poḍatarè, *s.* The side-bone of the scull.

ಪೊಡವಿ poḍavi, *s.* The earth; *cf.* ಪೃಥ್ವಿ.

ಪೊಡಸ್ poḍasu, *s.* The scales of fish.

ಪೊಡಿ poḍi, *s.* Powder, dust, crumbs. 2. flour. 3. snuff. –ಕಲ್ಲ್ gravel. –ಮುಕ್ಕೆ a miser, *abus.* –ಕ್ ಬಿತ್ತುನಿ to sow in dry land. –ಪಾರುನಿ, –ರಟ್ಟುನಿ dust to rise up *or* be dispersed. –ಮಳ್ಪುನಿ to pulverize, powder.

ಪೊಡಿತ್ತಾವುನಿ poḍittāvuni, *see* ಪೋಡಿಯಾವುನಿ.

ಪೊಡಿಯುನಿ poḍiyuni (ಪೊಡಿ), *v. a.* To powder, pulverize.

ಪೊಡುಂಬು poḍumbu, *adj.* Stupid, stolid. 2. cowardly. 3. sneakish. *s.* Cowardliness.

ಪೊಡುಂಬೆ poḍumbe, *s.* A stupid, *or* spiritless man.

ಪೊಡೆ poḍè, *see* ಪುಡೆ.

ಪೊಡೆಕುನಿ poḍekuni (ಪೊಡೆಕ್), *v. a.* To regret, repent. 2. to be envious.

ಪೊಡೆಪುನಿ poḍepuni, *see* ಪುಡೆಪುನಿ.

ಪೊಡ್ಡ poḍḍa, *adj.* Foolish.

ಪೊಡ್ಪೆಲೆ poḍpele, *see* ಪೊಡುಂಬೆ.

ಪೊಣಕೆ poṇakè, *see* ಪಣಕೆ.

ಪೊಣಕ್ಕೆ poṇakkè, *s.* A scab, scurf.

ಪೊಣಲುನಿ poṇaluni, *see* ಪುಲಾವುನಿ.

ಪೊಣೆ poṇè, *see* ಪುಣೆ.

ಪೊಣ್ಜವು, ಪೊಣ್ಜೆವು poṇjavu, poṇjevu, *s.* A female in general; a grown up woman. —ಆಪಿನಿ to become pubescent. *Four classes of females are enumerated by Hindus; namely:* ಕಾಮಿನಿ, ಮೋಹಿನಿ, ಶಂಕಿನಿ, ಪದ್ಮಿನಿ, *or* ಹಸ್ತಿನಿ, ಚಿತ್ರಿನಿ, ಶಂಕಿನಿ, ಪದ್ಮಿನಿ, *or* ಡಂಕಿನಿ, ಲಂಕಿನಿ, ಸಂಕಿನಿ, ಪದ್ಮಿನಿ.

ಪೊತ್ತ potta, *adj.* Hot, burning.

ಪೊತ್ತಾರಿ pottāri, *s.* A burnt cocoanut tree.

ಪೊತ್ತಾವುನಿ, ಪೊತ್ತಾಡ್ರುನಿ pottāvuni, pottāḍruni, *c. v.* (*of* ಪೊತ್ತುನಿ) To light, kindle, burn. ತುಡರ್— to light a lamp.

ಪೊತ್ತುನಿ pottuni (ಪೊತ್ತ್), *v. n.* To burn.

ಪೊತ್ತುರುನಿ, ಪೊತ್ರುನಿ potturuni, potruni (ಪೊತ್ತುರ್, ಪೊತ್ರ್), *v. a.* To kindle, set fire. 2. to incite to a quarrel.

ಪೊತ್ತೆಂಗ್ರಿ potteṅgri, *s.* Burnt trees.

ಪೊತ್ತೆಲ್ pottelu, *s.* The testicles. —ಮಾರಿ scrotal eczema. —ಗುದ್ದುನಿ to castrate. ಅಜ್ಜ— a vulgar name for ಬೊಂಡೊಲು. —ಕೆರೆಂಗ್ wild kind of yam.

ಪೊದ್‌ಕೋಲ್ poduköḷu, *see* ಪೊಹುಕೋಲು.

ಪೊದಕೆ podakè, *s.* The eye lashes.

ಪೊದಲುನಿ podaluni (ಪೊದಲ್), *v. n.* To come out, rise up.

ಪೊದಿಕೆ podikè, *s.* Stale food, food prepared for a journey. 2. hoarded money, savings. —ಕಟ್ಟುನಿ to put up food for a journey; to hoard money.

ಪೊದಿಪುನಿ podipuni, *see* ಪೊದೆಪುನಿ.

ಪೊದಿಯುನಿ podiyuni, *see* ಪೊದ್ದಯುನಿ.

ಪೊದು podu, *s.* Relationship *or* connection by marriage. —ಪಾತೆರುನಿ to propose an alliance by marriage.

ಪೊದುಂಕುಲು, ಪೊದುಂಕ್ಲು, ಪೊದುಕು, ಪೊದುಕ್ಲು poduṅkulu, poduṅklu, poduku, poduklu, *s.* A tuft; a handful of grass, *etc.*

ಪೊದುಂಬಟ್ಟ್ podumbaṭṭu, *see* ಬೊದುಂಬಟ್ಟ್.

ಪೊದುಂಬು podumbu, *see* ಕೊದುಂಬು.

ಪೊದುಕೋಲ್ podukōlu, *s.* A small broom for broiling ಪೊರಿ.

ಪೊದುಪುನಿ podupuni (ಪೊ), *v. a.* To broil, parch. ಪೊದುಕರ, ಪೊದುಪಿಕರ a broiling pan.

ಪೊದುಪೆಲ್ podupelu, *s.* Parching. *adj.* Parched, broiled. —ಬಾರ್ parched paddy.

ಪೊದೆಪಾವುನಿ podepāvuni, *c. v.* (*of* ಪೊದೆಪುನಿ) To cause to put on clothes, to dress.

ಪೊದೆಪು podepu, *s.* Wearing apparel; *also* ತುತ್ತುಪೊದೆಪು.

ಪೊದೆಪುನಿ podepuni (ಪೊದೆ), *v. a.* To put on clothes. 2. to brood, as a hen her chickens.

ಪೊದ್ದಾನ poddāna, *s.* A distant relationship; *also* ಪೊದಾನಪೊಪು.

ಪೊದ್ದಿಕೆ poddikè, *see* ಪೊದೆಪು.

ಪೊದ್ದಿಯುನಿ, ಪೊದ್ದುನಿ, poddiyuni, podduni, (ಪೊದ್ದು), *v. a.* To roll, cover, wrap. 2. to encircle, wind, twine.

ಪೊದ್ದು poddu, *see* ಪೊಮು.

ಪೊದ್ದೆ podde, *s.* A relative, kindred. —ರಿಷ್ಟೆರ್ relations and friends.

ಪೊದ್ದೊಲ್, ಪೊದ್ದೊಳು poddolu, poddoḷu, *s.* Broiled grain; *cf.* ಪೊರಿ.

ಪೊದ್ಪಾವುನಿ podpāvuni, *c. v.* (*of* ಪೊದ್ಪುನಿ) To roast, broil, toast, parch.

ಪೊದ್ಪುನಿ podpuni, *see* ಪೊದುಪುನಿ.

ಪೊದ್ಬಟ್ಟ್ podbaṭṭu, *see* ಬೊದುಂಬಟ್ಟೆ.

ಪೊದ್ಯುನಿ podyuni, *see* ಪೊದ್ದಿಯುನಿ.

ಪೊದ್ದ್ಯಾವುನಿ poddyāvuni, *c. v.* (*of* ಪೊದ್ದಿಯುನಿ) To cause to roll, cover, encircle.

ಪೊನಿಕೆ, ಪೊನ್ಕೆ ponikè, ponkè, *see* ಪಣಿಕೆ.

ಪೊಪ್ಪಳ poppala, *see* ಪಪ್ಪಡ.

ಪೊಪ್ಪಿ poppi, *see* ಪುಪ್ಪಿ.

ಪೊಯಿಕಂಣ್ poyikaṇṇu, *s.* A veil *or* mask. *adj.* Short-sighted.

ಪೊಯಿಪಿನಿ poyipini (ಪೊಯಿ), *v. a.* To twist, as a rope. 2. to tap with a horn, as the tender blossoms of a cocoanut tree for toddy-drawing.

ಪೊಯಿಮಾರ್ poyimāru, *s.* Violence, force. 2. extortion, pillage. —ಶೀಮೆ an anarchical province.

ಪೊಯಿಮುಸುಲು poyimusulu, *see* ಕೊಯಿಂಬುಸುಲು.

ಪೊಯಿಲ್ poyilu, *s.* An abscess. 2. tapping. —ಪಾಡುನಿ to tap the tender blossoms of a palm-bud in toddy-drawing.

ಪೊಯಿಸಲ್ poyisalu, *see* ಪೊಯಿಸಲ್.

ಪೊಯ್ಯಮನೆ poyyamanè, *see* ಪೊಲಿಮನೆ.

ಪೊಯ್ಯುನಿ poyyuni (ಪೊಯ್ಯ್), *v. n.* To sit cross-legged; *bet.* ಅಟ್ಟ ಪೊಯ್ಯುನಿ. 2. *see* ಪಾಯುನಿ.

ಪೊಯ್ಯುಸುಲು poyyusulu, *see* ಕೊಯಿಂಬುಸುಲು.

ಪೊಯ್ಯೆ poyyè, *s.* Sand. ಕಲ್ಲ— coarse sand. —ಪಕ್ಕುನಿ to be afflicted with small measles.

ಪೊರಂಜಾಲ್ porañjālu, *see* ಪೊರಲ್.

ಪೊರಂಟ್ poraṇṭu, *see* ಪರಂಟೆ. 2. *see* ಪೊಂಬಾಟ.

ಪೊರಕಲುನಿ porakaluni, *see* ಪೊರ್ಕಲ್ಯುನಿ.

ಪೊರಜನ porajana, *see* ಪ್ರಯೋಜನ.

ಪೊರಜೆ porajè, *see* ಪ್ರಜೆ.

ಪೊರಲ್ poralų, *s.* A fife, flute.

ಪೊರಲ್, ಪೊರಳ್ poralų, poraḷų, *s.* Fishy smell.

ಪೊರಿ pori, *s.* A harrow. 2. a spark. 3. *see* ಪೊದ್ದೊಲ್. –ಕಂಡೆ the whole root of a tree. –ಕಟ್ಟುನಿ to harrow. –ಆಪಿನಿ to lose in the game of ಚನ್ನೆಮಣೆ. –ಪೋಪಿನಿ to get broiled, as grain. –ಮಳ್ಪುನಿ to broil grain.

ಪೊರಿಪುನಿ poripuni (ಪೊರಿ), *v. a.* To broil, parch.

ಪೊರಿಯುನಿ poriyuni (ಪೊರಿ), *v. n.* To be broiled, parched.

ಪೊರುಂಕು poruṅku, *see* ಪೊಂರ್ಕ್.

ಪೊರುವೆ poruvè, *see* ಪೊರ್ವೆ.

ಪೊರುವೆಲ್ poruvelų, *s.* The under part of a fowl's wings. 2. the side, flank.

ಪೊರೆ porè, *see* ಪುರೆ.

ಪೊರೆಂಚುನಿ porenčuni, *see* ಪುಂಚುರ್ನಿ.

ಪೊರೆಡುನಿ poreḍuni, *see* ಪುರೆಲುನಿ.

ಪೊರೆಪುನಿ porepuni, *see* ಪುರೆಪುನಿ.

ಪೊರೆಲ್ porelų, *s.* Reeling.

ಪೊರೆಲುನಿ poreluni, *see* ಪುರೆಲುನಿ.

ಪೊರೆಲ್ಪುನಿ porelpuni, *see* ಪುರೆಪುನಿ.

ಪೊರೆಸುನಿ poresuni, *see* ಪುರೆಸುನಿ.

ಪೊರ್ಕಲ್ಯುನಿ, ಪೊರ್ಕೆಲ್ಯುನಿ porkalyuni, porkeluni (ಪೊರ್ಕಲ್, ಪೊರ್ಕೆಲ್), *v. n.* A boil to form *or* suppurate.

ಪೊರ್ಕೆಲ್ porkelų, *see* ಪೊಂರ್ಕೆಲ್.

ಪೊರ್ಕೆಲೆ porkele, *see* ಪೊಂರ್ಕೆ.

ಪೊರ್ಚುನಿ porčuni, *see* ಪೊರ್ದುನಿ.

ಪೊರ್ತಿಂಗೊಳು portiṅgoḷu, *see* ಪೊರ್ತೆಲ್.

ಪೊರ್ತು portu, *s.* Time, daylight; the sun. –ಅಂತರಿಯುನಿ the sun about to set. –ಕಂತುನಿ the sun to set. –ಪೋಪಿನಿ time to pass, to be late. –ಮೂಡುನಿ the sun to rise.

ಪೊರ್ತೆಲ್, ಪೊರ್ತ್ಯೊಳು portelų, portyoḷu, *s.* The month *or* time of birth.

ಪೊರ್ದಾವುನಿ pordāvuni, *c. v.* (*of* ಪೊರ್ದುನಿ) To bring together, make friends; to familiarize; to reconcile.

ಪೊರ್ದು pordu, *s.* Inclination, leaning of the mind. 2. battle, combat.

ಪೊರ್ದುನಿ porduni (ಪೊರ್ದ್), *v. n.* To approach, draw near; to be attached, adhered. 2. to be accessible, sociable, familiar. 3. to be in harmony; to be reconciled. ಎಂಕ್ ಆಯಡ ಪೊರ್ದುಜಿ I cannot cope with him. ಆಯಗ್ ಶಾಪ ಪೊರ್ದುಂಡು the curse cleaves to him.

ಪೊರ್ನನ pornana, *see* ಪೊಂರ್ದನ.

ಪೊರ್ಪುನಿ porpuni (ಪೊರ್), *v. a.* To pull, pluck off, root up *or* out.

ಪೊರ್ಲು porlu, *s.* Beauty, comeliness. *adj.* Beautiful, handsome, fair, pleasant, fine.

–ಆಣ್ a handsome boy. –ಪಾತೆರ a pleasant word. –ಕಂಟಿ very beautiful.

ಪೊರ್ಲೆ porle, *s.* A handsome man.

ಪೊರ್ವೆ porvè, *s.* A wild duck.

ಪೊರ್ವೆಲ್ porvelụ, *see* ಪೊರುವೆಲ್.

ಪೊಲಂಪುನಿ polampuni (ಪೊಲಂ), *v. a.* To clean, wash, rinse. 2. *see* ಪುಲಾವುನಿ.

ಪೊಲಬು polabu, *s.* Acquaintance. 2. familiarity, friendship. 3. exercise, practice. 4. ability. 5. the outline *or* plan of a work.

ಪೊಲಸ್ polasụ, *adj.* Dirty, unclean; *cf.* ಹೊಲಸ್. *s. see* ಪೊಲ್ಲುಸು.

ಪೊಲಿ poli, *s.* Interest in kind. 2. increase, abundance. –ಬಡ್ಡಾವುನಿ a farmer to bring home a sheaf of the first crop, shouting ಪೊಲಿಪೊಲಿ ಹೆಚ್ಚುಲ (increase! multiply! –ಗ್ ಕೊಪ್ಪಿನಿ to lend rice before the harvest and receive it back with 25 per cent after the season. –ಪಾಡುನಿ, –ಲೆಪ್ಪುನಿ to shout ಪೊಲಿಪೊಲಿ ಹೆಚ್ಚುಲ, while gathering corn in a barn. –ಬಳಿನಿ to increase.

ಪೊಲಿಕೆ, ಪೊಲಿಗೆ polikè, poligè, *see* ಪೊಲ್ಲಿಗೆ. 2. *see* ಪೊಳಿಂಕೆ.

ಪೊಲಿಪುನಿ polipuni (ಪೊಲಿ), *v. a.* To break. 2. *see* ಪೊಲ್ಪುನಿ.

ಪೊಲಿಮಣೆ polimaṇè, *s.* A wooden instrument for levelling and smoothening the flooring of a building, *etc.*

ಪೊಲಿಯುನಿ poliyuni (ಪೊಲಿ), *v. n.* To break, be broken.

ಪೊಲಿಸ್ polisụ, *see* ಪುಲಿಸ್.

ಪೊಲುವೆ poluvè, *see* ಪೊಲ್ಲಿಗೆ.

ಪೊಲುಸು polusu, *see* ಪೊಲ್ಲುಸು.

ಪೊಲೆ polè, *s.* Pollution, defilement.

ಪೊಲ್ಕೆ polkè, *see* ಪೊಳಿಂಕೆ.

ಪೊಲ್ಪುನಿ polpuni (ಪೊಲ್), *v. a.* To level and smoothen, as the flooring of a building, *etc.*, with a wooden instrument. *cf.* ಪೊಲಿಪುನಿ. ಜಾಲ್– to level a courtyard so.

ಪೊಲ್ಲಕಟ್ಟ್ pollakaṭṭụ, *s.* Mending upon mending, patch upon patch.

ಪೊಲ್ಲಾವುನಿ pollāvuni, *c. v.* (*of* ಪೊಲ್ಲುನಿ) To cause to sew *or* stitch.

ಪೊಲ್ಲಿಗೆ polligè, *s.* Sewing, stitching, needle-work.

ಪೊಲ್ಲಿಯುನಿ, ಪೊಲ್ಲುನಿ polliyuni, polluni (ಪೊಲ್ಲ್), *v. a.* To sew, stitch, knit. 2. to slander, backbite.

ಪೊಲ್ಲು pollu, *adj.* Devoid of pulp, *or* kernel, as a fruit. 2. empty, void. 3. timid, spiritless.

ಪೊಲ್ಲುನಾಯೆ, ಪೊಲ್ವೆದಾಯೆ pollunāye, polvedāye, *s.* A tailor. 2. a slanderer.

ಪೊಲ್ಲುವೆ polluvè, *see* ಪೊಲ್ಲಿಗೆ.

ಪೊಲ್ಲುಸು pollusu, *s.* Interest, gain, profit. 2. luck, good fortune. 3. money in reserve.

ಪೊಲ್ಲೆ pollè, *see* ಪುಲ್ಲೆ. 2. *see* ಪೊಲ್ಲಿಗೆ.

ಪೊಲ್ಲೆ pollè, *s.* Slander, talebearing. –ದ ಪೊಟ್ಟಿ a slanderer, tale-bearer.

ಪೊಲ್ವೆ polvè, *see* ಪೊಲ್ಲಿಗೆ.

ಪೊಲ್ಸು polsu, *see* ಪೊಲ್ಲುಸು.

ಪೊಸ posa, *adj.* New, novel. 2. fresh, recent. 3. strange, wonderful, unheard of. –ಒಡಂಬಡಿಕೆ the New Testament, *Chr.* –ಅರಿ rice of the new crop. –ಕುಂಟು a new cloth. –ನರಮಾನಿ a stranger. –ಸರಿ new kind; a new path. –ರಿವಾಜಿ a new custom, an innovation. –ವರ್ಷ a new year. –ಸುದ್ದಿ strange *or* wonderful news.

ಪೊಸಂಟೆ posaṇṭe, *see* ಪೊಸತಾಯೆ.

ಪೊಸತ್ posatụ, *s.* That which is new, fresh, *etc.* *adv.* Newly. –ಉಣ್ಪುನಿ to observe the harvest feast.

ಪೊಸತಾಯೆ, ಪೊಸಬೆ posatāye, posabe, *s.* A new man, novice.

ಪೊಸಾಗಮೆ posāgamè, *see* ಹೊಸಾಗಮೆ.

ಪೊಸುರುನಿ posuruni, *see* ಪೊತ್ತುರುನಿ.

ಪೊಸ್ಕೆ poskè, *see* ಪೊಡಿಕೆ.

ಪೊಳಂಕುನಿ poḷaṅkuni (ಪೊಳಂಕ್), *v. n.* To be in distress. 2. to have pity.

ಪೊಳಿ poḷi, *see* ಪೊಲಿ.

ಪೊಳಿಂಕೆ, ಪೊಳಿಕೆ poḷiṅkè, poḷikè, *s.* A present in cash to an actor. 2. bark, skin, peel, crust.

ಪೊಳಿಪುನಿ poḷipuni, *see* ಪೊಲಿಪುನಿ.

ಪೊಳ್ತು poḷtu, *see* ಪೊತುರ್.

ಪೊಳ್ಳ, ಪೊಳ್ಳು poḷḷa, poḷḷu, *see* ಪೊಲ್ಲು.

ಪೋಂಕರ pōnkara, *adj.* Dirty.

ಪೋಂಕುರು, ಪೋಂಕ್ರು pōṅkuru, pōṅkru, *s.* Slough, mire. *adj.* Miry. 2. dirty. –ಜನ nasty people. –ನೀರ್ muddy water. –ಮೂರಿ a dirty smell. –ಕೊಡಿಪುನಿ, –ಪತ್ತುನಿ to be covered with mire.

ಪೋಂಕ್ರೆ pōṅkrè, *see* ಪೋಕ್ರೆ.

ಪೋಕ್ರಿ pōkụri, *see* ಪೋಕಿರಿ.

ಪೋಕ pōka, *adj.* Profligate, debaucherous. 2. mischievous, turbulent. 3. jocose, droll. –ಜನ profligate, *or* debaucherous people.

ಪೋಕತನ, ಪೋಕಾಟಿಗೆ pōkatana, pōkāṭigè, *s.* Profligacy, debauchery. 2. mischief. 3. waggery, drollery.

ಪೋಕಾಲ pōkāla, *s.* Perdition, ruin.

ಪೋಕಿರಿ pōkiri, *s.* *Diminutive of* ಪೋಕೆ. *adj. see* ಪೋಕ.

ಪೋಕು pōku, *s.* Means; end. 2. passing off.

ಪೋಕುಲ್ pōkulụ, *see* ಪೊಕ್ಲ.

ಪೋಕೆ pōke, *s.* A profligate, debauchee. 2. a mischievous person. 3. *see* ಪುಕ್ಕೆ. 4. a wag, wit; *cf.* ಪೋಕಿರಿ.

ಪೋಕ್ತನ pōktana, *see* ಪೋಕತನ.

ಪೋಟಾಪೋಟಿ, ಪೋಟಿ pōṭāpōṭi, pōṭi, *s.* Rivalry, emulation, competition.

ಪೋಟಿ, ಪೋಟೆ pōṭi, pōṭè, *s.* A woman with a beard.

ಪೋಟುನಿ pōṭuni (ಪೋಟೆ), *v. a.* To embrace sexually, *vlg.*

ಪೋಡಿಗೆ **pōḍigè**, *s.* Fear, fright, terror. —ಕಟ್ಟಾವುನಿ, —ಪಟ್ಟಾವುನಿ to frighten, intimidate, threaten.

ಪೋಡಿಯಾವುನಿ, ಪೋಡಿಪಾವುನಿ **pōḍiyāvuni, pōḍipāvuni**, *c. v.* (*of* ಪೋಡಿಯುನಿ) To frighten, threaten, terrify.

ಪೋಡಿಯುನಿ **pōḍiyuni** (ಪೋಡಿ), *v. n.* To fear, be afraid. ಪೋಡೆದ್ ಪೋಪಿನಿ to be alarmed, frightened, terrified.

ಪೋತ್ರ **pōtra**, *s.* Coincidence in measurement, agreement, likeness. *adj.* Right, correct, equal, uniform; *cf.* ಪೋರಿಗೆ.

ಪೋಪಿನಿ **pōpini** (ಪೋ), *v. n.* To go, go off *or* away. 2. to be lost, disappear. 3. to pass, depart, start. ಇಲ್ಲ್— a house to be ruined. ದಿನ— to pass time; to support one's self *or* his family. ಪೋಪರಿ when going. ಪೋಪರಿ ಬರ್ಪರಿ when going and coming. ಪೋಡು ಬರ್ಪೆ let me take leave. ಪೋವಂದಿಲೆಕ್ಕ not to go, so as not to be lost. ಒಡೆಗ್ ಪೋತ where had you been? ಪೋನಗನೇ just when going. ಈ ಪೋವರೆ ಬಲ್ಲ you cannot go. ಈ ಪೋವೊಡು you must go.

ಪೋರ, ಪೋರೆ **pōra, pōre**, *s.* A lad.

ಪೋರಿ **pōri**, *s.* A lass. 2. *see* ಪೋಲಿ.

ಪೋರಿಗೆ **pōrigè**, *s.* Full *or* correct measurement of grain, *etc.* —ಆಪಿನಿ to measure correctly, measurement to be correct. —ಮಳ್ಪುನಿ to give a correct measure of grain, *etc.*, as a seller to a purchaser.

ಪೋರಿಯುನಿ **pōriyuni** (ಪೋರಿ), *v. a.* To give a correct measure of grain, *etc.* 2. to tease, trouble, annoy. 3. to wrestle, quarrel. ಅಂಜೊತ್ತು— to wrestle from insolence.

ಪೋರೊಟು **pōroṭu**, *s.* The side slips of a piece of timber.

ಪೋರ್ಯಾವುನಿ **pōryāvuni**, *c. v.* (*of* ಪೋರಿಯುನಿ) To cause to measure correctly, as grain.

ಪೋಲಿ **pōli**, *s.* Speaking irrelevently. 2. plunder, extortion. *adj.* Irrelevent, impertinent. 2. plundering, extortionate. —ಮಳ್ಪುನಿ to plunder.

ಪೋಲೆ **pōlè**, *see* ಪೋಳೆ.

ಪೋಲ್ಯೆ **pōlyè**, *s.* A small kind of basket.

ಪೋಷ, ಪೋಷಣ, ಪೋಷಣೆ **pōsha, pōshaṇa, pōshaṇè**, *s.* Nourishment, maintenance, feeding.

ಪೋಸ **pōsa**, *s.* Sunset, evening. —ದ ಪೊರ್ತು evening time. —ದಾಯಿ one who observes the custom of taking his supper before sunset, as a Jain. 2. *see* ಪೋಷ

ಪೋಸ್ರ **pōsra**, *s.* Urine.

ಪೋಸ್ರಳದಾಯೆ **pōsraḷadāye**, *s.* A demon so called.

ಪೋಳೆ **pōḷè**, *s.* A cake of rice flour, *etc.*, baked on a potsherd *or* iron plate.

ಪೋಳೆಕಾಯಿ pōḷekāyi, *s.* Writing a large, crooked hand, as children do.

ಪೌ pou, *see* ಪಾವು. 2. *see* ಪೂ.

ಪೌಂಚಿ pouñci, *see* ಪವುಂಚಿ.

ಪೌಂಜಿ, ಪೌಜಿ pouñji, pouji, *see* ಪವುಂಜಿ. [ಛವಜಿ.

ಪೌಜಿ, ಪೌಜು pouji, pouju, *see*

ಪೌಣಟ್ಟು, ಪೌನಟ್ಟು pouṇaṭṭu, pounaṭṭu, *s.* Doing things by halves. —ಕೆಲಸ a work done by half.

ಪೌತ್ರಿ poutri, *s.* A grand daughter.

ಪೌರುಷ pourusha, *s.* Heroism, manliness. 2. boast, brag.

ಪ್ಯಾದೆ pyādè, *see* ಪೇದೆ.

ಪ್ರ pra, *A Sans. prefix implying* Progressive motion. 2. excess. 3. excellence.

ಪ್ರಕಟ prakaṭa, *adj.* Displayed, unfolded, revealed, manifest, public. —ಮಾಡ್ಳುನ to proclaim, make public.

ಪ್ರಕಟಣೆ prakaṭaṇè, *s.* Revelation, manifestation.

ಪ್ರಕರಣ prakaraṇa, *s.* A chapter, section. 2. an introduction, prologue, prelude.

ಪ್ರಕಾರ prakāra, *s.* Manner, method, mode. *adv.* According to, conformably with.

ಪ್ರಕಾಶ prakāśa, *s.* Sunshine, lustre, light, splendour. 2. expansion, diffusion, manifestation. —ಆಪಿನ to shine. —ಉಪ್ಪುನಿ to have lustre. —ತೋಜುನಿ light *or* splendour to appear. —ಪೋಪಿನ light to fade away; light to shed forth.

ಪ್ರಕೃತ prakruta, *s.* The present, this time. —ಗು for the present.

ಪ್ರಕೃತಿ prakruti, *s.* Nature. 2. the natural state of anything. 3. the root. 4. cause, origin.

ಪ್ರಖ್ಯಾತ prakhyāta, *adj.* Celebrated, famous; notorious.

ಪ್ರಖ್ಯಾತಿ prakhyāti, *s.* Publicity, fame, notoriety.

ಪ್ರಚಂಡ pračaṇḍa, *adj.* Intolerable, insupportable. 2. bold confident, presumptuous. 3. violent, fierce. —ಘಾಳಿ tempest, storm. —ನರಮಾನಿ a bold, valiant *or* fierce man.

ಪ್ರಚಾರ pračāra, *s.* Precept, observance.

ಪ್ರಜಾಪತಿ prajāpati, *s.* Brahma, the creator. 2. a king. 3. a decent term for the *membrum virile.*

ಪ್ರಜೆ prajè, *s.* People, subjects. 2. offspring, progeny.

ಪ್ರಜೋತ್ಪತ್ತಿ prajōtpatti, *s.* The fifth year in the Hindu cycle of sixty.

ಪ್ರಜ್ವಲಿಸುನಿ prajvalisuni (ಪ್ರಜ್ವಾಲಿಸ್), *v. n.* To shine, glitter. 2. to blaze, be inflamed.

ಪ್ರಜ್ವಾಲೆ prajvālè, *s.* Shining, glitter, blaze. [affection.

ಪ್ರಣಯ praṇaya, *s.* Friendship,

ಪ್ರತಾಪ pratāpa, *s.* Dignity, majesty. 2. valour, prowess.

ಪ್ರತಾಪು pratāpu, *s.* An old Indian coin equivalent to one rupee.

ಪ್ರತಿ prati, *A Sans. prefix implying* Substitution. 2. several, in order. 3. direction, designation. 4. belonging to. 5. exchange, return. *s.* A substitute; a copy. *adj.* Each, every. –ದಿನ every day. –ನರ ಮಾನಿ each man. –ದೆಪ್ಪುನಿ to take a copy.

ಪ್ರತಿಕಾರ pratikāra, *s.* A remedy, antidote. 2. a return of offices either good *or* bad. –ಮಳ್ಪುನಿ to revenge, retaliate.

ಪ್ರತಿಕೂಲ pratikūla, *s.* Opposition, clashing, disagreement. *adj.* Adverse, contrary.

ಪ್ರತಿಜ್ಞೆ pratijñè, *s.* Promise, assent. 2. resolution, vow.

ಪ್ರತಿಧ್ವನಿ pratidhvani, *s.* An echo.

ಪ್ರತಿನಿಧಿ pratinidhi, *s.* A resemblance of a real figure, image, picture. 2. a representative, proxy. 3. a surety.

ಪ್ರತಿನೇಮ pratinēma, *s.* Daily religious observance.

ಪ್ರತಿಪಕ್ಷ pratipaksha, *s.* The opposite side *or* party.

ಪ್ರತಿಫಲ pratiphala, *s.* Reward; return, requital.

ಪ್ರತಿಬಂಧ pratibandha, *s.* Obstacle, impediment.

ಪ್ರತಿಬಂಧನೆ pratibandhanè, *s.* A demoniacal possession. 2. binding.

ಪ್ರತಿಬಿಂಬ pratibimba, *s.* A reflection, resemblance *or* counterpart of a real form, as a picture, image, shadow.

ಪ್ರತಿಮೆ pratimè, *s.* An image, idol, puppet.

ಪ್ರತಿರೂಪು pratirūpu, *s.* A picture, image, counterpart.

ಪ್ರತಿಲಾಭ pratilābha, *s.* Twofold gain, profit.

ಪ್ರತಿವಚನ, ಪ್ರತಿವಾಕ್ಯ prativačana, prativākya, *s.* A reply, answer.

ಪ್ರತಿವಾದಿ prativādi, *s.* A defendant, respondent.

ಪ್ರತಿಷ್ಠೆ pratishṭhè, *s.* Fame, celebrity. 2. consecration. 3. endowment. 4. staying, standing, fixation. –ಆಪಿನಿ to be consecrated. –ಮಳ್ಪುನಿ to consecrate.

ಪ್ರತೀಕಾರ pratīkāra, *see* ಪ್ರತಿಕಾರ.

ಪ್ರತೀಕ್ಷೆ pratīkshè, *s.* Hope, expectation.

ಪ್ರತ್ಯಯ pratyaya, *s.* An affix.

ಪ್ರತ್ಯಕ್ಷ pratyaksha, *adj.* Perceptible, perceivable, present. –ತೆ appearance, advent.

ಪ್ರತ್ಯುತ್ತರ pratyuttara, *s.* An answer, reply.

ಪ್ರತ್ಯುಪಕಾರ pratyupakāra, *s.* Reciprocated favour, return of good offices.

ಪ್ರತ್ಯೇಕ pratyēka, *adj.* Separate, distinct. ಪ್ರತ್ಯ– one by one.

ಪ್ರತ್ಯೇಕಿಪುನಿ, ಪ್ರತ್ಯೇಕಿಸುನಿ pratyēkipuni, pratyēkisuni (ಪ್ರತ್ಯೇಕಿ, ಪ್ರತ್ಯೇಕಿನ್), *v. a.* To separate.

ಪ್ರಥಮ prathama, *adj.* First, prior. 2. chief, principal. –ಪುರುಷ the third person, *gram.* –ವಿಭಕ್ತಿ the nominative case. –ತ at first.

ಪ್ರಥಮೆ prathame, *s.* The first lunar day.

ಪ್ರದರ್ಶನ **pradarśana,** *s.* Showing. 2. explaining.

ಪ್ರದಕ್ಷಣ, ಪ್ರದಕ್ಷಣೆ, ಪ್ರದಕ್ಷಿಣ **pradakshaṇa, pradakshaṇė pradakshiṇa,** *s.* Reverential circumambulation around an object of worship.

ಪ್ರದಾನ **pradāna,** *s.* A gift, donation.

ಪ್ರದೇಶ **pradēśa,** *s.* A place in general. 2. a country, district.

ಪ್ರದೋಷ **pradōsha,** *s.* The first part of the night.

ಪ್ರಧಾನ **pradhāna,** *adj.* Principal, chief, superior. –ಯಾಜಕ a high priest.

ಪ್ರಧಾನಿ **pradhāni,** *s.* A prime minister.

ಪ್ರಪಂಚ **prapañća,** *s.* The world, universe. 2. illusion, delusion. 3. partiality. *adj.* Worldly, secular. –ಮಳ್ಪುನಿ to be partial. ಪಂತಿಡ್ ಪರಪಂಚ ಇಜ್ಜಿ there is no distinction at a dinner table.

ಪ್ರಪಾತ **prapāta,** *s.* A cliff, precipice. 2. a water-fall. 3. a bank, shore.

ಪ್ರಬಂಧ **prabandha,** *s.* An essay, literary composition, connected discourse.

ಪ್ರಬಲ **prabala,** *adj.* Strong, powerful. 2. abounding, prevailing. –ಆಪಿನಿ to become powerful; to prevail; to spread widely.

ಪ್ರಭವ **prabhava,** *s.* The first year in the Hindu cycle of sixty.

ಪ್ರಭಾವ **prabhāva,** *s.* Majesty, dignity. 2. power, energy.

ಪ್ರಭಾವಳೆ **prabhāvaḷė,** *s.* The shrine of an idol.

ಪ್ರಭು **prabhu,** *s.* A lord, master, prince. –ತ್ವ power, authority, government.

ಪ್ರಭೆ **prabhė,** *s.* Light, splendour, radiance.

ಪ್ರಮತ್ತ **pramatta,** *adj.* Intoxicated. 2. infatuated, proud.

ಪ್ರಮಥೆ **pramathe,** *s.* An attendant on Śiva.

ಪ್ರಮದ **pramada,** *see* ಪ್ರಮೋದ.

ಪ್ರಮಾಣ **pramāṇa,** *s.* Measure, size, dimension, quantity. 2. proof, testimony. 3. an oath. 4. limit. –ಮುಚ್ಚಳಿಕೆ a document containing the terms of an oath. –ಮಳ್ಪುನಿ to take an oath.

ಪ್ರಮಾಣಿ **pramāṇi,** *s.* A head-man, chief.

ಪ್ರಮಾಣಿಕ **pramāṇika,** *see* ಪ್ರಾಮಾಣಿಕ.

ಪ್ರಮಾದ **pramāda,** *s.* Mistake, inaccuracy. 2. carelessness.

ಪ್ರಮಾದಿ **pramādi,** *s.* The thirteenth year in the Hindu cycle of sixty.

ಪ್ರಮಾದೀಚ **pramādīća,** *s.* The forty-seventh year in the Hindu cycle of sixty.

ಪ್ರಮುಖ **pramukha,** *adj.* Chief, principal, first. 2. excellent, best.

ಪ್ರಮೇಯ **pramēya,** *s.* Opportunity, occasion. 2. the subject *or* topic of a conversation.

ಪ್ರಮೇಸ್ರಿನೋಟು pramēsrinōṭu, *s.* A promissory note.

ಪ್ರಮೇಹ pramēha, *s.* The venereal disease.

ಪ್ರಮೋದ pramōda, *s.* Joy, gladness, happiness, delight.

ಪ್ರಮೋದೂತ pramōdūta, *s.* The fourth year in the Hindu cycle of sixty.

ಪ್ರಯತ್ನ prayatna, *s.* Endeavour, effort. 2. act, action. –ಮಾಡ್ಬುನಿ to try, endeavour.

ಪ್ರಯಾಗ prayāga, *s.* Sacrifice, oblation. 2. the confluence of the Ganges and Yamuna at Allahabad.

ಪ್ರಯಾಣ prayāṇa, *s.* Journey, march. –ದಾಯಿ, –ಸ್ತ a passenger, traveller. –ಮಳ್ಪುನಿ to travel, journey.

ಪ್ರಯಾಸ prayāsa, *s.* Labour, trouble, fatigue 2. difficulty, embarrassment. 3. pain.

ಪ್ರಯುಕ್ತ prayukta, *adj.* Endowed with, possessing, as an attribute. *postpo.* For, on account of.

ಪ್ರಯೋಗ prayōga, *s.* Consequence, result. 2. the operation *or* effect of magical *or* mysterious rites. 3. effort, exertion. 4. act, action. 5. use of a word. 6. the administration *or* prescription of medicine. –ಉಪ್ಪುನಿ to be in use, as a word. –ಮಳ್ಪುನಿ, ಪ್ರಯೋಗಿಪುನಿ to perform any magical rites, *etc.*; to administer, as medicine, poison, *etc.*; to use, make use of.

ಪ್ರಯೋಜಕೆ prayōjake, *s.* A clever man. ಅ–, ನಿಷ್– a worthless man.

ಪ್ರಯೋಜನ prayōjana, *s.* Cause. 2. motive. 3. result. 4. occupation, business. 5. profit, use, advantage. –ಆಪಿನಿ to be of use. ದಾನೆ– of what use is it? –ದಾಂತಿ useless, worthless.

ಪ್ರಲಯ pralaya, *s.* A general deluge, the world's destruction. ಜಲ– the deluge.

ಪ್ರಲಾಪ pralāpa, *s.* Sorrow, lamentation.

ಪ್ರವರ್ತಕೆ pravartake, *s.* An author. 2. an arbiter, judge.

ಪ್ರವರ್ತನ pravartana, *s.* Action, business. 2. conduct, behaviour.

ಪ್ರವರ್ತಿಸುನಿ pravartisuni (ಪ್ರವರ್ತಿಸ್), *v. n.* To be going on, to be in a state of action. 2. to behave, conduct one's self.

ಪ್ರವರ್ಧನೆ pravardhanè, *s.* Increasing, thriving.

ಪ್ರವರ್ಧಿಸುನಿ pravardhisuni (ಪ್ರವರ್ಧಿಸ್), *v. n.* To increase, prosper, thrive.

ಪ್ರವಾದ pravāda, *s.* Report, rumour.

ಪ್ರವಾದನೆ pravādanè, *s.* Prophecy, prediction. –ಪಣ್ಪುನಿ, ಪ್ರವಾದಿಸುನಿ to prophesy, foretell.

ಪ್ರವಾದಿ pravādi, *s.* A prophet.

ಪ್ರವಾಸ pravāsa, *see* ಪರವಾಸ.

ಪ್ರವಾಹ pravāha, *s.* A stream current; the flowing *or* course of any thing.

ಪ್ರವಾಳ **pravāḷa,** *s.* Coral. —ಭಸ್ಮ calcination of coral.

ಪ್ರವೀಣ **pravīṇa,** *adj.* Skilful, clever. —ತೆ cleverness, skill.

ಪ್ರವೀಣೆ **pravīṇe,** *s.* A skilful man, a clever man.

ಪ್ರವೃತ್ತಿ **pravṛutti,** *s.* Activity, occupation.

ಪ್ರವೃದ್ಧ **pravṛuddha,** *adj.* Full grown, expanded, spread abroad, dispersed, increased, more.

ಪ್ರವೇಶ **pravēśa,** *s.* Entrance. 2. arrival. 3. commencement, as of learning. —ಆಗು to interfere. —ಮಾಡು, ಪ್ರವೇಶಿಸು to enter; to commence.

ಪ್ರಶಂಸ **praśaṁśa,** *s.* Praise, flattery. 2. subject, matter. —ತೆಗೆ to refer to a matter. —ಮಾಡು to praise, flatter; to speak on a matter.

ಪ್ರಶಸ್ತ **praśasta,** *adj.* Good, commendable, excellent, illustrious, famous. 2. convenient, commodious.

ಪ್ರಶ್ನೆ **praśne,** *s.* A question, interrogation. 2. soothsaying. —ನೋಡು to consult stars on a matter *or* event; to make an astrological calculation. —ಮಾಡು to ask, question.

ಪ್ರಶ್ನೋತ್ತರ **praśnōttara,** *s.* A dialogue, catechism,

ಪ್ರಸಂಗ **prasaṅga,** *s.* A sermon, preaching. 2. a discourse, lecture. 3. a Hindu drama. ಪ್ರಸಂಗಿ a preacher. —ಮಾಡು to preach, discourse.

ಪ್ರಸನ್ನ **prasanna,** *adj.* Pleased, delighted, gracious, favourable, auspicious. —ಆಗು to be pleased, favourable. —ಮಾಡಿಕೊಳ್ಳು to win over.

ಪ್ರಸವ **prasava,** *s.* Bringing forth *or* bearing young. 2. birth, production. —ವೇದನೆ the travail of childbirth.

ಪ್ರಸಾದ **prasāda,** *s.* Favour, kindness, propitiousness. 2. food, *etc.*, offered to a deity *or* to a guru. ದೇವರ— God's favour; what is offered *or* consecrated to God.

ಪ್ರಸಾದನ **prasādana,** *s.* Cooked rice.

ಪ್ರಸಾಧನೆ **prasādhane,** *s.* Dress, decoration.

ಪ್ರಸಿದ್ಧ **prasiddha,** *adj.* Famous, celebrated, public, notorious. —ಆಗು to become famous *or* notorious. —ಮಾಡು to publish.

ಪ್ರಸಿದ್ಧಿ **prasiddhi,** *s.* Fame, notoriety, celebrity.

ಪ್ರಸೂತಿ **prasūti,** *s.* Bringing forth as young. 2. birth.

ಪ್ರಸ್ತ **prasta,** *s.* Any auspicious ceremony. 2. marriage. ಶೋಭನ— consummation of a marriage.

ಪ್ರಸ್ತಾಪ **prastāpa,** *s.* Opportunity. 2. incidental reference to a person *or* thing. —ಮಾಡು, ಪ್ರಸ್ತಾಪಿಸು to speak on an affair; to seize an opportunity.

ಪ್ರಸ್ತಾವನೆ **prastāvanè**, *s.* Commencement, introduction.

ಪ್ರಹರ **prahara**, *s.* A watch, *or* the eighth part of an entire day and night. 2. a weapon. 3. a blow.

ಪ್ರಹ್ಲಾದೆ **prahlāde**, *s.* A pious son of Hiraṇyakašipu.

ಪ್ರಳಯು **pralaya**, *see* ಪ್ರಲಯು.

ಪ್ರಕ್ಷಾಳನೆ **prakshālanè**, *s.* Washing, cleaning.

ಪ್ರಾಂತ, ಪ್ರಾಂತ್ಯ **prānta, prāntya**, *s.* Edge, border, frontier, part, neighbourhood. *adj.* Near, adjacent.

ಪ್ರಾಕ್ **prākụ**, *adj.* Before, prior, old, preceding. 2. past. –ಅರಭ್ಯ from past time. –ಲೆಖ್ಖ an old account. –ಡ formerly.

ಪ್ರಾಕೃತ **prākrụta**, *adj.* Natural. 2. low, vulgar. *s.* A peculiar dialect of Sanskrit.

ಪ್ರಾಚೀನ **prāćīna**, *adj.* Former, prior, ancient, old.

ಪ್ರಾಜ್ಞ **prājña**, *adj.* Clever, intelligent. –ನರಮಾನಿ, ಪ್ರಾಜ್ಞಿ a clever man.

ಪ್ರಾಣ **prāṇa**, *s.* Life, vitality. 2. air inhaled, breath. –ಯಿಷ್ಟ, –ಸ್ನೇಹಿತ, ಪ್ರಾಣಾಪ್ತ an intimate friend. –ಘಾತಕ a murderer. –ಪ್ರತಿಷ್ಠೆ consecration of an idol. –ಸಂಕಟ dangerous illness. –ಹೋಪಿನಿ to die. –ಬೆಂಜಿಸೋಲುನಿ to be weary of life; to consume one's self. ಪಂಚಪ್ರಾಣೊಲು the five vital airs, *or* modes of inspiration and respiration.

ಪ್ರಾಣಿ **prāṇi**, *s.* A living being, an animal.

ಪ್ರಾತಃಕಾಲ, ಪ್ರಾತಸ್ಕಾಲ **prātaḥkāla, prātaskāla**, *s.* The dawn, morning.

ಪ್ರಾಪ್ತ **prāpta**, *adj.* Obtained, gained, received. 2. proficient, efficient. –ಆದುಪ್ಪುನಿ to be competent.

ಪ್ರಾಪ್ತಿ **prāpti**, *s.* Gain, profit. 2. acquiring, obtaining. 3. success, improvement. 4. power *or* faculty of acquiring. 5. luck, fate, fortune. –ಆಪಿನಿ to happen; to be obtained. –ಉಪ್ಪುನಿ to be able *or* lucky.

ಪ್ರಾಮಾಣಿಕ **prāmāṇika**, *adj.* True, of great force, credit, *or* authority.

ಪ್ರಾಯ **prāya**, *s.* A state *or* condition of life, as age, youth, *etc.* –ಯೇತ್ how old are you? ನಡು– middle age, prime of life. –ಸ್ತ್ರ a young man. –ಆಪಿನಿ to be old; to come to age. *There is a saying about the different stages of human life; namely:*—ಪತ್ತೆಡ್ ಮರ್ಲ್, ಇರ್ವೊಡು ಪೊರ್ಲು, ಮುಪ್ಪೊಡು ಯವನ, ನಾಲ್ಪೊಡು ಜವನ, ಐವೊಡು ಅಜಕೆ, ಅಜ್ಪೊಡು ಬಯಕೆ, ಎಳ್ಪೊಡು ದಂಟೆ, ಎಣ್ಪೊಡು ಕುಂಟೆ, ಸೊಣ್ಪೊಡು ಶಯನ, ನೂದೆಡ್ ಪಯಣ childishness at ten (years), beauty at twenty, youth at thirty, manhood at forty, dotage at fifty, longing at sixty, a stick at seventy, cripple at eighty, prostration at ninety, and departure at hundred.

ಪ್ರಾಯಶ್ಚಿತ್ತ prāyaścitta, *s.* Punishment. 2. expiation, penance, atonement. –ಕೊಡಿಗನಿ to pay a fine. –ಮಳ್ಪುನಿ to punish, fine; to atone, expiate.

ಪ್ರಾರಂಭ prārambha, *s.* Commencement, beginning.

ಪ್ರಾರಂಭಿಸುನಿ prārambhisuni (ಪ್ರಾರಂಭಿಸಿ), *v. a.* To begin, commence.

ಪ್ರಾರಬ್ಧ, ಪ್ರಾಲಬ್ಧ prārabdha, prālabdha, *s.* Destiny, fortune, fate, luck.

ಪ್ರಾರ್ಥನೆ prārthanè, *s.* Prayer, supplication, asking. 2. divine service. –ಮಳ್ಪುನಿ, ಪ್ರಾರ್ಥಿಸುನಿ to pray.

ಪ್ರಾಶನ prāśana, *s.* Feeding, eating. –ಮಳ್ಪುನಿ to eat; to drink.

ಪ್ರಾಸ prāsa, *s.* Alliteration, rhyme.

ಪ್ರಾಸ್ತೆ prāste, *s.* A prime minister.

ಪ್ರಿಯ priya, *adj.* Dear, beloved, desired. 2. dear, high in price. 3. *see* ಪಿರಿಯ. –ಸಖೆ a beloved companion.

ಪ್ರೀತಿ prīti, *s.* Love, affection, regard. 2. delight, pleasure. 3. the second of the twenty-seven astronomical yōgas. –ಕಾರ, –ಭಾವ an affectionate disposition. –ತೋಜಾವುನಿ –ಮಳ್ಪುನಿ to love. –ದೀಪಿನಿ to be affectionate.

ಪ್ರೇತ prēta, *s.* A corpse. 2. a ghost, goblin.

ಪ್ರೇಮ prēma, *s.* Affection, kindness. 2. pleasure, sport, pastime, joy. –ವಾದ a friendly discussion.

ಪ್ರೇರಕೆ prērake, *s.* An inciter, mover, instigator.

ಪ್ರೇರಣೆ, ಪ್ರೇರೇಪಣೆ prēraṇè, prērēpaṇè, *s.* Sending, direction, passion *or* operation of the organs of sense. 2. incitement, instigation. 3. inspiration. –ಮಳ್ಪುನಿ, ಪ್ರೇರೇಪಿಸುನಿ to inspire; to incite, induce.

ಪ್ರೇರಿತ prērita, *adj.* Sent, directed; inspired.

ಪ್ರೋಚನ, ಪ್ರೋಕ್ಷಣ prōčana, prōkshaṇa, *s.* Sprinkling. –ಮಳ್ಪುನಿ, ಪ್ರೋಕ್ಷಿಸುನಿ to sprinkle.

ಪ್ರೌಢ prouḍha, *adj.* Skilful, clever.

ಪ್ರೌಢೆ prouḍhe, *s.* A skilful *or* clever man.

ಪ್ಲವ plava, *s.* The thirty-fifth year in the Hindu cycle of sixty.

ಪ್ಲವಂಗ plavaṅga, *s.* The forty-first year in the Hindu cycle of sixty.

ಫ Ph

ಫ pha, The thirty-fifth letter of the alphabet.

ಫಕೀರೆ phakīre, *s.* A dervise, Mussulman mendicant. 2. a destitute man. 3. a solitary man.

ಫಕ್ಕನೆ phakkanè, *adv.* Suddenly, unexpectedly.

ಫಜೀತಿ phajīti, *see* ಪಜೀತಿ.

ಫಟಿಂಗ phatinga, *adj.* Rude, ill-behaved, unsteady, dissipated. 2. dishonest. —ತನ dissipation; dishonesty.

ಫಟಿಂಗೆ phatinge, *s.* A rake, profligate. 2. a dishonest man.

ಫಡಿಚ, ಫಡ್ಚ phaḍiča, phaḍča, *s.* Settlement, adjustment. 2. determination, decision. —ಆಪಿನಿ to be settled; to be decided. —ಮಳ್ಪುನಿ to settle; to determine.

ಫಡ್ಪೋಸ್, ಫಡ್ಪೋಸಿ phaḍpōsu, phaḍpōsi, *s.* Carelessness, perfunctoriness. 2. answering without thinking. 3. getting through a business by hook or by crook. *adj.* Superficial, careless; *also* ಪಡ್ಪೊಸ್. —ಕೆಲಸ a work done anyhow. —ನರಮಾನಿ a superficial man. —ಪಾತೆರುನಿ to say more than one knows; to speak at random.

ಫಡಾಯಿ phaḍāyi, *s.* Difficulty, great distress.

ಫಣಿ phaṇi, *s.* A serpent, cobra. —ಮಂಡಲ a festive ceremony in the name of the serpent-god; *also* ನಾಗಮಂಡಲ.

ಫಣೆ phaṇè, *see* ಪಣೆ.

ಫತ್ತೆ phattè, *see* ಪತ್ತೆ.

ಫಯಿಸಲ್ phayisalu, *see* ಫೈಸಲ್.

ಫರಕ್ pharaku, *s.* Discrimination, distinction. 2. recognition, identification; *cf.* ಪರೀಕ್ಷೆ. —ಮಳ್ಪುನಿ to discriminate. —ಪತ್ತುನಿ to recognise, identify; to inquire.

ಫರಾಖತ್ pharākhatu, *adj.* Free, unrestricted, well off.

ಫರಾರಿ pharāri, *s.* Running away. —ಆಪಿನಿ to abscond, desert.

ಫರ್ಮಾನೆ pharmānè, *s.* A mandate, order.

ಫಲ phala, *s.* A fruit in general, the fruit of any plant. 2. result, produce, consequence. 3. prosperity, thriving. 4. gain, profit, advantage. —ವಸ್ತು fruits. —ಆಪಿನಿ to be fruitful. —ಕೊರ್ಪಿನಿ to yield fruit. —ತೋಜುನಿ to see the consequence of an act.

ಫಲಾನೆ phalānè, *pron.* Such a one, such and such. —ಕೆಲಸ such a work.

ಫಲಾರ phalāra, *s.* A slight repast of fruits *or* sweets, collation. 2. any food except rice. —ಮಳ್ಳುನಿ to take some light food.

ಫಲಿತ phalita, *adj.* Fruitful. 2. profitable. 3. prosperous, thriving. 4. effectual.

ಫಲಿಪುನಿ, ಫಲಿಸುನಿ phalipuni, phalisuni (ಫಲಿ), *v. n.* To yield fruit, be productive. 2. to be successful, profitable. 3. to come to pass, fulfill, as a prediction.

ಫಸಲಿ, ಫಸ್ಲಿ phasali, phasli, *s.* The current revenue year. (from July to June).

ಫವುಜಿ phavuji, *s.* An army, troops, host.

ಫಾಯಿದೆ phāyidè, *see* ಪಾಯಿದ.

ಫಾರಿಖತ್ phārikhatu, *s.* Receipt, acquittance, divorce. 2. payment of a debt.

ಫಾಲ್ಗುಣ phālguṇa, *s.* The twelfth lunar month.

ಫಿತೂರಿ phitūri, *s.* Any secret, deceitful *or* underhand proceeding, intrigue, conspiracy. 2. instigation, incitement. —ಕೊರ್ಪುನಿ to incite. —ಮಳ್ಪುನಿ to intrigue; to betray.

ಫಿರಂಗಿ phirangi, *see* ಪಿರಂಗಿ.

ಫಿರಿಯಾದಿ, ಫಿರ್ಯಾದಿ phiriyādi, phiryādi, *s.* A complaint, an accusation in law.

ಫೀಸ್ phīsu, *s.* Fees, remuneration.

ಫುರೋಕ್ತು phurōktu, *s.* Sale, particularly of stamps.

ಫೈಲ್ pheilu, *s.* A register, file.

ಫೈಸಲ್ pheisalu, *see* ಪೈಸಲ್.

ಬ B

ಬ ba, The thirty-sixth letter of the alphabet.

ಬಂಕಿ banki, *see* ಬಾಂಕೆ.

ಬಂಕಿನಾಯಕೆ bankināyake, *s.* A honorific title amongst Billavars.

ಬಂಗ, ಬಂಙ banga, banna, *see* ಭಂಗ.

ಬಂಗಲೆ bangalè, *see* ಬಂಗ್ಲೆ.

ಬಂಗಾಟ bangāṭa, *see* ಭಂಗಾಟ.

ಬಂಗಾರ್, ಬಂಗಾರ bangāru, bangāra, *see* ಭಂಗಾರ್.

ಬಂಗಾರಕಾಯಿ bangārakāyi, *s.* The Indian acalypha, *Acalypha Indica.*

ಬಂಗಾಳ bangāḷa, *s.* Bengal.

ಬಂಗಾಳಿ bangāḷi, *s.* Jugglery, legerdemain, trickery, imposture. 2. an impostor, cheat.

ಬಂಗಿ bangi, *s.* Hemp, *Cannabis sativa.* —ಬೀಡಿ one addicted to hemp smoking. —ಪತ್ತುನಿ to become intoxicated with hemp. —ಪೈಪುನಿ to smoke hemp.

ಬಂಗುಡೆ bangudè, *s.* The mackerel.

ಬಂಗುರ bangura, *see* ಬಿಂಗುರಿ.

ಬಂಗುಳೆ bangulè, *see* ಬಂಗ್ಲೆ.

ಬಂಗೆರ್ bangeru, *s.* A title of

certain old chieftains. 2. a family name amongst the Bants and Billavars.

ಬಂಗ್ರ, ಬಂಗ್ರಿ **bangra, bangri,** *see* ಬಿಂಗಾರಿ.

ಬಂಗ್ಲೆ **banglè,** *s.* A bangalow, residence of an European.

ಬಂಘಿ, ಬಂಘಿಟಪ್ಪಾಲ್ **banghi, banghiṭappālu,** *s.* Parcel *or* packet post.

ಬಂಙ **banna,** *see* ಭಂಗ.

ಬಂಜನತಾಯೆ **banjanatāye,** *s.* A demon so called.

ಬಂಚನೆ **bančanè,** *see* ವಂಚನೆ.

ಬಂಚುನಿ **bančuni,** *see* ವಂಚಿಪುನಿ.

ಬಂಜರ **banjara,** *see* ಪಂಜರ.

ಬಂಜರ **banjara,** *adj.* Sterile, barren. —ಭೂಮಿ uncultivated land; waste land. —ಬೂರುನಿ to remain uncultivated.

ಬಂಜಾರ **banjāra,** *adv.* Heartily, freely, largely. —ಆಪಿನಿ to have a hearty meal. —ಉಣ್ಪುನಿ to eat heartily. —ಪಾಡುನಿ to serve food profusely.

ಬಂಜಿ **banji,** *s.* The stomach. 2. the belly. 3. the womb. 4. the interior *or* inner part, as of a tree, *etc.* 5. the thinner portion of the shell of a cocoanut. 6. the mind, heart. ಮಲ್ಲ ಬಂಜಿದಾಯೆ a corpulent *or* clumsy man. —ಮರಿ a long worm infecting the bowel. —ಮಲ್ಲ voracious, eager; patient, long suffering. —ಗ್ ಇಜ್ಜಿ there is nothing to eat. —ಬೇನೆ colic, gripes; *fig.* envy. —ದ ಕರ the stomach. —ದ ಕೊಟಲೆ want o food, starvation. —ಅಲುಗ್ನಿ to be hungry; to be distressed. ತೂರಿ— a big belly, potbelly. ಪೊಟ್ಟ— pregnancy by illicit intercourse. ಮೇಲ್— an early stage of pregnancy. —ಆಪಿನಿ to be pregnant. —ಇರ್ಗುನಿ the belly to subside. —ಇರಿಯುನಿ, —ಉಬ್ಬುನಿ, —ಯೆರ್ಗುನಿ the belly to distend. —ಕರಪುನಿ to miscarry, cause an abortion. —ಕರಾವುನಿ to digest. —ಕುರೆವುನಿ, —ಪಿರೆವುನಿ to feel a griping pain in the bowels. —ದಿಂಜುನಿ to fill the belly, to have a hearty meal, hunger to be appeased. —ಪೊತ್ತುನಿ to be aggrieved. —ಬರ್ಪಿನಿ, —ಮಳ್ತೊಣುನಿ to become pregnant through illicit intercourse. —ಮಗ್ಪುನಿ, —ಮಡಿಪುನಿ to retch, to have nausea, qualm. —ಮಳ್ಪುನಿ to cause pregnancy through illicit intercourse. —ಡ್ಡ ಪೋಪಿನಿ to have looseness in the bowels, to purge.

ಬಂಜಿನ, ಬಂಜಿನವು **banjina, banjinavu,** *s.* Pregnancy. 2. stools. *adj.* Pregnant. —ಕುಳ್ಳುನಿ, ಬಂಜಿನಡೆಗ್ ಪೋಪಿನಿ to go to stool.

ಬಂಜಿನಡಿ **banjinaḍi,** *s.* The belly of a beast *or* fish.

ಬಂಜಿನಾಳ್ **banjināḷu,** *s.* A pregnant woman.

ಬಂಜಿಬೈರೆ **banjibeire,** *s.* A glutton.

ಬಂಜಿರುನಿ **banjiruni** (ಬಂಜಿರ್), *v. a.* The (distended) belly to subside.

ಬಂಜೆ banje, *s.* A barren woman. *adj.* Barren, sterile.

ಬಂಜೆಲೆ banjele, *s.* A glutton.

ಬಂಜೆಲ್ತನ banjeltana, *s.* Gluttony.

ಬಂಜೊತ್ತು banjottu, *see* ಬಂಜರ.

ಬಂಟ್ bantu, *s.* Pride, vanity. 2. bragging, boasting.

ಬಂಟಾಟ, ಬಂಟಾಟಿಗೆ bantāta, bantātigè, *see* ಭಂಡಾಟ.

ಬಂಟು bantu, *see* ಬಂಟ್. 2. heroic, courageous. 3. glutinous. —ತನ courage, pride.

ಬಂಟೆ bante, *s.* A man belonging to the principal class of cultivators, called Bants. 2. a servant. 3. a demon so called. ಭೂತದ— a demon priest.

ಬಂಡ್ handu, *see* ಭಂಡ್.

ಬಂಡಸ್ bandasu, *s.* A kind of fish.

ಬಂಡಸಾಲೆ bandasālè, *s.* A storehouse, warehouse, granary.

ಬಂಡಸೆ bendasè, *see* ಬಂಡಸ್.

ಬಂಡಾಟ, ಬಂಡಾಟಿಗೆ bandāta, bandātigè, *see* ಭಂಡಾಟಿಗೆ.

ಬಂಡಾಯಿ bandāyi, *s.* Conspiracy.

ಬಂಡಾರ bandāra, *see* ಭಂಡಾರ.

ಬಂಡಾರಿ bandāri, *see* ಭಂಡಾರಿ.

ಬಂಡಿ bandi, *see* ಭಂಡಿ.

ಬಂಡು, ಬಂಡುತನ bandu, banduta-na, *see* ಭಂಡ್.

ಬಂಡೆ bande, *see* ಭಂಡೆ.

ಬಣ್ಣ banna, *s.* Colour, paint, dye. 2. exaggeration. 3. a degree of fineness, touch in metallurgy. —ಗಾರೆ a painter, dyer; *fig.* a man given to exaggeration. —ಕೊಪಿಸ್ಸಿನಿ, —ದೆಪ್ಪನಿ, —ಪಾಡುನಿ to colour, paint, dye; to exaggerate. —ಪೋಪಿನಿ colour to fade.

ಬಣ್ಣಂಗಾಯಿ bannangāyi, *s.* A half grown cocoanut.

ಬಣ್ಣಟಿಗೆ, ಬಣ್ಣಾಟಿಗೆ bannatigè, bannātigè, *s.* A piece of wood driven through rafters to keep them fast. 2. carving, engraving.

ಬಣ್ಣನಿಗೆ bannanigè, *see* ಬಂದನಿಗೆ.

ಬಣ್ಣಸರ bannasara, *s.* A coral necklace.

ಬಣ್ಣಿಗೆ bannige, *s.* A painter.

ಬಂದ್ bandu, *s.* Shutting, closing. 2. stoppage, suspension, ceasing. 3. prohibition, forbidding. —ಆಪಿನಿ to be shut; to cease, stop. —ಕಟ್ಟ್, *see* ಬಂದುಕಟ್. —ಮಳ್ಪುನಿ to shut, close; to secure; to prohibit; to cease.

ಬಂದ banda, *s.* Dough. —ಪುಳಿ leaven. —ಕಲಪುನಿ, —ಮಳ್ಪುನಿ to knead flour to dough.

ಬಂದ banda, *see* ಬಂಧ.

ಬಂದಡ್ಡೆ bandaddye, *s.* Half baked *or* boiled cake.

ಬಂದದ ಮರ bandada-mara, *s.* The wild mangosteen tree, *Diospyros embroypteris.*

ಬಂದಗಿ bandagi, *s.* Slavery, servitude.

ಬಂದನ, ಬಂದನೆ bandana, bandanè, *see* ಬಂಧ.

ಬಂದನಿಗೆ bandanigè, *s.* A parasitic [plant.

ಬಂದರ್ bandaru, *s.* A port, harbour. —ಮಳ್ಪುನಿ to make a port, to anchor.

ಬಂದಿ **bandi,** *s.* A kind of neck-ornament of gold.

ಬಂದಿ **bandi,** *s.* Imprisonment, confinement. ನಜರ— temporary confinement. —ಕಾನೆ, —ಖಾನೆ a prison, jail, imprisonment, confinement.

ಬಂದಿಕೋಲು **bandikōlu,** *s.* A pair of cudgels used by a gymnast.

ಬಂದಿವಾನೆ **bandivāne,** *s.* A prisoner. 2. a criminal, culprit.

ಬಂದು, ಬಂದೆ **bandu, bande,** *see* ಬಂಧು.

ಬಂದುಕ್ **banduku,** ಬಂದೂಕ್.

ಬಂದುಕಟ್ **bandukaṭu,** *s.* Securing, making fast. 2. compactness, union. 3. fineness, nicety. *adj.* Secure, fast. 2. compact. 3. fine, nice.

ಬಂದೂಕ್ **bandūku,** *s.* A gun.

ಬಂದೆಲ್ **bandelu,** *s.* A residence, house.

ಬಂದೋಬಸ್ತ್ **bandōbastu,** *s.* Settlement, arrangement, management. 2. safety, security. —ಮಳ್ಪುನಿ to settle; to secure.

ಬಂಧ, ಬಂಧನ, ಬಂಧನೆ **bandha, bandhana, bandhanè,** *s.* Binding, tying. 2. imprisonment, confinement.

ಬಂಧು **bandhu,** *s.* A kinsman, relation. —ಬಳಗ relations, in the aggregate. —ಸ್ನೇಹ love of relatives.

ಬಂನನ **bannana,** *s.* Trouble, calamity, affliction, torment. 2. *see* ಬಂಧ. —ದಾಯೆ a tormenter. —ತಿನ್ಪಿನಿ, —ಪಡೆವುನಿ, ಬಂನನೊಸು ಬೂರುನಿ to be afflicted. —ಬರ್ಪಿನಿ to be involved in troubles. —ಮಳ್ಪುನಿ to afflict, torment, trouble.

ಬಂನಾಟಿಗೆ **bannāṭigè,** *see* ಬಂಚಾಟಿಗೆ.

ಬಂನನಿಗೆ **bannanigè,** *see* ಬಂದನಿಗೆ.

ಬಂನಾಳ್ **bannāḷu,** *see* ಮುದ್ಯಲ. 2. a family name. 3. lineage.

ಬಂನಿಮರ, ಬಂನೆಮರ **bannimara, bannemara,** *s.* The tree *Mimosa suma.*

ಬಂಪೆಲ್ **bampelu,** *see* ಜಾಂಪೆಲ್.

ಬಂಬಯಿ **bambayi,** *s.* The thorny part of a palmyra branch.

ಬಂಬು **bambu,** *s.* Layers of the fibrous coverings of a plantain tree. 2. the bamboo.

ಬಂಬುರಿ **bamburi,** *s.* A small kind of oyster.

ಬಂಬೆ **bambè,** *s.* The core or inside stalk of a plantain tree. 2. flattery, false praise. 3. prattling. —ದೊಳಿ the rind of a plantain. —ಕಡೆಯುನಿ to work for nothing *or* in vain.

ಬಂಮನ **bammana,** *s.* Slander, backbiting. —ಪಣ್ಪನಿ, —ಪಾತೆರುನಿ —ಮಳ್ಪುನಿ, ಬಂಮನಿಪುನಿ to backbite.

ಬಂಮನಿಯುನಿ **bammaniyuni,** *see* ಬಾಮಿಯುನಿ.

ಬಕ **baka,** *s.* A crane. —ನ ಬಾಯಿ a loud talking person. —ಮಾರಿ a glutton.

ಬಕಬಕ **bakabaka,** *adv.* Voraciously, eagerly. —ತಿನ್ಪಿನಿ to swallow eagerly.

ಬಕಲ **bakala,** *s.* A gash, deep incision. —ಆಪಿನಿ to be gashed.

ಬಕಲಮರ bakalamara, *s.* The tree *Mimusops elengi*; *also* ರೆಂಜಿರ್ ಮರ.

ಬಕಾಸುರೆ bakāsure, *s.* A monster so called. 2. a glutton.

ಬಕಿರೆ bakire, *see* ಫಕೀರೆ.

ಬಕೀಟಿ bakīṭi, *see* ಬಕೇಡಿ.

ಬಕೀಲ್ bakīlu, *s.* A glutton.

ಬಕು, ಬಕುಮಾರಿ, ಬಕೆ baku, bakumāri, bake, *see* ಬಕಾಸುರೆ.

ಬಕೇಡಿ bakēḍi, *s.* Loss from bad debts, insolvency. 2. difficulty, distress. 3. necessity, want. —ನರಮಾನಿ a needy man; an insolvent.

ಬಕ್ಕ bakka, *see* ಪಕ್ಕ.

ಬಕ್ಕನಿಪುನಿ, ಬಕ್ಕನ್ಯುನಿ bakkanipuni, bakkanyuni (ಬಕ್ಕನಿ, ಬಕ್ಕನ್), *v. a.* To ask repeatedly.

ಬಕ್ಕರ್ bakkaru, *s.* A stride.

ಬಕ್ಕಸ್ bakkasu, *see* ಜೊಕ್ಕಸ.

ಬಕ್ಕಾಸುನಿ bakkāsuni (ಬಕ್ಕಾಸ್), *v. a.* To devour.

ಬಕ್ಕೊಣುನಿ bakkoṇuni, *see* ಬಯಕುನಿ.

ಬಕ್ತಲೆ, ಬಗ್ತಲೆ baktalė, bagutalė, *s.* Parting the hair in the middle of the head by combing. 2. combing the hair into curls. 3. the crown of the head. 4. a chaplet.

ಬಕ್ರ bakra, *s.* A sheep, jungle sheep.

ಬಗ್ತಿ bagụti, *see* ಭಕ್ತಿ.

ಬಗ್ಲ್ bagụlu, *see* ಬಗಲ್. 2. *see* ಬಗಳು.

ಬಗಂದರ, ಬಗಂದಳ bagandara, bagandaḷa, *s.* A carbuncle, malignant abscess on the back.

ಬಗಟುನಿ bagaṭuni (ಬಗಟಿ), *v. n.* To straddle, stand astride.

ಬಗದತ್ತೆ bagadattė, *s.* The name of a giant.

ಬಗಬಗ bagabaga, *s.* The crackling noise of conflagration. —ಅಲುನಿ fire to blaze with a noise. ಬಾಯಿಡ್ ಬಲ್ಲ ಮಗಾ, ಬಂಜಿಡ್ ಬಗ ಬಗಾ (he says) "come son", while inwardly regards you with jealousy.

ಬಗರ್ bagaru, *see* ಬಕ್ಕರ್.

ಬಗರ bagara, *s.* A bow.

ಬಗಲ್ bagalu, *s.* The armpit, the side from the armpit to the hip. —ಗ್ ಪಾಡುನಿ to put *or* keep under the arm; to misappropriate.

ಬಗಲುನಿ bagaluni, *see* ಬಗಳುನಿ.

ಬಗಲೆ bagalė, *s.* An Arabian ship. —ಬಾಯಿ a large mouth; a glutton.

ಬಗಳಾಟ bagaḷāṭa, *s.* Barking. 2. clamouring, vociferation. —ಮಳ್ಪುನಿ, *see* ಬಗಳುನಿ.

ಬಗಳು bagaḷu, *s.* Raving, wandering in mind, talking irrationally. —ಸಂನಿ delirium, insanity.

ಬಗಳುನಿ bagaḷuni (ಬಗಳ್), *v. n.* To bark, clamour, vociferate. 2. to rave, talk irrationally.

ಬಗಳೆ bagaḷė, *s.* Distress, anguish, sorrow. 2. trouble, difficulties. —ದಾಯೆ a man in trouble.

ಬಗಾರ್ bagāru, *s.* Seasoning.

ಬಗಾಸುನಿ bagāsuni (ಬಗಾಸ್) *v. a.* To desire.

ಬಗು bagu, *see* ಬಗ್ಗ್.

ಬಗುತಲೆ bagutalè, *see* ಬಕ್ತಲೆ.

ಬಗುಲುನಿ, ಬಗುಳುನಿ baguluni, baguḷuni, *see* ಬಗಳುನಿ.

ಬಗೆ bagè, *s.* Kind, manner, way, species. 2. means, resource, income. —ಉಪ್ಪುನಿ to have property, stock, means, *or* substance. —ಮಳ್ಪುನಿ to acquire wealth; to pay off; to do a favour; to commit mischief.

ಬಗೆಬಗೆ bagebagè, *s.* Rank, grade, class. *adj.* Diverse, various. —ಸಾಮಾನ್ a variety of goods.

ಬಗೆಯುನಿ, ಬಗೆವುನಿ bageyuni, bagevuni (ಬಗೆ), *v. a.* To think, suppose, guess, imagine. ರಡ್ಡ— to deceive, intend evil, play the traitor. ಯೆಂಕ್ ರಡ್ಡ ಬಗೆಯಿ he intended to ruin me.

ಬಗ್ಗ್, ಬಗ್ಗು baggu, baggu, *s.* Flattery, praise. 2. backbiting, tale-bearing. —ಪಾತೆರುನಿ to flatter; to bear tales.

ಬಗ್ಗಾವುನಿ baggāvuni, *c. v.* (*of* ಬಗ್ಗುನಿ) To cause to stoop, make bend, cower.

ಬಗ್ಗಿ baggi, *s.* An iron hook pointed at its both ends.

ಬಗ್ಗುನಿ bagguni (ಬಗ್ಗ್), *v. n.* To bend, bow, stoop. 2. to yield, submit.

ಬಗ್ಗೆಲೆ baggele, *s.* A bending *or* crouching man.

ಬಗ್ತಲೆ bagtalè, *see* ಬಕ್ತಲೆ.

ಬಗ್ತೆ bagte, *see* ಭಕ್ತೆ.

ಬಗ್ಯೆ bagyè, *postp.* For, on account of.

ಬಚಾವು bačāvu, *s.* Protection, deliverance, escape. —ಆಪಿನಿ to escape. —ತೂಪಿನಿ to seek protection. —ಮಳ್ಪುನಿ to protect, save.

ಬಚ್ಚ bačča, *s.* A fault, mistake. 2. a young, as of an animal. 3. *see* ಭಕ್ಷ್ಯ. —ಕಂಜಿ a calf of not more than a year. —ಪಾಡುನಿ to pay a fine.

ಬಚ್ಚಂಗಾಯಿ baččangāyi, *s.* The water-melon, *Cucumis citrullus.*

ಬಚ್ಚಂಗೆಲ್ baččangelu, *s.* Tiredness, fatigue.

ಬಚ್ಚನೆ baččanè, *see* ಬರ್ಚನೆ.

ಬಚ್ಚಲೆ, ಬಚ್ಚಳೆ baččalè, baččaḷè, *see* ಬಸಳೆ.

ಬಚ್ಚಾವುನಿ baččāvuni, *c. v.* (*of* ಬಚ್ಚುನಿ) To cause to dry, fade, stunt. 2. to tire, fatigue.

ಬಚ್ಚಿರೆ baččirè, *s.* The betel leaf. —ದ ಬಟ್ಟಲ್ a betel salver. —ದ ಮರಿ a venomous insect found on betel leaves. —ದ ಸೂಡಿ a bundle of about one hundred betel leaves. —ತಿನ್ಪುನಿ to chew betel leaves; to make peace. ಕರುವಳಿ— *or* ಕರೊಲಿ—, ನಾಗವಳಿ— *or* ನಾಗೊಲಿ—, ಪಂಚವಳಿ— *or* ಪಂಚೊಲಿ, ಮುಂಡವಳಿ— *or* ಮುಂಡೊಲಿ— are varieties of betel leaves.

ಬಚ್ಚುನಿ baččuni (ಬಚ್ಚ್), *v. n.* To become lean, thin. 2. to dry up, evaporate. 3. to be weary, tired, fatigued. ಕೈಕಾರ್– the hands and legs to be tired. ನಾಲಾಯಿ– to falter in speaking; to be thirsty. ಬಚ್ಚೆದ್ಪೋಪಿನಿ to get tired; to grow lean; to be dried up, as a well.

ಬಚ್ಚೆಲ್ bačcelụ, *s.* Fatigue, weariness, tiredness. 2. leanness. 3. ebb; *cf.* ಜಪ್ಪೆಲ್. –ದೆಪ್ಪುನಿ to take rest, refresh one's self.

ಬಚ್ಚೆಲೆ baččele, *s.* A thin man.

ಬಜ bajа, *see* ಬಜಾವು.

ಬಜನ್, ಬಜನ, ಬಜನೆ bajanụ, bajana, bajanè, *see* ಭಜನ.

ಬಜಬಜ bajabaja, *adj.* Moist, moderately wet *or* softened with water. –ಮೋರಿ cattle-fodder soaked in water.

ಬಜವು bajavu, *see* ಬಜಾವು.

ಬಜಾಣಿ, ಬಜಾಣಿಗೆ bajāṇi, bajāṇigè, *s.* A broom, besom. 2. cleanliness, freedom from dirt, *etc.* 3. a plain, open ground; *cf.* ಮೈದಾನ್. –ಮಳ್ಪುನಿ to sweep, clean.

ಬಜಾಣ್ಯುನಿ bajāṇyuni (ಬಜಾನ್), *v. a.* To long, wish; be greedy.

ಬಜಾಯಿಸುನಿ, ಬಜಾಸುನಿ bajāyisuni, bajāsuni (ಬಜಾಯಿಸ್, ಬಜಾಸ್), *v. a.* To beat, strike. 2. to eat heartily. 3. to do anything freely, without restraint.

ಬಜಾರಿ bajāri, *s.* A harlot, whore, prostitute. 2. an immodest *or* indecent woman.

ಬಜಾವು bajāvu, *s.* Dried leaves *etc.*, used as fuel. 2. beating

ಬಜಿ baji, *adj.* Empty, mere, only. 2. vain, useless, false. –ಕೈ an empty hand. –ಸುಳ್ಳು an utter falsehood; an unfounded report, *etc.*

ಬಜಿಪುನಿ bajipuni, *see* ಭಜಿಸುನಿ.

ಬಜಿಲ್ bajilụ, *s.* Paddy, moistened, dried, broiled, and beaten into wafers in a mortar. –ಪಂತಿ a kind of grass. –ಸರ a kind of wreath made of similar wafers of gold.

ಬಜೆ bajè, *s.* Sweet-flag, *Acorus calamus.* –ಬೆಣ್ಣೆ a mixture of sweet-flag and butter. ಬಜೆನ್ ನಾಲಾಯಿಗ್ ನಕ್ಕಾವುನಿ to apply the paste of sweet-flag to the tongue (of children to improve articulation).

ಬಜ್ಜಣಿಗೆ bajjaṇigè, *see* ಬಜಾಣಿ.

ಬಜ್ಜಿ bajji, *s.* A mode of preparing certain vegetables by baking them in embers, a kind of condiment. –ಪಿಜಕುನಿ, –ಮಳ್ಪುನಿ to prepare the above.

ಬಜ್ಜೇಯಿ bajjēyi, *s.* The areca-nut, betel-nut.

ಬಜ್ರ bajra, *see* ಬಾಜಾರ್.

ಬಟ್ವಾಡೆ, ಬಟವಾಡೆ baṭụvāḍè, baṭavāḍè, *s.* Distribution of money, *etc.*

ಬಟ, ಬಟಾ baṭa, baṭā, *adj.* Open, wide. –ಬೈಲ್ an open plain. –ಮಾರ್ಗ a highway.

ಬಟಾಟೆ baṭāṭè, *s.* A potato.

ಬಟಾಣಿ baṭāṇi, *s.* A kind of pease, *Pisum sativum.* —ಬೇಳೆ —ಸಲಾಯಿ split pease.

ಬಟುವಡಿ baṭuvaḍi, *see* ಬಟವಾಡೆ.

ಬಟುವೆ baṭuvè, *s.* A bag, purse, satchel; *cf.* ಕಲ್ಲಿತ್ತಿ.

ಬಟೊಳು baṭoḷu, *s.* A sack, bag. 2. *see* ಬಟ್ಟಲ್.

ಬಟ್ಟ್ baṭṭu, *s.* The foreskin. —ಕುದುಪುನಿ to circumcise.

ಬಟ್ಟ baṭṭa, *s.* A globe, sphere. *adj* Circular, round. 2. *see* ಭ್ರಷ್ಟ. —ಎರು an ox with circular horns. —ತರೆ a bald head.

ಬಟ್ಟಲ್ baṭṭalu, *s.* A plate, *esp.* of bell-metal.

ಬಟ್ಟಿ baṭṭi, *s.* A ratan basket. 2. a still, kiln, distillery. 3. distillation. 4. a kind of scolopendra. —ಕಟ್ಟುನಿ to distill.

ಬಟ್ಟೆ baṭṭè, *s.* A cloth in general, garment. 2. a road, path.

ಬಟ್ಟೆ baṭṭe, *see* ಭಟ್ಟ.

ಬಟ್ಟೊಳು baṭṭoḷu, *see* ಬಟ್ಟಲ್.

ಬಟ್ವಾಡೆ baṭvāḍè, *see* ಬಟವಾಡೆ.

ಬಟ್ವೆ baṭvè, *see* ಬಟುವೆ.

ಬಡ್ತರುನಿ, ಬಡ್ತುರುನಿ, ಬಡ್ತ್ರುನಿ, ಬಡ್ಪುನಿ baḍụtaruni, baḍụturuni, baḍụtruni, baḍụpuni (ಬಡ್ತರ್, ಬಡ್ತುರ್, ಬಡ್ತ್ರ್, ಬಡ್), *v. n.* To ascend, climb, mount. ಗುಡ್ಡೆಗ್— to ascend a hill. ಮರಕ್— to climb a tree.

ಬಡ baḍa, *adj.* Poor, indigent. 2. lean, thin. —ತನ, —ಪತ್ತಿ, —ಸ್ತನ poverty, indigence, leanness. —ವೆ a poor man, pauper.

ಬಡಂತರುನಿ badantaruni, *see* ಬಡ್ತರುನಿ.

ಬಡಕಾಯಿ baḍakāyi, *s.* The North, *adj.* North, northern. —ದಿಕ್ಕ್ the north point.

ಬಡಕ್ಕ baḍakka, *adj.* Sudden, abrupt.

ಬಡತನ baḍatana, *s.* A marriage, wedding among Pariahs; *cf.* ಬಡ.

ಬಡತರುನಿ, ಬಡಪುನಿ baḍataruni, baḍapuni, *see* ಬಡ್ತರುನಿ.

ಬಡಬಡ baḍabaḍa, *s.* The noise of a drum. 2. babbling garrulity. —ಪಾತೆರುನಿ to babble.

ಬಡವು baḍavu, *s.* Hunger, appetite. —ಆಪಿನಿ to be hungry.

ಬಡವೆ, ಬಡಸ್ತನ baḍave, baḍastana, *see under* ಬಡ.

ಬಡಾಯಿ baḍāyi, *s.* Boasting, bragging. —ಪಾತೆರುನಿ to boast, brag.

ಬಡಾಯಿಸುನಿ, ಬಡಾಸುನಿ, baḍāyisuni, baḍāsuni (ಬಡಾಯಿಸ್, ಬಡಾಸ್), *v. a.* To augment, increase, enlarge. *v. n.* To increase, thrive, prosper.

ಬಡಾಲ baḍāla, *see* ಬಡಕ್ಕ.

ಬಡಾವು baḍāvu, *see* ಬಡವು.

ಬಡಿ baḍi, *s.* The fold of a garment. *adj.* Folded. ಇರ್— double, two-fold.

ಬಡಿಕಲ್ಲ್ baḍikallu, *s.* A stone slab on which a washerman washes his clothes. 2. an anvil.

ಬಡಿಗೆ baḍigè, *s.* Carpentry. 2. a carpenter; *also* ಬಡಿಗೆದಾಯಿ.

ಬಡಿಪುನಿ, ಬಡಿಯುನಿ baḍipuni, baḍiyuni (ಬಡಿ), *v. a.* To strike, beat, thrash.

ಬಡಿವಾರ baḍivāra, *see* ಬಡಾಯಿ.

ಬಡು baḍu, *s.* A stick, cudgel. —ಪಾಡುನಿ, —ಟ ಹಾಕುನಿ to beat, flog.

ಬಡುಪುನಿ baḍupuni (ಬಡು), *v. a.* To climb; *cf.* ಬಡ್ತರುನಿ.

ಬಡುವೆ baḍuve, *s.* A pimp, procurer. 2. *see* ಬಡವೆ.

ಬಡೆ baḍè, *adj.* Thin, lean. —ಕಟ್ಟುನಿ to become thin.

ಬಡೆಕಾನೆ baḍekānè, *s.* A large coffer, cash-box.

ಬಡೆಸೋಪು baḍesōpu, *s.* Sweet-fennel, *Anisum fœniculum.*

ಬಡ್ಡ್ baḍḍu, *adj.* Blunt, edgeless. 2. dull, stupid, obtuse. *s.* Bluntness, dulness, stupidity. —ಕತ್ತಿ a blunt knife. —ಆಪಿನಿ to become blunt. —ಕಟ್ಟುನಿ to get dull *or* obtuse.

ಬಡ್ಡ್‌ಪುಳಿ baḍḍupuḷi, *see* ಪುಣರಪುಳಿ.

ಬಡ್ಡ bdda, *see* ಬಡಕ್ಕ.

ಬಡ್ಡಿ baḍḍi, *s.* Interest on money. ಅಸಲ್— principal and interest. —ಗ ಬಡ್ಡಿ compound interest. —ಕೊರ್ಪಿನಿ to pay interest. —ಗ ಕೊರ್ಪಿನಿ to lend on interest.

ಬಡ್ಡಿಯುನಿ baḍḍiyuni (ಬಡ್ಡ್), *v. n.* To fly, run away.

ಬಡ್ಡೆ baḍḍe, *s.* A stupid man, dunce. 2. a refractory man.

ಬಡ್ತರುನಿ baḍtaruni, *see* ಬಡ್ತರುನಿ.

ಬಡ್ಯುನಿ baḍyuni, *see* ಬಡ್ಡಿಯುನಿ.

ಬಣ್ಂಪು baṇumpu, *s.* A kind of timber tree, *Terminalia coriacea.*

ಬಣ baṇa, *see* ಬನ.

ಬಣಂಗಾಯಿ baṇaṅgāyi, *see* ಬಂಣಂ[ಗಾಯಿ.

ಬಣಜಿಗೆ baṇajige, *s.* A Lingait merchant. 2. a Lingait.

ಬಣಬೆ baṇabè, *adj.* Light, not heavy. 2. weak, imbecile. *s.* A stack.

ಬಣಲೆ baṇalè, *see* ಬನಲೆ.

ಬಣಾರಿ baṇāri, *s.* A tear, sob.

ಬಣಿ baṇi, *s.* Colour, hue; *cf.* ಬಂಣ. 2. breed, kind. 3. wages.

ಬಣುಪು, ಬಣ್ಪು baṇupu, baṇpu, *see* ಬಣ್ಂಪು.

ಬಣ್ಣ baṇṇa, *see* ಬಂಣ.

ಬತ್ತ್ battu, *s.* A gander, duck. ನುಪ್ಪಡ— well boiled rice; a glutton. —ಭಂಗಾರ್ all kinds of metals.

ಬತ್ತ batta, *see* ಭತ್ತ. 2. *see* ಬಡ.

ಬತ್ತಡ battaḍa, *see* ಬಸ್ತ್ರ.

ಬತ್ತಲೆ battalè, *adj.* Naked, uncovered, without clothes. —ತನ nakedness.

ಬತ್ತಳಿಗೆ battaḷigè *s.* A quiver.

ಬತ್ತಾಯಿ battāyi, *s.* An inferior kind of tobacco.

ಬತ್ತಾಸ್ battāsu, *s.* A kind of sweetemat.

ಬತ್ತಿ batti, *s.* A wick, candle, match. 2. a cigar, cheroot. ಮಾಯಣದ— a wax-candle. —ಕ

ಟ್ಟುನಿ to make a cigar. —ಮುಳ್ಪುನಿ to twist the wick of a lamp. —ವೈಪುನಿ to smoke a cigar.

ಬತ್ತಿಕಜ್ಜ **battikajja**, *s.* The business on which one has come.

ಬತ್ತಿಮೀನ್ **battiminu**, *s.* A kind of fish; *also* ಓಟುಬತ್ತಿ.

ಬತ್ತುನಿ **battuni**, *see* ಬಜ್ಜುನಿ.

ಬತ್ತೆ **battė**, *see* ಭತ್ತೆ.

ಬತ್ತೆಲ್ **battelu**, *see* ಬಜ್ಜೆಲ್.

ಬದ್ಕ್ **badu̥ku̥**, *s.* Living, livelihood. 2. estate, wealth, property. —ಭಾಗ್ಯ a comfortable living. —ಶೊಲಗುನಿ to be impoverished, reduced to poverty. —ಮುಳ್ಪುನಿ to acquire wealth.

ಬದ್ಕಾವುನಿ **badu̥kāvuni**, *c. v.* (*of* ಬದ್ಕುನಿ) To cause to live, to save, protect. 2. to heal, cure.

ಬದ್ಕುನಿ **badu̥kuni** (ಬದ್ಕ್), To live, exist, subsist. 2. to survive, recover, be saved.

ಬದ **bada**, *see* ಬದು.

ಬದಂಗಲ **badaṅgala**, *s.* A large sore. 2. a carbuncle; *cf.* ಅರಸುಕುರಿ.

ಬದಂಬ, ಬದಂಬಟ್ಟೆ **badamba, badambaṭṭė**, *adj.* Flabby, not strong.

ಬದನಾಮೆ **badanāme**, *see* ಬದಲಮ್.

ಬದನೆ **badanė**, *s.* The brinjal plant, *Solanum esculentum, or S. melongona*; *cf.* ಗುಳ್ಳ. ಮುಳ್ಳು— the love-apple.

ಬದಬದ **badabada**, *adj.* Loosely, not tightly. —ತುತ್ತುನಿ to dress loosely.

ಬದರಿ **badari**, *see* ಜೊಗೊರಿ.

ಬದರಿ, ಬದರಿಕಾಶ್ರಮ **badari, badarikāśrama**, *s.* The residence of Vyāsa.

ಬದರಿಕೆ **badarikė**, *see* ಭದ್ರಿಕೆ.

ಬದರಿತನ **badaritana**, *s.* Dishonour, defamation.

ಬದಲ್ **badalu̥**, *s.* Exchange, compensation; *cf.* ಅದಲ್‌ಬದಲ್. *pro.* Other, another. *adj.* Substituted, acting for another. *adv.* Instead of. —ಗ in lieu of, instead of. ಬದಲ್‌ಗ ಬದಲ್ tit for tat, retaliation. —ಪಾತೆರ a contradiction. —ಮುಳ್ಪುನಿ, *see* ಬದಲಾಯಿಸುನಿ.

ಬದಲಮ್, ಬದಲಾಮು **badalamu̥, badalāmu**, *s.* Disrepute, ignominy. 2. responsibility, risk. 3. a false accusation.

ಬದಲಾಯಿಸುನಿ **badalāyisuni** (ಬದಲಾಯಿಸ್), *v. a.* To change, alter. 2. to exchange, substitute, barter.

ಬದಲಿ **badali**, *s.* A substitute; *cf.* ಬದಲ್. *adj.* Acting. —ಕೆಲಸ an acting appointment.

ಬದಾಮು **badāmu**, *s.* Almonds.

ಬದಾಲ್ **badālu̥**, *see* ಬದಲ್.

ಬದಿ **badi**, *s.* A dowry.

ಬದಿ **badi**, *see* ಬರಿ.

ಬದಿಯೆಲ್ **badiyelu̥**, *s.* A side-bone, rib.

ಬದಿರೆ **badirė**, *adj.* Deaf. ಬದಿರತನ deafness.

ಬದಿರೆಂಗಿ badireṅgi, *see* ಮದಿರೆಂಗಿ.

ಬದು badu, *adj.* Thin, watery; *also* ಬಡಬಡ.

ಬದುಕಾವುನಿ badukāvuni, *see* ಬದ್‌ಕಾವುನಿ.

ಬದುಕುನಿ badukuni, *see* ಬದ್‌ಕುನಿ.

ಬದೆಂಕುನಿ badeṅkuni (ಬದೆಂಕ್), *v.n.* To dangle, as a weak limb.

ಬದೆಂಗಲ badeṅgala, *see* ಬಡಂಗಲ.

ಬದ್ದ, badda, *adj.* True, certain. 2. bound.

ಬದ್ರ badra, *see* ಭದ್ರ.

ಬದ್ರಮುಷ್ಟಿ badramushṭi, *see* ಭದ್ರಮುಷ್ಟಿ.

ಬದ್ರಿ badri, *see* ಬದರಿ.

ಬದ್ರಿಕೆ, ಬದ್ರಿಗೆ badrikè, badrigè, *see* ಭದ್ರಿಕೆ.

ಬದ್ಧ baddha, *adj.* Tied, bound. 2. astringent.

ಬದ್ಲಾಮ್ badḷāmu, *see* ಬದಲಮ್.

ಬನ bana, *s.* A grove, pleasure garden. ನಾಗ– a thicket haunted by serpents.

ಬನಂಪು banampu, *see* ಬಗೆಂಪು.

ಬನಲೆ banalè, *s.* A kind of frying pan. *adj.* Thin. –ಕುಂಟು a thin kind of cloth.

ಬನಾತ್ banātu, *s.* Woollen cloth, broad cloth.

ಬನಾಯಿಸುನಿ banāyisuni (ಬನಾಯಿಸ್), *v.a.* To invent, forge, fabricate, as a false document, *etc.* 2. to prepare, as a dish.

ಬನಾರಿ banāri, *s.* Saliva *or* juice of fruits drivelling about the corners of the mouth, *etc.*

ಬನಾವಣೆ, ಬನಾವನಿ banāvaṇè, banāvani, *s.* Invention, forgery, fabrication. *adj.* Forged, fabricated, false, fictitious. –ಮಳ್ಪುನಿ to forge, fabricate.

ಬನಾವು banāvu, *s.* Agreement, concord.

ಬನಿ bani, *see* ಬಣಿ.

ಬನೆಕೆರಿ banekeri, *see* ಬನಾರಿ.

ಬಪ್ಪಂಗಾಯಿ, ಬಪ್ಪಾಯಿ bappaṅgāyi, bappāyi, *s.* The papaw fruit, *Carica papaya.*

ಬಪ್ಪರ್ bapparu, *s.* Obscenity. *adj.* Obscene. –ಪಾತೆರ obscene language.

ಬಪ್ಪು bappu, *s.* Stupidity, senselessness. *adj.* Stupid, simple.

ಬಪ್ಪೆ bappe, *s.* A simpleton, stupid man, glutton.

ಬಬ್ಬರಿಮಾಂಜಿ babbarimāñji, *s.* A kind of fish.

ಬಬ್ಬರ್ಯೆ babbarye, *s.* A demon so called. –ಕೊಟ್ಯ its shrine.

ಬಬ್ರಾಪುರಿ babrāpuri, *s.* Disorder, confusion.

ಬಮನ bamana, *s.* Backbiting.

ಬಮನಿಪುನಿ bamanipuni (ಬಮನಿ), *v.n.* To backbite.

ಬಯ baya, *see* ಭಯ.

ಬಯಂಬು bayambu, *s.* Chaff, shell. 2. a hollow, hole. *adj.* Hollow. –ಆಪಿನಿ to become hollow.

ಬಯಕುನಿ ಬಯಸುನಿ bayakuni, bayasuni (ಬಯಕ್, ಬಯಸ್), *v.a.* To long for, desire eagerly.

ಬಯಕೆ bayakè, *s.* Desire, especially the longing occasioned by pregnancy. –ಪಾಡುನಿ to entertain sumptuously a pregnant woman. —ಮದಮೆ a ceremony observed in the fourth *or* sixth month of pregnancy.

ಬಯಿ **bayi**, *see* ಬೈ.

ಬಯಿತಡ್ **bayitaḍu**, *see* ಬೈತಡ.

ಬಯಿನೆ **bayinè**, *see* ಬೈನೆ.

ಬಯಿರಾಸ್ **bayirāsu**, *see* ಬೈರಾಸ್.

ಬಯಿಲ್ **bayilu**, *see* ಬೈಲ್.

ಬಯಿಲರೆ **bayilarè**, *s.* Very low fields which are under water in the rainy season and yield only one crop.

ಬಯ್ಯ **bayya**, *s.* Evening, eventide; *also* ಬೈಯು.

ಬಯ್ಯಾಟ **bayyāṭa**, *s.* Abusing.

ಬಯ್ಯುನಿ **bayyuni** (ಬಯ್ಯ್), *v. a.* To perch, roost.

ಬಯ್ಯೆಲ್ **bayyelu**, *s.* Running. 2. riding. —ಇಡ್ಪಾವುನಿ to ride a horse, *etc.* —ಇಡ್ಪಿನಿ to run, as cattle, *etc.*

ಬಯ್ಯೊಳಿ **bayyoḷi**, *s.* A walk. —ಗ ಪಿದಾಡುನಿ to take a walk.

ಬರ **bara**, *s.* Famine, scarcity. 2. coming. 3. weakness. —ಗಾಲ, ಬರೆಗಾಲ a time of famine, dearth.

ಬರ **bara**, *s.* Divorce, dissolution of marriage. —ಪಣ್ಪುನಿ to divorce a wife.

ಬರಂಕಣೆ **baraṅkaṇè**, *adj.* Steep, sloping.

ಬರಂಗಯಿ **baraṅgayi**, *s.* Boundary, limit, shore.

ಬರಂಟ್ **baranṭu**, *s.* Scurf, leanness. *adj.* Scurfy, scabby. 2. scaly, as the skin. 3. lean, thin. —ಕಾಮಿಲಿ, —ರೋಗ a scurfy jaundice, scurvy. —ತಾಮರೆ a disease of children. —ಕಟ್ಟುನಿ to grow thin, scabby.

ಬರಂಟುನಿ **baranṭuni** (ಬರಂಟ್), *v. n.* To grow dry, become lean *or* thin. 2. a sore to heal.

ಬರಂಬು **barambu**, *see* ಬೊರಂಬು.

ಬರಕ್ **baraku**, *adj.* Full, filled, complete.

ಬರಕತ್ತ್ **barakattu**, *s.* Success, prosperity, thriving, blessing, fortune, luck.

ಬರಕಲ, ಬರಕಳ **barakala, barakaḷa**, *see* ಅರಿಕಲ.

ಬರಕೆಲ್ **barakelu**, *s.* Inundation. 2. *see* ಬರ.

ಬರಡ್, ಬರಡು **baraḍu, baraḍu**, *adj.* Useless, unprofitable, vain. 2. barren, childless. 3. (*imperat. of* ಬರ್ಪಿನಿ) let (him, *etc*). come; *see* ಬರ್ಪಿನಿ. —ಯೆರ್ಮೆ an old she-buffalo past milking.

ಬರಣಿ, ಬರಣೆ **baraṇi, baraṇè**, *s.* A china jar. 2. the trough of a water-lift.

ಬರತ **barata**, *see* ಭರ್ತ.

ಬರತಿ **barati**, *see* ಭರ್ತಿ.

ಬರನ **barana**, *adj.* Scarcely coming *or* occurring; rare, unusual.

ಬರನ್ಯುನಿ **baranyuni** (ಬರನ್), *v. a.* To curse. 2. *see* ಬರ್ಗೊತ್ತುನಿ. *v. n. see* ಬರೆಲುನಿ.

ಬರಪೂರು **barapūru**, *adj.* Full, plenty, ample, brimful.

ಬರಬರ **barabara**, *s.* A noise, as of rain pouring on a palm-leaf umbrella, *or* of parching paddy over a fire.

ಬರಬು **barabu**, *s.* A boundary.

ಬರಮು **baramu**, *s.* Respect, honour, reputation.

ಬರವಣಿಗೆ **baravaṇigè**, *s.* Composition, style.

ಬರವಸ **baravasa**, *see* ಭರವಸ.

ಬರವು **baravu**, *s.* A small excavation in a well *or* tank for water to collect in. 2. *see* ಬರಾವು. –ಕಡ್ಪುನಿ to make such an excavation.

ಬರವುನಿ **baravuni**, *see* ಬರಾವುನಿ.

ಬರಹ **baraha**, *see* ಬರಾವು.

ಬರಾಟ **barāṭa**, *s.* A kind of fire-work.

ಬರಾಣಿಗೆ **barāṇigè**, *s.* Agreement, coincidence, as between any two measures of grain, *etc.* 2. fulness, completeness. 3. *see* ಬರವಣಿಗೆ.

ಬರಾದಿ **barādi**, *s.* Coming, haste.

ಬರಾಬರಿ **barābari**, *adj.* Right, proper, just. *s.* Equality. 2. good order *or* arrangement.

ಬರಾವು **barāvu**, *s.* Writing, manuscript. 2. learning. –ಸರಾವು ಬರ್ಪಿನಿ to be able to read and write.

ಬರಾವುನಿ **barāvuni** (ಬರಾ), *v. n.* To be benumbed. ಕಾರ್– the foot *or* leg to sleep, to have numbness.

ಬರಾಸ್ **barāsu**, *s.* A carpenter's forked instrument.

ಬರಿ **bari**, *s.* Side, border.

ಬರಿ **bari**, *see* ಬಜಿ.

ಬರಿ **bari**, *s.* Lineage, descent, family, race, tribe. –ಬಂಡ, –ಬಂಲ, –ಬಂದ್ರು relations.

ಬರಿಂಕ **bariṅka**, *s.* A small kind of deer.

ಬರಿಕ, ಬರಿಕೆ **karika, barikè**, *adj.* Hard (distinguished from soft), as the pulp of a fruit. –ಕುಕ್ಕು a hard kind of mango.

ಬರಿತ **barita**, *see* ಭರ್ತ.

ಬರಿಪಂದ್ **bariparndu**, *adj.* Almost ripe.

ಬರಿಪುನಿ **baripuni** (ಬರಿ), *v. a.* To gash, cut, scratch. 2. to trim, as the border of a field.

ಬರಿಮೀನ್ **barimīnu**, *s.* A kind of fish.

ಬರಿಯುನಿ **bariyuni** (ಬರಿ), *v. n.* To encase a bottle, jar, *etc.*, in a kind of net-work.

ಬರೀತ **barīta**, *adj.* Full, complete.

ಬರು **baru**, *s.* Boast, brag. *adj.* *see* ಜೋರು.

ಬರುವೆ **baruvè**, *see* ಬಲ್ದ. 2. *see* [ಬರ್ಪಿನಿ.

ಬರೆ **barè**, *s.* A mud-wall round the premises. –ಯೇರಾವುನಿ to erect such a wall.

ಬರೆ **barè**, *s.* Branding the arm, *etc.*, with a piece of red-hot copper in certain diseases. –ಪಾಡುನಿ, –ವೈಪುನಿ to brand in this way.

ಬರೆ, ಬರೇ **barè, barē**, *see* ಬಜಿ.

ಬರೆಗಾಲ **baregāla**, *see under* ಬರ.

ಬರೆಜನ **barejana**, *s.* Low caste people. 2. talkativeness.

ಬರೆತ bareta, *s.* A line, mark, scar. 2. a wale, stripe. ಅಂಗೈದ– creases in the hand.

ಬರೆಪಾವುನಿ barepāvuni, *c. v.* (*of* ಬರೆಪಿನಿ) To dictate, cause to write. ಬರೆಪಾವುನಾಯೆ a schoolmaster.

ಬರೆಪಿನಿ barepini (ಬರೆ), *v. a.* To write, draw.

ಬರೆಲುನಿ bareluni (ಬರೆಲ್), *v. n.* To starve.

ಬರೆಲ್ಪುನಿ barelpuni, *c. v.* (*of* ಬರೆಲುನಿ) To cause to starve.

ಬರೋಣಿ baroṇi, *see* ಬರಣಿ.

ಬರೋಬರಿ barōbari, *see* ಬರಾಬರಿ.

ಬರ್ಕ barka, *adj.* The noise of rending a cloth.

ಬರ್ಕತ್ barkatu, *s.* Prosperity, thriving.

ಬರ್ಕಳ barkaḷa, *see* ಅರಿಕಲ.

ಬರ್ಕಾಸ್ barkāsu, *adj.* Bad, mean, base, vile; unpromising.

ಬರ್ಕಾಸ್ತ್ barkāstu, *s.* Rising, breaking up, as an assembly.

ಬರ್ಕೆ barkè, *s.* A title among the Bants. 2. *see* ಬರಿಕ.

ಬರ್ಕೆನ barkena, *adj.* Solid, fast; 2. *see* ಬರಿಕ.

ಬರ್ಗಟ್ಟ್ bargaṭṭu, *adj.* Reduced, weak.

ಬರ್ಗಟ್ಟಾವುನಿ bargaṭṭāvuni, *c. v.* (*of* ಬರ್ಗಟ್ಟುನಿ) To neglect, waste.

ಬರ್ಗಟ್ಟುನಿ bargaṭṭuni (ಬರ್ಗಟ್ಟ್), *v. n.* To run waste, be ruined.

ಬರ್ಗೊತ್ತು bargottu, *s.* Threatening, menacing. 2. frowning.

ಬರ್ಗೊತ್ತುನಿ bargottuni (ಬರ್ಗೊತ್ತ್), *v. n.* To threaten, menace 2. to frown.

ಬರ್ಚನೆ barcanè, *s.* A comb.

ಬರ್ಚಿ barci, *s.* A spear.

ಬರ್ಚುನಿ barćuni (ಬರ್ಚ್), *v. a.* To comb.

ಬರ್ಚೆಲೆ barčele, *s.* One who devours food in haste.

ಬರ್ಜುನಿ barjuni (ಬರ್ಜ್), *v. a.* To strike, beat. 2. to reprove, rebuke. *v. n.* To be obstinate, stubborn. ಬರ್ಜಿದ್ ಕುಳ್ಳುನಿ to refuse obstinately to do a thing.

ಬರ್ತ barta, *see* ಭರ್ತ.

ಬರ್ತಿ barti, *see* ಭರ್ತಿ.

ಬರ್ದಾಶ್ bardāshu, *s.* Consolation, comfort.

ಬರ್ಪಾವುನಿ barpāvuni, *c. v.* (*of* ಬರ್ಪಿನಿ), To let come, cause to bring. ಭಂಗ– to give trouble, tease, vex.

ಬರ್ಪಿನಿ barpini *v. n.* To come, arrive, arise. 2. to bring. 3. to happen, befall. *c. dat.* To acquire, get; to understand. 2. can. ಆಯಗ್ ಬುದ್ಧಿ ಬರು he will be wise. ಯೆಂಕ್ ತುಳು ಬರ್ಪುಂಡು I understand Tuḷu. ಯೆಂಕ್ ಬರವು ಬರ್ಪುಂಡು I can read and write.

ಬರ್ಪುಡುನಿ barpuḍuni, *see* ಬರ್ಪಾವುನಿ.

ಬರ್ಪುನಿ barpuni, *see* ಬರಿಪುನಿ.

ಬರ್ಪೂರ, ಬರ್ಪೂರು barpūra, *see* ಬರಪೂರು.

ಬರ್ಫಿ barphi, *s.* A kind of sweetmeat.

ಬರ್ಬರ್ barbaru, *s.* Noise, bustle.

ಬರ್ಮು barmu, *see* ಬರಮು.

ಬರ್ಮುಂಡೆ barmuṇḍè, *s.* A very poor widow.

ಬರ್ಲುನಿ barluni, *see* ಬರೆಲುನಿ.

ಬರ್ವೆ barvè, *s.* A kind of fish.

ಬರ್ಸ barsa, *s.* Rain. —ದೊರಿಯುನಿ rain to pour. —ಬರ್ಪಿನ to rain.

ಬಲ್ತ್ರುನಿ balutruni, *see* ಬಲಿಪ್ಪುನಿ.

ಬಲ bala, *s.* Strength, power, might, force, influence. —ತ ಅಡ್ಯೆ, —ತಡ್ಯೆ cakes prepared on the preceding day of a festival; the day preceding a festival. —ವಂತೆ a powerful man. ಅಗ್ನಿ— digestion. —ಆಪಿನಿ to become strong. —ತಪ್ಪಾವುನಿ to weaken, invalidate. —ಮಳ್ಪುನಿ to strengthen. —ಮ ಕೊತ್ತುನಿ to take courage, stand firmly. —ಮುರಿಯುನಿ to subjugate, put down, break down.

ಬಲ bala, *s.* A coarse net-work of rope, in which pots and other vessels are suspended from the beams of a house. —ಕಣ a noose to tighten the vessels so suspended.

ಬಲಂಕ್ balaṅku, *s.* A day of fasting previous to Krushṇa's birthday. —ಬಲಂಕ reduced.

ಬಲಂಜುನಿ balañjuni (ಬಲಂಜ್), *v. a.* To roll up.

ಬಲಂಟುನಿ balaṇṭuni (ಬಲಂಟ್), *v. a.* To grope, search in darkness; to feel, stroke.

ಬಲಂಬಾಯಿ balambāyi, *s.* Wide mouth. 2. *see* ಬಲಬಾಯಿ.

ಬಲಕಣ balakaṇa, *see* ಬಲ.

ಬಲಕಾಯಿಸುನಿ balakāyisuni (ಬಲಕಾಯಿಸ್), *v. a.* To secure, protect. 2. to augment, increase.

ಬಲಕೆ balakè, *see* ಬಳಕೆ.

ಬಲತ್ balatu, *s.* The right side.

ಬಲತ balata, *adj.* Right. —ಕೈ the right hand. —ಮಗ್ಗಲ್ the right side.

ಬಲತ್ಕಾರ balatkāra, *s.* Force, violence, constraint, exaction.

ಬಲಪುನಿ balapuni, *see* ಬಳಪುನಿ.

ಬಲಬಾಯಿ balabāyi, *s.* The bamboo of a roof just above the entrance of a house. —ನೇಲುನಿ to hang upon it.

ಬಲಭದ್ರೆ balabhadre, *s.* Krushṇa's elder brother.

ಬಲಮುರಿ balamuri, *s.* Turning to the right hand. —ಶಂಖ a rare conch that winds to the right.

ಬಲಯಿ balayi, *see* ಬಲಾಯಿ.

ಬಲರಾಮೆ balarāme, *s.* Krushṇa's elder brother.

ಬಲವಂತಿಗೆ balavantigè, *s.* Force, violence, compulsion, pressure.

ಬಲವಂತೆ balavante, *s.* A strong, *or* powerful man.

ಬಲವತ್ತೆ balavatte, *s.* An unequal pair.

ಬಲವು balavu, *s.* Potstone, glimmer, slate; *also* ಬಲವುದ ಕಲ್ಲ್. —ದ ಕಡ್ಡಿ a slate pencil.

ಬಲಸ್ balasu, *adj.* Loose, slack; phlegmatic. –ಆಪಿನಿ to become loose.

ಬಲಸುನಿ balasuni (ಬಲಸ್), *v. a.* To serve food.

ಬಲಹೀನ balahīna, *adj.* Weak, impotent. –ತೆ, –ತ್ವ weakness. ಬಲಹೀನೆ a weak man.

ಬಲಾಂಡಿ balāṇḍi, *s.* A female demon.

ಬಲಾಡಿಗೆ, ಬಲಾಢ್ಯೆ balāḍige, balāḍhye, *see* ಬಲವಂತೆ.

ಬಲಾತ್ಕಾರ balātkāra, *see* ಬಲತ್ಕಾರ.

ಬಲಾಪಿನಿ balāpini (ಬಲಾ), *v. n.* To gain strength; to recover health.

ಬಲಾಬಲ, ಬಲಾಬಲಿಕೆ balābala, balābalikè, *s.* Strength and weakness. 2. the strong and weak points of a case.

ಬಲಾಬಲ್ಮೆ baḷābalmè, *s.* Strength.

ಬಲಾಯಿ balāyi, *s.* A pestle used for pounding. 2. arrogance.

ಬಲಾಯಿಸುನಿ balayisuni (ಬಲಾಯಿಸ್), *v. a.* To transgress.

ಬಲಾರ balāra, *s.* The rounding of the edges of a table *or* other wood-work. 2. *see* ಬಳರ.

ಬಲಾಲ್ balālu, *adj.* Useless. *s.* *see* ಇಲಾಲ್. –ತಟ್ಟ a frame of bamboo sticks with torch-lights at their tops, carried in a procession.

ಬಲಾಸ್ balāsu, *adj.* Loose, not tight.

ಬಲಾಸ balāsa, *s.* The phlegmatic temperament.

ಬಲಾಳೆ balāḷè, *see* ಬಲ್ಲಾಳೆ.

ಬಲಿ bali, *s.* An offering, oblation, sacrifice; a victim. –ಅರ್ಪಣೆ an offering. –ಅರ್ಪಣೆ ಮಳ್ಪುನಿ to offer sacrifice, make an offering. –ಪಿದಾಡುನಿ to go in procession.

ಬಲಿ bali, *s.* The name of a king; *also* ಬಲಿಚಕ್ರವರ್ತಿ. –ಪರ್ಬ, –ಪಾಡ್ಯ a Hindu feast in memory of Vishṇu's treading him down.

ಬಲಿಕೆ balikè, *s.* Prowess, strength, hardness. 2. toughness. *adj.* Strong.

ಬಲಿಗೆ, ಬಲಿಗೆಮರ baligè, baligemara, *s.* A jungle tree used as strong timber.

ಬಲಿತರುನಿ balitaruni, *see* ಬಲಿಯುನಿ.

ಬಲಿಪಂ balipam, *s.* A marble.

ಬಲಿಪಬೂರು balipabūru *s.* The creeper *Gloriosa superba.*

ಬಲಿಪೀಠ balipīṭha, *s.* An altar.

ಬಲಿಪು balipu, *s.* A rope fastened over a thatched roof to keep the thatch compact. –ಕಟ್ಟುನಿ to fasten a rope in this way.

ಬಲಿಪುನಿ balipuni (ಬಲಿ), *v. n.* To decamp, scamper. *v. a.* To stick, adhere, hold fast.

ಬಲಿಪೆ, balipe, *s.* A royal tiger, leopard. 2. prowess, strength. 3. *see* ಬಲಿಪು.

ಬಲಿಮೆ balimè, *s.* Strength, might. 2. *see* ಬಲ್ಮೆ.

ಬಲಿಯುನಿ baliyuni (ಬಲಿ), *v. n.* To stick fast, as a poultice, plaster, *etc.*

ಬಲಿರುನಿ baliruni (ಬಲಿರ್), *v. n.* To develop, as the fetus, in the womb.

ಬಲಿಷ್ಟ balishṭa, *adj.* Strong, firm, powerful. —ಜನ strong, powerful people. ಬಲಿಷ್ಟೆ a powerful man.

ಬಲು balu, *adj.* Very, large, great. 2. severe, violent. —ಆಪಿನಿ to be powerful; to be violent.

ಬಲುಕಡೆ balukaḍè, *see* ಬಲ್ಕಡಿ.

ಬಲುಮರ balumara, *s.* A palm which does not yield toddy.

ಬಲುಮೆ balumè, *see* ಬಲ್ಮೆ.

ಬಲುಮೀನ್ balumīnu, *s.* A kind of fish.

ಬಲೆ balè, *s.* A net, web, snare. ತಾಲ್ಯ— a spider's web. —ಬೀಪುನಿ to cast a net. ಐಬುರ್ಲೆ, ಕಂಡಟ್ಲಿ, ಕಂತಲೆ, ಗೋರಲೆ, ತಿಕ್ಕಲೆ, ದೆಬ್ಬಲೆ, ಪತ್ತಿರ್ಲೆ, ಪಾರ್ಲೆ, ಬುದ್ದಲೆ, ಮೂರಿಬಲೆ are the names of different kinds of nets.

ಬಲೆ balè, *s.* The rapiers of bamboos fastened cross-wise to the rafters of a roof. 2. *see.* ಬಳಿ.

ಬಲೆಂಕ್ರಿ baleṅkri, *see* ಬನಾರಿ.

ಬಲೆಪು balepu, *s.* Closing an opening *or* passage in hunting, by which a beast can escape.

ಬಲೆಪುನಿ balepuni (ಬಲೆ), *v. a.* To enclose, surround. 2. to besiege. 3. to hem. *v. n.* To be distressed, vexed. ಬಲೆತ ದೀಪಿನಿ to ensnare. ಬಲೆತೊಲುನಿ to entangle one's self *or* to get entangled.

ಬಲೆವೋಡು balevōḍu, *s.* A kind of fish. 2. the broken mouth of a vessel.

ಬಲೇಂದ್ರಿಯೆ, ಬಲೇಂದ್ರೆ balēndriye, balēndre, *s.* A celebrated king of giants.

ಬಲ್ಕಡಿ, ಬಲ್ಗಡಿ balkaḍi, balgaḍi, *adj.* Firm, strong. *s.* Strength, prowess.

ಬಲ್ಕತ್ತಿ balkatti, *s.* A large knife. 2. *see* ಓಂಟಿಪುಳಿ.

ಬಲ್ಕೆ balkè, *see* ಬಳಿಕೆ. 2. *see* ಬಲಿಕೆ.

ಬಲ್ಗೆ balgè, *see* ಬಲಿಗೆ.

ಬಲ್ಚಟ್ balčaṭu, *s.* A kind of fish. 2. a coarse kind of bread offered to demons.

ಬಲ್ದೆ, ಬಲ್ದೆಮೀನ್ baldè, baldemīnu, *s.* A kind of fish.

ಬಲ್ಮಣ balmaṇa, *s.* Preparation. 2. decoration. ತಂಮಣ— a sumptuous dinner. —ಆಪಿನಿ to be ready for eating; to be decorated.

ಬಲ್ಮೆ balmè, *s.* Strength, prowess, might. 2. soothsaying, augury. —ದಾಯಿ, ಬಲ್ಯಾಯಿ a soothsayer, augurer. —ಕೇಣುನಿ to consult an augurer. —ಪಣ್ಪುನಿ to augur.

ಬಲ್ಯ balya, *s.* A turn to the right course. —ಕಲ್ಯಸಂಕಟ a doubtful sickness.

ಬಲ್ಯಾಯೆ balyāye, *see under* ಬಲ್ಮೆ.

ಬಲ್ಯಾರ್ balyāru, *s.* A shark. ಯಿಕ್ಕ—, ಯಿರ್ಮೆ—, ಯಿಟ್ಟ—, ಕೊಂಬು—, ಕೋರಿ— are different varieties of shark.

ಬಲ್ಲ್ ballu, *s.* A rope, cord.

ಬಲ್ಲ balla, *see* ಬಳ್ಳ. 2. *see* ಬರ್ಬೆನಿ.

ಬಲ್ಲಾಳ್, ಬಲ್ಲಾಳೆ ballālu, ballāle, *s.* A baron *or* nobleman.

ಬಲ್ಲಿ balli, *def. v. neg.* Cannot. (*posit.* ಬಲಿ) ಯೆಂಕ್– I cannot. ತೂವೆರೆ– cannot see.

ಬಲ್ಲೆ ballè, *s.* A thicket, bush. 2. *see* ಭಲ್ಲೆ.

ಬವ, ಬವಣ, ಬವಣೆ bava, bavaṇa, bavaṇè, *s.* Birth, origin, existance.

ಬವಟೆ bavaṭè, *see* ಬಾವಟೆ.

ಬವನ bavana, *s.* Cooked rice.

ಬವರೋಗ bavarōga, *see* ಭವರೋಗ.

ಬವು bavu, *s.* Barking. 2. *see* ಬಾವು.

ಬವುರುನಿ, ಬವುರೊತ್ತುನಿ bavuruni, bavurottuni, *see* ಬರ್ಗೊತ್ತುನಿ

ಬವುಸ bavusa, *see* ಭವಿಷ್ಯ.

ಬಸ basa, *s.* Strength, the marrow *or* serum of the flesh. *adv.* At once. –ಕುಂದುನಿ to become weak. –ಪಾಡುನಿ to put at once *or* suddenly.

ಬಸಕ್ಕ್, ಬಸಲ್ basakku, basalu, *adv.* Forcibly, violently. –ವೈ ಪುನಿ to draw violently.

ಬಸಬಸ basabasa, *s.* Gushing, flowing in a stream. –ನೆತ್ತೆರ್ ಕಕ್ಕುನಿ to throw up much blood.

ಬಸರೂರು basarūru, *s.* A village near Kundāpur. –ಪಂಚಾತಿಗೆ *lit.* the arbitration of Basrūru; an indefinite *or* unsettled arrangement, *pro.*

ಬಸಲೆ basalè, *s.* The Malabar nightshade, *Basella alba.*

ಬಸವ, ಬಸವೆ basava, basave, *s.* An ox; Šiva's steed.

ಬಸಾಲ್, ಬಸಾಲ basālu, basāla, *adv.* At once. –ತಮೆಪುನಿ, –ವೈ ಪುನಿ to throw, pour *or* cast at once.

ಬಸಿ basi, *s.* A porcelain dish *or* plate.

ಬಸಿಯುನಿ basiyuni, *see* ಬಚ್ಚುನಿ.

ಬಸುರಿ, ಬಸುರು basuri, basuru, *s.* Pregnancy.

ಬಸೂಲ basūla, *s.* A wale, stripe.

ಬಸೆ basè, *see* ಬಸ. 2. *see* ಬಸವ.

ಬಸ್ತ basta, *adv.* At once; *cf.* ಬಸ.

ಬಸ್ತಡೆ bastaḍè, *s.* An abode. 2. an inferior kind of fane.

ಬಸ್ತಿ basti, *s.* A Jain temple. 2. an abode, lodging. –ಮಳ್ಪುನಿ to people, colonize.

ಬಸ್ಮ basma, *see* ಭಸ್ಮ.

ಬಸ್ಸ bassa, *s.* Overflowing.

ಬಹದೂರು, ಬಹಾದರ್ bahadūru, bahādaru, *s.* A hero, warrior; a noble *or* high-minded man. 2. a title of honour; *cf.* ಬಾದರ್. ಬಹದರಿ ವರಾಹ a gold pagoda.

ಬಹಳ bahaḷa, *adj.* Abundant, much, many, numerous. *adv.* Abundantly. –ಸರ್ತಿ often, many times.

ಬಹಿ bahi, *adj.* Without. –ರಂಗ public, abroad, outside. –ರಂಗ ಆಪಿನಿ to become public. ಬಹಿರ್ಭಾಗ outside.

ಬಹಿಷ್ಕಾರ bahishkāra, *s.* Expulsion, ban, excommunication. –ಮಳ್ಪುನಿ to excommunicate.

ಬಹು bahu, *adj.* Much, numerous, many. 2. severe, violent. —ಕೆಲಸ much work. —ತರ many sorts *or* ways. —ಶೋಕಾಗ very nice. —ದೇವಾರ್ಚನೆ polytheism.

ಬಹುಧಾನ್ಯ bahudhānya, *s.* The twelfth year in the Hindu cycle of sixty.

ಬಹುಮಾನ bahumāna, *s.* A gift by a superior to an inferior. 2. reward, recompense. 3. honour. *adj.* Honourable, respectable.

ಬಹುಮೂತ್ರ bahumūtra, *s.* Diabetes.

ಬಹುವಚನ bahuvačana, *s.* The plural number.

ಬಹುಶಾ bahušā, *adv.* Probably, perhaps. 2. often, in many ways, for the most part.

ಬಹುಳ bahuḷa, *s.* The dark lunar fortnight.

ಬಳ baḷa, *see* ಬಲ. 2. *see* ಬಳ್ವ.

ಬಳಂಟುನಿ baḷaṇṭuni, *see* ಬಲಂಟುನಿ.

ಬಳಕಣಿ baḷakaṇi, *s.* Meshes of a net; a noose for tightening the vessels suspended in a net-work of rope.

ಬಳಕುನಿ baḷakuni (ಬಳಕ್), *v. n.* To quake, shake, shiver. 2. to bend, curve, stoop. 3. *see* ಬೊಳಕುನಿ.

ಬಳಕೆ baḷakè, *s.* Boasting. 2. *see* ಬಳಕೆ. 3. *see* ಬಾಳಕೆ.

ಬಳಕ್ಕ baḷakka, *s.* The sound of vomiting. 2. a large piece of a cocoanut kernel.

ಬಳಗ baḷaga, *s.* A quantity, heap, multitude, body. ಬಂಧು— relations.

ಬಳನಿಕೆ baḷanikè, *see* ಬಾಳಿಕೆ.

ಬಳಪ baḷapa, *see* ಬಲಪು.

ಬಳಪಾವುನಿ baḷapāvuni, *c. v.* (*of* ಬಳಪುನಿ) To make grow, rear, bring up.

ಬಳಪು baḷapu, *s.* Growth, growing.

ಬಳಪುನಿ baḷapuni (ಬಳ), *v. n.* To grow, shoot up, be enlarged.

ಬಳರ baḷara, *s.* A kind of cornice, ornamenting the beam on a wall, window *or* door-sill.

ಬಳಲಿಕೆ baḷalikè, *s.* Tiredness, fatigue, exhaustion.

ಬಳವಳಿ baḷavaḷi, *see* ಬಳುವಳಿ.

ಬಳಸುನಿ baḷasuni (ಬಳಸ್), *v. a.* To serve out food. 2. to use, have in common use.

ಬಳಿ baḷi, *see* ಬರಿ. 2. *see* ಬಲಿ.

ಬಳಿಕೆ baḷikè, *s.* Familiarity, acquaintance, intimacy, common use. *adj.* Common, familiar, usual.

ಬಳಿಕೊಟ್ಟು baḷikoṭṭu, *see* ಬರಿ.

ಬಳಿವಳಿ baḷivaḷi, *see* ಬಳುವಳಿ.

ಬಳುಂಬೂರು baḷumbūru, *s.* A kind of creeper.

ಬಳುಕುನಿ baḷukuni, *see* ಬಳಕುನಿ.

ಬಳುವಳಿ baḷuvaḷi, *s.* A wife's dower, bridal gift. 2. pursuing. —ಕೊರ್ಪಿನಿ to give dowry.

ಬಳುವಿಕೆ baḷuvikè, *see* ಬಾಳಿಕೆ.

ಬಳೆ baḷè, *s.* A bracelet. 2. a hoop. 2. the edge *or* rim of a vessel. 3. the reepers *or* slips of bamboos used to fasten the rafters of roof. ಇರ್‌– double reepers. ಒರ್– a single reeper. –ಜಾಯಿ, *see* ಬಲಜಾಯಿ.

ಬಳೆಪುನಿ baḷepuni, *see* ಬಲೆಪುನಿ.

ಬಳ್ಯಾರ್ baḷyāru, *see* ಬಲ್ಯಾರ್.

ಬಳ್ಳ್ ballu, *see* ಬಲ್ಲ್.

ಬಳ್ಳ baḷḷa, *s.* A seer, measure of capacity equal to about one seer *or* eighty tolas; *in comp.* ಒರ್ಳ, ಇರ್ಳ, ಮೂವಳ, ನಾವಲ, ಅಯ್ಯೊಲ, ಆಜಲ, ಏವಳ (ಏರ್ಳ), ಎಡ್ಂಬಳ, ಒಂಬ್ರಲ, ಪೈಂಬಳ are the modes of reckoning from one to ten seers.

ಬಳ್ಳಾಯೆ baḷḷāye, *s.* A master.

ಬಳ್ಳಾಳೆ baḷḷāḷe, *see* ಬಲ್ಲಾಳ್.

ಬಳ್ಳಿ baḷḷi, *s.* A creeper, particularly the betel vine. –ನಡ್ಪಿನಿ to plant betel vine.

ಬಾಂಕ್ bāṇku, *s.* A poniard, dagger.

ಬಾಂಕ bāṅka, *adj.* Huge, gaudy. –ಪಕಡಿ a gaudy turban.

ಬಾಂಕಡೆ bāṅkaḍè, *s.* Retching. –ಬರ್ಪಿನಿ to retch, be qualmish.

ಬಾಂಕಿ, ಬಾಂಕೆ bāṅki, bāṅkè, *s.* A trumpet, horn. –ಉರಿಪುನಿ to blow a trumpet. –ದಾಯೆ a trumpeter.

ಬಾಂಕು bāṅku, *s.* A bench.

ಬಾಂಕು, ಬಾಂಗ್, ಬಾಂಗ, ಬಾಂಗು bāṅku, bāṅgu, bāṅga, bāṅgu, *s.* A call for prayer among Mussulmans. –ಕೊರ್ಪಿನಿ to cry out, call for prayer.

ಬಾಂಗಾವುನಿ bāṅgāvuni, *c. v.* (*of* ಬಾಂಗುನಿ) To cause to bow *or* stoop.

ಬಾಂಗುನಿ bāṅguni (ಬಾಂಗಿ), *v. n.* To bow, stoop, lean on one side; *cf.* ಬಗ್ಗುನಿ.

ಬಾಂಡ bāṇḍa, *see* ಭಾಂಡ.

ಬಾಂಡು bāṇḍu, *see* ಬಾಂಡ್.

ಬಾಂತಿ, ಬಾಂತೆ bānti, bāntè, *see* ವಾಂತಿ.

ಬಾಂದ್ bāndu, *s.* An embankment, mound. 2. a boundary stone. –ಕಟ್ಟುನಿ to raise a mound.

ಬಾಂಧವೆ bāndhave, *s.* A relation, kinsman.

ಬಾಂಧಿಕೆ bāndhike, *see* ಬಾಧ್ಯಸ್ಥೆ; *cf.* ಸಂಮಂಧ.

ಬಾಂಪೆಲ್ bāmpelu, *see* ಬಾಪೆಲ್.

ಬಾಂಬೆ bāmbè, *see* ಬಂಬೆ.

ಬಾಂಬೆಲ್ bāmbelu, *s.* A crack, crevice, hole. 2. a large mouth. –ಕೆಬಿ a wide ear.

ಬಾಕರ್ bākaru, *s.* A walking stick, with a curved top.

ಬಾಕಾಯಿ bākāyi, *see* ಕೋಕಾಯಿ.

ಬಾಕಿ bāki, *s.* Balance, remainder, rest, surplus.

ಬಾಕಿಮಾರ್, ಬಾಕ್ಯಾರ್ bākimāru, bākyāru, *s.* A large open field in front of a house.

ಬಾಕಿಲ್ bākilu, *s.* A door, gate. ಆನೆ– a large gate. ಕುರು– a wicket, small gate. –ದ ಇರಿಯ door-hinges. –ಜಪ್ಪುನಿ, –ದೆಪ್ಪುನಿ to open the door. –ಪಾಡುನಿ, –ಮುಚ್ಚುನಿ to shut the door.

ಬಾಕುಡೆ bākuḍe; *s.* A Pariah husband.

ಬಾಗ್ bāgu, *s.* A garden.

ಬಾಗ bāga, *see* ಭಾಗ.

ಬಾಗಾದಿಗೆ, ಬಾಗಿ bāgādige, bāgi, *s.* A coparcener, shareholder. ಸಮ– equal sharer.

ಬಾಗಾಯಿತಿ, ಬಾಗಾಯಿತು bāgāyiti, bāgāyitu, *s.* A garden.

ಬಾಗಿಕಲ್ಲ್ bāgikallu, *s.* A resting place.

ಬಾಗೆಮರ bāgemara, *s.* The sirissa tree, *Acacia speciosa.*

ಬಾಗುನಿ bāguni (ಬಾಗಿ), *v. n.* To bow, stoop, lean.

ಬಾಚ bāča, *see* ಬಾಚಿ.

ಬಾಚಣಿಗೆ bāčaṇigė, *s.* A comb.

ಬಾಚಿ bāči, *s.* A wedge. 2. *see* ಬಾಜಿ. ರಾಶಿದ್ದ ಬಾಚಿ ದೆಪ್ಪುನಿ to take a little from a heap.

ಬಾಚಿಂಗ bāčinga, *see* ಬಾಶಿಂಗ.

ಬಾಚಿಂಗೆ bāčinge, *s.* A clown, rustic, simpleton.

ಬಾಚುನಿ bāčuni (ಬಾಚ್), *v. a.* To scoop *or* gather up. 2. to cut lengthwise. 3. to trim a palm leaf. 4. *see* ಬಚುರ್ನಿ.

ಬಾಚೆ bāče, *adj.* Curved in front. 2. oblique. *adv.* Obliquely. –ಕೊಂಬು a horn curved in front. –ಕೆತ್ತುನಿ to chip.

ಬಾಜನ bājana, *s.* Any vessel, as a pot, cup; a dish.

ಬಾಜಾರ್, ಬಾಜಾರ bājāru, bājāra, *s.* A bazaar, market place.

ಬಾಜಿ bāji, *s.* An adze, a carpenter's axe.

ಬಾಜಿಗೆ, ಬಾಜಿದಾಯೆ bājige, bājidāye, *s.* A musician.

ಬಾಜಿರ bājira, (*corrup. of* ಬಾಜಾರ್) A bazaar, shop, *etc.* –ದ ಪಲಯಿ the counter of a native shop.

ಬಾಜಿರಾಪು bājirāpu, *adj.* Very much. –ಉದ್ದ about eight feet long; very long.

ಬಾಜಿರಾಯೆ bājirāye, *s.* An eminent man.

ಬಾಜು bāju, *s.* The arm. 2. side. –ಬಂದಿ, –ಬಂದು an armlet. –ಬುದ್ಪಿನಿ to get out of the way, make way, step aside.

ಬಾಜೆ bājė, *s.* Music; a musical instrument.

ಬಾಜೆಲ್ bājelu, *s.* Thirst. 2. a drink. –ದ ಬಬ್ಬು the head of a Pariah gang, who has the honor of taking round the pot of toddy at a drinking party. –ಆಪಿನಿ to be thirsty. –ಕೊರ್ಪಿನಿ to give to drink. –ಪರ್ಪಿನಿ to drink.

ಬಾಜ್ರ bājra, *see* ಬಾಜಾರ್.

ಬಾಜ್ರೆ bājre, *s.* A rich merchant.

ಬಾಟಂಣೆ, ಬಾಟಣೆ bāṭaṇṇė, bāṭaṇė, *s.* Food, meat, provision. –ದೀಪಿನಿ to place food for a demon. [*vlg.*

ಬಾಟು bāṭu, *s.* A pimp, procurer,

ಬಾಡಂಕೆಲ್, ಬಾಡಂಗೆಲ್, ಬಾಡಂತೆಲ್ bāḍankelu, bāḍangelu, bāḍantelu, *s.* Withering, leanness; dejection; paleness; decay. *adj.* Withered, dejected.

ಬಾಡಣೆ bāḍaṇė, *s.* A bribe. 2. drying in shade; *cf.* ಬಾಟಂಣೆ. –ದ ಬಾರ್ partially dried paddy;

cf. ಪೊಲ್ಲಿ. —ಕೊರ್ಪಿನಿ to bribe. —ಮಲ್ಪುನಿ to dry.

ಬಾಡಾಯಿ **bāḍāyi**, *s*. Rent, hire, freight. —ಗ ಕೊರ್ಪಿನಿ to let. —ಮಲ್ಪುನಿ to fix rent, hire, *or* freight.

ಬಾಡಾವುನಿ **bāḍāvuni**, *c. v.* (*of* ಬಾಡುನಿ) To make dry *or* fade.

ಬಾಡಿ **bāḍi**, *adj*. Faded, withered.

ಬಾಡಿಗೆ **bāḍigè**, *see* ಬಾಡಾಯಿ.

ಬಾಡು **bāḍu**, *see* ಬಾಡು.

ಬಾಡುನಿ **bāḍuni** (ಬಾಡ್), *v. n.* To fade, shrivel, wither, die; *also* ಬಾಡ್‌ದ್‌ಪೋಪಿನಿ.

ಬಾಣ **bāṇa**, *s*. The sky, heaven, air. 2. an arrow. 3. a bow. 4. a rocket. 5. a water vessel. *adj*. Striped. —ಕಾಯಿ, —ಕಾರೊಳು a bitter kind of fruit. —ಪಕ್ಕಿ a swallow. —ಬಿರು a rainbow. —ಶೀರೆ a female's striped cloth. ಆಕಾಶ— a sky rocket. ಚಕ್ರ— a rocket, wheel-fire-work. —ಬುಡ್ಪಿನಿ to throw rockets, let off fire-work. —ಹಾಕುನಿ to shoot an arrow. ಬಾಣೊಡು ಎಂಣೆಪರಿಯ *lit*. an earthen oil-pot in the sky, (*riddle*); a palm fruit. ಬಾಣೊಡು ಬಲ್ಯತ್ತಿ *lit*. a knife in the sky (*riddle*); a tamarind pod.

ಬಾಣಂತಿ **bāṇanti**, *s*. A lying-in woman. —ಕುತ್ತ puerperal disorder.

ಬಾಣಕಂಣ್ **bāṇakaṇṇu**, *s*. A side-glance, blinking. —ದಾಯಿ one who blinks.

ಬಾಣಲ್, ಬಾಣಾಲ್ **bāṇalu, bāṇālu**, *s*. Darkness. 2. blindness, dimness.

ಬಾಣಲೆ **bāṇale**, *s*. A dim sighted man.

ಬಾಣಾಸುರೆ **bāṇāsure**, *s*. A giant destroyed by Kṛushṇa. 2. an archer.

ಬಾಣಿ **bāṇi**, *s*. A border, edge, as of a boat. 2. *see* ಪಾಣಿ.

ಬಾಣೆ **bāṇe**, *see* ಬಾನೆ.

ಬಾತ್ **bātu**, *see* ಬತ್ತಿ. 2. *see* ಬಾಪುನಿ.

ಬಾತ **bāta**, *see* ಪಾತ.

ಬಾತಿ **bāti**, *s*. Resemblance. 2. *see* ಬಾದಿ.

ಬಾತುಮೆ **bātumè**, *s*. Spying.

ಬಾದ **bāda**, *s*. Affliction, distress, torment.

ಬಾದರ್ **bādaru**, *see* ಬಹದೂರ್. *adj*. Heroic; excellent. —ಗಡ a small island near Uḍapi.

ಬಾದರಬೆಟ್ಟೆ **bādarabeṭṭè**, *s*. The nut of taliput palm.

ಬಾದರಾಯಣೆ **bādarāyaṇe**, *s*. Vyāsa, the compiler of the Vēdas.

ಬಾದಾಮ್ **bādāmu**, *s*. An almond, *Terminalia catappa*.

ಬಾದಿ **bādi**, *adj*. Heavy. —ಆಪಿನಿ to become heavy.

ಬಾದು **bādu**, *s*. A fence, file.

ಬಾದುರು **bāduru**, *see* ಬಹದೂರ್.

ಬಾದೆ **bādè**, *s*. A kind of drum, used by Pariahs.

ಬಾದ್ಬಕ್ಕನ **bādbakkana**, *s*. Making distinction in common affairs.

ಬಾದ್ರಿ **bādri**, *s*. A kind of barley

ಬಾದ್ಲಿ **bādli**, *see* ಬಾಧಳ.

ಬಾಧಕ **bādhaka,** *s.* Inconvenience, annoyance. –ಆಪಿನಿ to be inconvenient.

ಬಾಧಳ **bādhaḷa,** *s.* A door.

ಬಾಧಿಪುನಿ **bādhipuni** (ಬಾಧಿ), *v. a.* To afflict, distress, torment.

ಬಾಧಿಯುನಿ **bādhiyuni** (ಬಾಧಿ), *v. n.* To be affected, as by one's sin, *etc.*

ಬಾಧೆ **bādhė,** *s.* Pain, affliction, torment. 2. *see* ಬಾಧ್ಯಸ್ತೆ.

ಬಾಧ್ಯ **bādhya,** *adj.* Related to, entitled to; incumbent on.

ಬಾಧ್ಯತೆ, ಬಾಧ್ಯಸ್ತಿಗೆ **bādhyatė, bādhyastigė,** *s.* Relationship. 2. right, title, *or* claim to possession.

ಬಾಧ್ಯಸ್ತೆ **bādhyaste,** *s.* An heir; a claimant.

ಬಾನ **bāna,** *see* ಬಾಣ.

ಬಾನೆ **bānė,** *s.* A hill, *or* jungle near a rice-field. –ಬೊಟ್ಟ a rice-field situated on a high ground.

ಬಾಪ್ **bāpu̥,** *s.* A father.

ಬಾಪಂಗೆಲ್, ಬಾಪೆಲ್ **bāpaṅgelu̥, bāpelu̥,** *s.* A swelling, inflammation, sore. *adj.* Swollen.

ಬಾಪಾವುನಿ **bāpāvuni,** *c. v.* (*of* ಬಾಪುನಿ) To cause to inflame.

ಬಾಪು **bāpu,** *s.* A swelling, tumor, abscess. ಎದೆ–, ಗಡ್ಡೆ– *or* ಕ್ಯೊ–, ದೆಂಜಿ–, ಪಲ್ಲೆ–, ಬಟ್ಟಲ್– are diferent kinds of abscess.

ಬಾಪುನಿ **bāpuni** (ಬಾ), *v. n.* To swell.

ಬಾಪೆಲ್ **bāpelu̥,** *s.* Swelling; *cf.* ಬಾಪು.

ಬಾಪೆಲು **bāpelu,** *s.* A plethoric woman. 2. an angry woman.

ಬಾಪೆಲೆ **bāpele,** *s.* A plethoric man. 2. an angry man.

ಬಾಬ್, ಬಾಬು **bābu̥, bābu,** *s.* A point, matter, subject, item. –ವಾರ್ the particulars *or* details of an item, *etc.*

ಬಾಬ್ತು **bābtu,** *s.* Account, head, article, item. ಅರಿತ ಬಾಬ್ತಿದ ಪಣವು money due on account of rice.

ಬಾಮ **bāma,** *s.* A bend, crook, arch. *adv.* So, like, after that way *or* manner. –ಬರ್ಪಿನಿ to have a bend, be crooked.

ಬಾಮಿನಿ **bāmini,** *see* ಭಾಮಿನಿ.

ಬಾಮಿಯುನಿ **bāmiyuni** (ಬಾಮಿ), *v. a.* To console, comfort, soothe. 2. to decline, refuse.

ಬಾಮೆ **bāmė,** *s.* A faithful wife.

ಬಾಯಕೆ **bāyakė,** *see* ಬಯಕೆ.

ಬಾಯನ **bāyana,** *see* ವಾಯನ.

ಬಾಯಲಿಂಕ **bāyaliṅka,** *s.* A quarrel, dispute.

ಬಾಯಲೆ **bāyale,** *s.* A noisy man; *cf.* ಬಾಯಾಡಿ.

ಬಾಯಾಡಿ **bāyāḍi,** *s.* A prattler, braggart. –ತನ prattling.

ಬಾಯಾರಿಗೆ **bāyārigė,** *see* ಬಾಜಿಲ್.

ಬಾಯಾರುನಿ **bāyāruni** (ಬಾಯಾರ್), *v. n.* To be thirsty.

ಬಾಯಾಳಿ **bāyāḷi** *see* ಬಾಯಾಡಿ.

ಬಾಯಿ **bāyi,** *s.* A Roman Catholic woman.

ಬಾಯಿ **bāyi,** *s.* The mouth. 2. the edge of a knife, sword, *etc.* 3. speech, utterance. 4. an opening. ಅರೆ—, *see* ಅರಬಾಯಿ. ಇರ್—, *see* ಇರ್ಬಾಯಿ. ಕಡೆ— the corners of the mouth. ಕೈ— hand and mouth. ಬಾಯೀ— a loud noise. ಬಿಸಳೆ— a large mouth. ಶಿರಿ— a harelip. —ಉಪಚಾರ flattery. —ಕತ್ತಿ a large knife. —ಕಿಂಟೆರ್ಲ್ an itchy mouthed man; a quarrelsome man. —ಕೈಪೆ bitterness of the mouth; hatred. —ತೀಪೆ sweetness of the mouth; flattery. —ದಾಯೆ a loquacious man. —ನೀರ್ spittle. —ಪಡೆ dispute, quarrel. —ಪಾಠ learning by heart. —ಪಾತೆರ an oral communication, verbal message; a promise. —ಪುಡಿ a sore mouth, ulceration of the mouth. —ಬಡಕೆ a clamorous man; an indiscreet man. —ಮಲ್ಲಿ talking loudly *or* haughtily. —ಮುಚ್ಚಿಲ್ a cover, the lid of a vessel. —ಮೂರಿ a fetid breath. —ರುಚಿ taste, appetite. —ಲೆಖ್ಖ mental arithmetic. —ಸಬಿ savoury, palatable. —ಅಂಗಾವುನಿ to open the mouth, yawn, gape. —ಅರ್ಲ್ಯನಿ, —ಉರಿಯುನಿ the mouth to burn. —ಇಗರ್ಾವುನಿ, —ಹಿಗರ್ಾವುನಿ to turn the mouth of a vessel. —ಕಟ್ಟಾವುನಿ to overcome in argument; to silence; to prescribe diet. —ಕಟ್ಟುನಿ to muzzle; to observe regimen; restrain the appetite; to shut the mouth; to fasten the mouth of a bag, *etc.* —ಕಲೆಪಿನಿ to vociferate, talk loudly; to open the mouth. —ಕಾಪುನಿ to guard one's mouth; to refrain from returning abuse. —ಕೂಡುನಿ to be of age, as an animal when it has got its complete set of teeth; a sore, *etc.*, to be perfectly heal. —ಗ್ ಕೊರ್ಪಿನಿ to feed, nourish. —ಗ್ ಪಾಡುನಿ to bribe; to poison one's meal. —ಡ್ ಬೂರುನಿ to be entangled in a plot, *etc.*, to fall a prey to one's rage. —ಡ್ಡ್ ಬೂರುನಿ to fix a price definitely; to pass word; to make a promise. —ಬರ್ಪಿನಿ to be able to speak. —ಬುಡುಪಾವುನಿ to make one speak out, cause to confess. —ಬುಡ್ಪಿನಿ to open the mouth; to speak out, disclose, reveal, confess; to cry, as in danger, *etc.* —ಬೂರುನಿ to cease to speak, as a dying man. —ಮರ್ಲ್ಯನಿ the mouth to itch; to be quarrelsome. —ಮಳ್ಪುನಿ to make an opening; to bawl out; to scold, rebuke. —ಮುಕ್ಕುಳಿಯುನಿ to rinse, gargle. —ಮುಚ್ಚುನಿ to shut the mouth, to hold the tongue. —ಹಾಕುನಿ to deceive, defraud.

ಬಾರ್ bāru, *s.* Paddy. —ತಲ *see* ಬಾರ್ತಲ.

ಬಾರ bāra, *s.* A thong, strap. 2. the upper leather work of sandals. 3. *see* ಪಾರ.

ಬಾರ **bāra**, *s.* Overgrowing, over-ripeness.

ಬಾರಗೆ **bārage**, *s.* A title of Bants.

ಬಾರಣೆ, ಬಾರನೆ **bāraṇè, bāranè**, *s.* Stripping the bark of a tree, *or* cutting it lengthwise. 2. a comb. 3. *see* ಬಾರ್ಣೆ.

ಬಾರದಾನ್ **bāradānu**, *s.* The difference of weight in the two scales of a balance.

ಬಾರಾಪಿನಿ **bārāpini** (ಬಾರಾ), *v. n.* To be fruitful.

ಬಾರಾವುನಿ **bārāvuni**, *c. v.* (*of* ಬಾರುನಿ) To cause to chip.

ಬಾರಿ **bāri**, *s.* Bamboo splits fastened lengthwise to the rafters of a roof from both sides.

ಬಾರಿ **bāri**, *see* ಭಾರಿ.

ಬಾರಿಸುನಿ **bārisuni** (ಬಾರಿಸ್), *v. a.* To play on a musical instrument.

ಬಾರುನಿ **bāruni** (ಬಾರ್), *v. a.* To cut, chip, trim. 2. to comb the hair.

ಬಾರೆ **bārè**, *s.* The plantain tree, *Musa paradisica.* —ದ ಇರೆ a plantain leaf. —ದ ಕಂಡೆ the stock of a plantain tree. —ಕಾಯಿ unripe plantains. —ದ ಕುರ್ಲೆ a young plantain tree. —ದ ಕೈಲ್ a bunch of plantains. —ದ ಪಂಣಿ a cluster *or* comb of plantains. —ದ ಪಂರ್ದ್ ripe plantains. —ದ ಪೂಂಬೆ the pod containing plantain flowers. —ಬಂಬೆ the round stalk inside a plantain tree. ಅವುಂಡ—, ಕದೊಳಿ—, ಕಲ್ಲ್—, ಗಾಳಿ—, ಚಂದ್ರ—, ದೇವ—, ದೇಂದ್ರ—, ಪೂ—, ಬೊಂಬ್ಯಾ—, ಮೈಸೂರ್—, ಸಿಂಗ— are some of the varieties of plantain.

ಬಾರ್ಕಲ **bārkala**, *s.* The thrashing floor, barn.

ಬಾರ್ಕೆ **bārkè**, *see* ಬಾರನೆ.

ಬಾರ್ಣೆ **bārṇè**, *s.* An offering of food to a demon. 2. a meal after fasting, breakfast.

ಬಾರ್ಪಣಿ **bārpaṇi**, *s.* A comb.

ಬಾರ್ದನ್ **bārdanu**, *see* ಬಾರದಾನ್.

ಬಾರ್ಲಿ **bārli**, *s.* Barley.

ಬಾಲ್ **bālu**, *s.* A razor. 2. a pointed, double edged, short knife tied to the foot of a cock in cock-fighting. ಕಿರ್ನಿ—, ಕೊಕ್ಕೆ—, ಕೋಲು—, ನಾಗರಕಿರ್ನಿ— are some of the varieties of the same. —ತುಂಬು, —ಸುಂಬು the long feather of a cock. —ಬಂಡಾರ the sword and other gear of a demon. —ಮುಟ್ಟು a barber's case containing his shaving instruments. —ಕಟ್ಟುನಿ to tie a short knife to the foot of a cock in cock-fighting.

ಬಾಲ **bāla**, *adj.* Young, tender. 2. childish. —ಕ್ರೀಡೆ, —ಲೀಲೆ childish sport. —ತನ childhood. —ಬೋಧನೆ instruction of youth. —ಬ್ರಹ್ಮಚಾರಿ a young bachelor.

ಬಾಲಕೆ **bālake**, *s.* A boy.

ಬಾಲಗ್ರಹ **bālagraha**, *s.* Convulsions, fits to which children are liable.

ಬಾಲಡೆ **bālaḍè**, *s.* A kind of fish.

ಬಾಲಚಂದ್ರೆ **bālačandre,** *s.* The new moon.

ಬಾಲನಕ್ಷತ್ರ **bālanakšatra,** *s.* A comet.

ಬಾಲಸರ **bālasara,** *s.* A female's earring.

ಬಾಲಸಾವುನಿ **bālasāvuni,** (ಬಾಲಸಾ), *v. a.* To dispise; *cf.* ಆಸರ್ಡಾವುನಿ.

ಬಾಲಹರಡೆ **bālaharaḍe,** *s.* A small variety of gall nut.

ಬಾಲಾವುನಿ **bālāvuni,** *c. v.* (*of* ಬಾಲುನಿ) To export. 2. to administrate, rule.

ಬಾಲುನಿ **bāluni** (ಬಾಲ್), *v. n.* To run over, go out. 2. *see* ಬಾಳುನಿ.

ಬಾಲೆ **bāle,** *s.* A child. ಪುರು– a new-born child.

ಬಾಲೆಮೀನ್ **bālemīnu,** *s.* A kind of fish.

ಬಾಲ್ಕೆ **bālke,** *s.* A companion, comrade.

ಬಾಲ್ಜಿ **bālji,** *s.* A demon so called.

ಬಾಲ್ದಿ **bāldi,** *s.* A bucket.

ಬಾಲ್ಯ **bālya,** *s.* Childhood, infancy; *also* –ಪ್ರಾಯ, –ತ್ವ. *adj.* Young, tender.

ಬಾವ **bāva,** *see* ಭಾವ.

ಬಾವಟೆ, ಬಾವುಟೆ **bāvaṭe, bāvuṭe,** *s.* A banner, flag, ensign.

ಬಾವಡೆ **bāvaḍe,** *s.* An earthen lid *or* covering of a vessel.

ಬಾವಡೆಪಟ್ಟಿ **bāvaḍepaṭṭi,** *s.* The marginal rapier of a roof, pole-plate.

ಬಾವನೆ **bāvane,** *see* ಭಾವನೆ.

ಬಾವಲಿ **bāvali,** *see* ಬಾವೊಲಿ.

ಬಾವು **bāvu,** *s.* Inequality of surface, unevenness, bend, curve, as of a plank, tree, *etc.* 2. *see* ಬಾಪು.

ಬಾವುಡುನಿ **bāvuḍuni,** *v. a.* (ಬಾವುಡ್) To turn up a rice-pot after the gruel has been strained off.

ಬಾವೆ **bāve,** *see* ಭಾವೆ.

ಬಾವೆ **bāve,** *s.* The cream of milk. 2. the pulpy kernel of a tender cocoanut. 3. a film on the eye. –ಮಂಣ್ fine earth floating on the water; *cf.* ಮುದರ್.

ಬಾವೊಲಿ **bāvoli,** *s.* A bat. 2. an ornament worn by women at the tip of the ear.

ಬಾಶಿ **bāši,** *adj.* Plain, unstamped. –ಕಾಗಜಿ a plain paper, in contrast to stamp-paper.

ಬಾಶಿಂಗ **bāšinga,** *s.* A nuptial crown.

ಬಾಶೆ, ಬಾಸೆ **bāše, bāse,** *see* ಭಾಷೆ.

ಬಾಸಟ **bāsaṭa,** *adj.* Talkative, eloquent.

ಬಾಸರೆವುನಿ **bāsarevuni** (ಬಾಸರೆ), *v. n.* To talk in sleep.

ಬಾಸಿಂಗ **bāsinga,** *see* ಬಾಶಿಂಗ.

ಬಾಹುಳ್ಯ **bāhulya,** *s.* Abundance.

ಬಾಳ್ **bāḷu,** *see* ಬಾಲ್.

ಬಾಳ್ಕ, ಬಾಳಕ **bāḷuka, bāḷaka,** *s.* Thin slices of plantains fried in oil, called sovereigns.

ಬಾಳ **bāḷa,** *see* ಬಹಳ.

ಬಾಳಾವುನಿ **bāḷāvuni,** *c. v.* (*of* ಬಾಳುನಿ) To make thrive, prosper.

ಬಾಳಿಕೆ **bāḷike,** *s.* Existence, subsistence. 2. prosperity, thriving.

ಬಾಳುಗ **bāḷuga,** *see* ಬಾಳಿಕ.

ಬಾಳುನಿ **bāḷuni** (ಬಾಳ್), *v. n.* To thrive, prosper. 2. to exist, subsist. 3. to last, endure. 4. to sow seed.

ಬಾಳು, ಬಾಳುವಿಕೆ, ಬಾಳುವೆ, ಬಾಳ್ಕೆ, ಬಾಳ್ತರ, ಬಾಳ್ತೆ, ಬಾಳ್ವೆ **bāḷu, bāḷuvikė, bāḷuvė, bāḷkė, bāḷtara, bāḷtė, bāḷvė,** *see* ಬಾಳಿಕೆ.

ಬಿಂಕ **biṅka,** *s.* Boldness, courage. 2. pride, haughtiness.

ಬಿಂಗ **biṅga,** *s.* Talc, soap-stone.

ಬಿಂಗಾರಿ **biṅgāri,** *s.* A battlement. 2. intoxication.

ಬಿಂಗಿರಿ, ಬಿಂಗ್ರಿ **biṅgiri, biṅgri,** *s.* Raving. 2. self-conceit. *adj.* Delirious; vain; *also* ಬಿಂಗಾರಿ, ಬಿಂಗಿ, ಬಿಂಗಿರಿಟ, ಬಿಂಗೆರೆ, ಬಿಂಗ್ರು, ಬಿಂಗ್ಲ. —ಪಾತೆರುನಿ to rave, talk irrationally, as a mad man. —ಕಟ್ಟುನಿ to be wild, furious, as a mad man.

ಬಿಂಡಿ **biṇḍi,** *s.* A kind of cake.

ಬಿಂದ್, ಬಿಂದ **binduֹ, binda,** *s.* A drop. 2. a dot, mark. 3. *semen virile.*

ಬಿಂದಿ **bindi,** *s.* A small earthen pot.

ಬಿಂನ **binna,** *see* ಭಿಂನ.

ಬಿಂನಣ **binnaṇa,** *adj.* Quick, fast, speedy. *adv.* Quickly, speedily. —ನಡಕೆ fast walking.

ಬಿಂನತಲೆ **binnatalė,** *s.* A written memorial, petition *or* letter addressed to a superior.

ಬಿಂನನ **binnana,** *s.* Work, labour.

ಬಿಂನಯ, ಬಿಂನಹ **binnaya, binnaha,** *s.* A request, petition.

ಬಿಂನೆ **binne,** *s.* A kinsman, relative. 2. a guest.

ಬಿಂಬ **bimba,** *s.* The disk of the sun *or* moon. 2. form, shape, figure. 3. a reflected *or* represented form, shadow. 4. *see* ಬಿಂಮ.

ಬಿಂಬಲಿ, ಬಿಂಬಿಲಿ, ಬಿಂಬುಲಿ **bimbali, bimbili, bimbuli,** *s.* The bilimbi tree, *Averrhoa Bilimbi.*

ಬಿಂಮ **bimma,** *s.* The lip. —ಕಡ್ತೆಲೆ a man with a harelip.

ಬಿಂಮಗೆ ಬಿಂಮನೆ **bimmagė, bimmanė,** *adv.* Tightly, firmly.

ಬಿಕಾರಿ **bikāri,** *s.* A beggar, pauper. *adj.* Poor, destitute. 2. low, mean.

ಬಿಕ್ಕ್ **bikkuֹ,** *s.* Holding one's breath, as when making a strong effort, straining. 2. a sob.

ಬಿಕ್ಕನಾಸಿ **bikkanāsi,** *see* ಬಿಕ್ಕೇಸಿ.

ಬಿಕ್ಕಾವುನಿ **bikkāvuni,** *c. v.* (*of* ಬಿಕ್ಕುನಿ) To cause to hold breath, as when making a strong effort; to strain.

ಬಿಕ್ಕುನಿ **bikkuni** (ಬಿಕ್ಕ್), *v. a.* To hold one's breath. 2. to give little by little. ಬಿಕ್ಕ್‌ದ್ ಪೋಪಿನಿ to happen with difficulty; to have a premature birth. ಬಿಕ್ಕ್‌ದ್ ಅರ್ಪಿನಿ to sob. ಬಿಕ್ಕಬಿಕ್ಕದ್ ಕೊಪಿನಿ to give reluctantly, little by little.

ಬಿಕ್ಕೆ **bikkė,** *see* ಭಿಕ್ಷೆ.

ಬಿಕ್ಕೆಲ್ bikkelụ, *adj.* Deficient. 2. rotten. –ತತ್ತಿ a useless *or* rotten egg (*prov.*).

ಬಿಕ್ಕೆಲೆ bikkele, *s.* A man who hesitates in speaking.

ಬಿಕ್ನೇಸಿ biknēsi, *s.* A beggar. 2. a man of mean disposition. 3. a mischief-maker. 4. an obstinate man.

ಬಿಗ್‍ತೆ bigụtè, *see* ಬಿಗಿಪು.

ಬಿಗ್‍ಪುನಿ bigụpuni, *see* ಬಿಗಿಪುನಿ.

ಬಿಗ್‍ರ್ಲ್ bigụrlụ, *adv.* Late in the night.

ಬಿಗ biga, *see* ಬೀಗ.

ಬಿಗಟ bigaṭa, *adj.* Tight.

ಬಿಗಡ್ bigaḍụ, *s.* Taking offence. 2. disagreement, difference, discord, disunion. –ಪಂಚಾಯಿತಿಕೆ adverse counsel *or* decision. –ಪಾತೆರುನಿ to talk adversely.

ಬಿಗಡುನಿ, ಬಿಗಾಡುನಿ bigaḍuni, bigāḍuni (ಬಿಗಡ್, ಬಿಗಾಡ್), *v. n.* To be offended, take offence. 2. to change, alter, as one's opinion *or* sentiment. 3. to abandon, forsake, as a side *or* part. ಬುದ್ಧಿ ಬಿಗಡ್ಡ್ ಪೋಂಡು the mind was disturbed.

ಬಿಗರ್ bigarụ, *see* ಜಿಗರ್.

ಬಿಗಲೆ bigalè, *see* ಬಗಳೆ.

ಬಿಗಿ bigi, *s.* Tightness, tension. *adj.* Tight, fast, rigid. 2. difficult, hard. 3. obstinate, stubborn. –ಕಟ್ಟುನಿ to tie fast; to rivet. –ಮಳ್ಪುನಿ to make fast *or* tight.

ಬಿಗಿಪಾವುನಿ bigipāvuni, *c. v.* (*of* ಬಿಗಿಪುನಿ) To cause to fasten.

ಬಿಗಿಪು bigipu, *s.* Fastening, tightening.

ಬಿಗಿಪುನಿ bigipuni (ಬಿಗಿ), *v. a.* To tie, fasten, tighten. ಬಿಗಿತ್ ಪತ್ತುನಿ to hold fast.

ಬಿಗಿಯುನಿ bigiyuni (ಬಿಗಿ), *v. n.* To become fast *or* tight.

ಬಿಗು bigu, *see* ಬಿಗಿ.

ಬಿಗುತ biguta, *s.* Tightness, tension. *adj.* Tight, fast.

ಬಿಚ್ಚ bičča, *adj.* Drawn, unsheathed, as a weapon.

ಬಿಚ್ಚ bičča, *see* ಭಿಕ್ಷ.

ಬಿಚ್ಚಣಿಗೆ biččaṇigè, *see* ಬಚ್ಚಣೆ.

ಬಿಚ್ಚಾಟ biččāṭa, *s.* Bursting, breaking *or* flying open.

ಬಿಚ್ಚಾವುನಿ biččāvuni, *c. v.* (*of* ಬಿಚ್ಚುನಿ) To open, unfasten. 2. to split.

ಬಿಚ್ಚುಕತ್ತಿ biččukatti, *s.* A drawn sword.

ಬಿಚ್ಚುನಿ biččuni (ಬಿಚ್ಚ್), *v. n.* To burst, fly open, become loosened; *also* ಬಿಚ್ಚಿದ್‍ಪೋಪಿನಿ.

ಬಿಚ್ಚೆಲ್ biččelụ, *adj.* Broken, split, cracked.

ಬಿಚ್ಚೋಲೆ biččōlè, *s.* A coiled piece of palmyra leaf put in the ear.

ಬಿಚ್ವ bićva, *s.* A double edged sword; *cf.* ಬಾಂಕ್.

ಬಿಛಾನೆ bichānè, *s.* A bedding, mat, carpet. 2. the straw bed of a horse.

ಬಿಜ bija, *see* ಬೀಜ.

ಬಿಜ **bija,** *see* ಬಿಜಿ.

ಬಿಜಂಟ್ **bijanṭu,** *see* ಬೆಜಂಟಿ.

ಬಿಜಕ್ರೆ **bijakrè,** *see* ಬೆಜಕಿರೆ.

ಬಿಜಗ್ರೆ **bijagrè,** *see* ಬಿಜಾಗ್ರಿ.

ಬಿಜಯ **bijaya,** *see* ವಿಜಯ.

ಬಿಜಲ **bijala,** *s.* A monstrous speech.

ಬಿಜಲು **bijalu,** *see* ಬಿಜಿಲ್.

ಬಿಜಲ್ದಿ **bijaldi,** *s.* A midwife.

ಬಿಜಾಗ್ರಿ **bijāgri,** *s.* The hinges on which the lid of a chest, *etc.*, turns; *also* ಬಿಜಾಕ್ರಿ.

ಬಿಜಿಕ್ **bijiku,** *s.* A clacking sound.

ಬಿಜಿಕ್ರೆ **bijikrè,** *see* ಬೆಜಕಿರೆ.

ಬಿಜಿಗೆ **bijigè,** *see* ಬಿದಿಗೆ.

ಬಿಜಿಗ್ರೆ **bijigrè,** *see* ಬಿಜಾಗ್ರಿ.

ಬಿಜಿಪು **bijipu,** *adj.* Thin, watery.

ಬಿಜಿಬಿಜಿ **bijibiji,** *adj.* Greasy, gummy, sticky.

ಬಿಜಿಲ್ **bijilu,** *s.* The matter of a sore, pus.

ಬಿಜಿಲುನಿ, ಬಿಜೆಲುನಿ **bijiluni, bijeluni** (ಬಿಜಿಲ್, ಬಿಜಿಲ್), *v. a.* To bear, bring forth, as a child. *v. n.* To suppurate.

ಬಿಜು **biju,** *see* ಬಿಜಿಪು.

ಬಿಜುನಿ **bijuni** (ಬಿಜ್), *v. n.* To ooze; *cf.* ಊಜುನಿ.

ಬಿಜೆ **bijè,** *s.* A kind of venetian blind made of split bamboo *or* cane.

ಬಿಜ್ಜಣಿಗೆ **bijjaṇigè,** *see* ಬೀಸಣಿಗೆ.

ಬಿಜ್ಜಾಯಿ **bijjāyi,** *see* ಬಿಜಿ.

ಬಿಜ್ಜೆಲ್ಯುನಿ **bijjelyuni,** *see* ಬಿಜಿಲುನಿ.

ಬಿಟ್ಟಿ **biṭṭi,** *see* ಬುಟ್ಟಿ.

ಬಿಟ್ಟೆ **biṭṭè,** *s.* The excrement of sheep, goats, rats, *etc.*

ಬಿಡವು **biḍavu,** *s.* A ruling instrument of carpenters.

ಬಿಡಾಯಿಸುನಿ **biḍāyisuni** (ಬಿಡಾಯಿಸ್), *v. a.* To enclose, put in, fill.

ಬಿಡಾರ **biḍāra,** *see* ಬುಡಾರ.

ಬಿಡಾಲೆ **biḍālè,** *s.* A cat.

ಬಿಡಿಕೆ, ಬಿಡಿಗೆ **biḍikè, biḍigè,** *see* ಬೀಡಿಕೆ.

ಬಿಡಿತ **biḍita,** *see* ಪಿಡಿತ.

ಬಿಡಿತೆ **biḍitè,** *s.* The chorus of a drum-beating to a vocal music. 2. intrigue. —ಪಾಡುನಿ to beat a drum; to put on a mask; to disguise.

ಬಿಡುಗಡೆ **biḍugaḍè,** *see* ಬುಡುಗಡೆ.

ಬಿಡುಗು **biḍugu,** *s.* A coquette.

ಬಿಡುಗುಬಜರ್ **biḍugubajaru,** *see* ಬಿನುಗುಬಾಜಾರ್.

ಬಿಡೆ **biḍè,** *s.* Shame, modesty.

ಬಿಡ್ತೆ **biḍtè,** *see* ಬಿಡಿತೆ.

ಬಿತ್ತ್ **bittu,** *s.* Seed. 2. the kernel of a nut. 3. the testicles. 4. progeny.

ಬಿತ್ತಿಗೆ **bittigè,** *s.* Sowing.

ಬಿತ್ತುನಿ **bittuni** (ಬಿತ್ತ್), *v. a.* To sow seed.

ಬಿತ್ತೆ **bittè,** *see* ಬಿತ್ತಿಗೆ.

ಬಿದ್ರ್ **bidru,** *see* ಬೆದ್ರ್.

ಬಿದ **bida,** *see* ಬಿದಿ.

ಬಿದಿ, ಬಿದಿಯೆ **bidi, bidiyè,** *see* ವಿಧಿ.

ಬಿದಿಗೆ **bidigè,** *s.* The second day in a lunar fortnight.

ಬಿದುರುನಿ **biduruni** (ಬಿದುರ್), *v. n.* To loosen by itself.

ಬಿದೆ **bidè**, *s.* A particular sort of seed. 2. sort, kind, class. —ತ ಆಸಿಗಾಸಿ management of cultivation.

ಬಿದೊಳಿಗೆ **bidoḷigè**, *s.* Letting out, out going.

ಬಿದ್ದ್‌ಕಂಣ್ **biddukaṇṇu**, *s.* A squint eye.

ಬಿದ್ದರ್ಸೆ **biddarse**, *s.* A squint eyed man.

ಬಿಧಾನ **bidhāna**, *see* ವಿಧಾನ.

ಬಿನಹ **binnaha**, *see* ಬಿಂನಯು.

ಬಿನುಗುಬಾಜಾರ್ **binugubājāru**, *s.* Household furniture, baggage.

ಬಿಯ **biya**, *s.* A kind of tree.

ಬಿಯಾಂ **biyām̃**, *see* ಬೀಯುಂ.

ಬಿರ **bira**, *s.* A kiss. —ಮಾನ್ಯುನಿ to kiss.

ಬಿರಕೆ **birakè**, *see* ಚಿರಕೆ.

ಬಿರಮಣೆ, ಬಿರಾಣೆ **biramaṇe**, **birāṇe**, *s.* A Brahman.

ಬಿರವುನಿ, ಬಿರಾವುನಿ **biravuni**, **birāvuni** (ಬಿರ, ಬಿರಾ), *v. a.* To mix, mingle, compound.

ಬಿರಸುನಿ **birasuni**, *see* ಚಿರಸುನಿ.

ಬಿರಿಂಜಿ **birinji**, *s.* Slender pieces of firewood.

ಬಿರಿಬಿರಿ **biribiri**, *s.* The noise of rending cloth, *etc.*

ಬಿರಿಮರ **birimara**, *s.* A door bar.

ಬಿರಿಯುನಿ **biriyuni** (ಬಿರಿ), *v. n.* To split, crack, burst; *also* ಬಿರಿದ್‌ಪೋಪಿನಿ.

ಬಿರು **biru**, *s.* A bow. 2. a curved spring, as of a gun, *etc.*, *adj.* Violent, severe, strong, quick. —ಘಾಳಿ a tempest, whirlwind.

ಬಿರುದು **birudu**, *see* ಬಿರ್ದ್.

ಬಿರುವೆ **biruve**, *see* ಬಿರ್ವೆ.

ಬಿರುಸು **birusu**, *see* ಬಿರ್ಸ್. 2. *see* ದುಸುರ್.

ಬಿರೆಲ್ **birelu**, *s.* A finger. ಅರೆ— half finger, *fig.* half mind. ಉಂಗಿಲ—, ಮುದ್ರಿದ— the ring finger. ಒತ್ತು—, ಕೊರಗ— the forefinger. ಕಿಂನಿ—, ಕಿನ್ನನ— the little finger. ಕೊಂಬು— the thumb. ನಡು— the middle finger.

ಬಿರ್ಕ್ **birku**, *see* ಬಿಕ್ಕ್; *cf.* ಬಿರ್ಕುನಿ.

ಬಿರ್ಕ **birka**, *s.* Overflowing, abundant.

ಬಿರ್ಕುನಿ **birkuni** (ಬಿರ್ಕ್), *v. a.* To scatter, disperse, shed.

ಬಿರ್ಕೆ **birkè**, *s.* A crack, chink, gap.

ಬಿರ್ಕೆಲೆ **birkele**, *s.* A scatterer.

ಬಿರ್ಗಾಳಿ **birgāḷi**, *s. lit.* A tempest. 2. a vagabond, wanderer.

ಬಿರ್ದ್, ಬಿರ್ದೊಲಿಗೆ **birdu**, **birdoligè**, *s.* A badge of honour. 2. show, display. 3. prestige. —ದ ಬಳೆ a bracelet worn as a badge of honour.

ಬಿರ್ವೆ **birve**, *s.* A toddy-drawer.

ಬಿರ್ಸ್ **birsu**, *s.* Velocity. 2. a kind of firework. *adj.* Clever, skilful, dexterous. 2. hard, stiff, rough.

ಬಿರ್ಸಾದಿಗೆ **birsādigè**, *s.* Cleverness, ability, prowess.

ಬಿರ್ಸೆ **birse**, *s.* A skilful man, an able man.

ಬಿಲ್ **bilu**, *s.* A bill. —ಬಾಸೆ a sign; *cf.* ಸೊಂನೆ.

ಬಿಲ **bila**, *s.* A hole, cave.

ಬಿಲಾರ **bilāra,** *s.* Tin; iron vessels plated with tin.

ಬಿಲಿಂಬಿ **bilimbi,** *see* ಬಿಂಬಲಿ.

ಬಿಲಾವರ **bilāvara,** *s.* Glass, porcelain.

ಬಿಲುಕುಲು, ಬಿಲ್ಕುಲ್ **bilukulu, bilkulu,** *adv.* Never, not at all, by no means. 2. universally, entirely.

ಬಿಲೆ **bilè,** *s.* Price, value, worth. –ಅಡೆವುನಿ to cost. –ಕಟ್ಟುನಿ to estimate, fix the price. –ಕ ದೆತ್ತೊಣುನಿ to buy, purchase.

ಬಿಲ್ಪತ್ರೆ, ಬಿಲ್ವಪತ್ರೆ **bilpatrè, bilvapatrè,** *s.* The bael tree, *Aegle marmelos.*

ಬಿಲ್ಲು **billu,** *see* ಬಿರು.

ಬಿಲ್ಲೆ **billè,** *s.* Anything made in a flat form, as a tablet *or* lozenge, a peon's badge, *etc.* 2. a pane, panel. ಗಂಧದ– a lozenge of sandal paste. –ದಾ ಯಿ a peon.

ಬಿಲ್ವ **bilva,** *see* ಬಿಲ್ಪತ್ರೆ.

ಬಿಶಿ **biši,** *see* ಬಿಸಿ.

ಬಿಸತ್ತಿ **bisatti,** *s.* A knife.

ಬಿಸರುನಿ **bisaruni** (ಬಿಸರ್), *v.n.* To slip, tumble.

ಬಿಸಲೆ, ಬಿಸಳೆ **bisalè, bisaḷè,** *s.* An earthen vessel. ಕಿಂನಿ– a small earthen vessel. ಬಿಂಡಿ– a large earthen vessel.

ಬಿಸಾತ್ **bisātu,** *s.* Regard, concern, care for. ನಿನ ಬಿಸಾತ್ ಯೆಂಕ್ ದಾನೆ what do I care for you?

ಬಿಸಾಯಿನೇನ್ **bisāyinēnu,** *s.* The cord of a fishing net.

ಬಿಸಿ **bisi,** *adj.* Heat, warmth, *esp.* of the sun. 2. *see* ಬೆಚ್ಚ.

ಬಿಸು **bisu,** *see* ವಿಷು.

ಬಿಸುಲು **bisulu,** *s.* Sunshine.

ಬಿಳಿ **biḷi,** *adj.* White.

ಬಿಕ್ಷೆ **bikshè,** *see* ಭಿಕ್ಷೆ.

ಬೀಂಪು **bīmpu,** *s.* A tail.

ಬೀಗ **bīga,** *s.* A lock. –ದ ಕೈ a key. ಕತ್ತರಿ– a cross-lock. –ಪಾ ಡುನಿ to lock, bolt.

ಬೀಗತನ **bīgatana,** *s.* Relationship by marriage.

ಬೀಗೆ **bīge,** *s.* A relative by marriage.

ಬೀಜ **bīja,** *s.* A seed; *cf.* ಬಿತ್ತ್. 2. origin, cause. 3. a cashew nut.

ಬೀಜಾಟ **bījāṭa,** *s.* Waving, swinging, fanning; brandishing.

ಬೀಜಾಡುನಿ, ಬೀಜಾವುನಿ **bījāḍuni, bījāvuni,** *c. v.* (*of* ಬೀಜುನಿ) To brandish, fan. 2. to wave, swing out, fling. ಕೈ– to wave the hand backwards and forwards in walking; *also* ಬೀಜಿ ದುಗನಿ.

ಬೀಜುನಿ **bījuni** (ಬೀಜ್), *v. n.* To swing, blow, as the wind. *v. a. see* ಬೀಸುನಿ.

ಬೀಟ್ **bīṭu,** *s.* The beat of a policeman. 2. *see* ಬೀಟಿ. 3. *see* ಬೀತ.

ಬೀಟಿ **bīṭi,** *s.* Blackwood. ಕರಿ– ebony, *Dalbergia latifolia.*

ಬೀಡ್ **bīḍu,** *s.* A gathering, assembly. 2. dross, alloy of iron. ಸಂತೆದ– stallage.

ಬೀಡಿ bīḍi, *s.* A cigarette.

ಬೀಡಿಕೆ bīḍikè, *s.* A herd of loaded cattle. 2. the pile of their burdens.

ಬೀಡು bīḍu, *see* ಬೀಡ್. 2. *see* ಬೂಡು.

ಬೀಡೆ bīḍè, *s.* Shame, modesty. 2. agitation, nervousness, fear.

ಬೀಣೆ bīṇè, *s.* The Indian lute. 2. a harmonium.

ಬೀಣೆ bīṇè, *adj.* Tough, indissoluble, as overboiled jaggory.

ಬೀತ್ bītụ, *s.* Intoxication. *adj.* Intoxicated, drunk. *intj.* O drunkard! —ಆಪಿನಿ to get drunk.

ಬೀತಿ bīti, *see* ಭೀತಿ.

ಬೀದಿ bīdi, *s.* A street, gate. ನಾಗ—, *see* ನಾಗಬೀದಿ.

ಬೀನೆ bīnè, *s.* A grumbler. 2. *see* ಬೀಣೆ.

ಬೀಪಾಳ್, ಬೀಪಾಳಿ bīpāḷụ, bīpāḷi, *s.* A fisherman.

ಬೀಪು bīpu, *s.* Casting, throwing. 2. blowing of wind. 3. waving hands. —ಬಲೆ a casting net.

ಬೀಪುನಿ bīpuni (ಬೀ), *v. a.* To cast a net. 2. to throw, sling, as a stone. 3. to throw up earth. 4. to wave the hand. 5. to wash *or* cleanse rice. *v. n.* To blow, as wind; *cf.* ಬೀಜುನಿ.

ಬೀಪೆ bīpe, *s.* A king, ruler; a cruel man.

ಬೀಬಿ bībi, *s.* A Mohammedan lady.

ಬೀಮೆ bīme, *see* ಭೀಮೆ.

ಬೀಮು bīmu, *s.* A beam.

ಬೀಯ bīya, *see* ಬಿಯ.

ಬೀಯಂ, ಬೀಯಮ್ bīyaṁ, bīyamụ, *s.* A jar, jug.

ಬೀರ್ bīrụ, *s.* Beer.

ಬೀರ್‌ದರಿ bīrụdari, *see* ಜೀರದರಿ.

ಬೀರ bīra, *s.* Vanity, conceit. 2. baseness, wickedness. 3. a panegyric, eulogy. 4. heroism, bravery. 5. mischievousness, trick, knavery. *adj.* Vain. 2. panegyrical. 3. mischievous. —ದ ಬಿತ್ತ a mischievous person. —ದೆಪ್ಪುನಿ to humble, humiliate. —ಪಣ್ಪುನಿ, —ಲೆಪ್ಪುನಿ to boast; to sing the panegyric of a demon. —ಪೋಪಿನಿ to lead a mischievous life; to get worse; to be troublesome.

ಬೀರಂಜುನಿ bīrañjuni (ಬೀರಂಜ್), *v. a.* To collect, heap up.

ಬೀರಾವುನಿ bīrāvuni, *see* ಬಿರವುನಿ.

ಬೀರಿ bīri, *s.* Conflagration of a jungle *or* hill. —ಬೂರುನಿ a forest *or* hill to be on fire.

ಬೀರುನಿ, ಬೀರ್ಯುನಿ bīruni, bīryuni (ಬೀರ್), *v. a.* To scatter, disperse. 2. to brag, boast, parade.

ಬೀರೆ bīre, *see* ವೀರೆ.

ಬೀಲ bīla, *s.* A tail. —ದ ಮುಂಚಿ cubebs, *or* Chinese pepper, *Piper cubeba.* —ಪತ್ತುನಿ to walk behind one; *cf.* ಬೆರಿಪತ್ತುನಿ.

ಬೀಸ bīsa, *adv.* Quickly, rapidly, fast; straightly. —ಪೋಪಿನಿ to go fast.

ಬೀಸಕಲ್ಲ್ bīsakallụ, *s.* A millstone; a hand-mill.

ಬೀಸಣಿಗೆ, ಬೀಸನಿಗೆ **bīsaṇigè, bīsanigè,** *s.* A fan.

ಬೀಸತ್ತಿ **bīsatti,** *see* ಬಿಸತ್ತಿ.

ಬೀಸನ, ಬೀಸನೆ **bīsana, bīsanè,** *s.* Fanning. 2. net-fishing. –ಗಾರೆ a fisher. –ಮಾಡುನಿ to fan.

ಬೀಸುನಿ **bīsuni** (ಬೀಸ್), *v. a.* To fan. 2. to grind. 3. to wave, swing. 4. to cast. *v. n.* To blow, wave; *cf.* ಬೀಜುನಿ.

ಬುಂಜಿಪುನಿ **buñjipuni** (ಬುಂಜಿ), *v. a.* To enjoy.

ಬುಂನು **bunnu,** *see* ಬೂಣು.

ಬುಕೀಟ್ **bukīṭu,** *s.* A fragrant powder used as a perfumery.

ಬುಕುಟಿ, ಬುಕುಣಿ, ಬುಕುನಿ, ಬುಕ್ಕುಡಿ **bukuṭi, bukuṇi, bukuni, bukkuḍi,** *s.* Anything reduced to a very fine powder, as flour, *etc.*

ಬುಕ್ಕು **bukku,** *s.* A handful. 2. *see* ಬಿಕ್ಕ್.

ಬುಕ್ಕುಡು **bukkuḍu,** *see* ಮುಕ್ಕುಡು.

ಬುಕ್ಕುಡೆ **bukkuḍè,** *see* ಮುಕ್ಕುಡೆ.

ಬುಕ್ಕುನಿ **bukkuni** (ಬುಕ್ಕ್), *v. a.* To pulverize, powder. *v. n. see* ಬಿಕ್ಕುನಿ.

ಬುಕ್ಕೆ **bukke,** *An affix showing the* condition, disposition *or* habit of a person; *as,* ಗಜ್ಜಿ– a man subject to itch. ಬಂಗಿ– a man who chews *or* smokes hemp leaves.

ಬುಕ್ತಿ **bukti,** *s.* Sacred ashes; –ದ ಕರಡಿಗೆ a box containing sacred ashes.

ಬುಗು **bugu,** *see* ಬಕ್ಕು.

ಬುಗುಡಿ **buguḍi,** *s.* A female's ornament worn in the tip of the ear. –ಪೂ a small flower plant with yellow blossoms.

ಬುಗುಬುಗು **bugubugu,** *see* ಬಗಬಗ.

ಬುಗುರಿ **buguri,** *see* ಬೊಗೊರಿ.

ಬುಗುಳುನಿ **buguḷuni** (ಬುಗುಳ್), *v. n.* To be grieved.

ಬುಜ **buja,** *see* ಭುಜ.

ಬುಜಂಗ **bujaṅga,** *see* ಭುಜಂಗ.

ಬುಜರಿಕೆ, ಬುಜರಿಗೆ **bujarikè, bujarigè,** *s.* Dignity, honour.

ಬುಜು **buju,** *adv.* Softly. –ಜುಂಬುನಿ to suck as children.

ಬುಟ್ಟಗೆ **buṭṭagè,** *adv.* In cash, ready money. 2. in a round sum.

ಬುಟ್ಟಿ **buṭṭi,** *s.* A basket.

ಬುಟ್ಟಿ **buṭṭi,** *s.* Compulsory *or* unrequited labour. –ದ ಕೆಲಸ, –ದ ಬೇಲೆ task work, forced labour, perfunctory work. –ಮಳ್ಪುನಿ, –ಸಾಗಾವುನಿ to do task work; to do a thing perfunctorily.

ಬುಡ **buḍa,** *s.* The bottom *or* stump of a tree. 2. origin, cause, foundation. ಕಾಲ– beginning. ಬುಡೊಕು ನೀರ್ ದೀಪಿನಿ to ruin one (*prov.*).

ಬುಡಂದೆ **buḍandè,** *adv.* Without intermission, incessantly; *cf.* ಬುಡುಪಿನಿ.

ಬುಡಕನೆ **buḍakanè,** *adv.* Suddenly. 2. heavily, with force; *cf.* ಬುಡ್ಕ. –ಬೂರುನಿ to fall heavily. –ಮುಕ್ರುನಿ to dive suddenly. –ಲಕ್ಕುನಿ to rise suddenly.

ಬುಡಕ್ಕ buḍakka, *see* ಬುಡಕನೆ.

ಬುಡಪತ್ತ buḍapatta, *adj.* Irregular. –ಜರ intermittent fever.

ಬುಡಲೆ buḍalè, *s.* Ease, freedom. 2. overgrowing.

ಬುಡಾರ buḍāra, *s.* A temporary abode, lodging. –ಮಳ್ಪುನಿ to take lodgings.

ಬುಡಿಬೇಲೆ buḍibēlè, *see* ಬುಡುಬೇಲೆ.

ಬುಡು, ಬುಡುಕಟ್ಟು, buḍu, buḍukaṭṭu, *see* ಬುಡುಗಡೆ.

ಬುಡುಂಬ buḍumba, *adv.* Hastily. –ಪಾಡುನಿ to throw down hastily.

ಬುಡುಕ್ಕ buḍukka, *adv.* Suddenly, unexpectedly.

ಬುಡುಗಡೆ buḍugaḍè, *s.* Liberty, release, freedom. 2. intermission. –ಆಪಿನಿ to be released. –ಮಳ್ಪುನಿ to release.

ಬುಡುದಾರೆ buḍudārè, *s.* The remarriage of a widow *or* of a divorced person. 2. a remarried wife.

ಬುಡುದಾಳಿ buḍudāḷi, *s.* A rover. 2. a libertine.

ಬುಡುಪಾವುನಿ buḍupāvuni, *c. v.* (*of* ಬುಡುಪಿನಿ) To loosen, untie. 2. to release, emancipate, deliver.

ಬುಡುಪಿನಿ buḍupini (ಬುಡ), *v. a.* To put forth, from *or* away from. 2. to leave, forsake, quit, give up. 3. to let go, leave alone. 4. to shoot, discharge. 5. to remit, dispense with, deduct, leave out. 6. to dismiss, send away. 7. to cease, desist, terminate. 8. to set to, set on, as men to work, dogs to fight, *etc.*; to appoint to a work. 9. to uncover, expose, make bare, as any part of the body. *v. n.* To become loose, dishevelled. ಕಂಣ್– to open the eyes. ಕಂಣ್ ಬಾಯಿ– to be in a perplexity. ಕುದ್ರೆ– to gallop a horse. ಕ್ರಯೊಡು– to reduce the price of a thing. ಜನ– to send a messenger. ಜೀವ– to expire. ದಾರಿ–, ಸಾದಿ– to make way, get out of the way. ಪೂ– to flower. ಬಾಯಿ– to gape, yawn; to confess, reveal. ಬೆಡಿ– to shoot a gun. *Added to the gerund or suspensive tense of other verbs, it expresses the completion of the action, and answers to* off, away, *etc.; as,* ಕೊರ್ದ್– to give away. ದೆತ್ತ್– to take away; to collect *or* recover fully, as a debt, *etc.* ಪರ್ದ್– to drink off.

ಬುಡುಬುಡು buḍubuḍu, *adv.* By drops. –ಬೂರುನಿ to fall by drops.

ಬುಡುಬೇಲೆ buḍubēlè, *s.* A journeyman's labour, job work.

ಬುಡೆದಿ buḍedi, *see* ಬೊಡೆದಿ.

ಬುಡ್ಕ buḍka, *see* ಬುಡಕನೆ.

ಬುಡ್ಡಲೆ buḍḍalè, *s.* A kind of fishing net.

ಬುಡ್ಡೆ buḍḍè, *s.* A pod, legume.

ಬುಡ್ಪಿನಿ buḍpini, *see* ಬುಡುಪಿನಿ.

ಬುಡ್ರುನಿ buḍruni, *see* ಬುಡುಪಿನಿ.

ಬುಣ **buṇa,** *s.* A peg.

ಬುಣುಪು **buṇupu,** *s.* A straight branch. –ಕೈಲ್ a handle made of such a branch.

ಬುಣುಪ್ಪು, ಬುಣ್ಪು **buṇuppu, buṇpu,** *s.* Heel-tendon. 2. *see* ಬುಙುಪು.

ಬುತ್ತ್ **buttụ,** *see* ಬಿತ್ತ್.

ಬುತ್ತಾಯಿ **buttāyi,** *see* ಬೊತಾಯಿ.

ಬುತ್ತಿ **butti,** *s.* Stale food. 2. food put up for a journey.

ಬುತ್ತುನಿ **buttuni,** *see* ಬಿತ್ತುನಿ.

ಬುತ್ತೆ **buttè,** *s.* *Semen virile.*

ಬುದ್ಲೆ **budụlè,** *see* ಬುದುಲೆ.

ಬುದ **buda,** *see* ಬುಧ.

ಬುದಲಿ **budali,** *see* ಬುದಲೆ.

ಬುದಾರ **budāra,** *see* ಬುಧವಾರ.

ಬುದುಬುದು **budubudu,** *s.* A bubbling *or* gushing noise of water.

ಬುದುಲೆ, ಬುದ್ದಲಿ, ಬುದ್ದೊಲಿ **budulè, buddali, buddoli,** *s.* A skin bottle.

ಬುದ್ಯಂತೆ, ಬುದ್ಯಂದೆ **budyante, budyande,** *s.* A wise, sensible, *or* prudent man.

ಬುಧ **budha,** *s.* The planet Mercury. –ದಶೆ the influence of Mercury on one's fortunes; good luck; prosperity.

ಬುಧವಾರ **budhavāra,** *s.* Wednesday.

ಬುದ್ಧಂತೆ **buddhante,** *see* ಬುದ್ಯಂತೆ.

ಬುದ್ಧಿ **buddhi,** *s.* Intellect, sense, understanding. 2. knowledge, wisdom. 3. advice, admonition, reprimand. *intj.* Sir, your honour. –ದಾಂತಿ stupid, senseless. –ಚಿರಂಟಿ senselessness. –ವಂತಿಗೆ wisdom, prudence, sense. –ವಂತೆ a wise man. –ಹೀನೆ a stupid, senseless fellow. –ಕಲ್ಪುನಿ to learn wisdom, take counsel. –ಪಣ್ಪುನಿ to advise, admonish. –ಬರ್ಪುನಿ to grow wise, learn prudence.

ಬುನಾದಿ **bunādi,** *s.* A foundation. 2. origin, cause. –ತೋಡುನಿ to dig a foundation. –ಕಟ್ಟುನಿ to build a foundation. –ಪಾಡುನಿ to lay a foundation.

ಬುನಿಪು **bunipu,** *see* ಬುಙುಪ್ಪು.

ಬುನು **bunu,** *see* ಬೂಙು.

ಬುರ್, ಬುರನೆ, ಬುರು, ಬುರುಬುರು **burụ, buranè, buru, buruburu,** *see* ಬುರ್ರ್.

ಬುರುಜಿ **buruji,** *see* ಬುರ್ಜಿ.

ಬುರುಜು **buruju,** *see* ಬುರ್ಜು.

ಬುರುಡೆ **buruḍè,** *s.* A bottle, made of the shell of a cocoanut, gourd, *etc.* 2. the skull. 3. an inkstand. 4. a snuff-box. –ರಟ್ಟಾವುನಿ *lit.* to behead; to cut off; to revenge.

ಬುರುದೆ **burudè,** *see* ಬುರ್ದೆ.

ಬುರುಸು **burusu,** *s.* A brush.

ಬುರೆಲ್ **burelụ,** *see* ಬಿರೆಲ್.

ಬುರ್ರ್, ಬುರ್ರನೆ, ಬುರ್ರು **burrụ, burranè, burru,** *s.* The noise of a bird's wings in flying, *etc.*

ಬುರ್ಕ್, ಬುರ್ಕು **burkụ, burku,** *s.* Sipping noise. 2. the noise of breaking wind downwards.

ಬುರ್ಕಾವುನಿ burkāvuni, *see* ಪುರ್ಕಾವುನಿ.

ಬುರ್ಜಿ burji, *s.* Confusion. —ಆಪಿನಿ to be confused.

ಬುರ್ಜು, ಬುರ್ದು burju, burdu, *s.* A stone-dam; bastion.

ಬುರ್ತಾವುನಿ burtāvuni, *see* ಬೂಪಾವುನಿ.

ಬುರ್ದೆ burde, *s.* Mud, mire.

ಬುರ್ನಾಸ್ burnāsu, *adj.* Tasteless, insipid. 2. decayed, spoiled. 3. useless, worthless. —ಅರಿ decayed *or* worthless rice. —ನರಮಾನಿ a worthless man.

ಬುರ್ನುಸ್ burnusu, *s.* A kind of leveller.

ಬುರ್ಮ, ಬುರ್ಮು burma, burmu, *s.* A gimlet.

ಬುರ್ಸು bursu, *see* ಬುರುಸು.

ಬುಲಕ್ bulaku, *see* ಬೊಳಕ್.

ಬುಲಕುನಿ bulakuni, *see* ಬೊಲಕುನಿ.

ಬುಲರ bulara, *adj.* White, striped with black.

ಬುಲರೆ, ಬುಲಾರೆ bulare, bulāre, *s.* An ox striped white and black.

ಬುಲಾಕ್ bulāku, *s.* A jewel, worn by females between their nostrils.

ಬುಲಾವುನಿ bulāvuni, *c. v.* (*of* ಬುಲುನಿ) To open wide, as the eyes.

ಬುಲಿಪುನಿ bulipuni, *see* ಬುಲ್ಪುನಿ.

ಬುಲುನಿ buluni, *v. n.* To be open.

ಬುಲೆ bule, *adj.* Fermenting. 2. *see* ಬುಳೆ.

ಬುಲೆಕಲಿ bulekali, *s.* Sour toddy.

ಬುಲೆತಿ buleti, *see* ಬುಳೆತಿ.

ಬುಲೆಪಿನಿ bulepini, *see* ಬುಳೆಪಿನಿ.

ಬುಲ್ಪಕ್ಕಿ, ಬುಲ್ಬುಲ್‌ಪಕ್ಕಿ bulpakki, bulbulpakki, *s.* A kind of bird.

ಬುಲ್ಪುನಿ bulpuni, *see* ಬುಳ್ಪುನಿ.

ಬುಲ್ಲಾವುನಿ bullāvuni, *c. v.* (*of* ಬುಲ್ಲುನಿ) To enlarge a sore, *etc.* 2. to split, make a crack.

ಬುಲ್ಲುನಿ bulluni (ಬುಲ್ಲ್), *v. n.* A sore *or* wound to enlarge. 2. to crack, slit.

ಬುವನ buvana, *see* ಭುವನ.

ಬುಸು, ಬುಸುಬುಸು, ಬುಸ್ಸು busu, busubusu, bussu, *s.* Gasping, panting. 2. hissing. *adj.* Sullen. —ಗುಟ್ಟುನಿ to hiss. ಮೋಣೆ ಬುಸುಬುಸು ಆಪಿನಿ the face to look sullen.

ಬುಸ್ಸು bussu, *s.* Hissing; the noise of pouring water from a water-lift; *also* ಬುಸ್ರು.

ಬುಳಂತೆ buḷante, *see* ಬೊಳಂತೆ.

ಬುಳಂಬು buḷambu, *see* ಬೊಜ್ಜ.

ಬುಳಕ್ buḷaku, *s.* Brightness, shining.

ಬುಳು buḷu, *see* ಬುಳ್ಪು.

ಬುಳುನಿ buḷuni, *see* ಬುಳೆಪಿನಿ. 2. *see* ಬುಲ್ಲುನಿ.

ಬುಳೆ buḷe, *s.* Standing, growing corn, a crop. —ಕಟಾವು reaping of a crop. —ಕಾಣಿಕೆ the present of a small quantity of new corn, *etc.*, made by a tenant to his landlord during the harvest season. —ಚಿಲ್ the harvest time. —ಕೊಯ್ಪಿನಿ to reap corn.

ಬುಳೆಚೆಲ್ buḷeċelu, *see* ಬೊಳ್ಚೆಲ್.

ಬುಳೆತಿ buḷeti, (*fr.* ಬುಳೆಪಿನಿ) *adj.* Full grown, ripe; *cf.* ಬುಲೆವುನಿ.

ಬುಳೆಪಾವುನಿ, ಬುಳೆಪುಡುನಿ buḷepāvuni, buḷepuḍuni, *c. v.* (*of* ಬುಳೆವುನಿ) To make grow, rear, raise, as a crop, *etc.*

ಬುಳೆಪಿನಿ, ಬುಳೆಪುನಿ, ಬುಳೆಯುನಿ, ಬುಳೆವುನಿ buḷepini, buḷepuni, buḷeyuni, buḷevuni (ಬುಳೆ), *v. n.* To grow, ripen, be ripe.

ಬುಳ್ಕ bulka, *see* ಬುಳಕ್.

ಬುಳ್ಕಡ್, ಬುಳ್ಕಾಡ್ bulkaḍu, bulkāḍu, *s.* Crying passionately; bawling. 2. clearness. *adj.* Open, public.

ಬುಳ್ಕಡುನಿ bulkaḍuni (ಬುಳ್ಕಡ್), *v. n.* To cry, as from fear *or* being possessed of a demon.

ಬುಳ್ಪು bulpu, *s.* A cry, lamentation. 2. the noise of any animal *or* bird. 3. clamour.

ಬುಳ್ಪುನಿ bulpuni (ಬುಳ್ಪ್), *v. n.* To cry aloud, shout, exclaim.

ಬುಳ್ಳುನಿ bulluni, *see* ಬುಲ್ಲುನಿ.

ಬೂ bū, *see* ಭೂ.

ಬೂಂದು būndu, *see* ಬೂಣು.

ಬೂಕು būku, *s.* A book.

ಬೂಚಿ, ಬೂಚು būči, būču, *s.* A cork, stopper.

ಬೂಚಿ, ಬೂಚು, ಬೂಜು būči, būču, būju, *s.* Mould, mildew.

ಬೂಟಂಗ, ಬೂಟಕತನ būṭanga, būṭakatana, *see* ಬೂಟಿ.

ಬೂಟಾವುನಿ būṭāvuni, *c. v.* (*of* ಬೂಟುನಿ) To make pay *or* retribute, to avenge, revenge.

ಬೂಟಿ, ಬೂಟು būṭi, būṭu, *s.* Empty boast, brag. —ಗಾರೆ, —ದಾಯೆ a boasting man. —ಪಾತೆರುನಿ to boast, brag.

ಬೂಟುನಿ būṭuni (ಬೂಟ್), *v. a.* To repay, give in return, avenge. 2. to boast, brag.

ಬೂಡು būḍu, *s.* A manor-house, mansion, residence of a headman. —ದಾಯೆ the squire of a manor-house.

ಬೂಣ būṇa, *s.* A wedge, peg. 2. a short stick driven into a jackfruit to ripen it soon. —ಜೊಟ್ಟುನಿ, —ಹಾಕುನಿ to drive in a stick.

ಬೂಣು būṇu, *s.* The coffee berry.

ಬೂತ būta, *see* ಭೂತ.

ಬೂತಳ būtaḷa, *see* ಭೂತಳ.

ಬೂತಾಯಿ būtāyi, *s.* Sardines, —ದ ಕಕ್ಕ the refuse of sardine fish.

ಬೂದಿ būdi, *s.* Ashes.

ಬೂದಿಂಗ, ಬೂದು būdinga, būdu, *adj.* Ash-coloured.

ಬೂನ būna, *see* ಬೂಣ. 2. *see* ಬೂಣು.

ಬೂಪಾಳಿ būpāḷi, *s.* A king. —ರೋಗ the kings'-evil.

ಬೂಬಿ būbi, *see* ಬೀಬಿ.

ಬೂಮಿ būmi, *see* ಭೂಮಿ.

ಬೂರಾಟ būrāṭa, *s.* Falling, crumbling; delapidation.

ಬೂರಾವುನಿ būrāvuni, *c. v.* (*of* ಬೂರುನಿ) To cause to fall, to fell. 2. to conquer.

ಬೂರಿ būri, *s.* An assemblage, congregation of people. —ಕೈಪ a curry intended for a grand entertainment. –ದಕ್ಷಿಣೆ a gift of money to a large number of mendicants. –ಪಕ್ಷ majority.

ಬೂರಿಗ್ būrigụ, *see* ಬೂರುಗ.

ಬೂರಿಗೆ **būrige**, *s.* A kind of sweetmeat.

ಬೂರು **būru**, *s.* A creeper, climbing shrub. ಕೆಬಿತ– the lower part of the ear. ದೊಂಪದ–, *see* ಬಸಲೆ. ದ್ರಾಕ್ಷೆ– vine.

ಬೂರುಗ **būruga**, *s.* The tree *Eriodendrum anfractuosum*; *also* ಬೋರದ ಮರ; *cf.* ಅಲ.

ಬೂರುಡುನಿ **būruḍuni**, *see* ಬೂರ್ಡುನಿ,

ಬೂರುತಾವುನಿ **būrutāvuni**, *see* ಬೂರಾವುನಿ.

ಬೂರುನಿ **būruni** (ಬೂರ್), *v. n.* To fall. 2. to be caught in a snare. 3. to be overthrown, defeated. 4. to die. ಅಡ್ಡ– to fall down, prostrate, salute. ಮುಂಡು– to fall on the knees. ಸಮ– to suit, agree; to consent.

ಬೂರೆಲೆ **būrele**, *s.* A weak-legged man.

ಬೂರ್ಡುನಿ **būrḍuni** (ಬೂರ್ಡ್), *v. a.* To spread evenly, as grain for drying, *or* earth to level the ground. 2. to level, flatten.

ಬೂರ್ತಾವುನಿ **būrtāvuni**, *see* ಬೂರಾವುನಿ.

ಬೂರ್ತೆ **būrtè**, *see* ಮುತ್ತೆ.

ಬೂರ್ಪಾವುನಿ **būrpāvuni**, *see* ಬೂರಾವುನಿ.

ಬೂಲ್ಯ, ಬೂಳ್ಯ **būlya, būḷya** (*corrupt. of* ವೀಳ್ಯ), Betel leaves. 2. sandal paste offered to a demon and distributed to the people assembled.

ಬೂಷಣ **būshaṇa**, *see* ಭೂಷಣ.

ಬೂಳು **būḷu**, *see* ಬೂರು.

ಬೃಹಸ್ಪತಿ **bṛuhaspati**, *s.* The planet Jupiter. 2. the preceptor of the gods. 3. the name of a law-giver. –ವಾರ Thursday.

ಬೆಂಗ್ **beṅgụ**, *s.* Malice, hatred, envy; revenge. 2. disparagement, detraction, censure. –ಬೂಟುನಿ to revenge.

ಬೆಂಗ **beṅga**, *s.* The red sandalwood *Pterocarpus santalinus.*

ಬೆಂಗರುಡುನಿ **beṅgaruḍuni,** *see* ಬೆಂಗುನಿ.

ಬೆಂಗರೆ, ಬೆಂಗ್ರೆ **beṅgarè, beṅgrè**, *s.* Bank, shore, margin. ಅಡ್ಡ– a shore resorted to by smugglers.

ಬೆಂಗಲಿ **beṅgali**, *s.* The dregs, refuse, lees. *adj.* Drunk, intoxicated. 2. capricious, whimsical. –ಕುಡಿಯ a drunkard, sot.

ಬೆಂಗಳಿ **beṅgaḷi**, *s.* Boiled toddy.

ಬೆಂಗಿರಿ **beṅgiri**, *see* ಬಿಂಗಿರಿ.

ಬೆಂಗುನಿ **beṅguni** (ಬೆಂಗ್), *v. n.* To repent, be sorry. 2. to feel pity, compassion, commiseration; *also* ಬೆಂಗೊಂಬುನಿ, ಬೆಂಜಿಕೊಳುನಿ.

ಬೆಂಗೊಡಿತೇಡೆ **bengoḍitēḍè**, *s.* A kind of fish.

ಬೆಂಙ beṅṅa, *see* ಬೆಂಗ.

ಬೆಂಜನ, ಬೆಂಞಾನ beṅjana, beṅṅana, *s.* Curds, curdled milk.

ಬೆಂಡ್, ಬೆಂಡು beṇḍu, beṇḍu, *s.* Pith, a light and spongy plant growing in water, *Aeschynomene aspera.* 2. thinness, leanness, lightness. *adj.* Thin, light; emaciated. —ಆಪಿನಿ to become lean, thin, light, emaciated.

ಬೆಂಡೆ beṇḍè, *s.* The esculent okra *Abelmoschus esculentus.* ಕಾಡ್— *Hibiscus abelmoschus.* —ಕಾಯಿ its fruit.

ಬೆಂಡೆಕ್ಕ್ beṇḍekku, *s.* The tree *Lagerstrœmia microcarpa.*

ಬೆಂಡೊಲಿ beṇḍoli, *s.* The bush *Physalis indica.*

ಬೆಂಡೋಲೆ beṇḍōlè, *s.* A hollow kind of gold ear-ornament.

ಬೆಂಣೆ beṇṇè, *s.* Butter.

ಬೆಂತರ್ bentaru, *see* ಬೇಂತರ.

ಬೆಂತೆ bente, *s.* A class of Pariahs.

ಬೆಂತೆರ್ benteru, *s.* High water tide.

ಬೆಂದ್ರ್, ಬೆಂದಿರ್, ಬೆಂನಿರ್ bendụru, bendiru, benniru, *s.* Hot water. 2. a tepid bath. 3. a bathroom; *also* —ಕೊಟ್ಯ. —ಮೀ ಪುನಿ to bathe in hot water.

ಬೆಂನಿ, ಬೆಂನೆ benni, bennè, *s.* Land under cultivation. 2. agriculture. —ಗುಡ್ಡೆಲೆ, —ದಾಯೆ a cultivator, farmer. —ಬೆಪ್ಪಿನಿ, —ಮ ಳ್ಪುನಿ to cultivate; to rent a land for cultivation. —ಮುಗಿ ಯುನಿ to finish cultivation.

ಬೆಂಬಲ bembala, *s.* Recommendation, help, patronage.

ಬೆಂಮೆ, ಬೆಂಮೆರ್ bemme, bemmeru, *see* ಬೆಮೆರ್.

ಬೆಕ್ಕ bekka, *see* ದಕ್ಕ.

ಬೆಕ್ಕಸ್ bekkasu, *s.* Surprise, wonder. 2. nausea, disgust. —ಪೋಪಿನಿ to be disgusted; to be astonished.

ಬೆಕ್ಕಸುನಿ bekkasuni (ಬೆಕ್ಕಸಿ), *v. n.* To wonder, be surprised. 2. to faint, be tired. 3. to feel satiated.

ಬೆಗಡುನಿ begaḍuni (ಬೆಗಡಿ), *v. n.* To be alarmed, bewildered.

ಬೆಗಡೆ begaḍè, *see* ಬೇಗಡೆ.

ಬೆಗಪು begapu, *see* ಬೆಗರ.

ಬೆಗಪುನಿ, ಬೆಗರುನಿ begapuni, begaruni (ಬೆಗ, ಬೆಗರ), *v. n.* To perspire, sweat.

ಬೆಗರ್ begaru, *s.* Perspiration, sweat. —ಪುಟ್ಟುನಿ, —ಬೀಜುನಿ, —ಸಿಂ ಟುನಿ to perspire.

ಬೆಚ್ಚ beċca, *s.* Heat, warmth. *adj.* Hot, warm. *adv.* Hotly, warmly. —ನೀರ್ hot water. —ಅರಪುನಿ to cool. —ಕೊರ್ಪಿನಿ, —ಮ ಳ್ಪುನಿ to warm, heat, make hot; to beat, flog.

ಬೆಚ್ಚನ beċċana, *s.* Warmth. 2. evening meal; *cf.* ತಂಞಾನ. —ದ ಇಲ್ಲ್ a warm habitation.

ಬೆಚ್ಚನೆ beccanè, *adv.* Hotly, warmly.

ಬೆಚ್ಚೆಲ್ beċcelu, *see* ಬಚ್ಚೆಲ್.

ಬೆಜಂಟ್ bejaṇṭu, *s.* A dried cake of cow-dung, used as fuel.

ಬೆಜಕಿರೆ, ಬೆಜಕ್ರೆ bejakirè, bejakrè, *s.* Dried leaves, used as fuel.

ಬೆಜಾರ್ bejāru, *see* ಬೇಜಾರ್.

ಬೆಟ್ಟುನಿ beṭṭuni (ಬೆಟ್ಟ್), *v. a.* To cut, circumcise.

ಬೆಟ್ಟೆ beṭṭé, *adj.* Middling. —ನರ ಮಾನಿ a timid or weak man.

ಬೆಡಂಗ್, ಬೆಡಗ್ beḍaṅgu, beḍagu, *s.* Surprise, wonder. 2. *see* ಕೇಲೆ.

ಬೆಡಗುನಿ beḍaguni (ಬೆಡಗ್) *v. n.* To wonder, be surprised. 2. to behave.

ಬೆಡಗೆ beḍage, *s.* A charming man.

ಬೆಡಿ beḍi, *s.* A gun. —ಉಪ್ಪು saltpetre. —ಮರ್ದ್ gunpowder. —ಅಡಕುನಿ, —ದಕ್ಕುನಿ, —ಬುಡ್ಪಿನಿ, —ಪಾಕುನಿ to fire a gun.

ಬೆಡಿಬೆಡಿ beḍebeḍè, *s.* The sound of a broken vessel.

ಬೆಣ್ಣೆ beṇṇè, *see* ಬೆಂಣೆ.

ಬೆತ್ತ್ bettu, *conj.* However, but. 2. afterwards. —ದಾನೆ what then? what news?

ಬೆತ್ತ betta, *s.* A rattan, stick, cane. —ದ ಪಟ್ಟಿಗೆ a rattan basket.

ಬೆತ್ತುನಿ, ಬೆತ್ತೊಣುನಿ bettuni, bettoṇuni, *see* ಬೆಪ್ಪುನಿ.

ಬೆದ್‍ಪು, ಬೆದುಪು bedupu, bedupu, *s.* Erysipelas, an inflammatory eruption.

ಬೆದ್‍ರ್ bedurụ, *s.* A bamboo. —ಸೊಪ್ಪು a kind of grass.

ಬೆದಂಕೆ bedaṅke, *see* ಪೆದಂಕೆ.

ಬೆದರ್, ಬೆದರಿಕೆ bedarụ, bedarikè, *s.* A start, fright, fear, alarm.

ಬೆದರುನಿ bedaruni (ಬೆದರ್), *v. n.* To be alarmed.

ಬೆದಿಯುನಿ bediyuni (ಬೆದ್), *v. n.* To be surprised.

ಬೆದೆ bedè, *s.* Surprise, astonishment, miracle. —ಬೇಂಕೆ fear. —ಆಪಿನಿ, —ಕಟ್ಟುನಿ, —ಪತ್ತುನಿ to be surprised, astonished.

ಬೆನಕೆ benake, *s.* Gaṇeśa. 2. the name of a man; *also* ಬೆನಕಯ್ಯೆ.

ಬೆನ್ನಿ benni, *see* ಬೆಂನಿ.

ಬೆನ್ಪಿನಿ benpini (ಬೆನ್), *v. a.* To labour, work. 2. to cultivate. ಬೆಂದ್ ತಿನ್ಪಿನಿ to support one's self by labour.

ಬೆಪ್ಪು beppu, *s.* Moderate heat, lukewarmness. 2. feverishness. *adj.* Lukewarm. 2. feverish. —ಕೊರ್ಪಿನಿ, —ಮಳ್ಪುನಿ to heaten.

ಬೆಪ್ಪುನಿ beppuni (ಬೆ), *v. a.* To stab.

ಬೆಪ್ಪೆ beppe, *see* ಬಪ್ಪೆ.

ಬೆಬ್ಬೆ bebbè, *s.* Inarticulateness, speaking in broken, indistinct accents.

ಬೆಮರ್ bèmarụ, *see* ಬೆಗರ್.

ಬೆಯಿಪಿನಿ beyipini, *see* ಬೇಪಿನಿ.

ಬೆಯಿಪೆಲ್ beyipelụ, *s.* Boiling. *adj.* Boiled.

ಬೆರಂಕ beraṅka, *s.* Cleft, chink.

ಬೆರಂಕಂಣ್, ಬೆರಂಕಂಣಿ, ಬೆರಕಂಣಿ, ಬೆರಕಣ್ beraṅkaṇṇụ, beraṅkaṇṇi, berakaṇṇi, berakaṇụ, *s.* Cracks on the sole of a foot.

ಬೆರಂಕಲ್ಲ್ beraṅkallụ, *s.* The backbone.

ಬೆರಂಗಡೆ beraṅgaḍè, *adv.* Late, afterwards.

ಬೆರಂಗಯಿ beraṅgayi, *adv.* Finally.

ಬೆರಂಟ್, ಬೆರಂತ್ beranṭu, berantu, *see* ಬೆರ್ಮೆ, ಭ್ರಮೆ. 2. *see* ಭ್ರಾಂತಿ.

ಬೆರಕ beraka, *see* ಬೆರಗ್.

ಬೆರಕೆ berakè, *s.* A mixture, compound. –ಮಳ್ಪುನಿ to mix.

ಬೆರಗ್ beragu, *s.* Wonder, amazement. –ಆಪಿನಿ to be amazed.

ಬೆರಗುನಿ beraguni (ಬೆರಗ್), *v. n.* To be amazed, astonished.

ಬೆರಣೆ beraṇe, *s.* A Brahman.

ಬೆರಮೆ beramè, *see* ಬೆರ್ಮೆ, ಭ್ರಮೆ.

ಬೆರವುನಿ beravuni, *v. n.* To be mixed, mingled.

ಬೆರಸ್ berasu, *s.* An admixture.

ಬೆರಸುನಿ berasuni (ಬೆರಸ್), *v. a.* To mix, mingle.

ಬೆರಿ beri, *s.* The back. –ಮಟ್ಟೆಲ್ the lap, a pouch formed on the back by the folds of a garment. –ನೀರ್ very loose bowels. –ಮುಳ್ಳು the backbone. –ಮೊಡಂಕೆಲ್ hump-backed. –ಸಹಾಯ, *see* ಬೆರಿಸಾಯ. –ಪತ್ತುನಿ to follow, pursue. –ಪಾಡುನಿ to turn back; to flee, run away; to backslide. –ಟೀ, –ಯೀ closely, at the heels, just behind. –ಯಿ ಬರ್ಪಿನಿ to follow closely.

ಬೆರಿಂಕಲ್ಲ್ beriṅkallu, *s.* The backbone.

ಬೆರಿಸಾಯ berisāya, *s.* Support, aid, patronage, strength.

ಬೆರು beru, *s.* A marten.

ಬೆರೆಸುನಿ beresuni, *see* ಬೆರಸುನಿ.

ಬೆರೆಳ್ bereḷu, *see* ಬಿರೆಲ್.

ಬೆರ್ಕೆ berkè, *see* ಬೆರಕೆ. 2. *see* ಬೇರ್. ತಾರೆದ– roots of a cocoanut tree.

ಬೆರ್ತಡಿ, ಬೆರ್ತಳಿ, ಬೆರ್ತಾಳಿ bertaḍi, bertaḷi, bertāḷi, *adv.* Closely behind.

ಬೆರ್ಪುನಿ berpuni, *see* ಬೆಪ್ಪುನಿ.

ಬೆರ್ಪುರಿ berpuri, *s.* A borer.

ಬೆರ್ಮರ bermara, *s.* The fulcrum of a country water-lift.

ಬೆರ್ಮಸ್ಥಾನ bermasthāna, *see* ಬ್ರಹ್ಮಸ್ಥಾನ.

ಬೆರ್ಮೆ bermè, *see* ಭ್ರಮೆ. ನಿನ– by thee (I swear). –ಆಪಿನಿ, –ಪತ್ತುನಿ to be amazed, astonished; to feel giddy.

ಬೆರ್ಮೆ, ಬೆರ್ಮೆರ್ berme, bermeru, *see* ಬ್ರಹ್ಮರೆ. ಬೆರ್ಮೆರೆಗುಡಿ the demon's shrine. ಬೆರ್ಮಸ್ಥಾನ a place haunted by *or* sacred to it.

ಬೆರ್ಮೆತಿ bermeti, *s.* Trouble, annoyance, pain. ರಾಮ– what a wonder!

ಬೆರ್ಸೊಲು, ಬೆರ್ಸೊಳು bersolu, bersoḷu, *s.* A beam resting on the king-post.

ಬೆಲೆ belè, *see* ಬಿಲೆ.

ಬೆಲ್ಚಡೆ belčaḍe, *s.* A devil-dancer; one possessed with Kāḷi.

ಬೆಲ್ಲ bella, *s.* Jaggory. ಅಚ್ಚ– jaggory in tablets, sugarcane-jaggory. ತಾಳೆ– palmyra jaggory. –ದ ರವೆ, –ದ ರಾವೆ syrup *or* boiled juice of sugarcane, treacle.

ಬೆಲ್ಲಪತ್ರೆ bellapatrè, *see* ಬಿಲ್ಪತ್ರೆ.

ಬೆಲ್ಲಮುಳ್ಳು bellamuḷḷu, *s.* A kind of tree.

ಬೆಲ್ಲೊಳ್ಳಿ bellolli, *s.* A tender leaf of a palmyra. 2. *see* ಬೊಳ್ಳುಳ್ಳಿ.

ಬೆವರ್ಶಿ bevarši, *see* ಬೇವಾರಿಶಿ.

ಬೆಸರ್ besarụ, *see* ಬೇಸರ್.

ಬೆಸರ್ಪು, ಬೆಸ್ರಪು, ಬೆಸ್ರುಪು besarpu, besrapu, besrupu, *see* ಬಿದ್ಪು.

ಬೆಸಿಗೆ besigè, *s.* Soldering gold *or* other metal. –ದ ನಗ a soldered ornament. –ಪಾಡುನಿ to solder.

ಬೆಸಿಯುನಿ, ಬೆಸೆಯುನಿ besiyuni, beseyuni (ಬೆಸ್), *v. n.* To get hot. 2. *fig.* to be angry *or* haughty.

ಬೆಸ್ಸುನಿ bessuni, *see* ಬೆಪ್ಪುನಿ.

ಬೆಳಕಾರ beḷakāra, *s.* Borax.

ಬೆಳಗ್ beḷagụ, *s.* Brightness, splendour.

ಬೆಳಗಾವುನಿ beḷagāvuni, *c. v.* (*of* ಬೆಳಗುನಿ) To make shine; to polish.

ಬೆಳಗುನಿ beḷaguni (ಬೆಳಗ್), *v. n.* To shine, glitter.

ಬೇ bē, *pref.* Without, dis–. –ಅಬುರು, –ಯುಬುರು disrespect, dishonour, *etc.*

ಬೇಂಕೆ bēṅkè, *s.* Heat, sultriness. –ಆಪಿನ to become sultry.

ಬೇಂಗರೆ bēṅgarè, *see* ಬಿಂಗರೆ.

ಬೇಂಙ bēṅṅa, *s.* The tree *Pterocarpus tantalinus.*

ಬೇಂಚಿ bēnči, *s.* A bench.

ಬೇಂಟೆ bēṇṭè, *see* ಬೋಂಟೆ.

ಬೇಂತರ್ bēntarụ, *s.* Change of smell *or* taste. *adj.* Unsavoury. –ಮೂರಿ a bad smell, offensive smell of the body.

ಬೇಕಿಲ್, ಬೇಕಿಲೆ, ಬೇಚಿಲ್ bēkilụ, bēkilè, bēčilụ, *s.* The upper part of a roof. –ಅಟ್ಟ the loft of a bath-room, used as a granary. –ಕೊಟ್ಯ a bath-room with such a granary. –ಬಿತ್ತ್ seed stored in such a granary.

ಬೇಖೂಬ್ bēkhūbụ, *adj.* Stupid, senseless. ಬೇಖೂಬಿ a stupid man.

ಬೇಗ bēga, *adv.* Speedily, quickly, soon. *s. see* ವೇಗ.

ಬೇಗಡೆ bēgaḍè, *s.* Tinsel, brass leaf *or* foil.

ಬೇಗಾರಿ bēgāri, *s.* Compulsory labour.

ಬೇಚ್, ಬೇಚು bēčụ, bēču, *see* ಬೇಸ್.

ಬೇಚಿಲ್ bēčilụ, *s.* A kind of pumpkin.

ಬೇಜಾ bējā, *adj.* Improper, inconsistent, unsuitable, bad. –ಕೆಲಸ an improper act.

ಬೇಜಾರ್ bējārụ, *s.* Weariness, fatigue. 2. disgust, offence, vexation, annoyance.

ಬೇಜ್ಞಿ bējñi, *see* ಬಿಂಗ.

ಬೇಟಿ bēṭi, *see* ಭೇಟಿ. 2. *see* ಬೋಂಟೆ.

ಬೇಡವೆ bēḍave, *s.* A fowler. 2. a poor man, beggar.

ಬೇಡಿ bēḍi, *s.* Fetters, chains, hand-cuffs. –ಪಾಡುನಿ to fetter.

ಬೇಡುನಿ bēḍuni (ಬೇಡ್), *v. a.* To beg, ask, beseech, entreat.

ಬೇಡೆ bēḍè, *s.* The keystone of an arch. 2. abounding in thorns.

ಮುಳ್ಳುದ– full of thorns. –ಪಾಡುನಿ to fix the keystone; to finish a work.

ಬೇತಲ್, ಬೇತಾಳ್ bētalu̥, bētāḷu̥, *adj.* Naked. *s.* Nakedness.

ಬೇತಾಳೆ bētāḷe, *s.* A demon supposed to haunt dead bodies and cemeteries.

ಬೇತೆ bētè, *adj.* Separate, different, distinct, other. –ಆಪಿನಿ to become separated. –ಮಳ್ಪುನಿ to separate; to change.

ಬೇದ್ bēdu̥, *s.* Secret information. –ಗಾರೆ, –ದಾಯಿ a spy. –ಕೊರ್ಪಿನಿ to give secret information. –ಗೆಪ್ಪುನಿ to spy, pry. –ಪಿನ್ಪುನಿ to know a secret.

ಬೇದ್, ಬೇದ bēdu̥, bēda, *see* ಭೇದ.

ಬೇದಬು, ಬೇದಾಬ್ bēdabu, bēdābu̥, *s.* Disrespect, incivility, insult. –ಮಳ್ತ್ದ್ ಪಾತೆರುನಿ to speak rudely, *or* insultingly.

ಬೇದಾನ bēdāna, *s.* A kind of medicinal seed.

ಬೇದಿ bēdi, *see* ಭೇದಿ.

ಬೇದಿಗೆ bēdigè, *see* ವೈದಿಕೆ.

ಬೇದುನಿ, ಬೇದ್ಯುನಿ bēduni, bēdyuni (ಬೇದಿ), *v. a.* To leaven dough with toddy. 2. to listen, give ear. ಮರ್ದ್– to apply a medicine.

ಬೇದೊಳಿಗೆ bēdoḷigè, *s.* Cultivated land, fertile land.

ಬೇದೆ bēdè, *see* ಬಿದೆ.

ಬೇನೆ bēnè, *s.* Ache, pain. ತರೆ– headache. ಕಡುಮುಟ್ಟು– severe pain. ಬಂಜಿ– the colic. –ಬರ್ಪಿನಿ to have labour pains.

ಬೇಪಾರ bēpāra, *see* ಬ್ಯಾರ, ವ್ಯಾಪಾರ.

ಬೇಪಾವುನಿ bēpāvuni, *c. v.* (*of* ಬೇಪಿನಿ, ಬೇಪುನಿ) To boil, seethe, cook. 2. to cause to thatch, get thatched, as a roof.

ಬೇಪಿನಿ bēpini (ಬೇ), *v. a.* & *n.* To boil; to be boiled, seethed, cooked.

ಬೇಪು bēpu, *s.* Lurking, spying. 2. a kind of angling.

ಬೇಪುನಿ bēpuni (ಬೇ), *v. a.* To lurk, watch, spy; to betray.

ಬೇಪುನಿ bēpuni (ಬೇ), *v. a.* To thatch the roof of a house, *etc.*

ಬೇಬಂದ್ bēbandu̥, *adj.* Unsettled, without order. 2. negligent, careless.

ಬೇಯಬುರು bēyaburu, *s.* Disrespect, dishonor, insult.

ಬೇಯಿಪಿನಿ bēyipini, *see* ಬೇಪಿನಿ.

ಬೇಯುನಿ bēyuni (ಬೇ), *v. n.* To boil, seethe, be cooked, baked.

ಬೇರ್ bēru̥, *s.* A root. 2. origin, cause. ತಾಯಿ– a root-stalk. ಕೈ– a kind of citron, used in medicine. –ಊರುನಿ, ಬೇರೂರುನಿ to take root, be fixed. –ಕೊರ್ಪಿನಿ to aid, help; to incite, instigate.

ಬೇರ bēra, *see* ಬ್ಯಾರ.

ಬೇರಾವುನಿ bērāvuni, *c. v.* (*of* ಬೇರುನಿ) To lift up the hand for striking. 2. to beck, make a sign with the hand. 3. to row a boat.

ಬೇರಿ bēri, *see* ಭೇರಿ.

ಬೇರುನಿ bēruni (ಬೇರ್), *v. n.* To be waved, lifted up, as the hand. *v. a.* To lift up, as the hand. ತುದರ್–, ನಿನೆ– to trim a light. ಮಂಣ್– to throw *or* pile up earth. ದಂಡ್–, ದೋಣಿ– to row a boat.

ಬೇರೆಂಗೆಟ್ಟಿ bērengeṭṭi, *s.* A large kind of lobster.

ಬೇರೆಜಿ, ಬೇರೋಜಿ bēreji, bērōji, *s.* Land-revenue. 2. amount of assessment.

ಬೇರೆದಮರ bēredamara, *s.* The croton tree. *Croton tiglium.*

ಬೇರ್ಪುರಿ bērpuri, *see* ಬಿರ್ಪುರಿ.

ಬೇಲಾಯುಧ bēlāyudha, *s.* A lance, pike.

ಬೇಲಿ bēli, *s.* A hedge, fence. –ದ ತೂಣ a post *or* pole of a hedge.

ಬೇಲೆ bēlè, *s.* Work, labour; *cf.* ಬೇಳೆ. –ದಾಯಿ a workman. –ಬೆಪ್ಪಿನಿ to work.

ಬೇವಾರಿಶಿ bēvāriši, *adj.* Unclaimed, without a claimant. –ಮಾಲ್ unclaimed property.

ಬೇವು bēvu, *s.* The Neem or margosa tree; *also* ಕೈಬೇವು. 2. *see* ಸೋವು.

ಬೇವುನಿ bēvuni, *see* ಬೇಯುನಿ.

ಬೇವೂರು bēvūru, *s.* A foreign country.

ಬೇಶ್ bēšu, *s.* ಬೇಸ್.

ಬೇಶ bēša, *s.* The second Tuḷu month. –ದ ಪನಿ the first rain. ಅರೆ– hot weather.

ಬೇಶಾಲ bēšāla, *s.* The hot season.

ಬೇಶ್ಯ, ಬೇಷ bēšya, bēsha, *see* ಬೇಶ.

ಬೇಸ್ bēsu, *adj.* Good, proper, well; excellent, agreeable.

ಬೇಸಪ್ಪು bēsappu, *see* ಬೇಸೊಪ್ಪು.

ಬೇಸರ್ bēsaru, *s.* Fatigue, weariness, vexation, disgust. *adj.* Fatigued, weary. –ಆಪಿನಿ to get tired, be weary. –ದೆಪ್ಪುನಿ to rest.

ಬೇಸಾಯ bēsāya, *s.* Cultivation, agriculture, farming; *bet.* ವ್ಯವಸಾಯ.

ಬೇಸಿ bēsi, *see* ಬೇಸ್.

ಬೇಸಿಗೆ, ಬೇಸ್ಯ bēsigè, bēsya, *see* ಬೇಶ.

ಬೇಸುರ್ಪು bēsurpu, *see* ಬಿದ್ಪು.

ಬೇಸೊಪ್ಪು bēsoppu, *s.* The curry leaf *Bergera kœnigii; cf.* ಬೇವು.

ಬೇಳೆ bēḷè, *s.* Split pulse. 2. one-eighth of a rupee. 3. a liquid measure of about six seers.

ಬೈ bei, *s.* Straw. –ತ ಮುಟ್ಟಿ a stack. 2. *see* ಬಾಯಿ. –ದರ್ಪುನಿ to thrash.

ಬೈಂಕು beinku, *adj.* Dull.

ಬೈಂಬಿಗೆ, ಬೈಂಬು beimbigè, beimbu, *s.* A reindear; a boar. 2. *see* ಬೈಮುಗ.

ಬೈಕ್ beiku, *s.* Delay, stay. *adj.* Soft, delicate. *adv.* (*abbrev. of* ಬಯ್ಯಗ್) In the evening.

ಬೈಕಡ್ಡಿ beikaḍḍi, *s.* A female demon so called.

ಬೈಕತ್ತೆ beikattè, *s.* A sickle.

ಬೈಕಲ್ಲ್ beikallu (ಬಾಯಿದಕಲ್ಲ್), *s.* The stone *or* stones at the mouth of a well.

ಬೈಕೆ beikè, *see* ಬಯಕೆ.

ಬೈಚೆರ್ beičeru, *s.* A Malabar physician.

ಬೈಟ್ beiṭu, *s.* Stay, sitting. –ಮಳ್ಪುನಿ to cause to sit.

ಬೈತಡ್ beitaḍu, *s.* A flail, thrashing stick.

ಬೈತಬಾರ್ beitabāru, *s.* An inferior kind of paddy, obtained by beating straw.

ಬೈತರಿ beitari, *s.* A very inferior kind of rice.

ಬೈತಲೆ beitalè, *s.* Vortex, top, summit.

ಬೈದಂಡೆ beidaṇḍè, *s.* A beam put across the mouth of a well to stand upon when drawing water.

ಬೈದುರ್ಳಿ beidurḷi, *see* ಬೈದೆರ್ಲು.

ಬೈದೆ beide, *s.* A toddy-drawer; *fem.* ಬೈದ್ಯೆದಿ.

ಬೈದೆರ್ಲು, ಬೈದೆರ್ಳು beiderlu, beiderḷu, *s.* The demons Kōṭi and Čennaya, said to have been the sons of a Billavar father by a Brahman wife.

ಬೈದ್ಯ beidya, *see* ವೈದ್ಯ.

ಬೈನ, ಬೈನಿ beina, beini, *s.* The bastard sago palm, *Caryota urens.*

ಬೈನಾಳಿ beināḷi, *s.* A demon so called.

ಬೈಪ beipa, *s.* Obliquity, slope. *adj.* Oblique, sloping.

ಬೈಪಣೆ beipaṇè, *s.* A manger.

ಬೈಪಿನಿ, ಬೈಪುನಿ beipini, beipuni (ಬೈ), *v. a.* To chip *or* pare obliquely. 2. to cut, reap. 3. *see* ಜೇಪಿನಿ. 4. *see* ಬೈಯುನಿ.

ಬೈಮುಗ, ಬೈಮುಗೆ beimuga, beimugè, *s.* Shyness; shying.

ಬೈಮೃಗ beimṛga, *s.* A lair.

ಬೈಯ, ಬೈಯ್ಯ beiya, beiyya, *s.* Evening. –ಗ್, –ಡಗ in the evening. –ಮಲ್ಲಿಗೆ the four-o'clock flower, *Mirabilis jalappa.*

ಬೈಯುನಿ beiyuni (ಬೈ), *v. n.* To perch, roost.

ಬೈಯೆಲಿ beiyeli, *s.* Riding. 2. skipping, romping, as boys.

ಬೈರಂಗ beiraṅga, *see* ಬಹಿರಂಗ.

ಬೈರಯೆ, ಬೈರವು, ಬೈರಿಗೆ beirayè, beiravu, beirigè, *s.* An instrument for boring; *cf.* ಬುರ್ಮು.

ಬೈರವೆ beirave, *see* ಭೈರವೆ.

ಬೈರಾಗಿ beirāgi, *s.* An ascetic, mendicant.

ಬೈರಾಸ್ beirāsu, *s.* An upper *or* over cloth, a bath-towel.

ಬೈರಿ beiri, *s.* A kind of kite.

ಬೈರೆ beire, *s.* A man belonging to a class of Pariahs.

ಬೈಲ್ beilu, *s.* A fertile kind of rice-field, situated in a low land which can be easily irrigated. *adj.* Public. –ಆಪಿನಿ to become public.

ಬೈಲಕರೆ, ಬೈಲರೆ, ಬೈಲಾರ್, ಬೈಲಾರೆ beilakarè, beilarè, beilāru, beilārè, *s.* A low land near the seashore.

ಬೈಲ್ಮಣ beilmaṇa, *see* ಬಲ್ಮಣ.

ಬೊಂಕ boṅka, *adj.* Big, large. –ಅಪ್ಪ a large swelling; *also* ಗೋಂತು ಶಿಪ್ಪಿ. –ಶಿಪ್ಪಿ a large cocoanut shell.

ಬೊಂಕಲಿಯುನಿ boṅkaliyuni, *see* ಬೊಂಕೆಲುನಿ.

ಬೊಂಕು boṅku, *adj.* Hollow, void, empty.

ಬೊಂಕುನಿ boṅkuni (ಬೊಂಕ್), *v. a.* To deny.

ಬೊಂಕೆಲುನಿ boṅkeluni (ಬೊಂಕೆಲ್), *v.n.* To swell.

ಬೊಂಗ್, ಬೊಂಗು boṅgu̥, boṅgu, *s.* The inner part of the tender shoot of a cocoanut. 2. a distended navel. 3. a protuberance on any part of the body. 4. a large flower-bud.

ಬೊಂಗುಡೆ boṅguḍè, *see* ಬಂಗುಡೆ.

ಬೊಂಗುನಿ boṅguni (ಬೊಂಗ್), *v. n.* To be distended, protuberate; *also* ಬೊಂಗುದುಪೋಪಿನಿ.

ಬೊಂಡ boṇḍa, *s.* A tender cocoanut. ಗೆಂದಾಳಿ– a red kind of the same.

ಬೊಂಡಲ boṇḍala, *see* ಬೊಂಡೊಲಿ.

ಬೊಂಡಿ boṇḍi, *see* ಬೊಡಿ.

ಬೊಂಡು boṇḍu, *s.* Marrow. 2. the brain. 3. pith. –ಅಲಂಕುನಿ to be stunned. –ಆಪಿನಿ to be emaciated, decayed, become thin.

ಬೊಂಡೊಲಿ boṇḍoli, *s. Physalis Indica.*

ಬೊಂಡೊಲು boṇḍolu, *s.* A kind of medicinal plant.

ಬೊಂಣೆಯಿ boṇṇeyi, (~~*corrup.*~~ = fenne *of* ಬೊಳ್ಳನೆಯಿ) Butter.

ಬೊಂಣ್ಯ boṇṇya, *s.* Ashes.

ಬೊಂತೆಲ್ bontelu̥, *s.* The seventh Tuḷu month; the sign *Libra.*

ಬೊಂದ್, ಬೊಂದು bondu̥, bondu, *s.* Weakness.

ಬೊಂದ, ಬೊಂದ್ಯ bonda, bondya, *s.* A tender branch of a palmyra.

ಬೊಂದೆ, ಬೊಂದೆನ bondè, bondena, *s.* A kind of sardine.

ಬೊಂಪಿರಿ bompiri, *see* ಬೊಂಬುರಿ. *adj.* White.

ಬೊಂಬದೊಟ್ಟೆ bombadoṭṭè, (*corrup. of* ಬೊಂಡದ ಪಟ್ಟೆ) *s.* A tender cocoanut which has been emptied of its contents. –ರಟ್ಟಾವುನಿ to throw it out; to smash, as one's head, *abus.*

ಬೊಂಬಾಯಿ bombāyi, *s.* Bombay.

ಬೊಂಬು bombu, *s.* A large cocoanut shell. 2. *see* ಬೋಂಬು.

ಬೊಂಬುರಿ bomburi, *s.* A small kind of oyster.

ಬೊಂಬುಲಿ bombuli, *s.* A kind of fish, called "Bombay-duck."

ಬೊಂಬುಳಿ bombuḷi, *s.* A mob.

ಬೊಂಬೆ bombè, *s.* A puppet, doll. 2. an image, idol. 3. a silver coin. –ಆಟ a puppet show.

ಬೊಂಮನ bommana, *see* ಬಂಮನ.

ಬೊಂಮರ್ತಾಯೆ bommaru̥tāye, *s.* A demon so called.

ಬೊಂಮಿ bommi, *s.* A stupid woman.

ಬೊಂಮು bommu, *see* ಬೋಂಬು.

ಬೊಂಮೆ bomme, *s.* A simpleton.

ಬೊಂಬಟ್, ಬೊಂಬು bormbaṭu, bormbu, *see* ಬೊಮ್ಮಂಬಟ್ಟೆ.

ಬೊಕ್ಕ bokka, *conj.* And, but. *adj.* Subsequent. *adv.* Afterwards, then, even. —ಲಾ again, again and again. —ದ ಆಲೋಚನೆ an after thought.

ಬೊಕ್ಕಣ bokkaṇa, *s.* A bag, pocket.

ಬೊಕ್ಕಸ bokkasa, *s.* A large bag. 2. a kind of portmanteau. 3. treasure, treasury.

ಬೊಕ್ಕಿ, ಬೊಕ್ಕೆ bokki, bokkè, *s.* An itch, pustule, pimple.

ಬೊಕ್ಕೆಲೆ bokkele, *s.* A provoker.

ಬೊಕ್ಕೊಂಜಿ bokkoñji, *pron., adj.* Another.

ಬೊಕ್ಕೊರಿ bokkori, *pron., adj.* Another.

ಬೊಗರಿ bogari, *s.* A spinning top. 2. *see* ಬೊಗೊರಿ. *adj. see* ಬೋಗರೆ.

ಬೊಗಳಾಟ bogaḷāṭa, *see* ಬಗಳಾಟ.

ಬೊಗಾರಿ bogāri, *s.* A coppersmith.

ಬೊಗೊರಿ bogori, *s.* The jujube tree, *Ziziphus zujuba.*

ಬೊಗೊರಿಮೀನ್ bogorimīnu, *s.* A kind of fish.

ಬೊಗ್ಗಿ boggi, *s.* A bitch.

ಬೊಗ್ಗುಲಿ, ಬೊಗ್ಗುಳಿ, ಬೊಗ್ಗುಳ್ಳಿ bogguli, bogguḷi, bogguḷḷi, *s.* The Indian squill, *Scilla Indica.*

ಬೊಗ್ರೆ bogre, *s.* A dog.

ಬೊಜ್ಜ bojja, *s.* A funeral ceremony *or* feast, funeral obsequies.

ಬೊಟ್ಟ boṭṭa, *s.* A spot, mark. 2. a drop. —ಪಾಡುನಿ to put a mark on the forehead.

ಬೊಟ್ಟಾನ boṭṭāna, *adv.* Excessively, exceedingly. —ಬೊಡಿಯುನಿ, —ಬೊಡಿಪೋಪಿನಿ to be very much exhausted.

ಬೊಟ್ಟಾವುನಿ boṭṭāvuni, *c. v.* (*of* ಬೊಟ್ಟುನಿ) To make beat, as a drum. 2. to cause to hammer, as metal. 3. to cause to knock, as a door.

ಬೊಟ್ಟಿಕಂಡ boṭṭikaṇḍa, *see* ಬೊಟ್ಟುಕಂಡ.

ಬೊಟ್ಟು boṭṭu, *s. see* ಬೊಟ್ಟ. *adj.* High, lofty. 2. dry, as land. —ಕಂಡ a high land, dry field. ತರೆನೀರ್— such a rice-field irrigated by a reservoir situated on a hill. ಬಾನೊ— a rice-field depending solely on rain water for its irrigation.

ಬೊಟ್ಟುನಿ boṭṭuni (ಬೊಟ್ಟಿ), *v. a.* To beat, as a drum. 2. to hammer, as metal. 3. to knock, as a door.

ಬೊಟ್ಟೆಲೆ boṭṭele, *s.* A drummer.

ಬೊಡ boḍa, *see* ಬಡ.

ಬೊಡಿ boḍi, *s.* Satiety, surfeit, loathing, disgust. 2. backwardness. 3. exhaustion, tiredness, fatigue.

ಬೊಡಿಪಾವುನಿ boḍipāvuni, *c. v.* (*of* ಬೊಡಿಯುನಿ) To satiate, cloy, surfeit. 2. to exhaust, tire.

ಬೊಡಿಯುನಿ boḍiyuni (ಬೊಡಿ), *v. n.* To be satiated, cloyed, surfeited. 2. to be tired, done up.

ಬೊಡು boḍu, *see* ಬಡು.

ಬೊಡೆದಿ boḍedi, *s.* A wife.

ಬೊಡ್ಜಿ boḍji, *d.v.* (*neg. of* ಬೋಡು). Must not, should not, do not.

ಬೊಡ್ಡೆ boḍḍe, *s.* A stout man. 2. a simpleton.

ಬೊಣ್ಯ bonya, *see* ಬೊಂಣ್ಯ.

ಬೊದುಂಬಟ್ಟ್ bodumbaṭṭu, *adj.* Stout, corpulent, unwieldy.

ಬೊದುಂಬೆ bodumbe, *s.* A corpulent man.

ಬೊದುಲುನಿ, ಬೊದೊಲುನಿ boduluni, bodoluni (ಬೊದುಲ್, ಬೊದೊಲ್), *v.n.* To soak, steep.

ಬೊನು bonu, *s.* Encompassing, enclosure. —ಗು ಪಾಡುನಿ to encompass.

ಬೊಪ್ಪರ್ bopparu, *see* ಬಪ್ಪರ್.

ಬೊಪ್ಪು, ಬೊಪ್ಪೆ boppu, boppè, *see* ಬಪ್ಪು, ಬಪ್ಪೆ.

ಬೊಪ್ಪೊಣಿ bopponi, *s.* A small kind of crab.

ಬೊಬ್ಬಾಟ, bobbāṭa, *s.* A loud noise of quarrelling, weeping, *or* lamentation; a shout.

ಬೊಬ್ಬುಳಿ bobbuḷi, *s.* A bubble.

ಬೊಬ್ಬುರ್ಸಿ bobbursi, *s.* A cook.

ಬೊಬ್ಬೆ bobbè, *s.* Crying, weeping; *cf.* ಬೊಬ್ಬಾಟ. —ಪಾಡುನಿ to cry out.

ಬೊಮ್ಮನ bommana, *see* ಬಂಮನ.

ಬೊರಂಬು borambu, *s.* A small kind of mat.

ಬೊರಿಪಿನಿ boripini (ಬೊರಿ), *v.a.* To milk.

ಬೊರಿಯುನಿ boriyuni (ಬೊರಿ), *v.n.* To yield milk. *v.a.* To pillage, plunder, rob.

ಬೊರು boru, *s.* Brag, boast. —ತಾಯಿ a braggart.

ಬೊರುಕಲ್ಲ್, ಬೊರ್ಕಲ್ಲ್ borukallu, borkallu, *see* ಬೊಳ್ಕಲ್ಲ್.

ಬೊರ್ಕುಡೆ, ಬೊರ್ಗುಡೆ borkuḍè, borguḍè, *see* ಬೊಲ್ಕುಡೆ.

ಬೊರ್ಚು borču, *see* ಬೊಳ್ಚಿ.

ಬೊರ್ದು bordu, *see* ಪೊರ್ದು.

ಬೊಲ್ bolu, *adj.* White, bright.

ಬೊಲ್ಂಬು bolumbu, *see* ಬೊಳುಂಬು.

ಬೊಲಂಕರುನಿ, ಬೊಲಂಕುರಿಯುನಿ bolaṅkaruni, bolaṅkuriyuni (ಬೊಲಂಕರ್, ಬೊಲಂಕುರ್), *v. n.* To be intoxicated, fascinated; to be lustful, proud.

ಬೊಲಕ್ bolaku, *see* ಬೊಳಕ್.

ಬೊಲಕುನಿ bolakuni (ಬೊಲಕ್), *v. a.* To weld, solder.

ಬೊಲ್ಕರ bolkara, *adj.* Whitish.

ಬೊಲ್ಕಲ್ಲ್ bolkallu, *see* ಬೊಳ್ಕಲ್ಲ್.

ಬೊಲ್ಕುಡೆ, ಬೊಲ್ಗುಡೆ bolkuḍè, bolguḍè, *s.* A small umbrella, used in demon worship.

ಬೊಲ್ಚಯಿ bolčayi, *adj.* Pale, wan.

ಬೊಲ್ಚಿ bolči, *adj.* White. 2. *see* ಬೊಳ್ಚಿ.

ಬೊಲ್ಚುನಿ bolčuni, *see* ಬೊಳ್ಚುನಿ.

ಬೊಲ್ಚೆಲ್ bolčèlu, *see* ಬೊಳ್ಚಿ.

ಬೊಲ್ದು boldu, *see* ಬೊಳ್ದು.

ಬೊಲ್ಯರಿ bolyari, *s.* A kind of rice.

ಬೊಲ್ಲಿ bolli, *s. see* ಬೊಳ್ಳಿ. *adj. see* ಬೊಲ್ದು.

ಬೊಲ್ಲೆ bollè, *s.* A white kind of lice, found on clothes.

ಬೊಳ್ boḷụ, *see* ಬೊಲ್.

ಬೊಳ್ಂಗರೆ boḷụṅgarè, *adj.* White.

ಬೊಳಂಕ್ boḷaṅkụ, *s.* Mire, mud.

ಬೊಳಂತೆ boḷanté, *s.* Rice from paddy that has not been boiled; *also* ಬೊಳಂತ್ಯರಿ.

ಬೊಳಂಬು boḷambu, *see* ಬೊಜ್ಜ.

ಬೊಳಕ್ boḷakụ, *s.* The fat of fish; fish-tar.

ಬೊಳಕರ್ boḷakarụ, *adj.* Partially *or* nearly ripe.

ಬೊಳಕುನಿ boḷakuni, *see* ಬೊಲಕುನಿ.

ಬೊಳಚ್ಚೆಲ್ boḷaččelụ, *s.* Shying. 2. ripening. 3. paleness.

ಬೊಳಜ್ಜಿ boḷajji, *see* ಬೊಜ್ಜಿ.

ಬೊಳಪು boḷapu, *s.* A mode of catching fish with a net fringed with palm leaves. –ವೈಪುನಿ to fish with such a net.

ಬೊಳಯೆ boḷaye, *s. lit.* A white man. 2. an epithet used by Pariahs in addressing higher castes of people.

ಬೊಳಸುನಿ boḷasuni, *see* ಬಳಸುನಿ.

ಬೊಳಿಂಜಿರ್ boḷiñjirụ, *s.* A small, white kind of fish, called *cara pao.* 2. a kind of grass.

ಬೊಳಿರ್ boḷirụ, *s.* A kind of bush. –ತಪ್ಪು its leaves used in medicine.

ಬೊಳಿರುನಿ boḷiruni (ಬೊಳಿರ್), *v. n.* To become white *or* clear.

ಬೊಳಿಸುನಿ boḷisuni, *see* ಬೋಳಿಸುನಿ.

ಬೊಳು boḷu, *see* ಬೊರು. 2. *see* ಬೊಳ್ದು.

ಬೊಳುಂಬು boḷumbu, *s.* Alburnum, sapwood.

ಬೊಳುಪ್ಪು boḷuppu, *s.* White salt.

ಬೊಳುಬೇನೆ boḷubēnè, *s.* Severe colic.

ಬೊಳೆನ boḷena, *see* ಬೊಳ್ಳೆನ.

ಬೊಳೆಪುನಿ boḷepuni, *see* ಬುಳೆಪುನಿ.

ಬೊಳೆರುನಿ boḷeruni (ಬೊಳೆರ್), *v. n.* To become pale, to fade.

ಬೊಳ್ಕಲ್ಲ್ boḷkallụ, *s.* White stone, quartz. 2. marble, alabaster.

ಬೊಳ್ಕಿರ್ boḷkirụ, *s.* Clearing of the sky from clouds; a peep of the sun after shower. –ಕಾಯುನಿ to have sunshine after rainy weather.

ಬೊಳ್ಕುಡೆ, ಬೊಳ್ಗುಡೆ boḷkuḍè, boḷguḍè, *see* ಬೊಲ್ಕುಡೆ.

ಬೊಳ್ಚಾವುನಿ boḷčāvuni, *c. v.* (*of* ಬೊಳ್ಚುನಿ) To make shy.

ಬೊಳ್ಚಿ boḷči, *s.* Shyness, starting aside suddenly.

ಬೊಳ್ಚುನಿ boḷčuni (ಬೊಳ್ಚಿ), *v. n.* To shy, start aside suddenly, as an animal.

ಬೊಳ್ಚೆಲ್ boḷčelụ, *see* ಬೊಳ್ಚಿ.

ಬೊಳ್ಜಾತಿ boḷjāti, *s.* High-caste people. 2. white people.

ಬೊಳ್ಜಿ boḷji, *s.* The middle layer of fibre of a cocoanut branch.

ಬೊಳ್ತು boḷtu, *adj.* Sapless. –ದ ಮರ a sapless tree *or* wood.

ಬೊಳ್ದು boḷdu, *s.* Whiteness, brightness. 2. whites. *adj.* White, bright. –ಕೊಪ್ಪ the white leprosy. —ಪೋಪಿನಿ to suffer from whites.

ಬೊಳ್ಪು bolpu, *s.* Light. 2. a wick *or* candle. —ಕೊಚ್ಚಾವುನಿ, —ಮಳ್ಪುನಿ to kindle a light, *etc.*

ಬೊಳ್ಯ bolya, *adj.* Light, white, clear. —ನೆಯಿ butter.

ಬೊಳ್ಯಂಬಿಗೆ bolyambigè, *s.* Fæces, excrement.

ಬೊಳ್ಳ bolla, *s.* Inundation, flood.

ಬೊಳ್ಳಕರ್ bollakaru, *see* ಬೊಳಕರ್.

ಬೊಳ್ಳಡ್ಡಿ bolladdi, *fem. of* ಬೊಳ್ಳಳ್.

ಬೊಳ್ಳರಮಾಣಿಗ bollaramāniga, *s.* A kind of bird.

ಬೊಳ್ಳರೆ bollarè, *adj.* White.

ಬೊಳ್ಳಳ್ bollalu, *see* ಬಲ್ಲಾಳ್. 2. a family-title.

ಬೊಳ್ಳಿ bolli, *s.* A star. 2. silver. 3. three annas. 4. a gray ox. —ನೂಲು silver thread *or* girdle.

ಬೊಳ್ಳುಕಲ್ಲ್ bollukallu, *see* ಬೊಳ್ಕಲ್ಲ್.

ಬೊಳ್ಳುಳ್ಳಿ bollulli, *s.* Garlic.

ಬೊಳ್ಳೆ bollè, *s.* A white cock. 2. a gray *or* white ox *or* buffalo. 3. a kind of medicinal plant, *Mussænda frondosa.* 4. *see* ಬೊಲ್ಲೆ.

ಬೊಳ್ಳೆಂತರಿ bollentari, *see* ಬೊಳಂತೆ.

ಬೊಳ್ಳೆಂತಿ bollenti, *adj.* White.

ಬೊಳ್ಳೆನ bollena, *s.* A white substance. *adj.* Whitish. —ದಾಯೆ a fair man.

ಬೊಳ್ಳೆರಡುನಿ bolleraduni (ಬೊಳ್ಳೆರಡ್), *v. n.* To be heated to a white point.

ಬೊಳ್ಳೆರಿ bolleri, *s.* A kind of leprosy.

ಬೋಂಕ bōnka, *adj.* Large, great. —ತಿಪ್ಪಿ a large cocoanut shell.

ಬೋಂಗು bōngu, *see* ಬೊಂಗ್.

ಬೋಂಜಿರ್ bōñjiru, *see* ಬೊಳಂಜಿರ್.

ಬೋಂಟೆ bōntè, *s.* Hunting, chase. —ದಾಯೆ a hunter. —ಬಾರ hunting of wild beasts. —ಮಳ್ಪುನಿ to hunt.

ಬೋಂತ್ರೆ bōntre, *s.* A head man.

ಬೋಂದಲೆ, ಬೋಂದೆ bōndale, bōnde, *s.* A stout, corpulent man.

ಬೋಂಬಿಲ್ bōmbilu, *s.* A hollow. —ಬೂರುನಿ to become hollow.

ಬೋಂಬು bōmbu, *s.* A fire-engine. 2. a metallic instrument for tapping bales of rice, *etc.*

ಬೋಗ bōga, *see* ಭೋಗ.

ಬೋಗರೆ bōgarè, *adj.* Not quite true, fictitious, unreal. —ದುಖ್ಖ unreal hardships. —ದುಖ್ಖಪಾತೆರುನಿ to speak of hardships which are not fully true.

ಬೋಗರೆ bōgare, *s.* A coppersmith.

ಬೋಗಿ bōgi, *see* ಭೋಗಿ.

ಬೋಗಿಯುನಿ bōgiyuni (ಬೋಗಿ), *v. n.* To be enjoyed.

ಬೋಗುಣಿ bōguni, *s.* A small saucepan.

ಬೋಜ bōja, *s.* Excellence, greatness, loftiness. 2. pride. 3. salutation, obeisance.

ಬೋಜನ bōjana, *see* ಭೋಜನ.

ಬೋಟೆ bōtè, *see* ಬೋಂಟೆ.

ಬೋಡು bōdu, *d. v., c. dat.* To want, wish, desire. 2. to be requisite, necessary, must.

ಎಂಕ್— I want. ದಾಯೆಗ್— why wanted? ಬೋಡಾದ್ for the sake of, on account of, purposely; obstinately. ಬೋಡಾಯಿ needful, required. ಬೋಡಾಪಿನಾತ್, ಬೋಡಾಯಿನಾತ್ sufficient, ample; *cf.* ಬೊಡ್ಡಿ.

ಬೋಡುಬಾಯಿ **bōḍubāyi,** *s.* A teethless mouth.

ಬೋಣಿ **bōṇi,** *s.* Handsel, the first money a trader receives *or* the first bargain he effects in the morning. —ಮಳ್ಪುನಿ to take handsel.

ಬೋಣು **bōṇu,** *see* ಬೊನು.

ಬೋತಿರಿ, ಬೋತ್ರಿ **bōtiri, bōtri,** *see* ಬೊಡ್ಡಿ.

ಬೋದ **bōda,** *see* ಬೋಧ.

ಬೋದಿಗೆ **bōdigè,** *s.* The capital of a pillar. 2. architrave.

ಬೋದು **bōdu,** *s.* The dung of an ox *or* buffalo; *also* ಬೋಮು ಅಂಬಿ.

ಬೋದೆ **bōde,** *see* ಬೋಂದಲೆ.

ಬೋಧ **bōdha,** *s.* Intellect, understanding. 2. awakening, arousing. —ತಪ್ಪುನಿ to swoon, be out of senses. —ಬರ್ಪಿನಿ to come to senses.

ಬೋಧಕೆ **bōdhake,** *s.* A teacher, preacher.

ಬೋಧನೆ **bōdhanè,** *s.* Instruction, teaching, advice, persuasion, exhortation, incitement, inducement.

ಬೋಧಿಪುನಿ, ಬೋಧಿಸುನಿ **bōdhipuni, bōdhisuni** (ಬೋಧಿ, ಬೋಧಿಸ್) *v. a.* To instruct, teach, advise, admonish, incite, induce, exhort.

ಬೋಧೆ **bōdhè,** *see* ಬೋಧನೆ.

ಬೋನ್ಗಿರಿ **bōnṇgiri,** *s.* A variety in kāṅgu cloth; *cf.* ಕಾಂಗ್.

ಬೋನ **bōna,** *s.* Food. 2. boiled rice and ashes mixed into a paste for applying to the left side of a finger-drum.

ಬೋನಿ **bōni,** *see* ಬೋಣಿ.

ಬೋನು **bōnu,** *see* ಬೊನ.

ಬೋಯಿ **bōyi,** *s.* A class of fishermen who are also palankin bearers.

ಬೋರ್ **bōrụ,** *see* ಬೋರು.

ಬೋರ **bōra,** *see* ಬೂರುಗ.

ಬೋರಪ್ಪ **bōrappa,** *adv.* All, fully.

ಬೋರಿ **bōri,** *s.* A bull *or* ox.

ಬೋರು **bōru,** *adj.* Bald, bare, shaven; uncovered. —ಗುಡ್ಡೆ a barren hill. —ಚೊಕ್ಕನ an empty bag. —ಮಂಡೆ a bald head.

ಬೋರುನಿ **bōruni** (ಬೊರ್), *v. a.* To shave, shear, strip off. ತರೆ— to shave the head. ಮರ— to strip the branches of a tree.

ಬೋರೆ **bōrè,** *s.* The top of a hill.

ಬೋರ್ಯುನಿ **bōryuni** (ಬೋರ್), *v. a.* To assault *or* butt, as an ox *or* wild beast.

ಬೋರ್ದು **bōrdu,** *s.* The side of a ship.

ಬೋರ್ನು **bōrnu,** *adj.* Sluggish, lazy.

ಬೋರ್ನೆ **bōrne**, *s*. A sluggard, *or* vagabond.

ಬೋರ್ಯುನಿ **bōryuni**, *see* ಬೋರ್ರ್ಯುನಿ.

ಬೋರ್ಲು **bōrlu**, (*pl. of* ಬೋರಿ). 2. *see* ಬೋರು.

ಬೋಲ **bōla**, *see* ಬೋಳ.

ಬೋಲಿ, ಬೋಲೆ **bōli, bōlè**, *see* ಬೋಳಿ, ಬೋಳೆ.

ಬೋವಿ **bōvi**, *see* ಬೋಯಿ.

ಬೋವು **bōvu**, *s*. The tree *Vatico bardifera*. ಕರಿ– black kind of the same. ಬೊಳ್ದು– a white kind of the same.

ಬೋಳ **bōḷa**, *s*. Myrrh. 2. a kind of medicine composed of ghee, jaggory, cocoanut milk, *etc*.

ಬೋಳಸುನಿ **bōḷasuni**, *see* ಬೋರುನಿ. 2. *see* ಬೋಳೈಸುನಿ.

ಬೋಳಿ **bōḷi**, *s*. A widow whose head has been shorn.

ಬೋಳಿಸುನಿ **bōḷisuni** (ಬೋಳಿಸ್), *v.a.* To shave, shear, strip off; *cf*. ಬೋರುನಿ.

ಬೋಳು **bōḷu**, *adj*. Bald, close shaven. 2. hornless, though of an age to have them.

ಬೋಳುನಿ **bōḷuni** (ಬೋಳ್), *v.n*. To become bald. 2. *see* ಬೋರುನಿ.

ಬೋಳೆ **bōḷè**, *s*. The seeds of a jack fruit. 2. a bald head. ಕಂಣ್ಣದ– the eyeball. –ಕಣ್ಣ್ large eyes. –ಪೀಂಕಾವುನಿ to remove the seeds of a jack fruit; to put out the eyes.

ಬೋಳೈಸುನಿ **bōḷeisuni** (ಬೋಳೈಸ್), *v.a.* To coax. 2. to strip; *cf*. ಬೋಳಿಸುನಿ.

ಬೋಳ್ಕಾಳ್ಮುಂಚಿ **bōḷkāḷumuñci**, *s*. A smooth species of pepper.

ಬೌಣೆ **bouṇè**, *see* ಬವ.

ಬೌಧೆ **boudhe**, *see* ಬುದ್ಧ.

ಬೌರು **bouru**, *s*. The snarling of dogs and cats. 2. frowning, threatening.

ಬೌರುನಿ, ಬೌರೊತ್ತುನಿ **bouruni, bourottuni** (ಬೌರ್, ಬೌರೊತ್ತ್), *v.n.* To snarl, as a dog *or* cat. 2. to frown, threaten; *cf*. ಬಿಗೊಣತ್ತುನಿ.

ಬೌಲಣೆ **boulaṇè**, *s*. Speaking loudly.

ಬೌಲಿ **bouli**, *see* ಬಾವೊಲಿ.

ಬೌಶ, ಬೌಸ್, ಬೌಸು **bouša, bousu, bousu**, *see* ಭವಿಷ್ಯ.

ಬೌಳ **bouḷa**, *see* ಬಹುಳ.

ಬ್ಯಾಬುರು **byāburu**, *see* ಬೇಯುಬುರು.

ಬ್ಯಾರ **byāra**, *s*. Trade. –ಮಳ್ಪುನಿ to trade.

ಬ್ಯಾರಿ **byāri**, *s*. A Māpla, a Malayālam speaking Mahommedan.

ಬ್ಯಾರಿಬಿತ್ತ್ **byāribittu**, *s*. The croton seed.

ಬ್ರಮಾಂಡ **bramāṇḍa**, *see* ಬ್ರಹ್ಮಾಂಡ.

ಬ್ರಮೆ **bramè**, *see* ಭ್ರಮೆ.

ಬ್ರಷ್ಟ **brashṭa**, *see* ಭ್ರಷ್ಟ.

ಬ್ರಹ್ಮ **brahma**, *s*. The Divine Cause *or* essence of the world, the unknown God. 2. sacred knowledge. –ಚಾರಿ a religious student; a bachelor of the twice-born class. –ಸ್ಥಾನ the vital part in the head.

ಬ್ರಹ್ಮರೆ **brahmare,** *s.* A demon of the brahmanical class; *also* ಬ್ರಹ್ಮರಾಕ್ಷಸಿ.

ಬ್ರಹ್ಮಸ್ಥಾನ **brahmasthāna,** *s.* A shrine of the Brahmara demon.

ಬ್ರಹ್ಮಾಂಡ **brahmāṇḍa,** *s.* The universe. *adj.* Very much, many, abundant, excessive, immense.

ಬ್ರಾಂಡಿ **brāṇḍi,** *s.* Brandy.

ಬ್ರಾಂತ್, ಬ್ರಾಂತಿ **brāntu, brānti,** *see* ಭ್ರಾಂತಿ.

ಬ್ರಾಂದಿ **brāndi,** *s.* A Brahman woman.

ಬ್ರಾಣೆ **brāṇe,** *s.* A Brahman.

ಭ Bh

ಭ **bha,** The thirty-seventh letter of the alphabet.

ಭಂಗ **bhaṅga,** *s.* Loss, injury. 2. affliction, trouble. 3. defeat, disgrace, degradation. ಮಾನ– loss of reputation, disgrace. –ಕೊಡ್ಪಿನಿ to annoy, afflict. –ಪಡೆಯುನಿ to be disgraced, molested, troubled.

ಭಂಗಾಟ **bhaṅgāṭa,** *s.* Affliction upon affliction, extreme distress.

ಭಂಗಾರ್, ಭಂಗಾರ **bhaṅgāru, bhaṅgāra,** *s.* Gold.

ಭಂಗಿ **bhaṅgi,** *s.* Hemp, *Cannabis sativa.*

ಭಂಗಿಟಪ್ಪಾಲ್ **bhaṅgiṭappālu,** *see* [ಬಂಘು.

ಭಂಙ **bhañña,** *see* ಭಂಗ.

ಭಂಜನೆ **bhañjanė,** *s.* Destruction. 2. breaking, splitting.

ಭಂಡ್ **bhaṇḍu,** *s.* Obscenity, rudeness.

ಭಂಡ **bhaṇḍa,** *adj.* Obscene, rude, filthy, impudent. –ತನ obscenity.

ಭಂಡಾಟಿಗೆ, ಭಂಡಾಟ **bhaṇḍāṭigė, bhaṇḍāṭa,** *s.* Obscenity, rudeness, impudence.

ಭಂಡಾರ **bhaṇḍāra,** *s.* A treasury; treasure.

ಭಂಡಾರಿ **bhaṇḍāri,** *s.* A treasurer. 2. a family-title.

ಭಂಡಿ **bhaṇḍi,** *s.* A cart. 2. a small car on which an idol is drawn.

ಭಂಡೆ **bhaṇḍe.** *s.* A rake, lewd man. 2. an indecent man.

ಭಕ್ತಿ **bhakti,** *s.* Devotion, piety, zeal, worship, faith, godliness. –ಹೀನತೆ, –ಹೀನತ್ವ ungodliness. –ಹೀನೆ an ungodly man. –ಮಳ್ಪುನಿ to be devoted to; to worship.

ಭಕ್ತೆ **bhakte,** *s.* A pious *or* devout [man.

ಭಗಂದಲ **bhagandala,** *see* ಬಗಂದರ.

ಭಗವಂತೆ **bhagavante,** *s.* God, the Supreme Being.

ಭಗವತ್‌ಗೀತೆ **bhagavatugītė,** *s.* A theosophical poem represented as spoken by Kṛushṇa.

ಭಗವತಿ **bhagavati**, *s.* A goddess. 2. Pārvati, *etc.*

ಭಗೀರಥ **bhagīratha**, *adj.* Of *or* pertaining to Bhagīratha. –ದಾಯಿ an enterprising man. –ಪ್ರಯತ್ನ great exertions like those of Bhagīratha.

ಭಗೀರಥೆ **bhagīrathe**, *s.* A king who is said to have, after great exertions brought the Ganges down from heaven.

ಭಗ್ತಲೆ **bhagtalè**, *see* ಬಕ್ತಲೆ.

ಭಗ್ನ **bhagna**, *adj.* Broken, ruptured. 2. overcome, defeated.

ಭಜಕೆ **bhajake**, *s.* A devoted man.

ಭಜನೆ **bhajanè**, *s.* Adoration, worship, homage. 2. a singing service.

ಭಜಭಜ **bhajabhaja**, *see* ಬಜಬಜ.

ಭಜಿಪುನಿ, ಭಜಿಸುನಿ **bhajipuni, bhājisuni** (ಭಜಿ), *v. a.* To adore, worship.

ಭಟೆ **bhaṭe**, *s.* A hero, valiant man.

ಭಟ್ಟಿ **bhaṭṭi**, *see* ಬಟ್ಟಿ.

ಭಟ್ಟೆ **bhaṭṭe**, *s.* A priest. 2. a soothsayer.

ಭತ್ತೆ, ಭತ್ಯ **bhattè, bhatya**, *s.* Extra allowance, batta; travelling allowance. –ಕೊರ್ಪಿನಿ to pay extra allowance. –ಲಪ್ಪುನಿ to pay the same in kind.

ಭದ್ರ **bhadra**, *s.* Care, precaution. 2. safety, security. *adj.* Careful, attentive. 2. safe, secure.

ಭದ್ರಕಾಳಿ **bhadrakāḷi**, *s.* A form of Kāḷi.

ಭದ್ರಮುಷ್ಟಿ **bhadramushṭi**, *s.* The aromatic grass-root, *Cyperus hexastachyus*, used in medicine.

ಭದ್ರಾಸನ **bhadrāsana**, *s.* A throne.

ಭದ್ರಿಕೆ **bhādrikè**, *see* ಭದ್ರ.

ಭಯ **bhaya**, *s.* Fear, alarm, fright, timidity. –ರಹಿತೆ a fearless man. –ಭರಿತ full of fear, alarmed, terrified. –ಪಡೆವುನಿ to be afraid.

ಭಯಂಕರ **bhayaṅkara**, *adj.* Frightful, formidable, terrific.

ಭರ **bhara**, *s.* Swiftness, speed. ನಡಪು– swiftness of walking.

ಭರಣ **bharaṇa**, *see* ಭರ್ತಿ.

ಭರಣಿ **bharaṇi**, *s.* The second lunar mansion. 2. *see* ಬರಣಿ.

ಭರತ **bharata**, *see* ಭರ್ತ.

ಭರತೆ **bharate**, *s.* A younger brother of Rāma. 2. a celebrated dramatist. 3. the son of Dušyanta by Šakuntala. ಭರತಖಂಡ India proper. ಭರತಶಾಸ್ತ್ರ a standard work on dramaturgy.

ಭರಪೂರ್ **bharapūrụ**, *adj.* Full; brimful; crowded.

ಭರವಸ **bharavasa**, *s.* Confidence, trust; assurance. –ಕೊರ್ಪಿನಿ to assure. –ದೀಪಿನಿ, –ಮಳ್ಪುನಿ to trust, confide in.

ಭರಿತ **bharita**, *adj.* Full, replete, completed.

ಭರ್ಕೆ **bharkè**, *see* ಬರ್ಕೆ.

ಭರ್ತ, ಭರ್ತಿ **bharta, bharti**, *s.* The high tide, flow.

ಭರ್ತಿ, ಭರ್ತೆ bharti, bhartè, *s.* Fulness, completion. *adj.* Full, complete.

ಭಲ್ಲೆ bhalle, *s.* A spear.

ಭವನ bhavana, *s.* A house, dwelling.

ಭವ bhava, *s.* Mundane existence. —ರೋಗ sickness of worldly pleasures.

ಭವಿಷ್ಯತ್ bhavishyatu, *s.* Future, about to be. —ಕಾಲ the future tense.

ಭಸ್ಮ bhasma, *s.* Ashes. 2. calx. —ಆಪಿನಿ to be burnt to ashes; to be digested, as food.

ಭಕ್ಷ, ಭಕ್ಷಣ bhaksha, bhakshaṇa, *s.* Feeding, eating.

ಭಕ್ಷ, ಭಕ್ಷ್ಯ bhaksha, bhakshya, *s.* Dressed food. 2. a cake.

ಭಕ್ಷಕೆ bhakshake, *s.* An eater. 2. a glutton. ನರ— a cannibal. ಮಾಂಸ— a meat-eater.

ಭಕ್ಷಿಪುನಿ, ಭಕ್ಷಿಸುನಿ bhakshipuni, bhakshisuni (ಭಕ್ಷಿ, ಭಕ್ಷಿಸ್), *v. a.* To eat, devour.

ಭಾಂಡ bhāṇḍa, *s.* Any earthen vessel. 2. a bundle, load. 3. capital, principal.

ಭಾಗ bhāga, *s.* Portion, share, part. 2. side, part. —ಮಳ್ಪುನಿ to divide, distribute.

ಭಾಗವತ bhāgavata, *s.* One of the Purāṇas.

ಭಾಗವತೆ bhāgavate, *s.* A pious man. 2. the manager of a theatre.

ಭಾಗಾಕಾರ bhāgākāra, *s.* Division, *arith.*

ಭಾಗಾತೆ, ಭಾಗಾಯತಿ bhāgātè, bhāgāyati, *see* ಬಾಗಾಯಿತಿ.

ಭಾಗಿಪುನಿ, ಭಾಗಿಸುನಿ bhāgipuni, bhāgisuni (ಭಾಗಿ, ಭಾಗಿಸ್), *v. a.* To divide, distribute.

ಭಾಗೀರಥಿ bhāgīrathi, *s.* The Ganges.

ಭಾಗ್ಯ bhāgya, *s.* Riches, wealth. 2. felicity; fortune. 3. bliss. —ವಂತೆ a rich man; a blissful man.

ಭಾಜಕ bhājaka, *s.* The divisor, *arith.*

ಭಾಜನ bhājana, *see* ಬಾಜನ.

ಭಾಜ್ಯ bhājya, *s.* The dividend, *arith.*

ಭಾದ್ರಪದ bhādrapada, *s.* The sixth lunar month.

ಭಾನು bhānu, *s.* The sun. —ವಾರ Sunday.

ಭಾಮಿನಿ bhāmini, *s.* A virtuous wife.

ಭಾರ bhāra, *s.* A weight, load, burden. 2. charge, *onus.* 3. oppression, heaviness, as in sickness. 4. importance, consequence. *adj.* Heavy. 2. responsible. 3. oppressive. 4. important. ರಾಜ್ಯ— government, administration.

ಭಾರತ bhārata, *s.* A great epic poem of the Hindus, treating of the adventures of the Pāṇḍus and Kurus, *etc.*

ಭಾರತಿ bhārati, *s.* Sarasvati, goddess of speech.

ಭಾರಿ bhāri, *adj.* Important, serious. 2. great, huge. *s. see* ಬಾರಿ. —ನರಮಾನಿ a great man.

ಭಾವ bhāva, *s.* The eighth year in the Hindu cycle of sixty. 2. nature, condition of being, disposition. 3. meaning, purpose, intention, mind.

ಭಾವನೆ bhāvanè, *s.* Mental perception.

ಭಾವಾರ್ಥ bhāvārtha, *s.* Design, purport, intention.

ಭಾವಿ bhāvi, *s.* A well. 2. future.

ಭಾವಿಪುನಿ, ಭಾವಿಸುನಿ bhāvipuni, bhāvisuni (ಭಾವಿ, ಭಾವಿಸ್), *v. a.* To think, imagine, intend.

ಭಾವೆ bhāve, *s.* A brother-inlaw.

ಭಾಶೆ, ಭಾಷೆ bhāšè, bhāshè, *s.* Speech, language. 2. reproof, reprimand. –ಪಣ್ಪುನಿ to reprove. –ಬರ್ಪಿನಿ to be able to speak.

ಭಾಷಾಂತರ bhāshāntara, *s.* A translation, interpretation. –ಮಳ್ಪುನಿ to translate.

ಭಾಷಿಂಗ bhāshinga, *see* ಬಾಶಿಂಗ.

ಭಿಂನ bhinna, *adj.* Split, broken, mutilated. 2. divided, distinguished, other, different.

ಭಿಕಾರಿ bhikāri, *s.* A beggar. 2. a pauper, vagabond.

ಭಿಕ್ಷ bhiksha, *see* ಭಿಕ್ಷೆ.

ಭಿಕ್ಷಾಟ, ಭಿಕ್ಷಾಟಣೆ bhikshāṭa, bhikshāṭaṇè, *s.* Begging, asking. 2. wandering in quest of charity.

ಭಿಕ್ಷೆ bhikshè, *s.* Alms, charity. 2. begging. –ಗಾರೆ a beggar. –ನಟ್ಟುನಿ to beg alms.

ಭೀಕರ bhīkara, *adj.* Terrible, fearful, formidable, frightful.

ಭೀತಿ bhīti, *s.* Fear.

ಭೀಮೆ bhīme, *s.* The second of the Pāṇḍu princes.

ಭುಕ್ತ bhukta, *adj.* Eaten. ಏಕ– taking only one meal a day.

ಭುಕ್ತಿ bhukti, *s.* Eating. 2. food, a meal. [Ashes.

ಭುಕ್ತಿ, ಭುಗ್ತಿ bhukti, bhugti, *s.*

ಭುಜ bhuja, *s.* The arm. –ಬಲ ability.

ಭುಜಂಗ bhujanga, *s.* A serpent. 2. a libertine.

ಭುಜಿಪುನಿ bhujipuni, *see* ಭಕ್ಷಿಪುನಿ.

ಭುವನ bhuvana, *s.* The world.

ಭುಸ್ಸು bhussu, *s.* The hissing of a serpent. 2. panting.

ಭೂ bhū, *s.* The earth. –ಕಂಪ, –ಕಂಪನ an earthquake. –ಗೋಳ, –ಮಂಡಲ the earth, terrestrial globe. –ನಾಗೆ a worm. –ಪಠ a map. –ಪತಿ, –ಪಾಲೆ, –ಪೆ a king.

ಭೂತ bhūta, *s.* A goblin, ghost. 2. matter of fact, what has really been. *adj.* Been, become. 2. gone, past. –ಕಂಕೆ, –ಕಾರ್, –ಕೈ, –ಬಗೆ medicinal plants so called respectively. –ಕಾಲ the past tense. –ದರಿಪು ನಾಯಿ a devil dancer. –ಪ್ರೊಲ್ a malignant abscess. –ವಿದ್ಯೆ necromancy.

ಭೂತಳ bhūtaḷa, *s.* The surface of the earth.

ಭೂತಾಳಪಾಂಡೆ bhūtāḷapāṇḍe, *s.* The promulgator of the law of nepotism *or* inheritance of a person's property by his sister's children. ಭೂತಾಳಪಾಂಡಿ ಕಟ್ಟು the law of nepotism.

ಭೂತಾಳಿ bhūtāḷi, *see* ಅಲಡೆ. 2. a species of aloe.

ಭೂಮಿ **bhūmi**, *s*. The earth *or* world. 2. land, soil, ground. 3. a place, site. 4. landed property.

ಭೂವನ **bhūvana**, *see* ಭುವನ.

ಭೂಷಣ **bhūshaṇa**, *s*. Ornament, embellishment. 2. a trinket *or* jewel. 3. flattery, praise, honour.

ಭೃತ್ತೆ, ಭೃತ್ಯೆ **bhṛutte, bhṛutye**, *s*. A hired servant. 2. a dependant *or* adherent.

ಭೇಟಿ **bhēṭi**, *s*. A visit, audience. –ಕೊರ್ಪಿನಿ to give an audience. –ಮಳ್ಪುನಿ to visit.

ಭೇದ್ **bhēdụ**, *see* ಬೇದ್.

ಭೇದ **bhēda**, *s*. Distinction, difference. 2. disunion, discord, strife. –ಮಳ್ಪುನಿ to make distinctions.

ಭೇದಿ **bhēdi**, *s*. Purging; a purgative.

ಭೇದಿಸುನಿ **bhēdisuni** (ಭೇದಿಸ್), *v. a*. To separate, disunite, tear, pierce.

ಭೇರಿ **bhēri**, *s*. A large drum; a kettledrum.

ಭೈರವೆ **bheirave**, *s*. Śiva. 2. an inferior manifestation of him.

ಭೋಗ **bhōga**, *s*. Enjoyment, pleasure.

ಭೋಗಿ **bhōgi**, *s*. A person brought up in luxury *or* enjoying it.

ಭೋಗಿಪುನಿ **bhōgipuni** (ಭೋಗಿ), *v. a*. To enjoy, especially any carnal *or* sensual pleasure.

ಭೋಗ್ಯ **bhōgya**, *s*. Enjoyment, usufruct. 2. a crop. ಭೋಗ್ಯಾದಿ, ಭೋಗ್ಯಾದಿ ಅಡವು a mortgage by which the interest of money lent on a house, land, *etc*., is regarded as an equivalent for the use; a usufructuary mortgage.

ಭೋಜನ **bhōjana**, *s*. Food. 2. a repast, meal, eating. –ಶಾಲೆ a dining hall. ರಾತ್ರಿ– the Lord's Supper.

ಭ್ರಮಣ, ಭ್ರಮಣೆ **bhramaṇa, bhramaṇè**, *s*. Whirling, wandering. 2. perplexity, confusion.

ಭ್ರಮಿಪುನಿ, ಭ್ರಮಿಸುನಿ **bhramipuni, bhramisuni** (ಭ್ರಮಿ, ಭ್ರಮಿಸ್), *v. a*. To confuse, perplex. *v. n*. To err, think erroneously.

ಭ್ರಮೆ **bhramè**, *s*. Whirling, going round. 2. error, ignorance, mistake, misapprehension, illusion. 3. confusion, perplexity of mind, giddiness. 4. a temporary aberration of reason, delirium. 5. astonishment, surprise. ಪಿತ್ತ– a bilious complaint. –ಆಪಿನಿ to be confused; to be astonished.

ಭ್ರಷ್ಟ **bhrashṭa**, *adj*. Fallen, depraved, defiled. –ಆಪಿನಿ to be depraved, defiled.

ಭ್ರಷ್ಟೆ **bhrashṭe**, *s*. A depraved *or* corrupt man. ಮತ– an apostate.

ಭ್ರಾಂತ್, ಭ್ರಾಂತಿ **bhrāntụ, bhrānti**, *s*. Delusion, mistake, blunder. 2. delirium.

ಭ್ರಾಂತೆ **bhrānte**, *s*. An idiot, fool.

ಮ

M

ಮ **ma,** The thirty-eighth letter of the alphabet.

ಮಂಕ್ಡಿ **maṅkḍi,** *s.* A wooden peg in a wall to support a roof, *or* a plank serving as a shelf.

ಮಂಕ, ಮಂಕು **maṅka, maṅku,** *s.* Dulness, stupidity. –ಮರ್ಲ್ half mad, foppish.

ಮಂಗ **maṅga,** *s.* A monkey. *adj.* Apish, foolish, senseless. –ಚೇಷ್ಟೆ the pranks of a monkey. –ಬುದ್ಧಿ silliness.

ಮಂಗಟ್ **maṅgaṭụ,** *s.* Coaxing, wheedling, cajolery.

ಮಂಗಟಾವುನಿ **maṅgaṭāvuni** (ಮಂಗಟಾ), *v. a.* To coax, cajole, hoax, wheedle, deceive.

ಮಂಗಣೆ, ಮಂಗನೆ **maṅgaṇè, maṅganè,** *s.* Affectation, coquetry, foppishness.

ಮಂಗಲ, ಮಂಗಳ **maṅgala, maṅgaḷa,** *s.* Happiness, auspiciousness, good fortune. 2. *see* ಮಂಗಳೆ. *adj.* Happy, auspicious, fortunate, prosperous. –ಕಾರ್ಯ an auspicious ceremony. –ಮಾಯಕ deceit. –ಸೂತ್ರ a female's marriage-badge worn round the neck. –ಆಪಿನಿ an auspicious ceremony to be concluded.

ಮಂಗಲಾರತಿ **maṅgalārati,** *see* ಮಂಗಳಾರತಿ.

ಮಂಗಳವಾರ **maṅgaḷavāra,** *s.* Tuesday.

ಮಂಗಳಾದೇವಿ, ಮಂಗಳಾವತಿ **maṅgaḷādēvi, maṅgaḷāvati,** *s.* The goddess after whom the town of Mangalore is called.

ಮಂಗಳಾರತಿ **maṅgaḷārati,** *s.* Waving a lamp before an idol, *etc.*

ಮಂಗಳಾಷ್ಟಕ **maṅgaḷāshṭaka,** *s.* Sanskrit verses sung when waving lamps before a bridal pair.

ಮಂಗಳಿ **maṅngaḷi,** *s.* A spotted cow. *adj.* Dapple, spotted.

ಮಂಗಳೂರು **maṅgaḷūru,** *s. lit.* A prosperous town. 2. the town of Mangalore.

ಮಂಗಳೆ **maṅgaḷe,** *s.* The planet Mars. 2. a spotted ox *or* bull. *adj.* Spotted, dapple.

ಮಂಗಳ್ಯ **maṅgaḷya,** *see* ಮಂಗಲ.

ಮಂಗಾಟ **maṅgāṭa,** *s.* The pranks of a monkey. 2. tricks, pranks. 3. *see* ಮಂಗಟ್.

ಮಂಗು **maṅgu,** *s.* A female cat. 2. a silly female. 3. a small insect. ನಿನ ಕಥೆ ಆಪಿನೆತ್ತ ಉಳಯಿ ಮಂಗು ಮದಮಾಳ್ ಆಪಳ್ *lit.* by the time you conclude your narrative the cat will be pubescent; *i. e.,* you are a slow coach, *pro.*

ಮಂಗೆ **maṅge,** *s.* A monkey, ape. 2. a silly fellow. ಮಂಗೆ– a small worm.

ಮಂಙಣೆ **maṅṅaṇè,** *see* ಮಂಗಣೆ.

ಮಂಚವು, ಮಂಚಾವು **mańčavu, mańčāvu,** *s.* A cot, bedstead.

ಮಂಚಿಪತ್ರೆ, ಮಂಜಪತ್ರೆ, ಮಂಜಿಪತ್ರೆ **mańčipatrè, mańjapatrè, mańjipatrè,** *s. Artemisea indica*, a pungent, bitter drug, said to be anthelmintic, stomachic, and a remover of phlegm and catarrh.

ಮಂಚಿಲ್ **mańčilu,** *s.* A kind of conveyance, resembling a hammock, made of sack cloth with an awning above, and and carried on the shoulders of men.

ಮಂಜ **mańja,** *s.* A fish-market; *also* ಮೀನಮಂಜ.

ಮಂಜನ **mańjana,** *see* ಅಂಜನ.

ಮಂಜರಿ **mańjari,** *s.* The spike, pedicle, *or* bunch of flowers and fruits.

ಮಂಜಲ್, ಮಂಜಳ್ **mańjalu, mańjaḷu,** *s.* Turmeric, *Curcuma longa*. 2. yellow colour. *adj.* Yellow. –ಅಡ್ಡೆ a kind of cake. –ತೇಡೆ a kind of fish. –ಕಸ್ತೂರಿ *Curcuma zerumbet*. –ಪಕ್ಕಿ a kind of bird. –ಪೂ a kind of flower. ಅಜ್ಜಿ–, ಆನೆ–, ಮರ– are several kinds of turmeric. ಮರ– *Curcuma xanthorrhiza*, a kind of medicinal root, applied to the eye.

ಮಂಜಲ **mańjala,** *adj.* Yellow.

ಮಂಜಲೆ, ಮಂಜಳೆ **mańjale, mańjaḷe,** *s.* A yellow *or* tawny coloured man. –ಕೋೞಿ a yellow cock.

ಮಂಜಿ **mańji,** *s.* A long boat. 2. a single masted country-vessel.

ಮಂಜಿ **mańji,** *s.* A kind of hemp. –ಮುಸ್ಕು, *see* ಪ್ಯೆಂಡ್‌ಮುಸ್ಕು.

ಮಂಜಿಷ್ಠ **mańjishṭha,** Bengal madder, *Rubia manjista.*

ಮಂಜು **mańju,** *see* ಮಂಜಿ. 2. *see* ಮಂದ. 3. *see* ಪ್ಯೆಂಡ್.

ಮಂಜೂರು **mańjūru,** *s.* Approval. 2. validity. *adj.* Authentic, valid, ratified. ನಾ– disapproved, invalid; rejected. –ಮಳ್ಪುನಿ to approve, ratify; autenticate, to make valid.

ಮಂಜೆ **mańjè,** *adj.* Barren, unfruitful.

ಮಂಜೆಟ್ಟಿ **mańjeṭṭi,** *s.* The arnotto tree, *Bixa orellana.* 2. the seed of it, used as a weight by goldsmiths.

ಮಂಜೆರ್ **mańjeru,** *adj.* Sterile, barren. –ಭೂಮಿ a barren field.

ಮಂಜೆರಾಯೆ **mańjerāye,** *s.* A demon so called.

ಮಂಜೆಲೆ **mańjele,** *see* ಮಂಜಳೆ.

ಮಂಜೊಟ್ಟಿ, ಮಂಜೋಟಿ **mańjoṭṭi, mańjōṭi,** *see* ಮಂಜೆಟ್ಟಿ.

ಮಂಜೊಟ್ಟೆ **mańjoṭṭè,** *s.* A raised bank at the end of a race-field.

ಮಂಜೊಳು **mańjoḷu,** *see* ಮಂಜಲ್, ಮಂಜಲ.

ಮಂಟಪ, ಮಂಟಮೆ, ಮಂಟವು **maṇṭapa, maṇṭamè, maṇṭavu,** *s.* An open shed *or* hall erected on marriage and other festive occasions. ಘಾಳಿ— an airy shed. ಮುಖ— a portico, porch.

ಮಂಟು maṇṭu, *see* ಮಟ್ಟು.

ಮಂಡ maṇḍa, *s.* The counter of a country shop; a low bench *or* platform on which a shop-keeper squats while transacting business.

ಮಂಡಲ, ಮುಂಡಳ maṇḍala, maṇḍala, *s.* The disk of the sun *or* moon. 2. an orb, ball, globe, circumference in general. 3. a province, region, district. 4. an empire. 5. a heap, quantity, multitude, assemblage. 6. the period of forty-eight days. —ಅಧಿಪತಿ, ಮಂಡಲಾಧಿಪತಿ an emperor. ಚಂದ್ರ— the disk of the moon; an idol car. ಚೋಳ— the Coromandel Coast. ಪರ— a foreign territory. ಭೂ— the earth. —ಪಾಡುನಿ to describe a circle.

ಮಂಡಲಿ maṇḍali, *s.* An assembly, congress. —ಕೆ a member of an assembly. —ಗುರ್ಕಾರೆ a president.

ಮಂಡಿ maṇḍi, *s.* The knee.

ಮಂಡಿಕುಟ್ಟೆ maṇḍikuṭṭe, *s.* A demon so called.

ಮಂಡಿಗೆ maṇḍigè, *s.* A kind of very thin cake. 2. the nasal passage into the month. 3. the name of a caste.

ಮಂಡೆ maṇḍè, *s.* The skull; the head. 2. a large earthen vessel. —ಕಕ್ಕೆ a large kind of crow. —ಕುಂಡೆ from head to buttocks. —ಕುತ್ತ hydrocephalus, dropsy of the head. —ತೆರಿಗೆ, —ವಂತಿಗೆ a capitation *or* poll tax. —ಪಿಜಿನ್ a royal ant. —ಮಂಡೆ ಬುದ್ಧಿ difference of opinion, disagreement. —ಕುಟ್ಟುನಿ to box the head *or* knock it against anything hard. —ಪಾಡುನಿ to take part; to interfere.

ಮಂಡೆಗೆ maṇḍege, *s.* The name of a caste; *also* ಮಂಡಿಗೆ.

ಮಂಡೆಬಳೆ maṇḍebaḷè, *s.* A straw covering of a vessel. 2. the pole-plate of a roof.

ಮಂಡೆಮಾರಿ maṇḍemāri, *s.* Swelling of the head, a cerebral disorder. 2. giddiness, intoxication. 3. a word of abuse.

ಮಂಡೆಲೆ maṇḍele, *see* ಮಂಡಲಿಕೆ *under* ಮಂಡಲಿ.

ಮಂಡೊಲಿಗಾರೆ maṇḍoligāre, *s.* The president of an assembly. 2. a member of an assembly.

ಮಂಣ್ maṇṇu, *s.* Earth, clay, soil. —ಮಸಣ (*lit.*) earth and cemetery; anything without order *or* discrimination. —ದ ಮುದ್ದೆ a lump of earth. —ಮುದ್ದೆ heavy. ಮಂಣಾಪಿನಿ, ಮಂಣಾದ್‌ಪೋಪಿನಿ to be reduced to earth; to die; to decay. ಬಾಯಿಗ್ ಮಂಣ್ ಬೂರುನಿ *lit.* earth to fall into the mouth; to be disappointed *or* deceived; to be afflicted with. —ತಿನ್ಪಿ ಬುದ್ಧಿ a grovelling disposition. —ಮುಕ್ಕುನಿ to swallow earth.

ಮಂಣಡಕೆ mannadakè, *s.* The sepistan plum tree, *Cordia myxa.*

ಮಂಣಡಿಕ್ mannadiku, *adv.* Under the earth, subterranean.

ಮಂಣಣೆ mannanè, *see* ಮುಂನಣೆ.

ಮಂಣಾಶೆ mannāšè, *s.* Earthly desire, worldly-mindedness.

ಮಂಣಿ manni, *s.* Rice flour and jaggory boiled with cocoanut juice, *etc.*, treacle. —ಮಾಜಾವುನಿ to boil down.

ಮಂಣುಪ್ಪು mannuppu, *s.* Bay salt.

ಮಂತ್, ಮಂತ manty, manta, *s.* A churning stick. 2. *see* ಮಾತ.

ಮಂತದಬೊಂಬೆ mantadabombè, *s.* A moving puppet.

ಮಂತರ್ಮೆ mantarmè, *s.* The back *or* railing of a cot.

ಮಂತಾನ mantāna, *s.* High birth, noble parentage.

ಮಂತ್ರ mantra, *s.* A mystical verse *or* incantation. 2. a formula sacred to any individual deity. 3. a charm. —ಗಾರೆ, —ದಾಯಿ a charmer, conjurer, magician. —ತಂತ್ರ charms and devices. —ಪಾಡುನಿ, —ಮಳ್ಪುನಿ to charm. —ಸಾಧ್ಯುನಿ to master the mysteries of a formula.

ಮಂತ್ರಾಕ್ಷತೆ mantrākshatè, *s.* Raw rice coloured with red powder, over which incantations have been pronounced.

ಮಂತ್ರಿ mantri, *s.* A minister, counsellor. 2. the queen in chess.

ಮಂತ್ರಿಯುನಿ mantriyuni (ಮಂತ್ರಿ), *v.a.* To charm, enchant. 2. to advise, persuade.

ಮಂಥ್, ಮಂಥನ manthu, manthana, *see* ಮಂತ.

ಮಂಥನ, ಮಂಥಾನ manthana, manthāna, *see* ಮಂತಾನ.

ಮಂದ manda, *s.* Slowness; dulness, stupidity. 2. thickness, density. 3. the planet Saturn. *adj.* Dim, dull. 2. stupid, senseless. 3. mild, moderate, gentle. 4. thickly spread, dense. —ಅಗ್ನಿ, ಮಂದಾಗ್ನಿ indigestion, want of appetite. —ಅಲೆ, ಮಂದಲೆ thick butter milk. —ಕಂಣ್ dim sight. —ಕಾಡ್ a dense forest. —ಗಮನ a slow walk. —ನೀರ್ turbid water. —ಬುದ್ಧಿ dull comprehension. —ವಾಯು a gentle breeze. —ವಾರ Saturday. —ಹಾಸ a gentle smile.

ಮಂದರ, ಮಂದಾರ mandara, mandāra, *s.* The tree *Bauhinia acuminata.* 2. a mythical mountain. —ಪೂ mandāra flower.

ಮಂದರೆ mandarè, *s.* A tell-tale woman. 2. an artful woman.

ಮಂದಾಮಸ್ತು mandāmastu, *see* ಮದಾಮಸ್ತು.

ಮಂದಾಕ್ಷ mandāksha, *s.* Modesty, bashfulness.

ಮಂದಿ mandi, *see* ಮಂಡೆ.

ಮಂದಿರ mandira, *s.* A house, habitation. ರಾಜ— a palace.

ಮಂದಿರಿ mandiri, *see* ಮಂದ್ರಿ.

ಮಂದಿಲ್ಲ್ mandillu, *see* ಮುಂದಿಲ್ಲ್.

ಮಂದೆ mandè, *s.* People, persons. ಪತ್ತ್— *lit.* ten people; the members of a parish, a presbytery. ಏತ್— how many persons? ಪತ್ತ್ ಮಂದೆ ಮುತ್ತುಗು ಸಮ *lit.* ten people are equal to pearl; there is wisdom in the counsel of an assembly, *pro.* ಪಾಕ— a few persons.

ಮಂದ್ರಿ mandri, *s.* A bed-sheet, covering garment. 2. a table cloth.

ಮಂಧನ mandhana, *see* ಮಂತಾನ.

ಮಂಧಿ, ಮಂಧೆ mandhi, mandhe, *see* ಮಂದೆ.

ಮಂನ manna, *s.* Suspense, postponement. 2. discontinuance, cessation. 3. prohibition, disallowance.

ಮಂನಣೆ mannaṇè, *s.* Respect, civility, politeness, attention.

ಮಂನಿ manni, *see* ಮಂಣಿ.

ಮಂನಿಪುನಿ, ಮಂನಿಸುನಿ mannipuni, mannisuni (ಮಂನಿ, ಮಂನಿಸ್), *v. a.* To forgive, pass over, overlook. 2. to regard, treat kindly. 3. to honour, show respect.

ಮಂಪುನಿ mampuni, *see* ಮಳ್ಪುನಿ.

ಮಂಮ mamma, *s.* The pap, breast.

ಮಂಮಟಿಕೊಟ್ಟು mammaṭikoṭṭu, *s.* A mamooty.

ಮಂಮತೆ mammatè, *see* ಮಮತೆ.

ಮಂಮೆ mammè, *s.* Longing, eagerness. 2. want, deficiency, scarcity. —ಮಾರುನಿ to desire eagerly. [tion.

ಮಕ maka, *s.* A sacrifice, oblaಮಕಮಾಲ್ makamālu, *s.* Velvet.

ಮಕರ್ makaru, *s.* Trick, artifice, cheat, deception.

ಮಕರ makara, *s.* An alligator. 2. *Capricornus*, sign of the zodiac. *adj.* Obstinate. —ಕೇತನೆ Cupid, whose banner bears the sign of an alligator. —ತನ obstinacy. —ತೋರಣ a wreath carried on poles. —ಸಂಕ್ರಾಂದಿ the passage of the sun from *Sagittarius* into *Capricornus*.

ಮಕರಿಯುನಿ, ಮಕರ್ಯುನಿ makariyuni, makaryuni (ಮಕರಿ), *v. n.* To be changed.

ಮಕುಟ makuṭa, *s.* A crown, crest, tiara.

ಮಕೆ, makè, *see* ಮಘೆ.

ಮಕ್ಕ್ makku, *s.* Awn *or* beard of grain, *etc.* *adj.* Bristly, rough. —ಆಪಿನಿ to be bristly, as a plant, *etc.*

ಮಕ್ಕ್ makku, *s.* Irritation in the throat. *adj.* Irritating. —ತಂಮ distressing cough. —ಮಕ್ಕ ಆಪಿನಿ, —ಪುಟ್ಟುನಿ to feel irritation in the throat.

ಮಕ್ಕರ್ makkaru, *see* ಮಕರ್.

ಮಕ್ಕರ makkara, *see* ಮಕರ.

ಮಕ್ಕಳಚೇಷ್ಟೆ makkaḷacēshṭè, *s.* Convulsions of children.

ಮಕ್ಕಳಸಂತಾನ makkaḷasantāna, *s.* Inheritance by one's sons, in contrast to inheritance by nephews (ಅಳಿಯಸಂತಾನ).

ಮಕ್ಕಳಾಟಿಗೆ makkaḷāṭigè, *s.* Childishness.

ಮಕ್ಕಿ makki, *s.* Irritation. 2. ploughing. –ಕಂಡ a ploughed field; a field of one crop. –ದಾಯಿ a ploughman. –ಮರ rough timber.

ಮಕ್ಕು makku, *see* ಮಕ್ಕ್.

ಮಕ್ಕುನಿ makkuni (ಮಕ್ಕ್), *v. n.* To feel irritation in the throat.

ಮಕ್ಕೆ makkè, *see* ಮಘೆ.

ಮಕ್ಕೆರಿ makkeri, *s.* A kind of wicker basket used for fishing. –ಒಡ್ಡುನಿ to fish with such a basket.

ಮಕ್ಕೆಲ್ makkelụ, *adj.* Irritating, as a rancid substance. 2. bristly, rough.

ಮಕ್ಮಾಲ್ makmālụ, *see* ಮಕಮಾಲ್.

ಮಖೆ makhè, *see* ಮಘೆ.

ಮಗ್ತೆ magụtè, *adj.* Again, a second time.

ಮಗ್ಪು magụpu, *s.* A turn.

ಮಗ್ಪುನಿ magụpuni (ಮಗ್), *v. a.* To turn, upset. ಬಂಜಿ– to retch.

ಮಗ್ರ್ magụrụ, *adj.* Next, following. *adv.* Again, once more. –ಕಾಲ next year. –ಪುಟ್ಟುನಿ, –ಮುಟ್ಟುನಿ to crop up again, to have a relapse.

ಮಗ್ರ್ನೆ magụrnè, *adj.* Next, following, succeeding. –ಕಾಲ the next year.

ಮಗ maga, *see* ಮಗೆ.

ಮಗಪುನಿ magapuni (ಮಗ), *v. a.* To draw and turn over. ನೀರ್– to draw water.

ಮಗರ್ magarụ, *see* ಮಗ್ರ್.

ಮಗರುನಿ magaruni, *see* ಮಗ್ರುನಿ.

ಮಗರೂರು magarūru, *see* ಮಗ್ರೂರು.

ಮಗಳ್ magaḷụ, *s.* A daughter. *pl.* ಮಗಳಾಡ್ಳು daughters.

ಮಗುಚುನಿ ಮಗುಪುನಿ magučuni, magupuni, *see* ಮಗ್ಪುನಿ.

ಮಗೆ mage, *s.* A son; *pl.* ಮಗಾಡ್ಳು sons.

ಮಗ್ಗ magga, *s.* A loom. –ದಾಯಿ a weaver. –ದಕ್ಕುನಿ to pass *or* shoot the shuttle through the warp in weaving, as country weavers do.

ಮಗ್ಗಿ maggi, *s.* Multiplication, the multiplication table. –ಪಪ್ಪುನಿ to repeat the same. –ಬಿರ್ಪಿನಿ to know the same.

ಮಗ್ಗಿನ maggina, *s.* An obstacle, impediment.

ಮಗ್ತೆ magtè, *see* ಮಗ್ತೆ.

ಮಗ್ನ magna, *adj.* Plunged, immersed, sunk. –ಆಪಿನಿ to be sunk, as in any vice.

ಮಗ್ಪು magpu, *see* ಮಗ್ಪು.

ಮಗ್ರಮ magrama, *adj.* Next, following. –ದಿನ next day, the following day.

ಮಗ್ರಾವೊಣುನಿ magrāvoṇuni, *v. refl.* (*of* ಮಗ್ರುನಿ) To prostrate.

ಮಗ್ರು magru, *see* ಮಗ್ರ್.

ಮಗ್ರುನಿ magruni, *v. n.* To fall, tumble. 2. to shake, be agitated. 3. to feel a reeling sensation. ಬಂಜಿ– to feel uneasiness in the belly.

ಮಗ್ರೂರು magrūru, *s.* Pride, arrogance, haughtiness. 2. rudeness, impertinence.

ಮಘೆ maghè, *s.* The tenth lunar asterism. –ಬರ್ಸ a season of much rain.

ಮಚ್ಚ mačča, *s.* A little piece of gold *or* silver kept as a sample *or* test.

ಮಚ್ಚ mačča, *s.* A strong, stinking smell.

ಮಚ್ಚಮೀನ್ maččamīnu, *s.* A kind of fish.

ಮಚ್ಚರ maččara, *see* ಮತ್ಸರ.

ಮಚ್ಚಿ mačči, *s.* A stone-cutter's chisel.

ಮಚ್ಚು mačču, *see* ಮಚ್ಚ.

ಮಚ್ಚೆ maččè, *s.* Likeness, resemblance. 2. ಮುಚ್ಚೆ.

ಮಜ maja, *see* ಮಜಿ.

ಮಜಂಟಿ majaṇṭi, *s.* A small kind of bee. 2. its wax.

ಮಜಕುನಿ majakuni (ಮಜಕ), *v. n.* To become dim. *v. a.* To scatter, huddle.

ಮಜಕೊಟೆಬೂರು majakoṭebūru, *s.* A kind of creeper.

ಮಜಡೆ majaḍe, *see* ಮುಜಡೆ.

ಮಜನೆ majanè, *s.* A kind of black scars on the body. –ಬೂರುನಿ to suffer from them.

ಮಜಬೂತ್ majabūtu, *see* ಮಜ್ಬೂತ್.

ಮಜಲ್ majalu, *s.* A stage in a journey, halting place. 2. a distance from nine to twelve miles.

ಮಜಲ್ majalu, *adj.* Of middle sort, as land. –ಕಂಡ a field of middle sort. –ತರ middle sort.

ಮಜಲೆ majalè, *s.* Rubbish washed on shore.

ಮಜಾಶಿಗೆ majāšigè, *see* ಮಜ್ಲಾಶಿಗೆ.

ಮಜಿ maji, *s.* Coal. 2. black powder. 3. ink.

ಮಜಿಕೋಲು majikōlu, *s.* A churning-stick.

ಮಜೂರಿ, ಮಜೂರು majūri, majūru, *s.* Hire, cooly, wages. –ಕೊಡ್ಪಿನಿ to pay hire.

ಮಜೆ majè, *s.* A natural speck, spot, freckle, mole.

ಮಜ್ಜಿ majji, *see* ಮಜಿ.

ಮಜ್ಕೂರ್ majkūru, *adj.* Beforementioned, aforesaid. *s.* Contents.

ಮಜ್ಬೂತ್ majbūtu, *adj.* Strong, firm, fixed.

ಮಜ್ಲಾಶಿಗೆ majlāšigè, *s.* Boast, brag.

ಮಟಿಗೆ maṭige, *see* ಮಟ್ಟು. *adv.* Till.

ಮಟ್ಟ್ maṭṭu, *see* ಮಟ್ಟು.

ಮಟ್ಟ maṭṭa, *s.* A carpenter's *or* bricklayer's square. 2. level, height, measure. ಜಲ– water level.

ಮಟ್ಟ maṭṭa, *s.* Toddling. *adv.* At full length. –ಮರಕಣಿ on the whole back. –ಮಟ್ಟ ನಡಪುನಿ to toddle, as a child.

ಮಟ್ಟರ್ maṭṭarụ, *s*. A place of cock-fighting. 2. a fair held in the month of May.

ಮಟ್ಟಿತೌತೆ maṭṭitoutè, *s*. A small kind of cucumber, gerkin.

ಮಟ್ಟು maṭṭu, *s*. Measure, extent, limit, capacity, ability. –ಕೊಂಡಾಪಿನಿ to understand a person's capacity.

ಮಟ್ಟೆ maṭṭè, *s*. A kind of tune.

ಮಟ್ಟೆಲ್ maṭṭelụ, *s*. The pouch in front formed by the folds of a female's garment and used as a pocket. 2. the bosom, lap. ಮಡಿ–, ಮರಿ– an under pouch so formed.

ಮಠ maṭha, *s*. The residence of a priest *or* spiritual guide; a monastery. 2. a school, college. ಅಷ್ಟ– the eight residences of the spiritual guides, connected with the Krụshṇa temple at Udipi, namely, ಪಲಿಮಾರ್–, ಕೃಷ್ಣಾಪುರ–, ಪುತ್ತಿಗೆ–, ಶೀರೂರು–, ಕಾಣ್ಯೂರು–, ಸೋದೆ–, ಅದಮಾರ್–, and ಪೇಜಾವರ–. ಕನ್ಯ– a nunnery. ಗುರು– the residence of a spiritual guide *or* minister. ಜಂಗಮ– the residence of a Liṅga priest. –ವಾಸಿ an inhabitant of a monastery.

ಮಡ್‌ಗುನಿ maḍụguni, *see* ಮಡಗುನಿ.

ಮಡ maḍa, *see* ಮಾಡ.

ಮಡಂಕ್ maḍaṅkụ, *see* ಮೊಡಂಕ್.

ಮಡಂತೆಲ್, ಮಡಂದೆಲ್ maḍantelụ, maḍandelụ, *s*. Rice plants sprouting again after they have been once reaped. 2. a kind of tree.

ಮಡಕೆ maḍakè, *s*. An earthen vessel for collecting toddy. –ದೆಂಜಿ a kind of crab. –ಪಂದ್ಯ a kind of fruit.

ಮಡಗುನಿ maḍaguni (ಮಡಗಿ), *v. a.* To lay down, put, place.

ಮಡತನ maḍatana, *see* ಮಡಸ್ತನ.

ಮಡತೆ maḍatè, *s*. A fold, crease.

ಮಡಲ್ maḍalụ, *s*. A palm branch. 2. a cocoanut branch with plaited leaves. ಅರೆ– a dried leaf of a palmyra tree. –ವಿಾನ್ a kind of fish. –ಮುಡೆಪಿನಿ to plait palm leaves.

ಮಡಸ್ತನ maḍastana, *s*. Rolling one's self round a temple *or* before an idol, in fulfilment of a vow. –ಪಾಡುನಿ to roll in such a way.

ಮಡಾಯಿಸುನಿ maḍāyisuni (ಮಡಾಯಿಸಿ), *v. a.* To bind, cover, as a book.

ಮಡಿ maḍi, *s*. A newly washed cloth, bleached cloth. 2. a garment of bark, silk, *or* wool, worn by Brạhmans and other high-caste people during meals *or* any ceremonies. 3. fold, the same quantity added; (*in comp. with* ಒರ *and* ಇರ್, ಮ *changes into* ಬ;) *as*, ಒಬ್ಬಡಿ a single fold; ಇರ್ಬಡಿ a double fold, *etc*. *adj*. Bleached, washed. –ಕುಂಟು a washed cloth. –ಕೋಂಪೆ a kind of toad. –ತಾಯಿ a washerman. –ಮಳ್ಪುನಿ to bleach, wash clothes. –ವಾ

ಫುನಿ to change a washed garment. –ಪಾಡುನಿ to become dirty.

ಮಡಿಕೆ maḍikè, *s.* Folding, doubling. 2. a wrinkle, crease. 3. a small earthen vessel. –ತೆಲ್ಲವು a kind of cake.

ಮಡಿಚೀರವು maḍičīravu, *s.* A kind of bag *or* purse.

ಮಡಿಪಾವುನಿ maḍipāvuni, *c. v.* (*of* ಮಡಿಪುನಿ) To make fold, cause to fold.

ಮಡಿಪು maḍipu, *s.* A fold, plait. –ಬೀಸತಿ a clasp knife.

ಮಡಿಪುನಿ maḍipuni (ಮಡಿ), *v. a.* To fold, plait, double up. ಬಂಜಿ– to feel loathing *or* disgust; to retch.

ಮಡಿಯುನಿ maḍiyuni (ಮಡಿ), *v. n.* To become folded, doubled up.

ಮಡಿವಳೆ maḍivaḷe, *see* ಮಡ್ಡೆಲೆ.

ಮಡೀರ್ maḍīrụ, *adj.* Second born. –ದಾಯೆ the second son.

ಮಡು maḍu, *s.* An axe, hatchet. –ತ ಕೈಲ್ the handle of an axe.

ಮಡುಗಡಿ maḍugaḍi, *see* ಮರಕಡಿ.

ಮಡುಗುನಿ maḍuguni, *see* ಮಡಗುನಿ.

ಮಡೆ maḍè, *s.* Orts, refuse, crumbs, *or* remains of victuals. 2. saliva, spittle. 3. whatever has come in contact with the mouth. –ಇರೆ a leaf-plate that has been used for a meal. –ಪುಡಿ ring worm. –ಮಳ್ಪುನಿ to defile anything by bringing in contact with the mouth.

ಮಡೆಂಚಿ maḍeñji, *s.* A kind of fish.

ಮಡ್ಕೆ maḍkè, *s.* A quantity of grass, *etc.*

ಮಡ್ಡಿ maḍḍi, *s.* Sediment, lees. 2. rice boiled with cocoanut and husk, for cattle.

ಮಡ್ಡೆಲಪಕ್ಕಿ maḍḍelapakki, *s.* A kind of bird.

ಮಡ್ಡೆಲೆ, ಮಡ್ಯೆಲೆ maḍḍele, maḍyele, *s.* A washerman.

ಮಡ್ಲು maḍlu, *see* ಮಡಲ್.

ಮಣ, ಮಣಕ್ maṇa, maṇakụ, *adj.* Viscous, sticky. –ಪತ್ತುನಿ, –ಮಜೊಗು ಕುಳ್ಳುನಿ to stick, adhere, become united.

ಮಣಂಗ್ maṇaṅgụ, *s.* Pilchard.

ಮಣಜೋಗು maṇajōgu, *s.* Giddiness, vertigo.

ಮಣಲಿ maṇali, *s.* A tune. 2. *see* ಮಜೊಲಿ.

ಮಣಶಿಲೆ maṇaśilè, *s.* Red arsenic.

ಮಣಾರ maṇāra, *see* ಮನೋಹರ.

ಮಣಿ maṇi, *s.* A bead. 2. a small bell. 3. a gem, pearl. ಕರ್ಯ– a small kind of black beads. –ಕಾರ್ a rib of a ship. –ಪಾತೆರ a prophesy. –ಸರ a necklace of beads. –ಸರಕ್ beads in general. –ತುರಿಯುನಿ, –ಸುರಿಯುನಿ to string beads.

ಮಣಿಗಂಟ್ maṇigaṇṭụ, *s.* The ankle.

ಮಣಿಗಾರೆ maṇigārè, *see* ಮಣಿಗಾರೆ.

ಮಣಿಪಂದೆ maṇipandè, *see under* ಮನಿಪುನಿ.

ಮಣಿಪು maṇipu, *s.* A strong, superior kind of coir.

ಮಣಿಪುನಿ maṇipuni, *see* ಮನಿಫುನಿ.

ಮಣು maṇu, *s.* A maund equal to 28 lbs.

ಮಣೆ maṇe, *s.* A low stool to sit upon. ಒಚ್ಚಿದ– a whetting board. ಕೊಟ್ಟು– a kind of stool furnished with a short handle. ಚಂಡೆ–, *see under* ಚಂಡೆ. –ಮರಾಯಿ wooden furniture.

ಮಣೆಗಾರೆ maṇegāre, *s.* A revenue inspector.

ಮಣೊಲಿ maṇoli, *s.* The vegetable *Coccinia indica.*

ಮತ mata, *s.* Purpose, intention, wish, mind. 2. religion; a religious sect. ಕ್ರೈಸ್ತ– the Christian religion. –ದಾಯಿ, –ಸ್ಥೆ a follower of a religion, a sectarian. ಬೌದ್ಧ– Buddhism. –ಭೇದ religious difference.

ಮತಲಪು, ಮತಲಬು matalapu, matalabu, *s.* The contents *or* purport of a writing *or* speech.

ಮತಾಯಿ matāyi, *s.* A wave.

ಮತಿ mati, *s.* Understanding, intellect, common sense. 2. the senses. –ದಾಂತಿ senseless. –ತಪ್ಪುನಿ to be out of senses.

ಮತ್ತ್ mattu, *see* ಮಸ್ತ್.

ಮತ್ತ matta, *adj.* Intoxicated. 2. furious, mad.

ಮತ್ತಿ matti, *s.* The tree *Terminalia tomentosa.*

ಮತ್ತೆ matte, *s.* An inebriate man; a mad man.

ಮತ್ಲಬು matlabu, *see* ಮತಲಪು.

ಮತ್ಸರ matsara, *s.* Envy, malice.

ಮತ್ಸ್ಯ matsya, *s.* A fish. ಮತ್ಸ್ಯಾವತಾರ the first incarnation of Vishṇu in the form of a fish.

ಮಥನ mathana, *s.* Churning.

ಮದ್ಮಾಯೆ madumāye, *s.* A bridegroom.

ಮದ್ಮಾಳ್ madumāḷu, *s.* A bride. 2. a pubescent female. –ಮೀನ್ a kind of fish. –ಕಪ್ಪೆ, *see* ಪನಿ ಕಪ್ಪೆ *under* ಪನಿ.

ಮದ್ಮೆ madume, *s.* A wedding, marriage. –ದ ದೊಂಪ a shed erected for nuptial ceremonies. –ದ ಫೊಣಸ್ a wedding feast. –ಆಪಿನಿ to become married. –ಮಳ್ಪುನಿ to marry.

ಮದ್ರೆ madure, *s.* Madura. –ರು ಮೂಲ್ a red kind of turban manufactured in Madura.

ಮದ್ರೆಂಗಿ madureṅgi, *see* ಮದ್ರಿಂಗಿ.

ಮದ್ಲ್ madulu, *s.* A roofed wall of a compound. –ಕಟ್ಟುನಿ to make a roofed wall.

ಮದ mada, *s.* Pride, arrogance. 2. insanity, madness, infatuation. 3. joy, pleasure. 4. rutting, as of an elephant. 5. inebriety, intoxication. 6. spiritous *or* vinous liquor. 7. desire, love.

ಮದಂತೆ madante, *see* ಮದಾಂತೆ.

ಮದಕರಿ madakari, *s.* Ulcerous leprosy. –ಪತ್ತುನಿ to be affected with leprosy.

ಮದಕುನಿ madakuni (ಮದಕ್), *v. n.* To go *or* move swiftly.

ಮದಗ madaga, *s.* A large natural tank.

ಮದಡ್ madaḍu, *adj.* Slothful, indolent. *s.* A log, trunk. –ನರಮಾನಿ an indolent fellow.

ಮದಡಿ madaḍi, *see* ಮದೊಡಿ.

ಮದಡು madaḍu, *s.* A lazy woman. *adj.* Lazy. 2. sloping.

ಮದಡೆ madaḍe, *s.* A blockhead. 2. a sluggard.

ಮದತ್ರುನಿ madatruni, *see* ಮದಪುನಿ.

ಮದನ, ಮದನೆ madana, madane, *s.* Cupid. 2. a man's name.

ಮದಪು madapu, *s.* Forgetfulness.

ಮದಪುನಿ madapuni (ಮದ), *v. a.* To forget.

ಮದಪೆಲೆ madapele, *s.* A forgetful man, absent-minded man.

ಮದರಿ madari, *see* ಮದಕರಿ.

ಮದರೆಂಗಿ madareṅgi, *see* ಮದ್ರೆಂಗಿ.

ಮದಲೆ, ಮದಳೆ madalè, madaḷè, *see* ಮದ್ದಳೆ.

ಮದಾಂತೆ, ಮದಾಂಧೆ madānte, madāndhe, *s.* A man blind with pride *or* passion; an arrogant *or* dissolute man. 2. a sluggard, lazy man.

ಮದಾಮಸ್ತ್ madāmastu, *adj.* Stout, robust, lusty.

ಮದಿಪು madipu, *s.* A consultation, deliberation. 2. settlement, resolution. –ಕಲೆಪಿನಿ, –ದೆಪ್ಪುನಿ to consult. –ಮಳ್ಪುನಿ to settle.

ಮದಿಪುನಿ madipuni (ಮದ), *v. a.* To consult, deliberate, settle.

ಮದಿಮುಟ್ಟೆಲ್ madimuṭṭelu, *s.* The first menstruation.

ಮದಿರೆಂಗಿ madireṅgi, *see* ಮದ್ರೆಂಗಿ.

ಮದಿಲ್ madilu, *see* ಮದಲ್.

ಮದು madu, *s.* Mediating *or* interceding with a devil-dancer as the spokesman of a community. –ಪಣ್ಪುನಿ to mediate so.

ಮದುರ madura, *see* ಮಧುರ.

ಮದೆ madè, *s.* A screen, blind. 2. a retired place, privacy. –ಆಪಿನಿ to be screened, sheltered. –ಮಳ್ಪುನಿ to screen, hide.

ಮದೆಪು madepu, *s.* Shade, shelter, retirement.

ಮದೆಪುನಿ madepuni (ಮದೆ), *v. a.* To screen, shelter, hide.

ಮದೆಯುನಿ madeyuni (ಮದೆ), *v. n.* To be out of sight, shut.

ಮದೊಡಿ madoḍi, *s.* A branch of a palmyra, stripped of its leaves.

ಮದ್ದ್ maddu, *see* ಮರ್ದ್.

ಮದ್ದಡ್ಕತಾಯೆ maddaḍkatāye, *s.* A demon so called.

ಮದ್ದಲೆ, ಮದ್ದಳೆ maddalè, maddaḷè, *see* ಮದ್ದೊಳಿ.

ಮದ್ದಾನೆ maddānè, *s.* A rutting elephant.

ಮದ್ದಿಮ maddima, *see* ಮಧ್ಯಮ.

ಮದ್ದೇಸ, ಮದ್ಯೇಸ maddēsa, madyēsa, *s.* Persuasion, inducement. 2. pacifying, appeasing. 3. mediation.

ಮದ್ದೊಳಿ maddoḷi, *s.* A finger-drum.

ಮದ್ಯ **madya,** *s.* Wine; spirituous *or* fermented liquor. 2. *see* ಮಧ್ಯ. –ಪಾನ taking liquor. –ಪಾನಿ a drunkard.

ಮದ್ರೆಂಗಿ **madreṅgi,** *s.* The henna plant, *Lawsonia spinosa.*

ಮಧ **madha,** *see* ಮದ.

ಮಧಾಂಡೆ, ಮಧಾಂಧೆ **madhāṇḍe, madhāndhe,** *see* ಮದಾಂತಿ.

ಮಧು **madhu,** *s.* Spirituous liquor, wine. 2. honey. 3. sugar. 4. sweetness in flavour, sound, *or* disposition.

ಮಧುರ **madhura,** *adj.* Sweet, pleasing, agreeable.

ಮಧ್ಯ **madhya,** *s.* The middle, centre. *adv.* Between; *cf.* ನಡು.

ಮಧ್ಯಮ **madhyama,** *adj.* Middling, of middle sort.

ಮಧ್ಯಸ್ತಗಾರೆ, ಮಧ್ಯಸ್ತೆ **madhyastagāre, madhyaste,** *s.* A mediator, arbitrator.

ಮಧ್ಯಸ್ತಿಗೆ **madhyastigè,** *s.* Arbitration.

ವಧ್ಯಾನ, ಮಧ್ಯಾಹ್ನ **madhyāna, madhyāhna,** *s.* Noon, the middle of the day.

ಮಧ್ಯೇಸ **madhyēsa,** *see* ಮದ್ದೇಸ.

ಮಧ್ವಾಚಾರ್ಯೆ **madhvācārye,** *s.* The founder of a Veishṇava sect.

ಮನ **mana,** *see* ಮನಸ್ಸ್.

ಮನಃಪೂರ್ತಿ ಮನಃಪೂರ್ವಕ **manahpūrti, manahpūrvaka,** *adj.* Voluntary, wilful, earnest. *adv.* Voluntarily, wilfully, earnestly.

ಮನಕಸರಿಗೆ **manakasarigè,** *s.* Ill-feeling; uncleanness of heart *or* mind.

ಮನದಾನಿ **manadāni,** *s.* The next day, following day.

ಮನರ **manara,** *see* ಮನೋಹರ.

ಮನವರಿಕೆ **manavarikè,** *s.* Knowledge, perception.

ಮನಸಾಂತರ **manasāntara,** *see* ಮಾನಸಾಂತರ.

ಮನಸ್ತಾಪ **manastāpa,** *s.* Heart-burning, grief. 2. contrition, repentance. ನಿಕ್ಕ್ ಆಯು ಮನಸ್ತಾಪ ತಟ್ಟ್ಂಡ್ his grief has cleaved unto you.

ಮನಸ್ಸ್ **manassu,** *s.* The mind; the heart. 2. desire, inclination, attention. –ದ ಸ್ಥಿತಿ the state of mind. –ಮಲ್ಲೆ magnanimous. ಅರೆ– vacillation, wavering; reluctance. ಎಡ್ಡೆ– an excellent mind, amiable disposition. ಕನ– dreaming and waking. ಕೆಟ್ಟ–, ಪಡಿಕೆ– an evil mind; a bad disposition. ಚಂಚಲ– fickle-mindedness. –ಆಪಿನಿ to will; to wish, desire. –ಇಜ್ಜಿ to have no mind; not to desire *or* like. –ಬತ್ತಿಲೆಕ್ಕ as one likes; indiscriminately, arbitrarily. –ದೀಪಿನಿ to covet; to be attentive. –ಮಳ್ಪುನಿ to will; to resolve, determine. –ಉಪ್ಪುನಿ to have mind; to covet; to like. –ಕನಿಪುನಿ to be grieved. –ಕರಗುನಿ to be moved, to relent; to feel pity. –ಕುಂದುನಿ to be dejected. –ಕೊರ್ಪಿನಿ to pay attention. –ಮ

ಳ್ಳುನಿ to be willing, to will, consent, determine. —ಸೋಲ್ಪುನಿ to shrink, recoil; to be disinclined; to be fascinated, enamoured.

ಮನಸ್ಸಾಕ್ಷಿ **manassākshi**, *s.* Conscience.

ಮನಿಪುನಿ **manipuni** (ಮನಿ), *v. a.* To speak, utter. *It is used chiefly in the negative; as,* ಮನಿಪುಜಿ (I) do not speak ಮನಿಪಡೆ do not speak. ಮನಿಪುಜಿ he does not speak. ಮನಿಪಂದೆ without speaking, quietly, silently. ಮನಿಪಂದೆ ಉಪ್ಪುನಿ to be silent.

ಮನು **manu**, *s.* The celebrated Hindu legislator. —ಧರ್ಮಶಾಸ್ತ್ರ the institutes of Manu.

ಮನುಜೆ, ಮನುಷ್ಯೆ **manuje, manushye**, *s.* Man, a man, mankind.

ಮನುಸೆ **manuse**, *see* ಮನ್ಸೆ.

ಮನೆ **manè**, *s.* A house, home. ಅರ— a palace. ಸೆರೆ— a prison, jail. —ತನ a household. —ಸಾರ್ household furniture; personal property. —ವಾರ್ತೆ, —ವಾರ್ತಿಗೆ household affairs, family concern.

ಮನೆಗಾರೆ **manegāre**, *see* ಮಣಿಗಾರೆ.

ಮನೆಪು **manepu**, *see* ಮೊಣೆಪು.

ಮನೊಳಿ **manoḷi**, *see* ಮಣೊಲಿ.

ಮನೋಗತ **manōgata**, *s.* State of mind, purpose, opinion.

ಮನೋಭಾವ **manōbhāva**, *s.* State of mind.

ಮನೋರಥ **manōratha**, *s.* Wish, desire.

ಮನೋವಾಕ್ಕಾಯ **manōvākkāya**, *s.* Thought, word and deed.

ಮನೋವೇಗ **manōvēga**, *s.* Swiftness of thought. ಮನೋವೇಗೊಡ್ಡು as quick as thought.

ಮನೋಹರ **manōhara**, *s.* Charming, delightful, agreeable, pleasant.

ಮನ್ನಡಕೆ **mannaḍakè**, *see* ಮಂಣಡಕೆ.

ಮನ್ನಿಪುನಿ **mannipuni**, *see* ಮಂಣಿಪುನಿ

ಮನ್ಮಥೆ **manmathe**, *s.* Cupid.

ಮನ್ವಂತರ **manvantara**, *s.* The reign of a Manu, a period equal to 306,720,000 years of the mortals *or* one day of Brahma.

ಮನ್ವಾರ್ **manvāru**, *s.* A man of war.

ಮನ್ಸೆ **manse**, *s.* A Pariah.

ಮಪ್ಪು **mappu**, *s.* Evening, twilight. —ಆಪಿನಿ to grow dark.

ಮಬ್ಬು **mabbu**, *adj.* Dim, dull, obscure.

ಮಮಕಾರ, ಮಮತೆ, ಮಮತ್ಕಾರ **mamakāra, mamatè, mamatkāra**, *s.* Affection, love.

ಮಯು **maya**, *s. A Sanskrit affix used in the formation of adjectives attributive of that of which a thing is chiefly made or consists; as,* ಜಲ— covered with water. ಸ್ವರ್ಣ— golden, all gold.

ಮಯಂತಿ **mayanti**, *s.* A demon so called.

ಮಯಂದ್ರುನಿ **mayandruni**, *see* ಮಾಯಂಗ್ರುನಿ.

ಮಯಕ **mayaka**, *see* ಮಾಯಕ.

ಮಯಕುನಿ mayakuni (ಮಯಕ್), *v. n.* To vanish, disappear. 2. to flicker, as a light.

ಮಯಣ mayaṇa, *see* ಮಾಯಣ.

ಮಯಮಯ mayamaya, *adj.* Dim, dull. –ಆಪಿನಿ to become dim, as the eyes.

ಮಯಲುನಿ mayaluni, *see* ಮೈಲುನಿ.

ಮಯಾಸುರೆ mayāsure, *s.* A titan, the architect of giants.

ಮಯಿ mayi, *see* ಮೈ.

ಮಯಿಲೋ mayilō, *see* ಮಾಯಿಲೊ *under* ಮಾಯುನಿ.

ಮಯ್ಯರ್ mayyarụ, *s.* A pair of compasses. 2. a circle. –ಪಾಡುನಿ to draw a circle.

ಮರ mara, *s.* A tree. 2. timber; wood. –ಕಾರ್ a stilt; a wooden leg. –ತದರ್ small branches of a tree. –ತ ಬೇಲೆದಾಯಿ a carpenter. –ತೇವು a kind of Acacia, *Arum viviparum.* –ಕಟ್ಟುನಿ to become stiff. –ಕಡೆಯುನಿ trees to be rubbed against each other. –ಕಡ್ಪುನಿ to cut *or* fell a tree.

ಮರಂಕಣೆ, ಮರಕಣೆ maraṅkaṇè, marakaṇè, *adj.* On the back; topsy-turvy. –ಜೆಪ್ಪುನಿ to lie on the back. –ಬೂರುನಿ to fall backward. ಕಂಕಣೆ ಮರಂಕಣೆ ಮಳ್ಪುನಿ to turn topsy-turvy; to confuse.

ಮರಂಗೆ maraṅgè, *see* ಮೊರಂಗೆ.

ಮರಂಟೆ maranṭè, *see* ಮೊರಂಟೆ.

ಮರಂಡಲ maranḍala, *see* ಮೊರಂಡಲ.

ಮರಂಪು marampu, *see* ಮೊರಂಪು.

ಮರಂಪೆ marampè, *see* ಮೊರಂಪೆ.

ಮರಕ maraka, *see* ಮರ್ಕ.

ಮರಕಟ್ marakaṭụ, *adj.* Rough, clumsy. –ಬೇಲೆ a clumsy work.

ಮರಕಡಿ marakaḍi, *adj.* Rough, half finished, as a work.

ಮರಕತ marakata, *s.* An emerald.

ಮರಕಲ್ marakalụ, *see* ಮರ್ಕಲ್.

ಮರಕಲೆ marakale, *s.* A fisherman, who is also a palankeen bearer; a steersman. *fem.* ಮರಕಲ್ದಿ.

ಮರಕಲ್ಮೆ marakalme, *s.* The headman of fishermen.

ಮರಕೆರೆಂಗ್ marakereṅgụ, *s.* Tapioca, *Jatropha manihot.*

ಮರಕೊಡಪ್ಪೆ marakoḍappe, *s.* A woodpecker.

ಮರಗುಪತ್ರೆ maragupatrè, *s.* Mint.

ಮರಜೆ marajè, *see* ಮೊರಜ.

ಮರಡ್, ಮರಡು maraḍụ, maraḍu, *s.* Barrenness, sterility. 2. a small trough; *cf.* ಮರಾಯಿ. *adj.* Barren.

ಮರಣ maraṇa, *s.* Death. ಜನನ– birth and death. –ಕಾಲ time of death. –ಜಾತಕ a horoscope predicting one's death. –ಪತ್ರಿಕೆ, –ಶಾಸನ a will *or* testament.

ಮರಣಾಂತಿಕ maraṇāntika, *adj.* Lasting, enduring, ending with death.

ಮರದೇವಿ maradēvi, *s.* A barren woman.

ಮರನೀರ್ maranīrụ, *s.* Toddy.

ಮರಪು marapu, *s.* Forgetfulness; *cf.* ಮಜಪು. 2. a mistake, omission.

ಮರಪುನಿ marapuni (ಮರ), *v. a.* To fell, pull down, as a wall, *etc.* 2. to set up what has been upset. 3. *see* ಮದಪುನಿ.

ಮರಮುಂಜಲ್, ಮರಮಂಜಳ್ marامañjalu, maramañjaḷu, *s.* The yellow sanders, *Morinda umbellata.*

ಮರಮರ maramara, *adj.* Sleepy, drowsy.

ಮರಮಾರಿ maramāri, *see* ಮಾರಾಮಾರಿ.

ಮರಮಾಸ maramāsa, *s.* Tough meat.

ಮರಯಿ marayi, *see* ಮರಾಯಿ.

ಮರಲುನಿ maraluni, *see* ಮಲ್ರ್ನಿ.

ಮರವ marava, *s.* The caste of Maravas. 2. *see* ಮರ.

ಮರವೊಳಿ maravoḷi, *s.* A kind of mistletoe. 2. a wild screw-pine.

ಮರಸನಿ marasani, *s.* A kind of jam from Ceylon.

ಮರಹಂಮತ್ marahammatu, *s.* Mending, repair. 2. engineering. —ಇಲಾಖೆ public works department. —ಮಳ್ಪುನಿ to mend, repair.

ಮರಳಿಕ್ಕೆ maraḷikkè, *s.* Hinge.

ಮರಾಯಿ marāyi, *s.* A trough *or* bowl. ಅರ್ಗಂಜಿದ— a cattle trough. ಓಡ—, ತೋಡ— a long trough. ಕಲ್ಲ— a stone trough. ತುಳು— a large trough with a handle on either side.

ಮರಿ mari, *s.* A serpent, snake. 2. a worm. 3. a young animal. —ತ ಕುಲೆ the young of a serpent. ಪಚಿ— a green whip-snake. ಪೆರ್ಮರಿ a boa-constrictor. ಬಂಜಿ— an intestinal worm. —ತ ಮಂಣ್ poisonous earth; unhealthy soil.

ಮರಿಮುಗುಡು marimuguḍu, *s.* A kind of fresh-water fish.

ಮರಿಯಾದಿ, ಮರಿಯಾದೆ mariyādi, mariyādè, *s.* Custom, usage. 2. propriety of conduct. 3. respect, civility, politeness. 3. a present. —ದಾಯೆ a polite man; a man of rank.

ಮರಿಯಾಳ mariyāḷa, *see* ಮರ್ಯಾಳ.

ಮರು maru, *s.* A particle, atom. *adj.* Following, next. —ದಿನ the next day. ಜನತ ಮರು ಇಜ್ಜಿ there is no body.

ಮರುವ maruva, *see* ಮರ್ವ.

ಮರುವಾಯಿ maruvāyi, *s.* The bivalve, a kind of oyster. ಕಕ್ಕೆ—, ಕೇಸ—, ಕೊಯ್ಯೊಲ್—, ಕೋಲು—, ದಡ್ಡ—, ಪುಚ್ಚೆ—, ಪೂ— are different kinds of it.

ಮರುಳು maruḷu, *see* ಮಲ್ರ.

ಮರೆ marè, *s.* A shelter, retreat; *cf.* ಮಡೆ. 2. the milky juice *or* sap of plants, fruits, *etc.*; gum. —ಜಪ್ಪುನಿ the milky juice to exude. —ರೆಂಕುನಿ to be covered with the same.

ಮರೆಡುನಿ mareḍuni, *see* ಮುಯೊರ್ಡುನಿ.

ಮರೆಪುನಿ marepuni, *see* ಮದಪುನಿ. 2. *see* ಮರಪುನಿ.

ಮರ್ಕ್ marku, *s.* Scum *or* sediment of oil.

ಮರ್ಕ marka, *adj.* Fainting. dejection, languor. —ಆಪಿನಿ to faint, feel dejected.

ಮರ್ಕಟ್ markaṭu, *see* ಮರಕಟ.

ಮರ್ಕಟೆ markaṭe, *s.* A monkey, ape. 2. a stupid fellow.

ಮರ್ಕಡಿ markaḍi, *see* ಮರಕಡಿ.

ಮರ್ಕಡೆ, ಮರ್ಕೊಡೆ markaḍè, markoḍè, *s.* A bad habit, improper behaviour, rudeness, naughtiness.

ಮರ್ಕಲ್ markaḷu, *s.* A measure of salt, equal to 28 pounds.

ಮರ್ಕುನಿ markuni (ಮರ್ಕ್), *v. n.* To groan, moan.

ಮರ್ಕೆಲ್ markeḷu, *s.* Groaning, moaning.

ಮರ್ಗ್ margu, *adj.* Dead. —ಆಪಿನಿ to die.

ಮರ್ಗಿ margi, *see* ಮರಾಯಿ.

ಮರ್ಗಿಲ್ margiḷu, *s.* The side, flank. ಬಲತ— the right side. ದತ್ತ— the left side.

ಮರ್ಚ marća, *s.* Enticement, seduction. 2. taming, domesticating.

ಮರ್ಚಾವುನಿ marćāvuni, *c. v.* (*of* ಮರ್ಚುನಿ) To entice, seduce. 2. to tame, domesticate.

ಮರ್ಚುನಿ marćuni (ಮರ್ಚ್), *v. n.* To be enticed, seduced. 2. to be tamed, domesticated.

ಮರ್ಚೆಲ್ marćeḷu, *adj.* Tamed. *s.* Tameness. ಕೈ— taming, as an animal.

ಮರ್ಜ marja, *see* ಮೊರಜ.

ಮರ್ಜಾವುನಿ marjāvuni, *c. v.* (*of* ಮರ್ಜುನಿ) To cover, shelter, as a hen its young ones under its wings.

ಮರ್ಜಿ marji, *s.* Opinion, sentiment. 2. disposition, inclination. 3. will, pleasure. 4. manner, way.

ಮರ್ಣ marṇa, *see* ಮರಣ.

ಮರ್ತಿ marti, *s.* A silly *or* simple woman.

ಮರ್ತೆ martè, *s.* Selling, bargain.

ಮರ್ದ್ mardu, *s.* Medicine. 2. gunpowder; *also* ಬೆದಿಮರ್ದ್. 3. decoy powder, philter. —ದಾಯೆ a physician. —ಕೊರ್ಪಿನಿ to administer medicine, treat a patient.

ಮರ್ದಡೆ mardaḍe, *s.* An honorary title among Jainas.

ಮರ್ದನ mardana, *s.* Rubbing, shampooing. 2. grinding. 3. killing. —ಮಳ್ಪುನಿ, ಮರ್ದಿಪುನಿ to rub, shampoo, grind.

ಮರ್ಪು marpu, *see* ಮಾರ್ಪು.

ಮರ್ಬು marbu, *see* ಮಬ್ಬು.

ಮರ್ಮ marma, *s.* A secret. 2. a vital part. 3. *see* ವರ್ಮ.

ಮರ್ಮಳೆ marmaḷè, *see* ಮರ್ಮಾಳೆ.

ಮರ್ಮಾಯೆ marmāye, *s.* A female's son-in-law, a nephew *or* a brother's son.

ಮರ್ಮಾಳ್ marmāḷu, *s.* A female's daughter-in-law, a niece *or* a brother's daughter.

ಮರ್ಯಾದಿ maryādi, *see* ಮರಿಯಾದಿ.

ಮಯ್ಯಾಳ maryāḷa, *s.* The rainy season, monsoon.

ಮಲ್ marlu̥, *s.* Madness, insanity. *adj.* Mad, insane, foolish. ಅರೆ– half-mad, crack-brained. ಇಲ್– dotage, senility; absent-mindedness. –ಪಿಜಿನ್ a small, red kind of ant. –ಪೂ premature blossoms of a plant. –ಆಪಿನಿ to be fascinated, enticed, seduced; to be exceedingly pleased, enchanted. –ಕಟ್ಟುನಿ to behave foolishly. –ಪತ್ತುನಿ to become mad. –ಮಳ್ಪುನಿ to seduce, fascinate.

ಮಲ್ಲಾಟ marlāṭa, *s.* Foolishness, silliness. 2. pranks, tricks.

ಮಲ್ಲಾವುನಿ marlāvuni, *c. v.* (*of* ಮಲ್ಲುನಿ) To entice, decoy, allure, seduce.

ಮಲ್ಲು marlu, *see* ಮತಿ.

ಮಲ್ಲುನಿ marluni (ಮಲ್), *v. n.* To be restless *or* over-active; to be intent upon doing mischief.

ಮಲ್ಲೆ marle, *s.* A mad man. –ದಿ a mad woman.

ಮರ್ವ marva, *s.* A kind of timber tree, *Lagerstrœmia reginæ.*

ಮರ್ವಯಿ, ಮರ್ವಾಯಿ marvayi, marvāyi, *see* ಮರುವಾಯಿ.

ಮರ್ವಾವುನಿ marvāvuni (ಮರ್ವಾ), *v. a.* To gnaw, nibble, bite slowly *or* with effort.

ಮಲ mala, *s.* Dirt, bodily excretion. 2. dross. 3. sin. –ಮೂತ್ರ fæces and urine. –ಬದ್ಧ constipation.

ಮಲಂಪು malampu, *see* ಮೊಲಂಪು.

ಮಲಕ್ malaku̥, *s.* A kind of necklace. ಜೊಟ್ಟ– a small kind of necklace.

ಮಲಕ malaka, *s.* A storm, tempest. –ಆಕ್ಯುನಿ to have a storm.

ಮಲಗುನಿ malaguni (ಮಲಗ್), *v. n.* To lie down, to sleep.

ಮಲತಂಕೆ malataṅkè, *s.* A hyena.

ಮಲಪುನಿ malapuni, *see* ಮಲೆಂಗುನಿ.

ಮಲಪೂಪ, ಮಲಪೂಪು malapūpa, malapūpu, *s.* An enclosure in a letter.

ಮಲಮಲ್ malamalu̥, *s.* Muslin.

ಮಲಮಾಸ malamāsa, *s.* An intercalary month.

ಮಲಯಾಳ malayāḷa, *s.* The province of Malabar. ಮಲಯಾಳಿ a man from Malabar.

ಮಲರಾಯೆ malarāye, *s.* A demon so called.

ಮಲವೆ malave, *s.* A man with squint eyes.

ಮಲಾಮು malāmu̥, *see* ಮುಲಾಮು.

ಮಲಾಮತ್ malāmatu̥, *s.* A strait, calamity, difficulty, dilemma. 2. reproach.

ಮಲಿನ malina, *adj.* Foul, filthy, dirty.

ಮಲಿಯುನಿ, ಮಲಿರುನಿ maliyuni, maliruni (ಮಲಿ), *v. n.* To slip *or* wear away, as a portion of earth *or* mud work; *also* ಮಲಿದ್ಪೋಪಿನಿ.

ಮಲೆ malè, *s.* A forest, jungle; a hill overgrown with forest. –ಕಂಡೊಡಿ a large viper. –ಕಾ

ಳಂಸೆ, –ಮರಿ a kind of serpent. –ಕಿರೆಂಗ್, –ಗಿರೆಂಗ್ a large kind of sweet potato.

ಮಲೆಂಗುನಿ maleṅguni (ಮಲೆಂಗ್), *v. n.* To recline, lean against.

ಮಲೆಜುಮಾದಿ malejumādi, *s.* A demon so called.

ಮಲೆಪಿನಿ malepini, *see* ಮಲೆಯುನಿ.

ಮಲೆಯಾಳ maleyāḷa, *see* ಮಲಯಾಳ.

ಮಲೆಯುನಿ, ಮಲೆವುನಿ maleyuni, malevuni (ಮಲೆ), *v. a.* To frown, scowl. 2. to stare.

ಮಲ್ಲ, ಮಲ್ಲವು, ಮಲ್ಲಾವು malla, mallavu, mallāvu, *adj.* Great, large, big, extensive. 2. chief, principal, important. 3. loud. –ಕಳುವೆ a down-right thief. –ಕಾರ್ಯ an important business. –ನರಮಾನಿ a great *or* respectable man. –ಭೂಮಿ an extensive land. –ಶಬ್ದ a loud noise.

ಮಲ್ಲಂಜಿ mallañji, *see* ಮೊರಜ.

ಮಲ್ಲಂಮ mallamma, *s.* A goddess so called.

ಮಲ್ಲಯುದ್ಧ mallayuddha, *s.* Boxing, wrestling. 2. a duel, combat.

ಮಲ್ಲರಾಯೆ mallarāye, *see* ಮಲರಾಯೆ.

ಮಲ್ಲಸ್ತಿಗೆ, ಮಲ್ಲಾದಿಗೆ mallastigė, mallādigė, *s.* Greatness, superiority, loftiness. 2. pride.

ಮಲ್ಲಾಯೆ mallāye, *s.* A man senior in age; a senior. 2. a rich man. 3. a grown up man. *fem.* ಮಲ್ಲಾಳ್ a female senior in age; a grown up woman; a rich woman.

ಮಲ್ಲಾವುನಿ mallāvuni, *c. v.* (*of* ಮಲ್ಲುನಿ) To make coincide.

ಮಲ್ಲಾಸ್ mallāsu, *s.* A kind of fish.

ಮಲ್ಲಿ malli, *s.* A lamp-bearer, a man who attends with a light. ದೀಪದ– a molten image holding a lamp in its hands.

ಮಲ್ಲಿಗೆ malligė, *s.* The creeper *Jasminum sambac.* ಚೆಂಡ್–, ಚೆಂಡು–, ಜಾಜಿ–, ಜೂಜಿ–, ದೊಡ್ಡ–, are different kinds of jasmin. ಬ್ಯಾಯ– the four-o-clock flower, *Mirabilis jalappa.*

ಮಲ್ಲಿಯುನಿ malliyuni, *see* ಮಲಿಯುನಿ.

ಮಲ್ಲಿವಾಳ್ mallivāḷu, *see* ಮುಡ್ಯೆಲ.

ಮಲ್ಲುನಿ malluni (ಮಲ್ಲ್), *v. n.* To coincide. 2. *see* ಮಲೆಯುನಿ

ಮಲ್ಲೆ mallė, *see* ಮಲ್ಲ.

ಮಲ್ಲೆ malle, *s.* A boxer, wrestler. 2. a barber. 3. a keeper. ನಾಯಿತ– a dog-keeper.

ಮಲ್ಲೊಲಿ malloli, *see* ಮಲ್ಲಿ.

ಮವುಪುನಿ mavupuni, *see* ಮಪ್ಪುನಿ.

ಮಶಕ mašaka, *see* ಮಸ್ಕ.

ಮಶಕಿ mašaki, *s.* A leather bag.

ಮಶಲ್, ಮಶಾಲ್ mašalu, mašālu, *s.* A torch.

ಮಶಿ maši, *s.* Ink. 2. charcoal. –ದೌತಿ, –ಬುರುಡೆ an inkstand.

ಮಶೀದಿ mašīdi, *s.* A mosque.

ಮಶೆ mašė, *s.* Little, few, scarce. 2. *with neg.* not at all. –ಬೂರುಜಿ there is no effect at all.

ಮಶೆವುನಿ maševuni, *see* ಮಸಿಯುನಿ.

ಮಸಕು masaku, *see* ಮುಸುಕು.

ಮಸಕುನಿ masakuni, *see* ಮುಸ್ಕುನಿ.

ಮಸಣ masaṇa, *s.* A cemetery. ಮಂಗ್— any thing without reference to its quality. ಮಂಗ್ಮಸಣ ತಿನ್ನಿನಿ to eat indiscriminately.

ಮಸಲತ್, ಮಸಲಾದಿಗೆ masalatu̥, masalādigè, *s.* Deliberation, counsel. 2. intrigue, plot.

ಮಸಲುನಿ masaluni (ಮಸಲ್), *v. n.* To change colour. 2. to become muddy *or* foul. ಕಂಗ್— eyes to turn red. ನೀರ್—water to become muddy.

ಮಸಲೆ, ಮಸಾಲೆ masalè, masālè, *s.* Curry powder; spicery. 2. horse medicine.

ಮಸಿಯುನಿ, ಮಸೆವುನಿ masiyuni, masevuni (ಮಸಿ, ಮಸೆ), *v. a.* To whet, sharpen. 2. to quarrel, fight.

ಮುಸುಕು, ಮುಸ್ಕ್ masuku, masku̥, *s.* Dimness, dulness; fading. —ಆಪಿನಿ to become dim, to fade.

ಮಸೆಲುನಿ maseluni, *see* ಮಸಲುನಿ.

ಮಸ್ಕತಿ maskati, *s.* A fine kind of rice made of boiled paddy.

ಮುಸ್ಕುನಿ maskuni (ಮುಸ್ಕ್), *v. n.* To fade; to become dim, wane.

ಮಸ್ತ್, ಮಸ್ತು mastu̥, mastu, *s. adj.* Fat, stout. 2. abundant, plentiful; ample, sufficient. 3. drunk.

ಮಸ್ತ, ಮಸ್ತಕ masta, mastaka, *s.* The head, scull.

ಮಸ್ತಿ masti, *s.* Intoxication, pride, lust. 2. the rut of an elephant, *etc.* —ತೋಜಾವುನಿ, —ಮಳ್ಪುನಿ to be overbearing; to be aggressive, quarrelsome.

ಮಹಂಕಾಳಿ mahaṅkāḷi, *see* ಮಹಾಕಾಳಿ.

ಮಹತ್ವ mahatva, *s.* Greatness, either in rank *or* bulk.

ಮಹಲ್ mahalu̥, *s.* A palace, mansion, hall. 2. an elephant's stable.

ಮಹಾ mahā, *adj.* Great, much, eminent. *adv.* Exceedingly, excessively, very. —ಜನ a large crowd *or* assembly of people. —ರೋಗ an incurable disease.

ಮಹಾಕಾಳಿ, ಮಹಾದೇವಿ mahākāḷi, mahādēvi, *s.* Durgi, wife of Šiva.

ಮಹಾತ್ಮೆ mahātme, *s.* A great man. 2. a prophet.

ಮಹಾನುಭಾವೆ mahānubhāve, *s.* A man eminent for wisdom.

ಮಹಾರಾಜ mahārāja, *adj.* Princely, royal, great. —ಪೂಜಿತ worthy of great respect. —ಶ್ರೀ possessed of great respect; an honorific prefix.

ಮಹಾರಾಜೆ, ಮಹಾರಾಯೆ mahārāje, mahārāye, *s.* A sovereign, emperor. 2. a gentleman.

ಮಹಾರಾಷ್ಟ, ಮಹಾರಾಷ್ಟ್ರ mahārāshṭa, mahārāshṭra, *s.* The Mahratta country.

ಮಹಾರ್ನೌಮಿ mahārnoumi, *s.* The ninth day of Dasara feast. 2. the Dasara feast.

ಮಹಾಲಯ, ಮಹಾಳ್ಯ mahālaya, mahāḷya, *s.* Offerings made to the manes of the departed ancestors, during the second fortnight of the 6th lunar month; *also* –ಪಕ್ಷ.

ಮಹಿ mahi, *s.* The earth; *also* ಮಹಿತಲ. –ಪತಿ a king, sovereign.

ಮಹಿತ mahita, *adj.* Proper, right. 2. reverenced.

ಮಹಿಮೆ mahimè, *s.* Glory, magnitude, majesty, greatness.

ಮಹಿಷಾಸುರೆ mahishāsure, *s.* A giant so called.

ಮಹಿಸಂದಾಯೆ mahisandāye, *s.* A demon so called.

ಮಹೇಶ್ವರೆ mahēśvare, *s.* A name of Śiva.

ಮಹೋಂನತ mahōnnata, *adj.* Very high, supreme. –ಪದವಿ supreme bliss. ಮಹೋಂನತೆ God the Great *or* High One.

ಮಹೋತ್ಸವ mahōtsava, *s.* Great festivity.

ಮಹೋದರ mahōdara, *s.* Ascites, a kind of dropsy.

ಮಳಂಪು maḷampu, *see* ಮೊಳಂಪು.

ಮಳಿಗೆ maḷigè, *s.* A store-house, wholesale shop. 2. a cloth-shop.

ಮಳೆ maḷè, *s.* Rain. –ಮದೆ, –ಮಾಡ್ a temporary, sloping shed.

ಮಳ್ಪುನಿ maḷpuni (ಮಳ್), *v. a.* To do, make, perform, cause, frame. ಉಪಕಾರ– to do a kind office. ಕೈದ್– to arrest; to close, finish. ಕ್ರಾದೆ– to frame rules. ಬೇನೆ– to cause *or* inflict pain. *Affixed to nouns it gives them a verbal signification*; *as*, ಅಟ್ಟಿಲ್– to cook. ಒಣಸ್– to eat. ತಡ– to delay. ಪ್ರೀತಿ– to love.

ಮಾಂಕ māṅka, *s.* Darkness; *cf.* ಮಂಕ.

ಮಾಂಕಾಳಿ māṅkāḷi, *see* ಮಹಾಕಾಳಿ.

ಮಾಂಗಾವುನಿ māṅgāvuni, *c. v.* (*of* ಮಾಂಗುನಿ) To avert the eyes. 2. to put out of sight. 3. *see* ಮಾಜಾವುನಿ.

ಮಾಂಗುನಿ māṅguni (ಮಾಂಗ್), *v. n.* To disappear, vanish.

ಮಾಂಜಿ māñji, *s.* The pomfret, a kind of fish. ಬೊಳ್ದು– *Stromateus candidus*.

ಮಾಂತ mānta, *see* ಮಾತ.

ಮಾಂದ್ರ māndra, *s.* Dried juice of mangoes. 2. sweetness.

ಮಾಂಪುನಿ māmpuni, *see* ಮಳ್ಪುನಿ.

ಮಾಂಫಲ māmphala, *see* ಮಾಪಲ.

ಮಾಂಬಲ, ಮಾಂಬಳ māmbala, māmbaḷa, *s.* A cake of fruits.

ಮಾಂಬ್ರ māmbra, *s.* A garland put upon the neck of a devil-dancer.

ಮಾಂಸ māmsa, *s.* Flesh; meat.

ಮಾಕಟೆ, ಮಾಕಡೆ mākaṭè, mākaḍè, *s.* A deceitful woman. *adj.* Deceitful, trickish, fraudulent. 2. worthless, useless, base.

ಮಾಕರಿಯುನಿ mākariyuni (ಮಾಕರ್), *v. n.* To become black.

ಮಾಕಲ್ದಿ **mākaldi**, *see* ಮಹಾಕಾಳಿ.

ಮಾಕಿ **māki**, *see* ಮಕ್ಕಿ.

ಮಾಕೀರಕಲ್ಲ್ **mākīrakallu**, *s.* A collyrium from the calx of brass, used for toothache.

ಮಾಗಣೆ **māgaṇè**, *s.* A division of a tāluk. –ಶೇನವೆ a village accountant and writer.

ಮಾಗಯಿ **māgayi**, *s.* An ear-ornament.

ಮಾಗುನಿ **māguni** (ಮಾಗ್), *v. n.* To ripen. 2. *see* ಮಾಂಗುನಿ.

ಮಾಘ **māgha**, *s.* The eleventh lunar month. 2. the name of a Sanskrit poem.

ಮಾಚಿಪತ್ರೆ **māčipatrè**, *s.* Wormwood, *Grangea maderaspatana.*

ಮಾಜಾವುನಿ **mājāvuni**, *c. v.* (*of* ಮಾಜುನಿ) To hide, conceal. 2. to erase, wipe, efface. 3. to dissipate, squander.

ಮಾಜಿ **māji**, *adj.* Late, former, recent.

ಮಾಜಿಮ್, ಮಾಜಿಮೆ, ಮಾಜುಮ್ **mājimu, mājimè, mājumu**, *s.* An intoxicating sweetmeat made of hemp-leaves, sugar, *etc.*

ಮಾಜಿರ್ **mājiru**, *s.* A statement of people present at an inquest, *etc.*

ಮಾಜುನಿ **mājuni** (ಮಾಜ್), *v. n.* To wear away, become dim, be effaced. 2. to vanish; *also* ಮಾಜಿದ್‌ಪೋಪಿನಿ. 3. *see* ಮಾಯುನಿ.

ಮಾಟ್ **māṭu**, *adj.* Unsuitable.

ಮಾಟ **māṭa**, *s.* Sorcery, witchcraft. 2. wickedness, mischief. –ದಾಯೆ a sorcerer; a mischievous fellow. –ಮಳ್ಪುನಿ to bewitch.

ಮಾಟಿ **māṭi**, *see* ಮಾದ್ರಿ.

ಮಾಟೆ **māṭè**, *s.* A hole, *or* cavity in earth, wood, *etc.* 2. a hole of snakes, scorpions, *etc.*

ಮಾಡ್ **māḍu**, *s.* The roof. ಅಂತರ್–, ಕಳ್ಳ–, ಪಕ್ಕಿ–, ಪುಚ್ಚೆ–, ಮಳೆ– are different varieties of roof.

ಮಾಡ **māḍa**, *s.* The shrine of a demon.

ಮಾಡವುನಿ, ಮಾಡಾವುನಿ **māḍavuni, māḍāvuni** (ಮಾಡ, ಮಾಡಾ), *v. a.* To cultivate, as land. 2. to display, parade. ಸೇಲೆ– to be foppish.

ಮಾಡು **māḍu**, *s.* A weapon made of a deer's horn.

ಮಾಣಾವುನಿ **māṇāvuni** (ಮಾಣಾ), *v. a.* To lull to sleep. 2. to lessen, decrease, abate.

ಮಾಣಿ **māṇi**, *s.* A Brahman boy. 2. *see* ಮಾನಿ. 3. *see* ಮಾಣ್ಯೆ.

ಮಾಣಿಕ **māṇika**, *s.* A ruby.

ಮಾಣ್ಯಾದಿಗೆ **māṇyādigè**, *s.* The position of a demon priest.

ಮಾಣ್ಯೆ **māṇye**, *s.* A demon priest.

ಮಾತ್‌ಕಥೆ **mātukathe**, *s.* Conversation. 2. intercourse. –ಇಜ್ಜಿ not being on good terms.

ಮಾತ **māta**, *s.* The whole, all, every thing. *pro.* All. *adv.* Completely, wholly, entirely. –ಲಾ altogether, entirely.

ಮಾತಬಾರಿ **mātabāri**, *adj.* Rich, respectable, of good rank.

–ಗೃಹಸ್ಥ a respectable gentleman.

ಮಾತಾಯಿ mātāyi, *see* ಮತಾಯಿ.

ಮಾತಿರಿ mātiri, *s.* Ebb, the reflux of the tide.

ಮಾತುನಿ mātuni (ಮಾತಿ), *v. n.* To lounge about, saunter.

ಮಾತೆರ್, ಮಾತೆರ್ಲಾ māteru, māterlā, *s.* All people.

ಮಾತ್ರ mātra, *adv.* Only, solely, simply, merely; alone. ಅವು– merely that. ಆಯಿ– only he, he alone. ಬಲ್ಲ– just come.

ಮಾತ್ರೆ mātrè, *s.* A pill. 2. a short vowel. 3. quantity in metre.

ಮಾತ್ರೆಫಲ mātrephala, *s.* A kind of citron.

ಮಾದ್ mādu, *s.* Turning about. 2. a small bridge.

ಮಾದರಫಲ mādaraphala, *s.* A large kind of citron.

ಮಾದರಿ mādari, *see* ಮಾದ್ರಿ.

ಮಾದಲ mādala, *see* ಮಾಪಲ.

ಮಾದವುನಿ, ಮಾದಾವುನಿ mādavuni, mādāvuni, *c. v.* (*of* ಮಾದುನಿ) To turn about, turn the face to another quarter.

ಮಾದಿಗೆ mādige, *s.* A chuckler; a class of Pariahs.

ಮಾದಿರ mādira, *s.* A kind of dancing.

ಮಾದಿರ, ಮಾದಿರ್ದಬೂರು mādira, mādirdabūru, *s.* A kind of creeper.

ಮಾದಿರಿ mādiri, *see* ಮಾದ್ರಿ.

ಮಾದುನಿ māduni (ಮಾದ್), *v. n.* To turn about.

ಮಾದೇವಿ mādēvi, *see* ಮಹಾದೇವಿ.

ಮಾದ್ರಿ mādri, *s.* A specimen, sample, pattern.

ಮಾನ māna, *s.* Honour, respect, civility. 2. measure in general. 3. a quarter seer. ಅಪ– disgrace. ಚಾಂದ್ರ– lunar measurement. –ಭಂಗ defamation. –ಮರಿಯಾದೆ honours and privileges. –ವಂತೆ, –ಸ್ಥ a respectable man. –ಸ್ಥಾನ a place of honour. –ಹಾನಿ loss of respect. –ಹೀನೆ a despised man. –ಕೊರ್ಪಿನಿ to honour.

ಮಾನಸಾಂತರ mānasāntara, *s.* Repentance.

ಮಾನಾವುನಿ mānāvuni, *see* ಮಾಣಾವುನಿ.

ಮಾನಿ māni, *s.* A man. 2. a messenger. 3. a servant; *cf.* ಮಾಣಿ.

ಮಾನಿಪುನಿ, ಮಾನಿಸುನಿ mānipuni, mānisuni (ಮಾನಿ, ಮಾನಿಸ್), *v. a.* To honour, respect.

ಮಾನ್ಯ mānya, *s.* A grant of lands. 2. respectability. *adj.* Respectable, venerable. ರಾಜ– of princely honours; royal.

ಮಾನ್ಯ mānya, *adj.* Human, pertaining to man. –ಸರ human voice. –ಕೆರ್ಪಿನಿ to murder.

ಮಾನ್ಯೆ mānye, *s.* A Pariah servant. 2. *see* ಮಾನಿ.

ಮಾಪಲ māpala, *s.* A large citron, *Citrus medica.*

ಮಾಪಾರಿ, ಮಾಪ್ಯಾರಿ māpāri, māpyāri, *s.* A public measurer, one who metes *or* measures grains, *etc.*

ಮಾಪಿಳೆ, ಮಾಪುಳೆ **māpiḷe, māpuḷe**, *s.* A descendant of Malabar Mahommedans; *cf.* ಬ್ಯಾರಿ.

ಮಾಪುನಿ **māpuni** (ಮಾ), *v. a.* To undress, divest of clothes. 2. to change dress. 3. *see* ಮಗಪುನಿ. ಕುಂಟು– to change dress.

ಮಾಫ್, ಮಾಫು **māphu, māphu**, *s.* Pardon, excuse; exemption, remission. –ಕೊರ್ಪಿನಿ to excuse, as a fault; to remit, as a debt, *etc.* –ನಡ್ಪೊಲುನಿ to beg pardon. –ಮಳ್ಪುನಿ to forgive.

ಮಾಫಕ್ **māphaku**, *adj.* According to, suitable, fit, proper.

ಮಾಫಲ **māphala**, *see* ಮಾಪಲ.

ಮಾಮಿ **māmi**, *s.* A paternal aunt. 2. a mother-in-law. 3. the wife of a maternal uncle.

ಮಾಮುಲ್, ಮಾಮೂಲು **māmulu, māmūlu**, *s.* Usage, established custom, prescription.

ಮಾಮೆ **māme**, *s.* A maternal uncle, mother's brother.

ಮಾಯ **māya**, *s.* Fraud, trick; infatuation; deception. 2. illusion; *cf.* ಮಯಕ. 3. juggling. 4. wickedness, villainy. 5. vanity, phantom, imagination. 6. idealism. 7. Pārvati, Lakshmi. –ಗೋಚರ a vision. –ತಂತ್ರ, –ವಿದ್ಯೆ jugglery, sleight of hand, legerdemain, magic. –ಆಪಿನಿ to disappear. –ಮಳ್ಪುನಿ to deceive, impose upon; to conceal, hide.

ಮಾಯಂಗ್ರುನಿ, ಮಾಯಂದ್ರುನಿ **māyaṅgruni, māyandruni** (ಮಾಯಂಗ್ರ್, ಮಾಯಂದ್ರ್), *v. n.* To become dirty *or* filthy; to become sticky from much soiling, as clothes, *etc.*

ಮಾಯಂದಾಯೆ **māyandāye**, *s.* A demon so called.

ಮಾಯಂದಾಳ್, ಮಾಯಳ್, ಮಾಯೆಲ್ದಿ **māyandāḷu, māyaḷu, māyeldi**, *s.* A female demon so called.

ಮಾಯಕ, ಮಾಯಿಕ **māyaka, māyika**, *s.* Vanishing, fleeting, passing away, disappearing. 2. *see* ಮಾಯ. –ಆಪಿನಿ to vanish. –ಮಳ್ಪುನಿ to conceal.

ಮಾಯಕೆ **māyake**, *s.* A great deceiver; *cf.* ಮಾಯಕ.

ಮಾಯಣ **māyaṇa**, *s.* Wax. –ಬತ್ತಿ a wax candle.

ಮಾಯತ್, ಮಾಯಿತಿ **māyatu, māyiti**, *see* ಮಾಹಿತಿ.

ಮಾಯಾಪಾಶ **māyāpāśa**, *s.* Family ties.

ಮಾಯಾಪ್ರಪಂಚ **māyāprapañća**, *s.* The world, as being an illusion.

ಮಾಯಾವಾದ **māyāvāda**, *s.* Idealism. 2. pantheism.

ಮಾಯಾವಾದಿ **māyāvādi**, *s.* An idealist. 2. a pantheist.

ಮಾಯಿ **māyi**, *s.* The eleventh Tuḷu month (Febr.-March).

ಮಾಯಿಫಲ **māyiphala**, *s.* Gallnut; *also* ಅಗ್ರಕಾಯಿ.

ಮಾಯಿಲೊ **māyilo**, *s.* A term of exorcism, coupled with ಕಂಗಿಲೊ; *cf.* ಕಂಗಿಲ್.

ಮಾಯುನಿ mâyuni (ಮಾಯ್), *v. n.* To be extinguished, put out. 2. to evaporate, as vapour *or* fumes. 3. to fall off, as corn, *etc.* from being over-ripe. ತೂ— fire to extinguish. ಪಂರ್ದ್— to drop down, as a fruit from being over-ripe.

ಮಾಯೆ mâyè, *see* ಮಾಯು.

ಮಾರ್ mâru, *s.* A fathom, the space to which a man can extend his arms. 2. twisting straw into a rope. 3. *see* ಮಾರಾಟ. 4. *see* ಮರ್ಗ. —ಪಾಡುನಿ to measure a rope, *etc.*, with the arms extended. —ಬುಡ್ಪಿನಿ, —ಮಳ್ಪುನಿ to twist a rope of straw.

ಮಾರ mâra, *s.* Cupid.

ಮಾರಂಪಡೆ mârampaḍè, *s.* A title among Jains.

ಮಾರಜೆ mârajè, *s.* A large kind of snake; *cf.* ಕೇರೆ.

ಮಾರಣ mâraṇa, *s.* Killing, destroying by charms *or* sorcery. 2. intrigue, cabal.

ಮಾರಯಿ mârayi, *see* ಮರುವಾಯಿ.

ಮಾರಾಟ mârâṭa, *s.* Sale; barter, exchange.

ಮಾರಾಟಿಗೆ mârâṭige, *s.* A Mahratta settler.

ಮಾರಾಮಾರಿ mârâmâri, *s.* Fighting, cuffing. 2. a riot, affrey. —ಮಳ್ಪುನಿ to fight.

ಮಾರಾಯೆ mârâye, *see* ಮಹಾರಾಜೆ.

ಮಾರಾವುನಿ mârâvuni, *c. v.* (*of* ಮಾರುನಿ) To cause to sell, get sold.

ಮಾರಾಷ್ಟ mârâshṭa, *see* ಮಹಾರಾಷ್ಟ್ರ.

ಮಾರಿ mâri, *s.* Durgi, presiding over epidemic diseases. 2. a plague, epidemic. 3. smallpox. 4. a bore, intolerable person. —ಕಿದೆ a large cowpen. —ಬಲೆ a large hand-net. —ಮಗ್ನ pestilence. —ರೋಗ an epidemic, *as* cholera, *etc.* —ಶೊಗ್ನನಿ an evil to happen suddenly.

ಮಾರಿಮನ್ಸೆ, ಮಾರಿಮನ್ಸೆ mârimanuse, mârimanse, *s.* A low class of Pariahs.

ಮಾರು mâru, *see* ಮಾರ್.

ಮಾರುನಿ mâruni (ಮಾರ್), *v. a.* To sell, dispose of.

ಮಾರುಬಲ mârubala, *see* ಮಾರ್ಬಲ.

ಮಾರೊಜಿ mâroji, *see* ಮಾರಜೆ.

ಮಾರ್ಗ mârga, *s.* A way, road, path. 2. means, manner, mode. 3. conduct. ಅಡ್ಡ— a cross-path; an improper course *or* conduct. ಉಳ— a foot-path, short cut, by-path. ರಾಜ— the highway, main road. —ಸ್ಥ a traveller. —ತೋಜಾವುನಿ to show the way *or* means. —ಮಳ್ಪುನಿ to construct a road; to devise means.

ಮಾರ್ಜನೆ mârjanè, *s.* Cleaning, particularly the floor of a house with cow-dung.

ಮಾರ್ನುಡಿ mârnuḍi, *s.* A reply.

ಮಾರ್ನೊಮಿ mârnomi, *see* ಮಹಾನೌಮಿ.

ಮಾರ್ಪಾಟ mārpāṭa, *s.* Change, alteration. –ಆಪಿನಿ to change, be altered.

ಮಾರ್ಪು mārpu, *s.* A fathom; *cf.* ಮಾರ್.

ಮಾರ್ಬಲ mārbala, *s.* An opposing, [army.

ಮಾಲ್ māḻu, *s.* Property, wealth. 2. goods, things, articles.

ಮಾಲ್ māḻu, *s.* Scum, refuse, lees. –ಉಂತುನಿ scum to accumulate. –ಲಕ್ಕುನಿ scum to float, to ferment.

ಮಾಲ māla, *s.* The mullet, *Mugil cephalotus.*

ಮಾಲಕಾರಿಯ, ಮಾಲಯ mālakāriya, mālaya, *see* ಮಹಾಲಯ.

ಮಾಲಪುರಿ mālapuri, *s.* A kind of sweetmeat.

ಮಾಲಾವುನಿ mālāvuni, *c. v.* (*of* ಮಾಲುನಿ) To make lean *or* incline, cause to lean. 2. to impute, charge with; to throw upon. ಪಾಪ– to charge with guilt.

ಮಾಲಿ māli, *s.* A gardener.

ಮಾಲಿಕಾನ್ mālikānu, *s.* An annual allowance to deposed kings.

ಮಾಲಿಕೆ mālike, *s.* An owner, possessor. 2. an heir.

ಮಾಲಿಸ್ mālisu, *s.* Rubbing, cleaning, as a horse, *etc.*, with a brush. –ಮಳ್ಪುನಿ to clean a horse.

ಮಾಲುನಿ māluni (ಮಾಲ್ದಿ), *v. n.* To lean, incline. 2. to reel, stagger, totter. 3. to be proved, established.

ಮಾಲೆ mālè, *s.* A garland, wreath of flowers. 2. a necklace. 3. a string of beads, a rosary. 4. cunning, trickery; *cf.* ಮಾಲಿ. –ದಾಯಿ a florist; a class of dancers. ಗಂಡ– the scrofula.

ಮಾಲೋಕೆ mālōke, *s.* A foreigner, an alien.

ಮಾಲ್ದಿ māldi, *s. fem. of* ಮಾಲಿ.

ಮಾಳ್ಯ māḷya, *see* ಮಾಳಿಗೆ.

ಮಾವತೆ, ಮಾವುತೆ māvate, māvute, *s.* An elephant driver, a mahout.

ಮಾವು māvu, *s.* A kind of tares. –ಕೊಡಿಪುನಿ tares to grow.

ಮಾವೆ māve, *s.* A father-in-law.

ಮಾಸ್ māsu, *s.* Fading, turbidity; soiling. *adj.* Faded; turbid; soiled. [ಮಾಂಸ.

ಮಾಸ māsa *s.* A month. 2. *see*

ಮಾಸಾದಿಗೆ māsādigè, *s.* Animal food, in contrast to vegetable food.

ಮಾಸಿಕ māsika, *s.* A monthly ceremony for a deceased ancestor, performed during the first year after his decease. *adj.* Monthly.

ಮಾಸುನಿ māsuni (ಮಾಸ್ಸಿ), *v. n.* To fade, lose colour. 2. to soil. ಪೂ– a flower to fade. ಮೋಣೆ– the face to become pale.

ಮಾಸೆ māsè, *s.* The after-birth.

ಮಾಸೆಲ್ māselu, *s.* Fading. 2. that which has faded *or* soiled.

ಮಾಸ್ತಿ māsti, *s.* The ghost of a suttee. –ಭಜನೆ worship of such a ghost.

ಮಾಹಿತಿ **māhiti,** *s.* Acquaintance, knowledge, experience.

ಮಾಳ್ **māḷu,** *see* ಮಾಲ್.

ಮಾಳ **māḷa,** *see* ಮಾಲ.

ಮಾಳ, ಮಾಳಯ **māḷa, māḷaya,** *see* ಮಹಾಲಯ.

ಮಾಳಿಗೆ **māḷigè,** *s.* An upper story; a terraced roof. ನೆಲ– a cellar. ಮುಂದು– a garret, loft.

ಮಾಳುನಿ **māḷuni,** *see* ಮಾಲುನಿ.

ಮಾಕ್ಷಿ **mākshi,** *see* ಮಾಸ್ತಿ.

ಮಿಂಚಿ **minči,** *see* ಮೆಂಚಿ.

ಮಿಂಚುನಿ **minčuni,** *see* ಮೆಂಚುನಿ.

ಮಿಂಜುನಿ **minjuni** (ಮಿಂಜ್), *v. n.* To be released, saved. 2. to escape. *v. a.* To exceed. 2. to spare. 3. to conquer, overcome.

ಮಿಂಡಕಾರೆ **minḍakāre,** *see* ಮಿಂಡೆ.

ಮಿಂಡಗಾರಿಗೆ, ಮಿಂಡಾಟಿಗೆ, ಮಿಂಡಾದಿಗೆ **minḍagārigè, minḍāṭigè, minḍādigè,** *s.* Unchastity, lewdness (applied to a female).

ಮಿಂಡಿ **minḍi,** *s.* An incontinent woman.

ಮಿಂಡೆ **minḍe,** *s.* A rake, paramour, whoremonger. –ಪತ್ತುನಿ to live in adultery.

ಮಿಂಣುಕುನಿ **minṇukuni,** *see* ಮೆಣ್ಕುನಿ.

ಮಿಂಪುರಿ **mimpuri,** *see* ಮೆಣ್ಪುರಿ.

ಮಿಕ್ಕ **mikka,** *adj.* Left, remaining. 2. other. –ವಿಷಯ other affairs, *etc.*

ಮಿಕ್ಕುನಿ **mikkuni** (ಮಿಕ್ಕ್), *v. a.* To surpass, exceed, transgress. *v. n.* To remain, be left.

ಮಿಗ್ತೆ, ಮಿಗಿತೆ **miguṭè, migitè,** *s.* Surplus, balance, remnant. 2. mesne profit.

ಮಿಗ **miga,** *s.* A deer; *cf.* ಮೃಗ.

ಮಿಗಿ, ಮಿಗಿಲ್ **migi, migilu,** *s.* Surpassing, excelling.

ಮಿಗಿಲುನಿ **migiluni** (ಮಿಗಿಲ್), *v. n.* To excel, surpass.

ಮಿಗು, ಮಿಗ್ಗಿ **migu, miggi,** *see* ಮಿಗಿ.

ಮಿಗ್ಗುನಿ **migguni,** *see* ಮಿಕ್ಕುನಿ.

ಮಿಜಾಕ್, ಮಿಜಾದ್, ಮಿಜಾಸ್ **mijāku, mijādu, mijāsu,** *s.* Display, ostentation, vain show. 2. pride, vanity.

ಮಿಜಿಪುನಿ, ಮಿಜಿಲುನಿ **mijipuni, mijiluni** (ಮಿಜಿ, ಮಿಜಿಲ್), *v. n.* To be full of worms, affected with worms.

ಮಿಜಿಮಿಜಿ, ಮಿಞಿಮಿಞಿ **mijimiji, miñimiñi,** *a.* Viscous, sticky.

ಮಿಟ್ಟಿ **miṭṭi,** *s.* Sweetness. 2. smacking. –ಹಾಕುನಿ to smack.

ಮಿಟ್ಟೆ **miṭṭè,** *adj.* Prominent, protruding. *s.* Pollen. ಕೇದಗೆದ– pollen of *Pandanus odoratissimus.*

ಮಿಠಾಯಿ **miṭhāyi,** *s.* Sweetmeat.

ಮಿಡಿ **miḍi,** *s.* Young, unripe fruit.

ಮಿಡು **miḍu,** *see* ಮುಡು.

ಮಿಣಿಮಿಣಿ **miṇimiṇi,** *adj.* Twinkling, glistening, dimly shining. –ತುದರ್ a lamp burning dimly. ಕಂಣ್ ಮಿಣಿಮಿಣಿ ಆಪಿನಿ eyes to glisten.

ಮಿಣುಕು **miṇuku,** *see* ಮೆಣುಕು.

ಮಿಣುಕುನಿ, ಮಿಣ್ಕುನಿ miṇukuni, miṇkuni (ಮಿಣುಕು, ಮಿಣ್ಕ್), *v. n.* To twinkle, glisten, sparkle.

ಮಿತ mita, *s.* Moderation, temperance, forbearance. 2. measure. 3. limitation, bounds. *adj.* Temperate, moderate.

ಮಿತರುನಿ mitaruni, *see* ಮಿತ್ತರುನಿ.

ಮಿತಾನುಭವ, ಮಿತಾನುಭೋಗ, mitānubhava, mitānubhōga, *s.* Temperance, moderate enjoyment, indulging moderately.

ಮಿತಾಮಿತ mitāmita, *adj.* Moderation and excess.

ಮಿತಿ miti, *s.* Limit, bound. 2. measure. 3. moderation. –ದಾಂತಿ boundless. –ಕಟ್ಟುನಿ to rate, estimate; to despise, undervalue. –ಮೀರುನಿ to transgress.

ಮಿತ್ತ್ mittu, *postp.* Above, upon, over, after. *adv.* Then, afterwards. –ಬರ್ಪಿನಿ to come up, to prosper; to be possessed, as with a demon. –ಬೂರುನಿ to get up; to assault.

ಮಿತ್ತಂತಾಯೆ mittantāye, *s.* A demon so called.

ಮಿತ್ತಟ್ಟ mittaṭṭa, *s.* The loft of a small upstair-room, an attic.

ಮಿತ್ತಡಿ mittaḍi, *s.* An offering to the manes.

ಮಿತ್ತಡ್ಡ್ಯ mittaḍḍya, *s.* The lintel of a door, *etc.*

ಮಿತ್ತರ mittara, *adj.* High, beyond reach of hand.

ಮಿತ್ತರುನಿ, ಮಿತ್ತಾವುನಿ mittaruni, mittāvuni (ಮಿತ್ತರ್, ಮಿತ್ತಾ), *v. a.* To ascend, mount, climb.

ಮಿತ್ತಾಚಾರ mittāčāra, *s.* Hatred.

ಮಿತ್ತಾಡುನಿ mittāḍuni (ಮಿತ್ತಾಡ್), *v. n.* To spring *or* leap over.

ಮಿತ್ತೇರುನಿ mittēruni, *see* ಮಿತ್ತರುನಿ.

ಮಿತ್ತೊಟ್ಟು mittoṭṭu, *see* ಮಿತ್ತಟ್ಟ.

ಮಿತ್ತೋಡಿ mittōḍi, *s.* The higher *or* upper part of a garden.

ಮಿತ್ರೆ mitre, *s.* A friend.

ಮಿಥುನ mithuna, *s.* The third solar month; the sign *Gemini.*

ಮಿನಯ minaya, *s.* Suspension, interdict.

ಮಿನಾಯಿ, ಮಿನಾಹಿ mināyi, mināhi, *s.* Abolition. 3. discharge, dismissal. –ಮಳ್ಪುನಿ to dispense with, dismiss.

ಮಿನಿ mini, *postp. Et cetera*, and so forth.

ಮಿನಿಮಿನಿ minimini, *see* ಮಿಣಿಮಿಣಿ.

ಮಿನುಕುನಿ minukuni, *see* ಮಿಣುಕುನಿ.

ಮಿಯಂಡೆ miyaṇḍe, *see* ಮಾಯಂಡೆ.

ಮಿರ mira, *see* ಮಾರ.

ಮಿರಿಮಿರಿ mirimiri, *adj.* Astringent, sharp.

ಮಿರೆ mire, *s.* The breast. 2. the nipple *or* teat of any animal. –ತ ಕಂಠಿ the nipple. –ತ ಪೇರ್ breast-milk. –ಕೊರ್ಪಿನಿ to suckle. –ತಿನ್ಪಿನಿ to suck. –ಬುಡುಪಾವುನಿ to wean.

ಮಿರೆವುನಿ mirevuni (ಮಿರೆ), *v. a.* To produce.

ಮಿಲಾಕತ್ milākatu, *s.* A common visit.

ಮಿಲಾಯಿಸುನಿ, ಮಿಲಾವುನಿ, ಮಿಲಾಸುನಿ milāyisuni, milāvuni, milāsuni

(ಮಿಲಾಯಿಸ್, ಮಿಲಾ, ಮಿಲಾಸ್), *v. a.* To mix, compound.

ಮಿಳಾವು, ಮಿಳವು **milāvu, miḷavu,** *s.* Steel.

ಮಿಶ್ರ **miśra,** *s.* Mixing, mixture, combination. *adj.* Mixed, compounded.

ಮಿಸಿಮಿ **misimi,** *s.* Valour; skill.

ಮಿಸ್ಕ್ **misku,** *s.* Scorn, despising. 2. confusion, dizziness. —ಆಪಿನಿ to be dizzy.

ಮಿಸ್ಕುನಿ **miskuni** (ಮಿಸ್ಕ್), *v. n.* To move, venture. 2. to interfere with, meddle. *It is used chiefly in a negative sense with* ಆವುಜಿ, ಆವಂದ್, ಬಲ್ಲಿ, *etc.*; *as,* ಅವುಳು ಮಿಸ್ಕೆರೆ ಬಲ್ಲಿ you cannot venture there. ಗಾಡಿಡ್ ಸಾಮಾನ ದಿಂಜಿದ್ ಮಿಸ್ಕೆರೆ ಬಲ್ಲಿ the cart being completely laden, there is no more room. ಉಂಡಿನವು ಹೆಚ್ಚ್ ಆದ್ ನನ ಮಿಸ್ಕೆರೆ ಆವುಜಿ my stomach being full, I can take nothing more. ಆತ್ ನೇಲ್ಯ ಮರಟೆ ಮಿಸ್ಕೆರೆ ಕಿಲುಜಿ it is difficult to climb upon such a large tree. ಆಕುಳೆ ನ್ಯಾಯೊಡು ಮಿಸ್ಕೆರೆ ಆವಂದ್ you should not interfere with their quarrel.

ಮಿಸ್ರ **misra,** *see* ಮಿಶ್ರ.

ಮಿಸ್ರಿ **misri,** *s.* A gold coin worth about 2½ rupees.

ಮಿಳ್ಳಿ **milli,** *s.* A small metallic vessel. ತೀರ್ಥದ— such a vessel containing holy water.

ಮೀಂಟುನಿ **mīṇṭuni** (ಮೀಂಟ್), *v. a.* To force up *or* out; to exert a pressure *or* sustain weight, as with a lever.

ಮೀಟ್ **mīṭu,** *adj.* Clever, smart, sharp.

ಮೀಟಾವುನಿ **mīṭāvuni,** *c. v.* (*of* ಮೀಟುನಿ) To cause to force up.

ಮೀಟುನಿ **mīṭuni,** *see* ಮೀಂಟುನಿ.

ಮೀನ್ **mīnu,** *s.* A fish. ಉಪ್ಪು— salted *or* preserved fish. ನುಂಗೆಲ್— dried fish. ಪಚಿ— fresh fish. —ದ ಬಲೆ a fishing net. —ಬಾಲಸರ, —ಬಾವಲಿ a kind of ear-ornaments.

ಮೀನ **mīna,** *s.* The 12th solar month; the sign *Pisces* in the zodiac.

ಮೀನಕಂಡ **mīnakaṇḍa,** *s.* The calf of the leg.

ಮೀನಮಂಜ **mīnamañja,** *s.* A fish-market.

ಮೀನವುನಿ **mīnavuni** (ಮೀನ), *v. a.* To behave coquettishly.

ಮೀನಾಂಕ **mīnānka,** *s.* A public fishing.

ಮೀಪಾಟ **mīpāṭa,** *s.* Bathing, a bath.

ಮೀಪಾವುನಿ **mīpāvuni,** *c. v.* (*of* ಮೀಪಿನಿ) To make *or* cause to bathe; to bathe, wash, give a bath.

ಮೀಪಿನಿ **mīpini** (ಮೀ), *v. n.* To take a bath, to wash one's self.

ಮೀಯಂಡೆ **mīyaṇḍe,** *s.* The throat, roof of the mouth.

ಮೀಯರ್ಪುನಿ **mīyarpuni** (ಮೀಯರ್), *v. a.* To wash a corpse.

ಮೀರ್ **mīru,** *adj.* Much, exceeding; *cf.* ಮೀರುನಿ.

ಮಿಾರ mīra, *s.* Sweet toddy.

ಮಿಾರವುನಿ, ಮಿಾರಾವುನಿ mīravuni, mīrāvuni, *c. v.* (*of* ಮಿಾರುನಿ) To cause to surpass or exceed.

ಮಿಾರಿಕೆ, ಮಿಾರಿಗೆ, ಮಿಾರುವಿಕೆ mīrikè, mīrigè, mīruvikè, *s.* Transgression, violation.

ಮಿಾರುನಿ mīruni (ಮಿಾರ್), *v. a.* To transgress, violate. 2. to exceed; *cf.* ಮಿಕ್ಕುನಿ.

ಮಿಾರ್ಣೆ mīrṇe, *s.* The sexton of a Roman Catholic church.

ಮಿಾಸೆ mīsè, *s.* Mustaches, whiskers. 2. feelers of an insect. –ಕರ್ಪತ್ತುನಿ the whiskers to appear. –ತಿರಿಂಗಾವುನಿ to trim the mustaches. –ನೈಪುನಿ to stroke the mustaches; to defy, challenge.

ಮು, ಮುಂ mu, muṁ, (*in comp.*) *adj.* Three, treble. ಮುಂಮಡಿ three fold. ಮುಕ್ಕಾಲ್ a three pie *or* quarter anna piece. ಮುಕ್ಕಲಿಗೆ a tripod, stool.

ಮುಂ muṁ, *adv.* Before, in front. –ಕಡೆ the front.

ಮುಂಕಂಣ್ muṅkaṇṇu, *see* ಮೂಂಕಣ್.

ಮುಂಕುದಿ muṅkudi, *see* ಮೂಕುತಿ.

ಮುಂಕೆಲಿ muṅkeli, *s.* A proud woman.

ಮುಂಕೆಲೆ muṅkele, *s.* A sickly man. 2. *see* ಮೂಕೆಲೆ.

ಮುಂಕೊರಳ್ muṅkoraḷu, *s.* A small spike of corn. 2. the first ear of corn.

ಮುಂಗಡ, ಮುಂಗಣ muṅgaḍa, muṅgaṇa, *s.* An advance in money. –ಕೊರ್ಪಿನಿ to pay in advance.

ಮುಂಗಯಿ muṅgayi, *see* ಮುಂಗೈ.

ಮುಂಗಲಿಯುನಿ muṅgaliyuni (ಮುಂಗಲಿ), *v. a.* To surpass.

ಮುಂಗಾರ್ muṅgāru, *s.* A hammer.

ಮುಂಗಿಲಿ, ಮುಂಗಿಲೆ, ಮುಂಗುಲಿ muṅgili, muṅgilè, muṅguli, *s.* A mungoose, ichneumon.

ಮುಂಗು muṅgu, *see* ಮುಂಗೆ.

ಮುಂಗುಡುನಿ muṅguḍuni (ಮುಂಗುಡ್), *v. n.* To be angry; *cf.* ಮುಕುಡುನಿ.

ಮುಂಗುಡೆ muṅguḍè, *see* ಮುಕ್ಕುಡೆ.

ಮುಂಗುದಿ muṅgudi, *see* ಮೂಕುತಿ.

ಮುಂಗುದುನಿ muṅguduni (ಮುಂಗುದ್), *v. n.* To dive, sink.

ಮುಂಗುಮುಸುಡು muṅgumusuḍu, *s.* A wry face.

ಮುಂಗುರ್ತ muṅgurta, *s.* Prognostication, foretoken.

ಮುಂಗೆ muṅgè, *s.* A shoot, bud, sprout.

ಮುಂಗೈ muṅgei, *s.* The fore arm. 2. the elbow. –ಸರಪೊಳಿ a chain bracelet. –ಒಡ್ಡುನಿ to hold out the fore-arm. –ಕುಟ್ಟುನಿ to box each other's fore arm in a kind of boxing match.

ಮುಂಙಣ muṅṅaṇa, *see* ಮುಂಗಡ.

ಮುಂಚಿ muńči, *s.* Red cayenne pepper, chilli, *Capsicum annuum.* ಎಡ್ಡೆ– pepper, *Piper nigrum.* ಗಾಂಧಾರಿ–, ಜೀರಿಗೆ–, ಲವಂಗ– a very sharp kind of chilli. –ತೊಟ್ಟು the stalk of a chilli. –ನೀರ್ pepper water.

ಮುಂಜ muńja, *s.* Circumcision.

ಮುಂಜಿ muńji, *s.* The grass *Saccharum munja.* 2. investiture with the sacred thread; *also* ಮುಂಜು. 2. circumcision of Mahommedans. —ಮಳ್ಪುನಿ to invest a boy with the sacred thread; to circumcise.

ಮುಂಞ, ಮುಂಞೆ muńńa, muńńè, *s.* The breast, as called by children. —ಕೊರ್ಪುನಿ to suckle.

ಮುಂಟು muṇṭu, *see* ಮೋಂಟು.

ಮುಂಡ muṇḍa, *s.* The forehead; *cf.* ಮುಂಡು. 2. the trunk. *adj.* Small.

ಮುಂಡಗೆ muṇḍagè, *see* ಮುಂಡೆಯಿ.

ಮುಂಡತಾಯೆ muṇḍatāye, *s.* A demon so called.

ಮುಂಡಲ್, ಮುಂಡಲ muṇḍalu̥, muṇḍala, *s.* A higher class of Pariahs. —ಮನ್ಸೆ a Pariah of this class.

ಮುಂಡಳ್ಳಿ muṇḍaḷḷi, *see* ಮುಂಡೊಲಿ.

ಮುಂಡಾಸ್ muṇḍāsu̥, *s.* A turban. —ಕಟ್ಟುನಿ to wind a turban.

ಮುಂಡಿ muṇḍi, *s.* The blue flowered tree *Memecylon tinctorium.* 2. a female's name.

ಮುಂಡಿಗೆ muṇḍigè, *s.* A small stool. 2. *see* ಮುಂಡೆಯಿ.

ಮುಂಡಿಡುನಿ muṇḍiḍuni (ಮುಂಡಿದಿ), *v. a.* To kneel; .to prostrate; *also* ಮುಂಡಿಡ್ಪಿನಿ.

ಮುಂಡಿಡ್ಪಾವುನಿ muṇḍiḍpāvuni, *c. v.* (*of* ಮುಂಡಿಡ್ಪಿನಿ) To make kneel, cause to kneel.

ಮುಂಡಿಲ muṇḍilḁ, *s.* A brush used by devil-dancers. 2. a kind of bush.

ಮುಂಡು muṇḍu, *s.* A young ox. 2. the vessel in which toddy is put. 3. a small upper garment. 4. the raised border of a veranda. 5. *see* ಮುಂಡ. —ಕೊಟ್ಟಿಗೆ an out-house. —ಪಾಡುನಿ, —ಬೂರುನಿ to prostrate. —ಪೊದೆಪುನಿ to wear a small garment. —ಬರಿಯುನಿ to fasten a toddy-vessel with a coir net-work.

ಮುಂಡುಪಚಾರ muṇḍupačāra, *s.* False civility.

ಮುಂಡುಮುಕ್ಕಲಿಗೆ muṇḍumukkaligè, *s.* A tripod, low stool.

ಮುಂಡೆ muṇḍè, *s.* A widow. 2. an abusive term. 3. a pestle. —ಪೆಲಕಾಯಿ a kind of jack fruit.

ಮುಂಡೆಯಿ muṇḍeyi, *s.* The screw-pine, *Pandanus odoratissimus.*

ಮುಂಡೊ muṇḍo, *see* ಮುಂಡ.

ಮುಂಡೊಲ muṇḍola, *see* ಮುಂಡಲ್.

ಮುಂಡೊಲಿ, ಮುಂಡೊಳಿ muṇḍoli, muṇḍoḷi, *s.* A rough kind of betel leaves. ಕುಕ್ಕುದ— a betel-vine trained upon a mango tree.

ಮುಂಣಿ muṇṇi, *s.* The folds of a male's cloth.

ಮುಂಣೆ muṇṇè, *see* ಮುಣೆ.

ಮುಂದಣ mundaṇa, *s.* Priority. *adj.* First, prior, future. —ಗತಿ future destiny.

ಮುಂದರಿಪುನಿ, ಮುಂದರಿಸುನಿ mundaripuni, mundarisuni (ಮುಂದರಿ, ಮುಂದರಿಸ್), *v. a.* To advance, march; to continue, carry on; *also* ಮುಂದರಿಯುನಿ.

ಮುಂದಲೆ mundalè, *s.* The front part of the head. 2. the hair above the forehead. 3. a head ornament. —ಬೊಟ್ಟು a plate set with jewels in its centre. ಮೂಕು— the whole face.

ಮುಂದಿರಿ mundiri, *s.* Settlement, adjustment. —ಲೆಖ್ಖ a settled account.

ಮುಂದಿಲ್ mundilụ, *s.* Export, exportation. 2. the court-yard of a house. ಒಳ— the inner courtyard of a square.

ಮುಂದುಕ, ಮುಂದುಕಟ್ಟ್, ಮುಂದೂಕು munduka, mundukaṭṭụ, mundūku, *s.* Dangerous illness.

ಮುಂದುರುನಿ munduruni *see* ಮುಡುರುನಿ.

ಮುಂದೆ mundè, *adj.* Before, in front.

ಮುಂದೆರಿಯುನಿ, ಮುಂದೆರುನಿ, ಮುಂದೆಸ್ಯನಿ munderiyuni, munderuni, mundersuni, *see* ಮುಂದರಿಪುನಿ.

ಮುಂನಡ್ munnaḍụ, *see* ಮುಂನೊಡು.

ಮುಂನಯ munnaya, *s.* Bezoar. 2. the bezoar root, *Dorstenia Drakena, Radix contrajervæ.*

ಮುಂನಿ munni, *s.* Tip, lappet.

ಮುಂನಿಗೆ munnigè, *s.* The hem of a dressing garment.

ಮುಂನೂದು munnūdu, *num.* Three hundred.

ಮುಂನೂಲು munnūlu, *s.* Three threads.

ಮುಂನೆ munnè, *see* ಮುನೆ.

ಮುಂನೊಡು munnoḍu, *adv.* Year before the last, two years ago.

ಮುಂಬರ mumbara, *s.* Calamity, distress.

ಮುಂಬಾಯಿ mumbāyi, *s.* Bombay.

ಮುಂಬು mumbu, *s.* The name of a caste. 2. dumb animals.

ಮುಂಮಡಿ mummaḍi, *adj.* Threefold.

ಮುಂಮನ mummana, *see* ಬಂಮನ.

ಮುಂಕಾವುನಿ muṁkāvuni, *see* ಮುಕಾವುನಿ.

ಮುಂಕುನಿ, ಮುಂಗುನಿ muṅkuni, muṅguni, *see* ಮುಕುನಿ.

ಮುಂಗೆಲೆ muṅgele, *see* ಘಂಕೆಲೆ.

ಮುಂಟ್ muṇṭụ, *see* ಮುರುಂಟು.

ಮುಂಡಲ muṇḍala, *see* ಮೊರಂಡೆ.

ಮುಕ muka, *see* ಮುಖ.

ಮುಕದಾಮ್ mukadāmụ, *s.* A head cooly *or* labourer, a maistry.

ಮುಕಬಾರೆ mukabārè, *s.* A kind of bush.

ಮುಕರಾವು, ಮುಕರೂಪು, ಮುಕಶಿರಿ mukarāvu, mukarūpu, mukaśiri, *see under* ಮುಖ.

ಮುಕಾರ್ mukārụ, *s.* Three legs. —ದೆತ್ತ್ ಪಾರುನಿ to run with three legs, as a lame quadruped.

ಮುಕಾರಿ mukāri, *s.* The headman of Pariahs.

ಮುಕಾಸ್ mukāsụ, *s.* Consideration, foresight. 2. *see* ಮುಕ್ಯಾಸ್.

ಮುಕಾಸ್ತೆ mukāste, *see* ಮುಖ್ಯಸ್ತೆ.

ಮುಕುಂಡ mukuṇḍa, *adv*. All over, around.

ಮುಕುಂದೆ mukunde, *s*. A name of Vishṇu.

ಮುಕುಟ, ಮುಕುಟಿ, ಮುಕುಟೆ mukuṭa, mukuṭi, mukuṭė, *s*. A crown, diadem.

ಮುಕುಡ mukuḍa, *s*. The coccyx.

ಮುಕುಡಿ mukuḍi, *see* ಮುಕ್ಕುಡಿ.

ಮುಕುಡು mukuḍu, *s*. Looking back.

ಮುಕುಡುನಿ mukuḍuni (ಮುಕುಡ್), *v. n*. To look back, turn the face.

ಮುಕುಡೆ mukuḍe, *see* ಮುಕ್ಕುಡೆ.

ಮುಕುತಿ mukuti, *see* ಮುಕ್ತಿ.

ಮುಕುತೆ mukutė, *see* ಮುಗಿತೆ.

ಮುಕುರುಕಪೋಲೆ mukurukapōlė, *s*. A very nice woman.

ಮುಕುರುನಿ mukuruni (ಮುಕುರು), *v. n*. To bud, germinate.

ಮುಕುರೂರು mukurūru, *see* ಮುಕ್ರೂರು.

ಮುಕುಳಿ mukuḷi, *see* ಮುಕ್ಕುಲಿ.

ಮುಕೂಬ್ mukūbu, *s*. Suspension, stoppage, adjournment.

ಮುಕೆ mukė, *see* ಮುಗ್ಗೆ. 2. *see* ಮುಂಗೆ. 3. *see* ಮುಖ್ಯಸ್ತೆ.

ಮುಕೊರಲ್ mukoralu, *see* ಮುಂಕೊರಳ್.

ಮುಕ್ಕ mukka, *s*. An abusive word. 2. *see* ಮುಖ. *adj*. Deformed. –ಬಾಲೆ a deformed child.

ಮುಕ್ಕಂಣೆ mukkaṇṇe, *s*. Śiva with three eyes. [ರಾಪು.

ಮುಕ್ಕರಾವು mukkarāvu, *see* ಮುಖ

ಮುಕ್ಕಲಿಗೆ, ಮುಕ್ಕಲೆ mukkaligė, mukkalė, *s*. A small stool *or* bench.

ಮುಕ್ಕಲ್ದಿ mukkaldi, *s*. The priest of the demon Koḍamandāye.

ಮುಕ್ಕಾಂಬೆ mukkāmbė, *see* ಮೂಕಾಂಬೆ.

ಮುಕ್ಕಾಣಿ mukkāṇi, *s*. Three-sixty-fourths. 2. a quarter anna.

ಮುಕ್ಕಾರ್ mukkāru, *s*. Three legs.

ಮುಕ್ಕಾರಿ mukkāri, *see* ಮುಕಾರಿ.

ಮುಕ್ಕಾಲ್ mukkālu, *s*. Three quarters. 2. a three-pie *or* quarter anna piece.

ಮುಕ್ಕಾಲಿ mukkāli, *see* ಮುಕ್ಕಲಿಗೆ.

ಮುಕ್ಕಾವುನಿ mukkāvuni, *c. v*. (*of* ಮುಕ್ಕುನಿ) To over-feed.

ಮುಕ್ಕಾಸ್ mukkāsu, *s*. Three cash.

ಮುಕ್ಕಿ mukki, *see* ಮುಖಿ.

ಮುಕ್ಕು mukku, *s*. A corner. 2. a narrow lane. 3. painting, dying. –ಪಾಡುನಿ to dye.

ಮುಕ್ಕುಡ mukkuḍa, *adj*. Stout, robust. 2. mute, speechless. –ಮೂರುನಿ to become stout.

ಮುಕ್ಕುಡಿ mukkuḍi, *s*. A taciturn *or* a reserved woman.

ಮುಕ್ಕುಡು mukkuḍu, *s*. Reserve. 2. taciturnity, reservation.

ಮುಕ್ಕುಡೆ mukkuḍe, *s*. A taciturn *or* reserved man.

ಮುಕ್ಕುನಿ mukkuni (ಮುಕ್ಕ್), *v. a*. To gobble, swallow, devour. ಮಂಣ್ ಮುಕ್ಕುದ್‌ಪೋಪಿನಿ *lit*. to deyour earth, to be ill-fated, ruined.

ಮುಕ್ಕುರಿ **mukkuri**, *see* ಮುಕ್ರಿ.

ಮುಕ್ಕುರಿಡ್ಪಿನಿ **mukkuridpini**, *see* ಮುಕ್ಕುರುನಿ.

ಮುಕ್ಕುರು **mukkuru**, *s.* Snorting, grunting, growling. –ದೆಂಜಿ a kind of crab. –ಇಡ್ಪಿನಿ, –ದಕ್ಕುನಿ, *see* ಮುಕ್ಕುರುನಿ.

ಮುಕ್ಕುರುನಿ **mukkuruni** (ಮುಕ್ಕುರ್), *v. a.* To challenge, defy. 2. to snort, grunt, growl.

ಮುಕ್ಕುರೂರು **mukkurūru**, *see* ಮುಕ್ರೂರು.

ಮುಕ್ಕುಲಿ, ಮುಕ್ಕುಳಿ **mukkuli, mukkuḷi**, *s.* A mouthful of any liquid.

ಮುಕ್ಕುಲಿಯುನಿ, ಮುಕ್ಕುಳಿಯುನಿ **mukkuliyuni, mukkuḷiyuni** (ಮುಕ್ಕುಲ್, ಮುಕ್ಕುಳ್), *v. a.* To gargle *or* rinse the mouth.

ಮುಕ್ಕೆ **mukke**, *s.* One of a class of fishermen. 2. *see* ಮುಂಗೆ.

ಮುಕ್ಕೆಲೆ **mukkele**, *s.* A voracious man.

ಮುಕ್ಕೊಂಡೆ **mukkoṇḍe**, *s.* Three quarters of a seer.

ಮುಕ್ಕೊಳು **mukkoḷu**, *adv.* Thrice. –ದಾಯೆ a menial servant; *cf.* ಓಲಿಯಿದಾಯೆ.

ಮುಕ್ಕೋಣ **mukkōṇa**, *s.* A triangle.

ಮುಕ್ತ **mukta**, *adj.* Released, liberated.

ಮುಕ್ತಾ **muktā**, *see* ಮೊಕ್ತಾ.

ಮುಕ್ತಾರ್, ಮುಕ್ತಾರಿ, ಮುಕ್ತ್ಯಾರಿ **muktāru, muktāri, muktyāri**, *s.* A power of attorney. 2. an assignment, transfer of title *or* interest by writing.

ಮುಕ್ತಾರೆ **muktāre**, *s.* An attorney, agent, assignee. 2. an owner, master.

ಮುಕ್ತಿ **mukti**, *s.* Manumission, absolution. 2. final beatitude.

ಮುಕ್ತೇಸ್ರೆ **muktēsre**, *see* ಮೊಕ್ತೇಸರೆ.

ಮುಕ್ಯೆಲ್ **mukyelu**, *see* ಮುಕ್ಕೊಳು.

ಮುಕ್ರಿ **mukri**, *s.* A reader of the Koran in a mosque.

ಮುಕ್ರೂರು **mukrūru**, *adj.* Established, fixed, certain. 2. appointed. –ಮಳ್ಪುನಿ to establish, determine; to appoint.

ಮುಖ **mukha**, *s.* The face, countenance. 2. a means, instrument. –ಛಾಯಿ, –ರಂಗ್ the complexion, colour of the face. –ದಾಕ್ಷಿಣ್ಯ attention, regard *or* civility inspired by a person's presence; partiality, respect, consideration. –ಪರ್ದ a veil; a wrapper. –ಭಾವ the expression of the countenance. –ರೂಪು resemblance of features. –ಸಾಲೆ a front veranda. –ಶಿರಿ, –ಸಿರಿ lustre of the countenance; betel leaves, eaten with areca nut, lime, *etc.*, which gives the mouth a deep red tinge. –ಸ್ತುತಿ flattery. –ಮುಟ್ಟುದು, ಮುಖಾಮುಖಿ face to face; –ಕೆಟ್ಟುನಿ to be satiated; to become disgusted.

ಮುಖರಾಪು, ಮುಖರಾವು **mukharāpu, mukharāvu**, *s.* Expression

of the features. 2. a metallic plate tied below the eyes of a racing buffalo.

ಮುಖಾಂತರ **mukhāntara,** *prep.* Through. *adv.* By reason of, by means of.

ಮುಖಾಬಿಲೆ **mukhābilè,** *s.* Collation, comparison; confronting. —ತೂಪಿನಿ to compare, collate. —ಮಳ್ಪುನಿ to confront.

ಮುಖಿ **mukhi,** *see* ಮುಖ್ಯಸ್ತೆ.

ಮುಖುಫ್ **mukhuphu,** *s.* Abolition, abrogation. 2. adjournment, postponement. —ಆಪಿನಿ to be abolished, adjourned.

ಮುಖುರೂಪು **mukhurūpu,** *see under* ಮುಖ.

ಮುಖೊಟು **mukhoṭu,** *see* ಮುಖಾಂತರ.

ಮುಖ್ಯ **mukhya,** *adj.* Chief, principal. ಮುಖ್ಯಾದ್ chiefly.

ಮುಖ್ಯಸ್ತೆ **mukhyaste,** *s.* A chief, head, principal.

ಮುಗ **muga,** *s.* A demon's head-gear made of silver, *etc.* 2. a mask, disguise.

ಮುಗಂಟೆ **mugaṇṭè,** *s.* The pials on either side of an entrance; to a house.

ಮುಗಡ್, ಮುಗಡ, ಮುಗಡೆ **mugaḍu, mugaḍa, mugaḍè,** *s.* The capsule of a cocoanut *or* other fruit.

ಮುಗಡೊರ **mugaḍora,** *adj.* Bottled.

ಮುಗಣ್ **mugaṇu,** *s.* The front.

ಮುಗಪತ್ತ್ **mugapattu,** *s.* The cramp of a lock.

ಮುಗಪುನಿ **mugapuni,** *see* ಮೊಗಪುನಿ.

ಮುಗಮೂರ್ತಿ **mugamūrti,** *s.* Utensils of demon-worship, especially of Jumādi.

ಮುಗಯಿ **mugayi,** *s.* A small earthen vessel.

ಮುಗರಾವು **mugarāvu,** *see* ಮುಖರಾವು.

ಮುಗಲ್, ಮುಗಳ್ **mugalu, mugaḷu,** *s.* A cloud. —ದೊಂಬು sultry heat. —ಕಬಿಯುನಿ, —ಕಬ್ಬಿಯುನಿ to become cloudy.

ಮುಗಲ್ತೆ **mugaltè,** *s.* Scent. —ದೆಪ್ಪುನಿ to scent, track.

ಮುಗಸ್, ಮುಗಸ **mugasu, mugasa,** *see* ಮೊಗಸ್ಟು.

ಮುಗಾಡರ **mugāḍara,** *see* ಮುಗಡೊರ.

ಮುಗಾಯಿ **mugāyi,** *see* ಮುಗಯಿ.

ಮುಗಿತ **mugita,** *see* ಮುಗಿತೆ.

ಮುಗಿತಲ **mugitala,** *s.* End, conclusion. *adj.* Final.

ಮುಗಿತಾಯೆ **mugitāye,** *see* ಮುಗುತಾಯೆ.

ಮುಗಿತುರುನಿ **mugituruni** (ಮುಗಿತುರ್), *v. a.* To accomplish, conclude, finish.

ಮುಗಿತೆ **mugitè,** *s.* A settlement, decision. 2. a contract, bargain. —ಬೇಲೆ a work given on contract. —ಗ್ ಕೊರ್ಪಿನಿ, ಮುಗಿತ್ ಕೊರ್ಪಿನಿ to give a work on contract. —ಗ್ ದೆತ್ತೊಣುನಿ, ಮುಗಿತ್ ದೆತ್ತೊಣುನಿ to undertake a work on contract.

ಮುಗಿನೊಲ್ದು **muginoldu,** *s.* A kind of paddy.

ಮುಗಿಪು **mugipu,** *see* ಮುಗಿತೆ.

ಮುಗಿಪುನಿ **mugipuni** (ಮುಗಿ), *v. a.* To finish.

ಮುಗಿಯುನಿ mugiyuni (ಮುಗಿ), *v.n.* To end, terminate, cease. 2. to close, contract, shut up. ಕೈ— to close hands in salutation, to salute without prostrating.

ಮುಗಿಲ್ mugilu, *s.* Planitude. 2. *see* ಮುಗಲ್.

ಮುಗಿಲಿ mugili, *s.* A turret, minaret, top, as of a temple.

ಮುಗು mugu, *s.* The fixed hire with board, lodging, and raiment of a labourer. —ಕು ಕುಳ್ಳುನಿ to serve under such a contract.

ಮುಗುಡು mugudu, *s.* A kind of fish. 2. *see* ಮುಗುರು. ಮರಿ— a kind of eel.

ಮುಗುಡೆ mugude, *see* ಮುಕ್ಕುಡೆ.

ಮುಗುತಾಯಿ mugutāyi, *s.* Completion, finishing.

ಮುಗುತಾಯೆ mugutāye, *s.* A servant engaged for fixed hire, boarding, *etc.*; *cf.* ಮುಗು.

ಮುಗುತಿ muguti, *see* ಮುಕ್ತಿ. 2. *see* ಮೂಕುತಿ.

ಮುಗುತೆ mugutè, *see* ಮುಗಿತೆ.

ಮುಗುರು muguru, *s.* A sprout, shoot, bud. *adj.* Tender, delicate. 2. gentle, not harsh. —ತೆಲಿಕೆ a gentle smile. —ಮಿರೆ a tender breast.

ಮುಗುರುನಿ muguruni (ಮುಗುರ್), *v.a.* To bud, sprout.

ಮುಗುರೂರು mugurūru, *see* ಮುಕ್ರೂರು.

ಮುಗುಲ್ mugulu, *see* ಮೊಗುಲ್.

ಮುಗುಲರಿ mugulari, *s.* Parboiled rice.

ಮುಗುಲಿ muguli, *s.* An odd number. ಸರಿ— odd and even numbers.

ಮುಗುಲೆ mugule, *s.* A Mogul.

ಮುಗುವಳಿ muguvali, *see* ಮುಗ್ಗೊಲಿ.

ಮುಗುಳಿ muguli, *s.* A bubble. 2. the pinnacle of a temple. 3. the top of a walking stick. 4. *see* ಮುಕ್ಕುಲಿ. 5. *see* ಮುಗುಲಿ.

ಮುಗುಳು mugulu, *see* ಮುಗುರು.

ಮುಗೆ mugè, *s.* A small earthen vessel.

ಮುಗೆರ್ mugeru, *s.* A hare, rabbit. 2. *see* ಮುಗ್ಗೆರ್.

ಮುಗೆರಾಯೆ mugerāye, *s.* A demon so called. 2. the name of a caste.

ಮುಗ್ಗೈ mugei, *see* ಮುಗಯಿ.

ಮುಗ್ಗ mugga, *s.* Mould, mustiness. 2. *see* ಮುಗು. *adj.* Musty. —ವಾಸನೆ a musty smell. —ಪತ್ತುನಿ to become mouldy.

ಮುಗ್ಗಣ್, ಮುಗ್ಗೆಣ mugganu, muggena, *s.* A narrow piece of cloth, used for covering the privities.

ಮುಗ್ಗಿಯುನಿ muggiyuni, *see* ಮುಗಿಯುನಿ.

ಮುಗ್ಗು muggu, *see* ಮುಗ್ಗ.

ಮುಗ್ಗೆ muggè, *s.* A flower bud, germ.

ಮುಗ್ಗೆರ್ muggeru, *s.* A Malayālam fisherman. 2. *see* ಮುಗೆರ್.

ಮುಗ್ಗೆರ್ಲು muggerlu, *s.* A class of Pariahs.

ಮುಗ್ಗೊಲಿ, ಮುಗ್ಗೊಳಿ muggoli, muggoḷi, *s.* A species of contribution *or* tax levied in the days of Hyder and Tippoo.

ಮುಗ್ತೆ mugtè, *see* ಮುಗಿತೆ.

ಮುಗ್ಯಾಟ mugyāṭa, *s.* Conclusion, termination.

ಮುಗ್ಲಿ mugli, *see* ಮುಗಿಲಿ.

ಮುಙ್ಙಣ್ munṅaṇu, *see* ಮುಂಗಡ.

ಮುಚ್ಚ mučča, *see* ಮುಚ್ಚಲ.

ಮುಚ್ಚಂಟೆ muččaṇṭè, *s.* A close mouth-piece.

ಮುಚ್ಚಟೆ muččaṭè, *s.* A festivity, great rejoicing.

ಮುಚ್ಚಲ muččala, *s.* The lid *or* stopper of a vessel.

ಮುಚ್ಚಲಿಗೆ muččaligè, *s.* An agreement in writing, deed of settlement.

ಮುಚ್ಚಾಟ muččāṭa, *s.* Blind-man's-[buff.

ಮುಚ್ಚಾವುನಿ muččāvuni, *c. v.* (*of* ಮುಚ್ಚುನಿ) To cause to shut, cover, close.

ಮುಚ್ಚಿ mučči, *see* ಮುಚ್ಚಲ.

ಮುಚ್ಚಿಗೆ muččigè, *s.* A lid, cover, wrapper. 2. the ceiling of a roof.

ಮುಚ್ಚಿಲ್ muččilu, *s.* A medicinal plant, *Elephantopas scaber*; *bet.* ನೆಲಮುಚ್ಚಿಲ್.

ಮುಚ್ಚಿಲಮೆ muččilamè, *s.* Ceremonial defilement of women on the third day after child-birth.

ಮುಚ್ಚು mučču, *see* ಮುಚ್ಚಲ. —ಮದೆ a disguise, mask, covering.

ಮುಚ್ಚುನಿ muččuni (ಮುಚ್ಚ್), *v. n.* & *a.* To shut, close, cover. 2. to screen, shelter. ಕಂಣ್— to shut the eyes. ಬಾಕಿಲ್— to shut the door. ಬಾಯಿ— to keep quiet.

ಮುಚ್ಚೆ, ಮುಚ್ಚೆಲ್ mučče, muččelu, *see* ಮುಚ್ಚಲ. 2. *see* ಮುಚ್ಚಿಲ್.

ಮುಚ್ಚೆಲೆ muččele, *s.* A conniver, one who pretends not to see what takes place before his eyes.

ಮುಜಂಗೆ, ಮುಜಂಙೆ mujaṅgè, mujaṅṅè, *see* ಮೊಜಂಙೆ.

ಮುಜಂಟೆ mujaṇṭè, *see* ಮೊಜಂಟೆ.

ಮುಜಡೆ mujaḍe, *s.* A toothless, *or* old man.

ಮುಜಿಪುನಿ mujipuni, *see* ಮುಯಿಪುನಿ.

ಮುಜಿರೆ, ಮುಜಿಲೆ mujirè, mujilè, *s.* Allowance, subtraction, reduction, remission. —ಕಲೆಪಿನಿ to deduct.

ಮುಜುಕ್ರೆ mujukre, *adj.* Old, worn out.

ಮುಜೆ mujè, *s.* A kind of tree.

ಮುಜೆಕುನಿ mujekuni, *see* ಮೊಜೆಕುನಿ.

ಮುಜ್ಜಿ, ಮುಜ್ಜು mujji, mujju, *s.* A black monkey.

ಮುಜ್ಜಿಂಟಿ mujjiṇṭi, *see* ಮೊಜಂಟಿ.

ಮುಟದಣೆ muṭadaṇè, *see* ಮುಟ್ಟದಣೆ.

ಮುಟ್ಟ muṭṭa, *s.* Proximity, nearness. *adv.* Near, close by, to, with, towards. *postp.* Till, until, as far as. —ಕಂಣ್ short-sighted. —ದಾಯೆ a relation; a man with whom one can associate. —ದಾಳ್ a female relation; a female with whom one can associate. —ಪೋಪಿನಿ to approach, go near. —ಬರ್ಪಿನಿ to come near; to be sufficient. —ಡ್, ಮುಟ್ಟೊಡು very near, near by. [scythe.

ಮುಟ್ಟತ್ತಿ muṭṭatti, s. A sickle,

ಮುಟ್ಟಡಣೆ, ಮುಟ್ಟದನೆ muṭṭadaṇè, muṭṭadanè, s. An instrument for mincing vegetables, *etc.*

ಮುಟ್ಟಲೆ, ಮುಟ್ಟಳೆ muṭṭalè, muṭṭaḷè, s. A cap made of the stalk of an areca-nut branch. ಅಡ್ಡ—, ಕೊಂಬು—, ನೆರಿ— are some of its varieties.

ಮುಟ್ಟಾವುನಿ muṭṭâvuni, c. v. (*of* ಮುಟ್ಟುನಿ) To cause to touch. 2. to accompany to one's destination; to cause to reach, to deliver. ಕಾಗಜಿ— to deliver a letter.

ಮುಟ್ಟಾಳ್ muṭṭâḷu, s. A very stupid *or* indigent man.

ಮುಟ್ಟಿ muṭṭi, s. A small kind of earthen pot equal to a pint, by which toddy is sold to customers. 2. *see* ಮುಷ್ಟಿ. —ಪತ್ತುನಿ to be unlucky *or* unfortunate. ಯೇಕ್ ಮುಟ್ಟಿ ಸರಾಸರಿ, ದೋ ಮುಟ್ಟಿ ಚರಾಚಿರಿ, ತೀನ್ ಮುಟ್ಟಿ ರಂಬಾರೂಟಿ one potful of toddy will make one light-hearted, two will make him talkative, three will make him turbulent.

ಮುಟ್ಟಿಕಲ್ಲ್ muṭṭikallu, s. A stepping stone.

ಮುಟ್ಟಿಬಿಸಲೆ muṭṭibisalè, s. A distilling vessel; *also* ಮುಟ್ಟು.

ಮುಟ್ಟು muṭṭu, s. A shoe, sandal. 2. a footstep. 3. steps, stairs. 4. a stool. —ಕೊಡಂಗೆ a hold, brace. ಶೇಮಯಿಬಿದ—, ಸೇಮಯಿಬಿದ— a stool *or* machine for preparing vermicelli. —ಗು ಪೋಪಿನಿ to walk step by step. —ಪಾಡುನಿ to put on sandals; to measure with the foot. —ಬೂರುನಿ cocks to fight.

ಮುಟ್ಟು muṭṭu, s. Menstruation. 2. ceremonial uncleanliness *or* defilement. —ಚಟ್ಟೆ, —ಚಿಟ್ಟು, —ಚೇಷ್ಟೆ, —ಸಂಕಡ flooding, excessive menstrual discharge, *lochia.*

ಮುಟ್ಟು muṭṭu, s. Touch, contact. 2. a distillery. *adj.* Touching. —ಕಡಿ, —ಗಡಿ a critical state; a dangerous illness; a narrow path; straitened circumstances. —ಜನ people of the same rank. —ಬಟ್ಟಲ್ the lid of a distillery.

ಮುಟ್ಟುನಿ muṭṭuni (ಮುಟ್ಟ್), v. a. To touch. 2. to attain, reach, arrive. *v. n.* To arrive at, be received, come to hand. 2. to cost. ಊರುಗ್— to reach one's native place. ಕಾಗಜಿ— to receive a letter. ಪಣವು— to receive money; to cost. ಮಾಡ್ಗ್— to touch the roof.

ಮುಟ್ಟುವಳಿ muṭṭuvaḷi, *see* ಮುಟ್ಟೊಳಿ.

ಮುಟ್ಟೆ muṭṭè, s. The head, as of fish *or* fowls. 2. a heap. 3. *see* ಮೊಂಟೆ. ಕೈತ— the fist. ಬೈತ— a stack of straw.

ಮುಟ್ಟೆ **muṭṭè**, *s.* The knuckles, joints of fingers. 2. *see* ಮುಟ್ಟಿ.

ಮುಟ್ಟೆಲ್ **muṭṭelu**, *see* ಮಟ್ಟೆಲ್.

ಮುಟ್ಟೊಳಿ **muṭṭoḷi**, *s.* Expense, cost.

ಮುಡ **muḍa**, *s.* Stiffness, rigidness. 2. emaciation, leanness. –ಮಯ್ಯೊರ್ stupidity, dulness. –ಕಟ್ಟುನಿ to become stiff; to be emaciated; to become stunted.

ಮುಡಂಕ್ **muḍaṅku**, *see* ಮೊಡಂಕ್.

ಮುಡಂದಲೆ **muḍandalè**, *see* ಮಡಂತಲ್.

ಮುಡಜಿಲ್ **muḍajilu**, *s.* Shrinking.

ಮುಡಯಿ, ಮುಡಾಯಿ **muḍayi, muḍāyi**, *s.* East, eastward.

ಮುಡವು **muḍavu**, *s.* A kind of fish.

ಮುಡಿ **muḍi**, *s.* A bundle of rice, *etc.*, packed in straw. 2. a lump of tamarind, *etc.*, packed in leaves. 3. a measure of grain, *etc.*, containing from forty to sixty seers. 4. a young, unripe mango, *etc.* ಇರ್– from the head to the toe, all over the body. –ಏರುನಿ, –ಕಟ್ಟುನಿ to pack rice, *etc.*, into a straw-bundle. –ಮಳ್ಪುನಿ to pack a lump into a bundle.

ಮುಡಿ **muḍi**, *s.* The mask (*or* ಅಣಿ) of the demon called Lekkēsiri.

ಮುಡಿಕೆ **muḍikè**, *s.* Roasted rice.

ಮುಡಿಪಲ್ಲೆ **muḍipallè**, *s.* A gold ornament for the head.

ಮುಡಿಪಾವುನಿ **muḍipāvuni**, *c. v.* (*of* ಮುಡಿಪುನಿ) To have a person's head dressed with flowers.

ಮುಡಿಪಿನಿ, ಮುಡಿಪುನಿ **muḍipini, muḍipuni** (ಮುಡಿ), *v. a.* To dress the head with flowers. 2. to make the top-knot tight.

ಮುಡಿಪು **muḍipu**, *s.* A bundle of money, jewels, *etc.*, put by, as devoted to some idol. –ಕಟ್ಟುನಿ to put by money in this way. –ಸಾದ್ಯುನಿ to present to some idol money *or* jewels thus consecrated.

ಮುಡಿಯುನಿ **muḍiyuni** (ಮುಡಿ), *v. n.* To be turned into a knot; to be knotty.

ಮುಡಿಯೆ **muḍiye**, *s.* A cock with a treble comb. –ಕೊಟ್ಟು such a comb of a cock.

ಮುಡಿರ್ **muḍiru**, *s.* Pregnancy without getting menses after the birth of the former child.

ಮುಡಿವಾಳ **muḍivāḷa**, *see* ಮುಡ್ಡೆಲ.

ಮುಡಿಸಲೆ **muḍisalè**, *see* ಮುಡಿಪಲ್ಲೆ.

ಮುಡಿಸುನಿ **muḍisuni**, *see* ಮುಡಿಪಾವುನಿ.

ಮುಡು **muḍu**, *s.* The shoulder joint.

ಮುಡುಂಬು **muḍumbu**, *s.* A side-piece. 2. *see* ಮೂಂಡು. 3. *see* ಮುರೆ. ಕಲೆಂಬಿದ– a side-piece of a coffer.

ಮುಡುಗು **muḍugu**, *s.* A kind of parched rice.

ಮುಡುತೊಣುನಿ **muḍutoṇuni**, *see* ಮುಡಿಪುನಿ

ಮುಡುನಿ **muḍuni**, *see* ಮುಡಿಯುನಿ.

ಮುಡುಪು, ಮುಡುಪೆಲ್ **muḍupu, muḍupelu**, *see* ಮುಡಿಪು.

ಮುಡುಬು **muḍubu**, *see* ಮುರೆ.

ಮುಡುಸಾವುನಿ, ಮುಡುಸುನಿ muḍusāvuni, muḍusuni (ಮುಡುಸ್), *v.a.* To eat up, consume.

ಮುಡೆ muḍè, *s.* A screen, made of cocoanut leaves. –ಕಟ್ಟುನಿ to put up such a screen.

ಮುಡೆಂಕ್ muḍeṅku, *see* ಮೊಡಂಕ್.

ಮುಡೆಪಿನಿ, ಮುಡೆಪುನಿ muḍepini, muḍepuni (ಮುಡೆ), *v. a.* To plait, braid, knit. 2. to bind.

ಮುಡೆಯುನಿ, ಮುಡೆವುನಿ muḍeyuni, muḍevuni (ಮುಡೆ), *v. n.* To be folded. 2. to get entangled. ರೆಂಕೆ– to pinion the wings of a bird.

ಮುಡ್ಡಿ muḍḍi, *s.* The buttock.

ಮುಡ್ಡಿಯೆ muḍḍiyè, *s.* A wild boar. 2. *see* ಮುದಿಯೆ.

ಮುಡ್ಡೆಲ, ಮುಡ್ಯಲ, ಮುಡ್ಯೆಲ muḍḍela, muḍyala, muḍyela, *s.* The cuscus grass, *Andropogon muricatum.* ಕರಿಯ– a dark kind of it. ಬೊಳ್ದು– a white kind of it.

ಮುಡ್ಯೆ muḍye, *see* ಮುದಿಯೆ.

ಮುಣಿ muṇi, *see* ಮುನಿ.

ಮುಣುಗುನಿ muṇuguni, *see* ಮುರ್ಕುನಿ.

ಮುಣುಚಿ muṇuči, *see* ಮುಣ್ಚಿ.

ಮುಣುಮುಣು muṇumuṇu, *s.* Muttering, mumbling.

ಮುಣೆ muṇè, *see* ಮುನೆ.

ಮುಣ್ಕುನಿ muṇkuni (ಮುಣ್ಕ್), *v. a.* To say ಹೂಂ, expressive of disapproval *or* unwillingness. 2. to cry, as a ghost.

ಮುಣ್ಕೆಲೆ muṇkele, *s.* A grumbler.

ಮುಣ್ಚಿ muṇči, *s.* Pepper. 2. chilli. ಗಂಧ–, ಚೀನ– cubebs. ಗಾಂಧಾರ–, ಲವಂಗ– a very small, hot kind of chilli. ಬೋಳಕಾಳ್– peeled pepper. ಯೆಡ್ಡೆ– black pepper.

ಮುತಾಲಿಕೆ mutālike, *s.* An agent, steward. 2. agency.

ಮುತ್ತ mutta, *s.* A kiss; *cf.* ಮುದ್ದು.

ಮುತ್ತಕ muttaka, *s.* The tree *Butea frondosa.*

ಮುತ್ತಜ್ಜಿ muttajji, *s.* A great grand mother.

ಮುತ್ತಜ್ಜೆ muttajje, *s.* A great grand father.

ಮುತ್ತಯಿದೆ muttayidè, *see* ಮುತ್ತೈದೆ.

ಮುತ್ತರಿಯುನಿ muttariyuni, *see* ಮಿತ್ತರುನಿ.

ಮುತ್ತರೆ muttarè, *s.* Three heads; three generations. –ತಾಯೆ Brahma; a man who has seen three generations.

ಮುತ್ತಾಡಿ muttāḍi, *s.* The fish *Triacanthus.*

ಮುತ್ತಾತೆ muttāte, *see* ಮುತ್ತಜ್ಜಿ.

ಮುತ್ತಾರ muttāra, *adv.* Three times.

ಮುತ್ತಾರಿ muttāri, *see* ಮುಕ್ತಾರ್.

ಮುತ್ತಾಲಿಕೆ muttālike, *see* ಮುತಾಲಿಕೆ.

ಮುತ್ತಾವುನಿ muttāvuni, *c. v.* (*of* ಮುತ್ತುನಿ) To ruin, desolate, destroy.

ಮುತ್ತಾಸ್ muttāsu, *see* ಮುತ್ತಜ್ಜಿ.

ಮುತ್ತಿ, ಮುತ್ತಿಗೆ mutti, muttigè, *s.* A siege, the act of besieging. ಜೀರ್–, ಜೋರ್– urging. –ಪಾಡುನಿ to besiege.

ಮುತ್ತಿಗಂಧ muttigandha, *s.* A female's head-ornament.

ಮುತ್ತು **muttu,** *s.* A pearl. 2. a drop. 3. *see* ಮುತ್ತ. –ದ ಮಾಲೆ, –ದ ಸರ a pearl necklace. –ದ ಪೋಲೆ a pearl earring. –ರತ್ನ a precious pearl. ಕೆಕ್ಕಿದ– the nape of the neck. –ಪತ್ಪಾವುನಿ, –ಸುರಿಯುನಿ to string *or* set with pearls.

ಮುತ್ತು **muttu,** *s.* A darling, dear child. *adj. see* ಮುದ್ದು.

ಮುತ್ತು **muttu,** *adj.* Desolate, waste. –ಪೋಪಿನಿ to become desolate *or* extinct.

ಮುತ್ತುನಿ **muttuni** (ಮುತ್ತಿ), *v. n.* To become extinct, be destroyed.

ಮುತ್ತುನಿ **muttuni** (ಮುತ್ತಿ), *v. a.* To surround, besiege, hem in, encompass.

ಮುತ್ತೆ **muttè,** *s.* A dear boy. 2. four cowries won in a game of ಚಂನೆಮಣಿ. –ಅಳಿಪುನಿ to lose the chance of winning the same.

ಮುತ್ತೆದಿ **muttedi,** *see* ಮುತ್ತೇಶಿ.

ಮುತ್ತೆರಿ **mutteri,** *s.* A kind of skin eruption. 2. a small ornamental knob in jewelry.

ಮುತ್ತೇಶಿ, ಮುತ್ತೇಸಿ **muttēši, muttēsi,** *s.* A woman whose husband is alive.

ಮುತ್ತೇಸ **muttēsa,** *s.* The five principal ornaments, constituting the badge of a woman whose husband is alive; namely, ಕರ್ಯಮಣಿ, ಬೊಟ್ಟು, ಮೂಕುತಿ, ಕಾಜಿ and ಕಾರ್ವುಂಗಿಲ 2. any instrument *or* implement.

ಮುತ್ತೈದೆ **mutteidè,** *see* ಮುತ್ತೇಶಿ.

ಮುತ್ರಡಿ **mutraḍi,** *adj.* Impudent, mischievous.

ಮುತ್ರಾಲಿ **mutrāli,** *s.* A prominent man.

ಮುತ್ಸದ್ದಿ **mutsaddi,** *s.* A writer, accountant, clerk. 2. a salt superintendent.

ಮುದ **muda,** *s.* Joy, pleasure.

ಮುದರ್ **mudaru̥,** *s.* Rubbish, debris. 2. *see* ಬಾವೆಮುಂಗ್ *under* ಬಾವೆ.

ಮುದರುನಿ **mudaruni,** *see* ಮುದುರುನಿ.

ಮುದಲೆ, ಮುದಳೆ **mudalè, mudaḷè,** *s.* An alligator, crocodile. ಪನಿ– its young. –ಬಾಯಿ a talkative person.

ಮುದಲೆಕರು, ಮುದಲೆಗರು **mudalekaru, mudalegaru,** *s.* A lateral rafter that supports the ridge-piece of a roof.

ಮುದಿ **mudi,** *adj.* Old, aged, ancient. –ತನ, –ಪ್ರಾಯ old age.

ಮುದಿಯುನಿ **mudiyuni** (ಮುದಿ), *v. n.* To feel a severe pain in the joints. 2. to be worn out.

ಮುದಿಯೆ **mudiye,** *s.* An old man. *adj.* Old, aged.

ಮುದಿಪುನಿ, ಮುದುಪುನಿ **mudipuni, mudupuni** (ಮುದಿ, ಮುದು), *v. a.* To pluck out, pull out.

ಮುದು **mudu,** *see* ಮುದಿ. 2. *see* ಮುದ್ದು.

ಮುದುಕೆ **muduke,** *s.* An old man.

ಮುದುರ್ **muduru̥,** *s.* Expansion, dilation.

ಮುದುರುನಿ muduruni (ಮುದುರ್), *v. n.* To expand, become dilated *or* enlarged.

ಮುದುಲು mudulu, *s.* A hawk.

ಮುದೆ mudè, *s.* Consanguinity.

ಮುದೆಪು mudepu, *s.* A screen, blind.

ಮುದೆಲ್ mudelu, *s.* The bottom. 2. stubble, stump of a tree. 3. origin, cause. 4. capital, principal.

ಮುದ್ದ mudda, *see* ಮುದ್ದು.

ಮುದ್ದಣ್, ಮುದ್ದನ್ muddaṇu, muddanu, *s.* Pimples *or* blotches on the face.

ಮುದ್ದಮ್, ಮುದ್ದಾಮ್, ಮುದ್ದಾಮು muddamu, muddāmu, muddāmu, *adj.* Own. *s.* An express sent on a particular errand. —ಜನ ಕಡಪುಡುನಿ to send an express *or* courier.

ಮುದ್ದಯಲೆ, ಮುದ್ದಾಯಲೆ muddayale, muddāyale, *s.* An accused person; a defendant, respondent.

ಮುದ್ದಾಡುನಿ muddāḍuni (ಮುದ್ದಾಡ್), *v. a.* To kiss mutually.

ಮುದ್ದಾನ್ muddānu, *see* ಮುದ್ದಣ್.

ಮುದ್ದಾಯಿ muddāyi, *see* ಮುದ್ದೈ.

ಮುದ್ದಾಲೆ muddāle, *see* ಮುದ್ದಯಲೆ.

ಮುದ್ದಿಲ್‌ನಾಯೆ muddilunāye, *s.* A demon so called.

ಮುದ್ದು muddu, *s.* A kiss. 2. affection, love. *adj.* Dear, pet, darling, favourite. —ಪ್ರಾಯ juvenility. —ಬಾಲೆ a dear child. —ಕೊರ್ಪಿನಿ to kiss, give a kiss.

ಮುದ್ದೆ muddè, *s.* A lump, unshapen mass. 2. consanguinity. ಮಂಗ್— useless. —ಕಟ್ಟುನಿ to be turned into a lump *or* mass. ಪಂಬದೆರೆಗ್ ಮುದ್ದೆ ಇಜ್ಜಿ the Pambadas observe no rules of consanguinity.

ಮುದ್ದೈ muddei, *s.* A complainant, prosecutor.

ಮುದ್ದೈಲೆ muddeile, *see* ಮುದ್ದಯಲೆ.

ಮುದ್ರ mudra, *see* ಮುದ್ರೆ.

ಮುದ್ರಾಕ್ಷರ mudrākshara, *s.* The printing type; typography.

ಮುದ್ರಿಕೆ mudrikè, *s.* Dedication of a literary work to a person. 2. hoarding *or* amassing wealth. 3. *see* ಮುದ್ರೆ. —ದ ಪದ a dedicatory stanza. —ದೀಪಿನಿ to dedicate. —ಮಳ್ಪುನಿ to lay out money.

ಮುದ್ರಿಪುನಿ mudripuni (ಮುದ್ರಿ), *v. a.* To seal, stamp, impress.

ಮುದ್ರೆ mudrè, *s.* A seal, signet. 2. a stamp, print, impression. —ಕಾಗಜಿ a stamp-paper. —ದುಂಗಿಲ a seal-ring. —ಪಾಡುನಿ, —ಮಳ್ಪುನಿ, —ಪೊತ್ತುನಿ to seal, stamp, impress. ಮುದ್ರಧಾರಣೆ, ಮುದ್ರಾಧಾರಣೆ applying sectarian seals among the Vaishṇavaits to the different parts of their body above the navel.

ಮುನ muna, *adj.* Half done; remaining, left, unfinished.

ಮುನಪೆ, ಮುನಾಫೆ munapè, munāphè, *s.* Profit, gain; saving.

ಮುನಸೀಫೆ **munasīphe,** *s.* The subordinate civil judge of a tāluk.

ಮುನಸೆ **munase,** *see* ಮುನ್ಸೆ.

ಮುನಾಸಬ್, ಮುನಾಸಬು **munāsabu, munāsabu,** *s.* Worth, value, estimate. 2. discretion, opinion. 3. circumstance, condition, position, state. –ತೋಜುನಿ to be of opinion; to be worth, seemly *or* appropriate.

ಮುನಿ **muni,** *s.* A sage, saint.

ಮುನಿಪು **munipu,** *s.* Anger. 2. hatred.

ಮುನಿಪಿನಿ **munipini** (ಮುನಿ), *v. a.* To detest, hate.

ಮುನಿಯುನಿ **muniyuni** (ಮುನಿ), *v. n.* To be in a passion, to hate.

ಮುನಿಯೆಸ್ರೆ **muniyesre,** *s.* A taciturn man. 2. *see* ಮುನೀಶ್ವರೆ.

ಮುನಿಷಿ **munishi,** *s.* A teacher of a language. 2. a translator. 3. a writer. 4. a secretary.

ಮುನೀಶ್ವರೆ **munīsvare,** *s.* The chief of sages, a great saint.

ಮುನುಕುನಿ **munukuni,** *see* ಮುಣ್ಕುನಿ.

ಮುನುಕೆಲೆ **munukele,** *see* ಮುಣ್ಕೆಲೆ.

ಮುನುಮು, ಮುನುಮೆ **munumu, munume,** *s.* A grumbler, one who murmurs.

ಮುನೆ **munè,** *s.* A point, end, extremity. 2. *see* ಮುನ. ಕಂಟಾ ವುದ– the point of an iron style. ಕುರಿತ– the opening *or* outlet of a boil. ದೂಜಿದ– the point of a needle. ನಾಯೆರ್‍ದ– a plough shaft. –ಕೊರ್ಪಿನಿ to bring the matter of a boil to the point; to incite, instigate. –ಮಳ್ಪುನಿ to make pointed.

ಮುನೆಕಾಮ **munekāma,** *s.* A knot, tie.

ಮುನೆತೋಣುನಿ, ಮುನೆಯುನಿ **munetoṇuni, muneyuni,** *see* ಮುನಿಯುನಿ.

ಮುನೆನಾಗಿ, ಮುನೆವಾಶಿ **munenāgi, munevāsi,** *s.* A disease of cattle.

ಮುನ್ಕುನಿ **munkuni,** *see* ಮುಣ್ಕುನಿ.

ಮುನ್ನಿ **munni,** *see* ಮುಂನಿ.

ಮುಪ್ಪ **muppa,** *num.* Thirty. –ತೊಂಬ್ಯ thirty-nine. –ನೆ thirtieth. –ಳ thirty seers, equal to about two kalase.

ಮುಪ್ಪಾಗ **muppāga,** *s.* Three-fourths of a fanam.

ಮುಪ್ಪಾವು **muppāvu,** *s.* Three-quarters of a seer.

ಮುಪ್ಪು **muppu,** *adj.* Old, aged. *s.* Old age. 2. misfortune, mischief, ruin, destruction. ಕೆಪ್ಪು– infirmities of old age, senility. ಕುಡ್ಕೆಲಗ್ ಪರ್ಪಿನವೇ ಮುಪ್ಪು drunkenness is the ruin of a drunkard. ಗೊಬ್ಬುನಾಯಗ್ ಜುಗಾರಿಯೇ ಮುಪ್ಪು gambling is the ruin of a gamester.

ಮುಪ್ಪುರಿ **muppuri,** *adj.* Composed of three twists. –ಬಳ್ಳಿ a threefold rope.

ಮುಬ್ಬು **mubbu,** *see* ಮುಪ್ಪು.

ಮುಯಿ **muyi,** *s.* A gift of money at a wedding.

ಮುಯಿತುರುನಿ, ಮುಯಿತ್ರುನಿ **muyituruni, muyitruni** (ಮುಯಿತುರ್, ಮುಯಿತ್ರ್), *v. a.* To put upside down, overturn; *cf.* ಪಕಾವುನಿ. 2. to strangle. 3. to finish.

ಮುಯಿಪುನಿ **muyipuni** (ಮುಯಿ), *v. a.* To pluck off. 2. *see* ಮುಗಪುನಿ.

ಮುಯೆರ್ **muyerụ**, *see* ಮುಗೆರ್.

ಮುಯ್ಯ **muyya**, *adj.* Returning. –ಪಾಡುನಿ to return, give back.

ಮುರ **mura**, *s.* A demon so called.

ಮುರ **mura**, *s.* A stone quarry; laterite stone. *adj.* Laterite. 2. stony, hard, strong. ಕಲ್ಲ– a medicine prepared of hard wood left by white ants and of earth from the ant-hole. –ಕಲ್ಲ a laterite stone, used for building purposes. –ನರಮಾನಿ a hard-hearted man.

ಮುರ, ಮುರಂಗೆ **mura, murangè**, *see* ಮೊರಂಗೆ.

ಮುರಂಡ, ಮುರಂಡೆ **muraṇḍa, muraṇḍè**, *s.* A swelling, protuberance.

ಮುರಂಪೆ **murampè**, *see* ಮೊರೆ.

ಮುರಜೆ **murajè**, *s.* A rope made of straw.

ಮುರಡಿ **muraḍi**, *adj.* Knotty.

ಮುರಳಿ **muraḷi**, *s.* A fife. 2. *see* ಮುರ್ಲಿ.

ಮುರಾಣಿ, ಮುರಾನಿ **murāṇi, murāni**, *see* ಮೊರಾಣಿ.

ಮುರಿ **muri**, *s.* Entreaty; *cf.* ಪಂಮುಯು. 2. an incision *or* notch. –ಪಡ್ಪುನಿ to swear. –ಪಾಡುನಿ to make a notch

ಮುರಿ **muri**, *s.* A curve, circle, ring, twist. 2. the creases of the hand, winding of a conch, *etc.* ಬಲ– *Helicteres Isora*, a conch that winds to the right.

ಮುರಿಗಿ **murigi**, *see* ಮುರ್ಗ.

ಮುರಿಗೆ **murigè**, *s.* Twist. 2. entanglement. –ಬುಡುಪಾವುನಿ to disentangle.

ಮುರಿಪಾವುನಿ **muripāvuni**, *c. v.* (*of* ಮುರಿಪುನಿ) To cause to burn, consume, as firewood for culinary purposes.

ಮುರಿಪುನಿ **muripuni** (ಮುರಿ), *v. a.* To burn, consume, as firewood for culinary purposes.

ಮುರಿಯ **muriya**, *s.* A cry, weeping; a loud noise. –ಪತ್ತಾವುನಿ to make one cry; to grieve, distress.

ಮುರಿಯಾಟ **muriyāṭa**, *s.* Lamentation, wailing.

ಮುರಿಯೆಡುನಿ, ಮುರಿಯೊಡುನಿ **muriyeḍuni, muriyoḍuni** (ಮುರಿಯೆಡ್, ಮುರಿಯೊಡ್), *v. n.* To weep, lament, bewail.

ಮುರಿಯೆಡ್ಪಿನಿ **muriyeḍpini** (ಮುರಿಯೆಡ್), *v. n.* To grumble, murmur.

ಮುರಿಯೋ **muriyō**, *intj.* Alas! *s.* Weeping loudly; a cry of lamentation, distress, *etc.*

ಮುರಿಸಂಕಡ **murisaṅkaḍa**, *s.* Severe illness; a crisis.

ಮುರು **muru**, *s.* An ear-ring. 2. fortitude, patience. –ಪಾಡುನಿ to endure quietly.

ಮುರುಂಟು **muruṇṭu**, *adj.* Shrunk, shrivelled.

ಮುರುಂಟುನಿ **muruṇṭuni** (ಮುರುಂಟ್), *v. n.* To shrink, shrivel.

ಮುರುಂಟೆಲ್ muruṇṭelu, *s.* Shrinking.

ಮುರುಕು muruku, *see* ಮುರ್ಕು.

ಮುರುಗ muruga, *see* ಮೃಗ.

ಮುರುಟು muruṭu, *see* ಮುರುಂಟು.

ಮುರುಡಿ, ಮುರುಡು muruḍi, muruḍu, *s.* Roughness, coarseness. *adj.* Rough, coarse.

ಮುರುಡುನಿ muruḍuni, *see* ಮುರುಂಟುನಿ.

ಮುರುದು murudu, *see* ಮೃದು.

ಮುರುಪಾವುನಿ murupāvuni, *see* ಮುರಿಪಾವುನಿ.

ಮುರುಪುನಿ murupuni, *see* ಮುರಿಪುನಿ.

ಮುರುಮೀನ್ murumīnu, *s.* A kind of fish.

ಮುರುಮುರ್ಚಂಡೆ murumurčaṇḍe, *s.* Perplexity. 2. demoniacal possession.

ಮುರುಮೂಕುತಿ murumūkuti, *s.* A woman's jewelry.

ಮುರೆ mure, *s.* A node, protuberance; swelling, bruise. –ಬರ್ಪಿನಿ to have a node, swelling.

ಮುರೆಡುನಿ mureḍuni, *see* ಮುರಿಯೆಡುನಿ.

ಮುರೆಪಿನಿ murepini, *see* ಮುರೆಲುನಿ.

ಮುರೆಪುನಿ murepuni, *see* ಮೊರೆಪುನಿ.

ಮುರೆಲ್ murelu, *s.* The thick part of a spade. ಕೆಕ್ಕಿಲದ– the nape of the neck. ಮುಟ್ಟು– the creaking of shoes.

ಮುರೆಲುನಿ, ಮುರೆವುನಿ mureluni, murevuni (ಮುರೆವ್), *v. n.* The fœtus to be formed. 2. to creak, as shoes. 3. *see* ಮುರೆಸುನಿ. 4. *see* ಮುಲುರ್ನಿ.

ಮುರೆಸುನಿ muresuni (ಮುರೆಸ್), *v. n.* To rumble, rattle, as thunder. 2. to contest, as in a game of foot-ball. ಚೆಂಡ್– to vie with another in kicking a foot-ball. ಗಿಡಿಲ್– to thunder.

ಮುರ್ಕ murka, *adj.* Full, brimful. 2. exceeding, very much. ತಟ್ಟೆ ಮುರ್ಕ ಪೇರ್ ಗೆತ್ತೊಣುನಿ to take milk (with rice) up to the forearm; to swallow very much milk. ತೇಕಮುರ್ಕ ಆಪಿನಿ to be very much exhausted, be done up.

ಮುರ್ಕಾವುನಿ murkāvuni, *c. v.* (*of* ಮುರ್ಕುನಿ) To cause to sink, dip, immerse. 2. to ruin, injure, spoil.

ಮುರ್ಕಿ murki, *s.* Fainting, swooning.

ಮುರ್ಕು murku, *s.* A fragment, piece, bit. 2. the young of an animal. ಪಂಜಿದ– a young pig. ಬಜ್ಜೆರೆದ– a bit of betel leaf.

ಮುರ್ಕುನಿ murkuni (ಮುರ್ಕ್), *v. n.* To sink, immerse. 2. to be ruined. 3. the sun to set.

ಮುರ್ಕ್ಯುನಿ murkyuni (ಮುರ್ಕ್) *v. n.* To swoon, faint. ಮುರ್ಕಿಡ್ ಬೂರುನಿ to sink into a fainting fit, as one possessed with a demon.

ಮುರ್ಖೆ murkhe, *see* ಮೂರ್ಖೆ.

ಮುರ್ಗ murga, *s.* Union, concord, especially between a married couple. 2. *see* ಮೃಗ.

ಮುರ್ಗಿ murgi, *s.* A twisted bangle *or* wristlet, generally made of silver; *also* ಮುರ್ಗಿನಸುತ್ತು.

ಮುಗ್ರುನಿ murguni (ಮುರ್ಗಿ), *v. n.* To mould, become musty. 2. *see* ಮುಕ್ರುನಿ.

ಮುಗ್ರೆಲ್ murgelu, *s.* Ducking, diving.

ಮುಗ್ರೇಶ್ರೆ murgēśrè, *see* ಮೃಗಶಿರ.

ಮುರ್ಚಂಡೆ, ಮುರ್ಚಿ murčaṇḍè, murči, *see* ಮೂರ್ಚನೆ.

ಮುರ್ಚುನಿ murčuni *see* ಮುಕ್ರ್ಯುನಿ.

ಮುರ್ಚೆ murčè, *see* ಮೂರ್ಚನೆ.

ಮುರ್ತ murta, *s.* Beginning. 2. *see* ಮುಹೂರ್ತ. 3. *see* ಮೃತ. —ಮಳ್ಪುನಿ to begin.

ಮುರ್ತಾಪ, ಮುರ್ತಾಮ murtāpa, murtāma, *s.* Haughtiness, arrogance, pride. 2. folly, foolishness. —ದ ದೋಲು a kind of kettle-drum. —ದ ಬಲಿ an offering accompanied with beating of a drum.

ಮುರ್ತಿ murti, *see* ಮೃತ್ಯು.

ಮುರ್ತಿಕ, ಮುರ್ತಿಗೆ murtika, murtigè, *see* ಮೃತ್ತಿಕೆ.

ಮುರ್ತೆ murtè, *s.* The act of drawing toddy; tapping a palm tree for toddy. 2. *see* ಮತ್ತೆ.

ಮುರ್ತೆಲ್ murtelu, *s.* Dry leaves, *etc.*, used for kindling fire.

ಮುರ್ದಾರಸಿಂಗಿ murdārasiṅgi, *s.* Semi-vitrified oxide of lead.

ಮುರ್ನಾಲಿ, ಮುರ್ನಾಳಿ murnāli, murnāḷi, *s.* A grooved instrument of metal for tapping a bundle of grain, *etc.*, in order to take out a sample of it.

ಮುರ್ಪಾವುನಿ murpāvuni, *see* ಮುರಿಪಾವುನಿ.

ಮುರ್ಪುನಿ murpuni, *see* ಮುರಿಪುನಿ.

ಮುರ್ಯ murya, *see* ಮುರಿಯ.

ಮುರ್ಲಡಿ murlaḍi, *s.* Trouble. 2. fashion, work, practice; *also* ಮುಟ್ಟುಮುರ್ಲು.

ಮುರ್ಲಿ murli, *s.* A quarrelsome woman; *also* ನ್ಯಾಯದ ಮುರ್ಲಿ. 2. *see* ಮುರಳಿ.

ಮುರ್ಲು murlu, *s.* Kindling fire into a blaze. 2. stretching of a limb. 3. *see* ಮುರ್ಲಡಿ.

ಮುರ್ಲುನಿ murluni (ಮುರ್ಲಿ), *v. n.* A spark to be kindled into a blaze. 2. to be stretched, as the limbs. 3. *see* ಮುರೆಲುನಿ.

ಮುರ್ಲೆ murle, *s.* A quarrelsome man.

ಮುರ್ಲೆ murlè, *adj.* Little, small; tender.

ಮುರ್ಸಾವುನಿ mursāvuni, *see* ಮುಡು[ಸಾವುನಿ.

ಮುಲಾಂ, ಮುಲಾಮ್ mulām, mulāmu, *s.* Cerate, plaster. 2. gilding.

ಮುಳಾಜಿ, ಮುಲಾಜೆ mulāji, mulājè, *s.* Respect, regard for.

ಮುಲಿ muli, *s.* Thatching grass. —ಕೆತ್ತುನಿ, —ಕೆರೆಜುನಿ to cut the same. —ಪಾಡುನಿ, —ಚೇಪಿನಿ to thatch the roof with the same. ತಿಂಡೆ—, ದರ್ಬೆ—, ನೆಯಿ—, ಯೆರು— are different kinds of grass.

ಮುಲ್ಲ mulla, *s.* A mullah, Mussulman doctor *or* preceptor of law.

ಮುಲ್ಲಂಕಲೆ mullaṅkalè, *see* ಮುಳ್ಳಂ[ಕಲೆ.

ಮುಲ್ಲದೊಂಕುನಿ mulladoṅkuni (ಮುಲ್ಲದೊಂಕಿ), *v. n.* A Pariah woman to become pubescent.

ಮುಲ್ಲವುನಿ, ಮುಲ್ಲಾವುನಿ **mullavuni, mullāvuni** (ಮುಲ್ಲ), *v. n.* To limp, hobble, as from dislocation of the hip-bone *or* other cause; *also* ಮುಲ್ಲಾಮುಲ್ಲಾ ನಡಪುನಿ. 2. to disregard, treat with indifference.

ಮುಲ್ಲಿ, ಮುಲ್ಲಿತರು **mulli, mullitaru,** *s.* A kind of very small fish.

ಮುಲ್ಲುದೊಂಕುನಿ **mulludoṅkuni,** *see* ಮುಲ್ಲದೊಂಕುನಿ.

ಮುಲ್ಲೆ **mullè,** *s.* The tail of a cock, *etc.* 2. *see* ಮೂಲೆ. ಕೊಂಡ– the lapwing. ಬಾಲ– the tail of a cock.

ಮುಲ್ಲೆಂಗಿ **mulleṅgi,** *see* ಮೂಲೆಂಗಿ.

ಮುವೊಡು **muvoḍu,** *see* ಮೂವೊಡು.

ಮುವೊಳು, ಮುವ್ವಳ್ **muvoḷu, muvvaḷu,** *see* ಮೂವಳ.

ಮುವ್ವೆ **muvvè,** *s.* A blossom.

ಮುವ್ವೆರ್ **muvveru,** *see* ಮೂವೆರ್.

ಮುವ್ವೆಲ್ **muvvelu,** *see* ಮೂವೆಲ್.

ಮುಷ್ಟಿ **mushṭi,** *s.* The fist. 2. a handful.

ಮುಸರೆ **musarè,** *s.* Anything boiled *or* dressed for eating. 2. uncleanness. *adj.* Boiled, dressed. 2. unclean, foul. –ಬಾಜನ a vessel in which rice has been boiled.

ಮುಸಲ್ **musalu,** *s.* A wooden pestle used in pounding rice.

ಮುಸಾಪಿರಿ, ಮುಸಾಫರಿ **musāpiri, musāphari,** *s.* A traveller, stranger. –ಬಂಗ್ಲೆ a traveller's bungalow.

ಮುಸೀಬತ್ **musībatu,** *s.* Trouble.

ಮುಸುಂಟು, ಮುಸುಂಡು **musuṇṭu, musuṇḍu,** *s.* The face, snout, muzzle. –ಮೋಣಿ a distorted face; an angry look.

ಮುಸುಂಡಿ, ಮುಸುಡಿ **musuṅḍi, musuḍi,** *s.* A shameless woman. 2. a kind of weapon. 3. *see* ಮುಸುಂಟು.

ಮುಸುಕು **musuku,** *see* ಮುಸ್ಕು.

ಮುಸುಡು **musuḍu,** *see* ಮುಸುಂಟು.

ಮುಸುಲ್ಮಾನೆ **musulmāne,** *s.* A Mussalman.

ಮುಸ್ಕ್ **musku,** *s.* Inefficacy. 2. disregard, disrespect. *adj.* Ineffective, fruitless. 2. obscure. 3. *see* ಮುಸ್ಕು.

ಮುಸ್ಕರ **muskara,** *see* ಮುಸ್ಕು.

ಮುಸ್ಕೀಲ್ **muskīlu,** *s.* Pain, trouble.

ಮುಸ್ಕು **musku,** *s.* A hood, veil. –ಪಾಡುನಿ to put on a hood *or* veil; the sky to be clouded.

ಮುಸ್ತೆ **mustè,** *s.* The grass *Cyperus rotandus.*

ಮುಸ್ರೆ **musrè,** *see* ಮುಸರೆ.

ಮುಹೂರ್ತ **muhūrta,** *s.* Time. 2. an English hour. 3. an hour of 48 minutes. 4. the time fixed for marriage *or* other auspicious ceremonies. –ದೀಪಿನಿ to fix such a time. –ಮಳ್ಪುನಿ to begin at such a time.

ಮುಳ **muḷa,** *see* ಮೊಳ.

ಮುಳಡಿ **muḷaḍi,** *see* ಮುಳ್ಳಡಿ.

ಮುಳಾವುನಿ **muḷāvuni,** *see* ಮುಲ್ಲವುನಿ.

ಮುಳಿ **muḷi,** *see* ಮುಲಿ.

ಮುಳಿಯುನಿ, ಮುಳೆಯುನಿ, ಮುಳೆವುನಿ **muḷiyuni, muḷeyuni, muḷevuni** (ಮುಳಿ, ಮುಳೆ), *v. n.* To germ, shoot, sprout.

ಮುಳುಗುನಿ **muḷuguni,** *see* ಮುಕರ್ುನಿ.

ಮುಳೆ **muḷè,** *s.* A nail, peg, wedge. 2. a germ, shoot. ಮುಳೆಟೆ ತೆರಿಯು ಬುಳೆ the out-turn of a crop may be estimated from the saplings.

ಮುಳೆಕುತ್ತಿ **muḷekutti,** *see* ಮೊಳೆಕುತ್ತಿ.

ಮುಳ್ತ **muḷta,** *adv.* Of here, belonging to this place. ಮುಳ್ತಾಯೆ a man of this place.

ಮುಳ್ಪ, ಮುಳ್ಳ **muḷpa, muḷḷa,** *adv.* Here.

ಮುಳ್ಳಂಕಲೆ, ಮುಳ್ಳಂಕೋಲೆ **muḷḷaṅkalè, muḷḷaṅkōlè,** *s.* The plant *Hugonia mystax.*

ಮುಳ್ಳಡಿ **muḷḷaḍi,** *s.* A thorny ground. —ಟೆ ಮುಳ್ಳು ಕೊಡಿಪು thorns will sprout on a thorny ground, *prov.*

ಮುಳ್ಳಪಂದ್ರ್ **muḷḷaparndu,** *s.* The fruit of a thorny plant.

ಮುಳ್ಳಪದ್ಪೆ, ಮುಳ್ಳುಪದ್ಪೆ **muḷḷapadpè, muḷḷupadpè,** *s.* A kind of orach, *Amarantus spinosus.*

ಮುಳ್ಳಾವುನಿ **muḷḷāvuni,** *see* ಮುಲ್ಲವುನಿ.

ಮುಳ್ಳು **muḷḷu,** *see* ಮೂಳು.

ಮುಳ್ಳು **muḷḷu,** *s.* A thorn, thorny bush, an iron prickle. 2. a spur. 3. the bone of a fish *or* a serpent. 4. the spine. 5. a fork. —ಅಬ್ಜಿಕಾಯಿ the soursop. —ಕೆರೆಂಗ್ a species of yam, *Dioscorea tomentosa.* —ಕೊಪ್ಪ a female's ear-ornament. —ಸೇವತಿಗೆ a kind of *Pyrethrum.* —ದ ಜೇಡೆ a place abounding in thorns, thicket. —ದ ಬೇಲಿ a thorn hedge. ಕಣಿತ— the thorn of a bamboo branch. ಕರ್ಗಡೆ—, ಕೊಯು—, ತೇಡಿ—, ತೇಡೆ— are different kinds of thorny plants. ಕೂರಿ— the astringent plant *Zizyphus ænoplia.* ನಂಜಿ— a poisonous thorn. —ಕಂತುನಿ a thorn to pierce. —ತಾಗುನಿ to be pricked by a thorn.

ಮುಳ್ಳುನಿ **muḷḷuni** (ಮುಳ್ಳಿ), *v. n.* To grunt.

ಮುಕ್ಷ **muksha,** *see* ಮುಖ್ಯ.

ಮೂಂಕಣ್ **mūṅkaṇu,** *s.* Small grits of rice *or* other grain.

ಮೂಂಕು **mūṅku,** *s.* The germ of corn. 2. the top, *or* space between the eyes of a cocoanut. 3. the extremity of a mango fruit. 4. *see* ಮೂಕು.

ಮೂಂಡಿ **mūṇḍi,** *see* ಮುಂಡಿ.

ಮೂಂಡಿಕಂಡೆ **mūṇḍikaṇḍè,** *s.* A big yam from Ceylon.

ಮೂಂಡು **mūṇḍu,** *s.* A pale to support a wooden bridge.

ಮೂಕಣ್ **mūkaṇu,** *see* ಮೂಂಕಣ್.

ಮೂಕಾಂಬೆ **mūkāmbè,** *s.* A dumb goddess.

ಮೂಕಿ **mūki,** *s.* A woman who snuffles *or* speaks through the nose.

ಮೂಕು **mūku,** *s.* The nose, bill, beak. —ದ ಮರ the bridge of the nose. —ದ ಮುತ್ತೇಸ the nose-jewel of a woman whose husband is alive. –ದೊಟ್ಟೆ the nostrils. –ಮುಟ್ಟ up to the nose. ನಂಡ್– a flat nose. ನಾಯರ್– a long nose. –ಕಟ್ಟುನಿ to stop the nose. –ಕುತ್ತುನಿ to bore the nose. –ಡು ಪಾತೆರುನಿ to snuffle, speak through the nose. –ಡು ಬಿರೆಲ್ ದೀಪಿನಿ to put the finger on the nose, as an indication of surprise *or* threat. –ಸುಯಿಂಪುನಿ, –ಸ್ಯೆಂಪುನಿ to blow the nose.

ಮೂಕುಡುನಿ **mūkuḍuni,** *see* ಮುಕುಡುನಿ.

ಮೂಕುತಿ, ಮೂಕುದಿ **mūkuti, mūkudi,** *s.* A nose-ornament of a married woman.

ಮೂಕೆ **mūke,** *s.* A man who snuffles *or* speaks through the nose.

ಮೂಕೆಲೆ **mūkele,** *s.* A proud man.

ಮೂಕೊರಲ್ **mūkoraḷu,** *see under* ಕೊರಲ್.

ಮೂಗು **mūgu,** *see* ಮೂಕು. 2. *see* ಮುಗು.

ಮೂಗುತಿ **mūguti,** *see* ಮೂಕುತಿ.

ಮೂಚೆ **mūčè,** *see* ಮೂಸೆ.

ಮೂಜಡಿ **mūǰaḍi** (ಮೂಜಿ ಅಡಿ), *s.* Three feet *or* steps.

ಮೂಜನೆ **mūǰanè,** *adj.* Third. –ದಾಯಿ a third man; a bail.

ಮೂಜಿ **mūǰi,** *num.* Three. –ಕಾಸ್ one and half pie; a trifle. –ಕಾಸ್‌ದಾಯಿ a worthless *or* penniless man. –ಪಾತೆರ thrice uttered, as an oath. –ಭಾಷೆ indistinct, unclear. –ಮರಿಯಳ destitution, poverty. –ಲೋಕ the three worlds.

ಮೂಡ **mūḍa,** *s.* A cloud. 2. adversity, affliction, misfortune. –ಕಟ್ಟುನಿ to be clouded, as the weather; to become dull. –ಪತ್ತುನಿ to be afflicted with adversity; to be unfortunate.

ಮೂಡ, ಮೂಡಾಯಿ **mūḍa, mūḍāyi,** *see* ಮುಡಯಿ.

ಮೂಡಾವುನಿ **mūḍāvuni,** *c. v.* (*of* ಮೂಡುನಿ) To originate, produce, cause to rise, cause to be born.

ಮೂಡು **mūḍu,** *s.* Support. 2. the east.

ಮೂಡುನಿ **mūḍuni** (ಮೂಡ್), *v. n.* To rise, be born. ಪೊಕ್ಕೆ– itch to break out.

ಮೂಡುಸಾವುನಿ **mūḍusāvuni,** *see* ಮುಡುಸಾವುನಿ.

ಮೂಡೆ **mūḍè,** *s.* A kind of rice cake *or* pudding boiled in steam. 2. a mould made of the leaves of screw-pine, into which the dough is poured.

ಮೂಢ **mūḍha,** *adj.* Ignorant, foolish, stupid. –ತನ, –ತ್ವ ignorance, stupidity. –ಭಕ್ತಿ superstition. ಮೂಢಾತ್ಮೆ, *see* ಮೂಢೆ.

ಮೂಢೆ **mūḍhe,** *s.* An ignorant man; a fool.

ಮೂತ್ರ **mūtra,** *s.* Urine. ಉರಿ– scalding urine; inflammation of the urethra. –ಕೃಚ್ಛ್ರ stoppage of urine, strangury. —ದ್ವಾರ urethra.

ಮೂದಲೆ mūdalè, *see* ಮುದಲೆ.

ಮೂನಿಯುನಿ mūniyuni, *see* ಮುನಿಯುನಿ.

ಮೂನೆ mūnè, *see* ಮುನೆ.

ಮೂಪು mūpu, *s.* Timber.

ಮೂಪುನಿ mūpuni, *see* ಶೊಗಪುನಿ. 2. *see* ಮುರಿಪುನಿ.

ಮೂಬದಲಿ mūbadali, *s.* A loan without interest. 2. anything lent to be returned.

ಮೂರ್ mūrụ, *adj.* Fat, stout, corpulent. —ಪೋಪಿನಿ to become fat, stout.

ಮೂರಿ mūri, *s.* A bad smell, stench. 2. stretching oneself. —ಪೂ *Lantana aculeata.* —ಕಳೆಪಿನಿ, —ದೆಪ್ಪುನಿ to stretch oneself. —ಬರ್ಪಿನಿ, —ಲಕ್ಕುನಿ to stink.

ಮೂರು mūru, *see* ಮೂರ್; *cf.* ಮೂರುನಿ.

ಮೂರುತಿ mūruti, *see* ಮೂರ್ತಿ.

ಮೂರುನಾಲಿ mūrunāli, *see* ಮುರ್ನಾಲಿ.

ಮೂರುನಿ mūruni (ಮೂರ್), *v. a.* To tap the blossoms of a palm tree for toddy. 2. to mince, cut up, as vegetables. ಕಾಯಿಕಜಿಪು— to mince vegetables. ಮೂರುನಾಯೆ a toddy-drawer.

ಮೂರುಸಾವುನಿ mūrusāvuni, *see* ಮುಡುಸಾವುನಿ.

ಮೂರೆ mūre, *s.* A man without moustaches. 2. *see* ಮುರೆ.

ಮೂರ್ಖ mūrkha, *adj.* Obstinate, wilful. 2. foolish, ignorant, stupid. —ತನ obstinacy, stupidity, ignorance.

ಮೂರ್ಖೆ mūrkhe, *s.* An obstinate man. 2. a fool, blockhead.

ಮೂರ್ಚನೆ, ಮೂರ್ಚೆ, ಮೂರ್ಛೆ mūrċanè, mūrċè, mūrċhè, *s.* Fainting, syncope, swooning. —ಆಪಿನಿ to swoon, faint.

ಮೂರ್ತ mūrta, *see* ಮುಹೂರ್ತ.

ಮೂರ್ತಿ mūrti, *s.* Matter, form, solidity. 2. the body. 3. the figure, form, any definite shape *or* image, an idol. 4. a god, emanation of a god. 5. *see* ಮೃತಿ. —ಪೂಜೆ idolatry. ಕಾರಣ— the first cause. ತ್ರಿ— the Hindu triad. ವೇದ— a respectful epithet used in addressing learned men *or* priests.

ಮೂರ್ತಿಮತ್ತ್ mūrtimattụ, *adj.* Substantial, material.

ಮೂರ್ತಿಲಾಯೆ mūrtilāye, *s.* A demon so called.

ಮೂರ್ತೆ mūrtè, *see* ಮುರ್ತೆ.

ಮೂರ್ದ, ಮೂರ್ಧ mūrda, mūrdha, *s.* The head, pate.

ಮೂರ್ದುನಿ mūrduni, *see* ಮುದುರುನಿ.

ಮೂರ್ಧನ್ಯ mūrdhanya, *adj.* Chief, principal.

ಮೂರ್ಧಾಭಿಷೇಕ mūrdhābhishēka, *s.* Anointing *or* crowning a sovereign.

ಮೂಲ mūla, *s.* A root. 2. origin. 3. commencement. 4. capital, principal. 5. the original text of a work. 6. means. 7. cause. 8. the nineteenth of the lunar mansions. *adj.* Main, principal, original. —ಕಾ

ರಣ the original cause. –ಗಾರೆ the owner *or* proprietor of a land. –ಗೇಣಿ a perpetual lease of land. –ಗ್ರಂಥ the original text of a work. –ದಮಾನ್ಯೆ, –ದಾಯಿ a Pariah attached to a land. –ಪಟ್ಟಿ, –ಸಾಧನ the title-deed of a land. –ಮಂತ್ರ a mystic formula, the Gāyatri. –ವ್ಯಾಧಿ the piles. –ಸ್ಥಾನ the metropolis, original habitation *or* abode, as of a tribe *or* demon; one's native place. ಸಾಲ– assets and liabilities.

ಮೂಲಂಗಿ mūlaṅgi, *see* ಮೂಲೆಂಗಿ.

ಮೂಲಾಜಿ mūlāji, *see* ಮುಲಾಜಿ.

ಮೂಲಿ mūli, *adj.* Original, principal. –ವರ್ಗ proprietary tenure of land.

ಮೂಲಿಕೆ, ಮೂಲಿಗೆ mūlikè, mūligè, *s.* Any medicinal drug *or* root. 2. a charm. –ಕಟ್ಟುನಿ to wear a charm on some part of the body. –ಮಳ್ಪುನಿ to charm; to administer a drug.

ಮೂಲಿಯೆ mūliye, *s.* A potter.

ಮೂಲೆ mūlè, *s.* A corner, angle. 2. a point of the compass, quarter, direction. –ಕಲ್ಲ್ a corner-stone. –ಗ ಬಂದಾವುನಿ to put *or* collect in a corner; to exclude; to degrade; to ignore. –ಡ್ ಬೂರುನಿ to be in a corner; to become an old maid; to remain neglected; to remain unemployed. –ಶೇರುನಿ to become weak, powerless.

ಮೂಲೆಂಗಿ mūleṅgi, *s.* A radish.

ಮೂಲೋಕ mūlōka, *s.* The three worlds.

ಮೂಲ್ಯ mūlya, *see* ಮೌಲ್ಯ.

ಮೂಲ್ಯೆ mūlye, *s.* A demon priest. 2. *see* ಮೂಲಿಯೆ.

ಮೂವಳ mūvaḷa, *s.* Three seers; *cf.* ಮುಕ್ಕೊಳು.

ಮೂವೆ mūvè, *adj.* Shrivelled, shrunk, contracted.

ಮೂವೆರ್, ಮೂವ್ವೆರ್ mūverụ, mūvverụ, *pron.* Three persons.

ಮೂವೆಲ್ mūvelụ, *s.* Three pairs of cattle.

ಮೂವೊಡು mūvoḍu, *s.* Last year.

ಮೂವೊಳ, ಮೂವೊಳು mūvoḷa, mūvoḷu, *see* ಮೂವಳ.

ಮೂಷಿಕೆ mūshike, *s.* A rat, [mouse.

ಮೂಷೆ mūshè, *see* ಮೂಸೆ.

ಮೂಸಲಿಯುನಿ mūsaliyuni (ಮೂಸಲಿ), *v. a.* To scent, trace, track. 2. to smell.

ಮೂಸಾವುನಿ mūsāvuni, *c. v.* (*of* ಮೂಸುನಿ) To make smell.

ಮೂಸು mūsu, *s.* Smell. 2. money.

ಮೂಸುನಿ mūsuni (ಮೂಸ್), *v. a.* To smell. 2. to take notice. ಮೂಸುತೂಪಿನಿ to sniff. ಆಯನ್ ಯೇರ್ಲಾ ಮೂಸುಜಿರ್ no one takes notice of him.

ಮೂಸೆ mūsè, *s.* A mould. 2. a crucible.

ಮೂಳಾವುನಿ mūḷāvuni, *see* ಮುಲ್ಲವುನಿ. 2. *see* ಮೌರಾವುನಿ. [ಮುಳ್ಪ.

ಮೂಳು mūḷu, *adv.* Here; *cf.* ಇಡೆ,

ಮೃಗ mṛga, *s.* An animal, beast, brute. *adj.* Brutish. –ಭಾವ brutishness.

ಮೃಗಶಿರ, ಮೃಗೇಶ್ರೆ mrụgašira, mrụgēšrè, *s.* The fifth of the lunar mansions; head of *Orion*.

ಮೃತ, ಮೃತಿ mrụta, mrụti, *adj.* Dead, deceased. –ಸಂಜೀವನ a life-restoring cordial.

ಮೃತ್ತಿಕೆ, ಮೃತ್ತಿಗೆ mrụttikè, mrụttigè, *s.* Earth, clay, soil.

ಮೃತಿಪತ್ರ mrụtipatra, *s.* A will, testament.

ಮೃತ್ಯು mrụtyu, *s.* Death.

ಮೃದಂಗ mrụdaṅga, *s.* A finger-drum, tabour. –ಬಾರಿಸುನಿ, –ಬೊಟ್ಟುನಿ to beat the same.

ಮೃದು mrụdu, *adj.* Mild, soft, bland; *cf.* ಮಿದು.

ಮೃಷ್ಟಾಂನ mrụshṭānna, *s.* Cooked rice well seasoned. 2. dainties, rich meal.

ಮೆಂಚಾವುನಿ meṅčāvuni, *c. v.* (*of* ಮೆಂಚುನಿ) To cause to shine. 2. to polish.

ಮೆಂಚಿ meṅči, *s.* Brightness, effulgence, glitter. 2. lightning. –ಇಡ್ಪಿನಿ to sparkle, glitter.

ಮೆಂಚುನ meṅčuna, *adj.* Bright, shining, sparkling.

ಮೆಂಚುನಿ meṅčuni (ಮೆಂಚ್), *v. n.* To sparkle, glitter; to flash, lighten.

ಮೆಂಡೆ meṇḍe, *see* ಮಿಂಡೆ.

ಮೆಂಣ್ meṇṇụ, *s.* A spark.

ಮೆಂತಿ, ಮೆಂತೆ menti, mentè, *see* ಮೆತ್ತೆ.

ಮೆಂನ್ mennụ, *see* ಮೆಂಣ್.

ಮೆಂನಟೆ mennaṭè, *s.* The handkerchief, used for covering the breast of a Pariah woman.

ಮೆಂನಾಟಿಗೆ mennāṭigè, *s.* Haughtiness.

ಮೆಂಪುರಿ mempuri, *see* ಮೆಣ್ಪುರಿ.

ಮೆಗ್ದಿ, ಮೆಗ್ದಿ megụdi, megdi, *s.* A female's younger sister.

ಮೆಗ್ಗೆ, ಮೆಗ್ಗ್ಯೆ megge, meggye, *s.* A younger brother; *also* ಮಿಗ್ಗೆ.

ಮೆಚ್ಚಮನೆ meččamanè, *s.* A privy.

ಮೆಚ್ಚಾವುನಿ meččāvuni, *c. v.* (*of* ಮೆಚ್ಚುನಿ) To please.

ಮೆಚ್ಚಿ mečči, *s.* A sacrifice to a demon.

ಮೆಚ್ಚಿಗೆ meččigè, *s.* Approval, approbation, applause.

ಮೆಚ್ಚುನಿ meččuni (ಮೆಚ್ಚ್), *v. n.* To approve, consent, be pleased.

ಮೆಟ್ಟಮನೆ meṭṭamanè, *see* ಮೆಚ್ಚಮನೆ.

ಮೆಣ್ meṇụ, *s.* Glitter, sparkle.

ಮೆಣ್ಕಾವುನಿ meṇụkāvuni, *c. v.* (*of* ಮೆಣ್ಕುನಿ) To make glitter, glimmer.

ಮೆಣ್ಕುನಿ meṇụkuni (ಮೆಣ್ಕ್), *v. n.* To glimmer, glitter.

ಮೆಣ್ಪುರಿ meṇụpuri, *see* ಮೆಣ್ಪುರಿ.

ಮೆಣ್ಪೆ meṇụpè, *s.* The kingfisher. ಕೋರಯಿ– a large species of the same. ಬಜ್ಜಯಿ– a small species of the same.

ಮೆಣಕ್ meṇakụ, *s.* Glitter, glimmer.

ಮೆಣಕಟೆ meṇakaṭè, *adj.* Gummy, adhesive. 2. *see* ಪುಣಕಟ್ಟೆ.

ಮೆಣಕಾವುನಿ meṇakāvuni, *see* ಮೆಣ್ಕಾವುನಿ.

ಮೆಣಕಿಪುನಿ meṇakipuni, *see* ಮೆಣ್ಕುನಿ.

ಮೆಣಿಪುನಿ meṇipuni, *see* ಮಿನಿಪುನಿ.

ಮೆಣುಕು meṇuku, *s.* Sparkling.

ಮೆಣ್ಕುನಿ meṇkuni, *see* ಮೆಣ್ಕುನಿ.

ಮೆಣ್ಕೊಳಿ, ಮೆಣ್ಪಕ್ಕಿ, ಮೆಣ್ಪೆ meṇkoḷi, meṇpakki, meṇpe, *see* ಮೆಣ್ಪೆ.

ಮೆಣ್ಪುರಿ meṇpuri, *s.* A glowworm.

ಮೆತ್ತಣ, ಮೆತ್ತನೆ mettaṇa, mettanè, *see* ಮೆತ್ತನ.

ಮೆತ್ತಲೆ, ಮೆತ್ತಿ mettalè, metti, *see* ಮೆತ್ತೆ.

ಮೆತ್ತಿಗೆ mettigè, *s.* The pavement *or* boards of the floor of an upper story; the ceiling of a house. —ಪಾಡುನಿ to pave *or* cover in this way.

ಮೆತ್ತುನಿ mettuni (ಮೆತ್ತ್), *v. a.* To fill up with earth. 2. to repair, as a dam, *etc.*

ಮೆತ್ತೆ mettè, *s.* Fenugreek, *Trigonella fœnum græcum.*

ಮೆತ್ತೆನ mettena, *adj.* Soft, pliant.

ಮೆತ್ತೆಸಲೆ mettesalè, *s.* A kind of fine rice.

ಮೆದ್ಲೆ, ಪೆದಲೆ meduḷè, medalè, *s.* A thread-worm, pin-worm.

ಮೆದ್ಪುನಿ meduṗuni, *see* ಮೆದ್ಪುನಿ.

ಮೆದಿ medi, *s.* A bush about a field.

ಮೆದಿಪುನಿ medipuni, *see* ಮೆದ್ಪುನಿ.

ಮೆದು medu, *adj.* Soft, pliant, gentle, ripe, yielding. —ಆಪಿನಿ to become soft, get ripe. —ಮಳ್ಪುನಿ to soften, make elastic.

ಮೆದುಕುನಿ medukuni (ಮೆದುಕ್), *v. n.* To move, be in motion.

ಮೆದುಪಾವುನಿ medupāvuni, *see* ಮೆದ್ಪಾವುನಿ.

ಮೆದುಪುನಿ medupuni, *see* ಮೆದ್ಪುನಿ.

ಮೆದುಲೆ medulè, *see* ಮೆದ್ಲೆ.

ಮೆದ್ಕುನಿ medkuni, *see* ಮೆದುಕುನಿ.

ಮೆದ್ಕೂಲಿ medkūli, *s.* Hire for cleaning rice.

ಮೆದ್ಪಾವುನಿ medpāvuni, *c. v.* (*of* ಮೆದ್ಪುನಿ) To cause to clean, as rice.

ಮೆದ್ಪುನಿ medpuni (ಮೆದ್), *v. a.* To clean by pounding, as rice, *etc.* 2. to full, mill.

ಮೆನ್ಕೋರಿ menukōri, *s.* A kingfisher.

ಮೆನತ್ menatu, *see* ಮೆಹನತ್.

ಮೆನಿಪುನಿ menipuni (ಮೆನಿ), *v. a.* To awake, rouse.

ಮೆನ್ಕಾವುನಿ menkāvuni, *see* ಮೆಣ್ಕಾವುನಿ.

ಮೆನ್ಕುನಿ menkuni, *see* ಮೆಣ್ಕುನಿ.

ಮೆನ್ಕೋಳಿ menkōḷi, *see* ಮೆನ್ಕೋರಿ.

ಮೆಪ್ಪುನಿ meppuni, *see* ಮೆದ್ಪುನಿ.

ಮೆಮ mema, *s.* An abusive term.

ಮೆಯರೆ meyarè, *see* ಮೇರೆ.

ಮೆಯಿ meyi, *see* ಮೈ.

ಮೆರಣಿಗೆ, ಮೆರವಣಿಗೆ meraṇigè, meravaṇigè, *s.* A procession. —ಬರ್ಪಿನಿ a procession to march; to be wandering about. —ಮಳ್ಪುನಿ to take in procession, as a bridal couple.

ಮೆರುವೆ meruvè, *s.* An ornamented post near a ಗುರ್ಜಿ.

ಮೆರೆ merè, *s.* Display, parade. —ತೋಪಿನಿ to make a display.

ಮೆರೆಪಾವುನಿ merepāvuni, *c. v.* (*of* ಮೆರೆಪಿನಿ) To make *or* cause to go in procession. 2. to make shine.

ಮೆರೆಪಿನಿ, ಮೆರೆಯುನಿ, ಮೆರೆವುನಿ merepini, mereyuni, merevuni (ಮೆರೆ), *v.n.* To go in procession. 2. to swagger, make an ostentatious display. 3. to shine.

ಮೆರ್ಪು merpu, *s.* Glitter, lustre.

ಮೆರ್ವೆ mervè, *see* ಮೆರುವೆ.

ಮೆಲರುನಿ, ಮೆಲಾರಿಯುನಿ, ಮೆಲಾರುನಿ melaruni, melāriyuni, melāruni (ಮೆಲರ್, ಮೆಲಾರ್), *v.n.* To attack, rush upon, fall upon. 2. to enter.

ಮೆಲಿಪುನಿ melipuni (ಮೆಲಿ), *v. a.* To knead, as dough; to tread into a well mixed mass, as earth. ಮೆಲಿತ್ತು ತೊರಿತ್ತು ಪೊಲಿತ್ತು ಸಮ ಆಂಡ ಕಲ್ಲಿಗೋಡೆಗ್ ಸಮ if a wall be made of mud, well mixed, well trodden, and well beaten, it will be as good as a stone wall.

ಮೆಲಿಪ್ಪು melippu, *s.* Kneading, mixing well into a mass. 2. macerating.

ಮೆಲಿಯುನಿ meliyuni (ಮೆಲಿ), *v. n.* To become well mixed. 2. to be reduced by sickness. 3. to become rich; *cf.* ಮೆಲಿಪುನಿ.

ಮೆಲ್ಕಯಿ melkayi, *s.* Upper-hand; victory. —ಆಪಿನಿ to be victorious.

ಮೆಲ್ಕೊಡ್ಡುನಿ melkoḍḍuni, *see* ಮೇಲೊಡ್ಡುನಿ.

ಮೆಲ್ಗ್ ಮೀನ್ melgụminụ, *s.* A flying fish.

ಮೆಲ್ಪತ್ತುನಿ melpattuni (ಮೆಲ್ಪತ್ತ್), *v. a.* To beat with the hand.

ಮೆಲ್ಪುನಿ melpuni, *see* ಮೆಲಿಪುನಿ.

ಮೆಲ್ಲ mella, *adj.* Slow, soft, gentle. *adv.* Slowly, softly, gently, slightly; *also* ಮೆಲ್ಲನೆ. —ಪಾತೆರುನಿ to speak softly. —ಪೋಪಿನಿ to go slowly.

ಮೆಲ್ಲಿ melli, *adj.* Bad, inferior. ಎಡ್ಡೆ— good and evil; auspicious and inauspicious occasions.

ಮೆಸ್ಪಾಕ್ mespākụ, *s.* A kind of sweetmeat.

ಮೆಹನತ್ mehanatụ, *s.* Labour, pains, effort, exertion. —ಮಳ್ಪುನಿ to exert.

ಮೇಂಕೆ mēṅkè, *see* ಮೇಕೆ.

ಮೇಂಟ್, ಮೇಂಟ mēṇṭụ, mēṇṭa, *adj.* Showy, boastful. 2. lewd, rakish. —ಗಾರಿಕೆ showiness, foppery; lewdness. —ಗಾರೆ a fop; a rake.

ಮೇಂಟಿಗೆ mēṇṭigè, *s.* Coupling, union. 2. a female's toe-ornament. 3. *see* ಮೇಂಟಗಾರಿಕೆ. *under* ಮೇಂಟ.

ಮೇಂಟೆ mēṇṭè, *s.* A couple.

ಮೇಕ್ mēkụ, *s.* A peg, wedge, nail. 2. malice, enmity. —ದಾಯೆ a malicious man, foe. —ಗ್ ಪಣ್ಪುನಿ to speak maliciously. ಮೇಕಾ— full of malice.

ಮೇಕೆ mēkè, *s.* A disease of cattle, caused from feeding on poisonous matter. 2. the craw *or* crop of birds. 3. *see* ಮೇವು. —ಮೇಪಿನಿ cattle to suffer from the above disease.

ಮೇಗ mēga, *see* ಮೇಘ.

ಮೇಗರೆ, ಮೇಗಲಿ, ಮೇಗಲೆ, ಮೇಗಳ, ಮೇಗೊಳೆ **mēgarè, mēgali, mēgalè, mēgaḷa, mēgōlè,** *s.* An imputation, accusation, false *or* malicious statement; *cf.* ಮೈಗಳ್ಳ.

ಮೇಗಿ **mēgi,** *adj.* Cloudy; relating to clouds. —ಲೋಕ heaven.

ಮೇಘ **mēgha,** *s.* A cloud. —ಮಂಡಲ, —ಲೋಕ the region of clouds.

ಮೇಚಿ, ಮೇಚು **mēci, mēcu,** *see* ಮೇಜಿ.

ಮೇಚೆಲ್ **mēcelụ,** *s.* Pasture, a meadow.

ಮೇಜವಾನಿ, ಮೇಜ್ವಾನಿ **mējavāni, mējvāni,** *s.* A treat, banquet, entertainment.

ಮೇಜಿ **mēji,** *s.* A table. 2. a meal, repast. —ದೆಪ್ಪುನಿ to clear a table after the repast is over. —ಪಾಡುನಿ to serve a meal.

ಮೇಜೆ **mējè,** *see* ಮೇಸೆ.

ಮೇಜೋಡು **mējōḍu,** *s.* Stockings, socks.

ಮೇಟಿ **mēṭi,** *s.* A mate, *or* assistant of a butler.

ಮೇಡೆ **mēḍè,** *s.* A bar of a door.

ಮೇಣ **mēṇa,** *see* ಜಾಯುಉ.

ಮೇಣಾಯೆ **mēṇaye,** *see* ಮೇಮನೆ.

ಮೇಣವೆ **mēṇave,** *s.* An oil-monger wearing the sacred thread.

ಮೇದಲೆ **mēdalè,** *s.* That part of a female's garment which passes over the breast and down the back. —ಸೆರಂಗ್ the upper part of a female's garment.

ಮೇಧ **mēdha,** *s.* A sacrifice, offering.

ಮೇನತ್ **mēnatụ,** *see* ಮೆಹನತ್.

ಮೇಪರಿ, ಮೇಪಲಿ. ಮೇಪಾಲಿ **mēpari, mēpali, mēpāli,** *s.* A grazier, one who tends cattle.

ಮೇಪಾವುನಿ **mēpāvuni,** *c. v.* (*of* ಮೇಪುನಿ) To cause to feed *or* graze cattle.

ಮೇಪಿನಿ **mēpini** (ಮೇ), *v. n.* To graze, eat grass, as cattle. 2. to spread, as a parasitic itch. ಶರ— the body to be infested with ring-worms.

ಮೇಪು **mēpu,** *see* ಮೇವು.

ಮೇಪುನಾಯೆ **mēpunāye,** *s.* A grazier, one who tends cattle.

ಮೇಪುನಿ **mēpuni** (ಮೇ), *v. a.* To feed *or* graze cattle; *cf.* ಮೇಪಿನಿ.

ಮೇಮನೆ **mēmane,** *s.* A Mahommedan native of Cutch.

ಮೇಯಿ **mēyi,** *see* ಮೈ.

ಮೇಯಿಕೆ **mēyikè,** *see* ಮೇಕೆ. 2. *see* ಮೇವು.

ಮೇಯುನಿ **mēyuni,** *see* ಮೇಪಿನಿ.

ಮೇರ್ **mērụ,** *pro.* (*honorific pl. of* ಇಂಬೆ) This person.

ಮೇರ್ **mērụ,** *s.* The pipe *or* tube of a hooka.

ಮೇರು **mēru,** *s.* The mount Mēru.

ಮೇರುವೆ **mēruvè,** *see* ಮೇರ್ವೆ.

ಮೇರೆ **mērè,** *s.* A boundary, limit.

ಮೇರೋಗ **mērōga,** *see* ಮೇಹ.

ಮೇರ್ವೆ **mērvè,** *s.* Manner, method. 2. conduct, act, behaviour.

ಮೇಲ್ **mēlụ,** *s.* The upper part of any thing. 2. superiority, excellence. 3. futurity, time to come. 4. success. *adj.* Upper, higher. 2. superior. 3. future. *adv.* Hereafter, at some future time. *postp.* After, upon, over, above, beyond. —ಕೀಳ್ good and evil, superior and inferior. —ಜಾತಿ a high caste. —ತರ, ಮೇಲ್ತರ superior kind, breed, *etc.* —ವಿಚಾರ superintendence. —ವಿಲಾಸ the address of a letter. —ದ ಸಂಗತಿ future event, what is to happen hereafter. —ಸೆರಂಗ್ the upper part of a female's garment. —ಗ್ in future, hereafter. —ಆಪಿನಿ to succeed, overcome. —ಡ್ ದೀಪಿನಿ to place above *or* over. —ಡ್ ಬೂರುನಿ to fall upon, attack, assault. ಕೈಬಾಯಿ ಮೇಲ್ ಮಳ್ಪುನಿ *lit.* to raise the hands and mouth; to grumble, growl; to gesticulate.

ಮೇಲ mēla, *see* ಮೇಳ.

ಮೇಲಂಟೆ mēlaṇṭe, *s.* A barber of fishermen.

ಮೇಲಧಿಕಾರ mēladhikāra, *s.* Supremacy; predominance. ಮೇಲಧಿಕಾರಿ a superintendent, a higher authority.

ಮೇಲಾಗ್ರ mēlāgra, *s.* Curried vegetables.

ಮೇಲಾಟ mēlāṭa, *s.* Out-bidding another; rivalry.

ಮೇಲಾಡಿಸುನಿ, ಮೇಲಾಡುನಿ mēlāḍisuni, mēlāḍuni, *see* ಮೇಲೊಡ್ಡುನಿ.

ಮೇಲಾರ mēlāra, *adj.* Superficial; upper. —ತಪ್ಪು the fibrous covering of a cocoanut.

ಮೇಲಾಳ್ mēlāḷu, *s.* An overseer, head coolie. —ಆದ್ ತೂಪಿನಿ to supervise.

ಮೇಲೆ mēlè, *see* ಮೇಲ್.

ಮೇಲೊಡ್ಡುನಿ mēloḍḍuni (ಮೇಲೊಡ್ಡ್), *v. a.* To outbid, vie with each other.

ಮೇಲೊಣುನಿ mēloṇuni (ಮೇಲೊಣ್), *v. refl.* To overreach, defraud. 2. to throng.

ಮೇಲೋಗರ mēlōgara, *see* ಮೇಲಾಗ್ರ.

ಮೇಲ್ಕರ್ಚಿ mēlkarči, *s.* Extra expense; sundry expense.

ಮೇಲ್ಕೊಡುನಿ mēlkoḍuni, *see* ಮೇಲೊಡ್ಡುನಿ.

ಮೇಲ್ಗೊಣುನಿ mēlgoṇuni (ಮೇಲ್ಗೊಣ್), *v. n.* To be cautious. 2. to win. 2. *see* ಮೇಲೊಣುನಿ.

ಮೇಲ್ತರ mēltara, *see under* ಮೇಲ್.

ಮೇವ mēva, *s.* A sweet kind of food; any thing eatable.

ಮೇವು mēvu, *s.* Food, fodder, pasturage.

ಮೇಷ mēsha, *s.* The first solar month. 2. the sign *Aries* in the zodiac. 3. a ram.

ಮೇಸೆ mēsè, *s.* A cleft *or* hollow in a tree.

ಮೇಸ್ತೆ mēste, *s.* A carpenter. 2. a stone-cutter, mason.

ಮೇಸ್ತ್ರಿ, ಮೇಸ್ತ್ರೆ mēstri, mēstre, *s.* An overseer, head labourer, maistry.

ಮೇಹ, ಮೇಹರೋಗ mēha, mēharōga, *s.* Urinary *or* venereal disease, gonorrhœa.

ಮೇಳ mēḷa, *s.* Concord in music, concert, harmony. 2. a set of musicians, dancers and actors. ತಾಳ— beating time to music. ಸಂ— a double drum. —ದಾಯಿ a musician; an actor. —ಪಾಡುನಿ to cut a dash, make a display. —ಕಟ್ಟುನಿ to get up a band of musicians, *etc.*; to mask, disguise.

ಮೇಳನ mēḷana, *s.* Union.

ಮೇಳಿ mēḷi, *s.* Marriage. 2. a bride, wife. 3. rutting.

ಮೇಳೆ mēḷe, *see* ಮೇಳ.

ಮೈ mei, *s.* The body, person. 2. *see* ಮೈಂಯಿ. ತಿರಿ— a thin *or* lean body. —ಕಟ್ಟ್ form, shape, model. —ಕಂಣ್ a painted eye; *cf.* ಮೈಕಂಣ್. —ಕಾವಲ, —ಗಾವಲ a body-guard. —ಗುಣ temperament, habit. —ಟಿ ಕೈಟಿ ornaments and cash, whatever one has got. —ನೀರ್ perspiration; urine. —ಇರ್ಗ್ಯುನಿ to become thin. —ಕಾಯುನಿ to be feverish. —ಕೊಡುನಿ to become stout, robust. —ಗ್ ಕೊಣ್ಪುನಿ the system to be affected, as with food, *etc.* —ಕೊರ್ಪಿನಿ to assist, help; to venture; to be attentive. —ಟ ಬರ್ಪಿನಿ to be possessed by a god *or* demon. —ದರ್ಪುನಿ the body to swell, suffer from dropsy. —ಪೆಚುರ್ನಿ to become fat. —ಬರ್ಪಿನಿ to suffer from fever. —ಡ್ ಪೋಪಿನಿ to suffer from leucorrhea, as a female. —ಮಾಸುನಿ the body to become dirty.

ಮೈಂದ್ meindu, *s.* Dew; mist, fog. —ಮುಸ್ಕು thick fog. —ಬೂರುನಿ dew to fall.

ಮೈಂದ್ರಜಾಲಿ meindrajāli, *s.* Legerdemain, conjuration.

ಮೈಕಂಣ್, ಮೈಕಾನ್ meikaṇṇu, meikānu, *s.* A kind of fish.

ಮೈಕುನಿ meikuni (ಮೈಕ್), *v. n.* To entice, persuade. 2. to perplex.

ಮೈಗಳ, ಮೈಗಳ್ಳ meigaḷa, meigaḷḷa, *adj.* Lazy. —ತನ laziness.

ಮೈಗಳ್ಳೆ meigaḷḷe, *s.* A lazy fellow, sluggard.

ಮೈಜೋಡು meijōḍu, *see* ಮೇಜೋಡು.

ಮೈತಳ meitaḷa, *s.* The plant *Ruellia ringens*, used in medicine and purifying salt.

ಮೈತಿದಿ, ಮೈತೆದಿ meitidi, meitedi, *s.* A sister-in-law, a father's sister's daughter, *or* a mother's brother's daughter.

ಮೈತಿನೆ meitine, *s.* A husband's younger brother; a son of a female's maternal uncle; the husband of a female's sister.

ಮೈದಾನ್, ಮೈದಾನ meidānu, meidāna, *s.* A plain, open field.

ಮೈದುನೆ meidune, *see* ಮೈತಿನೆ.

ಮೈನ meina, *s.* The bird Mina.

ಮೈಪಾಕ್ meipāku, *s.* Exercise.

ಮೈಪಾವುನಿ meipāvuni, *c. v.* (*of* ಮೈಪುನಿ) To make *or* cause to pour.

ಮೈಪು meipu, *s.* A broom *or* besom made of the ribs of palm-leaves. ಕುಂಟಿ– a worn-out broom; the stump of a broom. ತಪ್ಪ– a new broom.

ಮೈಪುನಿ meipuni (ಮೈ), *v. a.* To pour. 2. to cast, as in a mould. ಬಾಯಿಗ್– to feed; to bait.

ಮೈಪೆ, ಮೈಪ್ಪೆ meipè, meippè, *s.* A black *or* dark-coloured fowl; *also* ಮೈಪೆಕೋರಿ.

ಮೈಮೆ meimè, *see* ಮಹಿಮೆ.

ಮೈಯರ್ meiyarụ, *see* ಮೈರ್.

ಮೈಯಿ meiyi, *s.* A kind of collyrium; *cf.* ಅಂಜನ.

ಮೈಯೆರೆಸುತ್ತು meiyeresuttu, *see* ಮೈರ್ಸುತ್ತು.

ಮೈರ್ meirụ, *s.* A compass.

ಮೈರ್ meirụ, *s.* A peacock. –ಕಂಣ್ಣ dim sight, weak eyes. –ದ ಕಂನದಿ the stars in a peacock's tail. –ದ ಪೀಲಿ a peacock's feather. –ಸುತ್ತು, *see* ಮೈರ್ಸುತ್ತು.

ಮೈರಂಬಳ meirambaḷa, *s.* A kind of plant.

ಮೈರಾಣ, ಮೈರ್ವಾಣ meirāṇa, meirvāṇa, *s.* Legerdemain, jugglery. –ಮಳ್ಪುನಿ to juggle, play tricks.

ಮೈರೆ meirè, *s.* A tawny coloured cow. 2. a female so called. *adj.* Dark yellow, tawny.

ಮೈರೋಜಿನ meirōjina, *s.* A kind of rush.

ಮೈರ್ಸುತ್ತು meirsuttu, *s.* Blue vitriol, sulphate of copper.

ಮೈಲ್ meilụ, *s.* A mile. –ಕಲ್ಲ್ a mile-stone.

ಮೈಲ್‌ತುತ್ತು meilụtuttu, *see* ಮೈರ್ಸುತ್ತು.

ಮೈಲಾಣ meilāṇa, *see* ಮೈರಾಣ.

ಮೈಲಾರ್ meilārụ, *s.* A Mopla priest. [ಮೈಲೆ.

ಮೈಲಿ, ಮೈಲಿಗೆ meili, meiligè, *see*

ಮೈಲುನಿ meiluni (ಮೈಲ್), *v. n.* To glimmer, shine *or* burn faintly.

ಮೈಲೆ meilè, *s.* Filth, pollution, dirtiness. *adj.* Dirty, filthy, foul. –ಕುಂಟು dirty clothes. –ಗಜ್ಜಿ the small-pox.. –ಆಪಿನಿ to become dirty. –ಮಳ್ಪುನಿ to make dirty.

ಮೈವರಿಪುನಿ meivaripuni (ಮೈವರಿ), *v. a.* To paint the eyes with antimony *or* collyrium.

ಮೈವಾನ meivāna, *see* ಮೈರಾಣ.

ಮೈಸಂದಾಯೆ meisandāye, *s.* A demon so called.

ಮೈಸಾಲ meisāla, *s.* A loan without pledge *or* mortgage. –ಪತ್ರ a simple bond.

ಮೈಸೂರು meisūru, *s.* The province *or* town of Mysore. –ಬಾರೆ a kind of plantains. –ಬಿಲ್ಲೆ cakes of sandal powder received from Mysore.

ಮೊಂಟಂಗೆಲ್ moṇṭaṅgelụ, *see* ಮೋಂಟಂಗೆಲ್.

ಮೊಂಟು moṇṭu, *see* ಮೋಂಟು.

ಮೊಂಟೆ moṇṭè, *s.* A grasshopper.

ಮೊಂಡು moṇḍu, *adj.* Blunt. 2. *see* ಮೋಂಟು.

ಮೊಕತಾ mokatā, *adv.* Face to face, personally. –ಪಾತೆರುನಿ to speak personally. –ಮಳ್ಪುನಿ to confront.

ಮೊಕದ್ದಮೆ mokaddamè, *s.* An affair. 2. a criminal proceeding.

ಮೊಕಮುಂಟಮೆ mokamaṇṭamè, *s.* The front porch, as of a temple. 2. a vestibule, portico.

ಮೊಕರೂರು mokarūru, *see* ಮೊಕ್ರೂರು.

ಮೊಕಸಾಲೆ mokasālè, *see* ಮೊಗಸಲೆ.

ಮೊಕಾಬಿಲಿ, ಮೊಕಾಬಿಲೆ mokābili, mokābilè, *s.* Confronting, comparison. –ಮಳ್ಪುನಿ to collate, compare, confront.

ಮೊಕಾಮು mōkāmu, *s.* A halting place in a journey, camp. 2. a dwelling, residence.

ಮೊಕ್ತಾ moktā, *see* ಮೊಕತಾ.

ಮೊಕ್ತಾರಿ, ಮೊಕ್ತ್ಯಾರಿ moktāri, moktyāri, *s.* A power of attorney; *also* ಮೊಕ್ತಾರಿನಾಮೆ. –ಕೊರ್ಪಿನಿ to empower, authorize.

ಮೊಕ್ತೇಸರೆ, ಮೊಕ್ತೇಸ್ರೆ moktēsare, moktēsre, *s.* A trustee, manager of a temple. 2. a principal resident of a village, *etc.*

ಮೊಕ್ರೂರು mokrūru, *s.* Appointment, nomination. 2. resolution, settlement. *adj.* Appointed. 2. settled. –ಆಪಿನಿ to be appointed; to be settled. –ಮಳ್ಪುನಿ to appoint; to settle.

ಮೊಖುಫ್ mokhuphu, *see* ಮುಖುಫ್.

ಮೊಖ್ತಾರಿ mokhtāri, *see* ಮೊಕ್ತಾರಿ.

ಮೊಗ moga, *s.* The front; *cf.* ಮುಖ.

ಮೊಗಂಟೆ mogaṇṭè, *see* ಮುಗಂಟೆ.

ಮೊಗಡೆ mogaḍè, *see* ಮುಗಡ.

ಮೊಗಪು mogapu, *s.* The clasp of a girdle.

ಮೊಗಪುನಿ mogapuni (ಮೊಗ), *v. a.* To turn, put. 2. to upset.

ಮೊಗರ್ mogaru, *adj.* Sandy. –ಕಂಡ a sandy rice-field.

ಮೊಗಸ್ mogasu, *s.* Surplus, remnant, balance. 2. orts, leavings. *adj.* Full, satisfied, pleasant, happy. –ಆಪಿನಿ to excel, surpass; to be glad. –ಮಳ್ಪುನಿ to satisfy.

ಮೊಗಸಲೆ, ಮೊಗಸಾಲೆ mogasalè, mogasālè, *s.* A veranda in front of a house *or* temple, a portico, porch.

ಮೊಗುಲ್ mogulu, *s.* Mogul.

ಮೊಗೇರೆ mogēre, *s.* A fisherman.

ಮೊಗ್ಗೆ moggè, *see* ಮುಗ್ಗೆ.

ಮೊಜಂಞೆ mojaññè, *s.* The head of a fish, jowl, jole.

ಮೊಜಂಟಿ mojaṇṭi, *s.* A small kind of bee. 2. a honeycomb.

ಮೊಜಡೆ mojaḍe, *see* ಮುಜಡೆ.

ಮೊಜೆಕುನಿ mojekuni (ಮೊಜಿಕ್), *v. a.* To mix, compound.

ಮೊಟ್ಟೆ moṭṭè, *s.* A bundle. 2. an egg; *cf.* ಮುಟ್ಟೆ.

ಮೊಡಂಕ್ moḍaṅku, *s.* Crookedness, obliquity. 2. a hump back. 3. perversity, obstinacy. *adj.* Crooked. 2. perverse. –ಪಾತೆರ speaking irrelevantly.

ಮೊಡಂಕುನಿ moḍaṅkuni (ಮೊಡಂಕ್), *v.n.* To become crooked. 2. to bow, bend.

ಮೊಡಂಕೆಲ್ moḍaṅkelu, *s.* Side, margin, edge. 2. *see* ಮೊಡಂಕ್. —ಕಾಯಿ a kind of oil fruit.

ಮೊಡಂಕೆಲೆ moḍaṅkele, *s.* A hump-backed man. 2. a perverse man.

ಮೊಡಂಗ್ modaṅgu, *s.* A kind of fish.

ಮೊಡಂದೆಲ್, ಮೊಡೆಂದೆಲ್ moḍandelu, moḍendelu, *see* ಮಡಂತೆಲ್.

ಮೊಡೆ moḍè, *adj.* Stiff.

ಮೊಡೆಪಿನಿ, ಮೊಡೆವುನಿ moḍepini, moḍevuni, *see* ಮುಡೆಪಿನಿ. 2. *see* ಮುಡೆಯುನಿ.

ಮೊಣೆ moṇè, *see* ಮುನೆ.

ಮೊಣೆಪು moṇepu, *s.* A small piece of land stretching into a river.

ಮೊದಡೆ modaḍè, *see* ಮುದಡೆ.

ಮೊನೆ monè, *see* ಮುನೆ.

ಮೊಪ್ಪೆ moppè, *s.* An old man.

ಮೊಬಲಗ್, ಮೊಬ್ಲಗ್ mobalagu, moblagu, *s.* A sum of money.

ಮೊಬಾದಿಲೆ mobādilè, *s.* Exchange, transfer. 2. advance; *also* ಮುಬಾದಿಲೆ.

ಮೊಬ್ಬು mobbu, *see* ಮಬ್ಬು.

ಮೊಮತೆ momatè, *see* ಮಮಕಾರ.

ಮೊಯಿಲಿ, ಮೊಯಿಲೆ moyili, moyile, *s.* One of a class of Šūdras, employed in the out-door service of temples and sometimes acting as musicians. 2. an oil-monger.

ಮೊರ mora, *see* ಮುರ.

ಮೊರಂಗೆ moraṅgè, *s.* A cubit from the elbow to the tip of the little finger, about seventeen inches.

ಮೊರಂಟೆ moraṇṭè, *s.* A kind of fish.

ಮೊರಂಡ, ಮೊರಂಡಲ, ಮೊರಂಡೆ moraṇḍa, moraṇḍala, moraṇḍè, *s.* A swelling on any part of the body; induration of the skin.

ಮೊರಂಪಾಯಿ morampāyi, *adj.* Knee-deep.

ಮೊರಂಪು morampu, *s.* The knee. 2. a cry, roaring. —ದ ಪಲ್ಲೆ the knee-pan. —ಊರುನಿ to kneel, bow the knee.

ಮೊರಂಪೆ morampè, *s.* A swelling *or* protuberance on any part of the body. —ಲಕ್ಕುನಿ to have a swelling.

ಮೊರಜ, ಮೊರಜೆ moraja, morajè, *see* ಮುರಜೆ.

ಮೊರಣೆ, ಮೊರಾನಿ moraṇi, morāni, *adv.* The day before yesterday.

ಮೊರು moru, *see* ಮುರು.

ಮೊರುಂಟು moruṇṭu, *see* ಮುರುಂಟು.

ಮೊರೆ morè, *s.* A cry. 2. *see* ಮುರೆ.

ಮೊರೆಂಜಿ moreṅji, *see* ಮುರಜೆ.

ಮೊರೆಡುನಿ moreḍuni, *see* ಮುರಿಯೆಡುನಿ.

ಮೊರೆಪಿನಿ, ಮೊರೆವುನಿ morepini, morepuni (ಮೊರೆ), *v. a.* To mix; to stir up.

ಮೊರೆಯೊಡುನಿ moreyoḍuni, *see* ಮುರಿಯೆಡುನಿ.

ಮೊರೆಲ್ morelu, *see* ಮುರೆಲ್.

ಮೊರೆಲುನಿ moreluni, *see* ಮುರೆಲುನಿ.

ಮೊರೆಸುನಿ **moresuni,** *see* ಮುರೆಸುನಿ.

ಮೊರೊಡು **moroḍu,** *adj.* Empty.

ಮೊಲ **mola,** *s.* A large hare.

ಮೊಲಂಪು **molampu,** *s.* Mire, mud; sediment.

ಮೊಲಂಕ್, ಮೊಲಂಕನ **molaṅkụ, molaṅkana,** *s.* The knee-pan.

ಮೊಲಾನಿ **molāni,** *see* ಮೊರಣಿ.

ಮೊಲಾಮ್ **molāmụ,** *see* ಮುಲಾಂ.

ಮೊಲೆ **molè,** *see* ಮುಳೆ.

ಮೊಸರು **mosaru,** *s.* Curds. –ಕುಡಿಕೆ a pot of curds; a festival in commemoration of Krushṇa's birthday and childhood.

ಮೊಸರೆ **mosarè,** *see* ಮುಸರೆ.

ಮೊಸಳೆ **mosaḷè,** *s.* An alligator, crocodile. –ಬಾಯಿ the ornamental top of the pole of a palankeen, *etc.*

ಮೊಹರ್, ಮೊಹರಿ **moharụ, mohari,** *s.* A gold mohur *or* pagoda. 2. *see* ಮೋರು.

ಮೊಹರಂ, ಮೊಹರಮ್ **moharam, moharamụ,** *s.* The first month of the Mahommedan year. 2. an annual Mussulman festival in commemoration of the death of the two brothers Hassan and Hussein.

ಮೊಹಸಮ್ **mohasamụ,** *s.* The trading season.

ಮೊಹುರು **mohuru,** *see* ಮೋರು.

ಮೊಳ **moḷa,** *see* ಮೊರಂಗೆ. 2. *see* ಮೊಲ.

ಮೊಳಂಪಾರ್ **moḷampārụ,** *see* ಮೊರಂಪಾಯಿ.

ಮೊಳಂಪು, ಮೊಳಂಬು **moḷampu, moḷambu,** *see* ಮೊಲಂಪು.

ಮೊಳಿಕೆ **moḷikè,** *s.* A bud, germ.

ಮೊಳಿಪುನಿ, ಮೊಳೆಪುನಿ **moḷipuni, moḷepuni** (ಮೊಳಿ, ಮೊಳೆ), *v. n.* To sprout, shoot, germ.

ಮೊಳೆ **moḷè,** *see* ಮುಳೆ.

ಮೊಳೆಕುತ್ತಿ **moḷekutti,** *s.* The hinge of a native door.

ಮೈಲಿ **moili,** *see* ಮೊಯಿಲಿ.

ಮೋಂಟ್, ಮೋಂಟ **mōṇṭụ, mōṇṭa,** *see* ಮೋಂಟು.

ಮೋಂಟಂಗೆಲ್ **mōṇṭaṅgelụ,** *adj.* Crooked, bent. 2. lame.

ಮೋಂಟಾವುನಿ **mōṇṭāvuni,** *c. v.* (*of* ಮೋಂಟುನಿ) To cause to bend. 2. to lame. 3. to limp, halt.

ಮೋಂಟಿ **mōṇṭi,** *s.* A lame woman.

ಮೋಂಟಿಯುನಿ **mōṇṭiyuni** (ಮೋಂಟಿ), *v. a.* To do mischief; to annoy, trouble.

ಮೋಂಟು **mōṇṭu,** *s.* Lameness. 2. crookedness, bend. 3. perverseness, obstinacy. *adj.* Lame, maimed, crooked, curved. 2. perverse. –ಕಾರ್ a lame leg. –ಕೊಂಬು a bent horn. –ಪಾತೆರ an irrelevant expression. ಕಾಂಟು–, *see* ಕಾಂಟೆ ಮೋಂಟೆ. –ನಡಪುನಿ, *see* ಮೋಂಟುನಿ. –ಮಳ್ಪುನಿ to be perverse.

ಮೋಂಟುನಿ **mōṇṭuni** (ಮೋಂಟೆ), *v. n.* To be lame; to limp. 2. to be crooked.

ಮೋಂಟೆ **mōṇṭe,** *s.* A cripple, lame man. ಕಾಂಜಿ– a very weak man; a cripple.

ಮೋಂದಲೆ mōndale, *s.* Shaving the face, *etc.*, particularly of a bridegroom. —ಜೆಪ್ಪಿನಿ to shave in this way.

ಮೋಂಬತ್ತಿ mōmbatti, *s.* A wax-candle.

ಮೋಕುಳು mōkuḷu, *pron.* (*plur. of* ಇಂಬೆ) These persons.

ಮೋಕೆ mōke, *s.* Love, affection. —ದಾಯಿ an affectionate man. —ಮಳ್ಪುನಿ to love, fondle.

ಮೋಖೂಫ್ mōkhūphu, *see* ಮುಖುಫ್.

ಮೋಗ mōga, *s.* Fragrance. 2. plenty. *adj.* Soft.

ಮೋಚನೆ mōcane, *see* ವಿಮೋಚನೆ.

ಮೋಚಿ mōči, *s.* A shoemaker. 2. a book-binder.

ಮೋಚೆ mōče, *s.* Country shoes.

ಮೋಜ, ಮೋಜಿ, ಮೋಜು mōǰa, mōǰi, mōǰu, *s.* Fun, sport, amusement, entertainment. —ಗಾರೆ a beau, gay man. —ಗಾರಿಕೆ gaiety, merriment.

ಮೋಟಿ mōṭi, *see* ಮೋಂಟಿ.

ಮೋಟೆ mōṭe, *see* ಮೋಂಟೆ.

ಮೋಡ mōḍa, *s.* A cloud. 2. obscurity, dullness. 3. *see* ಮೋದ.

ಮೋಡಾತ್ಮೆ mōḍātme, *see* ಮೂಢೆ.

ಮೋಡಿ mōḍi, *s.* Hooking the fingers one into the other. 2. any thing placed by a conjurer to try the ability of another. 2. conjuration, delusion, sorcery. 3. a running hand, illegible writing. —ಗಾರೆ a sorcerer, conjurer. —ಪಾತೆರ provincialism. —ಬರವು a running hand, illegible writing. —ವಿದ್ಯೆ sorcery, conjuration, trick.

ಮೋಡು mōḍu, *adj.* Cloudy. *s.* A hill. —ಪಲ್ಲ, —ಪಳ್ಳ hill and dale.

ಮೋಡೆ mōḍe, *s.* An ignorant man, silly fellow. ಯೇಪಾ— a simpleton, witless fellow; an instigator.

ಮೋಡೆ mōḍe, *adj.* Curved, bent. *s.* An ox *or* buffalo with curved horns. —ಕೊಂಬು a curved horn.

ಮೋಣೆ mōṇe, *s.* The face, countenance. 2. the front of a house. ತೆಂಪೆಲ್— a small face. ದೂಜಿ—, ಮುಂಗುಲಿ— a long face. ಬಾಪೆಲ್— a plump face; an angry face. ಸುಡು— a stern face. —ಕೆಪ್ಪು ಮಳ್ಪುನಿ, —ಕಾಂಗಾವುನಿ to be dejected. —ಗ್ ತಕ್ಕ ಪಾತೆರುನಿ to flatter. —ಗ್ ದರ್ಪುನಿ to slap on the face; to be over-sweet; to nauseate, as over-sweet food. —ತೂಪಿನಿ to regard, show partiality. —ದರ್ಪುನಿ the face to swell. —ಪಿಂಟುನಿ the face to be distorted *or* deformed. —ಪುಳಿಪಾವುನಿ to be sour-faced. —ಬಾಡುನಿ the face to become pale *or* reduced.

ಮೋತಯಿ mōtayi, *see* ಮತಾಯಿ.

ಮೋತ್ರ mōtra, *see* ಮೂತ್ರ.

ಮೋದ mōda, *s.* A wave, billow, surge.

ಮೋದ **mōda**, *s.* Joy, delight.

ಮೋದಂಡ **mōdaṇḍa**, *s.* Doubt, uncertainty. *adj.* Doubtful, uncertain. —ಪಾತೆರ a doubtful word, speaking undecidedly.

ಮೋದು **mōdu**, *s.* A stripe, a wale.

ಮೋನ **mōna**, *see* ಮೋಹ.

ಮೋನಿ **mōni**, *s.* A daughter.

ಮೋನು **mōnu**, *s.* A son.

ಮೋನೆ **mōnė**, *see* ಮೋಣೆ.

ಮೋಪು **mōpu**, *see* ಮೂಪು.

ಮೋರ **mōra**, *s.* Beginning, outset, commencement. 2. *see* ಮೋರು. *adv.* Immediately, instantly. ಪೊಸ— commencing a new business, a new undertaking; a new broom. ಬರ್ಸದ— commencement of the monsoon. ಬತ್ತಿ ಮೋರೊಗು ಆಯಿ ಕೆಲಸ ಆಂಡ್ the moment he came his business was done.

ಮೋರಿ **mōri**, *s.* Fodder for cattle. 2. a channel, drain, kennel. 3. a public dunghill.

ಮೋರಿಸ್ **mōrisụ**, *s.* Mauritius. —ಸಕ್ಕರೆ refined sugar.

ಮೋರು **mōru**, *s.* A seal, stamp. —ಪಾಡುನಿ to seal; *cf.* ಮೊಹರ್.

ಮೋರೆ **mōrė**, *s.* The face, visage. 2. a person without moustaches.

ಮೋರ್ಚ, ಮೋರ್ಜ, ಮೋಹರ್ಜೆ **mōrča, mōrǰa, mōharǰė**, *s.* A battery where cannons are mounted.

ಮೋರ್ತ **mōrta**, *see* ಮುಹೂರ್ತ.

ಮೋರ್ತಿ **mōrti**, *see* ಮೂರ್ತಿ.

ಮೋಲ್ **mōlụ**, *s.* Price, value.

ಮೋಲ **mōla**, *s.* Coupling *or* coming together, as serpents, cats, *etc.* —ಇಪ್ಪಿನಿ cats to couple. —ಪೊಡ್ಡುನಿ, ಮೋಲೊಡ್ಡುನಿ reptiles to couple.

ಮೋಲಿ **mōli**, *s.* A kind of pepper-water.

ಮೋಸ **mōsa**, *s.* Fraud, trick, deceit, dissimulation, treachery. 2. fault, mistake. 3. danger, risk. —ಗಾರೆ a deceiver, hypocrite. —ಆಪಿನಿ, ಮೋಸಾದ್ ಪೋಪಿನಿ to make a mistake. —ಬರ್ಪಿನಿ to be exposed to danger, to run a risk. —ಮಳ್ಪುನಿ to deceive. ಮೋಸೊಡು ತಿಕ್ಕುನಿ to be deceived. ಮೋಸೊಡು ಪಾಡುನಿ to mislead; to deceive. ಮೋಸೊಡು ಬೂರುನಿ to be mistaken; to run a risk.

ಮೋಸಂ **mōsam**, *see* ಮೊಹಸಮ್.

ಮೋಹ **mōha**, *s.* Love, lust, carnal affection. 2. fascination, allurement. —ಉಪ್ಪುನಿ to be affectionate, to love; to covet.

ಮೋಹನ **mōhana**, *s.* The overpowering of reason by worldly allurements, fascination. —ಮಾಲೆ a necklace of gold beads.

ಮೋಹರ್ **mōharụ**, *see* ಮೊಹರ್.

ಮೋಹಿನಿ **mōhini**, *s.* A fairy; a fascinating woman.

ಮೋಹಿಪುನಿ, ಮೋಹಿಸುನಿ **mōhipuni, mōhisuni** (ಮೋಹಿ, ಮೋಹಿಸ್), *v. a.* To love. 2. to fascinate.

ಮೋಳಿ mōḷi, *see* ಮೋರಿ. 2. *see* ಮೋಲಿ.

ಮೋಳು mōḷu, *pron.* She, this female.

ಮೋಕ್ಷ mōksha, *s.* Deliverance, setting free. 2. heaven, beatitude, bliss, salvation. –ಪ್ರಾಪ್ತಿ attainment of salvation. –ಮಾರ್ಗ the way of salvation.

ಮೌನ mouna, *s.* Silence, taciturnity. –ಧರಿಪುನಿ to be silent.

ಮೌಪುನಿ moupuni (ಮೌ), *v. a.* To upset, turn; *cf.* ಮಗಪುನಿ.

ಮೌರಾವುನಿ mourāvuni, *c. v.* (*of* ಮೌರುನಿ) To mumble, chew softly. 2. *fig.* to make a thing easy.

ಮೌರುನಿ mouruni (ಮೌರ್), *v. a.* To masticate, chew.

ಮೌಲಾವುನಿ moulāvuni, *c. v.* (*of* ಮೌಲುನಿ) To cause to desire, long for. 2. *see* ಮೌರಾವುನಿ.

ಮೌಲು, ಮೌಳು moulu, mouḷu, *s.* Desire, wish.

ಮೌಲುನಿ mouluni (ಮೌಲ್), *v. a.* To desire.

ಮೌಲ್ಯ moulya, *s.* Price, value.

ಮ್ಯಾಂವು myam̃vu, *s.* The mewing of a cat.

ಮ್ಲೇಂಚ್ಛ mlēn̆ččha, *adj.* Barbarian, outcaste, unclean. –ತನ barbarism, abomination, uncleanness.

ಮ್ಲೇಂಚ್ಛೆ mlēn̆čche, *s.* A barbarian. 2. an out-caste.

ಯ Y

ಯ ya, The thirty-ninth letter of the alphabet.

For words beginning with ಯ, ಯಿ, *etc.*, *not found here*, *see under* ಎ.

ಯಂತ್ರ yantra, *s.* An implement, engine, mill, apparatus, machine. 2. a necklace, talisman, amulet, charm. 3. a diagram of a mystical character. 4. restraining, checking, controling. ಜಲ– a water pump *or* lift. –ಕಟ್ಟುನಿ to append to the arm, *etc.*, a talisman; to avert evil by charms.

ಯಂತ್ರಿ yantri, *s.* A charmer.

ಯಕ್ಕಂದೆಲ್ yakkandeḷu, *s.* Being beyond reach *or* means. 2. want, insufficiency.

ಯಕ್ಕಂಬೆ, ಯಕ್ಕಂಬೆರ್, ಯಕ್ಕಂಬೆಲ್, yakkambè, yakkamberu̥, yakkambelu̥, *see* ಎಕ್ಕಮಲೆ.

ಯಜಮಾನಿ yajamāni, *s.* A mistress, wife; *also* ಯಜಮಾನ್ದಿ.

ಯಜಮಾನೆ yajamāne, *s.* A master, lord, proprietor, owner. 2. a husband.

ಯಜ್ಞ yajn̄ya, *s.* A sacrifice, ceremony in which oblations are presented.

ಯಡ yaḍa, *adj.* Left. –ಕೈ the left hand. –ತರ inferior sort.

ಯಡಂಬು yaḍambu, *s.* The left side. —ಬೆಡಂಬು ತೂಪಿಸಿ *lit.* to look to the right and left; to use the right hand instead of the left.

ಯತಾ yatā, *see* ಯಥಾ.

ಯತಿ yati, *s.* A sage whose passions are under complete subjection; a religious mendicant.

ಯಥಾ yathā, *adv.* As, according to, to the extent of. *adj.* Usual, customary; *also* ಎಥಾ.

ಯಥಾರ್ಥ yathārtha, *s.* Truth, verity. *adj.* True, real. *adv.* Truly, really. —ತ್ವ simplicity.

ಯಥಾಸ್ತಿಗೆ yathāstigė, *s.* Truthfulness, veracity.

ಯಥಾಸ್ಥಿತಿ yathāsthiti, *adj.* As before, as it was. 2. true, certain. *s.* Usual state; truth, fact.

ಯಥೇಚ್ಛ, ಯಥೇಷ್ಟ yatheċċa, yathēshṭa, *adj.* Agreeably to wish *or* desire, as required, as wished. 2. ample.

ಯಮಲೋಕ yamalōka, *s.* The infernal regions.

ಯಮರ್ಗೆ yamargė, *see* ಎಮರಿಕೆ.

ಯಮೆ yame, *s.* Yama the god of the infernal regions and judge of departed souls.

ಯವಂಚಿ yavañċi, *see* ಐವಂಚಿ.

ಯವನ yavana, *s.* Greece. 2. *see* ಯಕಾವನ. ಯವನೆರ್ the Greeks.

ಯಕ್ಷ yaksha, *s.* A demi-god, attendant on Kubēra.

ಯಕ್ಷಿ, ಯಕ್ಷಿಣಿ yakshi, yakshiṇi, *s.* A sort of female fiend, attached to the service of Durgi, and frequently maintaining, like a fairy, intercourse with mortals. —ಭಜನೆ worship of these spirits. —ಮಂತ್ರ a magical charm.

ಯಾ yā, *conj.* Or. *adv.* Otherwise.

ಯಾಗ yāga, *s.* A sacrifice.

ಯಾಚಕೆ yāċake, *s.* A beggar, mendicant.

ಯಾಜಕೆ yājake, *s.* A priest, any officiating Brahman who conducts any part of a sacrifice.

ಯಾತ yāta, *s.* An engine for drawing water.

ಯಾತನೆ yātanė, *s.* Pain, agony. 2. the pains of hell.

ಯಾತ್ರೆ yātrė, *s.* Pilgrimage. 2. *see* ಜಾತ್ರೆ. ಕಾಶಿ— pilgrimage to Benares. ತೀರ್ಥ— pilgrimage to a holy place for bathing, *etc.* —ಗ್ ಪೋಪಿನಿ, —ಮಲ್ಪುನಿ to go on pilgrimage.

ಯಾದಾಸ್ತ್ yādāstụ, *s.* A memorandum, note.

ಯಾನ್ yānụ, *pron.* I. ಯಾನಾ is it I? ಯಾನೇ I myself. ಯೆಂಕ್ to me. ಯೆಂಕುಳು we. ಯೆಂನವು mine. ಯೆನ my. ಯೆನನ್ me.

ಯಾಲ್ನಿ yālni, *intj.* of surprise.

ಯಾವತ್ತ್, ಯಾವಸ್ತ್ yāvattụ, yāvastụ, *s.* The whole. *adj.* Whole, entire.

ಯಿ, ಯೀ yi, yī, *For words beginning with these letters see under* ಇ *and* ಈ.

ಯುಕ್ತ yukta, *adj.* Right, fit, proper. 2. possessed of, endowed with, as virtue, qualities, *etc.*

ಯುಕ್ತಿ yukti, *s.* Fitness, propriety. 2. an excellent expedient, happy thought. 3. advice, counsel. –ದಾಯಿ, –ವಂತ a schemer, contriver. ಕು– a bad contrivance, foolish device. –ಹೇಳು to suggest an expedient. –ಮಾಡು to contrive.

ಯುಗ yuga, *s.* An age of the world, of which four are enumerated, namely, ಕೃತ– the primeval *or* golden age. ತ್ರೇತಾ– the second *or* silver age. ದ್ವಾಪರ– the third *or* brass age. ಕಲಿ– the fourth *or* iron age. –ಪಗರುವ the shape *or* state of any thing to change.

ಯುಗಾಂತ್ರ yugāntra, *s.* Change of ages; another age of the world.

ಯುಗಾದಿ yugādi, *s.* The new year's day.

ಯುಧಿಷ್ಠಿರೆ yudhishṭhire, *s.* Dharmarāya, the eldest of the Pāṇḍu princes.

ಯುದ್ಧ yuddha, *s.* War, battle, conflict.

ಯುವ yuva, *s.* The ninth year in the Hindu cycle of sixty. *adj.* Young, youthful.

ಯೆ ye, *see the remark under* ಯ.

ಯೆಕ್ಕುಬಲ್ಯಾರ್ yekkụbalyārụ, *s.* A species of shark.

ಯೆಕ್ಕೇರಿಗಂಟ್ yekkēriganṭụ, *s.* Consecrated money.

ಯೆಡ, ಯೆಡಂಬು, ಯೆಡತ್ತ್ yeḍa, yeḍambu, yeḍattụ, *see* ಯಡ. 2. *see* ಯಡಂಬು.

ಯೆಡುಮ, ಯೆಡ್ಮ yeḍuma, yeḍma, *see* ಎಡ್ಮ.

ಯೆರಸಾರ yerasāra, *see* ವ್ಯಾಪಾರ.

ಯೆವುರ yevura, *see* ವೈರ.

ಯೆಲಂಪು yelampu, *see* ಲಂಬು.

ಯೇಕನಾಲಿ yēkanāli, *s.* Indigestion.

ಯೇಗ yēga, *see* ಯೋಗ.

ಯೇಲಿ yēli, *see* ಎಲಿ.

ಯೇಷ್ಟಿ yēshti, *s.* A white garment with coloured borders worn by males.

ಯೇಸು yēsu, *s.* Jesus.

ಯೋ yō, *intj.* of surprise.

ಯೋಗ yōga, *s.* Junction, connexion, combination, association, conflux. 2. a religious and abstract meditation. 3. lucky conjuncture; *cf.* ಜೋಗ. –ಧ್ಯಾನ meditating abstractedly *or* deeply.

ಯೋಗಜ yōgaja, *s.* Wonder, surprise.

ಯೋಗಿ yōgi, *s.* A devotee, ascetic. 2. one who performs worldly actions and ceremonies without regard to their results, and keeps his mind fixed upon Brahma alone. 3. one devoted to abstract meditation.

ಯೋಗ್ಯ yōgya, *adj.* Fit, proper, worthy, suitable. 3. powerful, able, capable. —ತೆ ability, merit, fitness, suitability. —ಆಗಿ fitly, worthily.

ಯೋಚನೆ yōcanè, *s.* Thought, reflection, deliberation. 2. anxiety, concern.

ಯೋಜನ yōjana, *s.* A distance of about ten *or* twelve miles.

ಯೋನಿ yōni, *s.* The vulva; womb. 2. place *or* site of birth *or* production in general. There are four kind of ಯೋನಿ, *viz.* ಅಂಡಜ oviparous. ಉದ್ಭಿಜ sprouting. ಸ್ವೇದಜ engendered by sweat, steam *or* vapour, as insects and worms. ಜರಾಯುಜ viviparous.

ಯೌವನ youvana, *s.* Youth, virility, manhood. *adj.* Juvenile; *also* ಜವ್ವನ.

ರ R

ರ ra, The fortieth letter of the alphabet.

ರಂಕ rañka, *s.* A large ladle *or* spoon. 2. a measure of fluids equal to about twelve rupees in weight.

ರಂಗ್, ರಂಗ rañgu, rañga, *s.* Paint, colour, tint, dye. 2. dancing, acting, singing, *etc.* 3. pleasure. 4. a place. —ಪೂಜೆ worshipping an idol with illuminations and sweet offerings. —ಮಂಟಪ the ornamented hall of an idol; the place in which a king sits at a public levee. —ರಂಗಿಳ a very nice person. —ವಲ್ಲಿ, —ವಾಲೆ, *see* ರಂಗೋಲೆ. —ಸ್ಥಲ, —ಸ್ಥಳ the place before an assembly in which actors, *etc.*, perform. ರಣ— a battle-field. ರಂಗಾಗಿಸು to sound sweetly to the ear. —ಹಾಕುಸು to paint; to please, delight.

ರಂಗಣಿ rañgaṇi, *s.* A child's plaything.

ರಂಗಣೆ rañgaṇè, *see* ರಂಜಣೆ.

ರಂಗಸಲೆ rañgasalè, *see* ಗಂಧಸಾಲೆ.

ರಂಗಾಣಿ rañgāni, *see* ರಂಗಣಿ.

ರಂಗೋಲೆ rañgōlè, *s.* Ornamenting the entrance and floor of a house with white sand *or* chalk.

ರಂಜಣೆ raññaṇè, *s.* Fascination, enchantment, captivation, bewitchment. —ಮಳ್ಪುನಿ to captivate.

ರಂಜ rañja, *see* ರಿಂಜ.

ರಂಜಕ rañjaka, *adj.* Charming, agreeable. *s.* Colouring, dying. 2. a stimulus, an inciter of affection. —ಆಗಿ agreeably.

ರಂಜಕೆ rañjake, *s.* A charming man.

ರಂಜನ rañjana, *s.* Colouring. 2. gladdening.

ರಂಜಿರ್ **ranjiru**, *see* ಕೆಂಜಿರ್.

ರಂಜಿಪುನಿ **ranjipuni** (ರಂಜಿಸ್), *v. a.* To gladden, please. *v. n.* To be glad, pleased.

ರಂಜೆಲೆ **ranjele**, *s.* A charmer.

ರಂಟುನಿ **ranṭuni**, *see* ಅರಂಟುನಿ.

ರಂಡಿ **ranḍi**, *s.* A fretful woman. 2. a whore. 3. *see* ರಂಡೆ.

ರಂಡೆ **ranḍè**, *s.* A widow. 2. an abusive term; *also* ರಂಡೆಮುಂಡೆ.

ರಂದಾವುನಿ **randāvuni**, *c. v.* (*of* ರಂದುನಿ) To make *or* cause to importune, tease.

ರಂದುನಿ **randuni** (ರಂದ್), *v. a.* To crave, importune, tease, dun. 2. to beseech, entreat.

ರಂದೆಲ್ **randelu**, *s.* Begging, entreating.

ರಂಧ್ರ, ರಂಧ್ರ **randra, randhra**, *s.* A hole, fissure, cavity.

ರಂಪಿ **rampi**, *s.* A shoemaker's knife.

ರಂಪೆ **rampè**, *s.* An eye-lid.

ರಂಪೊಣಿ **ramponi**, *s.* A large casting net.

ರಂಬಾರೂಟಿ, ರಂಬಾರೊಟಿ **rambārūṭi, rambāroṭi**, *s.* Clamour, outcry. 2. diffusion, extension. 3. squandering, dissipating. ಅರಬ್ ರಂಬಾರೂಟಿ ಮಳ್ಪುನಿ to cry bitterly. ಬಿರ್ಗದ್ ರಂಬಾರೂಟಿ ಆಪಿನಿ to be scattered, thrown about. ಊರು ಪೊರ್ಲುಡು ರಂಬಾರೂಟಿ ಮಳ್ಪುನಿ to spread, publish abroad.

ರಂಬೆ, ರಂಭೆ **rambè, rambhè**, *s.* A celestial courtezan. 2. a beautiful woman. —ನಾಟಕ dancing.

ರಂಭಾಟ, ರಂಭಾರೂಟಿ **rambhāṭa, rambhārūṭi**, *see* ರಂಬಾರೂಟಿ.

ರಕ್ **raku**, *s.* Guard, guarding.

ರಕ್‌ವಾಲೆ **rakuvālè**, *s.* A guard, watch, keeper.

ರಕಣೆ **rakaṇè**, *see* ರಕ್ಷಣೆ.

ರಕಮ್, ರಕಮು **rakamu, rakamu**, *s.* The whole quantity; wholesale.

ರಕ್ಕ **rakka**, *see* ರೊಕ್ಕ.

ರಕ್ಕಣೆ **rakkaṇè**, *see* ರಕ್ಷಣೆ.

ರಕ್ಕಸಿ **rakkasi**, *s.* A giantess.

ರಕ್ಕಸೆ **rakkase**, *s.* A giant.

ರಕ್ಕೆ **rakkè**, *s.* A charm, amulet; *cf.* ರಕ್ಷೆ. 2. anything very thin *or* light.

ರಕ್ತ **rakta**, *s.* Blood. *adj.* Bloody; crimson. —ಪಿತ್ತ scurvy. —ಪ್ರಮೇಹ, —ಮೇಹ bloody urine, hematuria. —ವರ್ಣ crimson colour. —ವಾತ a rheumatic swelling of the veins. —ಸಾಕ್ಷಿ a martyr; martyrdom. —ಸ್ರಾವ the bloody flux.

ರಕ್ತಬೋಳ **raktabōḷa**, *s.* Myrrh, aloes.

ರಕ್ತಾಂಬರ **raktāmbara**, *s.* A red cloth.

ರಕ್ತಾಕ್ಷಿ **raktākshi**, *s.* The fifty-eighth year in the Hindu cycle of sixty.

ರಕ್ತೇಶ್ವರಿ **raktēsvari**, *s.* A female demon so called.

ರಖ್ವಾಲೆ **rakhvālè**, *see* ರಕ್‌ವಾಲೆ.

ರಗರಗ **ragaraga**, *adj.* Beautiful, handsome, pretty. —ಬೊಂಬೆ a nice picture. —ರಂಬೆ a beautiful female, belle.

ರಗಳೆ ragaḷè, *s.* Gabble, incoherent talk. 2. a confused state of things. 3. trouble, bother, annoyance. —ಬಾಯಿ a gabbler, prater. —ಡ್ ಬೂರುನಿ to be in a confused state; to be involved in troubles. —ಮಳ್ಪುನಿ to trouble.

ರಗ್ತ ragta, *see* ರಕ್ತ.

ರಘು raghu, *s.* The name of a sovereign of Ayōdhya. 2. a hero.

ರಚನೆ raċanè, *s.* Literary composition. 2. making *or* preparing anything. —ಮಳ್ಪುನಿ, ರಚೆಸುನಿ to compose, write; to make, fabricate.

ರಚ್ಚಣೆ raċċaṇè, *see* ರಕ್ಷಣೆ.

ರಚ್ಚೆ raċċè, *s.* The thorny rind of a jack fruit. —ಪಚ್ಚೆ ಅಪಿನಿ to fly from alarm.

ರಜ, ರಜೆ raja, rajè, *s.* Leave of absence; permission. 2. a holiday.

ರಜತಪೀಠ rajatapīṭha, *s.* A silver throne of the god Kr̥shṇa at Uḍapi. 2. a name of Uḍapi.

ರಜಪುತ್ರೆ rajaputre, *s.* A Rajpoot.

ರಜಬಂದಿಗೆ, ರಜವಂತಿಗೆ rajabandigè, rajavantigè, *s.* A compromise, composition. —ಮಳ್ಪುನಿ, —ಗೆಡ ತೀರಿಸಾವುನಿ to compromise a matter in dispute, to settle amicably.

ರಜಾರಪ್ತು rajāraptu, *s.* Absence on leave. —ಆಪಿನಿ to be absent on leave.

ರಜ್ಜು rajju, *s.* A rope, cord.

ರಟ್ಟ್ raṭṭu, *s.* Sacking, cânvas.

ರಟ್ಟಾವುನಿ raṭṭāvuni, *c. v.* (*of* ರಟ್ಟುನಿ) To strike *or* kindle fire. 2. to raise, as dust. 3. to shed, as blood. 4. to scatter.

ರಟ್ಟುನಿ raṭṭuni (ರಟ್ಟಿ), *v. n.* To splash, as mud. 2. to rise, as dust. 3. to fly, run away. 4. to be scattered.

ರಟ್ಟೆ raṭṭè, *s.* The arm.

ರಡೆ raḍe, *s.* Retreat, flight. —ದೆ ತ್ತೋಜುನಿ to run away, backslide.

ರಡ್ಡ್ raḍḍu, *num.* Two. —ಜೀವೆದಾಳ್ a pregnant woman. —ಎಂಜುನಿ, —ನೆನೆಪುನಿ to betray, be treacherous. ಒಂಜಿಕ್ ರಡ್ಡ್ ಪಣ್ಪುನಿ to exaggerate, misrepresent. ಒಂಜಿಕ್ ರಡ್ಡ್ ಮಳ್ಪುನಿ to improve, better, as one's fortune; to break, as a vessel, *etc.*

ರಡ್ಡನೆ raḍḍanè, *adj.* Second. 2. middling.

ರಣ raṇa, *s.* Battle, war. —ಕಹಳೆ a war trumpet, horn. —ಭೂಮಿ, —ಮಂಡಲ, —ರಂಗ, —ರಣಾಂಗಣ a battle-field. —ವೀರೆ, —ಶೂರೆ a valiant hero. —ಹೇಡಿ a runaway, coward.

ರಣರಣ raṇaraṇa, *s.* The glare *or* heat of the sun.

ರಣಾಗ್ರ raṇāgra, *s.* The front of a battle; a sanguinary battle. —ಮಳ್ಪುನಿ to fight.

ರತಲ್ ratalu, *s.* A weight, one pound *or* forty tolas.

ರತಿ **rati,** *s.* The wife of Cupid. 2. passion, desire. 3. sport, dalliance. 4. a weight, one-eighth of a pagoda, used in weighing diamonds and emeralds. –ಕ್ರೀಡೆ dalliance, sexual intercourse. –ಪತಿ Cupid. –ಕೊಡಾವುನಿ to enlarge, to make much of a trifle.

ರತಿಪ **ratipa,** *s.* Increase, multiplying. –ಕೊಡುನಿ to put *or* join together.

ರತಿಪೆ **ratipe,** *s.* A witty man.

ರತ್ನ **ratna,** *s.* A jewel, gem. ನವ– the nine kinds of precious stones. –ಕಂಬಳಿ a fine sort of rug used to sleep on, *etc.*

ರತ್ನಗಂಧಿ **ratnagandhi,** *s.* The Barbadoes flower-fence, *Cæsalpinia pulcherrima.*

ರತ್ನಗರ್ಭೆ **ratnagarbhe,** *s.* Kubēra the god of wealth. ರತ್ನಗರ್ಭ the ocean; the earth.

ರಥ **ratha,** *s.* A car, carriage, chariot. –ಉತ್ಸವ, ರಥೋತ್ಸವ the festivity of a car drawn in procession. ರಥಾರೋಹಣ ascending a car.

ರಥಿಕೆ **rathike,** *s.* A charioteer. 2. an able man.

ರದ್ದ್, ರದ್ದು **raddụ, raddu,** *s.* Repeal, cancelment, rejection. *adj.* Null, void. –ಆಪಿನಿ, ರದ್ದಾಪಿನಿ to be repealed, cancelled; to be void. –ಮಳ್ಪುನಿ to abrogate, abolish, cancel, revoke, reject.

ರನರನ **ranarana,** *see* ರಣರಣ.

ರಪ್‌ರಪ್ **rapụrapụ,** *s.* Drubbing, cudgeling; beating soundly. –ಹಾಕುನಿ to beat in this way.

ರಪ್ಪ **rappa,** *s.* A noise of beating; slapping suddenly; *also* ರಪ್ಪನೆ. –ಹಾಕುನಿ to beat suddenly, give a violent blow.

ರಪ್ಪು **rappu,** *s.* Darning. –ಪಾಡುನಿ, –ಮಳ್ಪುನಿ to darn.

ರಫ್ತು **raphtu,** *s.* Export. ಆಮದ್– import and export; sailing of a vessel to and fro. –ಆಪಿನಿ to be exported. –ಮಳ್ಪುನಿ to export.

ರಬಸ **rabasa,** *see* ರವಸ.

ರಮಣಿ **ramaṇi,** *s.* A woman, wife, mistress. 2. an agreeable woman. ರಮಣೀಯ beautiful, pleasing.

ರಮಣೆ **ramaṇe,** *s.* A husband.

ರಮಿಪುನಿ, ರಮಿಸುನಿ **ramipuni, ramisuni** (ರಮಿ, ರಮಿಸ್), *v. a.* To associate; to copulate with.

ರಮ್ಯ **ramya,** *adj.* Pleasing, delightful, agreeable, charming. –ವನ a delightful garden. –ವಾದ್ಯ charming music.

ರಯಿತೆ **rayite,** *see* ರೈತೆ.

ರವಕೆ **ravakè,** *s.* A bodice.

ರವಲವ **ravalava,** *s.* Ardent attachment, devotedness to some object *or* pursuit. 2. strong excitement.

ರವಸ **ravasa,** *s.* Speed, velocity. 2. a loud, rattling sound.

ರವಾನಿಸುನಿ ravānisuni (ರವಾನಿಸ್), *v. a.* To send, forward, despatch.

ರವಾನೆ ravānè, *s.* Sending, despatching. —ಮಳ್ಪುನಿ to send, despatch.

ರವಿ ravi, *s.* The sun. —ಮಂಡಲ the solar disk.

ರವೆ ravè, *s.* Molasses, syrup. 2. a small particle of anything, grit, groat. 3. a small shot.

ರಶೀದಿ rašīdi, *s.* A receipt.

ರಸ rasa, *s.* Flavour, taste. 2. taste, sentiment, emotion, as an object of composition. 3. affection of the mind, passion. 4. juice, exudation, liquid. 5. a mineral *or* metallic salt. 6. quicksilver. —ಕರ್ಪೂರ crude calomel. —ತಾಳಿ, *see* ರಸ್ತಾರಿ. —ಮಾಯನ, *see* ರಸಾಯನ. —ಬಾರೆ a kind of plantains.

ರಸನೆ rasanè, *s.* The tongue.

ರಸಾಯನ rasāyana, *s.* A dainty. 2. medicine in a state of fluid, elixir. 3. chemistry.

ರಸವಾದ rasavāda, *s.* Alchimy.

ರಸಾಲ್ rasālụ, *see* ಇರಸಾಲ್.

ರಸಿಕ rasika, *adj.* Tasteful, agreeable, sociable, sensible, full of good sense. —ನರಮಾನಿ an agreeable man; a sensible man. —ಪಾತೆರ an agreeable speech.

ರಸೀದಿ rasīdi, *see* ರಶೀದಿ.

ರಸೊಳಿ rasoḷi, *s.* A kind of plantains.

ರಸ್ತಾರಿ, ರಸ್ತಾಳಿ rastāri, rastāḷi *s.* A fine, soft kind of sugarcane; *also* ರಸ್ತಾಳಿ ಕಂಬುಲ.

ರಸ್ತೆ rastè, *s.* A road, way, path.

ರಹದಾರಿ rahadāri, *s.* A passport; an intimation to a village officer to provide a traveller with necessary supplies. —ಮಳ್ಪುನಿ to issue a passport.

ರಹಸ್ಯ rahasya, *adj.* Private, secret. *s.* A secret, mystery. —ದ ಪಾತೆರ a secret word.

ರಹಾರಿ rahāri, *s.* Pleasing.

ರಹಿತೆ rahite, *see* ರೈತೆ.

ರಕ್ಷಕೆ rakshake, *s.* A saviour, protector; a guardian.

ರಕ್ಷಣೆ rakshaṇè, *s.* Salvation, redemption; saving, protecting. —ಮಳ್ಪುನಿ to save.

ರಕ್ಷಸೆ rakshase, *see* ರಾಕ್ಷಸೆ.

ರಕ್ಷಿಪುನಿ, ರಕ್ಷಿಸುನಿ rakshipuni, rakshisuni (ರಕ್ಷಿ, ರಕ್ಷಿಸ್), *v. a.* To save, protect, defend.

ರಕ್ಷೆ rakshè, *s.* Preserving, protecting, saving. 2. a talisman, amulet, charm. ಅಂಗ— a jacket, coat. ಪಾದ— a pair of shoes. —ಮಳ್ಪುನಿ to charm.

ರಾಂಕುನಿ rāṅkuni (ರಾಂಕ್), *v. n.* To adulterate.

ರಾಕ್ rākụ, *see* ಅರಕ್.

ರಾಕಟಿ, ರಾಕಡಿ, ರಾಕುಟಿ rākaṭi, rākaḍi, rākuṭi, *s.* A circular ornamented plate of gold, worn by females on their topknot.

ರಾಕಸೆ rākase, *see* ರಾಕ್ಷಸೆ.

ರಾಕಿ, ರಾಕೆ rāki, rākè, *see* ರವಕೆ.

ರಾಗ rāga, *s.* Tune, music, singing. 2. mental affection in general, as joy, sorrow, passion. 3. envy. 4. *see* ರಂಗ. –ದ್ವೇಷ envy and hatred. –ಮಾಲಿಕೆ, –ಮಾಲಿಕೆದ ಪೆಟ್ಟಿಗೆ an organ *or* pianoforte. –ಮಳ್ಪುನಿ, –ಪ್ಯೊಪುನಿ to sing.

ರಾಗಿ rāgi, *s.* The common grain rāgi, *Eleusine coracana.* –ದ ಗಂಜಿ rāgi gruel.

ರಾಜ rāja, *adj.* Royal, denoting excellence *or* eminence. 2. chief, supreme. –ಅಂಙಣ, *see* ರಾಜಾಂಙಣ. –ಕಾರ್ಯ a public affair. –ಕುರು a carbuncle. –ತ್ವ kingship. –ಧರ್ಮ duty incumbent on a king. –ಧಾನಿ a capital, metropolis. –ನೀತಿ politics. –ಪೂಜಿತ ರಾಜಮಾನ್ಯರಾಜೇಶ್ರೀ kingly in respect, reverence, and wealth; a respectful mode of address. –ಬೀದಿ, –ಮಾರ್ಗ a highway. –ಯೋಗ royalty, royal dignity. –ಸಭೆ a royal assembly *or* court. –ಕ್ಷಯ a pulmonary consumption.

ರಾಜನೆ rājanè, *s.* The core of a bamboo.

ರಾಜಸ್, ರಾಜಸ rājasu, rājasa, *s.* The predominence of passion, pride, arrogance, presumption *or* anger.

ರಾಜಾಂಙಣ rājāṅṅaṇa, *s.* The court-yard of a palace.

ರಾಜಾಟ, ರಾಜಾಟಿಗೆ rājāṭa, rājāṭigè, *s.* Intermeddling; boasting. 2. royalty.

ರಾಜಿ rāji, *s.* A compromise *or* adjustment of differences. 2. reconciliation, pacification. 3. pleasure, good will. *adj.* Contented, satisfied, agreed, pleased, willing. –ಕಬೂಲಿ a written agreement to a compromise. –ನಾಮೆ a deed of compromise of matters in dispute; resignation of an employment. –ಆಪಿನಿ to come to terms, be compromised *or* adjusted; to consent, agree. –ಉಪ್ಪುನಿ to like, be willing; to be on good terms. –ಕೊರ್ಪಿನಿ to resign, as an employment *or* post. –ಮಳ್ಪುನಿ to compromise, reconcile.

ರಾಜಿಸ್ rājisu, *adj.* Manufactured by Rodgers, as a knife.

ರಾಜೆ rāje, *s.* A king, sovereign, prince. ಮಹಾ– an emperor, great king; a nobleman.

ರಾಜೆಶ್ರಿ, ರಾಜೇಶ್ರಿ rājeśri, rājēśri, *see under* ರಾಜ.

ರಾಜೇಂದ್ರೆ rājēndre, *s.* An emperor, king of kings.

ರಾಜ್ಯ rājya, *s.* A government, kingdom, province, country. 2. the administration of government. –ಭಾರ rule, government.

ರಾಟೆ rāṭè, *see* ಲಾಟಿ.

ರಾಡ್ rāḍu, *see* ಲಾಡ್.

ರಾಡಿ rāḍi, *adj.* Foul, turbid.

ರಾಡೆ rāḍè, *see* ನಾಡೆ.

ರಾಣ rāṇa, *s.* Brightness. 2. *see* ರಾಣ್ಯ.

ರಾಣಿ rāṇi, *s.* A queen.

ರಾಣ್ಯ rāṇya, *s.* An army. 2. a low class of Pariahs; *also* ರಾಣುವೆ. –ದಾಯೆ a man belonging to this class.

ರಾತಲ್, ರಾತೆಲ್ rātalụ, rātelụ, *see* ರತಲ್.

ರಾತ್ರಿ, ರಾತ್ರೆ rātri, rātrè, *s.* Night. ಅರ್ಧ–, ನಡು–, ಮಧ್ಯ– midnight. –ಪಗೆಲ್ night and day. –ಭೋಜನ the Lord's Supper. ರಾತಾರಾತ್ರಿಗ್, ರಾತಾರಾತ್ರಿಡ್ by night, before daybreak. ರಾತಾರಾತ್ರಿಗೇ ಆಯೆ ಬತ್ತ್‌ದ್ ಪೋಯೆ he came and went away before daybreak.

ರಾದ್ rādụ, *s.* A way; *cf.* ರಾಪುನಿ.

ರಾದಾರಿ rādāri, *see* ರಹದಾರಿ.

ರಾಪಾವುನಿ rāpāvuni, *c. v.* (*of* ರಾಪುನಿ) To make *or* cause to fly. 2. to blow up.

ರಾಪಿನಿ rāpini, *see* ರಾಪುನಿ.

ರಾಪು rāpu, *s.* Lustre, splendour, effulgence. 2. beauty, comeliness. 3. pride, arrogance, haughtiness. –ದಾಯೆ a proud man. ಪಣವುದ– pride of money.

ರಾಪುನಿ rāpuni (ರಾ), *v. n.* To fly. 2. to leap, jump, skip. 3. to behave haughtily.

ರಾಮ rāma, *s. see* ರಾಮೆ. *adj.* Of *or* pertaining to Rāma. –ದೂತೆ, –ಬಂಟೆ Hanumanta, the faithful messenger of Rāma. –ವಾಶ್ಯ Rāma's monkey-troops. –ಬಾಣ Rāma's arrow, which had the peculiar property of hitting the mark and then returning to the quiver; a kind of fire-work. –ರಾಮ್ a term of salutation among the Hindus. –ವಾಕ್ಯ a faithful promise.

ರಾಮಚ್ಚ rāmačča, *s.* The cuscus grass, *Andropogon muricatum.*

ರಾಮಾಯಣ rāmāyaṇa, *s.* The epic poem, containing the history of Rāma. ಅಧ್ಯಾತ್ಮ–, ಪಾತಾಳ–, ಬಾಲ–, ವಾಲ್ಮೀಕ– are some of the works on the same subject.

ರಾಮಾರಕ್ತ rāmārakta, *s.* Bleeding profusely.

ರಾಮೆ rāme, *s.* Rāma, the seventh incarnation of Vishṇu.

ರಾಮೇಶ್ವರ rāmēšvara, *s.* The celebrated place of pilgrimage in Madura.

ರಾಯ, ರಾಯೆ rāya, rāye, *s.* An honorific affix to the names of Brahmans, *etc.* 2. a Tahsildar. 3. *see* ರಾಜೆ.

ರಾಯಭಾರಿ rāyabhāri, *s.* An ambassador, envoy.

ರಾಯರೆ rāyarè, *s.* The moon.

ರಾಯಸ rāyasa, *s.* A letter addressed by a sovereign *or* a spiritual guide to his subjects *or* followers. –ಬರೆಪಿನಿ to write *or* address such a letter.

ರಾರಿ rāri, *s.* Cheerfulness, animation, good spirits. –ಉಪ್ಪು

ಸು to be cheerful *or* in good spirits.

ರಾಲಿ rāli, *see* ಲಾಲಿ.

ರಾವ್ rāvụ, *see* ರಾಯ.

ರಾವಕಿ rāvaki, *see* ರವಕೆ.

ರಾವಣ, ರಾವಣೆ rāvaṇa, rāvaṇe, *s.* The king of Lanka *or* Ceylon, who was destroyed by Rāma; *also* ರಾವಣೇಶ್ವರೆ.

ರಾವಲೆ, ರಾವಲ್ಯೆ rāvale, rāvalye, *s.* A greedy man.

ರಾವು rāvu, *see* ರಾಯ. 2. *see* ರಾಹು.

ರಾವುತೆ rāvute, *s.* A horseman, trooper.

ರಾವುನಿ rāvuni, *see* ರಾವುನಿ.

ರಾವೆ rāvè, *s.* Syrup made of sugarcane juice.

ರಾಶಿ rāśi, *s.* A heap, quantity. 2. abundance, plenty. 3. a sign of the zodiac; a month. —ಜನ a crowd of people. —ಪೂಜೆ a grand festival. ಚರ—, ಅಚರ— *or* ಸ್ಥಿರ—, and ಉಭಯ— are different positions of constellations interpreted in astrology. —ನೋಪಿನಿ to consult astrology about one's fortune. —ಪಾಡುನಿ to pile, heap up.

ರಾಶ್ಯ rāśya, *see* ರಹಸ್ಯ.

ರಾಷ್ಟ್ರ rāshṭra, *s.* An inhabited country, realm *or* region. ಮಹಾ— the Mahratta country.

ರಾಹು rāhu, *s.* The ascending node *or caput draconis.* 3. a sudden fit of apoplexy *or* paralysis. 4. a curse, deprecation. 5. voracity, ravenousness. —ಬಿತ್ತ್ *Elæocarpus dicera.* —ಮುಖ the diurnal situation of the ascending node; a fierce countenance. —ಕಟ್ಟುನಿ, —ಪತ್ತುನಿ to be voracious. —ಹಾಕುನಿ to be seized with a sudden fit of apoplexy *or* paralysis.

ರಾಹುತೆ rāhute, *see* ರಾವುತೆ.

ರಾಳ rāḷa, *s.* Pitch, resin.

ರಾಕ್ಷಸೆ rākshase, *s.* An evil spirit, giant, demon, fiend.

ರಿಕಾಬ್ rikābụ, *s.* A stirrup.

ರಿಜ rija, *s.* Punishment. —ಕೊರ್ಪಿನಿ to chastise, punish.

ರಿಟ್ಲೆಕಾಯಿ riṭlekāyi, *see* ನುರೆಕಾಯಿ.

ರಿತಿ riti, *s.* Taste, relish, sweetness. *adj.* Palatable, savoury. —ಆಪಿನಿ to be tasteful; to relish, like. —ಉಪ್ಪುನಿ to have a relish for. —ತಾಗುನಿ, —ಪತ್ತುನಿ to acquire a taste for; to attract one's attention. —ತೂಪಿನಿ to taste, try.

ರಿತು ritu, *see* ಋತು.

ರಿಪ್ಪೆ rippè, *see* ರೆಪ್ಪೆ. 2. *see* ಪುಂಡಿ.

ರಿಯಾತ್, ರಿಯಾತಿ, ರಿಯಾಯಿತಿ riyātụ, riyāti, riyāyiti, *s.* Remission, abatement, as of revenue. 2. lenity, moderation, forbearance. —ಡ್ ನಡಪಾವುನಿ to treat leniently, as one's subordinates. —ಮಳ್ಪುನಿ to abate in a demand, to be lenient in enforcing a penalty, *etc.*

ರಿವಾಜಿ rivāji, *s.* Custom, usage practice.

ರಿಷಿ rishi, *see* ಋಶಿ.

ರಿಸಾಲ್ risālu, *see* ಇರ್ಸಾಲ್.

ರೀಕ್ rīku, *s.* A mystical prayer.

ರೀತಿ rīti, *s.* Usage, custom, practice. 2. method, way, manner.

ರೀನ್ rīnu, *see* ಋಣ.

ರೀಪು rīpu, *s.* A reaper, lathe.

ರುಂಡ, ರುಂಡು, ರುಂಡೆ ruṇḍa, ruṇḍu, ruṇḍè, *s.* A skull. 2. the head severed from the body. –ಮಾಲೆ a necklace of skulls. –ಪೋಂ ದಲಾ ಬುಡಯೆ he will not yield even at the risk of his head.

ರುಂಡಾರಪಂಜುರ್ಲಿ ruṇḍārapañjurli, *s.* A demon so called.

ರುಂದಾರೆ, ರುಂದಾವನ rundārè, rundāvana, *see* ವೃಂದಾವನ.

ರುಂದಾ, ರುಂದಿ rundā, rundi, *s.* Width, breadth. *adj.* Broad.

ರುಂಧ, ರುಂಧಿ rundha, rundhi, *s.* The grave of a Svāmi.

ರುಂಬಾಧಿ rumbādhi, *s.* The front of a crowd.

ರುಂಬಾಲಿ rumbāli, *s.* The name of a tribe.

ರುಂಬಾವುನಿ rumbāvuni, *c. v.* (*of* ರುಂಬುನಿ) To make *or* cause to strip off, pluck off.

ರುಂಬು rumbu, *s.* Galloping, running with speed. 2. stripping, plucking. –ಕಟ್ಟುನಿ, –ಕಟ್ಟೆದ್ ಬಲಿ ಪುನಿ to decamp, take to one's heels.

ರುಂಬುನಿ rumbuni (ರುಂಬ್), *v. a.* To strip off, pluck off, as leaves from a stalk.

ರುಂಭ, ರುಂಭು rumbha, rumbhu, *see* ರುಂಬು.

ರುಂಮ rumma, *adv.* With violence. –ದಕ್ಕುನಿ to shoot *or* throw with violence.

ರುಂಮುನಿ rummuni (ರುಮ್), *v. n.* To move hastily. 2. *see* ರುಂ ಬುನಿ.

ರುಕ್ಮಿಣಿ, ರುಗ್ಮಿಣಿ rukmiṇi, rugmiṇi, *s.* The first wife of Krushṇa.

ರುಗ್ರುಜೆ rugruje, *s.* One beginning to learn the Vēdas.

ರುಗ್ವೇದ rugvēda, *s.* The first of the four Vēdas.

ರುಚಿ ruči, *s.* Taste, relish, sweetness; *cf.* ರಿತಿ.

ರುಜಿ, ರುಜು ruji, ruju, *s.* A signature. 2. proof; *also* ರುಜುವಾತ್. 3. assent, admission. *adj.* True. –ಆಪಿನಿ to be proved; to be brought home to; to be convicted. –ಪಾಡುನಿ to sign. –ಮಳ್ಪುನಿ to prove.

ರುಟ್ಟಿ ruṭṭi, *see* ರೊಟ್ಟಿ.

ರುಣ ruṇa, *s.* Debt, obligation. –ಪಾತಕ the sin of indebtedness. –ಬೂಟುನಿ, –ಸಂದುನಿ to discharge a debt. ರುಣೊಟು ಬೂರುನಿ to be indebted *or* under obligation. ಪುಣ ಸುಡ್ಂಡಲಾ ರುಣ ಸುಡಂದ್ the cremation of a person's remains cannot cancel his debt.

ರುತ ruta, *s.* Improvement, bettering, turning to good account; *cf.* ಕೃತ. 2. *see* ವ್ರತ. –ಆ ಪಿನಿ to be improved; to prosper.

–ಮಳ್ಪುನಿ to improve, make productive *or* profitable.

ರುತು **rutu,** *s.* A season. 2. the menses. ವಸಂತ–, ಗ್ರೀಷ್ಮ–, ವರ್ಷ–, ಶರದ್–, ಹಿಮವಂತ–, ಶಿಶಿರ– are the six seasons of a year.

ರುದ್ರ **rudra,** *adj.* Pertaining to ರುದ್ರೆ. 2. parched, hot, dried. –ಭೂಮಿ a cemetery; parched land. –ವಾಯು apoplexy.

ರುದ್ರಾಕ್ಷ, ರುದ್ರಾಕ್ಷಿ, ರುದ್ರಾಕ್ಷೆ **rudrāksha, rudrākshi, rudrākshè,** *s.* The berries of the *Elæocarpus lanceolatus.* –ಸರ, –ಮಾಲೆ a rosary made with its berries.

ರುದ್ರಿ **rudri,** *s.* One of the six Brahmans who take part in performing the sacrifice of ಯಾಗ.

ರುದ್ರೆ **rudre,** *s.* Śiva, the disperser of tears of mortals. 2. a demi-god.

ರುಧಿರೋದ್ಗಾರಿ **rudhirōdgāri,** *s.* The fifty-seventh year in the Hindu cycle of sixty.

ರುಪಾಯಿ, ರುಪ್ಯಾ **rupāyi, rupāi,** *s.* A rupee.

ರುಮ್‌ರುಮ್ **rumụrumụ,** *s.* A whirling sound, as of wind blowing violently. –ಗಾಳಿ ಬೀಜುನಿ wind to blow violently.

ರುಮಾಲ್ **rumālụ,** *s.* A turban. 2. a handkerchief.

ರುಯ್ಯ **ruyya,** *adv.* Noisily, with noise.

ರುಯಿ, ರುವಿ **ruyi, ruvi,** *s.* A pie.

ರುಶಿ, ರುಷಿ **ruši, rushi,** *s.* A sage, saint.

ರುಸುಂ, ರುಸುಮ್ **rusum, rusumụ,** *s.* Fees, remuneration. 3. lawyer's fees.

ರೂಡಣೆ, ರೂಡಿಗೆ **rūḍaṇè, rūḍigè,** *s.* Laying out in profitable investments, turning to good account, as money. –ಮಳ್ಪುನಿ to invest money profitably.

ರೂಡಿ, ರೂಢಿ **rūḍi, rūḍhi,** *s.* Custom, practice. –ಆಪಿನಿ to be accustomed, come into use, be established. –ಉಪ್ಪುನಿ a custom to prevail; to be in use.

ರೂಢಿಸುನಿ **rūḍhisuni** (ರೂಢಿಸ್), *v. a.* To improve, turn to profit; to establish.

ರೂಪ **rūpa,** *s.* Form, figure, shape; an image, reflection, *or* resemblance of any real object. 2. beauty. 3. declension, conjugation. –ವಂತೆ a beautiful man. –ವತಿ a beautiful female. –ಮಳ್ಪುನಿ to form, shape, model.

ರೂಪಾಂತ್ರ **rūpāntra,** *s.* Change of shape *or* figure, transformation, transfiguration.

ರೂಪಾಯಿ **rūpāyi,** *see* ರುಪಾಯಿ.

ರೂಪಾರೂಪು **rūpārūpu,** *see* ರೂಪು ರೂಪು.

ರೂಪಿತ **rūpita,** *s.* Economy, frugality. *adj.* Economical. –ಗಾರೆ a frugal man. –ಮಳ್ಪುನಿ to manage economically.

ರೂಪಿಸುನಿ **rūpisuni** (ರೂಪಿಸ್), *v. a.* To sketch, form, shape, model. 2. to describe.

ರೂಪು **rūpu,** *see* ರೂಪ.

ರೂಪುರೂಪು, ರೂಬಾರೂಪು, ರೂಬುರೂಬು **rūpurūpu, rūbārūpu, rūburūbu,** *adv.* Face to face, in one's presence. —ಕೇಳುನಿ to ask in person. —ಮಳ್ಪುನಿ to confront. —ತೂಪಿನಿ to see in person. —ಪಾತೆರುನಿ to speak personally.

ರೂಮಿ **rūmi,** *s.* A cheat, rogue, hypocrite. ಅಸಲ್— a downright rascal.

ರೂಸು **rūsu,** *s.* Hardness, stiffness.

ರೆಂಕಾವುನಿ **reṅkāvuni,** *c. v.* (*of* ರೆಂಕುನಿ) To smear, soil. 2. to perform slowly; to delay, put off.

ರೆಂಕುನಿ **reṅkuni** (ರೆಂಕ್), *v. n.* To be smeared, soiled. 2. to be dilatory, performed slowly; to linger, procrastinate. 3. to be delayed, put off.

ರೆಂಕೆ **reṅkè,** *s.* A wing of a bird. —ಕಟ್ಟುನಿ to pinion the wings. —ಬರ್ಪುನಿ to be fledged, as a bird. —ಮಾಲುನಿ to fade, faint, be exhausted.

ರೆಂಕೆರಾಗಿ **reṅkerāgi,** *s.* An inferior kind of rāgi.

ರೆಂಕೆಲೆ **reṅkele,** *s.* An invalid, cripple, *etc.* 2. a slow coach. 3. a procrastinator.

ರೆಂಚಿ **reñci,** *see* ಲೆಂಚಿ.

ರೆಂಜ, ರೆಂಜಿ, ರೆಂಜಿರ್, ರೆಂಜೆ, ರೆಂಜೆಯಿ, ರೆಂಜೆವು **reñja, reñji, reñjiru, reñjè, reñjeyi, reñjevu,** *s.* The tree *Mimusops elengi.*

ರೆಂಜುನಿ **reñjuni** (ರೆಂಜ್), *v. n.* To dissolve, decay. 2. to roll, wallow, as in mire.

ರೆಕ್ಕೆ **rekkè,** *s.* A weaving apparatus. 2. *see* ರೆಂಕೆ.

ರೆಚ್ಚೆವು **reććevu,** *s. Caladium esculentum.* —ದ ಕಂಡೆ the bulb of the same. ಕರಿಯ— a dark species of it.

ರೆಟ್ಟೆ **reṭṭè,** *see* ರಟ್ಟೆ. 2. *see* ರಟ್ಟೆ.

ರೆಪ್ಪುನಿ **reppuni,** *see* ಲೆಪ್ಪುನಿ.

ರೆಪ್ಪೆ **reppè,** *s.* The eyelash, eyelid. —ಪಾಡುನಿ to wink.

ರೆಸ **resa,** *see* ರಸ.

ರೆಕ್ಷೆ **rekshè,** *see* ರಕ್ಷೆ.

ರೇ **rē,** *intj.* Oh! halloo!

ರೇಂಜಿ **rēñji,** *s.* A kind of conveyance resembling a hammock, a litter. —ಡ್ ಕುಳ್ಳುನಿ to get into a litter. —ಡ್ ಪೋಪಿನಿ to travel in a litter.

ರೇಂಟಿ, ರೇಂಟಿಕಾಯಿ **rēṇṭi, rēṇṭikāyi,** *see* ಸುರೆಕಾಯಿ.

ರೇಕೆ, ರೇಖೆ **rēkè, rēkhè,** *s.* A line, streak, stroke. —ಶಾಸ್ತ್ರ geometry. ಹಸ್ತ— creases in the hand.

ರೇಗಿಯುನಿ **rēgiyuni** (ರೇಗಿ), *v. n.* To be excited.

ರೇಚನ **rēčana,** *see* ವಿರೇಚನೆ.

ರೇಡ್ **rēḍu,** *s.* Debt; *cf.* ಸಾಲ.

ರೇಣು **rēṇu,** *s.* Dust, powder.

ರೇತಸ್ಸ್ **rētassu,** *s. Semen virile.*

ರೇತಿ **rēti,** *s.* Fine, black sand. —ದಾನಿ a sand *or* pounce box.

ರೇಫ **rēpha,** *s.* The letter ೯ *or* ರ.

ರೇಭಾಂತ **rēbhānta,** *adj.* Described, stated.

ರೇಯತಿ rēyati, *see* ರಿಯಾತ್. 2. *see* ರೇವತಿ.

ರೇವಣಿ, ರೇವನಿ rēvaṇi, rēvani, *s.* Revenue, assessment. 2. the revenue department.

ರೇವತಿ rēvati, *s.* Balarāma's wife. 2. the twenty-seventh lunar asterism.

ರೇವು rēvu, *s.* A harbour, port.

ರೇವುಣಿ rēvuṇi, *see* ರೇವಣಿ.

ರೇಶಿ rēši, *s.* Pus, matter of a boil, *etc.*

ರೇಶಿಮಿ, ರೇಷ್ಮಿ rēšimi, rēshmi, *s.* Silk. —ದ ತುಂಡು a silk cloth.

ರೇಸ rēsa, *see* ರಸ.

ರೈತೆ reite, *s.* A farmer, cultivator, ryot; *also* ರಹಿತ.

ರೈಸ್ reisu, *s.* A small coin; a cash; *cf.* ಲೈಸ್.

ರೈಸುನಿ reisuni (ರೈಸ್), *v. n.* To be clear, evident; to shine.

ರೊಕೋಟಿ rokōṭi, *see* ರೋಕ.

ರೊಕ್ಕ rokka, *s.* Money, wealth. 2. ready money, cash, small money *or* change.

ರೊಚ್ಚು roccu, *see* ನೊಚ್ಚು.

ರೊಜ roja, *s.* Anything very little *or* small, a bit, trifle. *adj.* Little, small, trifling.

ರೊಟ್ಟಿ roṭṭi, *s.* Bread, a loaf. —ಗಾರೆ, —ದಾಯೆ a baker. —ಕಾಯಾವುನಿ, —ಸುಡ್ಪಿನಿ to bake. ರೊಟ್ಟಿ ದೆಕ್ಕ್‌ದ್ ನೀರ್ ಪರಿಲೆಕ್ಕ *pro.* wash the bread and drink the water, *i. e.*, preserve the capital and live on the profit.

ರೋಂಟು rōṇṭu, *s.* Leanness. —ಕಟ್ಟುನಿ to become thin, be emaciated.

ರೋಂದು rōndu, *s.* Patrolling, going the rounds, as a guard. —ದಾಯೆ a patrole, watchman.

ರೋಕ, ರೋಕಟಿ, ರೋಕಿ, ರೋಕೊಟಿ rōka, rōkaṭi, rōki, rōkoṭi, *adj.* In cash *or* ready money.

ರೋಗ rōga, *s.* Sickness, disease, indisposition. —ದಾಯೆ, ರೋಗಿಷ್ಠೆ a sick man; a leper. —ಆಪಿನಿ to get sick; to have syphilis. —ಪತ್ತುನಿ, ರೋಗೊಡು ಬೂರುನಿ to be sick.

ರೋಗನ್ rōganu, *s.* Varnish. —ಕೊರ್ಪಿನಿ, —ಶಾಗಾವುನಿ, —ದೆಪ್ಪುನಿ, —ಪಾಡುನಿ to varnish.

ರೋಚ rōca, *s.* Movement, motion.

ರೋಚನ rōcana, *s.* A yellow pigment used as medicine, dye *or* perfume; bezoar. 2. a stomachic; a carminative.

ರೋಜ rōja, *see* ರೊಜ.

ರೋಜಿ rōji, *s.* A day. 2. daily work. —ಗಾರಿಕೆ earning, service, employment. —ಗಾರೆ a workman, servant.

ರೋಜಿಪಿನಿ rōjipini (ರೋಜಿ), *v. n.* To be employed.

ರೋಟು rōṭu, *s.* Trouble, annoyance.

ರೋಡು rōḍu, *see* ಲೋಡು.

ರೋತ್ರಿ rōtri, *s.* A deceiver.

ರೋದನ, ರೋದನೆ rōdana, rōdanè, *s.* Weeping, lamentation, crying.

ರೋಪಣ rōpaṇa, *s.* Bewildering of the mind, confusion of ideas.

ರೋಮ rōma, *s.* The hair about the body. 2. hair, wool. ಕುರಿ— wool.

ರೋಮನ್ rōmanu, *adj.* Roman. —ದಾಯಿ a Roman Catholic.

ರೋಷ rōsha, *s.* Wrath, fury, anger.

ರೋಷನ್ rōshanu, *s.* Shine, glitter.

ರೋಹಿಣಿ rōhiṇi, *s.* The mother of Balarāma. 2. the fourth lunar asterism.

ರೋಹಿತ rōhita, *adj.* Red.

ರೋಹಿತೆ rōhite, *s.* A well-wisher.

ರೌಕುಳ roukuḷa, *see* ಓಕಳಿ.

ರೌದ್ರ roudra, *s.* Wrath, rage. *adj.* Fearful, formidable, terrific. 2. acute, violent. ರೌದ್ರಾಕಾರ a terrible form.

ರೌದ್ರಿ roudri, *s.* The fifty-fourth year in the Hindu cycle of sixty.

ರೌರವ rourava, *s.* One of the divisions of Tartarus, hell; *also* ರೌರವನರಕ.

ರೌಲು roulu, *s.* A mode of drum-beating.

ರೌವನೆ rouvanè, *adv.* Suddenly; *cf.* ರಪ್ಪ.

ರೌಸ್ rousu, *see* ರವಸು.

ಲ L

ಲ la, The forty-first letter of the alphabet.

ಲಂಕ, ಲಂಕೆ laṅka, laṅkè, *s.* Ceylon, the ancient capital of Rāvaṇa; *also* ಲಂಕಾದ್ವೀಪ, ಲಂಕಾಪಟ್ಣ.

ಲಂಕೆ laṅka, *see* ರಂಕೆ.

ಲಂಕಿನಿ laṅkini, A giantess who defended Laṅka. 2. a fierce, passionate woman.

ಲಂಗ್ಡೆ, ಲಂಗಡೆ laṅguḍe, laṅgaḍe, *s.* A cripple, lame man.

ಲಂಗ laṅga, *s.* A gown.

ಲಂಗರ್ laṅgaru, *s.* An anchor.

ಲಂಗೋಟಿ laṅgōṭi, *s.* A cloth covering the privities.

ಲಂಘನೆ laṅghanè *s.* Fasting. 2. leaping, jumping.

ಲಂಚ್ laṅću, *s.* Taming. —ಮಾಕುನಿ to tame a wild horse.

ಲಂಚ laṅća, *s.* Bribery, a bribe. —ಕೊರ್ಪಿನಿ to give bribes. —ತಿಪ್ಪಿನಿ to take bribes.

ಲಂಡ್, ಲಂಡ laṇḍu, laṇḍa, *s.* Obscenity, rudeness. 2. evil, wickedness; *also* ಲಂಡತನ. *adj.* Obscene, rude. 2. evil, wicked.

ಲಂಡೆ laṇḍe, *s.* A rude *or* wicked man.

ಲಂದುನಿ landuni (ಲಂದಿ), *v. a.* To lead a vagabond's life.

ಲಂದೆಲ್ landelu, *see* ರಂದೆಲ್.

ಲಂದೆಲೆ landele, *s.* A vagabond, vagrant.

ಲಂಪಟ lampaṭa, *s.* Eagerness, desire for. ವಿಷಯ– indulging in carnal appetites.

ಲಂಬ, ಲಂಬಾಸ್ lamba, lambāsu, *adj.* Long, tall. 2. suspended. 3. expanded. ಲಂಬಾಸ್ ನರಮಾನಿ a tall man.

ಲಂಬನ lambana, *s.* Hanging on, depending. 2. *see* ಲಂಜಿ.

ಲಂಬಾಡಿ, ಲಂಬಾಣಿ lambāḍi, lambāṇi, *see* ಲವಾಣಿ.

ಲಂಬಾಣುಗೆ lambāṇugė, *s.* Length.

ಲಂಬು lambu, *adj.* Tender.

ಲಂಬೆ lambė, *s.* A tender fruit.

ಲಂಬೋದರೆ lambōdare, *s. lit.* Large paunched. 2. Gaṇēśa.

ಲಂವ್ಡಿ lañvḍi,, *see* ಲಾಂಡಿ.

ಲಕ್‌ಲಕ್ lakulaku, *adj.* Shining, glittering, brilliant. –ಆಪಿನಿ to shine, glitter.

ಲಕೋಟೆ lakōṭė, *see* ಲಖೋಟೆ.

ಲಕ್ಕ lakka, *s.* A kind of dove.

ಲಕ್ಕಣಿಗೆ lakkaṇigė, *s.* A reed pen.

ಲಕ್ಕಾವುನಿ lakkāvuni, *c. v.* (*of* ಲಕ್ಕುನಿ.) To lift, raise. 2. to wake, rouse. 3. to steal, pilfer.

ಲಕ್ಕಿ lakki, *s.* A kind of medicinal plant. ಕಿರ್ಲಕ್ಕಿ a dark variety of this plant; a water-fowl.

ಲಕ್ಕಿಮಿ lakkimi, *see* ಲಕ್ಷ್ಮಿ.

ಲಕ್ಕುನಿ lakkuni (ಲಕ್ಯ್), *v. n.* To rise, get up. 2. to stand up, arise. 3. to depart, start. ಲಕ್ಕದ್ ಪೋಪಿನಿ to get away; to become loose.

ಲಕ್ಕೆ lakkė, *s.* A measure; a mark. –ದ ಬಳ್ಳ a seer for measuring.

ಲಖೋಟೆ lakhōṭė, *s.* A folded letter. 2. an envelope, cover. 3. a small packet. 4. a pouch. –ಡ್ ಪಾಡುನಿ to enclose in a cover; to put into a pouch. –ಮಳ್ಪುನಿ to fold a letter; to prepare an envelope.

ಲಗ್‌ಬಗ್ lagubagu, *adv.* About, nearly, approximately.

ಲಗ laga, *s.* Taking *or* seizing, as a fort.

ಲಗನ lagana, *see* ಲಗ್ನ.

ಲಗಬಗ lagabaga, *s.* Hurry, haste.

ಲಗಾಡ್ lagāḍu, *s.* Rubbing.

ಲಗಾಡ್, ಲಗಾಡಿ lagāḍu, lagāḍi, *s.* Intercourse, interference, connexion. 2. trouble, annoyance, difficulty. 3. wickedness, mischief. 4. ruin. –ದೆಪ್ಪುನಿ to annoy, dun; to ruin, eradicate, destroy. –ಗ್ ಪೋಪಿನಿ to interfere with.

ಲಗಾಮ್, ಲಗಾಮು lagāmu, lagāmu, *s.* A bridle.

ಲಗಾಸ್ lagāsu, *s.* Devouring. 2. flogging.

ಲಗಾಸುನಿ lagāsuni (ಲಗಾಸ್), *v. a.* To eat, devour. 2. to beat, flog.

ಲಗು lagu, *see* ಲಘು.

ಲಗ್ಗ lagga, *s.* Compensation. 2. *see* ಲಗ.

ಲಗ್ಗೆ laggė, *s.* Crowding, thronging, assembling. 2. scaling.

ಲಗ್ನ lagna, *s.* The period selected for any auspicious ceremony, as the celebration of a marriage, *etc.* 2. the rising of a sign, its appearance above the horizon. 3. the celebration of a wedding *or* of investiture with the sacred thread. ಚಂದ್ರ— the rising of the moon in a constellation. ಜನ್ಮ— a natal star. —ಆಪಿನಿ to be married, *etc.* —ತೂಪಿನಿ to fix a time for marriage, *etc.* —ಮುಳ್ಪುನಿ to marry, *etc.*

ಲಘು **laghu,** *s.* A short vowel. 2. sleight of hand, dexterity. *adj.* Light; slight, trifling. 2. abating, on the decrease.

ಲಚ್ಚ **lačča,** *see* ಲಕ್ಷ.

ಲಚ್ಚಣ **laččaṇa,** *see* ಲಕ್ಷಣ.

ಲಚ್ಚಿಮಿ **laččimi,** *see* ಲಕ್ಷ್ಮಿ.

ಲಚ್ಚಿಲ್ **laččilu,** *s.* A pasture ground; a brushwood.

ಲಚ್ಚೆ **lačče,** *see* ಲಕ್ಷ್ಯ.

ಲಜ್ಜ, ಲಜ್ಜೆ **lajja, lajjè,** *s.* Shame, modesty, bashfulness.

ಲಜ್ಜಂಡೆ **lajjaṇḍe,** *s.* A shameless fellow.

ಲಟ್ಪಟ್, ಲಟಪಟ **laṭupaṭu, laṭapaṭa,** *s.* A noise of breaking sticks, *etc.* 2. fighting, quarrelling. 3. slapping; *cf.* ಚಟಚಟ.

ಲಟ್ಟ್, ಲಟ್ಟು **laṭṭu, laṭṭu,** *s.* A top. 2. a stick, rod.

ಲಟ್ಟೆ **laṭṭè,** *s.* The arm. 2. a staff, cudgel.

ಲಡಾಯಿ **laḍāyi,** *s.* A battle, fight, contest. —ಮಳ್ಪುನಿ to fight, quarrel.

ಲಡ್ಡ್, ಲಡ್ಡಿಗೆ, ಲಡ್ಡು **laḍḍu, laḍḍigè, laḍḍu,** *s.* A ball of sweetmeat.

ಲತಡ್, ಲತಾಡ್ **latadu, latādu,** *s.* Pressure, urgency. 2. press, thronging. 3. difficulty, perplexity, trouble, hardship, annoyance. ಕೆಲಸದ— pressure of work. ಪಣವುದ— need of money, being pressed for money. —ಕೋಪಿನಿ to be overworked. ಲತಾಡ್ಡ್ ಬೂರುನಿ to be involved in difficulties.

ಲತಾವಳಿ **latāvaḷi,** *s.* Obstacles. 2. pain.

ಲತ್ತ್ **lattu,** *adj.* Young, tender, unripe, green. 2. imperfect, rough. —ಕುಕ್ಕು a tender mango. —ಪ್ರಾಯ tender age. —ಬುದ್ಧಿ immature understanding, thoughtlessness. ಆಯಿ ಲತ್ತ್ ಮಳ್ತ್ he acted imprudently, he was hasty. ಕೆಲಸ ಲತ್ತ್ ಆಂಡ್ the thing did not succeed; the business spoiled.

ಲತ್ತ **latta,** *s.* A creeper.

ಲತ್ತಂಡೆ, ಲತ್ತನೆ **lattaṇḍè, lattanè,** *s.* Lentil, *Dolichos catjang.*

ಲತ್ತೆ **lattè,** *s.* A die; a game of dice. 2. a blow. —ಗೊಬ್ಬು playing at dice. —ಕೊರ್ಪಿನಿ to give a blow.

ಲದ್ದಾ **laddā,** *adv.* Wholly.

ಲದ್ದಿ **laddi,** *s.* The dung of a horse, elephant, *etc.* —ಪಾಡುನಿ to void excrement.

ಲಪ್ಪಾವುನಿ **lappāvuni,** *c. v.* (*of* ಲಪ್ಪುನಿ) To make *or* cause to measure.

ಲಪ್ಪು lappu, *s.* Measurement. *adj.* Measuring. —ಕೋಲು a measuring rod.

ಲಪ್ಪುನಿ lappuni (ಲ), *v. a.* To measure, mete. *v. n.* To cough. 2. to sneeze. ಅರಿ— to measure rice. ತಂಮು— to cough. ಸುಂಬಿಲ್— to sneeze.

ಲಪ್ರಮ್ lapramụ, *s.* A pulley.

ಲಬ laba, *s.* Fear.

ಲಬಲಬ labalaba, *s.* A noise made by crying and beating the mouth. 2. crying, lamentation, weeping. —ಮಳ್ಪುನಿ a confused noise of talking loudly *or* indistinctly. —ಡಾ ಕೋಲುನಿ to beat the mouth while crying.

ಲಬಾಡಿ labāḍi, *s.* Dissimulation, hypocrisy, deceit, pretence, fraud. 2. a false promise. 3. a hyprocrite, cheat, rogue. —ಮಳ್ಪುನಿ to deceive, cheat, dissimulate; *also* ಲಬಾಡಿಯುನಿ.

ಲಬ್ಧ labdha, *s.* The product, *arith.* 2. profit, gain.

ಲಬ್ಬೆ labbe, *s.* One of a class of Tamil Mahommedans. 2. a Mahommedan weaver.

ಲಯ laya, *s.* Loss, destruction, ruin. —ಆಪಿನಿ to perish, be destroyed, ruined.

ಲಯಿಸ್ layisụ, *adj.* Accomplished. 2. ready.

ಲಲಂತಿಗೆ lalantigè, *s.* A necklace.

ಲಲನೆ lalanè, *s.* A woman.

ಲಲಾಟ lalāṭa, *s.* The forehead. —ರೇಖೆ, —ಲಿಖಿತ a line on the forehead; fate.

ಲಲ್ಲ, ಲಲ್ಲೆ lalla, lallè, *s.* Insincere love, pretended affection; *also* ಲಲ್ಲಗಾರಿಕೆ. —ಮಳ್ಪುನಿ to fondle; to flirt.

ಲವ lava, *s.* The sixtieth part of the twinkling of an eye. 2. an atom, mote. *adj.* Small, little, minute; *also* —ಕಾಲ. —ಲಾಂಛನ a small streak, a minute portion of anything.

ಲವಂಗ lavaṅga, *s.* The clove tree; cloves. —ಪತ್ರಿ mace.

ಲವಡಿ, ಲವುಡಿ lavaḍi, lavuḍi, *see* ಲಾಂಡಿ.

ಲವಣ lavaṇa, *s.* Salt.

ಲವಣಿ lavaṇi, *see* ಲವಾನೆ.

ಲವಾದನ lavādana, *s.* A moment.

ಲವಾದಿ lavādi, *see* ಲೇವಾದಿ.

ಲವಾನೆ lavāne, *s.* A man of the Brinjari caste. —ರ್ the Brinjari people.

ಲವೆ lave, *s.* A son of Rāma. 2. *see* ಲವ.

ಲಸ್ಕರ್ laskarụ, *s.* A camp-follower. 2. a soldier; a sailor.

ಲಹರಿ lahari, *s.* Intoxication, drunkenness.

ಲಕ್ಷ laksha, *s.* A lac, one hundred thousand. 2. *see* ಲಕ್ಷ್ಯ. ಲಕ್ಷಾಂತರ, ಲಕ್ಷಾಂತ್ರ more than a lac, many lacs.

ಲಕ್ಷಣ lakshaṇa, *s.* A property, peculiarity, indication, *or* predicate. 2. mark, sign. 3. beauty, neatness, perfection, in outward shape *or* form.

4. fortune. ಅವ—, ಪಡಿಕೆ— a bad sign.

ಲಕ್ಷದೀಪ lakshadīpa, *s.* A general illumination festival in honour of an idol.

ಲಕ್ಷಪೂಜೆ lakshapūjè, *s.* Worshipping an idol with a profusion of flowers.

ಲಕ್ಷಿಪುನಿ, ಲಕ್ಷಿಸುನಿ lakshipuni, lakshisuni (ಲಕ್ಷಿ), *v. a.* To esteem, regard, care for. 2. to aim.

ಲಕ್ಷೆ lakshè, *see* ಲಕ್ಷ್ಯ.

ಲಕ್ಷ್ಮಣೆ lakshmaṇe, *s.* Rāma's younger brother. 2. the name of a man.

ಲಕ್ಷ್ಮಿ lakshmi, *s.* The wife of Vishṇu, the goddess of wealth and property. 2. success, fortune, prosperity, riches, wealth. ಧನ—, ಭಾಗ್ಯ— rich in wealth. ಧೈರ್ಯ— rich in courage.

ಲಕ್ಷ್ಯ lakshya, *s.* Regard, respect, care for. —ಉಪ್ಪುನಿ to care for, be provident. —ಮಳ್ಪುನಿ, ಲಕ್ಷ್ಯೊಡು ದೀಪಿನಿ to regard.

ಲಾ lā, *A conjunctive affix meaning* and, also; *as*, ಇಲ್ಲ್ ಲಾ ಬಿತ್ತ್ ಲ್ ಲಾ house and garden; ಉಂದುಲಾ ಅವುಲಾ this and that; ನನಲಾ still, yet; ಏಪಲಾ always; ಆಂಡಲಾ though it be, but, nevertheless; ಮೂಳುಲಾ ಔಳುಲಾ here and there.

ಲಾಂಚನ, ಲಾಂಛನ, ಲಾಂಛೆ lāñcana, lāñchana, lāñchè, *s.* A mark, sign. 2. a spot; a bit. *adj.* Very little *or* small.

ಲಾಂಟನ್, ಲಾಂದರ್ lāṇṭanu, lāndaru, *see* ಲಾಟನ್.

ಲಾಂಬಿ lāmbi, *s.* Length. 2. hitting the ball from above in a game of cricket, *etc.*

ಲಾಂಬು lāmbu, *s.* A mushroom, toad-stool, fungus. 2. nonage. *adj.* Tender. ತೆತ್ತಿ—, ನಂಜಿ—, ನಿಯಿ—, ಪರೆಲ್—, ಪೆಗ್ಗುಡೆ—, ಪೆಲ— are different species of fungus.

ಲಾಕಿ lāki, *s.* A half-grown hen. 2. *see* ಲಾವಕ್ಕಿ.

ಲಾಗ, ಲಾಗ್ಯ lāga, lāgya, *s.* A summerset, jump, leap. —ಪಾಡುನಿ to make a summerset.

ಲಾಗ್ಗಾಟ, ಲಾಗ್ಯಾಟ lāggāṭa, lāgyāṭa, *s.* Jumping, leaping.

ಲಾಗಾಯಿತು, ಲಾಗ್ಯಾತ್ lāgāyitu, lāgāitu, *s.* Beginning, commencement.

ಲಾಗಿಯುನಿ, ಲಾಗ್ಯುನಿ lāgiyuni, lāgyuni (ಲಾಗಿ), *v. n.* To leap, jump, skip.

ಲಾಚಾರ್, ಲಾಚಾರಿ lāčāru, lāčāri, *adj.* Reduced, helpless, in difficult circumstances. 2. weak, debilitated. —ತನ difficulty, helplessness. —ಆಪಿನಿ to be in difficulty. —ಬೂರುನಿ to become weak, as from sickness.

ಲಾಚಿ lāči, *adj.* Tender, soft.

ಲಾಟ್ lāṭu, *adj.* Inexact, not precise, superficial, loose. —ಗ ಲಾಟಿ superficial work. —ಗ ಲಾ

ಟೆ ಮಳ್ಪುನಿ to do a thing superficially.

ಲಾಟನ್ lāṭanu, *s.* A lantern.

ಲಾಟೆ lāṭè, *s.* A spinning wheel. 2. a pulley used for drawing water.

ಲಾಡ್ lāḍu, *s.* A line, row, group.

ಲಾಡ lāḍa, *s.* A horse shoe.

ಲಾಡಿ, ಲಾಡೆ lāḍi, lāḍè, *see* ನಾಡೆ.

ಲಾತ್ lātu, *s.* A kick. 2. disgrace; reproof.

ಲಾಭ lābha, *s.* Gain, profit, advantage. ಲಾಭೊಡು ಪಗೆ ಇಜ್ಜಿ there is no enmity where an advantage is concerned.

ಲಾಯ lāya, *s.* A stable. ಕುದುರೆ– a horse-stable.

ಲಾಯಕ್, ಲಾಯಿಕ್ lāyaku, lāyiku, *adj.* Suitable, proper, fit, convenient, commodious. 2. nice, pretty.

ಲಾಲ್ lālu, *adj.* Red, crimson. 2. flushed with inebriation, drunk. –ಆಪಿನಿ to be drunk.

ಲಾಲ್, ಲಾಲ lālu, lāla, *see* ನಾಲ್.

ಲಾಲ್‌ದಾಯೆ lāludāye, *s.* A farrier.

ಲಾಲನೆ lālanè, *s.* Caressing, fondling. –ಮಳ್ಪುನಿ to fondle, caress, dandle.

ಲಾಲಿ lāli, *s.* Walking to and fro; frequenting. 2. wandering. 3. *see* ಲಾಳಿ. –ಪಾಡುನಿ to frequent, walk to and fro.

ಲಾಲಿಪುನಿ, ಲಾಲಿಸುನಿ lālipuni, lālisuni (ಲಾಲಿ, ಲಾಲಿಸ್), *v. a.* To listen, attend to. 2. to fondle, caress.

ಲಾವಂಗ lāvaṅga, *see* ಲವಂಗ.

ಲಾವಂಚ lāvañċa, *s.* The grass *Andropogon muricatum.*

ಲಾವಕ್ಕಿ lāvakki, *s.* The quail; *also* ಲಾವಕ್ಕಿಪಕ್ಕಿ.

ಲಾವಣಿ, ಲಾವಣೆ lāvaṇi, lāvaṇè, *s.* A tune so called. 2. a ballad.

ಲಾಳಿ lāḷi, *s.* A weaver's shuttle. 2. *see* ನಾಲಿ. 3. *see* ಲಾಲಿ.

ಲಾಳು lāḷu, *see* ಲಾಲ್.

ಲಾಕ್ಷ lāksha, *s.* Shell lac.

ಲಿಂಗ liṅga, *s.* The penis. 2. the phalus, *or* Śiva under that form *or* emblem. 3. gender, *gram.* –ವಂತೆ a Lingait, one who wears the liṅga. ನಪುಂಸಕ– the neuter gender. ಪುಲ್ಲಿಂಗ the masculine gender. ಸ್ತ್ರೀ– the feminine gender. –ಕಟ್ಟುನಿ to wear the liṅga.

ಲಿಂಗಿ liṅgi, *see* ಲುಂಗಿ.

ಲಿಂಬಿ, ಲಿಂಬೆ limbi, limbè, *s.* The lemon fruit, *Citrus bergamia; also* ಲಿಂಬೆಪುಲಿ.

ಲಿಖಿತ likhita, *adj.* Written. *s. see* ಲೇಖನ. ಬ್ರಹ್ಮ–, ಲಲಾಟ– fate, as supposed to have been inscribed upon the scull by Brahma.

ಲಿಪಿ lipi, *s.* Hand-writing, a written paper, *etc.* 2. destiny. ಬ್ರಹ್ಮ– fate; an act which is irrevocable *or* unalterable.

ಲೀಲೆ līlè, *s.* Play, sport, pastime, frolic. ಬಾಲ– children's sport.

ಲುಂಗಿ luṅgi, *s.* A checkered garment worn by a Mussalman.

ಲುಂಡ **luṇḍa**, *adj.* Confused, confounded, mingled. *s. see* ರುಂಡ.

ಲುಂಡೆ **luṇḍe**, *see* ಲೆಂಡೆ.

ಲುಂಬಾವುನಿ **lumbāvuni**, *c. v.* (*of* ಲುಂಬುನಿ) To cause to plunge, wash, rinse.

ಲುಂಬುನಿ **lumbuni** (ಲುಂಬಿ), *v. a.* To plunge, wash, rinse.

ಲುಕಾಲ್ **lukālụ**, *see* ಉಕಾಲ್.

ಲುಕ್ಸಾನ್ **luksānụ**, *s.* Loss, damage. —ಕಟ್ಟೋರಿ an ale-house, liquor shop, *slg.*

ಲುಚ್ಚ **lučča**, *adj.* Mean, base, low, worthless. —ತನ, ಲುಚ್ಚಾಟಿಗೆ meanness, baseness, vulgarity,

ಲುಚ್ಚೆ **lučče**, *s.* A base fellow.

ಲುಟಾಯಿಸುನಿ **luṭāyisuni** (ಲುಟಾಯಿಸಿ), *v. a.* To pillage, sack, plunder.

ಲುಟುಕ **luṭuka**, *s.* The cracking of the fingers.

ಲುಬ್ಧ **lubdha**, *adj.* Covetous, greedy. ಲುಬ್ಧಿ a miser, covetous man.

ಲೂಟಾಲೂಟಿ **lūṭālūṭi**, *s.* Plundering, sacking. 2. mischief, harm.

ಲೂಟಿ **lūṭi**, *s.* Mischief, misbehaviour. 2. plunder, pillage. —ಗಾರೆ a mischief-maker; a plunderer. —ಮಳ್ಪುನಿ to make *or* cause mischief; to plunder, extort.

ಲೂತಿ **lūti**, *s.* A cutaneous disease; *also* ಲೂತಿರೋಗ. —ಕಾಯಿ a kind of nut used in medicine for this disease.

ಲೆಂಕಿ **leṅki**, *adj.* Timid. —ಜನ timid people.

ಲೆಂಕಿನ್ **leṅkinụ**, *s.* A dark cloth.

ಲೆಂಕಿನಿ **leṅkini**, *see* ಲಂಕಿನಿ.

ಲೆಂಕಿರ್, ಲೆಂಕಿರಿ **leṅkirụ, leṅkiri**, *s.* A thin kind of bamboo.

ಲೆಂಕುನಿ **leṅkuni**, *see* ರೆಂಕುನಿ.

ಲೆಂಕೆ **leṅke**, *s.* A slave, servant.

ಲೆಂಚ **leñča**, *see* ಲಂಚ.

ಲೆಂಚಿ **leñči**, *s.* A ladder, flight of stairs.

ಲೆಂಡ **leṇḍa**, *adj.* Wicked, evil.

ಲೆಂಡೆ **leṇḍe**, *s.* A topknot, tuft of hair, tresses. 2. a lump of dung. —ಕಟ್ಟುನಿ, —ಪಾಡುನಿ to tie the hair into a knot.

ಲೆಕ್ಕ **lekka**, *conj.* That, in order that. *adv.* As, like, according to; *also* ಲೆಕ್ಕನೆ. *s. see* ಲೆಖ್ಖ. ಬರ್ಪಿ ಲೆಕ್ಕ ತೂಲ try to come. ಇಂಚಿ ಆಯ ಲೆಕ್ಕನೆ ಉಳ್ಳೆ he resembles that man.

ಲೆಕ್ಕಂದ **lekkanda**, *see* ಲಕ್ಕೆ. 2. *see* ಲೆಖ್ಖ.

ಲೆಕ್ಕಣಿ, ಲೆಕ್ಕಣಿಗೆ **lekkaṇi, lekkaṇigè**, *see* ಲಕ್ಕಣಿಗೆ.

ಲೆಕ್ಕಿಯುನಿ **lekkiyuni** (ಲೆಕ್ಕಿ), *v. a.* To count, reckon up. 2. to estimate, regard, esteem.

ಲೆಕ್ಕೆಸಿರಿ **lekkesiri**, *s.* A demon so called.

ಲೆಖ್ಖ **lekkha**, *s.* An account, reckoning, arithmetic. 2. concern. —ತೂಪಿನಿ to examine *or* audit an account. —ಬರೆಪಿನಿ to write out an account. —ಮಳ್ಪುನಿ to count. ಲೆಖ್ಖೊಗು ಬರೆಪಿನಿ to charge *or* enter to one's account.

ಲೆಖ್ಖಾಚಾರ **lekkhāčāra,** *s.* Accounts. 2. money transactions.

ಲೆಜ್ಜಂಡೆ **lejjaṇḍe,** *see* ಲಜ್ಜಂಡೆ.

ಲೆಜ್ಜಿ, ಲೆಜ್ಜೆ **lejji, lejjè,** *see* ಲಜ್ಜಿ.

ಲೆಪ್ಪಾವುನಿ **leppāvuni,** *c.v.* (*of* ಲೆಪ್ಪುನಿ) To cause to call, to send for.

ಲೆಪ್ಪು **leppu,** *s.* A call. 2. the distance at which a loud cry can be heard.

ಲೆಪ್ಪುಡಾವುನಿ, ಲೆಪ್ಪುಡುನಿ **leppuḍāvuni, leppuḍuni,** *see* ಲೆಪ್ಪಾವುನಿ.

ಲೆಪ್ಪುನಿ **leppuni** (ಲೆ), *v. a.* To call. 2. to invite to an entertainment.

ಲೆಬ್ಬೆ **lebbe,** *see* ಲಬ್ಬೆ.

ಲೇಖಣಿ, ಲೇಖಣಿಗೆ **lēkhaṇi, lēkhaṇigè,** *see* ಲಕ್ಕಣಿಗೆ.

ಲೇಖನ **lēkhana,** *s.* Writing, scripture. 2. an epistle, letter.

ಲೇಖೆ **lēkhè,** *see* ರೇಖೆ.

ಲೇಝುಮ್ **lējhamu,** *s.* A kind of arrow.

ಲೇದ್, ಲೇದೆ **lēdu, lēdè,** *s.* Denying. —ಪಾಡುನಿ to deny.

ಲೇಪ, ಲೇಪನ **lēpa, lēpana,** *s.* Smearing, plastering. 2. a liniment, salve, ointment. —ಪಾಡುನಿ, —ಪೂಜುನಿ to apply a liniment *or* ointment.

ಲೇರ್ **lēru,** *see* ಲಹರಿ.

ಲೇಲೆ **lēle,** *s.* Dancing of the Pariahs.

ಲೇವಡಿ **lēvaḍi,** *s.* A kind of sweetmeat.

ಲೇವಾದಿ, ಲೇವಾದೇವಿ **lēvādi, lēvādēvi,** *s.* Borrowing and lending, usury; dealing.

ಲೇವು **lēvu,** *s.* A cry. —ಪಾಡುನಿ to cry.

ಲೇವೆ **lēve,** *s.* A kind of decoration.

ಲೇಶ **lēša,** *s.* A bit, small quantity. *adj.* Small, little. —ಮಾತ್ರ only a little.

ಲೇಸ್, ಲೇಸು **lēsu, lēsu,** *s.* An auspicious ceremony *or* event. 2. a handkerchief. *adj.* Excellent, good; *cf.* ಲೈಸ್, ಜೇಸ್. —ಕರ್ತವೆ a host, one who receives *or* entertains guests. —ಆಪಿನಿ to be excellent; to be well done. —ದೆಪ್ಪುನಿ, —ಮಳ್ಪುನಿ to perform an auspicious ceremony.

ಲೇಹ **lēha,** *s.* An electuary in medicine.

ಲೈಪುನಿ **leipuni** (ಲೈ), *v. n.* To jump, leap; *also* ಲಾಗಯುನಿ; *cf.* ಲಪ್ಪುನಿ, ಲೆಪ್ಪುನಿ.

ಲೈಲಾಮ್ **leilāmu,** *s.* Auction. —ಮಳ್ಪುನಿ to sell by auction.

ಲೈಸ್ **leisu,** *s.* Preparing, providing, making ready, completing, finishing. —ಆಪಿನಿ to be ready; to be accomplished, finished. —ಮಳ್ಪುನಿ to prepare, make ready; to accomplish, finish.

ಲೊಟ್ಟುಲೊಟ್ಟು **loṭṭuloṭṭu,** *see* ಲಟಿಪಟಿ.

ಲೊಟ್ಟೆ **loṭṭè,** *s.* A lie, falsehood, fib. *adj.* False, untrue.

ಲೊಡ loḍa, *adj.* Loose. 2. unreserved. –ಬಡ open, frank; public.

ಲೋಕ lōka, *s.* A division of the universe; an inhabited place, region, world. 2. the world of people, mankind. ಮೂಜಿ– the three worlds, namely: ಪರ– heaven, ಭೂ– earth, and ಪಾತಾಳ– hell. –ನಾಥ, –ಪಾಲಕ an earthly ruler, king.

ಲೋಕಾಂತ lōkānta, *adj.* Public, spread abroad. –ಆಪಿನಿ to transpire, become public.

ಲೋಕಾಂತರ lōkāntara, *s.* Another world. –ಶೋಪಿನಿ to die.

ಲೋಕಾಂತ್ಯ lōkāntya, *s.* The end of the world.

ಲೋಕಾಚಾರ lōkāċāra, *s.* The manner of the world; worldly custom *or* practice.

ಲೋಚನ lōčana, *s.* The eye. 2. sight, seeing.

ಲೋಟ, ಲೋಟು lōṭa, lōṭu, *s.* A crowd *or* throng of people; over-crowdedness.

ಲೋಡು lōḍu, *s.* A cushion to lean the back against. –ದೀಪಿನಿ, –ಪಾಡುನಿ to place such a cushion.

ಲೋಪ lōpa, *s.* Rejection, expunging, cutting off in general. 2. elision, ellipsis, *gram.* ಅಕ್ಷರ– the dropping of a letter. ಕ್ರಿಯಾ– omitting part of one's duty. ದ್ರವ್ಯ– deficiency in wealth. –ಆಪಿನಿ to be left out *or* dropped; to decrease, become less and less, be wasted. –ಮಳ್ಪುನಿ to omit, drop; to waste.

ಲೋಪಿಸುನಿ lōpisuni (ಲೋಪಿಸ್), *v. a.* To omit, drop. *v. n.* To be omitted; to suffer elision. 2. to disappear.

ಲೋಭ lōbha, *s.* Covetousness, avarice, stinginess. –ತ್ವ parsimony, avarice.

ಲೋಭಾನ lōbhāna, *s.* A fragrant resin, incense. ಕಾಡಿ– myrrh. ಸೇರಿ– frankincense, resin of *Boswellia thurifera; also* ವಿ ಶೇಷಧೂಪ.

ಲೋಭಿ, ಲೋಭಿಷ್ಟೆ, lōbhi, lōbhishṭe, *s.* An avaricious man, miser.

ಲೋಮ lōma, *see* ರೋಮ.

ಲೋಲ, ಲೋಲೆ lōla, lōlè, *adj.* Desirous, wishing, bent on, fond of. 2. moving, shaking.

ಲೋಲಿಸರ lōlisara, *see* ಇಲೋಲಿಸರ *under* ಇಲೋಲಿ.

ಲೋವೆ lōvè, *s.* Steel. 2. *see* [ಲೋಹ.

ಲೋಹ lōha, *s.* Metal. –ಮಾರ್ಗ a rail-way.

ಲೋಳಿ, ಲೋಳೆ lōḷi, lōḷè, *see* ಇಲೋಲಿ.

ಲೌಂಡಿ louṇḍi, *s.* A strumpet, whore, harlot.

ಲೌಂತರ್, ಲೌಂತರಿ lountaru, lountari, *s.* The penis, *obsc.*

ಲೌಕಿಕ, ಲೌಕೀಕ loukika, loukīka, *adj.* Worldly, secular.

ಲೌಕಿಕೆ loukike, *s.* A worldly man; a layman.

ಲೌಡಿ louḍi, *see* ಲೌಂಡಿ.

ವ V

ವ va, The forty-second letter of the alphabet.

For words not found under this initial see under ಬ.

ವಂಕಿ vaṅki, *s.* A fimbriated gold ornament.

ವಂಗ vaṅga, *s.* The white oxide of lead. 2. tin. 3. the ancient province of Bengal. –ಭಸ್ಮ calcined oxide of lead, sugar of lead.

ವಂಚಕೆ vañčake, *s.* A cheat, deceiver, hypocrite.

ವಂಚನೆ vañcanè, *s.* Deceit, deception, delusion, fraud, hoax, hypocrisy.

ವಂಚಿಪುನಿ, ವಂಚಿಸುನಿ vañčipuni, vañčisuni (ವಂಚಿ, ವಂಚಿಸ್), *v. a.* To deceive, defraud.

ವಂಜಿ vañji, *see* ಬಂಜಿ.

ವಂತಕಾರಿ vantakāri, *see* ಬಂತಗಾರೆ.

ವಂತೆ, ವಂತೆದಿ vante, vantedi, *Masculine and feminine affixes implying the possession of certain dispositions, qualities, etc.* ಬುದ್ಧಿವಂತೆ a wise man. ನೀತಿವಂತೆ a righteous man. ರೂಪವಂತೆದಿ a handsome woman.

ವಂದನೆ vandanè, *s.* A bow, obeisance, reverence, worshipping, salutation. –ಮಳ್ಪುನಿ to reverence, salute.

ವಂದಿಪುನಿ, ವಂದಿಸುನಿ vandipuni, vandisuni (ವಂದಿ, ವಂದಿಸ್), *v. a.* To reverence, worship, salute.

ವಂಮುಖ vammukha, *see* ಬಂಮುಖ.

ವಂಕುರ್ varṅku, *see* ಬಂಕುರ್.

ವಂಬುರ್ನಿ varmbuni (ವಂಬ್ರ್), *v. n.* To quarrel, fight. 2. to grasp.

ವಂಶ, ವಂಸ vaṁśa, vaṁsa, *s.* A race, generation, lineage, family.

ವಂಶಾವಳಿ vaṁśāvaḷi, *s.* A genealogy, line of descent.

ವಕಾಲತ್, ವಕಾಲಾತ್ vakālatu, vakālātu, *s.* A power of attorney, commission, agency.

ವಕೀಲೆ vakīle, *s.* A pleader, vakil, advocate, agent.

ವಕ್ಕಣೆ, ವಕ್ಕನೆ vakkaṇè, vakkanè, *s.* The style of a letter. 2. a literary composition, diction.

ವಕ್ರ vakra, *adj.* Bent, awry, crooked. 2. malignant, cruel.

ವಗೈರೆ vageirè, *postp. Et cetera,* and so forth.

ವಚನ vačana, *s.* A word, speech, sentence, dictum, aphorism. ಏಕ– the singular number. ಬಹು– the plural number.

ವಚಿಪುನಿ vačipuni (ವಚಿ), *v. a.* To speak.

ವಜ, ವಜಾ vaja, vajā, *s.* Deduction, subtraction, remission; *also* ಬಜ. –ಪಾಡುನಿ, –ಮಳ್ಪುನಿ to deduct, remit.

ವಜಯ vajaya, *s.* Paying, payment; *cf.* ವಜ.

ವಜಯ vajaya, *s.* Form, shape. ಒಂಜೇ– of like form *or* shape, a chip of the old block.

ವಜಿರ vajira, *see* ವಜ್ರ.

ವಜೀರ್, ವಜೀರೆ vajīru, vajīre, *s.* A prime minister. 2. the queen, in cards.

ವಜ್ರ vajra, *s.* A diamond. 2. one of the astronomical yōgas. *adj.* Hard, strong. —ಕಾಯ a strong constitution of body. —ಕವಚ a coat of mail. —ಮುಷ್ಟಿ a hard blow. ವಜ್ರಾಯುಧ the weapon of Indra; a thunderbolt.

ವಜ್ರಾಯುಸ್ಸು, ವಜ್ರೌಸ vajrāyussu, vajrousa, *s.* Longevity, long life.

ವಟ vaṭa, *s.* The large banyan, *Ficus religiosa.* —ಪತ್ರ the leaf of it.

ವಟಾರ vaṭāra, *s.* The compound *or* enclosure of a house, vicinity.

ವಟ್ಟಮ್ vaṭṭamu, *see* ಒಟ್ಟಂ.

ವಡೆ vaḍe, *s.* A kind of cake.

ವಡ್ಡ್ಯನ vaḍḍyana, *see* ಒಡ್ಯಾಣ.

ವಣಂಜನ vaṇaññana, *s.* A kind of vegetable, *Alternanthera sessilis.*

ವಣಸ್ vaṇasu, *see* ಉಣಸ್.

ವತ್ತಸ್ vattasu, *see* ಒತ್ತಯ.

ವತ್ತಿ vatti, *see* ಒತ್ತಿ. 2. *see* ಒತ್ತೆ.

ವತ್ಸನಾಬಿ, ವತ್ಸನಾಭಿ vatsanābi, vatsanābhi, *s.* An active vegetable poison, *Aconitum ferox.*

ವತ್ಸರ vatsara, *s.* A year; *also* ಸಂವತ್ಸರ.

ವತ್ಸಲೆ vatsale, *s.* A kind, affectionate man. ಭಕ್ತ— God who is gracious to His devotees.

ವದನ vadana, *s.* The mouth, visage, face, countenance.

ವಧು vadhu, *s.* A woman, bride, wife. —ವರರ್ bride and bridegroom.

ವಧೆ vadhe, *s.* Killing, murder. —ಮಳ್ಪುನಿ to kill.

ವನ vana, *s.* A grove, garden, park, forest, wood. —ವಾಸ residence in a forest for religious purposes. —ವಾಸಿ one who resides in a forest, a hermit. ಉದ್ಯಾ— a pleasure garden. ಉಪ— a garden near a house *or* town.

ವಮನ vamana, *s.* Oblation. 2. vomiting.

ವಯನ vayana, *s.* Manner, circumstance, way; the art of doing a thing. 2. a device, scheme, expedient. 3. artifice, dodge.

ವಯಲುನಿ vayaluni (ವಯಲ್), *v. n.* To totter, reel, stagger. 2. to shake, be agitated.

ವಯಸ್, ವಯಸು vayasu, vayasu, *s.* Age, time of life.

ವಯಿನ vayina, *see* ವಯನ.

ವಯಿಲ್ vayilu, *see* ವೈಲ್.

ವಯ್ಯರ vayyara, *see* ಒಯ್ಯಾರ.

ವರ vara, *s.* A blessing, boon, gift. 2. a bridegroom. *adj.* Best, excellent.

ವರಂಟ್ varaṇṭu, *s.* Envy, rancour, deep animosity, hatred. *adj.* Malicious, vicious. ಒಡ್ಡು— obstruction of business from malice *or* spite. –ಪತ್ತುನಿ to bear malice.

ವರಂಡ **varaṇḍa**, *s*. A veranda.

ವರಕ್, ವರಕ **varakụ, varaka**, *s*. Gilt, gold leaf.

ವರಕ **varaka**, *s*. A fountain, spring.

ವರಟುನಿ **varaṭuni** (ವರಟಿ), *v. a*. To chaffer. 2. to trouble, dun; *cf*. ಬಿರಗುನಿ.

ವರಟೆ **varaṭè**, *see* ಹರಟೆ.

ವರಟೆಲೆ **varaṭele**, *s*. A haggler, one who chaffers. 2. a teasing fellow.

ವರಣ್, ವರಾಣ್ **varaṇụ, varāṇụ**, *s*. A pagoda, four rupees; *also* ಬರಣ್.

ವರದ **varada**, *adj*. Favorable.

ವರದಿ **varadi**, *see* ವರ್ದಿ.

ವರಹ **varaha**, *see* ಬರಣ್.

ವರುಣ, ವರುಣೆ **varuṇa, varuṇe**, *s*. Uranus, the Hindu Neptune, regent of the west, the god of water and rain.

ವರುಷ **varusha**, *see* ವರ್ಷ.

ವರ್ಗ **varga**, *s*. A class, tribe. 2. a chapter, section. 3. transfer, removal to another place. 4. tenure of land, proprietary right; *also* ಬರ್ಗ. –ಮೂಲ the square root. –ಮಳ್ಪುನಿ to transfer.

ವರ್ಗಿಪುನಿ, ವರ್ಗಿಸುನಿ **vargipuni, vargisuni** (ವರ್ಗಿ, ವರ್ಗಿಸ್), *v. a*. To square, multiply a number by itself; *also* ಬರ್ಗಿಪುನಿ.

ವರ್ಜ, ವರ್ಜನ, ವರ್ಜನೆ **varja, varjana, varjanè**, *s*. Abandonment, relinquishment, quitting. –ಮಳ್ಪುನಿ to abandon.

ವರ್ಜಿತ **varjita**, *adj*. Abandoned, relinquished.

ವರ್ಜಿಪುನಿ, ವರ್ಜಿಸುನಿ **varjipuni, varjisuni** (ವರ್ಜಿಸ್), *v. a*. To relinquish, abandon, give up.

ವರ್ಣ **varṇa**, *s*. A class, tribe, caste. 2. colour, tint, hue.

ವರ್ಣನೆ **varṇanè**, *s*. Description, explaining, pointing out qualities *or* excellencies.

ವರ್ಣಿಪುನಿ, ವರ್ಣಿಸುನಿ **varṇipuni, varṇisuni** (ವರ್ಣಿಸ್), *v. a*. To describe, point out qualities *or* excellencies.

ವರ್ತ **varta**, *s*. Fountain, spring.

ವರ್ತಕೆ **vartake**, *s*. A merchant, trader.

ವರ್ತನೆ **vartanè**, *s*. Occupation, profession, living, livelihood.

ವರ್ತಮಾನ **vartamāna**, *s*. News, intelligence, information, intimation. 2. the present tense, *gram*.

ವರ್ತಿಸುನಿ **vartisuni** (ವರ್ತಿಸ್), *v. a*. To act. 2. to thrive on.

ವರ್ತೆ **vartè**, *s*. A female demon so called.

ವರ್ದಿ **vardi**, *s*. News, report, intelligence; *also* ಬರ್ದಿ.

ವರ್ಧಂತಿ **vardhanti**, *s*. A birthday.

ವರ್ಧನ **vardhana**, *s*. Increase.

ವರ್ಧಿಸುನಿ **vardhisuni** (ವರ್ಧಿಸ್), *v. n*. To grow, prosper, thrive.

ವರ್ಮ varma, *s.* Rancour, grudge, spite. 2. *see* ಬರ್ಮ. –ಕಳೆ a vital point. –ಪತ್ತುನಿ, –ಸಾಧ್ಯುನಿ to pursue with rancour.

ವರ್ಮಲತಾಯೆ varmalatāye, *s.* A demon so called.

ವರ್ಷ, ವರ್ಸ varsha, varsa, *s.* A year. 2. rain; *cf.* ಬರ್ಸ.

ವಲೆಗುನಿ valeguni (ವಲೆಗ್), *v. n.* To be possessed by a demon.

ವಲ್ಲಭೆ vallabhe, *s.* A lover, husband. 2. a superintendent, overseer.

ವಶ, ವಸ vaša, vasa, *s.* Submission. 2. charge; *also* ಬಶ. ಕಾಲ– time of death. –ಆಪಿನಿ to be subject to, be possessed of. –ಮಳ್ಪುನಿ to subdue; to deliver, make over.

ವಸ vasa, *s.* Marrow, fat. 2. an offering to fire.

ವಸಂತ vasanta, *s.* The season of spring.

ವಸತಿ vasati, *s.* An abode, dwelling.

ವಸನ vasana, *s.* Cloth, garment, clothes.

ವಸಲ್ vasalu, *s.* Alacrity. 2. *see* ಬಸರ್.

ವಸಾವುನಿ vasāvuni (ವಸಾ), *v. a.* To sit, stay.

ವಸೀಲ್, ವಸೀಲಿ vasīlu, vasīli, *see* ಬಶೀಲ್.

ವಸು vasu, *s.* A kind of demi-god.

ವಸೂಲ್, ವಸೂಲಿ, ವಸೂಲು vasūlu, vasūlj, vasūlu, *s.* Collection of a debt, *etc.* –ಮಳ್ಪುನಿ to collect.

ವಸ್ತ್, ವಸ್ತು vastu, vastu, *s.* A thing, matter, substance.

ವಸ್ತಿ vasti, *s.* Halting, sojourning. 2. *see* ವಸತಿ. –ಮಳ್ಪುನಿ to halt, stay.

ವಸ್ತ್ರ vastra, *s.* Cloth, raiment.

ವಕ್ಷ vaksha, *s.* The heart.

ವಾ vā, *interrog. pron.* Which? what? *cf.* ದಾ. –ನರಮಾನಿ which person? –ವಾ whatever.

ವಾಂಕ್ vāṅku, *s.* The felloe, outer rim of a wheel; jaunt.

ವಾಂಕಡೆ vāṅkadè, *see* ಓಂಕಡೆ.

ವಾಂಗ್ಮೂಲ vāṅgmūla, *s.* A deposition, statement.

ವಾಂತಿ, ವಾಂತೆ vānti, vāntè, *s.* Vomiting. –ಬರ್ಪಿನಿ to retch, feel nausea. –ಭೇದಿ cholera. –ಮಳ್ಪುನಿ to vomit.

ವಾಕ್, ವಾಕು vāku, vāku, *s.* A word, speech. 2. a rule. 3. an imprecation, curse. 4. an imaginary danger *or* risk. –ಕಂತುನಿ, –ತಟ್ಟುನಿ, –ಮುಟ್ಟುನಿ a curse to cleave; to be affected with an imprecation. –ಕೊರ್ಪಿನಿ to curse, imprecate. –ಗ್ ತಿಕ್ಕುನಿ to incur the risk of ordering *or* assenting to a delicate proceeding. –ದೀಪಿನಿ to curse, denounce. –ಪಿರಿಪುನಿ to absolve from a curse.

ವಾಕ್ಚಾತುರ್ಯ vākcāturya, *s.* Eloquence. –ದಾಯೆ an eloquent man.

ವಾಕ್ಮೂಲ vākmūla, *see* ವಾಂಗ್ಮೂಲ.

ವಾಕ್ಯ vākya, *s.* A sentence. 2. a rule.

ವಾಗ್ದಂಡ vāgdaṇḍa, *s.* Reproof, reprimand.

ವಾಗ್ದತ್ತ, ವಾಗ್ದಾನ vāgdatta, vāgdāna, *s.* A promise.

ವಾಗ್ವಾದ vāgvāda, *s.* Quarrel, dispute.

ವಾಚಕ, ವಾಚನ vāčaka, vāčana, *s.* Facility in reading; reading. —ಮಳ್ಪುನಿ to read.

ವಾಚಾಟ, ವಾಚ್ಚಾಟ vāčāṭa, vāččāṭa, *s.* Quarrel, dispute. —ಮಳ್ಪುನಿ to quarrel, dispute.

ವಾಚಾಡುನಿ vāčāḍuni (ವಾಚಾಡಿ), *v. a.* To quarrel,. dispute.

ವಾಚಾಲಕೆ vāčālake, *s.* A great talker, eloquent man.

ವಾಚಿತ vācita, *s.* Reading.

ವಾಚೌಲೆ vāčoule, *s.* Talkativeness, loquacity.

ವಾಚ್ಯ vācya, *adj.* Fit to be uttered. 2. *see* ವಾಕ್ಯ. ಅ— improper to be spoken.

ವಾಜ vāja, *s.* Speed, haste, swiftness.

ವಾಜಬಿ, ವಾಜ್ಮಿ vājabi, vājmi, *adj.* Reasonable, proper, right, just. —ಕ್ರಯ reasonable price. —ಪಾತೆರ a proper, true word.

ವಾಟ vāṭa, *see* ಓಟ.

ವಾಟೆಪುಳಿ vāṭepuḷi, *see* ಓಂಟೆಪುಳಿ.

ವಾಡಿಕೆ, ವಾಡಿಗೆ vāḍikè, vāḍigè, *s.* Custom, usage, practice.

ವಾತ vāta, *s.* Rheumatism; gout, arthritis. 2. *see* ವಾಯು. ಗಂಟಿ—, ಸಂದ— gout; swelling of the joints. ಪಕ್ಷ— paralysis. ಸಂಧಿ— inflammation of the joints. —ಆಪಿನಿ to suffer from rheumatism.

ವಾತ್ಸಲ್ಯ vātsalya, *s.* Parental affection, love, tenderness; sympathy. 2. home-sickness.

ವಾದ್ vādu, *s.* Way, road.

ವಾದ್, ವಾದ vādu, vāda, *s.* A dissertation, discourse, dispute, contention, discussion. —ಮಳ್ಪುನಿ to discuss, dispute.

ವಾದಿ vādi, *s.* A plaintiff. ಪ್ರತಿ— a defendant, respondant.

ವಾದಿಕೆ vādikè, *see* ವಾದ್.

ವಾದಿಪುನಿ, ವಾದಿಸುನಿ vadipuni, vādisuni (ವಾದಿ, ವಾದಿಸ್), *v. n.* To argue, discuss, dispute.

ವಾದ್ಯ vādya, *s.* Instrumental music. 2. any musical instrument. —ದಾಯೆ a musician. ಕೊಂಬು— a wind-instrument. —ಮಳ್ಪುನಿ to play on a musical instrument.

ವಾನಪ್ರಸ್ಥೆ vānaprasthe, *s.* A hermit, anchorite.

ವಾನರೆ vānare, *s.* An ape *or* monkey.

ವಾಪಾಸ್ vāpāsu, *adv.* Again, behind, back, returning. *s.* Return. —ಮಳ್ಪುನಿ to return, give back.

ವಾಮನೆ vāmane, *s.* A dwarf. ವಾಮನವತಾರ the fifth incarnation of Vishṇu.

ವಾಯವ್ಯ vāyavya, *s.* The north-west quarter. *adj.* Relating to the wind.

ವಾಯಿ vāyi, *s.* Flatulence, windiness. 2. gout, rheumatism. 3. *see* ವಾಯು.

ವಾಯಿದ, ವಾಯಿದೆ **vāyida, vāyidè,** *s.* An instalment, term of payment.

ವಾಯಿಲಾಂಗ್, ವಾಯಿವಿಲಂಗ **vāyilāṅgụ, vāyivilaṅga,** *s.* The seeds of *Erycibe paniculata.*

ವಾಯು **vāyu,** *s.* Wind, air. 2. *see* ವಾಯಿ.

ವಾರ್ **vārụ,** *s.* Auction. 2. a rod, yard. –ಗ್ ಪಾಡುನಿ, –ಲೆಪ್ಪುನಿ to put to auction.

ವಾರ **vāra,** *s.* A time. ಇರ್ವಾರ twice; ಒರ್ವಾರ once.

ವಾರ **vāra,** *s.* A week day. 2. a week. ಆದಿತ್ಯ–, ಐತ್ವಾರ, ಐತಾರ Sunday; ಸೋಮ–, ಸೋಮಾರ Monday; ಅಂಗಾರೆ Tuesday; ಬುಧ–, ಬುದಾರ Wednesday; ಗುರು– Thursday; ಶುಕ್ರ–, ಸುಕ್ರಾರ Friday; ಶನಿ–, ಸನಿಯಾರ Saturday. ವಾ– on what day? ಈ ವಾರೊಡು ಆಪುಜಿ it cannot be this week. ವಾರೊಡ್ದು ವಾರ from week to week.

ವಾರಂಟ್ **vāraṇṭụ,** *s.* A warrant to seize an offender, goods, *etc.*

ವಾರಟೆ **vāraṭè,** *see* ಹರಟೆ.

ವಾರಿಸ್ **vārisụ,** *s.* Heirship, ownership; a claim. –ಶಾರೆ, –ದಾರೆ an heir, proprietor, owner, claimant.

ವಾರು **vāru,** *see* ವಾರ್.

ವಾರೆ **vārè,** *see* ಓರೆ.

ವಾರ್ಜಿಕ ವಾರ್ಜಿಗೆ **vārjika, vārjigè,** *s.* Haggling, chaffering, higgling, as in a bargain. –ಮಳ್ಪುನಿ to haggle.

ವಾರ್ಜಿತ **vārjita,** *see* ವರ್ಜಿತ.

ವಾರ್ತೆ **vārtè,** *s.* Tidings, news. ಶುಭ– good news, gospel.

ವಾಲಗ **vālaga,** *see* ಓಲಗ.

ವಾಲೆ **vālè,** *see* ಓಲೆ.

ವಾಲೆಮಣಂಗ್ **vālemaṇaṅgụ,** *see* ಓಲೆಮಣಂಗ್.

ವಾಲೈಸುನಿ **vāleisuni** (ವಾಲೈಸ್), *v. a.* To do homage. 2. to serve.

ವಾಲ್ಮೀಕಿ **vālmīki,** *s.* A sage, the author of Rāmāyaṇa.

ವಾವಾ **vāvā,** *see under* ವಾ.

ವಾಶಿ **vāśi,** *adj.* Improved, better, either in health *or* quality; preferable. *s.* Health, recovering. 2. preference. 3. fame. 4. *an affix added to words denoting fractions, as a mere expletive; as,* ಅರೆ– half; ಕಾಲ್– one-fourth. ಕೈತ– virtue of the hand; skill. ತಟ್ಟೆ– unequal balances. ನಾಲಯಿದ–, *see under* ನಾಲಯಿ. –ಆಪಿನಿ to be cured. –ಮಳ್ಪುನಿ to cure. ಐಡ್ದಲಾ ಉಂದು ವಾಶಿ this is preferable to that.

ವಾಸ, ವಾಸತೆ **vāsa, vāsatè,** *s.* An abode, dwelling, habitation. –ಮಳ್ಪುನಿ to dwell, abide.

ವಾಸನೆ **vāsanè,** *s.* Scent, smell, odour. ದುರ್– a stench, disagreeable smell. ಸು– a good smell, fragrance.

ವಾಸುದೇವೆ **vāsudēve,** *s.* A name of Kṛushṇa. 2. a proper name.

ವಾಸಿ **vāsi,** *s.* An inhabitant. 2. *see* ವಾಶಿ.

ವಾಸಿಪುನಿ, ವಾಸಿಸುನಿ vāsipuni, vāsisuni (ವಾಸಿಸ್), *v. a.* To dwell, reside.

ವಾಸ್ತವ್ಯ vāstavya, *s.* Dwelling, residence. –ಮಳ್ಪುನಿ to dwell.

ವಾಹನ vāhana, *s.* A conveyance, vehicle, chariot, waggon.

ವಾಹ್ವಾ vāhvā, *intj.* of approbation. –ಪಣ್ಪುನಿ to applaud.

ವಾಳ, ವಾಳೆ, ವಾಳ್ಯ vāḷa, vāḷè, vāḷya, *s.* A protuberance, swelling. 2. a bubo produced by venereal affection; *also* ತುಡೆವಳೆ, ತೊಡೆಬಾಳೆ.

ವಾಕ್ಷ vāksha, *see* ವಾಕ್ಯ.

ವಿಂಗಡ viṅgaḍa, *s.* Separation, parting. *adj.* Separate, distinct, apart. –ಮಳ್ಪುನಿ, ವಿಂಗಡಿಪುನಿ to separate, divide, set apart.

ವಿಂಧ್ಯ vindhya, *s.* A range of mountains so called.

ವಿಕಟ vikaṭa, *adj.* Terrific, awful, frightful. 2. austere, severe. –ರೂಪು a frightful form.

ವಿಕಲ್ಪ vikalpa, *s.* Doubt, indecision. 2. alternative. 3. offence, displeasure. –ಬರ್ಪಿನಿ to disagree, be at variance.

ವಿಕಾರ vikāra, *s.* Transformation, alteration, change. 2. sickness. *adj.* Ugly. 2. unnatural. –ಗುಣ an unnatural disposition. –ನರಮಾನಿ an ugly man.

ವಿಕಾರಿ vikāri, *s.* The twenty-third year in the Hindu cycle of sixty.

ವಿಕಾಸ vikāsa, *s.* Expansion; *cf.* ವಿಶಾಲ.

ವಿಕೀರ್ಣ vikīrṇa, *adj.* Scattered, diffused, spread about. 2. dissolved.

ವಿಕೃತ vikruta, *adj.* Changed. 2. ugly.

ವಿಕೃತಿ vikruti, *s.* The twenty-fourth year in the Hindu cycle of sixty. 2. change. *adj.* Wicked.

ವಿಕ್ರಮ vikrama, *s.* Heroism, valour, strength. 2. the fourteenth year in the Hindu cycle of sixty.

ವಿಕ್ರಮಾದಿತ್ಯೆ, ವಿಕ್ರಮಾರ್ಕೆ vikramāditye, vikramārke, *s.* A celebrated sovereign.

ವಿಕ್ರಯ vikraya, *s.* Selling, vending.

ವಿಗಡ vigaḍa, *adj.* Terriffic, severe. 2. opposed, contrary.

ವಿಗ್ರಹ vigraha, *s.* An idol, image. –ಆರಾಧಕೆ, ವಿಗ್ರಹಾರಾಧಕೆ an idolator. –ಆರಾಧನೆ, ವಿಗ್ರಹಾರಾಧನೆ idolatry.

ವಿಘಳಿಗೆ vighaligè, *s.* The sixtieth part of a ಘಳಿಗೆ.

ವಿಘಾತ vighāta, *s.* A hinderance, obstacle; a prohibition.

ವಿಘ್ನ vighna, *s.* An impediment, obstacle.

ವಿಘ್ನೇಶ್ವರೆ vighnēšvare, *s.* Gaṇēša, the remover of obstacles.

ವಿಚಕ್ಷಣ viċakshaṇa, *adj.* Clever, able, wise. ವಿಚಕ್ಷಣೆ a clever man.

ವಿಚಾರ vičāra, *s.* Investigation, consideration, judging. 2. solicitude, anxiety. –ಮಳ್ಪುನಿ to investigate. ವಿಚಾರೊಡು ಉಪ್ಪುನಿ to be solicitous.

ವಿಚಾರ, ವಿಚಾರಣೆ vičāra, vičāraṇè, *s.* Investigation, examination, inquiry. 2. consideration, thought. 3. superintendence, management; *also* ಮೇಲ್ವಿಚಾರ. –ಮಳ್ಪುನಿ to examine; to superintend; to inquire.

ವಿಚಾರಿಪುನಿ vičāripuni (ವಿಚಾರಿ), *v. a.* To investigate, examine, inquire.

ವಿಚಿತ್ರ vičitra, *s.* A curiosity, wonderful thing. *adj.* Beautiful, wonderful, variegated, curious. –ಕೆಲಸ a wonderful act *or* workmanship. –ರೂಪ a beautiful form.

ವಿಚೀರ್ಣ, ವಿಚ್ಚೀರ್ಣ vičīrṇa, viččirṇa, *s.* Agreeableness. *adj.* Pleasant, beautiful. 2. wonderful.

ವಿಜಯ vijaya, *s.* Victory, conquest, triumph. 2. the twenty-seventh year in the Hindu cycle of sixty. –ನಗರ Bijāpur.

ವಿಜಾರ್ vijārụ, *s.* Trowsers.

ವಿಜ್ಞಾಪನೆ vijṅāpanè, *s.* A petition, application, solicitation. –ಮಳ್ಪುನಿ to solicit, request.

ವಿಟ viṭa, *s.* Whoredom, lewdness, gallantry. –ಪುರುಷೆ a gallant, seducer, lewd man; a fop.

ವಿಡಂಬನೆ viḍambanè, *s.* Mimicry, mockery. 2. affecting.

ವಿಡೂರ, ವಿಡ್ಡೂರ viḍūra, viḍḍūra, *s.* Hinderance, obstacle.

ವಿತಲ vitala, *s.* The second world below the earth.

ವಿತ್ತ vitta, *s.* Substance, property, wealth.

ವಿತ್ಯಾಸ vityāsa, *see* ವ್ಯತ್ಯಾಸ.

ವಿದಾನ vidāna, *see* ವಿಧಾನ.

ವಿದಾರಣ, ವಿದಾರಣೆ vidāraṇa, vidāraṇè, *s.* Tearing, breaking, rending, splitting.

ವಿದ್ಯ vidya, *s.* Learning, science, knowledge. 2. an art. 3. juggling. ಧನುರ್– archery. ಶಸ್ತ್ರ– the art of using arms. ಶಿಲ್ಪ– sculpture, architecture. –ಕಲ್ಪಾವುನಿ to impart knowledge. –ಕಲ್ಪುನಿ to acquire knowledge.

ವಿದ್ಯಮಾನ vidyamāna, *s.* Circumstances, situation, condition.

ವಿದ್ಯವಂತೆ vidyavante, *see* ವಿದ್ಯಾವಂತೆ.

ವಿದ್ಯಾಧರೆ vidyādhare, *s.* A demi-god so called.

ವಿದ್ಯಾಭ್ಯಾಸ vidyābhyāsa, *s.* Study, learning.

ವಿದ್ಯಾರ್ಥಿ vidyārthi, *s.* A student.

ವಿದ್ಯಾವಂತೆ vidyāvante, *s.* A learned man. 2. a skilful man.

ವಿದ್ಯಾಶಾಲೆ vidyāśālè, *s.* An academy, school.

ವಿದ್ಯೆ vidyè, *see* ವಿದ್ಯ.

ವಿದ್ವಾಂಸೆ vidvāṁse, *s.* A learned man, philosopher.

ವಿಧ vidha, *s.* Form, formula, rule. 2. manner, kind, sort. —ವಿಧ various, of different sorts.

ವಿಧವೆ vidhavè, *s.* A widow.

ವಿಧಾನ vidhāna, *s.* Rule, precept. 2. form, mode, manner.

ವಿಧಿ vidhi, *s.* Fate, luck, destiny. 2. rule, precept, formula. 3. text. 4. order, command. 5. the imperative mood, *gram.*

ವಿಧುರ vidhura, *s.* Separation. *adj.* Confused.

ವಿಧುರೆ vidhure, *s.* A widower.

ವಿಧೇಯ vidhēya, *adj.* Obedient, pliant, tractable. —ತೆ, —ತ್ವ obedience, submission. —ಆ ದುತ್ತುನಿ to be obedient.

ವಿನಂತಿ vinanti, *s.* Petition, request.

ವಿನಯ vinaya, *s.* Modesty, affability, humility, mildness. 2. reverence, obeisance. 3. decorum. 4. *see* ವಿನಹ. —ದ ಪಾ ತೆರ speaking modestly. —ಪೂರ್ವ ಕ reverently, respectfully.

ವಿನಹಾ, ವಿನಾ vinahā, vinā, *adv.* Without, except.

ವಿನಾಯಕೆ vināyake, *s.* Gaṇēša. ವಿನಾಯಕಚೌತಿ a feast on the fourth day of the sixth lunar month, in commemoration of Gaṇēša's going to call his mother Pārvati.

ವಿನಾಯಿಸುನಿ vināyisuni (ವಿನಾಯಿಸ್), *v. a.* To except, exempt, exclude.

ವಿನಾಶ vināša, *s.* Destruction, annihilation, ruin. 2. loss.

ವಿನಿಯೋಗ viniyōga, *s.* Sharing any thing sacred. 2. appropriation, as of money, *etc.*, for any purpose. 3. giving or parting with any thing. —ಮಾ ಡು to divide, share, distribute.

ವಿನೋದ vinōda, *s.* Sport, play, pastime.

ವಿಪತ್ತ್, ವಿಪತ್ತು vipattụ, vipattu, *s.* Calamity, distress, adversity, danger.

ವಿಪರೀತ viparīta, *adj.* Contrary, reverse, perverse, opposite. —ಕೆಲಸ an unusual *or* improper act. —ಸಂಗತಿ an unusual event *or* circumstance.

ವಿಪ್ರೆ vipre, *s.* A Brahman.

ವಿಭಕ್ತ vibhakta, *adj.* Divided, apportioned. 2. parted, separated. ಅ— undivided.

ವಿಭಕ್ತಿ vibhakti, *s.* The inflection *or* case of a noun. ಪ್ರಥಮ— the nominative case.

ವಿಭಕ್ತೆ vibhakte, *s.* A divided member of a family.

ವಿಭವ vibhava, *s.* Property, substance. 2. magnanimity. 3. display, pomp. 4. the second year in the Hindu cycle of sixty.

ವಿಭಾಗ vibhāga, *s.* Part, share, portion. —ಮಳ್ಪುನಿ, ವಿಭಾಗಿಸುನಿ to divide, share, distribute.

ವಿಭೂತಿ vibhūti, *s.* Sacred ashes with which the followers of

Šiva smear themselves. 2. superhuman power. 3. divine grace, manifestation, glory.

ವಿಮರ್ಶೆ **vimaršè,** *s.* Investigation, inquiry. ಪುನರ್— review, as of a decree.

ವಿಮಾನ **vimāna,** *s.* A kind of air balloon *or* car, self-directed and self-moving. 2. a chariot of the gods.

ವಿಮುಕ್ತಿ **vimukti,** *s.* Liberation, final emancipation from future births.

ವಿಮೋಚನೆ **vimōčanè,** *s.* Pardoning, absolving, cancelling. 2. releasing, quitting. 3. redemption, liberation. —ಮಳ್ಪುನಿ, ವಿಮೋಚಿಸುನಿ to pardon, release, absolve; to deliver.

ವಿಯೋಗ **viyōga,** *s.* Separation, disunion. 2. bereavement, loss. 3. subtraction.

ವಿರಹಿತ **virahita,** *adj.* Left, abandoned, diverted. —ಮಳ್ಪುನಿ to exclude, discard.

ವಿರಾಗ **virāga,** *s.* Disregard of all carnal enjoyments, absence of passion.

ವಿರುದ್ಧ **viruddha,** *adj.* Opposed, hindered; contrary, opposite.

ವಿರೂಪ **virūpa,** *adj.* Deformed, ugly.

ವಿರೂಪಾಕ್ಷೆ **virūpākshe,** *s.* Šiva, having an unusual eye in the centre of his forehead.

ವಿರೇಚನೆ **virēčanè,** *s.* Purging; evacuation; *also* ವಿರೋಚನೆ.

ವಿರೋಧ **virōdha,** *s.* Animosity, opposition, contradiction. 2. prevention, hinderance. —ಗಾರೆ, —ಬಾಯಿ, *see* ವಿರೋಧಿ. —ಅದ್ ಪಾತೆರುನಿ to speak against. —ಮಳ್ಪುನಿ, ವಿರೋಧಿಸುನಿ to oppose.

ವಿರೋಧಿ **virōdhi,** *s.* An opponent, adversary, enemy. 2. the twenty-third year in the Hindu cycle of sixty.

ವಿರೋಧಿಕೃತು **virōdhikrutu,** *s.* The forty-fifth year in the Hindu cycle of sixty.

ವಿಲಂಬ **vilamba,** *see* ವಿಳಂಬ.

ವಿಲಂಬಿ **vilambi,** *s.* The thirty-second year in the Hindu cycle of sixty.

ವಿಲಯತಿ, ವಿಲಾಯತಿ **vilayati, vilāyati,** *s.* Europe. *adj.* European. —ಸುಂಣ chalk.

ವಿಲಕ್ಷಣ **vilakshaṇa,** *adj.* Extraordinary, unprecedented, peculiar.

ವಿಲಾಸ್ **vilāsu,** *s.* Superscription, mark *or* direction. 2. the price of a cloth, *etc.*, marked on it. ಮೇಲ್— the address of a letter.

ವಿಲಾಸ **vilāsa,** *s.* Sport, pastime. 2. dalliance, wantonness, coquetry.

ವಿಲೆ, ವಿಲೆವಾರಿ **vilè, vilevāri,** *s.* Distribution, apportioning, arranging.

ವಿವರ, ವಿವರಣೆ **vivara, vivaraṇè,** *s.* Explanation, particulars, detail. 2. circumstances, matter, affair.

ವಿವರಿಪುನಿ vivaripuni (ವಿವರಿ), *v. a.* To explain at large; to describe distinctly.

ವಿವಾಕ vivâka, *see* ವಿವೇಕ.

ವಿವಾದ vivāda, *s.* Dispute, quarrel, law-suit.

ವಿವಾಹ vivāha, *s.* A wedding, marriage, matrimony.

ವಿವಿಧ vividha, *adj.* Diverse, various.

ವಿವೇಕ vivēka, *s.* Judgment, discernment, discrimination. 2. reconciliation. –ಆಪಿನಿ to be reconciled. –ಮಳ್ಪುನಿ to reconcile.

ವಿವೇಕಿ vivēki, *s.* A sensible man.

ವಿಶ viša, *see* ವಿಷ.

ವಿಶಯ višaya, *see* ವಿಷಯ.

ವಿಶಾಖೆ višākhè, *s.* The sixteenth lunar mansion.

ವಿಶಾಲ višāla, *s.* Diffusion, extension. 2. the firmament. *adj.* Wide, roomy, capacious, spacious.

ವಿಶಿಷ್ಟ višishṭa, *adj.* All.

ವಿಶು višu, *see* ವಿಷು.

ವಿಶುದ್ಧ višuddha, *adj.* Pure, clean. 2. pious, virtuous.

ವಿಶೇಷ višēsha, *s.* Sort, kind, manner. 2. distinction, difference. 3. eminence. 4. any thing unusual. *adj.* Distinct, different. 2. unusual, extraordinary. 3. much, great. –ದಿನ a festive day. –ಬುದ್ಧಿ superior talents. –ಸಂಗತಿ an extraordinary affair, something unusual. –ಮಳ್ಪುನಿ to distinguish; to make much of.

ವಿಶೇಷಣ višēshaṇa, *s.* An attribute *or* adjective. 2. distinguishing, discriminating. ಕ್ರಿಯಾ– an adverb.

ವಿಶ್ರಮ višrama, *s.* Repose, rest.

ವಿಶ್ರಮಿಪುನಿ, ವಿಶ್ರಮಿಸುನಿ višramipuni, višramisuni (ವಿಶ್ರಮಿ, ವಿಶ್ರಮಿಸ್), *v. n.* To rest, repose.

ವಿಶ್ರಾಂತಿ višrānti, *s.* Repose, rest. –ಮಳ್ಪುನಿ to repose, rest.

ವಿಶ್ವ višva, *s.* The world, universe; all. –ನಾಥೆ Lord of the world; Šiva; a proper name.

ವಿಶ್ವಾಮಿತ್ರೆ višvāmitre, *s.* A monarch who became a Brahmarushi.

ವಿಶ್ವಾವಸು višvāvasu, *s.* The thirty-ninth year in the Hindu cycle of sixty.

ವಿಶ್ವಾಸ višvâsa, *s.* Faith, confidence, belief. 2. kindness, intimacy, favour. –ಘಾತಕೆ a betrayer of trust or confidence.

ವಿಶ್ವಾಸಿಸುನಿ višvāsisuni (ವಿಶ್ವಾಸಿಸ್), *v. a.* To believe, trust.

ವಿಶ್ವೆ višve, *s.* The heavenly architect.

ವಿಷ visha, *s.* Poison, venom. –ಕಲ್ಲ್ a famous remedy for snake-bite. –ಜಂತು a poisonous creature. –ಮುಂಗುಲಿ the shrub *Crinum deflexum.* –ಮೂಲಿ a kind of water-lily. ಕೈ–, *see* ಕೈಮಾಸ್. –ಪಾಡುನಿ to poison.

ವಿಷಮ vishama, *adj.* Odd (in numbers). 2. uneven, rough. 3. painful, difficult, troublesome.

ವಿಷಯ vishaya, *s.* Any object of sense, any thing perceived by the sense; any object in general. 2. reference, relation, as to a person, place, *etc.* 3. the topic *or* subject of a discourse, *etc.* 4. *semen virile.* *postps.* Respecting, regarding. ಈ ವಿಷಯೊಡು in this respect. ವಾ ವಿಷಯೊಡು in what respect? on what subject? ಆ ವಿಷಯ ಎಂಕ್ ಗೊತ್ತಿಜ್ಜಿ I am ignorant of that subject. ವಿಷಯಾತುರ uxorious. ವಿಷಯಾಸಕ್ತಿ inordinate devotion to women; lewdness.

ವಿಷು vishu, *s.* The fifteenth year in the Hindu cycle of sixty. 2. the vernal equinox; the feast observed on that day.

ವಿಷ್ಣು vishṇu, *s.* The second of the Hindu triad.

ವಿಷ್ಣುಕ್ರಾಂತಿ vishṇukrānti, *s.* The plant *Evolvulus alsinoides*, used as a decoction in fevers.

ವಿಸ visa, *see* ವಿಷ.

ವಿಸರ್ಗ visarga, *s.* The soft aspirate ಃ.

ವಿಸರ್ಜನೆ visarjanè, *s.* Quitting, relinquishing; dismissing.

ವಿಸರ್ಜಿಸುನಿ visarjisuni (ವಿಸರ್ಜಿಸ್), *v. a.* To relinquish, abandon.

ವಿಸೇಸ visēsa, *see* ವಿಶೇಷ.

ವಿಸ್ತರಿಪುನಿ vistaripuni (ವಿಸ್ತರಿ), *v. a.* To make prolix; to diffuse, publish.

ವಿಸ್ತಾರ vistāra, *s.* Diffusion, extension. 2. abundance, plenty. 3. prolixity. –ಆಪಿನಿ to become diffused, spread abroad; to extend, expand, dilate; to transpire, become public. –ಮಲ್ಪುನಿ, *see* ವಿಸ್ತರಿಪುನಿ.

ವಿಸ್ತೀರ್ಣ vistīrṇa, *adj.* Spread, extended, expanded. 2. large, great. *s.* Area, space, extent.

ವಿಸ್ಮಯ vismaya, *s.* Wonder, surprise. –ಆಪಿನಿ to be surprised.

ವಿಸ್ಮೃತಿ vismṛuti, *s.* Forgetfulness.

ವಿಹಿತ vihita, *adj.* Friendly, amiable. 2. fit, proper. 3. true, certain. –ಸಂಗತಿ a fact. –ಮಾರ್ಗ a friendly *or* proper manner.

ವಿಳಂಬ viḷamba, *s.* Slowness, tardiness; delay, procrastination.

ವಿಳಂಬಿ viḷambi, *see* ವಿಲಂಬಿ.

ವಿಳಾಸ viḷāsa, *see* ವಿಲಾಸ್.

ವೀಣೆ vīṇè, *s.* The Indian lute.

ವೀರ vīra, *adj.* Brave, valiant, strong, powerful. –ತನ, –ತ್ವ heroism, bravery.

ವೀರಭದ್ರೆ vīrabhadre, *s.* One of Śiva's attendants.

ವೀರೆ vīre, *s.* A hero, champion, warrior, brave man. ವೀರಧ್ವೀರೆ, ವೀರಾಧ್ವೀರೆ a great hero, very brave man.

ವೀರ್ಯ **vīrya**, *s.* Heroism. 2. strength, vigour. 3. fortitude, firmness. 4. *semen virile.*

ವೀಸ್, ವೀಸ **vīsụ, vīsa**, *s.* A sixteenth. 2. a weight of gold equal to a grain of rice.

ವೀಳೆ, ವೀಳ್ಯ **vīḷè, vīḷya**, *s.* The betel leaf.

ವು, ವೂ **u, ū**, *For words beginning with these letters see under* ಉ, ಊ.

ವೃಂದಾವನ **vrụndāvana**, *s.* A basin round the purple stalked basil, sacred to Vishṇu. 2. the shrine *or* tomb of a spiritual guide.

ವೃತ **vrụta**, *see* ವ್ರತ.

ವೃತ್ತ **vrụtta**, *s.* Verse, metre.

ವೃತ್ತಾಂತ **vrụttānta**, *s.* News, intelligence, tidings. 2. an event, occurrence.

ವೃತ್ತಿ **vrụtti**, *s.* Livelihood, profession, occupation.

ವೃಥಾ **vrụthā**, *adj.* Useless, fruitless. 2. incorrect. *adv.* In vain.

ವೃದ್ಧ **vrụddha**, *adj.* Old, aged, ancient. 2. wise, learned.

ವೃದ್ಧಾಪ್ಯ **vrụddhāpya**, *s.* Old age.

ವೃದ್ಧಿ **vrụddhi**, *s.* Enlargement, increase, augmentation, extension. 2. prosperity, success.

ವೃದ್ಧೆ **vrụddhe**, *s.* An old man; an experienced man.

ವೃಯ **vrụya**, *see* ವ್ರಯ.

ವೃಶ್ಚಿಕ **vrụščika**, *s.* A scorpion. 2. the sign *Scorpio*; the eighth solar month when the sun is in *Scorpio.*

ವೃಷಭ **vrụshabha**, *s.* A bull. 2. the sign *Taurus*; the second solar month when the sun is in *Taurus.*

ವೃಷ್ಟಿ **vrụshṭi**, *s.* Rain. ಅನಾ– drought. ಕನಕ– a shower of gold; a good shower of rain. ಪುಷ್ಪ– a shower of flowers.

ವೃಕ್ಷ **vrụksha**, *s.* A tree.

ವೆಂಕಟಗಿರಿ **veṅkaṭagiri**, *s.* The sacred hill of Tirupati.

ವೆಂಕಟರಮಣೆ **veṅkaṭaramaṇe**, *s.* Vishṇu worshipped at Tirupati, *etc.*, under this designation.

ವೆಚ್ಚ **večča**, *s.* Expenditure, expense. ಆದಾಯ– income and expense.

ವೆಜ್ಜ, ವೆಝ್ಝ **vejja, vejhjha**, *see* ಎಜ್ಜ.

ವೆತ್ಯಾಸ **vetyāsa**, *see* ವ್ಯತ್ಯಾಸ.

ವೆಥೆ **vethè**, *see* ವ್ಯಥೆ.

ವೆದ್ದೆ **veddè**, *adj.* Moist, wet.

ವೆರ್ತ **verta**, *see* ವ್ಯರ್ಥ.

ವೇಗ **vēga**, *s.* Speed, velocity, quickness. *adj.* Quick, speedy.

ವೇಜ್ಯ **vējya**, *see* ವ್ಯಾಜ್ಯ.

ವೇದ **vēda**, *s.* The principal sacred writings of the Hindus, which are four in number, namely, ಋಗ್ವೇದ, ಯಜುರ್ವೇದ, ಸಾಮವೇದ, and ಅಥರ್ವಣವೇದ. ಉಪ– supplementary Vēdas. ಸತ್ಯ– the true Vēda, the Bible.

ವೇದನೆ, ವೇಧನೆ vēdanè, vēdhanè, *s* Pain, agony, distress. 2. sensation, perception.

ವೇದಾಂಗ vēdānga, *s.* A subordinate part of the Vēdas.

ವೇದಾಂತ vēdānta, *s.* The Upanishads *or* theological part of the Vēdas.

ವೇದಾಂತಿ vēdānti, *s.* An adherent to the Vēdānta system.

ವೇದಿ, ವೇದಿಕೆ vēdi, vēdikè, *s.* A raised floor, especially one used as an altar. 2. a pulpit.

ವೇಲೆ vēlè, *see* ವೇಳೆ.

ವೇಶ್ಯಾಸ್ತ್ರೀ, ವೇಶ್ಯೆ vēšyāstrī, vēšyè, *s.* A professional dancing girl, prostitute, harlot.

ವೇಷ, ವೇಸ vēsha, vēsa, *s.* A mask, disguise. 2. ornament, dress, decoration. —ಪಾಡುನಿ to disguise one's self.

ವೇಷ್ಟಿ vēshṭi, *see* ಯೇಷ್ಟಿ.

ವೇಳೆ, ವೇಳ್ಯ vēḷè, vēḷya, *s.* Time, period, opportunity.

ವೈ vei, *see* ಪೊೖ.

ವೈಕ್ veikụ (*dat. of* ವಾ), *pron.* For what?

ವೈಕುಂಠ veikuṇṭha, *s.* The paradise of Vishṇu.

ವೈಚರ್ veičarụ, *see* ಬೈಚೆರ್.

ವೈಜಯಂತಿ veiǰayanti, *s.* The garland of Vishṇu. 2. a flag.

ವೈಡೂರ್ಯ, ವೈಢೂರ್ಯ veiḍūrya, veiḍhūrya, *s.* A gem of a fine azure-blue colour, *Lapis lazuli*, beryl.

ವೈದಿಕ veidika, *adj.* Conformable to the Vēdas; scriptural. 2. spiritual.

ವೈದಿಕೆ veidike, *s.* A Brahman well versed in the Vēdas. 2. a priest. 3. a doctor of law.

ವೈದ್ಯ veidya, *s.* The science of medicine; *also* ವೈದ್ಯಶಾಸ್ತ್ರ. 2. medical aid, advice *or* prescription. —ಬೆಪ್ಪುನಿ to give medicine.

ವೈದ್ಯೆ veidye, *s.* A physician; *also* ವೈದ್ಯದಾಯಿ.

ವೈಧವ್ಯ veidhavya, *s.* Widowhood.

ವೈನ್ veinụ, *see* ವಾ.

ವೈನ veina, *see* ವಯನ.

ವೈಪ, ವೈಪು veipa, veipu, *s.* Elongation, enlargement, growing long. —ಗಂಟಿ a loop, noose. —ನೂಲು a waist cord.

ವೈಪುನಿ veipuni, *see* ಬಯಿಪುನಿ.

ವೈಭವ, ವೈಭೋಗ veibhava, veibhōga, *s.* Happiness, enjoyment. 2. wealth, riches. 3. majesty, glory. —ಮಳ್ಪುನಿ to enjoy.

ವೈಮನಸ್ veimanasụ, *s.* Sadness, dislike, sorrow, disinclination, offence.

ವೈಮಾಲೆ veimālè, *s.* Fiction, invention. 2. *see* ಬಯಿಮಾಲೆ. *adj.* Fictitious, invented. —ಪಾಡೆರು ನಿ to invent a story.

ವೈಮಾಳಿಗೆ veimāḷigè, *s.* An open upstair room.

ವೈಮೆ veimè, *s.* Straightness, fitness, rectitude. 2. *see* ಪೊಂಯಿಮೆ. —ಮರ a straight tree.

ವೈಯಪುರೆ, ವೈಯಾಪುರೆ veiyapurè, veiyāpurè, *s.* A temporary roof. –ಕಟ್ಟುನಿ to build a temporary roof.

ವೈಯಾರ veiyāra, *see* ಒಯ್ಯಾರ.

ವೈಯಿ veiyi, *see* ವೈ.

ವೈರ, ವೈರತ್ವ veira, veiratva, *s.* Enmity, hostility, natural antipathy. –ಮಳ್ಪುನಿ to hate.

ವೈರಾಗಿ veirāgi, *s.* An ascetic, devotee, mendicant.

ವೈರಾಗ್ಯ veirāgya, *s.* The absence of worldly passion *or* desire, want of affection, self-renunciation.

ವೈರಿ veiri, *s.* An enemy, adversary, foe. ಷಡ್ವೈರಿಲು six properties of fallen humanity, namely, ಕಾಮ lust, ಕ್ರೋಧ anger, ಲೋಭ avarice, ಮೋಹ love, ಮದ pride, and ಮತ್ಸರ envy, hatred.

ವೈಲ್ veilų, *s.* A whirlpool, eddy; a strong current of water.

ವೈಲತ್ veilatų, *s.* Danger, difficulty.

ವೈಶಾಖ veiṡākha, *s.* The second lunar month. 2. mid-summer.

ವೈಶ್ಯ veiṡya, *s.* The agricultural and mercantile tribe. ವೈಶ್ಯೆ a man of such a tribe.

ವೈಷಮ್ಯ veishamya, *s.* Inequality, unevenness. 2. prejudice, bias, prepossession. –ಮಳ್ಪುನಿ to be biassed.

ವೈಷ್ಣವೆ veishṇave, *s.* A follower of Vishṇu.

ವೈಸ್‌ಲ್ veisųlų, *see* ಒಶೀಲ್.

ವೈಸಲ್ಮೆ veisalmè, *s.* Partiality; favouritism; bias, prepossession.

ವೈಸಾಣ್ veisāṇų, *s.* Acceptation, taking charge of.

ವೈಸುನಿ, ವೈಸೊಣುನಿ veisuni, veisoṇuni. (ವೈಸ್, ವೈಸೊ), *v. a.* To sustain, support, bear. 2. to take charge *or* responsibility of.

ವೊ, ವೋ vo, vō, *For words beginning with these letters, not found here, see under* ಉ, ಒ, ಓ.

ವೊಟ್ವಸ್ voṭvasų, *s.* Whitewash. –ಕೊರ್ಪುನಿ to whitewash.

ವೊಡುಂಗೆಲುನಿ voḍuṅgeluni (ವೊಡುಂಗೆಲ್), *v. n.* To fade, wither.

ವೊಡ್ಡು voḍḍu, *s.* Obstinacy, stubbornness. –ವರಂಟೆ ಮಳ್ಪುನಿ to importunate obstinately.

ವೊಯಿಪುನಿ voyipuni, *see* ಒಯಿಪುನಿ.

ವೊಯಿಮೆ voyimè, *s.* Artful, skillful, dexterous. 3. *see* ವೈಮೆ. –ದ ಪಾತೆರ speaking artfully.

ವೊಯಿಸ್‌ಲ್ voyisųlų, *see* ಒಶೀಲ್.

ವೊಯ್ಯಕೈಯ್ಯ voyyakeiyya, *s.* Struggle, wrangling.

ವೊರ vora, *see* ಒರ.

ವೊರಟುನಿ voraṭuni, *see* ಒರಟುನಿ.

ವೊರತೆ voratè, *s.* Source, spring, fountain.

ವೊರಾತ vorāta, *see* ಒರತ.

ವೊರಿಯಾಕರಿಯಾ voriyākariyā, *s.* A precarious condition. *adj.* Precarious, critical, uncertain.

ವೊರುಂಕು voruṅku, *see* ಒುಂಕುರ್.

ವೊರುವ, ವೊರುವೆ voruva, voruvė, *see* ಒುರ್ದ್.

ವೊರೆಟುನಿ voreṭuni (ವೊರೆಟ), *v. n.* To stick in the mire, as a wheel; to clog. 2. to be in a strait. 3. *see* ಒರಟುನಿ.

ವೊರೋಣೆ vorōṇė, *adv.* At once; *cf.* ಒರ.

ವೊರ್ಕಡಿ vorkaḍi, *see* ಒರ್ಕಡಿ. 2. *see* ಒುರ್ಗೆ.

ವೊಲುಮೆ volumė, *see* ಒಲುಮೆ. 2. *see* ಜೋಲುವೆ.

ವೋಕುಳಿ vōkuḷi, *see* ಓಕಳಿ.

ವೋಡುರಿಮಾಡ vōḍurimāḍa, *s.* A very small demon shrine.

ವೌಸ್ vousụ, *s.* Prosperity, good luck.

ವೈ voi, *s.* A small log of wood, a stake used for a hedge; *cf.* ತೂನ. –ಕೆಪ್ಪುನಿ to cut and prepare stakes for a hedge.

ವೈಪುನಿ voipuni, *see* ಒಯಿಪುನಿ.

ವ್ಯಂಜನ vyañjana, *s.* A consonant.

ವ್ಯಕ್ತ vyakta, *adj.* Clear, plain, evident. 2. individual, specific. ವ್ಯಕ್ತಿ individuality.

ವ್ಯತಿರಿಕ್ತ vyatirikta, *adj.* Different, distinct. –ಆದ್ ನಡಪುನಿ to behave differently from what one ought.

ವ್ಯತ್ಯಾಸ vyatyāsa, *s.* Contrariety, opposition, reverse; difference. 2. inverted *or* retrograde order. –ಮಳ್ಪುನಿ to make a difference.

ವ್ಯತೆ, ವ್ಯಥೆ vyatė, vyathė, *s.* Pain; distress. 2. fear, alarm. –ಆಪಿನಿ to be in pain, to be distressed. –ಟ ಉಪ್ಪುನಿ to be in distress.

ವ್ಯಭಿಚಾರ vyabhićāra, *s.* Adultery, prostitution. 2. erring, straying. –ಮಳ್ಪುನಿ to commit adultery.

ವ್ಯಭಿಚಾರಿ vyabhićāri, *s.* An adulterer. 2. an adulteress. 3. one who is going astray.

ವ್ಯಯ vyaya, *s.* The twentieth year in the Hindu cycle of sixty. 2. expenditure, spending. –ಮಳ್ಪುನಿ to spend.

ವ್ಯರ್ಥ vyartha, *adj.* Useless, vain, unprofitable, unmeaning. –ತೆ vanity. –ಆದ್ in vain.

ವ್ಯವಧಾನ vyavadhāna, *s.* Leisure, opportunity.

ವ್ಯವಸಾಯ vyavasāya, *s.* Cultivation. 2. exertion, effort, perseverance, industry.

ವ್ಯವಸ್ಥೆ vyavasthė, *s.* A decree, decision. 2. settlement, disposition.

ವ್ಯವಹಾರ vyavahāra, *s.* Litigation, law-suit. –ಮಳ್ಪುನಿ, ವ್ಯವಹರಿಸುನಿ to litigate, contest.

ವ್ಯಸನ vyasana, *s.* Grief, sorrow. 2. care, thought, concern. 3. calamity, misfortune. 4. fault, vice, frailty. ಪರ್– the vice of drunkenness. ಪುಗೆರೆದ– the vice of chewing tobacco. –ಆಪಿನಿ to be grieved. ವ್ಯಸನೊಡುಪ್ಪುನಿ to be in sorrow.

ವ್ಯಾಕರಣ vyākaraṇa, *s.* Grammar.

ವ್ಯಾಕುಲ **vyākula,** *adj.* Perplexed, confused, bewildered. *s.* Distress, perplexity, grief; *also* ವ್ಯಾಕುಲತೆ.

ವ್ಯಾಖ್ಯಾನ **vyākhyāna,** *s.* An explanation, exposition, gloss, commentary.

ವ್ಯಾಘ್ರ **vyāghra,** *s.* A tiger.

ವ್ಯಾಜ್ಯ **vyājya,** *s.* A law-suit, dispute, quarrel. –ಮಳ್ಪುನಿ to dispute; to sue.

ವ್ಯಾಧಿ **vyādhi,** *s.* Sickness, disease, plague.

ವ್ಯಾಪಕ **vyāpaka,** *adj.* Diffusive, pervading, comprehensive. –ಆಪುನಿ to diffuse, spread.

ವ್ಯಾಪಕೆ **vyāpake,** *s.* A ruler, superior person.

ವ್ಯಾಪಾರ **vyāpāra,** *s.* Occupation, business, commerce, trade; *cf.* ಬ್ಯಾರ. –ಮಳ್ಪುನಿ to trade.

ವ್ಯಾಪಿಸುನಿ **vyāpisuni** (ವ್ಯಾಪಿಸಿ), *v. n.* To pervade, extend, spread.

ವ್ಯಾಸ **vyāsa,** *s.* The diameter in geometry. 2. division.

ವ್ಯಾಸಂಗ **vyāsaṅga,** *s.* Knowledge *or* experience in learning. 2. state, circumstances.

ವ್ಯಾಸೆ **vyāse,** *s.* The original compiler *or* arranger of the Vēdas; a sage.

ವ್ರಣ **vraṇa,** *s.* An ulcer, sore, wound.

ವ್ರತ **vrata,** *s.* A vow, any meritorious act of devotion, the voluntary *or* vowed observance of any penance, austerity, *etc.* –ಮಳ್ಪುನಿ to observe a vow; to perform some act of piety.

ವ್ರಯ **vraya,** *s.* Expense, expenditure. 2. waste.

ವ್ಹಾ, ವ್ಹಾವ್ಹಾ **vhā, vhāvhā,** *intj.* Bravo! well done!

ಶ Š

ಶ **ša,** The forty-third letter of the alphabet.

ಶಂಕ್ **šaṅkụ,** *see* ಶಂಕೆ.

ಶಂಕ **šaṅka,** *s.* The conch-shell, used as a horn, and for offering libations. –ಪುಷ್ಪ a flower of the creeper *Clitorea ternatea.* ಬಲಮುರಿ– a conch winding to the right. ಎಡಮುರಿ– a conch winding to the left. –ಊರಿಪುನಿ to blow a conch.

ಶಂಕರೆ **šaṅkare,** *s.* Šiva, he who makes happy.

ಶಂಕಿನಿ **šaṅkini,** *s.* One of the four classes of females.

ಶಂಕಿಯುನಿ **šaṅkiyuni** (ಶಂಕಿ), *v. n.* To doubt, fear, be alarmed.

ಶಂಕೆ **šaṅkė,** *s.* Terror, fear, apprehension. 2. doubt, suspicion, uncertainty. 3. envy, jealousy.

ಶಂಖ śaṅkha, *see* ಶಂಕ.

ಶಂಖಪಾಷಾಣ śaṅkhapāshāṇa, *s.* Rats-bane, arsenic.

ಶಂಭು śambhu, *s.* Śiva.

ಶಕ śaka, *s.* An epoch, era.

ಶಕುತಿ śakuti, *see* ಶಕ್ತಿ.

ಶಕುನ śakuna, *s.* An omen, augury. 2. an ominous bird. –ದಾಯಿ an interpreter of omens. ಅಪ– a bad omen. ಶುಭ– a good omen. –ತೂಗಿನಿ to consult an omen.

ಶಕೆ śakè, *see* ಶಕೆ.

ಶಕ್ಕು śakkụ, *s.* Apprehension, suspicion, doubt. –ಆಗಿನಿ, –ಉಪ್ಪುನಿ to have doubt. –ಮಳ್ಪುನಿ to suspect, doubt.

ಶಕ್ಕರೆ śakkarè, *see* ಸಕ್ಕರೆ.

ಶಕ್ತ śakta, *adj.* Able, strong, powerful, capable.

ಶಕ್ತಿ śakti, *s.* Power, strength, prowess. 2. an iron spear *or* dart. 3. the energy *or* active power of the deity, personified as his wife. ಅ– impotence, weakness. ಶಕ್ತ್ಯರ್ಥ the potential mood.

ಶಕ್ತೆ śakte, *s.* A strong *or* powerful man.

ಶಕ್ಯ śakya, *adj.* Practical, possible. ಅ– impracticable.

ಶಕ್ಯಮುನಿ śakyamụni, *s.* Goutama the founder of Buddhism.

ಶಗ್ತಿ śagti, *s.* Extravagance. 2. *see* ಶಕ್ತಿ. 3. *see* ಸಕ್ತಿ.

ಶತ śata, *adj.* A hundred. 2. many. –ಪ್ರಯತ್ನ a great effort. –ಮಾನ a century. –ಸಂವತ್ಸರ a hundred years; a long life.

ಶತಭಿಷ śatabhisha, *s.* The twenty-fourth lunar mansion.

ಶತ್ರು śatru, *s.* An adversary, foe, enemy.

ಶನಿ, ಶನಿಸ್ರೆ, ಶನೀಶ್ವರೆ śani, śanisre, śanīśvare, *s.* The planet Saturn *or* its regent. 2. distress, calamity. ಶನಿವಾರ Saturday. ಶನಿಪತ್ತುನಿ to be in distress.

ಶಪಥ śapatha, *s.* An oath, protestation, asseveration by 2. an imprecation, curse, oath. –ಮಳ್ಪುನಿ to swear, take an oath; to resolve solemnly.

ಶಪಿಸುನಿ śapisuni (ಶಪಿಸ್), *v. a.* To curse, adjure.

ಶಬಾಸ್ śabāsụ, *intj.* Bravo! well done!

ಶಬ್ದ śabda, *s.* Sound, a sound. 2. a word. ಅಪ– an ungrammatical expression, speaking irrelevantly *or* improperly. ನಿಶ್ಶಬ್ದ noiseless, silent, still. ಶಬ್ದಾರ್ಥ literal meaning. –ಆಪಿನಿ to sound, a sound to be made. –ಮಳ್ಪುನಿ to sound, make a noise.

ಶಮ, ಶಮನ śama, śamana, *s.* Mental tranquillity, calmness. 2. subduing, pacifying, quenching. ಉಪ– refreshing, cooling.

ಶಮಿಸುನಿ šamisuni (ಶಮಿಸ್), *v. n.* To pacify, appease.

ಶಯನ šayana, *s.* Sleep, lying down, reposing. –ಮಳ್ಪುನಿ to sleep; to lie down.

ಶರ šara, *s.* An arrow.

ಶರಂಗ್ šarangu, *see* ಸಿರಂಗ್.

ಶರಣ šaraṇa, *s.* Protection, refuge, shelter. ಶರಣಾಗತೆ, ಶರಣಾರ್ಥಿ a refugee, one who seeks protection.

ಶರಣು šaraṇu, *s.* Obeisance, reverence, salutation. –ಮಳ್ಪುನಿ to salute.

ಶರತ್ಕಾಲ, ಶರದ್ರುತು šaratkāla, šaradrutu, *s.* Autumn.

ಶರಭ šarabha, *s.* A fabulous animal.

ಶರಾಬ್ šarābu, *s.* Brandy, liquor, spirit.

ಶರಾರತ್ šarāratu, *s.* Force, violence. 2. mischief, hurt.

ಶರೀರ šarīra, *s.* The body. *adj.* Bodily, corporeal. –ಪ್ರಕೃತಿ the constitution. ಕಫ–, ಪಿತ್ತ–, ವಾತ– are the different constitutions of the body.

ಶರೀರಿ šarīri, *s.* An animal *or* sentient being.

ಶರೆ šarè, *see* ಶೆರೆ.

ಶರ್ತ್, ಶರ್ತ šartu, šarta, *s.* A condition, stipulation, clause. 2. an agreement, compact. 3. a bet *or* wager. –ಮಳ್ಪುನಿ to bet.

ಶಲ್ಯ šalya, *s.* The shrub *Vanguerea spinosa.*

ಶಲ್ಯ, ಶಲ್ಲೆ šalya, šallè, *s.* A thin upper cloth, generally without border; *cf.* ಶೇಲೆ. *adj.* Thin, fine. –ಕುಂಟು a fine cloth.

ಶವ šava, *s.* A corpse, dead body.

ಶಶಿ šaši, *s.* The moon.

ಶಸ್ತ್ರ šastra, *s.* A weapon. 2. a surgical instrument. –ಪ್ರಯೋಗ discharging a weapon; surgical operation.

ಶಹರ್, ಶಹಾರ್ šaharu, šahāru, *s.* A city, town. 2. a bazaar.

ಶಾಂತ šānta, *adj.* Calm, patient, tranquil. –ಗುಣ quietness, meekness, patience. ಶಾಂತಾಸನ mercy-seat. –ಆಪಿನಿ to be calm, quiet, appeased; to abate, as fever, *etc.* –ಮಳ್ಪುನಿ to appease, quench.

ಶಾಂತಿ šānti, *s.* Tranquillity, quiet, peace. 2. patience. 3. mildness. 4. rest, repose. 5. preliminary ceremonies to prevent inauspicious accidents at any religious ceremonies. 6. remission, alleviation. 7. removing the effects of unhappy stars, inauspicious omens, *etc.* ಗ್ರಾಮ– a ceremony performed to avert a plague, *etc.* ನವಗ್ರಹ– a ceremony performed to propitiate the nine principal planets.

ಶಾಂತಿಮರ šāntimara, *s.* The tree *Terminalia bellerica*; *also* ಅಕ್ಷವೃಕ್ಷ.

ಶಾಖೆ šākhe, *s*. A part, branch, subdivision.

ಶಾನಭೋಗೆ šānabhōge, *see* ಶೇಣಬಾವೆ.

ಶಾನೆ šāne, *s*. A clever man. 2. *see* ಸಾಣೆ.

ಶಾಪ šāpa, *s*. Curse, imprecation, malediction; abuse. –ಗ್ರಸ್ತ an accursed man. –ನಿರ್ಣಯ condemnation. –ವಿಮೋಚನೆ deliverance from a curse. –ಕೊಡಿಸು to curse.

ಶಾಪಿಯುನಿ, ಶಾಪ್ಯುನಿ šāpiyuni, šāpyuni (ಶಾಪಿ), *v.a.* To curse.

ಶಾಬಸ್, ಶಾಬಾಸ್ šābasu, šābāsu, *see* ಶಬಾಸ್.

ಶಾಯಿ šāyi, *s*. Ink. –ದಪ್ಪಿ, –ದೌತಿ an inkstand.

ಶಾಯಿದಿ šāyidi, *s*. A witness. 2. evidence.

ಶಾರ್ šāru, *s*. A town.

ಶಾರದೆ šāradè, *s*. Sarasvati, the goddess of speech and knowledge in general.

ಶಾರ್ದೂಲ šārdūla, *s*. The royal tiger. *adj*. Excellent, superior.

ಶಾರ್ವರಿ šārvari, *s*. The thirty-fourth year in the Hindu cycle of sixty.

ಶಾಲ್ šālu, *see* ಶಾಲು.

ಶಾಲಿ šāli, *adj*. (*in comp.*) Possessing, having. ಜಯ– a conqueror. ಬುದ್ಧಿ– a wise man.

ಶಾಲಿವಾಹನೆ šālivāhane, *s*. An ancient king and institutor of the era called the Šālivāhanašaka, which commences A. D. 78.

ಶಾಲು šālu, *s*. A shawl.

ಶಾಲೆ šālè, *s*. A hall, room, chamber. 2. a school. ಗೋ– a cow-pen. ವಿದ್ಯಾ– a college.

ಶಾವಂತಿ, ಶಾವಂತಿಗೆ šāvanti, šāvantigè, *see* ಶೇಮತ್ತಿಗೆ.

ಶಾಶ್ವತ, ಶಾಶ್ವಿತ šāšvata, šāšvita, *adj*. Perpetual, eternal. 2. fixed, stable, permanent, durable. –ಕೆಲಸ durable work. –ಪದವಿ eternal bliss. –ಆದ್ permanently.

ಶಾಸನ šāsana, *s*. A charter, grant, usually inscribed on stone *or* copper. 2. a deed, written contract. ತಾಂಬ್ರ– an inscription on copper. ಮರಣ– a will, testament.

ಶಾಸ್ತ್ರ šāstra, *s*. Scripture, science, institutes of religion, law, *or* letters. 2. any work of literature *or* science in general. ಗಣಿತ– arithmetic. ಜ್ಯೋತಿಃ– astronomy, astrology. ಧರ್ಮ– a code of laws.

ಶಾಸ್ತ್ರಿ šāstri, *s*. A pundit, teacher of sacred science, *or* one skilled in it.

ಶಾಸ್ತ್ರೋಕ್ತ šāstrōkta, *adj*. According to scripture, agreeably to science.

ಶಿ ši, *Words not found beginning with this letter must be sought under* ಶಿ *or* ಸಿ.

ಶಿ ši, *intj. denoting* disgust, loathing, *etc*. Fie!

ಶಿಂಕದಂಡಣೆ šiṅkadaṇḍaṇè, *s*. Capital punishment.

ಶೀಂಕಿರಿ **šiṅkiri**, *see* ಸೀಂಕಿರಿ.

ಶಿಂಗರಿಪುನಿ **šiṅgaripuni**, *see* ಶೃಂಗರಿಪುನಿ.

ಶಿಂಗಾರ **šiṅgāra**, *see* ಶೃಂಗಾರ.

ಶಿಂಗಿ **šiṅgi**, *see* ಸಿಂಗಿ.

ಶಿಂಗಿರಿ **šiṅgiri**, *s.* A kind of fish.

ಶಿಂದ್ **šindụ**, *adj.* True, established; valid.

ಶಿಂಹ **šiṁha**, *see* ಸಿಂಹ.

ಶಿಕಸ್ತ್, ಶಿಕಸ್ತು **šikastụ, šikastu**, *s.* Doubling a paper into folds before writing upon it.

ಶಿಕಾರ್, ಶಿಕಾರಿ **šikārụ, šikāri**, *s.* Hunting. —ಮಳ್ಪುನಿ to hunt.

ಶಿಕೆ, ಶಿಖೆ **šikè, šikhè**, *s.* Heat.

ಶಿಕ್ಕುನಿ **šikkuni**, *see* ಶಿಕ್ಯುನಿ.

ಶಿಕ್ಕೆಯುನಿ **šikkeyuni** (ಶಿಕ್ಕೆ), *v. n.* To end, be complete.

ಶಿಖೆಯುನಿ **šikheyuni** (ಶಿಖೆ), *v.n.* To be hot, sultry.

ಶಿಗುರು **šiguru**, *s.* A sprout, germ.

ಶಿಗುರುನಿ **šiguruni**, *see* ಚಿಗುರುನಿ.

ಶಿಟ್ಟು **šiṭṭu**, *s.* Anger, displeasure.

ಶಿಟ್ಟೇಶಿ **šiṭṭēši**, *s.* Trouble.

ಶಿಡಿಕೆ, ಶಿಡಿಗೆ **šiḍikè, šiḍigè**, *see* ಕಿಡಿತ.

ಶಿಡಿಪುನಿ **šiḍipuni**, *see* ಕಿಡಿಪಿನಿ.

ಶಿಡಿಬು, ಶಿಡುಬು **šiḍibu, šiḍubu**, *s.* The pustule of small-pox.

ಶಿಡಿಲ್ **šiḍilụ**, *see* ಕಿಡಿಲ್.

ಶಿದಿ **šidi**, *see* ಸಿದ.

ಶಿದಿಗೋಳಿ **šidigōḷi**, *s.* The tree *Urostigma pisiferum*.

ಶಿದ್ದಿ **šiddi**, *see* ಶಿದ್ಧ.

ಶಿದ್ದಿಗೆ, ಶಿದ್ದೆ **šiddigè, šiddè**, *s.* A quarter seer.

ಶಿಪರಸ್, ಶಿಪಾರಸ್ **šiparasụ, šipārasụ**, *s.* Recommendation, commendation. —ಕಾಗಜಿ a certificate, testimonial. —ಕೊರ್ಪಿನಿ to commend. —ಮಳ್ಪುನಿ to recommend.

ಶಿಪಾಯಿ **šipāyi**, *s.* A soldier, sepoy.

ಶಿಬ್ಬ, ಶಿಬ್ಬು **šibba, šibbu**, *see* ಸುಬ್ಬ.

ಶಿಮ **šima**, *s.* Cold, moistness.

ಶಿಮುದ್ರೆ **šimudrè**, *see* ಶ್ರೀಮುದ್ರೆ.

ಶಿಯಮ್ **šiyamụ**, *adj.* Third, inferior. —ತರ third sort *or* quality.

ಶಿರ, ಶಿರಸ್ಸ್ **šira, širassụ**, *s.* The head. ಶಿರಚ್ಛೇದನ decapitation. ಶಿರಸಾವಹಿಸುನಿ to carry on the head; to obey implicitly.

ಶಿರಿ **širi**, *see* ಶ್ರೀ. 2. *see* ತಿರಿ.

ಶಿರಿಪೊಂನೆ **širiponnè**, *s.* The poon tree, *Calophyllum apetalum*.

ಶಿರೆ **širè**, *see* ಕಿರೆ.

ಶಿರೋಮಣಿ **širōmaṇi**, *s.* A crest gem. 2. a headman; a leader.

ಶಿರ್ದುನಿ **širduni** (ಶಿರ್ದ್), *v. a.* To correct, reform, alter, rectify. 2. to afflict, grieve, torment, trouble. 3. to reproach.

ಶಿರ್ಬೆ **širbè**, *see* ತಿರ್ಬೆ.

ಶಿರ್ವ **širva**, *see* ತಿರ್ವ.

ಶಿಲಾ **šilā**, *adj.* Of stone, made of stone. —ಮಯ made of, *or* abounding in stone. —ಮೂರ್ತಿ a stone image. —ಶಾಸನ a charter inscribed on stone.

ಶಿಲೆ **šilè**, *s.* A stone; *also* ಶಿಲೆಕಲ್ಲ್.

ಶಿಲೆ **šilè**, *s.* A fishing rod. —ಕೊರ್ಪಿನಿ to stir up, incite.

ಶಿಲ್ಪ, ಶಿಲ್ಪಿ **šilpa, šilpi,** *s.* Any manual *or* mechanical art. —ಶಾಸ್ತ್ರ architecture, sculpture.

ಶಿವ, ಶಿವೆ **šiva, šive,** *s.* Šiva, the third of the Hindu triad, the destroyer. ಶಿವಪುರಾಣ Šiva's history. ಶಿವಪೂಜೆ adoration of Šiva. ಶಿವಭಕ್ತ a follower of Šiva. ಶಿವರಾತ್ರಿ the thirteenth night of the second fortnight of the eleventh lunar month observed in honour of Šiva's birth.

ಶಿವಾಯಿ, ಶಿವ್ವಾ **šivāyi, šivāi,** *adv.* Besides, except. *adj.* Excluded, exempted.

ಶಿಶ್ಯೆ, ಶಿಷ್ಯೆ **šišše, šishye,** *s.* A pupil, disciple, follower.

ಶಿಸ್ತ್, ಶಿಸ್ತು **šistu, šistu,** *s.* A land-tax. 2. a mark, aim.

ಶಿಕ್ಷಕೆ **šikshake,** *s.* An instructor.

ಶಿಕ್ಷಿಸುನಿ **šikshisuni** (ಶಿಕ್ಷಿಸ್), *v. a.* To punish, fine, correct.

ಶಿಕ್ಷೆ **šikshè,** *s.* Punishment, correction, chastisement. 2. instruction. —ರಕ್ಷೆ punishment and protection. —ಕೊರ್ಪಿನಿ to punish.

ಶೀ **šī,** *adj.* Sweet. —ಕರ sweet and hot, sweetish, not sufficiently hot, as a dish.

ಶೀಂಕಿರಿ **šīṅkiri,** *see* ಸೀಂಕಿರಿ.

ಶೀಂಟುನಿ **šīṇṭuni,** *see* ಸೀಂಟುನಿ.

ಶೀಂತಿರಿ **šīntiri,** *s.* Sprinkling.

ಶೀಂತೆಲ್ **šīntelu,** *see* ಸೀಂತೆಲ್.

ಶೀಗ್ರ, ಶೀಘ್ರ **šīgra, šīghra,** *adj.* Quick, swift, speedy. *adv.* Quickly.

ಶೀಗೆ **šīgè,** *see* ಸೀಗೆ.

ಶೀಗೊಂಡೆ **šīgoṇḍè,** *see* ಶೀಮೆಗೊಂಡೆ *under* ಶೀಮೆ.

ಶೀತ **šīta,** *s.* Cold, chillness, catarrh. *adj.* Cold, chill. —ಜರ ague. —ಆಪಿನಿ to be cold; to catch cold, suffer from cold.

ಶೀತಾಫಲ **šītāphala,** *s.* The white custard-apple.

ಶೀತಾಳಿ **šītāḷi,** *s.* A white species of cocoanut. 2. *see* ಶ್ರೀತಾಳಿ.

ಶೀತೆ **šītè,** *see* ಸೀತೆ.

ಶೀತೋಷ್ಣ **šītōshṇa,** *s.* Cold and heat. *adj.* Cold and hot.

ಶೀದ **šīda,** *see* ಸೀದ.

ಶೀಪೆ **šīpè,** *s.* Sweetness, pleasantness. *adj.* Sweet, pleasant, agreeable. —ಗಡ್ಡಿ liquorice.

ಶೀಮೆ **šīmè,** *s.* A country. 2. England. —ಗೊಂಡೆ a kind of red flower. —ಸುಂಣ chalk.

ಶೀಯಮ್ **šīyamu,** *see* ಶಿಯಮು.

ಶೀರ್ **šīru,** *see* ಶೀರ್.

ಶೀರೆ **šīrè,** *s.* A female's garment. ಕೆಂಪುಳಿ—, ಕಸ್ತುರಿಗತ್ತಿ—, ಕಾಂಗ್—, ಕೊಟ್ಟಗಾರ—, ಗರ್ಭಸುತ್ತಿ—, ಪಟ್ಟೆ—, ಪೈತಣಿ—, ಬಾಣ—, ರಾಗವಳಿ— are different sorts of it.

ಶೀಲ **šīla,** *s.* Conduct, virtue. 2. nature, quality, disposition. ದು— bad nature *or* disposition. ಸು— good nature *or* disposition. ಆಯ ಶೀಲ ಪಿಂಟೆ I know his disposition.

ಶೀಲೆ šīlè, *see* ಶಿಲೆ.

ಶೀಶೀ šīšī, *intj.* Fie! fie! *cf.* ಛಿ.

ಶೀಸ šīsa, *see* ಸೀಸ.

ಶೀಸ, ಶೀಸೆ šīsa, šīsè, *s.* A glass bottle.

ಶೀಳ್ šīḷụ, *see* ಸೀಳ್.

ಶುಂಠಿ šuṇṭhi, *s.* Ginger, dry ginger; *also* ಸೂಂಟಿ.

ಶುಕ್ರ, ಶುಕ್ರೆ šukra, šukre, *s.* Venus. 2. the name of a man; *also* ತುಕ್ರೆ. ಶುಕ್ರವಾರ Friday.

ಶುಕ್ಲ šukla, *s.* White colour. 2. the third year in the Hindu cycle of sixty. 3. *semen virile.* *adj.* White. –ಪಕ್ಷ the bright lunar fortnight.

ಶುಚಿ šuči, *s.* Purity, purification. *adj.* Pure, ceremoniously pure. 2. clean, purified. 3. faultless.

ಶುದ್ಧ šuddha, *adj.* Clean, pure, cleansed, purified. 2. faultless, correct. 3. entire, complete. *s.* The bright lunar fortnight. –ತ್ವ cleanliness, purity, cleanness. –ಪ್ರತಿ a correct copy. –ಬೊಳ್ದು entirely white. –ಸುಳ್ಳು altogether false. –ಆಪಿನಿ to be clean, ceremoniously clean. –ಮಳ್ಪುನಿ to purify.

ಶುದ್ಧಿ šuddhi, *s.* Purity. ಶುದ್ಧೀಕರಣ sanctification.

ಶುಭ šubha, *adj.* Auspicious, fortunate, happy, prosperous. *s.* Any auspicious ceremony; *also* ಶುಭಕಾರ್ಯ. ಅ– inauspicious. –ದಿನ a lucky day; a holiday. –ವಾರ್ತೆ good news. –ಆಪಿನಿ to prosper, thrive. –ಮಸ್ತು let it prosper.

ಶುಭಕೃತ್ತು šubhakṛuttu, *s.* The thirty-sixth year in the Hindu cycle of sixty.

ಶುಭಾಷಿತ šubhāshita, *see* ಸುಭಾಷಿತ.

ಶುಭ್ರ šubhra, *adj.* White. 2. pure, clean. –ಕಂಠ, –ದೃಷ್ಟಿ clear eye-sight. –ಆಪಿನಿ to be clean.

ಶುಮಾರ್ šumārụ, *see* ಸುಮಾರ್.

ಶುರು šuru, *see* ಸುರು.

ಶೂ šū, *s.* A sound, used in exorcism. –ಮಂತ್ರ exorcism. –ಮಂತ್ರ ಮಳ್ಪುನಿ to exorcise.

ಶೂಂಠಿ šūṇṭhi, *see* ಶುಂಠಿ.

ಶೂದ್ರ šūdra, *adj.* Of *or* belonging to the fourth pure Hindu tribe.

ಶೂದ್ರೆ šūdre, *s.* A Šūdra, a man of the servile caste.

ಶೂನ್ಯ šūnya, *adj.* Empty, blank, void, vacant. –ದಿನ an unoccupied day. –ವಾದಿ an atheist. –ಆಪಿನಿ to turn blank, prove unsuccessful. –ಮಳ್ಪುನಿ to make blank; to disappoint; to annihilate.

ಶೂರ šūra, *adj.* Heroic, valiant, brave. –ತನ heroism.

ಶೂರೆ šūre, *s.* A hero, champion, brave man.

ಶೂರ್ಪನಖಿ šūrpanakhi, *s.* A giantess, Rāvaṇa's younger sister.

ಶೂಲ šūla, *s.* A weapon, pike, dart. 2. a stake for impaling criminals. ತ್ರಿ– a trident. ಶೂಲೊಗು ಪಾಡುನಿ to impale a criminal.

ಶೂಲ, ಶೂಲೆ šūla, šūlè, *s.* Sharp pain in general. 2. the colic. ಗರ್ಭ– painful menses, dysmenorrhœa.

ಶೂಸ್ತ್ರ šūstra, *see* ಸೂತ್ರ.

ಶೃಂಗರಿಪುನಿ šrụṅgaripuni (ಶೃಂಗರಿ), *v. a.* To decorate, garnish, ornament.

ಶೃಂಗಾರ šrụṅgāra, *s.* Ornament, decoration. 2. beauty. 3. the sentiment of love, as in poetry. –ಮಳ್ಪುನಿ to decorate.

ಶೃಂಗೇರಿ šrụṅgēri, *s.* A village in Mysore, containing the monastery of Šaṅkarāčārya and his successors.

ಶೆ šè, *Words not found beginning with this letter, must be sought under* ಕೆ *or* ಸೆ.

ಶೆಂಟುನಿ šeṇṭuni (ಶೆಂಟಿ), *v. n.* To stumble.

ಶೆಕೆ šekè, *s.* Heat, warmth.

ಶೆಟ್ಟ್ šeṭṭụ, *see* ಕೆಟ್ಟ್.

ಶೆಟ್ಟಾವುನಿ šeṭṭāvuni, *c. v.* (*of* ಶೆಟ್ಟುನಿ) To spoil, destroy, ruin.

ಶೆಟ್ಟಿ šēṭṭi, *s.* A title of Jains, Bants, *etc.* 2. the headman of a village, *etc.*

ಶೆಟ್ಟಿ šeṭṭi, *adj.* Spoiled, ruined. ಶೆಟ್ಟಿ ಬೊಕ್ಕ ಬುದ್ಧಿ to become wise when too late.

ಶೆಟ್ಟಿವಾಳ್ šeṭṭivāḷụ, *s.* A title of some Bants.

ಶೆಟ್ಟುನಿ šeṭṭuni (ಶೆಟ್ಟಿ), *v. n.* To decay, be spoiled.

ಶೆಟ್ಟೆ šeṭṭè, *see* ಕೆಟ್ಟ್.

ಶೆಡ್ತರುನಿ šeḍụtaruni (ಶೆಡ್ತರ್), *v. n.* To feel a throbbing pain. ತರೆ– the head to ache severely.

ಶೆಡವು šeḍavu, *s.* Pride, haughtiness, affectation, coquetry.

ಶೆಡಿ šeḍi, *s.* Sprinkling. 2. boxing with fingers. 3. *see* ಕೆಡಿತ. –ವಾತ a kind of cattle-desease.

ಶೆಡಿತ šeḍita, *s.* Throbbing pain.

ಶೆಡಿಪಿನಿ, ಶೆಡ್ಡ್ಯುನಿ šeḍipini, šeḍḍyuni (ಶೆಡಿ, ಶೆಡ್ಡ್ಯ), *v. a.* To sprinkle with fingers, as water, *etc.* 2. to box with fingers, as the ear, *etc.* *v. n.* To feel a throbbing pain; *cf.* ಶೆಡ್ತರುನಿ.

ಶೆಡಿಲ್ šeḍilụ, *see* ಕೆಡಿಲ್.

ಶೆಡ್ತರುನಿ šeḍtaruni, *see* ಶೆಡ್ತರುನಿ.

ಶೆರಂಗ್ šeraṅgụ, *see* ಸೆರಂಗ್.

ಶೆರೆ šerè, *s.* Imprisonment, captivity. 2. a prison; *also* ಶೆರೆಮನೆ. 3. indebtedness, obligation. 4. liability, answerableness. 5. *see* ಸೆರೆ. –ಬುಡ್ಪಿನಿ to excuse *or* release from an obligation; to absolve from a liability.

ಶೆರೆ šerè, *s.* A wave, billow.

ಶೆರ್ಗೆ šergè, *see* ಜರಿಗೆ.

ಶೆಲ್ಲೆ šellè, *see* ಶಲ್ಯ.

ಶೇಂಕಡ šēṅkaḍa, *see* ಶೇಕಡ.

ಶೇಂಕುನಿ šēṅkuni, *see* ಸೇಂಕುನಿ.

ಶೇಂಟ್, ಶೇಂಟ šēṇṭụ, šēṇṭa, *s.* The hair about the privities.

ಶೇಂದಿ šēndi, *s.* Toddy. –ಗುತ್ತಿಗೆ toddy-contract.

ಶೇಕ šēka, *s.* A salutary heat; fomentation; *cf.* ಶೆಕೆ. –ಪೊತ್ತುನಿ, –ಕೊರ್ಪಿನಿ to foment; to beat.

ಶೇಕಡ šēkada, *adv.* Per cent, hundred. *s.* Percentage. –ದ ಪಣವು a percentage.

ಶೇಟ್ šēṭu, *see* ಸೇಟ್.

ಶೇಟೆ šēṭè, *see* ಚೇಷ್ಟೆ.

ಶೇಡ್, ಶೇಡಿ šēḍu, šēḍi, *see* ಜೇಡಿ.

ಶೇಣವೆ, ಶೇನವೆ šēṇave, šēnave, *s.* A village clerk, writer, accountant.

ಶೇತು, ಶೇತುವೆ, ಶೇದು šētu, šētuvè, šēdu, *see* ಸೇತು.

ಶೇದುನಿ, ಶೇಪುನಿ šēduni, šēpuni, *see* ಶೇಪುನಿ.

ಶೇಬಿ šēbi, *adj.* Open. 2. wide.

ಶೇಬೆ šēbè, *see* ಶೋಭೆ.

ಶೇಮತ್ತಿಗೆ šēmattigè, *s.* A fragrant flower of *Pyrethrum Indicum*.

ಶೇಮಗೆ, ಶೇಮಯಿ šēmagè, šēmayi, *see* ಸೇಮೆಯಿದಡ್ಡೆ.

ಶೇರಾವುನಿ šērāvuni, *c. v.* (*of* ಶೇರುನಿ) To join, unite, mix, combine, include, accumulate. 2. to admit, as a member into any sect, class, *or* profession. 3. to find, provide with occupation *or* employment.

ಶೇರಿಗಾರೆ, ಶೇರುಗಾರೆ šērigāre, šērugāre, *s.* A man of the musicians' caste, a musician; *also* ವಾದ್ಯದಾಯೆ. 2. a man of a warrior-caste speaking Canarese; *also* ಕೋಟಿದಾಯೆ.

ಶೇರಿಗೆ šērigè, *s.* Union, inclusion. 2. influence, power. ಕುಲೆ ಭೂತದ ಶೇರಿಗೆಡ್ ಉಂಡು the ghost is in the power of a demon.

ಶೇರಿಸಾವುನಿ šērisāvuni, *c. v.* (*of* ಶೇರಿಸುನಿ) To cause to arrive, join. 2. to injure, harm, ruin.

ಶೇರಿಸುನಿ šērisuni *see* ಶೇರಿಸಾವುನಿ, ಶೇರಾವುನಿ.

ಶೇರುನಿ šēruni (ಶೇರ್), *v. n.* To arrive, reach. 2. to be added *or* joined to. 3. to be included in. 4. to enter, as a member into any sect, class *or* profession. 5. to be in harmony, to agree together. 6. to be relished, liked, to agree with, as a particular food *or* dish. 7. to adhere to, be attached to. ಇಲ್ಲ್– to reach home. ಜುಗಾರಿದಾಕುಳೆಡೊಪ್ಪ– to keep company with gamblers. ಪಾದ್ರಿ ಪಾಲ್ಗ್– to become a Christian. ಪೋಲಿಸ್ಡ್– to be enlisted in the police force. ಲೆಕ್ಕೊಡು– to be included in an account. ಆಯಗ್ ಮೀನ್ ಶೇರುಜಿ he does not like fish; fish does not agree with him.

ಶೇರ್ಗ šērga, *s.* A lot.

ಶೇರ್ವೆ šērvè, *see* ಶೇರಿಗೆ.

ಶೇರ್ಸಾವುನಿ šērsāvuni, *see* ಶೇರಿಸಾವುನಿ.

ಶೇಲೆ šēlè, *s.* Boast, brag. 2. coquetry, affectation, haughtiness. 3. display, show. *adj.* Boasting; showy; affected; haughty. –ದಾಯೆ a braggart;

a fop. –ದಾಳ್, –ಬಿಡುಗು a very coquettish woman. –ತೂಪಾವುನಿ to brag, be showy, affected, copuettish. –ಮಳ್ಪುನಿ, –ಮಾಡಾವುನಿ to make a display.

ಶೇಷ šēsha, *s.* The rest, remainder, residue. –ವಾನಿ what has remained.

ಶೇಷೆ šēshe, *s.* The chief of the serpent race; the couch and canopy of Vishṇu, and upholder of the world.

ಶೈತ್ಯ šeitya, *adj.* Cold, cooling. *s.* A cold.

ಶೈವ šeiva, *adj.* Belonging to the sect of Šiva.

ಶೈವೆ šeive, *s.* A follower of Šiva.

ಶೋಕ šōka, *s.* Sorrow, grief, afliction.

ಶೋಕು šōku, *s.* Pleasure, gaiety, merriment. 2. proclivity, addictedness to vice. –ದಾಯಿ a pleasure-hunter; a gay fellow. ಪರ್ಬ– indulgence in liquor.

ಶೋಕೆಲೆ šōkele, *s.* A gay man.

ಶೋಧಕೆ šōdhake, *s.* An inquirer, examiner, critic. 2. a tempter.

ಶೋಧನೆ šōdhanė, *s.* Search, research, examination. 2. temptation, trial. 3. correcting. 4. cleaning, cleansing, purifying. ಜಲ–filtering water. –ಮಳ್ಪುನಿ to search; to try; to correct; to filter, strain.

ಶೋಧಿಪುನಿ, ಶೋಧಿಯುನಿ šōdhipuni, šōdhiyuni (ಶೋಧ), *v. a.* To search, examine. 2. to try, assay, tempt. 3. to sift, strain, filter. 4. to purify, clean.

ಶೋಭಕೃತ್ತು šōbhakrụttu, *s.* The thirty-seventh year in the Hindu cycle of sixty.

ಶೋಭನ šōbhana, *s.* The consummation of a marriage, when the parties come together.

ಶೋಭಾನೆ šōbhānė, *s.* A festive song. –ಪಣ್ಪುನಿ to recite a festive song.

ಶೋಭಿಸುನಿ šōbhisuni (ಶೋಭಿಸ), *v. n.* To shine. 2. to be adorned.

ಶೋಭೆ šōbhė, *s.* Lustre, radiance, light. 2. beauty. –ಉಪ್ಪುನಿ to be beautiful.

ಶೌಚ šouča, *s.* Cleansing, purification. 2. easing nature.

ಶೌರ್ಯ šourya, *s.* Heroism, valour.

ಶ್ಮಶಾನ šmašāna, *s.* A cemetery.

ಶ್ರದ್ಧೆ šraddhė, *s.* Faith, devotion, confidence. 2. esteem, regard, care for. –ದಾಯಿ, –ಇತ್ತಿನಾಯೆ, ಶ್ರದ್ಧಾವಂತೆ a devout man. ಅ– negligence.

ಶ್ರಮ, ಶ್ರಮೆ šrama, šramė, *s.* Toil, labour, fatigue, distress, trouble, suffering. –ತಾಳುನಿ to endure hardships. –ಪಡೆಯುನಿ to be in trouble. –ಮಳ್ಪುನಿ to labour, toil; to be industrious.

ಶ್ರವಣ šravaṇa, *s.* The ear. 2. hearing. 3. the twenty-second lunar mansion. –ಮಳ್ಪುನಿ to listen to.

ಶ್ರಾದ್ಧ **śrāddha,** *s.* A funeral ceremony, performed for recently deceased relations and continued annually.

ಶ್ರಾವಕ **śrāvaka,** *s.* A sect of Jains.

ಶ್ರಾವಣ **śrāvaṇa,** *s.* The fifth lunar month.

ಶ್ರಿಂಗಾರ **śriṅgāra,** *see* ಶೃಂಗಾರ.

ಶ್ರೀ **śrī,** *s.* Lakshmi, wife of Vishṇu and goddess of plenty and prosperity. 2. fortune, prosperity, thriving. 3. wealth, riches. 4. a prefix to proper names of deities.

ಶ್ರೀಗಂಧ **śrīgandha,** *s.* Scented sandal.

ಶ್ರೀತಾಳಿ **śrītāḷi,** *s.* The taliput *or* fan-palm, *Corypha umbraculifera.*

ಶ್ರೀಮಂತ **śrīmanta,** *adj.* Noble, princely, wealthy.

ಶ್ರೀಮಂತೆ **śrīmante,** *s.* A prince; a nobleman; a very rich man.

ಶ್ರೀಮುಖ **śrīmukha,** *s.* The seventh year in the Hindu cycle of sixty.

ಶ್ರೀಮುದ್ರೆ **śrīmudrè,** *s.* The five sectarian seals used by Mādhva Brahmans in marking the face, *etc.* 2. the impression of these seals.

ಶ್ರೀವೇಷ **śrīvēsha,** *see* ಸ್ತ್ರೀವೇಷ *under* ಸ್ತ್ರೀ.

ಶ್ರುತ **śruta,** *s.* Holy writ, sacred science. *adj.* Heard. —ಆಪಿಸಿ to be heard *or* known. —ಪಡಿಸುಸಿ to inform, make known.

ಶ್ರುತಿ **śruti,** *s.* A sort of drone corresponding to that used with the bagpipes. 2. the Vēdas. 3. the ear; hearing.

ಶ್ರೇಯಸ್ಸು **śrēyassu,** *s.* Virtue, moral merit. 2. good fortune.

ಶ್ರೇಷ್ಠ **śrēshṭha,** *adj.* Pre-eminent, excellent, chief. —ತ್ವ excellence, pre-eminence.

ಶ್ರೇಷ್ಠೆ **śrēshṭhe,** *s.* An excellent man, a pre-eminent man.

ಶ್ಲೇಷ್ಮ **ślēshma,** *s.* Phlegm, phlegmatic humour.

ಶ್ಲೋಕ **ślōka,** *s.* A couplet, distich, stanza *or* verse.

ಶ್ವಾನ **śvāna,** *s.* A dog.

ಶ್ವಾಸ **śvāsa,** *s.* Breath, breathing. ಉ— breath inhaled. ಊರ್ಧ್ವ— labouring for breath, as a dying man. —ಕಟ್ಟುಸಿ to be choked, unable to breathe. —ತೆಪ್ಪುಸಿ to breathe in. —ಬುಡ್ಡಿಸಿ to breathe out, exhale; to pant. —ಆಕ್ಕುಸಿ to heave a sigh; to be jealous. —ನ್ಯೆಪುಸಿ to gasp, pant; to breathe one's last; to be in a hurry.

ಷ SH

ಷ sha, The forty-fourth letter of the alphabet.

ಷಷ್ಟಿ shashṭi, *s.* The sixth lunar day of either fortnight. *adj.* Sixth. —ವಿಭಕ್ತಿ the genitive case. ಸುಬ್ರಮಣ್ಯ— a festival observed on the sixth day of the ninth lunar month in honour of Kārtikēya.

ಷುಮಾರ್ shumāru, *see* ಸುಮಾರ್.

ಸ S

ಸ sa, The forty-fifth letter of the alphabet.

ಸಂ sam, *pref.* With, together with.

ಸಂಕ saṅka, *s.* A bridge. 2. the liver. 3. *see* ಶಂಕ.

ಸಂಕಟ, ಸಂಕಡ saṅkaṭa, saṅkaḍa, *s.* Illness, sickness. 2. distress, difficulty. —ದಾಯಿ a sick man. ಪ್ರಾಣ— dangerous illness. ಮರ್ಛ—fainting, swooning. —ಆಪಿನಿ, ಸಂಕಡೊಟು ಬೂರುನಿ to be sick, laid up.

ಸಂಕಣ saṅkaṇa, *see* ಸಕ್ಯಣ.

ಸಂಕಪಾಷಣ saṅkapāshaṇa, *see* ಶಂಖಪಾಷಾಣ.

ಸಂಕಮಾಲೆ saṅkamālè, *s.* A kind of serpent.

ಸಂಕಲೆ saṅkalè, *s.* Fetter, chain.

ಸಂಕಲೆಗುಳಿಗೆ saṅkaleguḷige, *s.* A demon so called.

ಸಂಕಲ್ಪ, ಸಂಕಲ್ಪನೆ saṅkalpa, saṅkalpanè, *s.* A resolve, determination, resolution. 2. a project, design. 3. a religious vow *or* declaration. —ಮಳ್ಪುನಿ to resolve, vow.

ಸಂಕಲ್ಪಿಸುನಿ saṅkalpisuni (ಸಂಕಲ್ಪಿಸ್), *v. n.* To resolve, determine. 2. to vow, declare solemnly.

ಸಂಕಲ್ಮೆ saṅkalmè, *s.* Doubt, suspicion.

ಸಂಕವಸನ saṅkavasana, *see* ಶಂಖಪಾಷಾಣ.

ಸಂಕಸ sankasa, *adj.* Like, similar.

ಸಂಕಸಾಲೆ saṅkasālè, *s.* A mint.

ಸಂಕಿಯುನಿ, ಸಂಕ್ಯುನಿ saṅkiyuni, saṅkyuni (ಸಂಕಿ), *v. n.* To hesitate, doubt, waver. 2. to be shy, *or* bashful; *also* ಶಂಕಿಯುನಿ.

ಸಂಕೀರ್ತನೆ saṅkīrtanè, *s.* Praising, hymning, celebrating. —ಮಳ್ಪುನಿ to sing the praises of God.

ಸಂಕೆ saṅkè, *see* ಶಂಕೆ.

ಸಂಕೆಲ್ಮೆ saṅkelmè, *see* ಸಂಕಲ್ಮೆ.

ಸಂಕೆಸ, ಸಂಕೇಸ saṅkesa, saṅkēsa, *s.* A residence. ಸ್ವಾಮಿ— the residence *or* seat of a swāmi.

ಸಂಕೊಲೆ, ಸಂಕೋಲೆ saṅkolè, saṅkōlè, *see* ಸಂಕಲೆ.

ಸಂಕೋಚ saṅkōća, *s.* Hesitation, doubt. 2. shrivelling up, contracting. 3. brevity, abridgment. —ಮಳ್ಳುನಿ to abridge.

ಸಂಕ್ಯಸೆ saṅkyasè, *see* ಸಂಕೆಸ.

ಸಂಕ್ರಮಣ, ಸಂಕ್ರಾಂತಿ saṅkramaṇa, saṅkrānti, *s.* The passage of the sun from one sign of the zodiac into another. 2. the first day of a solar month.

ಸಂಖೆ, ಸಂಖ್ಯೆ saṅkhè, saṅkhyè, *s.* Number in general. 2. a number *or* numeral. 3. counting.

ಸಂಗ saṅga, *s.* Union, junction, confluence. 2. association, company. ಸಜ್ಜನ— good company. ಸ್ತ್ರೀ— sexual embrace.

ಸಂಗಡ saṅgaḍa, *s.* Fastening two boats together. —ಕಟ್ಟುನಿ to fasten in this way.

ಸಂಗಡ saṅgaḍa, *see* ಸಂಗದ.

ಸಂಗಡಿ saṅgaḍi, *see* ತಂಗಡಿ.

ಸಂಗಡಿಗೆ saṅgaḍige, *s.* An associate, companion. 2. a colleague.

ಸಂಗತಿ saṅgati, *s.* Company, association, union. 2. subject, affair, matter, business, circumstance, occurrence, contents of a writing. ಆಯಿ ಸಂಗತಿ ಬೊಡ್ಚಿ have nothing to do with him. ದಾನೆ— what is the matter?

ಸಂಗದ saṅgada, *postp.* With, together with, accompanying.

ಸಂಗಮ saṅgama, *s.* Junction, meeting. 2. confluence, as of rivers.

ಸಂಗಾತೆ saṅgāte, *see* ಸಂಗಡಿಗೆ.

ಸಂಗೀತ saṅgīta, *s.* A song, psalm, singing, vocal music.

ಸಂಗ್ಮಾನ saṅgmāna, *see* ಸನ್ಮಾನ.

ಸಂಗ್ರಮ saṅgrama, *s.* Storing, piling, heaping, collecting together. 2. *see below.* —ಮಳ್ಪುನಿ to store.

ಸಂಗ್ರಹ saṅgraha, *s.* Acquisition, amassing, collection. 2. compilation. 3. abridgment. 4. taking, receiving, seizing. ನ್ಯಾಯು— a compendium of laws. ಪುಸ್ತಕ— a library. —ಮಳ್ಪುನಿ, ಸಂಗ್ರಹಿಪುನಿ to amass, acquire.

ಸಂಘ saṅgha, *s.* A number *or* multitude of living beings. 2. an association, society.

ಸಂಘಟನ, ಸಂಘಟನೆ saṅghaṭana, saṅghaṭanè, *s.* Occurrence, happening. 2. encountering, meeting. 3. success, achieving. —ಆಪಿನಿ to occur; to meet; to succeed.

ಸಂಚ sanća, *s.* Collection, mass, heap. 2. a hold, support.

ಸಂಚ, ಸಂಚಸಂಚ sanca, sanćasanća, *s.* Difficulty of breathing. —ವೈಪುನಿ to be choked, to gasp.

ಸಂಚಕಾರ sancakāra, *s.* Earnest money, advance. —ಕೊರ್ಪಿನಿ to advance.

ಸಂಚಯನ sańčayana, *s.* Throwing the ashes and bones of the dead into a sacred river.

ಸಂಚರಿಪುನಿ, ಸಂಚರಿಸುನಿ sańčaripuni, sańčarisuni (ಸಂಚರಿ, ಸಂಚರಿಸ್), *v.n.* To wander, roam, travel.

ಸಂಚಾರ sańčāra, *s.* Roaming, wandering, travelling, journeying. –ಮಳ್ಪುನಿ to wander, travel.

ಸಂಚಿ sańči, *see* ತಂಚಿ. 2. *see* ಸಂಚು.

ಸಂಚಿಗಾರ sańčigāra, *see* ಸಂಚಕಾರ.

ಸಂಚಿತ sańčita, *adj.* Acquired, obtained, got. *s.* What has been acquired, as wealth, merit, sin, *etc.*

ಸಂಚು sańču, *s.* Intrigue, plotting. 2. artifice, stratagem. 3. spying. ಉಳ– secret plotting, collusion. –ಗಾರೆ an intriguer. –ದೀಪಿನಿ to spy.

ಸಂಚೆಮಿ sańčemi, *see* ಸಂತೆಮಿ.

ಸಂಚೆಸರಕ್ sańčesaraku, *see* ತಟ್ಟಿ ಸರಕ್ *under* ತಟ್ಟಿ.

ಸಂಜ, ಸಂಜೆ sańja, sańjė, *see* ತಂಜ.

ಸಂಜಿ sańji, *see* ತಂಜಿ.

ಸಂಜೀವನ sańjīvana, *s.* A life-restoring medicine.

ಸಂಜ್ಞೆ sańjńė, *s.* A hint, gesture, sign; *cf.* ಸೊಂಡೆ.

ಸಂಟೆ saṇṭė, *see* ತಂಟೆ.

ಸಂಡಿಗೆ saṇḍigė, *s.* A condiment *or* seasoning made with chillies, asafœtida, cummin seed, *etc.*

ಸಂಣ saṇṇa, *adj.* Small, little. 2. fine, delicate, thin. 3. narrow.

ಸಂಣಿ saṇṇi, *s.* A kind of silk cloth, worn during prayers and meals.

ಸಂತತಿ, ಸಂತಾನ santati, santāna, *s.* Family, progeny, offspring, issue. 2. lineage, race.

ಸಂತರ್ಪಣೆ santarpaṇė, *s.* The ceremony of feeding Brahmans.

ಸಂತಾಪ santāpa, *s.* Burning heat. 2. torment, pain, distress. –ಆಪಿನಿ to be distressed.

ಸಂತುಷ್ಟ santushṭa, *adj.* Pleased, delighted, satisfied. –ಆಪಿನಿ to be satisfied, contented.

ಸಂತುಷ್ಟಿ santushṭi, *s.* Satisfaction, contentedness. –ಉಪ್ಪುನಿ to have contentment.

ಸಂತೃಪ್ತಿ santrupti, *s.* Fulness, satiety, satisfaction. –ಆಪಿನಿ to be satiated, satisfied.

ಸಂತೆ santė, *s.* A market, fair. –ಸರಕ್ goods taken to *or* purchased in a market. –ದೀಪಿನಿ to hold a fair.

ಸಂತೆಮಿ santemi, *s.* The wild mustard, *Cleome icosandra*; *cf.* ದಾಸೆಮಿ.

ಸಂತೆರುನಿ, ಸಂತೆರಿಪುನಿ, ಸಂತೆರಿಸುನಿ santeruni, santeripuni, santerisuni (ಸಂತೆರ್, ಸಂತೆರಿಸ್), *v.a.* To comfort, console, calm, pacify.

ಸಂತೇಸಿ santēsi, *see* ಸಂತತಿ.

ಸಂತೋಲ santōla, *see* ಸತ್ತಿಕಲ್ಲ್ *under* ಸತ್ತಿ.

ಸಂತೋಷ santōsha, *s.* Delight, gladness, joy, pleasure, happiness. –ಆಪಿನಿ to be glad, pleased. —ಮಳ್ಪುನಿ to please. ಸಂತೋಷೊಡುಪ್ಪುನಿ to be happy.

ಸಂದ್ sandụ, *s.* A cleft, fissure, opening. 2. a joint, joining, junction. 3. an interval of time. —ಕಟ್ಟ a crisis, critical time; an opportunity. —ಬೂರು the creeper *Cissus quadrangularis.* —ವಾತ, —ವಾಯು gout, arthritis, rheumatism of the joints. —ಕೂಡಾವುನಿ to rabbet, cement, join, as a fissure. —ಬುಡ್ಪಿನಿ to leave a gap; to crack. —ಮುಟ್ಟುನಿ to be polluted by an unclean contact.

ಸಂದರ್ಪು, ಸಂದರ್ಭ sandarpu, sandarbha, *s.* Convenience, feasibility. 2. opportunity. —ಆಪಿನಿ to be convenient, feasible; to have an opportunity; to get, obtain. —ಮಳ್ಪುನಿ to try for something. —ಮಳ್ತ್ ಕೊರ್ಪಿನಿ to procure.

ಸಂದರ್ಶನ sandarśana, *s.* Seeing; inspection. 2. a visit. —ಮಳ್ಪುನಿ to visit.

ಸಂದಾನ sandāna, *see* ಸಂಧಾನ.

ಸಂದಾಯ sandāya, *s.* Delivering over, making payment. —ಕೊರ್ಪಿನಿ to make a set-off. —ಪಣ್ಪುನಿ to make excuses; to justify. —ಮಳ್ಪುನಿ to pay off; to deliver over.

ಸಂದಾವುನಿ sandāvuni, *c. v.* (*of* ಸಂದುನಿ) To pay, liquidate. 2. to perform, accomplish. 3. to retort. ಗೇಣಿ— to pay rent. ಪರಕೆ— to perform a vow; to do a thing superficially. ಭಾಷೆ— to accomplish a resolution; to fulfil a promise. ಋಣ— to pay a debt; to perform an obligation, *or* to free one's self from it.

ಸಂದಿ sandi, *s.* A call, promise. 2. *see* ಸಂಧಿ. —ಪಾಡುನಿ to call.

ಸಂದು sandu, *see* ಸಂದ್.

ಸಂದುನಿ sanduni (ಸಂದ್), *v. n.* To pass, as time. 2. to pass from this world, die. 3. to be due, indebted. 4. to be paid, liquidated. 5. to come to pass, be accomplished. ಕಾಲ—, ದಿನ— time to pass. ಕೈಲಾಸೊಗು— to depart this life. ಪರಕೆ— a vow to be performed. ಸಾಲ— a debt to be paid. ಆಯಗ್ ಯೆನಡ್ದ ಸಂದುನವು ಉಂಡು I owe him something.

ಸಂದೇಹ sandēha, *s.* Suspicion, doubt, hesitation, scruple. —ಉಪ್ಪುನಿ to feel doubt *or* scruple.

ಸಂದ್ಯುನಿ sandyuni (ಸಂದ್ಯ), *v. a.* To join, unite; to bring in close contact.

ಸಂದ್ಯೆ sandyè, *see* ಸಂದ್.

ಸಂದ್ರಪು sandrapu, *see* ಸಂದರ್ಪು.

ಸಂಧಾನ sandhāna, *s.* Mediation, pacification. —ಮಳ್ಪುನಿ to mediate, go between.

ಸಂಧಿ sandhi, *s.* Junction, union, combination. 2. an interval, pause, rest. 3. the union of letters either at the end *or* beginning of different words *or* in the middle of compound terms, to avoid dissonance *or* hiatus. 4. a chapter. 5. a eulogistic narrative of a great personage.

ಸಂಧಿಪುನಿ **sandhipuni**, *see* ಸಂದ್ಯುನಿ.

ಸಂಧ್ಯಾವಂದನೆ **sandhyāvandanè**, *s.* The daily ceremonies and prayers of the Brahmans.

ಸಂನ್ **sannu**, *s. Anno domini.*

ಸಂನ **sanna**, *see* ಸಂಣ.

ಸಂನದ್, ಸಂನದು **sannadu**, **sannadu**, *s.* An order, a written authority for holding land *or* office. 3. a certificate enrolling a person as a pleader.

ಸಂನದ್ಧ **sannaddha**, *adj.* Ready, arranged.

ಸಂನಯ, ಸಂನಾಯ, ಸಂನಾಹ **sannaya**, **sannāya**, **sannāha**, *s.* Preparation. 2. materials required for a specific purpose. —ಮಳ್ಪುನಿ to prepare.

ಸಂನಿ **sanni**, *s.* Morbid state of the three humours, bile, wind and phlegm. 2. cholera; *also* ಸಂನಿರೋಗ. 3. epilepsy, convulsions. 4. typhus fever; delirium, as in fever; *also* ಸಂನಿಪಾತ. ಬಗ್ಳ್— raving, as in a fit of epilepsy.

ಸಂನಿಧಾನ, ಸಂನಿಧಿ **sannidhāna**, **sannidhi**, *s.* Presence, perceptibility, appearance. 2. proximity. ಸಂನಿಧಾನೊಡು in presence of, before.

ಸಂನಿವಾರ **sannivāra**, *see* ಶನಿವಾರ.

ಸಂನೆ **sannè**, *see* ಸಂಜ್ಞೆ.

ಸಂನ್ಯಾಸ, ಸಂನ್ಯಾಸಿಗೆ **sannyāsa**, **sannyāsigè**, *see* ಸನ್ಯಾಸ.

ಸಂಪಗೆ **sampagè**, *see* ಸಂಪಿಗೆ.

ಸಂಪತ್ತ್ **sampattu**, *s.* Riches, wealth, increase, prosperity; *also* ಸಂಪಟೆ, ಸಂಪಟ, ಸಂಪದ. —ಉಪ್ಪುನಿ to be prosperous.

ಸಂಪಂನ **sampanna**, *adj.* Possessed of, having. 2. accomplished, completed, effected, obtained. 3. prosperous, fortunate, thriving. ಸಂಪಂನೆ a prosperous man.

ಸಂಪಯ **sampaya**, *see* ಸಂಪು.

ಸಂಪಯಿ **sampayi**, *see* ಸಂಪಿಗೆ.

ಸಂಪರ್ಕ **samparka**, *s.* Union, mixture. 2. meeting, contact. —ಆಪಿನಿ to associate with, mix.

ಸಂಪಲ **sampala**, *see* ಸಫಲ. 2. *see* ಸಂಬಳ.

ಸಂಪಲಿಪುನಿ, ಸಂಪಲಿಯುನಿ **sampalipuni**, **sampaliyuni** (ಸಂಪಲಿ), *v. a.* To gain, acquire, attain, earn.

ಸಂಪಾದನೆ **sampādanè**, *s.* Gaining, acquiring, attaining. —ಮಳ್ಪುನಿ, ಸಂಪಾದಿಸುನಿ to gain, acquire.

ಸಂಪಾವುನಿ **sampāvuni** (ಸಂಪಾ), *v. n.* To become calm *or* cool.

ಸಂಪಿಗೆ **sampigè**, *s.* The strong smelling flower *Michelia champaca.* ಕಾಟ್—, ಗೋ— a wild sort of the same, *Plumeria acuminata.* ಕೆಂಪು— a red sort of it. ಗೆಜ್ಜೆ— another sort in the form of a bell. ನಾಗ—,

ಬೊಳ್ಪು– the white sort, *Mesua speciosa*. ನೆಲ– a sweet cented sort, *Kaempferia rotunda*. –ಎಂಣೆ champaca oil.

ಸಂಪಿಗೆತಾಯೆ **sampigetāye**, *s.* A demon so called.

ಸಂಪು **sampu**, *s.* Coolness, coldness. 2. sufficiency, competency. 3. plenty, abundance; *cf.* ತಂಪು. *adj.* Cold, cool, refreshing, pleasant, mild. 2. sufficient. 3. plenty. *adv.* Coolly, gently. –ಮಳ್ಪುನಿ to appease, refresh.

ಸಂಪೂರ್ಣ **sampūrṇa**, *adj.* Whole, entire. 2. complete, finished. –ತೆ completeness, perfection. –ಮಳ್ಪುನಿ to finish.

ಸಂಪೂರ್ತಿ **sampūrti**, *s.* Completion. 2. fulness, satiety. 3. abundance. –ಮಳ್ಪುನಿ to accomplish.

ಸಂಪೊತ್ತು, ಸಂಪೋದು **sampottu, sampōdu**, *see* ಸಂಪತ್ತು.

ಸಂಪ್ರದಾಯ **sampradāya**, *s.* Custom, practice, usage. 2. tradition.

ಸಂಪ್ರಯೋಗ **samprayōga**, *s.* Relation, dependence, association.

ಸಂಪ್ರೀತಿ **samprīti**, *s.* Great love.

ಸಂಪ್ರೋಕ್ಷಣೆ **samprōkshaṇė**, *s.* The ceremonial purification of an idol with milk, ghee, honey, *etc.*; *cf.* ಪ್ರೋಕ್ಷಣೆ.

ಸಂಫಲ **samphala**, *see* ಸಫಲ.

ಸಂಬಂಧ **sambandha**, *s.* Connection, relation, affinity.

ಸಂಬಡ **sambaḍa**, *see* ತಂಬಡ.

ಸಂಬರ **sambara**, *s.* Spicery, seasoning. –ಬಳ್ಳಿ the thick-leaved lavender, *Anisochilus carnosus*. [ಬಾಳಿಸುನಿ.

ಸಂಬಲಿಯುನಿ **sambaliyuni**, *see* ಸಂ

ಸಂಬಳ **sambaḷa**, *s.* Pay, salary, wages. –ದಾಯೆ a man in one's pay. –ಕೊರ್ಪಿನಿ to pay wages.

ಸಂಬಾರ **sambāra**, *see* ಸಂಬರ.

ಸಂಬಾಳಿಸುನಿ **sambāḷisuni** (ಸಂಬಾಳಿ ಸಿ), *v. a.* To sustain, bear, support; to appease. 2. to manage, control. ಕೋಪ– to control one's temper. ಬೇನೆ– to endure pain.

ಸಂಬಿ **sambi**, *s.* Secrets; spying; *cf.* ಬೇಡ. –ಪಾಡುನಿ to spy.

ಸಂಬುರ್ಮ **samburma**, *see* ಸಂಭ್ರಮ.

ಸಂಬೋಧನೆ **sambōdhanė**, *s.* Addressing, calling. 2. the vocative case, *gram.*

ಸಂಭವ **sambhava**, *s.* Birth, production. 2. cause, origin. 3. possibility, occurrence.

ಸಂಭವಿಪುನಿ **sambhavipuni** (ಸಂಭವಿ), *v. n.* To be born, befall, happen.

ಸಂಭಾವನೆ **sambhāvanė**, *s.* Honour, respect, respectability. 2. a present, reward.

ಸಂಭಾವಿಕೆ, ಸಂಭಾವಿತೆ **sambhāvike, sambhāvite**, *s.* A respectable man.

ಸಂಭಾಷಣೆ **sambhāshaṇė**, *s.* Dialogue, conversation, discourse. –ಮಳ್ಪುನಿ to converse.

ಸಂಭೋಗ **sambhōga**, *s.* Sexual pleasure; sexual embrace. 2. enjoyment, delight, luxury.

ಸಂಭ್ರಮ sambhrama, *s.* Joy, delight, pleasure. 2. grandeur.

ಸಂಮಂಧ sammandha, *s.* Connection by affinity, connection in general; *cf.* ಸಂಬಂಧ. *adj.* Connected with, endowed with, belonging to, possessing. ಸಂಮಂಧಕೆ a relative. –ಉಪ್ಪುನಿ to be related to.

ಸಂಮಗಾರೆ sammagāre, *see* ಸಮ್ಮಗಾರೆ.

ಸಂಮತ, ಸಂಮತಿ sammata, sammati, *s.* Assent, agreement; acquiescence; *also* ಸಮ್ಮಂತ. –ಆಪಿನಿ to assent, agree, yield, comply. –ಉಪ್ಪುನಿ to agree to, to be willing, to acquiesce in. –ಮಳ್ಪುನಿ to consent, agree to, accept. –ಕೊರ್ಪಿನಿ to give consent. –ಗೆತೊಣುನಿ to receive assent.

ಸಂಮನ sammana, *see* ತಂಮಣ.

ಸಂಮನಿಯುನಿ sammaniyuni, *see* ತಂಮಣೆಪುನಿ.

ಸಂಮಲೆ sammalè, *see* ತಂಮಲೆ.

ಸಂಮಾನ sammāna, *see* ಸನ್ಮಾನ. 2. *see* ತಂಮಣ.

ಸಂಮರ sammara, *see* ಸಂಹಾರ.

ಸಂಮುಖ sammukha, *adj.* Encountering, opposite, facing. ಸಂಮುಖೊಡು in front of, in the presence of.

ಸಂಮೇಳ sammēḷa, *s.* A double drum. 2. mixing, blending; union.

ಸಂಯುಕ್ತ saṁyukta, *adj.* Endowed with, possessed of. 2. united, joined, annexed. 3. compound.

ಸಂಯೋಗ saṁyōga, *s.* Intimate union, contact, communion, association. 2. copulation, sexual embrace. –ಮಳ್ಪುನಿ to copulate.

ಸಂರಕ್ಷಕೆ saṁrakshake, *s.* A saviour, protector, nourisher.

ಸಂರಕ್ಷಣೆ saṁrakshaṇè, *s.* Maintenance, support, protection, nourishment, care of. –ಮಳ್ಪುನಿ, ಸಂರಕ್ಷಿಪುನಿ to protect, nourish.

ಸಂಗೊಡೆ saṅgoḍe, *s.* A slender man.

ಸಂವತ್ಸರ saṁvatsara, *s.* A year, especially of the Hindu cycle of sixty.

ಸಂವಾದ saṁvāda, *s.* Dialogue.

ಸಂವಾರ saṁvāra, *see* ಸಂಹಾರ.

ಸಂಶಯ saṁśaya, *s.* Doubt, uncertainty, suspicion, scruple, hesitation. –ಉಪ್ಪುನಿ to have scruples *or* doubt. –ಮಳ್ಪುನಿ to doubt, hesitate.

ಸಂಸರ್ಗ saṁsarga, *s.* Union, proximity, contact. 2. acquaintance, intercourse, familiarity. –ಉಪ್ಪುನಿ to have intercourse. –ಮಳ್ಪುನಿ to associate with.

ಸಂಸಾರ saṁsāra, *s.* A family, household. 3. the world *or* habitation of mortals. –ತಾಪತ್ರಯ family cares. –ಪಾಶ family ties. –ಸಾಗರ the whole family. –ಸುಖ worldly happiness. –ಮಳ್ಪುನಿ to be a family-man, to keep house. ಸಂಸಾರಿಕೆ a family-man.

ಸಂಸ್ಕಾರ saṁskāra, *s.* A purificatory rite *or* ceremony. 2. burning *or* burying a dead body. –ಮಾಳ್ಪುನಿ to burn *or* bury a dead body.

ಸಂಸ್ಕೃತ saṁskṛuta, *s.* The Sanskrit language.

ಸಂಸ್ಥಾನ saṁsthāna, *s.* A seat of government, the royal city. 2. a kingdom, state, presidency. ಮದ್ರಾಸ್– the Madras presidency.

ಸಂಹಾರ saṁhāra, *s.* Destruction, killing, annihilation. –ಮಾಳ್ಪುನಿ, ಸಂಹರಿಪುನಿ to destroy, kill, annihilate.

ಸಂಹಿತೆ saṁhitė, *s.* An arrangement of the text of the Vēdas into short sentences. 2. a code, digest.

ಸಂಕ್ಷಿಪ್ತ saṅkshipta, *adj.* Abbreviated, abridged, brief.

ಸಂಕ್ಷೇಪ saṅkshēpa, *s.* Abridgment, brevity. –ಆದ್ ಪಣ್ಪುನಿ to say briefly. –ಮಾಳ್ಪುನಿ, ಸಂಕ್ಷೇಪಿಸುನಿ to abridge.

ಸಕ saka, *see* ಸಾಸ.

ಸಕಣ sakaṇa, *s.* An omen; *bet.* ಶಕುನ. –ಕ್ಕಿ an ominous bird.

ಸಕತಿ sakati, *see* ಶಕ್ತಿ.

ಸಕಲ sakala, *s.* The aggregate, whole. *adj.* All, entire, whole. –ಸಂಗತಿ all facts.

ಸಕಲಾತಿ, ಸಕಲಾತು sakalāti, sakalātu, *s.* Superior woollen stuffs.

ಸಕಾಯ sakāya, *s.* Easiness. 2. *see* ಸಹಾಯ.

ಸಕಿ saki, *see* ಸಖಿ.

ಸಕಿಯುನಿ sakiyuni (ಸಕ್), *v. a.* To submit.

ಸಕೆ, ಸಕ್ಕ್, ಸಕ್ಕೆ sakė, sakku, sakkė, *see* ಶಕ್ಕ್.

ಸಕ್ಕಣ sakkaṇa, *s.* A small mat. 2. a net. 2. *see* ಶಕ್ಕಣ. 3. *see* ಸಕಣ.

ಸಕ್ಕರೆ sakkarė, *s.* Sugar. ಕಂಚಿ– the pumplemose fruit. ಕಲ್ಲ್– sugar candy. ಚೀನಿ– China sugar. ಮೋರಿಸ್– Mauritius sugar.

ಸಕ್ಕೆಲ್ sakkelu, *see* ಸಜ್ಜ.

ಸಕ್ಕೆಲ sakkela, *s.* A proper *or* suitable time.

ಸಕ್ತಿ sakti, *s.* Force, constraint, exaction. 2. *see* ಶಕ್ತಿ.

ಸಕ್ರ sakra, *see* ಚಕ್ರ.

ಸಖಾಯ sakhāya, *see* ಸಕಾಯ.

ಸಖಿ sakhi, *s.* A female friend.

ಸಖೆ sakhe, *s.* A male friend.

ಸಖ್ಯ sakhya, *s.* Friendship, amity, intimacy. 2. *see* ಶಕ್ಯ.

ಸಗುತಿ saguti, *see* ಶಕ್ತಿ.

ಸಗುಳೆ sagulė, *see* ತಗುಳೆ.

ಸಗೆ sage, *see* ತಗೆ.

ಸಗೋತ್ರೆ sagōtre, *s.* A distant kinsman descended from a common ancestor of the same family-name, as among Brahmans; *also* ಸಗೋತ್ರದಾಯಿ. ಸಗೋತ್ರ a relationship of this description.

ಸಗ್ತಿ sagti, *see* ಶಕ್ತಿ.

ಸಗ್ಮೆ sagme, *see* ತಗ್ಮೆ.

ಸಚಲಸ್ನಾನ, ಸಚೇಲಸ್ನಾನ sacalasnāna, sacēlasnāna, *s.* Bathing with all one's clothes on. —ಮಳ್ಪುನಿ to bathe in this way.

ಸಚ್ಚ sacca, *see* ಸತ್ಯ.

ಸಚ್ಚಿದಾನಂದೆ saccidānande, *s.* God, the eternal source of wisdom and happiness.

ಸಚ್ಯ sacya, *s.* Expense. —ಪಾಲ್ಯುನಿ to pay expenses.

ಸಜ saja, *see* ಸಜಾ.

ಸಜಪು sajapu, *see* ತಜಪು.

ಸಜಾ sajā, *s.* Punishment, fine. 2. annoyance, trouble. —ಆಪಿನಿ to be punished. —ಕೊರ್ಪಿನಿ to punish.

ಸಜಾಬ್ sajābụ, *see* ಸದಾಪು.

ಸಜಿಬಿಜಿ sajibiji, *see* ತಜಿಬಿಜಿ.

ಸಜೀವ sajīva, *adj.* Animate, lively.

ಸಜ್ಜ sajja, *s.* A short time. *adj.* Instant, temporary. ಸಜ್ಜೊಗು presently, now, recently, lately; shortly; temporarily. ಸಜ್ಜೊಗು ಆದ್ for the present use; temporarily, *etc.* ಸಜ್ಜೊಗು ಬೇಲೆ ಉಜ್ಜಿ there is no work for the present. ಸಜ್ಜೊಗು ಬರ್ಪಳ್ she will come shortly.

ಸಜ್ಜಂದಿ sajjandi, *s.* A good woman, gentle woman.

ಸಜ್ಜನ sajjana, *adj.* Virtuous, good. 2. gentle.

ಸಜ್ಜನಿಗೆ sajjanigè, *s.* Virtue, goodness. 2. gentleness, meekness.

ಸಜ್ಜನೆ sajjane, *s.* A good man; a gentle man.

ಸಜ್ಜಲ್ಮೆ sajjalmè, *see* ಸಜ್ಜನಿಗೆ.

ಸಜ್ಜಿ sajji, *adj.* Good, well, proper, fine, excellent. 2. healthy. *adv.* Well, nicely, properly. —ದ ಆಣ್ a fine lad. —ದ ನಡತೆ a good behaviour. —ದ ಪಾತೆರ a proper speech. —ಡ್ ಉಪ್ಪುನಿ to enjoy good health, be well. —ಡ್ ಕೇಣುನಿ to hear attentively. —ಡ್ ತಿನ್ಪುನಿ to eat heartily. —ಡ್ ನೋಂಪುನಿ to thrash soundly. —ಮಳ್ಪುನಿ to make a thing well.

ಸಜ್ಜಿಗೆ sajjigè, *s.* Rolong *or* wheaten grits.

ಸಟಾಸಟಿ saṭāsaṭi, *adj.* Grating, harsh. *adv.* Harshly, severely. —ಪಾತೆರುನಿ to speak harshly.

ಸಟೆ saṭè, *s.* Falsehood; *also* ಸಟೆಸಟೆ.

ಸಟ್ಟ saṭṭa, *see* ಚಟ್ಟ.

ಸಟ್ಟಿ saṭṭi, *s.* A kind of wooden laddle. 2. *see* ಷಷ್ಟಿ. 3. a feast on the night of the sixth day of a child's birth.

ಸಟ್ಟುಗ saṭṭuga, *see* ತಟ್ಟುಗ.

ಸಡಗ saḍaga, *adj.* Hard.

ಸಡಗರ saḍagara, *see* ಸಿಡಗರ.

ಸಡಿತ saḍita, *s.* A purpose, vow, resolution. 2. a bet, wager.

ಸಡಿಲ್ saḍilụ, *adj.* Loose, slack, loosened. —ಆಪಿನಿ to become loose. —ಬುಡ್ಪಿನಿ to let loose. —ಮಳ್ಪುನಿ to loosen, slacken.

ಸಡ್ಡ್ saḍḍụ, *s.* Disdain, inattention, negligence. 2. satiety, indifference. 3. facility, ease. ಆ ಕೆಲಸ ಸಡ್ಡಿಗ ಸಮು he can do the work with the greatest ease. ಆ ಸಾದಿ ಸಡ್ಡಿಗ ಸಮು it is nothing to him to go by that road. ಪಂಡಿ ಪಾತೆರ ಸಡ್ಡಿಗ ಸಮು he would not listen to what he was told.

ಸಡ್ಡ್ಕೆ saḍḍụke, *s.* The relation in which the husbands of two sisters stand to each other.

ಸಡ್ಡೆ saḍḍè, *see* ಸಡ್ಡ್.

ಸಡ್ಸುಡು saḍsuḍu, *see* ಸುಡ್ಸುಡು.

ಸಣಿಪುನಿ, ಸನಿಯುನಿ saṇipuni, saniyuni (ಸಣಿ, ಸನಿ), *v. n.* To cool, grow calm, be mitigated.

ಸಣೆ saṇè, *s.* A fine cloth; *cf.* ಸಂಣೆ. 2. *see* ಸನಿ.

ಸಣ್ಣ saṇṇa, *see* ಸಂಣ.

ಸತ್ satụ, *adj.* (*in comp.*) True, good, virtuous, excellent, right, proper. –ಕಥೆ a true story. –ಕರ್ಮ, –ಕಾರ್ಯ a good action. –ಪಾತ್ರ worthiness. –ಪಾತ್ರೆ, –ಪುರುಷೆ a worthy man. –ಪುತ್ರೆ an excellent son.

ಸತಿ sati, *s.* A virtuous woman. 2. a woman in general.

ಸತು, ಸತುವ satu, satuva, *see* ಸತ್ವ.

ಸತ್ಕಾರ satkāra, *s.* Politeness, honour, respect. –ಮಳ್ಪುನಿ, ಸತ್ಕರಿಪುನಿ to show respect.

ಸತ್ತಿ satti (*corrup. of* ಶಕ್ತಿ), *s.* Power, strength. –ಕಲ್ಲ್ a heavy stone to be lifted up to try one's strength. –ಕೋಲು a stick to try one's strength with another in wrestling.

ಸತ್ತಿಗೆ sattigè, *s.* An umbrella, a parasol.

ಸತ್ತೀಕೆ sattīke, *see* ಸಾಕ್ಷಿಕೆ.

ಸತ್ಯ satya, *s.* Truth. 2. justice, honesty. *adj.* True, sincere, honest. –ತ್ವ truth; credibility. –ವಂತೆ a truthful man; a sincere man. –ಆಪಿನಿ truth to prevail; justice to be done. –ಜೆಪ್ಪಿನಿ, –ಮಳ್ಪುನಿ to do justice. –ಮುನಿಯುನಿ to be cursed.

ಸತ್ಯೆ satyè, *s.* An umbrella.

ಸತ್ವ satva, *s.* Life, vitality. 2. power, strength. 3. essence, substance. –ದಾಂತಿ powerless. –ಉಪ್ಪುನಿ to be strong *or* vigorous.

ಸದ್ sadụ, *see* ಸದು. 2. *see* ಸತ್.

ಸದ್ರ್, ಸದ್ರಂಗ sadụrụ, sadụraṅga, *s.* The front. 2. spreading abroad, becoming public. –ಗ ಬರ್ಪಿನಿ to come to the front; to appear before the public; to become published.

ಸದರ್, ಸದರು sadarụ, sadaru, *s.* A throne. 2. a mattress, carpet. 3. *see* ಸದ್ರ್.

ಸದರಮೀನೆ sadaramīne, *s.* A subordinate judge.

ಸದರಿ sadari, *see* ಸದ್ರಿ.

ಸದಾ sadā, *adv.* Always, at all times, perpetually, for ever. –ಕಾಲ, –ಕಾಲೊಗು for ever. –ತ್ಮೆ the eternal Spirit.

ಸದಾಚಾರ sadâčâra, *s.* Regular observance of all duties, good conduct.

ಸದಾಪು, ಸದಾಬು sadâpu, sadâbu, *s.* The rue plant, *Ruta graveolens.* [2. *see* ಚದಿ.

ಸದಿ sadi, *s.* Striking, beating.

ಸದು sadu, *s.* Sound, noise. 2. answer, reply. 3. rebutting. –ಕೊರ್ಪಿನಿ to answer. ಆಯ ಪಾತೆ ರೊಗು ಸದು ಇಜ್ಜಿ his words are unimpeachable.

ಸದುರಂಗ sadurañga, *see* ಸದರ್.

ಸದೃಶ sadruša, *adj.* Like, similar, resembling.

ಸದೆವುನಿ sadevuni (ಸದೆ), *v. n.* To get hardened. 2. to wear away, as an earthen vessel.

ಸದೊಳಿಗೆ sadoligè, *s.* Course, way.

ಸದ್ಗತಿ sadgati, *s.* Heaven, bliss. –ಅಕ್ಕುನಿ to attain bliss.

ಸದ್ಗುಣ sadguṇa, *s.* An excellent nature *or* disposition.

ಸದ್ಗುರು sadguru *s.* A virtuous spiritual guide.

ಸದ್ದು saddu, *see* ಸದು. [ಸಜ್ಜ.

ಸದ್ಯ, ಸದ್ಯೋಗು sadya, sadyogu, *see*

ಸದ್ರಂಗ sadrañga, *see* ಸದರ್.

ಸದ್ರಿ sadri, *adj.* Aforesaid, abovementioned.

ಸದ್ರೂಪ sadrûpa, *adv.* As it is, in an axact *or* true form. 2. face to face.

ಸನ್ sanu, *see* ಸಂನ್.

ಸನಂಗ್, ಸನಗ್ sanañgu, sanagu, *s.* A thing, article. 2. a piece of cloth brought to the market.

ಸನಮತ sanamata, *see* ಸಂಮತ.

ಸನಾನಿ sanâni, *see* ಚನಾನಿ.

ಸನಿ sani, *see* ಶನಿ. 2. *see* ಸಂನಿ.

ಸನಿಯಾರ saniyâra, *s.* Saturday.

ಸನಿಪ sanipa, *see* ಸಮೀಪ.

ಸನಿಪಾವುನಿ sanipâvuni, *c. v.* (*of* ಸನಿಪುನಿ) To make cold *or* cool. 2. to pacify, conciliate, comfort.

ಸನಿಪುನಿ sanipuni (ಸನಿ), *v. a.* To cool, render cold. 2. to refresh; to set at ease.

ಸನಿಯ saniya, *see* ಸಮೀಪ.

ಸನಿಯುನಿ saniyuni (ಸನಿ), *v. n.* To become cold; to be cool; to be softened.

ಸನಿಯೆಸ್ರೆ saniyesre, *see* ಶನಿ.

ಸನಿಲ್ sanilu, *s.* A bayonet.

ಸನೀಪ sanîpa, *see* ಸಮೀಪ.

ಸನು sanu, *see* ತನು.

ಸನೆ sanè, *see* ತನೆ.

ಸನ್ನ sanna, *see* ಸಂಣ.

ಸನ್ಮಾನ sanmâna, *s.* Respect, honour, politeness. –ಮಳ್ಪುನಿ, ಸನ್ಮಾನಿಸುನಿ to show respect, treat politely.

ಸನ್ಮಾರ್ಗ sanmârga, *s.* Morality, good conduct, true way.

ಸನ್ಯಾಸ sanyâsa, *s.* Asceticism.

ಸನ್ಯಾಸಿ sanyâsi, *s.* An ascetic.

ಸಪ sapa, *s.* Polish, smoothness. –ಸಾರ sap. –ಇಜ್ಜಿ there is no polish.

ಸಪತ sapata, *see* ಶಪಥ.

ಸಪಲ sapala, *see* ಸಫಲ. 2. *see* ತಪಲ.

ಸಪಲಿಯೆ, ಸಪಲೆ **sapaliye, sapale,** *see* ಸಪಲ್ಯೆ.

ಸಪಲೆ, ಸಪ್ಪಲೆ **sapalè, sappalè,** *see* ತಪಲೆ.

ಸಪಲ್ಯೆ, ಸಪಳೆ **sapalye, sapaḷe,** *s. lit.* A spearman. 2. a fisherman.

ಸಪಸಾರ **sapasāra,** *s.* Taste.

ಸಪಾಯಿ **sapāyi,** *adj.* Even, level, smooth. —ಆಪಿನಿ to become smooth. —ಮಳ್ಪುನಿ to make smooth.

ಸಪಾರ್ಣೆ **sapārṇè,** *s.* Fasting.

ಸಪುರ, ಸಪೂರ **sapura, sapūra,** *adj.* Delicate, thin, fine, narrow.

ಸಪೆ **sapè,** *s.* A page.

ಸಪೇತ್ **sapētu̥,** *see* ಸಫೇತ್.

ಸಪ್ತ **sapta,** *adj.* Seven. —ಸ್ವರ the seven notes of the gamut.

ಸಪ್ತಮ **saptama,** *adj.* Seventh. ಸಪ್ತಮಿ the seventh day of the lunar fortnight.

ಸಪ್ಪ **sappa,** *see* ಚಪ್ಪೆ.

ಸಪ್ಪಳ **sappaḷa,** *see* ತಪ್ಪಳ.

ಸಪ್ಪು **sappu,** *see* ತಪ್ಪು.

ಸಪ್ಪೆ **sappè,** *see* ಚಪ್ಪೆ.

ಸಫಲ **saphala,** *s.* Success, prosperity, reward. —ಆಪಿನಿ to be successful. —ಮಳ್ಪುನಿ to make successful.

ಸಫೇತ್ **saphētu̥,** *adj.* White. *s.* White lead. —ಬಂಣ white colour.

ಸಬಕು **sabaku,** *see* ತಬಕ್.

ಸಬಟ್ **sabaṭu̥,** *see* ತಬಟ.

ಸಬಟುನಿ **sabaṭuni,** *see* ತಬಟುನಿ.

ಸಬಟೆ **sabaṭè,** *see* ತಬಟೆ.

ಸಬಬ್, ಸಬಾಬ್ **sababu̥, sabābu̥,** *s.* Cause, reason, ground.

ಸಬರ **sabara,** *s.* A pack-saddle.

ಸಬಾಪುನಿ **sabāpuni,** *see* ಸಬಾಸುನಿ.

ಸಬಾಸುನಿ **sabāsuni** (ಸಬಾಸ್), *v. a.* To please, satisfy.

ಸಬಾಸ್ **sabāsu̥,** *see* ಶಬಾಸ್.

ಸಬಿ **sabi,** *s.* Flavour, taste. *adj.* Savoury, palatable, pleasant, sweet.

ಸಬಿಪುನಿ **sabipuni** (ಸಬಿ), *v. a.* To taste, try the flavour.

ಸಬುಕಾರ **sabukāra,** *s.* Soap.

ಸಬುರು **saburu,** *s.* Halt; delay. 2. *see* ತಬುರು.

ಸಬುಲಿ **sabuli,** *see* ತಬ್ಬುಲಿ.

ಸಬೆಪುನಿ **sabepuni,** *see* ತಬೆಪುನಿ.

ಸಬ್ಬಳ್ **sabbaḷu̥,** *s.* A crow-bar used for digging.

ಸಬ್ಬುಲಿ **sabbuli,** *see* ತಬ್ಬುಲಿ.

ಸಭೆ **sabhè,** *s.* A convocation, assembly, meeting. 2. a royal court; a council-hall. ಸಭಾಪತಿ the president of an assembly. ಸಭಾಲಯ the place of public meeting; a church, chapel. ಸಭಾಶಿಕ್ಷೆ church-discipline. —ತ ಕ್ರಮ church rules. —ತ ಹಿರಿಯೆ an elder, church-warden. —ತಾಯೆ a church-member; a councillor, member of an assembly. —ಅಗಪುನಿ an assembly to disperse. —ಕೂಡುನಿ an assembly to meet. —ಕ ಸೇರುನಿ to join a church (by baptism *or* confirmation). –ಡ್ದ ತಿರ್ ದೀಪಿನಿ, –ಡ್ದ ಬಹಿಷ್ಕಾರ ಮಳ್ಪುನಿ to excommunicate.

ಸಮ್‌ಗಾರೆ **samugāre,** *s.* A chuckler, shoemaker.

ಸಮ **sama,** *adj.* Like, similar. 2. same, even, equal. 3. uniform, equable. 4. right, just, proper. –ಕ್ರಯ proper value. –ಪಾಲ್ equal shares. –ರಾತ್ರಿ midnight. –ತೂಪಿನಿ to compare. –ಬೂರುನಿ to agree, coincide; to fit, suit. –ಮಳ್ಪುನಿ to make level; to put right; to make equal; to correct, rectify.

ಸಮಂತ **samanta,** *adj.* All, whole; ಸಮಂತೆರ್ all people.

ಸಮಕಟ್ಟ್ **samakaṭṭu,** *s.* Proportion, fitness, suitability. 2. level, smoothness of surface. –ಆಯಿ ನೆಲ a level, even surface. –ಉಪ್ಪುನಿ to fit, agree.

ಸಮಗಾರೆ **samagāre,** *see* ಸಮ್‌ಗಾರೆ.

ಸಮಗ್ರ **samagra,** *adj.* All, entire, full, complete.

ಸಮಜಯಿಸಿಗೆ, ಸಮಜೈಸಿಗೆ **samajayisigè, samajeisigè,** *s.* Pacification, satisfaction, consolation. –ಮಳ್ಪುನಿ to calm, appease.

ಸಮಜಯಿಸುನಿ, ಸಮಜೈಸುನಿ **samajayisuni, samajeisuni** (ಸಮಜೈಸ್), *v. a.* To appease, calm, pacify. 2. to comfort, console.

ಸಮತೆ, ಸಮತ್ವ **samatè, samatva,** *s.* Equality, proportion. 2. similarity.

ಸಮನಿಸುನಿ **samanisuni** *see* ತಂಮಣಿಪುನಿ.

ಸಮಯ **samaya,** *s.* Time, season, opportunity. 2. leisure. –ಉಪ್ಪುನಿ to have time; to be at leisure. –ಕಾಪುನಿ, –ತೂಪಿನಿ to watch for an opportunity. –ಕೊರ್ಪಿನಿ to allow time.

ಸಮರ **samara,** *s.* Conflict, war.

ಸಮರ್ಥ **samartha,** *adj.* Strong, powerful. 2. able, capable.

ಸಮರ್ಥಿಗೆ **samarthigè,** *see* ಸಾಮರ್ಥಿಗೆ.

ಸಮರ್ಥಿಪುನಿ **samarthipuni** (ಸಮರ್ಥ್), *v. a.* To overcome any difficulty; to succeed.

ಸಮರ್ಥೆ **samarthe,** *s.* An able man, powerful man.

ಸಮರ್ಧನೆ **samardhanè,** *see* ಸಮಾರಾಧನೆ.

ಸಮರ್ಪಕ **samarpaka,** *adj.* Proper, fit, appropriate; pertinent. –ಜವಾಬು a proper answer. –ಆದ್ ಪಣ್ಪುನಿ to speak pertinently.

ಸಮರ್ಪಣೆ **samarpaṇè,** *s.* An offering. –ಮಳ್ಪುನಿ, ಸಮರ್ಪಿಸುನಿ to offer, sacrifice.

ಸಮಸ್ತ **samasta,** *adj.* All, whole, entire.

ಸಮಕ್ಷ, ಸಮಕ್ಷಮ **samaksha, samakshama,** *adv.* Before, in presence *or* sight of. *s.* Presence, sight. ಆಯ ಸಮಕ್ಷಮೊಡು in his presence.

ಸಮಾಗಮ **samāgama,** *s.* Union, junction. 2. coming, arriving.

ಸಮಾಚಾರ **samācāra,** *s.* Tidings, news, intelligence, information. 2. a message. ಕ್ಷೇಮ– the intelligence of one's welfare.

ಸಮಾಜ samāja, *s.* A multitude, assembly. 2. a society, association.

ಸಮಾಧಾನ samādhāna, *s.* Peace, tranquillity. 2. conciliation, consent, agreement. 3. reconciling differences. 4. welfare, well-being. –ಆಪಿನಿ to be reconciled; to agree, consent; a sickness to become subdued. –ಉಪ್ಪುನಿ to have peace; to feel better. –ಮಳ್ಪುನಿ to reconcile, console, appease.

ಸಮಾಧಿ samādhi, *s.* A grave, tomb. 2. deep meditation. 3. silence. –ಡ್ ಉಪ್ಪುನಿ to be absorbed in meditation.

ಸಮಾನ samāna, *adj.* Like, similar, analogous. 2. equal. 3. one, uniform, same; *cf.* ಸಮ, ಸಾಮಾನ್. –ತ್ವ equality. –ವಸ್ತುಳು similar things. –ಸ್ಥ an equal person.

ಸಮಾಪ್ತ samāpta, *adj.* Finished, completed.

ಸಮಾಪ್ತಿ samāpti, *s.* Completion, finishing, end. 2. killing, destroying. –ಆಪಿನಿ to be completed. –ಮಳ್ಪುನಿ to complete, finish.

ಸಮಾರ samāra, *see* ಸಂಹಾರ.

ಸಮಾರಾಧನೆ samārādhanè, *s.* Worship, reverence. 2. a public feast to Brahmans.

ಸಮಾಸ samāsa, *s.* Composition of words, formation of compound terms, *gram.*

ಸಮಿಧೆ samidhè, *s.* Short sticks of particular trees used in burnt offerings.

ಸಮೀಪ samīpa, *s.* Neighbourhood, proximity. *adj.* Near, close by.

ಸಮುಖ samukha, *s.* Presence, proximity. ಸಮುಖೊಗ್, ಸಮುಖೊಡ್ near to, in the presence of.

ಸಮುಗಾರೆ samugāre, *see* ಸಮ್ಗಾರೆ.

ಸಮುಚ್ಚಯ samuččaya, *s.* Collection, assemblage. 2. conjunction of words *or* sentences, *gram.*

ಸಮುದಯ, ಸಮುದಾಯ samudaya, samudāya, *s.* Assemblage, heap, multitude, number, quantity. ಜನ– a multitude of persons. ಸಮುದಾಯೊಡು generally, on the whole.

ಸಮುದ್ರ samudra, *s.* The ocean, sea. –ಸ್ನಾನ a ceremony of bathing in the sea at new moon in the month Āṭi. –ಫಲ the fruit of the tree *Borringtonia racemosa*; fish.

ಸಮೂಹ samūha, *s.* Aggregate, assemblage, multitude.

ಸಮೃದ್ಧಿ samṛddhi, *s.* Prosperity, success. 2. increase, thriving. ಬುಳೆತ– an abundance of crop. –ಆಪಿನಿ to prosper.

ಸಮೇತ samēta, *adj.* Accompanied by, associated with, possessing.

ಸಯನ sayana, *see* ಶಯನ.

ಸಯಿ sayi, *see* ಸೈ.

ಸಯಿಪಿನಿ sayipini, *see* ಸೈಪಿನಿ.

ಸಯಿಲೆ sayilè, *s.* A ghost, goblin.

ಸಯಿಸುನಿ sayisuni, *see* ಸಹಿಸುನಿ.

ಸರ sara, *s.* A string of beads *or* pearls; a wreath, garland; a necklace. ಜಪ– a rosary. ನಾಣ್ಯದ– a necklace of coins.

ಸರ sara, *see* ಸ್ವರ.

ಸರಂಕ್ saranku, *s.* A kind of suffocation caused while swallowing any liquid.

ಸರಂಕಲ್ಲ್ sarankallu, *see* ಸರೆಂಕಲ್ಲ್.

ಸರಂಗ್ sarangu, *s.* A trench, mine, hole, tunnel. 2. a rat's hole.

ಸರಂಜಾಮ್ saranjāmu, *s.* Tools, implements, goods. 2. furniture. –ಮಳ್ಪುನಿ to prepare, furnish.

ಸರಕ್ saraku, *s.* Articles, goods, commodity. –ಜಪ್ಪುಡುನಿ, –ದೆಪ್ಪುನಿ to unlade; to land goods. –ದಿಂಜಾವುನಿ, –ಪಾಡುನಿ to lade, load; to freight.

ಸರಕ್ saraku, *intj.* Get out of the way! slip aside!

ಸರಕಾರ್ sarakāru, *s.* Government. –ಕೆಲಸ the government service. –ದ ಪಣವು the public money, assessment, revenue.

ಸರಕೊಣುನಿ sarakoṇuni, *see* ತರಕೊಣುನಿ.

ಸರದ್ saradu, *see* ಸರಹದ್ದ್.

ಸರದಾನಿ saradāni, *s.* A cry, noise.

ಸರದಾರ್, ಸರದಾರೆ saradāru, saradāre, *s.* A European. 2. a person of superior rank.

ಸರದಿ saradi, *s.* Cold, catarrh.

ಸರಪಣಿ, ಸರಪಳಿ, sarapaṇi, sarapaḷi, *see* ಸರಪೊಳಿ.

ಸರಪತಿ sarapati, *see* ಸರ್ಪತಿ.

ಸರಪಿತ sarapita, *see* ಸರ್ಪಿತ.

ಸರಪೊಳಿ sarapoḷi, *s.* A chain of any metal.

ಸರಬರಾಯಿ sarabarāyi, *s.* Furnishing supplies, preparation. –ಕೊರ್ಪಿನಿ, –ಮಳ್ಪುನಿ to furnish supplies.

ಸರಯಿ sarayi, *see* ಸಾರಾಯಿ.

ಸರಲ್ saralu, *see* ಸರಳ್.

ಸರಲೆ saralè, *see* ತರಳೆ.

ಸರಸ್ sarasu, *s.* A joke. 2. merriment. *adj.* Tasty, sapid. 2. jocose, merry.

ಸರಸರ sarasara, *adj.* Hastily, quickly, speedily.

ಸರಸ್ವತಿ sarasvati, *s.* Brahma's wife, the goddess of speech, learning, music, *etc.*

ಸರಹದ್ದ್ sarahaddu, *s.* Limit, boundary, frontier.

ಸರಳ್ saraḷu, *s.* A bar of iron.

ಸರಳ saraḷa, *adj* Straight. 2. sincere. 3. easy.

ಸರಳಜುಮಾದಿ saraḷajumādi, *s.* A demon so called.

ಸರಳಿ sarali, *see* ಸರೊಳಿ.

ಸರಳೆ saraḷè, *see* ತರಳೆ.

ಸರಾಗ್, ಸರಾಗ sarāgu, sarāga, *adj.* Easy, facile, convenient. 2. free, unobstructed. –ಮಾರ್ಗ

a straight road. —ಪೋಪಿನಿ to go straightly. ಈ ಆಯನ ಸರಾಗ ಪಾತೆರೊಲಿ you can freely speak to him. —ಆದ್ easily, freely.

ಸರಾನೆ sarānè, *adv.* Directly, straightly. —ಪೋಪಿನಿ to go straightly without lingering in the way.

ಸರಾಫೆ sarāphe, *s.* A jeweller. 2. a money-changer.

ಸರಾಬು sarābu, *see* ಶರಾಬ್.

ಸರಾಯಿ sarāyi, *see* ಸುರಾಯಿ.

ಸರಾರಿಯುನಿ sarāriyuni (ಸರಾರಿ), *v.n.* To be exact.

ಸರಾಸರಿ sarāsari, *adv.* Equally, alike. *adj.* Right, proper. *s.* An average. —ಕೊರ್ಪಿನಿ to give alike. —ತೂಪಿನಿ to find out an average.

ಸರಿ sari, *adj.* Equal, like. 2. just, right, proper, fit. 3. even, not odd. 4. full; *cf.* ಸಮ. *adv.* Good, very well, it is right. —ಬೆರಕೆ mixing different ingredients in equal parts. —ಮುಗುಲಿ evens and odds. —ಆಪಿನಿ to be right, equal, even, complete. —ಬೂರುನಿ to suit, fit; to be proper; to agree with, to be on good terms.

ಸರಿ sari, *s.* Spending, consuming, exhausting. —ಮಳ್ಪುನಿ to spend, exhaust.

ಸರಿಕೆ sarikè, *adj.* Right, fit, proper. 2. level, even. 3. plenty, abundant. 4. complete, full. —ಆಪಿನಿ to be properly arranged, to be well done. —ಉಣ್ಪಿನಿ to eat heartily. —ಬರ್ಪಿನಿ to be of age, as cattle. —ಮಳ್ಪುನಿ to arrange, put in order; to level; to do *or* execute anything well.

ಸರಿಗೆ sarigè, *s.* A wire, gold *or* silver thread. 2. a gold *or* silver armlet; *also* ತೋಳಸರಿಗೆ. 3. a thin wire of any metal.

ಸರಿಯ sariya, *see* ಸರ. 2. *see* ಸರಿಗೆ.

ಸರಿಸಮಾನ sarisamāna, *adj.* Equal, same, on a par with.

ಸರುಗುರು saruguru, *see* ಗುರುಗುರು.

ಸರುತ, ಸರೂತ saruta, sarūta, *see* ಸರ್ತ.

ಸರೆ sarè, *see* ತರೆ.

ಸರೆಂಕಲ್ಲ್ sareṅkallu, *s.* The shaft of an arrow.

ಸರೊಳಿ saroḷi, *adj.* Of superior breed, as cattle. 2. *see* ತರೊಳಿ. —ಯೆರ್ಮೆ a buffalo of superior breed yielding much milk.

ಸರೋನೆ sarōne, *see* ಸರಾನೆ.

ಸರೋವರ sarōvara, *s.* A lake.

ಸರ್ರ sarra, *see* ಸರಾನೆ.

ಸರ್ಕ sarka, *see* ತರ್ಕ. 2. *see* ಚರ್ಕ.

ಸರ್ಕತ್ತಿ sarkatti, *see* ಕತ್ತರಿ.

ಸರ್ಕಾರ್ sarkāru, *see* ಸರಕಾರ್.

ಸರ್ಕಿಯುನಿ sarkiyuni (ಸರ್ಕಿ), *v. n.* To consent, submit. 2. to get out of the way.

ಸರ್ಕೆ sarkè, *see* ಸರಿಕೆ.

ಸರ್ಕೆಣಿಪ್ಪುನಿ sarkeṇipuni (ಸರ್ಕೆಣಿ), *v. a.* To examine.

ಸರ್ಕೊಡ್ಡುನಿ sarkoḍḍuni (ಸರ್ಕೊಡ್ಡ್), *v. a.* To oppose, gainsay.

ಸರ್ಕೊಣುನಿ sarkoṇuni, *see* ತರಕೊಣುನಿ.

ಸರ್ಗ sarga, *s.* A chapter, section.

ಸರ್ಗೆ sargè, *see* ಸರಿಗೆ.

ಸರ್ತ sarta, *adj.* Straight, direct, upright. *adv.* Straightly, directly. –ನರಮಾನಿ a straightforward man. –ಸಾದಿ a straight road. –ಪೋಪಿನಿ to go straightly.

ಸರ್ತಿ sarti, *s.* A time, turn, rotation. ಒಂಜಿ– once. ಮಸ್ತ್– many times, often. ನಿನ– your turn. –ಪ್ರಕಾರ in turn.

ಸರ್ದಾರೆ sardāre, *see* ಸರದಾರೆ.

ಸರ್ದಿ sardi, *see* ಸರದಿ.

ಸರ್ಪ sarpa, *s.* A serpent, snake. –ಅಸ್ಯ a malignant sore mouth. –ಜಾತಿ the serpent kind. –ಬುದ್ಧಿ rancour, hatred. –ಶಾಪ barrenness supposed to be due to injury done to serpents. –ಸುತ್ತು a serpent's coil.

ಸರ್ಪತಿ sarpati, *s.* A train, line of gunpowder. –ದೀಪಿನಿ to lay a train.

ಸರ್ಪಳಿ sarpaḷi, *see* ಸರಪೊಳಿ.

ಸರ್ಪಿತ sarpita, *s.* Occurring, happening, befalling. 2. encountering, meeting. –ಆಪಿನಿ to occur; to meet.

ಸರ್ಪೆ sarpe, *see* ಸರ್ಪ.

ಸರ್ಬರಾಯಿ sarbarāyi, *see* ಸರಬರಾಯಿ.

ಸರ್ವ sarva, *adj.* All, entire, complete. –ಜ್ಞಾನ omniscience. –ಶಕ್ತಿ omnipotence. –ಶಕ್ತ the Almighty God. –ಸ್ವ all, everything.

ಸರ್ವಜಿತ್ತು sarvajittu, *s.* The twenty-first year in the Hindu cycle of sixty.

ಸರ್ವತಾ, ಸರ್ವಥಾ sarvatā, sarvathā, *adv.* In all ways, by all means, at any rate. 2. assuredly, certainly.

ಸರ್ವತ್ರ sarvatra, *adv.* Everywhere, at all times, in all places. –ಒಂಜೇ ಲೆಕ್ಕ ನಡಪುನಿ to behave alike at all times *or* in all places.

ಸರ್ವದಾ sarvadā, *adv.* Always, for ever.

ಸರ್ವಧಾರಿ sarvadhāri, *s.* The twenty-second year in the Hindu cycle of sixty.

ಸರ್ವನಾಮ sarvanāma, *s.* A pronoun.

ಸರ್ವಾಂಗ sarvāṅga, *s.* The whole body. –ಬೇನೆ feeling pain all over the body. –ಪೂಜುನಿ to rub the whole body, as with oil, *etc.*

ಸರ್ವಾತ್ಮೆ sarvātme, *s.* The all-pervading God.

ಸರ್ವೇಶ, ಸರ್ವೇಶ್ವ sarvēśa, sarvēśva, *s.* All. ಸರ್ವೇಶೆ, ಸರ್ವೇಶ್ವರೆ God, the Supreme Being.

ಸಲಕ್ salakụ, *see* ಬಾಲಾಕ್.

ಸಲಕೆ salakè, *see* ತಲಕೆ.

ಸಲಗೆ salagè, *see* ಸಲಿಗೆ.

ಸಲಗುನಿ salaguni (ಸಲಗ್), *v. a.* To nourish, succour, shelter, protect, take care of.

ಸಲಯಿ salayi, *s.* A hundred sheaves of straw. 2. a measure of paddy varying from five to twelve muḍas of rice. 3. ruin. 4. *see* ಸಲಾಯಿ. ಒಂಜಿ ಸಲಯಿ ಬೈ a hundred sheaves of straw. —ಆಪಿನಿ to be ruined.

ಸಲಹತ್ರ salahatra, *adv.* Near.

ಸಲಾಂ, ಸಲಾಮ್, ಸಲಾಮು salām, salāmụ, salāmu, *s.* A mode of salutation accompanied with the raising of the hand to the head. —ಮಳ್ಪುನಿ to salute in this way; to thank.

ಸಲಾಕಿ salāki, *adj.* Full grown. *s.* A log.

ಸಲಾಯಿ salāyi, *s.* Split pulse. ತೊಗರಿ— split *Cytisus cajan*, dhal.

ಸಲಾಯಿಸುನಿ salāyisuni (ಸಲಾಯಿಸ್), *v. a.* To clear, liquidate, as a debt.

ಸಲಾವಣಿ salāvaṇi, *see* ಚಲಾವಣಿ.

ಸಲಿ sali, *see* ಚಳಿ.

ಸಲಿಗೆ saligè, *s.* Friendship, amity, familiarity, indulgence. 2. freedom, liberty. —ಕೊರ್ಪಿನಿ to allow freedom, be indulgent. —ಡ ಉಪ್ಪುನಿ to be familiar.

ಸಲೀಮು salīma, *s.* Sardonyx.

ಸಲೀಸ್ salīsa, *adj.* Easy.

ಸಲೆ salè, *see* ತಲೆ.

ಸಲೆಯುನಿ saleyuni (ಸಲೆ), *v. a.* To bear, suffer, endure.

ಸಲೈಸುನಿ saleisuni, *see* ಸಲಾಯಿಸುನಿ.

ಸಲ್ಕಾವುನಿ salkāvuni, *c.v.* (*of* ಸಲ್ಕುನಿ) To entangle.

ಸಲ್ಕುನಿ salkuni (ಸಲ್ಕ್), *v. n.* To be entangled.

ಸಲ್ಮ salma, *see* ಸೊಲ್ಮ.

ಸಲ್ಮಂತ salmanta, *s.* Assent, agreement, acquiescence, compliance; *bet.* ಸಂಮತ.

ಸಲ್ಲಂದಿ, ಸಲ್ಲಾಂಜಿ, ಸಲ್ಲಾಂದಿ sallandi, sallāñji, sallāndi, *adj.* Exorbitant, extravagant, excessive. 2. unlawful, improper. —ಬಿಲೆ an exorbitant price. —ಬೇಲೆ excessive work.

ಸಲ್ಲಾನ sallāna, *adj.* Much, plenty, many.

ಸಲ್ಲಿ salli, *see* ತಳ್ಳಿ.

ಸಲ್ಲುನಿ salluni (ಸಲ್ಲ್), *v. n.* To be valid, fit, proper. 2. *see* ಸಂದುನಿ.

ಸವಕಾಶ savakāša, *see* ಸಾವಕಾಶ.

ಸವಣ savaṇa, *see* ಶ್ರವಣ.

ಸವಣೆ savaṇè, *adj.* Agreeable, suitable, convenient.

ಸವತಿ savati, *s.* The relationship which a man's two wives bear to each other. —ಮತ್ಸರ the enmity between a man's two wives.

ಸವಬೆ savabè, *see* ಸಭೆ.

ಸವರಿಯುನಿ savariyuni (ಸವರಿ), *v. n.* To walk up and down, move about.

ಸವಾದ್ರೆ savādre, *see* ಸಹೋದರೆ.

ಸವಾರಿ savāri, *s.* Riding. 2. any mode of conveyance. 3. going out of doors *or* abroad.

ಸವಾರೆ savāre, *s.* A rider.

ಸವಾಲ್ savālụ, *s.* Question, interrogation, inquiry, proposition. —ಉಪ್ಪುನಿ to have some thing to say. —ಪಾಡುನಿ to ask a question; to make a proposal.

ಸವಿ **savi**, *see* ಸಬಿ.

ಸವಿಪುನಿ **savipuni** (ಸವಿ), *v. n.* To be tasteful, savoury, palatable, sweet. 2. to abrade.

ಸವುತೆ **savutè**, *see* ತಾತೆ.

ಸಸಾರ **sasāra**, *adj.* Easy, light, trifling. *s.* Easiness, ease. —ಮಳ್ಪುನಿ to slight, make light of; to render easy.

ಸಸಿ **sasi**, *s.* A young plant.

ಸಸೆ **sasè**, *see* ಶಸೆ.

ಸಸೂತ್ರ **sasūtra**, *see* ಸುಸೂತ್ರ.

ಸಹ **saha**, *adj.* With, together with. 2. even, also. —ಕುಟುಂಬ the whole family.

ಸಹಗಮನ **sahagamana**, *s.* Accompanying; the self-immolation of a woman with the corpse of her husband.

ಸಹಜ **sahaja**, *adj.* Inherent, innate, natural. 2. proper. 3. true. 4. co-existent, born together. —ಗುಣ natural disposition. —ಆದ್ ಪಣ್ಪುನಿ to speak truly *or* sincerely.

ಸಹಜೆ **sahaje**, *s.* A brother of whole blood.

ಸಹನ **sahana**, *s.* Patience. *adj.* Patient, enduring, bearing. —ಮಳ್ಪುನಿ to have patience; to endure, as pain.

ಸಹಮೂಲ **sahamūla**, *adv.* With the root; completely, entirely.

ಸಹವಾಸ **sahavāsa**, *s.* Association, company. 2. sexual intercourse.

ಸಹಸ **sahasa**, *see* ಸಾಸ.

ಸಹಸ್ರ **sahasra**, *s.* A thousand. —ನಾಮ a thousand names, as of a deity. ಸಹಸ್ರಾಧಿಪತಿ a general, commandant.

ಸಹಾಯ **sahāya**, *s.* Help, aid, assistance, succour. 2. protection. —ಕೆ a helper, assistant. —ಮಳ್ಪುನಿ to help, assist.

ಸಹಿ **sahi**, *adj.* Proper, correct, right. 2. a signature. 3. *see* ಸೈ.

ಸಹಿತ **sahita**, *adj.* Accompanied by, in company with. 2. also. 3. with.

ಸಹಿಸುನಿ **sahisuni** (ಸಹಿಸ್), *v. a.* To endure, bear, suffer, support. 2. to forgive. ಬೇನೆ— to endure pain.

ಸಹೋದರಿ **sahōdari**, *s.* A sister.

ಸಹೋದರೆ **sahōdare**, *s.* A brother.

ಸಹ್ಯ **sahya**, *adj.* Bearable, tolerable. 2. agreeable. ಅ— unbearable; disgusting.

ಸಳಸಳ, ಸಳಸಳನೆ **saḷasaḷa, saḷasaḷanè**, *s.* A noise caused in pouring water, *etc.*

ಸಳಿ **saḷi**, *see* ಚಳಿ.

ಸಳೆ **saḷè**, *s.* A sling. 2. a snare.

ಸಳ್ಳಿ **saḷḷi**, *see* ತಳ್ಳಿ.

ಸಾಂಕಣೆ **sāṅkaṇè**, *s.* Fostering, nursing, nourishing, bringing up. 2. adoption of a boy *or* girl into another family.

–ದ ಅಪ್ಪೆ an adoptive mother. –ದ ಅಮ್ಮೆ an adoptive father. –ಮಗೆ an adopted son. –ಗ್ ದೆ ತ್ತೊಣುನಿ to adopt.

ಸಾಂಕಾವುನಿ sāṅkāvuni, *c.v.* (*of* ಸಾಂಕುನಿ) To cause to foster, bring up, nourish, nurse.

ಸಾಂಕುನಿ sāṅkuni (ಸಾಂಕ್), *v. a.* To foster, nourish, nurse, bring up, take care of, protect, shelter.

ಸಾಂಖ್ಯ sāṅkhya, *s.* A system of philosophy by Kapila.

ಸಾಂಗ್‌ಸರುವೆಲ್ sāṅgusaruvelu, *see* ಶಾಂಗ್‌ತರ್ವೆಲ್ *under* ಶಾಂಗ್.

ಸಾಂಗ, ಸಾಂಗ್ಯ sāṅga, sāṅgya, *adj.* Complete, perfect. –ಆಪಿನಿ to be accomplished, finished. –ಮಳ್ಪುನಿ to accomplish, complete.

ಸಾಂಚ sāñca, *adj.* Genuine, true. 2. upright.

ಸಾಂತ sānta, *adj.* Holy, saintly. 2. *see* ಶಾಂತ.

ಸಾಂತಿ sānti, *see* ಶಾಂತಿ.

ಸಾಂತಿಮರ sāntimara, *see* ಶಾಂತಿಮರ.

ಸಾಂತೆರ್ sānteru, *s.* The saints, *Rom.*

ಸಾಂಪ್ರದಾಯ sāmpradāya, *see* ಸಂಪ್ರದಾಯ.

ಸಾಂಬ್ರಾಣಿ sāmbrāṇi, *s.* Benzoin.

ಸಾಂಬ್ರಾಳಿ sāmbrāḷi, *see* ಸಂಬರಬಳ್ಳಿ *under* ಸಂಬರ.

ಸಾಕ್ sāku, *def. v.* To suffice. 2. to be wearied of. –ಆಪಿನಿ to be wearied of, done up. ಆಯಗ್ ಉಂಡ್‌ದ್ ಸಾಕ್ ಆಂಡ್ he ate to satiety. ಈ ಕೆಲಸೊಡ್ದು ಎಂಕ್ ಸಾಕಾಂಡ್ I am tired of this work. –ಸಾಕ್ ಆಪಿನಿ to be quite done up; to be exhausted.

ಸಾಕರ್ಮಿ sākarmi, *s.* A great sinner; a consort of sinners.

ಸಾಕಿ sāki, *see* ಸಾಕ್ಷಿ.

ಸಾಕಿ sāki, *adj.* Superficial. –ಗ್ ಸಾಕಿ speaking at random; doing a thing in a superficial manner.

ಸಾಗ್ sāgu, *see* ಸಾಗು.

ಸಾಗರ sāgara, *s.* The sea, ocean.

ಸಾಗಾರ sāgāra, *s.* Sauce, condiment. ಬಡವುಗು ಸಾಗಾರ ಬೊಡ್ಚಿ hunger requires no sauce. ಮೋಲ್– confection, dessert.

ಸಾಗಾವುನಿ sāgāvuni, *c. v.* (*of* ಸಾಗುನಿ) To expedite, as work. 2. to send, despatch, as goods. 3. to do a thing perfunctorily. ಸಾಗಾದ್ ಕಡಪುಡುನಿ to send away respectfully, as a friend, by accompanying him a short distance; to follow the remains of one's relatives, *etc.*, to the grave.

ಸಾಗು sāgu, *s.* Prosecution, progress, as of work.

ಸಾಗುನಿ sāguni (ಸಾಗ್), *v. n.* To proceed, progress, as work. 2. to be despatched, as goods. 3. to move forward, advance. ಏತ ನಡತೆಂಡಲಾ ಸಾದಿ ಸಾಗುಜಿ with all your speed you make no progress in your journey.

ಸಾಗುವಳಿ, ಸಾಗೊಳಿ, ಸಾಗ್ವಳಿ sāguvaḷi, sāgoḷi, sāgvaḷi, *s.* Farming, tillage, cultivation of land. —ಮಳ್ಪುನಿ to cultivate.

ಸಾಜ, ಸಾಜಿ sāja, sāji, *see* ಸಹಜ.

ಸಾಟ್ sāṭu, *s.* Barter, exchange. —ಮಳ್ಪುನಿ to barter.

ಸಾಟಿ sāṭe, *s.* A bargain, contract. —ದ ಪಣವು money paid under a contract. —ಮಳ್ಪುನಿ to strike a bargain.

ಸಾಣೆ, ಸಾಣೆಕಲ್ಲ್ sāṇe, sāṇekallu, *s.* A grind-stone. 2. a whet-stone. —ಪತ್ತುನಿ to grind, sharpen.

ಸಾತ್ sātu, *s.* A moment, instant. —ಗ immediately, instantly.

ಸಾತ್ರ sātra, *see* ಶಾಸ್ತ್ರ. 2. *see* ಸಾತ್ರಿ.

ಸಾತ್ರಿ sātri, *see* ಶಾಸ್ತ್ರಿ.

ಸಾತ್ರೆ sātre, *s.* A white cock with a thick comb; *also* ಸಾತ್ರಪೂಂಜಿ.

ಸಾತ್ವಿಕ, ಸಾತ್ವೀಕ sātvika, sātvīka, *adj.* Ingenuous, open, frank. 2. honest, true, good, gentle, amiable. —ಗುಣ a gentle disposition. —ತನ, —ತ್ವ openness, sincerity, honesty.

ಸಾತ್ವಿಕೆ sātvike, *s.* An honest, frank, sincere man.

ಸಾದ್ sādu, *see* ಶಾಸ್.

ಸಾದ sāda, *adj.* Plain, simple. *adv.* Throughout, wholly. 2. *see* ಸೀದ. —ಕಪ್ಪು wholly black. —ರುಮಾಲ್ a plain handkerchief.

ಸಾದ sāda, *s.* Purity.

ಸಾದಗ sādaga, *see* ಸಾಧಕ.

ಸಾದನ sādana, *see* ಸಾಧನ.

ಸಾದರ್ sādaru, *adj.* Received, arrived. ಹುಕುಮ್ ಸಾದರ್ ಆಯಿಜಿ the order is not received.

ಸಾದಲ್ವಾರ್ sādaluvāru, *s.* The sundry charges of a public office, contingent charges. 2. stationery.

ಸಾದಾ sādā, *see* ಸಾದ.

ಸಾದಿ sādi, *s.* A road, way, path. —ಕಟ್ಟುನಿ to stop the road; shut up a passage; to obstruct, hinder. —ತಪ್ಪುನಿ, —ತಪ್ಪಿಪೋಪಿನಿ to miss the way, go astray. —ತೋಜಾವುನಿ to lead, show the way. —ಬುಡ್ಪಿನಿ to make *or* give way. —ಮಳ್ಪುನಿ to make way; to devise means.

ಸಾದಿಕೆ sādike, *s.* Smearing. —ಆಪಿನಿ to besmear.

ಸಾದಿಯುನಿ sādiyuni, *see* ಸಾಧಿಯುನಿ.

ಸಾದು sādu, *see* ಸಾಧು.

ಸಾದೃಷೆ sādrushe, *s.* Manifestation.

ಸಾದೃಶ್ಯ sādruśya, *s.* Resemblance, similarity.

ಸಾದೆ sāde, *see* ಸಾದ.

ಸಾದೇವಿ sādēvi, *s.* The ash-coloured fleabane, *Vernonia cinerea.*

ಸಾದೊಳಿಗೆ sādoḷige, *s.* A water-course, channel.

ಸಾದ್ಯೆ sādye, *adv.* On the road, by the road. —ನಡಪುನಾಯೆ, —ಪೋಪಿನಾಯೆ a wayfarer, one walking on the road.

ಸಾಧಕ sādhaka, *s.* Exercise, practice. 2. gymnastics. —ಮಳ್ಪುನಿ to practise gymnastics.

ಸಾಧನ, ಸಾಧನೆ **sādhana, sādhanè**, *s.* Accomplishing, effecting. 2. means, expedient. 3. persevering. 4. instrument, agent. 5. a document, deed. ಕ್ರಯ– a deed of sale. ಧರ್ಮ– a deed of gift. ಮರಣ– a testament, will. –ಮಲ್ಪಿನಿ to try, aim, aspire after. –ಮಳ್ಪುನಿ to persevere; to accomplish.

ಸಾಧಾರಣ **sādhāraṇa**, *adj.* Common, ordinary, general, universal. *s.* The forty-fourth year in the Hindu cycle of sixty.

ಸಾಧಿಪುನಿ, ಸಾಧಿಯುನಿ **sādhipuni, sādhiyuui** (ಸಾಧಿ), *v. a.* To achieve, accomplish, persevere. 2. to retain malice long. 3. to take, conquer. 4. to assert, allege. 5. to prove, establish. 6. to charge upon another. ಪಗೆ– to harbour malice.

ಸಾಧು **sādhu**, *adj.* Tame, docile. 2. good, virtuous, pious. –ಮಳ್ಪುನಿ to tame.

ಸಾಧ್ಯ **sādhya**, *adj.* Curable. 2. possible, practicable. –ಕೆಲಸ a practicable work. –ಆಪಿನಿ to succeed, be accomplished. –ಮಳ್ಪುನಿ to accomplish.

ಸಾಧ್ಯುನಿ **sādhyuni**, *see* ಸಾಧಿಪುನಿ.

ಸಾನ್ **sānụ**, *adj.* Even. *adv.* Also.

ಸಾನ **sāna**, *s.* A demon shrine; *cf.* ಸ್ಥಾನ.

ಸಾನಾದಿಗೆ **sānādigè**, *s.* A native lamp; a lamp-stand.

ಸಾನಿ **sāni**, *s.* An affix to the names of respectable ladies. ಧೊರೆ– a lady.

ಸಾನೆ **sānè**, *see* ಸಾಣೆ.

ಸಾಪ್, ಸಾಪು **sāpụ, sāpu**, *adj.* Clear, pure, clean. *adv.* Entirely; plainly; smoothly. –ಕೆಲಸ clean work. –ಆಪಿನಿ to be clean, smooth, *or* level. –ಪಣ್ಪುನಿ to speak plainly. –ಮಳ್ಪುನಿ to make clean, smooth, *or* level.

ಸಾಪ **sāpa**, *see* ಶಾಪ.

ಸಾಫಲ್ಯ **sāphalya**, *s.* Productiveness, fruitfulness. 2. a reward. –ಆಪಿನಿ to succeed, be fruitful. –ಮಳ್ಪುನಿ to prosper, render successful.

ಸಾಬ್ **sābụ**, *see* ಸಾಯಿಬೆ.

ಸಾಬಾಸ್ **sābāsụ**, *see* ಶಬಾಸ್.

ಸಾಬೀತ್, ಸಾಬೂತ್ **sābītụ, sābūtụ**, *adj.* Proved, established, as guilt, *etc.* –ಆಪಿನಿ to be proved guilty. –ಮಳ್ಪುನಿ to prove guilty.

ಸಾಬುನು **sābunu**, *s.* Soap.

ಸಾಮ **sāma**, *s.* Reconciliation, appeasing. –ವೇದ the third Vēda.

ಸಾಮಗ್ರಿ **sāmagri**, *s.* A thing, article, ingredient, material.

ಸಾಮತಿ **sāmati**, *s.* A comparison, simile, proverb.

ಸಾಮರ್ಥಿಗೆ, ಸಾಮರ್ಥ್ಯ **sāmarthigè, sāmarthya**, *s.* Power, strength. 2. ability, capability. –ಉಪ್ಪುನಿ to possess strength, be able.

ಸಾಮಾದಿಗೆ sāmādige, *s.* Membership of an assembly *or* society.

ಸಾಮಾನ್ sāmānu, *s.* Baggage, goods and chattels. 2. things, furniture, tools, instruments.

ಸಾಮಾನ್ಯ sāmānya, *adj.* Common, general. 2. ordinary, indifferent, middling.

ಸಾಮಿ sāmi, *see* ಸ್ವಾಮಿ.

ಸಾಮೀಪ್ಯ sāmīpya, *s.* Proximity.

ಸಾಮೀಲ್ sāmīlu, *s.* Complicity, confederacy. 2. interference.

ಸಾಮೂಲ sāmūla, *see* ಸಹಮೂಲ.

ಸಾಮೆ sāmè, *s.* Millet, *Panicum miliaceum.* –ಜರಿ *Panicum frumentaceum.*

ಸಾಮ್ಯ sāmya, *s.* Equality. 2. likeness. 3. a comparison, parable, similitude, allegory, proverb. 4. one's due, as fees, *etc.*

ಸಾಮ್ರಾಜ್ಯ sāmrājya, *s.* Imperial rule, universal dominion.

ಸಾಯ sāya, *see* ಸಹಾಯ.

ಸಾಯಂಕಾಲ sāyankāla, *s.* Eventide, evening.

ಸಾಯನ sāyana, *s.* Help, aid.

ಸಾಯನೆ sāyane, *s.* A helper.

ಸಾಯರ್ sāyaru, *s.* Custom, duties, tax levied on imports and exports. ಅಳುವೆ– sea-customs. –ಕಟ್ಟೆ a custom-house.

ಸಾಯಸ sāyasa, *s.* Support, aid; *cf.* ಸಾಸ. –ಮಾಡುನಿ to help, support.

ಸಾಯಿತ್ಯ sāyitya, *see* ಸಾಹಿತೆ.

ಸಾಯಿದಿ sāyidi, *see* ಕಾಯಿದಿ.

ಸಾಯಿಬೆ sāyibe, *s.* A Mussulman of Arab descent; *bet.* ಸಾಹಿಬ್.

ಸಾಯಿರ sāyira, *see* ಸಾರ. 2. *see* ಸಾಯರ್.

ಸಾಯುಜ್ಯ sāyujya, *s.* Absorption in Brahma, union with the deity.

ಸಾಯೆತಿ sāyeti, *see* ಸಾಹಿತ್ಯ.

ಸಾರ್, ಸಾರ sāru, sāra, *s.* The essence of anything. 2. marrow. 3. the sap of trees. 4. strength, vigour. 5. soup, broth. –ದಾಂತಿ sapless; useless. ಬೇರ– merchandise, goods.

ಸಾರ sāra, *s.* One thousand. –ಸರ್ತಿ a thousand times.

ಸಾರಂಗಿ sārangi, *s.* A kind of fiddle with five strings.

ಸಾರಂಬಳ್ಳ sāramballa, *s. lit.* A thousand seers. 2. an offering to a demon.

ಸಾರಟ್ sāraṭu, *s* A chariot, carriage.

ಸಾರಣೆ sāraṇè, *s.* A sieve. 2. smearing, as a wall *or* floor with earth, cowdung, *etc.*, plastering. –ಅಂಡೆ a kind of sweetmeat. –ಮಳ್ಪುನಿ to plaster; *cf.* ಸಾರಿಸುನಿ.

ಸಾರತಿ sārati, *see* ಸಾರಥಿ.

ಸಾರತೆ sārate, *see* ಸಾರ್ತೆ.

ಸಾರಥಿ, sārathi, *s.* A charioteer.

ಸಾರದೆ sāradè, *see* ಶಾರದೆ.

ಸಾರಸ, ಸಾರಸ್ಯ sārasa, sārasya, *see* ಸ್ವಾರಸ್ಯ.

ಸಾರಸ್ವತ sārasvata, *s.* The north-west part of Delhi.

ಸಾರಸ್ವತೆ sārasvate, *s.* A Sārasvata Brahman.

ಸಾರಳಿ sārali, *s.* Smearing, plastering.

ಸಾರಾಂಶ sārāṁśa, *s.* The substance, essence, pith, purport. —ಪಣ್ಪುನಿ to give the purport.

ಸಾರಾಮಹಂಕಾಳಿ sārāmahaṅkāḷi, *s.* A demon so called.

ಸಾರಾಯಿ sārāyi, *s.* Arrack, spirit, liquor.

ಸಾರಿ sāri, *s.* A time, turn; *cf.* ಸರ್ತಿ. 2. a cowrie; *also* ಬಲ್ಕೆದ ಸಾರಿ. *adv.* Up and down, to and fro. ಒಂಜಿ— once. —ನಡಪು ನಿ to walk to and fro.

ಸಾರಿಂಗ sāriṅga, *see* ಸಾರಂಗ.

ಸಾರಿಯಾವುನಿ sāriyāvuni, *c. v.* (*of* ಸಾರಿಯುನಿ) To cause to proclaim *or* publish.

ಸಾರಿಯುನಿ sāriyuni (ಸಾರಿ), *v. a.* To proclaim, publish, preach. 2. to warn. 3. to sift. 4. to smear, plaster.

ಸಾರಿಸುನಿ sārisuni (ಸಾರಿಸ್), *v. a.* To smear, plaster. 2. *see* ಸಾರಿಯಾವುನಿ.

ಸಾರುನಿ sāruni (ಸಾರ್), *v. a.* To sift. 2. to smooth, polish. 3. *see* ಸಾರಿಯುನಿ.

ಸಾರೂಪ್ಯ sārūpya, *s.* Obtaining the image *or* form of God.

ಸಾರೆಂಗಿ sāreṅgi, *see* ಸಾರಂಗಿ.

ಸಾರೆತಿ sāreti, *see* ಸಾರ್ತಿ.

ಸಾರೆಸ sāresa, *see* ಸ್ವಾರಸ್ಯ.

ಸಾರೊಟು sāroṭu, *see* ಸಾರಟಿ.

ಸಾರೊಳಿ sāroḷi, *see* ಸಾರಳಿ.

ಸಾರ್ಯುನಿ sāryuni, *see* ಸಾರಿಯುನಿ.

ಸಾರ್ಣೆ sārṇè, *see* ಸಾರಣೆ.

ಸಾರ್ತಿ sārti, *s.* Encountering, meeting. 2. happening, occurring. —ಆಪಿನಿ to encounter; to happen.

ಸಾರ್ತೆ sārtè, *s.* Proclamation.

ಸಾರ್ಥಕ, ಸಾರ್ಥುಕ sārthaka, sārthuka, *adj.* Prospered, succeeded. —ಕೆಲಸ a meritorious act. —ಆಪಿನಿ to succeed, prosper.

ಸಾರ್ಲ, ಸಾರ್ಲಾ sārla, sārlā, *s.* Success, completion, achievement. —ಆಪಿನಿ to be successful.

ಸಾರ್ಲುನಿ sārluni (ಸಾರ್ಲ್), *v. n.* To proceed. 2. to become finished.

ಸಾಲ್ sāḷu, *s.* A line, row, furrow. —ಮರ an avenue, grove.

ಸಾಲ sāla, *s.* Debt. —ಗಾರೆ a debtor. —ದಾಯೆ a creditor; a debtor. —ಮೂಲ assets and liabilities. ಮೈ— a loan without mortgage. —ಎಪ್ಪುನಿ to recover a debt. —ಕೊರ್ಪಿನಿ to lend. —ತೀರ್ಸಾವುನಿ, —ಬೂಳುನಿ to pay a debt. —ದೆಪ್ಪುನಿ, —ಮಳ್ಪುನಿ to borrow, contract a debt. ಸಾಲೊಡು ಬೂರುನಿ to be in debt. —ಮುರ್ಕುನಿ a debt to be lost.

ಸಾಲಗ್ರಾಮ sālagrāma, *s.* A schistous stone containing the impression of one *or* more ammonites, imagined to represent Vishṇu.

ಸಾಲಾಮಿಸ್ರಿ **sālāmisri,** *s.* The salep misiri, *Orchis mascula.*

ಸಾಲಾವಳಿ **sālāvaḷi,** *s.* Luckiness of a horoscope. 2. agreement, amity.

ಸಾಲಿ **sāli,** *s.* Failure, loss, disappointment. 2. *see* ಶಾಲಿ.

ಸಾಲಿತ **sālita,** *adj.* Punctual, accurate, exact. 2. clear, as eye-sight.

ಸಾಲಿಯೆ **sāliye,** *see* ಶಾಲ್ಯೆ.

ಸಾಲೆ **sālè,** *see* ಶಾಲೆ.

ಸಾಲೋಕ್ಯ **sālōkya,** *s.* Obtaining existence in the very place where the deity resides.

ಸಾಲ್ಯ **sālya,** *s.* Sight. ಕಂಣ್ಣಿದ ಸಾಲ್ಯ ತೋಜುಜಿ the eye-sight is not clear.

ಸಾಲ್ಯುನಿ **sālyuni** (ಸಾಲ್ಯಿ), *v. a.* To smell.

ಸಾಲ್ಯೆ **sālye,** *see* ಶಾಲ್ಯೆ.

ಸಾವಕಾರೆ **sāvakāre,** *see* ಸೌಕಾರೆ.

ಸಾವಕಾಶ **sāvakāša,** *s.* Leisure, respite; delay. —ಉಪ್ಪುನಿ to be at leisure. —ಮಳ್ಪುನಿ to delay, be dilatory.

ಸಾವಜಿ **sāvaji,** *see* ಶಾವಜಿ.

ಸಾವಧಾನ **sāvadhāna,** *s.* Caution, deliberation. 2. diligence.

ಸಾವಾಸ **sāvāsa,** *see* ಸಹವಾಸ.

ಸಾವಿರ **sāvira,** *see* ಸಾರ.

ಸಾವು **sāvu,** *s.* Death. 2. a mourning feast. —ಮಳ್ಪುನಿ to celebrate a mourning feast.

ಸಾವುಕಾರೆ **sāvukāre,** *see* ಸೌಕಾರೆ.

ಸಾವೆ **sāvè,** *see* ಸಾಮೆ.

ಸಾಷ್ಟಾಂಗ **sāshṭāṅga,** *s.* A mode of salutation by prostrating one's self. —ನಮಸ್ಕಾರ such a mode of reverence. —ಬೂರುನಿ, —ಮಳ್ಪುನಿ to prostrate.

ಸಾಸ **sāsa,** *s.* Boldness, prowess. 2. energy, effort, exertion. —ಮಳ್ಪುನಿ, ಸಾಸಿಯುನಿ to exert one's self, be enterprising.

ಸಾಸನ **sāsana,** *adj.* Durable, lasting; *cf.* ಶಾಸನ. —ಕೆಲಸ durable work.

ಸಾಸಿ **sāsi,** *s.* A bold, adventurous man.

ಸಾಸಿಮೆ, ಸಾಸೆಮಿ **sāsimè, sāsemi,** *s.* Mustard, *Sinapis juncea; cf.* ದಾಸೆಮಿ.

ಸಾಸಿಯುನಿ **sāsiyuni,** *see under* ಸಾಸ.

ಸಾಸ್ತ್ರೆ **sāstre,** *see* ಸಾತ್ರೆ.

ಸಾಹಸ **sāhasa,** *see* ಸಾಸ.

ಸಾಹಸ್ರ, ಸಾಸ್ರ **sāhasra, sāsra,** *s.* An aggregate of many thousands; an army of a thousand strong.

ಸಾಹಿತೆ, ಸಾಹಿತ್ಯ, ಸಾಹೆತಿ **sāhitè, sāhitya, sāheti,** *s.* An implement. 2. an ingredient, material.

ಸಾಹೀಬ್, ಸಾಹೇಬ್ **sāhibu, sāhēbu,** *s.* A title of a respectable European. 2. *see* ಸಾಯಿಬೆ.

ಸಾಕ್ಷಾತ್ **sākshātu,** *adj.* Visible, present, manifest. *adv.* Evidently, manifestly.

ಸಾಕ್ಷಿ **sākshi,** *s.* Evidence, testimony, witness. —ಗಾರೆ, —ದಾಯೆ a witness. —ವಾಂಗ್ಮೂಲ a deposition of evidence. ದೇವೆರೆ– swearing by God. ರಕ್ತ– a martyr. –ಪಣ್ಪುನಿ to give evidence, testify. [ದಂಡಣೆ.

ಸಿಂಕದಂಡಣೆ sinkadandaṇè, *see* ಶಿಂಕ

ಸಿಂಕಿರಿ sinkiri, *see* ಸೀಂಕಿರಿ.

ಸಿಂಕೆ sinkè, *see* ಶಿಕೆ.

ಸಿಂಗ singa, *see* ಸಿಂಹ.

ಸಿಂಗಬಾರೆ singabärè, *s.* A sort of plantain.

ಸಿಂಗರ, ಸಿಂಗಾರ singara, singāra, *see* ಶೃಂಗಾರ.

ಸಿಂಗರಿಪುನಿ, ಸಿಂಗರಿಯುನಿ singaripuni, singariyuni, *see* ಶೃಂಗರಿಪುನಿ.

ಸಿಂಗಳಪುರಿ singaḷapuri, *see* ಶಿಂಗಪುರಿ.

ಸಿಂಗಿ singi, *s.* Poison; *also* ಶಿಂಗಿ. 2. a pungent taste. *adj.* Cross, perverse.

ಸಿಂಗಿರಿ singiri, *see* ಶಿಂಗಿರಿ.

ಸಿಂಗೊಡೆ singoḍè, *see* ಶಿಂಗೊಡೆ.

ಸಿಂಟು sinṭu, *see* ಶಿಟ್ಟು.

ಸಿಂಧು sindhu, *s.* The river Indus. 2. the province of Scinde.

ಸಿಂಧೂರ sindhūra, *s.* Red lead, *oxidum plumbi.*

ಸಿಂಬುಳು simbuḷu, *see* ಶಿಂಬುಳು.

ಸಿಂಮ simma, *adj.* Cold. 2. *see* ಸಿಂಹ.

ಸಿಂಮೆ simmè, *s.* The eyelash.

ಸಿರ್ಂಟುನಿ, ಸಿರ್ಂದುನಿ sirnṭuni, sirnduni (ಸಿರ್ಂಟ್, ಸಿರ್ಂದ್), *v. n.* To contract, shrivel.

ಸಿಂಹ simha, *s.* A lion. 2. the sign *Leo* in the zodiac; the fifth solar month.

ಸಿಂಹಳ simhaḷa, *s.* Ceylon.

ಸಿಂಹಾಸನ simhāsana, *s.* A throne, royal seat.

ಸಿಕಾರ್ sikāru, *see* ಶಿಕಾರ್.

ಸಿಕೆ sikè, *see* ಶಿಕೆ.

ಸಿಕೆಪಾವುನಿ sikepāvuni, *c. v.* (*of* ಸಿಕೆಪಿನಿ) To half-boil, as fruits for preserving.

ಸಿಕೆಪಿನಿ, ಸಿಕೆಯುನಿ, ಸಿಕೆವುನಿ sikepini, sikeyuni, sikevuni (ಸಿಕೆ), *v. n.* To be hot, feel hot.

ಸಿಕ್ಕ್ sikku, *see* ಶಿಕ್ಕ್.

ಸಿಕ್ಕ sikka, *s.* A net-work; *also* ಶಿಕ್ಕ.

ಸಿಕ್ಕಟ್ಟ್ sikkaṭṭu, *see* ಶಿಕ್ಕಟ್ಟ್.

ಸಿಕ್ಕಾವುನಿ sikkāvuni, *see* ಶಿಕ್ಕಾವುನಿ.

ಸಿಕ್ಕುನಿ sikkuni, *see* ಶಿಕ್ಕುನಿ.

ಸಿಗ್ಪುನಿ sigupuni, *see* ಶಿಗಿಪುನಿ.

ಸಿಗ siga, *see* ಶಿಗ.

ಸಿಗಲೆ sigalè, *see* ಶಿಗಲೆ.

ಸಿಗುರುನಿ siguruni, *see* ಶಿಗುರುನಿ.

ಸಿಟ್ಟು siṭṭu, *see* ಶಿಟ್ಟು.

ಸಿಟ್ಟೇಸಿ siṭṭēsi, *see* ಶಿಟ್ಟೇಸಿ.

ಸಿಡಿ siḍi, *see* ಸಿದಿ.

ಸಿಡಿಲ್ siḍilu, *see* ಶಿಡಿಲ್.

ಸಿಡುಬು siḍubu, *see* ಶಿಡಿಬು.

ಸಿತಾರ್ sitāru, *s.* Fortune, luck. 2. a stringed instrument.

ಸಿತ್ತ sitta, *see* ಚಿತ್ತ.

ಸಿದಿ, ಸಿದೆ sidi, sidè, *s.* Bellows. –ದೈಪುನಿ, –ಪಂದಾವುನಿ to blow bellows.

ಸಿದಿಗೋಲಿ sidigōli, *see* ಶಿದಿಗೋಳಿ.

ಸಿದ್ದಿ siddi, *s.* A Negro, an Arab. 2. *see* ಸಿದ್ಧಿ.

ಸಿದ್ದಿಗೆ, ಸಿದ್ದೆ siddigè, siddè, *s*. A leathern bottle. 2. *see* ಶಿದ್ದಿಗೆ.

ಸಿದ್ಧ siddha, *adj*. Ready, prepared. —ತ್ವ readiness. —ಆಪಿನಿ to be ready. —ಮಳ್ಪುನಿ to make ready, prepare.

ಸಿದ್ಧಾಂತ siddhānta, *s*. Demonstrated conclusion, established truth. 2. firm conviction. 3. the system of the Mīmāṁsa philosophy. 4. a work on astronomy. —ಮಳ್ಪುನಿ to demonstrate, prove.

ಸಿದ್ಧಾಂತಿ siddhānti, *s*. A follower of the Mīmāṁsa philosophy. 2. an astronomer.

ಸಿದ್ಧಾರ್ತಿ siddhārti, *see* ಸಿದ್ಧ್ಯಾರ್ಥಿ.

ಸಿದ್ಧಿ siddhi, *s*. Accomplishment, fulfilment, achievement, success. 2. the acquirement of supernatural powers. —ಆಪಿನಿ to be accomplished, achieved. —ಮಳ್ಪುನಿ to accomplish, achieve.

ಸಿದ್ಧೆ siddhe, *s*. An inspired *or* prophetic writer, seer. 2. an adept. 3. an ascetic.

ಸಿದ್ಧ್ಯಾರ್ಥಿ siddhyārthi, *s*. The fifty-third year in the Hindu cycle of sixty.

ಸಿನೆ sinè, *s*. A fence 2. *see* ಶಿನಿ. —ಕೋಲು a thin stick.

ಸಿಪಂಗಿ, ಸಿಪಾಂಗಿ sipaṅgi, sipāṅgi, *s*. Brag, boast. —ಓದುನಿ, —ಪಾತೆರುನಿ to brag.

ಸಿಪಾಯಿ sipāyi, *see* ಶಿಪಾಯಿ.

ಸಿಪಾರಸ್, ಸಿಫರಾಸ್ sipārasu, sipharāsu, *see* ಶಿಪರಸ್.

ಸಿಪ್ಪಿ sippi, *see* ತಿಪ್ಪಿ.

ಸಿಪ್ಪು, ಸಿಪ್ಪೆ sippu, sippè, *see* ತಿಪ್ಪೆ.

ಸಿಬಂದಿ sibandi, *s*. An establishment of clerks, peons, *etc*.

ಸಿಬ್ಬು sibbu, *see* ಸುಬ್ಬ.

ಸಿಮ sima, *s*. Cold, chill.

ಸಿಮೆ simè, *see* ಸಿಂಮೆ.

ಸಿರಸ್ರೆ sirasrè, *see* ಸೆರಸರೆ.

ಸಿರಿ siri, *see* ತಿರಿ. 2. *see* ಶ್ರೀ.

ಸಿರಿಂಟುನಿ, ಸಿರುಂಟುನಿ sirinṭuni, siruṇṭuni, *see* ಸಿಂಟುರ್ನಿ.

ಸಿರಿಗುಂಡು, ಸಿರಿಮುಡಿ sirigunḍu, sirimuḍi, *s*. The tuft *or* top-knot.

ಸಿರ್ಕ್ sirku, *s*. Fading, shrivelling. 2. weakness, faintness; *cf*. ತಿರ್ಕ್.

ಸಿರ್ಕ sirka, *s*. Vinegar.

ಸಿರ್ಕಾವುನಿ sirkāvuni, *c. v*. (*of* ಸಿರ್ಕುನಿ) To cause to fade; to make lean; to weaken; *also* ತಿರ್ಕಾವುನಿ.

ಸಿರ್ಕುನಿ sirkuni (ಸಿರ್ಕ್), *v. n*. To fade; to shrivel. 2. to become weak, lean. 3. to fall off; *also* ಸಿರ್ಕ್‌ದ್‌ಪೋಪಿನಿ, ತಿರ್ಕುನಿ.

ಸಿರ್ಕೆ sirkè, *see* ತಿರ್ಕೆ.

ಸಿರ್ದುನಿ sirduni, *see* ಶಿರ್ದುನಿ.

ಸಿಲಾ silā, *see* ಶಿಲಾ.

ಸಿಲೆ silè, *see* ಶಿಲೆ.

ಸಿಲ್ಕ್ silku, *adj*. Remaining. *s*. Remainder. —ಬಾಕಿ a remaining balance.

ಸಿಲ್ಕುನಿ silkuni (ಸಿಲ್ಕ್), *v. n*. To be entangled. 2. to be perplexed.

ಸಿಲ್ಪ, ಸಿಲ್ಪಿ silpa, silpi, *see* ಶಿಲ್ಪ.

ಸಿಲ್ಲಾನ, ಸಿಲ್ವಾನ sillāna, silvāna, *see* ಜಿಲುವಾನ.

ಸಿಲ್ಲುನಿ silluni (ಸಿಲ್ಲ್), *v. a.* To spurn, trample upon; *also* ಜಿಲ್ಲುನಿ.

ಸಿಲ್ಲೊಡುನಿ silloḍuni (ಸಿಲ್ಲೊಡ್), *v. a.* To push.

ಸಿಸ್ತ್ sistu, *see* ಶಿಸ್ತ್.

ಸಿಳಿಸಿಳಿ siḷisiḷi, *s.* Hissing.

ಸೀ sī, *see* ಶೀ.

ಸೀಂಕಿರಿ sīṅkiri, *s.* A thin stalk of a palm leaf. 2. a thin split of a bamboo, *etc.* 3. *see* ಶೀಂಕಿರಿ. *adj.* Thin, lean.

ಸೀಂಟ್ sīṇṭu, *adj.* Last; youngest. —ಮ್ಯೊಪೊಲು a last born daughter. —ಮ್ಯೊಪೊಲೆ a last born son.

ಸೀಂಟಾಟ, ಸೀಂಟಾಟಿಗೆ, ಸೀಂಟು sīṇṭāṭa, sīṇṭāṭigè, sīṇṭu, *s.* Scraping.

ಸೀಂಟುನಿ sīṇṭuni (ಸೀಂಟ್), *v. a.* To scrape, rub, wipe.

ಸೀಂಟೆಲ್ sīṇṭelu, *s.* Scraping, wiping.

ಸೀಂತಾವುನಿ sīntāvuni, *see* ಶೀಂತಾವುನಿ.

ಸೀಂತುನಿ sīntuni, *see* ಶೀಂತುನಿ.

ಸೀಂತೆಲ್ sīntelu, *adj.* Stinking. —ಮೂರಿ a stinking smell, stench.

ಸೀಂತೆಲು sīntelu, *s.* A dirty woman.

ಸೀಂದುನಿ sīnduni (ಸೀಂದ್), *v. n,* To have a disagreeable smell.

ಸೀಂಪಿ sīmpi, *see* ಜೀಂಪಿ.

ಸೀಂಪುನಿ sīmpuni, *see* ಸುಯಿಂಪುನಿ.

ಸೀಕ್ sīku, *adj.* Sick.

ಸೀಕೋಲ್ sīkōlu, *s.* Liquorice.

ಸೀಗೆ sīgè, *s.* The pods of *Mimosa abstergens* reduced to fine powder and used as soap for cleansing, *etc.*; soap-nut; *also* ಸೀಗೆಕಾಯಿ.

ಸೀತ sīta, *see* ಶೀತ. 2. *see* ಸೀತೆ.

ಸೀತಾಫಲ sītāphala, *see* ಶೀತಾಫಲ.

ಸೀತಾಳಿ sītāḷi, *see* ಶೀತಾಳಿ.

ಸೀತೆ sītè, *s.* Sīta, the wife of Rāma. —ಕಾರ್, ಸೀತಾದೇವಿಕಾರ್ a kind of fern.

ಸೀದ, ಸೀದಾ sīda, sīdā, *adj.* Straight, direct. 2. straightforward, upright, honest. —ನರಮಾನಿ an upright man. —ಮಾರ್ಗ a straight way.

ಸೀಪೆ sīpè, *see* ಶೀಪೆ.

ಸೀಪು sīpu, *see* ಜೀಪು.

ಸೀಮಂತ sīmanta, *s.* A purificatory ceremony performed in the sixth *or* eighth month of a female's first gestation.

ಸೀಮುಳ್ಳು, sīmuḷḷu, *see* ಶೀಮುಳ್ಳು.

ಸೀಮೆ sīmè, *see* ಶೀಮೆ. 2. *see* ಸಿಂಮೆ.

ಸೀಮೆಕೋಲು sīmekōlu, *s.* A fine kind of bamboo stick, as that of a Chinese umbrella.

ಸೀಯಮ್ sīyamu, *see* ಶಿಯಮ್.

ಸೀರುನಿ sīruni (ಸೀರ್), *v. n.* To hiss.

ಸೀರೆ sīrè, *see* ಶೀರೆ.

ಸೀರ್ತ sīrta, *see* ಶೀರ್ಪ.

ಸೀಲ sīla, *see* ಶೀಲ.

ಸೀವರಿಪುನಿ sīvaripuni (ಸೀವರಿ), *v. a.* To entice, allure.

ಸೀಸ sīsa, *s.* Lead. —ದ ಕಡ್ಡಿ, —ದ ಬಳಪು a lead pencil.

ಸೀಸ, ಸೀಸೆ sīsa, sīsè, *see* ಶೀಸ.

ಸೀಳ್ sīḷụ, *s.* A crack, crash, split. –ಮಳ್ಪುನಿ to split, divide, crack.

ಸು su, *A particle and prefix signifying* good, well, prosperous.

ಸುಂಕ suṅka, *s.* Toll, custom, duty on goods. –ದ ಕಟ್ಟೆ a custom-house. –ದ ಬಾಕಿಲ್ a toll-gate. –ಕೊರ್ಪಿನಿ to pay duty.

ಸುಂಕಣ suṅkaṇa, *see* ತೂಂಕಣ.

ಸುಂಕಾಣಿ suṅkāṇi, *see* ಚುಕಾಣಿ. 2. *see* ಚುಂಗಾಣಿ.

ಸುಂಕು suṅku, *see* ಸೋಂಕು.

ಸುಂಟಯಿ suṇṭayi, *see* ಸೂಂಟಯಿ.

ಸುಂಟಿ suṇṭi, *see* ಸೂಂಟಿ.

ಸುಂಟೆ suṇṭe, *see* ತುಂಟೆ.

ಸುಂಡಿಲ್ suṇḍilụ, *s.* An elephant's proboscis.

ಸುಂಡು suṇḍu, *see* ತುಂಡು.

ಸುಂಡೆಲಿ suṇḍeli, *s.* A muskrat.

ಸುಂಣ suṇṇa, *s.* Lime, chunam, mortar. –ದ ಕಾಯಿ, –ಜನ a small metallic box for keeping in chunam to eat with betel leaf. –ದ ಗಾರೆ lime mortar, stucco; whitewash. –ದೆಪ್ಪುನಿ to whitewash. –ಮೆದ್ಪುನಿ, –ಮೆಲ್ಪುನಿ to prepare lime mortar. –ಸುದ್ಪಿನಿ to burn lime.

ಸುಂದರ sundara, *adj.* Comely, handsome, beautiful.

ಸುಂದಾವುನಿ sundāvuni, *c. v.* (*of* ಸುಂದುನಿ) To cause to wind, as thread.

ಸುಂದಿಲ್ sundilụ, *see* ಸುಂಡಿಲ್.

ಸುಂದು sundu, *s.* Depression of mind.

ಸುಂದುನಿ sunduni (ಸುಂದ್), *v. a.* To wind, roll; to spool.

ಸುಂನತಿ sunnati, *s.* Circumcision; *cf.* ಮುಂಜಿ. –ಮಳ್ಪುನಿ to circumcise.

ಸುಂನಮುಖಿ sunnamukhi, *s.* Senna leaves.

ಸುಂನಲಿ sunnali, *see* ಸುಂಡೆಲಿ.

ಸುಂಬಿಲ್ sumbilụ, *see* ತುಂಬಿಲ್.

ಸುಂಬು sumbu, *see* ಸೂಂಬು.

ಸುಂಬೆ sumbè, *s.* A small hole in a wall.

ಸುಕ suka, *see* ಸುಖ.

ಸುಕುಟೆ sukuṭe, *s.* A smart man.

ಸುಕೃತ sukṛuta, *s.* Fortune, auspiciousness. 2. virtue, moral merit. *adj.* Virtuous.

ಸುಕ್ಣುಂಡೆ sukṇuṇḍè, *s.* A kind of sweet cake fried in ghee *or* oil.

ಸುಕ್ತಿ sukti, *s.* Ebb, low tide.

ಸುಕ್ರಮ sukrama, *s.* Good order.

ಸುಕ್ರ sukra, *see* ಶುಕ್ರ.

ಸುಖ sukha, *s.* Delight, happiness, joy, pleasure. 2. health, welfare, safety. *adj.* Happy, joyful, delighted. 2. healthy. –ದುಃಖ joy and grief; vicissitudes of life. –ಸುಮಾನ unexpectedly, unreasonably, without sufficient cause. –ಕೊರ್ಪಿನಿ to make happy. –ತಿಂಪಿನಿ, –ಪಡೆಯುನಿ to enjoy happiness. –ದುಃಖ ಪಣ್ಪಿನಿ to relate one's circumstances. –ಸುಮಾನ ನೆರ್ಪಿನಿ to scold unreasonably.

ಸುಗಂಧ sugandha, *s.* Fragrance, perfume. *adj.* Fragrant, scented, perfumed.

ಸುಗಂಧಿ sugandhi, *s.* A fragrant drug. 2. amethyst. –ಪೂ a kind of fragrant flower. –ಬೂರು sarsaparilla root.

ಸುಗತಿ sugati, *s.* A good *or* happy condition.

ಸುಗಿಪುನಿ sugipuni, *see* ಸ್ತುತಿಪುನಿ.

ಸುಗುಣ suguṇa, *s.* An amiable disposition. 2. morality.

ಸುಗುರುನಿ suguruni (ಸುಗುರ್), *v. a.* To uncoil, unwind. 2. to oppose. 3. to improve, better. ಸುಗುರುದು ಉಂತುನಿ to lift one's head; to oppose; to defy.

ಸುಗ್ಗಿ suggi, *s.* The twelfth Tuḷu month (March-April). 2. the second rice crop. 3. harvest. –ಅರಿ rice of the second crop.

ಸುಚಿ suči, *see* ಶುಚಿ.

ಸುಚ್ಚಾಲ್ suččālu, *s.* A swing.

ಸುಜಾತ್ sujātu, *adj.* Fine, nice.

ಸುಜ್ಜಿ sujji, *see* ಸುದ್ದಿ.

ಸುಟಿ suṭi, *see* ಚುಟಿ.

ಸುಡರ್ suḍaru, *see* ತುಡರ್. 2. *see* ಸೊಡರ್.

ಸುಡಲೆ suḍalè, *s.* Burning a dead body. –ದ ಜಾಗ a cemetery, burning ground. –ದ ನುಪ್ಪು a funeral repast.

ಸುಡು suḍu, *s.* The act of burning. –ಕಾಡ್, –ಗಾಡ್ a cemetery, burning ground. –ಗಾಳಿ hot wind. –ಬೊಗ್ಗು ashes of a burnt corpse. –ಮಂಣ್ burnt manure. –ಮೋಣೆ an angry face. –ಸುಡು very hot; *see* ಸುಡ್ಸುಡು. –ಸೂಕರ total ruin.

ಸುಡುಪಿನಿ, ಸುಡ್ಪಿನಿ suḍupini, suḍpini (ಸುಡ್), *v. n.* To burn, be hot *or* sultry. *v. a.* To burn. 2. to bake, toast, roast.

ಸುಡ್ಸುಡು suḍsuḍu, *s.* A burning sensation in the throat, as after vomiting, *etc.*

ಸುಣ್ಣ suṇṇa, *see* ಸುಂಣ.

ಸುತಿ suti, *see* ಸ್ತುತಿ. 2. *see* ಶ್ರುತಿ.

ಸುತುಲಿ, ಸುತ್ತಲಿ sutuli, suttali, *see* ಸುತ್ತೊಲಿ.

ಸುತೆ sute, *s.* A son.

ಸುತ್ತ sutta, *s.* Circumference; circuit. *postp.* Around, about. –ಮುತ್ತ round about. –ಮುತ್ತಿಗೆ besieging. –ಕಟ್ಟುನಿ, –ಪಾಡುನಿ to surround, besiege. –ಬಲೆಪುನಿ to enclose, fence, encompass.

ಸುತ್ತಾವುನಿ suttāvuni, *c. v.* (*of* ಸುತ್ತುನಿ) To cause to wind.

ಸುತ್ತಿ sutti, *see* ಶ್ರುತಿ. 2. *see* ಸುಸ್ತಿ.

ಸುತ್ತಿ, ಸುತ್ತಿಗೆ, ಸುತ್ತಿಯೆ, ಸುತ್ತೆ, ಸುತ್ಯೆ sutti, suttigè, suttiyè, suttè, suttyè, *s.* A hammer.

ಸುತ್ತು suttu, *see* ಸುತ್ತ.

ಸುತ್ತುನಿ suttuni (ಸುತ್ತು), *v. a.* To wind, roll, wrap. 2. to surround.

ಸುತ್ತೆ suttè, *see* ಸುತ್ಯೆ.

ಸುತ್ತೊಲಿ, ಸುತ್ತೊಳಿ suttoli, suttoḷi, *s.* Twine, pack-thread.

ಸುತ್ಯೆ sutyè, *s.* An offering of rice and cocoanut to a

demon. 2. *see* ಸುತ್ತಿ. —ದೀಪಿನಿ to make such an offering.

ಸುದ, ಸುದಾ **suda, sudā,** *adv.* Also. 2. even.

ಸುದರಿಪುನಿ **sudaripuni,** *see* ಸುದಾರಿಪುನಿ.

ಸುದರ್ಶನ **sudaršana,** *s.* Vishṇu's discus. *adj.* Handsome.

ಸುದಾರಣೆ, ಸುದಾರಿಗೆ **sudāraṇè, sudārigè,** *s.* Appeasing, comforting. 2. forbearance. 3. pardon. 4. shifting with, managing.

ಸುದಾರಿಪುನಿ, ಸುದಾರಿಸುನಿ **sudāripuni, sudārisuni** (ಸುದಾರಿ, ಸುದಾರಿಸ್), *v. a.* To appease, calm. 2. to comfort, compose. 3. to forgive. 4. to shift *or* manage with. 5. to support, maintain.

ಸುದಿ **sudi,** *see* ತುದಿ.

ಸುದುರೂಪ **sudurūpa,** *see* ಸದ್ರೂಪ.

ಸುದೆ **sudè,** *see* ತುದೆ.

ಸುದ್ದಿ **suddi,** *s.* Rumour, news, information, intelligence. —ಆಪಿನಿ to transpire, become public. —ಸುಲೇಕ, —ಶ್ಲೋಕ news, tidings. —ಮಳ್ಪುನಿ to publish, inform.

ಸುದ್ದುರುನಿ **sudduruni** (ಸುದ್ದುರ್), *v. n.* To get loose. 2. to get rid of.

ಸುಧಾ **sudhā,** *see* ಸುಧ.

ಸುಧೆ **sudhè,** *s.* Nectar, ambrosia. 2. *see* ತುದೆ.

ಸುನಾಮುಖಿ **sunāmukhi,** *see* ಸುಂನ [ಮುಖಿ.

ಸುನಾವಣಿ **sunāvaṇi,** *see* ಸುಲಾವಣಿ.

ಸುನೆ **sunè,** *see* ತುನೆ.

ಸುಪವತನ **supavatana,** *s.* Honesty.

ಸುಪವೆ **supave,** *s.* An honest man.

ಸುಪ್ತಿ **supti,** *s.* Sleep.

ಸುಫಲ **suphala,** *s.* Good fruit, happy result. *adj.* Bearing good fruit.

ಸುಬ **suba,** *s.* Proof, evidence.

ಸುಬಗೆ **subage,** *see* ಸುಪವೆ.

ಸುಬೆದಾರ್ **subedāru,** *see* ಸುಭೆದಾರ್.

ಸುಬೋಧನೆ **subōdhanè,** *s.* Moral instruction.

ಸುಬ್ಬ **subba,** *s.* A blotch, discolouring of the skin.

ಸುಬ್ಬರಾಯೆ **subbarāye,** *s.* The serpent-god. 2. a proper name.

ಸುಬ್ಬು **subbu,** *see* ಸುಬ್ಬ.

ಸುಬ್ಯಂಮ **subyamma,** *s.* A female demon so called.

ಸುಬ್ರಮಣ್ಯ **subramaṇya,** *s.* A celebrated place of pilgrimage in Uppinangadi Taluk.

ಸುಬ್ರಹ್ಮಣ್ಯೆ, ಸುಬ್ರಾಯೆ, **subrahmaṇye, subrāye,** *see* ಸುಬ್ಬರಾಯೆ.

ಸುಭವೆ **subhave,** *see* ಸುಪವೆ.

ಸುಭಾವ **subhāva,** *see* ಸ್ವಭಾವ.

ಸುಭಾಷಿತ **subhāshita,** *s.* Moral aphorisms *or* sayings. *adj.* Well spoken.

ಸುಭಿಕ್ಷೆ **subhikshè,** *s.* Abundance, plenty. —ಆಪಿನಿ to thrive.

ಸುಭೆದಾರ್, ಸುಭೆದಾರೆ **subhedāru, subhedāre,** *s.* A chief native military officer.

ಸುಮಂಗಲ, ಸುಮಂಗಳ **sumaṅgala, sumaṅgaḷa,** *adj.* Very auspicious. ಸುಮಂಗಲೆ a married woman.

ಸುಮಾನ **sumāna,** *s.* Arbitrariness, capriciousness. *adj.* Arbitrary, capricious, whimsical.

ಸುಮಾರ್ **sumāru**, *s.* Conjecture, guess, estimate. *adj.* Middling, moderate, tolerable. 2. better, well. *adv.* About. —ತರದ of middling sort. —ಆಪಿನಿ to abate, become less; to improve. ಸುಮಾರೊಗು approximately, probably.

ಸುಮಾಲಿ **sumāli**, *s.* A giant so called.

ಸುಮುಹೂರ್ತ **sumuhūrta**, *s.* A very auspicious time.

ಸುಯಿಂಪುನಿ, ಸುಯಿಂಬುನಿ **suyimpuni, suyimbuni** (ಸುಯಿಂ), *v. a.* To blow the nose. 2. to hiss, snort, bellow, fizz, grunt, *etc.*

ಸುಯಿಲ್, ಸುಯ್ಯು **suyilu, suyyu,** *s.* Breath, respiration; *also* ಸುಯಿಲಾಸ. 2. sighing, a sigh, sob. —ಕಟ್ಟುನಿ to hold one's breath, feel difficulty in breathing. —ಪಾಡುನಿ to blow; to whistle. —ಬುಡ್ಪಿನಿ to breathe out; to sigh.

ಸುಯ್ಯುನಿ **suyyuni,** *see* ಸುಯಿಂಪುನಿ.

ಸುರ **sura,** *adj.* Of *or* belonging to the gods. —ಪುರ the capital of Indra.

ಸುರಂಗ **suranga,** *see* ಸರಂಗ.

ಸುರಗಿ, ಸುರಗೆ **suragi, suragè,** *see* ಸೊರಗೆ.

ಸುರತ **surata,** *s.* Sexual embrace.

ಸುರಬೆ **surabè,** *s.* A gluttonous female.

ಸುರಲೆ **suralè,** *see* ತೊರಲೆ.

ಸುರಸ **surasa,** *adj.* Sweet. 2. well flavoured, juicy.

ಸುರಸುರನೆ **surasuranè,** *s.* Drinking liquids with a sipping noise. —ಪರ್ಪಿನಿ to drink in this way.

ಸುರಳಿ **surali,** *s.* A coil, roll of any thing. —ಮಳ್ಪುನಿ to coil, roll.

ಸುರಾಕಾರ **surākāra,** *s.* Saltpetre.

ಸುರಾಪಾನ **surāpāna,** *s.* Wine *or* spirit drinking.

ಸುರಾಯಿ **surāyi,** *see* ತುರಾಯಿ.

ಸುರಾಸುರೆ **surāsure,** *s.* A demi-god. 2. a giant.

ಸುರಿಗೆ **surigè,** *see* ಸೊರಗೆ.

ಸುರಿಪುನಿ **suripuni,** *see* ತುರಿಪಿನಿ.

ಸುರಿಯ **suriya,** *s.* A demon's straight sword.

ಸುರಿಯಾರುನಿ **suriyāruni** (ಸುರಿಯಾರ್), *v. n.* To wander, roam.

ಸುರಿಯುನಿ **suriyuni,** *see* ತುರಿಯುನಿ.

ಸುರಿಯೆ **suriyè,** *see* ಸುರಿಯ.

ಸುರು **suru,** *s.* Commencement, beginning. —ಮಳ್ಪುನಿ to begin.

ಸುರುಂಟು **suruntu,** *s.* Contraction, shrivelling.

ಸುರುಂಟುನಿ **suruntuni** (ಸುರುಂಟೆ), *v. n.* To shrivel, contract, shrink.

ಸುರುಗಿ **surugi,** *see* ಸೊರಗೆ.

ಸುರುಗು **surugu,** *s.* Sinking. 2. sliding.

ಸುರುಟು **surutu,** *see* ಸುರುಂಟು.

ಸುರುಟುನಿ **surutuni,** *see* ಸುರುಂಟುನಿ.

ಸುರುಪ **surupa,** *see* ಸ್ವರೂಪ. 2. *see* ಸುರೂಪ. 3. *see* ಸುರ್ಪ.

ಸುರುಪು **surupu,** *s.* Instigation, encouragement. —ಕೊರ್ಪಿನಿ to instigate.

ಸುರುಮ suruma, *s.* A collyrium for the eyes.

ಸುರುಮೈ surumei, *s.* A kind of dried fish.

ಸುರುಳು, ಸುರುಳೆ surulu, surulè, *see* ಸುರಳಿ.

ಸುರೂಪ surūpa, *s.* A beautiful form. *adj.* Handsome; *cf.* ಸ್ವರೂಪ.

ಸುರೆ surè, *see* ತುರೆ.

ಸುರೆ sure, *s.* A god.

ಸುರ್ಕ surka, *see* ಚರ್ಕ.

ಸುರ್ತಿ surti, *see* ಸುತ್ತಿ.

ಸುರ್ಪ surpa, *see* ಸ್ವರೂಪ.

ಸುರ್ಪು surpu, *s.* Beginning. 2. *see* ಸುರುಪು.

ಸುರ್ಲುಕಾಂಡಯಿ surlukāṇḍayi, *s.* A kind of fish.

ಸುರ್ಳುನಿ surḷuni, *see* ಸುಲಿಪಿನಿ. 2. *see* ತುರಿಪಿನಿ.

ಸುಲಗಿತ್ತಿ sulagitti, *see* ಸೂಲಗಿತ್ತಿ.

ಸುಲಬರ sulabara, *see* ತುಲೆಬಾರ.

ಸುಲಭ sulabha, *adj.* Easy, feasible, attainable. 2. easy of access, condescending. 3. cheap. 4. light, not heavy.

ಸುಲಯಿ sulayi, *s.* A rudder.

ಸುಲಯಿಸುನಿ sulayisuni, *see* ಸುಲಾವುನಿ. 2. *see* ಸುಲಿಯುನಿ.

ಸುಲಕ್ಷಣ sulakshaṇa, *s.* A good sign, auspiciousness. 2. beauty. *adj.* Respectable. 2. handsome, comely. 2. auspicious.

ಸುಲಾವಣೆ sulāvaṇi, *s.* Listening; hearing, acquaintance with. –ಆಪಿನಿ to be heard; to become familiar with the merits of a case. –ಮಳ್ಪುನಿ to cause a superior to hear, as the reading of the papers of a case; to interpret.

ಸುಲಾವುನಿ sulāvuni (ಸುಲಾ), *v. a.* To row a boat.

ಸುಲಿ suli, *see* ಸುಳಿ.

ಸುಲಿಗೆ suligè, *s.* Pillaging, plundering, robbing. –ಮಳ್ಪುನಿ to plunder, rob, pillage.

ಸುಲಿಪಿನಿ, ಸುಲಿಪುನಿ sulipini, sulipuni (ಸುಲಿ), *v. a.* To peel, flay, skin, pare off. 2. *see* ಸುಲಿಯುನಿ. *v. n.* To whirl, go around; *cf.* ತುಲಿಪುನಿ.

ಸುಲಿಪು sulipu, *see* ಸುಳಿ.

ಸುಲಿಯರುನಿ suliyaruni, *see* ಸುರಿಯಾರುನಿ.

ಸುಲಿಯಾವುನಿ suliyāvuni, *c. v.* (*of* ಸುಲಿಯುನಿ) To give up to plunder.

ಸುಲಿಯುನಿ suliyuni (ಸುಲಿ), *v. a.* To pillage, plunder, rob; *cf.* ಸುಲಿಪಿನಿ.

ಸುಲುಗೆ sulugè, *see* ಸುಲಿಗೆ.

ಸುಲೇಕ sulēka, *see* ಶ್ಲೋಕ.

ಸುಲೈಸುನಿ suleisuni, *see* ಸುಲಾವುನಿ.

ಸುಲೋಮಣಿ sulōmaṇi, *s.* An interpreter.

ಸುವರ್ಣ suvarṇa, *s.* Gold. *adj.* Fine coloured, golden.

ಸುವರ್ತಮಾನ, ಸುವಾರ್ತೆ suvartamāna, suvārtè, *s.* Good news. 2. a gospel.

ಸುವಾಸಿನಿ suvāsini, *s.* A married woman.

ಸುಶೀಲ suśīla, *adj.* Well disposed, of good temper. –ತೆ amiability, virtue. —ದಾಯಿ a good-natured man.

ಸುಷ್ಟಿ sushṭi, *see* ಸೃಷ್ಟಿ.

ಸುಸೂತ್ರ susūtra, *adj.* Free, clear, straight-forward. 2. unobstructed, easy, settled. 3. determined, decided. —ಪಣ್ಪುನಿ to speak decidedly, give a decided answer.

ಸುಸ್ತಿ susti, *s.* Delay. 2. sloth, laziness, indolence. —ಉಪ್ಪುನಿ to have leisure. —ಮಳ್ಪುನಿ to delay.

ಸುಸ್ತಿಗೆ sustigè, *see* ಸುತ್ಯೆ.

ಸುಳಿ suḷi, *s.* An eddy, whirlpool. 2. an ominous curve on the person. 3. a tender shoot, germ *or* bud. 4. the soft part on the crown of a young child's head. 5. a hinge. —ಕುತ್ತಿ, *see* ಮೊಳೆಕುತ್ತಿ. —ಗಾಳಿ whirlwind. —ಮರಾಯಿ a round trough.

ಸುಳಿಪುನಿ suḷipuni (ಸುಳಿ), *v. a.* To shake, agitate. 2. to churn. 3. to turn in a lathe. 4. *see* ಸುಲಿಪಿನಿ.

ಸುಳಿಯುನಿ suḷiyuni (ಸುಳಿ), *v.n.* To shake, be agitated, as water. 2. to overflow. 3. *see* ಸುಲಿಯುನಿ.

ಸುಳು suḷu, *s.* Devise, hint.

ಸುಳ್ಳು suḷḷu, *s.* A lie, falsehood, fib. *adj.* False, untrue. —ಕಥೆ a fable, fiction. —ಗಾರೆ a liar. —ಸಾಧನ a false document; a false claim; a false plea. —ಸಾಕ್ಷಿ a false witness; giving false evidence. —ಕೊಚ್ಚುನಿ to brag. —ಪಣ್ಪುನಿ to tell lies.

ಸೂ sū, *see* ತೂ.

ಸೂಂಕಣ sūṅkaṇa, *see* ತೂಂಕಣ.

ಸೂಂಕುನಿ sūṅkuni, *see* ತೂಂಕುನಿ.

ಸೂಂಕೆ sūṅkè, *see* ಸೂಕೆ.

ಸೂಂಗು sūṅgu, *see* ತೂಂಗು.

ಸೂಂಟಯಿ sūṇṭayi, *s.* The fatty part of pork.

ಸೂಂಟಿ, ಸೂಂಠಿ sūṇṭi, sūṇṭhi, *s.* Ginger, dry ginger, *Zingiber officinale.*

ಸೂಂಬು sūmbu, *s.* A sluice, gutter.

ಸೂಂಬೊ sūmbo, *s.* A term used for suspending a game. 2. a reserved place in a game.

ಸೂಕ sūka, *see* ತೂಕ.

ಸೂಕಣ sūkaṇa, *see* ತೂಂಕಣ.

ಸೂಕತ್ತೇರಿ sūkatteri, *s.* A demon so called.

ಸೂಕರ sūkara, *s.* Ruin. 2. a pig.

ಸೂಕೆ sūkè, *s.* Perception, cognition, apprehension. —ಆಪಿನಿ to perceive.

ಸೂಕ್ತ sūkta, *s.* A good word. 2. a hymn of the Vēdas.

ಸೂಕ್ರಮ sūkrama, *adj.* Delicate, fine, nice; *cf.* ಸುಕ್ರಮ. —ದ ಕೆಲಸ fine work. —ದಾಯಿ a man of fine discrimination.

ಸೂಚಕೆ sūčake, *s.* A spy, informer.

ಸೂಚನೆ sūčanè, *s.* A hint, intimation, gesture. 2. a note; a summary, contents of a book *or* chapter. —ಕೊಡಿಸು to hint, make a sign.

ಸೂಚಿಪುನಿ, ಸೂಚಿಸುನಿ sūcipuni, sūčisuni (ಸೂಚಿ, ಸೂಚಿಸ್), *v. a.* To hint, intimate, make a sign.

ಸೂಜಿ sūji, *see* ದೂಜಿ.

ಸೂಜಿಕಲ್ಲ್ sūjikallu, *s.* A loadstone.

ಸೂಟಣ್ sūṭaṇu, *see* ತೂಟಣ್.

ಸೂಟೆ sūṭè, *see* ತೂಟೆ.

ಸೂಡಿ sūḍi, *s.* A sheaf. 2. a bundle. 3. a faggot. —ಕಟ್ಟುನಿ to bind sheaves.

ಸೂಡು sūḍu, *see* ಸುಡು.

ಸೂಣ್ಯ sūṇya, *s.* Commencement, beginning.

ಸೂತಕ, ಸೂತಗ sūtaka, sūtaga, *s.* Ceremonial impurity from child-birth *or* death of a relation. 2. menstruation.

ಸೂತರಿ sūtari, *s.* A Šūdra woman.

ಸೂತಿ, ಸೂತಿಗ sūti, sūtiga, *s.* A scheme. 2. cleverness. 3. *see* ಸೂತಕ.

ಸೂತ್ರ sūtra, *s.* A rule, precept. 2. an axiom. 3. an expedient, contrivance. 4. a thread in general. 5. the spring, wire, *or* thread by which a puppet is moved. 6. the art, knack, key, *etc.*, in a curious piece of mechanism. —ದಾಯೆ, —ಧಾರಿ a puppet-showman; the principal actor or manager of a theatre. —ದ ಗೊಂಬೆ a puppet moved by wires, *etc.* —ಪಟ್ಟಿ an outer frame of a door. —ಬಲ್ಲ್ a carpenter's chalk line. —ದ ಚೇಲೆ fine work; mechanical workmanship. —ಪಾಡುನಿ to mark a plank, *etc.*, with chalk line.

ಸೂದ sūda, *see* ಸುದ.

ಸೂದ್ರೆ sūdre, *see* ಶೂದ್ರೆ.

ಸೂನ sūna, *s.* A place for sacrifice of animals.

ಸೂಪ sūpa, *s.* Sauce, soup. 2. cooking.

ಸೂರ sūra, *s.* A chapter of the Koran.

ಸೂರಂಟೆ sūraṇṭè, *s.* *Hydnocarpus inebrians.*

ಸೂರಣ sūraṇa, *s.* The Telinga potato, *Arum campanulatum.*

ಸೂರು sūru, *see* ಚೂರು.

ಸೂರೆ sūrè, *s.* Plundering, ransacking, pillaging. —ಬುಡುಪಿನಿ to give up to plunder. —ಮುಳ್ಪುನಿ to pillage, plunder.

ಸೂರೆ sūre, *see* ಶೂರೆ.

ಸೂರೊಳ್ sūroḷu, *s.* Rattan, *Calamus rotang.* —ದ ಬೆತ್ತ a rattan stick.

ಸೂರ್ಣ sūrṇa, *see* ಸೂರಣ. 2. *see* ಚೂರ್ಣ.

ಸೂರ್ತಿ sūrti, *s.* Surat. —ರೂಪಾಯಿ a Surat rupee.

ಸೂರ್ಯ, ಸೂರ್ಯೆ sūrya, sūrye, *s.* The sun. —ಕಾಂತಿ sunshine. —ಕಾಂತಿ ಪೂ the sun-flower, *Helianthus annuus.* —ಕಿರಣ a sunbeam. —ಗ್ರಹಣ an eclipse of the sun. —ನಮಸ್ಕಾರ prostration to the sun. —ಪುಟ

calcination of metals, medicines, *etc.*, by exposing them to the sun. —ಬಿಂಬ the disk of the sun. —ಮಂಡಲ the sun's orb. —ವಂಶ Rāma's generation. —ಕಂತುನಿ the sun to set. —ಮೂಡುನಿ the sun to rise.

ಸೂಲ **sūla,** *see* ಶೂಲ.

ಸೂಲಗಿತ್ತಿ **sūlagitti,** *s.* A midwife.

ಸೂಲಿ **sūli,** *s.* Skin, bark, rind; *cf.* ಚೋಲಿ.

ಸೂಲು **sūlu,** *s.* Swearing.

ಸೂಲೆ **sūlè,** *see* ಶೂಲೆ.

ಸೂಲೆಂಗಿ **sūleṅgi,** *s.* An instrument for peeling the fibrous covering of a cocoanut. 2. a small crowbar.

ಸೂವತ್ತಿ **sūvatti,** *s.* A good woman.

ಸೂಸಿ **sūsi,** *s.* A female's ordinary garment.

ಸೂಸು **sūsu,** *s.* A noise made for driving away birds, *etc.*

ಸೂಸ್ರ, ಸೂಸ್ತ **sūsra, sūstra,** *see* ಸೂತ್ರ.

ಸೂಳಗಿತ್ತಿ **sūḷagitti,** *see* ಸೂಲಗಿತ್ತಿ.

ಸೂಳಿ **sūḷi,** *see* ಚೂಲಿ. 2. *see* ಸುಳಿ.

ಸೂಳೆ **sūḷè,** *s.* A whore, harlot. —ಗಾರಿಗೆ whoredom. —ಗಾರೆ a whoremonger. —ಮಗೆ a whore's son; an abusive term, *vlg.*

ಸೂಳೆಬೊಟ್ಟು **sūḷeboṭṭu,** *s.* The shrub *Pavetta indica.*

ಸೂಕ್ಷ್ಮ **sūkshma,** *adj.* Fine, thin, subtle, delicate. 2. very small, minute, atomic. 3. clever, smart, quick. —ಕೆಲಸ delicate work. —ದೃಷ್ಟಿ quick sight. —ಬುದ್ಧಿ a refined mind, sagacity. —ವಸ್ತು a very fine thing; an atom, particle. —ಶರೀರ a delicate body.

ಸೃಂಗಾರ **sṛuṅgāra,** *see* ಶೃಂಗಾರ.

ಸೃಷ್ಟಿ **sṛushṭi,** *s.* Creation, creating. 2. the world, universe. —ಕರ್ತವೆ, —ಮಳ್ತಿನಾಯೆ the Creator. —ಮಳ್ಪುನಿ, ಸೃಷ್ಟಿಪುನಿ, ಸೃಷ್ಟಿಸುನಿ to create, give birth to; to forge, manufacture.

ಸೆಂಟ್ರುಣಿ **serṇṭuni,** *see* ತೆಕೆಂಟುನಿ.

ಸೆಕೆ **sekè,** *see* ಸಿಕೆ.

ಸೆಟ್ಟಿವಾಳ್ **seṭṭivāḷu,** *see* ಶೆಟ್ಟಿವಾಳ್.

ಸೆಡಗರ, ಸೆಡವು **seḍagara, seḍavu,** *s.* Egotism, vanity, conceit, ostentation. 2. squeamishness, over-nicety.

ಸೆಡಾಸುನಿ **seḍāsuni,** *see* ಚಡಾಯಿಸುನಿ.

ಸೆಡಿ **seḍi,** *s.* Swinging, in fulfilment of a vow to a goddess, suspended by an iron hook passed through the large tendons of the back, to one end of a lever which is raised on the top of a high pole *or* fulcrum, and whirled round by means of a rope fixed to the other end. 2. *see* ಶಿಡಿ. —ಪೂಜೆ the swinging feast. —ದೈಪುನಿ to suspend a person as described above.

ಸೆಡಿ **seḍi,** *adj.* Strong, affecting the smell powerfully. —ವಾಸನೆ a strong scent.

ಸೆಡಿತ **seḍita,** *see* ಕೆಡಿತ.

ಸೆಡಿತರುನಿ **seḍitaruni,** *see* ಕೆಡ್‌ತರುನಿ.

ಸೆಡಿಪಿನಿ, ಸೆಡಿಪುನಿ seḍipini, seḍipuni, *see* ಕೆಡಿಪಿನಿ.

ಸೆಡಿಲ್ seḍilu, *see* ಕೆಡಿಲ್.

ಸೆಡ್ಡಿಯುನಿ seḍḍiyuni (ಸೆಡ್ಡಿ), *v. n.* To throb. 2. *see* ಕೆಡಿಪಿನಿ.

ಸೆದೆ sedè, *s.* Sweeping, rubbish.

ಸೆಮತಿಗೆ sematigè, *see* ಕೇಮತ್ತಿಗೆ.

ಸೆರಂಗ್ serangu, *s.* The end *or* edge of a female's garment. ಕೀಲ್—, ಗೇಲ್— the lower edge of a garment. ತೋಪು— the silk edge of a garment. ಮೇ ದಲೆ—, ಮೇಲ್— the upper edge of the same.

ಸೆರಕಯಿ serakayi, *see* ಕರಕಯಿ.

ಸೆರಸರೆ, ಸೆರಸ್ರೆ serasarè, serasrè, *s.* A curtain, screen. —ಕಟ್ಟುನಿ to put up a curtain.

ಸೆರೆ serè, *see* ಕೆರೆ.

ಸೆರೆ serè, *s.* A wave. 2. the palm of the hand bent so as to hold anything. 3. *see* ಸೆರಸರೆ. —ಅರಿ a handful of rice. —ಗಂ ಡಿಪುನಿ to hold fast.

ಸೆಲಡಿಯುನಿ seladiyuni (ಸೆಲಡ್), *v. n.* To be folded. 2. to be tired. 3. to loathe.

ಸೆಲಡ್ಡುನಿ, ಸೆಲಾಡ್ರುನಿ seladduni, seladruni (ಸೆಲಡ್ಡ್), *v. n.* To move aside, get away; *cf.* ಕೆಲವುನಿ.

ಸೆಲಿ seli, *s.* A prepossessing appearance. *adj.* Clear, pure, filtered. —ನೀರ್ pure water.

ಸೆಲಿಪುನಿ selipuni (ಸೆಲಿ), *v. a.* To filter; to cleanse.

ಸೆಲಿಯುನಿ, ಸೆಲ್ಲಿಯುನಿ seliyuni, selliyuni (ಸೆಲಿ, ಸೆಲ್ಲಿ), *v. n.* To become clear, pure.

ಸೆಳೆ selè, *s.* A chink, crack, flaw, as in a stone.

ಸೆಳ್ಟುನಿ selṭuni, *see* ಕೆಳ್ಂಟುನಿ.

ಸೆಲ್ಬಿ selbi, *see* ಚೆಲುವೆ.

ಸೆಸೆ sesè, *see* ದೆಸೆ.

ಸೆಳೆ seḷè, *s.* Force. 2. *see* ಸಳೆ. *adj.* Strong.

ಸಳೆಯುನಿ seḷeyuni (ಸೆಳೆ), *v. n.* To go round; *cf.* ತಿಂಗುರುನಿ.

ಸೇಂಕುಡ sēṅkuḍa, *see* ಸೇಂಕೆ.

ಸೇಂಕುನಿ sēṅkuni (ಸೇಂಕ್), *v. n.* To pant, breathe quickly *or* heavily.

ಸೇಂಕೆ, ಸೇಂಕೆಲ್ sēṅkè, sēṅkelu, *s.* Panting, breathing quickly.

ಸೇಂಟ sēṇṭa, *see* ಸೇಟ.

ಸೇಂದಿ sēndi, *see* ಕೇಂದಿ.

ಸೇಂದಾವುನಿ sēndāvuni, *c. v.* (*of* ಸೇಂದುನಿ) To sprinkle. 2. to float.

ಸೇಂದುನಿ sēnduni (ಸೇಂದ್), *v. n.* To splash.

ಸೇಕ sēka, *see* ಕೇಕ.

ಸೇಕಡ sēkaḍa, *see* ಕೇಕಡ.

ಸೇಕೆ sēkè, *see* ತೇಕೆ.

ಸೇಜ sēja, *see* ತೇಜ.

ಸೇಜ, ಸೇಜಿ sēja, sēji, *s.* A present, gift; raw rice sprinkled on persons attending a marriage, *etc.* ಕೊರಾ— a novel gift; a rare *or* costly present.

ಸೇಜುನಿ sējuni (ಸೇಜ್), *v. a.* To sharpen, whet, polish.

ಸೇಟ್ sēṭu, *s.* The beard of the thatching grass. 2. *see* ಸೇಟ.

ಸೇಟ sēṭa, *s.* The hair about the privities.

ಸೇಟಿ, ಸೇಟು sēṭi, sēṭu, *s.* A Bombay merchant, a native of Guzerat *or* Cutch.

ಸೇಟುನಿ sēṭuni (ಸೇಟಿ), *v. a.* To stab.

ಸೇಡಿ sēḍi, *see* ಶೇಡಿ.

ಸೇಡು sēḍu, *s.* A slice, piece.

ಸೇಡೆ sēḍè, *see* ತೇಡೆ.

ಸೇಣವೆ sēṇave, *see* ಕೇಣವೆ

ಸೇತಿ sēti, *s.* A kind of silk cloth.

ಸೇತು, ಸೇತುವೆ sētu, sētuvè, *s.* A bridge. 2. Adam's bridge. –ಸ್ನಾನ bathing at Adam's bridge near Rāmēšvaram.

ಸೇದುನಿ sēduni (ಸೇದ್), *v. a.* To throb. 2. to draw, as water; *cf.* ತೇಪುನಿ.

ಸೇನೆ sēnè, *see* ಸೈನ್ಯ.

ಸೇಬಿ sēbi, *adj.* White.

ಸೇಮತಿಗೆ sēmatige, *see* ಕೇಮತ್ತಿಗೆ.

ಸೇಮಯಿದಡ್ಡ್ಯೆ sēmayidaḍḍyè, *s.* A kind of vermicelli made of wheat *or* other grain.

ಸೇಮೆ sēmè, *s.* A sharp kind of vermicelli. 2. a kind of crab.

ಸೇರ್ sērụ, *s.* A seer, measure of capacity equal to about eighty rupees in weight. 2. a weight equal to about twenty-four rupees.

ಸೇರಾವುನಿ sērāvuni, *see* ಕೇರಾವುನಿ.

ಸೇರಿಗಾರೆ, ಸೇರೆಗಾರೆ sērigāre, sēregāre, *see* ಕೇರಿಗಾರೆ.

ಸೇರಿಗೆ sērigè, *see* ಕೇರಿಗೆ.

ಸೇರು sēru, *see* ಸೇರ್.

ಸೇರೆ sērè, *see* ಸೆರೆ.

ಸೇರ್ಲೋಭಾನ sērlōbhāna, *s.* A kind of incense.

ಸೇಲೆ sēlè, *see* ಕೇಲೆ. 2. *see* ಶಲ್ಯ.

ಸೇವಂತಿಗೆ sēvantigè, *see* ಕೇಮತ್ತಿಗೆ.

ಸೇವಕೆ sēvake, *s.* A servant, attendant.

ಸೇವು sēvu, *see* ತೇವು.

ಸೇವೆ sēvè, *s.* Service, servitude. 2. homage, worship, devotion.

ಸೇಸ, ಸೇಸೆ sēsa, sēsè, *adv.* A time, turn. 2. *see* ಸೇಜ. ಮೂಜಿ– three times.

ಸೇಳೆ sēḷè, *see* ಕೇಲೆ.

ಸೈ sei, *adv.* It is right, it is well, indeed, aye. –ಬುದ್ಪಿನಿ to consent, assent, approve.

ಸೈಂಕೋಲು, ಸೈಂಗೊಲೆ, ಸೈಂಗೋಲು seiṅkōlu, seiṅgolè, seiṅgōlu, *s.* A crowbar.

ಸೈಂದವೆ seindave, *s.* A native of Sindh; a giant so called. 2. a stalwart man.

ಸೈಂದುಪ್ಪು, ಸೈಂದುರ್ಲವಣ seinduppu, seindurlavaṇa, *s.* Rocksalt.

ಸೈತನ seitana, *see* ಚೈತನ.

ಸೈತಾನ್, ಸೈತಾನೆ seitānụ, seitāne, *s.* The satan, devil.

ಸೈತ್ಯ seitya, *s.* Cold, a cold. *adj.* Cool, fresh, cooling.

ಸೈನ್ seinụ, *s.* A superior kind of long cloth.

ಸೈನಿಕೆ seinike, *s.* A soldier.

ಸೈನ್ಯ seinya, *s.* An army.

ಸೈನ್ಯಾಧಿಪತಿ seinyādhipati, *s.* The general *or* commander of an army.

ಸೈಪಿನಿ seipini (ಸೈ), *v. n.* To die, expire. 2. to be starved.

ಸೈರಣೆ seiraṇè, *s.* Patience, forbearance, endurance. —ಮಲ್ಪುನಿ to take patience, forbear, endure.

ಸೈರಿಪುನಿ, ಸೈರಿಸುನಿ seiripuni, seirisuni (ಸೈರಿ, ಸೈರಿಸ್), *v. a.* To bear, endure, suffer, put up with.

ಸೈಲೆ seilè, *s.* A ghost, an apparition.

ಸೈಲೇಂದ್ರಿ, ಸೈಳೇಂದ್ರಿ seilēndri, seiḷēndri, *s.* A female servant *or* attendant. 2. a name assumed by Droupadi, when serving in Virāṭarāja's household.

ಸೊಂಕುನಿ soṅkuni, *see* ಸೋಂಕುನಿ.

ಸೊಂಟ soṇṭa, *s.* The loins, hip, waist. —ಬೇನೆ lumbago. —ಕಟ್ಟುನಿ to gird the loins; to set to work; set out on a journey; to be equipped.

ಸೊಂಟಿ soṇṭi, *s.* A deformed woman.

ಸೊಂಡಿಲ್ soṇḍilu, *see* ಸುಂಡಿಲ್.

ಸೊಂಣ soṇṇa, *s.* Gold. —ಗಾರೆ, *see* ಸೊಣ್ಣಗಾರೆ.

ಸೊಂಣಮೆ soṇṇamè, *see* ಘಂಣಮೆ.

ಸೊಂತ sonta, *see* ಸ್ವಂತ.

ಸೊಂದು sondu, *s.* Exertion, effort.

ಸೊಂದುನಿ sonduni (ಸೊಂದು), *v. n.* To exert, labour, work hard.

ಸೊಂನಗಾರೆ sonnagāre, *see* ಸೊಣ್ಣಗಾರೆ.

ಸೊಂನೆ sonnè, *s.* The nought, cipher. 2. the medial letter ೦. 3. a sign. 4. a demon so called. ಕಂಣ್– winking. ಕೈ– beckoning with the hand.

ಸೊಂಪು sompu, *see* ಸಂಪು.

ಸೊಂಪೇರುನಿ somperuni (ಸೊಂಪೇರ್), *v. n.* To be refreshed, invigorated; to revive. 2. to improve, mend, as one's condition.

ಸೊಂಬ somba, *see* ಸಂಪಿಗೆ.

ಸೊಂಬ somba, *s.* Collection, mass, assemblage.

ಸೊಂಬರ sombara, *adj.* Full, complete, abundant. 2. *see* ಸಂಬರ.

ಸೊಂಕುರ್ನಿ, ಸೊಕ್ಕುನಿ soṅkuni, sokkuni, *see* ಸೊಕ್ರ್ನಿ.

ಸೊಕ್ಕು sokku, *see* ಸೊಕ್ರ್.

ಸೊಖ sokha, *see* ಸುಖ.

ಸೊಗಪುನಿ, ಸೊಗಸುನಿ sogapuni, sogasuni (ಸೊಗ, ಸೊಗಸ್), *v. n.* To be tasteful, agreeable, pleasant. *v. a.* To praise, commend.

ಸೊಗಸ್ sogasu, *s.* Relish, savouriness, agreeableness. 2. fastidiousness, squeamishness. 3. praise, commendation. *adj.* Savoury. 2. fastidious. 3. commendable.

ಸೊಗೊರಿ sogori, *see* ಜೊಗರಿ.

ಸೊಚ್ಚ socca, *see* ಸ್ವಚ್ಛ.

ಸೊಜ್ಜಿಗೆ sojjigè, *see* ಸೋಜಿ.

ಸೊಟ್ಟ soṭṭa, *see* ಚೊಟ್ಟ.

ಸೊಡರ್ soḍaru, *s.* The smell of burning; *also* ಸೊಡರ್ ಕಮ್ಮೆನ. *adj.* Smoky, fumid, noisome.

ಸೊಣಂಗ್ soṇaṅgu, *see* ನಾಯಿಸೊಣಂಗ್.

ಸೊಣಗಾರೆ, ಸೊಙ್ಗಾರೆ soṇagāre, soṅgāre, *s.* A Koṅkaṇi speaking goldsmith.

ಸೊಣ್ಕೆ soṇkè, *see* ಚೊಣಂಕೆ.

ಸೊಣ್ಪ soṇpa, *num.* Ninety.

ಸೊತಂತ್ರ sotantra, *see* ಸ್ವತಂತ್ರ.

ಸೊಪ್ನ sopna, *see* ಸ್ವಪ್ನ.

ಸೊಪ್ಪು soppu, *see* ತಪ್ಪು.

ಸೊಬ soba, *see* ಶುಭ.

ಸೊಬಗ್ sobagu̥, *adj.* Pleasing, well-looking.

ಸೊಬಗೆ sobage, *see* ಸುಪಮೆ.

ಸೊಯ soya, *see* ಸ್ವಯ.

ಸೊಯಿರೆ soyire, *s.* A eunuch.

ಸೊರ sora, *see* ಸ್ವರ.

ಸೊರಂಗ soraṅga, *see* ಸರಂಗ.

ಸೊರಗಿಬಳೆ soragibaḷè, *s.* A kind of bracelet.

ಸೊರಗೆ soragè, *s.* A small, sweet scented yellow flower. —ಮರ its tree.

ಸೊರಿ sori, *adj.* Sufficient for one year. —ಅರಿ rice sufficient from one harvest to the next.

ಸೊರೂಪ sorūpa, *see* ಸ್ವರೂಪ.

ಸೊರ್ಕ್, ಸೊರ್ಕು sorku̥, sorku, *s.* Fat; vigour. 2. rankness, luxuriance. 3. lust, inordinate affection. 4. pride, insolence.

ಸೊರ್ಕಲಿಯುನಿ sorkaliyuni, *see* ಸೊರ್ಕೆಲುನಿ.

ಸೊರ್ಕಾವುನಿ sorkāvuni, *c.v.* (*of* ಸೊರ್ಕುನಿ) To make fat, vigorous, *or* rank. 2. to give undue indulgence.

ಸೊರ್ಕುನಿ sorkuni (ಸೊರ್ಕ್), *v. n.* To become fat, vigorous. 2. to be rank, luxuriant. 3. to be lustful, sensual. 4. to be proud, insolent.

ಸೊರ್ಕೆಲ್ sorkeḷu̥, *s.* Lust, rutting, as an animal. 2. *see* ಸೊರ್ಕ್. 3. narcosis. *adj.* Vigorous, rank, lustful. 2. narcotic, as a dry piece of betel nut.

ಸೊರ್ಕೆಲುನಿ sorkeluni (ಸೊರ್ಕೆಲ್), *v. n.* To be in rut, to lust after, seek copulation, as an animal. 2. to be narcotic, as an areca nut.

ಸೊರ್ಗ sorga, *see* ಸ್ವರ್ಗ.

ಸೊಲಬರ solabara, *s.* Weighing one's self against gold, *etc.*, in fulfilment of a vow; *bet.* ತುಲೆಬಾರ.

ಸೊಲಭ solabha, *see* ಸುಲಭ.

ಸೊಲಾವುನಿ solāvuni, *see* ಸುಲಾವುನಿ.

ಸೊಲಿಕೆ solikè, *s.* The scab of itch. 2. a piece of plantain leaf.

ಸೊಲಿಗೆ soligè, *see* ಸುಲಿಗೆ.

ಸೊಲೇಕ solēka, *see* ಶ್ಲೋಕ.

ಸೊಲ್ಪ solpa, *see* ಸ್ವಲ್ಪ.

ಸೊಲ್ಪಾವುನಿ solpāvuni, *see* ಸೋಪಾವುನಿ.

ಸೊಲ್ಪುದ್ದರ್ solpuddaru̥, *s.* New rice boiled with milk *or* old rice and eaten at the harvest feast.

ಸೊಲ್ಪುನಿ solpuni, *see* ಸೋಪುನಿ.

ಸೊಲ್ಮ, ಸೊಲ್ಮೆ solma, solmè, *s.* Salutation, making obeisance, as a low-caste man does to one of a superior caste. 2. submission, yielding, as a defeated party. —ಪಾಡುನಿ to salute, to yield.

ಸೊಲ್ಮಿಯುನಿ solmiyuni (ಸೊಲ್ಮಿ), *v. a.* To salute. 2. to submit, yield, please.

ಸೋಂಕಣೆ sōṅkaṇè, *see* ಸಾಂಕಣೆ.

ಸೋಂಕು sōṅku, *s.* An epidemic, infection; a contagious disease; *also* ಸೋಂಕು ರೋಗ. 2. a fit of epilepsy *or* apoplexy. 3. paralysis. 4. *see* ಚೋಕು. —ದ ಪೊಯ್ಯೊ sand said to be thrown by a demon at a person to make him sick of such a disease.

ಸೋಂಕುನಿ, ಸೋಂಕುಡ್ರುನಿ, ಸೋಂಗುನಿ sōṅkuni, sōṅkuḍruni, sōṅguni (ಸೋಂಕ್, ಸೋಂಗ್), *v. a.* To affect, as a disease. 2. to touch, come into contact; to infect, affect.

ಸೋಂಗೆ sōṅgè, *s.* A furrow, a small channel. —ಕಡ್ಪುನಿ to make a furrow.

ಸೋಂಟ, ಸೋಂಟೆ sōṇṭa, sōṇṭè, *s.* A cudgel, club. 2. firewood.

ಸೋಂಟುನಿ sōṇṭuni (ಸೋಂಟ್), *v. a.* To box with the knuckle of the fingers.

ಸೋರ್ಂಟೆ sōrṇṭè, *s.* A kind of solanum.

ಸೋಕು sōku, *see* ಸೋಂಕು.

ಸೋಕುನಿ sōkuni, *see* ಸೋಂಕುನಿ.

ಸೋಗೆ sōgè, *s.* The peculiar branch *or* leaf of the palm species.

ಸೋಜಿ sōji, *s.* Rolong *or* wheaten grits.

ಸೋಜಿಗ sōjiga, *see* ಸೋದ್ಯ.

ಸೋಜುನಿ sōjuni, *see* ತೋಜುನಿ.

ಸೋಟ, ಸೋಟೆ sōṭa, sōṭè, *see* ಸೋಂಟ.

ಸೋಡ್ತಿ sōḍti, *s.* Lottery, raffle. —ಪಾಡುನಿ to raffle; to bet.

ಸೋಣ sōṇa, *s.* The fifth Tuḷu month (about August). —ಪೂ *Balsamina.*

ಸೋದರೆ sōdare, *see* ಸಹೋದರೆ.

ಸೋದಿಯುನಿ sōdiyuni, *see* ಶೋಧಿಯುನಿ.

ಸೋದೆ sōde, *s.* A rake. 2. a pimp.

ಸೋದ್ಯ sōdya, *s.* Wonder, surprise.

ಸೋದ್ರೆ sōdrè, *s.* An incontinent woman.

ಸೋನ sōna, *see* ಸೂನ.

ಸೋಪ sōpa, *see* ಸೋಪು.

ಸೋಪಣ sōpaṇa, *s.* A drain, sluice.

ಸೋಪಾಡುನಿ sōpāḍuni (ಸೋಪಾಡ್), *v. a.* To sway to and fro, as a devil-dancer.

ಸೋಪಾಣ sōpāṇa, *s.* A kind of gram.

ಸೋಪಾವುನಿ sōpāvuni, *c. v.* (*of* ಸೋಪುನಿ) To make one lose at a game. 2. to defeat, overcome, conquer. 3. to charm, allure, captivate.

ಸೋಪು sōpu, *s.* Defeat, discomfiture. 2. soap. *adj.* Defeated, overcome. 2. unclean. 3. rough.

ಸೋವುನಿ sōpuni (ಸೋ), *v. n.* To lose at a game. 2. to be defeated, overcome. 3. to be charmed, allured, to have the heart *or* affections won over to an object.

ಸೋಬಾನ sōbāna, *see* ಶೋಭಾನ.

ಸೋಬೆ sōbè, *see* ಶೋಭೆ.

ಸೋಮ sōma, *see* ಸೋಮೆ.

ಸೋಮನಾಥಕಲ್ಲ್ sōmanāthakallu, *s.* Marble-stone.

ಸೋಮನಾಥೆ sōmanāthe, *s.* Šiva.

ಸೋಮನಾಧಿಕಾಯಿ sōmanādhikāyi, *s.* Asafœtida.

ಸೋಮರಬೇರ್ sōmarabēru, *s.* The root of a medicinal plant so called.

ಸೋಮವಾರ, ಸೋಮಾರ sōmavāra, sōmāra, *s.* Monday.

ಸೋಮಸಾಲೆ sōmasālè, *s.* A kind of rice.

ಸೋಮಾರಿ sōmāri, *s.* A lazy man. *adj.* Lazy, indolent. —ತನ laziness, indolence.

ಸೋಮೆ sōme, *s.* The moon. 2. the name of a man.

ಸೋರಿಕೆ sōrikè, *see* ತೋರಿಕೆ.

ಸೋರುನಿ sōruni, *see* ತೋರುನಿ.

ಸೋರೆ sōrè, *adj.* Tender, unripe; *also* ಚೋರೆ.

ಸೋರ್ತೆ sōrtè, *s.* Oozing; *cf.* ತೋರುನಿ.

ಸೋಲ sōla, *s.* Defeat, failure, disappointment. —ಗೆಲವು loss and gain, defeat and success; a kind of game.

ಸೋಲಾವುನಿ sōlāvuni, *see* ಸೋಪಾವುನಿ.

ಸೋಲಿ sōli, *see* ಸೋರಿ.

ಸೋಲುನಿ sōluni, *see* ಸೋಪುನಿ.

ಸೋಲೆ sōlè, *see* ಚೊಲ್ಲೆ.

ಸೋಲ್ಪು sōlpu, *see* ಸೋಪು.

ಸೋವು sōvu, *s.* Spying, watching, observing secretly. 2. trace, mark, sign. 3. private intelligence, secret information. —ದಾಯಿ a spy. —ತೂಪಿನಿ to spy, trace. —ಪಾಡುನಿ to keep watch, lie in wait.

ಸೋಳು sōḷu, *see* ತೋಳು.

ಸ್ವೈಂಪಾಕ soimpāka, *see under* ಸ್ವಯಂ.

ಸೌಂಟು souṇṭu, *s.* A spoon *or* ladle.

ಸೌಂದರಿ, ಸೌಂದರ್ಯ soundari, soundarya, *s.* Comeliness, beauty.

ಸೌಕಾರ soukāra, *s.* Soap.

ಸೌಕಾರೆ soukāre, *s.* A merchant, trader.

ಸೌಕಾಶ soukāša, *see* ಸಾವಕಾಶ.

ಸೌಖ್ಯ soukhya, *s.* Pleasure, happiness, ease. —ಜಾಗ್ a comfortable place. ಉಣಿಯೆರೆ ತಿನಿಯೆರೆ ಸೌಖ್ಯ to have plenty to eat, *etc.*; to be in easy circumstances. ಜೀವೊದು ಸೌಖ್ಯ ಉಪ್ಪುನಿ to enjoy good health.

ಸೌಜನ್ಯ soujanya, *s.* Mildness, goodness.

ಸೌಜ್ಞೆ soujñè, *s.* A hint, sign, gesture. —ಮಳ್ಪುನಿ to make a sign.

ಸೌಟು souṭu, *see* ಸೌಂಟು.

ಸೌತೆ soutè, *see* ತೌತೆ.

ಸೌದ souda, *see* ಶಬ್ದ.

ಸೌದಿ soudi, *s.* Firewood.

ಸೌಭಾಗ್ಯ **soubhāgya,** *s.* Luckiness, auspiciousness, good fortune. –ವತಿ a woman whose husband is alive.

ಸೌಮ್ಯ **soumya,** *s.* The forty-third year in the Hindu cycle of sixty. *adj.* Handsome, pleasing. 2. gentle, mild, placid. –ಗುಣ a mild disposition. –ವಾರ Wednesday.

ಸೌರ **soura,** *s.* A solar month. –ಮಾನ measured by the sun, solar; day, year, time.

ಸೌರು **souru,** *s.* Heroism. 2. provoking language.

ಸೌರುನಿ **souruni,** *see* ಶೌರುನಿ.

ಸೌಳು **soulu,** *adj.* Brackish. –ನೀರ್ brackish water. –ಭೂಮಿ salt ground, unfruitful soil.

ಸೌಳಿ **souli,** *see* ಚೌಳಿ.

ಸ್ಕಂದ **skanda,** *s.* A chapter, section.

ಸ್ತಂಬ, ಸ್ತಂಭ **stamba, stambha,** *s.* A post, pillar. 2. stoppage, suppression, as of urine, *etc.* by incantation, medicine, *etc.*; *also* ಸ್ತಂಭನ.

ಸ್ತನ **stana,** *s.* The female breast. –ಪಾನಮಳ್ಪುನಿ to suck the breast.

ಸ್ತಬ್ಧ **stabdha,** *adj.* Stopped, blocked up. –ಆಪಿನಿ to be spell-bound; to be silent.

ಸ್ತುತಿ, ಸ್ತೋತ್ರ **stuti, stōtra,** *s.* Praise, eulogy. 2. adoration. ಮುಖ– flattery. –ಮಳ್ಪುನಿ, ಸ್ತುತಿಪುನಿ to praise, eulogize.

ಸ್ತೋಮ **stōma,** *s.* A heap, mass, quantity, assemblage, multitude. 2. a body, company, gang. ಜನ– a crowd of people.

ಸ್ತ್ರೀ **strī,** *s.* A woman. *adj.* Feminine, female. –ಧನ a woman's separate property; her dower. –ಬುದ್ಧಿ a weak, effeminate mind; indecision. –ಲಿಂಗ the feminine gender. –ವೇಷ the guise of a woman.

ಸ್ಥಲ, ಸ್ಥಳ **sthala, sthaḷa,** *s.* A place, site, spot, locality, residence. 2. room, lieu, stead. 3. an office, situation, station. 4. soil.

ಸ್ಥಳಾಂತರ **sthaḷāntara,** *s.* Change of place.

ಸ್ಥಾನ **sthāna,** *s.* A place, spot, situation, local position. 2. a habitation, dwelling, station. 3. likeness, resemblance. ದೇವ– a temple, God's dwelling. ಪಿತೃ– a father's place. ವಾಸ– a dwelling-place, residence. –ಮರಿಯಾದೆ a local privilege *or* custom.

ಸ್ಥಾನಿಕೆ **sthānike,** *s.* One belonging to a caste so called. 2. the steward *or* head servant of a temple employed in its outer service.

ಸ್ಥಾಪನೆ **sthāpanè,** *s.* Establishing, founding, fixing, erecting. 2. settling, determining, appointing, proving, verifying, confirming. –ಮಳ್ಪುನಿ, ಸ್ಥಾಪಿಸುನಿ to establish; to determine.

ಸ್ಥಾವರ **sthāvara,** *adj.* Immovable, fixed, stationary. –ಜಂಗಮ immovable and movable.

ಸ್ಥಿತಿ **sthiti,** *s.* An estate, wealth, property. 2. state, condition. 3. continuance, being; existence. –ಗತಿ one's condition *or* state. ಭೂ– landed property. –ವಂತ a wealthy man. ಸೃಷ್ಟಿ, ಸ್ಥಿತಿ, ಲಯ creation, existence, and destruction of the universe.

ಸ್ಥಿರ **sthira,** *adj.* Steady, stable, firm, fixed. 2. permanent, continuing, lasting. –ಚರ immovable and movable. –ದಾಂತಿನಾಯಿ an unsteady man. –ಬುದ್ಧಿ a steady disposition, decision of character. –ಆಪಿನಿ to be firm, fixed. –ಮಳ್ಪುನಿ to confirm.

ಸ್ಥೂಲ **sthūla,** *adj.* Great, large, thick. 2. gross, corpulent, huge, coarse. 3. dense, not attenuate *or* subtil. 4. doltish, stupid, thick-headed. –ದೇಹ a corpulent body. –ಬುದ್ಧಿ dull sense. –ವಸ್ತು a gross substance. –ವಿಚಾರ a superficial view of a case.

ಸ್ನಾನ **snāna,** *s.* Ablution, bathing. 2. ceremonial purification of the body through ablution, *etc.* 3. baptism. –ಕೊರ್ಪಿನಿ to baptise. –ಮಳ್ಪುನಿ to bathe. –ಹೊಂದುನಿ to be baptised.

ಸ್ನೇಹ **snēha,** *s.* Affection, attachment, friendship, love. ಪ್ರಾಣ– intimacy, intimate friendship. –ಮಳ್ಪುನಿ, ಸ್ನೇಹಿಪುನಿ to love, be attached. ಸ್ನೇಹಾಚಾರ friendship; intercourse, commerce.

ಸ್ನೇಹಿತೆ **snēhite,** *s.* A friend.

ಸ್ಪಟಿಕಾರ **spatikāra,** *s.* Alum.

ಸ್ಪರ್ಶ, ಸ್ಪರ್ಶನ **sparša, sparšana,** *s.* Touch, contact. 2. the sense of touch. 3. wind, air. –ಆಪಿನಿ to be touched. –ಮಳ್ಪುನಿ, ಸ್ಪರ್ಶಿಸುನಿ to touch.

ಸ್ಪಷ್ಟ **spashṭa,** *adj.* Clear, plain, distinct, apparent, open, manifest, evident, intelligible. –ಆಪಿನಿ to be plain, intelligible. –ಮಳ್ಪುನಿ to make plain.

ಸ್ಫಟಿಕ **sphaṭika,** *s.* A crystal.

ಸ್ಪುಟ, ಸ್ಫುಟ **spuṭa, sphuṭa,** *adj.* Open, clear, manifest. 2. revealed, explained, as a horoscope. *s. see* ಪುಟ. –ಮಳ್ಪುನಿ to elucidate a horoscope.

ಸ್ಮರಣೆ **smaraṇe,** *s.* Recollecting, reminiscence, recollection. 2. remembrance. 3. memory. 4. mental recitation of the name *or* names of a deity. –ಉಪ್ಪುನಿ to remember; to be conscious of. –ಮಳ್ಪುನಿ, ಸ್ಮರಿಪುನಿ to recollect, call to mind; to recite the names of a deity.

ಸ್ಮಶಾನ **smašāna,** *see* ಶ್ಮಶಾನ.

ಸ್ಮಾರ್ತೆ **smārte,** *s.* A follower of the doctrine of Šaṅkarāčārya.

ಸ್ಮೃತಿ **smṛuti,** *s.* Recollection, reminiscence, memory. 2. the body of the Hindu law, as committed to writing from recollection by the pupils of the law-givers. 3. any book, canon *or* portion of this law.

ಸ್ಯದ syada, *s.* Swiftness, speed.

ಸ್ರವ, ಸ್ರಾವ srava, srāva, *s.* Oozing, trickling. 2. exudation. 3. miscarriage, premature birth.

ಸ್ವ sva, *s.* Self, own soul *or* individuality. 2. property, wealth. *adj.* Own, proper, peculiar. –ಕಾರ್ಯ one's private business *or* interest. –ಬುದ್ಧಿ self-will. ದೇವ– God's property, church-property.

ಸ್ವಂತ svanta, *adj.* Own, private, peculiar. –ಆಸ್ತಿ one's own property.

ಸ್ವಚ್ಚ, ಸ್ವಚ್ಛ svaćca, svaććha, *adj.* Exceedingly pure *or* clean, spotless, stainless.

ಸ್ವತಂತ್ರ svatantra, *s.* Independence, freedom of will. *adj.* Independent, free, uncontrolled, absolute. –ನರಮಾನಿ an independent man.

ಸ್ವತಃ, ಸ್ವತಾ svataḥ, svatā, *adv.* Of one's own accord. 2. personally, in person.

ಸ್ವಪ್ನ svapna, *s.* A dream, dreaming. ಸ್ವಪ್ನಾವಸ್ಥೆ the state of dreaming. ಸ್ವಪ್ನೇಂದ್ರಿಯ nightly emissions.

ಸ್ವಭಾವ svabhāva, *s.* Own *or* native state *or* quality; nature, natural temper, disposition *or* constitution. –ಗುಣ natural temper.

ಸ್ವಯ svaya, *s.* Recollection, recollecting; memory, remembrance. –ದಾಂತಿನಾಯ an absent-minded man.

ಸ್ವಯಂ svayam, *adv.* Of one's own self *or* accord, spontaneously. –ಕೃತ self-formed. –ಪಾಕ cooking with one's own hands; cooking in general. –ಪಾಕಿ a cook. –ಭೂ God, the self-existent. –ವರ choosing one's own husband.

ಸ್ವರ svara, *s.* Voice, sound. 2. a note in music. 3. an accent. 4. a vowel. 5. air breathed through a nostril. –ಪಂದುಜಿ (his) voice is faint.

ಸ್ವರೂಪ svarūpa, *s.* One's own proper figure, general appearance, countenance, features. 2. nature, natural constitution, quality *or* condition. –ದಾಂತಿ senseless, shameless. ನಿನ ಸ್ವರೂಪ ಯಾನ್ ಪಿಂಚೆ I know your whole character.

ಸ್ವರ್ಗ svarga, *s.* The sky *or* heaven in general. 2. Indra's paradise. 3. bliss, beatitude. –ಲೋಕ the kingdom of heaven. ಸ್ವರ್ಗಾರೋಹಣ ascension, going to heaven.

ಸ್ವಲ್ಪ svalpa, *adj.* Little, few, small, trifling.

ಸ್ವಲ್ಮ svalma, *see* ಸೊಲ್ಮ.

ಸ್ವಸ್ತ, ಸ್ವಸ್ಥ svasta, svastha, *s.* Bodily health *or* ease. 2. mental composure. *adj.* Easy, quiet, composed, comfortable. ಅ– disease, sickness. –ಚಿತ್ತ

mind at ease. —ಆಪಿಸು to become well, recover, get better. —ಉಪ್ಪಸು to be at ease *or* healthy. —ಮಾಳ್ಪಸು to cure, heal. ಸ್ವಸ್ಥೊಡುಪ್ಪಸು to be well, quiet.

ಸ್ವಸ್ತಿ svasti, *s. A particle of benediction*, May it be well with you. 2. so be it, amen. —ಪಣ್ಪಸು to wish well, bless. —ಪಾಡುಸು to yield, acquiesce in.

ಸ್ವಾಡಿ svāḍi, *s.* A kind of fish. 2. a game.

ಸ್ವಾತಿ svāti, *s. Arcturus*, the fifteenth lunar asterism.

ಸ್ವಾದ್, ಸ್ವಾದು svādu, svādu, *s.* Taste, flavour. 2. tasting. *adj.* Sweet, agreeable, delightful. —ಉಪ್ಪಸು to be tasteful, sweet. —ಕೊರ್ಪಿನ to give taste. —ತೂಪಿನ to taste.

ಸ್ವಾಧಿನ, ಸ್ವಾಧೀನ svādhina, svādhīna, *adj.* Absolute, free, independent. 2. in the custody *or* keeping of. 3. under the control *or* command of. ಪರ— dependent on *or* subject to another; alienation, as of property. —ಆಪಿಸು to come into one's possession. —ಮಳ್ಪುನಿ to give possession, as of property.

ಸ್ವಾನುಭವ, ಸ್ವಾನುಭಾವ svānubhava, svānubhāva, *s.* One's own experience *or* observation.

ಸ್ವಾಮಿ svāmi, *s.* Owner, lord, master, chief, king. 2. a husband. 3. God. —ಕಾರ್ಯ one's master's business *or* interests. —ದ್ರೋಹ treachery, treason. —ದ್ರೋಹಿ a traitor.

ಸ್ವಾರಸ್ಯ, ಸ್ವಾರೆಸ svārasya, svāresa, *s.* Sweetness, savouriness. 2. pathos, spirit. 3. goodness, excellence. *adj.* Pleasing, delicious, excellent, good. —ಉಪ್ಪಸು to be pleasing, excellent.

ಸ್ವಾರ್ಜಿತ svārjita, *adj.* Self-acquired.

ಸ್ವಾರ್ತ svārta, *s.* Success. 2. possession. 3. *see* ಸ್ವಾರ್ಥ.

ಸ್ವಾರ್ತೆ svārtè, *see* ಸುವಾರ್ತೆ.

ಸ್ವಾರ್ತೂಕ svārtūka, *see* ಸಾರ್ಥಕ.

ಸ್ವಾರ್ಥ svārtha, *s.* Self-interest, selfishness. 2. inherent *or* real-meaning. —ದ ಪಾತೆರ a selfish word. —ಮಳ್ಪುನಿ to be selfish.

ಸ್ವಾಸ svāsa, *see* ಶ್ವಾಸ.

ಸ್ವಾಸ್ತಿ, ಸ್ವಾಸ್ಥ್ಯ svāsti, svāsthya, *s.* An estate, property, especially endowed for religious *or* charitable objects; a foundation. —ಬುಡ್ಪಿನ to endow a religious *or* charitable institution with property.

ಸ್ವಾಸ್ತಿಕ svāstika, *adj.* Everlasting. *s. see* ತಸ್ತಿಕ.

ಸ್ವೀಕಾರ svīkāra, *s.* Claiming, acknowledging; affirming *or* admitting to be one's own. 2. adoption. ಪುತ್ರ— adoption of a son. —ಮಳ್ಪುನ to adopt; to ackowledge, admit.

ಸ್ವೇದ svēda, *s.* Sweat 2. steam, —ಜ, *see under* ಯೋನಿ.

ಹ H

ಹ **ha,** The forty-sixth letter of the alphabet.

ಹಂಕಾರ **haṅkāra,** *see* ಅಹಂಕಾರ.

ಹಂಗ್ **haṅgų,** *s.* Obligation; the state of being in the power of another; duty. –ದಾಯಿ one who is under obligation *or* power of another; a dependant, adherent. –ಡ ಉಪ್ಪುನಿ to be under obligation to, *or* in the power of, another.

ಹಂಗ್ಸಾವುನಿ **haṅgųsāvuni** (ಹಂಗ್ ಸಾ), *v. a.* To upbraid, rebuke, charge contemptuously with any thing.

ಹಂಗಾಮಿ, ಹಂಗಾಮು **haṅgāmi, haṅgāmu,** *s.* Season, time, period. *adj.* Temporary, for the time being. –ಉದ್ಯೋಗ, –ಕೆಲಸ a temporary employment.

ಹಂಗಿಪುನಿ **haṅgipuni,** *see* ಹಂಗ್ಸಾವುನಿ.

ಹಂಚಿ **hańci,** *see* ತಂಚಿ.

ಹಂಚು **hańcu,** *s.* A tile.

ಹಂಚುನಿ **hańcuni** (ಹಂಚ್), *v. a.* To distribute, divide.

ಹಂಡಿ **haṇḍi,** *see* ಚಂಡಿ.

ಹಂಡೆ **haṇḍè,** *s.* A large copper vessel, caldron. 2. *see* ಅಂಡೆ.

ಹಂಣುಕಾಯಿ **haṇṇukāyi,** *see* ಅಂಣುಕಾಯಿ.

ಹಂತಾಯಿ **hantāyi,** *s.* Mustard.

ಹಂತಿ **hanti,** *see* ತಂತಿ. 2. *see* ಪಂತಿ.

ಹಂಬಲ್ **hambalų,** *s.* Solicitous thought; the mind absorbed in thought. –ಡ ಉಪ್ಪುನಿ to think anxiously respecting some thing, to brood over a subject.

ಹಂಬಲ್ **hambalų,** *see* ಅಂಬಲ್.

ಹಂಬೊತ್ತು **hambottu,** *see* ಅಂಬೊತ್ತು.

ಹಂಮತ್ತು **hammattu,** *see* ಹಂಮು.

ಹಂಮಲೆ **hammalè,** *see* ತಂಮಲೆ.

ಹಂಮಿಣಿ **hammiṇi,** *see* ಹಿಂಮಿಣಿ.

ಹಂಮು, ಹಂಮೊತ್ತು **hammu, hammottu,** *s.* Egotism, vanity, pride. –ಉಂತಾವುನಿ to humiliate. –ಉಂತುನಿ to be humiliated. –ತೋಜಾವುನಿ to be insolent.

ಹಂಸ, ಹಂಸೆ **haṁsa, haṁsè,** *s.* A swan, goose; a fabulous bird so called; *also* ಹಂಸಪಕ್ಷಿ.

ಹಂಸಪಾದ **haṁsapāda,** *s.* An asterisk. 2. a prop. 3. a caret.

ಹಂಸಾಣಿ **hamsāṇi,** *see* ಅಮುಸಾಣಿ.

ಹಕೀಕ್ **hakīkų,** *s.* A kind of bead.

ಹಕೀಕತ್, ಹಕೀಕತು **hakīkatų, hakīkatu,** *s.* A statement *or* representation of occurrences, affairs, *etc.* 2. affairs, events, facts. –ಪಣ್ಪುನಿ to state one's affairs, *etc.*

ಹಕೀಮೆ **hakīme,** *s.* A Mahommedan physician.

ಹಕ್ಕ್ **hakkų,** *s.* Right, title, claim. 2. share, portion. –ದಾಯಿ, –ದಾರೆ a claimant, the holder of a share; one who has a right. ನಾ— without right *or* reason.

ಹಕ್ಕಲ್ **hakkalu**, *s.* Gleanings of corn. 2. *see* ಅಕ್ಕಲ್.

ಹಕ್ಕಿ **hakki**, *see* ಪಕ್ಕಿ.

ಹಕ್ಕಿಲ್ **hakkilu**, *see* ಅರ್ಕಿಲ್.

ಹಕ್ಕು **hakku**, *see* ಹಕ್ಕ್.

ಹಗಲ್ **hagalu**, *s.* The daytime; *cf.* ಪಗೆಲ್. —ಬತ್ತಿ a large kind of blue light.

ಹಗುರ **hagura**, *adj.* Light, not heavy. 2. slow, dilatory. *adv.* Gently, slowly, leisurely. —ಪುದೆ a light load. —ಮನಸ್ fickleness, indifference. —ಮಳ್ಪುನಿ to make light, treat lightly; to act *or* work slowly.

ಹಗೆ **hagè**, *see* ಪಗೆ.

ಹಚ **haca**, *see* ಹತೊ.

ಹಚ್ಚ **hacca**, *see* ಅಚ್ಚ.

ಹಚ್ಚಡೆ **haccadè**, *see* ಪಚ್ಚಡೆ.

ಹಚ್ಚುನಿ **haccuni** (ಹಚ್ಚ್), *v. a.* To affix, attach. 2. to smear, daub, anoint, plaster. 3. to paste *or* glue on.

ಹಜಾಮೆ **hajāme**, *s.* A barber.

ಹಜೂರ್, **hajūru**, *s.* The head collector's office; *also* ಹಜೂರ್ ಕಚ್ಚೇರಿ.

ಹಟ, ಹಠ **haṭa, haṭha**, *s.* Obstinacy. 2. violence, severity. 3. a grudge, spite against. —ಗಾರೆ, —ದಾಯೆ, —ಮಾರಿ, —ವಾದಿ an obstinate man. —ಮಳ್ಪುನಿ to be obstinate.

ಹಡಕುನಿ **haḍakuni**, *see* ಅಡಕುನಿ.

ಹಡಗ **haḍaga**, *s.* A ship, sailing vessel.

ಹಡಪ **haḍapa**, *s.* A barber's dressing case; *cf.* ಬಾಲಿಮುಟ್ಟು.

ಹಡಪುನಿ **haḍapuni**, *see* ಅಡಪುನಿ.

ಹಡಬೆ **haḍabè**, *s.* A bastard; *also* ಅಡಬೆ.

ಹಡೆಪು **haḍepu**, *see* ಅಡೆಪು.

ಹಣ **haṇa**, *see* ಪಣವು.

ಹಣಾಹಣಿ **haṇāhaṇi**, *see* ಹಾಣಾಹಾಣಿ.

ಹಣಿತ **haṇita**, *see* ಪಣಿತ.

ಹಣೆ **haṇè**, *s.* The forehead, scull. —ಬರವು lot, fate, destiny, fortune.

ಹತ **hata**, *adj.* Struck, hit. 2. killed. —ಮಳ್ಪುನಿ to slay, kill.

ಹತೊ **hato**, *intj.* An exclamation used to set on, as a dog to pursue an animal, *etc.*

ಹತ್ತರ **hattara**, *adv.* Near, close by. *s.* Nearness, proximity.

ಹತ್ತಿ **hatti**, *see* ಪತ್ತಿ.

ಹತ್ತುನಿ **hattuni**, *see* ಪತ್ತುನಿ.

ಹತ್ಯ **hatya**, *s.* Killing, murder.

ಹತ್ರ **hatra**, *see* ಹತ್ತರ.

ಹದ್ **hadu**, *see* ಪತ್ತ್. 2. *see* ಪದ್.

ಹದ **hada**, *s.* The proper condition of things. 2. sharpness, as of a knife, *etc.* 3. forming, as metals to proper degree of hardness. 4. boiling *or* cooking to the proper point. —ಆದುಪ್ಪುನಿ to be fit for use; to be temperate. —ಆಪಿನಿ to become fit for use; to become sharp. —ಗೆಪ್ಪುನಿ to take a due proportion of ingredients; to harass, tire, exhaust. —ತೂಪಿನಿ to taste *or* try any thing to see whether it is duly done. —ಮಳ್ಪುನಿ to sharpen; to temper.

ಹದ್ದ್ **haddu,** *s.* A limit, border, boundary. ಸರ— neighbourhood, jurisdiction, extent of power. —ಗ ಪಣ್ಪುನಿ to guess. —ಮೀರುನಿ to violate a prescribed bound.

ಹನಿ **hani,** *see* ಪನಿ.

ಹನುಮಂತೆ, ಹನುಮಾನ್, ಹನುಮೆ **hanumante, hanumānu, hanume,** *s.* The deified monkey chief, friend, ally and spy of Rāma.

ಹಪ್ಪಳ **happaḷa,** *see* ಅಪ್ಪಳ.

ಹಬಡ್ **habaḍu,** *see* ಅಬಡ್.

ಹಬಲಿ **habali,** *see* ತಬ್ಬುಲಿ.

ಹಬೆ **habè,** *see* ಉಬೆ.

ಹಬ್ಬ **habba,** *see* ಪರ್ಬ.

ಹಮರುನಿ **hamaruni,** *see* ಅಮರುನಿ.

ಹಮೀರ **hamīre,** *s.* A nobleman, grandee.

ಹಮುಸಾಣಿ **hamusāṇi,** *see* ಅಮುಸಣಿ.

ಹರ **hara,** *s.* Breadth. *adj.* Broad.

ಹರ **hara,** *s.* Śiva. 2. expelling, as poison; counteracting, as evil spirits, *etc.*

ಹರಕ್ **haraku,** *see* ಹರ್ಕ.

ಹರಕತ್ **harakatu,** *see* ಹರ್ಕತ್.

ಹರಕೆ **harakè,** *see* ಪರಕೆ.

ಹರಗೋಲ್ **haragōlu,** *s.* A round wicker-boat covered with leather.

ಹರಟುನಿ **haraṭuni** (ಹರಟಿ), *v. a.* To prate, blabber, talk nonsense.

ಹರಟೆ **haraṭè,** *s.* Prate, jabber. 2. teasing, vexing, troubling. —ದಾಯೆ a prater, idle talker. —ಪಾತೆರುನಿ to prate, babble. —ಮಳ್ಪುನಿ to tease.

ಹರಡುನಿ **haraḍuni,** *see* ಪರಡುನಿ.

ಹರಡೆ **haraḍè,** *s.* Gallnut, inknut, *Terminalia chebula.*

ಹರಣ, ಹರಣೆ **haraṇa, haraṇè,** *s.* Removing, carrying, bearing off, as of pain, disease, sin, trouble, *etc.* 2. passing time; sustenance, maintenance. ದಿನ ಹರಣ ಮಳ್ಪುನಿ to pass away time; to live, sustain; to put off with vain excuses.

ಹರತ **harata,** *see* ಹಠ.

ಹರದಾರಿ **haradāri,** *s.* A distance of about three English miles.

ಹರದೆ **harade,** *see* ಅರದೆ.

ಹರವಂಚಿ **haravañci,** *s.* Embezzlement, defalcation, as of public money.

ಹರಸುನಿ **harasuni** (ಹರಸಿ); *v. a.* To bless, wish well.

ಹರಾಮ್, ಹರಾಮಿ **harāmu, harāmi,** *adj.* Wild, untamed, vicious. 2. wicked, iniquitous, vile, base. —ಕುದುರೆ a vicious horse. ನಂಮಕ್— treachery to a master.

ಹರಿ **hari,** *s.* Vishṇu.

ಹರಿಗೀಸ್ **harigīsu,** *see* ಅರಗೀಸ್.

ಹರಿಯಾಣ, ಹರಿವಾಣ hariyāṇa, harivāṇa, *s.* A flat, metal dish.

ಹರಿಯುನಿ hariyuni, *see* ಪರಿಯುನಿ. 2. *see* ಪರವುನಿ.

ಹರಿವಾತ harivāta, *s.* A kind of gout.

ಹರುಷ harusha, *see* ಹರ್ಷ.

ಹರ್ಕ್ harkụ, *adj.* Torn, rent, tattered.

ಹರ್ಕತ್ harkatụ, *s.* Opposition, hinderance. –ಮಳ್ಪುನಿ to oppose, hinder, obstruct.

ಹರ್ಕತ್ತಿ harkatti, *see* ತರ್ಕತ್ತಿ.

ಹರ್ಪುನಿ harpuni, *see* ತರ್ಪುನಿ. 2. *see* ಹರ್ಪುನಿ.

ಹರ್ಪುಡುನಿ harpuḍuni, *see* ತರ್ಪಾವುನಿ.

ಹರ್ಷ harsha, *s.* Happiness, delight, joy. –ಮಳ್ಪುನಿ, ಹರ್ಷಿಪುನಿ, ಹರ್ಷಿಸುನಿ to rejoice, be glad, delighted.

ಹಲವ halava, *see* ಹಲವು.

ಹಲವಂಗ halavaṅga, *adj.* Diverse, various. 2. much, great, many. –ತರದ of diverse sorts. –ವಿಧಾನೊಡು in various ways.

ಹಲವು halavu, *pron.* Many, much. 2. some. –ಜಾತಿ several castes *or* classes.

ಹಲಸ್ halasụ, *see* ಅಲಸ್.

ಹಲಾಕ್ halākụ, *s.* Loss, waste, desolation. 2. disorder, –ಆಪಿನಿ to be wasted, destroyed; to become weak. –ಮಳ್ಪುನಿ to destroy; to waste, spend.

ಹಲಿಕಿ haliki *see* ಹಲ್ಕ್.

ಹಲೆಪುನಿ halepuni, *see* ತಲೆಪುನಿ.

ಹಲ್ಕ್, ಹಲ್ಕ, ಹಲ್ಕಿ halkụ, halka, halki, *adj.* Inferior, low, mean, base. 2. cheap. 3. easy. –ಕುಂಟು a cheap *or* inferior sort of cloth. –ಕೆಲಸ a mean act. –ಜನ low people. –ನರಮಾನಿ a mean person. –ವಾತೆರ a low word. –ಮಳ್ಪುನಿ to depreciate; to slander, defame.

ಹಲ್ಕುನಿ halkuni, *see* ಅಲ್ಕುನಿ.

ಹಲ್ಲ್‌ಕಡ್ಡಿ hallụkaḍḍi, *s.* A tooth-pick.

ಹಲ್ಲಿ halli, *see* ಪಲ್ಲಿ.

ಹವಲ್‌ದಾರೆ, ಹವಲದಾರೆ havalụdāre, havaladāre, *see* ಹವಾಲ್ದಾರೆ.

ಹವನ havana, *s.* Sacrifice, offering to the gods.

ಹವಲೆ havalè, *see* ಅವಲೆ.

ಹವಳ havaḷa, *s.* Coral.

ಹವಾಲ್, ಹವಾಲಿ, ಹವಾಲ್ತೆ havālụ, havāli, havāltè, *s.* Charge, trust, care; commission, security. –ಕೊರ್ಪಿನಿ to give security. –ಮಳ್ಪುನಿ to commission.

ಹವಾಲ್ದಾರೆ havāldāre, *s.* A non-commissioned military native officer.

ಹವೆ havè, *s.* Air, wind; climate.

ಹವೇಲಿ havēli, *s.* A large house, mansion, villa. 2. the upper story of a house.

ಹಸ್ತ hasta, *s.* The hand. 2. the thirteenth lunar asterism; *also* ಹಸ್ತನಕ್ಷತ್ರ. –ಲಾಗ legerdemain, sleight of hand.

ಹಳ haḷa, *see* ಪಳ.

ಹಳಬೆ haḷabe, *s.* An old man; an old inhabitant; *cf.* ಪರಬೆ.

ಹಳ್ಮೆ haḷmè, *s.* A race, contest in running.

ಹಳ್ಳಿ haḷḷi, *s.* A hamlet, small village.

ಹಾ hā, *intj.* Ah! oh!

ಹಾಂಕಾರ hāṅkāra, *see* ಅಹಂಕಾರ.

ಹಾಕ್‌ಜೋಕ್ hākųjōkų, *see* ತಾಕು ತೋಕು.

ಹಾಕುನಿ hākuni (ಹಾಕ್), *v. a.* To beat, strike, smite, flog, lash, cuff.

ಹಾಗ್ hāgų, *s.* Accomplishment, completion.

ಹಾಗ hāga, *s.* A quarter of a gold fanam.

ಹಾಗುನಿ hāguni, *see* ತಾಗುನಿ.

ಹಾಜರ್, ಹಾಜಿರಿ hājarų, hājiri, *s.* Presence, attendance. 2. mustering; muster. *adj.* Present, at hand. —ಜಾಮೀನ್ the bail. —ಪಟ್ಟಿ a muster roll. —ಆಪಿನಿ to be present; to be in attendance. —ಮಳ್ಪುನಿ to produce, as an offender, *etc.*

ಹಾಡ್ hāḍų, *s.* Practice, exercise, familiarity.

ಹಾಡಿ hāḍi, *s.* An underwood near a farmhouse, scrub.

ಹಾಣಾಹಾಣಿ hāṇāhāṇi, *adj.* Severe, as a contest.

ಹಾಣಿ hāṇi, *see* ಹಾನಿ.

ಹಾದರ, ಹಾದ್ರ hādara, hādra, *s.* Adultery, fornication. —ಗಿತ್ತಿ an adulteress, whore. —ತನ whoredom, adultery. —ದಾಯೆ an adulterer, fornicator. —ಮಳ್ಪುನಿ to commit adultery.

ಹಾದಿ hādi, *see* ಸಾದಿ.

ಹಾನಿ hāni, *s.* Loss, injury, harm, detriment. *adj.* Damaged, injured. —ಮಳ್ಪುನಿ to ruin.

ಹಾನೆ hānè, *s.* A grain measure of eighty rupees weight.

ಹಾಯಿಮಾಲೆ hāyimālè, *see* ವೈಮಾಲೆ.

ಹಾಯುನಿ hāyuni (ಹಾಯ್), *v. a.* To cross, ford; *cf.* ಆಯುನಿ.

ಹಾರ hāra, *s.* A necklace, garland, chaplet. 2. *see* ಆಹಾರ.

ಹಾರಗೆ, ಹಾರಾಯಿ hāragè, hārāyi, *see* ತಾರಾಯಿ.

ಹಾರುನಿ hāruni, *see* ಪಾರುನಿ.

ಹಾರೆ hārè, *see* ತಾರೆ.

ಹಾರೈಸುನಿ hāreisuni (ಹಾರೈಸ್), *v. a.* To desire, wish, be anxious about. ಸಮಯ— to wish for an opportunity.

ಹಾಲ್ hālų, *s.* State, condition, affair.

ಹಾಲ್‌ಪಕ್ಕಿ hālųpakki, *s.* A bird of ill omen. 2. a mendicant who professes to interpret such omens. —ನುಡಿಪುನಿ this bird to utter its ominous notes.

ಹಾಲ್‌ಹವಾಲ್ hālųhavālų, *s.* Particulars of one's circumstances. —ಪಣ್ಪುನಿ to represent one's circumstances.

ಹಾಲಿ hāli, *adv.* Now, at the present time.

ಹಾಲಿತ hālita, *see* ಹಾಳಿತ.

ಹಾವಳಿ hāvaḷi, *s.* Trouble, difficulty. 2. evil.

ಹಾವು **hāvu**, *s.* A snake, serpent. —ಮೀನ್ the cockle fish.

ಹಾಶಿಗೆ **hāśigè**, *see* ಹಾಸಿಗೆ.

ಹಾಸ್ **hāsu̧**, *see* ಆಸ್.

ಹಾಸ್‌ಕಲ್ಲ್, ಹಾಸಿಕಲ್ಲ್ **hāsu̧kallu̧, hāsikallu̧**, *s.* A paving stone.

ಹಾಸ್‌ಪಾಸ್, ಹಾಸ್‌ಪೀಸ್ **hāsu̧pāsu̧, hāsu̧pīsu̧**, *see* ಆಸ್‌ಪಾಸ್.

ಹಾಸರಕತ್ತೆ **hāsarakattè**, *s.* A mule.

ಹಾಸಿಗೆ **hāsigè**, *s.* A bed, mattress. —ಹಾಸುನಿ to spread out a bed.

ಹಾಸಿಯುನಿ **hāsiyuni** (ಹಾಸಿ), *v. a.* To ridicule.

ಹಾಸುನಿ **hāsuni** (ಹಾಸ್), *v. a.* To spread out. 2. to pave.

ಹಾಸ್ಯ **hāsya**, *s.* Laughing at, ridicule, derision. 2. laughter. ಅಪ— derision, irony; mimicry. —ಗಾರೆ a jester, mocker. —ಮಳ್ಪುನಿ to jest, jeer, sport, mock.

ಹಾಹಾ **hāhā**, *intj.* of pain, grief, *or* surprise. 2. ah! woe!

ಹಾಳ್ **hāḷu̧**, *s.* Ruin, destruction, desolation, annihilation. *adj.* Desolate, waste, ruined, destroyed. —ಆಪಿನಿ, —ಆದ್‌ಪೋಪಿನಿ to go to ruin, to be waste. —ಮಳ್ಪುನಿ to ruin, spoil, destroy; to spend, waste.

ಹಾಳಿತ **hāḷita**, *s.* An exact measurement, dimension, quantity. *adj.* Exactly fitting, proper. 2. tempered, of due temperature. 3. of a proper heat. ಕಂಕ್—, ಗುಂಡು— a rough estimate, *etc.* —ಆಪಿನಿ to fit. —ಗೆಪ್ಪುನಿ to take an exact measurement, *etc.*; to take a due proportion of ingredients. —ತೂಪಿನಿ to see whether a given measurement, *etc.*, is correct.

ಹಾಳ್ಮೆ **hāḷmè**, *see* ತಾಳ್ಮೆ.

ಹಿಂಗ್ **hiṅgu̧**, *s.* Asafoetida. 2. abatement, allaying.

ಹಿಂಗರ **hiṅgara**, *see* ಪಿಂಗರ.

ಹಿಂಗರ **hiṅgara**, *adj.* Latter; following, subsequent. ಬರ್ಸ the latter rain. —ಬುಳೆ the second crop.

ಹಿಂಗರನೆ **hiṅgaranè**, *adv.* Behind, backward. —ಮುಂಗರನೆ ಲಾಗ making sommersets backward and forward.

ಹಿಂಗುನಿ **hiṅguni** (ಹಿಂಗ್), *v. n.* To be unsteady. 2. to be allayed, as thirst. 3. to be subdued, to abate, as sorrow; ಆಯೆ ಹಿಂಗಯೆ he will not shrink; he is firm, steady.

ಹಿಂಡಿ **hiṇḍi**, *s.* The remains of any thing from which the juice has been expressed; *cf.* ಪುಂಡಿ.

ಹಿಂದು **hindu**, *s.* A Hindu. 2. an Indian. *adj.* Indian, of India. —ಜನ the Hindu people. —ಜಾತಿ the Hindu castes. —ಸ್ಥಾನ India.

ಹಿಂಮತ್ **himmatu̧**, *s.* Boldness, courage, intrepidity, spirit, resolution.

ಹಿಂಮಿನಿ, ಹಿಂಮುನಿ **himmini, himmuni**, *see* ಹಿಮಿನಿ.

ಹಿಂಮೆಟ್ಟುನಿ himeṭṭuni (ಹಿಂಮೆಟ್ಟ್), *v. n.* To abate, be subdued, mitigated. 2. to be humbled. 3. to shrink, turn back.

ಹಿಂಗುರ್ನಿ hiṅguni, *see* ತಿಂಗುರ್ನಿ.

ಹಿಂಸೆ him̃sè, *s.* Persecuting, hurting, injuring. 2. slaying, killing. –ಮಳ್ಪುನಿ, ಹಿಂಸಿಸುನಿ to persecute, injure; to kill.

ಹಿಕ್ಮತ್ hikụmatụ, *s.* Skill, ingenuity, cunning. 2. knack, expedient, contrivance, device, project.

ಹಿಕ್ಕಡಿ, ಹಿಕ್ಡಿ hikkaḍi, hikḍi, *s.* Trick, stratagem, wile, juggle.

ಹಿಕ್ಕುನಿ hikkuni, *see* ತಿಕ್ಕುನಿ.

ಹಿಕ್ಮತ್, ಹಿಕ್ಮತಿ hikmatụ, hikmati, *see* ಹಿಕ್ಮತ್.

ಹಿಗ higa, *see* ತಿಗ.

ಹಿಗಲೆ higalè, *see* ತಿಗಲೆ.

ಹಿಜ hij̃a, *see* ಇಜ.

ಹಿಜರಿ, ಹಿಜ್ರಿ hij̃ari, hij̃ri, *s.* The Mohammedan era, which commences A. D. 622.

ಹಿಜಿಡೆ hij̃iḍe, *s.* A eunuch.

ಹಿಟ್ಟ್ hiṭṭụ, *s.* Porridge.

ಹಿಡಿ hiḍi, *s.* A hold, gripe, grasp. 2. a handful. 3. a handle, hilt. –ತ holding, grasping; obstinacy, stubbornness. ಕೈ– a warrant to seize an offender.

ಹಿತ hita, *s.* Advantage, profit, good, gain. *adj.* Beneficial, refreshing, wholesome, good, pleasant. –ವಂತೆ a well-wisher, benefactor. –ಆಪಿನಿ to be agreeable, refreshing *or* wholesome, as food; to be edifying.

ಹಿತಂತ್ರ hitantra, *s.* Enmity.

ಹಿತಬಾರ್ hitabārụ, *see* ಇತಬಾರ್.

ಹಿತ್ತಳೆ hittaḷè, *see* ಪಿತ್ತಳೆ.

ಹಿತ್ತುನಿ hittuni, *see* ಬಿತ್ತುನಿ.

ಹಿತ್ಲ್ hitlụ, *s.* A garden; *bet.* ಬಿತ್ತಲ್.

ಹಿದ್ಯ hidya, *see* ತಿದ್ಯ.

ಹಿನ್ಪಿನಿ hinpini, *see* ತಿನ್ಪಿನಿ.

ಹಿಪ್ಪಲಿ hippali, *see* ಇಪ್ಪಿಲಿ.

ಹಿಮ hima, *s.* Snow, hoar-frost, dew. 2. cold. *adj.* Frigid, cold, frosty. –ಕಾಲ the cold season, winter.

ಹಿಮಾಚಲ, ಹಿಮಾಲಯ himāćala, himālaya, *s.* The range of Himālaya mountains.

ಹಿಮಿನಿ himini, *s.* A purse, bag, pocket.

ಹಿರಣ್ಯ hiraṇya, *s.* Gold. 2. wealth, property.

ಹಿರಿ hiri, *adj.* Great, elder, senior, superior. –ಕಿರಿ, –ಪಿರಿ old and young, superior and inferior. –ಕೂಟ a presbytery. –ಯತನ eldership, seniority. –ಮಣಿ the monitor in a school; –ಯಾದಿಗೆ superiority, greatness; power, authority. –ಯಾಯೆ, –ಯೆ an ancestor, senior, elder, presbyter.

ಹಿರಿದ್ hiridụ, *see* ಹಿದ್ರ್.

ಹಿರಿಯುನಿ hiriyuni, *see* ಇರಿಯುನಿ.

ಹಿರಿಯೆ hiriye, *see under* ಹಿರಿ.

ಹಿರೆ hirè, *see* ಹಿರಿ.

ಹಿರ್ತ್ hirtu, *see* ಶಿರ್ತ್.

ಹಿರ್ದ್ hirdu, *adj.* Pre-eminent, best, superior, excellent. —ಕುಂಟು a superior cloth.

ಹಿರ್ದುನಿ hirduni, *see* ಶಿರ್ದುನಿ.

ಹಿಲಾಲ್ hilālu, *see* ಇಲಾಲ್.

ಹಿಲೆ hilè, *s.* An offering of betel-leaves to a demon. 2. *see* ಇಲೆ. 3. *see* ಶಿಲೆ.

ಹಿಲ್ಲೆ hillè, *s.* A false excuse, difficulties made to evade the payment of a debt *or* the performance of a task. —ಪಿಲ್ಲೆ ಪಣ್ಪುನಿ to plead a false excuse.

ಹಿಶೆ, ಹಿಸೆ hišè, hisè, *s.* Part, portion, share. —ಕೊರ್ಪಿನಿ to give a share. —ದೀಪಿನಿ, —ಮಳ್ಪುನಿ to divide, share, apportion.

ಹಿಷಾರೆ hishārè, *s.* A sign; a hint.

ಹಿಸಾಬ್ hisābu, *s.* An account.

ಹೀಂಕರಿಪುನಿ hīnkaripuni (ಹೀಂಕರಿ), *v. a.* To find fault with, blame, despise, scorn.

ಹೀಂತ್ರುನಿ, ಹೀಂಪುನಿ hīntruni, hīmpuni (ಹೀಂತ್ರಿ, ಹಿಂ), *v. a.* To blow the nose.

ಹೀನ hīna, *adj.* Deficient, defective, wanting. 2. base, vile, mean, abject. 3. abandoned, left. —ತೆ, —ತ್ವ meanness. —ಜಾತಿ a low caste. ಕುಲ— of low birth. ಬಲ— weak. ಬುದ್ಧಿ—, ಮತಿ— senseless, foolish, stupid. ಭಾಗ್ಯ— poor, destitute; unfortunate, unlucky. ಮಾನ— disgraced. ರೂಪ— deformed. ಲಜ್ಜಾ— shameless.

ಹೀನೆ hīne, *s.* A base fellow. 2. a weak man. ಬುದ್ಧಿ— a stupid man, fool.

ಹೀನೈಸುನಿ hīneisuni (ಹೀನೈಸಿ), *v. a.* To despise, disgrace, disregard.

ಹೀರುನಿ hīruni, *see* ತೀರುನಿ.

ಹೀರೆ hīrè, *see* ಪೀರೆ.

ಹುಂ hum, *intj.* of response, approbation *or* assent. —ಕುಟ್ಟುನಿ to answer, as a call; to approve; to assent; to pay attention to a story, *etc.*

ಹುಂಡಿ hundi, *s.* A bill of exchange; a money order.

ಹುಂಣಮೆ hunnamè, *see* ಪುಂಣಮೆ.

ಹುಂನರ್ hunnaru, *s.* An art, a resource *or* power of skill *or* cunning; ability for contriving, devising *or* effecting. —ಗಾರೆ, —ದಾಯಿ a schemer, a shrewd *or* ingenious man; an artist; an alchymist; an athlete *or* gymnast. —ತೋಜಾವುನಿ to devise, contrive; to show one's skill *or* ability.

ಹುಕುಮ್ hukumu, *s.* An order, command. 2. leave, permission. —ಕೊರ್ಪಿನಿ to command, order; to permit.

ಹುಕ್ಕಾ hukkā, *s.* A hooka, smoking apparatus.

ಹುಜ್ಜತ್ hujjatu, *s.* Constraint, force, compulsion. —ಮಳ್ಪುನಿ to force, compel.

ಹುಟ್ಟು huttu, *s.* Birth, origin, production. 2. nature, natural state. 3. profit, gain. *adj.* Natural, inherent. —ಚೇರ್ one's antecedents *or* circumstances.

ಹುಟ್ಟೊಳಿ huṭṭoḷi, *s.* The produce of a garden *or* field. 2. mesne profit *or* rent.

ಹುಡರ್ huḍarụ, *see* ತುಡರ್.

ಹುಡಿಗೆ, ಹುಡುಗೆ huḍige, huḍuge, *s.* A youngster.

ಹುಡುಗಾಟಿಗೆ huḍugāṭigè, *s.* Childishness, puerility.

ಹುಣ್ಣ huṇṇa, *see* ಸುಂಣ.

ಹುತೊ huto, *see* ಹತೊ.

ಹುದೆ hudè, *see* ತುದೆ.

ಹುಬ್ಬು hubbu, *s.* The eyebrow.

ಹುಬ್ಬೆ hubbè, *s.* The eleventh lunar asterism. 2. *see* ಉಟೆ.

ಹುಯಿಂಪುನಿ huyimpuni, *see* ಸುಯಿಂಪುನಿ.

ಹುರಿ huri, *see* ಪುರಿ.

ಹುರ್ಬು hurbu, *see* ಉರ್ಬು.

ಹುಲ್ಲು hullu, *s.* Grass. —ಕಡ್ಡಿ a handful of grass given by a cattle dealer to a purchaser as a ratification of bargain.

ಹುಶಿ huši, *s.* A lie, falsehood. 2. failure, omission, miscarriage. —ಆಪಿನಿ to fail *or* miscarry. —ಮಳ್ಪುನಿ to omit *or* neglect.

ಹುಷಾರ್, ಹುಷಾರಿ hushārụ, hushāri, *s.* Smartness, intelligence. 2. attentiveness, wakefulness, wariness. 3. freshness, briskness. *adj.* Smart. 2. awake, alert, cautious. —ಆದುಪ್ಪುನಿ, —ಉಪ್ಪುನಿ to be alert, watchful, careful. —ಆಪಿನಿ to be refreshed *or* invigorated; to be brisk.

ಹುಸಿ husi, *see* ಹುಶಿ.

ಹುಳಿ huḷi, *s.* Sauce, condiments *or* curds seasoned with spices *or* mixed with acids. 2. *see* ಪುಳಿ.

ಹೂ hū, *see* ಪೂ.

ಹೂಂ, ಹೂಂಕಾರ hūṁ, hūṅkāra, *s.* Menacing, threatening, defiance. 2. neighing.

ಹೂಂಕುಟ್ಟುನಿ hūṅkuṭṭuni (ಹೂಂಕುಟ್ಟು), *v. a.* To threaten. 2. to defy, menace, challenge.

ಹೂಜಿ hūji, *see* ದೂಜಿ.

ಹೂಜೆ hūjè, *see* ಕೂಜೆ.

ಹೂಣಿಗೆ hūṇigè, *s.* A soldier. 2. a hero.

ಹೂಣೆ hūṇè, *s.* A vow, promise.

ಹೂನ hūna, *see* ಊನ.

ಹೂಪಿನಿ hūpini, *see* ತೂಪಿನಿ.

ಹೃದ್, ಹೃದಯ hrụdụ, hrụdaya, *s.* The heart, mind, bosom, breast.

ಹೃದ್ಗತ hrụdgata, *adj. lit.* Gone to the heart *or* mind; impressed; remembered, got by heart.

ಹೆಂಗಸು heṅgasu, *s.* A woman.

ಹೆಂಟೆ heṇṭè, *see* ಎಂಟೆ.

ಹೆಂಡ heṇḍa, *s.* Toddy, palm-wine. —ಕುಡ್ಕೆ a drunkard, wine-bibber.

ಹೆಂಮ hemma, *adj.* Abundant, plenty, much, many.

ಹೆಂಮೆ hemmè, *s.* Pride, insolence,

arrogance, haughtiness. —ದಾಯಿ an insolent man. —ತೋಜಾವುನಿ to be haughty.

ಹೆಂಮೆಟ್ಟುನಿ hemmeṭṭuni, *see* ಹಿಂಮೆಟ್ಟುನಿ.

ಹೆಕ್ಕರ್ಮೆ hekkarmè, *s.* A kind of cucumber.

ಹೆಕ್ಕುನಿ hekkuni, *see* ಎಕ್ಕುನಿ.

ಹೆಗ್ಗಡೆ heggaḍè, *s.* A chief, chieftain, headman. 2. a family name; *cf.* ಪೆರ್ಗಡೆ.

ಹೆಚ್ಚ heċċa, *adj.* More, better. 2. high, superior. 3. excessive, superfluous, copious. —ಆಪಿನಿ to increase, augment, multiply, prosper. —ಮಳ್ಪುನಿ to promote, increase, enlarge, exalt; to exaggerate.

ಹೆಚ್ಚಲ್ಮೆ, ಹೆಚ್ಚಳ, ಹೆಚ್ಚಳ್ಮೆ heċċalmè, heċċaḷa, heċċaḷmè, *s.* Exaltation, greatness. 2. brag, boast. —ಮಳ್ಪುನಿ to praise, vaunt, boast.

ಹೆಚ್ಚಾವುನಿ heċċāvuni, *c. v.* (*of* ಹೆಚ್ಚುನಿ) To increase, enlarge, exalt, promote. 2. to spoil, vitiate, as a child, *etc.*, by over-indulgence; *also* ಹೆಚ್ಚಾದ್ ದೀಪಿನಿ.

ಹೆಚ್ಚಿ, ಹೆಚ್ಚಿಗೆ heċċi, heċċigè, *s.* Increase. 2. promotion, advancement. 3. excess, superfluity. 4. eminence, excellence. 5. any thing unusual. —ಪಾತೆರ a superfluous word. —ದ ಸಂಗತಿ an unusual occurrence; further particulars. —ಆಪಿನಿ to increase, augment; to be promoted. —ಮಳ್ಪುನಿ to raise, as rent, *etc.*; to increase, promote.

ಹೆಚ್ಚಿಕಡಮೆ, ಹೆಚ್ಚುಕಡಮೆ heċċikaḍamè, heċċukaḍamè, *s.* Difference, variation. *adj.* About, more *or* less. —ಆಪಿನಿ some difference to occur; to be a little indiscreet; a mistake to occur. —ಇಜ್ಜಿ there is no difference. —ಪಾತೆರುನಿ to speak without due regard; to abuse. —ಮಳ್ಪುನಿ to make a mistake; to make a difference; to make partiality.

ಹೆಚ್ಚುಗಾರಿಗೆ heċċugārigè, *see* ಹೆಚ್ಚಳ್ತೆ.

ಹೆಚ್ಚುನಿ heċċuni (ಹೆಚ್ಚ್), *v. n.* To increase, augment. ಬುದ್ಧಿ— to be overwise. ರೋಗ— a disease to aggravate. ಆಯಿ ಹೆಚ್ಚಿದೆ he has become conceited.

ಹೆಚ್ಚೆಲ್ heċċelu, *see* ಹೆಚ್ಚಿ.

ಹೆಜ್ಜೆ hejjè, *see* ಅಜೆ. 2. *see* ಎಜ್ಜ.

ಹೆಟ್ಟ್ heṭṭu, *see* ತಟ್ಟ್.

ಹೆಟ್ಟುನಿ heṭṭuni, *see* ಎಟ್ಟುನಿ.

ಹೆಡಮುಡಿ heḍamuḍi, *adj.* Pinioned, as the arms. —ಕಟ್ಟುನಿ to pinion.

ಹೆಡ್ಡ್, ಹೆಡ್ಡ heḍḍu, heḍḍa, *adj.* Dull, stupid, foolish, ignorant. —ತನ ignorance, foolishness. —ನರಮಾನಿ a stupid man. ಹೆಡ್ಡಿ a stupid woman.

ಹೆಡ್ಡೆ heḍḍe, *s.* A dolt, blockhead, stupid man.

ಹೆಡ್ಡ್ಯುನಿ, ಹೆಡ್ತರುನಿ, ಹೆಡ್ಪಿನಿ **heḍḍyuni, heḍtaruni, heḍpini,** *see* ಕೆಡಿಪಿನಿ, ಕೆಡ್‌ತರುನಿ.

ಹೆದರಿಕೆ **hedarikè,** *s.* Fear.

ಹೆದ್ದ **hedda,** *adj.* Great, large, spacious, chief, principal.

ಹೆದ್ದಾರಿ **heddāri,** *s.* A highway, great road.

ಹೆಬ್ಬರೆ **hebbare,** *s.* A dolt, blockhead, ignorant man.

ಹೆಬ್ಬಾಕಿಲ್ **hebbākilụ,** *s.* A town gate, chief entrance. 2. the front door of a house.

ಹೆಬ್ಬಾರೆ **hebbāre,** *s.* A family name. 2. a member of this family.

ಹೆಬ್ಬಾವು **hebbāvu,** *s.* The boa constrictor.

ಹೆರಂಗಡೆ **herangaḍè,** *s.* Exclusion, expulsion, interdict. –ದೀಪಿನಿ to interdict, excommunicate.

ಹೆರಿಯ **heriya,** *see* ಹಿರಿ.

ಹೆರುನಿ, ಹೆರ್ದುನಿ **heruni, herduni** (ಹೆರ್), *v. a.* To bring forth, as a child.

ಹೆರ್ಪುನಿ **herpuni,** *see* ದೆರ್ಪುನಿ.

ಹೆಲಿ **heli,** *see* ತೆಲಿ.

ಹೆಲಿಕೆ **helikè,** *see* ಕೆಲಿಕೆ.

ಹೇಗ **hēga,** *see* ಯೋಗ.

ಹೇಜ **hēja,** *see* ತೇಜ.

ಹೇಡಿ, ಹೇಡೆ **hēḍi, hēḍe,** *s.* A coward, poltroon. *adj.* Timid. –ತನ timidity, cowardice.

ಹೇತು **hētu,** *s.* Cause, reason, occasion, motive, purpose.

ಹೇನ್ **hēnụ,** *see* ಪೇನ್.

ಹೇಮ **hēma,** *s.* Gold.

ಹೇಮಂತರುತು **hēmantarutu,** *s.* The cold season.

ಹೇಮಲಂಬಿ **hēmalambi,** *see* ಹೇವಿಳಂಬಿ.

ಹೇರ್ **hērụ,** *s.* A sack of corn, *etc.* –ದಿಂಜಾವುನಿ to fill a sack.

ಹೇರಳ **hēraḷa,** *adj.* Much, many.

ಹೇರಾವುನಿ **hērāvuni,** *see* ಏರಾವುನಿ.

ಹೇರುನಿ **hēruni,** *see* ಏರುನಿ.

ಹೇರ್ಸಾವುನಿ **hērsāvuni,** *see* ಏರ್ಸಾವುನಿ.

ಹೇವಿಳಂಬಿ **hēviḷambi,** *s.* The thirty-first year in the Hindu cycle of sixty.

ಹೇಶಿಗೆ, ಹೇಸಿಗೆ **hēśigè, hēsigè,** *see* ಪೇಶಿಗೆ.

ಹೇಸುನಿ **hēsuni,** *see* ಪೇಶಿಯುನಿ.

ಹೇಳಿಕೆ **hēḷikè,** *s.* A statement, representation. 2. direction, instruction, order. –ದ ಪಾತೆರ hearsay. –ದುಪ್ಪುನಿ to be dependent upon. –ದ ಪ್ರಕಾರ ನಡಪುನಿ to obey one's instructions.

ಹೈಗೆ **heige,** *s.* A person belonging to a class of Brāhmans so called.

ಹೈಪಿನಿ **heipini,** *see* ಸೈಪಿನಿ.

ಹೈದ್ರಿ **heidri,** *adj.* Of the time of Hyder Ali. –ವರಾಹ a gold coin so called.

ಹೈರಾಣ್, ಹೈರಾಣ **heirāṇụ, heirāṇa,** *adj.* Perturbed, disturbed, distressed, discomposed, as through sickness, fatigue, *etc.* *s.* Distress, perturbation, discomposure. –ಆಪಿನಿ to be exhausted, done up.

ಹೊಂಗರೆ **hongarè,** *see* ತೊಂಗರೆ.

ಹೊಂದಿಕೆ hondikè, *s.* Union, attachment.

ಹೊಂದುನಿ honduni (ಹೊಂದ್), *v. a.* To get, attain, obtain, acquire. 2. to suffer, sustain, as loss *or* pain. 3. to enjoy, as happiness, *etc.* 4. to join, unite, attach to. *v. n.* To be agreeable, fit; to be on good terms.

ಹೊಂನೆ honnè, *see* ಪೊಂನೆ.

ಹೊಂಮುತ hommuta, *see* ಒಂಮುತ.

ಹೊಗಳುನಿ hogaḷuni, *see* ಪುಗರುನಿ.

ಹೊಗ್ಗುನಿ hogguni, *see* ಪೊಗ್ಗುನಿ.

ಹೊಟ್ಟು hoṭṭu, *see* ಪೊಟ್ಟು.

ಹೊಟ್ಟೆ hoṭṭè, *s.* The stomach, belly. –ಕಿಚ್ಚ್, –ಕಿಚ್ಚೆ envy, malice. –ಕಿಚ್ಚ್ ಮಳ್ಪುನಿ to envy.

ಹೊಡಂಕ್ hoḍaṅkụ, *see* ತೊಡಂಕ್.

ಹೊಡತ hoḍata, *s.* A stroke, beating.

ಹೊಡರ್ hoḍarụ, *see* ತೊಡರ್.

ಹೊಣಂಗಣಿ hoṇaṅgaṇi, *see* ಪೊಂನಾಂಕಣಿ.

ಹೊಣೆ hoṇè, *see* ಪುಣೆ.

ಹೊತ್ತುನಿ hottuni, *see* ಪೊತ್ತುನಿ.

ಹೊದ್ದಿಯುನಿ hoddiyuni, *see* ಪೊದ್ದಿಯುನಿ.

ಹೊಯ್ಯೊ hoyyo, *intj.* of encouragement, used especially when drawing *or* pulling any thing heavy.

ಹೊರಳುನಿ horaḷuni, *see* ಪುರೆಲುನಿ.

ಹೊರೆ horè, *s.* A load, burden.

ಹೊರೆಸುನಿ horesuni (ಹೊರೆಸ್), *v. a.* To load, burden. 2. to accuse, impute, charge with. 3. *see* ಒರೆಸುನಿ.

ಹೊರ್ತಂದೆ, ಹೊರ್ತು hortandè, hortu, *adv.* Unless, except. 2. besides. ಅವು– besides that.

ಹೊಲಸ್ holasụ, *adj.* Fetid, stinking, dirty. 2. unpleasant,

ಹೊಲೆ holè, *s.* Pollution, defilement. 2. menses. 3. ceremonial uncleanness. *adj.* Obscene, filthy.

ಹೊಲ್ವೆ holvè, *s.* A road, way. 2. *see* ಹೋಲುವೆ.

ಹೊಸ hosa, *see* ಪೊಸ.

ಹೊಸಗೆ hosagè, *see* ಬಸಗೆ.

ಹೊಳೆ hoḷè, *s.* A river.

ಹೊಳೆಪು hoḷepu, *s.* Brightness, radiance, lustre.

ಹೋಕ್, ಹೋಕು hōkụ, hōku, *s.* A defect, flaw, injury. 2. loss, detriment; *cf.* ಪೋಕು.

ಹೋಜುನಿ hōjuni, *see* ತೋಜುನಿ.

ಹೋಡು hōḍu, *see* ತೋಡು.

ಹೋಮ hōma, *s.* A burnt sacrifice, offering to the gods. ಉಚ್ಛಿಷ್ಟ–, ಕೃತ್ರಿಮ–, ಗಣ–, ಮಾರಣ–, ಶುದ್ಧದ– are different kinds of burnt sacrifices. ನೀರ್‍ಡ್‍ಗ್ ಹೋಮ ದೀಯಿಲೆಕ್ಕ useless, efforts, *prov.*

ಹೋರಾಟ hōrāṭa, *s.* Mutual wrangling, contention, fight.

ಹೋರಾಡುನಿ hōrāḍuni (ಹೋರಾಡ್), *v. a.* To wrangle, contend, fight.

ಹೋರಿ hōri, *see* ಜೋರಿ.

ಹೋಲಿ, ಹೋಳಿ hōli, hōḷi, *s.* A feast celebrated at the full-moon of the month of Phālguṇa, when Cupid is burnt in effigy.

ಹೋಲಿಕೆ hōlikè, *s.* Resemblance, similarity, likeness.

ಹೋಲುವೆ, ಹೋಲ್ವೆ hōluvè, hōlvè, *s.* Probability, likelihood. 2. resemblance.

ಹೋಳಿಗೆ hōḷigè, *s.* A broad, round cake of wheat flour, and filled with boiled split pulse and jaggory.

ಹೋಳೆ hōḷè, *see* ಹೊಳೆ.

ಹೌಳಿ houḷi, *see* ಚೌಳಿ.

ಳ Ḷ

ಳ ḷa, The forty-seventh letter of the alphabet. No words begin with this letter.

ಕ್ಷ KŠ

ಕ್ಷ ksha, The forty-eighth letter of the alphabet, compounded of ಕ and ಷ.

ಕ್ಷಣ kshaṇa, *s.* A measure of time equal to four minutes. 2. a moment, instant. —ತ ಲುಳ ರು in a moment.

ಕ್ಷತ್ರಿ kshatri, *s.* The second of the four classes of Hindus. —ಯ a man of the royal *or* military caste.

ಕ್ಷಮಿಪುನಿ, ಕ್ಷಮಿಸುನಿ kshamipuni, kshamisuni (ಕ್ಷಮಿ, ಕ್ಷಮಿಸ್), *v. a.* To pardon, forgive. 2. to bear with.

ಕ್ಷಮೆ kshamè, *s.* Forgiveness, pardon, forbearing, bearing with. 2. patience, endurance.

ಕ್ಷಯ kshaya, *s.* Waste, decline, decay, consumption. 2. destruction, extinction, annihilation. 3. decrease of the digits of the sun *or* moon. 4. the sixtieth year of the Hindu cycle of sixty. —ಚಂದ್ರ moon on the wane. —ರೋಗ phthisis, consumption. —ಆಪಿನಿ to be consumed, destroyed.

ಕ್ಷಾಮ kshāma, *s.* A famine, scarcity of provisions. —ಕಾಲ a time of famine.

ಕ್ಷೀಣ kshīṇa, *adj.* Wasted, emaciated. 2. destroyed, extinguished. 3. thin, lean. —ದೇಹ an emaciated body. —ನರಮಾನಿ, ಕ್ಷೀಣ a thin man.

ಕ್ಷೀರ **kshīra,** *s.* Milk.

ಕ್ಷೀರ್ಣ **kshīrṇa,** *s.* Digestion.

ಕ್ಷುದ್ರ **kshudra,** *adj.* Small, little. 2. low, mean. 3. avaricious. 4. cruel. *s.* Fault, folly, defect. 2. slander, calumny. 3. sorcery. —ಕೆಲಸ an intrigue; a mean act. —ದಾಯಿ an intriguer; a slanderer; a sorcerer. —ಪಾತೆರ a calumny. —ಮಳ್ಪುನಿ to bewitch.

ಕ್ಷುಧೆ **kshudhe,** *s.* Hunger, appetite.

ಕ್ಷೇತ್ರ **kshētra,** *s.* A sacred spot, place of pilgrimage, holy land. 2. a plane, superficies. —ಪಾಲಕೆ a demon so called. —ಫಲ land measure, area. ಪುಣ್ಯ— a holy place *or* shrine.

ಕ್ಷೇಮ **kshēma,** *s.* Welfare, well-being, happiness, health. *adj.* Well, happy. —ವಾರ್ತೆ, —ಸಮಾಚಾರ news about one's welfare.

ಕ್ಷೌರ **kshoura,** *s.* Shaving the head. —ಕೆ, —ದಾಯಿ a barber. —ಮಳ್ಪುನಿ, ಕ್ಷೌರಿಪುನಿ to shave.

SUPPLEMENT.

ಅಂನ್ಯಾರೆ annyāre, *see* ಅಂಣೆ.

ಅಂಬಾರಿ ambāri, ... 2. *see* ಸಂಬರ.

ಅಕ್ಕಲ್‌ಕಾರ akkalkāra *s.* A kind of medicinal root.

ಅಕ್ಕೊಸ akkosa, *see* ಆಕಾಶ.

ಅಚ್ಚಿ ačči, *s.* ....3. a gold coin, pagoda.............

ಅಟ್ಟಳಿಗೆ aṭṭaḷigè, *see* ಅಟ್ಟೊಳಿಗೆ. 2. *see* ಅಟ್ಟಳು

ಅಪ್ಪವಾಸ್ appavāsu, *s.* A kind of fish.

ಅರಿಕುಟ್ಟಿಲ್ arikuṭṭilu, *s.* A cook-room in a temple.

ಅಲ್ಕಡೆ alkaḍè, *see* ಅರ್ಕಡೆ.

ಅವ್ವಾಂಡು avvāṇḍu, *see* ಅವುಂಟು.

ಆಂಡುನಿ āṇḍuni (ಆಂಡ್), *v. a.* To do; *cf.* ಮುಳ್ಪುನಿ.

ಆರಿಯುನಿ āriyuni, *see* ಆರುನಿ.

ಆಲಂದ ālanda, *see* ಆಲಡೆ.

ಆವಾರ āvara, *see* ಆಹಾರ.

ಆಸಿಗಾಸಿ āsigāsi, *s.* Risk, responsibility, care; *cf.* ಜಾಕ್‌ಜೋಕ್.

ಇಟ್ಟೊರೆ iṭṭorè, *see* ಇಟ್ಟರೆ.

ಇಡಕತ್ತಿ, ಇಡೆಕತ್ತಿ iḍakatti, iḍekatti, *see* ಅಡ್ಡಕತ್ತರಿ.

ಇಡೆಪಿನಿ iḍepini, *see* ಇಡ್ಪಿನಿ.

ಇನಾಸರೆ ināsarè, *s.* Embracing.

ಇರೊಳು iroḷu, *see* ಇರ್ವೊಳು.

ಉಂಬರ umbara, *s.* Danger.

ಉಗುಡು uguḍu, *see* ಉಗ್ರ.

ಉಗೆ ugè, *see* ಉಜೆ.

ಉಚ್ಛಿಷ್ಟ uččhishṭa, *s.* Orts, leavings. *adj.* Left, rejected, as food.

ಉಡ uḍa, *see* ಕುಡ.

ಉಡಾಜಯ uḍājaya, *s.* A great victory.

ಉಡಾಪ್ಯ, ಉಡಾಫಿ uḍāpya, uḍāphi, *adj.* Evasive, as a reply. 2. denying. 3. contradictory.

ಉಡುಸ್ರೆ uḍusrè, *s.* A bed. 2. clothing; a female's garment.

ಉಣಿಲೆ uṇilè, *s.* A tender mango. 2. a kind of poison. 3. *see* ಕೊಣಲೆ. *adj.* ....

ಉದ್ನ udna, *see* ಉರ್ದು.

ಉಪಸಾರ upasāra, *see* ಉಪಚಾರ.

ಉಪಾಧ್ಯೆ upādhye, *s.* A teacher, schoolmaster. 2. a family-priest.

ಉಪ್ಪಾರೆ uppāre, *s.* A salt manufacturer.

ಉಬ್ಬುಳ್ಳು ubbuḷḷu, *adj.* Hairy.

ಉರ ura, *adj.* Exact.

ಉರಣೆ uraṇè, *s.* A kind of comb.

ಉಲಿಪೆ ulipè, *see* ಒಲಿಪೆ.

ಉಳ್ಳಾನ uḷḷāna, *adv.* As long as.

ಉಳ್ಳೆಲ್ uḷḷelu, *see* ತುಳ್ಳೆಲ್.

ಎಚ್ಚ್ಯ yeččya, *see* ವೆಚ್ಚ. —ಸಚ್ಚ general expenditure.

ಎಡುಮ yeḍuma, *see* ಎಡ್ಮ.

ಎತ್ತ್, ಎತ್ತ yettu, yetta, *s.* A game at dice.

ಎತ್ತೊಳಿ yettoli, *see* ಎತ್ತುವಳಿ.

ಎಸಗುನಿ yesaguni (ಎಸಗ್), *v. a.* To discharge. 2. to help. 3. to begin.

ಒತ್ತೊಳಿ vottoli, *see* ಒತ್ತಯು.

ಒರ್ಕಟ್ಟ vorkatta, *adj.* Single, alone.

ಒರ್ಬ vorba, *see* ಒರ್ಮೆ.

ಒಲ್ಮಣ volmana, *see* ಒಪ್ಪಿಸೆ.

ಓಡುರಿಮಾಡ vodurimada, *see* ವೋಡುರಿಮಾಡ.

ಕಂಡಡ kandada, *see* ಕೊಂಡಡ.

ಕಂದ kanda, *see* ಕಂದ್.

ಕಂಬಳ kambala, *see* ಕಂಬುಲ.

ಕಡಂಜಿಗೆ kadañjigè, *s.* Kneading; *cf.* ಕಡೆಂಚುನಿ.

ಕಡಾವುನಿ kadāvuni, *see* ಕಡವುಡುನಿ.

ಕಡೆಂಜಿಕಾಯಿ kadeñjikāyi, *see* ಕಕ್ಕೆ; *also* ಕಕ್ಕೆಟಿ.

ಕಡ್ಡೆಸ kaddesa, *see* ಕೆಡ್ಡಸ.

ಕಮಡ್, ಕಮರ್ kamadu, kamaru, *s.* Dregs. 2. smell of burnt oil, *etc.* *adj.* Old.

ಕಲಾವು kalāvu, *s.* A scar, mark. 2. *see* ಕಳವು.

ಕಲಿಜಿಗ, ಕಲ್ಜಿಗ kalijiga, kaljiga, *see* ಕಲಿಯುಗ.

ಕಲ್ಪಾದಿ kalpādi, *s.* A learned man, sophist. 2. a hypocrite.

ಕಲ್ಪೆ kalpè, *s.* Learning.

ಕಸವಡೆ kasavadè, *s.* A gown.

ಕಳಾಟ್ kalātu, *s.* A fixed place.

ಕಳ್ಳಾವು kallāvu, *see* ಕಲಾವು.

ಕಾಂಡಾಯ kāndāya, *s.* A large vessel for boiling.

ಕಾಂಡಾಯಿ kāndāyi, ...2. *see* ಕಾಂಡೆಲ್.

ಕಾಣ್ಮೆ kānmè, *s.* Appearance, show.

ಕಾಲಗ kālaga, *see* ಕಾಳಗ.

ಕಿಲ್ಲಾರ killāra, *s.* A frame-work. 2. the stomach.

ಕೀರಿವೊತ್ತುನಿ kīrivottuni, *see* ಕೀರೊತ್ತುನಿ.

ಕುಂಚಲ kuñčala, *see* ಕುಂಚ.

ಕುಂತೆ kunte, *see* ಕೊಂಕೆ.

ಕುಂಮುಡುನಿ kummuduni, *see* ಕುಮಿವುನಿ.

ಕುಕ್ಕುಟ kukkuta, *s.* A fowl.

ಕುಡ್ಡೆ kudde, *see* ಕುಂಟೆ.

ಕುದುಂಟೆ kuduntè, *s.* A lump of dung. 2. *see* ಕೊದಂಟೆ.

ಕುದ್ರು kudru, *see* ಕುದುರು.

ಕುರ್ದುನಿ kurduni, *see* ಕುದುರುನಿ.

ಕುರ್ಮ kurma, *s.* A kind of tree.

ಕೂಕ್ರು kūkru, *adj.* Young, small. ನಾಯಿತ— a cub, young dog. —ದೆಂಜಿ a kind of small crab.

ಕೂರಂದ kūranda, *see* ಕೂರಂಗೆಲ್.

ಕೂರ್ಚ kūrča, *s.* An enclosure. 2. a tassel.

ಕೆಡ್ಡೆಸ keddesa, *see* ಕೆಡ್ಡಸ.

ಕೆಪ್ಪ keppa, *see* ಕೆಪ್ಪು.

ಕೆಪ್ಪಾರ್ kepparu, *s.* A kind of cap; *cf.* ಮುಟ್ಟಳೆ.

ಕೇದಗೆ kēdagè, *see* ಕೇದಯಿ.

ಕೈಕುನಿ keikuni (ಕೈಕ್), *v. a.* To wash the hands.

ಕೈಪುನಿ keipuni, *v. a.* To fasten, bind tight.

ಕೊಂಡಡ kondada, *adj.* Beloved, dear. *s. see* ಕೊಂಡಾಟ.

ಕೊಂಬಾಗೆ kombāgè, *s.* A kind of umbrella.

ಕೊಜಂಞೆ kojaññè, *s.* A thicket.

ಕೊಪ್ಪಂದ koppanda, *s.* A female's ornament.

ಕೊರಣ koraṇa, *adj.* Unconferable; rare, as a gift.

ಕೊರ್ನಿ korni, *see* ಕುರ್ನಿ.

ಗಂದಂದ gandanda, *adj.* Small, fine.

ಗಂಡಾರ್ಳ್ garṇḍāḷu, *s.* A stalwart man, giant.

ಗಟ್ಯ gaṭya, *see* ಗಟ್ಟಿ.

ಗಡಿಪು, ಗಡಿಯ gaḍipu, gaḍiya, *adv.* Wholly; *cf.* ಗಟ್ಟಿ.

ಗಲಿ gali, *s.* Small pieces of light wood fastened to a net.

ಗವನ gavana, *s.* Desire, wish.

ಗಾನುನಿ gānuni, *see* ಗಾಣುನಿ.

ಗಿಂಡೆ giṇḍè, *see* ಗಿಂಡಿ.

ಗಿರಿಯ giriya, *s.* A hinge, as of a door.

ಗುಂಡಿ guṇḍi, *s.* . . . . *adj.* Deep, sunken.

ಗುಜ್ಜಿ gujji, *adj.* Short, thick, of little stature. —ತಾರೆ a short, thick cocoanut tree.

ಗುಡ್ಡಳುನಿ guḍḍaḷuni (ಗುಡ್ಡಳ್), *v. a.* To work hard.

ಗುಡ್ಡಳೆ guḍḍaḷe, *see* ಗುದ್ದಲಿ.

ಗುರ್ಮವಾಯು gurmavāyu, *see* ಗುಲ್ಮ.

ಗುವೆ guvè, *see* ಗುವೆಲ್.

ಗೆಲ್ಲಂದ್ gellandu, *s.* Success, victory, triumph; *cf.* ಗೆಂದುನಿ.

ಗೈರಯತ್ geirayatu, *s.* Absence.

ಚಂದಗಿಡಿ čandagiḍi, *s.* Haughtiness. 2. a man's name.

ಚಟಾಲ್ čaṭālu, *see* ಚಟೀಲ.

ಚಮಕ್ čamaku, *s.* Lustre; brandishment, flourish. 2. haughtiness.

ಚರಕಜೆ čarakaǰè, *s.* Dishevelled hair.

ಚಿಂಗಣಿ čiṅgaṇi, *see* ಚುಂಗಾಣಿ.

ಚಿಟ್ನೇಸಿ čiṭnēsi, *see* ತಿಟ್ನೇಸಿ.

ಚಿಲ್ಲೊಡುನಿ čilloḍuni, *see* ಸಿಲ್ಲೊಡುನಿ. 2. ತಿಲ್ಲಾಡುನಿ

ಚೋರೆ čōrè, *adj.* Tender, unripe, as a fruit.

ಛಾಪಖಾನೆ čhāpakhānè, *see* ಛಾಪು.

ಜಂತ್ರಿ ǰantri, *see* ತಂತ್ರಿ.

ಜಲ್ಮುಂಡೆ ǰalmuṇḍè, *adj.* Nice, fine. —ಪೆಲಕಾಯಿ a kind of jackfruit.

ಜಾಂಬುಮೂರಿ ǰāmbumūri, *s.* A peculiar smell.

ಜಾತಗ ǰātaga, *s.* Walking. —ಕೋಲು a walking stick.

ಜಾಮೂರಿ ǰāmūri, *see* ಜಾಂಬುಮೂರಿ.

ಜಾವರ ǰāvara, *see* ಜಾಗರ.

ಜುವಾನ ǰuvāna, *see* ಜೀವನ.

ಜೊಕ್ಕೆ, ಜೊಗ ǰokkè, ǰoga, *see* ಜಕ್ಕೆ. 2. *see* ದೊಕ್ಕೆ.

ಜೊಗಟೆ ǰogaṭè, *see* ಜೋಗಟ್ಟಿ.

ಜ್ವಲಿಪುನಿ ǰvalipuni, *v. n.* To burn, shine.

ಜ್ಯೋಕೆರಾಕೆ ǰyōkerākè, *see* ಜೋಕೆ.

ಡಲಗುನಿ ḍalaguni (ಡಲಗಿ), *v. a.* To shine.

ಡವಣೆ ḍavaṇè, *s.* A whirlpool; *also* ನೀರಡವಣೆ.

ತಕ್ಕೈರ್ takeiru, *see* ತಗ್ಗೈರ.

ತಟಿಮುಟಿ taṭimuṭi, *s.* Strait, dilemma. 2. *see* ತಟ್ಟಿಮುಟ್ಟಿ.

ತರಿಯ tariya, *see* ತಡವು.

ತರ್ತೆ tartè, *adj.* Deep; *cf.* ತಪ್ಪನಿ, ಶಾರುನಿ.

ತಲ್ಲಾರ tallāra, *see* ತಲರ.

ತಾಳೆ tāḷè, *s.* Comparison; proof; agreement.

ತಿಗ್ರ್ tigṛu, *s.* A sprout, bud, germ. 2. a split, crack.

ತಿಪ್ಪರ್ tipparu, *s.* A knotted root. 2. confusion, hurlyburly.

ತಿರುಡಿ tiruḍi, *s.* A vice, an instrument for holding and griping things. 2. *see* ತಿರುಳಿ.

ತಿರುಸೋಲು tirusōlu, *see* ತ್ರಿಶೂಲ.

ತುನೆ tunè, *s.* A stick. 2. *see* ತುಣಿ.

ತೇದುನಿ tēduni (ತೇದ್), *v. a.* To grind, macerate, bray.

ತೆಮುಲೆ temulè, *see* ತೆವಲ್.

ತೇಗು tēgu, *see* ತೇಗ್.

ತೋರಂಟೆ tōraṇṭè, *s.* A kind of *solanum.*

ತೋಳರ tōḷara, *adv.* With the arms extended.

ಥಲ್ಲಿ; ಥಲ್ಲೆ thalli, thallè, *s.* A cloth used in offerings to demons, at weddings, *etc.*

ದಮಣೆ damaṇè, *see* ದವಣಿ.

ದಳ್ಳಿಯ, ದಳ್ಳ್ಯ daḷḷiya, daḷḷya, *s.* A kind of cloth.

ದೀವಲ dīvala, *see* ದೀಪಾಳಿ.

ದೀವಾರೆ dīvārè, *s.* Fixing a day.

ದುಂದುನಿ dunduni, *see* ತೊಂದುನಿ.

ದುಕ್ಕಿ dukki, *s.* The left side of a finger-drum.

ದೇಂತಡೆ dēntaḍè, *see* ದೇವಸ್ಥಾನ.

ದೇವ dēva, *s.* . . . . . 3. *see* ದೇವೆರ್. 4. *see* ದಿವ್ಯ.

ದೇಸ, ದೇಸೆ dēsa, dēsè, *s.* Raw rice used on auspicious occasions for sprinkling upon a married couple, *etc.*; *cf.* ಸೇಜ. 2. *see* ದೇಶ. —ಪಾಡುನಿ to sprinkle rice in this way.

ದೊಡ್ಡುಳಿ, ದೊಡ್ರೆಯಿಪುಳಿ doḍḍuḷi, doḍreyipuḷi, *see* ಜೊಡ್ಡೆ.

ನಂಞುಡ naññuḍa, *see* ನಗಡ್.

ನಂದ್ nandu, *see* ನಂಡ್.

ನಂದಳಿಗೆ nandaḷigè, *see* ನಂದಾದೀಪ.

ನಾಗಜಾಪು nāgajāpu, *s.* A kind of cloth worn by males; *cf.* ದೋತ್ರ.

ನಾಟ nāṭa, *s.* Seeking, search.

ನಾಡ nāḍa, *adv.* Soon, speedily. *s.* A falsehood.

ನಾಞ್ಯುನಿ nāñyuni, *see* ನಾನುನಿ.

ನಾಪೆ nāpè, *see* ನಾಪಸ್.

ನಾಲಾವುನಿ nālāvuni, *see* ಮಾಲಾವುನಿ.

ನಿಲೆಪುನಿ nilepuni (ನಿಲೆ), *v. a.* To establish, found.

ಪಟ್ಲುಪ್ಪು paṭluppu, *s.* Salpetre.

ಪಡಕರ paḍakara, *see* ಪದಂಕರ.

ಪಡಾವು paḍāvu, *s.* . . . 2. a ship.

ಪಡಿತಡೆ paḍitaḍè, *s.* A temporary dwelling.

ಪದಾಂಪು padāmpu, *s.* Moisture. *adj.* Moist, wet.

ಪದಾಂಪುನಿ padāmpuni (ಪದಾಂ), *v. a.* To moisten, wet.

ಪರಿಪಾಡ್ paripāḍu, *s.* Fate. 2. trouble.

ಪರಿವಾಳ parivāḷa, *s.* Food. 2. *see* ಪರಿವಾರ.

ಪಾಂಬಳೆ pāmbaḷè, *s.* A kind of ornament

ಪಾಂಬೊಳು, pāmboḷu, *see* ಪಾಂಬೊಲ್.

ಪಿಡಿಬಾಳ್ piḍibāḷu, *s.* . . . 2. a demon's sword.

ಪಿದುಕಂಣ್ pidukaṇṇu, *s.* Blinking, twinkling of the eyes.

ಪಿರವತ್ತ್ piravattu, *see* ಪಿರಪ.

ಪಿರ್ನಾಲ್ pirnālu, *s.* A gift.

ಪೀನರಿ pīnari, *see* ಪೀನಾರಿ.

ಪುದಗಲ pudagala, *s.* The body.

ಪುರಪು purapu, *s.* Circumstances.

ಪುಲಿ puli, *s.* . . . –ಕೊದ್ದೆಲ್ a kind of sour sauce *or* condiment.

ಪೂಂಚ pūñča, *s.* An ant-hill.

ಪೂಗಾರೆ pūgārė, *s.* A temporary shed covered with awnings erected during the funeral ceremonies of a deceased Šūdra.

ಪೆರ್ನ perna, *see* ಪ್ರಾಣ.

ಪೊಂಚೊಳಿಗೆ, ಪೊಂಣೊಳಿಗೆ poñčoḷigė, poṇṇoḷigė, *see* ಪೊಂಣಳಿಗೆ.

ಪೊಟ್ಟುಳು poṭṭuḷu, *s.* A rotten seed.

ಪೋಕ್ರೆ pōkre, *s.* A nasty man.

ಪೋಟ್ಲ pōṭla, *s.* A pustule, blister, sore. 2. a kind of parasite.

ಪ್ರಾಣ prāṇa, *s.* . . . . . . –ಬೆಪ್ಪುನಿ to work hard. –ಬೆಂದೋಣುನಿ to commit suicide.

ಬಕ್ಕಣೆ bakkaṇė, *s.* A quarrel.

ಬಪಿಪುನಿ, ಬಬಿಪುನಿ bapipuni, babipuni (ಬಪಿ, ಬಬಿ), *v. a.* To put out of the way.

ಬಿತ್ತ್ಲ್ bittulu, *s.* A garden, compound.

ಬಿಸಾರ್ bisāru, *s.* A stroke, blow, cut.

ಬೆಂಕ್ beṅku, *s.* Disturbance, confusion, disorder. 2. entanglement. –ಬುಡುಪಾವುನಿ to disentangle.

ಬೆಂಕುನಿ beṅkuni (ಬೆಂಕ್), *v. n.* To be complicated, entangled.

ಬೆಂಬನ bembana, *s.* Work.

ಬೇದಗ bēdaga, *s.* Medicine for a woman in childbed.

ಮಲ್ಲಯಿಲ್ mallayilu, *s.* A large ladle.

ಮಾಂಬ್ರ māmbra, *s.* A cry, shout. –ಕುಟ್ಟುನಿ to cry, shout, call.

ಮಿಜಟ್ mijaṭu, *see* ಮಿಜಾಕ್.

ಮುಗಲಿಯುನಿ mugaliyuni (ಮುಗಲಿ), *v. n.* To become cloudy, as the sky.

ಮುಜುಡು mujuḍu, *s.* An old person.

ಮುದಾವುನಿ mudāvuni (ಮುದಾ), *v. a.* To draw near.

ರೆಸ resa, *s.* A kind of pepper water *or* sauce.

ಲೆಚ್ಚಲೆ leččalė, *adj.* Wide, broad.

ವಾಯನ vāyana, *s.* Offerings of cocoanuts made by a married woman to the goddess Gouri.

ವಾಯೊಲ vāyola, *s.* Any statement *or* account written on palm-leaves.

ಸೀನೆ sīnė, *s.* A flute, fife.

Errata.

Page 32 *under* ಅರ್ಸಯು	*for* (ದಾಸಯ್ಯ)	*read* (ದಾಸಯು).
„ 53 „ ಆಸ್	„ *cf.* ಹಾಸ್‌ಪಾಸ್	„ *cf.* ಆಸ್‌ಪಾಸ್.
„ 56 „ ಇಗಡ	„ ವಿಗಡ	„ ವಿಂಗಡ.
„ 61 „ ಇರ್ವೊಳು	„ ಇರೊಳು	„ ಈರೊಳ್.
„ 65 „ ಉಂಬುಗೆ	„ ಉಂಮತ	„ ಉಂಮುತ.
„ 72 „ ಉರ	„ to hold or	„ *or*
„ 106 „ ಕಂಣೊಂಬರ	„ **kaṇṇumberu**	„ **kaṇṇumbara**
„ 108 „ ಕಂರ್ಕ	„ being to burnt	„ being burnt
„ 129 „ ಕಶ್ಯಪ	„ of deified	„ of a deified
„ 144 „ ಕುಂಕುಮ	„ *see* ಕೇಸರ	„ *see* ಕೇಸರಿ.
„ 147 „ ಕುಜಲುನಿ	„ ಕೊಜೆಲುನಿ	„ ಕೊಜಲನಿ.
„ 178 „ ಕೋರೆ	„ *cf.* ವೋರೆ	„ ಓರೆ.
„ 188 „ ಗಡ್ಸ್ವತನ	„ ಗಡಸ್	„ ಗಡಿಸ್.
„ 196 „ ಗಿದಿಪುನಿ	„ ಗೆದಿಪುನಿ	„ ಗೆದಿಯುನಿ.
„ 213 „ ಘುಂಮ್	„ **ghamu**	„ **ghammu.**
„ 216 „ ಚಕ್ಕ್	„ ನಂದ್‌ಮೂಕು	„ ನಂಡ್‌ಮೂಕು *under* ನಂಡ್.
„ 220 „ ಚರಿಗೆ	„ ಚುರ್ಯ	„ ಚರ್ಯ
„ 221 „ ಚಲಪಲ	„ ತಳಬಳ	„ ತಳಬಲ.
„ „ „ ಚಲ್ಲ	„ a fall	„ falling
„ 228 „ ಚೇಂಕರಿ	„ splitters	„ splinters
„ 253 „	ಜೋಗಿಪಂದ್ರ	„ ಜೋಗಿಪಂದ್ರ.
„ 340 „ ನಕಾರಿ	„ *adj.* Inferior	„ 2. inferior.
„ 343 „ ನಬಾಬ್	„ ನವಾಬ್	„ ನವಾಬೆ.
„ 362 „ ನಿಲ್ಲಾವುನಿ	„ ಪಿಲ್ಯಾವುನಿ	„ ಪಿಲ್ಲಿಯಾವುನಿ.
„ 370 „ ನೆಲ	„ im-precate	„ imprecate.
„ 378 „ ಪಂತಿ	„ dauble	„ double
„ 414 „ ಪಿದುಕೋಣುನಿ	„ (ಪಿದುಕೊ)	„ (ಪಿದುಕೊಣ್)
„ 418 „ ಪೀತ	„ of Udipi	„ of the Udipi
„ „ „ ಪೀಡಣಿ	*omit* *cf.* ಪೀಡೆ.	
„ 432 „ ಪೆದಮಾಲೆ	*for* *see* ಪಿದಮಾಲೆ	„ *s.* A hill so called.
„ 459 „ ಬಜನ್	„ ಭಜನ	„ ಭಜನೆ.
„ 496 „ ಬ್ಯೆಂಬಿಗೆ	„ reindear	„ reindeer
„ 500 „ ಬೊಲ್ಲಿ	„ ಬೊಲ್ದು	„ ಬೊಳ್ದು.
„ 503 „ ಬೋನು	„ ಬೊನ	„ ಬೊನು.
„ 616 „ ಶೀಂಕಿರಿ	„ ಶೀಂಕಿರಿ	„ ಶಿಂಕಿರಿ.